WILLIAM SHAKESPEARE

BEST LOVED PLAYS

OF

WILLIAM SHAKESPEARE

EDITED BY

MARY COWDEN CLARKE

AUTHOR OF THE "COMPLETE CONCORD-
ANCE TO SHAKESPEARE", ETC. ETC.

*"His fame folds in
This orb o' the earth."*

SHAKESPEARE

THE SPENCER PRESS

RR2759
S57d

THE SPENCER PRESS

The avowed purpose of the Spencer Press is to publish classics which have survived the test of time. In the quest for enduring titles more than fifty famous lists of the finest books ever written were consulted. The findings were then tabulated and the list was found to include more than one thousand titles, some of which have been mentioned in the recommendations of as many as thirty-five different authorities. The first hundred titles which were most often mentioned by the critics, were selected on the assumption that any book which had been chosen so often and by so many eminent authorities must be exceptionally fine. Upon considering these titles, thirty books were discarded because they were either too heavy in style or subject matter to find popular favor.

The next problem was to select those twenty books which would form the cornerstone of a fine home library for people of discriminating taste; books with a cultural and educational background that would tend to broaden the vision and develop the inner resources of the reader . . . books that were sufficiently thrilling and popular in their appeal to capture the imagination and interest of every member of the family.

It seems significant to mention here that when the final list of twenty volumes was compiled it contained books which had been mentioned on almost every list of worthwhile reading. The titles of this set are submitted with the confidence that each and every volume merits the label "World's Greatest Literature."

The next problem of importance was the designing of a format worthy of the name "Spencer." The services of Mr. Leonard Mounteney, a master craftsman who had served for twenty years as a binder in the studios of Robert Riviere & Sons of London, England, were engaged for this artistic undertaking. Mounteney has in the last ten years won for himself considerable acclaim as one of the world's most eminent binders. He approached the task of designing these books with all the fervor and interest of a skilled artisan who loves his work, applying the same thought to these volumes as is usually accorded the bindings of museum masterpieces, incunabula and priceless first editions. Mounteney was well aware that the name "Spencer" had become identified with handsome illustration, fine printing and exquisite binding and he was most anxious to create books of surpassing beauty.

"The Spencer Press" is named in honor of and as a tribute to the memory of William Augustus Spencer, the son of Lorillard Spencer and Sarah Johnson Griswold. Spencer was born in New York, was educated in Europe and made his home in Paris, frequently visiting the United States. Spencer became an inveterate book collector, specializing in fine French bindings. He soon became a patron of the fine binders of his day and his collection, now on permanent exhibition at the New York Public Library, is rated as one of the finest of modern collections. Unfortunately, Spencer perished in the sinking of the Titanic in 1912 cutting short a career of great promise.

The books collected by Spencer were mostly nineteenth century works. These volumes represent a definite advancement in many spheres of book production. The authors, publishers, printers, engravers and bookbinders are all representative of what is modern in their several arts, for Spencer was a true collector who insisted upon a high state of perfection in every creative phase of the bookmaking art.

This type of publishing depends more than anything else upon patronage for its existence. The history of fine bookmaking is linked with the social history of the countries where it is practised. The wealthy nobility were usually the patrons of this fine art. The Kings of France were notable collectors forming libraries of considerable merit. Jean Grolier, Viscount d'Aguisy (1479-1565), Treasurer-General of the Duchy of Milan, friend of Francis I, and ambassador to Pope Clement VII, friend of Aldus, the great printer, was perhaps the most lavish patron of the art of binding and collecting books. To Grolier is accorded the first place among all the great names in book collecting history, and to him is owed the dignified standing in which book collecting is esteemed among the gentler arts. To Grolier also goes the honor for creating a most important and fundamental style in the decoration of book covers.

From Grolier to Spencer we find the names of many illustrious notables who have fostered and patronized the advancement of this art. Jean Baptiste Colbert, statesman and minister of finance under Louis XIV, was the founder of the Academy of Inscriptions which concerned itself greatly with book decoration. Then there was Mazarin, Italian and French cardinal and statesman, who founded one of the great libraries of the world which bears his name. During the intervening years there have been thousands of collectors who have patronized the art. In America one thinks of such great names as Weidner, Morgan, Huntington and Hay in this connection.

Such affluent patronage has given aid to many different interpretations of beauty. Books have been handsomely bound in paper, in wood, in parchment, in cloth and fine leathers. They have been inlaid with materials of contrasting colors, hand painted, encrusted with rare and valuable jewels. They have contained gorgeous end papers and fancy doublures. Men have spent years in the binding, tooling and decoration of a single volume.

These bibliophiles collected not only fine titles, bindings and illustrations but fine printing as well. Gutenberg, the father of fine printing, set an early standard which has been difficult if not impossible to excel. The books created by Gutenberg still rank as among the finest examples of book ornamentation ever produced. Then came the handsome volumes of the East with their arabesques, graceful lines and fleurons which found many an eager collector among the gentlemen of Venice. Aldus, the printer, patronized by Grolier, created many examples of fine printing influenced by these same Eastern designs.

The history of fine binding and bookmaking is a long and interesting one filled with many glorious stories of exquisite books. In the creation of this set of the "World's Greatest Literature," Mounteney has copied the designs of Roger Payne, the one truly great English binder of the nineteenth century. Payne's work was known to have a French influence, a delicate decorative scheme of dots, lines and simple designs. Mounteney has added certain elegant refinements of his own and has endeavored to create a set of books that would be a credit to the memory and name of one of the greatest of all modern collectors . . . a set of books within the reach of the true book-lover so that the appreciation of fine and beautiful books need no longer be a kingly prerogative alone.

The publishers do not claim or even dare to hope that these books are to be compared for richness of binding or makeup with the volumes in the Spencer Library, for some of those books cost thousands of dollars and occupied many years in the lives of master craftsmen. It is true, however, that Mounteney in his careful designing has created books possessing rare beauty of design and exquisite good taste which vie in appearance and handsomeness with the Spencer masterpieces. It should be remembered that the original Spencer volumes were designed by hand, tooled by hand, and often printed by hand, whereas these books were created by one of the world's greatest printers employing every advancement of modern science and efficiency to bring to you books you will treasure over the years . . . books that will add to the richness and fullness of your life.

Reading, Pa. 1936.   LEONARD S. DAVIDOW.

CONTENTS

CONTENTS.

Spirits hunting Caliban, Stephano, and Trinculo. Prospero and Ariel setting them on.
Act IV. S. 1

THE TEMPEST

DRAMATIS PERSONÆ.

ALONSO, *King of* Naples.
SEBASTIAN, *his brother.*
PROSPERO, *the rightful Duke of* Milan.
ANTONIO, *his brother, the usurping Duke of*
Milan.
FERDINAND, *son to the King of* Naples.
GONZALO, *an honest old Counsellor.*
ADRIAN, } *Lords.*
FRANCISCO, }
CALIBAN, *a savage and deformed Slave.*
TRINCULO, *a Jester.*

STEPHANO, *a drunken Butler.*
Master of a Ship, Boatswain, and Mariners.
MIRANDA, *daughter to* PROSPERO.
ARIEL, *an airy Spirit.*
IRIS,
CERES,
JUNO, } *Spirits.*
NYMPHS,
REAPERS,
· *Other Spirits attending on* PROSPERO.

SCENE,—*The Sea, with a Ship; afterwards an uninhabited Island.*

ACT I.

SCENE I.—*On a Ship at Sea.—A Storm
with Thunder and Lightning.*
Enter a Ship-master *and a* Boatswain.
MASTER. Boatswain!
BOATS. Here, master: what cheer?
MAST. Good, speak to the mariners: fall
to't yarely, or we run ourselves aground:
bestir, bestir. [*Exit.*
Enter Mariners.
BOATS. Heigh, my hearts! cheerly, cheer-

ly, my hearts! yare, yare: take in the top-
sail; tend to the master's whistle.—Blow,
till thou burst thy wind, if room enough!
Enter ALONSO, SEBASTIAN, ANTONIO, FER-
DINAND, GONZALO, *and Others.*
ALON. Good boatswain, have care. Where's
the master? Play the men.
BOATS. I pray now, keep below.
ANT. Where is the master, boatswain?
BOATS. Do you not hear him? You mar
our labour: keep your cabins: you do
assist the storm.

1

GON. Nay, good, be patient.

BOATS. When the sea is. Hence! What care these roarers for the name of king? To cabin: silence! trouble us not.

GON. Good; yet remember whom thou hast aboard.

BOATS. None that I more love than myself. You are a counsellor: if you can command these elements to silence, and work the peace of the present, we will not hand a rope more; use your authority: if you cannot, give thanks you have lived so long, and make yourself ready in your cabin for the mischance of the hour, if it so hap.— Cheerly, good hearts!—Out of our way, I say.   [Exit.

GON. I have great comfort from this fellow: methinks he hath no drowning mark upon him; his complexion is perfect gallows. Stand fast, good fate, to his hanging! make the rope of his destiny our cable, for our own doth little advantage! If he be not born to be hanged, our case is miserable.   [Exeunt.

Re-enter Boatswain.

BOATS. Down with the top-mast: yare; lower, lower! Bring her to try with main-course. [A cry within.] A plague upon this howling! they are louder than the weather, or our office.—

Re-enter SEBASTIAN, ANTONIO, and GONZALO.

Yet again! what do you here? Shall we give o'er, and drown? Have you a mind to sink?

SEB. A pox o' your throat, you bawling, blasphemous, incharitable dog!

BOATS. Work you, then.

ANT. Hang, cur, hang! you whoreson, insolent noise-maker, we are less afraid to be drowned than thou art.

GON. I'll warrant him for drowning; though the ship were no stronger than a nutshell, and as leaky as an unstanched wench.

BOATS. Lay her a-hold, a-hold! Set her two courses: off to sea again; lay her off.

Re-enter Mariners, wet.

MAR. All lost! to prayers, to prayers! all lost!   [Exeunt.

BOATS. What, must our mouths be cold?

GON. The king and prince at prayers! let us assist them,

SEB. I am out of patience.

ANT. We are merely cheated of our lives by drunkards.—

This wide-chapp'd rascal, — would thou might'st lie drowning,

The washing of ten tides! [Exit Boatswain.

GON.   He'll be hanged yet,

Though every drop of water swear against it,

And gape at wid'st to glut him. [A confused noise within,—"Mercy on us!"—

"We split, we split!"—"Farewell, my wife and children!"—

"Farewell, brother!"—"We split, we split, we split!"—]

ANT. Let's all sink with the king. [Exit.

SEB. Let's take leave of him.   [Exit.

GON. Now would I give a thousand furlongs of sea for an acre of barren ground; long heath, brown furze, any thing. The wills above be done! but I would fain die a dry death.   [Exit.

_____

SCENE II.—The Island: before the Cell of PROSPERO.

Enter PROSPERO and MIRANDA.

MIRA. If by your art, my dearest father, you have

Put the wild waters in this roar, allay them.

The sky, it seems, would pour down stinking pitch,

But that the sea, mounting to the welkin's cheek,

Dashes the fire out. O, I have suffer'd

With those that I saw suffer! a brave vessel,

Who had, no doubt, some noble creatures in her,

Dash'd all to pieces. O, the cry did knock

Against my very heart! Poor souls! they perish'd.

Had I been any god of power, I would

Have sunk the sea within the earth, or e'er

It should the good ship so have swallow'd, and

The fraughting souls within her.

PRO.   Be collected:

No more amazement. Tell your piteous heart,

There's no harm done.

MIRA.   O, woe the day!

PRO.   No harm.

I have done nothing but in care of thee,

(Of thee, my dear one! thee, my daughter!) who

Art ignorant of what thou art, naught knowing

Of whence I am; nor that I am more better

Than Prospero, master of a full poor cell,

And thy no greater father.

MIRA.   More to know

Did never meddle with my thoughts.

PRO.   'Tis time

I should inform thee farther. Lend thy hand,

And pluck my magic garment from me.—

So: [*Lays down his robe.*
Lie there, my art.—Wipe thou thine eyes;
      have comfort.
The direful spectacle of the wreck, which
      touch'd
The very virtue of compassion in thee,
I have with such provision in mine art
So safely order'd, that there is no soul—
No, not so much perdition as a hair,
Betid to any creature in the vessel
Which thou heard'st cry, which thou saw'st
      sink.
            Sit down;
For thou must now know farther.
MIRA.   You have often
Begun to tell me what I am; but stopp'd,
And left me to a bootless inquisition,
Concluding, "Stay, not yet."
PRO.   The hour's now come;
The very minute bids thee ope thine ear:
Obey, and be attentive. Canst thou re-
      member
A time before we came unto this cell?
I do not think thou canst, for then thou
      wast not
Out three years old.
MIRA.   Certainly, Sir, I can.
PRO. By what? by any other house, or
      person?
Of any thing the image tell me, that
Hath kept with thy remembrance.
MIRA.   'Tis far off;
And rather like a dream, than an assurance
That my remembrance warrants. Had I not
Four or five women once, that tended me?
PRO. Thou hadst, and more, Miranda. But
      how is it,
That this lives in thy mind? What seest
      thou else
In the dark backward and abysm of time?
If thou remember'st aught, ere thou cam'st
      here,
How thou cam'st here, thou may'st.
MIRA.   But that I do not.
PRO. Twelve year since, Miranda, twelve
      year since,
Thy father was the duke of Milan, and
A prince of power.
MIRA. Sir, are not you my father?
PRO. Thy mother was a piece of virtue,
      and
She said thou wast my daughter; and thy
      father
Was duke of Milan; and his only heir
A princess,—no worse issu'd.
MIRA.   O, the heavens! [thence?
What foul play had we, that we came from
Or blessed was't, we did?
PRO.   Both, both, my girl: [thence;
By foul play, as thou say'st, were we heav'd

But blessedly holp hither.
MIRA.   O! my heart bleeds
To think o' the teen that I have turn'd
      you to,
Which is from my remembrance. Please
      you, farther.
PRO. My brother, and thy uncle, call'd
      Antonio,—
I pray thee, mark me,—that a brother
      should
Be so perfidious!—he whom, next thyself,
Of all the world I lov'd, and to him put
The manage of my state; as, at that time,
Through all the signiories it was the first,
(And Prospero the prime duke, being so
      reputed
In dignity) and, for the liberal arts,
Without a parallel: those being all my
      study,
The government I cast upon my brother,
And to my state grew stranger, being
      transported,
And rapt in secret studies. Thy false
Dost thou attend me?   [uncle—
MIRA.   Sir, most heedfully.
PRO. Being once perfected how to grant
      suits,
How to deny them, whom t' advance, and
      whom
To trash for over-topping, new created
The creatures that were mine, I say, or
      chang'd them,
Or else new form'd them: having both the
      key
Of officer and office, set all hearts i' the
      state
To what tune pleas'd his ear; that now he
      was
The ivy, which had hid my princely trunk,
And suck'd my verdure out on't.—Thou
      attend'st not.
MIRA. O, good Sir, I do.
PRO.   I pray thee, mark me.
I, thus neglecting worldly ends, all dedi-
      cated
To closeness, and the bettering of my mind
With that, which, but by being so retir'd,
O'er-priz'd all popular rate, in my false
      brother
Awak'd an evil nature; and my trust,
Like a good parent, did beget of him
A falsehood, in its contrary as great
As my trust was; which had, indeed, no
      limit,
A confidence sans bound. He being thus
      lorded,
Not only with what my revenue yielded,
But what my power might else exact,—
      like one,
Who having, unto truth, by telling of it,

Made such a sinner of his memory,
To credit his own lie,—he did believe
He was indeed the duke; out o' the sub-
    stitution,
And executing th' outward face of royalty,
With all prerogative:—hence his ambition
Growing,—Dost thou hear?
MIRA. Your tale, Sir, would cure deaf-
ness.
PRO. To have no screen between this
    part he play'd,
And him he play'd it for, he needs will be
Absolute Milan. Me, poor man, my library
Was dukedom large enough: of temporal
    royalties
He thinks me now incapable; confederates
(So dry he was for sway) with the king of
    Naples   [age,
To give him annual tribute, do him hom-
Subject his coronet to his crown, and bend
The dukedom, yet unbow'd, (alas, poor
To most ignoble stooping.   [Milan!)
MIRA.   O the heavens!
PRO. Mark his condition, and th' event;
If this might be a brother. [then tell me
MIRA.   I should sin
To think but nobly of my grandmother:
Good wombs have borne bad sons.
PRO.   Now the condition.
This king of Naples, being an enemy
To me inveterate, hearkens my brother's
    suit;
Which was, that he, in lieu o' the prem-
    ises,—
Of homage, and I know not how much
    tribute,—
Should presently extirpate me and mine
Out of the dukedom, and confer fair Milan,
With all the honours, on my brother:
    whereon,
A treacherous army levied, one midnight
Fated to the purpose, did Antonio open
The gates of Milan; and, i' the dead of
    darkness,
The ministers for the purpose hurried
Me, and thy crying self.   [thence
MIRA.   Alack, for pity!
I, not rememb'ring how I cried out then,
Will cry it o'er again: it is a hint
That wrings mine eyes to't.
PRO.   Hear a little farther,
And then I'll bring thee to the present
    business
Which now's upon's; without the which,
Were most impertinent.   [this story
MIRA.   Wherefore did they not
That hour destroy us?
PRO.   Well demanded, wench:
My tale provokes that question. Dear, they
    durst not,—

So dear the love my people bore me,—nor
    set
A mark so bloody on the business; but
With colours fairer painted their foul ends.
In few, they hurried us aboard a bark,
Bore us some leagues to sea; where they
    prepar'd
A rotten carcass of a boat, not rigg'd,
Nor tackle, sail, nor mast; the very rats
Instinctively have quit it: there they hoist
    us,
To cry to the sea that roar'd to us; to sigh
To the winds, whose pity, sighing back
Did us but loving wrong.   [again,
MIRA.   Alack, what trouble
Was I then to you!
PRO.   O, a cherubin
Thou wast, that did preserve me! Thou
    didst smile,
Infused with a fortitude from heaven,
When I have deck'd the sea with drops
    full salt,
Under my burden groan'd; which rais'd in
An undergoing stomach, to bear up [me
Against what should ensue.
MIRA.   How came we ashore?
PRO. By Providence divine.
Some food we had, and some fresh water,
A noble Neapolitan, Gonzalo,   [that
Out of his charity, (who being then ap-
    pointed
Master of this design) did give us; with
Rich garments, linens, stuffs, and neces-
    saries,
Which since have steaded much: so, of his
    gentleness,
Knowing I lov'd my books, he furnish'd me,
From mine own library, with volumes that
I prize above my dukedom.
MIRA.   Would I might
But ever see that man!
PRO.   Now I arise:—
    [Puts on his robe again.
Sit still, and hear the last of our sea-sorrow.
Here in this island we arriv'd; and here
Have I, thy schoolmaster, made thee more
    profit
Than other princess' can, that have more
    time
For vainer hours, and tutors not so careful.
MIRA. Heavens thank you for't! And
    now, I pray you, Sir,—
For still 'tis beating in my mind,—your
For raising this sea-storm?   [reason
PRO.   Know thus far forth.
By accident most strange, bountiful for-
    tune—
Now my dear lady—hath mine enemies
Brought to this shore; and by my prescience
I find my zenith doth depend upon

A most auspicious star, whose influence
If now I court not, but omit, my fortunes
Will ever after droop. Here cease more
    questions:
Thou art inclin'd to sleep; 'tis a good
    dulness,
And give it way:—I know thou canst not
    choose.—   [MIRANDA *sleeps*.
Come away, servant, come! I am ready
Approach, my Ariel; come!   [now:
        Enter ARIEL.
ARI. All hail, great master! grave Sir,
    hail! I come
To answer thy best pleasure; be't to fly,
To swim, to dive into the fire, to ride
On the curl'd clouds: to thy strong bidding
Ariel, and all his quality.   [task
PRO.   Hast thou, spirit,
Perform'd to point the tempest that I bade
    thee?
ARI. To every article.
I boarded the king's ship; now on the beak,
Now in the waist, the deck, in every cabin,
I flam'd amazement: sometime I'd divide,
And burn in many places; on the topmast,
The yards, and bowsprit, would I flame
    distinctly,
Then meet, and join. Jove's lightnings, the
    precursors
O' the dreadful thunder-claps, more mo-
    mentary
And sight-outrunning were not: the fire,
    and cracks
Of sulphurous roaring, the most mighty
    Neptune
Seem to besiege, and make his bold waves
    tremble,
Yea, his dread trident shake.
PRO.   My brave spirit!
Who was so firm, so constant, that this coil
Would not infect his reason?
ARI.   Not a soul
But felt a fever of the mad, and play'd
Some tricks of desperation. All, but mari-
    ners,
Plunged in the foaming brine, and quit the
    vessel,
Then all a-fire with me: the king's son,
    Ferdinand,
With hair up-staring (then like reeds, not
    hair)
Was the first man that leap'd; cried, "Hell
    is empty,
And all the devils are here."
PRO.   Why, that's my spirit!
But was not this nigh shore?
ARI.   Close by, my master.
PRO. But are they, Ariel, safe?
ARI.   Not a hair perish'd;
On their sustaining garments not a blemish,

But fresher than before: and, as thou bad'st
    me,
In troops I have dispers'd them 'bout the
    isle.
The king's son have I landed by himself;
Whom I left cooling of the air with sighs
In an odd angle of the isle, and sitting,
His arms in this sad knot.
PRO.   Of the king's ship
The mariners, say how thou hast dispos'd,
And all the rest o' the fleet.
ARI.   Safely in harbour
Is the king's ship; in the deep nook, where
    once
Thou call'dst me up at midnight to fetch
    dew
From the still-vex'd Bermoothes, there she's
    hid:
The mariners all under hatches stow'd;
Whom, with a charm join'd to their suffer'd
    labour,
I have left asleep: and for the rest o' the
    fleet
Which I dispers'd, they all have met again,
And are upon the Mediterranean flote,
Bound sadly home for Naples;
Supposing that they saw the king's ship
    wreck'd,
And his great person perish.
PRO.   Ariel, thy charge
Exactly is perform'd; but there's more
What is the time o' the day?   [work.
ARI.   Past the mid season.
PRO. At least two glasses. The time
    'twixt six and now
Must by us both be spent most preciously.
ARI. Is there more toil? Since thou dost
    give me pains,
Let me remember thee what thou hast
    promis'd,
Which is not yet perform'd me.
PRO.   How now! moody?
What is't thou canst demand?
ARI.   My liberty.
PRO. Before the time be out? no more!
ARI.   I prithee,
Remember I have done thee worthy service;
Told thee no lies, made no mistakings,
    serv'd
Without or grudge or grumblings: thou
To bate me a full year.   [didst promise
PRO.   Dost thou forget
From what a torment I did free thee?
ARI.   No.
PRO. Thou dost; and think'st it much,
Of the salt deep,   [to tread the ooze
To run upon the sharp wind of the north,
To do me business in the veins o' th' earth,
When it is bak'd with frost.
ARI.   I do not, Sir.

PRO. Thou liest, malignant thing! Hast thou forgot
The foul witch Sycorax, who, with age and envy,
Was grown into a hoop? hast thou forgot
ARI. No, Sir.   [her?
PRO. Thou hast. Where was she born? speak; tell me.
ARI. Sir, in Argier.
PRO.   O, was she so? I must,
Once in a month, recount what thou hast been,
Which thou forget'st. This damn'd witch, Sycorax,
For mischiefs manifold, and sorceries terrible
To enter human hearing, from Argier,
Thou know'st, was banish'd: for one thing she did,
They would not take her life. Is not this
ARI. Aye, Sir.   [true?
PRO. This blue-ey'd hag was hither brought with child,
And here was left by the sailors. Thou, my slave,
As thou report'st thyself, wast then her servant:
And, for thou wast a spirit too delicate
To act her earthy and abhorr'd commands,
Refusing her grand hests, she did confine thee,
By help of her more potent ministers,
And in her most unmitigable rage,
Into a cloven pine; within which rift
Imprison'd, thou didst painfully remain
A dozen years; within which space she died,   [thy groans
And left thee there; where thou didst vent
As fast as mill-wheels strike. Then was this island
(Save for the son that she did litter here,
A freckled whelp, hag-born) not honour'd
A human shape.   [with
ARI.   Yes; Caliban, her son.
PRO. Dull thing, I say so; he, that Caliban,
Whom now I keep in service. Thou best know'st
What torment I did find thee in; thy groans
Did make wolves howl, and penetrate the breasts
Of ever-angry bears: it was a torment
To lay upon the damn'd, which Sycorax
Could not again undo. It was mine art,
When I arriv'd and heard thee, that made
The pine, and let thee out.   [gape
ARI.   I thank thee, master.
PRO. If thou more murmur'st, I will rend an oak,
And peg thee in his knotty entrails, till
Thou hast howl'd away twelve winters.

ARI.   Pardon, master:
I will be correspondent to command,
And do my spriting gently.
PRO.   Do so; and after two days
I will discharge thee.
ARI.   That's my noble master!
What shall I do? say what; what shall I do?
PRO. Go make thyself like a nymph o' the sea: be subject
To no sight but thine and mine; invisible
To every eyeball else. Go take this shape,
And hither come in't: go, hence with diligence.   [*Exit* ARIEL.
Awake, dear heart, awake! thou hast slept
Awake!   [well;
MIRA. The strangeness of your story put
Heaviness in me.
PRO.   Shake it off, Come on;
We'll visit Caliban, my slave, who never
Yields us kind answer.
MIRA.   'Tis a villain, Sir,
I do not love to look on.
PRO.   But, as 'tis,
We cannot miss him: he does make our fire,
Fetch in our wood, and serves in offices
That profit us.—What ho! slave! Caliban!
Thou earth, thou! speak.
CAL. [*Within.*] There's wood enough within.
PRO. Come forth, I say; there's other business for thee:
Come, thou tortoise! when?
        Re-enter ARIEL, *like a water-nymph.*
Fine apparition! My quaint Ariel!
Hark in thine ear.
ARI. My lord, it shall be done. [*Exit.*
PRO. Thou poisonous slave, got by the devil himself
Upon thy wicked dam, come forth!
            Enter CALIBAN
CAL. As wicked dew as e'er my mother brush'd
With raven's feather from unwholesome fen,
Drop on you both! a south-west blow on ye,
And blister you all o'er!
PRO. For this, be sure, to-night thou shalt have cramps,
Side-stitches that shall pen thy breath up; urchins
Shall, for that vast of night that they may work,
All exercise on thee: thou shalt be pinch'd
As thick as honey-comb, each pinch more stinging
Than bees that made them.
CAL.   I must eat my dinner.
This island's mine, by Sycorax my mother,
Which thou tak'st from me. When thou

camest first,
Thou strok'dst me, and mad'st much of me;
     would'st give me
Water with berries in't; and teach me how
To name the bigger light, and how the less,
That burn by day and night: and then I
     lov'd thee,
And show'd thee all the qualities o' th' isle,
The fresh springs, brine-pits, barren place
     and fertile.
Cursed be I that did so!—All the charms
Of Sycorax, toads, beetles, bats, light on
     you!
For I am all the subjects that you have,
Which first was mine own king; and here
     you sty me
In this hard rock, whiles you do keep from
The rest o' th' island.   [me
PRO.   Thou most lying slave,
Whom stripes may move, not kindness: I
     have us'd thee,
Filth as thou art, with human care; and
     lodg'd thee
In mine own cell, till thou didst seek to
The honour of my child.   [violate
CAL.   O ho, O ho!—would it had
     been done!
Thou didst prevent me; I had peopled else
This isle with Calibans.
PRO.   Abhorred slave,
Which any print of goodness will not take,
Being capable of all ill! I pitied thee,
Took pains to make thee speak, taught thee
     each hour
One thing or other: when thou didst not,
     savage,
Know thine own meaning, but would'st
     gabble like
A thing most brutish, I endow'd thy pur-
     poses
With words that made them known: but
     thy vile race,   [good natures
Though thou didst learn, had that in't which
Could not abide to be with; therefore wast
Deservedly confin'd into this rock,   [thou
Who hadst deserv'd more than a prison.
CAL. You taught me language; and my
     profit on't
Is, I know how to curse. The red plague
     rid you,
For learning me your language!
PRO.   Hag-seed, hence!
Fetch us in fuel; and be quick, thou'rt
     best,
To answer other business. Shrug'st thou,
     malice?
If thou neglect'st, or dost unwillingly
What I command, I'll rack thee with old
     cramps,
Fill all thy bones with aches, make thee
     roar,

That beasts shall tremble at thy din.
CAL.   No, pray thee!—
[*Aside.*] I must obey: his art is of such
     power,
It would control my dam's god, Setebos,
And make a vassal of him.
PRO.   So, slave; hence!
                              [*Exit* CALIBAN.
Re-enter ARIEL, *invisible, playing and sing-
     ing;* FERDINAND *following him.*

ARIEL'S SONG.
Come unto these yellow sands,
     And then take hands:
Court'sied when you have, and kiss'd
     The wild waves whist,
Foot it featly here and there;
And, sweet sprites, the burden bear.
     Hark, hark!
Burden. Bowgh, wowgh. [*Dispersedly.*
     The watch-dogs bark:
Burden. Bowgh, wowgh. [*Dispersedly.*
     Hark, hark! I hear
The strain of strutting chanticleer
Cry, Cock-a-doodle-doo.

FER. Where should this music be? i' th'
     air, or th' earth?—
It sounds no more;—and sure, it waits
     upon
Some god o' th' island. Sitting on a bank,
Weeping again the king my father's wreck,
This music crept by me upon the waters,
Allaying both their fury, and my passion,
With its sweet air: thence I have followed
     it,
Or it hath drawn me rather:—but 'tis
No, it begins again.   [gone.—

ARIEL *sings.*
Full fathom five thy father lies;
     Of his bones are coral made;
Those are pearls that were his eyes:
     Nothing of him that doth fade,
But doth suffer a sea-change
Into something rich and strange.
Sea-nymphs hourly ring his knell:
                    [*Burden:* ding-dong.
Hark! now I hear them,—ding-dong,
     bell.

FER. The ditty does remember my drown'd
     father.—
This is no mortal business, nor no sound
That the earth owes:—I hear it now above
     me.
PRO. The fringed curtains of thine eye
     advance,
And say, what thou seest yond'.
MIRA.   What is't? a spirit?
Lord, how it looks about! Believe me, Sir,

It carries a brave form:—but 'tis a spirit.
PRO. No, wench; it eats, and sleeps, and
hath such senses
As we have; such. This gallant, which
thou see'st,
Was in the wreck; and, but he's something
stain'd
With grief, that's beauty's canker, thou
might'st call him
A goodly person. He hath lost his fellows,
And strays about to find them.
MIRA. I might call him
A thing divine; for nothing natural
I ever saw so noble.
PRO. [Aside.] It goes on, I see,
As my soul prompts it.—Spirit, fine spirit!
I'll free thee
Within two days for this.
FER. Most sure, the goddess
On whom these airs attend!—Vouchsafe,
my prayer
May know if you remain upon this island;
And that you will some good instruction
give,
How I may bear me here: my prime
request,
Which I do last pronounce, is,—O you
If you be maid, or no? [wonder!—
MIRA. No wonder, Sir;
But certainly a maid.
FER. My language! heavens!—
I am the best of them that speak this
Were I but where 'tis spoken. [speech,
PRO. How, the best?
What wert thou, if the king of Naples
heard thee?
FER. A single thing, as I am now, that
wonders
To hear thee speak of Naples. He does
hear me;
And, that he does, I weep: myself am
Naples;
Who with mine eyes, ne'er since at ebb,
The king, my father, wreck'd. [beheld
MIRA. Alack, for mercy!
FER. Yes, faith, and all his lords; the
duke of Milan,
And his brave son, being twain.
PRO. [Aside.] The duke of Milan,
And his more braver daughter, could con-
trol thee,
If now 'twere fit to do't.—At the first sight
They have chang'd eyes:—delicate Ariel.
I'll set thee free for this!—[To FER.] A
word, good Sir;
I fear you have done yourself some wrong:
a word.
MIRA. Why speaks my father so ungently?
This
Is the third man that e'er I saw; the first
That e'er I sigh'd for: pity move my father

To be inclin'd my way!
FER. O! if a virgin,
And your affection not gone forth, I'll make
The queen of Naples. [you
PRO. Soft, Sir: one word more.—
[Aside.] They are both in either's powers:
but this swift business
I must uneasy make, lest too light winning
Make the prize light.—[To FER.] One word
I charge thee, [more:
That thou attend me. Thou dost here
usurp
The name thou ow'st not; and hast put
thyself
Upon this island as a spy, to win it
From me, the lord on't.
FER. No, as I am a man.
MIRA. There's nothing ill can dwell in
such a temple:
If the ill spirit have so fair a house,
Good things will strive to dwell with't.
PRO. [To FER.] Follow me.—[To MIRA.]
Speak not you for him; he's a traitor.—
[To FER.] Come;
I'll manacle thy neck and feet together:
Sea-water shalt thou drink; thy food shall
be
The fresh-brook muscles, wither'd roots,
and husks
Wherein the acorn cradled. Follow.
FER. No;
I will resist such entertainment, till
Mine enemy has more power.
[He draws, and is charmed from moving.
MIRA. O, dear father!
Make not too rash a trial of him, for
He's gentle, and not fearful.
PRO. What! I say:
My foot my tutor?—Put thy sword up,
traitor;
Who mak'st a show, but dar'st not strike,
thy conscience
Is so possess'd with guilt: come from thy
ward;
For I can here disarm thee with this stick,
And make thy weapon drop.
MIRA. Beseech you, father!
PRO. Hence! hang not on my garments.
MIRA. Sir, have pity:
I'll be his surety.
PRO. Silence! one word more
Shall make me chide thee, if not hate thee.
What!
An advocate for an impostor? hush!
Thou think'st there are no more such
shapes as he,
Having seen but him and Caliban: foolish
wench!
To the most of men this is a Caliban,
And they to him are angels.
MIRA. My affections

Are then most humble: I have no ambition
To see a goodlier man.
PRO. [*To* FER.]   Come on; obey:
Thy nerves are in their infancy again,
And have no vigour in them.
FER.   So they are:
My spirits, as in a dream, are all bound up.
My father's loss, the weakness which I feel,
The wreck of all my friends, nor this man's
   threats,
To whom I am subdued, are but light to
   me,
Might I but through my prison once a day
Behold this maid: all corners else o' th'
   earth
Let liberty make use of; space enough
Have I in such a prison.
PRO. [*Aside.*] It works.—[*To* FER.]
Come on.—
Thou hast done well, fine Ariel!—[*To*
FER.] Follow me.—
[*To* ARIEL.] Hark, what thou else shalt do
MIRA.   Be of comfort: [me.
My father's of a better nature, Sir,
Than he appears by speech: this is un-
Which now came from him.   [wonted,
PRO.   Thou shalt be as free
As mountain winds; but then, exactly do
All points of my command.
ARI.   To the syllable.
PRO. [*To* FER.] Come, follow.—[*To*
MIRA.] Speak not for him.   [*Exeunt.*

ACT II.

SCENE I.—*Another part of the Island.*
Enter ALONSO, SEBASTIAN, ANTONIO, GON-
ZALO, ADRIAN, FRANCISCO, *and Others.*
GON. Beseech you, Sir, be merry: you
   have cause
(So have we all) of joy; for our escape
Is much beyond our loss. Our hint of woe
Is common: every day, some sailor's wife,
The masters of some merchant, and the
   merchant,
Have just our theme of woe; but for the
   miracle,
I mean our preservation, few in millions
Can speak like us: then, wisely, good Sir,
   weigh
Our sorrow with our comfort.
ALON.   Pr'ythee, peace.
SEB. He receives comfort like cold por-
ridge.
ANT. The visitor will not give him o'er so.
SEB. Look, he's winding up the watch of
his wit; by and by it will strike.
GON. Sir,—
SEB. One:—tell.   [that's offer'd,
GON. When every grief is entertain'd
Comes to the entertainer—
SEB. A dollar.

GON. Dolour comes to him, indeed: you
have spoken truer than you purposed.
SEB. You have taken it wiselier than I
meant you should.
GON. Therefore, my lord,—
ANT. Fie, what a spendthrift is he of his
tongue!
ALON. I pr'ythee, spare.
GON. Well, I have done; but yet—
SEB. He will be talking.
ANT. Which, or he or Adrian, for a good
wager, first begins to crow?
SEB. The old cock.
ANT. The cockrel.
SEB. Done. The wager?
ANT. A laughter.
SEB. A match.
ADR. Though this island seem to be des-
ert,—
SEB. Ha, ha, ha!
ANT. So, you're paid.
ADR. Uninhabitable, and almost inacces-
sible,—
SEB. Yet—
ADR. Yet—
ANT. He could not miss it.
ADR. It must needs be of subtle, tender,
and delicate temperance.
ANT. Temperance was a delicate wench.
SEB. Ay, and a subtle; as he most learn-
edly delivered.
ADR. The air breathes upon us here most
sweetly,
SEB. As if it had lungs, and rotten ones.
ANT. Or as 'twere perfumed by a fen.
GON. Here is every thing advantageous to
life.
ANT. True; save means to live.
SEB. Of that there's none, or little.
GON. How lush and lusty the grass looks!
how green!
ANT. The ground, indeed, is tawny.
SEB. With an eye of green in't.
ANT. He misses not much.
SEB. No; he doth but mistake the truth
totally.
GON. But the rarity of it is, (which is
indeed almost beyond credit)—
SEB. As many vouch'd rarities are.
GON. That our garments, being, as they
were, drenched in the sea, hold, notwith-
standing, their freshness and glosses; being
rather new dyed, than stain'd with salt
water.
ANT. If but one of his pockets could
speak, would it not say, he lies?
SEB. Ay, or very falsely pocket up his
report.
GON. Methinks, our garments are now as
fresh as when we put them on first in
Afric, at the marriage of the king's fair

daughter Claribel to the king of Tunis.

SEB. 'Twas a sweet marriage, and we prosper well in our return.

ADR. Tunis was never graced before with such a paragon to their queen.

GON. Not since widow Dido's time.

ANT. Widow? a pox o' that! How came that widow in? Widow Dido!

SEB. What if he had said, widower Æneas too? good lord, how you take it!

ADR. Widow Dido, said you? you make me study of that: she was of Carthage, not of Tunis.

GON. This Tunis, Sir, was Carthage.

ADR. Carthage?

GON. I assure you, Carthage.

ANT. His word is more than the miraculous harp.

SEB. He hath rais'd the wall and houses too.

ANT. What impossible matter will he make easy next?

SEB. I think he will carry this island home in his pocket, and give it his son for an apple.

ANT. And, sowing the kernels of it in the sea, bring forth more islands.

GON. Ay?

ANT. Why, in good time.

GON. Sir, we were talking, that our garments seem now as fresh, as when we were at Tunis at the marriage of your daughter, who is now queen.

ANT. And the rarest that e'er came there.

SEB. Bate, I beeseech you, widow Dido.

ANT. O! widow Dido; ay, widow Dido.

GON. Is not, Sir, my doublet as fresh as the first day I wore it? I mean, in a sort.

ANT. That sort was well fish'd for.

GON. When I wore it at your daughter's marriage?

ALON. You cram these words into mine ears, against
The stomach of my sense. Would I had never
Married my daughter there! for, coming thence,
My son is lost; and, in my rate, she too,
Who is so far from Italy remov'd,
I ne'er again shall see her. O thou, mine heir
Of Naples and of Milan! what strange fish
Hath made his meal on thee?

FRAN.   Sir, he may live.
I saw him beat the surges under him,
And ride upon their backs: he trod the water,
Whose enmity he flung aside, and breasted
The surge most swoln that met him: his bold head   [oar'd
'Bove the contentious waves he kept, and

Himself with his good arms in lusty stroke
To the shore, that o'er his wave-worn basis bow'd,
As stooping to relieve him. I not doubt,
He came alive to land.

ALON.   No, no; he's gone.

SEB. Sir, you may thank yourself for this great loss,
That would not bless our Europe with your daughter,
But rather lose her to an African;
Where she, at least, is banish'd from your eye,
Who hath cause to wet the grief on't.

ALON.   Pr'ythee, peace.

SEB. You were kneel'd to, and importun'd otherwise
By all of us; and the fair soul herself
Weigh'd, between loathness and obedience, at
Which end o' the beam she'd bow. We have lost your son,
I fear, for ever: Milan and Naples have
More widows in them, of this business' making,
Than we bring men to comfort them: the fault's
Your own.   [fault's

ALON. So is the dearest of the loss.

GON.   My lord Sebastian,
The truth you speak doth lack some gentleness,
And time to speak it in; you rub the sore,
When you should bring the plaster.

SEB.   Very well.

ANT. And most chirurgeonly.

GON. It is foul weather in us all, good Sir,
When you are cloudy.

SEB.   Foul weather!

ANT.   Very foul.

GON. Had I plantation of this isle, my lord,—

ANT. He'd sow't with nettle-seed.

SEB.   Or docks, or mallows.

GON. And were the king on't, what would I do?

SEB. 'Scape being drunk, for want of wine.

GON. I' the commonwealth I would by contraries
Execute all things; for no kind of traffic
Would I admit; no name of magistrate;
Letters should not be known; riches, poverty,
And use of service, none; contract, succession,
Bourn, bound of land, tilth, vineyard, none;
No use of metal, corn, or wine, or oil;
No occupation; all men idle, all;
And women too, but innocent and pure;

No sovereignty,—

SEB.   Yet he would be king on't.

ANT. The latter end of his commonwealth forgets the beginning.

GON. All things in common nature should
produce,

Without sweat or endeavour: treason,
felony,

Sword, pike, knife, gun, or need of any
engine,

Would I not have; but nature should bring
forth,

Of its own kind, all foison, all abundance,

To feed my innocent people.

SEB. No marrying 'mong his subjects?

ANT. None, man; all idle; whores, and
knaves.

GON. I would with such perfection govern, Sir,

To excel the golden age.

SEB.   'Save his majesty!

ANT. Long live Gonzalo!

GON.   And, do you mark me, Sir?—

ALON. Pr'ythee, no more: thou dost talk
nothing to me.

GON. I do well believe your highness;
and did it to minister occasion to these
gentlemen, who are of such sensible and
nimble lungs, that they always use to laugh
at nothing.

ANT. 'Twas you we laugh'd at.

GON. Who, in this kind of merry fooling,
am nothing to you: so you may continue,
and laugh at nothing still.

ANT. What a blow was there given!

SEB. An it had not fallen flat-long.

GON. You are gentlemen of brave mettle:
you would lift the moon out of her sphere,
if she would continue in it five weeks without changing.

Enter ARIEL *invisible, playing solemn
music.*

SEB. We would so, and then go a bat-
fowling.

ANT. Nay, good my lord, be not angry.

GON. No, I warrant you; I will not adventure my discretion so weakly. Will you
laugh me asleep; for I am very heavy?

ANT. Go sleep; and hear us.

          [*All sleep but* ALON., SEB. *and* ANT.

ALON. What! all so soon asleep? I wish
mine eyes

Would, with themselves, shut up my
thoughts: I find,

They are inclin'd to do so.

SEB.   Please you, Sir,

Do not omit the heavy offer of it:

It seldom visits sorrow; when it doth,

It is a comforter.

ANT.   We two, my lord,   [your rest,

Will guard your person while you take

And watch your safety.

ALON.   Thank you.—Wondrous heavy.

          [ALONSO *sleeps. Exit* ARIEL.

SEB. What a strange drowsiness possesses
them!

ANT. It is the quality o' the climate.

SEB.   Why

Doth it not, then, our eye-lids sink? I

Myself dispos'd to sleep.   [find not

ANT.   Nor I: my spirits are nimble.

They fell together all, as by consent;

They dropp'd, as by a thunder-stroke. What
might,

Worthy Sebastian?—O! what might?—No
more:—

And yet, methinks, I see it in thy face,

What thou should'st be. Th' occasion
speaks thee; and

My strong imagination sees a crown

Dropping upon thy head.

SEB.   What! art thou waking?

ANT. Do you not hear me speak?

SEB.   I do; and surely,

It is a sleepy language, and thou speak'st

Out of thy sleep. What is it thou didst say?

This is a strange repose, to be asleep

With eyes wide open; standing, speaking,
moving,

And yet so fast asleep.

ANT.   Noble Sebastian,

Thou let'st thy fortune sleep—die, rather;

Whiles thou art waking.   [wink'st

SEB.   Thou dost snore distinctly:

There's meaning in thy snores.

ANT. I am more serious than my custom:
you

Must be so too, if heed me; which to do,

Trebles thee o'er.

SEB.   Well; I am standing water.

ANT. I'll teach you how to flow.

SEB.   Do so: to ebb

Hereditary sloth instructs me.

ANT.   O,

If you but knew, how you the purpose
cherish,   [it,

Whiles thus you mock it! how, in stripping

You more invest it! Ebbing men, indeed,

Most often do so near the bottom run

By their own fear, or sloth.

SEB.   Pr'ythee, say on:

The setting of thine eye, and cheek, proclaim

A matter from thee; and a birth, indeed,

Which throes thee much to yield.

ANT.   Thus, Sir:

Although this lord of weak remembrance,

(Who shall be of as little memory,   [this

When he is earth'd) hath here almost persuaded

(For he's a spirit of persuasion, only

Professes to persuade) the king, his son's
alive,—
'Tis as impossible that he's undrown'd,
As he that sleeps here, swims.
SEB.   I have no hope
That he's undrown'd.
ANT.   O, out of that no hope,
What great hope have you! no hope, that
way, is
Another way so high a hope, that even
Ambition cannot pierce a wink beyond,
But doubts discovery there. Will you grant,
That Ferdinand is drown'd?   [with me,
SEB.   He's gone.
ANT.   Then, tell me,
Who's the next heir of Naples?
SEB.   Claribel.
ANT. She that is queen of Tunis; she
that dwells
Ten leagues beyond man's life; she that
from Naples
Can have no note, unless the sun were post,
(The man i' the moon's too slow) till new-
born chins
Be rough and razorable; she, for whom
We all were sea-swallow'd, though some
cast again;
And, by that destiny to perform an act,
Whereof what's past is prologue, what to
In yours and my discharge.—   [come,
SEB. What stuff is this!—How say you?
'Tis true, my brother's daughter's queen of
Tunis;
So is she heir of Naples; 'twixt which
There is some space.   [regions
ANT.   A space whose every cubit
Seems to cry out, "How shall that Claribel
Measure us back to Naples?"—Keep in
Tunis,
And let Sebastian wake!—Say, this were
death
That now hath seiz'd them; why, they were
no worse
Than now they are. There be, that can
rule Naples
As well as he that sleeps; lords that can
As amply, and unnecessarily,   [prate
As this Gonzalo; I myself could make
A chough of as deep chat. O, that you bore
The mind that I do! what a sleep were this
For your advancement! Do you under-
SEB. Methinks, I do.   [stand me?
ANT.   And how does your content
Tender your own good fortune?
SEB.   I remember,
You did supplant your brother Prospero.
ANT.   True:
And look how well my garments sit upon
me;
Much feater than before. My brother's
servants

Were then my fellows; now they are my
SEB. But, for your conscience,—   [men.
ANT. Ay, Sir; where lies that? if it were
a kibe,
'Twould put me to my slipper; but I feel
not
This deity in my bosom: twenty con-
sciences,
That stand 'twixt me and Milan, candied
be they,
And melt, ere they molest! Here lies your
brother,
No better than the earth he lies upon,
If he were that which now he's like, that's
dead,
Whom I, with this obedient steel, three
inches of it,
Can lay to bed for ever; whiles you, doing
thus,
To the perpetual wink for aye might put
This ancient morsel, this sir Prudence,
who
Should not upbraid our course. For all the
rest,
They'll take suggestion as a cat laps milk;
They'll tell the clock to any business that
We say befits the hour.
SEB.   Thy case, dear friend,
Shall be my precedent; as thou got'st
Milan,
I'll come by Naples. Draw thy sword: one
stroke
Shall free thee from the tribute which thou
And I the king shall love thee.   [pay'st,
ANT.   Draw together:
And when I rear my hand, do you the like,
To fall it on Gonzalo.
SEB. O, but one word.
             [*They converse apart.*
Music. Re-enter ARIEL, *invisible.*
ARI. My master through his art fore-
sees the danger
That you, his friend, are in; and sends me
forth
(For else his project dies) to keep thee
living   [*Sings in* GONZALO'S *ear.*

    While you here do snoring lie,
    Open-ey'd conspiracy
      His time doth take.
    If of life you keep a care,
    Shake off slumber, and beware:
      Awake! Awake!

ANT. Then let us both be sudden.
GON. Now, good angels, preserve the king.
               [*They wake.*
ALON. Why, how now! ho, awake! Why
are you drawn?
Wherefore this ghastly looking?
GON.   What's the matter?

SEB. Whiles we stood here securing your repose,
Even now, we heard a hollow burst of bellowing
Like bulls, or rather lions: did it not wake you?
It struck mine ear most terribly. [you?
ALON. I heard nothing.
ANT. O, 'twas a din to fright a monster's ear,
To make an earthquake! sure, it was the roar
Of a whole herd of lions. [roar
ALON. Heard you this, Gonzalo?
GON. Upon mine honour, Sir, I heard a humming,
And that a strange one too, which did awake me.
I shak'd you, Sir, and cry'd; as mine eyes open'd,
I saw their weapons drawn:—there was a noise,
That's verity. 'Tis best we stand upon our guard,
Or that we quit this place: let's draw our weapons.
ALON. Lead off this ground, and let's make farther search
For my poor son. [make farther search
GON. Heavens keep him from these beasts!
For he is, sure, i' the island. [beasts!
ALON. Lead away. [*Exit with the others.*
ARI. Prospero, my lord, shall know what I have done:
So, king, go safely on to seek thy son.
[*Exit.*

SCENE II.—*Another part of the Island.*

Enter CALIBAN, *with a burden of wood.
A noise of thunder heard.*

CAL. All the infections that the sun sucks up
From bogs, fens, flats, on Prosper fall, and make him
By inch-meal a disease! His spirits hear me,
And yet I needs must curse. But they'll nor pinch,
Fright me with urchin shows, pitch me i' the mire,
Nor lead me, like a fire-brand, in the dark
Out of my way, unless he bid 'em; but
For every trifle are they set upon me:
Sometime like apes, that moe and chatter at me,
And after, bite me; then like hedge-hogs, which
Lie tumbling in my bare-foot way, and mount
Their pricks at my foot-fall: sometime am I
All wound with adders, who with cloven tongues
Do hiss me into madness.—Lo, now! lo!

Here comes a spirit of his, and to torment me
For bringing wood in slowly: I'll fall flat;
Perchance, he will not mind me.
Enter TRINCULO.
TRIN. Here's neither bush nor shrub to bear off any weather at all, and another storm brewing; I hear it sing i' the wind: yond' same black cloud, yond' huge one, looks like a foul bombard that would shed his liquor. If it should thunder, as it did before, I know not where to hide my head: yond' same cloud cannot choose but fall by pailfuls.—What have we here? a man or a fish? Dead or alive? A fish: he smells like a fish: a very ancient and fish-like smell; a kind of, not of the newest, Poor-John. A strange fish! Were I in England now, (as once I was,) and had but this fish painted, not a holiday fool there but would give a piece of silver: there would this monster make a man: any strange beast there makes a man. When they will not give a doit to relieve a lame beggar, they will lay out ten to see a dead Indian. Legg'd like a man! and his fins like arms! Warm, o' my troth! I do now let loose my opinion, hold it no longer; this is no fish, but an islander, that hath lately suffered by a thunder-bolt. [*Thunder.*] Alas! the storm is come again: my best way is to creep under his gaberdine; there is no other shelter hereabout: misery acquaints a man with strange bed-fellows. I will here shroud, till the dregs of the storm be past.
Enter STEPHANO, *singing; a bottle in his hand.*
STE. I shall no more to sea, to sea,
    Here shall I die a-shore:—
This is a very scurvy tune to sing at a man's funeral:
Well, here's my comfort. [*Drinks.*
    The master, the swabber, the boatswain, and I,
        The gunner, and his mate,
    Lov'd Mall, Meg, and Marian, and Margery,
        But none of us car'd for Kate;
        For she had a tongue with a tang,
        Would cry to a sailor, Go, hang!
    She lov'd not the savour of tar nor of pitch,
    Yet a tailor might scratch her where-e'er she did itch:
        Then, to sea, boys, and let her go hang.
This is a scurvy tune too; but here's my comfort. [*Drinks.*
CAL. Do not torment me: O!
STE. What's the matter? Have we devils here? Do you put tricks upon us

with savages, and men of Inde? Ha! I have not 'scaped drowning, to be afeard now of your four legs; for it hath been said, as proper a man as ever went on four legs cannot make him give ground; and it shall be said so again, while Stephano breathes at nostrils.

CAL. The spirit torments me: O!

STE. This is some monster of the isle, with four legs, who hath got, as I take it, an ague. Where the devil should he learn our language? I will give him some relief, if it be but for that. If I can recover him, and keep him tame, and get to Naples with him, he's a present for any emperor that ever trod on neat's-leather.

CAL. Do not torment me, pr'ythee: I'll bring my wood home faster.

STE. He's in his fit now, and does not talk after the wisest. He shall taste of my bottle: if he have never drunk wine afore, it will go near to remove his fit. If I can recover him, and keep him tame, I will not take too much for him: he shall pay for him that hath him, and that soundly.

CAL. Thou dost me yet but little hurt; thou wilt anon, I know it by thy trembling: now Prosper works upon thee.

STE. Come on your ways: open your mouth; here is that which will give language to you, cat. Open your mouth; this will shake your shaking, I can tell you, and that soundly: you cannot tell who's your friend; open your chaps again.

TRIN. I should know that voice: it should be—but he is drowned, and these are devils. O! defend me!

STE. Four legs, and two voices,—a most delicate monster! His forward voice, now, is to speak well of his friend; his backward voice is to utter foul speeches, and to detract. If all the wine in my bottle will recover him, I will help his ague. Come, —Amen! I will pour some in thy other mouth.

TRIN. Stephano!

STE. Doth thy other mouth call me? Mercy! mercy! This is a devil, and no monster: I will leave him; I have no long spoon.

TRIN. Stephano!—if thou beest Stephano, touch me, and speak to me; for I am Trinculo:—be not afeard,—thy good friend Trinculo.

STE. If thou beest Trinculo, come forth. I'll pull thee by the lesser legs: if any be Trinculo's legs, these are they. Thou art very Trinculo, indeed! How cam'st thou to be the siege of this moon-calf? Can he vent Trinculos?

TRIN. I took him to be killed with a thunder-stroke.—But art thou not drowned, Stephano? I hope now, thou art not drowned. Is the storm overblown? I hid me under the dead moon-calf's gaberdine for fear of the storm. And art thou living, Stephano? O Stephano! two Neapolitans 'scaped?

STE. Pr'ythee, do not turn me about: my stomach is not constant.

CAL. [*Aside.*] These be fine things, an if they be not sprites.
That's a brave god, and bears celestial liquor:
I will kneel to him.

STE. How didst thou 'scape? How cam'st thou hither? swear by this bottle, how thou cam'st hither. I escaped upon a butt of sack, which the sailors heaved over-board, by this bottle! which I made of the bark of a tree, with mine own hands, since I was cast a-shore.

CAL. I'll swear, upon that bottle, to be thy true subject; for the liquor is not earthly.

STE. Here: swear, then, how thou escapedst.

TRIN. Swam a-shore, man, like a duck: I can swim like a duck, I'll be sworn.

STE. Here, kiss the book. Though thou canst swim like a duck, thou art made like a goose.

TRIN. O Stephano! hast any more of this?

STE. The whole butt, man: my cellar is in a rock by the sea-side, where my wine is hid. How now, moon-calf! how does thine ague?

CAL. Hast thou not dropped from heaven?

STE. Out o' the moon, I do assure thee: I was the man in the moon, when time was.

CAL. I have seen thee in her, and I do adore thee: my mistress showed me thee, and thy dog, and thy bush.

STE. Come, swear to that; kiss the book. I will furnish it anon with new contents. Swear.

TRIN. By this good light, this is a very shallow monster:—I afeard of him?—a very weak monster!—The man i' the moon! —a most poor credulous monster!—Well drawn, monster, in good sooth.

CAL. I'll show thee every fertile inch o' the island; and I will kiss thy foot. I pr'ythee, be my god.

TRIN. By this light, a most perfidious and drunken monster: when his god's asleep, he'll rob his bottle.

CAL. I'll kiss thy foot; I'll swear myself thy subject.

STE. Come on, then; down, and swear.

TRIN. I shall laugh myself to death at this puppy-headed monster. A most scurvy monster! I could find in my heart to beat him,—

STE. Come, kiss.

TRIN.—But that the poor monster's in drink. An abominable monster!

CAL. I'll show thee the best springs; I'll pluck thee berries;
I'll fish for thee, and get thee wood enough.
A plague upon the tyrant that I serve!
I'll bear him no more sticks, but follow thee,
Thou wondrous man.

TRIN. A most ridiculous monster, to make a wonder of a poor drunkard!

CAL. I pr'ythee, let me bring thee where crabs grow;
And I with my long nails will dig thee pig-nuts;
Show thee a jay's nest, and instruct thee how
To snare the nimble marmozet: I'll bring thee
To clustering filberds, and sometimes I'll get thee
Young sea-mells from the rock. Wilt thou go with me?

STE. I pr'ythee now, lead the way, without any more talking.—Trinculo, the king and all our company else being drowned, we will inherit here.—[*To Cal.*] Here; bear my bottle.—Fellow Trinculo, we'll fill him by and by again.

CAL. Farewell, master; farewell, farewell. [*Sings drunkenly.*

TRIN. A howling monster; a drunken monster.

CAL. No more dams I'll make for fish;
Nor fetch in firing
At requiring,
Nor scrape trencher, nor wash dish;
'Ban, 'Ban, Ca—Caliban,
Has a new master—Get a new man.

Freedom, hey-day! hey-day, freedom! freedom! hey-day, freedom!

STE. O brave monster! lead the way.
[*Exeunt.*

ACT III.

SCENE I.—*Before* PROSPERO's *Cell.*
Enter FERDINAND, *bearing a log.*

FER. There be some sports are painful, and their labour
Delight in them sets off: some kinds of baseness
Are nobly undergone; and most poor matters
Point to rich ends. This my mean task
Would be as heavy to me, as odious; but
The mistress which I serve quickens what's dead,

And makes my labours pleasures: O! she is
Ten times more gentle than her father's crabbed;
And he's composed of harshness. I must remove
Some thousands of these logs, and pile them up,
Upon a sore injunction: my sweet mistress
Weeps when she sees me work; and says, such baseness
Had never like executor. I forget:
But these sweet thoughts do even refresh my labours;
Most busy, least when I do it.

Enter MIRANDA; *and* PROSPERO
at a distance.

MIRA.   Alas! now, pray you,
Work not so hard: I would, the lightning had
Burnt up those logs that you are enjoin'd to pile.
Pray, set it down, and rest you: when this burns,
'Twill weep for having wearied you. My father
Is hard at study; pray now, rest yourself:
He's safe for these three hours.

FER.   O, most dear mistress!
The sun will set, before I shall discharge
What I must strive to do.

MIRA.   If you'll sit down,
I'll bear your logs the while. Pray, give me that;
I'll carry it to the pile.

FER.   No, precious creature;
I had rather crack my sinews, break my back,
Than you should such dishonour undergo,
While I sit lazy by.

MIRA.   It would become me
As well as it does you: and I should do it
With much more ease; for my good will
And yours it is against.   [is to it,

PRO. [*Aside.*] Poor worm! thou art
This visitation shows it.   [infected;

MIRA.   You look wearily.

FER. No, noble mistress, 'tis fresh morning with me,
When you are by at night. I do beseech you,—
Chiefly that I might set it in my prayers,—
What is your name?

MIRA.   Miranda.—O my father!
I have broke your hest to say so.

FER.   Admir'd Miranda!
Indeed, the top of admiration; worth
What's dearest to the world! Full many a lady
I have ey'd with best regard; and many a time

The harmony of their tongues hath into
bondage
Brought my too diligent ear: for several
virtues
Have I liked several women; never any
With so full soul, but some defect in her
Did quarrel with the noblest grace she
ow'd,
And put it to the foil: but you, O you!
So perfect, and so peerless, are created
Of every creature's best.

MIRA.   I do not know
One of my sex; no woman's face remember,
Save, from my glass, mine own; nor have
I seen
More that I may call men, than you, good
friend,
And my dear father: how features are
abroad,
I am skill-less of; but, by my modesty,
(The jewel in my dower) I would not wish
Any companion in the world but you;
Nor can imagination form a shape,
Besides yourself, to like of. But I prattle
Something too wildly, and my father's pre-
I therein do forget.   [cepts

FER.   I am, in my condition,
A prince, Miranda; I do think, a king;
(I would, not so!) and would no more en-
This wooden slavery, than to suffer   [dure
The flesh-fly blow my mouth.—Hear my
soul speak:
The very instant that I saw you, did
My heart fly to your service; there resides,
To make me slave to it; and for your sake,
Am I this patient log-man.

MIRA.   Do you love me?

FER. O heaven! O earth! bear witness
to this sound,
And crown what I profess with kind event,
If I speak true; if hollowly, invert
What best is boded me to mischief! I,
Beyond all limit of what else i' the world,
Do love, prize, honour you.

MIRA.   I am a fool
To weep at what I'm glad of.

PRO. [*Aside.*]   Fair encounter
Of two most rare affections! Heavens rain
grace
On that which breeds between them!

FER.   Wherefore weep you?

MIRA. At mine unworthiness, that dare
not offer
What I desire to give; and much less take
What I shall die to want. But this is
trifling;
And all the more it seeks to hide itself,
The bigger bulk it shows. Hence, bashful
cunning!
And prompt me, plain and holy innocence!
I am your wife, if you will marry me;

If not, I'll die your maid: to be your fellow
You may deny me; but I'll be your servant,
Whether you will or no.

FER.   My mistress, dearest,
And I thus humble ever.

MIRA.   My husband, then?

FER. Ay, with a heart as willing
As bondage e'er of freedom: here's my
hand.

MIRA. And mine, with my heart in't:
and now farewell,
Till half an hour hence.

FER.   A thousand thousand!
[*Exeunt* FER. *and* MIR.

PRO. So glad of this as they, I cannot
be,
Who are surpris'd with all; but my re-
joicing
At nothing can be more. I'll to my book;
For yet, ere supper time, must I perform
Much business appertaining.   [*Exit.*

SCENE II.—*Another part of the Island.*
Enter CALIBAN, *with a bottle;*
STEPHANO, *and* TRINCULO.

STE. Tell not me:—when the butt is
out, we will drink water; not a drop before: therefore bear up, and board 'em.—
Servant-monster, drink to me.

TRIN. Servant-monster? the folly of
this island! they say, there's but five upon
this isle: we are three of them; if the other
two be brained like us, the state totters.

STE. Drink servant-monster, when I bid
thee: thy eyes are almost set in thy head.

TRIN. Where should they be set else?
he were a brave monster indeed, if they
were set in his tail.

STE. My man-monster hath drowned his
tongue in sack: for my part, the sea cannot drown me; I swam, ere I could recover
the shore, five-and-thirty leagues, off and
on, by this light.—Thou shalt be my lieutenant, monster, or my standard.

TRIN. Your lieutenant, if you list; he's
no standard.

STE. We'll not run, monsieur monster.

TRIN. Nor go neither: but you'll lie,
like dogs; and yet say nothing neither.

STE. Moon-calf, speak once in thy life,
if thou beest a good moon-calf.

CAL. How does thy honour? Let me lick
thy shoe. I'll not serve him, he is not
valiant.

TRIN. Thou liest, most ignorant monster: I am in case to justle a constable.
Why, thou deboshed fish thou, was there
ever man a coward, that hath drunk so
much sack as I to-day? Wilt thou tell a
monstrous lie, being but half a fish, and
half a monster?

CAL. Lo, how he mocks me! wilt thou let him, my lord?

TRIN. Lord, quoth he!—that a monster should be such a natural!

CAL. Lo, lo, again! bite him to death, I pr'ythee.

STE. Trinculo, keep a good tongue in your head: if you prove a mutineer, the next tree—The poor monster's my subject, and he shall not suffer indignity.

CAL. I thank my noble lord. Wilt thou be pleas'd to hearken once again to the suit I made to thee?

STE. Marry, will I; kneel and repeat it: I will stand, and so shall Trinculo.

Enter ARIEL, *invisible.*

CAL. As I told thee before, I am subject to a tyrant; a sorcerer, that by his cunning hath cheated me of the island.

ARI. Thou liest.   [thou;

CAL. Thou liest, thou jesting monkey, I would, my valiant master would destroy I do not lie.   [thee:

STE. Trinculo, if you trouble him any more in his tale, by this hand, I will supplant some of your teeth.

TRIN. Why, I said nothing.

STE. Mum then, and no more.—[*To* CALIBAN.] Proceed.

CAL. I say by sorcery he got this isle; From me he got it: if thy greatness will, Revenge it on him—for, I know, thou But this thing dare not,—   [dar'st;

STE. That's most certain.

CAL. Thou shalt be lord of it, and I'll serve thee.

STE. How, now, shall this be compassed? Canst thou bring me to the party?

CAL. Yea, yea, my lord: I'll yield him thee asleep, Where thou may'st knock a nail into his head.

ARI. Thou liest; thou canst not.

CAL. What a pied ninny's this; Thou scurvy patch!— I do beseech thy greatness, give him blows, And take his bottle from him: when that's gone, He shall drink naught but brine; for I'll not show him Where the quick freshes are.

STE. Trinculo, run into no farther danger: interrupt the monster one word farther, and, by this hand, I'll turn my mercy out of doors, and make a stock-fish of thee.

TRIN. Why, what did I? I did nothing. I'll go farther off.

STE. Didst thou not say he lied?

ARI. Thou liest.

STE. Do I so? take thou that. [*Strikes him.*] As you like this, give me the lie another time.

TRIN. I did not give the lie.—Out o' your wits, and hearing too?—A pox o' your bottle! this can sack and drinking do. —A murrain on your monster, and the devil take your fingers!

CAL. Ha, ha, ha!

STE. Now, forward with your tale.— Pr'ythee stand farther off.

CAL. Beat him enough: after a little I'll beat him too.   [time,

STE. Stand farther.—Come, proceed.

CAL. Why, as I told thee, 'tis a custom with him I' the afternoon to sleep: then thou may'st brain him, Having first seiz'd his books; or with a log Batter his skull, or paunch him with a stake, Or cut his wezand with thy knife. Remember, First to possess his books; for without them He's but a sot, as I am, nor hath not One spirit to command: they all do hate him, As rootedly as I. Burn but his books. He has brave utensils, (for so he calls them) Which, when he has a house, he'll deck withal: And that most deeply to consider is The beauty of his daughter; he himself Calls her a nonpareil: I never saw a woman But only Sycorax my dam, and she;   [an, But she as far surpasseth Sycorax, As great'st does least.

STE.   Is it so brave a lass?

CAL. Ay, lord; she will become thy bed, I warrant, And bring thee forth brave brood.

STE. Monster, I will kill this man: his daughter and I will be king and queen, (save our graces!) and Trinculo and thyself shall be viceroys.—Dost thou like the plot, Trinculo?

TRIN. Excellent.

STE. Give me thy hand: I am sorry I beat thee; but, while thou livest, keep a good tongue in thy head.

CAL. Within this half hour will he be Wilt thou destroy him then?   [asleep;

STE.   Ay, on mine honour.

ARI. This will I tell my master.

CAL. Thou mak'st me merry: I am full of pleasure. Let us be jocund: will you troll the catch You taught me but while-ere?

STE. At thy request, monster, I will do reason, any reason. Come on, Trinculo, let us sing.   [*Sings.*

Flout 'em, and skout 'em; and skout
   'em, and flout 'em;
     Thought is free.
CAL. That's not the tune.
[ARIEL *plays the tune on a Tabor and Pipe.*
STE. What is this same?
TRIN. This is the tune of our catch,
played by the picture of Nobody.
STE. If thou beest a man, show thyself
in thy likeness: if thou beest a devil, take't
as thou list.
TRIN. O, forgive me my sins!
STE. He that dies, pays all debts: I defy
thee.—Mercy upon us!
CAL. Art thou afeard?
STE. No, monster, not I.
CAL. Be not afeard: the isle is full of
   noises,
Sounds, and sweet airs, that give delight,
   and hurt not.
Sometimes a thousand twangling instru-
   ments
Will hum about mine ears; and some-
   times voices,
That, if I then had wak'd after long sleep,
Will make me sleep again: and then, in
   dreaming,
The clouds, methought, would open, and
   show riches
Ready to drop upon me; that, when I
I cried to dream again.   [waked,
STE. This will prove a brave kingdom
to me, where I shall have my music for
nothing.
CAL. When Prospero is destroyed.
STE. That shall be by and by: I remem-
ber the story.
TRIN. The sound is going away: let's
follow it, and after do our work.
STE. Lead, monster; we'll follow.—I would
I could see this taborer! he lays it on.
TRIN. Wilt come? I'll follow, Stephano.
                  [*Exeunt.*

SCENE III.—*Another part of the Island.*

Enter ALONSO, SEBASTIAN, ANTONIO,
GONZALO, ADRIAN, FRANCISCO, *and Others.*
GON. By'r la'kin, I can go no farther,
   Sir;
My old bones ache: here's a maze trod,
   indeed,
Through forth-rights, and meanders! by
I needs must rest me.   [your patience,
ALON. Old lord, I cannot blame thee,
Who am myself attach'd with weariness,
To the dulling of my spirits: sit down,
   and rest.
Even here I will put off my hope, and keep
   it
No longer for my flatterer: he is drown'd,

Whom thus we stray to find; and the sea
   mocks
Our frustrate search on land. Well, let
   him go.
ANT. [*Aside to* SEB.] I am right glad
   that he's so out of hope.
Do not, for one repulse, forego the purpose
That you resolv'd to effect.
SEB. [*Aside to* ANT.]   The next
Will we take throughly.   [advantage
ANT. [*Aside to* SEB.] Let it be to-night;
For, now they are oppress'd with travel,
   they
Will not, nor cannot, use such vigilance,
As when they are fresh.
SEB. [*Aside to* ANT.] I say, to-night:
   no more.
Solemn and strange music; and PROSPERO
   above, invisible. Enter several strange
   Shapes, bringing in a banquet: they
   dance about it with gentle actions of
   salutation; and, inviting the King, &c., to
   eat, they depart.
ALON. What harmony is this? my good
   friends, hark!
GON. Marvellous sweet music!
ALON. Give us kind keepers, heavens!
              What were these?
SEB. A living drollery. Now I will be-
   lieve
That there are unicorns; that in Arabia
There is one tree, the phœnix' throne; one
   phœnix
At this hour reigning there.
ANT.   I'll believe both;
And what does else want credit, come to
   me,
And I'll be sworn 'tis true: travellers ne'er
   did lie,
Though fools at home condemn them.
GON.   If in Naples
I should report this now, would they be-
   lieve me?
If I should say, I saw such islanders,
(For, certes, these are people of the is-
   land)
Who, though they are of monstrous shape,
   yet, note,
Their manners are more gentle-kind, than
Our human generation you shall find   [of
Many, nay, almost any.
PRO. [*Aside.*]   Honest lord,
Thou hast said well; for some of you there
Are worse than devils.   [present,
ALON.   I cannot too much muse,
Such shapes, such gesture, and such sound,
   expressing
(Although they want the use of tongue) a
Of excellent dumb discourse.   [kind
PRO. [*Aside.*]   Praise in departing.
FRAN. They vanish'd strangely.

SEB.   No matter, since
They have left their viands behind; for we
  have stomachs.—
Will't please you taste of what is here?
ALON.   Not I.
GON. Faith, Sir, you need not fear. When
  we were boys,
Who would believe that there were moun-
  taineers
Dew-lapp'd like bulls, whose throats had
  hanging at them
Wallets of flesh? or that there were such
  men,
Whose heads stood in their breasts? which
  now we find,
Each putter-out of five for one will bring
Good warrant of.   [us
ALON.   I will stand to, and feed,
Although my last: no matter, since I feel
The best is past.—Brother, my lord the
Stand to, and do as we.   [duke,
Thunder and lightning. Enter ARIEL *like a
  harpy; claps his wings upon the table;
  and, with a quaint device, the banquet
  vanishes.*
ARI. You are three men of sin, whom
  destiny
(That hath to instrument this lower world,
And what is in't) the never-surfeited sea
Hath caused to belch up; and on this
  island,
Where man doth not inhabit; you 'mongst
  men
Being most unfit to live. I have made you
  mad;
          [*Seeing* ALON., SEB., &c., *draw
                          their swords.*
And even with such like valour men hang
  and drown
Their proper selves. You fools! I and my
  fellows
Are ministers of fate: the elements,
Of whom your swords are temper'd, may
  as well
Wound the loud winds, or with bemock'd-
  at stabs
Kill the still-closing waters, as diminish
One dowle that's in my plume: my fellow-
  ministers
Are like invulnerable. If you could hurt,
Your swords are now too massy for your
  strengths,
And will not be uplifted. But, remember,
(For that's my business to you) that you
  three
From Milan did supplant good Prospero;
Expos'd unto the sea, (which hath requit
  it)
Him, and his innocent child: for which
  foul deed
The powers, delaying, not forgetting, have

Incens'd the seas and shores, yea, all the
  creatures,
Against your peace. Thee, of thy son,
  Alonso,
They have bereft; and do pronounce, by
  me,
Lingering perdition (worse than any death
Can be at once) shall step by step attend
You, and your ways; whose wraths to guard
  you from
(Which here, in this most desolate isle,
  else falls
Upon your heads) is nothing, but heart's
And a clear life ensuing.   [sorrow,
*He vanishes in thunder: then, to soft mu-
  sic, enter the Shapes again, and dance
  with mocks and mowes, and carry out
  the table.*
PRO. [*Aside.*] Bravely the figure of this
  harpy hast thou
Perform'd, my Ariel; a grace it had, de-
  vouring.
Of my instruction hast thou nothing 'bated,
In what thou hadst to say: so, with good
  life
And observation strange, my meaner minis-
  ters
Their several kinds have done. My high
  charms work,
And these, mine enemies, are all knit up
In their distractions: they now are in my
  power;
And in these fits I leave them, while I visit
Young Ferdinand, (whom they suppose is
  drown'd)
And his and my lov'd darling.
                              [*Exit above.*
GON. I' the name of something holy,
  Sir, why stand you
In this strange stare?
ALON. O, it is monstrous! monstrous!
Methought, the billows spoke, and told me
  of it;
The winds did sing it to me; and the
  thunder,
That deep and dreadful organ-pipe, pro-
  nounc'd
The name of Prosper: it did base my
  trespass.
Therefore my son i' the ooze is bedded; and
I'll seek him deeper than e'er plummet
  sounded,
And with him there lie mudded.   [*Exit.*
SEB.   But one fiend at a time,
I'll fight their legions o'er.
ANT.   I'll be thy second.
                  [*Exeunt* SEB. *and* ANT.
GON. All three of them are desperate:
  their great guilt,
Like poison given to work a great time
  after,

Now 'gins to bite the spirits.—I do beseech you,
That are of suppler joints, follow them swiftly,
And hinder them from what this ecstasy
May now provoke them to.
ADR.   Follow, I pray you. [*Exeunt.*

ACT IV.

SCENE I.—*Before* PROSPERO'S *Cell.*

Enter PROSPERO, FERDINAND, *and* MIRANDA.
PRO. If I have too austerely punish'd you,
Your compensation makes amends; for I
Have given you here a thread of mine own life,
Or that for which I live; whom once again
I tender to thy hand. All thy vexations
Were but my trials of thy love, and thou
Hast strangely stood the test: here, afore Heaven,
I ratify this my rich gift. O Ferdinand!
Do not smile at me that I boast her off,
For thou shalt find she will outstrip all praise,
And make it halt behind her.
FER.   I do believe it
Against an oracle.
PRO. Then, as my gift, and thine own acquisition
Worthily purchas'd, take my daughter: but
If thou dost break her virgin knot before
All sanctimonious ceremonies may
With full and holy rite be minister'd,
No sweet aspersion shall the heavens let fall
To make this contract grow; but barren hate,
Sour-ey'd disdain, and discord, shall bestrew
The union of your bed with weeds so loathly,
That you shall hate it both: therefore, take heed,
As Hymen's lamps shall light you.
FER.   As I hope
For quiet days, fair issue, and long life,
With such love as 'tis now, the murkiest den,
The most oppórtune place, the strong'st suggestion
Our worser genius can, shall never melt
Mine honour into lust, to take away
The edge of that day's celebration,
When I shall think, or Phœbus' steeds are founder'd,
Or night kept chain'd below.
PRO.   Fairly spoke,
Sit then, and talk with her; she is thine own.—

What, Ariel! my industrious servant, Ariel!
Enter ARIEL.
ARI. What would my potent master? here I am.
PRO. Thou and thy meaner fellows your last service
Did worthily perform, and I must use you
In such another trick. Go, bring the rabble,
O'er whom I give thee power, here, to this place:
Incite them to quick motion; for I must
Bestow upon the eyes of this young couple
Some vanity of mine art: it is my promise,
And they expect it from me.
ARI.   Presently?
PRO. Ay, with a twink.
ARI. Before you can say, "Come" and "go,"
And breathe twice, and cry, "so so,"
Each one, tripping on his toe,
Will be here with mop and mow.
Do you love me, master? no?
PRO. Dearly, my delicate Ariel. Do not approach
Till thou dost hear me call.
ARI.   Well I conceive. [*Exit.*
PRO. Look, thou be true. Do not give dalliance
Too much the rein: the strongest oaths are straw
To the fire i' the blood. Be more abstemious,
Or else, good night, your vow.
FER.   I warrant you, Sir;
The white-cold virgin snow upon my heart
Abates the ardour of my liver.
PRO.   Well.—
Now come, my Ariel! bring a corollary,
Rather than want a spirit: appear, and pertly.—
No tongue, all eyes; be silent.
            [*Soft music.*
A Masque. Enter IRIS.
IRIS. Ceres, most bounteous lady, thy rich leas
Of wheat, rye, barley, vetches, oats, and peas;
Thy turfy mountains, where live nibbling sheep,
And flat meads thatch'd with stover, them to keep;
Thy banks with peonied and lilied brims,
Which spungy April at thy hest betrims,
To make cold nymphs chaste crowns; and thy broom groves,
Whose shadow the dismissed bachelor loves,
Being lass-lorn; thy pole-clipt vineyard;
And thy sea-marge, sterile, and rocky-hard,
Where thou thyself dost air: the queen o' the sky,
Whose watery arch and messenger am I,

Bids thee leave these; and with her sov-
　ereign grace,
Here on this grass-plot, in this very place,
To come and sport. Her peacocks fly
　amain:
Approach, rich Ceres, her to entertain.
　　　　　　Enter CERES.
CER. Hail, many-colour'd messenger, that
　ne'er
Dost disobey the wife of Jupiter;
Who, with thy saffron wings, upon my
　flowers
Diffusest honey-drops, refreshing showers;
And with each end of thy blue bow dost
　crown
My bosky acres, and my unshrubb'd down,
Rich scarf to my proud earth; why hath
　thy queen
Summon'd me hither, to this short-grass'd
　green?
IRIS. A contract of true love to celebrate,
And some donation freely to estate
On the bless'd lovers.
CER.　　　　Tell me, heavenly bow,
If Venus, or her son, as thou dost know,
Do now attend the queen? since they did
　plot
The means that dusky Dis my daughter
　got,
Her and her blind boy's scandal'd com-
I have forsworn.　　　　　　[pany
IRIS.　　　　　　Of her society
Be not afraid: I met her deity
Cutting the clouds towards Paphos, and
　her son
Dove-drawn with her. Here thought they
　to have done
Some wanton charm upon this man and
　maid,
Whose vows are, that no bed-rite shall be
　paid
Till Hymen's torch be lighted; but in
　vain:
Mars's hot minion is return'd again,
Her waspish-headed son has broke his ar-
　rows,
Swears he will shoot no more, but play
And be a boy right out.　　[with sparrows,
CER.　　　　Highest queen of state,
Great Juno comes; I know her by her gait.
　　　　　　Enter JUNO.
JUN. How does my bounteous sister? Go
　with me
To bless this twain, that they may pros-
　perous be,
And honour'd in their issue.

JUNO.　　　　SONG
　Honour, riches, marriage-blessing,
　Long continuance, and increasing,
　Hourly joys be still upon you!

Juno sings her blessings on you.
CER.
　Earth's increase, foison plenty,
　Barns and garners never empty;
　Vines, with clust'ring bunches growing;
　Plants, with goodly burden bowing;
　Spring come to you, at the farthest,
　In the very end of harvest!
　Scarcity and want shall shun you;
　Ceres' blessing so is on you.

FER. This is a most majestic vision, and
Harmonious charmingly. May I be bold
To think these spirits?
PRO.　　　　Spirits, which by mine art
I have from their confines call'd to enact
My present fancies.
FER.　　　　Let me live here ever:
So rare a wonder'd father, and a wife,
Make this place Paradise.
　　　[JUNO *and* CERES *whisper, and*
　　　　　　send IRIS *on employment.*
PRO. Sweet now, silence!
Juno and Ceres whisper seriously;
There's something else to do: hush, and be
Or else our spell is marr'd.　　[mute,
IRIS. You nymphs, call'd Naiads, of the
　winding brooks,
With your sedg'd crowns, and ever-harm-
　less looks,
Leave your crisp channels, and on this
　green land
Answer your summons: Juno does com-
　mand.
Come, temperate nymphs, and help to
　celebrate
A contract of true love: be not too late.
　　　　Enter certain Nymphs.
You sun-burn'd sicklemen, of August
　weary,
Come hither from the furrow, and be
　merry:
Make holiday: your rye-straw hats put on,
And these fresh nymphs encounter every
In country footing.　　　　　　[one
Enter certain Reapers, *properly habited:
they join with the* Nymphs *in a grace-
ful dance; towards the end whereof*
PROSPERO *starts suddenly, and speaks;
after which, to a strange, hollow, and
confused noise, they heavily vanish.*
PRO. [*Aside.*] I had forgot that foul
　conspiracy
Of the beast Caliban, and his confederates,
Against my life: the minute of their plot
Is almost come.—[*To the* Spirits.] Well
　done:—avoid,—no more.
FER. This is strange: your father's in some
　passion
That works him strongly.
MIRA.　　　　Never till this day,

Saw I him touch'd with anger so distemper'd.

PRO. You do look, my son, in a mov'd sort,
As if you were dismay'd: be cheerful, Sir.
Our revels now are ended. These our actors,
As I foretold you, were all spirits, and
Are melted into air, into thin air:
And, like the baseless fabric of this vision,
The cloud-capp'd towers, the gorgeous palaces,
The solemn temples, the great globe itself,
Yea, all which it inherit, shall dissolve,
And, like this insubstantial pageant faded,
Leave not a rack behind. We are such stuff
As dreams are made of, and our little life
Is rounded with a sleep.—Sir, I am vex'd:
Bear with my weakness; my old brain is troubled:
Be not disturb'd with my infirmity.
If you be pleas'd, retire into my cell,
And there repose: a turn or two I'll walk,
To still my beating mind.

FER. MIRA.　　　　　We wish your peace.
　　　　　　　　　　　　　　　　[*Exeunt.*

PRO. Come with a thought!—I thank you.—Ariel, come!

　　　　　Enter ARIEL.

ARI. Thy thoughts I cleave to. What's thy pleasure?

PRO.　　　　　　Spirit,
We must prepare to meet with Caliban.

ARI. Ay, my commander: when I presented Ceres,
I thought to have told thee of it; but I fear'd,
Lest I might anger thee.

PRO. Say again, where didst thou leave these varlets?

ARI. I told you, Sir, they were red-hot with drinking:
So full of valour, that they smote the air
For breathing in their faces; beat the ground
For kissing of their feet; yet always bending
Towards their project. Then I beat my tabor;
At which, like unback'd colts, they prick'd their ears,
Advanc'd their eye-lids, lifted up their noses,
As they smelt music: so I charm'd their ears,
That, calf-like, they my lowing follow'd through
Tooth'd briers, sharp furzes, pricking goss, and thorns,
Which enter'd their frail shins: at last I left them

I' the filthy mantled pool beyond your cell,
There dancing up to the chins, that the
O'erstunk their feet.　　　　　[foul lake

PRO.　　　　This was well done, my bird.
Thy shape invisible retain thou still:
The trumpery in my house, go, bring it hither,
For stale to catch these thieves.

ARI.　　　　　　I go, I go. [*Exit.*

PRO. A devil, a born devil, on whose nature
Nurture can never stick; on whom my pains,
Humanely taken, all, all lost, quite lost;
And as with age his body uglier grows,
So his mind cankers. I will plague them all,

　　Re-enter ARIEL, *loaden with glistering apparel, &c*

Even to roaring.—Come, hang them on this line.

PROSPERO *and* ARIEL *remain unseen. Enter* CALIBAN, STEPHANO, *and* TRINCULO, *all wet.*

CAL. Pray you, tread softly, that the blind mole may not
Hear a foot fall: we now are near his cell.

STE. Monster, your fairy, which you say is a harmless fairy, has done little better than played the Jack with us.

TRIN. Monster, I do smell all horse-piss; at which my nose is in great indignation.

STE. So is mine.—Do you hear, monster? If I should take a displeasure against you, look you,—

TRIN. Thou wert but a lost monster.

CAL. Good my lord, give me thy favour still.
Be patient, for the prize I'll bring thee to
Shall hood-wink this mischance: therefore speak softly;
All's hush'd as midnight yet.

TRIN. Ay, but to lose our bottles in the pool,—

STE. There is not only disgrace and dishonour in that, monster, but an infinite loss.

TRIN. That's more to me than my wetting: yet this is your harmless fairy, monster.

STE. I will fetch off my bottle, though I be o'er ears for my labour.

CAL. Pr'ythee, my king, be quiet. Seest thou here,
This is the mouth o' the cell: no noise, and enter.　　　　　[this island
Do that good mischief, which may make
Thine own for ever, and I, thy Caliban,
For aye thy foot-licker.

STE. Give me thy hand. I do begin to have bloody thoughts.

TRIN. O king Stephano! O peer! O worthy Stephano! look, what a wardrobe here is for thee!

CAL. Let it alone, thou fool; it is but trash.

TRIN. O, ho, monster! we know what belongs to a frippery.—O king Stephano!

STE. Put off that gown, Trinculo; by this hand, I'll have that gown.

TRIN. Thy grace shall have it.

CAL. The dropsy drown this fool! what do you mean,
To doat thus on such luggage? Let's along,
And do the murder first: if he awake,
From toe to crown he'll fill our skins with pinches,
Make us strange stuff.

STE. Be you quiet, monster. — Mistress line, is not this my jerkin? Now is the jerkin under the line: now, jerkin, you are like to lose your hair, and prove a bald jerkin.

TRIN. Do, do: we steal by line and level, and't like your grace.

STE. I thank thee for that jest; here's a garment for't: wit shall not go unrewarded, while I am king of this country. "Steal by line and level," is an excellent pass of pate; here's another garment for't.

TRIN. Monster, come, put some lime upon your fingers, and away with the rest.

CAL. I will have none on't: we shall lose our time,
And all be turn'd to barnacles, or to apes
With foreheads villainous low.

STE. Monster, lay-to your fingers: help, to bear this away, where my hogshead of wine is, or I'll turn you out of my kingdom. Go to; carry this.

TRIN. And this.

STE. Ay, and this.

A noise of hunters heard. Enter divers Spirits, in shape of hounds, and hunt them about; PROSPERO and ARIEL setting them on.

PRO. Hey, Mountain, hey!

ARI. Silver! there it goes, Silver!

PRO. Fury! Fury! there Tyrant, there! hark, hark!

　　[CAL., STE., *and* TRIN. *are driven out.*
Go, charge my goblins that they grind their joints
With dry convulsions; shorten up their sinews
With aged cramps; and more pinch-spotted make them,
Than pard, or cat o' mountain.

ARI. 　　　　　Hark! they roar.

PRO. Let them be hunted soundly. At this hour

Lie at my mercy all mine enemies:
Shortly shall all my labours end, and thou
Shalt have the air at freedom: for a little,
Follow, and do me service. 　　　[*Exeunt.*

ACT V.

SCENE I.—*Before the Cell of* PROSPERO.

Enter PROSPERO *in his magic robes; and* ARIEL.

PRO. Now does my project gather to a head:
My charms crack not; my spirits obey; and time 　　　　　　　　[day?
Goes upright with his carriage. How's the

ARI. On the sixth hour; at which time, You said our work should cease. [my lord,

PRO. 　　　　　I did say so,
When first I rais'd the tempest. Say, my spirit,
How fares the king and's followers?

ARI. 　　　　Confin'd together
In the same fashion as you gave in charge;
Just as you left them: all prisoners, Sir,
In the line-grove which weather-fends your cell;
They cannot budge till your release. The king,
His brothers, and yours, abide all three distracted;
And the remainder mourning over them,
Brimful of sorrow and dismay; but chiefly
Him that you term'd, Sir, "the good old lord Gonzalo:"
His tears run down his beard, like winter's drops
From eaves of reeds. Your charm so strong-ly works them,
That if you now beheld them, your affec- [tions
Would become tender. 　　　[tions

PRO. 　　　Dost thou think so, spirit?

ARI. Mine would, Sir, were I human.

PRO. 　　　　　　And mine shall.
Hast thou, which art but air, a touch, a feeling
Of their afflictions, and shall not myself,
One of their kind, that relish all as sharply,
Passion as they, be kindlier mov'd than thou art?
Though with their high wrongs I am struck to the quick,
Yet, with my nobler reason, 'gainst my fury
Do I take part. The rarer action is
In virtue, than in vengeance: they being penitent,
The sole drift of my purpose doth extend
Not a frown farther. Go, release them, Ariel.
My charms I'll break, their senses I'll re- [store,
And they shall be themselves. 　　　[store,

ARI. 　　　　I'll fetch them, Sir. [*Exit.*

PRO. Ye elves of hills, brooks, standing lakes, and groves;
And ye, that on the sands with printless foot
Do chase the ebbing Neptune, and do fly him,
When he comes back; you demy-puppets, that
By moonshine do the green-sour ringlets make,
Whereof the ewe not bites; and you, whose pastime
Is to make midnight mushrooms; that rejoice
To hear the solemn curfew; by whose aid
(Weak masters though ye be) I have bedimm'd
The noontide sun, call'd forth the mutinous winds,
And 'twixt the green sea and the azur'd vault
Set roaring war: to the dread rattling thunder
Have I given fire, and rifted Jove's stout oak
With his own bolt: the strong-bas'd promontory
Have I made shake; and by the spurs pluck'd up
The pine and cedar: graves, at my command,
Have waked their sleepers; oped, and let them forth
By my so potent art. But this rough magic
I here abjure; and, when I have requir'd
Some heavenly music, (which even now I do)
To work mine end upon their senses, that
This airy charm is for, I'll break my staff,
Bury it certain fathoms in the earth,
And, deeper than did ever plummet sound,
I'll drown my book.   [*Solemn music.*

Re-enter ARIEL: *after him,* ALONSO, *with a frantic gesture, attended by* GONZALO; SEBASTIAN *and* ANTONIO *in like manner, attended by* ADRIAN *and* FRANCISCO: *they all enter the circle which* PROSPERO *had made, and there stand charmed; which* PROSPERO *observing, speaks.*

A solemn air, and the best comforter
To an unsettled fancy, cure thy brains,
Now useless, boil'd within thy skull! There
For you are spell-stopp'd.—   [stand,
Holy Gonzalo, honourable man,
Mine eyes, even sociable to the show of thine,
Fall fellowly drops.—The charm dissolves apace;
And as the morning steals upon the night,
Melting the darkness, so their rising senses

Begin to chase the ignorant fumes tha mantle
Their clearer reason.—O good Gonzalo!
My true preserver, and a loyal Sir
To him thou follow'st, I will pay thy grace
Home, both in word and deed.—Mos cruelly
Didst thou, Alonso, use me and m daughter:
Thy brother was a fartherer in the act;—
Thou'rt pinch'd for't now, Sebastian.—Fles and blood,
You brother mine, that entertain'd ambitio
Expell'd remorse and nature; who, wit Sebastian,
(Whose inward pinches therefore are mos strong)
Would here have kill'd your king; I d forgive thee,
Unnatural though thou art.—Their under standing
Begins to swell, and the approaching tide
Will shortly fill the reasonable shores,
That now lie foul and muddy. Not one o them
That yet looks on me, or would know me.— Ariel,
Fetch me the hat and rapier in my cell:—
            [*Exit* ARIEL
I will dis-case me, and myself present,
As I was sometime Milan.—Quickly, spirit
Thou shalt ere long be free.

ARIEL *re-enters, singing, and helps t attire* PROSPERO.
ARI.

Where the bee sucks, there suck I:
In a cowslip's bell I lie;
There I couch when owls do cry.
On the bat's back I do fly
After summer, merrily.
Merrily, merrily shall I live now,
Under the blossom that hangs on th bough.

PRO. Why, that's my dainty Ariel! shall miss thee;
But yet thou shalt have freedom:—so, so so.—
To the king's ship, invisible as thou art:
There shalt thou find the mariners asleep
Under the hatches; the master and th boatswain
Being awake, enforce them to this place,
And presently, I pr'ythee.
ARI. I drink the air before me, and retur
Or e'er your pulse twice beat.   [*Exit*
GON. All torment, trouble, wonder, and amazement
Inhabit here: some heavenly power guide u
Out of this fearful country!
PRO.   Behold, sir king

The wronged duke of Milan, Prospero.
For more assurance that a living prince
Does now speak to thee, I embrace thy
　body;
And to thee and thy company, I bid
A hearty welcome.
ALON.　　Whe'r thou beest he, or no,
Or some enchanted trifle to abuse me,
As late I have been, I not know: thy pulse
Beats, as of flesh and blood; and, since
　I saw thee,
Th' affliction of my mind amends, with
　which,
I fear, a madness held me. This must crave
(An if this be at all) a most strange story.
Thy dukedom I resign; and do entreat
Thou pardon me my wrongs.—But how
Be living, and be here?　[should Prospero
PRO.　　　　　First, noble friend,
Let me embrace thine age, whose honour
Be measur'd, or confin'd.　　　　[cannot
GON.　　　　　Whether this be,
Or be not, I'll not swear.
PRO.　　　　You do yet taste
Some subtilties o' the isle, that will not
　let you
Believe　things　certain. — Welcome,　my
　friends all:—
[*Aside to* SEB. *and* ANT.] But you, my brace
　of lords, were I so minded,
I here could pluck his highness' frown
　upon you,
And justify you traitors: at this time
I will tell no tales.
SEB. [*Aside.*] The devil speaks in him.
PRO.　　　　　　　　No.—
For you, most wicked Sir, whom to call
　brother
Would even infect my mouth, I do forgive
Thy rankest fault; all of them; and require
My dukedom of thee, which, perforce, I
Thou must restore.　　　　　　[know,
ALON.　　　If thou beest Prospero,
Give us particulars of thy preservation:
How thou hast met us here, who three hours
　since
Were wreck'd upon this shore; where I
　have lost,
(How sharp the point of this remembrance
My dear son Ferdinand.　　　　　[is!)
PRO.　　　I am woe for't, Sir.
ALON. Irreparable is the loss; and
Says it is past her cure.　　　[patience
PRO.　　　I rather think,
You have not sought her help; of whose
　soft grace,
For the like loss I have her sovereign aid,
And rest myself content.
ALON.　　You the like loss?
PRO. As great to me, as late; and, sup-
portable

To make the dear loss, have I means much
　weaker
Than you may call to comfort you; for I
Have lost my daughter.
ALON.　　　　　A daughter?
O heavens! that they were living both in
　Naples,
The king and queen there! that they were,
　I wish
Myself were mudded in that oozy bed
Where my son lies. When did you lose your
　daughter?
PRO. In this last tempest. I perceive,
　these lords
At this encounter do so much admire,
That they devour their reason, and scarce
　think
Their eyes do offices of truth, their words
Are natural breath: but, howsoe'er you have
Been justled from your senses, know for
　certain,
That I am Prospero, and that very duke
Which was thrust forth of Milan; who most
　strangely
Upon this shore, where you were wreck'd,
　was landed,
To be the lord on't. No more yet of this;
For 'tis a chronicle of day by day,
Not a relation for a breakfast, nor
Befitting this first meeting. Welcome, Sir;
This cell's my court: here have I few
　attendants,
And subjects none abroad: pray you, look in.
My dukedom since you have given me again,
I will requite you with as good a thing;
At least, bring forth a wonder, to content ye
As much as me my dukedom.
*The entrance of the Cell opens, and dis-
covers* FERDINAND *and* MIRANDA *playing
at chess.*
MIRA. Sweet lord, you play me false.
FER.　　　No, my dearest love,
I would not for the world.
MIRA. Yes, for a score of kingdoms you
　should wrangle,
And I would call it fair play.
ALON.　　　　If this prove
A vision of the island, one dear son
Shall I twice lose.
SEB.　　　A most high miracle!
FER. Though the seas threaten, they are
　merciful:
I have curs'd them without cause.
　　　　　　　[FERD. *kneels to* ALON.
ALON.　　Now, all the blessings
Of a glad father compass thee about!
Arise, and say how thou cam'st here.
MIRA.　　　　　O, wonder!
How many goodly creatures are there here!
How beauteous mankind is! O, brave new
That has such people in't!　　　[world,

PRO.   'Tis new to thee.
ALON. What is this maid, with whom
  thou wast at play?
Your eld'st acquaintance cannot be three
  hours:
Is she the goddess that hath sever'd us,
And brought us thus together?
FER.   Sir, she is mortal;
But, by immortal providence, she's mine:
I chose her, when I could not ask my father
For his advice, nor thought I had one. She
Is daughter to this famous duke of Milan,
Of whom so often I have heard renown,
But never saw before; of whom I have
Received a second life; and second father
This lady makes him to me.
ALON.   I am hers.
But O! how oddly will it sound, that I
Must ask my child forgiveness.
PRO.   There, Sir, stop:
Let us not burden our remembrances
With a heaviness that's gone.
GON.   I have inly wept,
Or should have spoke ere this.—Look down,
  you gods,
And on this couple drop a blessed crown!
For it is you that have chalk'd forth the
Which brought us hither.   [way,
ALON.   I say, Amen, Gonzalo!
GON. Was Milan thrust from Milan, that
  his issue
Should become kings of Naples? O! rejoice
Beyond a common joy, and set it down
With gold on lasting pillars: in one voyage
Did Claribel her husband find at Tunis;
And Ferdinand, her brother, found a wife
Where he himself was lost; Prospero, his
  dukedom
In a poor isle; and all of us, ourselves
When no man was his own.
ALON. [*To* FER. *and* MIR.] Give me your
  hands:
Let grief and sorrow still embrace his heart,
That doth not wish you joy!
GON.   Be it so: Amen!
Re-enter ARIEL, *with the* Master *and* Boat-
  swain *amazedly following.*
O look, Sir! look, Sir! heer are more of us.
I prophesied, if a gallows were on land,
This fellow could not drown.—Now,
  blasphemy,
That swear'st grace o'erboard, not an oath
  on shore?
Hast thou no mouth by land? What is the
  news?
BOATS. The best news is, that we have
  safely found
Our king and company: the next, our
  ship,—
Which, but three glasses since, we gave
  out split,—

Is tight, and yare, and bravely rigg'd, as
We first put out to sea.   [when
ARI. [*Aside to* PRO.] Sir, all this service
Have I done since I went.
PRO. [*Aside to* ARI.] My tricksy spirit!
ALON. These are not natural events;
  they strengthen
From strange to stranger.—Say, how came
  you hither?
BOATS. If I did think, Sir, I were well
  awake,
I'd strive to tell you. We were dead of
  sleep,
And (how we know not) all clapp'd under
  hatches,
Where, but even now, with strange and
  several noises
Of roaring, shrieking, howling, jingling
  chains,
And more diversity of sounds, all horrible,
We were awak'd; straightway, at liberty:
Where we, in all her trim, freshly beheld
Our royal, good, and gallant ship; our
  master
Capering to eye her: on a trice, so please
  you,
Even in a dream, were we divided from
And were brought moping hither.   [them,
ARI. [*Aside to* PRO.] Was't well done?
PRO. [*Aside to* ARI.] Bravely, my dili-
  gence! Thou shalt be free.
ALON. This is as strange a maze as e'er
  men trod;
And there is in this business more than
Was ever conduct of: some oracle   [nature
Must rectify our knowledge.
PRO.   Sir, my liege,
Do not infest your mind with beating on
The strangeness of this business: at pick'd
  leisure,
Which shall be shortly, single I'll resolve
  you
(Which to you shall seem probable) of
  every
These happen'd accidents; till when, be
  cheerful.
And think of each thing well.—   [*Aside to*
  ARI.] Come hither, spirit:
Set Caliban and his companions free;
Untie the spell. [*Exit* ARIEL.] How fares
  my gracious Sir?
There are yet missing of your company
Some few odd lads, that you remember not.
Re-enter ARIEL, *driving in* CALIBAN, STE-
  PHANO, *and* TRINCULO, *in their stolen
  apparel.*
STE. Every man shift for all the rest,
and let no man take care for himself, for
all is but fortune.—Coragio! bully-monster,
coragio!

TRIN. If these be true spies which I wear
in my head, here's a goodly sight.
CAL. O Setebos! these be brave spirits,
indeed.
How fine my master is! I am afraid
He will chastise me.
SEB.   Ha, ha!
What things are these, my lord Antonio?
Will money buy them?
ANT.   Very like; one of them
Is a plain fish, and, no doubt, marketable.
PRO. Mark but the badges of these men,
my lords,
Then say, if they be true.—This mis-shapen
knave,
His mother was a witch; and one so strong
That could control the moon, make flows
and ebbs,
And deal in her command, without her
power.
These three have robb'd me; and this demi-
devil
(For he's a bastard one) had plotted with
them
To take my life: two of these fellows you
Must know, and own; this thing of dark-
Acknowledge mine.   [ness I
CAL.   I shall be pinch'd to death.
ALON. Is not this Stephano, my drunken
butler?
SEB. He is drunk now: where had he
wine?
ALON. And Trinculo is reeling ripe;
where should they
Find this grand liquor that hath gilded
How cam'st thou in this pickle? [them?—
TRIN. I have been in such a pickle,
since I saw you last, that, I fear me, will
never out of my bones: I shall not fear
fly-blowing.
SEB. Why, how now, Stephano!
STE! O! touch me not: I am not Ste-
phano, but a cramp.
PRO. You'd be king of the isle, sirrah?
STE. I should have been a sore one, then.
ALON. This is as strange a thing as e'er
I looked on.   [*Pointing to* CALIBAN.
PRO. He is as disproportion'd in his
manners,
As in his shape.—Go, sirrah, to my cell;
Take with you your companions: as you
look
To have my pardon, trim it handsomely.
CAL. Ay, that I will; and I'll be wise
hereafter,
And seek for grace. What a thrice-double
ass

Was I, to take this drunkard for a god,
And worship this dull fool!
PRO.   Go to; away!
ALON. Hence, and bestow your luggage
where you found it.
SEB. Or stole it, rather
              [*Exeunt* CAL., STE., *and* TRIN.
PRO. Sir, I invite your highness, and
your train,
To my poor cell, where you shall take your
rest
For this one night; which, part of it, I'll
waste
With such discourse, as, I not doubt, shall
make it
Go quick away; the story of my life,
And the particular accidents gone by,
Since I came to this isle: and in the morn
I'll bring you to your ship, and so to Naples,
Where I have hope to see the nuptial
Of these our dear-beloved solemniz d;
And thence retire me to my Milan, where
Every third thought shall be my grave.
ALON.   I long
To hear the story of your life, which must
Take the ear strangely.
PRO.   I'll deliver all;
And promise you calm seas, auspicious
gales,
And sail so expeditious, that shall catch
Your royal fleet far off.—[*Aside to* ARI.]
              My Ariel;—chick,—
That is thy charge: then to the elements
Be free, and fare thou well!—Please you,
draw near.   [*Exeunt.*

EPILOGUE. Spoken by PROSPERO.
Now my charms are all o'erthrown,
And what strength I have's mine own,—
Which is most faint: now, 'tis true,
I must be here confin'd by you,
Or sent to Naples. Let me not,
Since I have my dukedom got,
And pardon'd the deceiver, dwell
In this bare island, by your spell;
But release me from my bands,
With the help of your good hands.

Gentle breath of yours my sails
Must fill, or else my project fails,
Which was to please. Now I want
Spirits to enforce, art to enchant;
And my ending is despair,
Unless I be reliev'd by prayer;
Which pierces so, that it assaults
Mercy itself, and frees all faults.
    As you from crimes would pardon'd be,
    Let your indulgence set me free.

Slender and Dr. Caius complaining to Page that they have been cozened by Anne Page.
Act V. S. 4.

MERRY WIVES OF WINDSOR

DRAMATIS PERSONÆ.

Sir JOHN FALSTAFF.
FENTON.
SHALLOW, *a Country Justice.*
SLENDER, *cousin to* SHALLOW.
FORD, ⎱ *two Gentlemen dwelling at*
PAGE, ⎰   Windsor
WILLIAM PAGE, *a Boy, son to* PAGE.
Sir HUGH EVANS, *a Welsh Parson.*
Dr. CAIUS, *a French Physician.*
Host of the Garter Inn.
BARDOLPH, ⎫
PISTOL,   ⎬ *followers of* FALSTAFF.
NYM,   ⎭

ROBIN, *page to* FALSTAFF.
SIMPLE, *servant to* SLENDER.
RUGBY, *servant to* Dr. CAIUS.

Mistress FORD.
Mistress PAGE.
ANNE PAGE, *her daughter, in love with*
    FENTON.
Mistress QUICKLY, *servant to* Dr. CAIUS.

Servants *to* PAGE, FORD, &c.

SCENE,—WINDSOR; *and the neighbourhood.*

ACT I.

SCENE I.—WINDSOR. *Before* PAGE'S *House.*

Enter Justice SHALLOW, SLENDER, *and Sir* HUGH EVANS.

SHAL. Sir Hugh, persuade me not; I will make a Star-chamber matter of it: if he were twenty Sir John Falstaffs, he shall not abuse Robert Shallow, Esquire.

SLEN. In the county of Gloster, justice of peace, and *coram.*

SHAL. Ay, cousin Slender, and *custalorum.*

SLEN. Ay, and *ratolorum* to; and a gentleman born, master parson; who writes himself *armigero,*—in any bill, warrant, quittance, or obligation, *armigero.*

SHAL. Ay, that I do; and have done any time these three hundred years.

SLEN. All his successors, gone before him, have don't; and all his ancestors, that

28

come after him, may: they may give the dozen white luces in their coat.

SHAL. It is an old coat.

EVA. The dozen white louses do become an old coat well; it agrees well, passant: it is a familiar beast to man, and signifies— love.

SHAL. The luce is the fresh fish; the salt fish is an old coat.

SLEN. I may quarter, coz?

SHAL. You may, by marrying.

EVA. It is marring, indeed, if he quarter it.

SHAL. Not a whit.

EVA. Yes, py'r lady; if he has a quarter of your coat, there is but three skirts for yourself, in my simple conjectures: but that is all one. If Sir John Falstaff have committed disparagements unto you, I am of the church, and will be glad to do my benevolence, to make atonements and com- promises between you.

SHAL. The council shall hear it: it is a riot.

EVA. It is not meet the council hear a riot; there is no fear of Got in a riot: the council, look you, shall desire to hear the fear of Got, and not to hear a riot; take your vizaments in that.

SHAL. Ha! o' my life, if I were young again, the sword should end it.

EVA. It is petter that friends is the sword, and end it: and there is also an- other device in my prain, which, peradven- ture, prings goot discretions with it: there is Anne Page, which is daughter to master George Page, which is pretty virginity.

SLEN. Mistress Anne Page? She has brown hair, and speaks small, like a woman.

EVA. It is that fery person for all the 'orld, as just as you will desire; and seven hundred pounds of monies, and gold, and silver, is her grandsire, upon his death's- bed, (Got deliver to a joyful resurrections!) give, when she is able to overtake seventeen years old. It were a goot motion if we leave our pribbles and prabbles, and desire a marriage between master Abraham and mis- tress Anne Page.

SHAL. Did her grandsire leave her seven hundred pound?

EVA. Ay, and her father is make her a petter penny.

SHAL. I know the young gentlewoman; she has good gifts.

EVA. Seven hundred pounds and possi- bilities, is good gifts.

SHAL. Well, let us see honest master Page. Is Falstaff there?

EVA. Shall I tell you a lie? I do despise a liar, as I do despise one that is false; or as I despise one that is not true. The knight, Sir John, is there; and, I beseech you, be ruled by your well-willers. I will peat the door for master Page. [*Knocks.*] What, ho! Got pless your house here!

PAGE. [*Within.*] Who's there?

EVA. Here is Got's plessing, and your friend, and justice Shallow; and here young master Slender, that peradventures, shall tell you another tale, if matters grow to your likings.

Enter PAGE.

PAGE. I am glad to see your worships well. I thank you for my venison, master Shallow.

SHAL. Master Page, I am glad to see you: much good do it your good heart! I wished your venison better; it was ill kill'd.—How doth good mistress Page?— and I thank you always with my heart, la; with my heart.

PAGE. Sir, I thank you.

SHAL. Sir, I thank you; by yea and no, I do.

PAGE. I am glad to see you, good master Slender.

SLEN. How does your fallow greyhound, Sir? I heard say, he was outrun on Cotsall.

PAGE. It could not be judged, Sir.

SLEN. You'll not confess, you'll not con- fess.

SHAL. That he will not:—'tis your fault, 'tis your fault:—'Tis a good dog.

PAGE. A cur, Sir.

SHAL. Sir, he's a good dog, and a fair dog; can there be more said? he is good, and fair.—Is Sir John Falstaff here?

PAGE. Sir, he is within; and I would I could do a good office between you.

EVA. It is spoke as a Christians ought to speak.

SHAL. He hath wronged me, master Page.

PAGE. Sir, he doth in some sort confess it.

SHAL. If it be confessed, it is not re- dressed: is not that so, master Page? He hath wronged me; indeed, he hath;—at a word, he hath;—believe me:—Robert Shal- low, Esquire, saith, he is wronged.

PAGE. Here comes Sir John.

Enter Sir JOHN FALSTAFF, BARDOLPH, NYM, *and* PISTOL.

FAL. Now, master Shallow,—you'll com- plain of me to the king?

SHAL. Knight, you have beaten my men, killed my deer, and broke open my lodge.

FAL. But not kissed your keeper's daugh- ter?

SHAL. Tut, a pin! this shall be answered.

FAL. I will answer it straight:—I have done all this.—That is now answered.

SHAL. The council shall know this.

FAL. 'Twere better for you, if it were known in counsel: you'll be laughed at.

EVA. *Pauca verba*, Sir John; goot worts.

FAL. Good worts! good cabbage.—Slender, I broke your head; what matter have you against me?

SLEN. Marry, Sir, I have matter in my head against you; and against your coney-catching rascals, Bardolph, Nym, and Pistol: they carried me to the tavern, and made me drunk, and afterwards picked my pocket.

BARD. You Banbury cheese!

SLEN. Ay, it is no matter.

PIST. How now, Mephostophilus!

SLEN. Ay, it is no matter.

NYM. Slice, I say! *pauca, pauca*; slice! that's my humour.

SLEN. Where's Simple, my man?—can you tell, cousin?

EVA. Peace, I pray you. Now let us understand: there is three umpires in this matter, as I understand; that is—master Page, *fidelicet*, master Page; and there is myself, *fidelicet*, myself; and the three party is, lastly and finally, mine host of the Garter.

PAGE. We three, to hear it, and end it between them.

EVA. Fery goot: I will make a prief of it in my note-book; and we will afterwards 'ork upon the cause, with as great discreetly as we can.

FAL. Pistol,—

PIST. He hears with ears.

EVA. The tevil and his tam! what phrase is this, "He hears with ear?" Why, it is affectations.

FAL. Pistol, did you pick master Slender's purse?

SLEN. Ay, by these gloves, did he,—or I would I might never come in mine own great chamber again else,—of seven groats in mill-sixpences, and two Edward shovel-boards, that cost me two shilling and two pence a-piece of Yead Miller, by these gloves.

FAL. Is this true, Pistol?

EVA. No; it is false, if it is a pick-purse.

PIST. Ha, thou mountain-foreigner!— Sir John and master mine,
I combat challenge of this latten bilbo.— Word of denial in thy labras here; Word of denial: froth and scum, thou liest.

SLEN. By these gloves, then, 'twas he.

NYM. Be advised, Sir, and pass good humours. I will say, "marry trap," with you, if you run the nuthook's humour on me; that is the very note of it.

SLEN. By this hat, then, he in the red face had it; for though I cannot remember what I did when you made me drunk, yet I am not altogether an ass.

FAL. What say you, Scarlet and John?

BARD. Why, Sir, for my part, I say, the gentleman had drunk himself out of his five sentences,—

EVA. It is his "five senses;" fie, what the ignorance is!

BARD. And being fap, Sir, was, as they say, cashier'd; and so conclusions pass'd the careires.

SLEN. Ay, you spake in Latin then too; but 'tis no matter: I'll ne'er be drunk whilst I live again, but in honest, civil, godly company, for this trick: if I be drunk, I'll be drunk with those that have the fear of God, and not with drunken knaves.

EVA. So Got 'udge me, that is a firtuous mind.

FAL. You hear all these matters denied, gentlemen; you hear it.

Enter ANNE PAGE *with Wine; Mistress* FORD *and Mistress* PAGE.

PAGE. Nay, daughter, carry the wine in; we'll drink within.   [*Exit* ANNE PAGE.

SLEN. O heaven! this is mistress Anne Page.

PAGE. How now, mistress Ford!

FAL. Mistress Ford, by my troth, you are very well met: by your leave, good mistress.   [*Kissing her.*

PAGE. Wife, bid these gentlemen welcome.—Come, we have a hot venison pasty to dinner: come, gentlemen, I hope we shall drink down all unkindness.

[*Exeunt all but* SHAL., SLEN., *and* EVANS.

SLEN. I had rather than forty shillings, I had my Book of Songs and Sonnets here.

Enter SIMPLE.

How now, Simple! Where have you been? I must wait on myself, must I? You have not the Book of riddles about you, have you?

SIM. Book of riddles! why, did you not lend it to Alice Shortcake upon Allhallowmas last, a fortnight afore Michaelmas?

SHAL. Come, coz; come, coz; we stay for you. A word with you, coz; marry, this, coz: there is, as 'twere, a tender, a kind of tender, made afar off by Sir Hugh here: do you understand me?

SLEN. Ay, Sir, you shall find me reasonable: if it be so, I shall do that that is reason.

SHAL. Nay, but understand me.

SLEN. So I do, Sir.

EVA. Give ear to his motions, master Slender: I will description the matter to you, if you be capacity of it.

SLEN. Nay, I will do as my cousin Shallow says: I pray you pardon me; he's a

justice of peace in his country, simple
though I stand here.

EVA. But that is not the question: the
question is concerning your marriage.

SHAL. Ay, there's the point, Sir.

EVE. Marry, is it; the very point of
it; to mistress Anne Page.

SLEN. Why, if it be so, I will marry her
upon any reasonable demands.

EVA. But can you affection the 'oman?
Let us command to know that of your
mouth, or of vour lips; for divers philoso-
phers hold, that the lips is parcel of the
mouth: therefore, precisely, can you carry
your good will to the maid?

SHAL. Cousin Abraham Slender, can you
love her?

SLEN. I hope, Sir, I will do as it shall
become one that would do reason.

EVA. Nay Got's lords and his ladies, you
must speak possitable, if you can carry her
your desires towards her.

SHAL. That you must. Will you, upon
good dowry marry her?

SLEN. I will do a greater thing than
that, upon your request, cousin, in any
reason.

SHAL. Nay, conceive me, conceive me,
sweet coz: what I do, is to pleasure you,
coz. Can you love the maid?

SLEN. I will marry her, Sir, at your request; but if there be no great love in the
beginning, yet heaven may decrease it upon
better acquaintance, when we are married,
and have more occasion to know one another: I hope, upon familiarity will grow
more contempt: but if you say, "marry
her," I will marry her; that I am freely
dissolved, and dissolutely.

EVA. It is a fery discretion answer:
save, the faul' is in the 'ort "dissolutely:"
the 'ort is, according to our meaning,
"resolutely."—His meaning is goot.

SHAL. Ay, I think my cousin meant well.

SLEN. Ay, or else I would I might be
hanged, la.

SHAL. Here comes fair mistress Anne.
—[*Re-enter* ANNE PAGE.] Would I were
young for your sake, mistress Anne!

ANNE. The dinner is on the table; my
father desires your worships' company.

SHAL. I will wait on him, fair mistress
Anne.

EVA. Od's plessed will! I will not be
absence at the grace.

[*Exeunt* SHALLOW *and* Sir H. EVANS.

ANNE. Will't please your worship to come
in, Sir?

SLEN. No, I thank you, forsooth, heartily; I am very well.

ANNE. The dinner attends you, Sir.

SLEN. I am not a-hungry, I thank you,
forsooth.—Go, sirrah, for all you are my
man, go, wait upon my cousin Shallow.
[*Exit* SIMPLE.] A justice of peace sometime may be beholden to his friend for a
man.—I keep but three men and a boy yet,
till my mother be dead; but what though?
yet I live like a poor gentleman born.

ANNE. I may not go in without your
worship: they will not sit till you come.

SLEN. I' faith, I'll eat nothing; I thank
you as much as though I did.

ANNE. I pray you, Sir, walk in.

SLEN. I had rather walk here, I thank
you. I bruised my shin the other day with
playing at sword and dagger with a master
of fence,—three veneys for a dish of stewed
prunes;—and, by my troth, I cannot abide
the smell of hot meat since.—Why do your
dogs bark so? be there bears i' the town?

ANNE. I think there are, Sir; I heard
them talked of.

SLEN. I love the sport well; but I shall
as soon quarrel at it as any man in England.—You are afraid, if you see the bear
loose, are you not?

ANNE. Ay, indeed, Sir.

SLEN. That's meat and drink to me,
now: I have seen Sackerson loose twenty
times, and have taken him by the chain;
but, I warrant you, the women have so
cried and shriek'd at it, that it passed: but
women, indeed, cannot abide 'em; they are
very ill-favoured rough things.

Re-enter PAGE.

PAGE. Come, gentle master Slender,
come; we stay for you.

SLEN. I'll eat nothing, I thank you, Sir.

PAGE. By cock and pye, you shall not
choose, Sir: come, come.

SLEN. Nay, pray you, lead the way.

PAGE. Come on, Sir.

SLEN. Mistress Anne, yourself shall go
first.

ANNE. Not I, Sir; pray you, keep on.

SLEN. Truly, I will not go first; truly,
la; I will not do you that wrong.

ANNE. I pray you, Sir.

SLEN. I'll rather be unmannerly, than
troublesome. You do yourself wrong, indeed, la. [*Exeunt.*

SCENE II.—*The Same.*

Enter Sir HUGH EVANS *and* SIMPLE.

EVA. Go your ways, and ask of Doctor
Caius' house, which is the way: and there
dwells one mistress Quickly, which is in the
manner of his nurse, or his dry nurse, or
his cook, or his laundry, his washer, and
his wringer.

SIM. Well, Sir.

EVA. Nay, it is petter yet.—Give her this letter; for it is a 'oman that altoget her's acquaintance with mistress Anne Page: and the letter is, to desire and require her to solicit your master's desires to mistress Anne Page. I pray you, be gone. I will make an end of my dinner; there's pippins and cheese to come.   [*Exeunt.*

SCENE III.—*A Room in the* Garter Inn.

Enter FALSTAFF, HOST, BARDOLPH, NYM, PISTOL, *and* ROBIN.

FAL. Mine host of the Garter,—

HOST. What says my bully-rook? Speak scholarly and wisely.

FAL. Truly, mine host, I must turn away some of my followers.

HOST. Discard, bully Hercules; cashier: let them wag; trot, trot.

FAL. I sit at ten pounds a week.

HOST. Thou'rt an emperor, Cæsar, Keisar, and Pheezar. I will entertain Bardolph; he shall draw, he shall tap: said I well, bully Hector?

FAL. Do so, good mine host.

HOST. I have spoke; let him follow.— Let me see thee froth and lime: I am at a word; follow.   [*Exit.*

FAL. Bardolph, follow him. A tapster is a good trade: an old cloak makes a new jerkin; a withered serving-man, a fresh tapster. Go; adieu.

BARD. It is a life that I have desired: I will thrive.

PIST. O base Gongarian wight! wilt thou the spigot wield?   [*Exit* BARD.

NYM. He was gotten in drink: is not the humour conceited? His mind is not heroic, and there's the humour of it.

FAL. I am glad I am so acquit of this tinder-box: his thefts were too open; his filching was like an unskilful singer,—he kept not time.

NYM. The good humour is to steal at a minim's rest.

PIST. "Convey," the wise it call. "Steal!" foh! a fico for the phrase!

FAL. Well, Sirs, I am almost out at heels.

PIST. Why, then, let kibes ensue.

FAL. There is no remedy; I must coneycatch; I must shift.

PIST. Young ravens must have food.

FAL. Which of you know Ford of this town?

PIST. I ken the wight: he is of substance good.

FAL. My honest lads, I will tell you what I am about.

PIST. Two yards, and more.

FAL. No quips now, Pistol; indeed, I am in the waist two yards about; but I am now about no waste; I am about thrift. Briefly, I do mean to make love to Ford's wife: I spy entertainment in her; she discourses, she carves, she gives the leer of invitation: I can construe the action of her familiar style; and the hardest voice of her behaviour, to be Englished rightly, is, "I am Sir John Falstaff's."

PIST. He hath studied her well, and translated her well,—out of honesty into English.

NYM. The anchor is deep: will that humour pass?

FAL. Now, the report goes, she has all the rule of her husband's purse; he hath a legion of angels.

PIST. As many devils entertain; and "To her, boy," say I.

NYM. The humour rises; it is good: humour me the angels.

FAL. I have writ me here a letter to her; and here another to Page's wife, who even now gave me good eyes too, examined my parts with most judicious eyeliads: sometimes the beam of her view gilded my foot, sometimes my portly belly.

PIST. Then did the sun on dunghill shine.

NYM. I thank thee for that humour.

FAL. O, she did so course o'er my exteriors with such a greedy intention, that the appetite of her eye did seem to scorch me up like a burning-glass! Here's another letter to her: she bears the purse too; she is a region in Guiana, all gold and bounty. I will be cheater to them both, and they shall be exchequers to me: they shall be my East and West Indies, and I will trade to them both. Go, bear thou this letter to mistress Page; and thou this to mistress Ford. We will thrive, lads, we will thrive.

PIST. Shall I Sir Pandarus of Troy become,
And by my side wear steel? then, Lucifer take all!

NYM. I will run no base humour: here, take the humour-letter. I will keep the 'haviour of reputation.

FAL. [*To* ROBIN.] Hold, sirrah, bear you these letters tightly:
Sail like my pinnace to these golden shores.—   [*Exit* ROBIN.
Rogues, hence! avaunt! vanish like hailstones, go;
Trudge, plod away o' the hoof; seek shelter, pack!
Falstaff will learn the humour of this age,
French thrift, you rogues; myself, and skirted page.   [*Exit.*

PIST. Let vultures gripe thy guts for
gourd and fullam holds.
And high and low beguile the rich and poor.
Tester I'll have in pouch, when thou shalt
Base Phrygian Turk!   [lack,
NYM. I have operations in my head,
which be humours of revenge.
PIST. Wilt thou revenge?
NYM. By welkin, and her stars!
PIST. With wit, or steel?
NYM. With both the humours, I:
I will discuss the humour of this love to
Page.
PIST. And I to Ford shall eke unfold,
How Falstaff, varlet vile,
His dove will prove, his gold will
hold,
And his soft couch defile.
NYM. My humour shall not cool: I will
incense Page to deal with poison; I will
possess him with yellowness, for the revolt
of mien is dangerous: that is my true
humour.
PIST. Thou art the Mars of malcontents:
I second thee; troop on.   [*Exeunt.*

SCENE IV.—*A Room in Dr.* CAIUS'S *House.*

Enter Mistress QUICKLY *and* SIMPLE.
QUICK. What, John Rugby! [*Enter*
RUGBY.] I pray there, go to the casement,
and see if you can see my master, master
Doctor Caius, coming: if he do, i' faith,
and find any body in the house, here will be
an old abusing of God's patience, and the
king's English.
RUG. I'll go watch.
QUICK. Go; and we'll have a posset
for't soon at night, in faith, at the latter
end of a sea-coal fire. [*Exit* RUGBY.] An
honest, willing, kind fellow, as ever servant
shall come in house withal; and, I warrant
you, no tell-tale, nor no breed-bate: his
worst fault is, that he is given to prayer;
he is something peevish that way: but nobody but has his fault; but let that pass.
—Peter Simple, you say your name is?
SIM. Ay, for fault of a better.
QUICK. And master Slender's your master?
SIM. Ay, forsooth.
QUICK. Does he not wear a great round
beard, like a glover's paring-knife?
SIM. No, forsooth: he hath but a little
wee face, with a little yellow beard,—a
cane-coloured beard.
QUICK. A softly-sprighted man, is he not?
SIM. Ay, forsooth; but he is as tall a
man of his hands, as any is between this
and his head: he hath fought with a war-
rener.

QUICK. How say you?—O, I should remember him: does he not hold up his head,
as it were, and strut in his gait?
SIM. Yes, indeed, does he.
QUICK. Well, heaven send Anne Page
no worse fortune! Tell master parson
Evans, I will do what I can for your master: Anne is a good girl, and I wish—
Re-enter RUGBY.
RUG. Out, alas! here comes my master.
QUICK. We shall all be shent.—Run in
here, good young man; go into this closet:
he will not stay long.—[*Shuts* SIMPLE *in
the Closet.*] What, John Rugby! John,
what, John, I say! Go, John, go enquire
for my master; I doubt, he be not well,
that he comes not home. [*Exit* RUGBY.]
[*Sings.*] "And down, down, adown-a," &c.
Enter Doctor CAIUS.
CAIUS. Vat is you sing? I do not like
dese toys. Pray you, go and vetch me in
my closet *un boitier verd;* a box, a green-a-
box: do intend vat I speak? a green-a box.
QUICK. Ay, forsooth; I'll fetch it you.
[*Aside.*] I am glad he went not in himself: if he had found the young man, he
would have been horn-mad.
CAIUS. Fe, fe, fe, fe! ma foi, il fait fort
chaud. Je m'en vais à la cour,—la grande
affaire.
QUICK. Is it this, Sir?
CAIUS. Oui; mette le au mor. pocket;
dépêche, quickly.—Vere is dat knave Rugby?
QUICK. What, John Rugby! John!
Re-enter RUGBY.
RUG. Here, Sir.
CAIUS. You are John Rugby, and you
are Jack Rugby: come, take-a your rapier,
and come after my heel to de court.
RUG. 'Tis ready, Sir, here in the porch.
CAIUS. By my trot, I tarry too long.—
Od's me! *Qu'ai-je oublié?* dere is some
simples in my closet, that I vill not for de
varld I shall leave behind.
QUICK. [*Aside.*] Ah me! he'll find the
young man there, and be mad.
CAIUS. O diable! diable! vat is in my
closet?—Villainy! *larron!* [*Pulling* SIMPLE
out.] Rugby, my rapier!
QUICK. Good master, be content.
CAIUS. Verefore shall I be content-a?
QUICK. The young man is an honest man.
CAIUS. Vat shall de honest man do in my
closet? dere is no honest man dat shall
come in my closet.
QUICK. I beseech you, be not so phleg-
matic. Hear the truth of it: he came of an
errand to me from parson Hugh.
CAIUS. Vell.

SIM. Ay, forsooth; to desire her to—
QUICK. Peace, I pray you.
CAIUS. Peace-a your tongue!—Speak-a your tale.
SIM. To desire this honest gentlewoman, your maid, to speak a good word to mistress Anne Page for my master, in the way of marriage.
QUICK. This is all, indeed, la; but I'll ne'er put my finger in the fire, and need not.
CAIUS. Sir Hugh send-a you?—Rugby, *baillez* me some paper.—Tarry you a little-a while.   [*Writes.*
QUICK. I am glad he is so quiet: if he had been thoroughly moved, you should have heard him so loud, and so melancholy. —But notwithstanding, man, I'll do your master what good I can; and the very yea and the no is, the French doctor, my master,—I may call him my master, look you, for I keep his house; and I wash, wring, brew, bake, scour, dress meat and drink, make the beds, and do all myself;—
SIM. 'Tis a great charge to come under one body's hand.
QUICK. Are you avis'd o' that? you shall find it a great charge: and to be up early and down late;—but notwithstanding,—to tell you in your ear,—I would have no words of it,—my master himself is in love with mistress Anne Page: but notwithstanding that, I know Anne's mind; that's neither here nor there.
CAIUS. You jack'nape, give-a dis letter to Sir Hugh; by gar, it is a shallenge: I vill cut his troat in de park; and I vill teach a scurvy jack-a-nape priest to meddle or make.—You may be gone; it is not good you tarry here:—by gar, I vill cut all his two stones; by gar, he shall not have a stone to trow at his dog.   [*Exit* SIMPLE.
QUICK. Alas! he speaks but for his friend.
CAIUS. It is no matter-a for dat:—do not you tell-a me, dat I shall have Anne Page for myself?—By gar, I vill kill de Jack priest; and I have appointed mine Host of de *Jarretière* to measure our weapon.—By gar, I vill myself have Anne Page.
QUICK. Sir, the maid loves you, and all shall be well. We must give folks leave to prate: what, the good-jer!
CAIUS. Rugby, come to the court vit me. —By gar, if I have not Anne Page, I shall turn your head out of my door.—Follow my heels, Rugby.
                        [*Exeunt* CAIUS *and* RUGBY.
QUICK. You shall have An fool's-head of your own. No, I know Anne's mind for that: never a woman in Windsor knows more of Anne's mind than I do; nor can

do more than I do with her, I thank heaven.
FENT. [*Within.*] Who's within there? ho!
QUICK. Who's there, I trow? Come near the house, I pray you.
                        Enter FENTON.
FENT. How now, good woman! how dost thou?
QUICK. The better, that it pleases your good worship to ask.
FENT. What news? how does pretty mistress Anne?
QUICK. In truth, Sir, and she is pretty, and honest, and gentle; and one that is your friend, I can tell you that by the way; I praise heaven for it.
FENT. Shall I do any good, thinkest thou? Shall I not lose my suit?
QUICK. Troth, Sir, all is in his hands above: but notwithstanding, master Fenton, I'll be sworn on a book, she loves you.—Have not your worship a wart above your eye?
FENT. Yes, marry, have I; what of that?
QUICK. Well, thereby hangs a tale.—Good faith, it is such another Nan;—but, I detest, an honest maid as ever broke bread: —we had an hour's talk of that wart.—I shall never laugh but in that maid's company;—but, indeed, she is given too much to allicholly and musing. But for you— well, go to.
FENT. Well, I shall see her to-day. Hold, there's money for thee; let me have thy voice in my behalf: if thou seest her before me, commend me—
QUICK. Will I? i' faith, that we will: and I will tell your worship more of the wart, the next time we have confidence; and of other wooers.
FENT. Well, farewell; I am in great haste now.
QUICK. Farewell to your worship.—[*Exit* FENTON.] Truly, an honest gentleman: but Anne loves him not; for I know Anne's mind as well as another does.—Out upon't! what have I forgot?   [*Exit.*

ACT II.

SCENE I.—*Before* PAGE'S *House.*

Enter Mistress PAGE, *with a Letter.*

MRS. PAGE. What! have I 'scaped love-letters in the holyday time of my beauty, and am I now a subject for them? Let me see.   [*Reads.*
"Ask me no reason why I love you; for though love use reason for his precisian, he admits him not for his counsellor. You are not young, no more am I; go to then, there's sympathy: you are merry, so am I; ha, ha! then, there's more sympathy: you

love sack, and so do I; would you desire better sympathy? Let it suffice thee, mistress Page,—at the least, if the love of a soldier can suffice,—that I love thee. I will not say, pity me,—'tis not a soldier-like phrase; but I say, love me. By me,

Thine own true knight,
By day or night,
Or any kind of light,
With all his might
For thee to fight,   JOHN FALSTAFF."

What a Herod of Jewry is this!—O wicked, wicked world!—one that is well nigh worn to pieces with age, to show himself a young gallant! What an unweighed behaviour hath this Flemish drunkard picked—with the devil's name—out of my conversation, that he dares in this manner assay me? Why, he hath not been thrice in my company!—What should I say to him?—I was then frugal of my mirth:—heaven forgive me!—Why, I'll exhibit a bill in the parliament for the putting down of men. How shall I be revenged on him? for revenged I will be, as sure as his guts are made of puddings.

Enter Mistress FORD.

MRS. FORD. Mistress Page! trust me, I was going to your house.

MRS. PAGE. And, trust me, I was coming to you. You look very ill.

MRS. FORD. Nay, I'll ne'er believe that: I have to show to the contrary.

MRS. PAGE. Faith, but you do, in my mind.

MRS. FORD. Well, I do then; yet, I say, I could show you to the contrary. O, mistress Page! give me some counsel.

MRS. PAGE. What's the matter, woman?

MRS. FORD. O woman! if it were not for one trifling respect, I could come to such honour.

MRS. PAGE. Hang the trifle, woman! take the honour. What is it?—dispense with trifles;—what is it?

MRS. FORD. If I would but go to hell for an eternal moment or so, I could be knighted.

MRS. PAGE. What? —thou liest. — Sir Alice Ford!—These knights will hack; and so, thou shouldst not alter the article of thy gentry.

MRS. FORD. We burn day-light:—here, read, read;—perceive how I might be knighted.—I shall think the worse of fat men, as long as I have an eye to make difference of men's liking: and yet he would not swear, praised women's modesty, and gave such orderly and well-behaved reproof to all uncomeliness, that I would have sworn his disposition would have

gone to the truth of his words; but they do no more adhere and keep place together, than the hundredth psalm to the tune of "Green Sleeves." What tempest, I trow, threw this whale, with so many tuns of oil in his belly, ashore at Windsor? How shall I be revenged on him? I think, the best way were to entertain him with hope, till the wicked fire of lust have melted him in his own grease.—Did you ever hear the like?

MRS. PAGE. Letter for letter, but that the name of Page and Ford differs!—To thy great comfort in this mystery of ill opinions, here's the twin-brother of thy letter: but let thine inherit first; for, I protest, mine never shall. I warrant, he hath a thousand of these letters, writ with blank space for different names,—sure, more,—and these are of the second edition. He will print them, out of doubt; for he cares not what he puts into the press, when he would put us two. I had rather be a giantess, and lie under mount Pelion. Well, I will find you twenty lascivious turtles, ere one chaste man.

MRS. FORD. Why, this is the very same; the very hand, the very words. What doth he think of us?

MRS. PAGE. Nay, I know not: it makes me almost ready to wrangle with mine own honesty. I'll entertain myself like one that I am not acquainted withal; for, sure, unless he know some strain in me, that I know not myself, he would never have boarded me in this fury.

MRS. FORD. Boarding, call you it? I'll be sure to keep him above deck.

MRS. PAGE. So will I: if he come under my hatches, I'll never to sea again. Let's be revenged on him: let's appoint him a meeting; give him a show of comfort in his suit; and lead him on with a fine-baited delay, till he hath pawned his horses to mine Host of the Garter.

MRS. FORD. Nay, I will consent to act any villainy against him, that may not sully the chariness of our honesty. O, that my husband saw this letter! it would give eternal food to his jealousy.

MRS. PAGE. Why, look, where he comes; and my good man too: he's as far from jealousy, as I am from giving him cause; and that, I hope, is an unmeasurable distance.

MRS. FORD. You are the happier woman.

MRS. PAGE. Let's consult together against this greasy knight. Come hither.

[*They retire.*

Enter FORD, PISTOL, PAGE, *and* NYM.

FORD. Well, I hope, it be not so.

PIST. Hope is a curtail dog in some af-
fairs: Sir John affects thy wife.
FORD. Why, Sir, my wife is not young.
PIST. He wooes both high and low, both
rich and poor,
Both young and old, one with another,
Ford:
He loves the gally-mawfry; Ford, perpend.
FORD. Love my wife? [go thou,
PIST. With liver burning hot: prevent, or
Like Sir Actæon he, with Ring-wood at thy
O, odious is the name! [heels.
FORD. What name, Sir?
PIST. The horn, I say. Farewell:
Take heed; have open eye; for thieves do
foot by night:
Take heed, ere summer, comes, or cuckoo-
birds do sing.—
Away, sir corporal Nym!—
Believe it, Page; he speaks sense.
[*Exit.*
FORD. [*Aside.*] I will be patient: I will
find out this.
NYM. [*To* PAGE.] And this is true; I like
not the humour of lying. He hath wronged
me in some humours: I should have borne
the humoured letter to her, but I have a
sword, and it shall bite upon my necessity.
He loves your wife; there's the short and
the long. My name is corporal Nym; I
speak, and I avouch 'tis true: my name is
Nym, and Falstaff loves your wife.—Adieu.
I love not the humour of bread and cheese;
and there's the humour of it. Adieu.
[*Exit.*
PAGE. [*Aside.*] "The humour of it,"
quoth 'a! here's a fellow frights humour
out of his wits.
FORD. [*Aside.*] I will seek out Falstaff.
PAGE. [*Aside.*] I never heard such a
drawling, affecting rogue.
FORD. [*Aside.*] If I do find it:—well.
PAGE. [*Aside.*] I will not believe such a
Cataian, though the priest o' the town
commended him for a true man.
FORD. [*Aside.*] 'Twas a good sensible
fellow:—well.
PAGE. How now, Meg!
MRS. PAGE. Whither go you, George?—
Hark you.
MRS. FORD. How now, sweet Frank!
why art thou melancholy?
FORD. I melancholy! I am not melan-
choly.—Get you home, go.
MRS. FORD. 'Faith, thou hast some crotch-
ets in thy head now.—Will you go, mistress
Page?
MRS. PAGE. Have with you.—You'll come
to dinner, George?—[*Aside to Mrs.* FORD.]
Look, who comes yonder: she shall be our
messenger to this paltry knight.

MRS. FORD. [*Aside to Mrs.* PAGE.] Trust
me, I thought on her: she'll fit it.
Enter Mrs. QUICKLY.
MRS. PAGE. You are come to see my
daughter Anne?
QUICK. Ay, forsooth; and, I pray, how
does good mistress Anne?
MRS. PAGE. Go in with us, and see: we
have an hour's talk with you.
[*Exeunt Mrs.* PAGE, *Mrs.* FORD,
and Mrs. QUICKLY.
PAGE. How now, master Ford!
FORD. You heard what this knave told
me, did you not?
PAGE. Yes; and you heard what the other
told me?
FORD. Do you think there is truth in
them?
PAGE. Hang 'em, slaves! I do not think
the knight would offer it: but these that
accuse him in his intent towards our
wives, are a yoke of his discarded men;
very rogues, now they be out of service.
FORD. Were they his men?
PAGE. Marry, were they.
FORD. I like it never the better for that.
—Does he lie at the Garter?
PAGE. Ay, marry, does he. If he should
intend this voyage towards my wife, I
would turn her loose to him; and what he
gets more of her than sharp words, let it
lie on my head.
FORD. I do not misdoubt my wife; but I
would be loath to turn them together. A
man may be too confident: I would have
nothing lie on my head: I cannot be thus
satisfied.
PAGE. Look, where my ranting Host of
the Garter comes. There is either liquor
in his pate, or money in his purse, when
he looks so merrily.—[*Enter* HOST.] How
now, mine host!
HOST. How now, bully-rook! thou'rt a
gentleman.—Cavalero-justice, I say!
Enter SHALLOW.
SHAL. I follow, mine host, I follow.—
Good even, and twenty, good master Page!
Master Page, will you go with us? we have
sport in hand.
HOST. Tell him, cavalero-justice; tell him,
bully-rook.
SHAL. Sir, there is a fray to be fought
between Sir Hugh, the Welsh priest, and
Caius, the French doctor.
FORD. Good mine Host o' the Garter, a
word with you.
HOST. What sayest thou, my bully-rook?
[*They go aside.*
SHAL. [*To* PAGE.] Will you go with us
to behold it? My merry host hath had the
measuring of their weapons; and, I think,

hath appointed them contrary places; for, believe me, I hear, the parson is no jester. Hark, I will tell you what our sport shall be. [*They go aside.*

HOST. Hast thou no suit against my knight, my guest-cavalier?

FORD. None, I protest: but I'll give you a pottle of burnt sack to give me recourse to him, and tell him my name is Brook; only for a jest.

HOST. My hand, bully: thou shalt have egress and regress; said I well? and thy name shall be Brook. It is a merry knight. —Will you go on, hearts?

SHAL. Have with you, mine host.

PAGE. I have heard, the Frenchman hath good skill in his rapier.

SHAL. Tut, Sir! I could have told you more. In these times you stand on distance, your passes, stoccadoes, and I know not what: 'tis the heart, master Page; 'tis here, 'tis here. I have seen the time, with my long sword, I would have made you four tall fellows skip like rats.

HOST. Here, boys, here, here! shall we wag?

PAGE. Have with you.—I had rather hear them scold than fight.

[*Exeunt* HOST, SHALLOW, *and* PAGE.

FORD. Though Page be a secure fool, and stands so firmly on his wife's frailty, yet I cannot put off my opinion so easily: she was in his company at Page's house; and what they made there, I know not. Well, I will look farther into't; and I have a disguise to sound Falstaff. If I find her honest, I lose not my labour; if she be otherwise, 'tis labour well bestowed.

[*Exit.*

SCENE II.—*A Room in the* Garter Inn.
Enter FALSTAFF *and* PISTOL

FAL. I will not lend thee a penny.

PIST. Why, then the world's mine oyster, Which I with sword will open.—
I will retort the sum in equipage.

FAL. Not a penny. I have been content, Sir, you should lay my countenance to pawn: I have grated upon my good friends for three reprieves for you and your coach-fellow, Nym; or else you had looked through the grate, like a gemini of ba-boons. I am damned in hell for swearing to gentlemen, my friends, you were good soldiers, and tall fellows: and when mis-tress Bridget lost the handle of her fan, I took't upon mine honour thou hadst it not.

PIST. Didst thou not share? hadst thou not fifteen pence?

FAL. Reason, you rogue, reason: thinkest thou, I'll endanger my soul gratis? At a word, hang no more about me; I am no gibbet for you:—go.—A short knife and a throng:—to your manor of Pickt-hatch, go. —You'll not bear a letter for me, you rogue!—you stand upon your honour!— Why, thou unconfinable baseness, it is as much as I can do, to keep the terms of my honour precise. I, I, I myself sometimes, leaving the fear of heaven on the left hand, and hiding mine honour in my necessity, am fain to shuffle, to hedge, and to lurch; and yet you, rogue, will ensconce your rags, your cat-a-mountain looks, your red-attice phrases, and your bold-beating oaths, under the shelter of your honour! You will not do it, you!

PIST. I do relent: what would'st thou more of man?

Enter ROBIN.

ROB. Sir, here's a woman would speak with you.

FAL. Let her approach.

Enter Mistress QUICKLY.

QUICK. Give your worship good-morrow.

FAL. Good-morrow, good wife.

QUICK. Not so, an't please your worship.

FAL. Good maid, then.

QUICK. I'll be sworn; as my mother was, the first hour I was born.

FAL. I do believe the swearer. What with me?

QUICK. Shall I vouchsafe your worship a word or two?

FAL. Two thousand, fair woman; and I'll vouchsafe thee the hearing.

QUICK. There is one mistress Ford, Sir: —I pray, come a little nearer this ways.— I myself dwell with master Doctor Caius,—

FAL. Well, on: Mistress Ford, you say,—

QUICK. Your worship says very true:—I pray your worship, come a little nearer this ways.

FAL. I warrant thee, nobody hears;— mine own people, mine own people.

QUICK. Are they so? Heaven bless them, and make them his servants!

FAL. Well: Mistress Ford;—What of her?

QUICK. Why, Sir, she's a good creature. Lord, lord! your worship's a wanton! Well, heaven forgive you, and all of us, I pray!

FAL. Mistress Ford; — come, mistress Ford,—

QUICK. Marry, this is the short and the long of it: you have brought her into such a canaries, as 'tis wonderful: the best courtier of them all, when the court lay at Windsor, could never have brought her to such a canary: yet there has been knights, and lords, and gentlemen, with their coaches; I warrant you, coach after coach, letter after letter, gift after gift; smelling so sweetly—all musk—and so rushling, I warrant you, in silk and gold; and in such alligant terms; and in such wine and sugar of the best, and the fairest, that would have won any woman's heart; and, I warrant you, they could never get an eye-wink of her.—I had myself twenty angels given me this morning; but I defy all angels, (in any such sort, as they say,) but in the way of honesty:—and, I warrant you, they could never get her so much as sip on a cup with the proudest of them all: and yet there has been earls, nay, which is more, pensioners; but, I warrant you, all is one with her.

FAL. But what says she to me? be brief, my good she Mercury.

QUICK. Marry, she hath received your letter; for the which she thanks you a thousand times; and she gives you to notify, that her husband will be absence from his house between ten and eleven.

FAL. Ten and eleven?

QUICK. Ay, forsooth; and then you may come and see the picture, she says, that you wot of:—master Ford, her husband, will be from home. Alas! the sweet woman leads an ill life with him; he's a very jealousy man; she leads a very frampold life with him, good heart.

FAL. Ten and eleven.—Woman, commend me to her; I will not fail her.

QUICK. Why, you say well. But I have another messenger to your worship. Mistress Page hath her hearty commendations to you, too:—and let me tell you in your ear, she's as fartuous a civil modest wife, and one (I tell you) that will not miss you morning nor evening prayer, as any is in Windsor, whoe'er be the other:—and she bade me tell your worship, that her husband is seldom from home; but, she hopes, there will come a time. I never knew a woman so dote upon a man: surely, I think you have charms, la; yes, in truth.

FAL. Not I, I assure thee: setting the attraction of my good parts aside, I have no other charms.

QUICK. Blessing on your heart for't!

FAL. But, I pray thee, tell me this: has Ford's wife, and Page's wife, acquainted each other how they love me?

QUICK. That were a jest, indeed!—they have not so little grace, I hope:—that were a trick, indeed!—But mistress Page would desire you to send her your little page, of all loves: her husband has a marvellous infection to the little page; and, truly, master Page is an honest man. Never a

wife in Windsor leads a better life than she does: do what she will, say what she will, take all, pay all, go to bed when she list, rise when she list, all is as she will: and, truly, she deserves it; for if there be a kind woman in Windsor, she is one. You must send her your page; no remedy.

FAL. Why, I will.

QUICK. Nay, but do so, then: and, look you, he may come and go between you both; and, in any case, have a nayword, that you may know one another's mind, and the boy never need to understand any thing; for 'tis not good that children should know any wickedness: old folks, you know, have discretion, as they say, and know the world.

FAL. Fare thee well: commend me to them both. There's my purse; I am yet thy debtor.—Boy, go along with this woman.—[*Exeunt* QUICKLY *and* ROBIN.] This news distracts me.

PIST. This punk is one of Cupid's carriers.—
Clap on more sails; pursue; up with your fights;
Give fire; she is my prize, or ocean whelm them all!   [*Exit.*

FAL. Sayest thou so, old Jack? go thy ways; I'll make more of thy old body than I have done. Will they yet look after thee? Wilt thou, after the expence of so much money, be now a gainer? Good body, I thank thee. Let them say, 'tis grossly done; so it be fairly done, no matter.

Enter BARDOLPH.

BARD. Sir John, there's one master Brook below would fain speak with you, and be acquainted with you; and hath sent your worship a morning's draught of sack.

FAL. Brook, is his name?

BARD. Ay, Sir.

FAL. Call him in. [*Exit* BARDOLPH.] Such Brooks are welcome to me, that o'erflow such liquor.—Ah, ha! mistress Ford and mistress Page, have I encompassed you? go to; *via!*

Re-enter BARDOLPH, *with* FORD *disguised.*

FORD. Bless you, Sir!

FAL. And you, Sir! would you speak with me?

FORD. I make bold, to press with so little preparation upon you.

FAL. You're welcome. What's your will? —Give us leave, drawer.   [*Exit* BARDOLPH.

FORD. Sir, I am a gentleman that have spent much: my name is Brook.

FAL. Good master Brook, I desire more acquaintance of you.

FORD. Good Sir John, I sue for yours:

not to charge you; for I must let you understand, I think myself in better plight for a lender than you are: the which hath something emboldened me to this unseasoned intrusion; for, they say, if money go before, all ways do lie open.

FAL. Money is a good soldier, Sir, and will on.

FORD. Troth, and I have a bag of money here troubles me: if you will help to bear it, Sir John, take all, or half, for easing me of the carriage.

FAL. Sir, I know not how I may deserve to be your porter.

FORD. I will tell you, Sir, if you will give me the hearing.

FAL. Speak, good master Brook; I shall be glad to be your servant.

FORD. Sir, I hear you are a scholar,—I will be brief with you;—and you have been a man long known to me, though I had never so good means, as desire, to make myself acquainted with you. I shall discover a thing to you, wherein I must very much lay open mine own imperfection: but, good Sir John, as you have one eye upon my follies, as you hear them unfolded, turn another into the register of your own, that I may pass with a reproof the easier, sith you yourself know how easy it is to be such an offender.

FAL. Very well, Sir; proceed.

FORD. There is a gentlewoman in this town, her husband's name is Ford.

FAL. Well, Sir.

FORD. I have long loved her, and, I protest to you, bestowed much on her; followed her with a doting observance; engrossed opportunities to meet her; fee'd every slight occasion that could but niggardly give me sight of her; not only bought many presents to give her, but have given largely to many, to know what she would have given. Briefly, I have pursued her as love hath pursued me; which hath been on the wing of all occasions. But whatsoever I have merited, either in my mind, or in my means, meed, I am sure, I have received none; unless experience be a jewel: that I have purchased at an infinite rate; and that hath taught me to say this,—

> Love like a shadow flies, when substance love pursues;
> Pursuing that that flies, and flying what pursues.

FAL. Have you received no promise of satisfaction at her hands?

FORD. Never.

FAL. Have you importuned her to such a purpose?

FORD. Never.

FAL. Of what quality was your love, then?

FORD. Like a fair house, built upon another man's ground; so that I have lost my edifice, by mistaking the place where I erected it.

FAL. To what purpose have you unfolded this to me?

FORD. When I have told you that, I have told you all. Some say, that though she appear honest to me, yet in other places she enlargeth her mirth so far, that there is shrewd construction made of her. Now, Sir John, here is the heart of my purpose: you are a gentleman of excellent breeding, admirable discourse, of great admittance, authentic in your place and person, generally allowed for your many war-like, court-like, and learned preparations.

FAL. O Sir!

FORD. Believe it, for you know it.—There is money; spend it, spend it; spend more; spend all I have; only give me so much of your time in exchange of it, as to lay an amiable siege to the honesty of this Ford's wife: use your art of wooing; win her to consent to you; if any man may, you may as soon as any.

FAL. Would it apply well to the vehemency of your affection, that I should win what you would enjoy? Methinks, you prescribe to yourself very preposterously.

FORD. O, understand my drift. She dwells so securely on the excellency of her honour, that the folly of my soul dares not present itself: she is too bright to be looked against. Now, could I come to her with any detection in my hand, my desires had instance and argument to commend themselves: I could drive her then from the ward of her purity, her reputation, her marriage vow, and a thousand other her defences, which now are too too strongly embattled against me. What say you to't, Sir John?

FAL. Master Brook, I will first make bold with your money; next, give me your hand; and last, as I am a gentleman, you shall, if you will, enjoy Ford's wife.

FORD. O good Sir!

FAL. I say you shall.

FORD. Want no money, Sir John; you shall want none.

FAL. Want no mistress Ford, master Brook; you shall want none. I shall be with her (I may tell you) by her own appointment; even as you came in to me, her assistant, or go-between, parted from me:

I say, I shall be with her between ten and eleven; for at that time the jealous rascally knave, her husband, will be forth. Come you to me at night; you shall know how I speed.

FORD. I am blest in your acquaintance. Do you know Ford, Sir?

FAL. Hang him, poor cuckoldly knave! I know him not.—Yet I wrong him, to call him poor: they say, the jealous wittolly knave hath masses of money; for the which, his wife seems to me well-favoured. I will use her as the key of the cuckoldly rogue's coffer; and there's my harvest-home.

FORD. I would you knew Ford, Sir, that you might avoid him, if you saw him.

FAL. Hang him, mechanical salt-butter rogue! I will stare him out of his wits; I will awe him with my cudgel,—it shall hang like a meteor o'er the cuckold's horns. Master Brook, thou shalt know I will predominate over the peasant, and thou shalt lie with his wife.—Come to me soon at night.—Ford's a knave, and I will aggravate his style; thou, master Brook, shalt know him for knave and cuckold.—Come to me soon at night.   [Exit.

FORD. What a damned Epicurean rascal is this!—My heart is ready to crack with impatience.—Who says this is improvident jealousy? my wife hath sent to him, the hour is fixed, the match is made. Would any man have thought this?—See the hell of having a false woman! My bed shall be abused, my coffers ransacked, my reputation gnawn at; and I shall not only receive this villainous wrong, but stand under the adoption of abominable terms, and by him that does me this wrong. Terms! names!—Amaimon sounds well; Lucifer, well; Barbason, well; yet they are devils' additions, the names of fiends: but cuckold! wittol cuckold! the devil himself hath not such a name. Page is an ass, a secure ass: he will trust his wife; he will not be jealous. I will rather trust a Fleming with my butter, parson Hugh the Welshman with my cheese, an Irishman with my aqua-vitæ bottle, or a thief to walk my ambling gelding, than my wife with herself: then she plots, then she ruminates, then she devises; and what they think in their hearts they may effect, they will break their hearts but they will effect. Heaven be praised for my jealousy!—Eleven o'clock the hour:—I will prevent this, detect my wife, be revenged on Falstaff, and laugh at Page. I will about it; better three hours too soon, than a minute too late. Fie, fie, fie! cuckold! cuckold! cuckold!   [Exit.

SCENE III.—Field near WINDSOR.

Enter CAIUS and RUGBY

CAIUS. Jack Rugby,—

RUG. Sir?

CAIUS. Vat is de clock, Jack?

RUG. 'Tis past the hour, Sir, that Sir Hugh promised to meet.

CAIUS. By gar, he has save his soul, dat he is no come: he has pray his Pible well, dat he is no come. By gar, Jack Rugby, he is dead already, if he be come.

RUG. He is wise, Sir; he knew your worship would kill him, if he came.

CAIUS. By gar, de herring is no dead, so as I vill kill him. Take your rapier, Jack; I vill tell you how I vill kill him.

RUG. Alas, Sir! I cannot fence.

CAIUS. Villainy! take your rapier.

RUG. Forbear; here's company.

Enter HOST, SHALLOW, SLENDER, and PAGE.

HOST. Bless thee, bully doctor!

SHAL. Save you, master doctor Caius!

PAGE. Now, good master doctor!

SLEN. Give you good-morrow, Sir.

CAIUS. Vat be all you, one, two, tree, four, come for?

HOST. To see thee fight, to see thee foin, to see thee traverse; to see thee here, to see thee there; to see thee pass thy punto, thy stock, thy reverse, thy distance, thy montant. Is he dead, my Ethiopian? is he dead, my Francisco? ha, bully! What says my Æsculapius? my Galen? my heart of elder? ha! is he dead, bully Stale? is he dead?

CAIUS. By gar, he is de coward Jack priest of de vorld; he is not show his face.

HOST. Thou art a Castillian, king Urinal! Hector of Greece, my boy!

CAIUS. I pray you, bear vitness that me have stay six or seven, two, tree hours for him, and he is no come.

SHAL. He is the wiser man, master doctor: he is a curer of souls, and you a curer of bodies; if you should fight, you go against the hair of your professions.—Is it not true, master Page?

PAGE. Master Shallow, you have yourself been a great fighter, though now a man of peace.

SHAL. Bodykins, master Page, though I now be old, and of the peace, if I see a sword out, my finger itches to make one. Though we are justices, and doctors, and churchmen, master Page, we have some salt of our youth in us; we are the sons of women, master Page.

PAGE. 'Tis true, master Shallow.

SHAL. It will be found so, master Page. —Master doctor Caius, I am come to fetch you home. I am sworn of the peace: you have showed yourself a wise physician, and Sir Hugh hath shown himself a wise and patient churchman. You must go with me, master doctor.

HOST. Pardon, guest-justice.—A word, monsieur Mock-water.

CAIUS. Mock-vater! vat is dat?

HOST. Mock-water, in our English tongue, is valour, bully.

CAIUS. By gar, den, I have as much mock-vater as de Englishman.—Scurvy jack-dog priest! by gar, me vill cut his ears.

HOST. He will clapper-claw thee tightly, bully.

CAIUS. Clapper-de-claw! vat is dat?

HOST. That is, he will make thee amends.

CAIUS. By gar, me do look, he shall clap-per-de-claw me; for, by gar, me vill have it.

HOST. And I will provoke him to't, or let him wag.

CAIUS. Me tank you for dat.

HOST. And moreover, bully,—But first, master guest, and master Page, and eke cavalero Slender, go you through the town to Frogmore.   [*Aside to them.*

PAGE. Sir Hugh is there, is he?

HOST. He is there: see what humour he is in; and I will bring the doctor about by the fields. Will it do well?

SHAL. We will do it.

PAGE, SHAL. and SLEN. Adieu, good master doctor.

[*Exeunt* PAGE, SHALLOW, *and* SLENDER.

CAIUS. By gar, me vill kill de priest; for he speak for a jack-an-ape to Anne Page.

HOST. Let him die: sheathe thy impatience; throw cold water on thy choler: go about the fields with me through Frogmore: I will bring thee where mistress Anne Page is, at a farm-house a-feasting; and thou shalt woo her. Cried I aim? said I well?

CAIUS. By gar, me tank you for dat: by gar, I love you; and I shall procure-a you de good guest, de earl, de knight, de lords, de gentlemen, my patients.

HOST. For the which I will be thy adversary toward Anne Page. Said I well?

CAIUS. By gar, 'tis good; vell said.

HOST. Let us wag, then.

CAIUS. Come at my heels, Jack Rugby.

[*Exeunt.*

ACT III.

SCENE I.—*A Field near* FROGMORE.

Enter Sir HUGH EVANS *and* SIMPLE.

EVA. I pray you now, good master Slen-

der's serving-man, and friend Simple by your name, which way have you looked for master Caius, that calls himself Doctor of Physic?

SIM. Marry, Sir, the pittie-ward, the park-ward, every way; old Windsor way, and every way but the town way.

EVA. I most fehemently desire you, you will also look that way.

SIM. I will, Sir.   [*Retiring.*

EVA. Pless my soul; how full of cholers I am, and trempling of mind!—I shall be glad, if he have deceived me.—How melancholies I am!—I will knog his urinals about his knave's costard, when I have goot opportunities for the 'ork: — pless my soul!—   [*Sings.*

    To shallow rivers, to whose falls
    Melodious birds sing madrigals;
    There will we make our peds of roses,
    And a thousand fragrant posies.
        To shallow—

Mercy on me! I have a great dispositions to cry.   [*Sings.*

    Melodious birds sing madrigals;—
    When as I sat in Pabylon,—
    And a thousand vagram posies.
        To shallow—

SIM. [*Coming forward.*] Yonder he is coming, this way, Sir Hugh.

EVA. He's welcome.—   [*Sings.*

    To shallow rivers, to whose falls—

Heaven prosper the right!—What weapons is he?

SIM. No weapons, Sir. There comes my master, master Shallow, and another gentleman, from Frogmore, over the stile, this way.

EVA. Pray you, give me my gown; or else keep it in your arms.

[*Reads in a book.*

Enter PAGE, SHALLOW, *and* SLENDER.

SHAL. How now, master parson! Good-morrow, good Sir Hugh. Keep a gamester from the dice, and a good student from his book, and it is wonderful.

SLEN. Ah, sweet Anne Page!

PAGE. Save you, good Sir Hugh!

EVA. Pless you from his mercy sake, all of you!

SHAL. What, the sword and the word! do you study them both, master parson?

PAGE. And youthful still, in your doublet and hose, this raw rheumatic day?

EVA. There is reasons and causes for it.

PAGE. We are come to you to do a good office, master parson.

EVA. Fery well: what is it?

PAGE. Yonder is a most reverend gentleman, who, belike having received wrong by some person, is at most odds with his own gravity and patience that ever you saw.

SHAL. I have lived fourscore years and upward; I never heard a man of his place, gravity, and learning, so wide of his own respect.

EVA. What is he?

PAGE. I think you know him; master doctor Caius, the renowned French physician.

EVA. Got's will, and his passion of my heart! I had as lief you would tell me of a mess of porridge.

PAGE. Why?

EVA. He has no more knowledge in Hibbocrates and Galen,—and he is a knave besides; a cowardly knave, as you would desires to be acquainted withal.

PAGE. I warrant you, he's the man should fight with him.

SLEN. O, sweet Anne Page!

SHAL. It appears so, by his weapons.— Keep them asunder:—here comes doctor Caius.

Enter HOST, CAIUS, *and* RUGBY.

PAGE. Nay, good master parson, keep in your weapon.

SHAL. So do you, good master doctor.

HOST. Disarm them, and let them question: let them keep their limbs whole, and hack our English.

CAIUS. I pray you, let-a me speak a word vit your ear: verefore vill you not meet-a me?

EVA. Pray you, use your patience: in goot time.

CAIUS. By gar, you are de coward, de Jack dog, John ape.

EVA. Pray you, let us not be laughing-stogs to other men's humours; I desire you in friendship, and I will one way or other make you amends:—I will knog your urinals about your knave's cogscomb for missing your meetings and appointments.

CAIUS. *Diable!* — Jack Rugby, — mine Host de *Jarretière*,—have I not stay for him to kill him? have I not, at de place I did appoint?

EVA. As I am a Christians soul, now, look you, this is the place appointed: I'll be judgment by mine Host of the Garter.

HOST. Peace, I say, Gallia and Guallia; French and Welsh; soul-curer and body-curer!

CAIUS. Ay, dat is very good; excellent.

HOST. Peace, I say! hear mine Host of the Garter. Am I politic? am I subtle? am I a Machiavel? Shall I lose my doctor? no; he gives me the potions, and the motions. Shall I lose my parson, my priest, my Sir Hugh? no; he gives me the proverbs and the noverbs.—Give me thy hand, terrestrial; so:—give me thy hand, celestial; so.—Boys of art, I have deceived you both; I have directed you to wrong places: your hearts are mighty, your skins are whole, and let burnt sack be the issue.— Come, lay their swords to pawn.—Follow me, lads of peace; follow, follow, follow.

SHAL. Trust me, a mad host!—Follow, gentlemen, follow.

SLEN. O, sweet Anne Page!

[*Exeunt* SHALLOW, SLENDER, PAGE, *and* HOST.

CAIUS. Ha, do I perceive dat? have you make-a de sot of us, ha, ha?

EVA. This is well; he has made us his vlouting-stog.—I desire you, that we may be friends; and let us knog our prains together to be revenge on this same scall, scurvy, cogging companion, the Host of the Garter.

CAIUS. By gar, vit all my heart. He promise to bring me vere is Anne Page: by gar, he deceive me too.

EVA. Well; I will smite his noddles.— Pray you, follow. [*Exeunt.*

SCENE II.—*A Street in* WINDSOR.

Enter Mistress PAGE *and* ROBIN.

MRS. PAGE. Nay, keep your way, little gallant: you were wont to be a follower, but now you are a leader. Whether had you rather, lead mine eyes, or eye your master's heels?

ROB. I had rather, forsooth, go before you like a man, than follow him like a dwarf.

MRS. PAGE. O, you are a flattering boy: now I see you'll be a courtier.

Enter FORD.

FORD. Well met, mistress Page. Whither go you?

MRS. PAGE. Truly, Sir, to see your wife: is she at home?

FORD. Ay; and as idle as she may hang together, for want of company. I think, if your husbands were dead, you two would marry.

MRS. PAGE. Be sure of that,—two other husbands.

FORD. Where had you this pretty weathercock?

MRS. PAGE. I cannot tell what the dickens his name is my husband had him of. —What do you call your knight's name, sirrah?

ROB. Sir John Falstaff.

FORD. Sir John Falstaff!

MRS. PAGE. He, he; I can never hit on's name.—There is such a league between my good man and he!—Is your wife at home, indeed?

FORD. Indeed, she is.

MRS. PAGE. By your leave, Sir: I am sick, till I see her.

    [*Exeunt* Mrs. PAGE *and* ROBIN.

FORD. Has Page any brains? hath he any eyes? hath he any thinking? Sure, they sleep; he hath no use of them. Why, this boy will carry a letter twenty miles, as easy as a cannon will shoot point-blank twelve score. He pieces-out his wife's inclination; he gives her folly motion and advantage: and now she's going to my wife, and Falstaff's boy with her:—a man may hear this shower sing in the wind:—and Falstaff's boy with her!—Good plots!—they are laid; and our revolted wives share damnation together. Well; I will take him, then torture my wife, pluck the borrowed veil of modesty from the so-seeming mistress Page, divulge Page himself for a secure and wilful Actæon; and to these violent proceedings all my neighbours shall cry aim. [*Clock strikes.*] The clock gives me my cue, and my assurance bids me search where I shall find Falstaff. I shall be rather praised for this, than mocked; for it is as positive as the earth is firm, that Falstaff is there: I will go.

Enter PAGE, SHALLOW, SLENDER, HOST, *Sir* HUGH EVANS, CAIUS, *and* RUGBY.

PAGE, SHAL. &c. Well met, master Ford.

FORD. Trust me, a good knot. I have good cheer at home; and I pray you all go with me.

SHAL. I must excuse myself, master Ford.

SLEN. And so must I, Sir: we have appointed to dine with mistress Anne, and I would not break with her for more money than I'll speak of.

SHAL. We have lingered about a match between Anne Page and my cousin Slender, and this day we shall have our answer.

SLEN. I hope I have your good will, father Page.

PAGE. You have, master Slender; I stand wholly for you:—but my wife, master doctor, is for you altogether.

CAIUS. Ay, by gar; and de maid is love-a me: my nursh-a Quickly tell me so mush.

HOST. What say you to young master Fenton? he capers, he dances, he has eyes of youth, he writes verses, he speaks holiday, he smells April and May: he will carry't, he will carry't; 'tis in his buttons; he will carry't.

PAGE. Not by my consent, I promise you. The gentleman is of no having: he kept company with the wild Prince and Poins; he is of too high a region; he knows too much. No, he shall not knit a knot in his fortunes with the finger of my substance: if he take her, let him take her simply; the wealth I have waits on my consent, and my consent goes not that way.

FORD. I beseech you, heartily, some of you go home with me to dinner: besides your cheer, you shall have sport; I will show you a monster.—Master Doctor, you shall go;—so shall you, master Page;—and you, Sir Hugh.

SHAL. Well, fare you well:—we shall have the freer wooing at master Page's.

    [*Exeunt* SHALLOW *and* SLENDER.

CAIUS. Go home, John Rugby; I come anon.

    [*Exit* RUGBY.

HOST. Farewell, my hearts: I will to my honest knight Falstaff, and drink canary with him.

    [*Exit* HOST.

FORD. [*Aside.*] I think, I shall drink in pipe-wine first with him; I'll make him dance.—Will you go, gentles?

ALL. Have with you, to see this monster.

    [*Exeunt.

SCENE III.—*A Room in* FORD'S *House.*

Enter Mistress FORD *and Mistress* PAGE.

MRS. FORD. What, John! what, Robert!

MRS. PAGE. Quickly, quickly:—Is the buck-basket—

MRS. FORD. I warrant.—What, Robin, I say!

Enter Servants with a large Basket.

MRS. PAGE. Come, come, come.

MRS. FORD. Here, set it down.

MRS. PAGE. Give your men the charge: we must be brief.

MRS. FORD. Marry, as I told you before, John, and Robert, be ready here hard by in the brew-house; and when I suddenly call you, come forth, and, without any pause or staggering, take this basket on your shoulders: that done, trudge with it in all haste, and carry it among the whitsters in Datchetmead, and there empty it in the muddy ditch, close by the Thames side.

MRS. PAGE. You will do it?

MRS. FORD. I have told them over and over; they lack no direction.—Be gone, and come when you are called.

    [*Exeunt* Servants.

MRS. PAGE. Here comes little Robin.

Enter ROBIN.

MRS. FORD. How now, my eyas-musket! what news with you?

ROB. My master, Sir John, is come in at

your back-door, mistress Ford, and requests your company.

MRS. PAGE. You little Jack-a-lent, have you been true to us?

ROB. Ay, I'll be sworn. My master knows not of your being here; and hath threatened to put me into everlasting liberty, if I tell you of it; for he swears he'll turn me away.

MRS. PAGE. Thou'rt a good boy; this secrecy of thine shall be a tailor to thee, and shall make thee a new doublet and hose.—I'll go hide me.

MRS. FORD. Do so.—Go tell thy master, I am alone.—Mistress Page, remember you your cue.   [*Exit* ROBIN.

MRS. PAGE. I warrant thee; if I do not act it, hiss me.

MRS. FORD. Go to, then: we'll use this unwholesome humidity, this gross watery pumpion; we'll teach him to know turtles from jays.

Enter FALSTAFF

FAL. "Have I caught my heavenly jewel?" Why, now let me die, for I have lived long enough; this is the period of my ambition: O this blessed hour!

MRS. FORD. O, sweet Sir John!

FAL. Mistress Ford, I cannot cog, I cannot prate, mistress Ford. Now shall I sin in my wish: I would thy husband were dead; I'll speak it before the best lord,—I would make thee my lady.

MRS. FORD. I, your lady, Sir John! alas, I should be a pitiful lady!

FAL. Let the court of France show me such another. I see how thine eye would emulate the diamond: thou hast the right arched beauty of the brow that becomes the ship-tire, the tire-valiant, or any tire of Venetian admittance.

MRS. FORD. A plain kerchief, Sir John: my brows become nothing else; nor that well neither.

FAL. By the Lord, thou art a traitor to say so: thou wouldst make an absolute courtier; and the firm fixure of thy foot would give an excellent motion to thy gait, in a semi-circled farthingale. I see what thou wert, if Fortune thy foe were not, Nature thy friend. Come, thou canst not hide it.

MRS. FORD. Believe me, there's no such thing in me.

FAL. What made me love thee? let that persuade thee, there's something extraordinary in thee. Come, I cannot cog, and say thou art this and that, like a many of these lisping hawthorn buds, that come like women in men's apparel, and smell like Bucklersbury in simple-time; I cannot: but

I love thee; none but thee; and thou deservest it.

MRS. FORD. Do not betray me, Sir. I fear you love mistress Page.

FAL. Thou might'st as well say, I love to walk by the Counter-gate, which is as hateful to me as the reek of a lime-kiln.

MRS. FORD. Well, heaven knows how I love you; and you shall one day find it.

FAL. Keep in that mind; I'll deserve it.

MRS. FORD. Nay, I must tell you, so you do; or else I could not be in that mind.

ROB. [*Within.*] Mistress Ford! mistress Ford! here's mistress Page at the door, sweating, and blowing, and looking wildly, and would needs speak with you presently.

FAL. She shall not see me: I will ensconce me behind the arras.

MRS. FORD. Pray you, do so: she's a very tattling woman.—

                [FALSTAFF *hides himself.*

Enter Mistress PAGE *and* ROBIN.

What's the matter? how now!

MRS. PAGE. O mistress Ford! what have you done? You're shamed, you are overthrown, you're undone for ever!

MRS. FORD. What's the matter, good mistress Page?

MRS. PAGE. O well-a-day, mistress Ford! having an honest man to your husband, to give him such cause of suspicion!

MRS. FORD. What cause of suspicion?

MRS. PAGE. What cause of suspicion?— Out upon you! how am I mistook in you?

MRS. FORD. Why, alas, what's the matter?

MRS. PAGE. Your husband's coming hither, woman, with all the officers in Windsor, to search for a gentleman, that he says, is here now in the house, by your consent, to take an ill advantage of his absence: you are undone.

MRS. FORD. 'Tis not so, I hope.

MRS. PAGE. Pray heaven it be not so, that you have such a man here! but 'tis most certain your husband's coming, with half Windsor at his heels, to search for such a one. I come before to tell you. If you know yourself clear, why, I am glad of it; but if you have a friend here, convey, convey him out. Be not amazed; call all your senses to you: defend your reputation, or bid farewell to your good life for ever.

MRS. FORD. What shall I do?—There is a gentleman, my dear friend; and I fear not mine own shame, so much as his peril: I had rather than a thousand pound, he were out of the house.

MRS. PAGE. For shame! never stand "you had rather," and "you had rather:" your husband's here at hand; bethink you of some conveyance: in the house you cannot hide him.—O, how have you deceived me! —Look, here is a basket: if he be of any reasonable stature, he may creep in here; and throw foul linen upon him, as if it were going to bucking: or, it is whiting-time, send him by your two men to Datchet-mead.

MRS. FORD. He's too big to go in there. What shall I do?

Re-enter FALSTAFF.

FAL. Let me see't, let me see't, O, let me see't! I'll in, I'll in:—follow your friend's counsel:—I'll in.

MRS. PAGE. What, Sir John Falstaff! Are these your letters, knight?

FAL. I love thee, and none but thee; help me away: let me creep in here. I'll never— [*He gets into the basket; they cover him with foul linen.*

MRS. PAGE. Help to cover your master, boy.—Call your men, mistress Ford.—You dissembling knight!   [*Exit* ROBIN.

MRS. FORD. What, John! Robert! John! [*Re-enter* Servants.] Go take up these clothes here quickly:—where's the cowl-staff? look, how you drumble! carry them to the laundress in Datchet-mead; quickly, come.

Enter FORD, PAGE, CAIUS, *and Sir* HUGH EVANS.

FORD. Pray you, come near: if I suspect without cause, why then make sport at me; then let me be your jest; I deserve it.— How now! what goes here? whither bear you this?

SERV. To the laundress, forsooth.

MRS. FORD. Why, what have you to do whither they bear it? You were best meddle with buck-washing.

FORD. Buck! I would I could wash myself of the buck! Buck, buck, buck? Ay, buck; I warrant you, buck and of the season too, it shall appear. [*Exeunt* Servants *with the basket.*] Gentlemen, I have dreamed to-night I'll tell you my dream. Here, here, here be my keys: ascend my chambers; search, seek, find out: I'll warrant we'll unkennel the fox.—Let me stop this way first.—So, now uncape.

PAGE. Good master Ford, be contented: you wrong yourself too much.

FORD. True, master Page.—Up, gentle-men you shall see sport anon: follow me, gentlemen.   [*Exit.*

EVA. This is fery fantastical humours and jealousies.

CAIUS. By gar, 'tis no de fashion of France it is not jealous in France.

PAGE. Nay, follow him, gentlemen; see the issue of his search.

[*Exeunt* PAGE, EVANS, *and* CAIUS.

MRS. PAGE. Is there not a double ex-cellency in this?

MRS. FORD. I know not which pleases me better, that my husband is deceived, or Sir John.

MRS. PAGE. What a taking was he in, when your husband asked what was in the basket!

MRS. FORD. I am half afraid he will have need of washing; so, throwing him into the water will do him a benefit.

MRS. PAGE. Hang him, dishonest rascal! I would all of the same strain were in the same distress.

MRS. FORD. I think, my husband hath some special suspicion of Falstaff's being here; for I never saw him so gross in his jealousy till now.

MRS. PAGE. I will lay a plot to try that; and we will yet have more tricks with Falstaff: his dissolute disease will scarce obey this medicine.

MRS. FORD. Shall we send that foolish carrion, mistress Quickly, to him, and excuse his throwing into the water; and give him another hope, to betray him to another punishment?

MRS. PAGE. We will do it: let him be sent for to-morrow eight o'clock, to have amends.

Re-enter FORD, PAGE, CAIUS, *and Sir* HUGH EVANS.

FORD. I cannot find him: may be, the knave bragged of that he could not compass.

MRS. PAGE. [*Aside to Mrs.* FORD.] Heard you that?

MRS. FORD. You use me well, master Ford, do you?

FORD. Ay, I do so.

MRS. FORD. Heaven make you better than your thoughts!

FORD. Amen!

MRS. PAGE. You do yourself mighty wrong, master Ford.

FORD. Ay, 'ay; I must bear it.

EVA. If there be any pody in the house, and in the chambers, and in the coffers, and in the presses, heaven forgive my sins at the day of judgment!

CAIUS. By gar, nor I too: dere is no bodies.

PAGE. Fie, fie, master Ford! are you not ashamed? What spirit, what devil suggests this imagination? I would not have your distemper in this kind for the wealth of Windsor Castle.

FORD. 'Tis my fault, master Page: I suffer for it.

EVA. You suffer for a pad conscience:

your wife is as honest a 'omans as I will
desires among five thousand, and five hundred too.

CAIUS. By gar, I see 'tis an honest woman.

FORD. Well; I promised you a dinner.—
Come, come, walk in the park: I pray you,
pardon me; I will hereafter make known
to you, why I have done this.—Come, wife;
—come, mistress Page. I pray you, pardon
me; pray heartily, pardon me.

PAGE. Let's go in, gentlemen; but, trust
me, we'll mock him. I do invite you to-
morrow morning to my house to breakfast:
after, we'll a birding together: I have a
fine hawk for the bush. Shall it be so?

FORD. Any thing.

EVA. If there is one, I shall make two in
the company.

CAIUS. If dere be one or two, I shall
make-a de turd.

FORD. Pray you go, master Page.

EVA. I pray you now, remembrance to-
morrow on the lousy knave, mine host.

CAIUS. Dat is good; by gar, vit all my
heart.

EVA. A lousy knave, to have his gibes,
and his mockeries!   [*Exeunt.*

SCENE IV.—*A Room in* PAGE'S *House.*

Enter FENTON *and* ANNE PAGE.

FENT. I see I cannot get thy father's love;
Therefore no more turn me to him, sweet
Nan.

ANNE. Alas! how then?

FENT.   Why, thou must be thyself.
He doth object, I am too great of birth;
And that my state being gall'd with my
expence,
I seek to heal it only by his wealth.
Besides these, other bars he lays before
My riots past, my wild societies;   [me,—
And tells me, 'tis a thing impossible
I should love thee, but as a property.

ANNE. May be, he tells you true.

FENT. No, heavens so speed me in my
time to come!
Albeit, I will confess, thy father's wealth
Was the first motive that I woo'd thee,
Anne:
Yet wooing thee, I found thee of more
value
Than stamps in gold, or sums in sealed
And 'tis the very riches of thyself   [bags;
That now I aim at.

ANNE.   Gentle master Fenton,
Yet seek my father's love; still seek it, Sir;
If opportunity and humblest suit
Cannot attain it, why then,—Hark you
hither.   [*They converse apart.*

Enter SHALLOW, SLENDER, *and Mrs.*
QUICKLY.

SHAL. Break their talk, mistress Quickly:
my kinsman shall speak for himself.

SLEN. I'll make a shaft or a bolt on't.
'Slid, 'tis but venturing.

SHAL. Be not dismayed.

SLEN. No, she shall not dismay me: I
care not for that,—but that I am afeard.

QUICK. Hark ye; master Slender would
speak a word with you.

ANNE. I come to him.—[*Aside.*] This is
my father's choice.
O, what a world of vile ill-favour'd faults
Looks handsome in three hundred pounds
a year!

QUICK. And how does good master Fenton? Pray you, a word with you.

SHAL. She's coming; to her, coz. O boy,
thou hadst a father!

SLEN. I had a father, mistress Anne;—
my uncle can tell you good jests of him.—
Pray you, uncle, tell mistress Anne the
jest, how my father stole two geese out of
a pen, good uncle.

SHAL. Mistress Anne, my cousin loves
you.

SLEN. Ay, that I do; as well as I love
any woman in Gloucestershire.

SHAL. He will maintain you like a gentlewoman.

SLEN. Ay, that I will, come cut and long-
tail, under the degree of a squire.

SHAL. He will make you a hundred and
fifty pounds jointure.

ANNE. Good master Shallow, let him woo
for himself.

SHAL. Marry, I thank you for it; I thank
you for that good comfort.—She calls you,
coz: I'll leave you.

ANNE. Now, master Slender,—

SLEN. Now, good mistress Anne,—

ANNE. What is your will?

SLEN. My will! od's heartlings, that's a
pretty jest, indeed! I ne'er made my will
yet, I thank heaven; I am not such a sickly
creature, I give heaven praise.

ANNE. I mean, master Slender, what
would you with me?

SLEN. Truly, for mine own part, I would
little or nothing with you. Your father, and
my uncle, have made motions: if it be my
luck, so; if not, happy man be his dole!
They can tell you how things go, better
than I can: you may ask your father; here
he comes.

Enter PAGE *and Mistress* PAGE.

PAGE. Now, master Slender:—love him,
daughter Anne.—
Why, how now! what does master Fenton
here?

You wrong me, Sir, thus still to haunt my
house:

I told you, Sir, my daughter is dispos'd of.

FENT. Nay, master Page, be not impatient.

MRS. PAGE. Good master Fenton, come
not to my child.

PAGE. She is no match for you.

FENT. Sir, will you hear me?

PAGE.   No, good master Fenton.—
Come, master Shallow;—come, son Slender; in.—

Knowing my mind, you wrong me, master
Fenton.

[*Exeunt* PAGE, SHALLOW, *and* SLENDER.

QUICK. Speak to mistress Page.

FENT. Good mistress Page, for that I love
your daughter

In such a righteous fashion as I do,

Perforce, against all checks, rebukes, and
manners,

I must advance the colours of my love,

And not retire: let me have your good will.

ANNE. Good mother, do not marry me to
yond' fool.

MRS. PAGE. I mean it not; I seek you a
better husband.

QUICK. That's my master, master doctor.

ANNE. Alas! I had rather be set quick i'
the earth,

And bowl'd to death with turnips!

MRS. PAGE. Come, trouble not yourself.
—Good master Fenton,

I will not be your friend, nor enemy:

My daughter will I question how she loves

And as I find her, so am I affected.   [you,

'Till then, farewell, Sir: she must needs

Her father will be angry.   [go in;

FENT. Farewell, gentle mistress:—farewell, Nan.

[*Exeunt Mrs.* PAGE *and* ANNE.

QUICK. This is my doing, now:—"Nay,"
said I, "will you cast away your child on
a fool, and a physician? look on master
Fenton:"—this is my doing.

FENT. I thank thee; and I pray thee, once
tonight

Give my sweet Nan this ring. There's for
thy pains.

QUICK. Now, heaven send thee good fortune! [*Exit* FENTON.] A kind heart he
hath: a woman would run through fire
and water for such a kind heart. But yet
I would my master had mistress Anne; or
I would master Slender had her; or, in
sooth, I would master Fenton had her: I
will do what I can for them all three; for
so I have promised, and I'll be as good
as my word; but speciously for master
Fenton. Well, I must of another errand to

Sir John Falstaff from my two mistresses:
what a beast am I to slack it!   [*Exit.*

SCENE V.—*A Room in the* Garter Inn.

Enter FALSTAFF *and* BARDOLPH.

FAL. Bardolph, I say,—

BARD. Here, Sir.

FAL. Go fetch me a quart of sack; put a
toast in't. [*Exit* BARD.] Have I lived to be
carried in a basket, like a barrow of butcher's offal, and to be thrown in the
Thames? Well, if I be served such another
trick, I'll have my brains ta'en out, and
buttered, and give them to a dog for a new
year's gift. The rogues slighted me into
the river with as little remorse as they
would have drowned a bitch's blind puppies,
fifteen i' the litter: and you may know by
my size, that I have a kind of alacrity in
sinking; if the bottom were as deep as
hell, I should down. I have been drowned,
but that the shore was shelvy and shallow;
a death that I abhor; for the water swells a
man; and what a thing should I have been
when I had been swelled! I should have
been a mountain of mummy.

Re-enter BARDOLPH, *with the Wine.*

BARD. Here's mistress Quickly, Sir, to
speak with you.

FAL. Come, let me pour in some sack to
the Thames water; for my belly's as cold
as if I had swallowed snow-balls for pills
to cool the reins. Call her in.

BARD. Come in, woman.

Enter Mrs. QUICKLY.

QUICK. By your leave; I cry your mercy:
—give your worship good-morrow.

FAL. Take away these chalices. Go brew
me a pottle of sack finely.

BARD. With eggs, Sir?

FAL. Simple of itself; I'll no pullet-sperm
in my brewage.—[*Exit* BARDOLPH.]—How
now!

QUICK. Marry, Sir, I come to your worship from mistress Ford.

FAL. Mistress Ford! I have had ford
enough: I was thrown into the ford; I have
my belly full of ford.

QUICK. Alas the day! good heart, that
was not her fault: she does so take on
with her men; they mistook their erection.

FAL. So did I mine, to build upon a foolish woman's promise.

QUICK. Well, she laments, Sir, for it, that
it would yearn your heart to see it. Her
husband goes this morning a birding: she
desires you once more to come to her between eight and nine. I must carry her
word quickly: she'll make you amends, I
warrant you.

FAL. Well, I will visit her: tell her so; and bid her think what a man is: let her consider his frailty, and then judge of my merit.

QUICK. I will tell her.

FAL. Do so. Between nine and ten, sayest thou?

QUICK. Eight and nine, Sir.

FAL. Well, be gone: I will not miss her.

QUICK. Peace be with you, Sir.   [*Exit.*

FAL. I marvel I hear not of master Brook: he sent me word to stay within. I like his money well.—O! here he comes.

Enter FORD.

FORD. Bless you, Sir.

FAL. Now, master Brook,—you come to know what hath passed between me and Ford's wife?

FORD. That, indeed, Sir John, is my business.

FAL. Master Brook, I will not lie to you: I was at her house the hour she appointed me.

FORD. And sped you, Sir?

FAL. Very ill-favouredly, master Brook.

FORD. How so, Sir? Did she change her determination?

FAL. No, master Brook; but the peaking cornuto her husband, master Brook, dwelling in a continual 'larum of jealousy, comes me in the instant of our encounter, after we had embraced, kissed, protested, and, as it were, spoke the prologue of our comedy; and at his heels a rabble of his companions, thither provoked and instigated by his distemper, and, forsooth, to search his house for his wife's love.

FORD. What! while you were there?

FAL. While I was there.

FORD. And did he search for you, and could not find you?

FAL. You shall hear. As good luck would have it, comes in one mistress Page; gives intelligence of Ford's approach; and in her invention, and Ford's wife's distraction, they conveyed me into a buck-basket.

FORD. A buck-basket!

FAL. By the Lord, a buck-basket!— rammed me in with foul shirts and smocks, socks, foul stockings, greasy napkins; that, master Brook, there was the rankest compound of villainous smell that ever offended nostril.

FORD. And how long lay you there?

FAL. Nay, you shall hear, master Brook, what I have suffered, to bring this woman to evil for your good. Being thus crammed in the basket, a couple of Ford's knaves, his hinds, were called forth by their mistress, to carry me in the name of foul clothes to Datchet-lane: they took me on their shoulders; met the jealous knave their master in the door, who asked them once or twice what they had in their basket. I quaked for fear, lest the lunatic knave would have searched it; but fate, ordaining he should be a cuckold, held his hand. Well; on went he for a search, and away went I for foul clothes. But mark the sequel, master Brook: I suffered the pangs of three several deaths: first, an intolerable fright, to be detected with a jealous rotten bell-wether: next, to be compassed, like a good bilbo, in the circumference of a peck, hilt to point, heel to head: and then, to be stopped in, like a strong distillation, with stinking clothes that fretted in their own grease: think of that,—a man of my kidney—think of that,—that am as subject to heat, as butter; a man of continual dissolution and thaw: it was a miracle, to 'scape suffocation. And in the height of this bath, when I was more than half stewed in grease, like a Dutch dish, to be thrown into the Thames, and cooled, glowing hot, in that surge, like a horseshoe; think of that,—hissing hot,—think of that, master Brook!

FORD. In good sadness, Sir, I am sorry that for my sake you have suffered all this. My suit, then, is desperate; you'll undertake her no more?

FAL. Master Brook, I will be thrown into Ætna, as I have been into Thames, ere I will leave her thus. Her husband is this morning gone a birding: I have received from her another embassy of meeting; 'twixt eight and nine is the hour, master Brook.

FORD. 'Tis past eight already, Sir.

FAL. Is it? I will then address me to my appointment. Come to me at your convenient leisure, and you shall know how I speed; and the conclusion shall be crowned with your enjoying her: adieu. You shall have her, master Brook; master Brook, you shall cuckold Ford.   [*Exit.*

FORD. Hum,—ha! is this a vision? is this a dream? do I sleep? Master Ford, awake! awake, master Ford! there's a hole made in your best coat, master Ford. This 'tis to be married! this 'tis to have linen, and buck-baskets!—Well, I will proclaim myself what I am: I will now take the lecher; he is at my house; he cannot 'scape me; 'tis impossible he should; he cannot creep into a half-penny purse, nor into a pepper-box: but, lest the devil that guides him should aid him, I will search impossible places. Though what I am I cannot avoid, yet to be what I would not, shall not make me tame: if I have horns to make me mad, let the proverb go with me, I'll be horn mad.   [*Exit.*

ACT IV.

SCENE I.—*The Street.*

Enter Mrs. PAGE, *Mrs.* QUICKLY, *and* WILLIAM.

MRS. PAGE. Is he at master Ford's already, thinkest thou?

QUICK. Sure, he is by this, or will be presently: but truly, he is very courageous mad about his throwing into the water. Mistress Ford desires you to come suddenly.

MRS. PAGE. I'll be with her by and by: I'll but bring my young man here to school. Look, where his master comes; 'tis a playing-day, I see.

Enter Sir HUGH EVANS.

How now, Sir Hugh! no school to-day?

EVA. No; master Slender is get the boys leave to play.

QUICK. Blessing of his heart!

MRS. PAGE. Sir Hugh, my husband says, my son profits nothing in the world at his book: I pray you, ask him some questions in his accidence.

EVA. Come hither, William: hold up your head; come.

MRS. PAGE. Come on, sirrah: hold up your head; answer your master, be not afraid.

EVA. William, how many numbers is in nouns?

WILL. Two.

QUICK. Truly, I thought there had been one number more, because they say, od's nouns.

EVA. Peace your tattlings.—What is *fair,* William?

WILL. Pulcher.

QUICK. Pole-cats! there are fairer things than pole-cats, sure.

EVA. You are a very simplicity 'oman: I pray you, peace.—What is *lapis,* William?

WILL. A stone.

EVA. And what is a stone, William?

WILL. A pebble.

EVA. No, it is *lapis*: I pray you remember in your prain.

WILL. Lapis.

EVA. That is a good William. What is he, William, that does lend articles?

WILL. Articles are borrowed of the pronoun; and be thus declined, *Singulariter, nominativo, hic hœc, hoc.*

EVA. *Nominativo, hig, hag, hog;*—pray you, mark: *genitivo, hujus.* Well, what is your accusative case?

WILL. *Accusativo, hunc.*

EVA. I pray you, have your remembrance, child; *accusativo, hung, hang, hog.*

QUICK. Hang hog is Latin for bacon, I warrant you.

EVA. Leave your prabbles, 'oman.—What is the focative case, William?

WILL. O,—*vocativo,* O.

EVA. Remember, William; focative is, *caret.*

QUICK. And that's a good root.

EVA. 'Oman, forbear.

MRS. PAGE. Peace!

EVA. What is your genitive case plural, William?

WILL. Genitive case?

EVA. Ay.

WILL. *Genitivo,—horum, harum, horum.*

QUICK. Vengeance of Jenny's case! fie on her!—Never name her, child, if she be a whore.

EVA. For shame, 'oman!

QUICK. You do ill to teach the child such words.—He teaches him to hick and to hack, which they'll do fast enough of themselves; and to call horum:—fie upon you!

EVA. 'Oman, art thou lunatics? hast thou no understandings for thy cases, and the numbers, and the genders? Thou art as foolish Christian creatures as I would desires.

MRS. PAGE. Pr'ythee, hold thy peace.

EVA. Show me now, William, some declensions of your pronouns.

WILL. Forsooth, I have forgot.

EVA. It is *qui, quœ, quod*; if you forget your *quis,* your *quœs,* and your *quods,* you must be preeches. Go your ways, and play; go.

MRS. PAGE. He is a better scholar than I thought he was.

EVA. He is a good sprag memory. Farewell, mistress Page.

MRS. PAGE. Adieu, good Sir Hugh. [*Exit Sir* HUGH.] Get you home, boy.—Come, we stay too long.   [*Exeunt.*

SCENE II.—*A Room in* FORD'S *House.*

Enter FALSTAFF *and Mrs.* FORD.

FAL. Mistress Ford, your sorrow hath eaten up my sufferance. I see you are obsequious in your love, and I profess requital to a hair's breadth; not only, Mrs. Ford, in the simple office of love, but in all the accoutrement, complement, and ceremony of it. But are you sure of your husband now?

MRS. FORD. He's a birding, sweet Sir John.

MRS. PAGE. [*Within.*] What ho, gossip Ford! what ho!

MRS. FORD. Step into the chamber, Sir
John.   [*Exit* FALSTAFF.
       Enter Mrs. PAGE.
MRS. PAGE. How now, sweetheart! who's
at home besides yourself?
MRS. FORD. Why, none but mine own
people.
MRS. PAGE. Indeed?
MRS. FORD. No, certainly.—[*Aside to
her.*] Speak louder.
MRS. PAGE. Truly, I am so glad you
have nobody here.
MRS. FORD. Why?
MRS. PAGE. Why, woman, your husband
is in his old lunes again: he so takes on
yonder with my husband; so rails against
all married mankind; so curses all Eve's
daughters, of what complexion soever; and
so buffets himself on the forehead, crying,
"Peer out, Peer out!" that any madness I
ever yet beheld seemed but tameness, civility, and patience, to this his distemper he is
in now. I am glad the fat knight is not
here.
MRS. FORD. Why, does he talk of him?
MRS. PAGE. Of none but him; and
swears he was carried out, the last time he
searched for him, in a basket: protests to
my husband he is now here; and hath
drawn him and the rest of their company
from their sport, to make another experiment of his suspicion. But I am glad the
knight is not here; now he shall see his
own foolery.
MRS. FORD. How near is he, mistress
Page?
MRS. PAGE. Hard by; at street end: he
will be here anon.
MRS. FORD. I am undone!—the knight
is here.
MRS. PAGE. Why then, you are utterly
shamed, and he's but a dead man. What a
woman are you!—Away with him, away
with him! better shame, than murder.
MRS. FORD. Which way should he go?
how should I bestow him? Shall I put him
into the basket again?
       Re-enter FALSTAFF.
FAL. No, I'll come no more i' the basket.
May I not go out, ere he come?
MRS. PAGE. Alas, three of master Ford's
brothers watch the door with pistols, that
none shall issue out; otherwise you might
slip away ere he came. But what make
you here?
FAL. What shall I do?—I'll creep up into
the chimney.
MRS. FORD. There they always use to
discharge their birding-pieces. Creep into
the kiln-hole.
FAL. Where is it?

MRS. FORD. He will seek there, on my
word. Neither press, coffer, chest, trunk,
well, vault, but he hath an abstract for the
remembrance of such places, and goes to
them by his note: there is no hiding you
in the house.
FAL. I'll go out, then.
MRS. PAGE. If you go out in your own
semblance, you die, Sir John. Unless you
go out disguised,—
MRS. FORD. How might we disguise him?
MRS. PAGE. Alas the day! I know not.
There is no woman's gown big enough for
him; otherwise, he might put on a hat,
a muffler, and a kerchief, and so escape.
FAL. Good hearts, devise something: any
extremity, rather than a mischief.
MRS. FORD. My maid's aunt, the fat
woman of Brentford, has a gown above.
MRS. PAGE. On my word, it will serve
him; she's as big as he is: and there's her
thrummed hat, and her muffler too.—Run
up, Sir John.
MRS. FORD. Go, go, sweet Sir John: mistress Page and I will look some linen for
your head.
MRS. PAGE. Quick, quick! we'll come
dress you straight: put on the gown the
while.   [*Exit* FALSTAFF.
MRS. FORD. I would my husband would
meet him in this shape: he cannot abide
the old woman of Brentford; he swears
she's a witch; forbade her my house, and
hath threatened to beat her.
MRS. PAGE. Heaven guide him to thy
husband's cudgel, and the devil guide his
cudgel afterwards!
MRS. FORD. But is my husband coming?
MRS. PAGE. Ay, in good sadness, is he;
and talks of the basket too, howsoever he
hath had intelligence.
MRS. FORD. We'll try that; for I'll appoint my men to carry the basket again, to
meet him at the door with it, as they did
last time.
MRS. PAGE. Nay, but he'll be here presently: let's go dress him like the witch of
Brentford.
MRS. FORD. I'll first direct my men what
they shall do with the basket. Go up; I'll
bring linen for him straight.   [*Exit.*
MRS. PAGE. Hang him, dishonest varlet!
we cannot misuse him enough.

  We'll leave a proof, by that which we
      will do,
Wives may be merry, and yet honest too:
We do not act, that often jest and laugh;
'Tis old, but true,—"Still swine eat all
      the draff."   [*Exit.*

Re-enter Mrs. FORD, *with two* Servants.

MRS. FORD. Go, Sirs, take the basket again on your shoulders: your master is hard at door; if he bid you set it down, obey him: quickly, despatch.   [*Exit*.

1 SERV. Come, come, take it up.

2 SERV. Pray heaven, it be not full of knight again.

1 SERV. I hope not; I had as lief bear so much lead.

Enter FORD, PAGE, SHALLOW, CAIUS, *and*
Sir HUGH EVANS.

FORD. Ay, but if it prove true, master Page, have you any way then to unfool me again?—Set down the basket, villains!—Somebody call my wife.—Youth in a basket! —O you panderly rascals! there's a knot, a ging, a pack, a conspiracy against me: now shall the devil be shamed.—What, wife, I say!—Come, come forth!—Behold what honest clothes you send forth to bleaching.

PAGE. Why, this passes! Master Ford, you are not to go loose any longer; you must be pinioned.

EVA. Why, this is lunatics! this is mad as a mad dog!

SHAL. Indeed, master Ford, this is not well; indeed.

FORD. So say I too, Sir.—[*Re-enter Mrs.* FORD.] Come hither, mistress Ford; mistress Ford, the honest woman, the modest wife, the virtuous creature, that hath the jealous fool to her husband!—I suspect without cause, mistress, do I?

MRS. FORD. Heaven be my witness, you do, if you suspect me in any dishonesty.

FORD. Well said, brazen-face! I hold it out.—Come forth, sirrah.
            [*Pulls the clothes out of the basket*.

PAGE. This passes!

MRS. FORD. Are you not ashamed? let the clothes alone.

FORD. I shall find you anon.

EVA. 'Tis unreasonable! Will you take up your wife's clothes? Come away.

FORD. Empty the basket, I say!

MRS. FORD. Why, man, why,—

FORD. Master Page, as I am a man, there was one conveyed out of my house yesterday in this basket: why may not he be there again? In my house I am sure he is: my intelligence is true; my jealousy is reasonable.—Pluck me out all the linen.

MRS. FORD. If you find a man there, he shall die a flea's death.

PAGE. Here's no man.

SHAL. By my fidelity, this is not well, master Ford; this wrongs you.

EVA. Master Ford, you must pray, and not follow the imaginations of your own heart: this is jealousies.

FORD. Well, he's not here I seek for.

PAGE. No, nor no where else, but in your brain.

FORD. Help to search my house this one time: if I find not what I seek, show no colour for my extremity; let me for ever be your table-sport; let them say of me, "As jealous as Ford, that searched a hollow walnut for his wife's leman." Satisfy me once more; once more search with me.

MRS. FORD. What ho, mistress Page! come you and the old woman down; my husband will come into the chamber.

FORD. Old woman! What old woman's that?

MRS. FORD. Why, it is my maid's aunt of Brentford.

FORD. A witch, a quean, an old cozening quean! Have I not forbid her my house? She comes of errands, does she? We are simple men; we do not know what's brought to pass under the profession of fortune-telling. She works by charms, by spells, by the figure, and such daubery as this is; beyond our element: we know nothing.—Come down, you witch, you hag, you; come down, I say!

MRS. FORD. Nay, good, sweet husband,— good gentlemen, let him not strike the old woman.

Enter FALSTAFF *in Women's Clothes, led*
by Mrs. PAGE.

MRS. PAGE. Come, mother Prat; come, give me your hand.

FORD. I'll "prat" her.—[*Beats him.*] Out of my door, you witch, you rag, you baggage, you pole-cat, you ronyon! out, out, I'll conjure you, I'll fortune-tell you.
            [*Exit* FALSTAFF.

MRS. PAGE. Are you not ashamed? I think you have killed the poor woman.

MRS. FORD. Nay, he will do it.—'Tis a goodly credit for you.

FORD. Hang her, witch!

EVA. By yea and no, I think the 'oman is a witch indeed: I like not when a 'oman has a great peard; I spy a great peard under her muffler.

FORD. Will you follow, gentlemen? I beseech you, follow: see but the issue of my jealousy. If I cry out thus upon no trail, never trust me when I open again.

PAGE. Let's obey his humour a little farther: come, gentlemen.
            [*Exeunt* FORD, PAGE, SHALLOW, CAIUS *and*
EVANS.]

MRS. PAGE. Trust me, he beat him most pitifully.

MRS. FORD. Nay, by the mass, that he did not; he beat him most unpitifully, methought.

MRS. PAGE. I'll have the cudgel hallowed, and hung o'er the altar; it hath done meritorious service.

MRS. FORD. What think you? May we, with the warrant of womanhood, and the witness of a good conscience, pursue him with any farther revenge?

MRS. PAGE. The spirit of wantonness is, sure, scared out of him: if the devil have him not in fee-simple, with fine and recovery, he will never, I think, in the way of waste, attempt us again.

MRS. FORD. Shall we tell our husbands how we have served him?

MRS. PAGE. Yes, by all means; if it be but to scrape the figures out of your husband's brains. If they can find in their hearts the poor unvirtuous fat knight shall be any farther afflicted, we two will still be the ministers.

MRS. FORD. I'll warrant, they'll have him publicly shamed; and methinks there would be no period to the jest, should he not be publicly shamed.

MRS. PAGE. Come, to the forge with it, then; shape it: I would not have things cool.   [Exeunt.

SCENE III.—A Room in the Garter Inn.

Enter Host and BARDOLPH.

BARD. Sir, the Germans desire to have three of your horses: the duke himself will be to-morrow at court, and they are going to meet him.

HOST. What duke should that be, comes so secretly? I hear not of him in the court. Let me speak with the gentlemen; they speak English?

BARD. Ay, Sir; I'll call them to you.

HOST. They shall have my horses; but I'll make them pay; I'll sauce them: they have had my house a week at command; I have turned away my other guests: they must come off; I'll sauce them. Come.   [Exeunt.

SCENE IV.—A Room in FORD'S House.

Enter PAGE, FORD, Mrs. PAGE, Mrs. FORD, and Sir HUGH EVANS.

EVA. 'Tis one of the pest discretions of a 'oman as ever I did look upon.

PAGE. And did he send you both these letters at an instant?

MRS. PAGE. Within a quarter of an hour.

FORD. Pardon me, wife. Henceforth do what thou wilt;

I rather will suspect the sun with cold,
Than thee with wantonness: now doth thy honour stand,
In him that was of late a heretic,
As firm as faith.

PAGE. 'Tis well, 'tis well; no more:
Be not as extreme in submission,
As in offence.
But let our plot go forward: let our wives
Yet once again, to make us public sport,
Appoint a meeting with this old fat fellow,
Where we may take him, and disgrace him for it.

FORD. There is no better way than that they spoke of.

PAGE. How! to send him word they'll meet him in the park at midnight? fie, fie! he'll never come.

EVA. You say, he has been thrown into the rivers, and has been grievously peaten, as as old 'oman: methinks there should be terrors in him, that he should not come; methinks his flesh is punished, he shall have no desires.

PAGE. So think I too.

MRS. FORD. Devise but how you'll use him when he comes,
And let us two devise to bring him thither.

MRS. PAGE. There is an old tale goes, that Herne the hunter,
Sometime a keeper here in Windsor forest,
Doth all the winter time, at still midnight,
Walk round about an oak, with great ragg'd horns;
And there he blasts the trees, and takes the cattle,
And makes milch-kine yield blood, and shakes a chain
In a most hideous and dreadful manner.
You have heard of such a spirit; and well you know,
The superstitious idle-headed eld
Received, and did deliver to our age,
This tale of Herne the hunter for a truth.

PAGE. Why, yet there want not many, that do fear
In deep of night to walk by this Herne's oak.
But what of this?   [oak.

MRS. FORD. Marry, this is our device;
That Falstaff at that oak shall meet with us,
Disguis'd like Herne, with huge horns on his head.

PAGE. Well, let it not be doubted but he'll come,
And in this shape: when you have brought him thither,
What shall be done with him? what is your plot?

MRS. PAGE. That likewise have we thought upon, and thus.

Nan Page my daughter, and my little son,
And three or four more of their growth, we'll dress
Like urchins, ouphes, and fairies, green and white,

With rounds of waxen tapers on their
  heads,
And rattles in their hands. Upon a sudden,
As Falstaff, she, and I, are newly met,
Let them from forth a saw-pit rush at once
With some diffused song: upon their sight,
We two in great amazedness will fly:
Then, let them all encircle him about,
And, fairy-like, to-pinch, the unclean
  knight;
And ask him, why, that hour of fairy revel,
In their so sacred paths he dares to tread
In shape profane.

MRS. FORD. And till he tell the truth,
Let the supposed fairies pinch him sound,
And burn him with their tapers.

MRS. PAGE.   The truth being known,
We'll all present ourselves, dis-horn the
  spirit,
And mock him home to Windsor.

FORD.   The children must
Be practis'd well to this, or they'll ne'er
do't.

EVA. I will teach the children their behaviours; I will be like a jack-an-apes also,
to burn the knight with my taber.

FORD. That will be excellent. I'll go buy
them vizards.

MRS. PAGE. My Nan shall be the queen
of all the fairies,
Finely attired in a robe of white.

PAGE. That silk will I go buy:—[*Aside.*]
and in that time
Shall master Slender steal my Nan away,
And marry her at Eton.—[*To them.*] Go,
send to Falstaff straight.

FORD. Nay, I'll to him again in name of
Brook:
He'll tell me all his purpose. Sure, he'll
come.

MRS. PAGE. Fear not you that. Go, get
us properties,
And tricking for our fairies.

EVA. Let us about it: it is admirable
pleasures, and fery honest knaveries.

[*Exeunt* PAGE, FORD, *and* EVANS.

MRS. PAGE. Go, mistress Ford,
Send Quickly to Sir John, to know his
mind.   [*Exit Mrs.* FORD.
I'll to the doctor: he hath my good will,
And none but he, to marry with Nan Page.
That Slender, though well landed, is an
idiot;
And him my husband best of all affects.
The doctor is well money'd, and his friends
Potent a court: he, none but he, shall have
her,
Though twenty thousand worthier come to
crave her.   [*Exit.*

SCENE V.—*A Room in the* Garter Inn.
Enter Host *and* SIMPLE.

HOST. What wouldst thou have, boor?
what, thick-skin, speak, breathe, discuss;
brief, short, quick, snap.

SIM. Marry, Sir, I come to speak with Sir
John Falstaff from master Slender.

HOST. There's his chamber, his house, his
castle, his standing-bed, and truckle-bed:
'tis painted about with the story of the
prodigal, fresh and new. Go, knock and
call; he'll speak like an Anthropophaginian
unto thee: knock, I say.

SIM. There's an old woman, a fat woman,
gone up into his chamber: I'll be so bold
as stay, Sir, till she come down; I come to
speak with her, indeed.

HOST. Ha! a fat woman? the knight may
be robbed: I'll call.—Bully knight! Bully
Sir John! speak from thy lungs military:
art thou there? it is thine host, thine
Ephesian, calls.

FAL. [*Above.*] How now, mine host!

HOST. Here's a Bohemian Tartar tarries
the coming down of thy fat woman. Let
her descend, bully, let her descend; my
chambers are honourable: fie! privacy? fie!

Enter FALSTAFF.

FAL. There was, mine host, an old fat
woman even now with me; but she's gone.

SIM. Pray you, Sir, was't not the wise
woman of Brentford?

FAL. Ay, marry, was it, muscle-shell:
what would you with her?

SIM. My master, Sir, master Slender, sent
to her, seeing her go through the streets, to
know, Sir, whether one Nym, Sir, that beguiled him of a chain, had the chain or no.

FAL. I spake with the old woman about it.

SIM. And what says she, I pray, Sir?

FAL. Marry, she says that the very same
man, that beguiled master Slender of his
chain, cozened him of it.

SIM. I would I could have spoken with
the woman herself; I had other things to
have spoken with her too, from him.

FAL. What are they? let us know.

HOST. Ay, come; quick.

SIM. I may not conceal them, Sir.

HOST. Conceal them, or thou diest.

SIM. Why, Sir, they were nothing but
about mistress Anne Page; to know, if it
were my master's fortune to have her, or
no.

FAL. 'Tis, 'tis his fortune.

SIM. What, Sir?

FAL. To have her,—or no. Go; say the
woman told me so.

SIM. May I be bold to say so, Sir?

FAL. Ay, Sir Tike, who more bold?

SIM. I thank your worship: I shall make my master glad with these tidings.   [*Exit.*
HOST. Thou art clerkly, thou art clerkly, Sir John. Was there a wise woman with thee?
FAL. Ay, that there was, mine host; one that hath taught me more wit than ever I learned before in my life; and I paid nothing for it neither, but was paid for my learning.

Enter BARDOLPH.

BARD. Out, alas, Sir! cozenage, mere cozenage!
HOST. Where be my horses? speak well of them, varletto.
BARD. Run away, with the cozeners: for so soon as I came beyond Eton, they threw me off, from behind one of them, in a slough of mire; and set spurs and away, like three German devils, three Doctor Faustuses.
HOST. They are gone but to meet the duke, villain: do not say they be fled; Germans are honest men.

Enter Sir HUGH EVANS.

EVA. Where is mine host?
HOST. What is the matter, Sir?
EVA. Have a care of your entertainments: there is a friend of mine come to town, tells me, there is three cousin germans, that has cozened all the hosts of Readings, of Maidenhead, of Colebrook, of horses and money. I tell you for good-will, look you: you are wise, and full of gibes and vlouting-stogs, and 'tis not convenient you should be cozened. Fare you well.   [*Exit.*

Enter Doctor CAIUS.

CAIUS. Vere is mine Host de *Jarretière?*
HOST. Here, master doctor, in perplexity, and doubtful dilemma.
CAIUS. I cannot tell vat is dat; but it is tell-a me, dat you make grand preparation for a duke de Jarmany: by my trot, dere is no duke dat de court is know to come. I tell you for good vill: adieu.   [*Exit.*
HOST. Hue and cry, villain! go.—Assist me, knight.—I am undone!—Fly, run, hue and cry, villain!—I am undone!

[*Exeunt* HOST *and* BARDOLPH

FAL. I would all the world might be cozened; for I have been cozened, and beaten too. If it should come to the ear of the court how I have been transformed, and how my transformation hath been washed and cudgelled, they would melt me out of my fat, drop by drop, and liquor fisher-men's boots with me: I warrant, they would whip me with their fine wits, till I were as crest-fallen as a dried pear. I never prospered since I forswore myself at pri-

mero. Well, if my wind were but long enough to say my prayers, I would repent.—

Enter Mistress QUICKLY.

Now, whence come you?
QUICK. From the two parties, forsooth.
FAL. The devil take one party, and his dam the other and so they shall be both bestowed. I have suffered more for their sakes, more than the villainous inconstancy of man's disposition is able to bear.
QUICK. And have not they suffered? Yes, I warrant; speciously one of them: mistress Ford, good heart, is beaten black and blue, that you cannot see a white spot about her.
FAL. What tellest thou me of black and blue? I was beaten myself into all the colours of the rainbow; and I was like to be apprehended for the witch of Brentford: but that my admirable dexterity of wit, my counterfeiting the action of an old woman, delivered me, the knave constable had set me i' the stocks, i' the common stocks, for a witch.
QUICK. Sir, let me speak with you in your chamber: you shall hear how things go; and, I warrant, to your content. Here is a letter will say somewhat. Good hearts, what ado here is to bring you together! Sure, one of you does not serve heaven well, that you are so crossed.
FAL. Come up into my chamber.

[*Exeunt.*

SCENE VI.—*Another Room in the* Garter Inn.

Enter FENTON *and* HOST.

HOST. Master Fenton, talk not to me; my mind is heavy: I will give over all.
FENT. Yet hear me speak. Assist me in my purpose,
And, as I am a gentleman, I'll give thee
A hundred pound in gold more than your loss.
HOST. I will hear you, master Fenton; and I will, at the least, keep your counsel.
FENT. From time to time I have acquaint-ed you
With the dear love I bear to fair Anne Page;
Who, mutually, hath answer'd my affection
(So far forth as herself might be her chooser)
Even to my wish. I have a letter from her
Of such contents as you will wonder at;
The mirth whereof so larded with my matter,
That neither, singly, can be manifested,
Without the show of both;—wherein fat Falstaff
Hath a great scene: the image of the jest
[*Pointing to the Letter.*

I'll show you here at large. Hark, good
mine host:
To-night at Herne's oak, just 'twixt twelve
and one,
Must my sweet Nan present the fairy
queen;
The purpose why, is here: [*Pointing to
Letter.*] in which disguise,
While other jests are something rank on
foot,
Her father hath commanded her to slip
Away with Slender, and with him at Eton
Immediately to marry: she hath consented.
Now, Sir,
Her mother, even strong against that match,
And firm for Dr. Caius, hath appointed
That he shall likewise shuffle her away,
While other sports are tasking of their
minds,
And at the deanery, where a priest attends,
Straight marry her: to this her mother's
plot
She, seemingly obedient, likewise hath
Made promise to the doctor.—Now, thus
it rests:
Her father means she shall be all in white;
And in that habit, when Slender sees his
time
To take her by the hand, and bid her go,
She shall go with him: her mother hath
intended,
The better to denote her to the doctor,
(For they must all be mask'd and vizarded)
That, quaint in green, she shall be loose
enrob'd,
With ribands pendent, flaring 'bout her
head;
And when the doctor spies his vantage ripe,
To pinch her by the hand, and on that
token,
The maid hath given consent to go with
him.
HOST. Which means she to deceive, father
or mother?
FENT. Both, my good host, to go along
with me:
And here it rests,—that you'll procure the
vicar
To stay for me at church 'twixt twelve
and one,
And, in the lawful name of marrying,
To give our hearts united ceremony.
HOST. Well, husband your device: I'll to
the vicar.
Bring you the maid, you shall not lack a
priest.
FENT. So shall I evermore be bound to
thee;
Besides, I'll make a present recompense.
[*Exeunt.*

ACT V.

SCENE I.—*A room in the* Garter Inn.

Enter FALSTAFF *and* Mrs. QUICKLY.

FAL. Pr'ythee, no more prattling;—go:—
I'll hold. This is the third time; I hope
good luck lies in odd numbers. Away, go.
They say there is divinity in odd numbers,
either in nativity, chance, or death.—
Away.
QUICK. I'll provide you a chain; and I'll
do what I can to get you a pair of horns.
FAL. Away, I say; time wears: hold up
your head, and mince. [*Exit Mrs.* QUICKLY.

Enter FORD

How now, master Brook! Master Brook,
the matter will be known to-night, or never.
Be you in the park about midnight, at
Herne's oak, and you shall see wonders.
FORD. Went you not to her yesterday,
Sir, as you told me you had appointed?
FAL. I went to her, master Brook, as you
see, like a poor old man: but I came from
her, master Brook, like a poor old woman.
That same knave Ford, her husband, hath
the finest mad devil of jealousy in him,
master Brook, that ever governed frenzy:—
I will tell you:—he beat me grievously, in
the shape of a woman; for in the shape of a
man, master Brook, I fear not Goliath with
a weaver's beam; because I know also, life
is a shuttle. I am in haste; go along with
me: I'll tell you all, master Brook. Since
plucked geese, played truant, and whipped
top, I knew not what it was to be beaten,
till lately. Follow me: I'll tell you strange
things of this knave Ford; on whom to-
night I will be revenged, and I will deliver
his wife into your hand.—Follow:—Strange
things in hand, master Brook:—follow.
[*Exeunt.*

SCENE II.—Windsor Park.

Enter PAGE, SHALLOW, *and* SLENDER.

PAGE. Come, come: we'll couch i' the cas-
tle-ditch, till we see the light of our fairies.
—Remember, son Slender, my daughter.
SLEN. Ay, forsooth; I have spoke with
her, and we have a nay-word, how to know
one another. I come to her in white, and
cry, "mum;" she cries, "budget;" and by
that we know one another.
SHAL. That's good too: but what needs
either your "mum," or her "budget?" the
white will decipher her well enough.—It
hath struck ten o'clock.
PAGE. The night is dark; light and   'ts
will become it well. Heaven prospe
sport! No man means evil but the

and we shall know him by his horns. Let's away; follow me.   [*Exeunt.*

SCENE III.—*The Street in* WINDSOR.

Enter Mrs. PAGE, *Mrs.* FORD, *and Dr.* CAIUS.
MRS. PAGE. Master Doctor, my daughter is in green: when you see your time, take her by the hand, away with her to the deanery, and despatch it quickly. Go before into the park: we two must go together.
CAIUS. I know vat I have to do. Adieu.
MRS. PAGE. Fare you well, Sir. [*Exit* CAIUS.] My husband will not rejoice so much at the abuse of Falstaff, as he will chafe at the doctor's marrying my daughter: but 'tis no matter; better a little chiding, than a great deal of heart-break.
MRS. FORD. Where is Nan now, and her troop of fairies? and the Welsh devil, Hugh?
MRS. PAGE. They are all couched in a pit hard by Herne's oak, with obscured lights; which, at the very instant of Falstaff's and our meeting, they will at once display to the night.
MRS. FORD. That cannot choose but amaze him.
MRS. PAGE. If he be not amazed, he will be mocked; if he be amazed, he will every way be mocked.
MRS. FORD. We'll betray him finely.
MRS. PAGE. Against such lewdsters, and their lechery,
Those that betray them do no treachery.
MRS. FORD. The hour draws on: to the oak, to the oak!   [*Exeunt.*

SCENE IV.—Windsor Park.

Enter Sir HUGH EVANS, *disguised as a Satyr, with* ANNE PAGE *and others as Fairies.*
EVA. Trib, trib, fairies: come; and remember your parts. Be pold, I pray you; follow me into the pit; and when I give the watch-'ords, do as I pid you: come, come; trib, trib.   [*Exeunt.*

SCENE V.—*Another part of the Park.*

Enter FALSTAFF *disguised as Herne, with a Buck's Head on.*
FAL. The Windsor bell hath struck twelve; the minute draws on. Now, the hot-blooded gods assist me!—remember, Jove, thou wast a bull for thy Europa; love set on thy horns:—O powerful love! that, in some respects, makes a beast a man; in some other, a man a beast.—You were also, Ju-

piter, a swan for the love of Leda:—O omnipotent love! how near the god drew to the complexion of a goose!—A fault done first in the form of a beast;—O Jove, a beastly fault! and then another fault in the semblance of a fowl: think on't, Jove; a foul fault.—When gods have hot backs, what shall poor men do? For me, I am here a Windsor stag; and the fattest, I think, i' the forest. Send me a cool ruttime, Jove, or who can blame me to piss my tallow?—Who comes here? my doe?
Enter Mrs. FORD *and Mrs.* PAGE.
MRS. FORD. Sir John, art thou there, my deer? my male deer?
FAL. My doe with the black scut!—Let the sky rain potatoes; let it thunder to the tune of "Green Sleeves;" hail kissing-comfits, and snow eringoes; let there come a tempest of provocation, I will shelter me here.   [*Embracing her.*
MRS. FORD. Mistress Page is come with me, sweetheart.
FAL. Divide me like a bribed buck, each a haunch: I will keep my sides to myself, my shoulders for the fellow of this walk, and my horns I bequeath your husbands. Am I woodman, ha? Speak I like Herne the hunter?—Why, now is Cupid a child of conscience; he makes restitution. As I am a rue spirit, welcome!   [*Noise within.*
MRS. PAGE. Alas! what noise?
MRS. FORD. Heaven forgive our sins!
FAL. What should this be?
MRS. FORD. }
MRS. PAGE. } Away, away!
      [*They run off.*
FAL. I think the devil will not have me damned, lest the oil that is in me should set hell on fire; he would never else cross me thus.
Enter Sir HUGH EVANS, *as a Satyr;* PISTOL, *as Hobgoblin;* ANNE PAGE, *as the Fairy Queen, attended by her brother and others, as fairies, with waxen tapers on their heads.*
QUEEN. Fairies, black, grey, green, and white,
You moonshine revellers, and shades of night,
You orphan-heirs of fixed destiny,
Attend your office and your quality.—
Crier Hobgoblin, make the fairy o-yes.
PIST. Elves, list your names; silence, you airy toys!
Cricket, to Windsor chimneys when thou'st leapt,
Where fires thou find'st unrak'd and hearths unswept,
There pinch the maids as blue as bilberry:
Our radiant queen hates sluts, and sluttery.

FAL. They are fairies; he that speaks to them, shall die:
I'll wink and couch: no man their works must eye.   [*Lies down upon his face.*
EVA. Where's Bede?—Go you, and where you find a maid,
That, ere she sleep, has thrice her prayers said,
Raise up the organs of her fantasy,
Sleep she as sound as careless infancy:
But those that sleep, and think not on their sins,
Pinch them, arms, legs, backs, shoulders, sides, and shins.
QUEEN. About, about!
Search Windsor castle, elves, within and out:
Strew good luck, ouphes, on every sacred room;
That it may stand till the perpetual doom,
In state as wholesome as in state 'tis fit;
Worthy the owner, and the owner it.
The several chairs of order look you scour
With juice of balm, and every precious flower:
Each fair instalment, coat, and several crest,
With loyal blazon, ever more be blest!
And nightly, meadow-fairies, look you sing,
Like to the Garter's compass, in a ring:
Th' expressure that it bears, green let it be,
More fertile-fresh than all the field to see;
And, *Honi soit qui mal y pense*, write,
In emerald tufts, flowers purple, blue, and white;
Like sapphire, pearl, and rich embroidery,
Buckled below fair knighthood's bending knee:—
Fairies use flowers for their charactery.
Away! disperse! But, till 'tis one o'clock,
Our dance of custom round about the oak
Of Herne the hunter, let us not forget.
EVA. Pray you, lock hand in hand; yourselves in order set;
And twenty glow-worms shall our lanterns be,
To guide our measure round about the tree.—
But, stay! I smell a man of middle earth.
FAL. Heavens defend me from that Welsh fairy, lest he transform me to a piece of cheese!
PIST. Vile worm, thou wast o'er-look'd, even in thy birth.
QUEEN. With trial-fire touch me his finger-end:
If he be chaste, the flame will back descend,
And turn him to no pain; but if he start,
It is the flesh of a corrupted heart.
PIST. A trial, come.

EVA.   Come, will this wood take fire?
[*They burn him with their tapers.*
FAL. Oh, oh, oh!
QUEEN. Corrupt, corrupt, and tainted in desire!—
About him, fairies; sing a scornful rhyme:
And, as you trip, still pinch him to your time.

SONG.

Fie on sinful fantasy!
Fie on lust and luxury!
Lust is but a bloody fire,
Kindled with unchaste desire,
Fed in heart; whose flames aspire,
As thoughts do blow them higher and higher.
Pinch him, fairies, mutually;
Pinch him for his villainy;
Pinch him, and burn him, and turn him about,
Till candles, and star-light, and moonshine be out.

During this song, the fairies pinch FALSTAFF. *Doctor* CAIUS *comes one way, and steals away a fairy in green;* SLENDER *another way, and takes off a fairy in white; and* FENTON *comes, and steals away* ANNE PAGE. *A noise of hunting is made within. The fairies run away.* FALSTAFF *pulls off his buck's head, and rises.*
Enter PAGE, FORD, MRS. PAGE, *and* MRS. FORD. *They lay hold on* FALSTAFF.
PAGE. Nay, do not fly: I think we have watch'd you now.
Will none but Herne the hunter serve your turn?
MRS. PAGE. I pray you come; hold up the jest no higher.—
Now, good Sir John, how like you Windsor wives?—
See you these, husband? do not these fair yokes
Become the forest better than the town?
FORD. Now, Sir, who's a cuckold now?—
Master Brook, Falstaff's a knave, a cuckoldly knave; here are his horns, master Brook: and, master Brook, he hath enjoyed nothing of Ford's but his buck-basket, his cudgel, and twenty pounds of money, which must be paid to master Brook; his horses are arrested for it, master Brook.
MRS. FORD. Sir John, we have had ill luck; we could never meet. I will never take you for my love again; but I will always count you my deer.
FAL. I do begin to perceive that I am made an ass.
FORD. Ay, and an ox too; both the proofs are extant.

FAL. And these are not fairies? I was three or four times in the thought, they were not fairies: and yet the guiltiness of my mind, the sudden surprise of my powers, drove the grossness of the foppery into a received belief, in despite of the teeth of all rhyme and reason, that they were fairies. See now, how wit may be made a Jack-a-lent, when 'tis upon ill employment!

EVA. Sir John Falstaff, serve Got, and leave your desires, and fairies will not pinse you.

FORD. Well said, fairy Hugh.

EVA. And leave you your jealousies too, I pray you.

FORD. I will never mistrust my wife again, till thou art able to woo her in good English.

FAL. Have I laid my brain in the sun, and dried it, that it wants matter to prevent so gross o'er-reaching as this? Am I ridden with a Welsh goat too? shall I have a coxcomb of frize? 'Tis time I were choked with a piece of toasted cheese.

EVA. Seese is not goot to give putter; your pelly is all putter.

FAL. Seese and putter! have I lived to stand at the taunt of one that makes fritters of English? This is enough to be the decay of lust, and late-walking, through the realm.

MRS. PAGE. Why, Sir John, do you think, though we would have thrust virtue out of our hearts by the head and shoulders, and have given ourselves without scruple to hell, that ever the devil could have made you our delight?

FORD. What, a hodge-pudding? a bag of flax?

MRS. PAGE. A puffed man?

PAGE. Old, cold, withered, and of intolerable entrails?

FORD. And one that is as slanderous as Satan?

PAGE. And as poor as Job?

FORD. And as wicked as his wife?

EVA. And given to fornications, and to taverns, and sack, and wine, and metheglins, and to drinkings, and swearings and starings, pribbles and prabbles?

FAL. Well, I am your theme: you have the start of me; I am dejected; I am not able to answer the Welsh flannel; ignorance itself is a plummet o'er me: use me as you will.

FORD. Marry, Sir, we'll bring you to Windsor, to one master Brook, that you have cozened of money, to whom you should have been a pander: over and above that you have suffered, I think, to repay that money will be a biting affliction.

PAGE. Yet be cheerful, knight: thou shalt eat a posset to-night at my house; where I will desire thee to laugh at my wife, that now laughs at thee: tell her, master Slender hath married her daughter.

MRS. PAGE. [*Aside.*] Doctors doubt that: if Anne Page be my daughter, she is, by this, doctor Caius' wife.

Enter SLENDER.

SLEN. Whoo, ho! ho! father Page!

PAGE. Son, how now! how now, son! have you despatched?

SLEN. Despatched—I'll make the best in Gloucestershire know on't; would I were hanged, la, else!

PAGE. Of what, son?

SLEN. I came yonder at Eton to marry mistress Anne Page, and she's a great lubberly boy. If it had not been i' the church, I would have swinged him, or he should have swinged me. If I did not think it had been Anne Page, would I might never stir!—and 'tis a post-master's boy.

PAGE. Upon my life, then, you took the wrong.

SLEN. What need you tell me that? I think so, when I took a boy for a girl. If I had been married to him, for all he was in woman's apparel, I would not have had him.

PAGE. Why, this is your own folly. Did not I tell you how you should know my daughter by her garments?

SLEN. I went to her in white, and cried, "mum," and she cried "budget," as Anne and I had appointed; and yet it was not Anne, but a post-master's boy.

MRS. PAGE. Good George, be not angry: I knew of your purpose; turned my daughter into green; and indeed, she is now with the doctor at the deanery, and there married.

Enter Doctor CAIUS.

CAIUS. Vere is mistress Page? By gar, I am cozened: I ha' married *un garçon*, a boy; *un paisan*, by gar, a boy; it is not Anne Page: by gar, I am cozened.

MRS. PAGE. Why, did you take her in green?

CAIUS. Ay, by gar, and 'tis a boy: by gar, I'll raise all Windsor.   [*Exit.*

FORD. This is strange. Who hath got the right Anne?

PAGE. My heart misgives me: here comes master Fenton.

Enter FENTON *and* ANNE PAGE.

How now, master Fenton!

ANNE. Pardon, good father!—good my mother, pardon!

PAGE. Now, mistress,—how chance you went not with master Slender?

MRS. PAGE. Why went you not with master doctor, maid?

FENT. You do amaze her: hear the truth of it.
You would have married her most shamefully,
Where there was no proportion held in love.
The truth is, she and I, long since contracted,   [us.
Are now so sure, that nothing can dissolve
The offence is holy that she has committed;
And this deceit loses the name of craft,
Of disobedience, or unduteous title;
Since therein she doth evitate and shun
A thousand irreligious cursed hours,
Which forced marriage would have brought upon her.

FORD. Stand not amaz'd; here is no remedy.—
In love, the heavens themselves do guide the state;

Money buys lands, and wives are sold by fate.

FAL. I am glad, though you have ta'en a special stand to strike at me, that your arrow hath glanced.

PAGE. Well, what remedy?—Fenton, heaven give thee joy!—
What cannot be eschew'd, must be embrac'd.

FAL. When night-dogs run, all sorts of deer are chas'd.

MRS. PAGE. Well, I will muse no farther.
—Master Fenton,
Heaven give you many, many merry days!—
Good husband, let us every one go home,
And laugh this sport o'er by a country fire;
Sir John and all.

FORD.   Let it be so.—Sir John,
To master Brook you yet shall hold your word;
For he, to-night, shall lie with mistress Ford.   [*Exeunt.*

The Watch bringing Borachio and Conrade before the Constables. Act IV. S. 2.

MUCH ADO ABOUT NOTHING

DRAMATIS PERSONÆ.

DON PEDRO, *Prince of* Arragon.
DON JOHN, *his bastard Brother.*
CLAUDIO, *a young Lord of* Florence.
BENEDICK, *a young Gentleman of* Padua.
LEONATO, *Governor of* Messina.
ANTONIO, *his Brother.*
BALTHAZAR, *attendant on* DON PEDRO.
BORACHIO, } *followers of* DON JOHN.
CONRADE, }
DOGBERRY, } *two foolish City-Officers.*
VERGES, }

FRIAR FRANCIS.
A Sexton.
A Boy.

HERO, *daughter to* LEONATO.
BEATRICE, *niece to* LEONATO.
MARGARET, } *Gentlewomen attending*
URSULA, } *on* HERO.

Messengers, Watchmen, Attendants, &c.

SCENE,—MESSINA.

ACT I.

SCENE I.—*Grounds adjoining* LEONATO'S *House.*

Enter LEONATO, HERO, *and* BEATRICE, *with a Messenger.*

LEON. I learn in this letter, that Don Pedro of Arragon comes this night to Messina.

MESS. He is very near by this: he was not three leagues off when I left him.

LEON. How many gentlemen have you lost in this action?

MESS. But few of any sort, and none of name.

LEON. A victory is twice itself, when the achiever brings home full numbers. I find here, that Don Pedro hath bestowed much honour on a young Florentine, called Claudio.

MESS. Much deserved on his part, and equally remembered by Don Pedro. He hath borne himself beyond the promise of his age; doing, in the figure of a lamb, the feats of a lion: he hath, indeed, better bettered expectation, than you must expect of me to tell you how.

LEON. He hath an uncle here in Messina will be very much glad of it.

MESS. I have already delivered him letters, and there appears much joy in him; even so much, that joy could not show itself modest enough without a badge of bitterness.

LEON. Did he break out into tears?

MESS. In great measure.

LEON. A kind overflow of kindness: there are no faces truer than those that are so washed. How much better is it to weep at joy, than to joy at weeping!

BEAT. I pray you, is signior Montanto returned from the wars, or no?

MESS. I know none of that name, lady: there was none such in the army of any sort.

LEON. What is he that you ask for, niece?

HERO. My cousin means signior Benedick of Padua.

MESS. O, he is returned; and as pleasant as ever he was.

BEAT. He set up his bills here in Messina, and challenged Cupid at the flight; and my uncle's fool, reading the challenge, subscribed for Cupid, and challenged him at the bird-bolt.—I pray you, how many hath he killed and eaten in these wars? But how many hath he killed? for, indeed, I promised to eat all of his killing.

LEON. Faith, niece, you tax signior Benedick too much; but he'll be meet with you, I doubt it not.

MESS. He hath done good service, lady, in these wars.

BEAT. You had musty victual, and he hath holp to eat it: he is a very valiant trencherman; he hath an excellent stomach.

MESS. And a good soldier too, lady.

BEAT. And a good soldier to a lady;—but what is he to a lord?

MESS. A lord to a lord, a man to a man; stuffed with all honourable virtues.

BEAT. It is so, indeed; he is no less than a stuffed man: but for the stuffing,—Well, we are all mortal.

LEON. You must not, Sir, mistake my niece. There is a kind of merry war betwixt signior Benedick and her: they never meet, but there's a skirmish of wit between them.

BEAT. Alas, he gets nothing by that! In our last conflict four of his five wits went halting off, and now is the whole man governed with one: so that if he have wit enough to keep himself warm, let him bear it for a difference between himself and his horse; for it is all the wealth that he hath left, to be known a reasonable creature.—Who is his companion now? He hath every month a new sworn brother.

MESS. Is't possible?

BEAT. Very easily possible: he wears his faith but as the fashion of his hat; it ever changes with the next block.

MESS. I see, lady, the gentleman is not in your books.

BEAT. No; an he were, I would burn my study. But I pray you, who is his companion? Is there no young squarer now, that will make a voyage with him to the devil?

MESS. He is most in the company of the right noble Claudio.

BEAT. O Lord! he will hang upon him like a disease: he is sooner caught than the pestilence, and the taker runs presently mad. God help the noble Claudio! if he have caught the Benedick, it will cost him a thousand pound ere he be cured.

MESS. I will hold friends with you, lady.

BEAT. Do, good friend.

LEON. You will never run mad, niece.

BEAT. No, not till a hot January.

MESS. Don Pedro is approached.

Enter Don PEDRO, Don JOHN, CLAUDIO, BENEDICK, and BALTHAZAR.

D. PEDRO. Good signior Leonato, you are come to meet your trouble: the fashion of the world is to avoid cost, and you encounter it.

LEON. Never came trouble to my house in the likeness of your grace: for trouble being gone, comfort should remain; but when you depart from me, sorrow abides, and happiness takes his leave.

D. PEDRO. You embrace your charge too willingly.—I think this is your daughter.

LEON. Her mother hath many times told me so.

BENE. Were you in doubt, Sir, that you asked her?

LEON. Signior Benedick, no; for then were you a child.

D. PEDRO. You have it full, Benedick: we may guess by this what you are, being a man.—Truly, the lady fathers herself.—Be happy, lady; for you are like an honourable father.

BENE. If signior Leonato be her father, she would not have his head on her shoulders for all Messina, as like him as she is.

BEAT. I wonder that you will still be talking, signior Benedick: nobody marks you.

BENE. What, my dear lady Disdain! are you yet living?

BEAT. Is it possible disdain should die, while she hath such meet food to feed it, as signior Benedick? Courtesy itself must convert to disdain, if you come in her presence.

BENE. Then is courtesy a turn-coat.—But it is certain I am loved of all ladies, only you excepted: and I would I could find in my heart that I had not a hard heart; for, truly, I love none.

BEAT. A dear happiness to women: they would else have been troubled with a pernicious suitor. I thank God and my cold blood, I am of your humour for that: I had rather hear my dog bark at a crow, than a man swear he loves me.

BENE. God keep your ladyship still in that mind! so some gentleman or other shall 'scape a predestinate scratched face.

BEAT. Scratching could not make it worse, an't were such a face as yours were.

BENE. Well, you are a rare parrot-teacher.

BEAT. A bird of my tongue is better than a beast of yours.

BENE. I would my horse had the speed of your tongue, and so good a continuer. But keep your way, o' God's name; I have done.

BEAT. You always end with a jade's trick: I know you of old.

D. PEDRO. This is the sum of all: Leonato,—signior Claudio, and signior Benedick,—my dear friend Leonato hath invited you all. I tell him we shall stay here at the least a month; and he heartily prays some occasion may detain us longer: I dare swear he is no hypocrite, but prays from his heart.

LEON. If you swear, my Lord, you shall not be forsworn.—Let me bid you welcome, my lord: being reconciled to the prince your brother, I owe you all duty.

D. JOHN. I thank you: I am not of many words, but I thank you.

LEON. Please it your grace lead on?

D. PEDRO. Your hand, Leonato; we will go together.

[*Exeunt all but* BENEDICK *and* CLAUDIO.

CLAUD. Benedick, didst thou note the daughter of signior Leonato?   [her.

BENE. I noted her not; but I looked on

CLAUD. Is she not a modest young lady?

BENE. Do you question me, as an honest man should do, for my simple true judgment; or would you have me speak after my custom, as being a professed tyrant to their sex?

CLAUD. No; I pray thee, speak in sober judgment.

BENE. Why, i' faith, methinks she's too low for a high praise, too brown for a fair praise, and too little for a great praise: only this commendation I can afford her,

—that were she other than she is, she were unhandsome; and being no other but as she is, I do not like her.

CLAUD. Thou thinkest, I am in sport: I pray thee, tell me truly how thou likest her.

BENE. Would you buy her, that you enquire after her?

CLAUD. Can the world buy such a jewel?

BENE. Yea, and a case to put it into. But speak you this with a sad brow? or do you play the flouting Jack, to tell us Cupid is a good hare-finder, and Vulcan a rare carpenter? Come, in what key shall a man take you, to go in the song?

CLAUD. In mine eye she is the sweetest lady that ever I looked on.

BENE. I can see yet without spectacles, and I see no such matter: there's her cousin, an she were not possessed with a fury, exceeds her as much in beauty, as the first of May doth the last of December. But I hope, you have no intent to turn husband, have you?

CLAUD. I would scarce trust myself, though I had sworn the contrary, if Hero would be my wife.

BENE. Is't come to this, i' faith? Hath not the world one man, but he will wear his cap with suspicion? Shall I never see a bachelor of threescore again? Go to, i' faith; an thou wilt needs thrust thy neck into a yoke, wear the print of it, and sigh away Sundays. Look; Don Pedro is returned to seek you.

Re-enter Don PEDRO.

D. PEDRO. What secret hath held you here, that you followed not to Leonato's?

BENE. I would your grace would constrain me to tell.

D. PEDRO. I charge thee on thy allegiance.

BENE. You hear, Count Claudio: I can be secret as a dumb man, I would have you think so; but on my allegiance,—mark you this, on my allegiance.—He is in love. With whom?—now that is your grace's part.—Mark, how short his answer is;—with Hero, Leonato's short daughter.

CLAUD. If this were so, so were it uttered.

BENE. Like the old tale, my lord: it is not so, nor 'twas not so; but, indeed, God forbid it should be so.

CLAUD. If my passion change not shortly, God forbid it should be otherwise.

D. PEDRO. Amen, if you love her; for the lady is very well worthy.

CLAUD. You speak this to fetch me in, my lord.

D. PEDRO. By my troth, I speak my thought.

CLAUD. And in faith, my lord, I spoke mine.

BENE. And by my two faiths and troths, my lord, I spoke mine.

CLAUD. That I love her, I feel.

D. PEDRO. That she is worthy, I know.

BENE. That I neither feel how she should be loved, nor know how she should be worthy, is the opinion that fire cannot melt out of me: I will die in it at the stake.

D. PEDRO. Thou wast ever an obstinate heretic in the despite of beauty.

CLAUD. And never could maintain his part, but in the force of his will.

BENE. That a woman conceived me, I thank her; that she brought me up, I likewise give her most humble thanks: but that I will have a recheat winded in my forehead, or hang my bugle in an invisible baldrick, all women shall pardon me. Because I will not do them the wrong to mistrust any, I will do myself the right to trust none; and the fine is, (for the which I may go the finer,) I will live a bachelor.

D. PEDRO. I shall see thee, ere I die, look pale with love.

BENE. With anger, with sickness, or with hunger, my lord; not with love: prove that ever I lose more blood with love than I will get again with drinking, pick out mine eyes with a ballad-maker's pen, and hang me up at the door of a brothel-house for the sign of blind Cupid.

D. PEDRO. Well, if ever thou dost fall from this faith, thou wilt prove a notable argument.

BENE. If I do, hang me in a bottle like a cat, and shoot at me; and he that hits me, let him be clapped on the shoulder, and called Adam.

D. PEDRO. Well, as time shall try: "In time the savage bull doth bear the yoke."

BENE. The savage bull may; but if ever the sensible Benedick bear it, pluck off the bull's horns, and set them in my forehead: and let me be vilely painted; and in such great letters as they write, "Here is good horse to hire," let them signify under my sign,—"Here you may see Benedick the married man."

CLAUD. If this should ever happen, thou would'st be horn-mad.

D. PEDRO. Nay, if Cupid have not spent all his quiver in Venice, thou wilt quake for this shortly.

BENE. I look for an earthquake too, then.

D. PEDRO. Well, you will temporize with the hours. In the meantime, good signior Benedick, repair to Leonato's: commend me to him, and tell him I will not fail him at supper; for indeed he hath made great preparation.

BENE. I have almost matter enough in me for such an embassage; and so I commit you—

CLAUD. To the tuition of God: from my house, if I had it,—

D. PEDRO. The sixth of July: your loving friend, Benedick.

BENE. Nay, mock not, mock not. The body of your discourse is sometime guarded with fragments, and the guards are but slightly basted on neither: ere you flout old ends any farther, examine your conscience: and so I leave you.   [*Exit.*

CLAUD. My liege, your highness now may do me good.

D. PEDRO. My love is thine to teach: teach it but how,
And thou shalt see how apt it is to learn
Any hard lesson that may do thee good.

CLAUD. Hath Leonato any son, my lord?

D. PETRO. No child but Hero; she's his only heir.
Dost thou affect her, Claudio?

CLAUD.   O, my lord,
When you went onward on this ended action,
I look'd upon her with a soldier's eye,
That lik'd, but had a rougher task in hand
Than to drive liking to the name of love:
But now I am return'd, and that war-thoughts
Have left their places vacant, in their rooms
Come thronging soft and delicate desires,
All prompting me how fair young Hero is,
Saying, I lik'd her ere I went to wars.

D. PEDRO. Thou wilt be like a lover presently,
And tire the hearer with a book of words.
If thou dost love fair Hero, cherish it;
And I will break with her, and with her father,
And thou shalt have her. Was't not to this end
That thou began'st to twist so fine a story?

CLAUD. How sweetly do you minister to love,
That know love's grief by his complexion!
But lest my liking might too sudden seem,
I would have salv'd it with a longer treatise.

D. PEDRO. What need the bridge much broader than the flood?
The fairest grant is the necessity.
Look, what will serve is fit: 'tis once, thou lovest;
And I will fit thee with the remedy.
I know we shall have reveling to-night:
I will assume thy part in some disguise,
And tell fair Hero I am Claudio;
And in her bosom I'll unclasp my heart,

And take her hearing prisoner with the force
And strong encounter of my amorous tale:
Then, after, to her father will I break;
And the conclusion is, she shall be thine.
In practice let us put it presently. [*Exeunt.*

SCENE II.—*A Room in* LEONATO'S *House.*
Enter LEONATO *and* ANTONIO.

LEON. How now, brother! Where is my cousin, your son? Hath he provided this music?
ANT. He is very busy about it. But, brother, I can tell you strange news, that you yet dreamt not of.
LEON. Are they good?
ANT. As the event stamps them: but they have a good cover; they show well outward. The prince and count Claudio, walking in a thick-pleached alley in my orchard, were thus much overheard by a man of mine: the prince discovered to Claudio that he loved my niece your daughter, and meant to acknowledge it this night in a dance; and, if he found her accordant, he meant to take the present time by the top, and instantly break with you of it.
LEON. Hath the fellow any wit that told you this?
ANT. A good sharp fellow: I will send for him; and question him yourself.
LEON. No, no; we will hold it as a dream, till it appear itself; but I will acquaint my daughter withal, that she may be the better prepared for an answer, if peradventure this be true. Go you, and tell her of it. [*Several persons cross the stage.*] Cousins, you know what you have to do.—O, I cry you mercy, friend; go you with me, and I will use your skill.—Good cousin, have a care this busy time. [*Exeunt.*

SCENE III.—*Another Room in* LEONATO'S *House.*
Enter Don JOHN *and* CONRADE.

CON. What the good-year, my lord! why are you thus out of measure sad?
D. JOHN. There is no measure in the occasion that breeds; therefore the sadness is without limit.
CON. You should hear reason.
D. JOHN. And when I have heard it, what blessing bringeth it?
CON. If not a present remedy, yet a patient sufferance.
D. JOHN. I wonder that thou, being (as thou say'st thou art) born under Saturn, goest about to apply a moral medicine to a mortifying mischief. I cannot hide what I am: I must be sad when I have cause, and smile at no man's jests; eat when I have stomach, and wait for no man's leisure; sleep when I am drowsy, and tend on no man's business; laugh when I am merry, and claw no man in his humour.
CON. Yea, but you must not make the full show of this, till you may do it without controlment. You have of late stood out against your brother, and he hath ta'en you newly into his grace; where it is impossible you should take true root, but by the fair weather that you make yourself: it is needful that you frame the season for your own harvest.
D. JOHN. I had rather be a canker in a hedge, than a rose in his grace; and it better fits my blood to be disdained of all, than to fashion a carriage to rob love from any: in this, though I cannot be said to be a flattering honest man, it must not be denied but I am a plain-dealing villain. I am trusted with a muzzle, and enfranchised with a clog; therefore I have decreed not to sing in my cage. If I had my mouth, I would bite; if I had my liberty, I would do my liking: in the meantime, let me be that I am, and seek not to alter me.
CON. Can you make no use of your discontent?
D. JOHN. I make all use of it, for I use it only.—Who comes here? [*Enter* BORACHIO.] What news, Borachio?
BORA. I came yonder from a great supper: the prince, your brother, is royally entertained by Leonato; and I can give you intelligence of an intended marriage.
D. JOHN. Will it serve for any model to build mischief on? What is he for a fool, that betroths himself to unquietness?
BORA. Marry, it is your brother's right hand.
D. JOHN. Who, the most exquisite Claudio?
BORA. Even he.
D. JOHN. A proper squire! And who, and who? which way looks he?
BORA. Marry, on Hero, the daughter and heir of Leonato.
D. JOHN. A very forward March-chick! How came you to this?
BORA. Being entertained for a perfumer, as I was smoking a musty room, comes me the prince and Claudio, hand in hand, in sad conference: I whipt me behind the arras; and there heard it agreed upon, that the prince should woo Hero for himself, and having obtained her, give her to count Claudio.
D. JOHN. Come, come, let us thither: this may prove food to my displeasure. That young start-up hath all the glory of my overthrow: if I can cross him any way, I

bless myself every way. You are both sure, and will assist me?

CON. To the death, my lord.

D. JOHN. Let us to the great supper; their cheer is the greater, that I am subdued. Would the cook were of my mind!—Shall we go prove what's to be done?

BORA. We'll wait upon your lordship.

[*Exeunt.*

ACT II.

SCENE I.—*A Hall in* LEONATO'S *House.*

Enter LEONATO, ANTONIO, HERO, BEATRICE, *and others.*

LEON. Was not count John here at supper?

ANT. I saw him not.

BEAT. How tartly that gentleman looks! I never can see him, but I am heart-burned an hour after.

HERO. He is of a very melancholy disposition.

BEAT. He were an excellent man, that were made just in the mid-way between him and Benedick: the one is too like an image, and says nothing; and the other too like my lady's eldest son, evermore tattling.

LEON. Then, half signior Benedick's tongue in count John's mouth, and half count John's melancholy in signior Benedick's face,—

BEAT. With a good leg, and a good foot, uncle, and money enough in his purse, such a man would win any woman in the world,—if he could get her good will.

LEON. By my troth, niece, thou wilt never get thee a husband, if thou be so shrewd of thy tongue.

ANT. In faith, she's too curst.

BEAT. Too curst is more than curst: I shall lessen God's sending that way; for it is said, "God sends a curst cow short horns;" but to a cow too curst he sends none.

LEON. So, by being too curst, God will send you no horns?

BEAT. Just, if he send me no husband; for the which blessing, I am at him upon my knees every morning and evening. Lord! I could not endure a husband with a beard on his face: I had rather lie in the woollen.

LEON. You may light on a husband that hath no beard.

BEAT. What should I do with him? dress him in my apparel, and make him my waiting-gentlewoman? He that hath a beard is more than a youth; and he that hath no beard is less than a man: and he that is more than a youth is not for me; and he that is less than a man, I am not for him: therefore I will even take sixpence in earnest of the bear-ward, and lead his apes into hell.

LEON. Well then, go you into hell?

BEAT. No; but to the gate; and there will the devil meet me, like an old cuckold, with horns on his head, and say, "Get you to heaven, Beatrice, get you to heaven; here's no place for you maids:" so, deliver I up my apes, and away to Saint Peter for the heavens: he shows me where the bachelors sit, and there live we as merry as the day is long.

ANT. [*To* HERO.] Well, niece, I trust you will be ruled by your father.

BEAT. Yes, faith; it is my cousin's duty to make court'sy, and say, "Father, as it please you:"—but yet for all that, cousin, let him be a handsome fellow, or else make another court'sy, and say, "Father, as it please me."

LEON. Well, niece, I hope to see you one day fitted with a husband.

BEAT. Not till God make men of some other metal than earth. Would it not grieve a woman to be over-mastered with a piece of valiant dust? to make an account of her life to a clod of wayward marl? No, uncle, I'll none: Adam's sons are my brethren; and truly, I hold it a sin to match in my kindred.

LEON. Daughter, remember what I told you: if the prince do solicit you in that kind, you know your answer.

BEAT. The fault will be in the music, cousin, if you be not wooed in good time: if the prince be too important, tell him there is measure in every thing, and so dance out the answer. For, hear me, Hero:—wooing, wedding, and repenting, is as a Scotch jig, a measure, and a cinque-pace: the first suit is hot and hasty, like a Scotch jig, and full as fantastical; the wedding, mannerly-modest, as a measure, full of state and ancientry; and then comes repentance, and, with his bad legs, falls into the cinque-pace faster and faster, till he sink into his grave.

LEON. Cousin, you apprehend passing shrewdly.

BEAT. I have a good eye, uncle; I can see a church by day-light.

LEON. The revellers are entering, brother: make good room!

Enter Don PEDRO, CLAUDIO, BENEDICK, BALTHAZAR, *Don* JOHN, BORACHIO, MARGARET, URSULA, *and others, masked.*

D. PEDRO. Lady, will you walk about with your friend?

HERO. So you walk softly, and look sweetly, and say nothing, I am yours for the walk; and especially when I walk away.

D. PEDRO. With me in your company?

HERO. I may say so, when I please.

D. PEDRO. And when please you to say so?

HERO. When I like your favour; for God defend the lute should be like the case!

D. PEDRO. My visor is Philemon's roof; within the house is Jove.

HERO. Why, then, your visor should be thatch'd.

D. PEDRO. Speak low, if you speak love.
                                    [*Takes her aside.*

BALTH. Well, I would you did like me.

MARG. So would not I, for your own sake; for I have many ill qualities.

BALTH. Which is one?

MARG. I say my prayers aloud.

BALTH. I love you the better; the hearers may cry Amen.

MARG. God match me with a good dancer!

BALTH. Amen.

MARG. And God keep him out of my sight, when the dance is done!—Answer, clerk.

BALTH. No more words: the clerk is answered.

URS. I know you well enough; you are signior Antonio.

ANT. At a word, I am not.

URS. I know you by the waggling of your head.

ANT. To tell you true, I counterfeit him.

URS. You could never do him so ill-well, unless you were the very man. Here's his dry hand up and down: you are he, you are he.

ANT. At a word, I am not.

URS. Come, come, do you think I do not know you by your excellent wit? Can virtue hide itself? Go to, mum, you are he: graces will appear, and, there's an end.

BEAT. Will you not tell me who told you so?

BENE. No, you shall pardon me.

BEAT. Nor will you not tell me who you are?

BENE. Not now.

BEAT. That I was disdainful, and that I had my good wit out of the "Hundred Merry Tales."—Well, this was signior Benedick that said so.

BENE. What's he?

BEAT. I am sure, you know him well enough.

BENE. Not I, believe me.

BEAT. Did he never make you laugh?

BENE. I pray you, what is he?

BEAT. Why, he is the prince's jester: a very dull fool; only his gift is in devising impossible slanders: none but libertines delight in him; and the commendation is not in his wit, but in his villany; for he both pleases men and angers them, and then they laugh at him and beat him. I am sure he is in the fleet; I would he had boarded me!

BENE. When I know the gentleman, I'll tell him what you say.

BEAT. Do, do: he'll but break a comparison or two on me; which, peradventure, not marked, or not laughed at, strikes him into melancholy; and then there's a partridge' wing saved, for the fool will eat no supper that night. [*Music within.*] We must follow the leaders.

BENE. In every good thing.

BEAT. Nay, if they lead to any ill, I will leave them at the next turning.

[*Dance; then, exeunt all but Don* JOHN, BORACHIO, *and* CLAUDIO.

D. JOHN. Sure, my brother is amorous on Hero, and hath withdrawn her father to break with him about it. The ladies follow her, and but one visor remains.

BORA. And that is Claudio: I know him by his bearing.

D. JOHN. Are not you signior Benedick?

CLAUD. You know me well: I am he.

D. JOHN. Signior, you are very near my brother in his love: he is enamoured on Hero. I pray you, dissuade him from her; she is no equal for his birth: you may do the part of an honest man in it.

CLAUD. How know you he loves her?

D. JOHN. I heard him swear his affection.

BORA. So did I too; and he swore he would marry her to-night.

D. JOHN. Come, let us to the banquet.

[*Exeunt Don* JOHN *and* BORACHIO.

CLAUD. Thus answer I in name of Benedick,

But hear these ill news with the ears of Claudio.

'Tis certain so:—the prince wooes for himself.

Friendship is constant in all other things,

Save in the office and affairs of love

Therefore, all hearts in love use their own tongues;

Let every eye negotiate for itself,

And trust no agent; for beauty is a witch,

Against whose charms faith melteth into blood.

This is an accident of hourly proof,

Which I mistrusted not. Farewell, therefore, Hero!

Re-enter BENEDICK.

BENE. Count Claudio?

CLAUD. Yea, the same.

BENE. Come, will you go with me?

CLAUD. Whither?

BENE. Even to the next willow, about

your own business, count. What fashion will you wear the garland of? About your neck, like a usurer's chain? or under your arm, like a lieutenant's scarf? You must wear it one way, for the prince hath got your Hero.

CLAUD. I wish him joy of her.

BENE. Why, that's spoken like an honest drover: so they sell bullocks. But did you think the prince would have served you thus?

CLAUD. I pray you, leave me.

BENE. Ho! now you strike like the blind man: 'twas the boy that stole your meat, and you'll beat the post.

CLAUD. If it will not be, I'll leave you. [*Exit.*

BENE. Alas, poor hurt fowl! Now will he creep into sedges.—But, that my lady Beatrice should know me, and not know me! The prince's fool!!—Ha! it may be I go under that title, because I am merry.—Yea, but so I am apt to do myself wrong; I am not so reputed: it is the base, though bitter disposition of Beatrice, that puts the world into her person, and so gives me out. Well, I'll be revenged as I may.

Re-enter Don PEDRO.

D. PEDRO. Now, signior, where's the count? Did you see him?

BENE. Troth, my lord, I have played the part of lady Fame. I found him here as melancholy as a lodge in a warren: I told him, and I think I told him true, that your grace had got the good-will of this young lady; and I offered him my company to a willow tree, either to make him a garland, as being forsaken, or to bind him up a rod, as being worthy to be whipped.

D. PEDRO. To be whipped! What's his fault?

BENE. The flat transgression of a school-boy; who, being overjoy'd with finding a bird's nest, shows it his companion, and he steals it.

D. PEDRO. Wilt thou make a trust a transgression? The transgression is in the stealer.

BENE. Yet it had not been amiss the rod had been made, and the garland too; for the garland he might have worn himself, and the rod he might have bestowed on you, who, as I take it, have stolen his bird's nest.

D. PEDRO. I will but teach them to sing, and restore them to the owner.

BENE. If their singing answer your saying, by my faith, you say honestly.

D. PEDRO. The lady Beatrice hath a quarrel to you: the gentleman that danced with her, told her she is much wronged by you.

BENE. O, she misused me past the endurance of a block! an oak, but with one green leaf on it, would have answered her; my very visor began to assume life, and scold with her. She told me,—not thinking I had been myself,—that I was the prince's jester; that I was duller than a great thaw; huddling jest upon jest, with such impossible conveyance, upon me, that I stood like a man at a mark, with a whole army shooting at me. She speaks poniards, and every word stabs: if her breath were as terrible as her terminations, there were no living near her; she would infect to the north star. I would not marry her, though she were endowed with all that Adam had left him before he transgressed: she would have made Hercules have turned spit, yea, and have cleft his club to make the fire too. Come, talk not of her; you shall find her the infernal Até in good apparel. I would to God some scholar would conjure her; for certainly, while she is here, a man may live as quiet in hell as in a sanctuary; and people sin upon purpose, because they would go thither; so, indeed, all disquiet, horror, and perturbation follow her.

D. PEDRO. Look, here she comes.

Re-enter CLAUDIO, BEATRICE, HERO, *and* LEONATO.

BENE. Will your grace command me any service to the world's end? I will go on the slightest errand now to the Antipodes that you can devise to send me on; I will fetch you a toothpicker now from the farthest inch of Asia; bring you the length of Prester John's foot; fetch you a hair off the great Cham's beard; do you any embassage to the Pigmies,—rather than hold three words' conference with this harpy. You have no employment for me?

D. PEDRO. None, but to desire your good company.

BENE. O God, Sir, here's a dish I love not: I cannot endure my lady Tongue. [*Exit.*

D. PEDRO. Come, lady, come; you have lost the heart of signior Benedick.

BEAT. Indeed, my lord, he lent it me a while; and I gave him use for it,—a double heart for his single one: marry, once before he won it of me with false dice, therefore your grace may well say I have lost it.

D. PEDRO. You have put him down, lady, you have put him down.

BEAT. So I would not he should do me, my lord, lest I should prove the mother of fools.—I have brought count Claudio, whom you sent me to seek.

D. PEDRO. Why, how now, count! wherefore are you sad?

CLAUD. Not sad, my lord.

D. PEDRO. How then? Sick?

CLAUD. Neither, my lord.

BEAT. The count is neither sad, nor sick, nor merry, nor well; but civil, count, —civil as an orange, and something of that jealous complexion.

D. PEDRO. I' faith, lady, I think your blazon to be true; though, I'll be sworn, if he be so, his conceit is false.—Here, Claudio, I have wooed in thy name, and fair Hero is won: I have broke with her father, and, his good will obtained, name the day of marriage, and God give thee joy!

LEON. Count, take of me my daughter, and with her my fortunes: his grace hath made the match, and all grace say Amen to it!

BEAT. Speak, count, 'tis your cue.

CLAUD. Silence is the perfectest herald of joy: I were but little happy, if I could say how much.—Lady, as you are mine, I am yours: I give away myself for you, and dote upon the exchange.

BEAT. Speak, cousin; or, if you cannot, stop his mouth with a kiss, and let not him speak neither.

D. PEDRO. In faith, lady, you have a merry heart.

BEAT. Yea, my lord; I thank it, poor fool, it keeps on the windy side of care.—My cousin tells him in his ear, that he is in her heart.

CLAUD. And so she doth, cousin.

BEAT. Good lord, for alliance! Thus goes every one to the world but I, and I am sunburned: I may sit in a corner, and cry heigh-ho for a husband!

D. PEDRO. Lady Beatrice, I will get you one.

BEAT. I would rather have one of your father's getting. Hath your grace ne'er a brother like you? Your father got excellent husbands, if a maid could come by them.

D. PEDRO. Will you have me, lady?

BEAT. No, my lord, unless I might have another for working-days: your grace is too costly to wear every day.—But, I beseech your grace, pardon me; I was born to speak all mirth, and no matter.

D. PEDRO. Your silence most offends me, and to be merry best becomes you; for, out of question, you were born in a merry hour.

BEAT. No, sure, my lord, my mother cried; but then there was a star danced, and under that was I born.—Cousins, God give you joy!

LEON. Niece, will you look to those things I told you of?

BEAT. I cry you mercy, uncle.—By your grace's pardon.   [*Exit.*

D. PEDRO. By my troth, a pleasant-spirited lady.

LEON. There's little of the melancholy element in her, my lord: she is never sad, but when she sleeps; and not ever sad then; for I have heard my daughter say, she hath often dreamed of unhappiness, and waked herself with laughing.

D. PEDRO. She cannot endure to hear tell of a husband.

LEON. O, by no means: she mocks all her wooers out of suit.

D. PEDRO. She were an excellent wife for Benedick.

LEON. O lord, my lord, if they were but a week married, they would talk themselves mad!

D. PEDRO. Count Claudio, when mean you to go to church?

CLAUD. To-morrow, my lord: time goes on crutches till love have all his rites.

LEON. Not till Monday, my dear son, which is hence a just seven-night; and a time too brief, too, to have all things answer my mind.

D. PEDRO. Come, you shake the head at so long a breathing: but, I warrant thee, Claudio, the time shall not go dully by us. I will, in the interim, undertake one of Hercules' labours; which is, to bring signior Benedick and the lady Beatrice into a mountain of affection, the one with the other. I would fain have it a match; and I doubt not but to fashion it, if you three will but minister such assistance as I shall give you direction.

LEON. My lord, I am for you, though it cost me ten nights' watchings.

CLAUD. And I, my lord.

D. PEDRO. And you too, gentle Hero?

HERO. I will do any modest office, my lord, to help my cousin to a good husband.

D. PEDRO. And Benedick is not the unhopefullest husband that I know. Thus far can I praise him; he is of a noble strain, of approved valour, and confirmed honesty. I will teach you how to humour your cousin, that she shall fall in love with Benedick;—and I, with your two helps, will so practise on Benedick, that, in despite of his quick wit and his queasy stomach, he shall fall in love with Beatrice. If we can do this, Cupid is no longer an archer: his glory shall be ours, for we are the only love-gods. Go in with me, and I will tell you my drift.   [*Exeunt.*

SCENE II.—*Another Room in* LEONATO'S *House.*

Enter Don JOHN *and* BORACHIO.

D. JOHN. It is so; the count Claudio shall marry the daughter of Leonato.

BORA. Yea, my lord; but I can cross it.

D. JOHN. Any bar, any cross, any impediment will be medicinable to me: I am sick in displeasure to him; and whatsoever comes athwart his affection, ranges evenly with mine. How canst thou cross this marriage?

BORA. Not honestly, my lord; but so covertly that no dishonesty shall appear in me.

D. JOHN. Show me briefly how.

BORA. I think I told your lordship, a year since, how much I am in the favour of Margaret, the waiting-gentlewoman to Hero.

D. JOHN. I remember.

BORA. I can, at any unseasonable instant of the night, appoint her to look out at her lady's chamber-window.

D. JOHN. What life is in that, to be the death of this marriage?

BORA. The poison of that lies in you to temper. Go you to the prince your brother; spare not to tell him, that he hath wronged his honour in marrying the renowned Claudio (whose estimation do you mightily hold up) to a contaminated stale, such a one as Hero.

D. JOHN. What proof shall I make of that?

BORA. Proof enough to misuse the prince, to vex Claudio, to undo Hero, and kill Leonato. Look you for any other issue?

D. JOHN. Only to despite them, I will endeavour any thing.

BORA. Go, then; find me a meet hour to draw Don Pedro and the count Claudio alone: tell them that you know that Hero loves me; intend a kind of zeal both to the prince and Claudio, as,—in love of your brother's honour, who hath made this match, and his friend's reputation, who is thus like to be cozened with the semblance of a maid,—that you have discovered thus. They will scarcely believe this without trial: offer them instances; which shall bear no less likelihood than to see me at her chamber-window; hear me call Margaret, Hero; hear Margaret term me, Claudio; and bring them to see this the very night before the intended wedding,— for in the meantime I will so fashion the matter that Hero shall be absent;—and there shall appear such seeming truth of Hero's disloyalty, that jealousy shall be called assurance, and all the preparation overthrown.

D. JOHN. Grow this to what adverse issue it can, I will put it in practice. Be cunning in the working this, and thy fee is a thousand ducats.

BORA. Be you constant in the accusation, and my cunning shall not shame me.

D. JOHN. I will presently go learn their day of marriage.   [*Exeunt.*

SCENE III.—LEONATO'S *Garden.*

Enter BENEDICK.

BENE. Boy!

Enter a Boy.

BOY. Signior?

BENE. In my chamber-window lies a book; bring it hither to me in the orchard.

BOY. I am here already, Sir.

BENE. I know that; but I would have thee hence, and here again. [*Exit* Boy.] I do much wonder, that one man, seeing how much another man is a fool when he dedicates his behaviours to love, will, after he hath laughed at such shallow follies in others, become the argument of his own scorn by falling in love: and such a man is Claudio. I have known, when there was no music with him but the drum and the fife; and now had he rather hear the tabor and the pipe: I have known, when he would have walked ten mile afoot to see a good armour; and now will he lie ten nights awake, carving the fashion of a new doublet. He was wont to speak plain, and to the purpose, like an honest man, and a soldier; and now is he turned orthographer; his words are a very fantastical banquet,—just so many strange dishes. May I be so converted, and see with these eyes? I cannot tell; I think not: I will not be sworn but love may transform me to an oyster; but I'll take my oath on it, till he have made an oyster of me, he shall never make me such a fool. One woman is fair, —yet I am well; another is wise,—yet I am well; another virtuous,—yet I am well: but till all graces be in one woman, one woman shall not come in my grace. Rich she shall be, that's certain; wise, or I'll none; virtuous, or I'll never cheapen her; fair, or I'll never look on her; mild, or come not near me; noble, or not I for an angel; of good discourse, an excellent musician, and her hair shall be of what colour it please God.—Ha! the prince and monsieur Love! I will hide me in the arbour.
[*Withdraws.*

Enter Don PEDRO, LEONATO, *and* CLAUDIO, *followed by* BALTHAZAR *and* Musicians.

D. PEDRO. Come, shall we hear this music?

CLAUD. Yea, my good lord.—How still the evening is,
As hush'd on purpose to grace harmony!

D. PEDRO. [*Aside to* CLAUD.] See you where Benedick hath hid himself?

CLAUD. [*Aside to D.* PEDRO.] O, very well, my lord: the music ended,
We'll fit the kid-fox with a penny-worth.

D. PEDRO. Come, Balthazar, we'll hear that song again.

BALTH. O, good my lord, tax not so bad a voice
To slander music any more than once.

D. PEDRO. It is the witness still of excellency,
To put a strange face on his own perfection:—
I pray thee, sing, and let me woo no more.

BALTH. Because you talk of wooing, I will sing;
Since many a wooer doth commence his suit
To her he thinks not worthy; yet he woos,
Yet will he swear, he loves.

D. PEDRO.   Nay, pray thee, come;
Or, if thou wilt hold longer argument,
Do it in notes.

BALTH.   Note this before my notes,—
There's not a note of mine that's worth the noting.

D. PEDRO. Why these are very crotchets that he speaks;
Note, notes, forsooth, and nothing!
                    [*Music.*

BENE. [*Aside.*] Now, divine air! now is his soul ravished!—Is it not strange, that sheeps' guts should hale souls out of men's bodies?—Well, a horn for my money, when all's done.

            BALTHAZAR *sings.*

Sigh no more, ladies, sigh no more,
    Men were deceivers ever;
One foot in sea, and one on shore;
    To one thing constant never:
        Then sigh not so,
        But let them go,
And be you blithe and bonny;
Converting all your sounds of woe
    Into, Hey nonny, nonny.

Sing no more ditties, sing no mo
    Of dumps so dull and heavy;
The fraud of men was ever so,
    Since summer first was leavy.
        Then sigh not so, &c.

D. PEDRO. By my troth, a good song.

BALTH. And an ill singer, my lord.

D. PEDRO. Ha? no, no, faith; thou singest well enough, for a shift.

BENE. [*Aside.*] An he had been a dog that should have howled thus, they would have hanged him; and I pray God, his bad voice bode no mischief! I had as lief have heard the night-raven, come what plague could have come after it.

D. PEDRO. [*To* CLAUDIO.] Yea, marry.—Dost thou hear, Balthazar? I pray thee, get us some excellent music; for to-morrow night we would have it at the lady Hero's chamber-window.

BALTH. The best I can, my lord.

D. PEDRO. Do so: farewell. [*Exeunt* BALTHAZAR *and* Musicians.] Come hither, Leonato: what was it you told me of to-day,—that your niece Beatrice was in love with signior Benedick?

CLAUD. O, ay:—[*Aside to* PEDRO.] Stalk on, stalk on; the fowl sits. [*Aloud.*] I did never think that lady would have loved any man.

LEON. No, nor I neither; but most wonderful, that she should so dote on signior Benedick, whom she hath in all outward behaviours seemed ever to abhor.

BENE. [*Aside.*] Is't possible? Sits the wind in that corner?

LEON. By my troth, my lord, I cannot tell what to think of it: but that she loves him with an enraged affection,—it is past the infinite of thought.

D. PEDRO. May be, she doth but counterfeit.

CLAUD. 'Faith, like enough.

LEON. O God! counterfeit! There was never counterfeit of passion came so near the life of passion as she discovers it.

D. PEDRO. Why, what effects of passion shows she?

CLAUD. [*Aside to them.*] Bait the hook well; this fish will bite.

LEON. What effects, my lord? She will sit you,—you heard my daughter tell you how.

CLAUD. She did, indeed.

D. PEDRO. How, how, I pray you? You amaze me: I would have thought her spirit had been invincible against all assaults of affection.

LEON. I would have sworn it had, my lord; especially against Benedick.

BENE. [*Aside.*] I should think this a gull, but that the white-bearded fellow speaks it: knavery cannot, sure, hide himself in such reverence.

CLAUD. [*Aside to them.*] He hath ta'en the infection: hold it up.

D. PEDRO. Hath she made her affection known to Benedick?

LEON. No; and swears she never will: that's her torment.

CLAUD. 'Tis true, indeed; so your daughter says: "Shall I," says she, "that have so oft encountered him with scorn, write to him that I love him?"

LEON. This says she now when she is beginning to write to him; for she'll be up twenty times a night; and there will she sit in her smock, till she have writ a sheet of paper:—my daughter tells us all.

CLAUD. Now you talk of a sheet of paper, I remember a pretty jest your daughter told us of.

LEON. O,—when she had writ it, and was reading it over, she found Benedick and Beatrice between the sheet?—

CLAUD. That.

LEON. O, she tore the letter into a thousand half-pence; railed at herself, that she should be so immodest to write to one that she knew would flout her: "I measure him," says she, "by my own spirit; for I should flout him, if he writ to me; yea, though I love him, I should."

CLAUD. Then down upon her knees she falls, weeps, sobs, beats her heart, tears her hair, prays, cries,—"O sweet Benedick! God give me patience!"

LEON. She doth indeed: my daughter says so: and the ecstasy hath so much overborne her, that my daughter is sometime afeard she will do a desperate outrage to herself: it is very true.

D. PEDRO. It were good, that Benedick knew of it by some other, if she will not discover it.

CLAUD. To what end? He would but make a sport of it, and torment the poor lady worse.

D. PEDRO. An he should, it were an alms to hang him. She's an excellent sweet lady; and, out of all suspicion she is virtuous.

CLAUD. And she is exceeding wise.

D. PEDRO. In every thing, but in loving Benedick.

LEON. O my lord, wisdom and blood combating in so tender a body, we have ten proofs to one, that blood hath the victory. I am sorry for her, as I have just cause, being her uncle and her guardian.

D. PEDRO. I would she had bestowed this dotage on me: I would have daffed all other respects, and made her half myself. I pray you, tell Benedick of it, and hear what he will say.

LEON. Were it good, think you?

CLAUD. Hero thinks surely she will die; for she says she will die if he love her not; and she will die, ere she make her love known; and she will die, if he woo her,

rather than she will bate one breath of her accustomed crossness.

D. PEDRO. She doth well: if she should make tender of her love 'tis very possible he'll scorn it; for the man, as you know all, hath a contemptible spirit.

CLAUD. He is a very proper man.

D. PEDRO. He hath indeed a good outward happiness.   [wise.

CLAUD. 'Fore God, and in my mind, very

D. PEDRO. He doth indeed show some sparks that are like wit.

LEON. And I take him to be valiant.

D. PEDRO. As Hector, I assure you: and in the managing of quarrels you may say he is wise; for either he avoids them with great discretion, or undertakes them with a most Christian-like fear.

LEON. If he do fear God, he must necessary keep peace: if he break the peace, he ought to enter into a quarrel with fear and trembling.

D. PEDRO. And so will he do; for the man doth fear God, howsoever it seems not in him by some large jests he will make. Well, I am sorry for your niece. Shall we go seek Benedick, and tell him of her love?

CLAUD. Never tell him, my lord: let her wear it out with good counsel.

LEON. Nay, that's impossible: she may wear her heart out first.

D. PEDRO. Well, we will hear farther of it by your daughter: let it cool the while. I love Benedick well; and I could wish he would modestly examine himself, to see how much he is unworthy to have so good a lady.

LEON. My lord, will you walk? dinner is ready.

CLAUD. [Aside to them.] If he do not dote on her upon this, I will never trust my expectation.

D. PEDRO. [Aside to LEONATO.] Let there be the same net spread for her; and that must your daughter and her gentlewoman carry. The sport will be, when they hold one an opinion of another's dotage, and no such matter: that's the scene that I would see, which will be merely a dumb show. Let us send her to call him in to dinner.

[*Exeunt Don* PEDRO, CLAUDIO, *and* LEONATO.

BENE. [Advancing from the arbour.] This can be no trick: the conference was sadly borne. They have the truth of this from Hero. They seem to pity the lady: it seems, her affections have their full bent. Love me! why, it must be requited. I hear how I am censured: they say I will bear myself proudly, if I perceive the love come from her: they say too, that she will

rather die than give any sign of affection.
—I did never think to marry.—I must not
seem proud.—Happy are they that hear
their detractions, and can put them to
mending. They say the lady is fair,—'tis a
truth, I can bear them witness; and virtuous,—'tis so, I cannot reprove it; and wise,
but for loving me: by my troth, it is no
addition to her wit; nor no great argument
of her folly,—for I will be horribly in love
with her. I may chance have some odd
quirks and remnants of wit broken on me,
because I have railed so long against marriage: but doth not the appetite alter? A
man loves the meat in his youth, that he
cannot endure in his age. Shall quips,
and sentences, and these paper bullets of
the brain, awe a man from the career of
his humour? No; the world must be
peopled. When I said I would die a bachelor, I did not think I should live till I
were married.—Here comes Beatrice. By
this day, she's a fair lady: I do spy some
marks of love in her.

Enter BEATRICE.

BEAT. Against my will, I am sent to bid
you come in to dinner.
BENE. Fair Beatrice, I thank you for your
pains.
BEAT. I took no more pains for those
thanks, than you take pains to thank me:
if it had been painful, I would not have
come.
BENE. You take pleasure, then, in the
message?
BEAT. Yea, just so much as you may
take upon a knife's point, and choke a daw
withal.—You have no stomach, signior:
fare you well.   [*Exit.*
BENE. Ha! "Against my will I am sent
to bid you come in to dinner,"—there's a
double meaning in that. "I took no more
pains for those thanks, than you took pains
to thank me,"—that's as much as to say,
Any pains that I take for you is as easy
as thanks.—If I do not take pity of her,
I am a villain: if I do not love her, I am
a Jew. I will go get her picture. [*Exit.*

ACT III.

SCENE I.—LEONATO'S *Garden.*

Enter HERO, MARGARET, *and* URSULA.
HERO. Good Margaret, run thee to the
parlour;
There shalt thou find my cousin Beatrice
Proposing with the Prince and Claudio:
Whisper her ear, and tell her, I and Ursula
Walk in the orchard, and our whole dis-
course

Is all of her: say that thou overheard'st us;
And bid her steal into the pleached bower,
Where honey-suckles, ripen'd by the sun,
Forbid the sun to enter;—like favourites,
Made proud by princes, that advance their
pride
Against that power that bred it:—there
will she hide her,
To listen our propose. This is thy office;
Bear thee well in it, and leave us alone.
MARG. I'll make her come, I warrant
you, presently.   [*Exit.*
HERO. Now, Ursula, when Beatrice doth
come,
As we do trace this alley up and down,
Our talk must only be of Benedick.
When I do name him, let it be thy part
To praise him more than ever man did
merit.
My talk to thee must be, how Benedick
Is sick in love with Beatrice. Of this mat-
ter
Is little Cupid's crafty arrow made,
That only wounds by hearsay. Now begin;

Enter BEATRICE, *behind.*

For look where Beatrice, like a lapwing,
runs
Close by the ground, to hear our confer-
ence.
URS. The pleasant'st angling is to see
the fish
Cut with her golden oars the silver stream,
And greedily devour the treacherous bait:
So angle we for Beatrice; who even now
Is couched in the woodbine coverture.
Fear you not my part of the dialogue.
HERO. Then go we near her, that her ear
lose nothing
Of the false sweet bait that we lay for it.—
            [*They advance to the bower.*
No, truly, Ursula, she is too disdainful;
I know her spirits are as coy and wild
As haggards of the rock.
URS.   But are you sure
That Benedick loves Beatrice so entirely?
HERO. So says the prince, and my new-
trothed lord.
URS. And did they bid you tell her of it,
madam?
HERO. They did entreat me to acquaint
her of it;
But I persuaded them, if they lov'd Bene-
dick,
To wish him wrestle with affection,
And never to let Beatrice know of it.
URS. Why did you so? Doth not the
gentleman
Deserve as full, as fortunate a bed,
As ever Beatrice shall couch upon?
HERO. O God of love! I know he doth
deserve

As much as may be yielded to a man:
But nature never fram'd a woman's heart
Of prouder stuff than that of Beatrice;
Disdain and scorn ride sparkling in her
   eyes,
Misprising what they look on; and her wit
Values itself so highly, that to her
All matter else seems weak: she cannot
   love,
Nor take no shape nor project of affection,
She is so self-endear'd.
URS.   Sure, I think so;
And therefore certainly it were not good
She knew his love, lest she make sport at it.
HERO. Why, you speak truth. I never yet
   saw man,
How wise, how noble, young, how rarely
   featur'd,
But she would spell him backward: if
   fair-fac'd,
She'd swear the gentleman should be her
   sister;
If black, why, nature, drawing of an an-
   tick,
Made a foul blot; if tall, a lance ill-
   headed;
If low, an agate very vilely cut;
If speaking, why, a vane blown with all
   winds;
If silent, why, a block moved with none.
So turns she every man the wrong side out;
And never gives to truth and virtue that
Which simpleness and merit purchaseth.
URS. Sure, sure, such carping is not com-
   mendable.
HERO. No; not to be so odd, and from
   all fashions,
As Beatrice is, cannot be commendable:
But who dare tell her so? If I should
   speak,
She would mock me into air; O, she would
   laugh me
Out of myself, press me to death with wit!
Therefore let Benedick, like cover'd fire,
Consume away in sighs, waste inwardly:
It were a better death than die with
   mocks,
Which is as bad as die with tickling.
URS. Yet, tell her of it: hear what she
   will say.
HERO. No; rather I will go to Benedick,
And counsel him to fight against his pas-
   sion.
And, truly, I'll devise some honest slan-
   ders
To stain my cousin with: one doth not
   know,
How much an ill word may empoison lik-
   ing.
URS. O, do not do your cousin such a
   wrong!

She cannot be so much without true judg-
   ment,
(Having so swift and excellent a wit
As she is priz'd to have) as to refuse
So rare a gentleman as signior Benedick.
HERO. He is the only man of Italy,—
Always excepted my dear Claudio.
URS. I pray you, be not angry with me,
   madam,
Speaking my fancy: signior Benedick,
For shape, for bearing, argument, and
   valour,
Goes foremost in report through Italy.
HERO. Indeed, he hath an excellent good
   name.
URS. His excellence did earn it, ere he
   had it.—
When are you married, madam?
HERO. Why, every day; — to-morrow.
   Come, go in:
I'll show thee some attires; and have thy
   counsel,
Which is the best to furnish me to-morrow.
URS. [*Aside.*] She's lim'd, I warrant
you: we have caught her, madam.
HERO. [*Aside.*] If it prove so, then lov-
ing goes by haps:
Some Cupid kills with arrows, some with
   traps.   [*Exeunt* HERO *and* URSULA.
BEAT. [*Advancing.*] What fire is in mine
ears? Can this be true?
Stand I condemn'd for pride and scorn so
much?
Contempt, farewell! and maiden pride,
   adieu!
No glory lives behind the back of such.
And, Benedick, love on: I will requite thee,
   Taming my wild heart to thy loving hand.
If thou dost love, my kindness shall incite
   thee
To bind our loves up in a holy band;
For others say thou dost deserve, and I
Believe it better than reportingly. [*Exit.*

SCENE II.—*A Room in* LEONATO'S *House.*
   Enter Don PEDRO, CLAUDIO, BENEDICK,
               and LEONATO.

D. PEDRO. I do but stay till your marriage be consummate, and then go I
toward Arragon.
CLAUD. I'll bring you thither, my lord,
if you'll vouchsafe me.
D. PEDRO. Nay, that would be as great
a soil in the new gloss of your marriage,
as to show a child his new coat, and forbid him to wear it. I will only be bold
with Benedick for his company; for, from
the crown of his head to the sole of his
foot, he is all mirth: he hath twice or
thrice cut Cupid's bow-string, and the little
hangman dare not shoot at him. He hath

a heart as sound as a bell, and his tongue is the clapper; for what his heart thinks, his tongue speaks.

BENE. Gallants, I am not as I have been.

LEON. So say I: methinks you are sadder.

CLAUD. I hope he be in love.

D. PEDRO. Hang him, truant! there's no true drop of blood in him, to be truly touched with love. If he be sad, he wants money.

BENE. I have the tooth-ache.

D. PEDRO. Draw it.

BENE. Hang it!

CLAUD. You must hang it first, and draw it afterwards.

D. PEDRO. What! sigh for the tooth-ache?

LEON. Where is but a humour, or a worm?

BENE. Well, every one can master a grief, but he that has it.

CLAUD. Yet say I, he is in love.

D. PEDRO. There is no appearance of fancy in him, unless it be a fancy that he hath to strange disguises; as, to be a Dutchman to-day, a Frenchman to-morrow; or in the shape of two countries at once; as, a German from the waist downward, all slops, and a Spaniard from the hip upward, no doublet. Unless he have a fancy to this foolery, as it appears he hath, he is no fool for fancy, as you would have it appear he is.

CLAUD. If he be not in love with some woman, there is no believing old signs: he brushes his hat o' mornings; what should that bode?

D. PEDRO. Hath any man seen him at the barber's?

CLAUD. No, but the barber's man hath been seen with him; and the old ornament of his cheek hath already stuffed tennis-balls.

LEON. Indeed, he looks younger than he did, by the loss of a beard.

D. PEDRO. Nay, he rubs himself with civet: can you smell him out by that?

CLAUD. That's as much as to say, the sweet youth's in love.

D. PEDRO. The greatest note of it is his melancholy.

CLAUD. And when was he wont to wash his face?

D. PEDRO. Yea, or to paint himself? for the which, I hear what they say of him.

CLAUD. Nay, but his jesting spirit; which is now crept into a lutestring, and now governed by stops.

D. PEDRO. Indeed, that tells a heavy tale for him. Conclude, conclude, he is in love.

CLAUD. Nay, but I know who loves him.

D. PEDRO. That would I know too: I warrant, one that knows him not.

CLAUD. Yes, and his ill conditions; and in despite of all, dies for him.

D. PEDRO. She shall be buried with her face upwards.

BENE. Yet is this no charm for the tooth-ache.—Old signior, walk aside with me: I have studied eight or nine wise words to speak to you, which these hobby-horses must not hear.

[*Exeunt* BENEDICK *and* LEONATO.

D. PEDRO. For my life, to break with him about Beatrice.

CLAUD. 'Tis even so. Hero and Margaret have by this, played their parts with Beatrice; and then the two bears will not bite one another when they meet.

Enter Don JOHN.

D. JOHN. My lord and brother, God save you.

D. PEDRO. Good den, brother.

D. JOHN. If your leisure served, I would speak with you.

D. PEDRO. In private?

D. JOHN. If it please you: yet count Claudio may hear; for what I would speak of concerns him.

D. PEDRO. What's the matter?

D. JOHN. [*To* CLAUDIO.] Means your lordship to be married to-morrow?

D. PEDRO. You know he does.

D. JOHN. I know not that, when he knows what I know.

CLAUD. If there be any impediment, I pray you discover it.

D. JOHN. You may think I love you not: let that appear hereafter, and aim better at me by that I now will manifest. For my brother, I think he holds you well; and in dearness of heart hath holp to effect your ensuing marriage,—surely, suit ill spent, and labour ill bestowed.

D. PEDRO. Why, what's the matter?

D. JOHN. I came hither to tell you; and, circumstances shortened, (for she hath been too long a talking of,) the lady is disloyal.

CLAUD. Who, Hero?

D. JOHN. Even she: Leonato's Hero, your Hero, every man's Hero.

CLAUD. Disloyal!

D. JOHN. The word is too good to paint out her wickedness: I could say, she were worse: think you of a worse title, and I will fit her to it. Wonder not till farther warrant: go but with me to-night, you shall see her chamber-window entered, even the night before her wedding-day: if you love her then, to-morrow wed her; but it would better fit your honour to change your mind.

CLAUD. May this be so?

D. PEDRO. I will not think it.

D. JOHN. If you dare not trust that you see, confess not that you know. If you will follow me, I will show you enough; and when you have seen more, and heard more, proceed accordingly.

CLAUD. If I see any thing to-night why I should not marry her to-morrow, in the congregation, where I should wed, there will I shame her.

D. PEDRO. And, as I wooed for thee to obtain her, I will join with thee to disgrace her.

D. JOHN. I will disparage her no farther, till you are my witnesses: bear it coldly but till midnight, and let the issue show itself.

D. PEDRO. O day untowardly turned!

CLAUD. O mischief strangely thwarting!

D. JOHN. O plague right well prevented! So will you say, when you have seen the sequel.   [*Exeunt.*

SCENE III.—*A Street.*

Enter DOGBERRY *and* VERGES,
with the Watch.

DOGB. Are you good men and true?

VERG. Yea, or else it were pity but they should suffer salvation, body and soul.

DOGB. Nay, that were a punishment too good for them, if they should have any allegiance in them, being chosen for the prince's watch.

VERG. Well, give them their charge, neighbour Dogberry.

DOGB. First, who think you the most desartless man to be constable?

1 WATCH. Hugh Oatcake, Sir, or George Seacoal; for they can write and read.

DOGB. Come hither, neighbour Seacoal. God hath blessed you with a good name: to be a well-favoured man is the gift of fortune; but to write and read comes by nature.

2 WATCH. Both which, master constable,—

DOGB. You have: I knew it would be your answer. Well, for your favour, Sir, why, give God thanks, and make no boast of it; and for your writing and reading, let that appear when there is no need of such vanity. You are thought here to be the most senseless and fit man for the constable of the watch; therefore bear you the lantern. This is your charge—you shall comprehend all vagrom men; you are to bid any man stand, in the prince's name.

2 WATCH. How if a' will not stand?

DOGB. Why then, take no note of him, but let him go; and presently call the rest of the watch together, and thank God you are rid of a knave.

VERG. If he will not stand when he is bidden, he is none of the prince's subjects.

DOGB. True, and they are to meddle with none but the prince's subjects.—You shall also make no noise in the streets; for, for the watch to babble and talk, is most tolerable and not to be endured.

2 WATCH. We will rather sleep than talk: we know what belongs to a watch.

DOGB. Why, you speak like an ancient and most quiet watchman; for I cannot see how sleeping should offend: only, have a care that your bills be not stolen.—Well, you are to call at all the ale-houses, and bid those that are drunk get them to bed.

2 WATCH. How if they will not?

DOGB. Why then, let them alone till they are sober: if they make you not then the better answer, you may say they are not the men you took them for.

2 WATCH. Well, Sir.

DOGB. If you meet a thief, you may suspect him, by virtue of your office, to be no true man; and, for such kind of men, the less you meddle or make with them, why, the more is for your honesty.

2 WATCH. If we know him to be a thief, shall we not lay hands on him?

DOGB. Truly, by your office, you may; but I think they that touch pitch will be defiled: the most peaceable way for you, if you do take a thief, is, to let him show himself what he is, and steal out of your company.

VERG. You have been always called a merciful man, partner.

DOGB. Truly, I would not hang a dog by my will; much more a man who hath any honesty in him.

VERG. If you hear a child cry in the night, you must call to the nurse, and bid her still it.

2 WATCH. How, if the nurse be asleep, and will not hear us?

DOGB. Why then, depart in peace, and let the child wake her with crying; for the ewe that will not hear her lamb when it baes, will never answer a calf when he bleats.

VERG. 'Tis very true.

DOGB. This is the end of the charge.— You, constable, are to present the prince's own person: if you meet the prince in the night, you may stay him.

VERG. Nay, by'r lady, that, I think, a' cannot.

DOGB. Five shillings to one on't, with any man that knows the statutes, he may stay him: marry, not without the prince be willing; for, indeed, the watch ought to offend no man; and it is an offence to stay a man against his will.

VERG. By'r lady, I think it be so.

DOGB. Ha, ha, ha! Well, masters, good night: an there be any matter of weight chances, call up me: keep your fellows' counsels and your own; and good night. —Come, neighbour.

2 WATCH. Well, masters, we hear our charge: let us go sit here upon the church-bench till two, and then all to bed.

DOGB. One word more, honest neighbours. I pray you, watch about signior Leonato's door; for the wedding being there to-morrow, there is a great coil to-night. Adieu, be vigitant, I beseech you.

[*Exeunt* DOGBERRY *and* VERGES.
Enter BORACHIO *and* CONRADE.

BORA. What, Conrade!

WATCH. [*Aside.*] Peace! stir not.

BORA. Conrade, I say!

CON. Here, man; I am at thy elbow.

BORA. Mass, and my elbow itched; I thought there would a scab follow.

CON. I will owe thee an answer for that: and now forward with thy tale.

BORA. Stand thee close, then, under this penthouse, for it drizzles rain; and I will, like a true drunkard, utter all to thee.

WATCH. [*Aside.*] Some treason, masters: yet stand close.

BORA. Therefore know, I have earned of Don John a thousand ducats.

CON. Is it possible that any villainy should be so dear?

BORA. Thou should'st rather ask, if it were possible any villainy should be so rich; for when rich villains have need of poor ones, poor ones may make what price they will.

CON. I wonder at it.

BORA. That shows thou art unconfirmed. Thou knowest, that the fashion of a doublet, or a hat, or a cloak, is nothing to a man.

CON. Yes, it is apparel.

BORA. I mean, the fashion.

CON. Yes, the fashion is the fashion.

BORA. Tush! I may as well say the fool's the fool. But seest thou not what a deformed thief this fashion is?

WATCH. [*Aside.*] I know that Deformed; a' has been a vile thief this seven year: a' goes up and down like a gentleman. I remember his name.

BORA. Didst thou not hear somebody?

CON. No; 'twas the vane on the house.

BORA. Seest thou not, I say, what a deformed thief this fashion is? how giddily he turns about all the hot bloods between fourteen and five and thirty? sometime, fashioning them like Pharaoh's soldiers in the reechy painting; sometime, like god Bel's priests in the old church window; sometime, like the shaven Hercules in the smirched worm-eaten tapestry,—where his cod-piece seems as massy as his club?

CON. All this I see; and I see that the fashion wears out more apparel than the man. But art not thou thyself giddy with the fashion too, that thou hast shifted out of thy tale into telling me of the fashion?

BORA. Not so, neither: but know, that I have to-night wooed Margaret, the lady Hero's gentlewoman, by the name of Hero: she leans me out at her mistress' chamber-window, bids me a thousand times good night,—I tell this tale vilely:—I should first tell thee how the prince, Claudio, and my master, planted and placed and possessed by my master Don John, saw afar off in the orchard this amiable encounter.

CON. And thought they Margaret was Hero?

BORA. Two of them did, the prince and Claudio; but the devil, my master, knew she was Margaret; and partly by his oaths, which first possessed them, partly by the dark night, which did deceive them, but chiefly by my villainy, which did confirm any slander that Don John had made, away went Claudio enraged; swore he would meet her, as he was appointed, next morning at the temple, and there, before the whole congregation, shame her with what he saw over-night, and send her home again without a husband.

1 WATCH. We charge you in the prince's name, stand!

2 WATCH. Call up the right master constable. We have here recovered the most dangerous piece of lechery that ever was known in the commonwealth.

1 WATCH. And one Deformed is one of them: I know him; a' wears a lock.

CON. Masters, masters,—

2 WATCH. You'll be made bring Deformed forth, I warrant you.

CON. Masters,—

1 WATCH. Never speak: we charge you, let us obey you to go with us.

BORA. We are like to prove a goodly commodity, being taken up of these men's bills.

CON. A commodity in question, I warrant you.—Come, we'll obey you.

[*Exeunt.*

SCENE IV.—*A Room in* LEONATO'S *House.*

Enter HERO, MARGARET, *and* URSULA.

HERO. Good Ursula, wake my cousin Beatrice, and desire her to rise.

URS. I will, lady.

HERO. And bid her come hither.

URS. Well.   [*Exit.*

MARG. Troth, I think your other rabato were better.

HERO. No, pray thee, good Meg, I'll wear this.

MARG. By my troth, it's not so good; and I warrant, your cousin will say so.

HERO. My cousin's a fool, and thou art another: I'll wear none but this.

MARG. I like the new tire within excellently, if the hair were a thought browner; and your gown's a most rare fashion, i' faith. I saw the duchess of Milan's gown, that they praise so.

HERO. O, that exceeds, they say.

MARG. By my troth, it's but a night-gown in respect of yours,—cloth o' gold, and cuts, and laced with silver, set with pearls down sleeves, side sleeves, and skirts round, underborne with a bluish tinsel: but for a fine, quaint, graceful, and excellent fashion, yours is worth ten on't.

HERO. God give me joy to wear it! for my heart is exceeding heavy!

MARG. 'Twill be heavier soon by the weight of a man.

HERO. Fie upon thee! art not ashamed?

MARG. Of what, lady? of speaking honourably? Is not marriage honourable in a beggar? Is not your lord honourable without marriage? I think you would have me say, saving your reverence,—"a husband:" an bad thinking do not wrest true speaking, I'll offend nobody. Is there any harm in —"the heavier for a husband?" None, I think, an it be the right husband, and the right wife; otherwise 'tis light, and not heavy: ask my lady Beatrice else; here she comes.

Enter BEATRICE.

HERO. Good-morrow, coz.

BEAT. Good-morrow, sweet Hero.

HERO. Why, how now! do you speak in the sick tune?

BEAT. I am out of all other tune, methinks.

MARG. Clap us into—"Light o' love;" that goes without a burden: do you sing it, and I'll dance it.

BEAT. Yea, "Light o' love," with your heels!—then, if your husband have stables enough, you'll see he shall lack no barns.

MARG. O illegitimate construction! I scorn that with my heels.

BEAT. 'Tis almost five o'clock, cousin; 'tis time you were ready.—By my troth, I am exceeding ill:—heigh-ho!

MARG. For a hawk, a horse, or a husband?

BEAT. For the letter that begins them all, H.

MARG. Well, an you be not turned Turk, there's no more sailing by the star.

BEAT. What means the fool, trow?

MARG. Nothing I; but God send every one their heart's desire!

HERO. These gloves the count sent me; they are an excellent perfume.

BEAT. I am stuffed, cousin, I cannot smell.

MARG. A maid, and stuffed! there's goodly catching of cold.

BEAT. O, God help me! God help me! how long have you professed apprehension?

MARG. Ever since you left it. Doth not my wit become me rarely?

BEAT. It is not seen enough, you should wear it in your cap.—By my troth, I am sick.

MARG. Get you some of this distilled Carduus Benedictus, and lay it to your heart: it is the only thing for a qualm.

HERO. There thou prick'st her with a thistle.

BEAT. Benedictus! why Benedictus? you have some moral in this Benedictus.

MARG. Moral? no, by my troth, I have no moral meaning; I meant, plain holy-thistle. You may think, perchance, that I think you are in love: nay, by'r lady, I am not such a fool to think what I list; nor I list not to think what I can; nor, indeed, I cannot think, if I would think my heart out of thinking, that you are in love, or that you will be in love, or that you can be in love. Yet Benedick was such another, and now is he become a man: he swore he would never marry; and yet now, in despite of his heart, he eats his meat without grudging: and how you may be converted, I know not; but methinks you look with your eyes as other women do.

BEAT. What pace is this that thy tongue keeps?

MARG. Not a false gallop.

Re-enter URSULA.

URS. Madam, withdraw: the prince, the count, signior Benedick, Don John, and all the gallants of the town, are come to fetch you to church.

HERO. Help to dress me, good coz, good Meg, good Ursula.   [*Exeunt.*

SCENE V.—*Another Room in* LEONATO'S *House.*

Enter LEONATO, *with* DOGBERRY *and* VERGES.

LEON. What would you with me, honest neighbour?

DOGB. Marry, Sir, I would have some confidence with you, that decerns you nearly.

LEON. Brief, I pray you; for you see it is a busy time with me.

DOGB. Marry, this it is, Sir.

VERG. Yes, in truth it is, Sir.

LEON. What is it, my good friends?

DOGB. Goodman Verges, Sir, speaks a little off the matter: an old man, Sir, and his wits are not so blunt, as, God help, I would desire they were; but, in faith, honest as the skin between his brows.

VERG. Yes, I thank God, I am as honest as any man living, that is an old man, and no honester than I.

DOGB. Comparisons are odorous: palabras, neighbour Verges.

LEON. Neighbours, you are tedious.

DOGB. It pleases your worship to say so, but we are the poor duke's officers; but truly, for mine own part, if I were as tedious as a king, I could find in my heart to bestow it all of your worship.

LEON. All thy tediousness on me, ha?

DOGB. Yea, an't were a thousand pound more than 'tis; for I hear as good exclamation on your worship, as of any man in the city; and though I be but a poor man, I am glad to hear it.

VERG. And so am I.

LEON. I would fain know what you have to say.

VERG. Marry, Sir, our watch to-night, excepting your worship's presence, have ta'en a couple of as arrant knaves as any in Messina.

DOGB. A good old man, Sir; he will be talking: as they say, when the age is in, the wit is out. God help us! it is a world to see!—Well said, i' faith, neighbour Verges:—well, God's a good man: an two men ride of a horse, one must ride behind. —An honest soul, i' faith, Sir; by my troth he is, as ever broke bread: but God is to be worshipped: all men are not alike;— alas, good neighbour!

LEON. Indeed, neighbour, he comes too short of you.

DOGB. Gifts that God gives.

LEON. I must leave you.

DOGB. One word, Sir: our watch, Sir, have indeed comprehended two aspicious persons, and we would have them this morning examined before your worship.

LEON. Take their examination yourself, and bring it me: I am now in great haste, as may appear unto you.

DOGB. It shall be suffigance.

LEON. Drink some wine ere you go: fare you well.

Enter a Messenger.

MESS. My lord, they stay for you to give your daughter to her husband.

LEON. I'll wait upon them: I am ready.

[*Exeunt* LEONATO *and* Messenger.

DOGB. Go, good partner, go, get you to Francis Seacoal; bid him bring his pen and inkhorn to the gaol: we are now to examination these men.

VERG. And we must do it wisely.

DOGB. We will spare for no wit, I warrant you; here's that shall drive some of them to a *non com:* only get the learned writer to set down our excommunication, and meet me at the gaol. [*Exeunt.*

ACT IV.

SCENE I.—*The Inside of a Church.*

Enter Don PEDRO, *Don* JOHN, LEONATO, *Friar* FRANCIS, CLAUDIO, BENEDICK, HERO, BEATRICE, *and others.*

LEON. Come, friar Francis, be brief; only to the plain form of marriage, and you shall recount their particular duties afterwards.

FRIAR. You come hither, my lord, to marry this lady?

CLAUD. No.

LEON. To be married to her: friar, you come to marry her.

FRIAR. Lady, you come hither to be married to this count?

HERO. I do.

FRIAR. If either of you know any inward impediment why you should not be conjoined, I charge you, on your souls, to utter it.

CLAUD. Know you any, Hero?

HERO. None, my lord.

FRIAR. Know you any, count?

LEON. I dare make his answer,—none.

CLAUD. O, what men dare do! what men may do! what men daily do, not knowing what they do!

BENE. How now! Interjections? Why then, some be of laughing, as ha! ha! he!

CLAUD. Stand thee by, friar.—Father, by your leave:

Will you with free and unconstrained soul Give me this maid, your daughter?

LEON. As freely, son, as God did give her me.

CLAUD. And what have I to give you back, whose worth
May counterpoise this rich and precious gift?
D. PEDRO. Nothing, unless you render her again.
CLAUD. Sweet prince, you learn me noble thankfulness.—
There, Leonato; take her back again:
Give not this rotten orange to your friend;
She's but the sign and semblance of her honour.—
Behold how like a maid she blushes here!
O, what authority and show of truth
Can cunning sin cover itself withal!
Comes not that blood as modest evidence
To witness simple virtue? Would you not swear,
All you that see her, that she were a maid,
By these exterior shows? But she is none:
She knows the heat of a luxurious bed;
Her blush is guiltiness, not modesty.
LEON. What do you mean, my lord?
CLAUD.   Not to be married;
Not to knit my soul to an approved wanton.
LEON. Dear my lord, if you, in your own proof,
Have vanquish'd the resistance of her youth,
And made defeat of her virginity,—
CLAUD. I know what you would say: if I have known her,
You'll say she did embrace me as a husband,
And so extentuate the 'forehand sin:
No, Leonato,
I never tempted her with word too large;
But, as a brother to his sister, show'd
Bashful sincerity and comely love.
HERO. And seem'd I ever otherwise to you?
CLAUD. Out on thy seeming! I will write against it,—
You seem to me as Dian in her orb,
As chaste as is the bud ere it be blown;
But you are more intemperate in your blood
Than Venus, or those pamper'd animals
That rage in savage sensuality.
HERO. Is my lord well, that he doth speak so wide?
LEON. Sweet prince, why speak not you?
D. PEDRO.   What should I speak?
I stand dishonour'd, that have gone about
To link my dear friend to a common stale.
LEON. Are these things spoken? or do I but dream?
D. JOHN. Sir, they are spoken, and these things are true.
BENE. This looks not like a nuptial.
HERO.   True! O God!
CLAUD. Leonato, stand I here?

Is this the prince? Is this the prince's brother?
Is this face Hero's? Are our eyes our own?
LEON. All this is so; but what of this, my lord?
CLAUD. Let me but move one question to your daughter;
And, by that fatherly and kindly power
That you have in her, bid her answer truly.
LEON. I charge thee do so, as thou art my child.
HERO. O, God defend me! how am I beset!—
What kind of catechizing call you this?
CLAUD. To make you answer truly to your name.
HERO. Is it not Hero? Who can blot that name
With any just reproach?
CLAUD.   Marry, that can Hero:
Hero itself can blot out Hero's virtue.
What man was he talk'd with you yesternight
Out at your window, betwixt twelve and one?
Now, if you are a maid, answer to this.
HERO. I talk'd with no man at that hour, my lord.
D. PEDRO. Why, then are you no maiden.
—Leonato,
I am sorry you must hear: upon mine honour,
Myself, my brother, and this grieved count,
Did see her, hear her, at that hour last night,
Talk with a ruffian at her chamber-window;
Who hath indeed, most like a liberal villain,
Confess'd the vile encounters they have had
A thousand times in secret.
D. JOHN. Fie, fie! they are not to be nam'd, my lord,
Not to be spoke of;
There is not chastity enough in language,
Without offence to utter them. Thus, pretty lady,
I am sorry for thy much misgovernment.
CLAUD. O Hero! what a Hero hadst thou been,
If half thy outward graces had been plac'd
About thy thoughts, and counsels of thy heart!
But fare thee well, most foul, most fair! farewell,
Thou pure impiety, and impious purity!
For thee I'll lock up all the gates of love,
And on my eye-lids shall conjecture hang,
To turn all beauty into thoughts of harm,
And never shall it more be gracious.
LEON. Hath no man's dagger here a point for me?   [HERO *swoons.*
BEAT. Why, how, now, cousin! wherefore sink you down?

D. JOHN. Come, let us go. These things, come thus to light,
Smother her spirits up.

[*Exeunt Don* PEDRO, *Don* JOHN, *and* CLAUDIO.

BENE. How doth the lady?
BEAT. Dead, I think:—help, uncle!— Hero! why, Hero!—Uncle!—signior Benedick!—friar!
LEON. O fate, take not away thy heavy hand!
Death is the fairest cover for her shame
That may be wish'd for.
BEAT.   How now, cousin Hero!
FRIAR. Have comfort, lady.
LEON. Dost thou look up?
FRIAR.   Yea, wherefore should she not?
LEON. Wherefore! Why, doth not every earthly thing
Cry shame upon her? Could she here deny
The story that is printed in her blood?—
Do not live, Hero; do not ope thine eyes:
For, did I think thou would'st not quickly die,
Thought I thy spirits were stronger than thy shames,
Myself would, on the rearward of reproaches,
Strike at thy life. Griev'd I, I had but one?
Chid I for that at frugal nature's frame?
O, one too much by thee! Why had I one?
Why ever wast thou lovely in my eyes?
Why had I not with charitable hand
Took up a beggar's issue at my gates;
Who smirched thus and mir'd with infamy,
I might have said, "No part of it is mine;
This shame derives itself from unknown loins?"
But mine, and mine I lov'd, and mine I prais'd,
And mine that I was proud on; mine so much,
That I myself was to myself not mine,
Valuing of her; why, she—O, she is fallen
Into a pit of ink, that the wide sea
Hath drops too few to wash her clean again,
And salt too little, which may season give
To her foul tainted flesh!
BENE.   Sir, Sir, be patient.
For my part, I am so attir'd in wonder,
I know not what to say.
BEAT. O, on my soul, my cousin is belied!
BENE. Lady, were you her bedfellow last night?
BEAT. No, truly, not; although, until last night,
I have this twelvemonth been her bedfellow.
LEON. Confirm'd, confirm'd! O, that is stronger made,
Which was before barr'd up with ribs of iron!

Would the two princes lie? and Claudio lie,
Who lov'd her so, that, speaking of her foulness,
Wash'd it with tears? Hence from her! let her die.
FRIAR. Hear me a little;
For I have only been silent so long,
And given way unto this course of fortune,
By noting of the lady: I have mark'd
A thousand blushing apparitions start
Into her face; a thousand innocent shames
n angel whiteness bear away those blushes;
And in her eye there hath appear'd a fire,
To burn the errors that these princes hold
Against her maiden truth. Call me a fool;
Trust not my reading nor my observation,
Which with experimental seal doth warrant
The tenour of my book; trust not my age,
My reverence, calling, nor divinity,
If this sweet lady lie not guiltless here
Under some biting error.
LEON.   Friar, it cannot be.
Thou seest that all the grace that she hath left,
Is, that she will not add to her damnation
A sin of perjury: she not denies it.
Why seek'st thou, then, to cover with excuse
That which appears in proper nakedness?
FRIAR. Lady, what man is he you are accus'd of of?
HERO. They know, that do accuse me; I know none:
If I know more of any man alive,
Than that which maiden modesty doth warrant,
Let all my sins lack mercy!—O, my father!
Prove you that any man with me convers'd
At hours unmeet, or that I yesternight
Maintain'd the change of words with any creature,
Refuse me, hate me, torture me to death.
FRIAR. There is some strange misprision in the princes.
BENE. Two of them have the very bent of honour;
And if their wisdoms be misled in this,
The practice of it lives in John the bastard,
Whose spirits toil in frame of villainies.
LEON. I know not. If they speak but truth of her,
These hands shall tear her: if they wrong her honour,
The proudest of them shall well hear of it.
Time hath not yet so dried this blood of mine,
Nor age so eat up my invention,
Nor fortune made such havock of my means,
Nor my bad life reft me so much of friends,

But they shall find, awak'd in such a kind,
Both strength of limb and policy of mind,
Ability in means and choice of friends,
To quit me of them throughly.

FRIAR. Pause a while,
And let my counsel sway you in this case.
Your daughter, here, the princes left for
dead:
Let her awhile be secretly kept in,
And publish it, that she is dead indeed;
Maintain a mourning ostentation,
And on your family's old monument
Hang mournful epitaphs, and do all rites
That appertain unto a burial.

LEON. What shall become of this? What
will this do?

FRIAR. Marry, this, well carried, shall on
her behalf
Change slander to remorse;—that is some
good:
But not for that dream I on this strange
course,
But on this travail look for greater birth.
She dying, as it must be so maintain'd,
Upon the instant that she was accus'd,
Shall be lamented, pitied, and excus'd
Of every hearer: for it so falls out,
That what we have we prize not to the
worth
Whiles we enjoy it; but being lack'd and
lost,
Why, then we rack the value, then we find
The virtue that possession would not show
us,
Whiles it was ours.—So will it fare with
Claudio:
When he shall hear she died upon his
words,
The idea of her life shall sweetly creep
Into his study of imagination;
And every lovely organ of her life
Shall come apparell'd in more precious
habit,
More moving delicate, and full of life,
Into the eye and prospect of his soul,
Than when she liv'd indeed:—then shall
he mourn,
(If ever love had interest in his liver)
And wish he had not so accused her,—
No, though he thought his accusation true.
Let this be so, and doubt not but success
Will fashion the event in better shape
Than I can lay it down in likelihood.
But if all aim but this be levell'd false,
The supposition of the lady's death
Will quench the wonder of her infamy:
And if it sort not well, you may conceal her
(As best befits her wounded reputation)
In some reclusive and religious life,

Out of all eyes, tongues, minds, and
injuries.

BENE. Signior Leonato, let the friar ad-
vise you:
And though you know my inwardness and
love
Are very much unto the prince and
Claudio,
Yet, by mine honour, I will deal in this
As secretly and justly, as your soul
Should with your body.

LEON. Being that I flow in grief,
The smallest twine may lead me.

FRIAR. 'Tis well consented: presently
away;
For to strange sores strangely they strain
the cure.—
Come, lady, die to live: this wedding day
Perhaps is but prolong'd: have patience,
and endure.
[*Exeunt Friar* FRANCIS, HERO *and* LEONATO.

BENE. Lady Beatrice, have you wept all
this while?

BEAT. Yea, and I will weep a while
longer.

BENE. I will not desire that.

BEAT. You have no reason; I do it freely.

BENE. Surely, I do believe your fair
cousin is wronged.

BEAT. Ah, how much might the man
deserve of me that would right her!

BENE. Is there any way to show such
friendship?

BEAT. A very even way, but no such
friend.

BENE. May a man do it?

BEAT. It's a man's office, but not yours.

BENE. I do love nothing in the world so
well as you: is not that strange?

BEAT. As strange as the thing I know not.
It were as possible for me to say I loved
nothing so well as you: but believe me
not; and yet I lie not; I confess nothing,
nor I deny nothing.—I am sorry for my
cousin.

BENE. By my sword, Beatrice, thou lovest
me.

BEAT. Do not swear by it, and eat it.

BENE. I will swear by it that you love
me; and I will make him eat it that says
I loved you not.

BEAT. Will you not eat your word?

BENE. With no sauce that can be devised
to it. I protest I love thee.

BEAT. Why then, God forgive me!

BENE. What offence, sweet Beatrice?

BEAT. You have stayed me in a happy
hour: I was about to protest I loved you.

BENE. And do it with all thy heart.

BEAT. I love you with so much of my heart, that none is left to protest.

BENE. Come, bid me do any thing for thee.

BEAT. Kill Claudio.

BENE. Ha! not for the wide world.

BEAT. You kill me to deny it. Farewell.

BENE. Tarry, sweet Beatrice.

BEAT. I am gone, though I am here:—there is no love in you.—Nay, I pray you, let me go.

BENE. Beatrice,—

BEAT. In faith, I will go.

BENE. We'll be friends first.

BEAT. You dare easier be friends with me, that fight with mine enemy.

BENE. Is Claudio thine enemy?

BEAT. Is he not approved in the height a villain, that hath slandered, scorned, dishonoured my kinswoman?—O that I were a man!—What! bear her in hand until they come to take hands; and then, with public accusation, uncovered slander, unmitigated rancour,—O God, that I were a man! I would eat his heart in the market-place.

BENE. Hear me, Beatrice,—

BEAT. Talk with a man out at a window!—a proper saying!

BENE. Nay, but Beatrice,—

BEAT. Sweet Hero!—she is wronged. she is slandered, she is undone.

BENE. Beat—

BEAT. Princes and counties! Surely, a princely testimony, a goodly count, count confect; a sweet gallant, surely! O that I were a man for his sake! or that I had any friend would be a man for my sake! But manhood is melted into courtesies, valour into compliment, and men are only turned into tongue, and trim ones too: he is now as valiant as Hercules that only tells a lie, and swears it.—I cannot be a man with wishing, therefore I will die a woman with grieving.

BENE. Tarry, good Beatrice. By this hand, I love thee.

BEAT. Use it for my love some other way than swearing by it.

BENE. Think you in your soul the count Claudio hath wronged Hero?

BEAT. Yea, as sure as I have a thought or a soul.

BENE. Enough! I am engaged; I will challenge him. I will kiss your hand, and so leave you. By this hand, Claudio shall render me a dear account. As you hear of me, so think of me. Go, comfort your cousin: I must say she is dead: and so, farewell.   [*Exeunt.*

SCENE II.—*A Prison.*

Enter DOGBERRY, VERGES, *and* SEXTON, *in gowns; and the* Watch, *with* CONRADE *and* BORACHIO.

DOGB. Is our whole dissembly appeared?

VERG. O, a stool and a cushion for the sexton.

SEXTON. Which be the malefactors?

DOGB. Marry, that am I and my partner.

VERG. Nay, that's certain: we have the exhibition to examine.

SEXTON. But which are the offenders that are to be examined? let them come before master constable.

DOGB. Yea, marry, let them come before me.—What is your name, friend?

BORA. Borachio.

DOGB. Pray — write down — Borachio.—Yours, sirrah?

CON. I am a gentleman, Sir, and my name is Conrade.

DOGB. Write down—master gentleman Conrade.—Masters, do you serve God?

CON., BORA. Yea, Sir, we hope.

DOGB. Write down—that they hope they serve God:—and write God first; for God defend but God should go before such villains!—Masters, it is proved already that you are little better than false knaves; and it will go near to be thought so shortly. How answer you for yourselves?

CON. Marry, Sir, we say we are none.

DOGB. A marvellous witty fellow, I assure you; but I will go about with him.—Come you hither, sirrah; a word in your ear, Sir: I say to you, it is thought you are false knaves.

BORA. Sir, I say to you, we are none.

DOGB. Well, stand aside.—'Fore God they are both in a tale. Have you writ down—that they are none?

SEXTON. Master constable, you go not the way to examine: you must call forth the watch that are their accusers.

DOGB. Yea, marry, that's the eftest way.—Let the watch come forth.—Masters, charge you, in the prince's name, accuse these men.

1 *WATCH.* This man said, Sir, that Don John, the prince's brother, was a villain.

DOGB. Write down—prince John a villain.—Why, this is flat perjury, to call a prince's brother villain.

BORA. Master constable,—

DOGB. Pray thee, fellow, peace: I do not like thy look, I promise thee.

SEXTON. What heard you him say else?

2 *WATCH.* Marry, that he had received a thousand ducats of Don John, for accusing the lady Hero wrongfully.

DOGB. Flat burglary as ever was committed.

VERG. Yea, by the mass, that it is.

SEXTON. What else, fellow?

1 WATCH. And that Count Claudio did mean, upon his words, to disgrace Hero before the whole assembly, and not marry her.

DOGB. O villain! thou wilt be condemned into everlasting redemption for this.

SEXTON. What else?

2 WATCH. This is all.

SEXTON. And this is more, masters, than you can deny. Prince John is this morning secretly stolen away: Hero was in this manner accused; in this very manner refused; and, upon the grief of this, suddenly died.—Master constable, let these men be bound, and brought to Leonato's: I will go before, and show him their examination.
[*Exit.*

DOGB. Come, let them be opinioned.

VERG. Let them be in the hands—

CON. Off, coxcomb!

DOGB. God's my life! where's the sexton? let him write down—the prince's officer, coxcomb.—Come, bind them.—Thou naughty varlet!

CON. Away! you are an ass, you are an ass.

DOGB. Dost thou not suspect my place? Dost thou not suspect my years?—O that he were here to write me down an ass!— but, masters, remember that I am an ass; though, it be not written down, yet forget not that I am an ass.—No, thou villain, thou art full of piety, as shall be proved upon thee by good witness. I am a wise fellow; and, which is more, an officer; and, which is more, a householder; and, which is more, as pretty a piece of flesh as any in Messina; and one that knows the law, go to; and a rich fellow enough, go to; and a fellow that hath had losses; and one that hath two gowns, and every thing handsome about him.—Bring him away.—O that I had been writ down an ass!
[*Exeunt.*

ACT V.

SCENE I.—*Before* LEONATO'S *House*
Enter LEONATO *and* ANTONIO.

ANT. If you go on thus, you will kill yourself;
And 'tis not wisdom thus to second grief
Against yourself.

LEON. I pray thee, cease thy counsel,
Which falls into mine ears as profitless
As water in a sieve: give not me counsel;
Nor let no comforter delight mine ear

But such a one whose wrongs do suit with mine.
Bring me a father that so lov'd his child,
Whose joy of her is overwhelm'd like mine,
And bid him speak of patience;
Measure his woe the length and breadth of mine,
And let it answer every strain for strain;
As thus for thus, and such a grief for such,
In every lineament, branch, shape, and form:—
If such a one will smile, and stroke his beard;
Cry "Sorrow, wag!" and hem, when he should groan;
Patch grief with proverbs; make misfortune drunk
With candle-wasters:—bring him yet to me,
And I of him will gather patience.
But there is no such man: for, brother, men
Can counsel, and speak comfort to that grief
Which they themselves not feel; but, tasting it,
Their counsel turns to passion, which before
Would give preceptial medicine to rage,
Fetter strong madness in a silken thread,
Charm ache with air, and agony with words:
No, no; 'tis all men's office to speak patience
To those that wring under the load of sorrow;
But no man's virtue, nor sufficiency,
To be so moral when he shall endure
The like himself. Therefore give me no counsel:
My griefs cry louder than advertisement.

ANT. Therein do men from children nothing differ.

LEON. I pray thee, peace! I will be flesh and blood;
For there was never yet philosopher
That could endure the tooth-ache patiently,
However they have writ the style of gods,
And made a push at chance and sufferance.

ANT. Yet bend not all the harm upon yourself;
Make those that do offend you suffer too.

LEON. There thou speak'st reason: nay, I will do so.
My soul doth tell me Hero is belied;
And that shall Claudio know; so shall the prince,
And all of them that thus dishonour her.

ANT. Here come the prince and Claudio hastily.

Enter Don PEDRO *and* CLAUDIO.

D. PEDRO. Good den, good den.

CLAUD.   Good day to both of you.
LEON. Hear you my lords,—
D. PEDRO. We have some haste, Leonato.
LEON. Some haste my lord!—well, fare
you well, my lord:—
Are you so hasty now?—well, all is one.
D. PEDRO. Nay, do not quarrel with us,
good old man.
ANT. If he could right himself with
quarrelling,
Some of us would lie low.
CLAUD.   Who wrongs him?
LEON. Marry, thou dost wrong me; thou,
dissembler, thou:—
Nay, never lay thy hand upon thy sword;
I fear thee not.
CLAUD.   Marry, beshrew my hand,
If it should give your age such cause of
fear:
In faith, my hand meant nothing to my
sword.
LEON. Tush, tush, man! never fleer and
jest at me:
I speak not like a dotard nor a fool,
As, under privilege of age, to brag
What I have done being young, or what
would do,
Were I not old. Know, Claudio, to thy
head,
Thou hast so wrong'd mine innocent child
and me,
That I am forc'd to lay my reverence by,
And, with grey hairs and bruise of many
days,
Do challenge thee to trial of a man.
I say thou hast belied mine innocent child:
Thy slander hath gone through and through
her heart,
And she lies buried with her ancestors,—
O, in a tomb where never scandal slept,
Save this of hers, fram'd by thy villainy!
CLAUD. My villainy!
LEON.   Thine Claudio; thine, I say.
D. PEDRO. You say not right, old man.
LEON.   My lord, my lord,
I'll prove it on his body, if he dare,
Despite his nice fence and his active
practice,
His May of youth and bloom of lustyhood.
CLAUD. Away! I will not have to do
with you.
LEON. Canst thou so daff me? Thou hast
kill'd my child:
If thou kill'st me, boy, thou shalt kill a man.
ANT. He shall kill two of us, and men
indeed:
But that's no matter; let him kill one
first:—
Win me and wear me,—let him answer me.—
Come, follow me, boy! come, sir boy, come,
follow me!

Sir boy, I'll whip you from your foining
Nay, as I am a gentleman, I will.   [fence;
LEON. Brother,—
ANT. Content yourself. God knows I lov'd
my niece;
And she is dead, slander'd to death by
villains,
That dare as well answer a man, indeed,
As I dare take a serpent by the tongue;
Boys, apes, braggarts, Jacks, milksops!—
LEON.   Brother Antony,—
ANT. Hold you content. What, man! I
know them, yea,
And what they weigh, even to the utmost
scruple,—
Scambling, out-facing, fashion-mong'ring
boys,
That lie, and cog, and flout, deprave, and
slander,
Go antickly, and show outward hideous-
ness,
And speak off half a dozen dangerous
words,
How they might hurt their enemies if
And this is all!   [they durst;
LEON. But, Brother Antony,—
ANT.   Come, 'tis no matter:
Do not you meddle; let me deal in this.
D. PEDRO. Gentlemen both, we will not
wake your patience,
My heart is sorry for your daughter's death:
But, on my honour, she was charg'd with
nothing
But what was true, and very full of proof.
LEON. My lord, my lord!—
D. PEDRO.   I will not hear you.
LEON.   No?—
Come, brother, away.—I will be heard.—
ANT. And shall, or some of us will smart
for it.   [Exeunt LEONATO and ANTONIO.
D. PEDRO. See, see; here comes the man
we went to seek.

Enter BENEDICK.

CLAUD. Now, signior, what news?
BENE. Good day, my lord.
D. PEDRO. Welcome, signior: you are
almost come to part almost a fray.
CLAUD. We had like to have had our two
noses snapped off with the two old men
without teeth.
D. PEDRO. Leonato and his brother. What
thinkest thou? Had we fought, I doubt,
we should have been too young for them.
BENE. In a false quarrel there is no true
valour. I came to seek you both.
CLAUD. We have been up and down to
seek thee; for we are high-proof melancholy, and would fain have it beaten away.
Wilt thou use my wit?
BENE. It is in my scabbard: shall I draw
it?

D. PEDRO. Dost thou wear thy wit by thy side?

CLAUD. Never any did so, though very many have been beside their wit.—I will bid thee draw, as we do the minstrels; draw, to pleasure us.

D. PEDRO. As I am an honest man, he looks pale.—Art thou sick, or angry?

CLAUD. What, courage man! What though care killed a cat, thou hast mettle enough in thee to kill care.

BENE. Sir, I shall meet your wit in the career, an you charge it against me. I pray you, choose another subject.

CLAUD. Nay then, give him another staff: this last was broke cross.

D. PEDRO. By this light, he changes more and more. I think he be angry indeed.

CLAUD. If he be, he knows how to turn his girdle.

BENE. Shall I speak a word in your ear?

CLAUD. God bless me from a challenge?

BENE. You are a villain;—I jest not:—I will make it good how you dare, with what you dare, and when you dare.—Do me right, or I will protest your cowardice. You have killed a sweet lady, and her death shall fall heavy on you. Let me hear from you.

CLAUD. Well, I will meet you, so I may have good cheer.

D. PEDRO. What, a feast? a feast?

CLAUD. I' faith, I thank him; he hath bid me to a calf's-head and a capon; the which if I do not carve most curiously, say my knife's naught.—Shall I not find a woodcock too?

BENE. Sir, your wit ambles well; it goes easily.

D. PEDRO. I'll tell thee how Beatrice praised thy wit the other day. I said, thou hadst a fine wit: "True," says she, "a fine little one." "No," said I, "a great wit:" "Right," says she, "a great gross one." "Nay," said I, "a good wit:" "Just," said she, "it hurts nobody." "Nay," said I, "the gentleman is wise:" "Certain," said she, "a wise gentleman." "Nay," said I, "he hath the tongues:" "That I believe," said she, "for he swore a thing to me on Monday night, which he forswore on Tuesday morning; there's a double tongue; there's two tongues." Thus did she, an hour together, trans-shape thy particular virtues: yet at last she concluded with a sigh, thou wast the properest man in Italy.

CLAUD. For the which she wept heartily, and said she cared not.

D. PEDRO. Yea, that she did; but yet, for all that, an if she did not hate him deadly, she would love him dearly: the old man's daughter told us all.

CLAUD. All, all; and moreover, God saw him when he was hid in the garden.

D. PEDRO. But when shall we set the savage bull's horns on the sensible Benedick's head?

CLAUD. Yea, and text underneath, "Here dwells Benedick the married man!"

BENE. Fare you well, boy: you know my mind. I will leave you now to your gossip-like humour: you break jests as braggarts do their blades, which, God be thanked, hurt not.—My lord, for your many courtesies I thank you: I must discontinue your company: your brother, the bastard, is fled from Messina: you have, among you, killed a sweet and innocent lady. For my lord Lack-beard there, he and I shall meet; and till then, peace be with him.   [*Exit.*]

D. PEDRO. He is in earnest.

CLAUD. In most profound earnest; and, I'll warrant you, for the love of Beatrice.

D. PEDRO. And hath challenged thee?

CLAUD. Most sincerely.

D. PEDRO. What a pretty thing man is when he goes in his doublet and hose, and leaves off his wit!

CLAUD. He is then a giant to an ape: but then is an ape a doctor to such a man.

D. PEDRO. But, soft you, let me be: pluck up, my heart, and be sad! Did he not say, my brother was fled?

Enter DOGBERRY, VERGES, *and the* Watch, *with* CONRADE *and* BORACHIO.

DOGB. Come, you, Sir: if justice cannot tame you, she shall ne'er weigh more reasons in her balance. Nay, an you be a cursing hypocrite once, you must be looked to.

D. PEDRO. How now! two of my brother's men bound? Borachio, one?

CLAUD. Hearken after their offence, my lord.

D. PEDRO. Officers, what offence have these men done?

DOGB. Marry, Sir, they have committed false report; moreover, they have spoken untruths; secondarily, they are slanders; sixth and lastly, they have belied a lady; thirdly, they have verified unjust things; and, to conclude, they are lying knaves.

D. PEDRO. First, I ask thee what they have done; thirdly, I ask thee what's their offence; sixth and lastly, why they are committed; and, to conclude, what you lay to their charge.

CLAUD. Rightly reasoned, and in his own division; and, by my troth, there's one meaning well suited.

D. PEDRO. Whom have you offended,

masters, that you are thus bound to your answer? this learned constable is too cunning to be understood: what's your offence?

BORA. Sweet prince, let me go no farther to mine answer: do you hear me, and let this count kill me. I have deceived even your very eyes: what your wisdoms could not discover, these shallow fools have brought to light; who, in the night, overheard me confessing to this man, how Don John your brother incensed me to slander the lady Hero; how you were brought into the orchard, and saw me court Margaret in Hero's garments; how you disgraced her, when you should marry her: my villainy they have upon record; which I had rather seal with my death, than repeat over to my shame. The lady is dead upon mine and my master's false accusation; and, briefly, I desire nothing but the reward of a villain.

D. PEDRO. Runs not this speech like iron through your blood?

CLAUD. I have drunk poison whiles he utter'd it.

D. PEDRO. But did my brother set thee on to this?

BORA. Yea; and paid me richly for the practice of it.

D. PEDRO. He is compos'd and fram'd of treachery:—
And fled he is upon this villainy.

CLAUD. Sweet Hero! now thy image doth appear
In the rare semblance that I lov'd it first.

DOGB. Come, bring away the plaintiffs: by this time our sexton hath reformed signior Leonato of the matter: and masters, do not forget to specify, when time and place shall serve, that I am an ass.

VERG. Here, here comes master signior Leonato, and the sexton too.

Re-enter LEONATO, ANTONIO, *and the* Sexton.

LEON. Which is the villain? Let me see his eyes,
That, when I note another man like him,
I may avoid him: which of these is he?

BORA. If you would know your wronger, look on me.

LEON. Art thou the slave that with thy breath has't kill'd
Mine innocent child?

BORA.   Yea, even I alone.

LEON. No, not so, villain; thou beliest thyself:
Here stand a pair of honourable men,
A third is fled, that had a hand in it.—
I thank you, princes, for my daughter's death:
Record it with your high and worthy deeds;

'Twas bravely done, if you bethink you of it.

CLAUD. I know not how to pray your patience;
Yet I must speak. Choose your revenge yourself;
Impose me to what penance your invention
Can lay upon my sin: yet sinn'd I not,
But in mistaking.

D. PEDRO.   By my soul, nor I:
And yet, to satisfy this good old man,
I would bend under any heavy weight
That he'll enjoin me to.

LEON. I cannot bid you bid my daughter live,—
That were impossible: but, I pray you both,
Possess the people in Messina here,
How innocent she died; and if your love
Can labour aught in sad invention,
Hang her an epitaph upon her tomb,
And sing it to her bones,—sing it tonight:—
To-morrow morning come you to my house;
And since you could not be my son-in-law,
Be yet my nephew: my brother hath a daughter,
Almost the copy of my child that's dead,
And she alone is heir to both of us:
Give her the right you should have given her cousin,
And so dies my revenge.

CLAUD.   O noble Sir!
Your over-kindness doth wring tears from me.
I do embrace your offer; and dispose
For henceforth of poor Claudio.

LEON. To-morrow, then, I will expect your coming;
To-night I take my leave.—This naughty man
Shall face to face be brought to Margaret,
Who, I believe, was pack'd in all this wrong,
Hir'd to it by your brother.

BORA.   No, by my soul, she was not;
Nor knew not what she did, when she spoke to me;
But always hath been just and virtuous,
In any thing that I do know by her.

DOGB. Moreover, Sir, (which, indeed, is not under white and black,) this plaintiff here, the offender, did call me ass: I beseech you, let it be remembered in his punishment. And also, the watch heard them talk of one Deformed: they say he wears a key in his ear, and a lock hanging by it; and borrows money in God's name, —the which he hath used so long, and never paid, that now men grow hardhearted, and will lend nothing for God's sake: pray you, examine him upon that point.

LEON. I thank thee for thy care and honest pains.

DOGB. Your worship speaks like a most thankful and reverend youth; and I praise God for you.

LEON. There's for thy pains.

DOGB. God save the foundation!

LEON. Go, I discharge thee of thy prisoner, and I thank thee.

DOGB. I leave an arrant knave with your worship; which I beseech your worship to correct yourself, for the example of others. God keep your worship! I wish your worship well; God restore you to health! I humbly give you leave to depart; and if a merry meeting may be wished, God prohibit it!—Come neighbour.

[Exeunt DOGBERRY, VERGES, and Watch.

LEON. Until to-morrow morning, lords, farewell.

ANT. Farewell, my lords: we look for you to-morrow.

D. PEDRO. We will not fail.

CLAUD. To-night I'll mourn with Hero.

[Exeunt Don PEDRO and CLAUDIO.

LEON. Bring you these fellows on. We'll talk with Margaret,
How her acquaintance grew with this lewd fellow.   [Exeunt.

SCENE II.—LEONATO'S Garden.

Enter BENEDICK and MARGARET, meeting.

BENE. Pray thee, sweet mistress Margaret, deserve well at my hands by helping me to the speech of Beatrice.

MARG. Will you, then, write me a sonnet in praise of my beauty?

BENE. In so high a style, Margaret, that no man living shall come over it; for, in most comely truth, thou deservest it.

MARG. To have no man come over me! why, shall I always keep below stairs?

BENE. Thy wit is as quick as the greyhound's mouth,—it catches.

MARG. And yours as blunt as the fencer's foils, which hit, but hurt not.

BENE. A most manly wit, Margaret; it will not hurt a woman: and so, I pray thee, call Beatrice: I give thee the bucklers.

MARG. Give us the swords; we have bucklers of our own.

BENE. If you use them, Margaret, you must put in the pikes with a vice; and they are dangerous weapons for maids.

MARG. Well, I will call Beatrice to you, who I think hath legs.

BENE. And therefore will come.

[Exit MARGARET.

[Singing.]   The god of love,
                That sits above,
       And knows me, and knows me,
          How pitiful I deserve,—

I mean, in singing; but in loving, Leander the good swimmer, Troilus the first employer of panders, and a whole book full of these quondam carpet-mongers, whose names yet run smoothly in the even road of a blank verse,—why, they were never so truly turned over and over as my poor self, in love. Marry, I cannot show it in rhyme; I have tried: I can find out no rhyme to "lady" but "baby,"—an innocent rhyme; for "scorn," "horn,"—a hard rhyme; for "school," "fool,"—a babbling rhyme; very ominous endings: no, I was not born under a rhyming planet, nor I cannot woo in festival terms.—

Enter BEATRICE.

Sweet Beatrice, would'st thou come when I called thee?

BEAT. Yea, signior; and depart when you bid me.

BENE. O, stay but till then!

BEAT. "Then" is spoken; fare you well now:—and yet, ere I go, let me go with that I came for; which is, with knowing what hath passed between you and Claudio.

BENE. Only foul words; and thereupon I will kiss thee.

BEAT. Foul words is but foul wind, and foul wind is but foul breath, and foul breath is noisome; therefore I will depart unkissed.

BENE. Thou hast frighted the word out of his right sense, so forcibly is thy wit. But I must tell thee plainly, Claudio undergoes my challenge; and either I must shortly hear from him, or I will subscribe him a coward. And, I pray thee now, tell me for which of my bad parts didst thou first fall in love with me?

BEAT. For them all together; which maintained so politic a state of evil, that they will not admit any good part to intermingle with them. But for which of my good parts did you first suffer love for me?

BENE. "Suffer love,"—a good epithet! I do suffer love indeed, for I love thee against my will.

BEAT. In spite of your heart, I think; alas, poor heart! If you spite it for my sake, I will spite it for yours; for I will never love that which my friend hates.

BENE. Thou and I are too wise to woo peaceably.

BEAT. It appears not in this confession: there's not one wise man among twenty that will praise himself.

BENE. An old, an old instance, Beatrice, that lived in the time of good neighbours. If a man do not erect in this age his own tomb ere he dies, he shall live no longer in monument, than the bell rings and the widow weeps.

BEAT. And how long is that, think you?

BENE. Question:—why, an hour in clamour, and a quarter in rheum: therefore is it most expedient for the wise (if Don Worm, his conscience, find no impediment to the contrary,) to be the trumpet of his own virtues, as I am to myself. So much for praising myself, who, I myself will bear witness, is praiseworthy. And now tell me, how doth your cousin?

BEAT. Very ill.

BENE. And how do you?

BEAT. Very ill too.

BENE. Serve God, love me, and mend. There will I leave you too, for here comes one in haste.

Enter URSULA.

URS. Madam, you must come to your uncle. Yonder's old coil at home: it is proved, my lady Hero hath been falsely accused, the prince and Claudio mightily abused; and Don John is the author of all, who is fled and gone. Will you come presently?

BEAT. Will you go hear this news, signior?

BENE. I will live in thy heart, die in thy lap, and be buried in thy eyes; and moreover, I will go with thee to thy uncle's.

[*Exeunt.*

———

SCENE III.—*The Inside of a Church.*

Enter Don PEDRO, CLAUDIO, *and* Attendants, *with music and tapers.*

CLAUD. Is this the monument of Leonato?

ATTEN. It is, my lord.

CLAUD. [*Reads from a scroll.*]
　Done to death by slanderous tongues
　　Was the Hero that here lies:
　Death, in guerdon of her wrongs,
　　Gives her fame which never dies.
　So the life, that died with shame,
　Lives in death with glorious fame.

　Hang thou there upon the tomb,
　　[*Appending it; as Epitaph.*
　Praising her when I am dumb.—

Now, music, sound; and sing your solemn hymn.

SONG.
　Pardon, goddess of the night,
　Those that slew thy virgin knight;
　For the which, with songs of woe,
　Round about her tomb they go.
　　Midnight, assist our moan;
　　Help us to sigh and groan,
　　　Heavily, heavily:
　　Graves, yawn, and yield your dead,
　　Till death be uttered,
　　　Heavily, heavily.

CLAUD. Now, unto thy bones good night! Yearly will I do this rite.

D. PEDRO. Good-morrow, masters; put your torches out:
The wolves have prey'd; and look, the gentle day,
Before the wheels of Phœbus, round about
Dapples the drowsy east with spots of grey.
Thanks to you all, and leave us: fare you well.

CLAUD. Good-morrow, masters: each his several way.

D. PEDRO. Come, let us hence, and put on other weeds:
And then to Leonato's we will go.

CLAUD. And Hymen now with luckier issue speeds,
Than this, for whom we render'd up this woe!　　　[*Exeunt.*

———

SCENE IV.—*A Room in* LEONATO'S *House.*
Enter LEONATO, ANTONIO, BENEDICK, BEATRICE, MARGARET, URSULA, *Friar* FRANCIS *and* HERO.

FRIAR. Did I not tell you she was innocent?

LEON. So are the prince and Claudio, who accus'd her.
Upon the error that you heard debated:
But Margaret was in some fault for this,
Although against her will, as it appears
In the true course of all the question.

ANT. Well, I am glad that all things sort so well.

BENE. And so am I, being else by faith enforc'd
To call young Claudio to a reckoning for it.

LEON. Well, daughter, and you gentlewomen all,
Withdraw into a chamber by yourselves,
And when I send for you, come hither mask'd:
The prince and Claudio promis'd by this hour
To visit me.—You know your office, brother;
You must be father to your brother's daughter,

And give her to young Claudio.
                              [*Exeunt ladies.*
ANT. Which I will do with confirm'd
    countenance.
BENE. Friar, I must entreat your pains,
    I think.
FRIAR. To do what, signior?
BENE. To bind me, or undo me; one of
    them.—
Signior Leonato, truth it is, good signior,
Your niece regards me with an eye of
    favour.
LEON. That eye my daughter lent her: 'tis
    most true.
BENE. And I do with an eye of love re-
    quite her.
LEON. The sight whereof, I think, you
    had from me,
From Claudio, and the prince: but what's
    your will?
BENE. Your answer, Sir, is enigmatical:
But, for my will, my will is, your good will
May stand with ours, this day to be con-
    join'd
In the state of honourable marriage:—
In which, good friar, I shall desire your
    help.
LEON. My heart is with your liking.
FRIAR.   And my help.—
Here come the prince and Claudio.

    Enter Don PEDRO *and* CLAUDIO, *with*
                Attendants.

D. PEDRO. Good-morrow to this fair
    assembly.
LEON. Good-morrow, prince; good-mor-
    row, Claudio:
We here attend you. Are you yet determin'd
To-day to marry with my brother's
    daughter?
CLAUD. I'll hold my mind, were she an
    Ethiop.
LEON. Call her forth, brother: here's the
    friar ready.   [*Exit* ANTONIO.
D. PEDRO. Good-morrow, Benedick. Why,
    what's the matter,
That you have such a February face,
So full of frost, of storm, and cloudiness?
CLAUD. I think, he thinks upon the sav-
    age bull.—
Tush! fear not, man; we'll tip thy horns
    with gold,
And all Europa shall rejoice at thee;
As once Europa did at lusty Jove,
When he would play the noble beast in
    love.
BENE. Bull Jove, Sir, had an amiable
    low;
And some such strange bull leap'd your
    father's cow,

And got a calf in that same noble feat,
Much like to you, for you have just his
    bleat.
CLAUD. For this I owe you: here come
    other reckonings.

    Re-enter ANTONIO, *with the ladies
                masked.*

Which is the lady I must seize upon?
ANT. This same is she, and I do give you
    her.
CLAUD. Why, then she's mine.—Sweet,
    let me see your face.   [her hand
LEON. No, that you shall not, till you take
Before this friar, and swear to marry her.
CLAUD. Give me your hand before this
    holy friar:
I am your husband, if you like of me.
HERO. And when I liv'd, I was your other
    wife: [*Unmasking.*
And when you lov'd, you were my other
CLAUD. Another Hero!   [husband.
HERO.   Nothing certainer:
One Hero died defil'd; but I do live,
And surely as I live, I am a maid.
D. PEDRO. The former Hero! Hero that
    is dead!
LEON. She died, my lord, but whiles her
    slander liv'd.
FRIAR. All this amazement can I qualify:
When after that the holy rites are ended,
I'll tell you largely of fair Hero's death:
Meantime, let wonder seem familiar,
And to the chapel let us presently.
BENE. Soft and fair, friar.—Which is
    Beatrice?
BEAT. [*Unmasking.*] I answer to that
    name. What is your will?
BENE. Do not you love me?
BEAT. Why, no; no more than reason.
BENE. Why, then, your uncle, and the
    prince, and Claudio.
Have been deceived; for they swore you
BEAT. Do not you love me?   [did.
BENE. Troth, no; no more than reason.
BEAT. Why, then, my cousin, Margaret,
    and Ursula,
Are much deceiv'd; for they did swear,
    you did.
BENE. They swore that you were almost
    sick for me.
BEAT. They swore that you were well-nigh
    dead for me.
BENE. 'Tis no such matter.—Then, you
    do not love me?
BEAT. No, truly, but in friendly recom-
    pense.
LEON. Come, cousin, I am sure you love
    the gentleman.
CLAUD. And I'll be sworn upon't that he
    loves her;

For here's a paper, written in his hand,
A halting sonnet of his own pure brain,
Fashion'd to Beatrice.
HERO.   And here's another,
Writ in my cousin's hand, stolen from her
pocket,
Containing her affection unto Benedick.
BENE. A miracle! here's our own hands
against our hearts.—Come, I will have thee;
but, by this light, I take thee for pity.
BEAT. I would not deny you;—but, by
this good day, I yield upon great persuasion; and partly to save your life, for I
was told you were in a consumption.
BENE. Peace! I will stop your mouth.
                              [*Kissing her.*
D. PEDRO. How dost thou, Benedick, the
married man?
BENE. I'll tell thee what, prince; a college of wit-crackers cannot flout me out of
my humour. Dost thou think I care for a
satire, or an epigram? No: if a man will
be beaten with brains, he shall wear nothing handsome about him. In brief, since
I do purpose to marry, I will think nothing to any purpose that the world can say
against it; and therefore never flout at me
for what I have said against it; for man
is a giddy thing, and this is my conclusion.
—For thy part, Claudio, I did think to have
beaten thee; but, in that thou art like to
be my kinsman, live unbruised, and love
my cousin.
CLAUD. I had well hoped thou wouldst
have denied Beatrice, that I might have
cudgelled thee out of thy single life, to
make thee a double-dealer; which, out of
question, thou wilt be, if my cousin do not
look exceeding narrowly to thee.
BENE. Come, come, we are friends.—Let's
have a dance ere we are married, that we
may lighten our own hearts, and our
wives' heels.
LEON. We'll have dancing afterward.
BENE. First, of my word; therefore play,
music!—Prince, thou art sad; get thee a
wife, get thee a wife: there is no staff more
reverend than one tipped with horn.

Enter a Messenger.

MESS. My lord, your brother John is
ta'en in flight,   [*Messina.*
And brought with armed men back to
BENE. Think not on him till to-morrow:
I'll devise thee brave punishments for him.
—Strike up, pipers!   [*Dance. Exeunt.*

Quince arranging the play. Act I. S. 2.

MIDSUMMER-NIGHT'S DREAM

DRAMATIS PERSONÆ

THESEUS, *Duke of* Athens.

EGEUS, *Father to* HERMIA.

LYSANDER,
DEMETRIUS, } *in love with* HERMIA.

PHILOSTRATE, *Master of the Revels to* THESEUS.

QUINCE, *a Carpenter.*

SNUG, *a Joiner.*

BOTTOM, *a Weaver.*

FLUTE, *a Bellows-mender.*

SNOUT, *a Tinker.*

STARVELING, *a Tailor.*

HIPPOLYTA, *Queen of the Amazons, betrothed to* THESEUS.

HERMIA, *in love with* LYSANDER.

HELENA, *in love with* DEMETRIUS.

OBERON, *King of the Fairies.*

TITANIA, *Queen of the Fairies.*

PUCK, *or* Robin-Goodfellow.

PEAS-BLOSSOM,
COBWEB,
MOTH,
MUSTARD-SEED, } *Fairies.*

PYRAMUS,
THISBE,
WALL,
MOONSHINE,
LION, } *Characters in the Interlude performed by the "rude mechanicals."*

Other Fairies attending their King and Queen.

Attendants on THESEUS *and* HIPPOLYTA.

SCENE,—ATHENS; *and a Wood near it.*

ACT I.

SCENE I.—ATHENS. *A Room in the Palace of* THESEUS.

Enter THESEUS, HIPPOLYTA, PHILOSTRATE, *and Attendants.*

THE. Now, fair Hippolyta, our nuptial hour

Draws on apace; four happy days bring in

Another moon: but, oh, methinks, how slow

This old moon wanes! she lingers my desires,

Like to a step-dame, or a dowager,

Long withering out a young man's revenue.

HIP. Four days will quickly steep themselves in nights;
Four nights will quickly dream away the time;
And then the moon, like to a silver bow
New bent in heaven, shall behold the night
Of our solemnities.

THE.   Go, Philostrate,
Stir up the Athenian youth to merriments;
Awake the pert and nimble spirit of mirth:
Turn melancholy forth to funerals,—
The pale companion is not for our pomp.—
                 [*Exit* PHILOSTRATE.
Hippolyta, I woo'd thee with my sword,
And won thy love, doing thee injuries;
But I will wed thee in another key,
With pomp, with triumph, and with revelling.

    Enter EGEUS, HERMIA, LYSANDER *and*
          DEMETRIUS.

EGE. Happy be Theseus, our renowned duke!

THE. Thanks, good Egeus: what's the news with thee?

EGE. Full of vexation come I, with complaint
Against my child, my daughter Hermia.—
Stand forth, Demetrius.—My noble lord,
This man hath my consent to marry her.—
Stand forth, Lysander:—and, my gracious duke,
This man hath bewitch'd the bosom of my child:—
Thou, thou, Lysander, thou hast given her rhymes,
And interchang'd love-tokens with my child:
Thou hast by moon-light at her window sung,
With feigning voice, verses of feigning love;
And stol'n th' impression of her fantasy
With bracelets of thy hair, rings, gawds, conceits,
Knacks, trifles, nosegays, sweet-meats (messengers
Of strong prevailment in unharden'd youth):
With cunning hast thou filch'd my daughter's heart;
Turn'd her obedience, which is due to me,
To stubborn harshness:—and, my gracious duke,
Be it so she will not here before your grace
Consent to marry with Demetrius,
I beg the ancient privilege of Athens,—
As she is mine, I may dispose of her:
Which shall be either to this gentleman,
Or to her death, according to our law
Immediately provided in that case.

THE. What say you, Hermia? be advis'd, fair maid:
To you your father should be as a god;
One that compos'd your beauties; yea, and one
To whom you are but as a form in wax,
By him imprinted, and within his power
To leave the figure, or disfigure it.
Demetrius is a worthy gentleman.

HER. So is Lysander.

THE.   In himself he is;
But, in this kind, wanting your father's voice,
The other must be held the worthier.

HER. I would my father look'd but with my eyes.

THE. Rather, your eyes must with his judgment look.

HER. I do entreat your grace to pardon me.
I know not by what power I am made bold,
Nor how it may concern my modesty,
In such a presence here, to plead my thoughts;
But I beseech your grace, that I may know
The worst that may befall me in this case,
If I refuse to wed Demetrius.

THE. Either to die the death, or to abjure
For ever the society of men.
Therefore, fair Hermia, question your desires;
Know of your youth, examine well your blood,
Whether, if you yield not to your father's choice,
You can endure the livery of a nun;
For aye to be in shady cloister mew'd,
To live a barren sister all your life,
Chanting faint hymns to the cold fruitless moon.
Thrice blessed they, that master so their blood,
To undergo such maiden pilgrimage;
But earthlier happy is the rose distill'd,
Than that which, withering on the virgin thorn,
Grows, lives, and dies, in single blessedness.

HER. So will I grow, so live, so die, my lord,
Ere I will yield my virgin patent up
Unto his lordship, whose unwished yoke
My soul consents not to give sovereignty.

THE. Take time to pause; and, by the next new moon,—
The sealing-day betwixt my love and me
For everlasting bond of fellowship,—

at day either prepare to die
obedience to your father's will,
e to wed Demetrius, as he would;
Diana's altar to protest,
ye, austerity and single life.
. Relent, sweet Hermia:—and, Ly-
nder, yield
y crazed title to my certain right.
YS. You have her father's love, Deme-
trius;
Let me have Hermia's: do you marry him.
EGE. Scornful Lysander! true, he hath
my love,—
And what is mine my love shall render
him;
And she is mine, and all my right of her
I do estate unto Demetrius.
LYS. I am, my lord, as well deriv'd as he,
As well possess'd; my love is more than
his;
My fortunes every way as fairly rank'd
(If not with vantage,) as Demetrius';
And, which is more than all these boasts
can be,
I am belov'd of beauteous Hermia:
Why should not I, then, prosecute my
right?
Demetrius, I'll avouch it to his head,
Made love to Nedar's daughter, Helena,
And won her soul; and she, sweet lady,
dotes,
Devoutly dotes, dotes in idolatry,
Upon this spotted and inconstant man.
THE. I must confess that I have heard
so much,
And with Demetrius thought to have
spoke thereof;
But, being over-full of self-affairs,
My mind did lose it.—But, Demetrius,
come;
And come, Egeus: you shall go with me,
I have some private schooling for you
both.—
For you, fair Hermia, look you arm your-
self
To fit your fancies to your father's will;
Or else the law of Athens yields you up
(Which by no means we may extenuate)
To death, or to a vow of single life.—
Come, my Hippolyta: what cheer, my
love?—
Demetrius, and Egeus, go along:
I must employ you in some business
Against our nuptial; and confer with you
Of something nearly that concerns your-
selves.
EGE. With duty and desire we follow you.
[*Exeunt* THES. HIP. EGE. DEM. *and train.*
LYS. How now, my love! Why is your
cheek so pale?

How chance the roses there do fade so
fast?
HER. Belike, for want of rain, which I
could well
Beteem them from the tempest of mine
eyes.
LYS. Ah me! for aught that ever I could
read,
Could ever hear by tale or history,
The course of true love never did run
smooth;
But, either it was different in blood,—
HER. O cross; too high to be enthrall'd
to low!
LYS. Or else misgraffed in respect of
years,—
HER. O spite! too told to be engag'd to
young!
LYS. Or else it stood upon the choice of
friends,—
HER. O hell! to choose love by another's
eye!
LYS. Or, if there were a sympathy in
choice,
War, death, or sickness, did lay siege to it,
Making it momentany as a sound,
Swift as a shadow, short as any dream;
Brief as the lightning in the collied night,
That, in a spleen, unfolds both heaven and
earth,
And ere a man hath power to say,—Be-
hold!
The jaws of darkness do devour it up:
So quick bright things come to confusion.
HER. If, then, true lovers have been ever
cross'd,
It stands as an edict in destiny:
Then let us teach our trial patience,
Because it is a customary cross,
As due to love as thoughts, and dreams,
and sighs,
Wishes, and tears, poor fancy's followers.
LYS. A good persuasion: therefore, hear
me, Hermia.
I have a widow aunt, a dowager
Of great revenue, and she hath no child:
From Athens is her house remote seven
leagues;
And she respects me as her only son.
There, gentle Hermia, may I marry thee;
And to that place the sharp Athenian law
Cannot pursue us. If thou lov'st me, then,
Steal forth thy father's house to-morrow
night;
And in the wood, a league without the
town,
Where I did meet thee once with Helena,
To do observance to a morn of May,
There will I stay for thee.
HER.   My good Lysander!

I swear to thee, by Cupid's strongest bow;
By his best arrow with the golden head;
By the simplicity of Venus' doves;
By that which knitteth souls and prospers loves,
And by that fire which burned the Carthage queen,
When the false Trojan under sail was seen;
By all the vows that ever men have broke,
In number more than ever women spoke;—
In that same place thou hast appointed me,
To-morrow truly will I meet with thee.

LYS. Keep promise, love. Look, here comes Helena.

Enter HELENA.

HER. God speed fair Helena! Whither away?

HEL. Call you me fair? that fair again unsay.
Demetrius loves your fair: O happy fair!
Your eyes are lode-stars; and your tongue's sweet air
More tuneable than lark to shepherd's ear,
When wheat is green, when hawthorn buds appear.
Sickness is catching: O, were favour so,
Yours would I catch, fair Hermia! ere I go,
My ear should catch your voice, my eye your eye,
My tongue should catch your tongue's sweet melody.
Were the world mine, Demetrius being bated,
The rest I'll give to be to you translated.
O, teach me how you look; and with what art
You sway the motion of Demetrius' heart!

HER. I frown upon him, yet he loves me still.

HEL. O that your frowns would teach my smiles such skill!

HER. I give him curses, yet he gives me love.

HEL. O that my prayers could such affection move!

HER. The more I hate, the more he follows me.

HEL. The more I love, the more he hateth me.

HER. His folly, Helena, is no fault of mine.

HEL. None, but your beauty: would that fault were mine!

HER. Take comfort: he no more shall see my face;
Lysander and myself will fly this place.—
Before the time I did Lysander see,

Seem'd Athens as a paradise to
O, then, what graces in my love
That he hath turn'd a heaven unto

LYS. Helen, to you our minds w unfold:
To-morrow night, when Phœbe dot hold
Her silver visage in the wat'ry glass,
Decking with liquid pearl the bladed gra
(A time that lovers' flights doth still conceal,)
Through Athens' gates have we devis'd to steal.

HER. And in the wood, where often you and I
Upon faint primrose-beds were wont to lie,
Emptying our bosoms of their counsel sweet,
There my Lysander and myself shall meet;
And thence from Athens turn away our eyes,
To seek new friends and stranger companies.
Farewell, sweet playfellow: pray thou for us;
And good luck grant thee thy Demetrius!—
Keep word, Lysander: we must starve our sight
From lovers' food till morrow deep midnight.

LYS. I will, my Hermia.—[*Exit* HERM.]
Helena, adieu:
As you on him, Demetrius dote on you!
                                    [*Exit.*

HEL. How happy some, o'er other some can be!
Through Athens I am thought as fair as she:
But what of that? Demetrius thinks not so;
He will not know, what all but he do know;
And as he errs, doting on Hermia's eyes,
So I, admiring of his qualities.
Things base and vile, holding no quantity,
Love can transpose to form and dignity:
Love looks not with the eyes, but with the mind;
And therefore is wing'd Cupid painted blind:
Nor hath Love's mind of any judgment taste;
Wings, and no eyes, figure unheedy haste:
And therefore is Love said to be a child,
Because in choice he is so oft beguil'd.
As waggish boys in game themselves forswear,
So the boy Love is perjur'd every where:
For ere Demetrius look'd on Hermia's eyne,

He hail'd down oaths that he was only
  mine;
And when this hail some heat from Hermia
  felt,
So he dissolv'd, and showers of oaths did
  melt.
I will go tell him of fair Hermia's flight:
Then to the wood will he, to-morrow night,
Pursue her; and for this intelligence
If I have thanks, it is a dear expense:
But herein mean I to enrich my pain,
To have his sight thither and back again.
                                    [*Exit.*

SCENE II.—*The Same. A Room in* QUINCE'S
              House.

Enter QUINCE, SNUG, BOTTOM, FLUTE,
    SNOUT, *and* STARVELING.

QUIN. Is all our company here?
BOT. You were best to call them generally,
man by man, according to the scrip.
QUIN. Here is the scroll of every man's
name, which is thought fit, through all
Athens, to play in our interlude before the
duke and the duchess on his wedding-day
at night.
BOT. First, good Peter Quince, say what
the play treats on; then read the names
of the actors; and so grow to a point.
QUIN. Marry, our play is—The most lamentable comedy, and most cruel death of
Pyramus and Thisby.
BOT. A very good piece of work, I assure
you, and a merry.—Now, good Peter Quince,
call forth your actors by the scroll.—Masters, spread yourselves.
QUIN. Answer, as I call you.—Nick Bottom, the weaver.
BOT. Ready. Name what part I am for,
and proceed.
QUIN. You, Nick Bottom, are set down
for Pyramus.
BOT. What is Pyramus? a lover, or a tyrant?
QUIN. A lover, that kills himself most
gallantly for love.
BOT. That will ask some tears in the true
performing of it: if I do it, let the audience
look to their eyes; I will move storms, I
will condole in some measure. To the rest:
—yet my chief humour is for a tyrant: I
could play Ercles rarely, or a part to tear a
cat in, to make all split.

      "The raging rocks
      And shivering shocks,
      Shall break the locks
        Of prison-gates;
      And Phibbus' car

          Shall shine from far,
          The foolish fates."
      And make and mar

This was lofty!—Now name the rest of the
players.—This is Ercles' vein, a tyrant's
vein;—a lover is more condoling.
QUIN. Francis Flute, the bellows-mender.
FLU. Here, Peter Quince.
QUIN. You must take Thisby on you.
FLU. What is Thisby? a wandering knight?
QUIN. It is the lady that Pyramus must
love.
FLU. Nay, faith, let not me play a woman;
I have a beard coming.
QUIN. That's all one: you shall play it in
a mask, and you may speak as small as
you will.
BOT. An I may hide my face, let me play
Thisby too: I'll speak in a monstrous little
voice;—"Thisne, Thisne"—"Ah, Pyramus,
my lover dear! thy Thisby dear, and lady
dear!"
QUIN. No, no; you must play Pyramus:—
and, Flute, you Thisby.
BOT. Well, proceed.
QUIN. Robin Starveling, the tailor.
STAR. Here, Peter Quince.
QUIN. Robin Starveling, you must play
Thisby's mother.—Tom Snout, the tinker.
SNOUT. Here, Peter Quince.
QUIN. You, Pyramus's father; — myself,
Thisby's father;—Snug, the joiner, you, the
lion's part:—and, I hope, here is a play
fitted.
SNUG. Have you the lion's part written?
pray you, if it be, give it me, for I am slow
of study.
QUIN. You may do it extempore, for it is
nothing but roaring.
BOT. Let me play the lion too: I will roar,
that I will do any man's heart good to hear
me; I will roar, that I will make the duke
say, "Let him roar again, let him roar
again."
QUIN. An you should do it too terribly,
you would fright the duchess and the ladies, that they would shriek; and that were
enough to hang us all.
ALL. That would hang us, every mother's
son.
BOT. I grant you, friends, if that you
should fright the ladies out of their wits,
they would have no more discretion but to
hang us: but I will aggravate my voice so,
that I will roar you as gently as any sucking dove; I will roar you an 'twere any
nightingale.
QUIN. You can play no part but Pyramus;
for Pyramus is a sweet-faced man; a proper

...e shall see in a summer's day; a
...vely, gentlemanlike man: therefore,
...ust needs play Pyramus.
...T. Well, I will undertake it. What
beard were I best to play it in?
QUIN. Why, what you will.
BOT. I will discharge it in either your
straw-colour beard, your orange-tawny
beard, your purple-in-grain beard, or your
French-crown-colour beard, your perfect
yellow.
QUIN. Some of your French crowns have
no hair at all, and then you will play bare-
faced.—But masters, here are your parts:
and I am to entreat you, request you, and
desire you, to con them by to-morrow
night; and meet me in the palace wood, a
mile without the town, by moon-light; there
will we rehearse,—for if we meet in the
city, we shall be dogged with company, and
our devices known. In the meantime, I
will draw a bill of properties, such as our
play wants. I pray you, fail me not.
BOT. We will meet; and there we may
rehearse more obscenely, and courageously.
Take pains; be perfect; adieu.
QUIN. At the duke's oak we meet.
BOT. Enough; hold, or cut bow-strings.
[*Exeunt.*

ACT II.

SCENE I.—*A Wood near* ATHENS.

Enter a Fairy *and* PUCK, *from opposite
sides.*

PUCK. How now, spirit! whither wander
you?
FAI. Over hill, over dale,
    Thorough bush, thorough brier,
Over park, over pale,
    Thorough flood, thorough fire,
I do wander every where,
Swifter than the moon's sphere;
And I serve the fairy queen,
To dew her orbs upon the green:
The cowslips tall her pensioners be;
In their gold coats spots you see;
Those be rubies, fairy favours,
In those freckles live their savours:
I must go seek some dew-drops here,
And hang a pearl in every cowslip's ear.
Farewell, thou lob of spirits; I'll be gone:
Our queen and all her elves come here anon.
PUCK. The king doth keep his revels here
to-night:
Take heed the queen come not within his
sight;
For Oberon is passing fell and wrath,
Because that she, as her attendant, hath
A lovely boy, stol'n from an Indian king;

She never had so sweet a changeling:
And jealous Oberon would have the child
Knight of his train, to trace the forests
wild;
But she, perforce, withholds the loved boy,
Crowns him with flowers, and makes him
all her joy:
And now they never meet in grove or green,
By fountain clear, or spangled star-light
sheen,
But they do square; that all their elves, for
fear,
Creep into acorn cups, and hide them there.
FAI. Either I mistake your shape and
making quite,
Or else you are that shrewd and knavish
sprite,
Call'd Robin Good-fellow: are you not he
That frights the maidens of the villagery;
Skims milk, and sometimes labours in the
quern,
And bootless makes the breathless house-
wife churn;
And sometime makes the drink to bear no
barm;
Misleads night-wanderers, laughing at their
harm?
Those that Hobgoblin call you, and sweet
Puck,
You do their work, and they shall have
good luck:
Are not you he?
PUCK.   Thou speak'st aright;
I am that merry wanderer of the night.
I jest to Oberon, and make him smile,
When I a fat and bean-fed horse beguile,
Neighing in likeness of a filly foal:
And sometime lurk I in a gossip's bowl,
In very likeness of a roasted crab;
And, when she drinks, against her lips I
bob,
And on her wither'd dew-lap pour the ale.
The wisest aunt, telling the saddest tale,
Sometime for three-foot stool mistaketh me;
Then slip I from her bum, down topples
she,
And "tailor" cries, and falls into a cough;
And then the whole quire hold their hips,
and loffe;
And waxen in their mirth, and neeze, and
swear
A merrier hour was never wasted there.—
But, room, Fairy! here comes Oberon.
FAI. And here my mistress.—Would that
he were gone!

SCENE II.—*The Same.*

Enter OBERON *from one side, with his train;
and* TITANIA *from the other, with hers.*

OBE. Ill met by moon-light, proud Titania.

TITA. What, jealous Oberon! Fairies, skip hence:
I have forsworn his bed and company.

OBE. Tarry, rash wanton: am not I thy lord?

TITA. Then, I must be thy lady: but I know
When thou hast stol'n away from fairy land,
And in the shape of Corin sat all day,
Playing on pipes of corn, and versing love
To amorous Phillida. Why art thou here,
Come from the farthest steep of India,
But that, forsooth, the bouncing Amazon,
Your buskin'd mistress and your warrior love,
To Theseus must be wedded? and you come
To give their bed joy and prosperity.

OBE. How canst thou thus, for shame, Titania,
Glance at my credit with Hippolyta,
Knowing I know thy love to Theseus?
Didst thou not lead him through the glimmering night
From Perigenia, whom he ravished?
And make him with fair Ægle break his faith,
With Ariadne, and Antiopa?

TITA. These are the forgeries of jealousy:
And never, since the middle summer's spring,
Met we on hill, in dale, forest, or mead,
By paved fountain, or by rushy brook,
Or on the beached margent of the sea,
To dance our ringlets to the whistling wind,
But with thy brawls thou hast disturb'd our sport.
Therefore the winds, piping to us in vain,
As in revenge, have suck'd up from the sea
Contagious fogs; which, falling in the land,
Have every pelting river made so proud,
That they have overborne their continents:
The ox hath therefore stretch'd his yoke in vain,
The ploughman lost his sweat; and the green corn
Hath rotted ere his youth attain'd a beard:
The fold stands empty in the drowned field,
And crows are fatted with the murrain flock;
The nine-men's morris is fill'd up with mud;
And the quaint mazes in the wanton green,
For lack of tread are undistinguishable:
The human mortals want their winter here;
No night is now with hymn or carol blest:—
Therefore the moon, the governess of floods,
Pale in her anger, washes all the air,
That rheumatic diseases do abound:

And thorough this distemperature we see
The seasons alter: hoary-headed frosts
Fall in the fresh lap of the crimson rose;
And on old Hyem's chin, and icy crown,
An odorous chaplet of sweet summer buds
Is, as in mockery, set. The spring, the summer,
The childing autumn, angry winter, change
Their wonted liveries; and the 'mazed world,
By their increase, now knows not which is which:
And this same progeny of evils comes
From our debate, from our dissension;
We are their parents and original.

OBE. Do you amend it, then; it lies in you:
Why should Titania cross her Oberon?
I do but beg a little changeling boy,
To be my henchman.

TITA.   Set your heart at rest:
The fairy land buys not the child of me.
His mother was a votaress of my order:
And, in the spiced Indian air, by night,
Full often hath she gossip'd by my side;
And sat with me on Neptune's yellow sands,
Marking th' embarked traders on the flood;
When we have laugh'd to see the sails conceive,
And grow big-bellied, with the wanton wind;
Which she, with pretty and with swimming gait
Following, (her womb then rich with my young squire)
Would imitate, and sail upon the land,
To fetch me trifles, and return again,
As from a voyage, rich with merchandise.
But she, being mortal, of that boy did die;
And for her sake I do rear up her boy;
And for her sake I will not part with him.

OBE. How long within this wood intend you stay?

TITA. Perchance till after Theseus' wedding-day.
If you will patiently dance in our round,
And see our moonlight revels, go with us;
If not, shun me, and I will spare your haunts.

OBE. Give me that boy, and I will go with thee.

TITA. Not for thy fairy kingdom.—Fairies, away!
We shall chide downright, if I longer stay.
                [*Exit* TITANIA, *with her train.*

OBE. Well, go thy way: thou shalt not from this grove,
Till I torment thee for this injury.—

My gentle Puck, come hither. Thou re-
    member'st
Since once I sat upon a promontory,
And heard a mermaid, on a dolphin's back,
Uttering such dulcet and harmonious breath,
That the rude sea grew civil at her song,
And certain stars shot madly from their
    spheres,
To hear the sea-maid's music.
PUCK.   I remember.
OBE. That very time I saw (but thou
    could'st not),
Flying between the cold moon and the
    earth,
Cupid all arm'd: a certain aim he took
At a fair vestal throned by the west,
And loos'd his love-shaft smartly from his
    bow,
As it should pierce a hundred thousand
    hearts:
But I might see young Cupid's fiery shaft
Quench'd in the chaste beams of the
    wat'ry moon,
And the imperial votaress passed on,
In maiden meditation, fancy-free.
Yet mark'd I where the bolt of Cupid fell:
It fell upon a little western flower,
Before milk-white, now purple with love's
    wound,
And maidens call it, love-in-idleness.
Fetch me that flower; the herb I show'd
    thee once:
The juice of it on sleeping eyelids laid,
Will make or man or woman madly dote
Upon the next live creature that it sees.
Fetch me this herb; and be thou here
    again,
Ere the leviathan can swim a league.
PUCK. I'll put a girdle round about the
    earth
In forty minutes.   [Exit.
OBE.   Having once this juice,
I'll watch Titania when she is asleep,
And drop the liquor of it in her eyes.
The next thing then she waking looks upon,
(Be it on lion, bear, or wolf, or bull,
On meddling monkey, or on busy ape,)
She shall pursue it with the soul of love:
And ere I take this charm off from her
    sight,
(As I can take it with another herb)
I'll make her render up her page to me.
But who comes here? I am invisible;
And I will over-hear their conference.
    Enter DEMETRIUS, HELENA following him.
DEM. I love thee not, therefore pursue me
    not.
Where is Lysander, and fair Hermia?
The one I'll slay, the other slayeth me.

Thou told'st me they were stol'n into this
    wood;
And here am I, and wood within this wood,
Because I cannot meet my Hermia.
Hence! get thee gone, and follow me no
    more.
HEL. You draw me, you hard-hearted
    adamant;
But yet you draw not iron, for my heart
Is true as steel: leave you your power to
    draw,
And I shall have no power to follow you.
DEM. Do I entice you? Do I speak you
    fair?
Or, rather, do I not in plainest truth
Tell you, I do not nor I cannot love you?
HEL. And even for that do I love you the
    more.
I am your spaniel; and, Demetrius,
The more you beat me, I will fawn on you:
Use me but as your spaniel, spurn me,
    strike me,
Neglect me, lose me; only give me leave,
Unworthy as I am, to follow you.
What worser place can I beg in your love,
(And yet a place of high respect with me,)
Than to be used as you use your dog?
DEM. Tempt not too much the hatred of
    my spirit;
For I am sick when I do look on thee.
HEL. And I am sick when I look not on
    you.
DEM. You do impeach your modesty too
    much,
To leave the city, and commit yourself
Into the hands of one that loves you not;
To trust the opportunity of night,
And the ill counsel of a desert place,
With the rich worth of your virginity.
HEL. Your virtue is my privilege for that.
It is not night when I do see your face,
Therefore I think I am not in the night;
Nor doth this wood lack worlds of com-
    pany,
For you, in my respect, are all the world:
Then how can it be said I am alone,
When all the world is here to look on me?
DEM. I'll run from thee and hide me in
    the brakes,
And leave thee to the mercy of wild beasts.
HEL. The wildest hath not such a heart as
    you.
Run when you will, the story shall be
    chang'd,—
Apollo flies, and Daphne holds the chase;
The dove pursues the griffin; the mild hind
Makes speed to catch the tiger,—bootless
    speed,
When cowardice pursues, and valour flies!

DEM. I will not stay thy questions; let me
go:
Or, if thou follow me, do not believe
But I shall do the mischief in the wood.
HEL. Ay, in the temple, in the town, the
field,
You do me mischief. Fie, Demetrius!
Your wrongs do set a scandal on my sex:
We cannot fight for love, as men may do;
We should be woo'd, and were not made
to woo.
I'll follow thee, and make a heaven of hell,
To die upon the hand I love so well.
            [*Exeunt* DEM. *and* HEL.
OBE. Fare thee well, nymph: ere he do
leave this grove,
Thou shalt fly him, and he shall seek thy
love.—

        Re-enter PUCK.

Hast thou the flower there? Welcome, wan-
derer.
PUCK. Ay, there it is.
OBE.   I pray thee, give it me.
I know a bank where the wild thyme blows,
Where ox-lips, and the nodding violet
grows;
Quite over-canopied with luscious wood-
bine,
With sweet musk-roses, and with eglantine:
There sleeps Titania some time of the
night,
Lull'd in these flowers with dances and
delight;
And there the snake throws her enamel'd
skin,
Weed wide enough to wrap a fairy in:
And with the juice of this I'll streak her
eyes,
And make her full of hateful fantasies.
Take thou some of it, and seek through this
grove:
A sweet Athenian lady is in love
With a disdainful youth: anoint his eyes;
But do it, when the next thing he espies
May be the lady. Thou shalt know the
man
By the Athenian garments he hath on.
Effect it with some care, that he may prove
More fond on her, than she upon her love:
And look thou meet me ere the first cock
crow.
PUCK. Fear not, my lord, your servant
shall do so.   [*Exeunt.*

SCENE III.—*Another part of the Wood*

        Enter TITANIA, *with her train.*

TITA. Come, now a roundel, and a fairy
song;
Then, for the third part of a minute,
hence;—

Some, to kill cankers in the musk-rose
buds;
Some, war with rear-mice for their leathern
wings,
To make my small elves coats; and some
keep back
The clamorous owl, that nightly hoots, an
wonders
At our quaint spirits. Sing me now asleep;
Then to your offices, and let me rest.

        SONG.

1 *FAI.* You spotted snakes, with double
tongue,
    Thorny hedge-hogs, be not seen;
Newts, and blind-worms, do no wrong;
    Come not near our fairy queen:

Chorus.

    Philomel, with melody,
    Sing in our sweet lullaby;
Lulla, lulla, lullaby; lulla, lulla,
    lullaby:
    Never harm,
    Nor spell nor charm,
    Come our lovely lady nigh;
    So, good night, with lullaby.

2 *FAI.* Weaving spiders, come not here;
    Hence, you long-legg'd spinners,
    hence!
Beetles black, approach not near;
    Worm, nor snail, do no offence.

Chorus.

    Philomel, with melody, &c.

1 *FAI.* Hence, away! now all is well.
    One, aloof, stand sentinel.
        [*Exeunt Fairies.* TITANIA *sleeps.*
            Enter OBERON.
OBE. What thou seest when thou dost
wake,
[*Squeezes the flower on* TITANIA's *eye-lids.*
Do it for thy true love take;
Love, and languish for his sake:
Be it ounce, or cat, or bear,
Pard, or boar with bristled hair,
In thy eye that shall appear
When thou wak'st, it is thy dear.
Wake when some vile thing is near. [*Exit.*
        Enter LYSANDER *and* HERMIA.
LYS. Fair love, you faint with wandering
in the wood;
And to speak troth, I have forgot our way:
We'll rest us, Hermia, if you think it good,
And tarry for the comfort of the day.
HER. Be it so, Lysander: find you out a
bed;
For I upon this bank will rest my head.

LYS. One turf shall serve as pillow for us both;
One heart, one bed, two bosoms, and one troth.

HER. Nay, good Lysander; for my sake, my dear,
~~ farther off yet; do not lie so near.

LYS. O, take the sense, sweet, of my innocence!
Love takes the meaning in love's conference.
I mean, that my heart unto yours is knit,
So that but one heart we can make of it:
Two bosoms interchained with an oath;
So then, two bosoms, and a single troth.
Then, by your side no bed-room me deny;
For, lying so, Hermia, I do not lie.

HER. Lysander riddles very prettily:—
Now much beshrew my manners and my pride,
If Hermia meant to say, Lysander lied.
But, gentle friend, for love and courtesy
Lie farther off; in human modesty,
Such separation as may well be said
Becomes a virtuous bachelor and a maid,—
So far be distant; and, good night, sweet friend.
Thy love ne'er alter till thy sweet life end!

LYS. Amen, amen, to that fair prayer, say I;
And then end life, when I end loyalty!
Here is my bed: sleep give thee all his rest!

HER. With half that wish the wisher's eyes be press'd!   [*They sleep.*

Enter PUCK.

PUCK.
Through the forest have I gone,
But Athenian found I none,
On whose eyes I might approve
This flower's force in stirring love.
Night and silence! who is here?
Weeds of Athens he doth wear:
This is he, my master said,
Despised the Athenian maid;
And here the maiden, sleeping sound,
On the dank and dirty ground:—
Pretty soul! she durst not lie
Near this lack-love, this kill-courtesy.
Churl, upon thy eyes I throw
[*Squeezes the flower on* LYSANDER's *eyelids.*
All the power this charm doth owe.
When thou wak'st, let love forbid
Sleep his seat on thy eyelid:
So awake when I am gone,
For I must now to Oberon.   [*Exit.*

Enter DEMETRIUS *and* HELENA, *running.*

HEL. Stay, though thou kill me, sweet Demetrius.

DEM. I charge thee, hence; and do not haunt me thus.

HEL. O, wilt thou darkling leave me? do not so.

DEM. Stay, on thy peril: I alone will go.
[*Exit* DEMETRIUS.

HEL. O, I am out of breath in this fond chase!
The more my prayer, the lesser is my grace.
Happy is Hermia, wheresoe'er she lies;
For she hath blessed and attractive eyes.
How came her eyes so bright? Not with salt tears:
If so, my eyes are oftener wash'd than hers.
No, no, I am as ugly as a bear;
For beasts that meet me, run away for fear:
Therefore no marvel though Demetrius
Do, as a monster, fly my presence thus.
What wicked and dissembling glass of mine
Made me compare with Hermia's sphery eyne?—
But who is here?—Lysander! on the ground!
Dead? or asleep?—I see no blood, no wound.—
Lysander, if you live, good Sir, awake.

LYS. [*Awaking.*] And run through fire I will, for thy sweet sake.
Transparent Helena! Nature here shows art,
That through thy bosom makes me see thy heart.
Where is Demetrius? O, how fit a word
Is that vile name to perish on my sword!

HEL. Do not say so, Lysander; say not so.
What though he love your Hermia? Lord, what though?
Yet Hermia still loves you: then be content.

LYS. Content with Hermia! No; I do repent
The tedious minutes I with her have spent.
Not Hermia, but Helena I love:
Who will not change a raven for a dove?
The will of man is by his reason sway'd;
And reason says you are the worthier maid.
Things growing are not ripe until their season:
So, I being young, till now ripe not to reason;
And touching now the point of human skill,
Reason becomes the marshal to my will,
And leads me to your eyes; where I o'erlook
Love's stories, written in love's richest book.

HEL. Wherefore was I to this keen mockery born?
When, at your hands, did I deserve this scorn?
Is't not enough, is't not enough, young man,
That I did never, no, nor never can,
Deserve a sweet look from Demetrius' eye,
But you must flout my insufficiency?
Good troth, you do me wrong,—good sooth, you do,—

In such disdainful manner me to woo.
But fare you well: perforce I must confess,
I thought you lord of more true gentleness.
O, that a lady, of one man refus'd,
Should of another therefore be abus'd!
                                            [*Exit.*
LYS. She sees not Hermia.—Hermia,
   sleep thou there:
And never may'st thou come Lysander
   near!
For, as a surfeit of the sweetest things
The deepest loathing to the stomach brings;
Or, as the heresies, that men do leave,
Are hated most of those they did deceive;
So thou, my surfeit and my heresy,
Of all be hated, but the most of me!
And, all my powers, address your love and
   might
To honour Helen, and to be her knight.
                                            [*Exit.*
HER. [*Awaking.*] Help me, Lysander, help
   me! do thy best
To pluck this crawling serpent from my
   breast!
Ah me, for pity!—what a dream was here!
Lysander, look how I do quake with fear:
Methought a serpent eat my heart away,
And you sat smiling at his cruel prey.—
Lysander — What, remov'd? — Lysander!
   lord!—
What, out of hearing? gone? no sound, no
   word?
Alack! where are you? speak, an if you
   hear;
Speak, of all loves! I swoon almost with
   fear.
No?—then I well perceive you are not
   nigh:
Either death, or you, I'll find immediately.
                                            [*Exit.*

ACT III.

SCENE I.—*The Wood.* TITANIA *lying asleep.*
Enter QUINCE, SNUG, BOTTOM, FLUTE,
   SNOUT, *and* STARVELING.

BOT. Are we all met?
QUIN. Pat, pat; and here's a marvellous
convenient place for our rehearsal. This
green plot shall be our stage, this hawthorn
brake our 'tiring-house; and we will do it in
action, as we will do it before the duke.
BOT. Peter Quince,—
QUIN. What say'st thou, bully Bottom?
BOT. There are things in this comedy of
"Pyramus and Thisby," that will never
please. First, Pyramus must draw a sword
to kill himself; which the ladies cannot
abide. How answer you that?
SNOUT. By'rlakin, a parlous fear.

STAR. I believe we must leave the killing
out, when all is done.
BOT. Not a whit: I have a device to make
all well. Write me a prologue; and let the
prologue seem to say, we will do no harm
with our swords, and that Pyramus is not
killed indeed; and, for the more better
assurance, that I, Pyramus, am not Pyramus, but Bottom the weaver. This will put
them out of fear.
QUIN. Well, we will have such a prologue; and it shall be written in eight and
six.
BOT. No, make it two more; let it be
written in eight and eight.
SNOUT. Will not the ladies be afeard of the
STAR. I fear it, I promise you.   [lion?
BOT. Masters, you ought to consider with
yourselves: to bring in,—God shield us!—
a lion among ladies, is a most dreadful
thing; for there is not a more fearful wild-
fowl than your lion, living; and we ought to
look to it.
SNOUT. Therefore, another prologue must
tell he is not a lion.
BOT. Nay, you must name his name, and
half his face must be seen through the
lion's neck; and he himself must speak
through, saying thus, or to the same defect,
—"Ladies,—or, fair ladies,—I would wish
you,—or, I would request you,—or, I would
entreat you,—not to fear, not to tremble:
my life for yours. If you think I come
hither as a lion, it were pity of my life: no,
I am no such thing; I am a man as other
men are:"—and there, indeed, let him name
his name, and tell them plainly, he is Snug,
the joiner.
QUIN. Well, it shall be so. But there is
two hard things,—that is, to bring the
moonlight into a chamber; for, you know,
Pyramus and Thisby meet by moonlight.
SNUG. Doth the moon shine that night we
play our play?
BOT. A calendar, a calendar! look in the
almanack; find out moonshine, find out
moonshine.
QUIN. Yes, it doth shine that night.
BOT. Why, then may you leave a casement
of the great chamber window, where we
play, open; and the moon may shine in at
the casement.
QUIN. Ay; or else one must come in with
a bush of thorns and a lanthorn, and say he
comes to disfigure, or to present, the person
of moonshine. Then there is another thing:
we must have a wall in the great chamber;
for Pyramus and Thisby, says the story,
did talk through the chink of a wall.
SNUG. You can never bring in a wall.—
What say you, Bottom?

BOT. Some man or other must present wall: and let him have some plaster, or some loam, or some rough-cast about him, to signify wall; and let him hold his fingers thus, and through that cranny shall Pyramus and Thisby whisper.

QUIN. If that may be, then all is well. Come, sit down, every mother's son, and rehearse your parts. Pyramus, you begin. When you have spoken your speech, enter into that brake;—and so every one according to his cue.

Enter PUCK *behind.*

PUCK. What hempen home-spuns have we swaggering here,
So near the cradle of the fairy queen?
What, a play toward! I'll be an auditor;
An actor too, perhaps, if I see cause.

QUIN. Speak, Pyramus.—Thisby, stand forth.

PYR. "Thisby, the flowers of odious savours sweet,"—

QUIN. "Odours," "odours."

PYR. —"odours savours sweet:
So hath thy breath, my dearest Thisby, dear.—
But hark, a voice! stay thou but here a while,
And by and by I will to thee appear." [*Exit.*

PUCK. [*Aside.*] A stranger Pyramus than e'er play'd here! [*Exit.*

THIS. Must I speak now?

QUIN. Ay, marry, must you; for you must understand, he goes but to see a noise that he heard, and is to come again.

THIS. "Most radiant Pyramus, most lily-white of hue,
Of colour like the red rose on triumphant brier,
Most briskly juvenal, and eke most lovely Jew,
As true as truest horse, that yet would never tire,
I'll meet thee, Pyramus, at Ninny's tomb."

QUIN. "Ninus' tomb," man. Why, you must not speak that yet; that you answer to Pyramus: you speak all your part at once, cues and all.—Pyramus, enter: your cue is past; it is, "never tire."

THIS. O,—"As true as truest horse, that yet would never tire."

Re-enter PUCK, *and* BOTTOM *with an ass's head.*

PYR. "If I were, fair Thisby, I were only thine:"—

QUIN. O monstrous! O strange! we are haunted.—Pray, masters! fly, masters!— Help!

Exit, with SNUG, FLUTE, SNOUT, *and* STARVELING.

PUCK. I'll follow you, I'll lead you about a round,
Through bog, through bush, through brake, through brier:
Sometime a horse I'll be, sometime a hound,
A hog, a headless bear, sometime a fire;
And neigh, and bark, and grunt, and roar, and burn,
Like horse, hound, hog, bear, fire, at every turn. [*Exit.*

BOT. Why do they run away? this is a knavery of them, to make me afeard.

Re-enter SNOUT.

SNOUT. O Bottom! thou art changed! what do I see on thee?

BOT. What do you see? you see an ass's head of your own, do you? [*Exit* SNOUT.

Re-enter QUINCE.

QUIN. Bless thee, Bottom! bless thee! thou art translated. [*Exit.*

BOT. I see their knavery: this is to make an ass of me, to fright me, if they could. But I will not stir from this place, do what they can: I will walk up and down here, and I will sing, that they shall hear I am not afraid. [*Sings.*

The ousel-cock, so black of hue,
  With orange-tawny bill,
The throstle with his note so true,
  The wren with little quill:—

TITA. [*Awaking.*] What angel wakes me from my flowery bed?

BOT. [*Sings.*]
The finch, the sparrow, and the lark,
  The plain-song cuckoo gray,
Whose note full many a man doth mark,
  And dares not answer, nay;—

for, indeed, who would set his wit to so foolish a bird? who would give a bird the lie, though he cry "cuckoo" never so?

TITA. I pray thee, gentle mortal, sing again:
Mine ear is much enamour'd of thy note;
So is mine eye enthralled to thy shape;
And thy fair virtue's force, perforce doth move me,
On the first view, to say, to swear, I love thee.

BOT. Methinks, mistress, you should have little reason for that: and yet, to say the truth, reason and love keep little company together now-a-days;— the more the pity, that some honest neighbours will not make them friends. Nay, I can gleek upon occasion.

TITA. Thou art as wise as thou art beautiful.

BOT. Not so, neither: but if I had wit enough to get out of this wood, I have enough to serve mine own turn.

TITA. Out of this wood do not desire to go:
Thou shalt remain here, whether thou wilt
I am a spirit of no common rate,— [or no.
The summer still doth tend upon my state;
And I do love thee: therefore go with me;
I'll give thee fairies to attend on thee;
And they shall fetch thee jewels from the deep,
And sing, while thou on pressed flowers dost sleep:
And I will purge thy mortal grossness so,
That thou shalt like an airy spirit go.—
Peas-blossom! Cobweb! Moth! and Mustard-seed!

Enter PEAS-BLOSSOM, COBWEB, MOTH,
and MUSTARD-SEED.

PEAS. Ready.
COB.   And I.
MOTH.   And I.
MUS.   And I.
ALL FOUR   Where shall we go?
TITA. Be kind and courteous to this gentleman:
Hop in his walks and gambol in his eyes;
Feed him with apricocks, and dewberries,
With purple grapes, green figs, and mulberries,
The honey-bags steal from the humble-bees,
And for night tapers crop their waxen thighs,
And light them at the fiery glow-worm's eyes,
To have my love to bed, and to arise;
And pluck the wings from painted butterflies,
To fan the moon-beams from his sleeping eyes:
Nod to him, elves, and do him courtesies.
PEAS. Hail, mortal!
COB. Hail!
MOTH. Hail!
MUS. Hail!
BOT. I cry your worship's mercy, heartily.
—I beseech your worship's name.
COB. Cobweb.
BOT. I shall desire you of more acquaintance, good master Cobweb: if I cut my finger, I shall make bold with you.—Your name, honest gentleman?
PEAS. Peas-blossom.
BOT. I pray you, commend me to mistress Squash, your mother, and to master Peascod, your father. Good master Peas-blossom, I shall desire you of more acquaintance too. —Your name, I beseech you, sir?
MUS. Mustard-seed.
BOT. Good master Mustard-seed, I know

your patience well: that same cowardly, giant-like ox-beef, hath devoured many a gentleman of your house: I promise you, your kindred hath made my eyes water ere now. I desire you of more acquaintance, good master Mustard-seed.
TITA. Come, wait upon him; lead him to my bower.
The moon, methinks, looks with a watery eye;
And when she weeps, weeps every little flower,
Lamenting some enforced chastity.
Tie up my love's tongue, bring him silently.
[*Exeunt.*

———

SCENE II.—*Another part of the Wood.*

Enter OBERON.

OBE. I wonder if Titania be awak'd;
Then, what it was that next came in her eye,
Which she must dote on in extremity.—
Here comes my messenger.—[*Enter* PUCK.]
How now, mad spirit!
What night-rule now about this haunted grove?
PUCK. My mistress with a monster is in love.
Near to her close and consecrated bower,
While she was in her dull and sleeping hour,
A crew of patches, rude mechanicals,
That work for bread upon Athenian stalls,
Were met together to rehearse a play,
Intended for great Theseus' nuptial day.
The shallowest thick-skin of that barren sort,
Who Pyramus presented, in their sport
Forsook his scene, and enter'd in a brake:
When I did him at this advantage take,
An ass's nowl I fixed on his head:
Anon his Thisbe must be answered,
And forth my mimic comes. When they him spy,
As wild geese that the creeping fowler eye,
Or russet-pated choughs, many in sort,
Rising and cawing at the gun's report,
Sever themselves, and madly sweep the sky;
So, at his sight, away his fellows fly;
And, at our stamp, here o'er and o'er one falls;
He murder cries, and help from Athens calls.
Their sense thus weak, lost with their fears thus strong,
Made senseless things begin to do them wrong;
For briers and thorns at their apparel snatch;

Some, sleeves,—some, hats,—from yielders all things catch.
I led them on in this distracted fear.
And left sweet Pyramus translated there:
When in that moment (so it came to pass,)
Titania wak'd, and straightway lov'd an ass.
OBE. This falls out better than I could devise.
But hast thou yet latch'd the Athenian's eyes
With the love-juice, as I did bid thee do?
PUCK. I took him sleeping, (that is finish'd too,)
And the Athenian woman by his side;
That, when he wak'd, of force she must be ey'd.

   Enter DEMETRIUS *and* HERMIA.

OBE. Stand close: this is the same Athenian.
PUCK. This is the woman; but not this the man.
DEM. O, why rebuke you him that loves you so?
Lay breath so bitter on your bitter foe.
HER. Now I but chide; but I should use thee worse,
For thou, I fear, hast given me cause to curse.
If thou hast slain Lysander in his sleep,
Being o'er shoes in blood, plunge in the deep,
And kill me too.   [deep,
The sun was not so true unto the day,
As he to me: would he have stol'n away
From sleeping Hermia? I'll believe as soon,
This whole earth may be bor'd; and that the moon
May through the centre creep, and so displease
Her brother's noon-tide with th' Antipodes.
It cannot be but thou hast murder'd him;
So should a murderer look,—so dead, so grim.
DEM. So should the murder'd look; and so should I,
Pierc'd through the heart with your stern cruelty:
Yet you, the murderer, look as bright, as clear,
As yonder Venus in her glimmering sphere.
HER. What's this to my Lysander? where is he?
Ah, good Demetrius, wilt thou give him me?
DEM. I had rather give his carcase to my hounds.
HER. Out, dog! out, cur! thou driv'st me past the bounds
Of maiden's patience. Hast thou slain him, then?
Henceforth be never number'd among men!
O, once tell true, tell true, e'en for my sake!

Durst thou have look'd upon him being awake,
And hast thou kill'd him sleeping? O brave touch!
Could not a worm, an adder, do so much?
An adder did it; for with doubler tongue
Than thine, thou serpent, never adder stung.
DEM. You spend your passion on a mispris'd mood:
I am not guilty of Lysander's blood;
Nor is he dead, for aught that I can tell.
HER. I pray thee, tell me, then, that he is well.
DEM. An if I could, what should I get therefore?
HER. A privilege, never to see me more:—
And from thy hated presence part I so:
See me no more, whether he be dead or no.
           [*Exit.*
DEM. There is no following her in this fierce vein:
Here therefore, for a while I will remain.
So sorrow's heaviness doth heavier grow
For debt that bankrupt sleep doth sorrow owe;
Which now in some slight measure it will pay,
If for his tender here I make some stay.
      [*Lies down and sleeps.*
OBE. What hast thou done? thou hast mistaken quite,
And laid the love-juice on some true-love's sight:
Of thy misprision must perforce ensue
Some true-love turn'd, and not a false turn'd true.
PUCK. Then fate o'er-rules; that, one man holding troth,
A million fail, confounding oath on oath.
OBE. About the wood go swifter than the wind,
And Helena of Athens look thou find:
All fancy-sick she is, and pale of cheer
With sighs of love, that cost the fresh blood dear:
By some illusion see thou bring her here:
I'll charm his eyes against she do appear.
PUCK. I go, I go; look how I go,
Swifter than arrow from the Tartar's bow.   [*Exit.*
OBE.
   Flower of this purple die,
   Hit with Cupid's archery,
Squeezes the flower on DEMETRIUS's *eyelids.*
   Sink in apple of his eye!
   When his love he doth espy,
   Let her shine as gloriously
   As the Venus of the sky.—
   When thou wak'st, if she be by,
   Beg of her for remedy.

Re-enter PUCK.

PUCK.
 Captain of our fairy band,
 Helena is here at hand;
 And the youth, mistook by me,
 Pleading for a lover's fee.
 Shall we their fond pageant see?
 Lord, what fools these mortals be!

OBE.
 Stand aside: the noise they make
 Will cause Demetrius to awake.

PUCK.
 Then will two at once woo one,—
 That must needs be sport alone;
 And those things do best please me,
 That befall preposterously.

Enter LYSANDER *and* HELENA.

LYS. Why should you think that I should
  woo in scorn?
Scorn and derision never come in tears:
Look, when I vow, I weep, and vows so
In their nativity all truth appears. [born,
How can these things in me seem scorn
  to you,
Bearing the badge of faith, to prove them
  true?
HEL. You do advance your cunning more
 and more.
When truth kills truth, O devilish-holy
 fray!
These vows are Hermia's: will you give her
 o'er?
Weigh oath with oath, and you will nothing
 weigh:
Your vows to her and me, put in two scales,
Will even weigh; and both as light as tales.
LYS. I had no judgment when to her I
 swore.
HEL. Nor none, in my mind, now you give
 her o'er.
LYS. Demetrius loves her, and he loves
 not you.
DEM. [*Awaking.*] O Helen, goddess,
 nymph, perfect, divine!
To what, my love, shall I compare thine
 eyne?
Crystal is muddy. O, how ripe in show
Thy lips, those kissing cherries, tempting
 grow!
That pure congealed white, high Taurus
 snow,
Fann'd with the eastern wind, turns to a
 crow
When thou hold'st up thy hand: O, let me
 kiss
This princess of pure white, this seal of
 bliss!
HEL. O spite! O hell! I see you all are
 bent

To set against me, for your merriment:
If you were civil, and knew courtesy,
You would not do me thus much injury.
Can you not hate me, as I know you do,
But you must join in souls to mock me too?
If you were men, as men you are in show,
You would not use a gentle lady so;
To vow, and swear, and superpraise my
 parts,
When I am sure you hate me with your
 hearts,
You both are rivals, and love Hermia;
And now both rivals, to mock Helena:
A trim exploit, a manly enterprise,
To conjure tears up in a poor maid's eyes
With your derision! none of noble sort
Would so offend a virgin, and extort
A poor soul's patience, all to make you
 sport.
LYS. You are unkind, Demetrius; be not
 so;
For you love Hermia;—this you know I
 know:
And here, with all good will, with all my
 heart,
In Hermia's love I yield you up my part;
And yours of Helena to me bequeath,
Whom I do love, and will do to my death.
HEL. Never did mockers waste more idle
 breath.
DEM. Lysander, keep thy Hermia; I will
 none:
If e'er I lov'd her, all that love is gone.
My heart to her but as guest-wise sojourn'd,
And now to Helen is it home return'd,
There to remain.
LYS.   Helen, it is not so.
DEM. Disparage not the faith thou dost
 not know,
Lest, to thy peril, thou aby it dear.—
Look, where thy love comes; yonder is thy
 dear.

Re-enter HERMIA.

HER. Dark night, that from the eye his
 function takes,
The ear more quick of apprehension makes;
Wherein it doth impair the seeing sense,
It pays the hearing double recompense.—
Thou art not by mine eye, Lysander, found;
Mine ear, I thank it, brought me to thy
 sound.
But why unkindly didst thou leave me so?
LYS. Why should he stay, whom love doth
 press to go?
HER. What love could press Lysander
 from my side?
LYS. Lysander's love, that would not let
 him bide,—
Fair Helena; who more engilds the night
Than all you fiery oes and eyes of light.

Why seek'st thou me? could not this make
  thee know,
The hate I bear thee made me leave thee
  so?
HER. You speak not as you think: it
  cannot be.
HEL. Lo, she is one of this confederacy!
Now I perceive they have conjoin'd, all
  three,
To fashion this false sport in spite of me.
Injurious Hermia! most ungrateful maid!
Have you conspir'd, have you with these
  contriv'd
To bait me with this foul derision?
Is all the counsel that we two have shar'd,
The sisters' vows, the hours that we have
  spent,
When we have chid the hasty-footed time
For parting us,—O! is all forgot?
All school-days' friendship, childhood in-
  nocence?
We, Hermia, like two artificial gods,
Have with our neelds created both one
  flower,
Both on one sampler, sitting on one cushion,
Both warbling of one song, both in one key;
As if our hands, our sides, voices, and
  minds,
Had been incorporate. So we grew together,
Like to a double cherry, seeming parted;
But yet a union in partition,
Two lovely berries moulded on one stem;
So, with two seeming bodies, but one heart;
Two of the first, like coats in heraldry,
Due but to one, and crowned with one
  crest.
And will you rent our ancient love asunder,
To join with men in scorning your poor
  friend?
It is not friendly, 'tis not maidenly:
Our sex, as well as I, may chide you for it,
Though I alone do feel the injury.
HER. I am amazed at your passionate
  words.
I scorn you not: it seems that you scorn
  me.
HEL. Have you not set Lysander, as in
  scorn,
To follow me, and praise my eyes and face?
And made your other love, Demetrius,
(Who even but now did spurn me with
  his foot,)
To call me goddess, nymph, divine, and
  rare,
Precious, celestial? Wherefore speaks he
  this
To her he hates? and wherefore doth
  Lysander
Deny your love, so rich within his soul,
And tender me, forsooth, affection,
But by your setting on, by your consent?

What though I be not so in grace as you,
So hung upon with love, so fortunate;
But miserable most to love unlov'd?
This you should pity, rather than despise.
HER. I understand not what you mean by
  this.
HEL. Ay, do, persever, counterfeit sad
  looks,
Make mouths upon me when I turn my
  back;
Wink each at other; hold the sweet jest up;
This sport, well carried, shall be chronicled.
If you have any pity, grace, or manners,
You would not make me such an argument.
But, fare ye well: 'tis partly mine own
  fault;
Which death, or absence, soon shall remedy.
LYS. Stay gentle Helena; hear my excuse:
My love, my life, my soul, fair Helena!
HEL. O excellent!
HER.   Sweet, do not scorn her so.
DEM. If she cannot entreat, I can compel.
LYS. Thou canst compel no more than she
  entreat:
Thy threats have no more strength than
  her weak prayers.—
Helen, I love thee; by my life, I do:
I swear by that which I will lose for thee,
To prove him false that says I love thee not.
DEM. I say I love thee more than he can
  do.
LYS. If thou say so, withdraw, and prove
  it too.
DEM. Quick, come!
HER. Lysander, whereto tends all this?
LYS. Away, you Ethiop!
DEM.   No, no, Sir:—
Seem to break loose; take on, as you would
  follow;
But yet come not: you are a tame man, go!
LYS. [*To* HERMIA.] Hang off, thou cat,
  thou burr! vile thing, let loose,
Or I will shake thee from me like a
  serpent!
HER. Why are you grown so rude? what
  change is this,
Sweet love?
LYS.   Thy love? out, tawny Tartar, out!
Out, loathed medicine! O hated potion
  hence
HER. Do you not jest?
HEL.   Yes, 'sooth; and so do you
LYS. Demetrius, I will keep my word with
  thee.
DEM. I would I had your bond, for I
  perceive
A weak bond holds you: I'll not trust your
  word.
LYS. What, should I hurt her, strike her
  kill her dead?
Although I hate her, I'll not harm her so

HER. What, can you do me greater harm
than hate?
Hate me! wherefore? O me! what news,
my love?
Am not I Hermia? Are not you Lysander?
I am as fair now, as I was erewhile.
Since night, you lov'd me; yet, since night
you left me:
Why, then you left me (O, the gods
In earnest, shall I say?   [forbid!)
LYS.   Ay, by my life;
And never did desire to see thee more.
Therefore be out of hope, of question, of
doubt:
Be certain, nothing truer; 'tis no jest,
That I do hate thee, and love Helena.
HER. O me!—you juggler! you canker-
blossom!
You thief of love! what, have you come by
night,
And stol'n my love's heart from him?
HEL.   Fine, i'faith!
Have you no modesty, no maiden shame,
No touch of bashfulness? What, will you
tear
Impatient answers from my gentle tongue?
Fie, fie! you counterfeit, you puppet you!
HER. Puppet! why, so: ay, that way goes
the game.
Now I perceive that she hath made compare
Between our statures; she hath urg'd her
height;
And with her personage, her tall personage,
Her height, forsooth, she hath prevail'd
with him.—
And are you grown so high in his esteem,
Because I am so dwarfish and so low?
How low am I, thou painted maypole?
speak;
How low am I? I am not yet so low,
But that my nails can reach unto thine
eyes.
HEL. I pray you, though you mock me,
gentlemen,
Let her not hurt me: I was never curst;
I have no gift at all in shrewishness;
I am a right maid for my cowardice:
Let her not strike me. You perhaps may
think,
Because she is something lower than myself,
That I can match her.
HER.   Lower! hark, again.
HEL. Good Hermia, do not be so bitter
with me.
I evermore did love you, Hermia,
Did ever keep your counsels, never wrong'd
you;
Save that, in love unto Demetrius,
I told him of your stealth unto this wood.
He follow'd you; for love, I follow'd him;

But he hath chid me hence, and threaten'd
me
To strike me, spurn me, nay, to kill me too:
And now, so you will let me quiet go,
To Athens will I bear my folly back,
And follow you no farther: let me go:
You see how simple and how fond I am.
HER. Why, get you gone: who is't that
hinders you?
HEL. A foolish heart, that I leave here
behind.
HER. What, with Lysander?
HEL.   With Demetrius.
LYS. Be not afraid; she shall not harm
thee, Helena.
DEM. No, Sir, she shall not, though you
take her part.
HEL. O, when she is angry, she is keen
and shrewd!
She was a vixen when she went to school;
And though she be but little, she is fierce.
HER. Little again! nothing but low and
little!—
Why will you suffer her to flout me thus?
Let me come to her.
LYS.   Get you gone, you dwarf!
You minimus, of hindering knot-grass
made;
You bead, you acorn!
DEM.   You are too officious
In her behalf that scorns your services.
Let her alone: speak not of Helena;
Take not her part; for, if thou dost intend
Never so little show of love to her,
Thou shalt aby it.
LYS.   Now she holds me not;
Now follow, if thou dar'st, to try whose
right,—
Or thine or mine,—is most in Helena.
DEM. Follow? nay, I'll go with thee, cheek
by jole.   [*Exeunt* Lys. *and* Dem.
HER. You, mistress, all this coil is 'long
of you:
Nay, go not back.
HEL.   I will not trust you, I,
Nor longer stay in your curst company.
Your hands, than mine, are quicker for a
fray;
My legs are longer though, to run away.
                              [*Exit.*
HER. I am amaz'd, and know not what
to say.   [*Exit.*
OBE. This is thy negligence: still thou
mistak'st,
Or else commit'st thy knaveries wilfully.
PUCK. Believe me, king of shadows, I
mistook.
Did not you tell me I should know the man
By the Athenian garments he had on?
And so far blameless proves my enterprise,

That I have 'nointed an Athenian's eyes;
And so far am I glad it so did sort,
As this their jangling I esteem a sport.
OBE. Thou seest, these lovers seek a place
to fight:
Hie therefore, Robin, overcast the night;
The starry welkin cover thou anon
With drooping fog, as black as Acheron;
And lead these testy rivals so astray,
As one come not within another's way.
Like to Lysander sometime frame thy
tongue,
Then stir Demetrius up with bitter wrong;
And sometime rail thou like Demetrius;
And from each other look thou lead them
thus,
Till o'er their brows death-counterfeiting
sleep
With leaden legs and batty wings doth
creep:
Then crush this herb into Lysander's eye;
Whose liquor hath this virtuous property,
To take from thence all error with his
might,
And make his eye-balls roll with wonted
sight.
When they next wake, all this derision
Shall seem a dream, and fruitless vision;
And back to Athens shall the lovers wend,
With league, whose date till death shall
never end.
Whiles I in this affair do thee employ,
I'll to my queen, and beg her Indian boy;
And then I will her charmed eye release
From monster's view, and all things shall
be peace.
PUCK. My fairy lord, this must be done
with haste,
For night's swift dragons cut the clouds
full fast,
And yonder shines Aurora's harbinger;
At whose approach, ghosts, wandering here
and there,
Troop home to church-yards: damned
spirits all,
That in cross-ways and floods have burial,
Already to their wormy beds are gone;
For fear lest day should look their shames
upon,
They wilfully themselves exile from light,
And must for aye consort with black-brow'd
night.
OBE. But we are spirits of another sort:
I with the morning's love have oft made
sport;
And, like a forester, the groves may tread,
Even till the eastern gate, all fiery-red,
Opening on Neptune with fair blessed
beams,
Turns into yellow gold his salt green
streams.

But, notwithstanding, haste; make no de-
lay:
We may effect this business yet ere day.
    [*Exit* OBERON.
PUCK.
    Up and down, up and down,
    I will lead them up and down:
    I am fear'd in field and town:
    Goblin, lead them up and down.
Here comes one.
        Re-enter LYSANDER.
LYS. Where art thou, proud Demetrius?
speak thou now.
PUCK. Here, villain! drawn and ready.
Where art thou?
LYS. I will be with thee straight.
PUCK.   Follow me, then,
To plainer ground.
        [*Exit* LYS. *as following the voice.*
        Re-enter DEMETRIUS.
DEM.   Lysander, speak again.
Thou runaway, thou coward, art thou fled?
Speak! In some bush? Where dost thou
hide thy head?
PUCK. Thou coward! art thou bragging
to the stars,
Telling the bushes that thou look'st for
wars,
And wilt not come? Come, recreant; come,
thou child;
I'll whip thee with a rod: he is defil'd
That draws a sword on thee.
DEM.   Yea, art thou there?
PUCK. Follow my voice: we'll try no
manhood here.   [*Exeunt.*
        Re-enter LYSANDER.
LYS. He goes before me, and still dares
me on:
When I come where he calls, then he is
gone.
The villain is much lighter-heel'd than I:
I follow'd fast, but faster he did fly;
That fallen am I in dark uneven way,
And here will rest me. [*Lies down.*] Come,
thou gentle day!
For if but once thou show me thy grey
light,
I'll find Demetrius, and revenge this spite.
        [*Sleeps.*
        Re-enter PUCK *and* DEMETRIUS.
PUCK. Ho! ho! ho! Coward, why com'st
thou not?
DEM. Abide me, if thou dar'st; for well
I wot
Thou runn'st before me, shifting every
place,
And dar'st not stand, nor look me in the
Where art thou now?   [face.
PUCK.   Come hither: I am here.
DEM. Nay, then, thou mock'st me. Thou
shalt 'by this dear,

If ever I thy face by day-light see:
Now, go thy way. Faintness constraineth
    me
To measure out my length on this cold bed.
By day's approach look to be visited.
            [*Lies down and sleeps.*

                Re-enter HELENA.

HEL. O weary night! O long and tedious
    night!
Abate thy hours: shine, comforts, from
    the east,
That I may back to Athens, by day-light,
From these that my poor company detest:
And sleep, that sometimes shuts up sor-
    row's eye,
Steal me a while from mine own company.
            [*Lies down and sleeps.*

PUCK.

    Yet but three? Come one more;
    Two of both kinds make up four.
    Here she comes, curst and sad:—
    Cupid is a knavish lad,
    Thus to make poor females mad.

                Re-enter HERMIA.

HER. Never so weary, never so in woe;
Bedabbled with the dew, and torn with
    briers;
I can no farther crawl, no farther go;
My legs can keep no pace with my desires.
Here will I rest me till the break of day.
Heavens shield Lysander, if they mean a
    fray!   [*Lies down and sleeps.*
PUCK. On the ground sleep sound:
    I'll apply to your eye,
    Gentle lover, remedy.
[*Squeezing the herb on* LYSANDER's *eyelids.*

    When thou wak'st, thou tak'st
    True delight in the sight
    Of thy former lady's eye:
    And the country proverb known,
    That every man should take his own,
    In your waking shall be shown:

        Jack shall have Jill;
        Naught shall go ill;

    The man shall have his mare again,
    And all shall be well.   [*Exit.*

ACT IV.

SCENE I.—*The Wood.*

Enter TITANIA *and* BOTTOM; LYSANDER,
DEMETRIUS, HERMIA, *and* HELENA,
still lying asleep. PEAS-BLOSSOM, COB-
WEB, MOTH, MUSTARD-SEED, *and other
Fairies attending;* OBERON *behind un-
seen.*

TITA. Come, sit thee down upon this
    flowery bed,
While I thy amiable cheeks do coy,
And stick musk-roses in thy sleek smooth
    head,
And kiss thy fair large ears, my gentle joy.
BOT. Where's Peas-blossom?
PEAS. Ready.
BOT. Scratch my head, Peas-blossom.—
Where's monsieur Cobweb?
COB. Ready.
BOT. Monsieur Cobweb, good monsieur,
get your weapons in your hand, and kill me
a red-hipped humble-bee on the top of a
thistle; and, good monsieur, bring me the
honey-bag. Do not fret yourself too much
in the action, monsieur; and, good monsieur, have a care the honey-bag break not;
I would be loath to have you overflown
with a honey-bag, signior.—Where's monsieur Mustard-seed?
MUST. Ready.
BOT. Give me your neif, monsieur Mustard-seed. Pray you, leave your courtesy,
good monsieur.
MUST. What's your will?
BOT. Nothing, good monsieur, but to help
cavalery Cobweb to scratch. I must to
the barber's, monsieur; for methinks I am
marvellous hairy about the face; and I
am such a tender ass, if my hair do but
tickle me, I must scratch.
TITA. What, wilt thou hear some music,
    my sweet love?
BOT. I have a reasonable good ear in
music: let us have the tongs and the
bones.
TITA. Or say, sweet love, what thou
    desir'st to eat.
BOT. Truly, a peck of provender: I could
munch your good dry oats. Methinks I
have a great desire to a bottle of hay:
good hay, sweet hay, hath no fellow.
TITA. I have a venturous fairy that shall
    seek
The squirrel's hoard, and fetch thee new
    nuts.
BOT. I had rather have a handful or two
of dried peas. But, I pray you, let none
of your people stir me: I have an exposi-
tion of sleep come upon me.
TITA. Sleep thou, and I will wind thee
    in my arms.—
Fairies, be gone, and be all ways away.—
                [*Exeunt Fairies.*
So doth the woodbine the sweet honey-
    suckle
Gently entwist: the female ivy so
Enrings the barky fingers of the elm.

O, how I love thee, how I dote on thee!
[*They sleep.*

Enter PUCK.

OBE. [*Advancing.*] Welcome, good Robin.
Seest thou this sweet sight?
Her dotage now I do begin to pity:
For, meeting her of late behind the wood,
Seeking sweet savours for this hateful fool,
I did upbraid her, and fall out with her;
For she his hairy temples then had rounded
With coronet of fresh and fragrant flowers;
And that same dew, which sometime on the
buds
Was wont to swell, like round and orient
pearls,
Stood now within the pretty flow'rets' eyes,
Like tears, that did their own disgrace
bewail.
When I had at my pleasure taunted her,
And she in mild terms begg'd my patience,
I then did ask of her her changeling child;
Which straight she gave me; and her
fairy sent
To bear him to my bower in fairy land.
And now I have the boy, I will undo
This hateful imperfection of her eyes:
And, gentle Puck, take this transformed
scalp
From off the head of this Athenian swain;
That he, awaking when the other do,
May all to Athens back again repair,
And think no more of this night's accidents,
But as the fierce vexation of a dream.
But first I will release the fairy queen.
Be, as thou wast wont to be;
[*Touching her eyes with a herb.*
See, as thou wast wont to see:
Dian's bud o'er Cupid's flower
Hath such force and blessed power.
Now, my Titania; wake you, my sweet
queen.
TITA. My Oberon! what visions have I
seen!
Methought I was enamour'd of an ass.
OBE. There lies your love.
TITA.   How came these things to pass?
O, how mine eyes do loathe his visage
now!
OBE. Silence, awhile.—Robin, take off this
head.—
Titania, music call; and strike more dead
Than common sleep, of all these five the
sense.
TITA. Music, ho! music! such as charm-
eth sleep.
PUCK. Now when thou wak'st, with thine
own fool's eyes peep.
OBE. Sound, music!—[*Still music.*] Come,
my queen, take hands with me,
And rock the ground whereon these sleep-
ers be.

Now thou and I are new in amity,
And will to-morrow midnight solemnly
Dance in Duke Theseus' house triumph-
antly.
And bless it to all fair prosperity.
There shall the pairs of faithful lovers be
Wedded, with Theseus, all in jollity.
PUCK. Fairy king, attend, and mark:
I do hear the morning lark.
OBE.   Then, my queen, in silence sad,
Trip we after the night's shade:
We the globe can compass soon,
Swifter than the wandering moon.
TITA. Come, my lord; and in our flight,
Tell me how it came this night,
That I sleeping here was found
With these mortals on the ground.
[*Exeunt. Horns sound within.*

Enter THESEUS, HIPPOLYTA, EGEUS, *and
train.*

THE. Go, one of you, find out the forester;
For now our observation is perform'd;
And since we have the vaward of the day,
My love shall hear the music of my hounds:
Uncouple in the western valley; let them
go:
Despatch, I say, and find the forester.—
[*Exit an* Attendant.
We will, fair queen, up to the mountain's
And mark the musical confusion   [top,
Of hounds and echo in conjunction.
HIP. I was with Hercules and Cadmus
once,
When in a wood of Crete they bay'd the
bear
With hounds of Sparta: never did I hear
Such gallant chiding; for, besides the
groves,
The skies, the fountains, every region near
Seem'd all one mutual cry: I never heard
So musical a discord, such sweet thunder.
THE. My hounds are bred out of the
Spartan kind,
So flew'd, so sanded; and their heads are
hung
With ears that sweep away the morning
dew;
Crook-knee'd, and dew-lapp'd like Thes-
salian bulls;
Slow in pursuit, but match'd in mouth like
bells,
Each under each. A cry more tuneable
Was never holla'd to, nor cheer'd with horn,
In Crete, in Sparta, nor in Thessaly:
Judge, when you hear.—But soft! what
nymphs are these?
EGE. My lord, this is my daughter here
asleep;
And this, Lysander; this Demetrius is;
This Helena, old Nedar's Helena:
I wonder of their being here together.

THE. No doubt they rose up early to observe
The rite of May; and, hearing our intent,
Came here in grace of our solemnity.—
But speak, Egeus; is not this the day
That Hermia should give answer of her choice?
EGE. It is, my lord.   [with their horns.
THE. Go, bid the huntsmen wake them
[*Exit an* Attendant. *Horns, and shout within.* LYSANDER, DEMETRIUS, HERMIA, *and* HELENA, *awake and start up.*
Good-morrow, friends. Saint Valentine is past:
Begin these wood-birds but to couple now?
LYS. Pardon, my lord.
                    [*He and the rest kneel.*
THE.   I pray you all, stand up.
I know you two are rival enemies:
How comes this gentle concord in the world,
That hatred is so far from jealousy,
To sleep by hate, and fear no enmity?
LYS. My lord, I shall reply amazedly,
Half sleep, half waking: but as yet, I swear,
I cannot truly say how I came here;
But, as I think, (for truly would I speak,—
And now I do bethink me, so it is)
I came with Hermia hither: our intent
Was to be gone from Athens, where we might,
Without the peril of the Athenian law—
EGE. Enough, enough, my lord; you have enough:
I beg the law, the law, upon his head.—
They would have stol'n away; they would,
Demetrius,
Thereby to have defeated you and me,
You of your wife, and me of my consent,—
Of my consent that she should be your wife.
DEM. My lord, fair Helen told me of their stealth,
Of this their purpose hither to this wood;
And I in fury hither follow'd them,
Fair Helena in fancy following me.
But, my good lord, I wot not by what power,
(But by some power it is,) my love to Hermia,
Melted as the snow, seems to me now
As the remembrance of an idle gawd,
Which in my childhood I did dote upon;
And all the faith, the virtue of my heart,
The object, and the pleasure of mine eye,
Is only Helena. To her, my lord,
Was I betroth'd ere I saw Hermia:
But, like in sickness, did I loath this food;
But, as in health, come to my natural taste,
Now do I wish it, love it, long for it,
And will for evermore be true to it.

THE. Fair lovers, you are fortunately met:
Of this discourse we more will hear anon.—
Egeus, I will overbear your will;
For in the temple, by and by, with us,
These couples shall eternally be knit.
And, for the morning now is something worn,
Our purpos'd hunting shall be set aside.
Away, with us, to Athens: three and three,
We'll hold a feast in great solemnity.—
Come, Hippolyta.
          [*Exeunt* THESEUS, HIPPOLYTA, EGEUS, *and train.*
DEM. These things seem small and undistinguishable,
Like far-off mountains turned into clouds.
HER. Methinks I see these things with parted eye,
When every thing seems double.
HEL.   So methinks:
And I have found Demetrius, like a jewel,
Mine own, and not mine own.
DEM.   Are you sure
That we are awake? It seems to me
That yet we sleep, we dream.—Do not you think
The duke was here, and bid us follow him?
HER. Yea; and my father.
HEL.   And Hippolyta.
LYS. And he did bid us follow to the temple.
DEM. Why then, we are awake: let's follow him;
And by the way let us recount our dreams.
          [*Exeunt* LYS. DEM. HER. *and* HEL.
BOT. [*Awaking.*] When my cue comes, call me, and I will answer:—my next is, "Most fair Pyramus."—Hey, ho!—Peter Quince! Flute, the bellows-mender! Snout, the tinker! Starveling!—God's my life! stolen hence, and left me asleep! I have had a most rare vision. I have had a dream, —past the wit of man to say what dream it was: man is but an ass, if he go about to expound this dream. Methought I was —there is no man can tell what. Methought I was, and methought I had,—but man is but a patched fool, if he will offer to say what methought I had. The eye of man hath not heard, the ear of man hath not seen, man's hand is not able to taste, his tongue to conceive, nor his heart to report, what my dream was. I will get Peter Quince to write a ballad of this dream: it shall be called Bottom's Dream, because it hath no bottom; and I will sing it in the latter end of a play, before the duke: peradventure, to make it the more gracious, I shall sing it at her death.
          [*Exit.*

SCENE II.—ATHENS. *A Room in* QUINCE'S
House.

Enter QUINCE, FLUTE, SNOUT, *and*
STARVELING.

QUIN. Have you sent to Bottom's house?
is he come home yet?

STAR. He cannot be heard of. Out of
doubt, he is transported.

FLU. If he come not, then the play is
marred: it goes not forward, doth it?

QUIN. It is not possible: you have not a
man in all Athens able to discharge Pyramus but he.

FLU. No, he hath simply the best wit of
any handycraft man in Athens.

QUIN. Yea, and the best person too; and
he is a very paramour for a sweet voice.

FLU. You must say, paragon: a paramour
is, God bless us! a thing of naught.

Enter SNUG.

SNUG. Masters, the duke is coming from
the temple, and there is two or three lords
and ladies more married: if our sport had
gone forward, we had all been made men.

FLU. O sweet bully Bottom! Thus hath
he lost sixpence a-day during his life; he
could not have 'scaped sixpence a-day: an
the duke had not given him sixpence a-day
for playing Pyramus, I'll be hanged; he
would have deserved it: sixpence a-day in
Pyramus, or nothing.

Enter BOTTOM.

BOT. Where are these lads? where are
these hearts?

QUIN. Bottom!—O most courageous day!
O most happy hour!

BOT. Masters, I am to discourse wonders:
but ask me not what; for if I tell you, I
am no true Athenian. I will tell you
everything, right as it fell out.

QUIN. Let us hear, sweet Bottom.

BOT. Not a word of me. All that I will
tell you is, that the duke hath dined. Get
your apparel together, good strings to your
beards, new ribbons to your pumps; meet
presently at the palace; every man look
o'er his part; for the short and the long
is, our play is preferred. In any case, let
Thisby have clean linen; and let not him
that plays the lion pare his nails, for they
shall hang out for the lion's claws. And,
most dear actors, eat no onions nor garlick,
for we are to utter sweet breath; and I
do not doubt but to hear them say, it is a
sweet comedy. No more words: away! go;
away!   [*Exeunt.*

ACT V.

SCENE I.—ATHENS. *An Apartment in the
Palace of* THESEUS.

Enter THESEUS, HIPPOLYTA, PHILOSTRATE,
LORDS, *and* Attendants.

HIP. 'Tis strange, my Theseus, that these
lovers speak of.

THE. More strange than true: I never may
believe
These antique fables, nor these fairy toys.
Lovers and madmen, have such seething
brains,
Such shaping fantasies, that apprehend
More than cool reason ever comprehends.
The lunatic, the lover, and the poet,
Are of imagination all compact:—
One sees more devils than vast hell can
hold,—
That is, the madman: the lover, all as
frantic,
Sees Helen's beauty in a brow of Egypt:
The poet's eye, in a fine frenzy rolling,
Doth glance from heaven to earth, from
earth to heaven;
And, as imagination bodies forth
The forms of things unknown, the poet's
pen
Turns them to shapes, and gives to airy
nothing
A local habitation and a name.
Such tricks hath strong imagination,
That, if it would but apprehend some joy,
It comprehends some bringer of that joy;
Or in the night, imagining some fear,
How easy is a bush suppos'd a bear!

HIP. But all the story of the night told
over,
And all their minds transfigur'd so together,
More witnesseth than fancy's images,
And grows to something of great con-
stancy;
But, howsoever, strange and admirable.

THE. Here come the lovers, full of joy
and mirth.

Enter LYSANDER, DEMETRIUS, HERMIA *and*
HELENA.

Joy, gentle friends! joy, and fresh days of
love,
Accompany your hearts!

LYS.   More than to us
Wait in your royal walks, your board,
your bed!

THE. Come now; what masks, what
dances shall we have,
To wear away this long age of three hours,
Between our after-supper, and bed-time?
Where is our usual manager of mirth?
What revels are in hand? Is there no play,
To ease the anguish of a torturing hour?
Call Philostrate.

PHILOST.   Here, mighty Theseus.

THE. Say, what abridgment have you for
this evening?

What mask? what music? How shall we
beguile
The lazy time, if not with some delight?
PHILOST. There is a brief how many
sports are ripe:
Make choice of which your highness will
see first. [*Giving a paper.*
THE. [*Reads.*] "The battle with the Cen-
taurs, to be sung
By an Athenian eunuch to the harp."—
We'll none of that: that have I told my
love,
In glory of my kinsman Hercules.—
Reads.] "The riot of the tipsy Bacchanals,
Tearing the Thracian singer in their
rage."—
That is an old device; and it was play'd
When I from Thebes came last a con-
queror.—
Reads.] "The thrice three Muses mourn-
ing for the death
Of learning, late deceas'd in beggary."—
That is some satire, keen and critical,
Not sorting with a nuptial ceremony.—
Reads.] "A tedious brief scene of young
Pyramus,
And his love Thisbe; very tragical
mirth."—
Merry and tragical! Tedious and brief!
That is, hot ice and wondrous strange
snow.
How shall we find the concord of this dis-
cord?
PHILOST. A play there is, my lord,
some ten words long,
Which is as brief as I have known a play;
But by ten words, my lord, it is too long,
Which makes it tedious; for in all the play
There is not one word apt, one player
fitted:
And tragical, my noble lord, it is;
For Pyramus therein doth kill himself.
Which, when I saw rehears'd, I must con-
fess,
Made mine eyes water; but more merry
tears
The passion of loud laughter never shed.
THE. What are they that do play it?
PHILOST. Hard-handed men, that work
in Athens here,
Which never labour'd their minds till now;
And now have toil'd their unbreath'd mem-
ories
With this same play, against your nuptial.
THE. And we will hear it.
PHILOST. No, my lord;
It is not for you: I have heard it over,
And it is nothing, nothing in the world;
Unless you can find sport in their intents,
Extremely stretch'd and conn'd with cruel
To do you service. [pain,

THE. I will hear that play;
For never any thing can be amiss,
When simpleness and duty tender it.
Go, bring them in:—and take your places,
ladies. [*Exit* PHILOSTRATE.
HIP. I love not to see wretchedness o'er-
charg'd,
And duty in his service perishing.
THE. Why, gentle sweet, you shall see
no such thing.
HIP. He says they can do nothing in this
kind.
THE. The kinder we, to give them thanks
for nothing.
Our sport shall be to take what they mis-
take:
And what poor duty cannot do,
Noble respect takes it in might, not merit.
Where I have come, great clerks have pur-
posed
To greet me with premeditated welcomes;
Where I have seen them shiver and look
pale,
Make periods in the midst of sentences,
Throttle their practis'd accent in their
fears,
And, in conclusion, dumbly have broke off,
Not paying me a welcome. Trust me,
sweet,
Out of this silence, yet, I pick'd a wel-
come;
And in the modesty of fearful duty
I read as much, as from the rattling tongue
Of saucy and audacious eloquence.
Love, therefore, and tongue-tied simplicity,
In least speak most, to my capacity.
Enter PHILOSTRATE.
PHILOST. So please your grace, the pro-
logue is addrest.
THE. Let him approach.
[*Flourish of trumpets.*
Enter PROLOGUE.
PROL. "If we offend, it is with our good
will.
That you should think, we come not to
offend,
But with good-will. To show our simple
skill,
That is the true beginning of our end.
Consider, then, we come but in despite.
We do not come as minding to content
you,
Our true intent is. All for your delight,
We are not here. That you should here
repent you,
The actors are at hand; and, by their show,
You shall know all, that you are like to
know."
THE. This fellow doth not stand upon
points.
LYS. He hath rid his prologue like a

rough colt; he knows not the stop. A good moral, my lord: it is not enough to speak, but to speak true.

HIP. Indeed, he hath played on his prologue, like a child on a recorder; a sound, but not in government.

THE. His speech was like a tangled chain; nothing impaired, but all disordered. Who is next?

Enter PYRAMUS *and* THISBE, Wall, Moonshine, *and* Lion, *as in dumb show.*

PROL. "Gentles, perchance you wonder at this show;
But wonder on, till truth make all things plain.
This man is Pyramus, if you would know;
This beauteous lady Thisby is, certain.
This man, with lime and rough-cast, doth present
Wall, that vile wall which did these lovers sunder;
And through wall's chink, poor souls, they are content
To whisper; at the which let no man wonder.
This man, with lantern, dog, and bush of thorn,
Presenteth moonshine; for, if you will know,
By moonshine did these lovers think no scorn
To meet at Ninus' tomb, there, there to woo.
This grisly beast, which lion hight by name,
The trusty Thisby, coming first by night,
Did scare away, or rather did affright;
And, as she fled, her mantle she did fall,
Which lion vile with bloody mouth did stain.
Anon comes Pyramus, sweet youth and tall,
And finds his trusty Thisby's mantle slain:
Whereat, with blade, with bloody blameful blade
He bravely broach'd his boiling bloody breast;
And Thisby, tarrying in mulberry shade,
His dagger drew, and died. For all the rest,
Let lion, moonshine, wall, and lovers twain,
At large discourse, while here they do remain."

[*Exeunt Prol.* THISBE, Lion, *and* Moonshine.

THE. I wonder, if the lion be to speak.

DEM. No wonder, my lord: One lion may, when many asses do.

WALL. "In this same interlude it doth befall,

That I, one Snout by name, present a wall;
And such a wall, as I would have you think,
That had in it a cranny'd hole or chink,
Through which the lovers, Pyramus and Thisby,
Did whisper often very secretly.
This lime, this rough-cast, and this stone, doth show
That I am that same wall; the truth is so:
And this the cranny is, right and sinister,
Through which the fearful lovers are to whisper."

THE. Would you desire lime and hair to speak better?

DEM. It is the wittiest partition that ever I heard discourse, my lord.

THE. Pyramus draws near the wall: silence!

Enter PYRAMUS.

PYR. "O grim-look'd night! O night with hue so black!
O night, which ever art when day is not!
O night, O night! alack, alack, alack!
I fear my Thisby's promise is forgot!—
And thou, O wall, O sweet, O lovely wall,
That stand'st between her father's ground and mine;
Thou wall, O wall, O sweet, and lovely wall,
Show me thy chink to blink through with mine eyne!
[*Wall holds up his fingers.*
Thanks, courteous wall: Jove shield thee well for this!
But what see I? No Thisby do I see.
O wicked wall, through whom I see no bliss!
Curst be thy stones for thus deceiving me!"

THE. The wall, methinks, being sensible, should curse again.

PYR. No, in truth, Sir, he should not. "Deceiving me," is Thisby's cue: she is to enter now, and I am to spy her through the wall. You shall see, it will fall pat as I told you.—Yonder she comes.

Enter THISBE.

THIS. "O wall, full often hast thou heard my moans,
For parting my fair Pyramus and me!
My cherry lips have often kiss'd thy stones,
Thy stones with lime and hair knit up in thee."

PYR. "I see a voice: now will I to the chink,
To spy an I can hear my Thisby's face.—
Thisby!"

THIS. "My love! thou art my love, I think."

PYR. "Think what thou wilt, I am thy
lover's grace;
And, like Limander, am I trusty still."
THIS. "And I like Helen, till the fates
me kill."
PYR. "Not Shafalus to Procrus was so
true."
THIS. "As Shafalus to Procrus, I to you."
PYR. "O! kiss me through the hole of
this vile wall!"
THIS. "I kiss the wall's hole, not your lips
at all."
PYR. "Wilt thou at Ninny's tomb meet
me straightway?"
THIS. "'Tide life, 'tide death, I come
without delay."

[*Exeunt* PYRAMUS *and* THISBE.

WALL. "Thus have I, wall, my part dis-
charged so;
And, being done, thus wall away doth go."
[*Exit.*

THE. Now is the mural down between the
two neighbours.
DEM. No remedy, my lord, when walls
are so wilful to hear without warning.
HIP. This is the silliest stuff that ever I
heard.
THE. The best in this kind are but
shadows; and the worst are no worse, if
imagination amend them.
HIP. It must be your imagination then,
and not theirs.
THE. If we imagine no worse of them
than they of themselves, they may pass for
excellent men.—Here come two noble
beasts in, a moon and a lion.

Enter Lion *and* Moonshine.

LION. "You, ladies, you, whose gentle
hearts do fear
The smallest monstrous mouse that creeps
on floor,
May now perchance both quake and
tremble here,
When lion rough in wildest rage doth
roar.
Then know that I, one Snug the joiner, am
No lion fell, nor else no lion's dam;
For, if I should as lion come in strife
Into this place, 'twere pity of my life."
THE. A very gentle beast, and of a good
conscience.
DEM. The very best at a beast, my lord,
that e'er I saw.
LYS. This lion is a very fox for his valour.
THE. True; and a goose for his discretion.
DEM. Not so, my lord; for his valour
cannot carry his discretion; and the fox
carries the goose.
THE. His discretion, I am sure, cannot
carry his valour; for the goose carries not

the fox. It is well: leave it to his discretion, and let us listen to the moon.
MOON. "This lantern doth the horned
moon present;'—
DEM. He should have worn the horns on
his head.
THE. He is no crescent, and his horns
are invisible within the circumference.
MOON. "This lantern doth the horned
moon present;
Myself the man i' the moon do seem to be."
THE. This is the greatest error of all the
rest: the man should be put into the lantern. How is it else the man i' the moon?
DEM. He dares not come there for the
candle; for, you see, it is already in snuff.
HIP. I am aweary of this moon: would
he would change!
THE. It appears, by his small light of
discretion, that he is in the wane; but yet,
in courtesy, in all reason, we must stay
the time.
LYS. Proceed, moon.
MOON. All that I have to say, is, to tell
you that the lantern is the moon; I, the
man in the moon; this thorn-bush, my
thorn-bush; and this dog, my dog.
DEM. Why, all these should be in the
lantern; for all these are in the moon.
But, silence! here comes Thisbe.

Enter THISBE.

THIS. "This is old Ninny's tomb. Where
is my love?"
LION. [*Roaring.*] "Oh—."
[THISBE *runs off.*

DEM. Well roared, lion.
THE. Well run, Thisbe.
HIP. Well shone, moon.—Truly, the moon
shines with a good grace.
[*The* Lion *tears* THISBE'S *mantle, and exit.*
THE. Well moused, lion.
DEM. And then came Pyramus.
LYS. And so the lion vanished.

Enter PYRAMUS.

PYR. "Sweet moon, I thank thee for thy
sunny beams;
I thank thee, moon, for shining now so
bright;
For, by thy gracious, golden, glittering
streams,
I trust to taste of truest Thisby's sight.

But stay,—O spite!—
But mark, poor knight,
What dreadful dole is here!
Eyes, do you see?
How can it be?
O dainty duck! O dear!
Thy mantle good,
What, stain'd with blood?

Approach, ye furies fell!
    O fates, come, come,
    Cut thread and thrum;
Quail, crush, conclude, and quell!"

THE. This passion, and the death of a
dear friend would go near to make a man
look sad.

HIP. Beshrew my heart, but I pity the
man.

PYR. "O wherefore, nature, didst thou
lions frame?
Since lion vile hath here deflower'd my
    dear:
Which is—no, no—which was the fairest
    dame
That liv'd, that lov'd, that lik'd, that
    look'd with cheer
    Come, tears, confound;
    Out, sword, and wound
The pap of Pyramus,—
    Ay, that left pap,
    Where heart doth hop:—
              [*Stabs himself.*
Thus die I, thus, thus, thus!
    Now am I dead,
    Now am I fled;
My soul is in the sky:
    Tongue, lose thy light!
    Moon, take thy flight!
            [*Exit Moonshine.*
Now die, die, die, die, die."   [*Dies.*

DEM. No die, but an ace, for him; for
he is but one.

LYS. Less than an ace, man; for he is
dead; he is nothing.

THE. With the help of a surgeon, he
might yet recover, and prove an ass.

HIP. How chance moonshine is gone, before Thisbe comes back and finds her
lover?

THE. She will find him by starlight.—
Here she comes; and her passion ends the
play.

Re-enter THISBE.

HIP. Methinks she should not use a long
one for such a Pyramus: I hope she will
be brief.

DEM. A mote will turn the balance, which
Pyramus, which Thisbe, is the better; he
for a man, God warrant us,—she for a woman, God bless us.

LYS. She hath spied him already with
those sweet eyes.

DEM. And thus she moans, *videlicet:*—

THIS. "Asleep, my love?
    What, dead, my dove?
    O Pyramus, arise!
    Speak, speak. Quite dumb?
    Dead, dead? A tomb

Must cover thy sweet eyes.
    These lily lips,
    This cherry nose,
These yellow cowslip cheeks,
    Are gone, are gone:
    Lovers, make moan:
His eyes were green as leeks.
    O, sisters three,
    Come, come to me,
With hands as pale as milk;
    Lay them in gore,
    Since you have shore
With shears his thread of silk.
    Tongue, not a word:
    Come, trusty sword;
Come, blade, my breast imbrue:
            [*Stabs herself.*
    And farewell, friends,—
    Thus Thisby ends,—
Adieu, adieu, adieu."   [*Dies.*

THE. Moonshine and Lion are left to
bury the dead.

DEM. Ay, and Wall too.

BOT. No, I assure you; the wall is down
that parted their fathers. Will it please
you to see the epilogue, or to hear a Bergomask dance between two of our company?

THE. No epilogue, I pray you; for your
play needs no excuse. Never excuse; for
when the players are all dead, there need
none to be blamed. Marry, if he that writ
it, had play'd Pyramus, and hanged himself
in Thisbe's garter, it would have been a
fine tragedy; and so it is, truly; and very
notably discharged. But come, your Bergomask: let your epilogue alone.   [*A dance.*
The iron tongue of midnight hath told
    twelve:—
Lovers, to bed; 'tis almost fairy time.
I fear we shall out-sleep the coming morn,
As much as we this night have overwatch'd.
This palpable gross play hath well beguil'd
The heavy gait of night.—Sweet friends, to
    bed.—
A fortnight hold we this solemnity,
In nightly revels, and new jollity.
                [*Exeunt.*

SCENE II.

Enter PUCK.

PUCK. Now the hungry lion roars,
    And the wolf behowls the moon;
Whilst the heavy ploughman snores,
    All with weary task fordone.
Now the wasted brands do glow,
    Whilst the screech-owl, screeching
        loud,
Puts the wretch that lies in woe,
    In remembrance of a shroud.

Now it is the time of night,
  that the graves, all gaping wide
Every one lets forth his sprite,
  In the church-way paths to glide:
And we fairies, that do run
  By the triple Hecate's team,
From the presence of the sun,
  Following darkness like a dream,
Now are frolic: not a mouse
Shall disturb this hallow'd house:
I am sent, with broom, before,
To sweep the dust behind the door.

Enter OBERON *and* TITANIA, *with their
    train.*

OBE. Through the house give glimmering
    light,
  By the dead and drowsy fire:
Every elf, and fairy sprite,
  Hop as light as bird from brier;
And this ditty, after me,
Sing, and dance it trippingly.

TITA. First, rehearse your song by rote,
  To each word a warbling note:
Hand in hand, with fairy grace,
Will we sing, and bless this place.
                      [*Song and dance.*

OBE. Now, until the break of day,
  Through this house each fairy stray.
To the best bride-bed will we,
  Which by us shall blessed be;
And the issue there create
Ever shall be fortunate.

So shall all the couples three
Ever true in loving be;
And the blots of nature's hand
Shall not in their issue stand;
Never mole, hare-lip, nor scar,
Nor mark prodigious, such as are
Despised in nativity,
Shall upon their children be.
With this field-dew consecrate,
Every fairy take his gait;
And each several chamber bless,
Through this palace, with sweet peace:
Ever shall in safety rest,
And the owner of it blest.
Trip away; make no stay;
Meet me all by break of day.
        [*Exeunt* OBERON, TITANIA, *and train.*

PUCK. If we shadows have offended,
Think but this, (and all is mended,)
That you have but slumber'd here,
While these visions did appear.
And this weak and idle theme,
No more yielding but a dream,
Gentles, do not reprehend:
If you pardon, we will mend.
And, as I'm an honest Puck,
If we have unearned luck
Now to 'scape the serpent's tongue,
We will make amends ere long;
Else the Puck a liar call:
So, good night unto you all.
Give me your hands, if we be friends,
And Robin shall restore amends. [*Exit.*

"All that glistens is not gold." Act II. S. 7.

MERCHANT OF VENICE

DRAMATIS PERSONÆ.

DUKE OF VENICE.
PRINCE OF MOROCCO, } *Suitors to* PORTIA.
PRINCE OF ARRAGON, }
ANTONIO, *the Merchant of* Venice.
BASSANIO, *his kinsman and friend.*
GRATIANO, } *Friends to* ANTONIO
SOLANIO, } *and* BASSANIO.
SALARINO, }
LORENZO, *in love with* JESSICA.
SHYLOCK, *a Jew.*
TUBAL, *a Jew, his friend.*
LAUNCELOT GOBBO, *a Clown, servant to*
SHYLOCK, *afterwards to* BASSANIO.

Old GOBBO, *Father to* LAUNCELOT.
LEONARDO, *Servant to* BASSANIO.
BALTHAZAR, } *Servants to* PORTIA.
STEPHANO, }

PORTIA, *a rich Heiress.*
NERISSA, *her Waiting-maid.*
JESSICA, *daughter to* SHYLOCK.

Magnificoes of Venice, Officers of the Court
of Justice, Gaoler, Servants, *and other*
Attendants.

SCENE,—*Partly at* VENICE, *and partly at* BELMONT, *the seat of Portia, on the Continent.*

ACT I.

SCENE I.—VENICE. *A Street.*

Enter ANTONIO, SALARIO, *and* SOLANIO.

ANT. In sooth, I know not why I am so
sad
It wearies me; you say it wearies you;
But how I caught it, found it, or came by it,
What stuff 'tis made of, whereof it is born,
I am to learn;
And such a want-wit sadness makes of me,
That I have much ado to know myself.

SALAR. Your mind is tossing on the
ocean;
There, where your argosies with portly
sail,—
Like signiors and rich burghers on the
flood,
Or, as it were, the pageants of the sea,—
Do overpeer the petty traffickers,
That court'sy to them, do them reverence,
As they fly by them with their woven wings.
SOLAN. Believe me, Sir, had I such ven-
ture forth,

The better part of my affections would
Be with my hopes abroad. I should be still
Plucking the grass, to know where sits the
　　wind;
Peering in maps for ports, and piers, and
　　roads;
And every object that might make me fear
Misfortune to my ventures, out of doubt
Would make me sad.
SALAR.　　　My wind, cooling my broth,
Would blow me to an ague, when I thought
What harm a wind too great might do at
　　sea,
I should not see the sandy hour-glass run,
But I should think of shallows and of flats;
And see my wealthy Andrew dock'd in
　　sand,
Vailing her high top lower than her ribs,
To kiss her burial. Should I go to church,
And see the holy edifice of stone,
And not bethink me straight of dangerous
　　rocks,
Which, touching but my gentle vessel's
　　side,
Would scatter all her spices on the stream;
Enrobe the roaring waters with my silks;
And, in a word, but even now worth this,
And now worth nothing? Shall I have the
　　thought
To think on this; and shall I lack the
　　thought,
That such a thing bechanc'd would make
　　me sad?
But tell not me; I know, Antonio
Is sad to think upon his merchandize.
ANT. Believe me, no: I thank my fortune
　　for it,
My ventures are not in one bottom trusted,
Nor to one place; nor is my whole estate
Upon the fortune of this present year:
Therefore, my merchandize makes me not
　　sad.
SALAR. Why, then you are in love.
ANT.　　　　　　　Fie, fie!
SALAR. Not in love neither? Then let's
　　say, you are sad,
Because you are not merry: and 'twere as
　　easy
For you to laugh, and leap, and say you
　　are merry,
Because you are not sad. Now, by two-
　　headed Janus,
Nature hath fram'd strange fellows in her
　　time:
Some that will evermore peep through their
　　eyes,
And laugh, like parrots, at a bag-piper;
And other of such vinegar aspect,
That they'll not show their teeth in way of
　　smile,
Though Nestor swear the jest be laughable.
SOLAN. Here comes Bassanio, your most
　　noble kinsman,

Gratiano, and Lorenzo. Fare you well:
We leave you now with better company.
SALAR. I would have stay'd till I had
　　made you merry,
If worthier friends had not prevented me.
ANT. Your worth is very dear in my regard.
I take it, your own business calls on you,
And you embrace the occasion to depart.
Enter BASSANIO, LORENZO, *and* GRATIANO.
SALAR. Good morrow, my good lords.
BASS. Good signiors both, when shall we
　　laugh? Say, when?
You grow exceeding strange: must it be so?
SALAR. We'll make our leisures to attend
　　on yours.
　　　　　　[*Exeunt* SALARINO *and* SOLANIO.
LOR. My lord Bassanio, since you have
　　found Antonio,
We two will leave you: but, at dinner-time,
I pray you, have in mind where we must
BASS. I will not fail you.　　　[meet.
GRA. You look not well, signior Antonio;
You have too much respect upon the world:
They lose it that do buy it with much care:
Believe me, you are marvellously chang'd.
ANT. I hold the world but as the world,
　　Gratiano;
A stage, where every man must play a part,
And mine a sad one.
GRA.　　　　Let me play the fool:
With mirth and laughter let old wrinkles
　　come;
And let my liver rather heat with wine,
Than my heart cool with mortifying groans.
Why should a man, whose blood is warm
　　within,
Sit like his grandsire cut in alabaster?
Sleep when he wakes? and creep into the
　　jaundice
By being peevish? I tell thee what, An-
　　tonio,—
I love thee, and it is my love that speaks,—
There are a sort of men, whose visages
Do cream and mantle like a standing pond;
And do a wilful stillness entertain,
With purpose to be dress'd in an opinion
Of wisdom, gravity, profound conceit;
As who should say, "I am Sir Oracle,
And, when I ope my lips, let no dog bark!"
O my Antonio, I do know of these,
That therefore only are reputed wise,
For saying nothing; when, I am very sure,
If they should speak, would almost damn
　　those ears,
Which, hearing them, would call their
　　brothers fools.
I'll tell thee more of this another time:
But fish not, with this melancholy bait,
For this fool-gudgeon, this opinion.—
Come, good Lorenzo.—Fare ye well, awhile:
I'll end my exhortation after dinner.

LOR. Well, we will leave you, then, till
   dinner-time: [men,
I must be one of these same dumb wise
For Gratiano never lets me speak.
GRA. Well, keep me company but two
   years more,
Thou shalt not know the sound of thine own
   tongue.
ANT. Farewell: I'll grow a talker for this
   gear.
GRA. Thanks, i' faith; for silence is only
   commendable
In a neat's tongue dried, and a maid not
   vendible.
      [*Exeunt* GRATIANO *and* LORENZO.
ANT. Is that any thing now?
BASS. Gratiano speaks an infinite deal of
nothing, more than any man in all Venice.
His reasons are as two grains of wheat hid
in two bushels of chaff: you shall seek all
day ere you find them; and, when you have
them, they are not worth the search.
ANT. Well; tell me now, what lady is the
   same
To whom you swore a secret pilgrimage,
That you to-day promis'd to tell me of?
BASS. 'Tis not unknown to you, Antonio,
How much I have disabled mine estate,
By something showing a more swelling port
Than my faint means would grant con-
   tinuance:
Nor do I now make moan to be abridg'd
From such a noble rate; but my chief care
Is, to come fairly off from the great debts,
Wherein my time, something too prodigal,
Hath left me gag'd. To you, Antonio,
I owe the most, in money and in love;
And from your love I have a warranty
To unburthen all my plots and purposes,
How to get clear of all the debts I owe.
ANT. I pray you, good Bassanio, let me
   know it;
And if it stand, as you yourself still do,
Within the eye of honour, be assur'd,
My purse, my person, my extremest means,
Lie all unlock'd to your occasions.
BASS. In my school-days, when I had lost
   one shaft,
I shot his fellow of the self-same flight
The self-same way with more advised watch,
To find the other forth; and by adventuring
   both,
I oft found both: I urge this childhood
   proof,
Because what follows is pure innocence.
I owe you much; and, like a wilful youth,
That which I owe is lost: but if you please
To shoot another arrow that self way
Which you did shoot the first, I do not
   doubt.
As I will watch the aim, or to find both,

Or bring your latter hazard back again,
And thankfully rest debtor for the first.
ANT. You know me well; and herein
   spend but time,
To wind about my love with circumstance;
And out of doubt you do me now more
   wrong
In making question of my uttermost,
Than if you had made waste of all I have:
Then do but say to me what I should do,
That in your knowledge may by me be
   done,
And I am prest unto it: therefore, speak.
BASS. In Belmont is a lady richly left;
And she is fair, and, fairer than that word,
Of wondrous virtues: sometimes from her
   eyes
I did receive fair speechless messages:
Her name is Portia; nothing undervalu'd
To Cato's daughter, Brutus' Portia:
Nor is the wide world ignorant of her
   worth;
For the four winds blow in from every coast
Renowned suitors: and her sunny locks
Hang on her temples like a golden fleece;
Which makes her seat of Belmont Colchos'
   strand,
And many Jasons come in quest of her.
O my Antonio! had I but the means
To hold a rival place with one of them,
I have a mind presages me such thrift,
That I should questionless be fortunate.
ANT. Thou know'st that all my fortunes
   are at sea;
Neither have I money, nor commodity
To raise a present sum: therefore go forth;
Try what my credit can in Venice do:
That shall be rack'd, even to the uttermost,
To furnish thee to Belmont, to fair Portia.
Go, presently enquire, and so will I,
Where money is; and I no question make,
To have it of my trust, or for my sake.
                 [*Exeunt.*

SCENE II.—BELMONT. *A Room in
      *PORTIA'S *Mansion.*

    Enter PORTIA *and* NERISSA.

POR. By my troth, Nerissa, my little body
is aweary of this great world.
NER. You would be, sweet madam, if
your miseries were in the same abundance
as your good fortunes are: and yet, for
aught I see, they are as sick that surfeit
with too much, as they that starve with
nothing: it is no mean happiness, therefore,
to be seated in the mean: superfluity comes
sooner by white hairs; but competency lives
longer.
POR. Good sentences, and well pronounced.

NER. They would be better, if well followed.

POR. If to do were as easy as to know what were good to do, chapels had been churches, and poor men's cottages princes' palaces. It is a good divine that follows his own instructions: I can easier teach twenty what were good to be done, than be one of the twenty to follow mine own teaching. The brain may devise laws for the blood; but a hot temper leaps o'er a cold decree: such a hare is madness, the youth, to skip o'er the meshes of good counsel, the cripple. But this reasoning is not in the fashion to choose me a husband:—O me, the word choose! I may neither choose whom I would, nor refuse whom I dislike; so is the will of a living daughter curbed by the will of a dead father.—Is it not hard, Nerissa, that I cannot choose one, nor refuse none?

NER. Your father was ever virtuous; and holy men, at their death, have good inspirations: therefore, the lottery, that he hath devised in these three chests of gold, silver, and lead (whereof who chooses his meaning, chooses you,) will, no doubt, never be chosen by any rightly, but one whom you shall rightly love. But what warmth is here in your affection towards any of these princely suitors that are already come?

POR. I pray thee, over-name them; and as thou namest them, I will describe them; and, according to my description, level at my affection.

NER. First, there is the Neapolitan prince.

POR. Ay, that's a colt, indeed, for he doth nothing but talk of his horse; and he makes it a great appropriation to his own good parts, that he can shoe him himself. I am much afraid, my lady his mother played false with a smith.

NER. Then is there the count Palatine.

POR. He doth nothing but frown; as who should say, "An you will not have me, choose." He hears merry tales, and smiles not: I fear he will prove the weeping philosopher when he grows old, being so full of unmannerly sadness in his youth. I had rather be married to a death's head with a bone in his mouth, than to either of these: —God defend me from these two!

NER. How say you by the French lord, Monsieur Le Bon?

POR. God made him, and therefore let him pass for a man. In truth, I know it is a sin to be a mocker: but, he!—why, he hath a horse better than the Neapolitan's; a better bad habit of frowning than the count Palatine: he is every man in no man; if a throstle sing, he falls straight a capering: he will fence with his own shadow.

If I should marry him, I should marry twenty husbands. If he would despise me, I would forgive him; for if he love me to madness, I shall never requite him.

NER. What say you, then, to Faulconbridge, the young baron of England?

POR. You know I say nothing to him; for he understands not me, nor I him: he hath neither Latin, French, nor Italian; and you will come into the court and swear that I have a poor penny-worth in the English. He is a proper man's picture; but, alas, who can converse with a dumb show? How oddly he is suited! I think he bought his doublet in Italy, his round hose in France, his bonnet in Germany, and his behaviour every where.

NER. What think you of the Scottish lord, his neighbour?

POR. That he hath a neighbourly charity in him; for he borrowed a box of the ear of the Englishman, and swore he would pay him again when he was able: I think the Frenchman became his surety, and sealed under for another.

NER. How like you the young German, the duke of Saxony's nephew?

POR. Very vilely in the morning, when he is sober; and most vilely in the afternoon, when he is drunk: when he is best, he is a little worse than a man; and when he is worst, he is little better than a beast. An the worst fall that ever fell, I hope I shall make shift to go without him.

NER. If he should offer to choose, and choose the right casket, you should refuse to perform your father's will, if you should refuse to accept him.

POR. Therefore, for fear of the worst, I pray thee, set a deep glass of Rhenish wine on the contrary casket; for, if the devil be within, and that temptation without, I know he will choose it. I will do any thing, Nerissa, ere I will be married to a sponge.

NER. You need not fear, lady, the having any of these lords: they have acquainted me with their determinations; which is, indeed, to return to their home, and to trouble you with no more suit, unless you may be won by some other sort than your father's imposition, depending on the caskets.

POR. If I live to be as old as Sibylla, I will die as chaste as Diana, unless I be obtained by the manner of my father's will. I am glad this parcel of wooers are so reasonable; for there is not one among them but I dote on his very absence; and I pray God grant them a fair departure.

NER. Do you not remember, lady, in your father's time, a Venetian, a scholar and a

soldier, that came hither in company of
the marquis of Montferrat?

POR. Yes, yes, it was Bassanio: as I think,
so was he called.

NER. True, madam: he, of all the men
that ever my foolish eyes looked upon, was
the best deserving a fair lady.

POR. I remember him well; and I remember him worthy of thy praise.—[*Enter a Servant.*] How now! what news?

SERV. The four strangers seek for you,
madam, to take their leave: and there is a
forerunner come from a fifth, the prince of
Morocco; who brings word, the prince his
master, will be here to-night.

POR. If I could bid the fifth welcome with
so good heart, as I can bid the other four
farewell, I should be glad of his approach:
if he have the condition of a saint, and the
complexion of a devil, I had rather he
should shrive me than wive me. Come,
Nerissa.—Sirrah, go before.—Whiles we
shut the gate upon one wooer, another
knocks at the door.   [*Exeunt.*

SCENE III.—VENICE. *A public Place.*

Enter BASSANIO *and* SHYLOCK.

SHY. Three thousand ducats,—well.

BASS. Ay, Sir, for three months.

SHY. For three months,—well.

BASS. For which, as I told you, Antonio
shall be bound.

SHY. Antonio shall become bound,—well.

BASS. May you stead me? Will you
pleasure me? Shall I know your answer?

SHY. Three thousand ducats for three
months, and Antonio bound.

BASS. Your answer to that.

SHY. Antonio is a good man.

BASS. Have you heard any imputation to
the contrary?

SHY. Oh no, no, no, no;—my meaning, in
saying he is a good man, is to have you
understand me, that he is sufficient. Yet
his means are in supposition: he hath an
argosy bound to Tripolis, another to the
Indies; I understand, moreover, upon the
Rialto, he hath a third at Mexico, a fourth
for England,—and other ventures he hath
squandered abroad. But ships are but
boards, sailors but men; there be land-rats
and water-rats, land-thieves and water-
thieves,—I mean pirates; and then, there is
the peril of waters, winds, and rocks. The
man is, notwithstanding, sufficient:—three
thousand ducats:—I think, I may take his
bond.

BASS. Be assured you may.

SHY. I will be assured I may; and, that

I may be assured, I will bethink me. May
I speak with Antonio?

BASS. If it please you to dine with us.

SHY. Yes, to smell pork; to eat of the
habitation which your prophet, the Nazarite,
conjured the devil into. I will buy with
you, sell with you, talk with you, walk with
you, and so following; but I will not eat
with you, drink with you, nor pray with
you. What news on the Rialto?—Who is he
comes here?

Enter ANTONIO.

BASS. This is signior Antonio.

SHY. [*Aside.*] How like a fawning publi-
can he looks!
I hate him for he is a Christian;
But more, for that, in low simplicity,
He lends out money gratis, and brings down
The rate of usance here with us in Venice.
If I can catch him once upon the hip,
I will feed fat the ancient grudge I bear
    him.
He hates our sacred nation; and he rails,
Even there where merchants most do con-
    gregate,
On me, my bargains, and my well-won
    thrift,
Which he calls interest. Cursed be my tribe,
If I forgive him!

BASS.   Shylock, do you hear?

SHY. I am debating of my present store;
And, by the near guess of my memory,
I cannot instantly raise up the gross
Of full three thousand ducats. What of
    that?
Tubal, a wealthy Hebrew of my tribe,
Will furnish me. But soft! how many
    months
Do you desire?—[*To* ANTONIO.] Rest you
    fair, good signior;
Your worship was the last man in our
    mouths.

ANT. Shylock, albeit I neither lend nor
    borrow,
By taking, nor by giving of excess,
Yet, to supply the ripe wants of my friend,
I'll break a custom.—[*To* BASSANIO.] Is he
    yet possess'd,
How much you would?

SHY.   Ay, ay, three thousand ducats.

ANT. And for three months.

SHY. I had forgot,—three months:—[*To*
    BASS.] you told me so.
[*To* ANT.] Well then, your bond; and let
    me see,—But hear you;
Methought you said you neither lend nor
Upon advantage.   [*borrow

ANT.   I do never use it.

SHY. When Jacob graz'd his uncle Laban's
    sheep,—
This Jacob from our holy Abraham was

(As his wise mother wrought in his behalf,)
The third possessor;—ay, he was the third,—

ANT. And what of him? did he take interest?

SHY. No, not take interest; not, as you would say,
Directly, interest:—mark what Jacob did.
When Laban and himself were compromis'd
That all the eanlings which were streak'd and pied
Should fall as Jacob's hire, the ewes, being rank,
In end of autumn turned to the rams;
And when the work of generation was
Between these woolly breeders in the act,
The skilful shepherd peel'd me certain wands,
And, in the doing of the deed of kind,
He stuck them up before the fulsome ewes,
Who, then conceiving, did in eaning time
Fall party-colour'd lambs, and those were Jacob's.
This was a way to thrive, and he was blest:
And thrift is blessing if men steal it not.

ANT. This was a venture, Sir, that Jacob serv'd for;
A thing not in his power to bring to pass,
But sway'd and fashion'd by the hand of heaven.
Was this inserted to make interest good?
Or is your gold and silver ewes and rams?

SHY. I cannot tell; I make it breed as fast.
But note me, signior.   [fast:—

ANT.   Mark you this, Bassanio,
The devil can cite scripture for his purpose.
An evil soul, producing holy witness,
Is like a villain with a smiling cheek;
A goodly apple rotten at the heart:
O, what a goodly outside falsehood hath!

SHY. Three thousand ducats,—'tis a good round sum.
Three months from twelve, then let me see the rate.

ANT. Well, Shylock, shall we be beholden to you?

SHY. Signior Antonio, many a time and oft
In the Rialto, you have rated me
About my monies and my usances:
Still have I borne it with a patient shrug;
For sufferance is the badge of all our tribe:
You call me misbeliever, cut-throat dog,
And spit upon my Jewish gaberdine,
And all for use of that which is mine own.
Well, then, it now appears you need my help:
Go to, then; you come to me, and you say,
"Shylock, we would have monies:"—you say so;

You, that did void your rheum upon my beard,
And foot me, as you spurn a stranger cur
Over your threshold: monies is your suit.
What should I say to you? Should I not
"Hath a dog money? Is it possible, [say
A cur can lend three thousand ducats?" or
Shall I bend low, and in a bondman's key,
With 'bated breath and whispering humble-
Say this,—   [ness,
"Fair Sir, you spit on me on Wednesday last;
You spurn'd me such a day; another time
You call'd me dog; and for these courtesies
I'll lend you thus much monies?"

ANT. I am as like to call thee so again,
To spit on thee again, to spurn thee too.
If thou wilt lend this money, lend it not
As to thy friends; (for when did friendship take
A breed for barren metal of his friend?)
But lend it rather to thine enemy;
Who if he break, thou may'st with better
Exact the penalty.   [face

SHY.   Why, look you, how you storm!
I would be friends with you, and have your love,
Forget the shames that you have stain'd me with,
Supply your present wants, and take no doit
Of usance for my monies,
And you'll not hear me: this is kind I

ANT. This were kindness.   [offer.

SHY.   This kindness will I show.—
Go with me to a notary, seal me there
Your single bond; and, in a merry sport,
If you repay me not on such a day,
In such a place, such sum or sums as are
Express'd in the condition, let the forfeit
Be nominated for an equal pound
Of your fair flesh, to be cut off and taken
In what part of your body pleaseth me.

ANT. Content, in faith: I'll seal to such a bond,
And say there is much kindness in the Jew.

BASS. You shall not seal to such a bond for me:
I'll rather dwell in my necessity.

ANT. Why, fear not, man; I will not forfeit it:
Within these two months,—that's a month before
This bond expires,—I do expect return
Of thrice three times the value of this bond.

SHY. O father Abraham! what these Christians are,
Whose own hard dealings teaches them suspect

The thoughts of others!—Pray you, tell me
this;
If he should break his day, what should I
By the exaction of the forfeiture?   [gain
A pound of man's flesh taken from a man,
Is not so estimable, profitable neither,
As flesh of muttons, beefs, or goats. I say,
To buy his favour, I extend this friendship:
If he will take it, so; if not, adieu;
And, for my love, I pray you wrong me not.
ANT. Yes, Shylock, I will seal unto this
bond.
SHY. Then meet me forthwith at the
notary's.—
Give him direction for this merry bond;
And I will go and purse the ducats straight;
See to my house, left in the fearful guard
Of an unthrifty knave; and presently
I will be with you.
ANT.   Hie thee, gentle Jew.
                [*Exit* SHYLOCK.
This Hebrew will turn Christian: he grows
kind.
BASS. I like not fair terms and a villain's
mind.
ANT. Come on: in this there can be no
dismay;
My ships come home a month before the
day.   [*Exeunt.*

ACT II.

SCENE I.—BELMONT. *A Room in* PORTIA'S
Mansion.

Flourish of cornets. Enter the PRINCE OF
MOROCCO, *and his train*; PORTIA,
NERISSA, *and other* Attendants.

MOR. Mislike me not for my complexion,
The shadow'd livery of the burnish'd sun,
To whom I am a neighbour, and near bred.
Bring me the fairest creature northward
born,
Where Phœbus' fire scarce thaws the icicles,
And let us make incision for your love,
To prove whose blood is reddest, his or
mine.
I tell thee, lady, this aspect of mine
Hath fear'd the valiant: by my love, I
swear
The best regarded virgins of our clime
Have lov'd it too: I would not change this
hue,
Except to steal your thoughts, my gentle
queen.
POR. In terms of choice I am not solely
By nice direction of a maiden's eyes;   [led
Besides, the lottery of my destiny
Bars me the right of voluntary choosing:
But, if my father had not scanted me,
And hedg'd me by his wit, to yield myself

His wife who wins me by that means I told
you,
Yourself, renowned prince, then stood as
fair
As any comer I have look'd on yet
For my affection.
MOR. Even for that I thank you:
Therefore, I pray you, lead me to the cas-
To try my fortune. By this scimitar,— [kets,
That slew the Sophy, and a Persian prince
That won three fields of Sultan Solyman,—
I would out-stare the sternest eyes that
look,
Out-brave the heart most daring on the
earth,
Pluck the young sucking cubs from the she-
bear,
Yea, mock the lion when he roars for prey,
To win thee, lady. But, alas the while!
If Hercules and Lichas play at dice
Which is the better man, the greater throw
May turn by fortune from the weaker hand:
So is Alcides beaten by his page;
And so may I, blind fortune leading me,
Miss that which one unworthier may attain,
And die with grieving.
POR.   You must take your chance;
And either not attempt to choose at all,
Or swear before you choose,—if you choose
Never to speak to lady afterward [wrong,
In way of marriage: therefore be advis'd.
MOR. Nor will not. Come, bring me unto
my chance.
POR. First, forward to the temple: after
Your hazard shall be made.   [dinner
MOR.   Good fortune then!
To make me blest or cursed'st among men!
                [*Cornets, and exeunt.*

SCENE II.—VENICE. *A Street.*
Enter LAUNCELOT GOBBO.

LAUN. Certainly, my conscience will serve
me to run from this Jew, my master. The
fiend is at mine elbow, and tempts me,
saying to me, "Gobbo, Launcelot Gobbo,
good Launcelot," or "good Gobbo," or
"good Launcelot Gobbo, use your legs, take
the start, run away." My conscience says,
"No; take heed, honest Launcelot; take
heed, honest Gobbo;" or, as aforesaid,
"honest Launcelot Gobbo; do not run;
scorn running with thy heels." Well, the
most courageous fiend bids me pack: "*Via!*"
says the fiend; "away!" says the fiend;
"for the heavens, rouse up a brave mind,"
says the fiend, "and run." Well, my conscience, hanging about the neck of my
heart, says very wisely to me, "My honest
friend Launcelot, being an honest man's
son,"—or rather an honest woman's son;

—for, indeed, my father did something smack, something grow to,—he had a kind of taste;—well, my conscience says, "Launcelot, budge not." "Budge," says the fiend. "Budge not," says my conscience. Conscience, say I, you counsel well; fiend, say I, you counsel well: to be ruled by my conscience, I should stay with the Jew my master, who (God bless the mark!) is a kind of devil; and, to run away from the Jew, I should be ruled by the fiend, who, saving your reverence, is the devil himself. Certainly, the Jew is the very devil incarnation; and, in my conscience, my conscience is but a kind of hard conscience, to offer to counsel me to stay with the Jew. The fiend gives the more friendly counsel: I will run, fiend; my heels are at your commandment; I will run.

Enter Old Gobbo, *with a basket.*

GOB. Master young man, you, I pray you, which is the way to master Jew's?

LAUN. [*Aside.*] O heavens, this is my true begotten father! who, being more than sand-blind, high-gravel blind, knows me not:—I will try confusions with him.

GOB. Master young gentleman, I pray you, which is the way to master Jew's?

LAUN. Turn up on your right hand at the next turning, but, at the next turning of all, on your left; marry, at the very next turning, turn of no hand, but turn down indirectly to the Jew's house.

GOB. By God's sonties, 'twill be a hard way to hit. Can you tell me whether one Launcelot, that dwells with him, dwell with him or no?

LAUN. Talk you of young master Launcelot?—[*Aside.*] Mark me now; now will I raise the waters.—[*To him.*] Talk you of young master Launcelot?

GOB. No master, Sir, but a poor man's son: his father, though I say it, is an honest exceeding poor man; and, God be thanked, well to live.

LAUN. Well, let his father be what a' will, we talk of young master Launcelot.

GOB. Your worship's friend, and Launcelot, Sir.

LAUN. But I pray you, *ergo,* old man, *ergo,* I beseech you, talk you of young master Launcelot?

GOB. Of Launcelot, an't please your mastership.

LAUN. Ergo, master Launcelot. Talk not of master Launcelot, father; for the young gentleman (according to fates and destinies, and such odd sayings, the sisters three, and such branches of learning,) is, indeed, deceased; or, as you would say in plain terms, gone to heaven.

GOB. Marry, God forbid! the boy was the very staff of my age, my very prop.

LAUN. [*Aside.*] Do I look like a cudgel or a hovel-post, a staff or a prop?—[*To him.*] Do you know me, father?

GOB. Alack the day! I know you not, young gentleman: but I pray you, tell me, is my boy, (God rest his soul!) alive or dead?

LAUN. Do you not know me, father?

GOB. Alack, Sir, I am sand-blind; I know you not.

LAUN. Nay, indeed, if you had your eyes, you might fail of the knowing me: it is a wise father that knows his own child. Well, old man, I will tell you news of your son. [*Kneels.*] Give me your blessing: truth will come to light; murder cannot be hid long,—a man's son may; but, in the end, truth will out.

GOB. Pray you, Sir, stand up: I am sure you are not Launcelot, my boy.

LAUN. Pray you, let's have no more fooling about it, but give me your blessing: I am Launcelot, your boy that was, your son that is, your child that shall be.

GOB. I cannot think you are my son.

LAUN. I know not what I shall think of that: but I am Launcelot, the Jew's man; and I am sure Margery, your wife, is my mother.

GOB. Her name is Margery, indeed: I'll be sworn, if thou be Launcelot, thou art mine own flesh and blood. Lord, worshipped might he be! what a beard hast thou got! thou hast got more hair on thy chin, than Dobbin my thill-horse has on his tail.

LAUN. It should seem, then, that Dobbin's tail grows backward: I am sure he had more hair of his tail, than I have of my face, when I last saw him.

GOB. Lord, how art thou changed! How dost thou and thy master agree? I have brought him a present. How 'gree you now?

LAUN. Well, well: but, for mine own part, as I have set up my rest to run away, so I will not rest till I have run some ground. My master's a ver' Jew: give him a present! give him a halter: I am famished in his service; you may tell every finger I have with my ribs. Father, I am glad you are come: give me your present to one master Bassanio, who, indeed, gives rare new liveries: if I serve not him, I will run as far as God has any ground.—O rare fortune! here comes the man:—to him, father; for I am a Jew, if I serve the Jew any longer.

Enter BASSANIO, *with* LEONARDO, *and other followers.*

BASS. You may do so;—but let it be so hasted, that supper be ready at the farthest by five of the clock. See these letters delivered; put the liveries to making; and desire Gratiano to come anon to my lodging.

[*Exit a* Servant.

LAUN. To him, father.

GOB. God bless your worship!

BASS. Gramercy: would'st thou aught with me?

GOB. Here's my son, Sir, a poor boy,—

LAUN. Not a poor boy, Sir, but the rich Jew's man; that would, Sir,—as my father shall specify,—

GOB. He hath a great infection, Sir, as one would say, to serve—

LAUN. Indeed, the short and the long is, I serve the Jew, and have a desire,—as my father shall specify,—

GOB. His master and he (saving your worship's reverence,) are scarce cater-cousins,—

LAUN. To be brief, the very truth is, that the Jew having done me wrong, doth cause me,—as my father, being, I hope, an old man, shall frutify unto you,—

GOB. I have here a dish of doves, that I would bestow upon your worship; and my suit is,—

LAUN. In very brief, the suit is impertinent to myself, as your lordship shall know by this honest old man; and, though I say it, though old man, yet, poor man, my father.

BASS. One speak for both.—What would you?

LAUN. Serve you, Sir.

GOB. That is the very defect of the matter, Sir.

BASS. I know thee well; thou hast obtain'd thy suit: [day,

Shylock, thy master, spoke with me this And hath preferr'd thee,—if it be preferment

To leave a rich Jew's service, to become The follower of so poor a gentleman.

LAUN. The old proverb is very well parted between my master Shylock and you, Sir: you have the grace of God, Sir, and he hath enough.

BASS. Thou speak'st it well.—Go, father, with thy son.—

Take leave of thy old master, and enquire My lodging out.—[*To his followers.*] Give him a livery

More guarded than his fellows': see it done.

LAUN. Father, in.—I cannot get a service, no; I have ne'er a tongue in my head. Well, [*Looking on his palm;*] if any man

in Italy have a fairer table, which doth offer to swear upon a book,—I shall have good fortune! Go to, here's a simple line of life! here's a small trifle of wives, alas, fifteen wives is nothing! eleven widows, and nine maids, is a simple coming-in for one man! and then, to 'scape drowning thrice, and to be in peril of my life with the edge of a feather-bed,—here are simple 'scapes! Well, if Fortune be a woman, she's a good wench for this gear.—Father, come; I'll take my leave of the Jew in the twinkling of an eye.

[*Exeunt* LAUNCELOT *and* Old GOBBO.

BASS. I pray thee, good Leonardo, think on this:

These things being bought, and orderly bestow'd,

Return in haste, for I do feast to-night [go,

My best-esteem'd acquaintance: hie thee,

LEON. My best endeavours shall be done herein.

Enter GRATIANO.

GRA. Where is your master?

LEON. Yonder, Sir, he walks.

GRA. Signior Bassanio,—   [*Exit.*

BASS. Gratiano!

GRA. I have a suit to you.

BASS.   You have obtain'd it.

GRA. You must not deny me: I must go with you to Belmont.

BASS. Why, then you must. But hear thee, Gratiano:

Thou art too wild, too rude, and bold of voice,—

Parts that become thee happily enough,

And in such eyes as ours appear not faults;

But where thou art not known, why, there they show   [pain

Something too liberal. Pray thee, take To allay with some cold drops of modesty Thy skipping spirit; lest, through thy wild behaviour,

I be misconstru'd in the place I go to,

And lose my hopes.

GRA.   Signior Bassanio, hear me:

If I do not put on a sober habit,   [then,

Talk with respect, and swear but now and Wear prayer-books in my pocket, look demurely;   [eyes

Nay more, while grace is saying, hood mine Thus with my hat, and sigh, and say amen; Use all the observance of civility,

Like one well studied in a sad ostent

To please his grandam,—never trust me more.

BASS. Well, we shall see your bearing.

GRA. Nay, but I bar to-night: you shall not gage me

By what we do to-night.

BASS.   No, that were pity:
I would entreat you rather to put on
Your boldest suit of mirth, for we have
  friends
That purpose merriment. But fare you
I have some business.   [well;
GRA. And I must to Lorenzo and the rest:
But we will visit you at supper-time.
                              [Exeunt.

SCENE III.—VENICE. A Room in SHYLOCK'S
          House.

      Enter JESSICA and LAUNCELOT.

JES. I am sorry thou wilt leave my father
  so:
Our house is hell; and thou, a merry devil,
Didst rob it of some taste of tediousness.
But fare thee well; there is a ducat for
  thee: [see
And, Launcelot, soon at supper shalt thou
Lorenzo, who is thy new master's guest:
Give him this letter; do it secretly;—
And so farewell: I would not have my
See me in talk with thee.   [father
LAUN. Adieu!—tears exhibit my tongue.
Most beautiful pagan,—most sweet Jew!
If a Christian do not play the knave, and
get thee, I am much deceived. But, adieu!
these foolish drops do somewhat drown
my manly spirit: adieu!
JES. Farewell, good Launcelot.—
                    [Exit LAUNCELOT.
Alack, what heinous sin is it in me,
To be asham'd to be my father's child!
But though I am a daughter to his blood,
I am not to his manners. O Lorenzo!
If thou keep promise, I shall end this
  strife,—
Become a Christian, and thy loving wife.
                              [Exit.

SCENE IV.—VENICE. A Street.

Enter GRATIANO, LORENZO, SALARINO,
        and SOLANIO.

LOR. Nay, we will slink away in supper-
  time,
Disguise us at my lodging, and return
All in an hour.
GRA. We have not made good preparation.
SALAR. We have not spoke us yet of
  torch-bearers.
SOLAN. 'Tis vile, unless it may be quaintly
  order'd,
And better, in my mind, not undertook.
LOR. 'Tis now but four o'clock: we have
To furnish us.—   [two hours
    Enter LAUNCELOT, with a letter.
  Friend Launcelot, what's the news?

LAUN. An it shall please you to break
up this, it shall seem to signify.
                    [Giving the letter.
LOR. I know the hand: in faith, 'tis a
  fair hand;
And whiter than the paper it writ on
Is the fair hand that writ.
GRA.   Love-news, in faith.
LAUN. By your leave, Sir.
LOR. Whither goest thou?
LAUN. Marry, Sir, to bid my old master,
the Jew, to sup to-night with my new mas-
ter, the Christian.
LOR. Hold here, take this:—tell gentle
  Jessica,
I will not fail her;—speak it privately;
Go.—Gentlemen,   [Exit LAUNCELOT.
Will you prepare you for this mask to-
I am provided of a torch-bearer. [night?
SALAR. Ay, marry, I'll be gone about it
SOLAN. And so will I.   [straight.
LOR.   Meet me and Gratiano
At Gratiano's lodging some hour hence.
SALAR. 'Tis good we do so.
          [Exeunt SALAR. and SOLAN.
GRA. Was not that letter from fair Jessica?
LOR. I must needs tell thee all. She hath
  directed
How I shall take her from her father's
  house;
What gold and jewels she is furnish'd
  with;
What page's suit she hath in readiness.
If e'er the Jew her father come to heaven,
It will be for his gentle daughter's sake:
And never dare misfortune cross her foot,
Unless she do it under this excuse,—
That she is issue to a faithless Jew.
Come, go with me: peruse this as thou
  goest.
Fair Jessica shall be my torch-bearer.
                              [Exeunt.

SCENE V.—VENICE. Before SHYLOCK'S
          House.

      Enter SHYLOCK and LAUNCELOT.

SHY. Well, thou shalt see; thy eyes shall
  be thy judge,   [sanio:—
The difference of old Shylock and Bas-
What, Jessica!—thou shalt not gormandize,
As thou hast done with me; — What,
  Jessica!—
And sleep and snore, and rend apparel
Why, Jessica, I say!   [out;—
LAUN.   Why, Jessica!
SHY. Who bids thee call? I do not bid
thee call.
LAUN. Your worship was wont to tell me
I could do nothing without bidding.

Enter JESSICA.

JES. Call you? What is your will?

SHY. I am bid forth to supper, Jessica:
There are my keys.—But wherefore should
I go?
I am not bid for love; they flatter me:
But yet I'll go in hate, to feed upon
The prodigal Christian.—Jessica, my girl,
Look to my house.—I am right loath to go:
There is some ill a brewing towards my
rest,
For I did dream of money-bags to-night.

LAUN. I beseech you, Sir, go: my young
master doth expect your reproach.

SHY. So do I his.

LAUN. And they have conspired together,
—I will not say you shall see a mask; but
if you do, then it was not for nothing that
my nose fell a bleeding on Black-Monday
last at six o'clock i' the morning, falling
out that year on Ash-Wednesday was four
year in the afternoon.   [me, Jessica:

SHY. What! are there masks?—Hear you
Lock up my doors; and when you hear the
drum,
And the vile squeaking of the wry-neck'd
fife,
Clamber not you up to the casements then,
Nor thrust your head into the public street
To gaze on Christian fools with varnish'd
faces;
But stop my house's ears,—I mean my
casements:
Let not the sound of shallow foppery enter
My sober house.—By Jacob's staff, I swear
I have no mind of feasting forth to-night:
But I will go.—Go you before me, sirrah;
Say I will come.

LAUN. I will go before, Sir.—[*Low, to*
JESSICA.]
Mistress, look out at window, for all this;
There will come a Christian by,
Will be worth a Jewess' eye.
                    [*Exit* LAUN.

SHY. What says that fool of Hagar's off-
spring, ha?   [nothing else.

JES. His words were, farewell, mistress;

SHY. The patch is kind enough; but a
huge feeder,
Snail-slow in profit, and he sleeps by day
More than the wild cat: drones hive not
with me;
Therefore I part with him; and part with
him
To one that I would have him help to waste
His borrow'd purse.—Well, Jessica, go in:
Perhaps I will return immediately:
Do as I bid you; shut doors after you:
Fast bind, fast find,—
A proverb never stale in thrifty mind.
                    [*Exit.*

JES. Farewell; and if my fortune be not
crost,
I have a father, you a daughter, lost. [*Exit.*

SCENE VI.—*The Same.*

Enter GRATIANO *and* SALARINO, *masked.*

GRA. This is the pent-house under which
Desir'd us to make stand.   [Lorenzo

SALAR.   His hour is almost past.

GRA. And it is marvel he out-dwells his
hour,
For lovers ever run before the clock.

SALAR. O, ten times faster Venus' pigeons
fly
To seal love's bonds new-made, than they
are wont
To keep obliged faith unforfeited!

GRA. That ever holds: who riseth from a
feast
With that keen appetite that he sits down?
Where is the horse that doth untread again
His tedious measures with the unbated fire
That he did pace them first? All things
that are,
Are with more spirit chased than enjoy'd.
How like a younker or a prodigal
The scarfed bark puts from her native bay,
Hugg'd and embraced by the strumpet
wind!
How like a prodigal doth she return,
With over-weather'd ribs and ragged sails,
Lean, rent, and beggar'd by the strumpet
wind!

SALAR. Here comes Lorenzo:—more of
this hereafter.

Enter LORENZO.

LOR. Sweet friends, your patience for my
long abode;
Not I, but my affairs, have made you wait:
When you shall please to play the thieves
for wives,
I'll watch as long for you then.—Approach;
Here dwells my father Jew.—Ho! who's
within?

Enter JESSICA *above, in boy's clothes.*

JES. Who are you? Tell me, for more
certainty,
Albeit I'll swear that I do know your

LOR. Lorenzo, and thy love.   [tongue.

JES. Lorenzo, certain; and my love, indeed,—
For whom love I so much? And now who
knows
But you, Lorenzo, whether I am yours?

LOR. Heaven and thy thoughts are witness that thou art.

JES. Here, catch this casket; it is worth
the pains.
I am glad 'tis night, you do not look on me,
For I am much asham'd of my exchange:

But love is blind, and lovers cannot see
The pretty follies that themselves commit:
For if they could, Cupid himself would
blush
To see me thus transformed to a boy.
LOR. Descend, for you must be my torch-
bearer.
JES. What, must I hold a candle to my
shames?
They in themselves, good sooth, are too too
light.
Why, 'tis an office of discovery, love;
And I should be obscur'd.
LOR.　　　　　So are you, sweet,
Even in the lovely garnish of a boy.
But come at once;
For the close night doth play the run-away,
And we are stay'd for at Bassiano's feast.
JES. I will make fast the doors, and gild
myself
With some more ducats, and be with you
straight.　　　　　　　[*Exit above.*
GRA. Now, by my hood, a Gentile, and no
Jew.
LOR. Beshrew me but I love her heartily;
For she is wise, if I can judge of her;
And fair she is, if that mine eyes be true;
And true she is, as she hath prov'd herself;
And therefore, like herself, wise, fair, and
true,
Shall she be placed in my constant soul.
　　　　　Enter JESSICA below.
What, art thou come?—On, gentlemen;
away!
Our masking mates by this time for us
stay. [*Exit with JESSICA and SALARINO.*
　　　　　Enter ANTONIO.
ANT. Who's there?
GRA. Signior Antonio?
ANT. Fie, fie, Gratiano! where are all the
rest?
'Tis nine o'clock; our friends all stay for
you.
No mask to-night: the wind is come about;
Bassanio presently will go aboard:
I have sent twenty out to seek for you.
GRA. I am glad on't: I desire no more
delight,
Than to be under sail, and gone to-night.
　　　　　　　　　　　　[*Exeunt.*

————

SCENE VII.—BELMONT. *A Room in*
PORTIA'S *Mansion.*

Flourish of cornets. Enter PORTIA, with the
PRINCE OF MOROCCO, *and their trains.*
POR. Go, draw aside the curtains, and
discover
The several caskets to this noble prince.—
Now make your choice. 　　[tion bears—
MOR. The first, of gold, who this inscrip-

"Who chooseth me shall gain what many
　men desire;"
The second, silver, which this promise car-
　ries,—
"Who chooseth me shall get as much as
　he deserves;"
This third, dull lead, with warning all as
　blunt,—
"Who chooseth me must give and hazard
　all he hath."—
How shall I know if I do choose the right?
POR. The one of them contains my pic-
　ture, prince:
If you choose that, then I am yours withal.
MOR. Some god direct my judgment! Let
　me see;
I will survey th' inscriptions back again.
What says this leaden casket?
"Who chooseth me must give and hazard
　all he hath." 　　　　　　[lead?
Must give,—For what? for lead? hazard for
This casket threatens: men that hazard all,
Do it in hope of fair advantages:
A golden mind stoops not to shows of
　dross;
I'll then nor give nor hazard aught for lead.
What says the silver, with her virgin hue?
"Who chooseth me, shall get as much as
　he deserves."
As much as he deserves!—Pause there,
　Morocco,
And weigh thy value with an even hand:
If thou be'st rated by thy estimation,
Thou dost deserve enough; and yet enough
May not extend so far as to the lady:
And yet to be afeard of my deserving
Were but a weak disabling of myself.
As much as I deserve!—Why, that's the
　lady:
I do in birth deserve her, and in fortunes,
In graces, and in qualities of breeding;
But more than these, in love I do deserve.
What if I stray'd no farther, but chose
　here?—
Let's see once more this saying grav'd in
　gold:
"Who chooseth me shall gain what many
　men desire."
Why, that's the lady; all the world desires
　her:
From the four corners of the earth they
　come,
To kiss this shrine, this mortal breathing
　saint:
The Hyrcanian deserts, and the vasty wilds
Of wide Arabia, are as through-fares now
For princes to come view fair Portia:
The wat'ry kingdom, whose ambitious head
Spits in the face of heaven, is no bar
To stop the foreign spirits; but they come,
As o'er a brook, to see fair Portia.

One of these three contains her heavenly
picture.
Is't like, that lead contains her? 'Twere
damnation
To think so base a thought: it were too
gross
To rib her cerecloth in the obscure grave.
Or shall I think in silver she's immur'd,
Being ten times undervalu'd to tried gold?
O sinful thought! Never so rich a gem
Was set in worse than gold. They have in
England
A coin, that bears the figure of an angel
Stamped in gold, — but that's insculp'd
upon;
But here an angel in a golden bed
Lies all within.—Deliver me the key:
Here do I choose, and thrive I as I may!
POR. There, take it, prince; and if my
form lie there,
Then I am yours.
                [*He opens the golden casket.*
MOR.   O hell! what have we here?
A carrion death, within whose empty eye
There is a written scroll! I'll read the
writing.
[*Reads.*] "All that glisters is not gold,—
    Often have you heard that told:
    Many a man his life hath sold,
    But my outside to behold:
    Gilded tombs do worms infold.
    Had you been as wise as bold,
    Young in limbs, in judgment old,
    Your answer had not been inscroll'd:
    Fare you well; your suit is cold."
Cold, indeed; and labour lost: [frost!—
Then,   farewell,   heat;   and   welcome,
Portia, adieu. I have too griev'd a heart
To take a tedious leave: thus losers part.
                [*Exit with his train. Cornets.*
POR. A gentle riddance.—Draw the cur-
tains: go.—
Let all of his complexion choose me so.
                                [*Exeunt.*

SCENE VIII.—VENICE. *A Street.*

Enter SALARINO *and* SOLANIO.

SALAR. Why man, I saw Bassanio under
With him is Gratiano gone along;   [sail:
And in their ship, I'm sure, Lorenzo is not.
SOLAN. The villain Jew with outcries
rais'd the duke;
Who went with him to search Bassanio's
ship.
SALAR. He came too late, the ship was
under sail:
But there the duke was given to understand,
That in a gondola were seen together
Lorenzo and his amorous Jessica.
Besides, Antonio certified the duke,

They were not with Bassanio in his ship.
SOLAN. I never heard a passion so con-
fus'd,
So strange, outrageous, and so variable,
As the dog Jew did utter in the streets:
"My daughter! — O my ducats! — O my
daughter!
Fled with a Christian!—O my Christian
ducats!—
Justice! the law! my ducats, and my
daughter!
A sealed bag, two sealed bags of ducats,
Of double ducats, stol'n from me by my
daughter!
And jewels,—two stones, two rich and
precious stones,
Stol'n by my daughter!—Justice! find the
girl!
She hath the stones upon her, and the
ducats!"
SALAR. Why, all the boys in Venice fol-
low him,
Crying,—his stones, his daughter, and his
ducats.
SOLAN. Let good Antonio look he keep
Or he shall pay for this.   [his day,
SALAR.   Marry, well remember'd.
I reason'd with a Frenchman yesterday,
Who told me,—in the narrow seas that part
The French and English, there miscarried
A vessel of our country, richly fraught:
I thought upon Antonio when he told me;
And wish'd in silence that it were not his.
SOLAN. You were best to tell Antonio
what you hear;
Yet do not suddenly, for it may grieve him.
SALAR. A kinder gentleman treads not the
earth.
I saw Bassanio and Antonio part:
Bassanio told him he would make some
speed
Of his return: he answer'd, "Do not so,—
Slubber not business for my sake, Bassanio,
But stay the very riping of the time;
And for the Jew's bond, which he hath of
me,
Let it not enter in your mind of love:
Be merry; and employ your chiefest
thoughts
To courtship, and such fair ostents of love
As shall conveniently become you there:"
And even there, his eye being big with
tears,   [him,
Turning his face, he put his hand behind
And with affection wondrous sensible,
He wrung Bassanio's hand; and so they
parted.   [for him.
SOLAN. I think, he only loves the world
I pray thee, let us go and find him out,

And quicken his embraced heaviness
With some delight or other.
SALAR.   Do we so.   [*Exeunt.*

Scene IX.—Belmont. *A Room in*
Portia's *Mansion.*
Enter Nerissa, *with a* Servant.
NER. Quick, quick, I pray thee; draw the
curtain straight:
The prince of Arragon hath ta'en his oath,
And comes to his election presently.
Flourish of cornets. Enter the Prince of
Arragon, Portia, *and their trains.*
POR. Behold, there stand the caskets,
noble prince:
If you choose that wherein I am contain'd,
Straight shall our nuptial rites be sol-
emniz'd;   [lord,
But if you fail, without more speech, my
You must be gone from hence immediately.
AR. I am enjoin'd by oath to observe
three things:—
First, never to unfold to any one
Which casket 'twas I chose; next, if I fail
Of the right casket, never in my life
To woo a maid in way of marriage; lastly,
If I do fail in fortune of my choice,
Immediately to leave you and be gone.
POR. To these injunctions every one doth
swear
That comes to hazard for my worthless self.
AR. And so have I address'd me. Fortune
now
To my heart's hope!—Gold, silver, and
base lead.
"Who chooseth me must give and hazard
all he hath."
You shall look fairer, ere I give or hazard.
What says the golden chest? ha! let me see:
"Who chooseth me shall gain what many
men desire."
What many men desire!—that many may
be meant
By the fool multitude, that choose by show,
Not learning more than the fond eye doth
teach;
Which pries not to th' interior, but, like
the martlet,
Builds in the weather, on the outward wall,
Even in the force and road of casualty.
I will not choose what many men desire,
Because I will not jump with common
spirits,
And rank me with the barbarous multitudes.
Why, then to thee, thou silver treasure-
house;
Tell me once more what title thou dost
bear:
"Who chooseth me shall get as much as
he deserves:"

And well said too; for who shall go about
To cozen fortune, and be honourable
Without the stamp of merit? Let none
presume
To wear an undeserved dignity.
O, that estates, degrees, and offices,
Were not deriv'd corruptly! and that clear
honour
Were purchas'd by the merit of the wearer!
How many then should cover, that stand
bare!
How many be commanded, that command!
How much low peasantry would then be
glean'd
From the true seed of honour! and how
much honour
Pick'd from the chaff and ruin of the
times,
To be new varnish'd! Well, but to my
choice:
"Who chooseth me shall get as much as he
deserves."   [this,
I will assume desert.—Give me a key for
And instantly unlock my fortunes here.
                    [*He opens the silver casket.*
POR. Too long a pause for that which you
find there.
AR. What's here? the portrait of a blink-
ing idiot,
Presenting me a schedule! I will read it.
How much unlike art thou to Portia!
How much unlike my hopes, and my de-
servings!
"Who chooseth me shall have as much as
he deserves."
Did I deserve no more than a fool's head?
Is that my prize? are my deserts no better?
POR. To offend, and judge, are distinct
offices,
And of opposed natures.
AR.   What is here?
[*Reads.*]
    "The fire seven times tried this.
    Seven times tried that judgment is,
    That did never choose amiss.
    Some there be that shadows kiss;
    Such have but a shadow's bliss:
    There be fools alive, I wis,
    Silver'd o'er; and so was this.
    Take what wife you will to bed,
    I will ever be your head:
    So be gone: you are sped."
    Still more fool I shall appear
    By the time I linger here:
    With one fool's head I came to woo,
    But I go away with two.—
    Sweet, adieu. I'll keep my oath,
    Patiently to bear my wroth.
                    [*Exit with his train.*
POR. Thus hath the candle sing'd the
moth.

O, these deliberate fools! when they do
choose,
They have the wisdom by their wit to lose.
NER. The ancient saying is no heresy,—
Hanging and wiving goes by destiny.
POR. Come, draw the curtain, Nerissa.
              Enter a Messenger.
MESS. Where is my lady?
POR.   Here; what would my lord?
MESS. Madam, there is alighted at your
gate
A young Venetian, one that comes before
To signify the approaching of his lord;
From whom he bringeth sensible re-
greets,—
To wit, (besides commends, and courteous
breath,)
Gifts of rich value: yet I have not seen
So likely an embassador of love.
A day in April never came so sweet,
To show how costly summer was at hand,
As this fore-spurrer comes before his lord.
POR. No more, I pray thee: I am half
afeard.
Thou wilt say anon he is some kin to thee,
Thou spend'st such high-day wit in prais-
ing him.—
Come, come, Nerissa; for I long to see
Quick Cupid's post, that comes so man-
nerly.
NER. Bassanio, lord Love, if thy will it
be!   [*Exeunt.*

ACT III.

SCENE I.—VENICE.   *A Street.*
          Enter SOLANIO *and* SALARINO.
SOLAN. Now, what news on the Rialto?
SALAR. Why, yet it lives there unchecked,
that Antonio hath a ship of rich lading
wrecked on the narrow seas; the Good-
wins, I think they call the place; a very
dangerous flat, and fatal, where the car-
casses of many a tall ship lie buried, as
they say, if my gossip, Report, be an honest woman of her word.
SOLAN. I would she were as lying a gossip in that, as ever knapped ginger, or
made her neighbours believe she wept for
the death of a third husband. But it is
true,—without any slips of prolixity, or
crossing the plain high-way of talk,—that
the good Antonio, the honest Antonio,—
O, that I had a title good enough to keep
his name company!—
SALAR. Come, the full stop.
SOLAN. Ha,—what say'st thou?—Why,
the end is, he hath lost a ship.
SALAR. I would it might prove the end
of his losses.

SOLAN. Let me say amen betimes, lest
the devil cross my prayer,—for here he
comes in the likeness of a Jew.—
              Enter SHYLOCK.
How now, Shylock! what news among the
merchants?
SHY. You knew, none so well, none so
well as you, of my daughter's flight.
SALAR. That's certain: I, for my part,
knew the tailor that made the wings she
flew withal.
SOLAN. And Shylock, for his own part,
knew the bird was fledged; and then, it is
the complexion of them all to leave the
dam.
SHY. She is damned for it.
SALAR. That's certain, if the devil may be
her judge.
SHY. My own flesh and blood to rebel!
SOLAN. Out upon it, old carrion! rebels
it at these years?
SHY. I say, my daughter is my flesh and
blood.
SALAR. There is more difference between
thy flesh and hers, than between jet and
ivory; more between your bloods, than
there is between red wine and rhenish.—
But tell us, do you hear whether Antonio
have had any loss at sea or no?
SHY. There I have another bad match: a
bankrupt, a prodigal, who dare scarce
show his head on the Rialto;—a beggar,
that used to come so smug upon the mart:
—let him look to his bond: he was wont
to call me usurer;—let him look to his
bond: he was wont to lend money for a
Christian courtesy;—let him look to his
bond.
SALAR. Why, I am sure, if he forfeit,
thou wilt not take his flesh: what's that
good for?
SHY. To bait fish withal: if it will feed
nothing else, it will feed my revenge. He
hath disgraced me, and hindered me half
a million; laughed at my losses, mocked
at my gains, scorned my nation, thwarted
my bargains, cooled my friends, heated
mine enemies; and what's his reason? I
am a Jew. Hath not a Jew eyes? hath not
a Jew hands, organs, dimensions, senses,
affections, passions? fed with the same
food, hurt with the same weapons, subject
to the same diseases, healed by the same
means, warmed and cooled by the same
winter and summer, as a Christian is? if
you prick us, do we not bleed? if you
tickle us, do we not laugh? if you poison
us, do we not die? and if you wrong us,
shall we not revenge? If we are like you
in the rest, we will resemble you in that.
If a Jew wrong a Christian, what is his

humility? revenge: if a Christian wrong
a Jew, what should his sufferance be by
Christian example? why, revenge. The villainy you teach me, I will execute; and it
shall go hard but I will better the instruction.

Enter a Servant.

SERV. Gentlemen, my master Antonio is
at his house, and desires to speak with you
both.

SALAR. We have been up and down to
seek him.

SOLAN. Here comes another of the tribe:
a third cannot be matched, unless the devil
himself turn Jew.

[*Exeunt* SOLAN. SALAR. *and* Servant.
Enter TUBAL.

SHY. How now, Tubal! what news from
Genoa? hast thou found my daughter?

TUB. I often came where I did hear of
her, but cannot find her.

SHY. Why there, there, there, there! a
diamond gone, cost me two thousand ducats
in Frankfort! The curse never fell upon
our nation till now; I never felt it till now:
—two thousand ducats in that; and other
precious, precious jewels.—I would my
daughter were dead at my foot, and the
jewels in her ear! would she were hearsed
at my foot, and the ducats in her coffin!
No news of them?—Why, so:—and I know
not what's spent in the search: Why thou
—loss upon loss! the thief gone with so
much, and so much to find the thief; and
no satisfaction, no revenge: nor no ill luck
stirring but what lights o' my shoulders;
no sighs but o' my breathing; no tears but
o' my shedding.

TUB. Yes, other men have ill luck too.
Antonio, as I heard in Genoa,—

SHY. What, what, what? ill luck, ill luck?

TUB. —hath an argosy cast away, coming from Tripolis.

SHY. I thank God! I thank God! Is it
true? is it true?

TUB. I spoke with some of the sailors that
escaped the wreck.

SHY. I thank thee, good Tubal.—Good
news, good news! ha, ha!—Where? in
Genoa?

TUB. Your daughter spent in Genoa, as I
heard, one night, fourscore ducats.

SHY. Thou stick'st a dagger in me:—I
shall never see my gold again: fourscore
ducats at a sitting! fourscore ducats!

TUB. There came divers of Antonio's
creditors in my company to Venice, that
swear he cannot choose but break.

SHY. I am very glad of it:—I'll plague
him; I'll torture him:—I am glad of it.

TUB. One of them showed me a ring, that

he had of your daughter for a monkey.

SHY. Out upon her! Thou torturest me,
Tubal: it was my turquoise; I had it of
Leah, when I was a bachelor: I would not
have given it for a wilderness of monkeys.

TUB. But Antonio is certainly undone.

SHY. Nay, that's true, that's very true.
Go, Tubal, fee me an officer; bespeak him
a fortnight before. I will have the heart
of him, if he forfeit; for, were he out of
Venice, I can make what merchandize I
will. Go, Tubal, and meet me at our
synagogue; go, good Tubal, at our synagogue, Tubal. [*Exeunt.*

SCENE II.—BELMONT. *A Room in*
PORTIA'S *Mansion.*

Enter BASSANIO, PORTIA, GRATIANO,
NERISSA, *and* Attendants.

POR. I pray you, tarry: pause a day or
two,
Before you hazard; for, in choosing wrong,
I lose your company: therefore, forbear a
while.
There's something tells me, (but it is not
love,)
I would not lose you; and you know your-
self,
Hate counsels not in such a quality.
But lest you should not understand me
well,
(And yet a maiden hath no tongue but
thought,)
I would detain you here some month or
two,
Before you venture for me. I could teach
you
How to choose right, but then I am for-
sworn;
So will I never be: so may you miss me;
But if you do, you'll make me wish a sin,
That I had been forsworn. Beshrew your
eyes,
They have o'er-look'd me, and divided me;
One half of me is yours, the other half
yours,—
Mine own, I would say; but if mine, then
yours,
And so all yours! O, these naughty times
Put bars between the owners and their
rights!
And so, though yours, not yours.—Prove
it so,
Let fortune go to hell for it,—not I.
I speak too long; but 'tis to peize the
time,
To eke it, and to draw it out in length,
To stay you from election.

BASS. Let me choose;
For, as I am, I live upon the rack.

POR. Upon the rack, Bassanio! then con-
fess
What treason there is mingled with your
love.
BASS. None but that ugly treason of mis-
trust,
Which makes me fear th' enjoying of my
love:
There may as well be amity and life
'Tween snow and fire, as treason and my
love.
POR. Ay, but I fear you speak upon the
rack,
Where men enforced do speak anything.
BASS. Promise me life, and I'll confess
the truth.
POR. Well then, confess, and live.
BASS.   Confess, and love,
Had been the very sum of my confession.
O happy torment, when my torturer
Doth teach me answers for deliverance!
But let me to my fortune and the caskets.
  [*Curtain drawn from before the caskets.*
POR. Away then. I am lock'd in one of
them:
If you do love me, you will find me out.—
Nerissa, and the rest, stand all aloof.—
Let music sound while he doth make his
choice;
Then, if he lose, he makes a swan-like end,
Fading in music: that the comparison
May stand more proper, my eye shall be
the stream,
And watery death-bed for him. He may
win;
And what is music then? then music is
Even as the flourish when true subjects
bow
To a new-crowned monarch: such it is,
As are those dulcet sounds in break of
day,
That creep into the dreaming bridegroom's
ear,
And summon him to marriage. Now he
goes,
With no less presence, but with much more
love,
Than young Alcides, when he did redeem
The virgin tribute paid by howling Troy
To the sea-monster: I stand for sacrifice;
The rest aloof are the Dardanian wives,
With bleared visages, come forth to view
The issue of th' exploit. Go, Hercules!
Live thou, I live:—with much, much more
dismay
I view the fight, than thou that mak'st the
fray.
  [*Music, and this* SONG, *whilst* BASSANIO
    comments on the caskets to himself.
    Tell me where is fancy bred,
    Or in the heart, or in the head?

How begot, how nourished?
    Reply, reply.
It is engender'd in the eyes,
With gazing fed; and fancy dies
In the cradle where it lies.
    Let us all ring fancy's knell;
    I'll begin it,—Ding, dong, bell.
All. Ding, dong, bell.
BASS. So may the outward shows be least
themselves:
The world is still deceiv'd with ornament.
In law, what plea so tainted and corrupt,
But, being season'd with a gracious voice,
Obscures the show of evil? In religion,
What damned error, but some sober brow
Will bless it, and approve it with a text,
Hiding the grossness with fair ornament?
There is no vice so simple, but assumes
Some mark of virtue on his outward parts:
How many cowards, whose hearts are all
as false
As stairs of sand, wear yet upon their chins
The beards of Hercules and frowning
Mars;
Who, inward search'd, have livers white
as milk;
And these assume but valour's excrement
To render them redoubted. Look on
beauty
And you shall see 'tis purchas'd by the
weight;
Which therein works a miracle in nature,
Making them lightest that wear most of it:
So are those crisped snaky golden locks,
Which make such wanton gambols with the
wind,
Upon supposed fairness, often known
To be the dowry of a second head,
The skull that bred them, in the sepulchre.
Thus ornament is but the guiled shore
To a most dangerous sea; the beauteous
scarf
Veiling an Indian beauty; in a word,
The seeming truth which cunning times
put on
To entrap the wisest. Therefore, thou
gaudy gold,
Hard food for Midas, I will none of thee;
Nor none of thee, thou pale and common
drudge
'Tween man and man: but thou, thou mea-
gre lead,
Which rather threat'nest than dost promise
aught,
Thy paleness moves me more than elo-
quence,
And here choose I: joy be the consequence!
POR. How all the other passions fleet to
air,—
As doubtful thoughts, and rash-embrac'd
despair,

And shuddering fear, and green-ey'd jeal-
ousy!
O love, be moderate; allay thy ecstasy;
In measure rain thy joy; scant this excess!
I feel too much thy blessing: make it less,
For fear I surfeit!
BASS.   What find I here?
        [Opening the leaden casket.
Fair Portia's counterfeit! What demi-god
Hath come so near creation? Move these
eyes?
Or whether, riding on the balls of mine,
Seem they in motion? Here are sever'd
lips,
Parted with sugar breath: so sweet a bar
Should sunder such sweet friends. Here,
in her hairs,
The painter plays the spider; and hath
woven
A golden mesh t' entrap the hearts of men,
Faster than gnats in cobwebs: but her
eyes,—
How could he see to do them? having made
one,
Methinks it should have power to steal
both his,
And leave itself unfurnish'd. Yet look,
how far
The substance of my praise doth wrong
this shadow
In underprizing it, so far this shadow
Doth limp behind the substance.—Here's
the scroll,
The continent and summary of my for-
tune.
[Reads.]
    "You that choose not by the view,
    Chance as fair, and choose as true!
    Since this fortune falls to you,
    Be content, and seek no new.
    If you be well pleas'd with this,
    And hold your fortune for your bliss,
    Turn you where your lady is,
    And claim her with a loving kiss."
A gentle scroll.—Fair lady, by your leave;
I come by note, to give, and to receive.
                        [Kissing her.
Like one of two contending in a prize,
That thinks he hath done well in people's
eyes,
Hearing applause and universal shout,
Giddy in spirit, still gazing, in a doubt
Whether those peals of praise be his or
no;
So, thrice fair lady, stand I, even so;
As doubtful whether what I see be true,
Until confirm'd, sign'd, ratified by you.
POR. You see me, lord Bassanio, where I
stand,
Such as I am: though for myself alone
I would not be ambitious in my wish,
To wish myself much better; yet, for you
I would be trebled twenty times myself;
A thousand times more fair, ten thousand
times more rich;
That only to stand high in your account,
I might in virtues, beauties, livings, friends,
Exceed account: but the full sum of me
Is sum of nothing; which, to term in gross,
Is an unlesson'd girl, unschool'd, unprac-
tis'd:
Happy in this, she is not yet so old
But she may learn; happier than this,
She is not bred so dull but she can learn;
Happiest of all, is, that her gentle spirit
Commits itself to yours to be directed,
As from her lord, her governor, her king.
Myself and what is mine, to you and yours
Is now converted: but now, I was the lord
Of this fair mansion, master of my serv-
ants,
Queen o'er myself; and even now, but
now,
This house, these servants, and this same
myself,
Are yours, my lord: I give them with this
ring;
Which when you part from, lose, or give
away,
Let it presage the ruin of your love,
And be my vantage to exclaim on you.
BASS. Madam, you have bereft me of all
words;
Only my blood speaks to you in my veins:
And there is such confusion in my powers,
As, after some oration fairly spoke
By a beloved prince, there doth appear
Among the buzzing pleased multitude;
Where every something, being blent to-
gether,
Turns to a wild of nothing, save of joy,
Express'd, and not express'd. But when
this ring
Parts from this finger, then parts life from
hence:
O, then be bold to say, Bassanio's dead!
NER. My lord and lady, it is now our
time,
That have stood by, and seen our wishes
prosper,
To cry, good joy. Good joy, my lord and
lady!
GRA. My lord Bassanio, and my gentle
lady,
I wish you all the joy that you can wish;
For I am sure you can wish none from
me:
And, when your honours mean to solemnize
The bargain of your faith, I do beseech
you,
Even at that time I may be married too.

BASS. With all my heart, so thou can'st
get a wife.
GRA. I thank your lordship, you have got
me one.
Mv eyes, my lord, can look as swift as
yours:
You saw the mistress, I beheld the maid;
You lov'd, I lov'd; for intermission
No more pertains to me, my lord, than you.
Your fortune stood upon the caskets there;
And so did mine too, as the matter falls;
For wooing here, until I sweat again,
And swearing, till my very roof was dry
With oaths of love, at last,—if promise
last,—
I got a promise of this fair one here,
To have her love, provided that your for-
tune
Achiev'd her mistress.
POR.   Is this true, Nerissa?
NER. Madam, it is, so you stand pleas'd
withal.
BASS. And do you, Gratiano, mean good
faith?
GRA. Yes, 'faith, my lord.
BASS. Our feast shall be much honour'd
in your marriage.
GRA. We'll play with them the first boy
for a thousand ducats.
NER. What, and stake down?
GRA. No; we shall ne'er win at that sport,
and stake down.—
But who comes here? Lorenzo and his
infidel?
What, and my old Venetian friend, Sola-
nio?
Enter LORENZO, JESSICA, *and* SOLANIO.
BASS. Lorenzo, and Solanio, welcome
hither;
If that the youth of my new interest here
Have power to bid you welcome.—By your
leave,
I bid my very friends and countrymen,
Sweet Portia, welcome.
POR.   So do I, my lord:
They are entirely welcome.
LOR. I thank your honour.—For my part,
my lord,
My purpose was not to have seen you here;
But meeting with Solanio by the way,
He did entreat me, past all saying nay,
To come with him along.
SOLAN.   I did, my lord;
And I have reason for it. Signior Antonio
Commends him to you.
          [*Gives* BASSANIO *a letter.*
BASS.   Ere I ope his letter,
I pray you, tell me how my good friend
doth.
SOLAN. Not sick, my lord, unless it be in
mind;

Nor well, unless in mind: his letter there
Will show you his estate.
          [BASSANIO *reads the letter.*
GRA. Nerissa, cheer yon stranger; bid her
welcome.—
Your hand, Solanio: what's the news from
Venice?
How doth that royal merchant, good An-
tonio?
I know he will be glad of our success;
We are the jasons, we have won the fleece.
SOLAN. I would you had won the fleece
that he hath lost!
POR. There are some shrewd contents in
yon same paper,
That steal the colour from Bassanio's
cheek:
Some dear friend dead; else nothing in the
world
Could turn so much the constitution
Of any constant man. What, worse and
worse!—
With leave, Bassanio; I am half yourself,
And I must freely have the half of any
thing
That this same paper brings you.
BASS.   O sweet Portia,
Here are a few of the unpleasant'st words
That ever blotted paper! Gentle lady,
When I did first impart my love to you,
I freely told you, all the wealth I had
Ran in my veins,—I was a gentleman;
And then I told you true: and yet, dear
lady,
Rating myself at nothing, you shall see
How much I was a braggart. When I told
you
My state was nothing, I should then have
told you
That I was worse than nothing; for, in-
deed,
I have engag'd myself to a dear friend,
Engag'd my friend to his mere enemy,
To feed my means. Here is a letter, lady,
The paper as the body of my friend,
And every word in it a gaping wound,
Issuing life-blood.—But is it true, Solanio?
Have all his ventures fail'd? What, not
one hit?
From Tripolis, from Mexico, and England,
From Lisbon, Barbary, and India?
And not one vessel 'scape the dreadful
touch
Of merchant-marring rocks?
SOLAN.   Not one, my lord.
Besides, it should appear, that if he had
The present money to discharge the Jew,
He would not take it. Never did I know
A creature, that did bear the shape of man,
So keen and greedy to confound a man:
He plies the duke at morning and at night;

And doth impeach the freedom of the
state,
If they deny him justice: twenty mer-
chants,
The duke himself, and the magnificoes
Of greatest port, have all persuaded with
him;
But none can drive him from the envious
plea
Of forfeiture, of justice, and his bond.
JES. When I was with him, I have heard
him swear,
To Tubal, and to Chus, his countrymen,
That he would rather have Antonio's flesh,
Than twenty times the value of the sum
That he did owe him: and I know, my lord,
If law, authority, and power deny not,
It will go hard with poor Antonio.
POR. Is it your dear friend that is thus
in trouble?
BASS. The dearest friend to me, the
kindest man,
The best condition'd and unwearied spirit
In doing courtesies; and one in whom
The ancient Roman honour more appears,
Than any that draws breath in Italy.
POR. What sum owes he the Jew?
BASS. For me, three thousand ducats.
POR.   What, no more?
Pay him six thousand, and deface the
bond;
Double six thousand, and then treble that,
Before a friend of this description
Shall lose a hair through Bassanio's fault.
First, go with me to church and call me
wife,
And then away to Venice to your friend;
For never shall you lie by Portia's side
With an unquiet soul. You shall have gold
To pay the petty debt twenty times over:
When it is paid, bring your true friend
along.
My maid Nerissa and myself, meantime,
Will live as maids and widows. Come,
away!
For you shall hence upon your wedding-
day:
Bid your friends welcome, show a merry
cheer:
Since you are dear bought, I will love you
dear.—
But let me hear the letter of your friend.
BASS. [Reads.] "Sweet Bassanio, my ships
have all miscarried, my creditors grow
cruel, my estate is very low, my bond to
the Jew is forfeit; and since in paying it,
it is impossible I should live, all debts are
cleared between you and I, if I might but
see you at my death. Notwithstanding, use
your pleasure: if your love do not persuade
you to come, let not my letter."

POR. O love, despatch all business, and
be gone!
BASS. Since I have your good leave to go
away,
I will make haste: but, till I come again,
No bed shall e'er be guilty of my stay,
Nor rest be interposer 'twixt us twain.
                                    [Exeunt.

───────

SCENE III.—VENICE. A Street.

Enter SHYLOCK, SALARINO, ANTONIO,
and Gaoler.

SHY. Gaoler, look to him:—tell not me of
mercy;—
This is the fool that lent out money gra-
tis:—
Gaoler, look to him.
ANT.   Hear me yet, good Shylock.
SHY. I'll have my bond; speak not against
my bond:
I have sworn an oath that I will have my
bond.
Thou call'st me dog before thou hadst a
cause:
But, since I am a dog, beware my fangs:
The duke shall grant me justice.—I do
wonder,
Thou naughty gaoler, that thou art so fond
To come abroad with him at his request.
ANT. I pray thee, hear me speak.
SHY. I'll have my bond; I will not hear
thee speak:
I'll have my bond; and therefore speak no
more.
I'll not be made a soft and dull-ey'd fool,
To shake the head, relent, and sigh, and
yield
To Christian intercessors. Follow not;
I'll have no speaking: I will have my bond.
                                    [Exit.
SALAR. It is the most impenetrable cur
That ever kept with men.
ANT.   Let him alone:
I'll follow him no more with bootless pray-
ers.
He seeks my life; his reason well I know:
I oft deliver'd from his forfeitures
Many that have at times made moan to me;
Therefore he hates me.
SALAR.   I am sure, the duke
Will never grant this forfeiture to hold.
ANT. The duke cannot deny the course of
law:
For the commodity that strangers have
With us in Venice, if it be denied,
Will much impeach the justice of the
state;
Since that the trade and profit of the city
Consisteth of all nations. Therefore, go:
These griefs and losses have so 'bated me,

That I shall hardly spare a pound of flesh
To-morrow to my bloody creditor.—
Well, gaoler, on.—Pray God, Bassanio come
To see me pay his debt,—and then I care
not!   [*Exeunt.*

SCENE IV.—BELMONT. *A Room in*
PORTIA'S *Mansion.*

Enter PORTIA, NERISSA, LORENZO, JESSICA,
and BALTHAZAR.

LOR. Madam, although I speak it in your
presence,
You have a noble and a true conceit
Of god-like amity; which appears most
strongly
In bearing thus the absence of your lord.
But if you knew to whom you show this
honour,
How true a gentleman you send relief,
How dear a lover of my lord, your hus-
band,
I know you would be prouder of the work,
Than customary bounty can enforce you.
POR. I never did repent for doing good,
Nor shall not now: for in companions
That do converse and waste the time to-
gether,
Whose souls do bear an equal yoke of love,
There must be needs a like proportion
Of lineaments, of manners, and of spirit;
Which makes me think that this Antonio,
Being the bosom lover of my lord,
Must needs be like my lord. If it be so,
How little is the cost I have bestow'd,
In purchasing the semblance of my soul
From out the state of hellish cruelty!
This comes too near the praising of myself;
Therefore, no more of it: hear other
things.—
Lorenzo, I commit into your hands
The husbandry and manage of my house,
Until my lord's return: for mine own part,
I have toward heaven breath'd a secret vow
To live in prayer and contemplation,
Only attended by Nerissa here,
Until her husband and my lord's return:
There is a monastery two miles off,
And there we will abide. I do desire you
Not to deny this imposition;
The which my love, and some necessity,
Now lays upon you.
LOR.   Madam, with all my heart;
I shall obey you in all fair commands.
POR. My people do already know my
mind,
And will acknowledge you and Jessica
In place of lord Bassanio and myself.
So fare you well, till we shall meet again.
LOR. Fair thoughts, and happy hours,
attend on you!

JES. I wish your ladyship all heart's con-
tent.
POR. I thank you for your wish, and am
well pleas'd.
To wish it back on you: fare you well,
Jessica.—
                [*Exeunt* JESSICA *and* LORENZO.
Now, Balthazar,
As I have ever found thee honest, true,
So let me find thee still. Take this same
letter,
And use thou all the endeavour of a man
In speed to Padua: see thou render this
Into my cousin's hand, doctor Bellario;
And, look, what notes and garments he
doth give thee,
Bring them, I pray thee, with imagin'd
speed
Unto the Tranect, to the common ferry
Which trades to Venice. Waste no time in
words,
But get thee gone: I shall be there before
thee.
BALTH. Madam, I go with all convenient
speed.   [*Exit.*
POR. Come on, Nerissa; I have work in
hand,
That you yet know not of: we'll see our
husbands,
Before they think of us.
NER.   Shall they see us?
POR. They shall, Nerissa; but in such a
habit,
That they shall think we are accomplished
With that we lack. I'll hold thee any wager,
When we are both accoutred like young
men,
I'll prove the prettier fellow of the two,
And wear my dagger with the braver
grace;
And speak between the change of man
and boy,
With a reed voice; and turn two mincing
steps
Into a manly stride; and speak of frays,
Like a fine bragging youth; and tell quaint
lies,
How honourable ladies sought my love,
Which I denying, they fell sick and died,—
I could not do withal;—then I'll repent,
And wish, for all that, that I had not kill'd
them:
And twenty of these puny lies I'll tell;
That men shall swear I have discontinu'd
school
Above a twelvemonth: I have within my
mind
A thousand raw tricks of these bragging
Jacks,
Which I will practise.

NER. Why, shall we turn to men?
POR. Fie, what a question's that,
If thou wert near a lewd interpreter!
But come, I'll tell thee all my whole device
When I am in my coach, which stays for us
At the park gate; and therefore haste away,
For we must measure twenty miles to-day.
[Exeunt.

SCENE V.—BELMONT. PORTIA'S *Garden*.

Enter LAUNCELOT *and* JESSICA.

LAUN. Yes, truly; for, look you, the sins of the father are to be laid upon the children: therefore, I promise you, I fear you. I was always plain with you, and so now I speak my agitation of the matter: therefore be of good cheer; for, truly, I think you are damned. There is but one hope in it that can do you any good; and that is but a kind of bastard hope neither.
JES. And what hope is that, I pray thee?
LAUN. Marry, you may partly hope that your father got you not,—that you are not the Jew's daughter.
JES. That were a kind of bastard hope, indeed: so the sins of my mother should be visited upon me.
LAUN. Truly, then, I fear you are damned both by father and mother: thus when I shun Scylla, your father, I fall into Charybdis, your mother: well, you are gone both ways.
JES. I shall be saved by my husband; he hath made me a Christian.
LAUN. Truly, the more to blame he: we were Christians enow before; e'en as many as could well live, one by another. This making of Christians will raise the price of hogs: if we grow all to be pork-eaters, we shall not shortly have a rasher on the coals for money.
JES. I'll tell my husband, Launcelot, what you say: here he comes.

Enter LORENZO.

LOR. I shall grow jealous of you shortly, Launcelot, if you thus get my wife into corners.
JES. Nay, you need not fear us, Lorenzo: Laucelot and I are out. He tells me flatly, there is no mercy for me in heaven, because I am a Jew's daughter: and he says, you are no good member of the commonwealth; for, in converting Jews to Christians, you raise the price of pork.
LOR. I shall answer that better to the commonwealth, than you can the getting up of the negro's belly: the Moor is with child by you, Launcelot.
LAUN. It is much, that the Moor should be more than reason: but if she be less than an honest woman, she is indeed more than I took her for.
LOR. How every fool can play upon the word! I think the best grace of wit will shortly turn into silence; and discourse grow commendable in none only but parrots.—Go in, sirrah; bid them prepare for dinner.
LAUN. That is done, Sir; they have all stomachs.
LOR. Goodly lord, what a wit-snapper are you! then, bid them prepare dinner.
LAUN. That is done too, Sir; only, cover is the word.
LOR. Will you cover, then, Sir?
LAUN. Not so, Sir, neither; I know my duty.
LOR. Yet more quarrelling with occasion! Wilt thou show the whole wealth of thy wit in an instant? I pray thee, understand a plain man in his plain meaning: go to thy fellow; bid them cover the table, serve in the meat, and we will come in to dinner.
LAUN. For the table, Sir, it shall be served in; for the meat, Sir, it shall be covered; for your coming in to dinner, Sir, why, let it be as humours and conceits shall govern. [Exit.
LOR. O dear discretion, how his words are suited!
The fool hath planted in his memory
An army of good words; and I do know
A many fools, that stand in better place,
Garnish'd like him, that for a tricksy word
Defy the matter.—How cheer'st thou, Jessica?
And now, good sweet, say thy opinion,—
How dost thou like the lord Bassanio's wife?
JES. Past all expressing. It is very meet,
The lord Bassanio lead an upright life;
For, having such a blessing in his lady,
He finds the joys of heaven here on earth;
And if on earth he do not mean it, then
In reason he should never come to heaven.
Why, if two gods should play some heavenly match,
And on the wager lay two earthly women,
And Portia one, there must be something else
Pawn'd with the other; for the poor rude world
Hath not her fellow.
LOR.   Even such a husband
Hast thou of me, as she is for a wife.
JES. Nay, but ask my opinion, too, of that.

LOR. I will anon: first, let us go to dinner.

JES. Nay, let me praise you, while I have a stomach.

LOR. No, pray thee, let it serve for table-talk;
Then, howsoe'er thou speak'st, 'mong other things
I shall digest it.

JES.   Well, I'll set you forth.

                                        [Exeunt.

ACT IV.

SCENE I.—VENICE. *A Court of Justice.*

Enter the DUKE; *the* Magnificoes; ANTONIO, BASSANIO, GRATIANO, SALARINO, SOLANIO, *and others.*

DUKE. What, is Antonio here?

ANT. Ready, so please your grace.

DUKE. I am sorry for thee: thou art come to answer
A stony adversary, an inhuman wretch
Uncapable of pity, void and empty
From any dram of mercy.

ANT.   I have heard,
Your grace hath ta'en great pains to qualify
His rigorous course; but since he stands obdurate,
And that no lawful means can carry me
Out of his envy's reach, I do oppose
My patience to his fury; and am arm'd
To suffer, with a quietness of spirit,
The very tyranny and rage of his.

DUKE. Go one, and call the Jew into the court.

SOLAN. He's ready at the door: he comes, my lord.

Enter SHYLOCK.

DUKE. Make room, and let him stand before our face.—
Shylock, the world thinks, and I think so too,
That thou but lead'st this fashion of thy malice
To the last hour of act; and then, 'tis thought,
Thou'lt show thy mercy and remorse, more strange
Than is thy strange apparent cruelty;
And where thou now exact'st the penalty,
(Which is a pound of this poor merchant's flesh,)
Thou wilt not only loose the forfeiture,
But, touch'd with human gentleness and love,
Forgive a moiety of the principal;
Glancing an eye of pity on his losses,
That have of late so huddled on his back,
Enow to press a royal merchant down,
And pluck commiseration of his state

From brassy bosoms and rough hearts of flint,
From stubborn Turks and Tartars, never train'd
To offices of tender courtesy.
We all expect a gentle answer, Jew.

SHY. I have possess'd your grace of what I purpose;
And by our holy Sabbath have I sworn
To have the due and forfeit of my bond:
If you deny it, let the danger light
Upon your charter and your city's freedom.
You'll ask me, why I rather choose to have
A weight of carrion flesh, than to receive
Three thousand ducats: I'll not answer that;
But say it is my humour: is it answer'd?
What if my house be troubled with a rat,
And I be pleas'd to give ten thousand ducats
To have it baned? What, are you answer'd yet?
Some men there are, love not a gaping pig;
Some, that are mad if they behold a cat;
And others, when the bag-pipe sings i' the nose,
Cannot contain their urine: for affection,
Master of passion, sways it to the mood
Of what it likes or loathes. Now, for your answer:
As there is no firm reason to be render'd,
Why he cannot abide a gaping pig;
Why he, a harmless necessary cat;
Why he, a swollen bag-pipe,—but of force
Must yield to such inevitable shame
As to offend, himself being offended;
So can I give no reason, nor I will not,
More than a lodg'd hate and a certain loathing
I bear Antonio, that I follow thus
A losing suit against him. Are you answer'd?

BASS. This is no answer, thou unfeeling man,
To excuse the current of thy cruelty.

SHY. I am not bound to please thee with my answer.

BASS. Do all men kill the things they do not love?

SHY. Hates any man the thing he would not kill?

BASS. Every offence is not a hate at first.

SHY. What, would'st thou have a serpent sting thee twice?

ANT. I pray you, think you question with the Jew:
You may as well go stand upon the beach,
And bid the main flood bate his usual height;

You may as well use question with the
wolf,
Why he hath made the ewe bleat for the
lamb;
You may as well forbid the mountain pines
To wag their high tops, and to make no
noise,
When they are fretted with the gusts of
heaven;
You may as well do any thing most hard,
As seek to soften that (than which what's
harder?)
His Jewish heart:—therefore, I do beseech
you,
Make no more offers, use no farther means,
But, with all brief and plain conveniency,
Let me have judgment, and the Jew his
will.

BASS. For thy three thousand ducats here
is six.

SHY. If every ducat in six thousand ducats
Were in six parts, and every part a ducat,
I would not draw them,—I would have my
bond.

DUKE. How shalt thou hope for mercy,
rendering none?

SHY. What judgment shall I dread, doing
no wrong?
You have among you many a purchas'd
slave,
Which, like your asses and your dogs and
mules,
You use in abject and in slavish parts,
Because you bought them:—shall I say to
you,
Let them be free, marry them to your
heirs?
Why sweat they under burdens? let their
beds
Be made as soft as yours, and let their
palates
Be season'd with such viands? You will
answer,
The slaves are ours:—so do I answer you:
The pound of flesh which I demand of
him,
Is dearly bought, 'tis mine, and I will have
it.
If you deny me, fie upon your law!
There is no force in the decrees of Venice.
I stand for judgment: answer,—shall I
have it?

DUKE. Upon my power I may dismiss
this court,
Unless Bellario, a learned doctor.
Whom I have sent for to determine this,
Come here to-day.

SALAR.　　My lord, here stays without
A messenger with letters from the doctor,
New come from Padua.

DUKE. Bring us the letters; call the messenger.

BASS. Good cheer, Antonio! What, man,
courage yet!
The Jew shall have my flesh, blood, bones,
and all,
Ere thou shalt lose for me one drop of
blood.

ANT. I am a tainted wether of the flock,
Meetest for death: the weakest kind of
fruit
Drops earliest to the ground; and so let
me:
You cannot better be employ'd, Bassanio,
Than to live still, and write mine epitaph.

Enter NERISSA, *dressed like a lawyer's clerk.*

DUKE. Came you from Padua, from Bellario?

NER. From both, my lord. Bellario greets
your grace.　　*[Presents a letter.*

BASS. Why dost thou whet thy knife so
earnestly?

SHY. To cut the forfeiture from that bankrupt there.

GRA. Not on thy sole, but on thy soul,
harsh Jew,
Thou mak'st thy knife keen; but no metal
can,
No, not the hangman's axe, bear half the
keenness
Of thy sharp envy. Can no prayers pierce
thee?

SHY. No, none that thou hast wit enough
to make.

GRA. O, be thou damn'd, inexorable dog!
And for thy life let justice be accus'd.
Thou almost mak'st me waver in my faith,
To hold opinion with Pythagoras,
That souls of animals infuse themselves
Into the trunks of men: thy currish spirit
Govern'd a wolf, who, hang'd for human
slaughter,
Even from the gallows did his fell soul fleet,
And, whilst thou lay'st in thy unhallow'd
dam,
Infus'd itself in thee; for thy desires
Are wolfish, bloody, starv'd, and ravenous.

SHY. Till thou can'st rail the seal from
off my bond,
Thou but offend'st thy lungs to speak so
loud:
Repair thy wit, good youth, or it will fall
To cureless ruin.—I stand here for law.

DUKE. This letter from Bellario doth
commend
A young and learned doctor to our court.—
Where is he?

NER.　　He attendeth here hard by,
To know your answer, whether you'll admit
him.

DUKE. With all my heart.—Some three or four of you,
Go give him courteous conduct to this place.
Meantime, the court shall hear Bellario's letter.
[*Clerk reads.*] "Your grace shall understand, that at the receipt of your letter I am very sick: but in the instant that your messenger came, in loving visitation was with me a young doctor of Rome; his name is Balthazar. I acquainted him with the cause in controversy between the Jew and Antonio the merchant: we turned o'er many books together: he is furnished with my opinion; which, bettered with his own learning, (the greatness whereof I cannot enough commend,) comes with him, at my importunity, to fill up your grace's request in my stead. I beseech you, let his lack of years be no impediment to let him lack a reverend estimation; for I never knew so young a body with so old a head. I leave him to your gracious acceptance, whose trial shall better publish his commendation."
DUKE. You hear the learn'd Bellario, what he writes:
And here, I take it, is the doctor come.—
Enter PORTIA, *dressed like a doctor of laws.*
Give me your hand. Came you from old Bellario?
POR. I did, my lord.
DUKE. You are welcome: take your place.
Are you acquainted with the difference
That holds this present question in the court?
POR. I am informed throughly of the cause.—
Which is the merchant here, and which the Jew?
DUKE. Antonio and old Shylock, both stand forth.
POR. Is your name Shylock?
SHY.   Shylock is my name.
POR. Of a strange nature is the suit you follow;
Yet in such rule, that the Venetian law
Cannot impugn you as you do proceed.—
[*To* ANTONIO.] You stand within his danger, do you not?
ANT. Ay, so he says.
POR.   Do you confess the bond?
ANT. I do.
POR.   Then must the Jew be merciful.
SHY. On what compulsion must I? tell me that.
POR. The quality of mercy is not strain'd,—
It droppeth as the gentle rain from heaven

Upon the place beneath: it is twice bless'd,—
It blesseth him that gives, and him that takes:
'Tis mightiest in the mightiest; it becomes
The throned monarch better than his crown;
His sceptre shows the force of temporal power,
The attribute to awe and majesty,
Wherein doth sit the dread and fear of kings:
But mercy is above this sceptred sway,—
It is enthroned in the hearts of kings,
It is an attribute to God himself;
And earthly power doth then show likest God's,
When mercy seasons justice. Therefore, Jew,
Though justice be thy plea, consider this,—
That, in the course of justice, none of us
Should see salvation: we do pray for mercy;
And that same prayer doth teach us all to render
The deeds of mercy. I have spoke thus much,
To mitigate the justice of thy plea;
Which if thou follow, this strict court of Venice
Must needs give sentence 'gainst the merchant there.
SHY. My deeds upon my head! I crave the law,
The penalty and forfeit of my bond.
POR. Is he not able to discharge the money?
BASS. Yes, here I tender it for him in the court;
Yea, twice the sum: if that will not suffice,
I will be bound to pay it ten times o'er,
On forfeit of my hands, my head, my heart:
If this will not suffice, it must appear
That malice bears down truth. And, I beseech you,
Wrest once the law to your authority:
To do a great right, do a little wrong;
And curb this cruel devil of his will.
POR. It must not be; there is no power in Venice
Can alter a decree established:
'Twill be recorded for a precedent;
And many an error, by the same example,
Will rush into the state: it cannot be.
SHY. A Daniel come to judgment! yea, a Daniel!—
O wise young judge, how I do honour thee!
POR. I pray you, let me look upon the bond.

SHY. Here 'tis, most reverend doctor, here it is.

POR. Shylock, there's thrice thy money offer'd thee.

SHY. An oath, an oath, I have an oath in heaven:
Shall I lay perjury upon my soul?
No, not for Venice.

POR.   Why, this bond is forfeit;
And lawfully by this the Jew may claim
A pound of flesh, to be by him cut off
Nearest the merchant's heart.—Be merciful:
Take thrice thy money; bid me tear the bond.

SHY. When it is paid according to the tenour.—
It doth appear you are a worthy judge;
You know the law, your exposition
Hath been most sound: I charge you by the law,
Whereof you are a well-deserving pillar,
Proceed to judgment: by my soul I swear
There is no power in the tongue of man
To alter me: I stay here on my bond.

ANT. Most heartily I do beseech the court
To give the judgment.

POR.   Why then, thus it is:—
You must prepare your bosom for his knife.

SHY. O noble judge! O excellent young man!

POR. For, the intent and purpose of the law
Hath full relation to the penalty,
Which here appeareth due upon the bond.

SHY. 'Tis very true: O wise and upright judge!
How much more elder art thou than thy looks!

POR. Therefore, lay bare your bosom.

SHY.   Ay, his breast;
So says the bond:—doth it not, noble judge?—
Nearest his heart: those are the very words.

POR. It is so. Are there balance here to weigh
The flesh?

SHY. I have them ready.

POR. Have by some surgeon, Shylock, on your charge,
To stop his wounds, lest he do bleed to death.

SHY. Is it so nominated in the bond?

POR. It is not so express'd; but what of that?
'Twere good you do so much for charity.

SHY. I cannot find it; 'tis not in the bond.

POR. Come, merchant, have you any thing to say?

ANT. But little: I am arm'd and well prepar'd.—

Give me your hand, Bassanio: fare you well!
Grieve not that I am fallen to this for you;
For herein Fortune shows herself more kind
Than is her custom: it is still her use
To let the wretched man out-live his wealth,
To view with hollow eye and wrinkled brow
An age of poverty; from which lingering penance
Of such misery doth she cut me off.
Commend me to your honourable wife:
Tell her the process of Antonio's end;
Say how I lov'd you, speak me fair in death;
And, when the tale is told, bid her be judge,
Whether Bassanio had not once a love.
Repent not you that you shall lose your friend,
And he repents not that he pays your debt;
For, if the Jew do cut but deep enough,
I'll pay it instantly with all my heart.

BASS. Antonio, I am married to a wife
Which is as dear to me as life itself;
But life itself, my wife, and all the world,
Are not with me esteem'd above thy life:
I would lose all, ay, sacrifice them all
Here to this devil, to deliver you.

POR. Your wife would give you little thanks for that,
If she were by, to hear you make the offer.

GRA. I have a wife, whom, I protest, I love:
I would she were in heaven, so she could
Entreat some power to change this currish Jew.

NER. 'Tis well you offer it behind her back;
The wish would make else an unquiet house.

SHY. [*Aside.*] These be the Christian husbands! I have a daughter;
Would any of the stock of Barrabas
Had been her husband, rather than a Christian!
[*Aloud.*] We trifle time: I pray thee, pursue sentence.

POR. A pound of that same merchant's flesh is thine:
The court awards it, and the law doth give it.

SHY. Most rightful judge!

POR. And you must cut this flesh from off his breast:
The law allows it, and the court awards it.

SHY. Most learned judge!—A sentence! come, prepare!

POR. Tarry a little: there is something else.
This bond doth give thee here no jot of blood;—

The words expressly are, a pound of flesh:
Take then thy bond, take thou thy pound
of flesh;
But, in the cutting it, if thou dost shed
One drop of Christian blood, thy lands
and goods
Are, by the laws of Venice, confiscate
Unto the state of Venice.
GRA. O upright judge!—Mark, Jew:—O
learned judge!
SHY. Is that the law?
POR.   Thyself shalt see the act:
For, as thou urgest justice, be assur'd
Thou shalt have justice, more than thou
desir'st.
GRA. O learned judge!—Mark, Jew:—a
learned judge!
SHY. I take this offer, then;—pay the
bond thrice,
And let the Christian go.
BASS.   Here is the money.
POR. Soft!
The Jew shall have all justice;—soft! no
haste:—
He shall have nothing but the penalty.
GRA. O Jew! an upright judge, a learned
judge!
POR. Therefore, prepare thee to cut off
the flesh.
Shed thou no blood; nor cut thou less, nor
more,
But just a pound of flesh: if thou tak'st
more,
Or less, than a just pound,—be it but so
much
As makes it light, or heavy, in the sub-
stance,
Or the division of the twentieth part
Of one poor scruple; nay, if the scale do
turn
But in the estimation of a hair,—
Thou diest, and all thy goods are confiscate.
GRA. A second Daniel, a Daniel, Jew!
Now, infidel, I have thee on the hip.
POR. Why doth the Jew pause? take thy
forfeiture.
SHY. Give me my principal, and let me
go.
BASS. I have it ready for thee; here it is.
POR. He hath refus'd it in the open court:
He shall have merely justice, and his bond.
GRA. A Daniel, still say I; a second
Daniel!—
I thank thee, Jew, for teaching me that
word.
SHY. Shall I not have barely my prin-
cipal?
POR. Thou shalt have nothing but the
forfeiture,
To be so taken at thy peril, Jew.

SHY. Why, then the devil give him good
of it!
I'll stay no longer question.
POR.   Tarry, Jew:
The law hath yet another hold on you.
It is enacted in the laws of Venice,—
If it be prov'd against an alien
That by direct or indirect attempts
He seek the life of any citizen,
The party 'gainst the which he doth con-
trive
Shall seize one half his goods; the other
half
Comes to the privy coffer of the state;
And the offender's life lies in the mercy
Of the duke only, 'gainst all other voice.
In which predicament, I say, thou stand'st;
For it appears, by manifest proceeding,
That indirectly, and directly too,
Thou hast contriv'd against the very life
Of the defendant; and thou hast incurr'd
The danger formerly by me rehears'd.
Down, therefore, and beg mercy of the
duke.
GRA. Beg that thou may'st have leave to
hang thyself:
And yet, thy wealth being forfeit to the
state,
Thou hast not left the value of a cord;
Therefore, thou must be hang'd at the
state's charge.
DUKE. That thou shalt see the difference
of our spirit,
I pardon thee thy life before thou ask it:
For half thy wealth, it is Antonio's;
The other half comes to the general state,
Which humbleness may drive unto a fine.
POR. Ay, for the state,—not for Antonio.
SHY. Nay, take my life and all; pardon
not that:
You take my house, when you do take the
prop
That doth sustain my house; you take my
life,
When you do take the means whereby I
live.
POR. What mercy can you render him,
Antonio?
GRA. A halter gratis; nothing else, for
God's sake!
ANT. So please my lord the duke, and all
the court,
To quit the fine for one half of his goods;
I am content, so he will let me have
The other half in use, to render it,
Upon his death, unto the gentleman
That lately stole his daughter:
Two things provided more,—that, for this
favour,
He presently become a Christian;
The other, that he do record a gift,

Here in the court, of all he dies possess'd,
Unto his son Lorenzo and his daughter.
DUKE. He shall do this; or else I do
recant
The pardon that I late pronounced here.
POR. Art thou contented, Jew? what dost
SHY. I am content.   [thou say?
POR.   Clerk, draw a deed of gift.
SHY. I pray you, give me leave to go
from hence;
I am not well: send the deed after me,
And I will sign it.
DUKE.   Get thee gone, but do it.
GRA. In christening thou shalt have two
godfathers:
Had I been judge, thou should'st have had
ten more,
To bring thee to the gallows, not the font.
                              [*Exit* SHYLOCK.
DUKE. Sir, I entreat you home with me
to dinner.
POR. I humbly do desire your grace of
pardon:
I must away this night toward Padua,
And it is meet I presently set forth.
DUKE. I am sorry that your leisure serves
you not.—
Antonio, gratify this gentleman;
For, in my mind, you are much bound to
him.
           [*Exeunt* DUKE, Magnificoes, *and train.*
BASS. Most worthy gentleman, I and my
friend
Have by your wisdom been this day
acquitted
Of grievous penalties; in lieu whereof,
Three thousand ducats, due unto the Jew,
We freely cope your courteous pains withal.
ANT. And stand indebted, over and above,
In love and service to you evermore.
POR. He is well paid that is well satisfied;
And I, delivering you, am satisfied,
And therein do account myself well paid:
My mind was never yet more mercenary.
I pray you, know me, when we meet again:
I wish you well, and so I take my leave.
BASS. Dear Sir, of force I must attempt
you farther:
Take some remembrance of us, as a tribute,
Not as a fee: grant me two things, I pray
you,—
Not to deny me, and to pardon me.
POR. You press me far, and therefore I
will yield.
Give me your gloves, I'll wear them for
your sake;
And, for your love, I'll take this ring from
you:—
Do not draw back your hand; I'll take
no more;
And you in love shall not deny me this.

BASS. This ring, good Sir,—alas, it is a
trifle!
I will not shame myself to give you this.
POR. I will have nothing else but only
this;
And now methinks I have a mind to it.
BASS. There's more depends on this, than
on the value.
The dearest ring in Venice will I give you,
And find it out by proclamation:
Only for this, I pray you, pardon me.
POR. I see, Sir, you are liberal in offers:
You taught me first to beg; and now me-
thinks
You teach me how a beggar should be
answer'd.
BASS. Good Sir, this ring was given me
by my wife;
And, when she put it on, she made me vow
That I should neither sell, nor give, nor
lose it.
POR. That 'scuse serves many men to save
their gifts.
And if your wife be not a mad woman,
And know how well I have deserv'd this
ring,
She would not hold out enemy for ever,
For giving it to me. Well, peace be with
you!   [*Exeunt* PORTIA *and* NERISSA.
ANT. My lord Bassanio, let him have the
ring:
Let his deservings, and my love withal,
Be valu'd 'gainst your wife's commandment.
BASS. Go, Gratiano, run and overtake
him;
Give him the ring; and bring him, if thou
canst,
Unto Antonio's house: away! make haste.
                              [*Exit* GRATIANO.
Come, you and I will thither presently;
And in the morning early will we both
Fly toward Belmont: come, Antonio.
                              [*Exeunt.*

SCENE II.—VENICE. *A Street.*

Enter PORTIA *and* NERISSA.

POR. Enquire the Jew's house out, give
him this deed,
And let him sign it: we'll away to-night,
And be a day before our husbands home:
This deed will be well welcome to Lorenzo.

Enter GRATIANO.

GRA. Fair Sir, you are well o'erta'en:
My lord Bassanio, upon more advice,
Hath sent you here this ring; and doth
Your company at dinner.   [entreat
POR.   That cannot be:
His ring I do accept most thankfully;
And so, I pray you, tell him: farthermore,

I pray you, show my youth old Shylock's
house.
GRA. That will I do.
NER.   Sir, I would speak with you.—
[Aside to PORTIA.] I'll see if I can get my
husband's ring,
Which I did make him swear to keep for
ever.
POR. Thou may'st, I warrant. We shall
have old swearing
That they did give the rings away to men;
But we'll outface them, and outswear them
too.
Away! make haste: thou know'st where I
will tarry.
NER. Come, good Sir, will you show me
to this house?   [Exeunt.

ACT V.

SCENE I.—BELMONT. *The Avenue to*
PORTIA'S *Mansion*.
Enter LORENZO *and* JESSICA.

LOR. The moon shines bright:—in such a
night as this,
When the sweet wind did gently kiss the
trees,
And they did make no noise,—in such a
night
Troilus methinks mounted the Trojan walls,
And sigh'd his soul toward the Grecian
tents,
Where Cressid lay that night.
JES.   In such a night
Did Thisbe fearfully o'ertrip the dew,
And saw the lion's shadow ere himself,
And ran dismay'd away.
LOR.   In such a night
Stood Dido with a willow in her hand
Upon the wild sea-banks, and waft her love
To come again to Carthage.
JES.   In such a night
Medea gather'd the enchanted herbs
That did renew old Æson.
LOR.   In such a night
Did Jessica steal from the wealthy Jew,
And with an unthrift love did run from
As far as Belmont.   [Venice,
JES.   In such a night
Did young Lorenzo swear he lov'd her well,
Stealing her soul with many vows of faith,
And ne'er a true one.
LOR.   In such a night
Did pretty Jessica, like a little shrew,
Slander her love, and he forgave it her.
JES. I would out-night you, did nobody
come;
But, hark, I hear the footing of a man.
Enter STEPHANO.
LOR. Who comes so fast in silence of the
STEPH. A friend.   [night?

LOR. A friend! what friend? your name,
I pray you, friend.
STEPH. Stephano is my name; and I
bring word,
My mistress will before the break of day
Be here at Belmont: she doth stray about
By holy crosses, where she kneels and prays
For happy wedlock hours.
LOR.   Who comes with her?
STEPH. None, but a holy hermit, and her
maid.
I pray you, is my master yet return'd?
LOR. He is not, nor we have not heard
from him.—
But go we in, I pray thee, Jessica,
And ceremoniously let us prepare
Some welcome for the mistress of the house.
Enter LAUNCELOT.
LAUN. Sola, sola! wo, ha, ho! sola, sola!
LOR. Who calls?
LAUN. Sola! did you see master Lorenzo
and mistress Lorenzo? sola, sola!
LOR. Leave hollaing, man:—here.
LAUN. Sola! where? where?
LOR. Here.
LAUN. Tell him there's a post come from
my master, with his horn full of good
news: my master will be here ere morning.
                                   [Exit.
LOR. Sweet soul, let's in, and there expect
their coming.
And yet no matter:—why should we go
in?—
My friend Stephano, signify, I pray you,
Within the house, your mistress is at hand;
And bring your music forth into the air.—
                           [Exit STEPHANO.
How sweet the moonlight sleeps upon this
bank!
Here will we sit, and let the sounds of
music
Creep in our ears: soft stillness, and the
night,
Become the touches of sweet harmony.
Sit, Jessica: look, how the floor of heaven
Is thick inlaid with patines of bright gold:
There's not the smallest orb which thou
behold'st,
But in his motion like an angel sings,
Still quiring to the young ey'd cherubins,—
Such harmony is in immortal souls;
But whilst this muddy vesture of decay
Doth grossly close it in, we cannot hear it.
Enter MUSICIANS.
Come, ho! and wake Diana with a hymn:
With sweetest touches pierce your mistress'
ear,
And draw her home with music.   [Music.
JES. I am never merry when I hear sweet
music.

LOR. The reason is, your spirits are attentive:
For do but not a wild and wanton herd,
Or race of youthful and unhandled colts,
Fetching mad bounds, bellowing, and neighing loud,
Which is the hot condition of their blood;
If they but hear perchance a trumpet sound,
Or any air of music touch their ears,
You shall perceive them make a mutual stand,
Their savage eyes turn'd to a modest gaze,
But the sweet power of music: therefore the poet
Did feign that Orpheus drew trees, stones, and floods;
Since naught so stockish, hard, and full of rage,
But music for the time doth change his nature.
The man that hath no music in himself,
Nor is not mov'd with concord of sweet sounds,
Is fit for treasons, stratagems, and spoils;
The motions of his spirit are dull as night,
And his affections dark as Erebus:
Let no such man be trusted.—Mark the music.

Enter PORTIA *and* NERISSA, *at a distance.*

POR. That light we see is burning in my hall.
How far that little candle throws his beams!
So shines a good deed in a naughty world.
NER. When the moon shone, we did not see the candle.
POR. So doth the greater glory dim the less:
A substitute shines brightly as a king,
Until a king be by; and then his state
Empties itself, as doth an inland brook
Into the main of waters.—Music! hark!
NER. It is your music, madam, of the house.
POR. Nothing is good, I see, without respect:
Methinks it sounds much sweeter than by day.
NER. Silence bestows that virtue on it, madam.
POR. The crow doth sing as sweetly as the lark,
When neither is attended; and I think
The nightingale, if she should sing by day,
When every goose is cackling, would be thought
No better a musician than the wren.
How many things by season season'd are
To their right praise and true perfection!—
Peace, ho! the moon sleeps with Endymion,
And would not be awak'd! [*Music ceases.*

LOR. That is the voice,
Or I am much deceiv'd, of Portia.
POR. He knows me, as the blind man knows the cuckoo,
By the bad voice.
LOR. Dear lady, welcome home.
POR. We have been praying for our husbands' welfare,
Which speed, we hope, the better for our words.
Are they return'd? [*words.*
LOR. Madam, they are not yet;
But there is come a messenger before,
To signify their coming.
POR. Go in, Nerissa;
Give order to my servants that they take
No note at all of our being absent hence;—
Nor you, Lorenzo;—Jessica, nor you.
[*A tucket sounds.*
LOR. Your husband is at hand; I hear his trumpet:
We are no tell-tales, madam; fear you not.
POR. This night methinks is but the daylight sick;
It looks a little paler: 'tis a day,
Such as the day is when the sun is hid.

Enter BASSANIO, ANTONIO, GRATIANO, *and their followers.*

BASS. We should hold day with the Antipodes,
If you would walk in absence of the sun.
POR. Let me give light, but let me not be light;
For a light wife doth make a heavy husband,
And never be Bassanio so for me:
But God sort all!—You are welcome home, my lord.
BASS. I thank you, madam: give welcome to my friend;
This is the man, this is Antonio,
To whom I am so infinitely bound.
POR. You should in all sense be much bound to him,
For, as I hear, he was much bound for you.
ANT. No more than I am well acquitted of.
POR. Sir, you are very welcome to our house:
It must appear in other ways than words,
Therefore I scant this breathing courtesy.
GRA. [*To* NERISSA.] By yonder moon I swear you do me wrong;
In faith, I gave it to the judge's clerk:
Would he were gelt that had it, for my part,
Since you do take it, love, so much at heart.
POR. A quarrel, ho, already! what's the matter?
GRA. About a hoop of gold, a paltry ring
That she did give me; whose posy was

For all the world like cutler's poetry
Upon a knife, "Love me, and leave me not."
NER. What talk you of the posy, or the
value?
You swore to me, when I did give it you,
That you would wear it till your hour of
death:
And that it should lie with you in your
grave:
Though not for me, yet for your vehement
oaths,
You should have been respective, and have
kept it.
Gave it a judge's clerk! no, God's my
judge,
The clerk will ne'er wear hair on's face
that had it.
GRA. He will, an if he live to be a man.
NER. Ay, if a woman live to be a man.
GRA. Now, by this hand, I gave it to a
youth,—
A kind of boy; a little scrubbed boy,
No higher than thyself, the judge's clerk;
A prating boy, that begg'd it as a fee:
I could not for my heart deny it him.
POR. You were to blame,—I must be plain
with you,—
To part so slightly with your wife's first
gift;
A thing stuck on with oaths upon your
finger,
And so riveted with faith unto your flesh.
I gave my love a ring, and made him swear
Never to part with it; and here he
stands,—
I dare be sworn for him, he would not
leave it,
Nor pluck it from his finger, for the wealth
That the world masters. Now, in faith,
Gratiano,
You give your wife too unkind a cause of
grief:
An 'twere to me, I should be mad at it.
BASS. [*Aside.*] Why, I were best to cut
my left hand off,
And swear I lost the ring defending it.
GRA. My lord Bassanio gave his ring away
Unto the judge that begg'd it, and indeed
Deserv'd it too; and then the boy, his clerk,
That took some pains in writing, he begg'd
mine:
And neither man nor master would take
But the two rings.   [*aught
POR.   What ring gave you, my lord?
Not that, I hope, which you receiv'd of me.
BASS. If I could add a lie unto a fault,
I would deny it; but you see, my finger
Hath not the ring upon it,—it is gone.
POR. Even so void is your false heart of
truth.

By heaven, I will ne'er come in your bed
Until I see the ring.
NER.   Nor I in yours,
Till I again see mine.
BASS.   Sweet Portia,
If you did know to whom I gave the ring,
If you did know for whom I gave the ring,
And would conceive for what I gave the
ring,
And how unwillingly I left the ring,
When naught would be accepted but the
ring,
You would abate the strength of your dis-
pleasure.
POR. If you had known the virtue of the
ring,
Or half her worthiness that gave the ring,
Or your own honour to contain the ring,
You would not then have parted with the
ring.
What man is there so much unreasonable,
If you had pleas'd to have defended it
With any terms of zeal, wanted the modesty
To urge the thing held as a ceremony?
Nerissa teaches me what to believe:
I'll die for't, but some woman had the
ring.
BASS. No, by mine honour, madam, by
my soul,
No woman had it, but a civil doctor,
Which did refuse three thousand ducats of
me,
And begg'd the ring; the which I did deny
him,
And suffer'd him to go displeas'd away,
Even he that had held up the very life
Of my dear friend. What should I say,
sweet lady?
I was enforc'd to send it after him;
I was beset with shame and courtesy;
My honour would not let ingratitude
So much besmear it. Pardon me, good
lady;
For, by these blessed candles of the night,
Had you been there, I think you would
have begg'd
The ring of me to give the worthy doctor.
POR. Let not that doctor e'er come near
my house:
Since he hath got the jewel that I lov'd,
And that which you did swear to keep for
I will become as liberal as you;   [me,
I'll not deny him any thing I have,
No, not my body, nor my husband's bed:
Know him I shall, I am well sure of it:
Lie not a night from home; watch me like
Argus:
If you do not, if I be left alone,
Now, by mine honour, which is yet mine
own,
I'll have that doctor for my bedfellow.

NER. And I his clerk; therefore be well advis'd
How you do leave me to mine own protection.
GRA. Well, do you so: let not me take him, then;
For if I do, I'll mar the young clerk's pen.
ANT. I am th' unhappy subject of these quarrels.
POR. Sir, grieve not you; you are welcome notwithstanding.
BASS. Portia, forgive me this enforced wrong;
And, in the hearing of these many friends,
I swear to thee, even by thine own fair eyes,
Wherein I see myself,—
POR.   Mark you but that!
In both my eyes he doubly sees himself;
In each eye, one:—swear by your double self,
And there's an oath of credit.
BASS.   Nay, but hear me:
Pardon this fault, and by my soul I swear,
I never more will break an oath with thee.
ANT. I once did lend my body for his wealth;
Which, but for him that had your husband's ring,
Had quite miscarried: I dare be bound again,
My soul upon the forfeit, that your lord
Will never more break faith advisedly.
POR. Then you shall be his surety. Give him this;
And bid him keep it better than the other.
ANT. Here, lord Bassanio; swear to keep this ring.
BASS. By heaven! it is the same I gave the doctor!
POR. I had it of him: pardon me, Bassanio;
For, by this ring, the doctor lay with me.
NER. And pardon me, my gentle Gratiano;
For that same scrubbed boy, the doctor's clerk,
In lieu of this last night did lie with me.
GRA. Why, this is like the mending of highways
In summer, when the ways are fair enough:
What, are we cuckolds ere we have deserv'd it?
POR. Speak not so grossly.—You are all amaz'd:
Here is a letter, read it at your leisure;
It comes from Padua, from Bellario:
There you shall find that Portia was the doctor;

Nerissa there, her clerk: Lorenzo, here,
Shall witness I set forth as soon as you,
And even but now return'd; I have not yet
Enter'd my house.—Antonio, you are welcome;
And I have better news in store for you
Than you expect: unseal this letter soon;
There you shall find, three of your argosies
Are richly come to harbour suddenly:
You shall not know by what strange accident
I chanced on this letter.
ANT.   I am dumb.
BASS. Were you the doctor, and I knew you not?
GRA. Were you the clerk that is to make me cuckold?
NER. Ay, but the clerk that never means to do it,
Unless he live until he be a man.
BASS. Sweet doctor, you shall be my bedfellow:
When I am absent, then, lie with my wife.
ANT. Sweet lady, you have given me life and living;
For here I read for certain that my ships
Are safely come to road.
POR.   How now, Lorenzo!
My clerk hath some good comforts, too, for you.
NER. Ay, and I'll give them him without a fee.—
There do I give to you and Jessica,
From the rich Jew, a special deed of gift,
After his death, of all he dies possess'd of.
LOR. Fair ladies, you drop manna in the way
Of starved people.
POR.   It is almost morning,
And yet I am sure you are not satisfied
Of these events at full. Let us go in;
And charge us there upon inter'gatories,
And we will answer all things faithfully.
GRA. Let it be so: the first inter'gatory
That my Nerissa shall be sworn on, is,
Whether till the next night she had rather stay,
Or go to bed now, being two hours to-day:
But were the day come, I should wish it dark,
That I were couching with the doctor's clerk.
Well, while I live, I'll fear no other thing
So sore, as keeping safe Nerissa's ring.
                              [*Exeunt.*

The banishment of Oliver. Act III. S. 1.

AS YOU LIKE IT

DRAMATIS PERSONÆ.

DUKE, *Senior, living in exile.*
FREDERICK, *his Brother, usurper of his*
           dominions.
AMIENS, } *Lords, attending upon the*
JAQUES, }   *exiled* DUKE.
LE BEAU, *a Courtier, attending upon*
   FREDERICK.
CHARLES, *a Wrestler.*
OLIVER,
JAQUES, } *Sons of Sir Rowland de Bois.*
ORLANDO,
ADAM, } *Servants to* OLIVER.
DENNIS,

TOUCHSTONE, *a Clown.*
SIR OLIVER MAR-TEXT, *a Vicar.*
CORIN, } *Shepherds.*
SILVIUS, }
WILLIAM, *a Country Fellow, in love with*
   AUDREY.
A person representing Hymen.
ROSALIND, *daughter to the exiled* DUKE.
CELIA, *daughter to* FREDERICK.
PHEBE, *a Shepherdess.*
AUDREY, *a Country Wench.*

Lords, Pages, Foresters, *and* Attendants.

SCENE.—*First, near* OLIVER'S *House; afterwards, in the Usurper's Court, and in the*
Forest of ARDEN.

ACT I.

SCENE I.—*An Orchard near* OLIVER'S *House.*

Enter ORLANDO *and* ADAM.

ORL. As I remember, Adam, it was upon this fashion,—bequeathed me by will but a poor thousand crowns and, as thou say'st, charged my brother, on his blessing, to breed me well: and there begins my sadness. My brother Jaques he keeps at school, and report speaks goldenly of his profit: for my part, he keeps me rustically at home, or, to speak more properly, stays me here at home unkept; for call you that keeping for a gentleman of my birth, that differs not from the stalling of an ox? His horses are bred better; for, besides that they are fair with their feeding, they are taught their manage, and to that end riders dearly hired: but I, his brother, gain noth-

150

ing under him but growth; for the which his animals on his dunghills are as much bound to him as I. Besides this nothing that he so plentifully gives me, the something that nature gave me, his countenance seems to take from me: he lets me feed with his hinds, bars me the place of a brother, and, as much as in him lies, mines my gentility with my education. This is it, Adam, that grieves me; and the spirit of my father, which I think is within me, begins to mutiny against this servitude: I will no longer endure it, though yet I know no wise remedy how to avoid it.

ADAM. Yonder comes my master, your brother.

ORL. Go apart, Adam, and thou shalt hear how he will shake me up.

Enter OLIVER.

OLI. Now, Sir! what make you here?

ORL. Nothing: I am not taught to make any thing.

OLI. What mar you then, Sir?

ORL. Marry, Sir, I am helping you to mar that which God made, a poor unworthy brother of yours, with idleness.

OLI. Marry, Sir, be better employed, and be naught awhile.

ORL. Shall I keep your hogs, and eat husks with them? What prodigal portion have I spent, that I should come to such penury?

OLI. Know you where you are, Sir?

ORL. O, Sir, very well: here in your orchard.

OLI. Know you before whom, Sir?

ORL. Ay, better than he I am before knows me. I know you are my eldest brother; and, in the gentle condition of blood, you should so know me. The courtesy of nations allows you my better, in that you are the first-born; but the same tradition takes not away my blood, were there twenty brothers betwixt us: I have as much of my father in me, as you; albeit, I confess, your coming before me is nearer to his reverence.

OLI. What, boy!

ORL. Come, come, elder brother, you are too young in this.

OLI. Wilt thou lay hands on me, villain?

ORL. I am no villain: I am the youngest son of Sir Rowland de Bois: he was my father; and he is thrice a villain that says such a father begot villains. Wert thou not my brother, I would not take this hand from thy throat, till this other had pulled out thy tongue for saying so: thou hast railed on thyself.

ADAM [Coming forward.] Sweet masters, be patient: for your father's remembrance, be at accord.

OLI. Let me go, I say.

ORL. I will not, till I please: you shall hear me. My father charged you in his will to give me good education: you have trained me like a peasant, obscuring and hiding from me all gentleman-like qualities. The spirit of my father grows strong in me, and will no longer endure it: therefore allow me such exercises as may become a gentleman, or give me the poor allottery my father left me by testament; with that I will go buy my fortunes.

OLI. And what wilt thou do? beg, when that is spent? Well, Sir, get you in: I will not long be troubled with you; you shall have some part of your will: I pray you, leave me.

ORL. I will no farther offend you than becomes me for my good.

OLI. Get you with him, you old dog.

ADAM. Is old dog my reward? Most true, I have lost my teeth in your service.—God be with my old master! he would not have spoken such a word.

[*Exeunt* ORLANDO *and* ADAM.

OLI. Is it even so? begin you to grow upon me? I will physic your rankness, and yet give no thousand crowns neither.—Hola, Dennis!

Enter DENNIS.

DEN. Calls your worship?

OLI. Was not Charles the duke's wrestler here to speak with me?

DEN. So please you, he is here at the door, and importunes access to you.

OLI. Call him in. [*Exit* DENNIS.]—'Twill be a good way; and to-morrow the wrestling is.

Enter CHARLES.

CHA. Good-morrow to your worship.

OLI. Good monsieur Charles, what's the new news at the new court?

CHA. There's no news at the court, Sir, but the old news: that is, the old duke is banished by his younger brother the new duke; and three or four loving lords have put themselves into voluntary exile with him, whose lands and revenues enrich the new duke; therefore he gives them good leave to wander.

OLI. Can you tell if Rosalind, the duke's daughter, be banished with her father?

CHA. O, no; for the duke's daughter, her cousin, so loves her,—being ever from their cradles bred together,—that she would have followed her exile, or have died to stay behind her. She is at the court, and no less beloved of her uncle than his own daughter; and never two ladies loved as they do.

OLI. Where will the old duke live?

CHA. They say, he is already in the forest of Arden, and a many merry men with him; and there they live like the old Robin Hood of England: they say, many young gentlemen flock to him every day, and fleet the time carelessly, as they did in the golden world.

OLI. What, you wrestle to-morrow before the new duke?

CHA. Marry, do I, Sir; and I came to acquaint you with a matter. I am given, Sir, secretly to understand that your younger brother, Orlando, hath a disposition to come in disguised against me to try a fall. To-morrow, Sir, I wrestle for my credit; and he that escapes me without some broken limb shall acquit him well. Your brother is but young and tender; and, for your love, I would be loath to foil him, as I must, for my own honour, if he come in: therefore, out of my love to you, I came hither to acquaint you withal; that either you might stay him from his intendment, or brook such disgrace well as he shall run into; in that it is a thing of his own search, and altogether against my will.

OLI. Charles, I thank thee for thy love to me, which, thou shalt find, I will most kindly requite. I had myself notice of my brother's purpose herein, and have by underhand means laboured to dissuade him from it; but he is resolute. I'll tell thee, Charles, it is the stubbornest young fellow of France; full of ambition, an envious emulator of every man's good parts, a secret and villanous contriver against me his natural brother: therefore use thy discretion: I had as lief thou didst break his neck as his finger: and thou wert best look to't; for if thou dost him any slight disgrace, or if he do not mightily grace himself on thee, he will practise against thee by poison, entrap thee by some treacherous device, and never leave thee till he hath ta'en thy life by some indirect means or other; for, I assure thee,—and almost with tears I speak it,—there is not one so young and so villanous this day living. I speak but brotherly of him; but should I anatomize him to thee as he is, I must blush and weep, and thou must look pale and wonder.

CHA. I am heartily glad I came hither to you. If he come to-morrow, I'll give him his payment: if ever he go alone again, I'll never wrestle for prize more: and so, God keep your worship!

OLI. Farewell, good Charles.— [Exit CHARLES.] Now will I stir this gamester: I hope I shall see an end of him; for my soul, yet I know not why, hates nothing more than he: yet he's gentle; never

schooled, and yet learned; full of noble device; of all sorts enchantingly beloved; and, indeed, so much in the heart of the world, and especially of my own people, who best know him, that I am altogether misprised: but it shall not be so long; this wrestler shall clear all: nothing remains but that I kindle the boy thither; which now I'll go about.   [Exit.

SCENE II.—A Lawn before the Duke's Palace.

Enter ROSALIND and CELIA.

CEL. I pray thee, Rosalind, sweet my coz, be merry.

ROS. Dear Celia, I show more mirth than I am mistress of; and would you yet I were merrier? Unless you could teach me to forget a banished father, you must not learn me how to remember any extraordinary pleasure.

CEL. Herein, I see, thou lovest me not with the full weight that I love thee. If my uncle, thy banished father, had banished thy uncle, the duke my father, so thou hadst been still with me, I could have taught my love to take thy father for mine: so would'st thou, if the truth of thy love to me were so righteously tempered as mine is to thee.

ROS. Well, I will forget the condition of my estate, to rejoice in yours.

CEL. You know my father hath no child but me, nor none is like to have: and, truly, when he dies, thou shalt be his heir; for what he hath taken away from thy father perforce, I will render thee again in affection; by mine honour, I will; and when I break that oath, let me turn monster: therefore, my sweet Rose, my dear Rose, be merry.

ROS. From henceforth I will, coz, and devise sports. Let me see; what think you of falling in love?

CEL. Marry, I pr'ythee, do, to make sport withal: but love no man in good earnest; nor no farther in sport neither, than with safety of a pure blush thou may'st in honour come off again.

ROS. What shall be our sport, then?

CEL. Let us sit and mock the good housewife Fortune from her wheel, that her gifts may henceforth be bestowed equally.

ROS. I would we could do so; for her benefits are mightily misplaced; and the bountiful blind woman doth most mistake in her gifts to women.

CEL. 'Tis true; for those that she make fair, she scarce makes honest; and thos

...that she makes honest, she makes very ill-favouredly.

ROS. Nay, now thou goest from Fortune's office to Nature's: Fortune reigns in gifts of the world, not in the lineaments of Nature.

CEL. No; when Nature hath made a fair creature, may she not by Fortune fall into the fire?—Though Nature hath given us wit to flout at Fortune, hath not Fortune sent in this fool to cut off the argument?

Enter TOUCHSTONE.

ROS. Indeed, there is Fortune too hard for Nature, when Fortune makes Nature's natural the cutter off of Nature's wit.

CEL. Peradventure this is not Fortune's work neither, but Nature's; who, perceiving our natural wits too dull to reason of such goddesses, hath sent this natural for our whetstone for always the dulness of the fool is the whetstone of the wits.—How now, wit! whither wander you?

TOUCH. Mistress, you must come away to your father.

CEL. Were you made the messenger?

TOUCH. No, by mine honour; but I was bid to come for you.

ROS. Where learned you that oath, fool?

TOUCH. Of a certain knight, that swore by his honour they were good pancakes, and swore by his honour the mustard was naught: now, I'll stand to it, the pancakes were naught, and the mustard was good; and yet was not the knight forsworn.

CEL. How prove you that, in the great heap of your knowledge?

ROS. Ay, marry, now unmuzzle your wisdom.

TOUCH. Stand you both forth now: stroke your chins, and swear by your beards that I am a knave.

CEL. By our beards, if we had them, thou art.

TOUCH. By my knavery, if I had it, then I were; but if you swear by that that is not, you are not forsworn: no more was this knight, swearing by his honour, for he never had any; or if he had, he had sworn it away before ever he saw those pancakes or that mustard.

CEL. Pr'ythee, who is't that thou meanest?

TOUCH. One that old Frederick, your father, loves.

CEL. My father's love is enough to honour him enough: speak no more of him; you'll be whipped for taxation one of these days.

TOUCH. The more pity, that fools may not speak wisely, what wise men do foolishly.

CEL. By my troth, thou sayest true; for since the little wit that fools have was silenced, the little foolery that wise men

have makes a great show.—Here comes Monsieur Le Beau.

ROS. With his mouth full of news.

CEL. Which he will put on us, as pigeons feed their young.

ROS. Then shall we be news-cramm'd.

CEL. All the better; we shall be the more marketable.—[*Enter* LE BEAU.] *Bon jour,* Monsieur Le Beau: what's the news?

LE BEAU. Fair princess, you have lost much good sport.

CEL. Sport! Of what colour?

LE BEAU. What colour, madam? How shall I answer you?

ROS. As wit and fortune will.

TOUCH. Or as the destinies decree.

CEL. Well said: that was laid on with a trowel.

TOUCH. Nay, if I keep not my rank,—

ROS. Thou losest thy old smell.

LE BEAU. You amaze me, ladies: I would have told you of good wrestling, which you have lost the sight of.

ROS. Yet tell us the manner of the wrestling.

LE BEAU. I will tell you the beginning; and, if it please your ladyships, you may see the end; for the best is yet to do; and here, where you are, they are coming to perform it.

CEL. Well,—the beginning, that is dead and buried.

LE BEAU. There comes an old man and his three sons,—

CEL. I could match this beginning with an old tale.

LE BEAU. Three proper young men, of excellent growth and presence;—

ROS. With bills on their necks,—"Be it known unto all men by these presents,"—

LE BEAU. The eldest of the three wrestled with Charles, the duke's wrestler; which Charles in a moment threw him, and broke three of his ribs, that there is little hope of life in him: so he served the second, and so the third. Yonder they lie; the poor old man, their father, making such pitiful dole over them, that all the beholders take his part with weeping.

ROS. Alas!

TOUCH. But what is the sport, monsieur, that the ladies have lost?

LE BEAU. Why, this that I speak of.

TOUCH. Thus men may grow wiser every day! it is the first time that ever I heard breaking of ribs was sport for ladies.

CEL. Or I, I promise thee.

ROS. But is there any else longs to see this broken music in his sides? is there yet another dotes upon rib-breaking?—Shall we see this wrestling, cousin?

LE BEAU. You must, if you stay here; for here is the place appointed for the wrestling, and they are ready to perform it.

CEL. Yonder, sure, they are coming: let us now stay and see it.

Flourish. Enter Duke FREDERICK, *Lords,* ORLANDO, CHARLES, *and* Attendants.

DUKE F. Come on: since the youth will not be entreated, his own peril on his forwardness.

ROS. Is yonder the man?

LE BEAU. Even he, madam.

CEL. Alas, he is too young! yet he looks successfully.

DUKE F. How now, daughter, and cousin! are you crept hither to see the wrestling?

ROS. Ay, my liege, so please you give us leave.

DUKE F. You will take little delight in it, I can tell you, there is such odds in the men. In pity of the challenger's youth, I would fain dissuade him, but he will not be entreated. Speak to him, ladies; see if you can move him.

CEL. Call him hither, good Monsieur Le Beau.

DUKE F. Do so: I'll not be by.

[*Duke goes apart.*

LE BEAU. Monsieur the challenger, the princesses call for you.

ORL. I attend them with all respect and duty.

ROS. Young man, have you challenged Charles the wrestler?

ORL. No, fair princess; he is the general challenger: I come but in, as others do, to try with him the strength of my youth.

CEL. Young gentleman, your spirits are too bold for your years. You have seen cruel proof of this man's strength: if you saw yourself with your eyes, or knew yourself with your judgment, the fear of your adventure would consel you to a more equal enterprise. We pray you, for your own sake, to embrace your own safety, and give over this attempt.

ROS. Do, young Sir; your reputation shall not therefore be misprised: we will make it our suit to the duke that the wrestling might not go forward.

ORL. I beseech you, punish me not with your hard thoughts; wherein I confess me much guilty, to deny so fair and excellent ladies any thing. But let your fair eyes and gentle wishes go with me to my trial: wherein if I be foiled, there is but one shamed that was never gracious; if killed, but one dead that is willing to be so: I shall do my friends no wrong, for I have none to lament me; the world no injury, for in it I have nothing; only in the world I

fill up a place, which may be better sup plied when I have made it empty.

ROS. The little strength that I have, would it were with you.

CEL. And mine, to eke out hers.

ROS. Fare you well: pray heaven, I l deceived in you!

CEL. Your heart's desires be with you!

CHA. Come, where is this young gallan that is so desirous to lie with his moth earth?

ORL. Ready, Sir; but his will hath in a more modest working.

DUKE F. You shall try but one fall.

CHA. No, I warrant your grace, you sha not entreat him to a second, that have mightily persuaded him from a first.

ORL. You mean to mock me after; yo should not have mocked me before: b come your ways.

ROS. Now Hercules be thy speed, your man!

CEL. I would I were invisible, to catch th strong fellow by the leg.

[CHARLES *and* ORLANDO *wrestl*

ROS. O excellent young man!

CEL. If I made a thunderbolt in mine ey I can tell who should down.

[CHARLES *is thrown. Shou*

DUKE F. No more, no more.

ORL. Yes, I beseech your grace: I am n yet well breathed.

DUKE F. How dost thou, Charles?

LE BEAU. He cannot speak, my lord.

DUKE F. Bear him away.

[CHARLES *is borne ou*

What is thy name, young man?

ORL. Orlando, my liege; the youngest so of Sir Rowland de Bois.

DUKE F. I would thou hadst been son t some man else:
The world esteem'd thy father honourabl
But I did find him still mine enemy:
Thou shouldst have better pleas'd me wit
    this deed,
Hadst thou descended from another hous
But fare thee well; thou art a gallar
    youth:
I would thou hadst told me of anothe
    father.

[*Exeunt Duke* FRED. *train, and* LE BEAU

CEL. Were I my father, coz, would I d this?

ORL. I am more proud to be Sir Rov land's son,
His youngest son;—and would not chang
    that calling,
To be adopted heir to Frederick.

ROS. My father lov'd Sir Rowland as h
    soul,

And all the world was of my father's mind;
Had I before known this young man his
  son,
I should have given him tears unto en-
  treaties,
Ere he should thus have ventur'd.
CEL.   Gentle cousin,
Let us go thank him and encourage him:
My father's rough and envious disposition
Sticks me at heart.—Sir, you have well de-
  serv'd;
If you do keep your promises in love
But justly, as you have exceeded all promise,
Your mistress shall be happy.
ROS.   Gentleman,
      [*Giving him a chain from her neck.*
Wear this for me, one out of suits with
  fortune,
That could give more, but that her hand
  lacks means.—
Shall we go, coz?
CEL. Ay.—Fare you well, fair gentleman.
ORL. Can I not say, I thank you? My bet-
  ter parts
Are all thrown down; and that which here
  stands up
Is but a quintain, a mere lifeless block.
ROS. He calls us back: my pride fell with
  my fortunes;
I'll ask him what he would.—Did you call,
  Sir?—
Sir, you have wrestled well, and overthrown
More than your enemies.
CEL.   Will you go, coz?
ROS. Have with you.—Fare you well.
          [*Exeunt* ROSALIND *and* CELIA.
ORL. What passion hangs these weights
  upon my tongue?
I cannot speak to her, yet she urg'd con-
  ference.
O poor Orlando, thou art overthrown!
Or Charles, or something weaker, masters
  thee.
          Re-enter LE BEAU.
LE BEAU. Good Sir, I do in friendship
  counsel you
To leave this place. Albeit you have de-
  serv'd
High commendation, true applause, and love,
Yet such is now the duke's condition,
That he misconstrues all that you have
  done.
The duke is humorous: what he is, indeed,
More suits you to conceive, than me to
  speak of.
ORL. I thank you, Sir: and, pray you, tell
  me this,—
Which of the two was daughter of the duke,
That here was at the wrestling?
LE BEAU. Neither his daughter, if we
  judge by manners;

But yet, indeed, the smaller is his daughter:
The other is daughter to the banish'd duke,
And here detain'd by her usurping uncle,
To keep his daughter company; whose
  loves
Are dearer than the natural bond of sisters.
But I can tell you, that of late this duke
Hath ta'en displeasure 'gainst his gentle
  niece,
Grounded upon no other argument,
But that the people praise her for her vir-
  tues,
And pity her for her good father's sake;
And, on my life, his malice 'gainst the lady
Will suddenly break forth.—Sir, fare you
  well:
Hereafter, in a better world than this,
I shall desire more love and knowledge of
  you.
ORL. I rest much bounden to you: fare
  you well.   [*Exit* LE BEAU.
Thus must I from the smoke into the
  smother;
From tyrant duke unto a tyrant brother:—
But heavenly Rosalind!   [*Exit.*

SCENE III.—*A Room in the Palace.*

Enter CELIA *and* ROSALIND.

CEL. Why, cousin; why, Rosalind;—Cupid
have mercy!—Not a word?
ROS. Not one to throw at a dog.
CEL. No, thy words are too precious to
be cast away upon curs, throw some of
them at me: come, lame me with reasons.
ROS. Then there were two cousins laid up,
when the one should be lamed with reasons, and the other mad without any.
CEL. But is all this for your father?
ROS. No, some of it for my father's child.
O, how full of briers is this working-day
world!
CEL. They are but burrs, cousin, thrown
upon thee in holiday foolery: if we walk
not in the trodden paths, our very petticoats
will catch them.
ROS. I could shake them off my coat:
these burrs are in my heart.
CEL. Hem them away.
ROS. I would try, if I could cry hem, and
have him.
CEL. Come, come, wrestle with thy affections.
ROS. O, they take the part of a better
wrestler than myself!
CEL. O, a good wish upon you! you will
try in time, in despite of a fall.—But, turning these jests out of service, let us talk in
good earnest: is it possible, on such a sudden, you should fall into so strong a liking
with old Sir Rowland's youngest son?

ROS. The duke my father lov'd his father dearly.

CEL. Doth it therefore ensue that you should love his son dearly? By this kind of chase, I should hate him, for my father hated his father dearly; yet I hate not Orlando.

ROS. No, 'faith, hate him not, for my sake.

CEL. Why should I not? doth he not deserve well?

ROS. Let me love him for that; and do you love him because I do.—Look, here comes the duke.

CEL. With his eyes full of anger.

     Enter Duke FREDERICK, *with* Lords.

DUKE F. Mistress, dispatch you with your safest haste,
And get you from our court.

ROS.   Me, uncle?

DUKE F.   You, cousin:
Within these ten days if that thou be'st found
So near our public court as twenty miles,
Thou diest for it.

ROS.   I do beseech your grace,
Let me the knowledge of my fault bear with me:
If with myself I hold intelligence,
Or have acquaintance with mine own desires;
If that I do not dream, or be not frantic,
(As do trust I am not) then, dear uncle,
Never so much as in a thought unborn
Did I offend your highness.

DUKE F.   Thus do all traitors:
If their purgation did consist in words,
They are as innocent as grace itself:—
Let it suffice thee, that I trust thee not.

ROS. Yet your mistrust cannot make me a traitor:
Tell me whereon the likelihood depends.

DUKE F. Thou art thy father's daughter; there's enough.

ROS. So was I when your highness took his dukedom;
So was I when your highness banish'd him.
Treason is not inherited, my lord;
Or, if we did derive it from our friends,
What's that to me? my father was no traitor:
Then, good my liege, mistake me not so much,
To think my poverty is treacherous.

CEL. Dear sovereign, hear me speak.

DUKE F. Ay, Celia; we stay'd her for your sake,
Else had she with her father rang'd along.

CEL. I did not then entreat to have her stay;
It was your pleasure, and your own remorse:

I was too young that time to value her;
But now I know her: if she be a traitor,
Why so am I; we still have slept together,
Rose at an instant, learn'd, play'd, eat together;
And whersoe'er we went, like Juno's swans,
Still we went coupled and inseparable.

DUKE F. She is too subtle for thee; and her smoothness,
Her very silence, and her patience,
Speak to the people, and they pity her.
Thou art a fool: she robs thee of thy name;
And thou wilt show more bright, and seem more virtuous,
When she is gone. Then, open not thy lips:
Firm and irrevocable is my doom
Which I have pass'd upon her;—she is banish'd.

CEL. Pronounce that sentence, then, on me, my liege:
I cannot live out of her company.

DUKE F. You are a fool.—You, niece, provide yourself:
If you out-stay the time, upon mine honour,
And in the greatness of my word, you die.

     [*Exeunt Duke* FREDERICK *and* Lords.

CEL. O my poor Rosalind! whither wilt thou go?
Wilt thou change fathers? I will give thee mine.
I charge thee, be not thou more griev'd than I am.

ROS. I have more cause.

CEL.   Thou hast not, cousin;
Pr'ythee, be cheerful: know'st thou not, the duke
Hath banished me, his daughter?

ROS.   That he hath not.

CEL. No? hath not? Rosalind lacks, then, the love
Which teacheth thee that thou and I am one.
Shall we be sunder'd? shall we part, sweet girl?
No: let my father seek another heir.
Therefore devise with me how we may fly,
Whither to go, and what to bear with us:
And do not seek to take your change upon you,
To bear your griefs yourself, and leave me out;
For, by this heaven, now at our sorrows pale,
Say what thou canst, I'll go along with thee.

ROS. Why, whither shall we go?

CEL.   To seek my uncle
In the forest of Arden.

ROS. Alas, what danger will it be to us,
Maids as we are, to travel forth so far!
Beauty provoketh thieves sooner than gold.

CEL. I'll put myself in poor and mean attire,
And with a kind of umber smirch my face;
The like do you: so shall we pass along,
And never stir assailants.

ROS.   Were it not better,
Because that I am more than common tall,
That I did suit me all points like a man?
A gallant curtle-ax upon my thigh,
A boar-spear in my hand; and (in my heart
Lie there what hidden woman's fear there will,)
We'll have a swashing and a martial outside;
As many other mannish cowards have,
That do outface it with their semblances.

CEL. What shall I call thee when thou art a man?

ROS. I'll have no worse a name than Jove's own page;
And therefore look you call me Ganymede.
But what will you be call'd?

CEL. Something that hath a reference to my state:
No longer Celia, but Aliena.

ROS. But, cousin, what if we assay'd to steal
The clownish fool out of your father's court?
Would he not be a comfort to our travel?

CEL. He'll go along o'er the wide world with me;
Leave me alone to woo him. Let's away,
And get our jewels and our wealth together;
Devise the fittest time and safest way
To hide us from pursuit that will be made
After my flight. Now go we in content
To liberty, and not to banishment.

[*Exeunt.*

ACT II.

Scene I.—*The Forest of* Arden.

Enter Duke Senior, Amiens, *and other*
Lords, *in the dress of Foresters.*

DUKE S. Now, my co-mates and brothers in exile,
Hath not old custom made this life more sweet
Than that of painted pomp? Are not these woods
More free from peril than the envious court?
Here feel we but the penalty of Adam,
The seasons' difference; as, the icy fang
And churlish chiding of the winter's wind,
Which, when it bites and blows upon my body,
Even till I shrink with cold, I smile, and say,

This is no flattery: these are counsellors
That feelingly persuade me what I am.
Sweet are the uses of adversity;
Which, like the toad, ugly and venomous,
Wears yet a precious jewel in his head:
And this our life, exempt from public haunt,
Finds tongues in trees, books in the running brooks,
Sermons in stones, and good in every thing.

AMI. I would not change it. Happy is your grace,
That can translate the stubbornness of fortune
Into so quiet and so sweet a style.

DUKE S. Come, shall we go and kill us venison?
And yet it irks me, the poor dappled fools,
Being native burghers of this desert city,
Should, in their own confines, with forked heads
Have their round haunches gor'd.

1 LORD. Indeed, my lord,
The melancholy Jaques grieves at that;
And, in that kind, swears you do more usurp
Than doth your brother that hath banish'd you.
To-day my lord of Amiens and myself
Did steal behind him, as he lay along
Under an oak, whose antique root peeps out
Upon the brook that brawls along this wood:
To the which place a poor sequester'd stag,
That from the hunters' aim had ta'en a hurt,
Did come to languish; and, indeed, my lord,
The wretched animal heav'd forth such groans,
That their discharge did stretch his leathern coat
Almost to bursting; and the big round tears
Cours'd one another down his innocent nose
In piteous chase: and thus the hairy fool,
Much marked of the melancholy Jaques,
Stood on the extremest verge of the swift brook,
Augmenting it with tears.

DUKE S.   But what said Jaques?
Did he not moralize this spectacle?

1 LORD. O, yes, into a thousand similes.
First, for his weeping into the needless stream;
"Poor deer," quoth he, "thou mak'st a testament
As wordlings do, giving thy sum of more
To that which had too much:" then, being there alone,
Left and abandon'd of his velvet friends;
"'Tis right," quoth he; "thus misery doth part

The flux of company:" anon, a careless
    herd,
Full of the pasture, jumps along by him,
And never stays to greet him; "Ay," quoth
    Jaques,
"Sweep on, you fat and greasy citizens;
'Tis just the fashion: wherefore do you look
Upon that poor and broken bankrupt
    there?"
Thus most invectively he pierceth through
The body of the country, city, court,
Yea, and of this our life: swearing that we
Are mere usurpers, tyrants, and what's
    worse,
To fright the animals, and to kill them up,
In their assign'd and native dwelling place.
DUKE S. And did you leave him in this
    contemplation?
2 LORD. We did, my lord, weeping and
    commenting
Upon the sobbing deer.
DUKE S.   Show me the place:
I love to cope him in these sullen fits,
For then he's full of matter.
2 LORD. I'll bring you to him straight.
                                    [*Exeunt.*

SCENE II.—*A Room in the Palace.*

Enter Duke FREDERICK, *Lords, and
    Attendants.*

DUKE F. Can it be possible that no man
    saw them?
It cannot be: some villains of my court
Are of consent and sufferance in this.
1 LORD. I cannot hear of any that did see
    her.
The ladies, her attendants of her chamber,
Saw her a-bed; and, in the morning early,
They found the bed untreasur'd of their
    mistress.
2 LORD. My lord, the roynish clown, at
    whom so oft
Your grace was wont to laugh, is also
    missing.
Hesperia, the princess' gentlewoman,
Confesses that she secretly o'er-heard
Your daughter and her cousin much com-
    mend
The parts and graces of the wrestler,
That did but lately foil the sinewy Charles;
And she believes, wherever they are gone,
That youth is surely in their company.
DUKE F. Send to his brother; fetch that
    gallant hither:
If he be absent, bring his brother to me;
I'll make him find him: do this suddenly;
And let not search and inquisition quail
To bring again these foolish runaways.
                                    [*Exeunt.*

SCENE III.—*Before* OLIVER'S *House.*

Enter ORLANDO *and* ADAM, *meeting.*

ORL. Who's there?
ADAM. What, my young master?—O my
    gentle master!
O my sweet master! O you memory
Of old Sir Rowland! why, what make you
    here?
Why are you virtuous? Why do people
    love you?
And wherefore are you gentle, strong, and
    valiant?
Why would you be so fond to overcome
The bony priser of the humorous duke?
Your praise is come too swiftly home be-
    fore you.
Know you not, master, to some kind of men
Their graces serve them but as enemies?
No more do yours: your virtues, gentle
    master,
Are sanctified and holy traitors to you.
O, what a world is this, when what is
    comely
Envenoms him that bears it!
ORL. Why, what's the matter?
ADAM.   O unhappy youth,
Come not within these doors! within this
    roof
The enemy of all your graces lives:
Your brother—(no, no brother; yet the
    son—
Yet not the son—I will not call him son—
Of him I was about to call his father,)—
Hath heard your praises; and this night he
    means
To burn the lodging where you use to lie,
And you within it: if he fail of that,
He will have other means to cut you off:
I overheard him, and his practices.
This is no place; this house is but a butch-
    ery:
Abhor it, fear it, do not enter it.
ORL. Why, whither, Adam, woulds't thou
    have me go?
ADAM. No matter whither, so you come
    not here.
ORL. What! would'st thou have me go and
    beg my food?
Or with a base and boisterous sword en-
    force
A thievish living on the common road?
This I must do, or know not what to do:
Yet this I will not do, do how I can;
I rather will subject me to the malice
Of a diverted blood, and bloody brother.
ADAM. But do not so. I have five hun-
    dred crowns,
The thrifty hire I sav'd under your father,
Which I did store, to be my foster-nurse

When service should in my old limbs lie
  lame,
And unregarded age in corners thrown:
Take that; and He that doth the ravens
  feed,
Yea, providently caters for the sparrow,
Be comfort to my age! Here is the gold;
All this I give you. Let me be your servant:
Though I look old, yet I am strong and
  lusty;
For in my youth I never did apply
Hot and rebellious liquors in my blood;
Nor did not with unbashful forehead woo
The means of weakness and debility;
Therefore my age is as a lusty winter,
Frosty, but kindly: let me go with you;
I'll do the service of a younger man
In all your business and necessities.
ORL. O good old man, how well in thee
  appears
The constant service of the antique world,
When service sweat for duty, not for meed!
Thou art not for the fashion of these times,
Where none will sweat but for promotion;
And having that, do choke their service up
Even with the having: it is not so with
  thee.
But, poor old man, thou prun'st a rotten
  tree,
That cannot so much as a blossom yield,
In lieu of all thy pains and husbandry.
But come thy ways; we'll go along together;
And ere we have thy youthful wages spent,
We'll light upon some settled low content.
ADAM. Master, go on, and I will follow
  thee,
To the last gasp, with truth and loyalty.—
From seventeen years, till now almost four-
  score,
Here lived I, but now live here no more.
At seventeen years many their fortunes
  seek;
But at fourscore it is too late a week:
Yet fortune cannot recompense me better,
Than to die well, and not my master's
  debtor.   [*Exeunt.*

SCENE IV.—*The Forest of* ARDEN.

Enter ROSALIND *dressed like a youth,* CELIA
  like a shepherdess, and TOUCHSTONE.
ROS. O Jupiter! how weary are my spirits!
TOUCH. I care not for my spirits, if my
legs were not weary.
ROS. I could find in my heart to disgrace
my man's apparel, and to cry like a woman;
but I must comfort the weaker vessel, as
doublet and hose ought to show itself
courageous to petticoat: therefore, courage,
good Aliena.

CEL. I pray you, bear with me; I can go
no farther.
TOUCH. For my part, I had rather bear
with you, than bear you: yet I should bear
no cross, if I did bear you; for I think you
have no money in your purse.
ROS. Well, this is the forest of Arden.
TOUCH. Ay, now am I in Arden; the
more fool I; when I was at home, I was
in a better place: but travellers must be
content.
ROS. Ay, be so, good Touchstone.—Look
you, who comes here; a young man, and an
old, in solemn talk.
          Enter CORIN *and* SILVIUS.
COR. That is the way to make her scorn
you still.
SIL. O Corin, that thou knew'st how I do
love her!
COR. I partly guess; for I have lov'd ere
now.
SIL. No, Corin, being old, thou canst not
guess;
Though in thy youth thou wast as true a
  lover
As ever sigh'd upon a midnight pillow:
But if thy love were ever like to mine,
(As sure I think did never man love so,)
How many actions most ridiculous
Hast thou been drawn to by thy fantasy?
COR. Into a thousand that I have forgot-
ten.
SIL. O, thou didst then ne'er love so
  heartily!
If thou remember'st not the slightest folly
That ever love did make thee run into,
Thou hast not lov'd:
Or if thou hast not sat, as I do now,
Wearying thy hearer in thy mistress' praise,
Thou hast not lov'd:
Or if thou hast not broke from company
Abruptly, as my passion now makes me,
Thou hast not lov'd.—O Phebe, Phebe,
  Phebe!   [*Exit.*
ROS. Alas, poor shepherd! searching of
thy wound,
I have by hard adventure found mine own.
TOUCH. And I mine. I remember, when I
was in love, I broke my sword upon a stone,
and bid him take that for coming a-night
to Jane Smile: and I remember the kissing
of her batlet, and the cow's dugs that her
pretty chopped hands had milked: and I
remember the wooing of a peascod instead
of her; from whom I took two cods, and
giving her them again, said with weeping
tears, "Wear these for my sake." We, that
are true lovers, run into strange capers;
but as all is mortal in nature, so is all nature in love mortal in folly.

ROS. Thou speakest wiser than thou art
'ware of.
TOUCH. Nay, I shall ne'er be 'ware of
mine own wit,
Till I break my shins against it.
ROS. Jove, Jove! this shepherd's passion
Is much upon my fashion.
TOUCH. And mine; but it grows some-
thing stale with me.
CEL. I pray you, one of you question yond'
man,
If he for gold will give us any food:
I faint almost to death.
TOUCH. Hola, you clown!
ROS. Peace, fool; hes not thy kinsman.
COR. Who calls?
TOUCH. Your betters, Sir.
COR. Else are they very wretched.
ROS.   Peace, I say.—
Good even to you, friend.
COR. And to you, gentle Sir, and to you
all.
ROS. I pr'ythee, shepherd, if that love or
gold
Can in this desert place buy entertainment,
Bring us where we may rest ourselves and
feed:
Here's a young maid with travel much
oppress'd,
And faints for succour.
COR.   Fair Sir, I pity her,
And wish, for her sake more than for mine
own,
My fortunes were more able to relieve her;
But I am shepherd to another man,
And do not shear the fleeces that I graze:
My master is of churlish disposition,
And little recks to find the way to heaven
By doing deeds of hospitality:
Besides, his cote, his flocks, and bounds
of feed,
Are now on sale; and at our sheepcote now,
By reason of his absence, there is nothing
That you will feed on; but what is, come
see,
And in my voice most welcome shall you
be.
ROS. What is he that shall buy his flock
and pasture?
COR. That young swain that you saw here
but erewhile,
That little cares for buying any thing.
ROS. I pray thee, if it stand with honesty,
Buy thou the cottage, pasture, and the
flock,
And thou shalt have to pay for it of us.
CEL. And we will mend thy wages. I like
this place,
And willingly could waste my time in it.
COR. Assuredly, the thing is to be sold:
Go with me: if you like, upon report,

The soil, the profit, and this kind of life,
I will your very faithful feeder be,
And buy it with your gold right suddenly.
                                   [*Exeunt.*

SCENE V.—*Another part of the Forest.*

Enter AMIENS, JAQUES, *and others.*

SONG.

AMI.

Under the greenwood tree
Who loves to lie with me,
And turn his merry note
Unto the sweet bird's throat,
Come hither, come hither, come hither:
Here shall he see
No enemy,
But winter and rough weather.

JAQ. More, more, I pr'ythee, more.
AMI. It will make you melancholy, monsieur Jaques.
JAQ. I thank it. More, I pr'ythee, more. I
can suck melancholy out of a song, as a
weasel sucks eggs. More, I pr'ythee, more.
AMI. My voice is ragged: I know I cannot
please you.
JAQ. I do not desire you to please me; I
do desire you to sing. Come, more; another stanza: call you them stanzas?
AMI. What you will, monsieur Jaques.
JAQ. Nay, I care not for their names; they
owe me nothing. Will you sing?
AMI. More at your request, than to please
myself.
JAQ. Well then, if ever I thank any man,
I'll thank you: but that they call compliment is like the encounter of two dog-
apes; and when a man thanks me heartily,
methinks I have given him a penny, and
he renders me the beggarly thanks. Come,
sing; and you that will not, hold your
tongues.
AMI. Well, I'll end the song.—Sirs, cover
the while; the duke will drink under this
tree.—He hath been all this day to look
you.
JAQ. And I have been all this day to
avoid him. He is too disputable for my
company: I think of as many matters as he;
but I give heaven thanks, and make no
boast of them. Come, warble, come.

SONG.

[*All together here.*]

Who doth ambition shun,
And loves to live i' the sun,
Seeking the food he eats,
And pleas'd with what he gets,

Come hither, come hither, come hither:
                    Here shall he see
                    No enemy,
But winter and rough weather.

JAQ. I'll give you a verse to this note, that I made yesterday in despite of my invention.
AMI. And I'll sing it.
JAQ. Thus it goes:—

If it do come to pass,
That any man turn ass,
Leaving his wealth and ease,
A stubborn will to please,
Ducdame, ducdame, ducdame:
                    Here shall he see,
                    Gross fools as he,
An if he will come to me.

AMI. What's that "ducdame?"
JAQ. 'Tis a Greek invocation, to call fools into a circle. I'll go sleep, if I can; if I cannot, I'll rail against all the first-born of Egypt.
AMI. And I'll go seek the duke: his banquet is prepared.   [*Exeunt severally.*

Scene VI.—*Another part of the Forest.*
Enter ORLANDO *and* ADAM.

ADAM. Dear master, I can go no farther: O, I die for food! Here lie I down, and measure out my grave. Farewell, kind master.
ORL. Why, how now, Adam! no greater heart in thee? Live a little; comfort a little; cheer thyself a little. If this uncouth forest yield any thing savage, I will either be food for it, or bring it for food to thee. Thy conceit is nearer death than thy powers. For my sake be comfortable: hold death awhile at the arm's end: I will here be with thee presently; and if I bring thee not something to eat, I will give thee leave to die: but if thou diest before I come, thou art a mocker in my labour. Well said! thou lookest cheerly; and I'll be with thee quickly.—Yet thou liest in the bleak air: come, I will bear thee to some shelter; and thou shalt not die for lack of a dinner, if there live anything in this desert. Cheerly good Adam.   [*Exeunt.*

Scene VII.—*Another part of the Forest.*
The same as Scene V.

A Table set out. Enter DUKE Senior, AMIENS, *Lords and others.*

DUKE S. I think he be transform'd into a beast:

For I can no where find him like a man.
1 LORD. My lord, he is but even now gone hence:
Here was he merry, hearing of a song.
DUKE S. If he, compact of jars grow musical,
We shall have shortly discord in the spheres.
Go, seek him: tell him I would speak with him.
1 LORD. He saves my labour by his own approach.

Enter JAQUES.

DUKE S. Why, how now, monsieur! what a life is this,
That your poor friends must woo your company!
What, you look merrily!
JAQ. A fool, a fool!—I met a fool i' the forest,
A motley fool;—a miserable world!—
As I do live by food, I met a fool;
Who laid him down and bask'd him in the sun,
And rail'd on lady Fortune in good terms,
In good set terms,—and yet a motley fool.
"Good-morrow, fool," quoth I. "No, Sir,"
quoth he,
"Call me not fool, till heaven hath sent me fortune."
And then he drew a dial from his poke
And, looking on it with lack-lustre eye,
Says very wisely, "It is ten o'clock:
Thus may we see," quoth he, "how the world wags:
'Tis but an hour ago since it was nine;
And after one hour more 'twill be eleven;
And so, from hour to hour, we ripe and ripe,
And then, from hour to hour, we rot and rot;
And thereby hangs a tale." When I did hear
The motley fool thus moral on the time,
My lungs began to crow like chanticleer,
That fools should be so deep contemplative;
And I did laugh, sans intermission,
An hour by his dial.—O noble fool!
A worthy fool!—Motley's the only wear.
DUKE S. What fool is this?
JAQ. O worthy fool!—One that hath been a courtier;
And says, if ladies be but young and fair,
They have the gift to know it: and in his brain,—
Which is as dry as the remainder biscuit
After a voyage,—he hath strange places cramm'd
With observation, the which he vents
In mangled forms.—O that I were a fool!
I am ambitious for a motley coat.

DUKE S. Thou shalt have one.
JAQ.   It is my only suit;
Provided, that you weed your better judgments
Of all opinion that grows rank in them,
That I am wise. I must have liberty
Withal, as large a charter as the wind,
To blow on whom I please; for so fools have:
And they that are most galled with my folly,
They most must laugh. And why, Sir, must they so?
The why is plain as way to parish church:
He, that a fool doth very wisely hit,
Doth very foolishly, although he smart,
Not to seem senseless of the bob: if not,
The wise man's folly is anatomiz'd,
Even by the squandering glances of the fool.
Invest me in my motley; give me leave
To speak my mind, and I will through and through
Cleanse the foul body of th' infected world,
If they will patiently receive my medicine.
DUKE S. Fie on thee! I can tell what thou wouldst do.
JAQ. What, for a counter, would I do, but good?
DUKE S. Most mischievous foul sin, in chiding sin:
For thou thyself hast been a libertine,
As sensual as the brutish sting itself;
And all th' embossed sores, and headed evils,
That thou with license of free foot hast caught,
Would'st thou disgorge into the general world.
JAQ. Why, who cries out on pride,
That can therein tax any private party?
Doth it not flow as hugely as the sea,
Till that the weary very means do ebb?
What woman in the city do I name,
When that I say, the city-woman bears
The cost of princes on unworthy shoulders?
Who can come in, and say that I mean her,
When such a one as she, such is her neigh-
Or what is he of basest function   [bour?
That says his bravery is not on my cost,
(Thinking that I mean him,) but therein suits
His folly to the mettle of my speech?
There then; how then? what then? Let me see wherein
My tongue hath wrong'd him: if it do him right,
Then he hath wrong'd himself; if he be free,
Why then, my taxing like a wild goose flies,

Unclaim'd of any man.—But who comes here?
Enter ORLANDO, with his sword drawn.
ORL. Forbear, and eat no more.
JAQ. Why, I have eat none yet.
ORL. Nor shalt not, till necessity be serv'd.
JAQ. Of what kind should this cock come of?
DUKE S. Art thou thus bolden'd, man, by thy distress,
Or else a rude despiser of good manners,
That in civility thou seem'st so empty?
ORL. You touch'd my vein at first: the thorny point
Of bare distress hath ta'en from me the show
Of smooth civility: yet I am inland bred,
And know some nurture. But forbear, I say:
He dies, that touches any of this fruit,
Till I and my affairs are answered.
JAQ. An you will not be answered with reason, I must die.   [reason,
DUKE S. What would you have? Your gentleness shall force,
More than your force move us to gentleness.
ORL. I almost die for food; and let me have it.
DUKE S. Sit down and feed, and welcome to our table.
ORL. Speak you so gently? Pardon me, I pray you:
I thought that all things had been savage here;
And therefore put I on the countenance
Of stern commandment. But whate'er you are,
That in this desert inaccessible,   [are,
Under the shade of melancholy boughs,
Lose and neglect the creeping hours of time;
If ever you have look'd on better days,
If ever been where bells have knoll'd to church,
If ever sat at any good man's feast,
If ever from your eye-lids wip'd a tear,
And know what 'tis to pity, and be pitied,—
Let gentleness my strong enforcement be:
In the which hope, I blush, and hide my sword.
DUKE S. True is it that we have seen better days,
And have with holy bell been knoll'd to church,
And sat at good men's feasts, and wip'd our eyes
Of drops that sacred pity hath engender'd:
And therefore sit you down in gentleness,

And take upon command what help we have,
That to your wanting may be minister'd.
ORL. Then, but forbear your food a little while,
Whiles, like a doe, I go to find my fawn,
And give it food. There is an old poor man,
Who after me hath many a weary step
Limp'd in pure love: till he be first suffic'd,—
Oppress'd with two weak evils, age and hunger,—
I will not touch a bit.   [*hunger,—*
DUKE S.   Go find him out,
And we will nothing waste till you return.
ORL. I thank ye; and be bless'd for your good comfort!   [*Exit.*
DUKE S. Thou seest, we are not all alone unhappy:
This wide and universal theatre
Presents more woful pageants, than the scene
Wherein we play in.   [*scene*
JAQ.   All the world's a stage,
And all the men and women merely players:
They have their exits and their entrances;
And one man in his time plays many parts,
His acts being seven ages. At first the infant,
Mewling and puking in the nurse's arms.
Then the whining school-boy, with his satchel,
And shining morning face, creeping like snail
Unwillingly to school. And then the lover,
Sighing like furnace, with a woful ballad
Made to his mistress' eye-brow. Then a soldier,
Full of strange oaths, and bearded like the pard,
Jealous in honour, sudden and quick in quarrel,
Seeking the bubble reputation
Even in the cannon's mouth. And then the justice,
In fair round belly with good capon lin'd,
With eyes severe, and beard of formal cut,
Full of wise saws and modern instances;
And so he plays his part. The sixth age shifts
Into the lean and slipper'd pantaloon,
With spectacles on nose, and pouch on side;
His youthful hose, well sav'd, a world too wide
For his shrunk shank; and his big manly voice,
Turning again toward childish treble, pipes
And whistles in his sound. Last scene of all,
That ends this strange eventful history,
Is second childishness, and mere oblivion,—

Sans teeth, sans eyes, sans taste, sans every thing.
Re-enter ORLANDO, *with* ADAM.
DUKE S. Welcome. Set down your venerable burden,
And let him feed.   [*able burden,*
ORL.   I thank you most for him.
ADAM. So had you need:—
I scarce can speak to thank you for myself.
DUKE S. Welcome; fall to: I will not trouble you
As yet, to question you about your fortunes.—
Give us some music; and, good cousin, sing.

SONG.

AMI.
    Blow, blow, thou winter wind,
        Thou art not so unkind
        As man's ingratitude;
        Thy tooth is not so keen,
        Because thou art not seen,
        Although thy breath be rude.
Heigh, ho! sing, heigh, ho! unto the green holly:
Most friendship is feigning, most loving mere folly:
        Then heigh, ho! the holly!
        This life is most jolly.

    Freeze, freeze, thou bitter sky,
        That dost not bite so nigh
        As benefits forgot:
        Though thou the waters warp,
        Thy sting is not so sharp,
        As friend remember'd not.
Heigh, ho! sing, &c.

DUKE S. If that you were the good Sir Rowland's son,—
As you have whisper'd faithfully you were,
And as mine eye doth his effigies witness
Most truly limn'd and living in your face,—
Be truly welcome hither: I am the duke,
That lov'd your father: the residue of your fortune,
Go to my cave and tell me.—Good old man,
Thou art right welcome as thy master is.—
Support him by the arm.—Give me your hand,
And let me all your fortunes understand.   [*Exeunt.*

ACT III.

SCENE I.—*A room in the Palace.*

Enter Duke FREDERICK, OLIVER, *Lords, and* Attendants.
DUKE F. Not see him since? Sir, Sir, that cannot be:

But were I not the better part made mercy,
I should not seek an absent argument
Of my revenge, thou present. But look to it:
Find out thy brother, wheresoe'er he is;
Seek him with candle; bring him, dead or
    living,
Within this twelvemonth, or turn thou no
To seek a living in our territory.   [more
Thy lands, and all things that thou dost
    call thine,
Worth seizure, do we seize into our hands,
Till thou canst quit thee by thy brother's
Of what we think against thee.   [mouth
OLI. O that your highness knew my heart
    in this!
I never lov'd my brother in my life.
DUKE F. More villain thou.—Well, push
    him out of doors;
And let my officers of such a nature
Make an extent upon his house and lands:
Do this expediently, and turn him going.
                                        [Exeunt.

SCENE II.—*The Forest of* ARDEN.

Enter ORLANDO, *with a paper.*

ORL. Hang there, my verse, in witness of
    my love;
And thou, thrice-crowned queen of night,
    survey
With thy chaste eye, from thy pale sphere
    above,
Thy huntress' name, that my full life doth
    sway.
O Rosalind! these trees shall be my books,
And in their barks my thoughts I'll char-
    acter;
That every eye, which in this forest looks,
Shall see thy virtue witness'd every where.
Run, run, Orlando; carve on every tree
The fair, the chaste, and unexpressive she.
                                        [Exit.

Enter CORIN *and* TOUCHSTONE.

COR. And how like you this shepherd's
life, master Touchstone?
TOUCH. Truly, shepherd, in respect of itself, it is a good life; but in respect that
it is a shepherd's life, it is naught. In
respect that it is solitary, I like it very well;
but in respect that it is private, it is a
very vile life. Now, in respect it is in the
fields, it pleaseth me well; but in respect
it is not in the court, it is tedious. As it
is a spare life, look you, it fits my humour
well; but as there is no more plenty in it,
it goes much against my stomach. Hast any
philosophy in thee, shepherd?
COR. No more but that I know, the more
one sickens, the worse at ease he is; and
that he that wants money, means, and con-

tent, is without three good friends; that
the property of rain is to wet, and fire to
burn; that good pasture makes fat sheep;
and that a great cause of the night, is
lack of the sun; that he that hath learned
no wit by nature nor art, may complain of
good breeding, or comes of a very dull
kindred.
TOUCH. Such a one is a natural philosopher. Wast ever in court, shepherd?
COR. No, truly.
TOUCH. Then thou art damned.
COR. Nay, I hope,—
TOUCH. Truly, thou art damned; like an
ill-roasted egg, all on one side.
COR. For not being at court? Your
reason.
TOUCH. Why, if thou never wast at court,
thou never sawest good manners; if thou
never sawest good manners, then thy manners must be wicked; and wickedness is
sin, and sin is damnation. Thou art in a
parlous state, shepherd.
COR. Not a whit, Touchstone: those that
are good manners at the court, are as ridiculous in the country, as the behaviour of
the country, is most mockable at the court.
You told me you salute not at the court,
but you kiss your hands: that courtesy
would be uncleanly, if courtiers were shepherds.
TOUCH. Instance, briefly; come, instance.
COR. Why, we are still handling our
ewes; and their fells, you know, are greasy.
TOUCH. Why, do not your courtier's
hands sweat? and is not the grease of a
mutton as wholesome as the sweat of a
man? Shallow, shallow. A better instance,
I say; come.
COR. Besides, our hands are hard.
TOUCH. Your lips will feel them the
sooner. Shallow again. A more sounder
instance; come.
COR. And they are often tarred over with
the surgery of our sheep; and would you
have us kiss tar? The courtier's hands are
perfumed with civet.
TOUCH. Most shallow man! Thou worms-
meat, in respect of a good piece of flesh,
indeed!—Learn of the wise, and perpend:
civet is of a baser birth than tar,—the very
uncleanly flux of a cat. Mend the instance,
shepherd.
COR. You have too courtly a wit for me:
I'll rest.
TOUCH. Wilt thou rest damned? God
help thee, shallow man! God make incision
in thee! thou art raw.
COR. Sir, I am a true labourer: I earn
that I eat, get that I wear; owe no man
hate, envy no man's happiness; glad of

other men's good, content with my harm;
and the greatest of my pride is, to see my
ewes graze, and my lambs suck.

TOUCH. That is another simple sin in
you; to bring the ewes and the rams together, and to offer to get your living by
the copulation of cattle; to be bawd to a
bell-wether; and to betray a she-lamb of a
twelvemonth, to a crooked-pated, old cuckoldly ram, out of all reasonable match.
If thou be'st not damned for this, the devil
himself will have no shepherds; I cannot
see else how thou shouldst 'scape.

COR. Here comes young master Ganymede, my new mistress's brother.

Enter ROSALIND, *reading a paper.*

ROS. [*Reads.*]
"From the east to western Ind,
No jewel is like Rosalind.
Her worth, being mounted on the wind,
Through all the world bears Rosalind.
All the pictures, fairest lin'd,
Are but black to Rosalind.
Let no face be kept in mind,
But the fair of Rosalind."

TOUCH. I'll rhyme you so, eight years
together, dinners, and suppers, and sleeping hours excepted: it is the right butter-
women's rank to market.

ROS. Out, fool!

TOUCH. For a taste:—

If a hart do lack a hind,
Let him seek out Rosalind.
If the cat will after kind,
So, be sure, will Rosalind.
Winter-garments must be lin'd,
So must slender Rosalind.
They that reap must sheaf and bind;
Then to cart with Rosalind.
Sweetest nut hath sourest rind,
Such a nut is Rosalind.
He that sweetest rose will find,
Must find love's prick, and Rosalind.

This is the very false gallop of verses: why
do you infect yourself with them?

ROS. Peace, you dull fool! I found them
on a tree.

TOUCH. Truly, the tree yields bad fruit.

ROS. I'll graff it with you, and then I
shall graff it with a medlar: then it will
be the earliest fruit i' the country; for
you'll be rotten e'er you be half ripe, and
that's the right virtue of the medlar.

TOUCH. You have said; but whether
wisely or no, let the forest judge.

Enter CELIA, *reading a paper.*

ROS. Peace!
Here comes my sister, reading: stand aside.

CEL. [*Reads.*]
"Why should this a desert be?
For it is unpeopled? No;
Tongues I'll hang on every tree,
That shall civil saying show:
Some, how brief the life of man
Runs his erring pilgrimage,
That the stretching of a span
Buckles in his sum of age;
Some, of violated vows
'Twixt the souls of friend and friend:
But upon the fairest boughs,
Or at every sentence' end,
Will I Rosalinda write;
Teaching all that read, to know
The quintessence of every sprite
Heaven would in little show.
Therefore heaven Nature charg'd
That one body should be fil'd
With all graces wide enlarg'd:
Nature presently distill'd
Helen's cheek, but not her heart;
Cleopatra's majesty;
Atalanta's better part;
Sad Lucretta's modesty.
Thus Rosalind of many parts
By heavenly synod was devis'd;
Of many faces, eyes, and hearts,
To have the touches dearest priz'd.
Heaven would that she these gifts
    should have,
And I to live and die her slave."

ROS. O most gentle Jupiter!—what tedious homily of love have you wearied your
parishioners withal, and never cried, "Have
patience, good people!"

CEL. How now! back, friends:—shepherd, go off a little:—go with him, sirrah.

TOUCH. Come, shepherd, let us make an
honourable retreat; though not with bag
and baggage, yet with scrip and scrippage.
[*Exeunt* CORIN *and* TOUCHSTONE.

CEL. Didst thou hear these verses?

ROS. O, yes, I heard them all, and more
too; for some of them had in them more
feet than the verses would bear.

CEL. That's no matter: the feet might
bear the verses.

ROS. Ay, but the feet were lame, and
could not bear themselves without the verse,
and therefore stood lamely in the verse.

CEL. But didst thou hear without won-
dering, how thy name should be hanged
and carved upon these trees?

ROS. I was seven of the nine days out
of the wonder before you came; for look
here what I found on a palm-tree:—I was
never so be-rhymed since Pythagoras' time,

that I was an Irish rat, which I can hardly remember.

CEL. Trow you who hath done this?

ROS. Is it a man?

CEL. And a chain, that you once wore, about his neck. Change your colour?

ROS. I pr'ythee, who?

CEL. O lord, lord! it is a hard matter for friends to meet; but mountains may be removed with earthquakes, and so encounter.

ROS. Nay, but who is it?

CEL. Is it possible?

ROS. Nay, I pr'ythee now, with most petitionary vehemence, tell me who it is.

CEL. O wonderful, wonderful, and most wonderful, wonderful! and yet again wonderful, and after that, out of all whooping!

ROS. Good my complexion! dost thou think, though I am caparison'd like a man, I have a doublet and hose in my disposition? One inch of delay more is a South-sea of discovery; I pr'ythee, tell me who is it quickly, and speak apace. I would thou couldst stammer, that thou might'st pour this concealed man out of thy mouth, as wine comes out of a narrow-mouth'd bottle,—either too much at once, or none at all. I pr'ythee, take the cork out of thy mouth, that I may drink thy tidings.

CEL. So you may put a man in your belly.

ROS. Is he of God's making? What manner of man? Is his head worth a hat, or his chin worth a beard?

CEL. Nay, he hath but a little beard.

ROS. Why, God will send more, if the man will be thankful: let me stay the growth of his beard, if thou delay me not the knowledge of his chin.

CEL. It is young Orlando, that tripped up the wrestler's heels and your heart, both, in an instant.

ROS. Nay, but the devil take mocking: speak sad brow, and true maid.

CEL. I' faith, coz, 'tis he.

ROS. Orlando?

CEL. Orlando.

ROS. Alas the day! what shall I do with my doublet and hose?—What did he, when thou sawest him? What said he? How looked he? Wherein went he? What makes he here? Did he ask for me? Where remains he? How parted he with thee? and when shalt thou see him again? Answer me in one word.

CEL. You must borrow me Gargantua's mouth first: 'tis a word too great for any mouth of this age's size. To say ay and no to these particulars, is more than to answer in a catechism.

ROS. But doth he know that I am in this forest, and in man's apparel? Looks he as freshly as he did the day he wrestled?

CEL. It is as easy to count atomies, as to resolve the propositions of a lover:—but take a taste of my finding him, and relish it with good observance. I found him under a tree, like a dropped acorn.

ROS. It may well be call'd Jove's tree, when it drops forth such fruit.

CEL. Give me audience, good madam.

ROS. Proceed.

CEL. There lay he, stretch'd along like a wounded knight.

ROS. Though it be pity to see such a sight, it well becomes the ground.

CEL. Cry, hola! to thy tongue, I pr'ythee; it curvets unseasonably. He was furnish'd like a hunter.

ROS. O, ominous! he comes to kill my heart.

CEL. I would sing my song without a burden: thou bringest me out of tune.

ROS. Do you not know I am a woman? when I think, I must speak. Sweet, say on.

CEL. You bring me out.—Soft! comes he not here?

ROS. 'Tis he: slink by, and note him.

[ROSALIND *and* CELIA *retire.*

Enter ORLANDO *and* JAQUES.

JAQ. I thank you for your company; but good faith, I had as lief have been myself alone.

ORL. And so had I; but yet, for fashion' sake, I thank you too for your society.

JAQ. God be wi' you: let's meet as little as we can.

ORL. I do desire we may be better strangers.

JAQ. I pray you, mar no more trees with writing love-songs in their barks.

ORL. I pray you, mar no more of my verses with reading them ill-favoredly.

JAQ. Rosalind is your love's name?

ORL. Yes, just.

JAQ. I do not like her name.

ORL. There was no thought of pleasing you when she was christened.

JAQ. What stature is she of?

ORL. Just as high as my heart.

JAQ. You are full of pretty answers. Have you not been acquainted with goldsmiths' wives, and conn'd them out of rings?

ORL. Not so; but I answer you right painted cloth, from whence you have studied your questions.

JAQ. You have a nimble wit: I think 'twas made of Atalanta's heels. Will you sit down with me? and we two will rail against our mistress the world, and all our misery.

ORL. I will chide no breather in the world but myself against whom I know most faults.

JAQ. The worst fault you have is to be in love.

ORL. 'Tis a fault I will not change for your best virtue. I am weary of you.

JAQ. By my troth, I was seeking for a fool when I found you.

ORL. He is drowned in the brook: look but in, and you shall see him.

JAQ. There I shall see mine own figure.

ORL. Which I take to be either a fool, or a cypher.

JAQ. I'll tarry no longer with you: farewell, good signior Love.

ORL. I am glad of your departure: adieu, good monsieur Melancholy.

[*Exit* JAQUES. ROSALIND *and* CELIA *come forward.*

ROS. [*Aside to* CELIA.] I will speak to him like a saucy lackey, and under that habit play the knave with him. [*To him.*] Do you hear, forester?

ORL. Very well: what would you?

ROS. I pray you, what is't o'clock?

ORL. You should ask me, what time o'day: there's no clock in the forest.

ROS. Then there is no true lover in the forest; else sighing every minute, and groaning every hour, would detect the lazy foot of Time as well as a clock.

ORL. And why not the swift foot of Time? had not that been as proper?

ROS. By no means, Sir. Time travels in divers paces with divers persons: I'll tell you who Time ambles withal, who Time trots withal, who Time gallops withal, and who he stands still withal.

ORL. I pr'ythee, who doth he trot withal?

ROS. Marry, he trots hard with a young maid, between the contract of her marriage, and the day it is solemnized: if the interim be but a se'nnight, Time's pace is so hard that it seems the length of seven years.

ORL. Who ambles Time withal?

ROS. With a priest that lacks Latin, and a rich man that hath not the gout; for the one sleeps easily, because he cannot study; and the other lives merrily, because he feels no pain: the one lacking the burden of lean and wasteful learning; the other knowing no burden of heavy tedious penury: these Time ambles withal.

ORL. Who doth he gallop withal?

ROS. With a thief to the gallows; for though he go as softly as foot can fall, he thinks himself too soon there.

ORL. Who stays it still withal?

ROS. With lawyers in the vacation; for they sleep between term and term, and then they perceive not how Time moves.

ORL. Where dwell you, pretty youth?

ROS. With this shepherdess, my sister; here in the skirts of the forest, like fringe upon a petticoat.

ORL. Are you native of this place?

ROS. As the coney, that you see dwell where she is kindled.

ORL. Your accent is something finer than you could purchase in so removed a dwelling.

ROS. I have been told so of many: but indeed an old religious uncle of mine taught me to speak, who was in his youth an inland man; one that knew courtship too well, for there he fell in love. I have heard him read many lectures against it; and I thank God, I am not a woman to be touched with so many giddy offenses, as he hath generally taxed their whole sex withal.

ORL. Can you remember any of the principal evils that he laid to the charge of women?

ROS. There were none principal: they were all like one another, as half-pence are; every one fault seeming monstrous, till his fellow fault came to match it.

ORL. I pr'ythee, recount some of them.

ROS. No, I will not cast away my physic, but on those that are sick. There is a man haunts the forest, that abuses our young plants with carving Rosalind on their barks; hangs odes upon hawthorns, and elegies on brambles; all, forsooth, deifying the name of Rosalind: if I could meet that fancy-monger, I would give him some good counsel, for he seems to have the quotidian of love upon him.

ORL. I am he that is so love-shaked. I pray you, tell me your remedy.

ROS. There is none of my uncle's marks upon you: he taught me how to know a man in love; in which cage of rushes I am sure you are not prisoner.

ORL. What were his marks?

ROS. A lean cheek,—which you have not; a blue eye, and sunken,—which you have not; an unquestionable spirit,—which you have not; a beard neglected,—which you have not;—but I pardon you for that; for, simply, your having in beard is a younger brother's revenue:—then, your hose should be ungarter'd, your bonnet unbanded, your sleeve unbuttoned, your shoe untied, and every thing about you demonstrating a careless desolation; but you are no such man,—you are rather point-device in your accoutrements, as loving yourself, than seeming the lover of any other.

ORL. Fair youth, I would I could make thee believe I love.

ROS. Me believe it! you may as soon make her that you love believe it; which, I warrant, she is apter to do, than to confess she does: that is one of the points in the which women still give the lie to their consciences. But, in good sooth, are you he that hangs the verses on the trees, wherein Rosalind is so admired?

ORL. I swear to thee, youth, by the white hand of Rosalind, I am that he, that unfortunate he.

ROS. But are you so much in love as your rhymes speak?

ORL. Neither rhyme nor reason can express how much.

ROS. Love is merely a madness; and, I tell you, deserves as well a dark house and a whip, as madmen do: and the reason why they are not so punished and cured, is, that the lunacy is so ordinary, that the whippers are in love too. Yet I profess curing it by counsel.

ORL. Did you ever cure any so?

ROS. Yes, one; and in this manner. He was to imagine me his love, his mistress; and I set him every day to woo me: at which time would I, being but a moonish youth, grieve, be effeminate, changeable, longing, and liking; proud, fantastical, apish, shallow, inconstant, full of tears, full of smiles; for every passion something, and for no passion truly any thing, as boys and women are, for the most part, cattle of this colour: would now like him, now loathe him; then entertain him, then forswear him; now weep for him, then spit at him; that I drave my suitor from is mad humour of love, to a living humour of madness; which was, to forswear the full stream of the world, and to live in a nook, merely monastic. And thus I cured him; and this way will I take upon me to wash your liver as clean as a sound sheep's heart, that there shall not be one spot of love in't.

ORL. I would not be cured, youth.

ROS. I would cure you, if you would but call me Rosalind, and come every day to my cote, and woo me.

ORL. Now, by the faith of my love, I will: tell me where it is.

ROS. Go with me to it, and I'll show it you: and, by the way, you shall tell me where in the forest you live. Will you go?

ORL. With all my heart, good youth.

ROS. Nay, you must call me Rosalind.— Come, sister, will you go?   [*Exeunt.*

SCENE III.—*Another part of the Forest.*

Enter TOUCHSTONE *and* AUDREY; JAQUES *behind.*

TOUCH. Come apace, good Audrey: I will fetch up your goats, Audrey. And how, Audrey? am I the man yet? Doth my simple feature content you?

AUD. Your features! Lord warrant us! what features?

TOUCH. I am here with thee and thy goats, as the most capricious poet, honest Ovid, was among the Goths.

JAQ. [*Aside.*] O knowledge ill-inhabited! worse than Jove in a thatch'd house!

TOUCH. When a man's verses cannot be understood, nor a man's good wit seconded with the forward child, understanding, it strikes a man more dead than a great reckoning in a little room.—Truly, I would the gods had made thee poetical.

AUD. I do not know what poetical is: is it honest in deed and word? Is it a true thing?

TOUCH. No, truly; for the truest poetry is the most feigning; and lovers are given to poetry; and what they swear in poetry, may be said, as lovers, they do feign.

AUD. Do you wish, then, that the gods had made me poetical?

TOUCH. I do, truly; for thou swearest to me thou art honest: now, if thou wert a poet, I might have some hope thou didst feign.

AUD. Would you not have me honest?

TOUCH. No, truly, unless thou wert hard-favor'd; for honesty coupled to beauty, is to have honey a sauce to sugar.

JAQ. [*Aside.*] A material fool!

AUD. Well, I am not fair; and therefore I pray the gods make me honest.

TOUCH. Truly, and to cast away honesty upon a foul slut, were to put good meat into an unclean dish.

AUD. I am not a slut, though I thank the gods I am foul.

TOUCH. Well, praised be the gods for thy foulness! sluttishness may come hereafter. But be it as it may be, I will marry thee: and to that end, I have been with Sir Oliver Mar-text, the vicar of the next village; who hath promised to meet me in this place of the forest, and to couple us.

JAQ. [*Aside.*] I would fain see this meeting.

AUD. Well, the gods give us joy!

TOUCH. Amen. A man may, if he were of a fearful heart, stagger in this attempt; for here we have no temple but the wood, no assembly but hornbeasts. But what though? Courage! As horns are odious, they are necessary. It is said,—many a man knows no end of his goods: right; many a man has good horns, and knows no end of them. Well, that is the dowry of his wife; 'tis none of his own getting. Horns? Even so:—Poor men alone?—No, no; the noblest deer hath them as huge as the rascal. Is the single man therefore blessed? No: as a walled town is more worthier than a village, so is the forehead of a married man more honourable than the bare brow of a bachelor; and by how much defense is better than no skill, by so much is a horn more precious than to want.—Here comes Sir Oliver.

Enter Sir OLIVER MAR-TEXT.

Sir Oliver Mar-text, you are well met: will you dispatch us here under this tree, or shall we go with you to your chapel?

SIR OLI. Is there none here to give the woman?

TOUCH. I will not take her on gift of any man.

SIR OLI. Truly, she must be given or the marriage is not lawful.

JAQ. [*Coming forward.*] Proceed, proceed: I'll give her.

TOUCH. Good even, good master Whatye-call't: how do you, Sir? You are very well met: God'ild you for your last company: I am very glad to see you:—even a toy in hand here, Sir:—nay, pray be covered.

JAQ. Will you be married, motley?

TOUCH. As the ox hath his bow, Sir, the horse his curb, and the falcon her bells, so man hath his desires; and as pigeons bill, so wedlock would be nibbling.

JAQ. And will you, being a man of your breeding, be married under a bush, like a beggar? Get you to church, and have a good priest that can tell you what marriage is: this fellow will but join you together as they join wainscot; then one of you will prove a shrunk panel, and like green timber, warp, warp.

TOUCH. [*Aside.*] I am not in the mind but I were better to be married of him than of another: for he is not like to marry me well; and not being well married, it will be a good excuse for me hereafter to leave my wife.

JAQ. Go thou with me, and let me counsel thee.

TOUCH. Come, sweet Audrey: We must be married, or we must live in bawdry.—

Farewell, good master Oliver:—not,—
         O sweet Oliver,
         O brave Oliver,
Leave me not behind thee:—
but,—   Wend away,
         Begone, I say,
will not to wedding with thee.
    [*Exeunt* JAQUES, TOUCHSTONE, *and*
                              AUDREY.

SIR OLI. 'Tis no matter: ne'er a fantastical knave of them all shall flout me out of my calling.   [*Exit.*

SCENE IV.—*A part of the Forest. Before a Cottage.*

Enter ROSALIND *and* CELIA.

ROS. Never talk to me; I will weep.

CEL. Do, I pr'ythee; but yet have the grace to consider, that tears do not become a man.

ROS. But have I not cause to weep?

CEL. As good cause as one would desire; therefore weep.

ROS. His very hair is of the dissembling colour.

CEL. Something browner than Judas's: marry, his kisses are Judas's own children.

ROS. I' faith, his hair is of a good colour.

CEL. An excellent colour: your chestnut was ever the only colour.

ROS. And his kissing is as full of sanctity as the touch of holy bread.

CEL. He hath bought a pair of cast lips of Diana: a nun of winter's sisterhood kisses not more religiously; the very ice of chastity is in them.

ROS. But why did he swear he would come this morning, and comes not?

CEL. Nay, certainly, there is no truth in him.

ROS. Do you think so?

CEL. Yes; I think he is not a pick-purse, nor a horse-stealer; but for his verity in love, I do think him as concave as a covered goblet, or a worm-eaten nut.

ROS. Not true in love?

CEL. Yes, when he is in; but I think he is not in.

ROS. You have heard him swear downright, he was.

CEL. "Was" is not "is:" besides, the oath of a lover is no stronger than the word of a tapster; they are both the confirmers of false reckonings. He attends here in the forest on the duke your father.

ROS. I met the duke yesterday, and had much question with him. He asked me, of what parentage I was; I told him, of as good as he; so he laughed and let me go. But what talk we of fathers, when there is such a man as Orlando?

CEL. O, that's a brave man! he writes brave verses, speaks brave words, swears

brave oaths, and breaks them bravely, quite
traverse, athwart the heart of his lover; as
a puny tilter, that spurs his horse but on
one side, breaks his staff like a noble
goose: but all's brave, that youth mounts,
and folly guides.—Who comes here?

Enter CORIN.

COR. Mistress, and master, you have oft
enquir'd
After the shepherd that complain'd of love,
Who you saw sitting by me on the turf,
Praising the proud disdainful shepherdess
That was his mistress.

CEL.   Well, and what of him?

COR. If you will see a pageant truly
play'd,
Between the pale complexion of true love,
And the red glow of scorn and proud disdain,
Go hence a little, and I shall conduct you,
If you will mark it.

ROS.   O, come, let us remove:
The sight of lovers feedeth those in love.—
Bring us to this sight, and you shall say
I'll prove a busy actor in their play.
                                    [*Exeunt.*

SCENE V.—*Another part of the Forest.*
Enter SILVIUS *and* PHEBE.

SIL. Sweet Phebe, do not scorn me; do
not, Phebe:
Say that you love me not; but say not so
In bitterness. The common executioner,
Whose heart th' accustom'd sight of death
makes hard,
Falls not the axe upon the humbled neck,
But first begs pardon: will you sterner be
Than he that dies and lives by bloody
drops?

Enter ROSALIND, CELIA, *and* CORIN, *behind.*

PHE. I would not be thy executioner:
I fly thee, for I would not injure thee.
Thou tell'st me there is murder in mine
eye:
'Tis pretty, sure, and very probable,
That eyes,—that are the frail'st and softest
things,
Who shut their coward gates on atomies,—
Should be call'd tyrants, butchers, murderers!
Now I do frown on thee with all my heart;
And, if mine eyes can wound, now let them
kill thee:
Now counterfeit to swoon; why, now fall
down;
Or, if thou canst not, O, for shame, for
shame!
Lie not, to say mine eyes are murderers.
Now show the wound mine eye hath made
in thee:

Scratch thee but with a pin, and there remains
Some scar of it; lean but upon a rush,
The cicatrice and capable impressure
Thy palm some moment keeps: but now
mine eyes,
Which I have darted at thee, hurt thee
not;
Nor, I am sure, there is no force in eyes
That can do hurt.

SIL.   O dear Phebe,
If ever, (as that ever may be near,)
You meet in some fresh cheek the power
of fancy,
Then shall you know the wounds invisible
That love's keen arrows make.

PHE.   But, till that time,
Come not thou near me: and, when that
time comes,
Afflict me with thy mocks, pity me not;
As, till that time, I shall not pity thee.

ROS. [*Advancing.*] And why, I pray you?
Who might be your mother,
That you insult, exult, and all at once,
Over the wretched? What though you have
no beauty,
(As, by my faith, I see no more in you
Than without candle may go dark to bed,)
Must you be therefore proud and pitiless?
Why, what means this? Why do you look
on me?
I see no more in you, than in the ordinary
Of nature's sale-work:—Od's my little life!
I think she means to tangle my eyes too.
No, 'faith, proud mistress, hope not after it:
'Tis not your inky brows, your black-silk
hair,
Your bugle eye-balls, nor your cheek of
cream,
That can entame my spirits to your worship.—
You foolish shepherd, wherefore do you
follow her,
Like foggy south, puffing with wind and
rain?
You are a thousand times a properer man,
Than she a woman: 'tis such fools as you,
That make the world full of ill-favour'd
children:
'Tis not her glass, but you, that flatters
her;
And out of you she sees herself more
proper,
Than any of her lineaments can show her.—
But, mistress, know yourself: down on your
knees,
And thank heaven, fasting, for a good
man's love:
For I must tell you friendly in your ear,—
Sell when you can: you are not for all
markets:

Cry the man mercy; love him; take his offer:
Foul is most foul, being foul to be a scoffer.—
So, take her to thee, shepherd:—fare you well.

PHE. Sweet youth, I pray you, chide a year together:
I had rather hear you chide, than this man woo.

ROS. He's fallen in love with your foulness:—[*To* Silvius.] and she'll fall in love with my anger. If it be so, as fast as she answers thee with frowning looks, I'll sauce her with bitter words.—[*To* Phebe.] Why look you so upon me?

PHE. For no ill will I bear you.

ROS. I pray you, do not fall in love with me,
For I am falser than vows made in wine:
Besides, I like you not.—If you will know my house,
'Tis at the tuft of olives, here hard by.—
Will you go, sister?—Shepherd, ply her hard.—
Come, sister.—Shepherdess, look on him better,
And be not proud: though all the world could see,
None could be so abus'd in sight as he.—
Come, to our flock.
    [*Exeunt* Rosalind, Celia, *and* Corin.

PHE. Dead shepherd, now I find thy saw of might,—
"Who ever lov'd, that lov'd not at first sight?"

SIL. Sweet Phebe,—
PHE.   Ha, what say'st thou, Silvius?
SIL. Sweet Phebe, pity me.
PHE. Why, I am sorry for thee, gentle Silvius.
SIL. Wherever sorrow is, relief would be:
If you do sorrow at my grief in love,
By giving love, your sorrow and my grief
Were both extermin'd.
PHE. Thou hast my love: is not that neighbourly?
SIL. I would have you.
PHE.   Why, that were covetousness.
Silvius, the time was, that I hated thee:
And yet it is not, that I bear thee love:
But since that thou canst talk of love so well,
Thy company, which erst was irksome to me,
I will endure; and I'll employ thee too:
But do not look for farther recompense
Than thine own gladness that thou art employ'd.
SIL. So holy and so perfect is my love,

And I in such a poverty of grace,
That I shall think it a most plenteous crop
To glean the broken ears after the man
That the main harvest reaps; loose now and then
A scatter'd smile, and that I'll live upon.

PHE. Know'st thou the youth that spoke to me erewhile?
SIL. Not very well, but I have met him oft;
And he hath bought the cottage and the bounds
That the old carlot once was master of.

PHE. Think not I love him, though I ask for him;
'Tis but a peevish boy:—yet he talks well;—
But what care I for words? yet words do well,
When he that speaks them pleases those that hear.
It is a pretty youth:—not very pretty:—
But, sure, he's proud; and yet his pride becomes him:
He'll make a proper man: the best thing in him
Is his complexion; and faster than his tongue
Did make offence, his eye did heal it up.
He is not very tall; yet for his years he's tall:
His leg is but so so; and yet 'tis well:
There was a pretty redness in his lip,
A little riper and more lusty red
Than that mix'd in his cheek; 'twas just the difference
Betwixt the constant red, and mingled damask.
There be some women, Silvius, had they mark'd him
In parcels, as I did, would have gone near
To fall in love with him: but, for my part,
I love him not, nor hate him not; and yet
I have more cause to hate him than to love him:
For what had he to do to chide at me?
He said mine eyes were black, and my hair black:
And, now I am remember'd, scorn'd at me:
I marvel why I answer'd not again:
But that's all one; omittance is no quittance.
I'll write to him a very taunting letter,
And thou shalt bear it: wilt thou, Silvius?
SIL. Phebe, with all my heart.
PHE.   I'll write it straight;
The matter's in my head, and in my heart:
I will be bitter with him, and passing short.
Go with me, Silvius.   [*Exeunt.*

ACT IV.

SCENE I.—*The Forest of* ARDEN.

Enter ROSALIND, CELIA, *and* JAQUES.

JAQ. I pr'ythee, pretty youth, let me be better acquainted with thee.

ROS. They say, you are a melancholy fellow.

JAQ. I am so; I do love it better than laughing.

ROS. Those that are in extremity of either are abominable fellows, and betray themselves to every modern censure worse than drunkards.

JAQ. Why, 'tis good to be sad and say nothing.

ROS. Why then, 'tis good to be a post.

JAQ. I have neither the scholar's melancholy, which is emulation; nor the musician's, which is fantastical; nor the courtier's, which is proud; nor the soldier's, which is ambitious; nor the lawyer's, which is politic; nor the lady's, which is nice; nor the lover's, which is all these; but it is a melancholy of mine own, compounded of many simples, extracted from many objects; and, indeed, the sundry contemplation of my travels; which, by often rumination, wraps me in a most humorous sadness.

ROS. A traveller! By my faith, you have great reason to be sad: I fear, you have sold your own lands, to see other men's; then, to have seen much, and to have nothing, is to have rich eyes and poor hands.

JAQ. Yes, I have gained my experience.

ROS. And your experience makes you sad: I had rather have a fool to make me merry, than experience to make me sad; and to travel for it too!

Enter ORLANDO.

ORL. Good day, and happiness, dear Rosalind!

JAC. Nay then, God be wi' you, an you talk in blank verse.

ROS. Farewell, monsieur Traveller: look you lisp, and wear strange suits; disable all the benefits of your own country; be out of love with your nativity, and almost chide God for making you that countenance you are; or I will scarce think you have swam in a gondola.—[*Exit* JAQUES.] Why, how now, Orlando! where have you been all this while? You a lover!—An you serve me such another trick, never come in my sight more.

ORL. My fair Rosalind, I come within an hour of my promise.

ROS. Break an hour's promise in love! He that will divide a minute into a thousand parts, and break but a part of the thousandth part of a minute in the affairs of love, it may be said of him, that Cupid hath clapped him o' the shoulder, but I'll warrant him heart-whole.

ORL. Pardon me, dear Rosalind.

ROS. Nay, an you be so tardy, come no more in my sight: I had as lief be woo'd of a snail.

ORL. Of a snail!

ROS. Ay, of a snail; for though he comes slowly, he carries his house on his head,—a better jointure, I think, than you make a woman: besides, he brings his destiny with him.

ORL. What's that?

ROS. Why, horns; which such as you are fain to be beholden to your wives for: but he comes armed in his fortune, and prevents the slander of his wife.

ORL. Virtue is no horn-maker; and my Rosalind is virtuous.

ROS. And I am your Rosalind.

CEL. It pleases him to call you so; but he hath a Rosalind of a better leer than you.

ROS. Come, woo me, woo me; for now I am in a holiday humour, and like enough to consent.—What would you say to me now, an I were your very very Rosalind?

ORL. I would kiss before I spoke.

ROS. Nay, you were better speak first; and when you were gravelled for lack of matter, you might take occasion to kiss. Very good orators, when they are out, they will spit; and for lovers, lacking (God warn us!) matter, the cleanliest shift is to kiss.

ORL. How if the kiss be denied?

ROS. Then she put you to entreaty, and there begins new matter.

ORL. Who could be out, being before his beloved mistress?

ROS. Marry, that should you, if I were your mistress; or I should think my honesty ranker than my wit.

ORL. What, of my suit?

ROS. Not out of your apparel, and yet out of your suit. Am not I your Rosalind?

ORL. I take some joy to say you are, because I would be talking of her.

ROS. Well, in her person, I say—I will not have you.

ORL. Then, in mine own person, I die.

ROS. No, 'faith, die by attorney. The poor world is almost six thousand years old, and in all this time there was not any man died in his own person, *videlicet,* in a love-cause. Troilus had his brains dashed out with a Grecian club; yet he did what he could to die before; and he is one of the patterns of love. Leander, he would have lived many a fair year, though Hero had turned nun, if it had not been for a hot midsummer night; for, good youth, he went but forth to wash him in the Hellespont, and, being taken with the cramp, was drowned: and the foolish chroniclers of that age found it was—Hero of Sestos. But these are all lies: men have died from time to time, and worms have eaten them, but not for love.

ORL. I would not have my right Rosalind of this mind; for, I protest, her frown might kill me.

ROS. By this hand, it will not kill a fly. But come, now I will be your Rosalind in a more coming-on disposition; and ask me what you will, I will grant it.

ORL. Then love me, Rosalind.

ROS. Yes, faith will I, Fridays and Saturdays and all.

ORL. And wilt thou have me?

ROS. Ay, and twenty such.

ORL. What sayest thou?

ROS. Are you not good?

ORL. I hope so.

ROS. Why, then, can one desire too much of a good thing?—Come, sister, you shall be the priest, and marry us.—Give me your hand, Orlando.—What do you say, sister?

ORL. Pray thee, marry us.

CEL. I cannot say the words.

ROS. You must begin,—"Will you, Orlando,"—

CEL. Go to.—Will you, Orlando, have to wife this Rosalind?

ORL. I will.

ROS. Ay, but when?   [us.

ORL. Why now; as fast as she can marry

ROS. Then you must say,—"I take thee, Rosalind, for wife."

ORL. I take thee, Rosalind, for wife.

ROS. I might ask you for your commission; but—I do take thee, Orlando, for my husband:—there's a girl goes before the priest; and, certainly, a woman's thought runs before her actions.   [winged.

ORL. So do all thoughts,—they are

ROS. Now tell me how long you would have her, after you have possessed her?

ORL. For ever and a day.

ROS. Say a day, without the ever. No, no, Orlando; men are April when they woo, December when they wed: maids are May when they are maids, but the sky changes when they are wives. I will be more jealous of thee than a Barbary cock-pigeon over his hen; more clamorous than a parrot against rain; more new-fangled than an ape; more giddy in my desires than a monkey: I will weep for nothing like Diana in the fountain, and I will do that when

you are disposed to be merry; I will laugh like a hyen, and that when thou art inclined to sleep.

ORL. But will my Rosalind do so?

ROS. By my life, she will do as I do.

ORL. O, but she is wise.

ROS. Or else she could not have the wit to do this: the wiser, the waywarder: make the doors upon a woman's wit, and it will out at the casement; shut that, and 'twill out at the key-hole; stop that, 'twill fly with the smoke out at the chimney.

ORL. A man that had a wife with such a wit, he might say,—"Wit, whither wilt?"

ROS. Nay, you might keep that check for it, till you met your wife's wit going to your neighbour's bed.   [excuse that?

ORL. And what wit could wit have to

ROS. Marry, to say,—she came to seek you there. You shall never take her without her answer, unless you take her without her tongue. O, that woman that cannot make her fault her husband's occasion, let her never nurse her child herself, for she will breed it like a fool.

ORL. For these two hours, Rosalind, I will leave thee.   [two hours!

ROS. Alas, dear love, I cannot lack thee

ORL. I must attend the duke at dinner: by two o'clock I will be with thee again.

ROS. Ay, go your ways, go your ways;— I knew what you would prove: my friends told me as much, and I thought no less:— that flattering tongue of yours won me:— 'tis but one cast away, and so,—come, death!—Two o'clock is your hour?

ORL. Ay, sweet Rosalind.

ROS. By my troth, and in good earnest, and so God mend me, and by all pretty oaths that are not dangerous, if you break one jot of your promise, or come one minute behind your hour, I will think you the most pathetical break-promise, and the most hollow lover, and the most unworthy of her you call Rosalind, that may be chosen out of the gross band of the unfaithful: therefore, beware my censure, and keep your promise.

ORL. With no less religion than if thou wert indeed my Rosalind: so, adieu.

ROS. Well, Time is the old justice that examines all such offenders, and let Time try: adieu.   [*Exit* ORLANDO.

CEL. You have simply misused our sex in your love-prate: we must have your doublet and hose plucked over your head, and show the world what the bird hath done to her own nest.

ROS. O coz, coz, coz, my pretty little coz, that thou didst know how many fathom deep I am in love! But it cannot be

sounded: my affection hath an unknown
bottom, like the bay of Portugal.

CEL. Or rather, bottomless; that as fast as
you pour affection in, it runs out.

ROS. No, that same wicked bastard of
Venus, that was begot of thought, conceived of spleen, and born of madness;
that blind rascally boy, that abuses every
one's eyes, because his own are out, let him
be judge how deep I am in love:—I'll tell
thee, Aliena, I cannot be out of the sight
of Orlando: I'll go find a shadow, and sigh
till he come.

CEL. And I'll sleep.   [*Exeunt.*

SCENE II.—*Another part of the Forest.*
Enter JAQUES *and* Lords.

JAQ. Which is he that killed the deer?

1 *LORD.* Sir, it was I.

JAQ. Let's present him to the duke, like
a Roman conqueror; and it would do well
to set the deer's horns upon his head, for
a branch of victory.—Have you no song,
forester, for this purpose?

2 *LORD.* Yes, Sir.

JAQ. Sing it: 'tis no matter how it be in
tune, so it make noise enough.

SONG.

What shall he have that kill'd the deer?
His leather skin, and horns to wear.
Take thou no scorn to wear the horn;
    (Then sing him home: the rest shall
        bear this burden.)
It was a crest ere thou wast born:
    Thy father's father wore it,
    And thy father bore it:
The horn, the horn, the lusty horn,
    Is not a thing to laugh to scorn.
                            [*Exeunt.*

SCENE III.—*Another part of the Forest.*
Enter ROSALIND *and* CELIA.

ROS. How say you now? Is it not past
two o'clock?
And here much Orlando!

CEL. I warrant you, with pure love and
troubled brain,   [gone forth—
He hath ta'en his bow and arrows, and is
To sleep. Look, who comes here.

Enter SILVIUS.

SIL. My errand is to you, fair youth;—
My gentle Phebe did bid me give you this:
                        [*Giving a letter.*
I know not the contents; but, as I guess
By the stern brow and waspish action
Which she did use as she was writing of it,
It bears an angry tenor: pardon me,
I am but as a guiltless messenger.

ROS. Patience herself would startle at this
letter,   [all:
And play the swaggerer; bear this, bear
She says I am not fair; that I lack man-
ners;   [not love me,
She calls me proud; and that she could
Were man as rare as Phœnix. Od's my
will!
Her love is not the hare that I do hunt:
Why writes she so to me?—Well, shepherd,
well,
This is a letter of your own device.

SIL. No, I protest, I know not the contents:
Phebe did write it.

ROS.   Come, come, you are a fool,
And turn'd into the extremity of love.
I saw her hand: she has a leathern hand,
A freestone-colour'd hand; I verily did
think   [hands:
That her old gloves were on, but 'twas her
She has a housewife's hand; but that's no
matter:
I say, she never did invent this letter;
This is a man's invention, and his hand.

SIL. Sure, it is hers.   [style,

ROS. Why, 'tis a boisterous and a cruel
A style for challengers; why, she defies me,
Like Turk to Christian: woman's gentle
brain   [tion,
Could not drop forth such giant-rude inven-
Such Ethiop words, blacker in their effect
Than in their countenance.—Will you hear
the letter?   [yet:

SIL. So please you, for I never heard it
Yet heard too much of Phebe's cruelty.

ROS. She Phebes me: mark how the ty-
rant writes.
[*Reads.*]
    "Are thou god to shepherd turn'd,
    That a maiden's heart hath burn'd?"—
Can a woman rail thus?

SIL. Call you this railing?

ROS. [*Reads.*]
    "Why, thy godhead laid apart,
    Warr'st thou with a woman's heart?"—
Did you ever hear such railing?—
[*Reads.*]
    "Whiles the eye of man did woo me,
    That could do no vengeance to me."—
Meaning me a beast.—
[*Reads.*]
    "If the scorn of your bright eyne
    Have power to raise such love in mine,
    Alack, in me what strange effect
    Would they work in mild aspect!
    Whiles you chid me, I did love;
    How then might your prayers move!
    He that brings this love to thee,
    Little knows this love in me:

And by him seal up thy mind;
Whether that thy youth and kind
Will the faithful offer take
Of me, and all that I can make;
Or else by him my love deny,
And then I'll study how to die."
SIL. Call you this chiding?
CEL. Alas, poor shepherd!
ROS.—Do you pity him? no, he deserves no
pity.—Wilt thou love such a woman?—
What, to make thee an instrument, and
play false strains upon thee! not to be
endured!—Well, go your way to her, (for
I see, love hath made thee a tame snake,)
and say this to her:—that if she love me,
I charge her to love thee; if she will not, I
will never have her, unless thou entreat
for her.—If you be a true lover, hence, and
not a word; for here comes more company.
                                [*Exit* SILVIUS.

                  Enter OLIVER.

OLI. Good morrow, fair ones: pray you,
  if you know,
Where in the purlieus of this forest stands
A sheepcote, fenc'd about with olive-trees?
CEL. West of this place, down in the
  neighbour bottom:
The rank of osiers, by the murmuring
  stream,   [place.
Left on your right hand, brings you to the
But at this hour the house doth keep itself;
There's none within.
OLI. If that an eye may profit by a tongue,
Then should I know you by description;
Such garments, and such years:—"The
  boy is fair,
Of female favour, and bestows himself
Like a ripe sister: but the woman low,
And browner than her brother." Are not
  you
The owner of the house I did enquire for?
CEL. It is no boast, being ask'd, to say
  we are.
OLI. Orlando doth commend him to you
  both;
And to that youth he calls his Rosalind,
He sends this bloody napkin:—are you he?
ROS. I am: what must we understand by
  this?
OLI. Some of my shame; if you will know
  of me
What man I am, and how, and why, and
  where
This handkerchief was stain'd.
CEL.   I pray you, tell it.
OLI. When last the young Orlando parted
  from you,
He left a promise to return again
Within an hour; and, pacing through the
  forest,

Chewing the food of sweet and bitter fancy,
Lo, what befel! he threw his eye aside,
And, mark, what object did present itself:
Under an old oak, whose boughs were
  mossed with age,
And high top bald with dry antiquity,
A wretched ragged man, o'ergrown with
  hair,
Lay sleeping on his back: about his neck
A green and gilded snake had wreath'd
  itself,
Who with her head, nimble in threats, ap-
  proach'd
The opening of his mouth; but suddenly,
Seeing Orlando, it unlink'd itself,
And with indented glides did slip away
Into a bush: under which bush's shade
A lioness, with udders all drawn dry,
Lay couching, head on ground, with catlike
  watch,   [for 'tis
When that the sleeping man should stir;
The royal disposition of that beast,
To prey on nothing that doth seem as
  dead:
This seen, Orlando did approach the man,
And found it was his brother, his elder
  brother.
CEL. O, I have heard him speak of that
  same brother;
And he did render him the most unnatural
That liv'd 'mongst men.
OLI.   And well he might so do,
For well I know he was unnatural.
ROS. But, to Orlando:—did he leave him
  there,
Food to the suck'd and hungry lioness?
OLI. Twice did he turn his back, and
  purpos'd so;
But kindness, nobler ever than revenge,
And nature, stronger than his just occasion,
Made him give battle to the lioness,
Who quickly fell before him: in which
  hurtling,
From miserable slumber I awak'd.
CEL. Are you his brother?
ROS.   Was it you he rescu'd?
CEL. Was't you that did so oft contrive
  to kill him?
OLI. 'Twas I; but 'tis not I: I do not
  shame
To tell you what I was, since my conversion
So sweetly tastes, being the thing I am.
ROS. But, for the bloody napkin?—
OLI.   By and by.
When from the first to last, betwixt us two,
Tears our recountments had most kindly
  bath'd,
As, how I came into that desert place;—
In brief, he led me to the gentle duke,
Who gave me fresh array and entertain-
  ment,

Committing me unto my brother's love;
Who led me instantly unto his cave,
There stripp'd himself, and here upon his
  arm
The lioness had torn some flesh away,
Which all this while had bled; and now
  he fainted,
And cried, in fainting, upon Rosalind.
Brief, I recover'd him, bound up his
  wound;
And, after some small space, being strong
  at heart,
He sent me hither, stranger as I am,
To tell this story, that you might excuse
His broken promise, and to give this nap-
  kin,
Dyed in his blood, unto the shepherd
  youth
That he in sport doth call his Rosalind.
CEL. Why, how now, Ganymede! sweet
  Ganymede!   [ROSALIND *swoons.*
OLI. Many will swoon when they do look
  on blood.
CEL. There is more in it.—Cousin!—
  Ganymede!
OLI. Look, he recovers.
ROS. I would I were at home.
CEL.   We'll lead you thither.—
I pray you, will you take him by the arm?
OLI. Be of good cheer, youth:—you a
  man? You lack
A man's heart.
ROS. I do so, I confess it. Ah, sirrah, a
body would think this was well counter-
feited: I pray you, tell your brother how
well I counterfeited.—Heigh ho!—
OLI. This was not counterfeit: there is
too great testimony in your complexion,
that it was a passion of earnest.
ROS. Counterfeit, I assure you.
OLI. Well then, take a good heart, and
counterfeit to be a man.
ROS. So I do: but, i' faith, I should have
been a woman by right.
CEL. Come, you look paler and paler:
pray you, draw homewards.—Good Sir, go
with us.
OLI. That will I, for I must bear answer
  back
How you excuse my brother, Rosalind.
ROS. I shall devise something. But, I
pray you, commend my counterfeiting to
him:—will you go?   [*Exeunt.*

ACT V.

SCENE I.—*The Forest of* ARDEN.
Enter TOUCHSTONE *and* AUDREY.

TOUCH. We shall find a time, Audrey;
patience, gentle Audrey.

AUD. 'Faith, the priest was good enough,
for all the old gentleman's saying.
TOUCH. A most wicked Sir Oliver, Audrey, a most vile Mar-text. But, Audrey,
there is a youth here in the forest lays
claim to you.
AUD. Ay, I know who 'tis: he hath no
interest in me in the world: here comes
the man you mean.
TOUCH. It is meat and drink to me to
see a clown: by my troth, we that have
good wits have much to answer for; we
shall be flouting; we cannot hold.
            Enter WILLIAM.
WILL. Good even, Audrey.
AUD. God ye good even, William.
WILL. And good even to you, Sir.
TOUCH. Good even, gentle friend. Cover
thy head, cover thy head; nay, pr'ythee,
be covered. How old are you, friend?
WILL. Five and twenty, Sir.
TOUCH. A ripe age. Is thy name Wil-
WILL. William, Sir.   [liam?
TOUCH. A fair name. Wast born i' the
forest here?
WILL. Ay, Sir, I thank God.
TOUCH. Thank God;—a good answer.
Art rich?
WILL. 'Faith, Sir, so so.
TOUCH. So so, is good, very good, very
excellent good:—and yet it is not; it is but
so so. Art thou wise?
WILL. Ay, Sir, I have a pretty wit.
TOUCH. Why, thou sayest well. I do
now remember a saying,—"The fool doth
think he is wise; but the wise man knows
himself to be a fool." The heathen philosopher, when he had a desire to eat a
grape, would open his lips when he put it
into his mouth; meaning thereby, that
grapes were made to eat, and lips to open.
You do love this maid?
WILL. I do, Sir.
TOUCH. Give me your hand. Art thou
WILL. No, Sir.   [learned?
TOUCH. Then learn this of me: to have,
is to have; for it is a figure in rhetoric,
that drink, being poured out of a cup into
a glass, by filling the one doth empty the
other; for all your writers do consent, that
ipse is he: now, you are not *ipse*, for I am
WILL. Which he, Sir?   [he.
TOUCH. He, Sir, that must marry this
woman. Therefore, you clown, abandon,—
which is in the vulgar, leave,—the society,
—which in the boorish is, company,—of
this female,—which in the common is,
woman; which together is, abandon the
society of this female, or, clown, thou
perishest; or, to thy better understanding,
diest; or, to wit, I kill thee, make thee

away, translate thy life into death, thy liberty into bondage: I will deal in poison with thee, or in bastinado, or in steel; I will bandy with thee in Faction; I will o'errun thee with policy; I will kill thee a hundred and fifty ways: therefore tremble and depart.

AUD. Do, good William.

WILL. God rest you merry, Sir.   [*Exit.*

Enter CORIN.

COR. Our master and mistress seek you; come, away, away!

TOUCH. Trip, Audrey, trip, Audrey.—I attend, I attend.   [*Exeunt.*

SCENE II.—*Another part of the Forest.*

Enter ORLANDO *and* OLIVER.

ORL. Is't possible, that on so little acquaintance you should like her? that, but seeing, you should love her? and, loving, woo? and, wooing, she should grant? and will you persever to enjoy her?

OLI. Neither call the giddiness of it in question, the poverty of her, the small acquaintance, my sudden wooing, nor her sudden consenting; but say with me, I love Aliena; say with her, that she loves me; consent with both, that we may enjoy each other: it shall be to your good; for my father's house, and all the revenue that was old Sir Rowland's, will I estate upon you, and here live and die a shepherd.

ORL. You have my consent. Let your wedding be to-morrow: thither will I invite the duke, and all his contented followers. Go you and prepare Aliena; for, look you, here comes my Rosalind.

Enter ROSALIND.

ROS. God save you, brother.

OLI. And you, fair sister.   [*Exit.*

ROS. O, my dear Orlando, how it grieves me to see thee wear thy heart in a scarf!

ORL. It is my arm.

ROS. I thought thy heart had been wounded with the claws of a lion.

ORL. Wounded it is, but with the eyes of a lady.

ROS. Did your brother tell you how I counterfeited to swoon, when he showed me your handkerchief?

ORL. Ay, and greater wonders than that.

ROS. O, I know where you are:—nay, 'tis true: there was never any thing so sudden, but the fight of two rams, and Cæsar's thrasonical brag of—"I came, saw, and overcame:" for your brother and my sister no sooner met, but they looked; no sooner looked, but they loved; no sooner loved, but they sighed; no sooner sighed, but they asked one another the reason; no

sooner knew the reason, but they sought the remedy: and in these degrees have they made a pair of stairs to marriage, which they will climb incontinent, or else be incontinent before marriage: they are in the very wrath of love, and they will together; clubs cannot part them.

ORL. They shall be married to-morrow; and I will bid the duke to the nuptial. But, O, how bitter a thing it is to look into happiness through another man's eyes! By so much the more shall I tomorrow be at the height of heart-heaviness, by how much I shall think my brother happy in having what he wishes for.

ROS. Why then, to-morrow I cannot serve your turn for Rosalind?

ORL. I can live no longer by thinking.

ROS. I will weary you, then, no longer with idle talking. Know of me, then, (for now I speak to some purpose,) that I know you are a gentleman of good conceit: I speak not this, that you should bear a good opinion of my knowledge, insomuch I say I know you are; neither do I labour for a greater esteem than may in some little measure draw a belief from you, to do yourself good, and not to grace me. Believe then, if you please, that I can do strange things: I have, since I was three years old, conversed with a magician, most profound in his art, and yet not damnable. If you do love Rosalind so near the heart as your gesture cries it out, when your brother marries Aliena, shall you marry her: I know into what straits of fortune she is driven; and it is not impossible to me, if it appear not inconvenient to you, to set her before your eyes to-morrow, human as she is, and without any danger.

ORL. Speakest thou in sober meanings?

ROS. By my life, I do; which I tender dearly, though I say I am a magician. Therefore, put you in your best array, bid your friends; for if you will be married to-morrow, you shall; and to Rosalind, if you will.—Look, here comes a lover of mine, and a lover of hers.

Enter SILVIUS *and* PHEBE.

PHE. Youth, you have done me much ungentleness,
To show the letter that I writ to you.

ROS. I care not, if I have: it is my study
To seem despiteful and ungentle to you:
You are there follow'd by a faithful shepherd;
Look upon him, love him; he worships you.

PHE. Good shepherd, tell this youth what 'tis to love.

SIL. It is to be all made of sighs and tears:—

And so am I for Phebe.

PHE. And I for Ganymede.

ORL. And I for Rosalind.

ROS. And I for no woman.

SIL. It is to be all made of faith and service;—

And so am I for Phebe.

PHE. And I for Ganymede.

ORL. And I for Rosalind.

ROS. And I for no woman.

SIL. It is to be all made of fantasy,

All made of passion, and all made of wishes;

All adoration, duty and observance;

All humbleness, all patience, and impatience;

All purity, all trial, all obedience;

And so am I for Phebe.

PHE. And so am I for Ganymede.

ORL. And so am I for Rosalind.

ROS. And so am I for no woman.

PHE. [*To* ROSALIND] If this be so, why blame you me to love you?

SIL. [*To* PHEBE] If this be so, why blame you me to love you?

ORL. If this be so, why blame you me to love you?

ROS. Whom do you speak to,—"why blame you me to love you?"

ORL. To her, that is not here, nor doth not hear.

ROS. Pray you, no more of this: 'tis like the howling of Irish wolves against the moon.—[*To* SILVIUS.] I will help you, if I can:—[*To* PHEBE.] I would love you, if I could.—To-morrow meet me all together.—[*To* PHEBE.] I will marry you, if ever I marry woman, and I'll be married to-morrow:—[*To* ORLANDO.] I will satisfy you, if ever I satisfied man, and you shall be married to-morrow:—[*To* SILVIUS.] I will content you, if what pleases you contents you, and you shall be married to-morrow.—[*To* ORLANDO.] As you love Rosalind, meet:—[*To* SILVIUS.] as you love Phebe, meet; and as I love no woman, I'll meet.—So, fare you well: I have left you commands.

SIL. I'll not fail, if I live.

PHE.   Nor I.

ORL.   Nor I.

[*Exeunt.*

SCENE III.—*Another part of the Forest.*

Enter TOUCHSTONE *and* AUDREY.

TOUCH. To-morrow is the joyful day, Audrey; to-morrow will we be married.

AUD. I do desire it with all my heart; and I hope it is no dishonest desire, to

desire to be a woman of the world. Here come two of the banished duke's pages.

Enter two Pages.

1 PAGE. Well met, honest gentleman.

TOUCH. By my troth, well met. Come, sit, sit, and a song.

2 PAGE. We are for you: sit i' the middle.

1 PAGE. Shall we clap into't roundly, without hawking, or spitting, or saying we are hoarse, which are the only prologues to a bad voice?

2 PAGE. I'faith, i'faith; and both in a tune, like two gypsies on a horse.

SONG.

It was a lover and his lass,
  With a hey, and a ho, and a hey nonino,
That o'er the green corn-field did pass
In the spring time, the only pretty ring time
When birds do sing, hey ding a ding, ding:
Sweet lovers love the spring.

Between the acres of the rye,
  With a hey, and a ho, and a hey nonino,
These pretty country folks would lie,
  In the spring time, &c.

This carol they began that hour,
  With a hey, and a ho, and a hey nonino,
How that a life was but a flower
  In the spring time, &c.

And therefore take the present time,
  With a hey, and a ho, and a hey nonino;
For love is crowned with the prime
  In the spring time, &c.

TOUCH. Truly, young gentlemen, though there was no great matter in the ditty, yet the note was very untuneable.

1 PAGE. You are deceived, Sir: we kept time, we lost not our time.

TOUCH. By my troth, yes; I count it but time lost to hear such a foolish song. God be wi' you; and God mend your voices!—Come, Audrey. [*Exeunt.*

SCENE IV.—*Another part of the Forest.*

Enter DUKE Senior, AMIENS, JAQUES, ORLANDO, OLIVER, *and* CELIA.

DUKE S. Dost thou believe, Orlando, that the boy
Can do all this that he hath promised?

ORL. I sometimes do believe, and sometimes do not;
As those that fear they hope, and know they fear.

Enter ROSALIND, SILVIUS, *and* PHEBE.

ROS. Patience once more, whiles our compact is urg'd:—

[*To the* Duke.] You say, if I bring in your Rosalind,
You will bestow her on Orlando here?
DUKE S. That would I, had I kingdoms to give with her.
ROS. [*To* Orlando.] And you say, you will have her, when I bring her?
ORL. That would I, were I of all kingdoms king.
ROS. [*To* Phebe.] You say, you'll marry me, if I be willing?
PHE. That will I, should I die the hour after.
ROS. But if you do refuse to marry me,
You'll give yourself to this most faithful shepherd?
PHE. So is the bargain.
ROS. [*To* Silvius.] You say, that you'll have Phebe, if she will?
SIL. Though to have her and death were both one thing.
ROS. I have promis'd to make all this matter even.
Keep you your word, O duke, to give your daughter;—
You yours, Orlando, to receive his daughter:—
Keep your word, Phebe, that you'll marry me,
Or else, refusing me, to wed this shepherd:—
Keep your word, Silvius, that you'll marry her,
If she refuse me:—and from hence I go,
To make these doubts all even.

       [*Exeunt* Rosalind *and* Celia.

DUKE S. I do remember in this shepherd boy
Some lively touches of my daughter's favour.
ORL. My lord, the first time that I ever saw him,
Methought he was a brother to your daughter:
But, my good lord, this boy is forest-born,
And hath been tutor'd in the rudiments
Of many desperate studies by his uncle,
Whom he reports to be a great magician,
Obscured in the circle of this forest.
JAQ. There is, sure, another flood toward, and these couples are coming to the ark. Here comes a pair of very strange beasts, which in all tongues are called fools.

       Enter Touchstone *and* Audrey.

TOUCH. Salutation and greeting to you all.
JAQ. Good my lord, bid him welcome: this is the motley-minded gentleman, that I have so often met in the forest: he hath been a courtier, he swears.

TOUCH. If any man doubt that, let him put me to my purgation. I have trod a measure; I have flattered a lady; I have been politic with my friend, smooth with mine enemy; I have undone three tailors; I have had four quarrels, and like to have fought one.
JAQ. And how was that ta'en up?
TOUCH. 'Faith, we met, and found the quarrel was upon the seventh cause.
JAQ. How seventh cause?—Good my lord, like this fellow.
DUKE S. I like him very well.
TOUCH. God'ild you, Sir; I desire you of the like. I press in here, Sir, amongst the rest of the country copulatives, to swear, and to forswear; according as marriage binds and blood breaks:—a poor virgin, Sir, an ill-favoured thing, Sir, but mine own; a poor humour of mine, Sir, to take that that no man else will: rich honesty dwells like a miser, Sir, in a poor house, as your pearl in your foul oyster.
DUKE S. By my faith, he is very swift and sententious.
TOUCH. According to the fool's bolt, Sir, and such dulcet diseases.
JAQ. But, for the seventh cause; how did you find the quarrel on the seventh cause?
TOUCH. Upon a lie seven times removed:
—bear your body more seeming, Audrey:—as thus, Sir. I did dislike the cut of a certain courtier's beard: he sent me word, if I said his beard was not cut well, he was in the mind it was: this is called the Retort courteous. If I sent him word again, it was not well cut, he would send me word, he cut it to please himself: this is called the Quip modest. If again, it was not well cut, he disabled my judgment: this is called the Reply churlish. If again, it was not well cut, he would answer, I spake not true: this is called the Reproof valiant. If again, it was not well cut, he would say, I lie: this is called the Countercheck quarrelsome: and so to the Lie circumstantial, and the Lie direct.
JAQ. And how oft did you say, his beard was not well cut?
TOUCH. I durst go no farther than the Lie circumstantial, nor he durst not give me the Lie direct; and so we measured swords, and parted.
JAQ. Can you nominate in order now the degrees of the lie?
TOUCH. O Sir, we quarrel in print, by the book; as you have books for good manners: I will name you the degrees. The first, the Retort courteous; the second, the Quip modest; the third, the Reply churlish; the fourth, the Reproof valiant; the fifth, the

Countercheck quarrelsome; the sixth, the Lie with circumstance; the seventh, the Lie direct. All these you may avoid, but the Lie direct; and you may avoid that too, with an "if." I knew when seven justices could not take up a quarrel; but when the parties were met themselves, one of them thought but of an "if," as "If you said so, then I said so;" and they shook hands, and swore brothers. Your "if" is the only peacemaker; much virtue in "if."

JAQ. Is not this a rare fellow, my lord? he's as good at any thing, and yet a fool.

DUKE S. He uses his folly like a stalking-horse, and under the presentation of that, he shoots his wit.

Still music. Enter HYMEN, *leading* ROSALIND *in woman's clothes; and* CELIA.

HYM. Then is there mirth in heaven,
    When earthly things made even
        Atone together.
Good duke, receive thy daughter:
Hymen from heaven brought her;
    Yea, brought her hither,
That thou might'st join her hand with his,
Whose heart within her bosom is.

ROS. [*To* DUKE S.] To you I give myself, for I am yours.—
[*To* ORLANDO.] To you I give myself, for I am yours.

DUKE S. If there be truth in sight, you are my daughter.

ORL. If there be truth in sight, you are my Rosalind.

PHE. If sight and shape be true,
    Why then,—my love adieu!

ROS. [*To* DUKE S.] I'll have no father, if you be not he:—
[*To* ORLANDO.] I'll have no husband, if you be not he:—
[*To* PHEBE.] Nor ne'er wed woman, if you be not she.

HYM. Peace, ho! I bar confusion:
'Tis I must make conclusion
    Of these most strange events:
Here's eight that must take hands
To join in Hymen's bands,
    If truth holds true contents.
[*To* ORLANDO *and* ROSALIND.] You and you no cross shall part:—
[*To* OLIVER *and* CELIA.] You and you are heart in heart:—
[*To* PHEBE.] You to his love must accord,
    Or have a woman to your lord:—
[*To* TOUCHSTONE *and* AUDREY.] You and you are sure together,
    As the winter to foul weather.
Whiles a wedlock-hymn we sing,

Feed yourselves with questioning;
That reason wonder may diminish,
How thus we met, and these things finish.

SONG.

Wedding is great Juno's crown:
    O blessed bond of board and bed!
'Tis Hymen peoples every town;
    High wedlock, then, be honoured:
Honour, high honour and renown,
To Hymen, god of every town!

DUKE S. O my dear niece, welcome thou art to me!
Even daughter, welcome in no less degree.

PHE. [*To* SILVIUS.] I will not eat my word, now thou art mine;
Thy faith my fancy to thee doth combine.

Enter JAQUES DE BOIS.

JAQ. DE B. Let me have audience for a word or two:
I am the second son of old Sir Rowland,
That bring these tidings to this fair assembly.—
Duke Frederick, hearing how that every day
Men of great worth resorted to this forest,
Address'd a mighty power; which were on foot,
In his own conduct, purposely to take
His brother here, and put him to the sword:
And to the skirts of this wild wood he came;
Where, meeting with an old religious man,
After some question with him, was converted
Both from his enterprise and from the world;
His crown bequeathing to his banish'd brother,
And all their lands restor'd to them again,
That were with him exil'd. This to be true,
I do engage my life.

DUKE S. Welcome, young man;
Thou offer'st fairly to thy brothers' wedding:
To one, his lands withheld; and to the other,
A land itself at large, a potent dukedom.
First, in this forest, let us do those ends
That here were well begun, and well begot:
And after, every of this happy number,
That have endur'd shrewd days and nights with us,
Shall share the good of our returned fortune,
According to the measure of their states.

Meantime, forget this new-fall'n dignity,
And fall into our rustic revelry.—
Play, music!—and you, brides and bride-
grooms all,
With measure heap'd in joy, to the meas-
ures fall.
JAQ. Sir, by your patience.—If I heard
you rightly,
The duke hath put on a religious life,
And thrown into neglect the pompous
court?
JAQ. DE B. He hath.
JAQ. To him will I: out of these con-
vertites
There is much matter to be heard and
learn'd.—
[*To* Duke S.] You to your former honour
I bequeath;
Your patience, and your virtue, well de-
serve it:—
[*To* Orlando.] You to a love, that your
true faith doth merit:—
[*To* Oliver.] You to your land, and love,
and great allies:—
[*To* Silvius.] You to a long and well-de-
served bed:—
[*To* Touchstone.] And you to wrangling;
for thy loving voyage
Is but for two months victual'd.—So, to
your pleasures:
I am for other than for dancing measures.
DUKE S. Stay, Jaques, stay.
JAQ. To see no pastime, I:—what you
would have,
I'll stay to know at your abandon'd cave.
[*Exit.*

DUKE S. Proceed, proceed: we will begin
these rites,
As we do trust they'll end, in true delights.

EPILOGUE.

ROS. It is not the fashion to see the lady
the epilogue; but it is no more unhandsome, than to see the lord the prologue.
If it be true that good wine needs no bush,
'tis true that a good play needs no epilogue: yet to good wine they do use good
bushes; and good plays prove the better by
the help of good epilogues. What a case am
I in, then, that am neither a good epilogue,
nor cannot insinuate with you in the behalf of a good play! I am not furnished
like a beggar, therefore to beg will not become me: my way is, to conjure you; and
I'll begin with the women. I charge you,
O women, for the love you bear to men, to
like as much of this play as please you:
and I charge you, O men, for the love you
bear to women, (as I perceive by your
simpering none of you hates them,) that
between you and the women, the play may
please. If I were a woman, I would kiss
as many of you as had beards that pleased
me, complexions that liked me, and breaths
that I defied not; and, I am sure, as many
as have good beards, or good faces, or
sweet breaths, will, for my kind offer, when
I make court'sy, bid me farewell.

[*Exeunt.*

Katharina breaking the lute over Hortensio's head. Act II. S.1.

TAMING OF THE SHREW

DRAMATIS PERSONÆ.

A Lord.
CHRISTOPHER SLY, *a Tinker.* }
Hostess, Page, Players,
  Huntsmen, *and* Servants. } *Persons in the Induction.*

BAPTISTA, *a rich Gentleman of* Padua.
VINCENTIO, *an old Gentleman of* Pisa.
LUCENTIO, *son to* VINCENTIO; *in love with* BIANCA.
PETRUCHIO, *a Gentleman of* Verona; *suitor to* KATHARINA.
GREMIO, }
HORTENSIO, } *suitors to* BIANCA.

TRANIO, }
BIONDELLO, } *servants to* LUCENTIO.
GRUMIO, }
CURTIS, } *servants to* PETRUCHIO.
Pedant.

KATHARINA, *the Shrew,* }
BIANCA, } *daughters to* BAPTISTA.
Widow.

Tailor, Haberdasher, *and* Servants *attending on* BAPTISTA *and* PETRUCHIO.

SCENE,—*Sometimes in* Padua; *and sometimes in* PETRUCHIO'S *House in the Country.*

INDUCTION.

SCENE I.—*Before an Alehouse on a Heath.*
Enter Hostess *and* SLY.

SLY. I'll pheese you, in faith.
HOST. A pair of stocks, you rogue!
SLY. Y' are a baggage: the Slys are no rogues; look in the chronicles, we came in with Richard Conqueror. Therefore, *paucas pallabris*; let the world slide: *Sessa!*
HOST. You will not pay for the glasses you have burst?

SLY. No, not a denier. Go by, Saint Jeronimy,—Go to thy cold bed, and warm thee.
HOST. I know my remedy: I must go fetch the thirdborough. [*Exit.*
SLY. Third, or fourth, or fifth borough, I'll answer him by law: I'll not budge an inch, boy: let him come, and kindly.
[*Lies down on the ground, and falls asleep.*
Wind Horns. Enter a Lord *from hunting, with* Huntsmen *and* Servants.

132

LORD. Huntsmen, I charge thee, tender well my hounds:

Trash Merriman,—the poor cur is emboss'd;
And couple Clowder with the deep-mouth'd brach.

Saw'st thou not, boy, how Silver made it good
At the hedge corner, in the coldest fault?
I would not lose the dog for twenty pound.

1 HUN. Why, Belman is as good as he, my lord;
He cried upon it at the merest loss,
And twice to-day pick'd out the dullest scent:

Trust me, I take him for the better dog.

LORD. Thou art a fool: if Echo were as fleet,
I would esteem him worth a dozen such.

But sup them well, and look unto them all:
To-morrow I intend to hunt again.

1 HUN. I will, my lord.

LORD. [Sees SLY.] What's here? one dead, or drunk? See, doth he breathe?

2 HUN. He breathes, my lord. Were he not warm'd with ale,
This were a bed but cold to sleep so soundly.

LORD. O monstrous beast! how like a swine he lies!—

Grim death, how foul and loathsome is thine image!—

Sirs, I will practise on this drunken man.
What think you, if he were convey'd to bed,
Wrapp'd in sweet clothes, rings put upon his fingers,
A most delicious banquet by his bed,
And brave attendants near him when he wakes,—

Would not the beggar then forget himself?

1 HUN. Believe me, lord, I think he cannot choose.

2 HUN. It would seem strange unto him when he wak'd.

LORD. Even as a flattering dream, or worthless fancy.

Then take him up, and manage well the jest:—

Carry him gently to my fairest chamber,
And hang it round with all my wanton pictures:

Balm his foul head in warm distilled waters,
And burn sweet wood to make the lodging sweet:

Procure me music ready when he wakes,
To make a dulcet and a heavenly sound:
And if he chance to speak, be ready straight,
And, with a low submissive reverence,

Say,—What is it your honour will command?

Let one attend him with a silver bason
Full of rose-water, and bestrew'd with flowers;

Another bear the ewer, the third a diaper,
And say,—Will't please your lordship cool your hands?

Some one be ready with a costly suit,
And ask him what apparel he will wear;
Another tell him of his hounds and horse,
And that his lady mourns at his disease:

Persuade him that he hath been lunatic;
And, when he says he is, say that he dreams,
For he is nothing but a mighty lord.

This do, and do it kindly, gentle Sirs:
It will be pastime passing excellent,
If it be husbanded with modesty.

1 HUN. My lord, I warrant you, we will play our part,
As he shall think, by our true diligence,
He is no less than what we say he is.

LORD. Take him up gently, and to bed with him;
And each one to his office when he wakes.—

[SLY is borne out. A trumpet sounds.

Sirrah, go see what trumpet 'tis that sounds:—   [Exit Servant.

Belike, some noble gentleman, that means,
Travelling some journey, to repose him here.—

Re-enter Servant.

How now! who is it?

SERV.   An it please your honour,
Players that offer service to your lordship.

LORD. Bid them come near.

Enter Players.

Now, fellows, you are welcome.

PLAYERS. We thank your honour.

LORD. Do you intend to stay with me to-night?

2 PLAY. So please your lordship to accept our duty.

LORD. With all my heart.—This fellow I remember,
Since once he play'd a farmer's eldest son:—

'Twas where you woo'd the gentlewoman so well:

I have forgot your name; but, sure, that part
Was aptly fitted and naturally perform'd.

1 PLAY. I think 'twas Soto that your honour means.

LORD. 'Tis very true: thou didst it excellent.—

Well, you are come to me in happy time;
The rather for I have some sport in hand,
Wherein your cunning can assist me much.

There is a lord will hear you play to-night:
But I am doubtful of your modesties;
Lest, over-eyeing of his odd behaviour,
(For yet his honour never heard a play,)
You break into some merry passion,
And so offend him; for I tell you, Sirs,
If you should smile, he grows impatient.
1 PLAY. Fear not, my lord: we can con-
tain ourselves,
Were he the veriest antick in the world.
LORD. Go, sirrah, take them to the
buttery,
And give them friendly welcome every one:
Let them want nothing that my house
affords.—
                    [Exeunt Servant and Players.
[To a Servant.] Sirrah, go you to Bar-
thol'mew my page,
And see him dress'd in all suits like a
lady:
That done, conduct him to the drunkard's
chamber;
And call him madam, do him obeisance.
Tell him from me, (as he will win my
love,)
He bear himself with honourable action,
Such as he hath observ'd in noble ladies
Unto their lords, by them accomplished:
Such duty to the drunkard let him do,
With soft low tongue and lowly courtesy;
And say,—what is't your honour will com-
mand,
Wherein your lady and your humble wife
May show her duty, and make known her
love?
And then,—with kind embracements,
tempting kisses,
And with declining head into his bosom,—
Bid him shed tears, as being overjoy'd
To see her noble lord restor'd to health,
Who for this seven years hath esteemed
him
No better than a poor and loathsome
beggar:
And if the boy have not a woman's gift
To rain a shower of commanded tears,
An onion will do well for such a shift;
Which, in a napkin being close convey'd,
Shall in despite enforce a watery eye.
See this despatch'd with all the haste thou
canst:
Anon I'll give thee more instructions.
                              [Exit Servant.
I know the boy will well usurp the grace,
Voice, gait, and action of a gentlewoman:
I long to hear him call the drunkard
husband;
And how my men will stay themselves from
laughter,
When they do homage to this simple
peasant.

I'll in to counsel them; haply my presence
May well abate the over-merry spleen,
Which otherwise would grow into extremes.
                              [Exeunt.

SCENE II.—A Bedchamber in the
Lord's House.

SLY is discovered in a rich night gown,
with Attendants; some with apparel,
others with bason, ewer, and appurte-
nances, others with wine and sweetmeats.
Enter Lord, dressed like a servant.
SLY. For God's sake, a pot of small ale.
1 SERV. Will't please your lordship drink
a cup of sack?
2 SERV. Will't please your honour taste
of these conserves?
3 SERV. What raiment will your honour
wear today?
SLY. I am Christophero Sly; call not me
honour, nor lordship: I ne'er drank sack
in my life; and if you give me any conserves, give me conserves of beef: ne'er
ask me what raiment I'll wear; for I
have no more doublets than backs, no more
stockings than legs, nor no more shoes than
feet,—nay, sometime more feet than shoes,
or such shoes as my toes look through the
overleather.
LORD. Heaven cease this idle humour in
your honour!
O, that a mighty man, of such descent,
Of such possessions, and so high esteem,
Should be infused with so foul a spirit!
SLY. What, would you make me mad? Am
not I Christopher Sly, old Sly's son, of
Burton-heath; by birth a pedlar, by education a card-maker, by transmutation a bear-
herd, and now by present profession a
tinker? Ask Marian Hacket, the fat ale-
wife of Wincot, if she know me not: if she
say I am not fourteen pence on the score
for sheer ale, score me up for the lyingest
knave in Christendom. What! I am not
bestraught: here's—
1 SERV. O, this it is that makes your lady
mourn.
2 SERV. O, this it is that makes your
servants droop.
LORD. Hence, comes it that your kindred
shun your house,
As beaten hence by your strange lunacy.
O noble lord, bethink thee of thy birth!
Call home thy ancient thoughts from
banishment,
And banish hence these abject lowly
dreams.
Look how thy servants do attend on thee,
Each in his office ready at thy beck.

Wilt thou have music? hark! Apollo plays,
And twenty caged nightingales do sing:
                                    [*Music.*
Or wilt thou sleep? we'll have thee to a
    couch
Softer and sweeter than the lustful bed
On purpose trimm'd up for Semiramis.
Say thou wilt walk; we wilt bestrew the
    ground:
Or wilt thou ride, thy horses shall be
    trapp'd,
Their harness studded all with gold and
    pearl.
Dost thou love hawking? thou hast hawks
    will soar
Above the morning lark: or wilt thou hunt?
Thy hounds shall make the welkin answer
    them,
And fetch shrill echoes from the hollow
    earth.
1 *SERV.* Say thou wilt course; thy grey-
    hounds are as swift
As breathed stags, ay, fleeter than the roe.
2 *SERV.* Dost thou love pictures? we will
    fetch thee straight
Adonis painted by a running brook,
And Cytherea all in sedges hid,
Which seem to move and wanton with her
    breath,
Even as the waving sedges play with wind.
LORD. We'll show thee Io as she was
    a maid,
And how she was beguiled and surpris'd,
As lively painted as the deed was done.
3 *SERV.* Or Daphne roaming through a
    thorny wood,
Scratching her legs, that one shall swear
    she bleeds,
And at that sight shall sad Apollo weep,
So workmanly the blood and tears are
    drawn.
LORD. Thou art a lord, and nothing but a
    lord:
Thou hast a lady far more beautiful
Than any woman in this waning age.
1 *SERV.* And, till the tears that she hath
    shed for thee,
Like envious floods, o'er-ran her lovely face,
She was the fairest creature in the world;
And yet she is inferior to none.
SLY. Am I a lord? and have I such a
    lady?
Or do I dream? or have I dream'd till
    now?
I do not sleep: I see, I hear, I speak;
I smell sweet savours; and I feel soft
    things:—
Upon my life, I am a lord, indeed;
And not a tinker, nor Christophero Sly.—
Well, bring our lady hither to our sight;
And once again, a pot o' the smallest ale.

2 *SERV.* Will't please your mightiness to
    wash your hands?
    [*Servants present an ewer, bason, and
                                    napkin.*
O, how we joy to see your wit restor'd!
O, that once more you knew but what
    you are!
These fifteen years you have been in a
    dream;
Or, when you wak'd, so wak'd as if you
    slept.
SLY. These fifteen years! by my fay, a
    goodly nap.
But did I never speak of all that time?
1 *SERV.* O, yes, my lord; but very idle
    words:
For though you lay here in this goodly
    chamber,
Yet would you say, ye were beaten out of
    door;
And rail upon the hostess of the house;
And say, you would present her at the
    leet,
Because she brought stone jugs and no
    seal'd quarts:
Sometimes you would call out for Cicely
    Hacket.
SLY. Ay, the woman's maid of the house.
3 *SERV.* Why, Sir, you know no house,
    nor no such maid;
Nor no such men, as you have reckon'd
    up,—
As Stephen Sly, and old John Naps of
    Greece,
And Peter Turf, and Henry Pimpernell;
And twenty more such names and men as
    these,
Which never were, nor no man ever saw.
SLY. Now, Lord be thanked for my good
    amends!
ALL. Amen.
SLY. I thank thee: thou shalt not lose
    by it.
Enter the Page, *as a lady, with* Attendants.
PAGE. How fares my noble lord?
SLY. Marry, I fare well; for here is cheer
Where is my wife?   [enough.
PAGE. Here, noble lord: what is thy will
    with her?
SLY. Are you my wife, and will not call
    me husband?
My men should call me lord: I am your
    goodman.
PAGE. My husband and my lord, my lord
    and husband;
I am your wife in all obedience.
SLY. I know it well.—What must I call
    her?
LORD. Madam.
SLY. Al'ce madam, or Joan madam?

LORD. Madam, and nothing else: so lords call ladies.

SLY. Madam wife, they say that I have dream'd,
And slept above some fifteen year or more.

PAGE. Ay, and the time seems thirty unto me,
Being all this time abandon'd from your bed.

SLY. 'Tis much.—Servants, leave me and her alone.—
Madam, undress you, and come now to bed.

PAGE. Thrice noble lord, let me entreat of you
To pardon me yet for a night or two;
Or, if not so, until the sun be set,
For your physicians have expressly charg'd,
In peril to incur your former malady,
That I should yet absent me from your bed:
I hope this reason stands for my excuse.

SLY. Ay, it stands so, that I may hardly tarry so long; but I would be loath to fall into my dreams again: I will therefore tarry, in spite of the flesh and the blood.

Enter a Servant.

SERV. Your honour's players, hearing your amendment,
Are come to play a pleasant comedy;
For so your doctors hold it very meet,
Seeing too much sadness hath congeal'd your blood,
And melancholy is the nurse of frenzy:
Therefore they thought it good you hear a play,
And frame your mind to mirth and merriment,
Which bars a thousand harms, and lengthens life.

SLY. Marry, I will; let them play it. Is not a commonty a Christmas gambol, or a tumbling-trick?

PAGE. No, my good lord: it is more pleasing stuff.

SLY. What, household stuff?

PAGE. It is a kind of history.

SLY. Well, we'll see't. Come, madam wife, sit by my side,
And let the world slip: we shall ne'er be younger.　　[*They sit down.*

ACT I.

SCENE I.—PADUA. *A public Place.*

Enter LUCENTIO *and* TRANIO.

LUC. Tranio, since, for the great desire I had
To see fair Padua, nursery of arts,
I am arriv'd for fruitful Lombardy,
The pleasant garden of great Italy;
And, by my father's love and leave, am arm'd
With his good will and thy good company,
My trusty servant, well approv'd in all;
Here let us breathe, and haply institute
A course of learning and ingenious studies.
Pisa, renowned for grave citizens,
Gave me my being; and my father first,
A merchant of great traffic through the world,
Vincentio, come of the Bentivolii.
Vincentio's son, brought up in Florence,
It shall become, to serve all hopes conceiv'd,
To deck his fortune with his virtuous deeds:
And therefore, Tranio, for the time I study,
Virtue, and that part of philosophy
Will I apply, that treats of happiness
By virtue specially to be achiev'd.
Tell me thy mind; for I have Pisa left,
And am to Padua come, as he that leaves
A shallow plash, to plunge him in the deep,
And with satiety seeks to quench his thirst.

TRA. *Mi perdonate*, gentle master mine,
I am in all affected as yourself;
Glad that you thus continue your resolve
To suck the sweets of sweet philosophy:
Only, good master, while we do admire
This virtue and this moral discipline,
Let's be no stoics nor no stocks, I pray;
Or so devote to Aristotle's ethics,
As Ovid be an outcast quite abjur'd:
Talk logic with acquaintance that you have,
And practise rhetoric in your common talk;
Music and poesy use to quicken you;
The mathematics and the metaphysics,
Fall to them, as you find your stomach serves you;
No profit grows, where is no pleasure ta'en:
In brief, Sir, study what you most affect.

LUC. Gramercies, Tranio, well dost thou advise.
If Biondello now were come ashore,
We could at once put us in readiness;
And take a lodging, fit to entertain
Such friends as time in Padua shall beget.
But stay a while: what company is this?

TRA. Master, some show, to welcome us to town.

Enter BAPTISTA, KATHARINA, BIANCA, GREMIO, *and* HORTENSIO. LUCENTIO *and* TRANIO *stand aside.*

BAP. Gentlemen, importune me no farther,
For how I firmly am resolv'd you know;
That is, not to bestow my youngest daughter
Before I have a husband for the elder:
If either of you both love Katharina,
Because I know you well and love you well,
Leave shall you have to court her at your pleasure.

GRE. To cart her rather: she's too rough for me.—

There, there, Hortensio, will you any wife?

KATH. [*To* BAP.] I pray you, Sir, is it your will
To make a stale of me amongst these mates?

HOR. Mates, maid! how mean you that? no mates for you,
Unless you were of gentler, milder mould.

KATH. I' faith, Sir, you shall never need to fear:
I wis, it is not half way to her heart;
But if it were, doubt not her care should be
To comb your noddle with a three-legg'd stool,
And paint your face, and use you like a fool.

HOR. From all such devils, good Lord deliver us!

GRE. And me too, good Lord!

TRA. Hush, master! here is some good pastime toward:
That wench is stark mad, or wonderful froward.

LUC. But in the other's silence do I see
Maids' mild behaviour, and sobriety.
Peace, Tranio!

TRA. Well said, master; mum! and gaze your fill.

BAP. Gentlemen, that I may soon make good
What I have said,—Bianca, get you in:
And let it not displease thee, good Bianca,
For I will love thee ne'er the less, my girl.

KATH. A pretty peat! it is best
Put finger in the eye,—an she knew why.

BIAN. Sister, content you in my discontent.—
Sir, to your pleasure humbly I subscribe:
My books and instruments shall be my company,
On them to look, and practise by myself.

LUC. Hark, Tranio! thou may'st hear Minerva speak.

HOR. Signior Baptista, will you be so strange?
Sorry am I, that our good will effects Bianca's grief.

GRE.   Why will you mew her up,
Signior Baptista, for this fiend of hell,
And make her bear the penance of her tongue?

BAP. Gentlemen, content ye; I am resolv'd:—
Go in, Bianca:—   [*Exit* BIANCA.
And for I know she taketh most delight
In music, instruments, and poetry,
Schoolmasters will I keep within my house,
Fit to instruct her youth.—If you, Hortensio,—

Or signior Gremio, you,—know any such,
Prefer them hither; for to cunning men
I will be very kind, and liberal
To mine own children in good bringing-up:
And so, farewell.—Katharina, you may stay:
For I have more to commune with Bianca.
                                   [*Exit.*

KATH. Why, and I trust I may go too, may I not? What, shall I be appointed hours; as though, belike, I knew not what to take, and what to leave, ha?   [*Exit.*

GRE. You may go to the devil's dam: your gifts are so good, here's none will hold you.—Their love is not so great, Hortensio, but we may blow our nails together, and fast it fairly out: our cake's dough on both sides. Farewell:—yet, for the love I bear my sweet Bianca, if I can by any means light on a fit man to teach her that wherein she delights, I will wish him to her father.

HOR. So will I, signior Gremio: but a word, I pray. Though the nature of our quarrel yet never brooked parle, know now, upon advice, it toucheth us both,—that we may yet again have access to our fair mistress, and be happy rivals in Bianca's love,—to labour and effect one thing 'specially.

GRE. What's that, I pray?

HOR. Marry, Sir, to get a husband for her sister.

GRE. A husband! a devil.

HOR. I say, a husband.

GRE. I say, a devil. Thinkest thou, Hortensio, though her father be very rich, any man is so very a fool to be married to hell?

HOR. Tush, Gremio! though it pass your patience and mine to endure her loud alarums, why, man, there be good fellows in the world, an a man could light on them, would take her with all faults, and money enough.

GRE. I cannot tell; but I had as lief take her dowry with this condition,—to be whipped at the high-cross every morning.

HOR. 'Faith, as you say, there's small choice in rotten apples. But, come; since this bar in law makes us friends, it shall be so far forth friendly maintained, till by helping Baptista's eldest daughter to a husband, we set his youngest free for a husband, and then have to't afresh.—Sweet Bianca!—Happy man be his dole! He that runs fastest gets the ring. How say you, signior Gremio?

GRE. I am agreed: and 'would I had given him the best horse in Padua to begin his wooing, that would thoroughly woo her,

wed her, and bed her, and rid the house
of her! Come on.

        [*Exeunt* GREMIO *and* HORTENSIO.

TRA. [*Advancing.*] I pray, Sir, tell me,—
is it possible
That love should of a sudden take such
hold?

LUC. O Tranio, till I found it to be true,
I never thought it possible or likely;
But see! while idly I stood looking on,
I found the effect of love in idleness:
And now in plainness do confess to thee,—
That art to me as secret and as dear
As Anna to the Queen of Carthage was,—
Tranio, I burn, I pine, I perish, Tranio,
If I achieve not this young modest girl.
Counsel me, Tranio, for I know thou canst;
Assist me, Tranio, for I know thou wilt.

TRA. Master, it is no time to chide you
now;
Affection is not rated from the heart:
If love have touch'd you, naught remains
but so,—
Redime te captum, quam queas minimo.

LUC. Gramercies, lad; go forward; this
contents:
The rest will comfort, for thy counsel's
sound.

TRA. Master, you look'd so longly on the
maid,
Perhaps you mark'd not what's the pith
of all.

LUC. O yes, I saw sweet beauty in her
face,
Such as the daughter of Agenor had,
That made great Jove to humble him to
her hand,
When with his knees he kiss'd the Cretan
strand.

TRA. Saw you no more? mark'd you not
how her sister
Began to scold, and raise up such a storm,
That mortal ears might hardly endure the
din?

LUC. Tranio, I saw her coral lips to move,
And with her breath, she did perfume the
air:
Sacred and sweet was all I saw in her.

TRA. Nay, then, 'tis time to stir him from
his trance.—
I pray, awake, Sir: if you love the maid,
Bend thoughts and wits to achieve her.
Thus it stands:—
Her elder sister is so curst and shrewd,
That, till the father rid his hands of her,
Master, your love must live a maid at
home;
And therefore has he closely mew'd her up,
Because she will not be annoy'd with
suitors.

LUC. Ah, Tranio, what a cruel father's he!
But art thou not advis'd, he took some care
To get her cunning schoolmasters to in-
struct her?

TRA. Ay, marry, am I, Sir; and now 'tis
plotted.

LUC. I have it, Tranio.

TRA.   Master, for my hand,
Both our inventions meet and jump in one.

LUC. Tell me thine first.

TRA.   You will be schoolmaster,
And undertake the teaching of the maid:
That's your device.

LUC.   It is: may it be done?

TRA. Not possible; for who shall bear
your part,
And be in Padua here Vincentio's son;
Keep house, and ply his book; welcome his
friends;
Visit his countrymen, and banquet them?

LUC. Basta; content thee; for I have it
full.
We have not yet been seen in any house;
Nor can we be distinguished, by our faces,
For man, or master: then, it follows thus;—
Thou shalt be master, Tranio, in my stead,
Keep house, and port, and servants, as I
should:
I will some other be; some Florentine,
Some Neapolitan, or meaner man of Pisa.
'Tis hatch'd, and shall be so:—Tranio, at
once
Uncase thee; take my colour'd hat and
cloak:
When Biondello comes, he waits on thee;
But I will charm him first to keep his
tongue.

TRA. So had you need.

        [*They exchange habits.*
In brief, Sir, sith it your pleasure is,
And I am tied to be obedient,
(For so your father charg'd me at our
parting,—
"Be serviceable to my son," quoth he,
Although I think 'twas in another sense,)
I am content to be Lucentio,
Because so well I love Lucentio.

LUC. Tranio, be so, because Lucentio
loves:
And let me be a slave, t' achieve that maid
Whose sudden sight hath thrall'd my
wounded eye.
Here comes the rogue.—[*Enter* BIONDELLO.]
Sirrah, where have you been?

BION. Where have I been! Nay, how now!
where are you?
Master, has my fellow Tranio stol'n your
clothes,
Or you stol'n his? or both? pray, what's the
news?

LUC. Sirrah, come hither: 'tis no time
to jest,
And therefore frame your manners to the
time.
Your fellow Tranio, here, to save my life,
Puts my apparel and my countenance on,
And I for my escape have put on his;
For in a quarrel, since I came ashore,
I kill'd a man, and fear I was descried:
Wait you on him, I charge you, as becomes,
While I make way from hence to save my
You understand me?   [life:
BION.   I, Sir! ne'er a whit.
LUC. And not a jot of Tranio in your
mouth:
Tranio is chang'd into Lucentio.
BION. The better for him: 'would I were
so too!
TRA. So would I, 'faith, boy, to have the
next wish after,   [est daughter.
That Lucentio indeed had Baptista's young-
But, sirrah,—not for my sake, but your
master's,—I advise
You use your manners discreetly in all kind
of companies:
When I am alone, why, then I am Tranio;
But in all places else, your master, Lucentio.
LUC. Tranio, let's go:—
One thing more rests, that thyself execute,—
To make one among these wooers: if thou
ask me why,—
Sufficeth, my reasons are both good and
weighty.   [*Exeunt.*

1 *SERV.* My lord, you nod; you do not
mind the play.
SLY. Yes, by saint Anne, do I. A good
matter, surely: comes there any more of it?
PAGE. My lord, 'tis but begun.
SLY. 'Tis a very excellent piece of work,
madam lady: would 'twere done!

SCENE II.—PADUA. *Before* HORTENSIO'S
House.
Enter PETRUCHIO *and* GRUMIO.

PET. Verona, for a while I take my leave,
To see my friends in Padua; but, of all,
My best beloved and approved friend,
Hortensio; and I trow this is his house.—
Here, sirrah Grumio; knock, I say.
GRU. Knock, Sir! whom should I knock?
is there any man has rebused your wor-
ship?
PET. Villain, I say, knock me here soundly.
GRU. Knock you here, Sir! why, Sir,
what am I, Sir, that I should knock you
here, Sir?
PET. Villain, I say, knock me at this
gate,   [pate.
And rap me well, or I'll knock your knave's

GRU. My master is grown quarrelsome.—
I should knock you first,
And then I know after who comes by the
PET. Will it not be?   [worst.
'Faith, sirrah, an you'll not knock, I'll
wring it;
I'll try how you can *sol, fa,* and sing it.
          [*He wrings* GRUMIO *by the ears.*
GRU. Help, masters, help! my master is
mad.   [villain!
PET. Now, knock when I bid you, sirrah
          Enter HORTENSIO.
HOR. How now! what's the matter?—My
old friend Grumio! and my good friend
Petruchio!—How do you all at Verona?
PET. Signior Hortensio, come you to part
the fray?
Con tutto il core ben trovato, may I say.
*HOR. Alla nostra casa ben venuto, molto
honorato signior mio Petruchio.*—
Rise, Grumio, rise: we will compound this
quarrel.
GRU. Nay, 'tis no matter, Sir, what he
'leges in Latin.—If this be not a lawful
cause for me to leave his service,—look
you, Sir,—he bid me knock him, and rap
him soundly, Sir: well, was it fit for a servant to use his master so; being, perhaps,
(for aught I see) two and thirty,—a pip
out?
Whom, 'would to God, I had well knock'd
at first,
Then had not Grumio come by the worst.
PET. A senseless villain!—Good Hortensio,
I bade the rascal knock upon your gate,
And could not get him for my heart to do it.
GRU. Knock at the gate!—O heavens!
Spake you not these words plain,—"Sirrah,
knock me here, rap me here, knock me
well, and knock me soundly?" And come
you now with—knocking at the gate?
PET. Sirrah, be gone, or talk not, I ad-
vise you.   [pledge:
HOR. Petruchio, patience; I am Grumio's
Why, this 's a heavy chance 'twixt him and
you,
Your ancient, trusty, pleasant servant
Grumio.   [gale
And tell me now, sweet friend, what happy
Blows you to Padua here, from old Verona?
PET. Such wind as scatters young men
through the world,
To seek their fortunes farther than at home,
Where small experience grows. But in a
few,
Signior Hortensio, thus it stands with me:—
Antonio, my father, is deceas'd;
And I have thrust myself into this maze,
Haply to wive and thrive as best I may:
Crowns in my purse I have, and goods at
home,

And so am come abroad to see the world.

HOR. Petruchio, shall I then come roundly
  to thee,   [wife?
And wish thee to a shrewd ill-favour'd
Thou'dst thank me but a little for my
  counsel:
And yet I'll promise thee she shall be rich,
And very rich:—but thou'rt too much my
And I'll not wish thee to her.   [friend,
PET. Signior Hortensio, 'twixt such friends
  as we,   [know
Few words suffice; and therefore, if thou
One rich enough to be Petruchio's wife,
(As wealth is burden of my wooing dance)
Be she as foul as was Florentius' love,
As old as Sybil, and as curst and shrewd
As Socrates' Xantippe, or a worse,
She moves me not, or not removes, at least,
Affection's edge in me,—were she as rough
As are the swelling Adriatic seas:
I come to wive it wealthily in Padua;
If wealthily, then happily in Padua.
GRU. Nay, look you, Sir, he tells you
flatly what his mind is: why, give him gold
enough, and marry him to a puppet or an
aglet-baby; or an old trot with ne'er a tooth
in her head, though she have as many dis-
eases as two and fifty horses: why, nothing
comes amiss, so money comes withal.
HOR. Petruchio, since we are stepp'd thus
far in,
I will continue that I broach'd in jest.
I can, Petruchio, help thee to a wife
With wealth enough, and young and beau-
  teous;   [woman:
Brought up as best becomes a gentle-
Her only fault, (and that is faults enough,)
Is,—that she is intolerable curst,
And shrewd, and froward; so beyond all
  measure,
That, were my state far worser than it is,
I would not wed her for a mine of gold.
PET. Hortensio, peace! thou knows't not
  gold's effect:—
Tell me her father's name, and 'tis enough;
For I will board her, though she chide as
  loud   [crack.
As thunder, when the clouds in autumn
HOR. Her father is Baptista Minola,
An affable and courteous gentleman:
Her name is Katharina Minola,
Renown'd in Padua for her scolding tongue.
PET. I know her father, though I know
  not her;
And he knew my deceased father well.
I will not sleep, Hortensio, till I see her;
And therefore let me be thus bold with you,
To give you over at this first encounter,
Unless you will accompany me thither.
GRU. I pray you, Sir, let him go while
the humour lasts. O' my word, an she knew

him as well as I do, she would think
scolding would do little good upon him: she
may, perhaps, call him half a score knaves,
or so: why, that's nothing; an he begin
once, he'll rail in his rope-tricks. I'll tell
you what, Sir,—an she stand him but a
little, he will throw a figure in her face,
and so disfigure her with it, that she shall
have no more eyes to see withal than a cat.
You know him not, Sir.
HOR. Tarry, Petruchio, I must go with
  thee;
For in Baptista's keep my treasure is:
He hath the jewel of my life in hold,
His youngest daughter, beautiful Bianca;
And her withholds from me, and other
  more,
Suitors to her, and rivals in my love;
Supposing it a thing impossible
(For those defects I have before rehears'd,)
That ever Katharina will be woo'd;
Therefore this order hath Baptista ta'en,
That none shall have access unto Bianca,
Till Katharine the curst have got a hus-
GRU. Katharine the curst!   [band.
A title for a maid, of all titles the worst.
HOR. Now shall my friend Petruchio do
  me grace;
And offer me, disguis'd in sober robes,
To old Baptista as a schoolmaster
Well seen in music, to instruct Bianca;
That so I may, by this device, at least
Have leave and leisure to make love to her,
And, unsuspected, court her by herself.
GRU. Here's no knavery! See, to beguile
the old folks, how the young folks lay their
heads together!—
Enter GREMIO; *and* LUCENTIO *disguised,
with books under his arm.*
Master, master, look about you: who goes
there, ha?
HOR. Peace, Grumio: 'tis the rival of my
Petruchio, stand by a while.   [love.
GRU. A proper stripling, and an amorous!
        [*They retire.*
GRE. O, very well; I have perus'd the note.
Hark you, Sir; I'll have them very fairly
  bound;
All books of love, see that at any hand;
And see you read no other lectures to her:
You understand me:—over and beside
Signior Baptista's liberality,
I'll mend it with a largess:—take your
  papers too,
And let me have them very well perfum'd;
For she is sweeter than perfume itself,
To whom they go. What will you read to
  her?   [for you,
LUC. Whate'er I read to her, I'll plead
As for my patron, (stand you so assur'd,)
As firmly as yourself were still in place:

Yea, and perhaps with more successful
  words
Than you, unless you were a scholar, Sir.
GRE. O this learning! what a thing it is!
GRU. O this woodcock! what an ass it is!
PET. Peace, sirrah!
HOR. Grumio, mum!—[Coming forward.]
God save you, signior Gremio!   [tensio.
GRE. And you are well met, signior Hor-
Know you whither I am going?—To Bap-
tista Minola.
  promis'd to enquire carefully
About a schoolmaster for the fair Bianca:
And by good fortune, I have lighted well
On this young man; for learning and be-
  haviour
Fit for her turn; well read in poetry,
And other books,—good ones, I warrant ye.
HOR. 'Tis well: and I have met a gentle-
  man
Hath promis'd me to help me to another,
A fine musician to instruct our mistress;
So shall I no whit be behind in duty
To fair Bianca, so belov'd of me.
GRE. Belov'd of me,—and that my deeds
  shall prove.
GRU. And that his bags shall prove.
HOR. Gremio, 'tis now no time to vent our
  love:
Listen to me; and if you speak me fair,
I'll tell you news indifferent good for
  either.
Here is a gentleman, whom by chance I
  met,
Upon agreement from us to his liking,
Will undertake to woo curst Katharine,
Yea, and to marry her, if her dowry please.
GRE. So said, so done, is well:—
Hortensio, have you told him all her faults?
PET. I know she is an irksome brawling
  scold:
If that be all, masters, I hear no harm.
GRE. No, say'st me so, friend? What
  countryman?
PET. Born in Verona, old Antonio's son:
My father is dead, my fortune lives for me;
And I do hope good days and long to see.
GRE. O Sir, such a life, with such a wife,
  were strange!   [name:
But if you have a stomach, to't o' God's
You shall have me assisting you in all.
But will you woo this wild cat?
PET.   Will I live?
GRU. Will he woo her? ay, or I'll hang
  her.
PET. Why came I hither, but to that
  intent?
Think you a little din can daunt mine ears?
Have I not in my time heard lions roar?
Have I not heard the sea, puff'd up with
  winds,

Rage like an angry boar chafed with sweat?
Have I not heard great ordnance in the
  field,
And heaven's artillery thunder in the skies?
Have I not in a pitched battle heard
Loud 'larums, neighing steeds, and trum-
  pet's clang?
And do you tell me of a woman's tongue;
That gives not half so great a blow to
As will a chestnut in a farmer's fire? [hear,
Tush, tush! fear boys with bugs.
GRU.   For he fears none.
GRE. Hortensio, hark:
This gentleman is happily arriv'd,   [ours.
My mind presumes, for his own good, and
HOR. I promis'd we would be contributors,
And bear his charge of wooing, whatsoe'er.
GRE. And so we will,—provided that he
  win her.   [dinner.
GRU. I would I were as sure of a good
  Enter TRANIO, bravely apparalled; and
  BIONDELLO.
TRA. Gentlemen, God save you! If I may
  be bold,   [iest way
Tell me, I beseech you, which is the read-
To the house of signior Baptista Minola?
BION. He that has the two fair daughters:
  —[To Tranio.] is't he you mean?
TRA. Even he, Biondello.
GRE. Hark you, Sir; you mean not her
  to—   [have you to do?
TRA. Perhaps him and her, Sir; what
PET. Not her that chides, Sir, at any hand,
  I pray.   [let's away.
TRA. I love no chiders. Sir.—Biondello,
LUC. [Aside.] Well begun, Tranio.
HOR. Sir, a word ere you go:—
Are you a suitor to the maid you talk of,
  yea or no?
TRA. An if I be, Sir, is it any offence?
GRE. No; if without more words you will
  get you hence.
TRA. Why, Sir, I pray, are not the streets
For me as for you?   [as free
GRE.   But so is not she.
TRA. For what reason, I beseech you?
GRE. For this reason, if you'll know,—
That she's the choice love of signior
  Gremio.   [Hortensio.
HOR. That she's the chosen of signior
TRA. Softly, my masters! if you be gentle-
  men,
Do me this right,—hear me with patience.
Baptista is a noble gentleman,
To whom my father is not all unknown;
And, were his daughter fairer than she is,
She may more suitors have, and me for one.
Fair Leda's daughter had a thousand
  wooers;
Then well one more may fair Bianca have:
And so she shall; Lucentio shall make one,

Though Paris came in hope to speed alone.

GRE. What, this gentleman will out-talk us all!

LUC. Sir, give him head: I know he'll prove a jade.

PET. Hortensio, to what end are all these words?

HOR. Sir, let me be so bold as ask you, Did you yet ever see Baptista's daughter?

TRA. No, sir; but hear I do, that he hath two;
The one as famous for a scolding tongue, As is the other for beauteous modesty.

PET. Sir, Sir, the first's for me; let her go by.

GRE. Yea, leave that labour to great Hercules;
And let it be more than Alcides' twelve.

PET. Sir, understand you this of me, in sooth;   [for,
The youngest daughter, whom you hearken
Her father keeps from all access of suitors;
And will not promise her to any man
Until the elder sister first be wed:
The younger then is free, and not before.

TRA. If it be so, Sir, that you are the man
Must stead us all, and me among the rest;
And if you break the ice, and do this feat,
Achieve the elder, set the younger free
For our access,—whose hap shall be to have her,
Will not so graceless be, to be ingrate.

HOR. Sir, you say well, and well you do conceive;
And since you do profess to be a suitor,
You must, as we do, gratify this gentleman,
To whom we all rest generally beholden.

TRA. Sir, I shall not be slack: in sign whereof,
Please ye we may contrive this afternoon,
And quaff carouses to our mistress' health;
And do as adversaries do in law,—
Strive mightily, but eat and drink as friends.

GRU. BION. O excellent motion! Fellows, let's be gone.   [so:—

HOR. The motion's good indeed, and be it Petruchio, I shall be your *ben venuto*.
          [*Exeunt.*

ACT II.

Scene I.—Padua. *A Room in* Baptista's *House.*

Enter Katharina *and* Bianca.

BIAN. Good sister, wrong me not, nor wrong yourself,
To make a bondmaid and a slave of me;
That I disdain: but for these other gawds,

Unbind my hands, I'll pull them off myself,
Yea, all my raiment, to my petticoat;
Or, what you will command me will I do,
So well I know my duty to my elders.

KATH. Of all thy suitors, here I charge thee, tell
Whom thou lov'st best: see thou dissemble not.

BIAN. Believe me, sister, of all the men
I never yet beheld that special face   [alive,
Which I could fancy more than any other.

KATH. Minion, thou liest: is't not Hortensio?   [swear.

BIAN. If you affect him, sister, here I
I'll plead for you myself, but you shall have him.   [more:

KATH. O then, belike, you fancy riches
You will have Gremio to keep you fair.

BIAN. Is it for him you do envy me so?
Nay, then you jest; and now I well perceive
You have but jested with me all this while:
I pr'ythee, sister Kate, untie my hands.

KATH. If that be jest, then all the rest was so.   [*Strikes her.*

Enter Baptista.

BAP. Why, how now, dame! whence grows this insolence?—
Bianca, stand aside:— poor girl! she weeps:—
Go ply thy needle; meddle not with her.—
For shame, thou hilding of a devilish spirit,
Why dost thou wrong her that did ne'er wrong thee?   [word?
When did she cross thee with a bitter

KATH. Her silence flouts me, and I'll be reveng'd.   [*Flies after* Bianca.

BAP. What! in my sight?—Bianca, get thee in.   [*Exit* Bianca.

KATH. What! will you not suffer me? Nay now I see
She is your treasure, she must have a husband;
I must dance barefoot on her wedding-day,
And, for your love to her, lead apes in hell.
Talk not to me: I will go sit and weep,
Till I can find occasion of revenge [*Exit.*

BAP. Was ever gentleman thus griev'd
But who comes here?   [as I?

Enter Gremio, *with* Lucentio, *in the habit of a mean man;* Petruchio, *with* Hortensio *as a Musician; and* Tranio, *with* Biondello *bearing a lute and books.*

GRE. Good-morrow, neighbour Baptista.

BAP. Good-morrow, neighbour Gremio.—
God save you, gentlemen!

PET. And you, good Sir. Pray, have you not a daughter
Call'd Katharina, fair and virtuous?

BAP. I have a daughter, Sir, call'd Katharina.

GRE. You are too blunt: go to it orderly.

PET. You wrong me, signior Gremio; give me leave.—

[*To* BAP.] I am a gentleman of Verona, Sir,
That,—hearing of her beauty and her wit,
Her affability and bashful modesty,
Her wondrous qualities and mild behaviour,—
Am bold to show myself a forward guest
Within your house, to make mine eye the witness
Of that report which I so oft have heard.
And, for an entrance to my entertainment,
I do present you with a man of mine,
                    [*Presenting* HORTENSIO.
Cunning in music and the mathematics,
To instruct her fully in those sciences,
Whereof I know she is not ignorant:
Accept of him, or else you do me wrong:
His name is Licio, born in Mantua.

BAP. You're welcome, Sir: and he, for your good sake.   [know,
But for my daughter Katharine,—this I
She is not for your turn, the more my grief.

PET. I see you do not mean to part with her;
Or else you like not of my company.

BAP. Mistake me not; I speak but as I find.   [your name?
Whence are you, Sir? what may I call

PET. Petruchio is my name; Antonio's son,
A man well known throughout all Italy.

BAP. I know him well: you are welcome for his sake.

GRE. Saving your tale, Petruchio, I pray,
Let us, that are poor petitioners, speak too:
Baccare! you are marvellous forward.

PET. O, pardon me, signior Gremio; I would fain be doing.

GRE. I doubt it not, Sir; but you will curse your wooing.—
Neighbour, this is a gift very grateful, I am sure of it. To express the like kindness myself, that have been more kindly beholden to you than any, I freely give unto you this young scholar, [*Presenting* LUCENTIO,] that hath been long studying at Rheims; as cunning in Greek, Latin, and other languages, as the other in music and mathematics: his name is Cambio; pray accept his service.

BAP. A thousand thanks, signior Gremio. Welcome, good Cambio.—[*To* TRANIO.] But, gentle Sir, methinks you walk like a stranger: may I be so bold to know the cause of your coming?   [own;

TRA. Pardon me, Sir, the boldness is mine
That, being a stranger in this city here,
Do make myself a suitor to your daughter,
Unto Bianca, fair and virtuous.
Nor is your firm resolve unknown to me,
In the preferment of the eldest sister.
This liberty is all that I request,—

That, upon knowledge of my parentage,
I may have welcome 'mongst the rest that woo,
And free access and favour as the rest:
And, toward the education of your daugh-
I here bestow a simple instrument,   [ters,
And this small packet of Greek and Latin books: [great.
If you accept them, then their worth is

BAP. Lucentio is your name,—of whence I pray?

TRA. Of Pisa, Sir; son to Vincentio.

BAP. A mighty man of Pisa; by report
I know him well: you are very welcome, Sir.—

[*To* HOR.] Take you the lute; [*To* LUC.] and you the set of books;
You shall go see your pupils presently.—
Hola, within!

                    Enter a Servant.
Sirrah, lead these gentlemen
To my daughters; and tell them both,
These are their tutors: bid them use them well.

          [*Exit* Servant, *with* HORTENSIO,
              LUCENTIO, *and* BIONDELLO.
We will go walk a little in the orchard,
And then to dinner. You are passing welcome,
And so I pray you all to think yourselves.

PET. Signior Baptista, my business asketh haste,
And every day I cannot come to woo.
You knew my father well; and in him, me,
Left solely heir to all his lands and goods,
Which I have better'd rather than decreas'd:
Then tell me,—if I get your daughter's love,
What dowry shall I have with her to wife?

BAP. After my death, the one half of my lands;
And, in possession, twenty thousand crowns.

PET. And, for that dowry, I'll assure her of
Her widowhood,—be it that she survive me,—
In all my lands and leases whatsoever:
Let specialties be therefore drawn between us,   [hand.
That covenants may be kept on either

BAP. Ay, when the special thing is well obtain'd,
That is, her love; for that is all in all.

PET. Why, that is nothing; for I tell you, father,
I am as peremptory as she proud-minded;
And where two raging fires meet together,
They do consume the thing that feeds their fury: [wind,
Though little fire grows great with little
Yet extreme gusts will blow out fire and all:
So I to her, and so she yields to me;   [all:

For I am rough, and woo not like a babe.

BAP. Well may'st thou woo, and happy be thy speed!
But be thou arm'd for some unhappy words.

PET. Ay, to the proof; as mountains are for winds,   [ually.
That shake not, though they blow perpet-

Re-enter HORTENSIO, *with his head broken.*

BAP. How now, my friend! why dost thou look so pale?

HOR. For fear, I promise you, if I look pale.   [good musician?

BAP. What, will my daughter prove a

HOR. I think she'll sooner prove a soldier: Iron may hold with her, but never lutes.

BAP. Why, then thou can'st not break her to the lute?

HOR. Why no; for she hath broke the lute to me.
I did but tell her she mistook her frets,
And bow'd her hand to teach her fingering:
When, with a most impatient devilish spirit,
"Frets, call you these?" quoth she; "I'll fume with them;"
And, with that word, she struck me on the head,   [way;
And through the instrument my pate made
And there I stood amazed for a while,
As on a pillory, looking through the lute;
While she did call me rascal fiddler,
And twangling Jack; with twenty such vile terms,
As she had studied to misuse me so.

PET. Now, by the world, it is a lusty wench!
I love her ten times more than e'er I did:
O, how I long to have some chat with her!

BAP. [*To* HOR.] Well, go with me, and be not so discomfited:
Proceed in practice with my younger daughter;   [turns.—
She's apt to learn, and thankful for good
Signior Petruchio, will you go with us,
Or shall I send my daughter Kate to you?

PET. I pray you do; I will attend her here,

[*Exeunt* BAPTISTA, GREMIO, TRANIO, *and* HORTENSIO.

And woo her with some spirit when she comes.   [plain,
Say, that she rail; why, then I'll tell her
She sings as sweetly as a nightingale:
Say, that she frown; I'll say she looks as clear
As morning roses newly wash'd with dew:
Say, she be mute, and will not speak a
Then I'll commend her volubility,   [word;
And say she uttereth piercing eloquence:
If she do bid me pack, I'll give her thanks,
As though she bid me stay by her a week:
If she deny to wed, I'll crave the day

When I shall ask the banns, and when be married.—   [speak.
But here she comes; and now, Petruchio,

Enter KATHARINA.

Good-morrow, Kate; for that's your name, I hear.

KATH. Well have you heard, but something hard of hearing:
They call me Katharine, that do talk of me.

PET. You lie, in faith; for you are call'd plain Kate,
And bonny Kate, and sometimes Kate the curst;
But, Kate, the prettiest Kate in Christendom,
Kate of Kate-Hall, my super-dainty Kate,
For dainties are all cates,—and therefore, Kate,
Take this of me, Kate of my consolation;—
Hearing thy mildness prais'd in every town,
Thy virtues spoke of, and thy beauty sounded,
(Yet not so deeply as to thee belongs,)
Myself am mov'd to woo thee for my wife.

KATH. Mov'd! in good time: let him that mov'd you hither,
Remove you hence: I knew you at the first,
You were a moveable.

PET.   Why, what's a moveable?

KATH. A joint-stool.

PET. Thou hast hit it: come, sit on me.

KATH. Asses are made to bear, and so are you.

PET. Women are made to bear, and so are you.   [you mean.

KATH. No such jade to bear you, if me

PET. Alas, good Kate! I will not burden thee;   [light,—
For, knowing thee to be but young and

KATH. Too light for such a swain as you to catch;
And yet as heavy as my weight should be.

PET. Should be! should buz.

KATH.   Well ta'en, and like a buzzard.

PET. O slow-wing'd turtle! shall a buzzard take thee?   [buzzard.

KATH. Ay, for a turtle,—as he takes a

PET. Come, come, you wasp; i' faith, you are too angry.

KATH. If I be waspish, best beware my sting.

PET. My remedy is, then, to pluck it out.

KATH. Ay, if the fool could find it where it lies.

PET. Who knows not where a wasp does In his tail.   [wear his sting?

KATH. In his tongue.

PET.   Whose tongue?

KATH. Yours, if you talk of tails; and so farewell.

PET. What! with my tongue in your tail?
    nay, come again,
Good Kate; I am a gentleman.
KATH.   That I'll try. [*Striking him.*
PET. I swear I'll cuff you, if you strike
    again.
KATH. So may you lose your arms:
If you strike me, you are no gentleman;
And if no gentleman, why then no arms.
PET. A herald, Kate? O, put me in thy
    books!
KATH. What is your crest? a coxcomb?
PET. A combless cock, so Kate will be my
    hen.   [like a craven.
KATH. No cock of mine; you crow too
PET. Nay, come, Kate, come; you must
    not look so sour.
KATH. It is my fashion, when I see a
    crab.   [look not sour.
PET. Why, here's no crab; and therefore
KATH. There is, there is.
PET. Then show it me.
KATH.   Had I a glass, I would.
PET. What, you mean my face?
KATH. Well aim'd of such a young one.
PET. Now, by Saint George, I am too
    young for you.
KATH. Yet you are wither'd.
PET.   'Tis with cares.
KATH.   I care not.
PET. Nay, hear you, Kate: in sooth, you
    'scape not so.
KATH. I chafe you, if I tarry: let me go.
PET. No, not a whit: I find you passing
    gentle.
'Twas told me, you were rough, and coy,
    and sullen,
And now I find report a very liar;
For thou art pleasant, gamesome, passing
    courteous,   [time flowers:
But slow in speech, yet sweet as spring-
Thou canst not frown, thou canst not look
    askance,
Nor bite the lip, as angry wenches will;
Nor hast thou pleasure to be cross in talk;
But thou with mildness entertain'st thy
    wooers,
With gentle conference, soft and affable.
Why does the world report that Kate doth
    limp?   [twig,
O slanderous world! Kate, like the hazel-
Is straight and slender; and as brown in
    hue
As hazel nuts, and sweeter than the kernels.
O! let me see thee walk: thou dost not
    halt.   [command.
KATH. Go, fool; and whom thou keep'st,
PET. Did ever Dian so become a grove,
As Kate this chamber with her princely
    gait?
O, be thou Dian, and let her be Kate;

And then let Kate be chaste, and Dian
    sportful!
KATH. Where did you study all this
    goodly speech?
PET. It is extempore, from my mother-
    wit.   [son.
KATH. A witty mother! witless else her
PET. Am I not wise?
KATH.   Yes; keep you warm.
PET. Marry, so I mean, sweet Katharine,
    in thy bed:
And therefore, setting all this chat aside,
Thus in plain terms:—your father hath
    consented   ['greed on;
That you shall be my wife; your dowry
And, will you, nill you, I will marry you.
Now, Kate, I am a husband for your turn;
For, by this light, whereby I see thy beauty,
(Thy beauty that doth make me like thee
    well,)
Thou must be married to no man but me:
For I am he, am born to tame you, Kate;
And bring you from a wild Kate to a Kate
Conformable, as other household Kates.
Here comes your father: never make denial;
I must and will have Katharine to my wife.
Re-enter BAPTISTA, GREMIO, *and* TRANIO.
BAP. Now, signior Petruchio, how speed
    you with my daughter?
PET. How but well, Sir? how but well?
It were impossible I should speed amiss.
BAP. Why, how now, daughter Katharine!
    in your dumps?
KATH. Call you me daughter? now, I
    promise you,
You have show'd a tender fatherly regard,
To wish me wed to one half lunatic;
A mad-cap ruffian, and a swearing Jack.
That thinks with oaths to face the matter
    out.   [the world,
PET. Father, 'tis thus:—yourself and all
That talk'd of her, have talk'd amiss of
If she be curst, it is for policy.   [her;
For she's not froward, but modest as the
    dove;
She is not hot, but temperate as the morn;
For patience she will prove a second Gris-
And Roman Lucrece for her chastity: [sel,
And to conclude,—we have 'greed so well
    together,
That upon Sunday is the wedding-day.
KATH. I'll see thee hang'd on Sunday first.
GRE. Hark, Petruchio; she says, she'll see
    thee hang'd first.
TRA. Is this your speeding? nay then,
    good night our part!   [for myself:
PET. Be patient, gentlemen; I choose her
If she and I be pleas'd, what's that to you?
'Tis bargain'd 'twixt us twain, being alone,
That she shall still be curst in company.
I tell you, 'tis incredible to believe

How much she loves me: O, the kindest
    Kate!
She hung about my neck; and kiss on kiss
She vied so fast, protesting oath on oath,
That in a twink she won me to her love.
O, you are novices! 'tis a world to see,
How tame, when men and women are alone,
A meacock wretch can make the curstest
    shrew.—
Give me thy hand, Kate: I will unto Venice,
To buy apparel 'gainst the wedding-day.—
Provide the feast, father, and bid the
    guests;
I will be sure my Katharine shall be fine.
BAP. I know not what to say: but give me
    your hands;
God send you joy, Petruchio! 'tis a match.
GRE. TRA. Amen, say we: we will be
    witnesses.   [adieu;
PET. Father, and wife, and gentlemen,
I will to Venice; Sunday comes apace.—
We will have rings, and things, and fine
    array,   [o' Sunday.
And kiss me Kate, we will be married
    [*Exeunt* PETRUCHIO *and* KATHARINA,
        severally.
GRE. Was ever match clapp'd up so sud-
    denly?
BAP. Faith, gentlemen, now I play a mer-
    chant's part.
And venture madly on a desperate mart.
TRA. 'Twas a commodity lay fretting by
    you: [seas.
'Twill bring you gain, or perish on the
BAP. The gain I seek is quiet in the
    match.
GRE. No doubt but he hath got a quiet
    catch.   [ter:
But now, Baptista, to your younger daugh-
Now is the day we long have looked for:
I am your neighbour, and was suitor first.
TRA. And I am one that love Bianca more
Than words can witness, or your thoughts
    can guess.
GRE. Youngling, thou canst not love so
    dear as I.
TRA. Grey-beard, thy love doth freeze.
GRE.   But thine doth fry.
Skipper, stand back: 'tis age that nourish-
    eth.   [isheth.
TRA. But youth in ladies' eyes that flour-
BAP. Content you, gentlemen; I'll com-
    pound this strife:
'Tis deeds must win the prize; and he, of
    both,   [dower.
That can assure my daughter greatest
Shall have my Bianca's love.—
Say, signior Gremio, what can you assure
    her?   [in the city
GRE. First, as you know, my house with-
Is richly furnished with plate and gold;

Basons and ewers, to lave her dainty hands;
My hangings all of Tyrian tapestry;
In ivory coffers I have stuff'd my crowns;
In cypress chests my arras, counterpoints,
Costly apparel, tents, and canopies,
Fine linen, Turkey cushions boss'd with
    pearl,
Valance of Venice gold in needle-work;
Pewter and brass, and all things that belong
To house or housekeeping: then, at my
    farm
I have a hundred milch-kine to the pail,
Six score fat oxen standing in my stalls,
And all things answerable to this portion.
Myself am struck in years, I must confess;
And if I die to-morrow, this is hers,
If whilst I live she will be only mine.
TRA. That "only" came well in.—Sir, list
    to me:
I am my father's heir and only son:
If I may have your daughter to my wife,
I'll leave her houses three or four as good,
Within rich Pisa walls, as any one
Old signior Gremio has in Padua;
Besides two thousand ducats by the year
Of fruitful land, all which shall be her
    jointure.—
What, have I pinch'd you, signior Gremio?
GRE. Two thousand ducats by the year of
    land!
My land amounts not to so much in all:
That she shall have; besides an argosy
That now is lying in Marseilles' road.—
What, have I chok'd you with an argosy?
TRA. Gremio, 'tis known, my father hath
    no less   [liasses,
Than three great argosies; besides two gal-
And twelve tight galleys: these I will assure
    her,   [next.
And twice as much, whate'er thou offer'st
GRE. Nay, I have offer'd all,—I have no
    more;
And she can have no more than all I
    have:—
If you like me, she shall have me and mine.
TRA. Why, then the maid is mine from all
    the world,
By your firm promise: Gremio is out-vied.
BAP. I must confess your offer is the best;
And, let your father make her the assur-
    ance;   [me:
She is your own; else, you must pardon
If you should die before him, where's her
    dower?
TRA. That's but a cavil: he is old, I young.
GRE. And may not young men die, as well
BAP. Well, gentlemen,   [as old?
I am thus resolv'd:—on Sunday next, you
    know,
My daughter Katharine is to be married:
Now, on the Sunday following, shall Bianca

Be bride to you, if you make this assurance;
If not, to signior Gremio:
And so, I take my leave, and thank you
both.
GRE. Adieu, good neighbour. [*Exit* BAP.]
Now I fear thee not:
Sirrah young gamester, your father were a
fool
To give thee all, and in his waning age
Set foot under thy table. Tut, a toy!
An old Italian fox is not so kind, my boy.
                                            [*Exit.*
TRA. A vengeance on your crafty wither'd
hide!
Yet I have faced it with a card of ten.
'Tis in my head to do my master good:—
I see no reason, but suppos'd Lucentio
Must get a father, call'd—suppos'd Vin-
centio;
And that's a wonder: fathers, commonly,
Do get their children; but in this case of
wooing,   [cunning.
A child shall get a sire, if I fail not of my
                                            [*Exit.*

ACT III.

SCENE I.—PADUA. *A Room in* BAPTISTA'S
House.

Enter LUCENTIO, HORTENSIO, *and* BIANCA.

LUC. Fiddler, forbear; you grow too for-
ward, Sir:
Have you so soon forgot the entertainment
Her sister Katharine welcom'd you withal?
HOR. But, wrangling pedant, this is
The patroness of heavenly harmony:
Then give me leave to have prerogative;
And when in music we have spent an hour,
Your lecture shall have leisure for as much.
LUC. Preposterous ass, that never read so
far
To know the cause why music was ordain'd!
Was it not to refresh the mind of man,
After his studies, or his usual pain?
Then give me leave to read philosophy,
And while I pause, serve in your harmony.
HOR. Sirrah, I will not bear these braves
of thine.   [ble wrong,
BIAN. Why, gentlemen, you do me dou-
To strive for that which resteth in my
choice:
I am no breeching scholar in the schools;
I'll not be tied to hours nor 'pointed times,
But learn my lessons as I please myself.
And, to cut off all strife, here sit we
down:—
Take you your instrument, play you the
whiles;
His lecture will be done, ere you have tun'd.

HOR. You'll leave his lecture when I am
in tune?   [HORTENSIO *retires.*
LUC. That will be never:—tune your in-
strument.
BIAN. Where left we last?
LUC. Here, madam:—
Hac ibat Simois; hic est Sigeia tellus;
Hic steterat Priami regia celsa senis.
BIAN. Construe them.
LUC. Hac ibat, as I told you before,—
Simois, I am Lucentio,—*hic est,* son unto
Vincentio of Pisa,—*Sigeia tellus,* disguised
thus to get your love;—*Hic steterat,* and
that Lucentio that comes a wooing,—
Priami, is my man Tranio,—*regia,* bearing
my port,—*celsa senis,* that we might be-
guile the old pantaloon.
HOR. [*Coming forward.*] Madam, my in-
strument's in tune.
BIAN. Let's hear.—   [HORTENSIO *plays.*
O fie! the treble jars.
LUC. Spit in the hole, man, and tune
again.   [HOR. *again retires.*
BIAN. Now let me see if I can construe
it:—*Hac ibat Simois,* I know you not,—
hic est Sigeia tellus, I trust you not;—*Hic
steterat Priami,* take heed he hear us not,
—*regia,* presume not;—*celsa senis,* des-
pair not.
HOR. [*Again coming forward.*] Madam,
'tis now in tune.
LUC.   All but the base.
HOR. The base is right; 'tis the base
knave that jars.
How fiery and forward our pedant is!
[*Aside.*] Now, for my life, the knave doth
court my love:
Pedascule, I'll watch you better yet.
BIAN. In time I may believe, yet I mis-
trust.
LUC. Mistrust it not; for, sure, Æacides
Was Ajax,—call'd so from his grandfather.
BIAN. I must believe my master; else, I
promise you,
I should be arguing still upon that doubt:
But let it rest.—Now, Licio, to you:—
Good masters, take it not unkindly, pray,
That I have been thus pleasant with you
both.
HOR. [*To* LUCENTIO.] You may go walk,
and give me leave awhile:
My lessons make no music in three parts.
LUC. Are you so formal, Sir? [*Aside.*]
Well, I must wait,
And watch withal; for, but I be deceiv'd,
Our fine musician groweth amorous.
HOR. Madam, before you touch the instru-
To learn the order of my fingering, [ment,
I must begin with rudiments of art;
To teach you gamut in a briefer sort,
More pleasant, pithy, and effectual,

Than hath been taught by any of my trade:
And there it is in writing, fairly drawn.

BIAN. Why, I am past my gamut long ago.

HOR. Yet read the gamut of Hortensio.

BIAN. [Reads.]

"*Gamut* I am, the ground of all accord,
    A re, to plead Hortensio's passion,
B mi, Bianca, take him for thy lord,
    C fa ut, that loves with all affection:
D sol re, one cliff, two notes have I:
E la mi, show pity, or I die."

Call you this gamut? tut! I like it not:
Old fashions please me best; I am not so nice,
To change true rules for odd inventions.
                Enter a Servant.

SERV. Mistress, your father prays you leave your books,
And help to dress your sister's chamber up:
You know, to-morrow is the wedding-day.

BIAN. Farewell, sweet masters, both; I must be gone.
        [*Exeunt* BIANCA *and* Servant.

LUC. 'Faith, mistress, then I have no cause to stay.   [*Exit.*

HOR. But I have cause to pry into this pedant: [*love:—*
Methinks he looks as though he were in love:—
Yet if thy thoughts, Bianca, be so humble,
To cast thy wandering eyes on every stale,
Seize thee that list: if once I find thee ranging,
Hortensio will be quit with thee by changing.   [*Exit.*

——

SCENE II.—PADUA. *Before* BAPTISTA'S *House.*

Enter BAPTISTA, GREMIO, TRANIO, KATHARINA, BIANCA, LUCENTIO, *and Attendants.*

BAP. [*To* TRANIO.] Signior Lucentio, this is the 'pointed day
That Katharine and Petruchio should be married,
And yet we hear not of our son-in-law.
What will be said? what mockery will it be,
To want the bridegroom, when the priest attends
To speak the ceremonial rites of marriage!
What says Lucentio to this shame of ours?

KATH. No shame but mine: I must, forsooth, be forc'd
To give my hand, oppos'd against my heart,
Unto a mad-brain rudesby, full of spleen;
Who woo'd in haste, and means to wed at leisure.
I told you, I, he was a frantic fool,
Hiding his bitter jests in blunt behaviour:
And, to be noted for a merry man,

He'll woo a thousand, 'point the day of marriage,
Make friends invited, and proclaim the banns;   [*woo'd.*
Yet never means to wed where he hath woo'd.
Now must the world point at poor Katharine,
And say,—"Lo, there is mad Petruchio's wife,
If it would please him come and marry her!"   [*tista too.*

TRA. Patience, good Katharine, and Baptista too.
Upon my life, Petruchio means but well,
Whatever fortune stays him from his word:
Though he be blunt, I know him passing wise;
Though he be merry, yet withal he's honest.

KATH. Would Katharine had never seen him though!
        [*Exit weeping, followed by* BIANCA
                and others.

BAP. Go girl; I cannot blame thee now to weep;
For such an injury would vex a very saint,
Much more a shrew of thy impatient humour.

                Enter BIONDELLO.

BION. Master, master! old news, and such news as you never heard of!

BAP. Is it new and old too? how may that be?

BION. Why, is it not news to hear of Petruchio's coming?

BAP. Is he come?

BION. Why, no, Sir.

BAP. What then?

BION. He is coming.

BAP. When will he be here?

BION. When he stands where I am, and sees you there.

TRA. But, say, what to thine old news?

BION. Why, Petruchio is coming, in a new hat and an old jerkin; a pair of old breeches thrice turned; a pair of boots that have been candle-cases, one buckled, another laced; an old rusty sword ta'en out of the town armoury, with a broken hilt, and chapeless; with two broken points: his horse hipped with an old mothy saddle, and stirrups of no kindred; besides, possessed with the glanders, and like to mose in the chine; troubled with the lampass, infected with the fashions, full of wind-galls, sped with spavins, raied with the yellows, past cure of the fives, stark spoiled with the staggers, begnawn with the bots, swayed in the back, and shoulder-shotten; ne'er-legged before, and with a half-checked bit, and a head-stall of sheep's leather, which being restrained to keep him from stumbling, hath been often burst, and now re-

paired with knots; one girth six times
pieced, and a woman's crupper of velure,
which hath two letters for her name fairly
set down in studs, and here and there
pieced with pack-thread.

BAP. Who comes with him?

BION. O, Sir, his lackey, for all the world
caparisoned like the horse; with a linen
stock on one leg, and a kersey boot-hose on
the other, gartered with a red and blue
list; an old hat, and The humour of forty
fancies pricked in't for a feather: a monster, a very monster in apparel; and not
like a Christian footboy, or a gentleman's
lackey.

TRA. 'Tis some odd humour pricks him
to this fashion;
Yet oftentimes he goes but mean apparell'd.

BAP. I am glad he is come, howsoe'er he
comes.

BION. Why, Sir, he comes not.

BAP. Didst thou not say, he comes?

BION. Who? that Petruchio came?

BAP. Ay, that Petruchio came.

BION. No, Sir; I say his horse comes,
with him on his back.

BAP. Why, that's all one.

BION. Nay, by Saint Jamy,
　　　I hold you a penny,
　　　　A horse and a man
　　　Is more than one,
　　　And yet not many.

Enter PETRUCHIO *and* GRUMIO.

PET. Come, where be these gallants? who
is at home?

BAP. You are welcome, Sir.

PET. 　　　　And yet I come not well.

BAP. And yet you halt not.

TRA. 　　　　Not so well apparell'd,
As I wish you were.

PET. Were it better, I should rush in thus.
But where is Kate? where is my lovely
bride?—　　　　　　　　[you frown:
How does my father?—Gentles, methinks
And wherefore gaze this goodly company,
As if they saw some wondrous monument,
Some comet, or unusual prodigy?

BAP. Why, Sir, you know this is your
wedding-day:　　　　　　　[come;
First were we sad, fearing you would not
Now sadder, that you come so unprovided.
Fie, doff this habit, shame to your estate,
An eye-sore to our solemn festival!

TRA. And tell us, what occasion of im-
port　　　　　　　　　　[wife,
Hath all so long detain'd you from your
And sent you hither so unlike yourself?

PET. Tedious it were to tell, and harsh
to hear:
Sufficeth, I am come to keep my word,
Though in some part enforced to digress;

Which, at more leisure, I will so excuse
As you shall well be satisfied withal.
But where is Kate? I stay too long from
her: The morning nears, 'tis time we
were at church.　　　　　　[ent robes:

TRA. See not your bride in these unrever-
Go to my chamber; put on clothes of mine.

PET. Not I, believe me: thus I'll visit her.

BAP. But thus, I trust, you will not marry
her.

PET. Good sooth, even thus; therefore
have done with words:
To me she's married, not unto my clothes:
Could I repair what she will wear in me,
As I can change these poor accoutrements,
'Twere well for Kate, and better for myself.
But what a fool am I to chat with you,
When I should bid good-morrow to my
bride,
And seal the title with a lovely kiss!

　　　　[*Exeunt* PETRUCHIO *and* GRUMIO.

TRA. He hath some meaning in his mad
attire.
We will persuade him, be it possible,
To put on better ere he go to church.

BAP. I'll after him, and see the event of
this.　　　[*Exeunt* BAP., GRE., *and* BION.

TRA. But, Sir, to love concerneth us to
add
Her father's liking: which to bring to pass,
As I before imparted to your worship,
I am to get a man,—whate'er he be,
It skills not much, we'll fit him to our
And he shall be Vincentio of Pisa; [turn,
And make assurance, here in Padua,
Of greater sums than I have promised.
So shall you quietly enjoy your hope,
And marry sweet Bianca with consent.

LUC. Were it not that my fellow school-
master
Doth watch Bianca's steps so narrowly,
'Twere good, methinks, to steal our mar-
riage;　　　　　　　　[say no,
Which once perform'd, let all the world
I'll keep mine own, despite of all the world.

TRA. That by degrees we mean to look
into,
And watch our vantage in this business:
We'll over-reach the grey-beard, Gremio,
The narrow-prying father, Minola,
The quaint musician, amorous Licio;
All for my master's sake, Lucentio.

Re-enter GREMIO.

Signior Gremio, came you from the church?

GRE. As willingly as e'er I came from
school.

TRA. And is the bride, and bridegroom,
coming home?

GRE. A bridegroom say you? 'tis a groom
indeed,　　　　　　　　[find.
A grumbling groom, and that the girl shall

TRA. Curster than she? why, 'tis impossible.

GRE. Why, he's a devil, a devil, a very fiend.

TRA. Why, she's a devil, a devil, the devil's dam.

GRE. Tut, she's a lamb, a dove, a fool to him!

I'll tell you, Sir Lucentio: when the priest
Should ask if Katharine should be his wife,
"Ay, by gogs-wouns!" quoth he; and swore so loud,
That, all amaz'd, the priest let fall the book;
And, as he stoop'd again to take it up,
The mad-brain'd bridegroom took him such
   a cuff,   [and priest:
That down fell priest and book, and book
"Now take them up," quoth he, "if any
   list."   [again?

TRA. What said the wench when he arose?

GRE. Trembled and shook; for why, he
   stamp'd and swore,
As if the vicar meant to cozen him.
But after many ceremonies done,
He calls for wine: "A health!" quoth he;
   as if   [mates
He had been aboard, carousing to his
After a storm: quaff'd off the muscadel,
And threw the sops all in the sexton's face;
Having no other reason   [gerly,
But that his beard grew thin and hun-
And seem'd to ask him sops as he was
   drinking.   [neck,
This done, he took the bride about the
And kiss'd her lips with such a clamorous
   smack;   [echo:
That, at the parting, all the church did
And I, seeing this, came thence for very
   shame;
And after me, I know, the rout is coming.
Such a mad marriage never was before:—
Hark, hark! I hear the minstrels play.
       [*Music.*

Re-enter PETRUCHIO, KATHARINA, BIANCA,
BAPTISTA, HORTENSIO, GRUMIO, *and train.*

PET. Gentlemen and friends, I thank you
   for your pains:
I know you think to dine with me to-day,
And have prepar'd great store of wedding
   cheer;
But so it is, my haste doth call me hence,
And therefore here I mean to take my
   leave.

BAP. Is't possible you will away to-night?

PET. I must away to-day, before night
   come:
Make it no wonder; if you knew my business,
You would entreat me rather go than
   stay.—
And, honest company, I thank you all,

That have beheld me give away myself
To this most patient, sweet, and virtuous
   wife:
Dine with my father, drink a health to me;
For I must hence; and farewell to you all.

TRA. Let us entreat you stay till after
   dinner.

PET. It may not be.

GRE.   Let me entreat you.

PET. It cannot be.

KATH.   Let me entreat you.

PET. I am content.

KATH.   Are you content to stay?

PET. I am content you shall entreat me
   stay;
But yet not stay, entreat me how you can.

KATH. Now, if you love me, stay.

PET.   Grumio, my horse!

GRU. Ay, Sir, they be ready: the oats
have eaten the horses.

KATH. Nay, then,
Do what thou canst, I will not go to-day;
No, nor to-morrow; not till I please my-
   self.
The door is open, Sir; there lies your way;
You may be jogging whiles your boots are
   green;
For me, I'll not be gone till I please my-
   self:
'Tis like you'll prove a jolly surly groom,
That take it on you at the first so roundly.

PET. O Kate, content thee; pr'ythee, be
   not angry.

KATH. I will be angry: what hast thou
   to do?—
Father, be quiet: he shall stay my leisure.

GRE. Ay, marry, Sir, now it begins to
   work.

KATH. Gentlemen, forward to the bridal
   dinner:
I see, a woman may be made a fool,
If she had not a spirit to resist.

PET. They shall go forward, Kate, at thy
   command.—
Obey the bride, you that attend on her;
Go to the feast, revel and domineer,
Carouse full measure to her maidenhead,
Be mad and merry,—or go hang your-
   selves:
But for my bonny Kate, she must with me.
Nay, look not big, nor stamp, nor stare,
   nor fret;
I will be master of what is mine own:
She is my goods, my chattels; she is my
   house,
My household-stuff, my field, my barn,
My horse, my ox, my ass, my any thing;
And here she stands, touch her whoever
   dare;
I'll bring mine action on the proudest he
That stops my way in Padua.—Grumio,

Draw forth thy weapon, we're beset with
thieves;
Rescue thy mistress, if thou be a man.—
Fear not, sweet wench, they shall not touch
thee, Kate:
I'll buckler thee against a million.
[*Exeunt* PETRUCHIO, KATHARINA,
and GRUMIO.

BAP. Nay, let them go, a couple of quiet
ones.

GRE. Went they not quickly, I should die
with laughing.

TRA. Of all mad matches never was the
like!

LUC. Mistress, what's your opinion of
your sister?

BIAN. That, being mad herself, she's
madly mated.

GRE. I warrant him, Petruchio is Kated.

BAP. Neighbours and friends, though
bride and bridegroom wants
For to supply the places at the table,
You know there wants no junkets at the
feast.—
Lucentio, you shall supply the bridegroom's
place;
And let Bianca take her sister's room.

TRA. Shall sweet Bianca practise how to
bride it?

BAP. She shall, Lucentio.—Come, gentlemen, let's go.   [*Exeunt.*

ACT IV.

SCENE I.—*A Hall in* PETRUCHIO'S
Country House.

Enter GRUMIO.

GRU. Fie, fie, on all tired jades, on all
mad masters, and all foul ways! Was ever
man so beaten? was ever man so rayed?
was ever man so weary? I am sent before
to make a fire, and they are coming after
to warm them. Now, were not I a little
pot, and soon hot, my very lips might freeze
to my teeth, my tongue to the roof of my
mouth, my heart in my belly, ere I should
come by a fire to thaw me; but I, with
blowing the fire, shall warm myself; for,
considering the weather, a taller man than
I will take cold. Hola, ho! Curtis!

Enter CURTIS.

CURT. Who is that calls so coldly?

GRU. A piece of ice: if thou doubt it,
thou may'st slide from my shoulder to my
heel, with no greater a run but my head
and my neck. A fire, good Curtis.

CURT. Is my master and his wife coming,
Grumio?

GRU. O, ay, Curtis, ay: and therefore fire,
fire; cast on no water.

CURT. Is she so hot a shrew as she's reported?

GRU. She was, good Curtis, before this
frost: but, thou knowest, winter tames man,
woman, and beast; for it hath tamed my
old master, and my new mistress, and myself, fellow Curtis.

CURT. Away, you three-inch fool! I am
no beast.

GRU. Am I but three inches? why, thy
horn is a foot: and so long am I at the
least. But wilt thou make a fire, or shall
I complain on thee to our mistress, whose
hand (she being now at hand) thou shalt
soon feel, to thy cold comfort, for being
slow in thy hot office?

CURT. I pr'ythee, good Grumio, tell me,
how goes the world?

GRU. A cold world, Curtis, in every office
but thine; and therefore, fire: do thy duty,
and have thy duty, for my master and
mistress are almost frozen to death.

CURT. There's fire ready; and therefore,
good Grumio, the news?

GRU. Why, "Jack, boy! ho, boy!" and
as much news as thou wilt.

CURT. Come, you are so full of coney-
catching!—

GRU. Why therefore, fire; for I have
caught extreme cold. Where's the cook? is
supper ready, the house trimmed, rushes
strewed, cobwebs swept; the serving-men
in their new fustian, their white stockings,
and every officer his wedding-garment on?
Be the Jacks fair within, the Jills fair
without, the carpets laid, and every thing
in order?

CURT. All ready; and therefore, I pray
thee, news?

GRU. First, know, my horse is tired; my
master and mistress fallen out.

CURT. How?

GRU. Out of their saddles into the dirt;
and thereby hangs a tale.

CURT. Let's ha't, good Grumio.

GRU. Lend thine ear.

CURT. Here.

GRU. [*Striking him.*] There.

CURT. This is to feel a tale, not to hear
a tale.

GRU. And therefore 'tis called a sensible
tale: and this cuff was but to knock at
your ear, and beseech listening. Now I
begin: *Imprimis*, we came down a foul
hill, my master riding behind my mistress:—

CURT. Both of one horse?

GRU. What's that to thee?

CURT. Why, a horse.

GRU. Tell thou the tale:—but hadst thou
not crossed me, thou should'st have heard

how her horse fell, and she under her
horse; thou should'st have heard, in how
miry a place; how she was bemoiled; how
he left her with the horse upon her; how
he beat me because her horse stumbled;
how she waded through the dirt to pluck
him off me; how he swore; how she prayed
—that never prayed before; how I cried;
how the horses ran away; how her bridle
was burst; how I lost my crupper;—with
many things of worthy memory, which now
shall die in oblivion, and thou return un-
experienced to thy grave.

CURT. By this reckoning, he is more
shrew than she.

GRU. Ay; and that, thou and the proudest of you all shall find, when he comes
home. But what talk I of this? Call forth
Nathaniel, Joseph, Nicholas, Philip,. Walter,
Sugarsop, and the rest: let their heads be
sleekly combed, their blue coats brushed,
and their garters of an indifferent knit:
let them court'sy with their left legs; and
not presume to touch a hair of my master's horse-tail, till they kiss their hands.
Are they all ready?

CURT. They are.

GRU. Call them forth.

CURT. Do you hear? ho! you must meet
my master, to countenance my mistress.

GRU. Why, she hath a face of her own.

CURT. Who knows not that?

GRU. Thou, it seems, that callest for company to countenance her.

CURT. I call them forth to credit her.

GRU. Why, she comes to borrow nothing
of them.

Enter several Servants.

NATH. Welcome home, Grumio!

PHIL. How now, Grumio!

JOS. What, Grumio!

NICH. Fellow Grumio!

NATH. How now, old lad?

GRU. Welcome, you;—how now, you;—
what, you;—fellow, you;—and thus much
for greeting. Now, my spruce companions,
is all ready, and all things neat?

NATH. All things is ready. How near is
our master?

GRU. E'en at hand, alighted by this; and
therefore be not,—Cock's passion, silence!
—I hear my master.

Enter PETRUCHIO *and* KATHARINA.

PET. Where be these knaves? What, no
man at door,
To hold my stirrup, nor to take my horse!
Where is Nathaniel, Gregory, Philip?—

ALL SERV. Here, here, Sir; here, Sir.

PET. Here, Sir! here, Sir! here, Sir!
here, Sir!
You logger-headed and unpolish'd grooms!

What, no attendance? no regard? no
duty?—
Where is the foolish knave I sent before?

GRU. Here, Sir; as foolish as I was before.

PET. You peasant swain! you whoreson
malt-horse drudge!
Did I not bid thee meet me in the park,
And bring along these rascal knaves with
thee?

GRU. Nathaniel's coat, Sir, was not fully
made,
And Gabriel's pumps were all unpink'd i'
the heel;
There was no link to colour Peter's hat,
And Walter's dagger was not come from
sheathing:
There were none fine but Adam, Ralph,
and Gregory;
The rest were ragged, old, and beggarly;
Yet, as they are, here are they come to
meet you.

PET. Go, rascals, go, and fetch my supper in.—   [*Exeunt some of the* Servants.
[*Sings.*] "Where is the life that late I
led"—
Where are those—? Sit down, Kate, and
welcome.—
Soud, soud, soud, soud!

Re-enter Servants, *with supper.*

Why, when, I say?—Nay, good sweet Kate,
be merry.—
Off with my boots, you rogues! you vil-
lains, when?
[*Sings.*] "It was the friar of orders grey,
As he forth walked on his way:"—
Out, you rogue! you pluck my foot awry:
[*Strikes him.*
Take that, and mend the plucking off the
other.—
Be merry, Kate.—Some water, here; what,
ho!—
Where's my spaniel Troilus?—Sirrah, get
you hence,
And bid my cousin Ferdinand come
hither:—   [*Exit* Servant.
One, Kate, that you must kiss, and be
acquainted with.—
Where are my slippers?—Shall I have some
water?

Enter a Servant, *with a bason and ewer.*

Come, Kate, and wash, and welcome heartily.—
[*Servant lets the ewer fall.* PETRUCHIO
strikes him.
You whorseson villain! will you let it fall?

KATH. Patience, I pray you; 'twas a fault
unwilling.

PET. A whoreson, beetleheaded, flap-ear'd
knave!—

Come, Kate, sit down; I know you have a
  stomach.
Will you give thanks, sweet Kate; or else
  shall I?—
What's this? mutton?
1 SERV.   Ay.
PET.   Who brought it?
1 SERV.   I.
PET. 'Tis burnt; and so is all the meat.
What dogs are these!—Where is the rascal
  cook?
How durst you, villains, bring it from the
  dresser,
And serve it thus to me that love it not?
          [Throws the meat, &c. at them.
There, take it to you, trenchers, cups, and
  all.
You heedless joltheads and unmanner'd
  slaves!
What, do you grumble? I'll be with you
  straight.
KATH. I pray you, husband, be not so
  disquiet:
The meat was well, if you were so con-
  tented.
PET. I tell thee, Kate, 'twas burnt and
  dried away;
And I expressly am forbid to touch it,
For it engenders choler, planteth anger;
And better 'twere, that both of us did
  fast,—
Since, of ourselves, ourselves are choleric,—
Than feed it with such over-roasted flesh.
Be patient; to-morrow't shall be mended,
And, for this night, we'll fast for com-
  pany:—
Come, I will bring thee to thy bridal
  chamber.
      [Exeunt PETRUCHIO, KATHARINA,
                        and CURTIS.
NATH. Peter, didst ever see the like?
PETER. He kills her in her own humour.
            Re-enter CURTIS
GRU. Where is he?
CURT. In her chamber,
Making a sermon of continency to her;
And rails, and swears, and rates, that she,
  poor soul,
Knows not which way to stand, to look,
  to speak,
And sits as one new-risen from a dream.
Away, away! for he is coming hither.
                        [Exeunt.
        Re-enter PETRUCHIO.
PET. Thus have I politicly begun my
  reign,
And 'tis my hope to end successfully.
My falcon now is sharp, and passing
  empty;
And, till she stoop, she must not be full-
  gorg'd,

For then she never looks upon her lure.
Another way I have to man my haggard,
To make her come, and know her keeper's
  call;
That is, to watch her, as we watch these
  kites
That bate, and beat, and will not be
  obedient.
She eat no meat to-day, nor none shall
  eat:
Last night she slept not, nor to-night she
  shall not;
As with the meat, some undeserved fault
I'll find about the making of the bed;
And here I'll fling the pillow, there the
  bolster,
This way the coverlet, another way the
  sheets:—
Ay, and amid this hurly, I intend
That all is done in reverend care of her;
And, in conclusion, she shall watch all
  night:
And, if she chance to nod, I'll rail and
  brawl,
And with the clamour keep her still awake.
This is a way to kill a wife with kindness;
And thus I'll curb her mad and headstrong
  humour.—
He that knows better how to tame a shrew,
Now let him speak: 'tis charity to show.
                        [Exit.

          ———

SCENE II.—PADUA. Before BAPTISTA'S
                  House.

    Enter TRANIO and HORTENSIO.
TRA. Is't possible, friend Licio, that mis-
  tress Bianca
Doth fancy any other but Lucentio?
I tell you, Sir, she bears me fair in hand.
HOR. Sir, to satisfy you in what I have
  said,
Stand by, and mark the manner of his
  teaching.   [They stand aside.
    Enter BIANCA and LUCENTIO.
LUC. Now, mistress, profit you in what
  you read?
BIAN. What, master, read you? first re-
  solve me that.
LUC. I read that I profess, the Art to
  Love.
BIAN. And may you prove, Sir, master
  of your art!
LUC. While you, sweet dear, prove mis-
  tress of my heart.   [They retire.
HOR. [Coming forward.] Quick proceed-
  ers, marry! Now, tell me, I pray,
You that durst swear that your mistress
  Bianca
Lov'd none in the world so well as Lu-
  centio.

TRA. O despiteful love! unconstant womankind!—
I tell thee, Licio, this is wonderful.
HOR. Mistake no more: I am not Licio,
Nor a musician, as I seem to be;
But one that scorns to live in this disguise,
For such a one as leaves a gentleman,
And makes a god of such a cullion:
Know, Sir, that I am call'd Hortensio.
TRA. Signior Hortensio, I have often heard
Of your entire affection to Bianca;
And since mine eyes are witness of her lightness,
I will with you,—if you be so contented,—
Forswear Bianca and her love for ever.
HOR. See, how they kiss and court!—
Signior Lucentio,
Here is my hand, and here I firmly vow
Never to woo her more; but do forswear her,
As one unworthy all the former favours
That I have fondly flatter'd her withal.
TRA. And here I take the like unfeigned oath,
Never to marry with her, though she would entreat:
Fie on her! see, how beastly she doth court him.
HOR. Would all the world, but he, had quite forsworn!
For me, that I may surely keep mine oath,
I will be married to a wealthy widow,
Ere three days pass, which hath as long lov'd me,
As I have lov'd this proud disdainful haggard.
And so farewell, signior Lucentio.—
Kindness in women, not their beauteous looks,
Shall win my love:—and so I take my leave,
In resolution as I swore before.
　　　　[*Exit* HORTENSIO. LUCENTIO *and*
　　　　　　BIANCA *advance.*
TRA. Mistress Bianca, bless you with such grace
As 'longeth to a lover's blessed case!
Nay, I have ta'en you napping, gentle love;
And have forsworn you, with Hortensio.
BIAN. Tranio, you jest: but have you both forsworn me?
TRA. Mistress, we have.
LUC. 　　　　Then we are rid of Licio.
TRA. I' faith, he'll have a lusty widow now,
That shall be woo'd and wedded in a day.
BIAN. God give him joy!
TRA. Ay, and he'll tame her.
BIAN. 　　　　He says so, Tranio.

TRA. 'Faith, he is gone unto the taming-school.
BIAN. The taming-school! what, is there such a place?
TRA. Ay, mistress, and Petruchio is the master;
That teacheth tricks eleven and twenty long,
To tame a shrew, and charm her chattering tongue.
　　　　　Enter BIONDELLO.
BION. O master, master, I have watch'd so long
That I'm dog-weary! but at last I spied
An ancient angel coming down the hill,
Will serve the turn.
TRA. 　　　　What is he, Biondello?
BION. Master, a mercatantè, or a pedant,
I know not what; but formal in apparel,
In gait and countenance surely like a father.
LUC. And what of him, Tranio?
TRA. If he be credulous, and trust my tale,
I'll make him glad to seem Vincentio;
And give assurance to Baptista Minola,
As if he were the right Vincentio.
Take in your love, and then let me alone.
　　　　[*Exeunt* LUCENTIO *and* BIANCA.
　　　　　Enter a Pedant.
PED. God save you, Sir!
TRA. 　　　　And you, Sir: you are welcome.
Travel you far on, or are you at the farthest?
PED. Sir, at the farthest for a week or two:
But then up farther, and as far as Rome,
And so to Tripoli, if God lend me life.
TRA. What countryman, I pray?
PED. 　　　　　　　　　Of Mantua.
TRA. Of Mantua, Sir?—marry, God forbid!
And come to Padua, careless of your life?
PED. My life, Sir! how, I pray? for that goes hard.
TRA. 'Tis death for any one in Mantua
To come to Padua. Know you not the cause?
Your ships are stay'd at Venice; and the duke,
For private quarrel 'twixt your duke and him,
Hath publish'd and proclaim'd it openly:
'Tis marvel; but that you are but newly come,
You might have heard it else proclaim'd about.
PED. Alas, Sir, it is worse for me than so!
For I have bills for money by exchange

From Florence, and must here deliver them.

TRA. Well, Sir, to do you courtesy,
This will I do, and this I will advise you:—
First, tell me, have you ever been at Pisa?

PED. Ay, Sir, in Pisa have I often been;
Pisa, renowned for grave citizens.

TRA. Among them, know you one Vincentio?

PED. I know him not, but I have heard of him;
A merchant of incomparable wealth.

TRA. He is my father, Sir; and, sooth to say,
In countenance somewhat doth resemble you.

BION. [*Aside.*] As much as an apple doth an oyster, and all one.

TRA. To save your life in this extremity,
This favour will I do you for his sake;
And think it not the worst of all your fortunes
That you are like to Sir Vincentio.
His name and credit shall you undertake,
And in my house you shall be friendly lodg'd:—
Look that you take upon you as you should;
You understand me, Sir:—so shall you stay
Till you have done your business in the city:
If this be courtesy, Sir, accept of it.

PED. O Sir, I do; and will repute you ever
The patron of my life and liberty.

TRA. Then go with me, to make the matter good.
This, by the way, I let you understand;
My father is here look'd for every day,
To pass assurance of a dower in marriage
'Twixt me and one Baptista's daughter here:
In all these circumstances I'll instruct you:
Go with me, to clothe you as becomes you.
[*Exeunt.*

SCENE III.—*A Room in* PETRUCHIO's *House.*

Enter KATHARINA *and* GRUMIO.

GRU. No, no, forsooth; I dare not, for my life.

KATH. The more my wrong, the more his spite appears:
What, did he marry me to famish me?
Beggars, that come unto my father's door,
Upon entreaty have a present alms;
If not, elsewhere they meet with charity:
But I,—who never knew how to entreat,
Nor never needed that I should entreat,—

Am starv'd for meat, giddy for lack of sleep;
With oaths kept waking, and with brawling fed:
And that which spites me more than all these wants,
He does it under name of perfect love;
As who should say, if I should sleep, or eat,
'Twere deadly sickness, or else present death.—
I pr'ythee go, and get me some repast;
I care not what, so it be wholesome food.

GRU. What say you to a neat's foot?

KATH. 'Tis passing good: I pr'ythee let me have it.

GRU. I fear it is too choleric a meat.
How say you to a fat tripe, finely broil'd?

KATH. I like it well: good Grumio, fetch it me.

GRU. I cannot tell; I fear 'tis choleric.
What say you to a piece of beef, and mustard?

KATH. A dish that I do love to feed upon.

GRU. Ay, but the mustard is too hot a little.

KATH. Why, then the beef, and let the mustard rest.

GRU. Nay, then I will not: you shall have the mustard,
Or else you get no beef of Grumio.

KATH. Then both, or one, or any thing thou wilt.

GRU. Why then, the mustard without the beef.

KATH. Go, get thee gone, thou false deluding slave, [*Beats him.*
That feed'st me with the very name of meat:
Sorrow on thee, and all the pack of you,
That triumph thus upon my misery!
Go, get thee gone, I say.

Enter PETRUCHIO *with a dish of meat; and* HORTENSIO.

PET. How fares my Kate? What, sweeting, all amort?

HOR. Mistress, what cheer?

KATH. 'Faith, as cold as can be.

PET. Pluck up thy spirits; look cheerfully upon me.
Here, love; thou seest how diligent I am,
To dress thy meat myself, and bring it thee: [*Sets the dish on a table.*
I am sure, sweet Kate, this kindness merits thanks.
What, not a word? Nay then, thou lov'st it not;
And all my pains is sorted to no proof.—
Here, take away this dish.

KATH. I pray you, let it stand.

PET. The poorest service is repaid with
thanks;
And so shall mine, before you touch the
meat.
KATH. I thank you, Sir.
HOR. Signior Petruchio, fie! you are to
blame.—
Come, mistress Kate, I'll bear you com-
pany.
PET. [Aside to him.] Eat it up all, Hor-
tensio, if thou lov'st me.—
[To her.] Much good do it unto thy gentle
heart!
Kate, eat apace:—and now, my honey love.
Will we return unto thy father's house,
And revel it as bravely as the best,
With silken coats, and caps, and golden
rings,
With ruffs, and cuffs, and farthingales, and
things;
With scarfs, and fans, and double change
of bravery,
With amber bracelets, beads, and all this
knavery.
What, hast thou din'd? The tailor stays
thy leisure,
To deck thy body with his ruffling treasure.
Enter Tailor.
Come, tailor, let us see these ornaments;
Lay forth the gown.—[Enter Haberdasher.]
What news with you, Sir?
HAB. Here is the cap your worship did
bespeak.
PET. Why, this was moulded on a por-
ringer;
A velvet dish:—fie, fie! 'tis lewd and
filthy:
Why, 'tis a cockle or a walnut shell,
A knack, a toy, a trick, a baby's cap:
Away with it! come, let me have a bigger.
KATH. I'll have no bigger: this doth fit
the time,
And gentlewomen wear such caps as these.
PET. When you are gentle, you shall have
one too;
And not till then.
HOR. [Aside.] That will not be in haste.
KATH. Why, Sir, I trust I may have leave
to speak;
And speak I will; I am no child, no babe:
Your betters have endur'd me say my
mind;
And if you cannot, best you stop your ears.
My tongue will tell the anger of my heart;
Or else my heart, concealing it, will break:
And rather than it shall, I will be free
Even to the uttermost, as I please, in words.
PET. Why, thou say'st true; it is a paltry
cap,
A custard-coffin, a bauble, a silken pie:
I love thee well, in that thou lik'st it not.

KATH. Love me or love me not, I like
the cap;
And it I will have, or I will have none.
PET. Thy gown? why, ay:—come, tailor,
let us see't.
O mercy, God! what masking stuff is here?
What's this? a sleeve? 'tis like a demi-
cannon:
What! up and down, carv'd like an apple-
tart?
Here's snip, and nip, and cut, and slish,
and slash,
Like to a censer in a barber's shop:—
Why, what, o' devil's name, tailor, call'st
thou this?
HOR. [Aside.] I see, she's like to have
neither cap nor gown.
TAI. You bid me make it orderly and
well,
According to the fashion, and the time.
PET. Marry, and did; but if you be re-
member'd,
I did not bid you mar it to the time,
Go, hop me over every kennel home,
For you shall hop without my custom, Sir:
I'll none of it: hence! make your best of it.
KATH. I never saw a better-fashion'd
gown,
More quaint, more pleasing, nor more com-
mendable:
Belike you mean to make a puppet of me.
PET. Why, true; he means to make a
puppet of thee.
TAI. She says, your worship means to
make a puppet of her.
PET. O monstrous arrogance! Thou liest,
Thou thimble,   [thou thread,
Thou yard, three-quarters, half-yard, quar-
ter, nail!
Thou flea, thou nit, thou winter cricket
thou!—
Brav'd in mine own house with a skein
of thread?
Away! thou rag, thou quantity, thou rem-
nant;
Or I shall so be-mete thee with thy yard,
As thou shalt think on prating whilst thou
liv'st!
I tell thee, I, that thou hast marr'd her
gown.
TAI. Your worship is deceiv'd; the gown
is made
Just as my master had direction:
Grumio gave order how it should be done.
GRU. I gave him no order; I gave him
the stuff.
TAI. But how did you desire it should be
made?
GRU. Marry, Sir, with needle and thread.
TAI. But did you not request to have it
cut?

GRU. Thou hast faced many things.

TAI. I have.

GRU. Face not me: thou hast braved many men; brave not me: I will neither be faced nor braved. I say unto thee,— I bid thy master cut out the gown; but I did not bid him cut it to pieces: *ergo*, thou liest.

TAI. Why, here is the note of the fashion to testify.

PET. Read it.

GRU. The note lies in's throat, if he say I said so.

TAI. [*Reads.*] *"Imprimis*, a loose-bodied gown:"—

GRU. Master, if ever I said loose-bodied gown, sew me in the skirts of it, and beat me to death with a bottom of brown thread: I said, a gown.

PET. Proceed.

TAI. [*Reads.*] "With a small compassed cape:"—

GRU. I confess the cape.

TAI. [*Reads.*] "With a trunk sleeve:"—

GRU. I confess two sleeves.

TAI. [*Reads.*] "The sleeves curiously cut."

PET. Ay, there's the villainy.

GRU. Error i' the bill, Sir; error i' the bill. I commanded the sleeves should be cut out, and sewed up again; and that I'll prove upon thee, though thy little finger be armed in a thimble.

TAI. This is true that I say: an I had thee in place where, thou should'st know it.

GRU. I am for thee straight take thou the bill, give me thy mete-yard, and spare not me.

HOR. God-a-mercy, Grumio! then he shall have no odds.

PET. Well, Sir, in brief, the gown is not for me.

GRU. You are i' the right, Sir: 'tis for my mistress.

PET. Go, take it up unto thy master's use.

GRU. Villain, not for thy life: take up my mistress' gown for thy master's use!

PET. Why, Sir, what's your conceit in that?

GRU. O, Sir, the conceit is deeper than you think for: Take up my mistress' gown to his master's use! [*use!*]

PET. [*Aside.*] Hortensio, say thou wilt see the tailor paid.—

[*To* Tailor.] Go take it hence; be gone, and say no more.

HOR. [*Aside to* Tailor.] Tailor, I'll pay thee for thy gown to-morrow: Take no unkindness of his hasty words:

Away, I say; commend me to thy master. [*Exeunt* Tailor *and* Haberdasher.

PET. Well, come, my Kate; we will unto your father's,
Even in these honest mean habiliments:
Our purses shall be proud, our garments poor;
For 'tis the mind that makes the body rich:
And as the sun breaks through the darkest clouds,
So honour peereth in the meanest habit.
What, is the jay more precious than the lark,
Because his feathers are more beautiful?
Or is the adder better than the eel,
Because his painted skin contents the eye?
O, no, good Kate; neither art thou the worse
For this poor furniture and mean array.
If thou account'st it shame, lay it on me;
And therefore frolic: we will hence forthwith,
To feast and sport us at thy father's house.—
Go, call my men, and let us straight to him;
And bring our horses unto Long-lane end;
There will we mount, and thither walk on foot:
Let's see; I think 'tis now some seven o'clock,
And well we may come there by dinner-time.

KATH. I dare assure you, Sir, 'tis almost two;
And 'twill be supper-time ere you come there.

PET. It shall be seven, ere I go to horse:
Look, what I speak, or do, or think to do,
You are still crossing it.—Sirs, let't alone:
I will not go to-day; and ere I do,
It shall be what o'clock I say it is.

HOR. Why, so! this gallant will command the sun. [*Exeunt.*

SCENE IV.—PADUA. *Before* BAPTISTA'S *House.*

Enter TRANIO, *and the* Pedant *dressed like* VINCENTIO.

TRA. Sir, this is the house: please it you, that I call?

PED. Ay, what else? and, but I be deceived,
Signior Baptista may remember me,
Near twenty years ago, in Genoa,
Where we were lodgers at the Pegasus.

TRA. 'Tis well; and hold your own, in any case,
With such austerity as 'longeth to a father.

PED. I warrant you. But, Sir, here comes your boy;
'Twere good, he were school'd.

Enter BIONDELLO.

TRA. Fear you not him.—Sirrah Biondello,
Now do your duty throughly, I advise you:
Imagine 'twere the right Vincentio.

BION. Tut! fear not me.

TRA. But hast thou done thy errand to Baptista?

BION. I told him that your father was at Venice;
And that you look'd for him this day in Padua.

TRA. Thou'rt a tall fellow: [*Gives money.*] hold thee that to drink.
Here comes Baptista:—Set your countenance, Sir.—

Enter BAPTISTA *and* LUCENTIO.

Signior Baptista, you are happily met.—
[*To the* Pedant.] Sir, this is the gentleman I told you of:
I pray you, stand good father to me now,
Give me Bianca for my patrimony.

PED. Soft, son!—
Sir, by your leave: having come to Padua
To gather in some debts, my son Lucentio
Made me acquainted with a weighty cause
Of love between your daughter and himself:
And,—for the good report I hear of you,
And for the love he beareth to your daughter,
And she to him,—to stay him not too long,
I am content, in a good father's care,
To have him match'd; and,—if you please to like
No worse than I,—upon some agreement,
Me shall you find ready and willing
With one consent to have her so bestow'd;
For curious I cannot be with you,
Signior Baptista, of whom I hear so well.

BAP. Sir, pardon me in what I have to say:
Your plainness and your shortness please me well.
Right true it is, your son Lucentio here
Doth love my daughter, and she loveth him,
Or both dissemble deeply their affections:
And therefore, if you say no more than this,
That like a father you will deal with him,
And pass my daughter a sufficient dower,
The match is made, and all is done:
Your son shall have my daughter with consent.

TRA. I thank you, Sir. Where, then, do you know best,
We be affied, and such assurance ta'en,

As shall with either part's agreement stand?

BAP. Not in my house, Lucentio; for, you know,
Pitchers have ears, and I have many servants:
Besides, old Gremio is hearkening still;
And, happily, we might be interrupted.

TRA. Then at my lodging, an it like you:
There doth my father lie; and there, this night,
We'll pass the business privately and well.
Send for your daughter by your servant here;
My boy shall fetch the scrivener presently.
The worst is this,—that, at so slender warning,
You're like to have a thin and slender pittance.

BAP. It likes me well.—Cambio, hie you home,
And bid Bianca make her ready straight;
And, if you will, tell what hath happened,—
Lucentio's father is arrived in Padua,
And how she's like to be Lucentio's wife.

LUC. I pray the gods she may with all my heart!

TRA. Dally not with the gods, but get thee gone.—
Signior Baptista, shall I lead the way?
Welcome! one mess is like to be your cheer:
Come, Sir; we will better it in Pisa.

BAP. I follow you.

[*Exeunt* TRANIO, Pedant, *and* BAPTISTA.

BION. Cambio!—

LUC. What say'st thou, Biondello?

BION. You saw my master wink and laugh upon you?

LUC. Biondello, what of that?

BION. 'Faith, nothing; but he has left me here behind, to expound the meaning or moral of his signs and tokens.

LUC. I pray thee, moralize them.

BION. Then thus. Baptista is safe, talking with the deceiving father of a deceitful son.

LUC. And what of him?

BION. His daughter is to be brought by you to the supper.

LUC. And then?—

BION. The old priest at St. Luke's church is at your command at all hours.

LUC. And what of all this?

BION. I cannot tell; expect they are busied about a counterfeit assurance: take you assurance of her, *cum privilegio ad imprimendum solum:* to the church;—take the priest, clerk, and some sufficient honest witnesses.

If this be not that you look for, I have no
  more to say,
But bid Bianca farewell for ever and a
  day.   [*Going.*
LUC. Hearest thou, Biondello?
BION. I cannot tarry: I knew a wench
married in an afternoon as she went to the
garden for parsley to stuff a rabbit; and
so may you, Sir: and so, adieu, Sir. My
master hath appointed me to go to St.
Luke's, to bid the priest be ready to come
against you come with your appendix.
                                   [*Exit.*
LUC. I may, and will, if she be so contented:
She will be pleas'd; then wherefore should
  I doubt?
Hap what hap may, I'll roundly go about
  her:
It shall go hard, if Cambio go without her.
                                   [*Exit.*

SCENE V.—*A public Road.*
Enter PETRUCHIO, KATHARINA, *and*
      HORTENSIO.

PET. Come on, o' God's name; once more
  toward our father's.
Good lord, how bright and goodly shines
  the moon!
KATH. The moon! the sun: it is not
  moonlight now.
PET. I say it is the moon that shines so
  bright.
KATH. I know it is the sun that shines
  so bright.
PET. Now, by my mother's son, and that's
  myself,
It shall be moon, or star, or what I list,
Or ere I journey to your father's house.—
Go on, and fetch our horses back again.—
Evermore cross'd, and cross'd; nothing but
  cross'd!
HOR. Say as he says, or we shall never
  go.
KATH. Forward, I pray, since we have
  come so far.
And be it moon, or sun, or what you
  please:
An if you please to call it a rush candle,
Henceforth, I vow, it shall be so for me.
PET. I say it is the moon.
KATH.   I know it is the moon.
PET. Nay, then you lie: it is the blessed
  sun.
KATH. Then God be bless'd, it is the
  blessed sun:—
But sun it is not, when you say it is not;
And the moon changes, even as your mind.
What you will have it nam'd, even that it
  is;

And so, it shall be so for Katharine.
HOR. Petruchio, go thy ways; the field is
  won.
PET. Well, forward, forward! thus the
  bowl should run,
And not unluckily against the bias.—
But soft! company is coming here.
      Enter VINCENTIO, *in a travelling dress.*
[*To* VINCENTIO.] Good-morrow, gentle mis-
  tress: where away?—
Tell me, sweet Kate, and tell me truly too,
Hast thou beheld a fresher gentlewoman?
Such war of white and red within her
  cheeks!
What stars do spangle heaven with such
  beauty,
As those two eyes become that heavenly
  face?—
Fair lovely maid, once more good day to
  thee.—
Sweet Kate, embrace her for her beauty
  sake.
HOR. 'A will make the man mad, to make
  a woman of him.
KATH. Young budding virgin, fair and
  fresh and sweet,
Whither away; or where is thy abode?
Happy the parents of so fair a child;
Happier the man, whom favourable stars
Allot thee for his lovely bed-fellow!
PET. Why, how now, Kate! I hope thou
  are not mad:
This is a man, old, wrinkled, faded,
  wither'd;
And not a maiden, as thou say'st he is.
KATH. Pardon, old father, my mistaking
  eyes,
That have been so bedazzled with the sun,
That every thing I look on seemeth green:
Now I perceive thou art a reverend father;
Pardon, I pray thee, for my mad mistak-
  ing.
PET. Do, good old grandsire; and withal
  make known
Which way thou travell'st: if along with
  us,
We shall be joyful of thy company.
VIN. Fair Sir, and you my merry mis-
  tress,
That with your strange encounter much
  amaz'd me,
My name is call'd Vincentio; my dwelling,
  Pisa;
And bound I am to Padua; there to visit
A son of mine, which long I have not seen.
PET. What is his name?
VIN.   Lucentio, gentle Sir.
PET. Happily met; the happier for thy
  son.
And now by law, as well as reverend age,
I may entitle thee my loving father:

The sister to my wife, this gentlewoman,
Thy son by this hath married. Wonder not,
Nor be not griev'd: she is of good esteem,
Her dowry wealthy, and of worthy birth;
Beside, so qualified as may beseem
The spouse of any noble gentleman.
Let me embrace with old Vincentio:
And wander we to see thy honest son,
Who will of thy arrival be full joyous.
VIN. But is this true? or is it else your pleasure,
Like pleasant travellers, to break a jest
Upon the company you overtake?
HOR. I do assure thee, father, so it is.
PET. Come, go along, and see the truth hereof;
For our first merriment hath made thee jealous.

[*Exeunt* PETRUCHIO, KATHARINA,
and VINCENTIO.

HOR. Well, Petruchio, this has put me in heart.
Have to my widow! and if she be froward,
Then hast thou taught Hortensio to be untoward.   [*Exit.*

ACT V.

SCENE I.—PADUA. *Before* LUCENTIO'S
House.

Enter on one side BIONDELLO, LUCENTIO,
and BIANCA; GREMIO *walking on
the other side.*

BION. Softly and swiftly, Sir; for the priest is ready.
LUC. I fly, Biondello: but they may chance to need thee at home; therefore leave us.
BION. Nay, faith, I'll see the church o' your back; and then come back to my master as soon as I can.

[*Exeunt* LUCENTIO, BIANCA, *and*
BIONDELLO.

GRE. I marvel Cambio comes not all this while.

Enter PETRUCHIO, KATHARINA, VINCENTIO,
and Attendants.

PET. Sir, here's the door, this is Lucentio's house:
My father's bears more toward the market-place;
Thither must I, and here I leave you, Sir.
VIN. You shall not choose but drink before you go:
I think I shall command your welcome here,
And, by all likelihood, some cheer is toward.   [*Knocks.*

GRE. They're busy within; you were best knock louder.

Enter Pedant *above, at a window.*

PED. What's he, that knocks as he would beat down the gate?
VIN. Is signior Lucentio within, Sir?
PED. He's within, Sir; but not to be spoken withal.
VIN. What if a man bring him a hundred pound or two, to make merry withal?
PED. Keep your hundred pounds to yourself: he shall need none, so long as I live.
PET. Nay, I told you your son was well beloved in Padua.—Do you hear, Sir?—to leave frivolous circumstances,—I pray you, tell signior Lucentio, that his father is come from Pisa, and is here at the door to speak with him.
PED. Thou liest: his father is come from Pisa, and here looking out at the window.
VIN. Art thou his father?
PED. Ay, Sir; so his mother says, if I may believe her.
PET. [*To* VINCEN.] Why, how now, gentleman! why, this is flat knavery, to take upon you another man's name.
PED. Lay hands on the villain. I believe, 'a means to cozen somebody in this city under my countenance.

Re-enter BIONDELLO.

BION. I have seen them in the church together: God send 'em good shipping!—But who is here? mine old master, Vincentio! now we are undone, and brought to nothing.
VIN. [*Seeing* BION.] Come hither, crack-hemp.
BION. I hope I may choose, Sir.
VIN. Come hither, you rogue. What, have you forgot me?
BION. Forgot you! no, Sir: I could not forget you, for I never saw you before in all my life.
VIN. What, you notorious villain, didst thou never see thy master's father, Vincentio?
BION. What, my old, worshipful old master? yes, marry, Sir: see where he looks out of the window.
VIN. Is't so, indeed?   [*Beats* BIONDELLO.
BION. Help, help, help! here's a madman will murder me.   [*Exit.*
PED. Help, son! help, signior Baptista!
[*Exit from the window.*
PET. Pr'ythee, Kate, let's stand aside, and see the end of this controversy.
[*They retire.*

Re-enter Pedant *below;* BAPTISTA,
TRANIO, *and* Servants.

TRA. Sir, what are you, that offer to beat my servant?

VIN. What am I, Sir! nay, what are you, Sir?—O immortal gods! O fine villain! A silken doublet! a velvet hose! a scarlet cloak! and a copatain hat!—O, I am undone! I am undone! while I play the good husband at home, my son and my servant spend all at the university.

TRA. How now! what's the matter?

BAP. What, is the man lunatic?

TRA. Sir, you seem a sober ancient gentleman by your habit, but your words show you a madman. Why, Sir, what 'cerns it you if I wear pearl and gold? I thank my good father, I am able to maintain it.

VIN. Thy father! O villain! he is a sailmaker in Bergamo.

BAP. You mistake, Sir, you mistake, Sir. Pray, what do you think is his name?

VIN. His name! as if I knew not his name: I have brought him up ever since he was three years old, and his name is Tranio.

PED. Away, away, mad ass! his name is Lucentio; and he is mine only son, and heir to the lands of me, signior Vincentio.

VIN. Lucentio! O, he hath murdered his master!—Lay hold on him, I charge you, in the duke's name.—O my son, my son!—tell me, thou villain, where is my son Lucentio?

TRA. Call forth an officer.

Enter one with an Officer.

Carry this mad knave to the jail.—Father Baptista, I charge you see that he be forthcoming.

VIN. Carry me to the jail!

GRE. Stay, officer: he shall not go to prison.

BAP. Talk not, signior Gremio: I say he shall go to prison.

GRE. Take heed, signior Baptista, lest you be coney-catched in this business: I dare swear this is the right Vincentio.

PED. Swear, if thou darest.

GRE. Nay, I dare not swear it.

TRA. Then thou wert best say, that I am not Lucentio.

GRE. Yes, I know thee to be signior Lucentio.

BAP. Away with the dotard! to the jail with him!

VIN. Thus strangers may be haled and abused:—O monstrous villain!

Re-enter BIONDELLO, *with* LUCENTIO *and* BIANCA.

BION. O, we are spoiled! and yonder he is: deny him, forswear him, or else we are all undone.

LUC. [*Kneeling.*] Pardon, sweet father.

VIN. Lives my sweet son?

[BIONDELLA, TRANIO, *and* Pedant *run out.*

BIAN. [*Kneeling.*] Pardon, dear father.

BAP. How hast thou offended?—Where is Lucentio?

LUC. Here's Lucentio, Right son to the right Vincentio; That have by marriage made thy daughter mine, While counterfeit suppose blear'd thine eyne.

GRE. Here's packing, with a witness, to deceive us all!

VIN. Where is that damned villain Tranio, That fac'd and brav'd me in this matter so?

BAP. Why, tell me, is not this my Cambio?

BIAN. Cambio is chang'd into Lucentio.

LUC. Love wrought these miracles. Bianca's love Made me exchange my state with Tranio, While he did bear my countenance in the town; And happily I have arrived at the last Unto the wished haven of my bliss. What Tranio did, myself enforc'd him to; Then pardon him, sweet father, for my sake.

VIN. I'll slit the villain's nose, that would have sent me to the jail.

BAP. [*To* LUCENTIO.] But do you hear, Sir? Have you married my daughter without asking my good-will?

VIN. Fear not, Baptista; we will content you, go to; but I will in, to be revenged for this villany. [*Exit.*

BAP. And I, to sound the depth of this knavery. [*Exit.*

LUC. Look not pale, Bianca; thy father will not frown. [*Exeunt* LUC. *and* BIAN.

GRE. My cake is dough: but I'll in among the rest; Out of hope of all, but my share of the feast. [*Exit.*

PETRUCHIO *and* KATHARINA *advance.*

KATH. Husband, let's follow, to see the end of this ado.

PET. First kiss me, Kate, and we will.

KATH. What, in the midst of the street?

PET. What, art thou ashamed of me?

KATH. No, Sir, God forbid; but ashamed to kiss.

PET. Why then, let's home again.—Come, sirrah, let's away.

KATH. Nay, I will give thee a kiss: now pray thee, love, stay.

PET. Is not this well?—Come, my sweet Kate: Better once than never, for never too late. [*Exeunt.*

SCENE II.—*A Room in* LUCENTIO'S *House.*

A Banquet set out. Enter BAPTISTA, VIN-
CENTIO, GREMIO, *the* Pedant, LUCENTIO,
BIANCA, PETRUCHIO, KATHARINA, HOR-
TENSIO, *and* Widow. TRANIO, BIONDELLA,
GRUMIO, *and others, attending.*

LUC. At last, though long, our jarring
notes agree:
And time it is, when raging war is done,
To smile at 'scapes and perils overblown.—
My fair Bianca, bid my father welcome,
While I with self-same kindness welcome
thine.—
Brother Petruchio,—sister Katharina,—
And thou, Hortensio, with thy loving
widow,—
Feast with the best, and welcome to my
house:
My banquet is to close our stomachs up,
After our great good cheer. Pray you, sit
down;
For now we sit to chat, as well as eat.
[*They sit at table.*

PET. Nothing but sit and sit, and eat
and eat!

BAP. Padua affords this kindness, son
Petruchio.

PET. Padua affords nothing but what is
kind.

HOR. For both our sakes, I would that
word were true.

PET. Now, for my life, Hortensio fears
his widow.

WID. Then never trust me, if I be afeard.

PET. You are very sensible, and yet you
miss my sense:
I mean, Hortensio is afeard of you.

WID. He that is giddy thinks the world
turns round.

PET. Roundly replied.

KATH. Mistress, how mean you that?

WID. Thus I conceive by him.

PET. Conceives by me!—How likes Hortensio that?

HOR. My widow says, thus she conceives
her tale.

PET. Very well mended.—Kiss him for
that, good widow.

KATH. He that is giddy thinks the world
turns round:—
I pray you, tell me what you meant by that.

WID. Your husband, being troubled with
a shrew,
Measures my husband's sorrow by his woe:
And now you know my meaning.

KATH. A very mean meaning.

WID. Right, I mean you.

KATH. And I am mean, indeed, respecting you.

PET. To her, Kate!

HOR. To her, widow!

PET. A hundred marks, my Kate does
put her down.

HOR. That's my office.

PET. Spoke like an officer:—Ha' to thee,
lad. [*Drinks to* HORTENSIO.

BAP. How likes Gremio these quick-witted
folks?

GRE. Believe me, Sir, they butt together
well.

BIAN. Head and butt! a hasty-witted
body
Would say, your head and butt were head
and horn.

VIN. Ay, mistress bride, hath that awa-
ken'd you?

BIAN. Ay, but not frighted me; therefore I'll sleep again.

PET. Nay, that you shall not: since you
have begun,
Have at you for a bitter jest or two.

BIAN. Am I your bird? I mean to shift
my bush,
And then pursue me as you draw your
bow.—
You are welcome all.
[*Exeunt* BIANCA, KATHARINA, *and* Widow.

PET. She hath prevented me.—Here,
signior Tranio,
This bird you aim'd at, though you hit her
not;
Therefore a health to all that shot and
miss'd.

TRA. O Sir, Lucentio slipp'd me like his
grey-hound,
Which runs himself, and catches for his
master.

PET. A good swift simile, but something
currish.

TRA. 'Tis well, Sir, that you hunted for
yourself:
'Tis thought your deer does hold you at a
bay.

BAP. O ho, Petruchio! Tranio hits you
now.

LUC. I thank thee for that gird, good
Tranio.

HOR. Confess, confess, hath he not hit
you here?

PET. 'A has a little gall'd me, I confess;
And, as the jest did glance away from me,
'Tis ten to one it maim'd you two outright.

BAP. Now, in good sadness, son Petruchio,
I think thou hast the veriest shrew of all.

PET. Well, I say no: and therefore, for
assurance,
Let's each one send unto his wife;
And he whose wife is most obedient.
To come at first when he doth send for her,
Shall win the wager which we will propose.

HOR. Content. What is the wager?
LUC.   Twenty crowns.
PET. Twenty crowns!
I'll venture so much of my hawk or hound,
But twenty times so much upon my wife.
LUC. A hundred then.
HOR.   Content.
PET.   A match! 'tis done.
HOR. Who shall begin?
LUC.   That will I.—
Go, Biondello, bid your mistress come to
me.
BION. I go.   [*Exit.*
BAP. Son, I will be your half, Bianca
comes.
LUC. I'll have no halves; I'll bear it all
myself.

   Re-enter BIONDELLO.
How now! what news?
BION.   Sir, my mistress sends you word
That she is busy, and she cannot come.
PET. How! she is busy, and she cannot
come!
Is that an answer?
GRE.   Ay, and a kind one too:
Pray God, Sir, your wife send you not a
worse.
PET. I hope, better.
HOR. Sirrah Biondello, go and entreat my
wife
To come to me forthwith. [*Exit* BIONDELLO.
PET.   O ho! entreat her!
Nay, then she must needs come.
HOR.   I am afraid, Sir,
Do what you can, yours will not be en-
treated.
   Re-enter BIONDELLO.
Now, where's my wife?
BION. She says you have some goodly
jest in hand:
She will not come; she bids you come to
her.
PET. Worse and worse; she will not
come! O vile,
Intolerable, not to be endur'd!—
Sirrah Grumio, go to your mistress; say,
I command her come to me.
                    [*Exit* GRUMIO.
HOR. I know her answer.
PET. What?
HOR. She will not.
PET. The fouler fortune mine, and there
an end.
BAP. Now, by my holidame, here comes
Katharina!
   Re-enter KATHARINA.
KATH. What is your will, Sir, that you
send for me?
PET. Where is your sister, and Hortensio's
wife?

KATH. They sit conferring by the parlour
fire.
PET. Go, fetch them hither: if they deny
to come,
Swinge me them soundly forth unto their
husbands:
Away, I say, and bring them hither
straight.   [*Exit* KATHARINA.
LUC. Here is a wonder, if you talk of a
wonder.
HOR. And so it is: I wonder what it
bodes.
PET. Marry, peace it bodes, and love,
and quiet life,
An awful rule, and right supremacy;
And, to be short, what not, that's sweet
and happy.
BAP. Now, fair befall thee, good Petru-
chio!
The wager thou hast won; and I will add
Unto their losses twenty thousand crowns;
Another dowry to another daughter,
For she is chang'd, as she had never been.
PET. Nay, I will win my wager better yet,
And show more sign of her obedience,
Her new-built virtue and obedience.
See, where she comes, and brings your
froward wives
As prisoners to her womanly persuasion.—
   Re-enter KATHARINA, *with* BIANCA
        and Widow.
Katharine, that cap of yours becomes you
not:
Off with that bauble, throw it under foot.
[KATHARINA *pulls off her cap, and throws
        it down.*
WID. Lord! let me never have a cause
to sigh,
Till I be brought to such a silly pass!
BIAN. Fie! what a foolish duty call you
this?
LUC. I would your duty were as foolish
too:
The wisdom of your duty, fair Bianca,
Hath cost me a hundred crowns since
supper-time.
BIAN. The more fool you, for laying on
my duty.
PET. Katharine, I charge thee, tell these
head-strong women
What duty they do owe their lords and
husbands.
WID. Come, come, you're mocking: we
will have no telling.
PET. Come on, I say; and first begin with
her.
WID. She shall not.
PET. I say she shall:—and first begin
with her.
KATH. Fie, fie! unknit that threatening
unkind brow;

And dart not scornful glances from those
eyes,
To wound thy lord, thy king, thy governor:
It blots thy beauty, as frosts do bite the
meads;
Confounds thy fame, as whirlwinds shake
fair buds;
And in no sense is meet or amiable.
A woman mov'd is like a fountain troubled,
Muddy, ill-seeming, thick, bereft of beauty;
And while it is so, none so dry or thirsty.
Will deign to sip, or touch one drop of it.
Thy husband is thy lord, thy life, thy
keeper,
Thy head, thy sovereign; one that cares
for thee,
And for thy maintenance; commits his body
To painful labour both by sea and land,
To watch the night in storms, the day in
cold,
Whilst thou liest warm at home, secure
and safe;
And craves no other tribute at thy hands,
But love, fair looks, and true obedience,—
Too little payment for so great a debt.
Such duty as the subject owes the prince,
Even such a woman oweth to her husband;
And when she's froward, peevish, sullen,
sour,
And not obedient to his honest will,
What is she but a foul contending rebel,
And graceless traitor to her loving lord?—
I am asham'd that women are so simple
To offer war, where they should kneel for
peace;
Or seek for rule, supremacy, and sway,
When they are bound to serve, love, and
obey.
Why are our bodies soft, and weak, and
smooth,

Unapt to toil and trouble in the world,
But that our soft conditions, and our hearts,
Should well agree with our external parts?
Come, come, you froward and unable
worms!
My mind hath been as big as one of yours,
My heart as great, my reason, haply, more,
To bandy word for word, and frown for
frown;
But now I see our lances are but straws;
Our strength as weak, our weakness past
compare,—
That seeming to be most, which we indeed
least are.
Then vail your stomachs, for it is no boot;
And place your hands below your husband's
foot:
In token of which duty, if he please,
My hand is ready, may it do him ease.

PET. Why, there's a wench!—Come on
and kiss me, Kate.

LUC. Well, go thy ways, old lad; for thou
shalt ha't.

VIN. 'Tis a good hearing, when children
are toward.

LUC. But a harsh hearing, when women
are froward.

PET. Come, Kate, we'll to bed.—
We three are married, but you two are
sped.
'Twas I won the wager. [*To* LUCENTIO.]
though you hit the white;
And, being a winner, God give you good
night!   [*Exeunt* PETRUCHIO *and* KATH.

HOR. Now, go thy ways; thou hast tam'd
a curst shrew.

LUC. 'Tis a wonder, by your leave, she
will be tam'd so.   [*Exeunt.*

*The Revel: Sir Toby Belch, Sir Andrew Ague-cheek, and the Clown sing a catch.—
Enter Maria. Act II. S. 3.*

TWELFTH-NIGHT: OR, WHAT YOU WILL

DRAMATIS PERSONÆ.

ORSINO, *Duke of* Illyria.

SEBASTIAN, *a young Gentleman, Brother to* VIOLA.

ANTONIO, *a Sea Captain, Friend to* SEBASTIAN.

A Sea Captain, *Friend to* VIOLA.

VALENTINE, } *Gentlemen attending on the*
CURIO, } *Duke.*

SIR TOBY BELCH, *Uncle to* OLIVIA.

SIR ANDREW AGUE-CHEEK.

MALVOLIO, *Steward to* OLIVIA.

FABIAN, }
FESTE, *a Clown,* } *Servants to* OLIVIA.

OLIVIA, *a rich Countess.*

VIOLA, *in love with the Duke.*

MARIA, OLIVIA'S *Waiting-woman.*

Lords, Priests, Sailors, Officers, Musicians, *and other* Attendants.

SCENE,—*A City in* ILLYRIA; *and the Sea-coast near it.*

ACT I.

SCENE I.—*An Apartment in the Duke's Palace.*

Enter Duke, CURIO, *Lords; Musicians attending.*

DUKE. If music be the food of love, play on;
Give me excess of it, that, surfeiting,
The appetite may sicken, and so die.—
That strain again;—it had a dying fall:
O, it came o'er my ear like the sweet south,
That breathes upon a bank of violets,
Stealing, and giving odour.—Enough; no more:
'Tis not so sweet now, as it was before.
O spirit of love, how quick and fresh art thou!
That, notwithstanding thy capacity
Receiveth as the sea, naught enters there,
Of what validity and pitch soe'er,
But falls into abatement and low price,
Even in a minute! so full of shapes is fancy,
That it alone is high-fantastical.
CUR. Will you go hunt, my lord?

DUKE.   What, Curio?
CUR.   The hart.
DUKE. Why, so I do, the noblest that I
have:
O, when mine eyes did see Olivia first,
Methought she purg'd the air of pestilence:
That instant was I turn'd into a hart;
And my desire, like fell and cruel hounds,
E'er since pursue me.—

Enter VALENTINE.
       How now! what news from her?
VAL. So please my lord, I might not be
admitted;
But from her handmaid do return this an-
swer:
The element itself, till seven years' heat,
Shall not behold her face at ample view;
But, like a cloistress, she will veiled walk,
And water once a day her chamber round
With eye-offending brine: all this, to season
A brother's dead love, which she would
keep fresh
And lasting in her sad remembrance.
DUKE. O, she that hath a heart of that
fine frame,
To pay this debt of love but to a brother,
How will she love, when the rich golden
shaft
Hath kill'd the flock of all affections else
That live in her,—when liver, brain, and
heart,
These sovereign thrones, are all supplied
and fill'd,
(Her sweet perfections) with one self
king!—
Away before me to sweet beds of flowers:
Love-thoughts lie rich, when canopied with
bowers.   [*Exeunt.*

SCENE II.—*The Sea-coast.*

Enter VIOLA, Captain, *and* Sailors.
VIO. What country, friends, is this?
CAP.   This is Illyria, lady.
VIO. And what should I do in Illyria?
My brother he is in Elysium.
Perchance, he is not drown'd:—what think
you, sailors?
CAP. It is perchance that you yourself
were sav'd.
VIO. O my poor brother! and so per-
chance may he be.
CAP. True, Madam: and, to comfort you
with chance,
Assure yourself, after our ship did split,
When you, and those poor number saved
with you,
Hung on our driving boat, I saw your
brother,
Most provident in peril, bind himself

(Courage and hope both teaching him the
practice)
To a strong mast, that lived upon the sea;
Where, like Arion on the dolphin's back,
I saw him hold acquaintance with the
waves
So long as I could see.
VIO.   For saying so, there's gold:
Mine own escape unfoldeth to my hope,
Whereto thy speech serves for authority,
The like of him. Know'st thou this
country?
CAP. Ay, Madam, well; for I was bred
and born
Not three hours' travel from this very place.
VIO. Who governs here?
CAP.   A noble duke, in nature
As in name.
VIO.   What is his name?
CAP.   Orsino.
VIO. Orsino! I have heard my father name
him:
He was a bachelor then.
CAP. And so is now, or was so very late;
For but a month ago I went from hence,
And then 'twas fresh in murmur, (as, you
know,
What great ones do, the less will prattle
of)
That he did seek the love of fair Olivia.
VIO. What's she?
CAP. A virtuous maid, the daughter of a
count
That died some twelvemonth since; then
leaving her
In the protection of his son, her brother,
Who shortly also died: for whose dear love,
They say, she hath abjur'd the company
And sight of men.
VIO.   O that I serv'd that lady!
And might not be delivered to the world,
Till I had made mine own occasion mellow,
What my estate is.
CAP.   That were hard to compass;
Because she will admit no kind of suit,
No, not the duke's.
VIO. There is a fair behaviour in thee,
captain;
And though that nature with a beauteous
wall
Doth oft close in pollution, yet of thee
I will believe, thou hast a mind that suits
With this thy fair and outward character.
I pr'ythee, (and I'll pay thee bounteously,)
Conceal me what I am; and be my aid
For such disguise as haply shall become
The form of my intent. I'll serve this duke
Thou shalt present me as a eunuch to him,
It may be worth thy pains; for I can sing
And speak to him in many sorts of music
That will allow me very worth his service

That else may hap, to time I will commit;
Only, shape thou thy silence to my wit.

CAP. Be you his eunuch, and your mute
I'll be:
When my tongue blabs, then let mine eyes
not see.

VIO. I thank thee: lead me on.

[*Exeunt.*

Scene III.—*A Room in* Olivia's *House.*

Enter Sir Toby Belch *and* Maria.

SIR TO. What a plague means my niece,
to take the death of her brother thus? I am
sure care's an enemy to life.

MAR. By my troth, Sir Toby, you must
come in earlier o' nights: your cousin, my
lady, takes great exceptions to your ill
hours.

SIR TO. Why, let her except before excepted.

MAR. Ay, but you must confine yourself
within the modest limits of order.

SIR TO. Confine! I'll confine myself no
finer than I am: these clothes are good
enough to drink in; and so be these boots
too; an they be not, let them hang themselves in their own straps.

MAR. That quaffing and drinking will undo you: I heard my lady talk of it yesterday; and of a foolish knight, that you
brought in one night here to be her wooer.

SIR TO. Who? Sir Andrew Ague-cheek?

MAR. Ay, he.

SIR TO. He's as tall a man as any's in
Illyria.

MAR. What's that to the purpose?

SIR TO. Why, he has three thousand ducats a year.

MAR. Ay, but he'll have but a year in all
these ducats; he's a very fool, and a prodigal.

SIR TO. Fie, that you'll say so! he plays
o' the viol-de-gamboys, and speaks three or
four languages word for word without book,
and hath all the good gifts of nature.

MAR. He hath, indeed,—almost natural:
for, besides that he's a fool, he's a great
quarreller; and, but that he hath the gift
of a coward to allay the gust he hath in
quarrelling, 'tis thought among the prudent
he would quickly have the gift of a grave.

SIR TO. By this hand, they are scoundrels
and substractors that say so of him. Who
are they?

MAR. They that add, moreover, he's drunk
nightly in your company.

SIR TO. With drinking healths to my
niece: I'll drink to her, as long as there is
a passage in my throat, and drink in Illyria.
He's a coward, and a coystril, that will not

drink to my niece, till his brains turn o'
the toe like a parish-top. What, wench!
Castiliano vulgo; for here comes Sir Andrew Ague-face.

Enter Sir Andrew Ague-cheek.

SIR AND. Sir Toby Belch, how now, Sir
Toby Belch!

SIR TO. Sweet Sir Andrew.

SIR AND. Bless you, fair shrew.

MAR. And you too, Sir.

SIR TO. Accost, Sir Andrew, accost.

SIR AND. What's that?

SIR TO. My niece's chamber-maid.

SIR AND. Good mistress Accost, I desire
better acquaintance.

MAR. My name is Mary, Sir.

SIR AND. Good mistress Mary Accost,—

SIR TO. You mistake, knight: accost, is,
front her, board her, woo her, assail her.

SIR AND. By my troth I would not undertake her in this company. Is that the meaning of accost?

MAR. Fare you well, gentlemen.

SIR TO. An thou let part so, Sir Andrew,
would thou might'st never draw sword
again!

SIR AND. An you part so, mistress, I
would I might never draw sword again.
Fair lady, do you think you have fools in
hand?

MAR. Sir, I have not you by the hand.

SIR AND. Marry, but you shall have; and
here's my hand.

MAR. Now, Sir, thought is free: I pray
you, bring your hand to the buttery-bar,
and let it drink.

SIR AND. Wherefore, sweet heart? what's
your metaphor?

MAR. It's dry, Sir.

SIR AND. Why, I think so: I am not such
an ass, but can keep my hand dry. But
what's your jest?

MAR. A dry jest, Sir.

SIR AND. Are you full of them?

MAR. Ay, Sir, I have them at my fingers'
ends: marry, now I let go your hand, I am
barren.   [*Exit.*

SIR TO. O knight! thou lackest a cup of
canary: when did I see thee so put down?

SIR AND. Never in your life, I think; unless you see canary put me down. Methinks
sometimes I have no more wit than a
Christian, or an ordinary man has: but I
am a great eater of beef, and I believe
that does harm to my wit.

SIR TO. No question.

SIR AND. An I thought that, I'd forswear it. I'll ride home to-morrow, Sir
Toby.

SIR TO. Pourquoi, my dear knight?

SIR AND. What is *pourquoi?* do or not

do? I would I had bestowed that time in
the tongues, that I have in fencing, dancing, and bear-baiting: O, had I but followed the arts!

SIR TO. Then hadst thou had an excellent head of hair.

SIR AND. Why, would that have mended
my hair?

SIR TO. Past question; for thou seest it
will not curl by nature.

SIR AND. But it becomes me well enough,
does't not?

SIR TO. Excellent; it hangs like flax on a
distaff; and I hope to see a housewife take
thee between her legs, and spin it off.

SIR AND. 'Faith, I'll home to-morrow, Sir
Toby: your niece will not be seen; or if
she be, it's four to one she'll none of me:
the count himself, here hard by, woos her.

SIR TO. She'll none o' the count: she'll
not match above her degree, neither in estate, years, nor wit; I have heard her swear
it. Tut, there's life in't, man.

SIR AND. I'll stay a month longer. I am
a fellow o' the strangest mind i' the world;
I delight in masks and revels sometimes
altogether.

SIR TO. Art thou good at these kick-
shaws, knight?

SIR AND. As any man in Illyria, whatsoever he be, under the degree of my betters;
and yet I will not compare with an old
man.

SIR TO. What is thy excellence in a galliard, knight?

SIR AND. 'Faith, I can cut a caper.

SIR TO. And I can cut the mutton to't.

SIR AND. And I think I have the back-
trick, simply as strong as any man in
Illyria.

SIR TO. Wherefore are these things hid?
wherefore have these gifts a curtain before them? are they like to take dust, like
mistress Mall's picture? why dost thou not
go to church in a galliard, and come home
in a coranto? My very walk should be a
jig: I would not so much as make water,
but in a sink-a-pace. What dost thou mean?
is it a world to hide virtues in? I did
think, by the excellent constitution of thy
leg, it was formed under the star of a
galliard.

SIR AND. Ay, 'tis strong, and it does indifferent well in a flame-coloured stock.
Shall we set about some revels?

SIR TO. What shall we do else? were we
not born under Taurus?

SIR AND. Taurus! that's sides and heart.

SIR TO. No, Sir; it is legs and thighs. Let
me see thee caper: ha! higher: ha, ha!—
excellent!   [Exeunt.

SCENE IV.—An Apartment in the Duke's
Palace.

Enter VALENTINE, and VIOLA in man's
attire.

VAL. If the duke continue these favours
toward you, Cesario, you are like to be
much advanced: he hath known you but
three days, and already you are no stranger.

VIO. You either fear his humour, or my
negligence, that you call in question the
continuance of his love: is he inconstant,
Sir, in his favours?

VAL. No, believe me.

VIO. I thank you. Here comes the count.

Enter Duke, CURIO, and Attendants.

DUKE. Who saw Cesario? ho!

VIO. On your attendance, my lord; here.

DUKE. Stand you awhile aloof.—Cesario,
Thou know'st no less but all; I have un-
clasp'd
To thee the book even of my secret soul:
Therefore, good youth, address thy gait
unto her;
Be not denied access, stand at her doors,
And tell them, there thy fixed foot shall
grow,
Till thou have audience.

VIO.   Sure, my noble lord,
If she be so abandon'd to her sorrow,
As it is spoke, she never will admit me.

DUKE. Be clamorous, and leap all civil
bounds,
Rather than make unprofited return.

VIO. Say I do speak with her, my lord,
what then?

DUKE. O, then unfold the passion of my
love,
Surprise her with discourse of my dear
faith:
It shall become thee well to act my woes;
She will attend it better in thy youth,
Than in a nuncio of more grave aspect.

VIO. I think not so, my lord.

DUKE.   Dear lad, believe it;
For they shall yet belie thy happy years,
That say thou art a man: Diana's lip
Is not more smooth and rubious; thy small
pipe
Is as the maiden's organ, shrill and sound;
And all is semblative a woman's part.
I know thy constitution is right apt
For this affair:—some four or five attend
him;
All, if you will; for I myself am best,
When least in company:—prosper well in
this,
And thou shalt live as freely as thy lord,
To call his fortunes thine.

VIO.   I'll do my best

To woo your lady: [*Aside*.] yet, a barful strife!

Whoe'er I woo, myself would be his wife.

[*Exeunt*.

Scene V.—*A Room in* Olivia's *House.*

Enter Maria *and* Clown.

MAR. Nay, either tell me where thou hast been, or I will not open my lips so wide as a bristle may enter in way of thy excuse: my lady will hang thee for thy absence.

CLO. Let her hang me: he that is well hanged in this world needs to fear no colours.

MAR. Make that good.

CLO. He shall see none to fear.

MAR. A good lenten answer: I can tell thee where that saying was born, of, I fear no colours.

CLO. Where, good mistress Mary?

MAR. In the wars; and that may you be bold to say in your foolery.

CLO. Well, God give them wisdom, that have it; and those that are fools, let them use their talents.

MAR. Yet you will be hanged for being so long absent; or, to be turned away: is not that as good as a hanging to you?

CLO. Many a good hanging prevents a bad marriage; and, for turning away, let summer bear it out.

MAR. You are resolute, then?

CLO. Not so, neither; but I am resolved on two points.

MAR. That if one break, the other will hold; or, if both break, your gaskins fall.

CLO. Apt, in good faith; very apt. Well, go thy way; if Sir Toby would leave drinking, thou wert as witty a piece of Eve's flesh as any in Illyria.

MAR. Peace, you rogue, no more o' that. Here comes my lady: make your excuse wisely, you were best.   [*Exit*.

CLO. Wit, an't be thy will, put me into good fooling! Those wits, that think they have thee, do very oft prove fools; and I, that am sure I lack thee, may pass for a wise man: for what says Quinapalus? Better a witty fool, than a foolish wit.—[*Enter* Olivia *and* Malvolio.] God bless thee, lady!

OLI. Take the fool away.

CLO. Do you not hear, fellows? Take away the lady.

OLI. Go to, you're a dry fool; I'll no more of you: besides, you grow dishonest.

CLO. Two faults, madonna, that drink and good counsel will amend: for give the dry fool drink, then is the fool not dry: bid the dishonest man mend himself; if he mend,

he is no longer dishonest; if he cannot, let the botcher mend him: any thing that's mended is but patched: virtue that transgresses is but patched with sin; and sin that amends is but patched with virtue: if that this simple syllogism will serve, so; if it will not, what remedy? As there is no true cuckold but calamity, so beauty's a flower.—The lady bade take away the fool; therefore, I say again, take her away.

OLI. Sir, I bade them take away you.

CLO. Misprision in the highest degree!—Lady, *cucullus non facit monachum*; that's as much as to say, I wear not motley in my brain. Good madonna, give me leave to prove you a fool.

OLI. Can you do it?

CLO. Dexteriously, good madonna.

OLI. Make your proof.

CLO. I must catechize you for it, madonna: good my mouse of virtue, answer me.

OLI. Well, Sir, for want of other idleness, I'll 'bide your proof.

CLO. Good madonna, why mournest thou?

OLI. Good fool, for my brother's death.

CLO. I think his soul is in hell, madonna.

OLI. I know his soul is in heaven, fool.

CLO. The more fool, madonna, to mourn for your brother's soul being in heaven.—Take away the fool, gentlemen.

OLI. What think you of this fool, Malvolio? doth he not mend?

MAL. Yes, and shall do, till the pangs of death shake him: infirmity, that decays the wise, doth ever make the better fool.

CLO. God send you, Sir, a speedy infirmity, for the better increasing your folly! Sir Toby will be sworn that I am no fox; but he will not pass his word for twopence that you are no fool.

OLI. How say you to that, Malvolio?

MAL. I marvel your ladyship takes delight in such a barren rascal: I saw him put down the other day with an ordinary fool, that has no more brain than a stone. Look you now, he's out of his guard already; unless you laugh and minister occasion to him, he is gagged. I protest, I take these wise men, that crow so at these set kind of fools, no better than the fools' zanies.

OLI. O, you are sick of self-love, Malvolio, and taste with a distempered appetite. To be generous, guiltless, and of free disposition, is to take those things for bird-bolts, that you deem cannon-bullets: there is no slander in an allowed fool, though he do nothing but rail; nor no railing in a known discreet man, though he do nothing but reprove.

CLO. Now, Mercury endue thee with leasing, for thou speakest well of fools!

Re-enter MARIA.

MAR. Madam, there is at the gate a young gentleman much desires to speak with you.

OLI. From the count Orsino, is it?

MAR. I know not, Madame: 'tis a fair young man, and well attended.

OLI. Who of my people hold him in delay?

MAR. Sir Toby, Madam, your kinsman.

OLI. Fetch him off, I pray you; he speaks nothing but madman: fie on him! [*Exit* MARIA.] Go you, Malvolio: if it be a suit from the count, I am sick, or not at home; what you will, to dismiss it. [*Exit* MALVOLIO.] Now you see, Sir, how your fooling grows old, and people dislike it.

CLO. Thou hast spoke for us, madonna, as if thy eldest son should be a fool,—whose skull Jove cram with brains! for here he comes, one of thy kin, has a most weak *pia mater*.

Enter Sir TOBY BELCH.

OLI. By mine honour, half drunk.—What is he at the gate, cousin?

SIR TO. A gentleman.

OLI. A gentleman! what gentleman?

SIR TO. 'Tis a gentleman here—a plague o' these pickle-herrings!—How now, sot!

CLO. Good Sir Toby!—

OLI. Cousin, cousin, how have you come so early by this lethargy?

SIR TO. Lechery! I defy lechery. There's one at the gate.

OLI. Ay, marry, what is he?

SIR TO. Let him be the devil, an he will, I care not: give me faith, say I. Well, it's all one. [*Exit.*

OLI. What's a drunken man like, fool?

CLO. Like a drown'd man, a fool, and a madman: one draught above heat makes him a fool; the second mads him; and a third drowns him.

OLI. Go thou and seek the coroner, and let him sit o' my coz; for he's in the third degree of drink,—he's drowned: go, look after him.

CLO. He is but mad yet, madonna; and the fool shall look to the madman. [*Exit.*

Re-enter MALVOLIO.

MAL. Madam, yond' young fellow swears he will speak with you. I told him you were sick; he takes on him to understand so much, and therefore comes to speak with you: I told him you were asleep; he seems to have a fore-knowledge of that too, and therefore comes to speak with

you. What is to be said to him, lady? he's fortified against any denial.

OLI. Tell him, he shall not speak with me.

MAL. He has been told so; and he says, he'll stand at your door like a sheriff's post, and be the supporter to a bench, but he'll speak with you.

OLI. What kind of man is he?

MAL. Why, of man kind.

OLI. What manner of man?

MAL. Of very ill manner; he'll speak with you, will you, or no.

OLI. Of what personage, and years is he?

MAL. Not yet old enough for a man, nor young enough for a boy; as a squash is before 'tis a peascod, or a codling when 'tis almost an apple: 'tis with him e'en standing water, between boy and man. He is very well-favoured, and he speaks very shrewishly; one would think, his mother's milk were scarce out of him.

OLI. Let him approach: call in my gentlewoman.

MAL. Gentlewoman, my lady calls. [*Exit.*

Re-enter MARIA.

OLI. Give me my veil: come, throw it o'er my face. We'll once more hear Orsino's embassy.

Enter VIOLA.

VIO. The honourable lady of the house, which is she?

OLI. Speak to me; I shall answer for her. Your will?

VIO. Most radiant, exquisite, and unmatchable beauty,—I pray you, tell me if this be the lady of the house, for I never saw her: I would be loath to cast away my speech; for, besides that it is excellently well penned, I have taken great pains to con it. Good beauties, let me sustain no scorn; I am very comptible, even to the least sinister usage.

OLI. Whence came you, Sir?

VIO. I can say little more than I have studied, and that question's out of my part. Good gentle one, give me modest assurance if you be the lady of the house, that I may proceed in my speech.

OLI. Are you a comedian?

VIO. No, my profound heart: and yet, by the very fangs of malice I swear, I am not that I play. Are you the lady of the house?

OLI. If I do not usurp myself, I am.

VIO. Most certain, if you are she, you do usurp yourself; for, what is yours to bestow, is not yours to reserve. But this is from my commission: I will on with my speech in your praise, and then show you the heart of my message.

OLI. Come to what is important in't: I forgive you the praise.

VIO. Alas, I took great pains to study it; and 'tis poetical.

OL. It is the more like to be feigned: I pray you, keep it in. I heard you were saucy at my gates; and allowed your approach, rather to wonder at you than to hear you. If you be not mad, be gone; if you have reason, be brief: 'tis not that time of moon with me to make one in so skipping a dialogue.

MAR. Will you hoist sail, Sir? here lies your way.

VIO. No, good swabber; I am to hull here a little longer.—Some mollification for your giant, sweet lady.

OLI. Tell me your mind.

VIO. I am a messenger.

OLI. Sure, you have some hideous matter to deliver, when the courtesy of it is so fearful. Speak your office.

VIO. It alone concerns your ear. I bring no overture of war, no taxation of homage: I hold the olive in my hand; my words are full of peace as matter.

OLI. Yet you began rudely. What are you? what would you?

VIO. The rudeness that hath appear'd in me, have I learn'd from my entertainment. What I am, and what I would, are as secret as maidenhead: to your ears, divinity; to any other's, profanation.

OLI. Give us the place alone: we will hear this divinity. [*Exit* MARIA.] Now, Sir, what is your text?

VIO. Most sweet lady,—

OLI. A comfortable doctrine, and much may be said of it. Where lies your text?

VIO. In Orsino's bosom.

OLI. In his bosom! In what chapter of his bosom?

VIO. To answer by the method, in the first of his heart.

OLI. O, I have read it: it is heresy. Have you no more to say?

VIO. Good Madam, let me see your face.

OLI. Have you any commission from your lord to negociate with my face? you are now out of your text: but we will draw the curtain, and show you the picture.[*Unveiling.*] Look you, Sir, such a one I was as this presents: is't not well done?

VIO. Excellently done, if God did all.

OLI. 'Tis in grain, Sir; 'twill endure wind and weather.

VIO. 'Tis beauty truly blent, whose red and white
Nature's own sweet and cunning hand laid
Lady, you are the cruell'st she alive, [on:

If you will lead these graces to the grave,
And leave the world no copy.

OLI. O, Sir, I will not be so hard-hearted;
I will give out divers schedules of my beauty: it shall be inventoried, and every particle and utensil labelled to my will:—as, item, two lips, indifferent red; item, two grey eyes, with lids to them; item, one neck, one chin, and so forth. Were you sent hither to praise me?

VIO. I see you what you are,—you are too proud;
But, if you were the devil, you are fair.
My lord and master loves you: O, such love
Could be but recompens'd, though you were crown'd
The nonpareil of beauty!

OLI.   How does he love me?

VIO. With adorations, with fertile tears,
With groans that thunder love, with sighs of fire.

OLI. Your lord does know my mind; I cannot love him:
Yet I suppose him virtuous, know him noble,
Of great estate, of fresh and stainless youth;
In voices well divulg'd, free, learn'd, and valiant;
And, in dimension and the shape of nature,
A gracious person but yet I cannot love him;
He might have took his answer long ago.

VIO. If I did love you in my master's flame,
With such a suffering, such a deadly life,
In your denial I would find no sense;
I would not understand it.

OLI.   Why, what would you?

VIO. Make me a willow cabin at your gate,
And call upon my soul within the house;
Write loyal cantons of contemned love,
And sing them loud even in the dead of night;
Hollo your name to the reverberate hills,
And make the babbling gossip of the air
Cry out, Olivia! O, you should not rest
Between the elements of air and earth,
But you should pity me!

OLI. You might do much. What is your parentage?

VIO. Above my fortunes, yet my state is
I am a gentleman.   [well:

OLI.   Get you to your lord;
I cannot love him: let him send no more;
Unless, perchance, you come to me again,
To tell me how he takes it. Fare you well:
I thank you for your pains: spend this for me.   [purse,

VIO. I am no fee'd post, lady; keep your

My master, not myself, lacks recompense.
Love make his heart of flint, that you shall
      love;
And let your fervour, like my master's, be
Plac'd in contempt! Farewell, fair cruelty.
                                        [*Exit.*
OLI. "What is your parentage?"
"Above my fortunes, yet my state is well:
I am a gentleman."—I'll be sworn thou art;
Thy tongue, thy face, thy limbs, actions,
      and spirit,
Do give thee five-fold blazon:—not too fast:
      —soft, soft!
Unless the master were the man.—How
      now!
Even so quickly may one catch the plague?
Methinks I feel this youth's perfections,
With an invisible and subtle stealth,
To creep in at mine eyes. Well, let it be.—
What ho, Malvolio!—
                Re-enter MALVOLIO.
MAL.   Here, Madam, at your service.
OLI. Run after that same peevish mes-
      senger,
The county's man: he left this ring behind
      him,
Would I, or not: tell him I'll none of it.
Desire him not to flatter with his lord,
Nor hold him up with hopes; I am not for
      him:
If that the youth will come this way to-
      morrow,
I'll give him reasons for't. Hie thee, Mal-
      volio.
MAL. Madam, I will   [*Exit.*
OLI. I do I know not what; and fear to
      find
Mine eye too great a flatterer for my mind.
Fate, show thy force: ourselves we do not
      owe;
What is decreed must be, and be this so!
                                        [*Exit.*

ACT II.

SCENE I.—*The Sea-coast.*

Enter ANTONIO *and* SEBASTIAN.

ANT. Will you stay no longer? nor will
you not that I go with you?
SEB. By your patience, no. My stars shine
darkly over me: the malignancy of my fate
might, perhaps, distemper yours; therefore
I shall crave of you your leave, that I may
bear my evils alone: it were a bad recompense for your love, to lay any of them on
you.
ANT. Let me yet know of you, whither
you are bound.
SEB. No, 'sooth, Sir: my determinate voyage is mere extravagancy. But I perceive

in you so excellent a touch of modesty, that
you will not extort from me what I am
willing to keep in; therefore, it charges
me in manners the rather to express myself.
You must know of me then, Antonio, my
name is Sebastian, which I called Roderigo.
My father was that Sebastian of Messaline,
whom I know you have heard of. He left
behind him myself and a sister, both born
in an hour: if the heavens had been
pleased, would we had so ended! but you,
Sir, altered that; for some hour before you
took me from the breach of the sea was my
sister drowned.
ANT. Alas, the day!
SEB. A lady, Sir, though it was said she
much resembled me, was yet of many accounted beautiful: but, though I could not
with such estimable wonder overfar believe
that, yet thus far I will boldly publish her,
—she bore a mind that envy could not but
call fair. She is drowned already, Sir, with
salt water, though I seem to drown her remembrance again with more.
ANT. Pardon me, Sir, your bad entertainment.
SEB. O good Antonio, forgive me your
trouble!
ANT. If you will not murder me for my
love, let me be your servant.
SEB. If you will not undo what you have
done, that is, kill him whom you have recovered, desire it not. Fare ye well at once:
my bosom is full of kindness; and I am yet
so near the manners of my mother, that,
upon the least occasion more, mine eyes
will tell tales of me. I am bound to the
count Orsino's court: farewell.   [*Exit.*
ANT. The gentleness of all the gods go
      with thee!
I have many enemies in Orsino's court,
Else would I very shortly see thee there:
But, come what may, I do adore thee so,
That danger shall seem sport, and I will go.
                                        [*Exit.*

SCENE II.—*A Street.*

Enter VIOLA; MALVOLIO *following.*

MAL. Were not you even now with the
countess Olivia?
VIO. Even now, Sir; on a moderate pace
I have since arrived but hither.
MAL. She returns this ring to you, Sir:
you might have saved me my pains, to have
taken it away yourself. She adds, moreover,
that you should put your lord into a desperate assurance she will none of him: and
one thing more,—that you be never so
hardy to come again in his affairs, unless
it be to report your lord's taking of this:
receive it so.

VIO. She took the ring of me;—I'll none of it.

MAL. Come, Sir, you peevishly threw it to her; and her will is, it should be so returned: if it be worth stooping for, there it lies in your eye; if not, be it his that finds it.   [*Exit.*

VIO. I left no ring with her: what means this lady?

Fortune forbid, my outside have not charm'd her!

She made good view of me; indeed, so much,

That methought her eyes had lost her tongue,

For she did speak in starts distractedly.

She loves me, sure; the cunning of her passion

Invites me in this churlish messenger.

None of my lord's ring! why, he sent her none.

I am the man:—if it be so,—as 'tis,—

Poor lady, she were better love a dream.

Disguise, I see, thou art a wickedness,

Wherein the pregnant enemy does much.

How easy is it for the proper-false

In women's waxen hearts to set their forms!

Alas, our frailty is the cause, not we!

For, such as we are made of, such we be.

How will this fadge? My master loves her dearly;

And I, poor monster, fond as much on him;

And she, mistaken, seems to dote on me.

What will become of this? As I am man,

My state is desperate for my master's love;

As I am woman,—now alas the day!—

What thriftless sighs shall poor Olivia breathe!

O time, thou must untangle this, not I;

It is too hard a knot for me t' untie.

                              [*Exit.*

———

SCENE III.—*A Room in* OLIVIA'S *House.*

Enter Sir TOBY BELCH *and Sir*
ANDREW AGUE-CHEEK.

SIR TO. Approach, Sir Andrew: not to be a-bed after midnight is to be up betimes; and *diluculo surgere,* thou knowst,—

SIR AND. Nay, by my troth, I know not: but I know, to be up late, is to be up late.

SIR TO. A false conclusion: I hate it as an unfilled can. To be up after midnight, and to go to bed then, is early: so that, to go to bed after midnight, is to go to bed betimes. Do not our lives consist of the four elements?

SIR AND. 'Faith, so they say; but, I think, it rather consists of eating and drinking.

SIR TO. Thou art a scholar; let us therefore eat and drink.—Marian, I say!—a stoop of wine!

SIR AND. Here comes the fool, i' faith.
                    Enter CLOWN.

CLO. How now, my hearts! Did you never see the picture of we three?

SIR TO. Welcome, ass. Now let's have a catch.

SIR AND. By my troth, the fool has an excellent breast. I had rather than forty shillings I had such a leg, and so sweet a breath to sing, as the fool has. In sooth, thou wast in very gracious fooling last night, when thou spokest of Pigrogromitus, of the Vapians passing the equinoctial of Queubus: 'twas very good, i' faith. I sent thee sixpence for thy leman: hadst it?

CLO. I did impeticos thy gratillity; for Malvolio's nose is no whipstock: my lady has a white hand, and the Myrmidons are no bottle-ale houses.

SIR AND. Excellent! Why, this is the best fooling, when all is done. Now, a song.

SIR TO. Come on; there is sixpence for you: let's have a song.

SIR AND. There's a testril of me too: if one knight give a—

CLO. Would you have a love-song, or a song of good life?

SIR TO. A love-song, a love-song.

SIR AND. Ay, ay; I care not for good life.

SONG.

CLO.

O mistress mine, where are you roaming?
O, stay and hear; your true love's coming,
    That can sing both high and low:
Trip no farther, pretty sweeting;
Journeys end in lovers' meeting,
    Every wise man's son doth know.

SIR AND. Excellent, good, i' faith.
SIR TO. Good, good.
CLO.

What is love? 'tis not hereafter;
Present mirth hath present laughter;
    What's to come is still unsure:
In delay there lies no plenty;
Then come kiss me, sweet and twenty,
    Youth's a stuff will not endure.

SIR AND. A mellifluous voice, as I am true knight.

SIR TO. A contagious breath.

SIR AND. Very sweet and contagious, i' faith.

SIR TO. To hear by the nose, it is dulcet in contagion. But shall we make the welkin dance indeed? Shall we rouse the night-owl in a catch, that will draw three souls out of one weaver? shall we do that?

SIR AND. An you love me, let's do't: I am dog at a catch.

CLO. By'r lady, Sir, and some dogs will catch well.

SIR AND. Most certain. Let our catch be, "Thou knave."

CLO. "Hold thy peace, thou knave," knight? I shall be constrain'd in't to call thee knave, knight.

SIR AND. 'Tis not the first time I have constrain'd one to call me knave. Begin, fool: it begins, "Hold thy peace."

CLO. I shall never begin, if I hold my peace.

SIR AND. Good, i' faith. Come, begin.
            [They sing a catch.

Enter MARIA.

MAR. What a caterwauling do you keep here! If my lady have not called up her steward, Malvolio, and bid him turn you out of doors, never trust me.

SIR TO. My lady's a Cataian, we are politicians; Malvolio's a Peg-a-Ramsey, and "Three merry men be we." Am not I consanguineous? am I not of her blood? Tillyvalley, lady! [Singing.] "There dwelt a man in Babylon, lady, lady!"

CLO. Beshrew me, the knight's in admirable fooling.

SIR AND. Ay, he does well enough, if he be disposed, and so do I too: he does it with a better grace, but I do it more natural.

SIR TO. [Singing.] "O, the twelfth day of December,"—

MAR. For the love o' God, peace!

Enter MALVOLIO.

MAL. My masters, are you mad? or what are you? Have you no wit, manners, nor honesty, but to gabble like tinkers at this time of night? Do ye make an alehouse of my lady's house, that ye squeak out your coziers' catches without any mitigation or remorse of voice? Is there no respect of place, persons, nor time, in you?

SIR TO. We did keep time, Sir, in our catches. Sneck up!

MAL. Sir Toby, I must be round with you. My lady bade me tell you, that, though she harbours you as her kinsman, she's nothing allied to your disorders. If you can separate yourself and your misdemeanours, you are welcome to the house; if not, an it would please you to take leave of her, she is very willing to bid you farewell.

SIR TO. [Singing.] "Farewell, dear heart, since I must needs be gone."

MAR. Nay, good Sir Toby.

CLO. [Singing.] "His eyes do show his days are almost done."

MAL. Is't even so?

SIR TO. [Singing.] "But I will never die."

CLO. Sir Toby, there you lie.

MAL. This is much credit to you.

SIR TO. [Singing.] "Shall I bid him go?"

CLO. [Singing.] "What an if you do?"

SIR TO. [Singing.] "Shall I bid him go, and spare not?"

CLO. [Singing.] "O! no, no, no, no, you dare not."

SIR TO. Out o' time, Sir? ye lie.—Art any more than a steward? Dost thou think, because thou art virtuous, there shall be no more cakes and ale?

CLO. Yes, by Saint Anne; and ginger shall be hot i' the mouth too.

SIR TO. Thou'rt i' the right.—Go, Sir, rub your chain with crumbs.—A stoop of wine, Maria!

MAL. Mistress Mary, if you prized my lady's favour at any thing more than contempt, you would not give means for this uncivil rule: she shall know of it, by this hand.   [Exit.

MAR. Go shake your ears.

SIR AND. 'Twere as good a deed as to drink when a man's a-hungry, to challenge him to the field, and then to break promise with him, and make a fool of him.

SIR TO. Do't, knight: I'll write thee a challenge; or I'll deliver thy indignation to him by word of mouth.

MAR. Sweet Sir Toby, be patient for tonight: since the youth of the count's was to-day with my lady, she is much out of quiet. For monsieur Malvolio, let me alone with him: if I do not gull him into a nayword, and make him a common recreation, do not think I have wit enough to lie straight in my bed: I know, I can do it.

SIR TO. Possess us, possess us; tell us something of him.

MAR. Marry, Sir, sometimes he is a kind of puritan.

SIR AND. O, if I thought that, I'd beat him like a dog!

SIR TO. What, for being a puritan? thy exquisite reason, dear knight?

SIR AND. I have no exquisite reason for't, but I have reason good enough.

MAR. The devil a puritan that he is, or any thing constantly, but a time-pleaser; an affectioned ass, that cons state without book, and utters it by great swaths: the best persuaded of himself, so crammed, as he thinks, with excellences, that it is his ground of faith, that all that look on him love him; and on that vice in him will my revenge find notable cause to work.

SIR TO. What wilt thou do?

MAR. I will drop in his way some obscure epistles of love; wherein, by the colour of his beard, the shape of his leg, the manner of his gait, the expressure of his eye, forehead, and complexion, he shall find himself most feelingly personated: I can write very like my lady, your niece; on a forgotten matter we can hardly make distinction of our hands.

SIR TO. Excellent! I smell a device.

SIR AND. I have't in my nose, too.

SIR TO. He shall think, by the letters that thou wilt drop, that they come from my niece, and that she is in love with him.

MAR. My purpose is, indeed, a horse of that colour.

SIR AND. And your horse, now, would make him an ass.

MAR. Ass, I doubt not.

SIR AND. O, 'twill be admirable!

MAR. Sport royal, I warrant you: I know my physic will work with him. I will plant you two and let the fool make a third, where he shall find the letter: observe his construction of it. For this night, to bed, and dream on the event. Farewell.

SIR TO. Good night, Penthesilea.

                              [*Exit* MARIA.

SIR AND. Before me, she's a good wench.

SIR TO. She's a beagle, true-bred, and one that adores me: what o' that?

SIR AND. I was adored once too.

SIR TO. Let's to bed, knight.—Thou hast need send for more money.

SIR AND. If I cannot recover your niece, I am a foul way out.

SIR TO. Send for money, knight: if thou hast her not i' the end, call me cut.

SIR AND. If I do not, never trust me, take it how you will.

SIR TO. Come, come; I'll go burn some sack, 'tis too late to go to bed now: come, knight; come, knight.   [*Exeunt.*

SCENE IV.—*An Apartment in the Duke's Palace.*

Enter DUKE, VIOLA, CURIO, *and others.*

DUKE. Give me some music:—now, good morrow, friends:—
Now, good Cesario, but that piece of song,
That old and antique song, we heard last night:
Methought it did relieve my passion much,
More than light airs, and recollected terms,
Of these most brisk and giddy-paced times:
Come, but one verse.

CUR. He is not here, so please your lordship, that should sing it.

DUKE. Who was it?

CUR. Feste, the jester, my lord; a fool, that the lady Olivia's father took much delight in: he is about the house.

DUKE. Seek him out:—and play the tune the while.   [*Exit* CURIO. *Music.*
Come hither, boy: if ever thou shalt love,
In the sweet pangs of it, remember me;
For such as I am, all true lovers are,—
Unstaid and skittish in all motions else,
Save in the constant image of the creature
That is belov'd.—How dost thou like this tune?

VIO. It gives a very echo to the seat
Where Love is thron'd.

DUKE.   Thou dost speak masterly:
My life upon't, young though thou art,
    thine eye
Hath stay'd upon some favour that it
    loves;—
Hath, it not, boy?

VIO.   A little, by your favour.

DUKE. What kind of woman is't?

VIO.   Of your complexion.

DUKE. She is not worth thee, then. What years, i' faith?

VIO. About your years, my lord.

DUKE. Too old, by heaven: let still the woman take
An elder than herself; so wears she to him,
So sways she level in her husband's heart:
For, boy, however we do praise ourselves,
Our fancies are more giddy and unfirm,
More longing, wavering, sooner lost and
    worn,
Than women's are.

VIO.   I think it well, my lord.

DUKE. Then, let thy love be younger than
    thyself,
Or thy affection cannot hold the bent;
For women are as roses, whose fair flower
Being once display'd, doth fall that very
    hour.

VIO. And so they are: alas, that they are
    so,—
To die, even when they to perfection grow!
Re-enter CURIO *with* Clown.

DUKE. O, fellow, come, the song we had
    last night.—
Mark it, Cesario; it is old and plain:
The spinsters and the knitters in the sun,
And the free maids that weave their thread
    with bones,
Do use to chaunt it: it is silly sooth,
And dallies with the innocence of love,
Like the old age.

CLO. Are you ready, Sir?

DUKE. Ay; pr'ythee, sing.   [*Music.*

SONG.

CLO. Come away, come away, death,
    And in sad cypress let me be laid;

Fly away, fly away, breath;
I am slain by a fair cruel maid.
My shroud of white, stuck all with
yew,
      O, prepare it!
My part of death no one so true
      Did share it.

Not a flower, not a flower sweet,
On my black coffin let there be strown;
Not a friend, not a friend greet
My poor corse, where my bones shall
be thrown:
A thousand thousand sighs to save,
      Lay me, O, where
Sad true lover never find my grave,
      To weep there!

DUKE. There's for thy pains.
CLO. No pains, Sir; I take pleasure in
singing, Sir.
DUKE. I'll pay thy pleasure then.
CLO. Truly, Sir, and pleasure will be paid,
one time or another.
DUKE. Give me now leave to leave thee.
CLO. Now, the melancholy god protect
thee; and the tailor make thy doublet of
changeable taffeta, for thy mind is a very
opal!—I would have men of such constancy
put to sea, that their business might be
every thing, and their intent every where;
for that's it, that always makes a good
voyage of nothing.—Farewell.   [*Exit.*
DUKE. Let all the rest give place.
    [*Exeunt* CURIO *and* Attendants.
             Once more, Cesario,
Get thee to yond' same sovereign cruelty:
Tell her, my love, more noble than the
world,
Prizes not quantity of dirty lands;
The parts that fortune hath bestow'd upon
her.
Tell her, I hold as giddily as fortune;
But 'tis that miracle and queen of gems,
That nature pranks her in, attracts my soul.
VIO. But, if she cannot love you, Sir?
DUKE. I cannot be so answer'd.
VIO.   Sooth, but you must.
Say, that some lady, as, perhaps, there is,
Hath for your love as great a pang of
heart
As you have for Olivia: you cannot love
her;
You tell her so; must she not, then, be
answer'd?
DUKE. There is no woman's sides
Can bide the beating of so strong a passion
As love doth give my heart; no woman's
heart
So big, to hold so much: they lack re-
tention.

Alas, their love may be call'd appetite,—
No motion of the liver, but the palate,—
That suffers surfeit, cloyment, and revolt;
But mine is all as hungry as the sea,
And can digest as much: makes no com-
pare
Between that love a woman can bear me,
And that I owe Olivia.
VIO.   Ay, but I know,—
DUKE. What dost thou know?
VIO. Too well what love women to men
may owe:
In faith, they are as true of heart as we.
My father had a daughter lov'd a man,
As it might be, perhaps, were I a woman,
I should your lordship.
DUKE.   And what's her history?
VIO. A blank, my lord. She never told
her love,
But let concealment, like a worm i' the
bud,
Feed on her damask cheek: she pin'd in
thought;
And, with a green and yellow melancholy,
She sat like patience on a monument,
Smiling at grief. Was not this love indeed?
We men may say more, swear more: but,
indeed,
Our shows are more than will; for still
we prove
Much in our vows, but little in our love.
DUKE. But died thy sister of her love, my
boy?
VIO. I am all the daughters of my father's
house,
And all the brothers too;— and yet I know
not.—
Sir, shall I to this lady?
DUKE.   Ay, that's the theme.
To her in haste; give her this jewel; say,
My love can give no place, bide no denay.
                    [*Exeunt.*

SCENE V.—OLIVIA's *Garden.*

Enter Sir TOBY BELCH, *Sir* ANDREW AGUE-
CHEEK, *and* FABIAN.

SIR TO. Come thy ways, signior Fabian.
FAB. Nay, I'll come: if I lose a scruple of
this sport, let me be boiled to death with
melancholy.
SIR TO. Would'st thou not be glad to
have the niggardly rascally sheep-biter come
by some notable shame?
FAB. I would exult, man: you know, he
brought me out o' favour with my lady
about a bear-baiting here.
SIR TO. To anger him, we'll have the bear
again; and we will fool him black and blue:
—shall we not, Sir Andrew?

SIR AND. An we do not, it is pity of our lives.

SIR TO. Here comes the little villain.— [*Enter* MARIA.] How now, my nettle of India!

MAR. Get ye all three into the box-tree: Malvolio's coming down this walk: he has been yonder i' the sun, practising behaviour to his own shadow this half hour: observe him, for the love of mockery; for I know this letter will make a contemplative idiot of him. Close, in the name of jesting! [*The men hide themselves.*] Lie thou there; [*Throws down a letter.*] for here comes the trout that must be caught with tickling.

Enter MALVOLIO.   [*Exit.*

MAL. 'Tis but fortune; all is fortune. Maria once told me she did affect me: and I have heard herself come thus near, that, should she fancy, it should be one of my complexion. Besides, she uses me with a more exalted respect than any one else that follows her. What should I think on't?

SIR TO. Here's an over-weening rogue!

FAB. O, peace! Contemplation makes a rare turkey-cock of him: how he jets under his advanced plumes!   [rogue!

SIR AND. 'Slight, I could so beat the

SIR TO. Peace! I say.

MAL. To be count Malvolio,—

SIR TO. Ah, rogue!

SIR AND. Pistol him, pistol him.

SIR TO. Peace, peace!

MAL. There is example for't; the lady of the Strachy married the yeoman of the wardrobe.

SIR AND. Fie on him, Jezebel!

FAB. O, peace! now he's deeply in: look how imagination blows him.

MAL. Having been three months married to her, sitting in my state,—

SIR TO. O, for a stone-bow, to hit him in the eye!

MAL. Calling my officers about me, in my branched velvet gown; having come from a day-bed, where I have left Olivia sleeping,—

SIR TO. Fire and brimstone!

FAB. O, peace, peace!

MAL. And then to have the humour of state; and after a demure travel of regard, —telling them I know my place, as I would they should do theirs,— to ask for my kinsman Toby,—

SIR TO. Bolts and shackles!

FAB. O, peace, peace, peace! now, now.

MAL. Seven of my people, with an obedient start, make out for him: I frown the while; and perchance wind up my watch, or play with some rich jewel. Toby approaches; court'sies there to me,—

SIR TO. Shall this fellow live?

FAB. Though our silence be drawn from us with cars, yet peace!

MAL. I extend my hand to him thus, quenching my familiar smile with an austere regard of control,—

SIR TO. And does not Toby take you a blow o' the lips then?

MAL. Saying, "Cousin Toby, my fortunes, having cast me on your niece, give me this prerogative of speech,"—

SIR TO. What, what?

MAL. "You must amend your drunkenness."

SIR TO. Out, scab!

FAB. Nay, patience, or we break the sinews of our plot.

MAL. "Besides, you waste the treasure of your time with a foolish knight,"—

SIR AND. That's me, I warrant you.

MAL. "One Sir Andrew,"—

SIR AND. I know 'twas I; for many do call me fool.

MAL. [*Seeing the letter.*] What employment have we here?

FAB. Now is the woodcock near the gin.
        [MAL. *Takes up the letter.*

SIR TO. O, peace! and the spirit of humours intimate reading aloud to him!

MAL. By my life, this is my lady's hand: these be her very C's, her U's, and her T's; and thus makes she her great P's. It is, in contempt of question, her hand.

SIR AND. Her C's, her U's, and her T's: why that?

MAL. [*Reads.*] "To the unknown beloved, this, and my good wishes:" her very phrases!—By your leave, wax.—Soft!—and the impressure her Lucrece, with which she uses to seal: 'tis my lady. To whom should this be?

FAB. This wins him, liver and all.

MAL. [*Reads.*] "Jove knows, I love:
        But who?
    Lips do not move;
    No man must know."

"No man must know."—What follows? the numbers altered!— "No man must know:" —if this should be thee, Malvolio?

SIR TO. Marry, hang thee, brock!

MAL. [*Reads.*] "I may command where I adore;
But silence, like a Lucrece knife,
With bloodless stroke my heart doth gore:
M, O, A, I, doth sway my life."

FAB. A fustian riddle!

SIR TO. Excellent wench, say I.

MAL. "M, O, A, I, doth sway my life."— Nay, but first, let me see,—let me see,— let me see.

FAB. What a dish of poison has she dressed him!

SIR TO. And with what wing the stannyel checks at it!

MAL. "I may command where I adore." Why, she may command me: I serve her; she is my lady. Why, this is evident to any formal capacity: there is no obstruction in this:—and the end,—what should that alphabetical position portend? if I could make that resemble something in me,—Softly!—M, O, A, I,—

SIR TO. O, ay, make up that:—he is now at a cold scent.

FAB. Sowter will cry upon't, for all this, though it be as rank as a fox.

MAL. M,—Malvolio;—M, why, that begins my name.

FAB. Did not I say he would work it out? the cur is excellent at faults.

MAL. M,—But then there is no consonancy in the sequel; that suffers under probation: A should follow, but O does.

FAB. And O shall end, I hope.

SIR TO. Ay, or I'll cudgel him, and make him cry, O!

MAL. And then I comes behind.

FAB. Ay, an you had any eye behind you, you might see more detraction at your heels, than fortunes before you.

MAL. M, O, A, I;—this simulation is not as the former:—and yet, to crush this a little, it would bow to me, for every one of these letters are in my name. Soft! here follows prose.—[*Reads.*] "If this fall into thy hand, revolve. In my stars I am above thee; but be not afraid of greatness: some are born great, some achieve greatness, and some have greatness thrust upon them. Thy fates open their hands; let thy blood and spirit embrace them. And, to inure thyself to what thou art like to be, cast thy humble slough, and appear fresh. Be opposite with a kinsman, surly with servants; let thy tongue tang arguments of state; put thyself into the trick of singularity: she thus advises thee, that sighs for thee. Remember who commended thy yellow stockings, and wished to see thee ever cross-gartered: I say, remember. Go to, thou art made, if thou desires to be so; if not, let me see thee a steward still, the fellow of servants, and not worthy to touch Fortune's fingers. Farewell. She that would alter services with thee,

The Fortunate Unhappy."

Day-light and champain discovers not more: this is open. I will be proud, I will read politic authors, I will baffle Sir Toby, I will wash off gross acquaintance, I will be point-device the very man. I do not now fool myself, to let imagination jade me; for every reason excites to this, that my lady loves me. She did commend my yellow stockings of late, she did praise my leg, being cross-gartered; and in this she manifests herself to my love, and, with a kind of injunction, drives me to these habits of her liking. I thank my stars, I am happy. I will be strange, stout, in yellow stockings, and cross-gartered, even with the swiftness of putting on. Jove and my stars be praised! —Here is yet a postscript. [*Reads.*] "Thou canst not choose but know who I am. If thou entertainest my love, let it appear in thy smiling: thy smiles become thee well; therefore in my presence still smile, dear my sweet, I pr'ythee."—Jove, I thank thee. —I will smile: I will do every thing that thou wilt have me.   [*Exit.*

FAB. I will not give my part of this sport for a pension of thousands to be paid from the Sophy.

SIR TO. I could marry this wench for this device,—

SIR AND. So could I too.

SIR TO. And ask no other dowry with her, but such another jest.

SIR AND. Nor I neither.

FAB. Here comes my noble gull-catcher.

Re-enter MARIA.

SIR TO. Wilt thou set thy foot o' my neck?

SIR AND. Or o' mine either?

SIR TO. Shall I play my freedom at tray-trip, and become thy bond-slave?

SIR AND. I' faith, or I either?

SIR TO. Why, thou hast put him in such a dream, that when the image of it leaves him, he must run mad.

MAR. Nay, but say true; does it work upon him?

SIR TO. Like aqua-vitæ with a midwife.

MAR. If you will, then, see the fruits of the sport, mark his first approach before my lady: he will come to her in yellow stockings, and 'tis a colour she abhors, and cross-gartered, a fashion she detests; and he will smile upon her, which will now be so unsuitable to her disposition, being addicted to a melancholy as she is, that it cannot but turn him into a notable contempt. If you will see it, follow me.

SIR TO. To the gates of Tartar, thou most excellent devil of wit!

SIR AND. I'll make one too.   [*Exeunt.*

ACT III.

Scene I.—Olivia's *Garden.*

Enter Viola, *and* Clown *with a tabor.*

VIO. Save thee, friend, and thy music: dost thou live by thy tabor?

CLO. No. Sir, I live by the church.

VIO. Art thou a churchman?

CLO. No such matter, Sir: I do live by the church; for I do live at my house, and my house doth stand by the church.

VIO. So thou may'st say, the king lies by a beggar, if a beggar dwell near him; or, the church stands by thy tabor, if thy tabor stands by the church.

CLO. You have said, Sir.—To see this age! —a sentence is but a cheveril glove to a good wit: how quickly the wrong side may be turned outward!

VIO. Nay, that's certain; they that dally nicely with words, may quickly make them wanton.

CLO. I would, therefore, my sister had had no name, Sir.

VIO. Why, man?

CLO. Why, Sir, her name's a word; and to dally with that word, might make my sister wanton. But, indeed, words are very rascals, since bonds disgraced them.

VIO. Thy reason, man?

CLO. Troth, Sir, I can yield you none without words; and words are grown so false, I am loath to prove reason with them.

VIO. I warrant thou art a merry fellow, and carest for nothing.

CLO. Not so, Sir, I do care for something; but in my conscience, Sir, I do not care for you: if that be to care for nothing, Sir, I would it would make you invisible.

VIO. Art not thou the lady Olivia's fool?

CLO. No, indeed, Sir; the lady Olivia has no folly: she will keep no fool, Sir, till she be married; and fools are as like husbands, as pilchards are to herrings,—the husband's the bigger: I am, indeed, not her fool, but her corrupter of words.

VIO. I saw thee late at the count Orsino's.

CLO. Foolery, Sir, does walk about the orb; like the sun, it shines every where. I would be sorry, Sir, but the fool should be as oft with your master, as with my mistress; I think I saw your wisdom there.

VIO. Nay, an thou pass upon me, I'll no more with thee. Hold, there's expenses for thee.   [*Gives a piece of money.*]

CLO. Now Jove, in his next commodity of hair, send thee a beard!

VIO. By my troth, I'll tell thee,—I am almost sick for one; though I would not have it grow on my chin. Is thy lady within?

CLO. [*Pointing to the coin.*] Would not a pair of these have bred, Sir?

VIO. Yes, being kept together, and put to use.

CLO. I would play lord Pandarus of Phrygia, Sir, to bring a Cressida to this Troilus.

VIO. I understand you, Sir; 'tis well begg'd.

CLO. The matter, I hope, is not great, Sir, begging but a beggar: Cressida was a beggar. My lady is within, Sir. I will construe to them whence you come; who you are, and what you would, are out of my welkin,—I might say element, but the word is overworn.   [*Exit.*]

VIO. This fellow's wise enough to play the fool;
And to do that well craves a kind of wit:
He must observe their mood on whom he jests,
The quality of persons, and the time;
Not, like the haggard, check at every feather
That comes before his eye. This is a practice
As full of labour as a wise man's art:
For folly, that he wisely shows, is fit;
But wise men folly-fallen, quite taint their wit.

Enter Sir TONY BELCH *and Sir* ANDREW AGUE-CHEEK.

SIR TO. Save you, gentleman.

VIO. And you, Sir.

SIR AND. Dieu vous garde, monsieur.

VIO. Et vous aussi; votre serviteur.

SIR AND. I hope, Sir, you are; and I am yours.

SIR TO. Will you encounter the house? my niece is desirous you should enter, if your trade be to her.

VIO. I am bound to your niece, Sir: I mean, she is the list of my voyage.

SIR TO. Taste your legs, Sir; put them to motion.

VIO. My legs do better understand me, Sir, than I understand what you mean by bidding me taste my legs.

SIR TO. I mean to go, Sir, to enter.

VIO. I will answer you with gait and entrance:—but we are prevented.

Enter OLIVIA *and* MARIA.

Most excellent accomplished lady, the heavens rain odours on you!

SIR AND. That youth's a rare courtier: "Rain odours!" well.

VIO. My matter hath no voice, lady, but to your own most pregnant and vouchsafed ear.

SIR AND. "Odours," "pregnant," and "vouchsafed:"—I'll get 'em all three all ready.

OLI. Let the garden door be shut, and leave me to my hearing.
[*Exeunt Sir* TOBY, *Sir* ANDREW, *and* MARIA.
Give me your hand, Sir.

VIO. My duty, Madam, and most humble service.

OLI. What is your name?

VIO. Cesario is your servant's name, fair
princess.
OLI. My servant, Sir! 'Twas never merry
world,
Since lowly feigning was call'd compliment:
You're servant to the count Orsino, youth.
VIO. And he is yours, and his must needs
be yours: Your servant's servant is your
servant, Madam.
OLI. For him, I think not on him: for his
thoughts,
'Would they were blanks, rather than fill'd
with me!
VIO. Madam, I come to whet your gentle
thoughts
On his behalf:—
OLI.   O, by your leave, I pray you,—
I bade you never speak again of him:
But, would you undertake another suit,
I had rather hear you to solicit that,
Than music from the spheres.
VIO. Dear lady,—
OLI. Give me leave, 'beseech you. I did
send,
After the last enchantment you did here,
A ring in chase of you: so did I abuse
Myself, my servant, and, I fear me, you:
Under your hard construction must I sit,
To force that on you, in a shameful cunning,
Which you knew none of yours: what might
you think?
Have you not set mine honour at the stake,
And baited it with all th' unmuzzled
thoughts
That tyrannous heart can think? To one
of your receiving,
Enough is shown: a cyprus, not a bosom,
Hides my heart. So, let me hear you speak.
VIO. I pity you.
OLI. That's a degree to love.
VIO. No, not a grise; for 'tis a vulgar
proof,
That very oft we pity enemies.
OLI. Why, then, methinks, 'tis time to
smile again.
O world, how apt the poor are to be proud!
If one should be a prey, how much the
better
To fall before the lion, than the wolf!
    [*Clock strikes.*
The clock upbraids me with the waste of
time.—
Be not afraid, good youth, I will not have
you:
And yet, when wit and youth is come to
harvest,
Your wife is like to reap a proper man:
There lies your way, due west.
VIO.   Then westward ho!
Grace and good disposition 'tend your lady-
ship!

You'll nothing, Madam, to my lord by me?
OLI. Stay:
I pr'ythee, tell me what thou think'st of me.
VIO. That you do think you are not what
you are.
OLI. If I think so, I think the same of
you.
VIO. Then think you right: I am not what
I am.
OLI. I would you were as I would have
you be!
VIO. Would it be better, Madam, than I
am,
I wish it might; for now I am your fool.
OLI. O, what a deal of scorn looks beau-
tiful
In the contempt and anger of his lip!
A murderous guilt shows not itself more
soon
Than love that would seem hid: love's night
is noon.
Cesario, by the roses of the spring,
By maidhood, honour, truth, and every
thing,
I love thee so, that, maugre all thy pride
Nor wit, nor reason, can my passion hide.
Do not extort thy reasons from this clause,
For that I woo, thou therefore hast no
cause;
But, rather, reason thus with reason fetter,—
Love sought is good, but given unsought is
better.
VIO. By innocence I swear, and by my
youth,
I have one heart, one bosom, and one
truth,—
And that no woman has; nor never none
Shall mistress be of it, save I alone.
And so, adieu, good Madam: never more
Will I my master's tears to you deplore.
OLI. Yet come again; for thou perhaps
may'st move
That heart, which now abhors, to like his
love.   [*Exeunt.*

SCENE II.—*A Room in* OLIVIA'S *House.*

Enter Sir TOBY BELCH, *Sir* ANDREW AGUE-
CHEEK, *and* FABIAN.

SIR AND. No, faith, I'll not stay a jot
longer.
SIR TO. Thy reason, dear venom, give thy
reason.
FAB. You must needs yield your reason,
Sir Andrew.
SIR AND. Marry, I saw your niece do more
favours to the count's serving man, than
ever she bestowed upon me; I saw't i' the
orchard.
SIR TO. Did she see thee the while, old
boy? tell me that.

SIR AND. As plain as I see you now.

FAB. This was a great argument of love in her toward you.

SIR AND. 'Slight, will you make an ass o' me?

FAB. I will prove it legitimate, Sir, upon the oaths of judgment and reason.

SIR TO. And they have been grand jurymen since before Noah was a sailor.

FAB. She did show favour to the youth in your sight only to exasperate you, to awake your dormouse valour, to put fire in your heart, and brimstone in your liver. You should then have accosted her; and with some excellent jests, fire-new from the mint, you should have banged the youth into dumbness. This was looked for at your hand, and this was baulked: the double gilt of this opportunity you let time wash off, and you are now sailed into the north of my lady's opinion; where you will hang like an icicle on a Dutchman's beard, unless you do redeem it by some laudable attempt, either of valour, or policy.

SIR AND. An't be any way, it must be with valour; for policy I hate: I had as lief be a Brownist as a politician.

SIR TO. Why, then, build me thy fortunes upon the basis of valour. Challenge me the count's youth to fight with him; hurt him in eleven places: my niece shall take note of it; and assure thyself, there is no love-broker in the world can more prevail in man's commendation with woman, than report of valour.

FAB. There is no way but this, Sir Andrew.

SIR AND. Will either of you bear me a challenge to him?

SIR TO. Go, write it in a martial hand; be curst and brief; it is no matter how witty, so it be eloquent, and full of invention: taunt him with the license of ink: if thou "thou'st" him some thrice, it shall not be amiss; and as many lies as will lie in thy sheet of paper, although the sheet were big enough for the bed of Ware in England, set 'em down: go, about it. Let there be gall enough in thy ink; though thou write with a goose-pen, no matter: about it.

SIR AND. Where shall I find you?

SIR TO. We'll call thee at the *cubiculo:* go.   [*Exit Sir* ANDREW.

FAB. This is a dear manakin to you, Sir Toby.

SIR TO. I have been dear to him, lad,— some two thousand strong, or so.

FAB. We shall have a rare letter from him: but you'll not deliver it.

SIR TO. Never trust me, then; and by all means stir on the youth to an answer. I think oxen and wainropes cannot hale them together. For Andrew, if he were opened, and you find so much blood in his liver as will clog the foot of a flea, I'll eat the rest of the anatomy.

FAB. And his opposite, the youth, bears in his visage no great presage of cruelty.

SIR TO. Look, where the youngest wren of nine comes.

Enter MARIA.

MAR. If you desire the spleen, and will laugh yourselves into stitches, follow me. Yond' gull Malvolio is turned heathen, a very renegado; for there is no Christian, that means to be saved by believing rightly, can ever believe such impossible passages of grossness. He's in yellow stockings.

SIR TO. And cross-gartered?

MAR. Most villanously; like a pedant that keeps a school i' the church.—I have dogged him like his murderer. He does obey every point of the letter that I dropped to betray him: he does smile his face into more lines, than are in the new map, with the augmentation of the Indies: you have not seen such a thing as 'tis; I can hardly forbear hurling things at him. I know my lady will strike him: if she do, he'll smile, and take't for a great favour.

SIR TO. Come, bring us, bring us where he is.   [*Exeunt.*

SCENE III.—*A Street.*

Enter SEBASTIAN *and* ANTONIO.

SEB. I would not, by my will, have troubled you;

But since you make your pleasure of your pains,

I will no farther chide you.

ANT. I could not stay behind you: my desire,

More sharp than filed steel, did spur me forth;

And not all love to see you, (though so much

As might have drawn one to a longer voyage)

But jealousy what might befall your travel,

Being skilless in these parts; which to a stranger,

Unguided and unfriended, often prove

Rough and unhospitable: my willing love,

The rather by these arguments of fear,

Set forth in your pursuit.

SEB.   My kind Antonio,

I can no other answer make, but thanks,

And thanks, and ever thanks; and oft good turns

Are shuffled off with such uncurrent pay:

But, were my worth, as is my conscience, firm,

You should find better dealing. What's to
    do?

Shall we go see the reliques of this town?

ANT. To-morrow, Sir: best first go see
    your lodging.

SEB. I am not weary, and 'tis long to
    night:

I pray you, let us satisfy our eyes

With the memorials, and the things of fame,

That do renown this city.

ANT.   'Would you'd pardon me;

I do not without danger walk these streets:

Once, in a sea-fight, 'gainst the count his
    galleys,

I did some service; of such note, indeed,

That, were I ta'en here, it would scarce be
    answer'd.

SEB. Belike, you slew great number of his
    people?

ANT. The offence is not of such a bloody
    nature;

Albeit the quality of the time, and quarrel,

Might well have given us bloody argument.

It might have since been answer'd in re-
    paying

What we took from them; which, for
    traffic's sake,

Most of our city did: only myself stood out;

For which, if I be lapsed in this place,

I shall pay dear.

SEB.   Do not, then, walk too open.

ANT. It doth not fit me. Hold, Sir, here's
    my purse.

In the south suburbs at the Elephant,

Is best to lodge: I will bespeak our diet,

Whiles you beguile the time, and feed your
    knowledge,

With viewing of the town: there shall you
    have me.

SEB. Why I your purse?

ANT. Haply your eye shall light upon
    some toy

You have desire to purchase; and your
    store,

I think, is not for idle markets, Sir.

SEB. I'll be your purse-bearer, and leave
    you for an hour.

ANT. To the Elephant.

SEB. I do remember.   [*Exeunt.*

SCENE IV.—*Grounds adjoining* OLIVIA's
    House.

Enter OLIVIA *and* MARIA.

OLI. I have sent after him: he says he'll
    come:

How shall I feast him? what bestow of
    him?

For youth is bought more oft, than begg'd,
    or borrow'd.

I speak too loud.—

Where is Malvolio?—he is sad and civil,

And suits well for a servant with my for-
    tunes:—

Where is Malvolio?

MAR. He's coming, Madam; but in very
    strange manner. He is, sure, possess'd,
    Madam.

OLI. Why, what's the matter? does he
    rave?

MAR. No, Madam, he does nothing but
    smile: your ladyship were best to have
    some guard about you, if he come; for,
    sure, the man is tainted in's wits.

OLI. Go call him hither.—[*Exit* MARIA.]

    I am as mad as he,

If sad and merry madness equal be.—

    Re-enter MARIA, *with* MALVOLIO.

How now, Malvolio!

MAL. [*Smiles fantastically.*] Sweet lady,
    ho, ho.

OLI. Smil'st thou?

I sent for thee upon a sad occasion.

MAL. Sad, lady? I could be sad: this
    does make some obstruction in the blood,
    this cross-gartering; but what of that? if it
    please the eye of one, it is with me as the
    very true sonnet is, "Please one, and please
    all."

OLI. Why, how dost thou, man? what is
    the matter with thee?

MAL. Not black in my mind, though yel-
    low in my legs. It did come to his hands,
    and commands shall be executed: I think
    we do know the sweet Roman hand.

OLI. Wilt thou go to bed, Malvolio?

MAL. To bed? ay, sweet-heart; and I'll
    come to thee.

OLI. God comfort thee! Why dost thou
    smile so, and kiss thy hand so oft?

MAR. How do you, Malvolio?

MAL. At your request! Yes; nightingales
    answer daws.

MAR. Why appear you with this ridicu-
    lous boldness before my lady?

MAL. "Be not afraid of greatness:"—
    'Twas well writ.

OLI. What meanest thou by that, Mal-

MAL. "Some are born great,"—   [volio?

OLI. Ha?

MAL. "Some achieve greatness,"—

OLI. What say'st thou?

MAL. "And some have greatness thrust
    upon them."

OLI. Heaven restore thee!

MAL. "Remember, who commended thy
    yellow stockings,"—

OLI. Thy yellow stockings!

MAL. "And wished to see thee cross-
    gartered."

OLI. Cross-gartered!

MAL. "Go to, thou art made, if thou desirest to be so;"—

OLI. Am I made?

MAL. "If not, let me see thee a servant still."

OLI. Why, this is very midsummer madness.

Enter Servant.

SER. Madam, the young gentleman of the count Orsino's is returned: I could hardly entreat him back: he attends your ladyship's pleasure.

OLI. I'll come to him. [*Exit* Servant.] Good Maria, let this fellow be looked to. Where's my cousin Toby? Let some of my people have a special care of him: I would not have him miscarry, for the half of my dowry.   [*Exeunt* OLIVIA *and* MARIA.

MAL. Oh, ho! do you come near me now? no worse man than Sir Toby to look to me? This concurs directly with the letter: she sends him on purpose, that I may appear stubborn to him; for she incites me to that in the letter. "Cast thy humble slough," says she; "be opposite with a kinsman, surly with servants; let thy tongue tang with arguments of state; put thyself into the trick of singularity;"—and consequently sets down the manner how; as, a sad face, a reverend carriage, a slow tongue, in the habit of some Sir of note, and so forth. I have limed her; but it is Jove's doing, and Jove make me thankful! And when she went away now, "Let this fellow be looked to:" fellow! not Malvolio, nor after my degree, but fellow. Why, every thing adheres together, that no dram of a scruple, no scruple of a scruple, no obstacle, no incredulous or unsafe circumstance—What can be said? Nothing, that can be, can come between me and the full prospect of my hopes. Well, Jove, not I, is the doer of this, and he is to be thanked.

Re-enter MARIA, *with* Sir TOBY BELCH *and* FABIAN.

SIR TO. Which way is he, in the name of sanctity? If all the devils of hell be drawn in little, and Legion himself possessed him, yet I'll speak to him.

FAB. Here he is, here he is.—How is't with you, Sir? how is't with you, man?

MAL. Go off; I discard you: let me enjoy my private: go off.

MAR. Lo, how hollow the fiend speaks within him! did not I tell you?—Sir Toby, my lady prays you to have a care of him.

MAL. Ah, ha! does she so?

SIR TO. Go to, go to; peace, peace! we must deal gently with him: let me alone.— How do you, Malvolio? how is't with you?

What, man! defy the devil: consider, he's an enemy to mankind.

MAL. Do you know what you say?

MAR. La you! an you speak ill of the devil, how he takes it at heart! Pray God, he be not bewitched!

FAB. Carry his water to the wise woman.

MAR. Marry, and it shall be done tomorrow morning, if I live. My lady would not lose him for more than I'll say.

MAL. How now, mistress!

MAR. O lord!

SIR TO. Pr'ythee, hold thy peace; this is not the way: do you not see you move him? let me alone with him.

FAB. No way but gentleness; gently, gently: the fiend is rough, and will not be roughly used.

SIR TO. Why, how now, my bawcock! how dost thou, chuck?

MAL. Sir!

SIR TO. Ay, Biddy, come with me. What, man! 'tis not for gravity to play at cherry-pit with Satan: hang him, foul collier!

MAR. Get him to say his prayers; good Sir Toby, get him to pray.

MAL. My prayers, minx!

MAR. No, I warrant you, he will not hear of godliness.

MAL. Go, hang yourselves all! you are idle shallow things: I am not of your element: you shall know more hereafter.
                                        [*Exit.*

SIR TO. Is't possible?

FAB. If this were played upon a stage now, I could condemn it as an improbable fiction.

SIR TO. His very genius hath taken the infection of the device, man.

MAR. Nay, pursue him now, lest the device take air, and taint.

FAB. Why, we shall make him mad indeed.

MAR. The house will be the quieter.

SIR TO. Come, we'll have him in a dark room, and bound. My niece is already in the belief that he's mad: we may carry it thus, for our pleasure and his penance, till our very pastime, tired out of breath, prompt us to have mercy on him; at which time, we will bring the device to the bar, and crown thee for a finder of madmen.— But see, but see.

FAB. More matter for a May morning.

Enter Sir ANDREW AGUE-CHEEK.

SIR AND. Here's the challenge, read it: I warrant there's vinegar and pepper in't.

FAB. Is't so saucy?

SIR AND. Ay, is't, I warrant him: do but read.

SIR TO. Give me. [*Reads.*] "Youth, whatsoever thou art, thou art but a scurvy fellow."

FAB. Good, and valiant.

SIR TO. [*Reads.*] "Wonder not, nor admire not in thy mind, why I do call thee so, for I will show thee no reason for't."

FAB. A good note: that keeps you from the blow of the law.

SIR TO. [*Reads.*] "Thou comest to the lady Olivia, and in my sight she uses thee kindly: but thou liest in thy throat; that is not the matter I challenge thee for."

FAB. Very brief, and exceeding good sense-less.

SIR TO. [*Reads.*] "I will way-lay thee going home; where, if it be thy chance to kill me,"—

FAB. Good.

SIR TO. [*Reads.*] "Thou killest me like a rogue and a villain."

FAB. Still you keep o' the windy side of the law: good.

SIR TO. [*Reads.*] "Fare thee well; and God have mercy upon one of our souls! He may have mercy upon mine; but my hope is better, and so look to thyself. Thy friend, as thou usest him, and thy sworn enemy, ANDREW AGUE-CHEEK." If this letter move him not, his legs cannot: I'll give't him.

MAR. You may have very fit occasion for't: he is now in some commerce with my lady, and will by and by depart.

SIR TO. Go, Sir Andrew; scout me for him at the corner of the orchard, like a bum-bailie: so soon as ever thou seest him, draw; and, as thou drawest, swear horrible, for it comes to pass oft, that a terrible oath, with a swaggering accent sharply twanged off, gives manhood more approbation than ever proof itself would have earned him. Away!

SIR AND. Nay, let me alone for swearing.
[*Exit.*

SIR TO. Now, will not I deliver his letter: for the behaviour of the young gentleman gives him out to be of good capacity and breeding; his employment between his lord and my niece confirms no less: therefore this letter, being so excellently ignorant, will breed no terror in the youth,—he will find it comes from a clodpole. But, Sir, I will deliver his challenge by word of mouth; set upon Ague-cheek a notable report of valour; and drive the gentleman (as I know his youth will aptly receive it,) into a most hideous opinion of his rage, skill, fury, and impetuosity. This will so fright them both, that they will kill one another by the look, like cockatrices.

FAB. Here he comes with your niece: give them way, till he take leave, and presently after him.

SIR TO. I will meditate the while upon some horrid message for a challenge.
[*Exeunt Sir* TOBY, FABIAN, *and* MARIA.
Re-enter OLIVIA, *with* VIOLA.

OLI. I have said too much unto a heart of stone,
And laid mine honour too unchary out:
There's something in me that reproves my fault;
But such a headstrong potent fault it is,
That it but mocks reproof.

VIO. With the same 'haviour that your passion bears,
Go on my master's griefs.

OLI. Here, wear this jewel for me,—'tis my picture;
Refuse it not; it hath no tongue to vex you:
And, I beseech you, come again to-morrow.
What shall you ask of me that I'll deny,
That honour, sav'd, may upon asking give?

VIO. Nothing but this,—your true love for my master.

OLI. How with mine honour may I give him that
Which I have given to you?

VIO.   I will acquit you.

OLI. Well, come again to-morrow: fare thee well:
A fiend like thee might bear my soul to hell.
[*Exit.*
Re-enter Sir TOBY BELCH *and* FABIAN.

SIR TO. Gentleman, God save thee.

VIO. And you, Sir.

SIR TO. That defence thou hast, betake thee to't: of what nature the wrongs are thou hast done him, I know not; but thy intercepter, full of despight, bloody as the hunter, attends thee at the orchard end: dismount thy tuck, be yare in thy preparation; for thy assailant is quick, skilful, and deadly.

VIO. You mistake, Sir, I am sure; no man hath any quarrel to me: my remembrance is very free and clear from any image of offence done to any man.

SIR TO. You'll find it otherwise, I assure you: therefore, if you hold your life at any price, betake you to your guard; for your opposite hath in him what youth, strength, skill, and wrath, can furnish man withal.

VIO. I pray you, Sir, what is he?

SIR TO. He is knight, dubbed with unhatch'd rapier, and on carpet consideration; but he is a devil in private brawl: souls and bodies hath he divorced three; and his incensement at this moment is so implacable, that satisfaction can be none but by pangs of death and sepulchre: hob, nob, is his word; giv't, or tak't.

VIO. I will return again into the house, and desire some conduct of the lady. I am no fighter. I have heard of some kind of men, that put quarrels purposely on others, to taste their valour: belike this is a man of that quirk.

SIR TO. Sir, no; his indignation derives itself out of a very competent injury: therefore, get you on, and give him his desire. Back you shall not to the house, unless you undertake that with me, which with as much safety you might answer him: therefore, on, or strip your sword stark naked; for meddle you must, that's certain, or forswear to wear iron about you.

VIO. This is as uncivil, as strange. I beseech you, do me this courteous office, as to know of the knight what my offence to him is: it is something of my negligence, nothing of my purpose.

SIR TO. I will do so.—Signior Fabian, stay you by this gentleman till my return.

                                   [*Exit.*

VIO. Pray you, Sir, do you know of this matter?

FAB. I know the knight is incensed against you, even to a mortal arbitrement; but nothing of the circumstance more.

VIO. I beseech you, what manner of man is he?

FAB. Nothing of that wonderful promise, to read him by his form, as you are like to find him in the proof of his valour. He is, indeed, Sir, the most skilful, bloody, and fatal opposite that you could possibly have found in any part of Illyria. Will you walk towards him? I will make your peace with him, if I can.

VIO. I shall be much bound to you for't: I am one that would rather go with sir priest, than sir knight: I care not who knows so much of my mettle.

Re-enter Sir TOBY, *with Sir* ANDREW.

SIR TO. Why, man, he's a very devil; I have not seen such a firago. I had a pass with him, rapier, scabbard, and all, and he gives me the stuck in, with such a mortal motion, that it is inevitable; and on the answer he pays you as surely as your feet hit the ground they step on: they say, he has been fencer to the Sophy.

SIR AND. Pox on't, I'll not meddle with him.

SIR TO. Ay, but he will not now be pacified: Fabian can scarce hold him yonder.

SIR AND. Plague on't, an I thought he had been valiant, and so cunning in fence,

I'd have seen him damned ere I'd have challenged him. Let him let the matter slip, and I'll give him my horse, grey Capilet.

SIR TO. I'll make the motion: stand here, make a good show on't: this shall end without the perdition of souls.—[*Aside.*] Marry, I'll ride your horse as well as I ride you.

Re-enter FABIAN *and* VIOLA.

[*To* FAB.] I have his horse to take up the quarrel:

I have persuaded him the youth's a devil.

FAB. [*To Sir* TOBY.] He is as horribly conceited of him; and pants, and looks pale, as if a bear were at his heels.

SIR TO. [*To* VIOLA.] There's no remedy, Sir; he will fight with you for's oath sake: marry, he hath better bethought him of his quarrel, and he finds that now scarce to be worth talking of: therefore draw, for the supportance of his vow; he protests he will not hurt you.

VIO. [*Aside.*] Pray God defend me! A little thing would make me tell them how much I lack of a man.

FAB. [*To* VIOLA.] Give ground, if you see him furious.

SIR TO. Come, Sir Andrew, there's no remedy; the gentleman will, for his honour's sake, have one bout with you; he cannot by the duello avoid it: but he has promised me, as he is a gentleman and a soldier, he will not hurt you. Come on; to't.

SIR AND. [*Aside.*] Pray God, he keep his oath!   [*Draws.*

VIO. [*To* FABIAN.] I do assure you, 'tis against my will.   [*Draws.*

Enter ANTONIO.

ANT. Put up your sword.—If this young gentleman

Have done offence, I take the fault on me:

If you offend him, I for him defy you.

                                   [*Drawing.*

SIR TO. You, Sir! why, what are you?

ANT. One, Sir, that for his love dares yet do more,

Than you have heard him brag to you he will.

SIR TO. Nay, if you be an undertaker, I am for you.   [*Draws.*

FAB. O, good Sir Toby, hold! here come the officers.

SIR TO. [*To* ANT.] I'll be with you anon.

VIO. [*To Sir* AND.] Pray, Sir, put your sword up, if you please.

SIR AND. Marry, will I, Sir;—and, for that I promised you, I'll be as good as my word: he will bear you easily, and reins well.

Enter Officers.

1 *OFF.* This is the man; do thy office.
2 *OFF.* Antonio, I arrest thee at the suit
Of count Orsino.
ANT.   You do mistake me, Sir.
1 *OFF.* No, Sir, no jot; I know your
favour well,
Though now you have no sea-cap on your
head.—
Take him away: he knows I know him
well.
ANT. I must obey.—[*To* VIOLA.] This
comes with seeking you:
But there's no remedy; I shall answer it.
What will you do, now my necessity
Makes me to ask you for my purse? It
grieves me
Much more for what I cannot do for you,
Than what befalls myself. You stand
amaz'd;
But be of comfort.
2 *OFF.* Come, Sir, away.
ANT. I must entreat of you some of that
money.
VIO. What money, Sir?
For the fair kindness you have show'd me
here,
And, part, being prompted by your present
trouble,
Out of my lean and low ability
I'll lend you something: my having is not
much;
I'll make division of my present with you:
Hold, there's half my coffer.
ANT.   Will you deny me now?
Is't possible that my deserts to you
Can lack persuasion? Do not tempt my
misery,
Lest that it make me so unsound a man,
As to upbraid you with those kindnesses
That I have done for you.
VIO.   I know of none;
Nor know I you by voice, or any feature:
I hate ingratitude more in a man
Than lying, vainness, babbling, drunken-
ness,
Or any taint of vice whose strong corrup-
tion
Inhabits our frail blood.
ANT.   O heavens themselves!
2 *OFF.* Come, Sir, I pray you, go.
ANT. Let me speak a little. This youth
that you see here
I snatch'd one half out of the jaws of
death;
Reliev'd him with such sanctity of love,—
And to his image, which methought did
promise
Most venerable worth, did I devotion.
1 *OFF.* What's that to us? The time
goes by: away!

ANT. But O how vile an idol proves this
god!—
Thou hast, Sebastian, done good feature
shame.—
In nature there's no blemish but the mind;
None can be call'd deform'd but the
unkind:
Virtue is beauty; but the beauteous evil
Are empty trunks, o'erflourish'd by the
devil.
1 *OFF.* The man grows mad: away with
him!—Come, come, Sir.
ANT. Lead me on.
          [*Exeunt* Officers *with* ANTONIO.
VIO. Methinks his words do from such
passion fly,
That he believes himself: so do not I.
Prove true, imagination, O, prove true,
That I, dear brother, be now ta'en for you!
SIR TO. Come hither, knight; come
hither, Fabian: we'll whisper o'er a couplet
or two of most sage saws.
VIO. He nam'd Sebastian: I my brother
know
Yet living in my glass; even such, and so,
In favour was my brother; and he went
Still in this fashion, colour, ornament,—
For him I imitate: O, if it prove,
Tempests are kind, and salt waves fresh in
love!   [*Exit.*
SIR TO. A very dishonest paltry boy, and
more a coward than a hare: his dishonesty
appears in leaving his friend here in neces-
sity, and denying him; and for his coward-
ship, ask Fabian.
FAB. A coward, a most devout coward,
religious in it.
SIR AND. 'Slid, I'll after him again, and
beat him.
SIR TO. Do; cuff him soundly, but never
draw thy sword.
SIR AND. An I do not,—   [*Exit.*
FAB. Come, let's see the event.
SIR TO. I dare lay any money 'twill be
nothing yet.   [*Exeunt.*

———

ACT IV.

SCENE I.—*Another part of the Grounds
adjoining* OLIVIA's *House.*

Enter SEBASTIAN *and* Clown.

CLO. Will you make me believe that I
am not sent for you?
SEB. Go to, go to, thou art a foolish
Let me be clear of thee.   [fellow:
CLO. Well held out, i' faith! No, I do
not know you; nor I am not sent to you
by my lady, to bid you come speak with
her; nor your name is not master Cesario;

nor this is not my nose neither.—Nothing that is so, is so.

SEB. I pr'ythee, vent thy folly somewhere else:

Thou know'st not me.

CLO. Vent my folly! He has heard that word of some great man, and now applies it to a fool: vent my folly! I am afraid this great lubber, the world, will prove a cockney.—I pr'ythee now, ungird thy strangeness, and tell me what I shall vent to my lady: shall I vent to her that thou art coming?

SEB. I pr'ythee, foolish Greek, depart from me:

There's money for thee: if you tarry longer,

I shall give worse payment.

CLO. By my troth, thou hast an open hand.—These wise men, that give fools money, get themselves a good report after fourteen years' purchase.

Enter Sir ANDREW AGUE-CHEEK.

SIR AND. Now, Sir, have I met you again? there's for you.

　　　　　　　[*Striking* SEBASTIAN.

SEB. Why, there's for thee, and there, and there.—[*Beating Sir* ANDREW.] Are all the people mad?

Enter Sir TOBY BELCH *and* FABIAN.

SIR TO. Hold, Sir, or I'll throw your dagger o'er the house.

CLO. This will I tell my lady straight: I would not be in some of your coats for two-pence.　　　　　　　[*Exit.*

SIR TO. [*Holding* SEBASTIAN.] Come on, Sir: hold!

SIR AND. Nay, let him alone: I'll go another way to work with him; I'll have an action of battery against him, if there be any law in Illyria: though I struck him first, yet it's no matter for that.

SEB. Let go thy hand.

SIR TO. Come, Sir, I will not let you go. Come, my young soldier, put up your iron: you are well fleshed; come on.

SEB. I will be free from thee. [*Disengaging himself.*] What would'st thou now?

If thou dar'st tempt me farther, draw thy sword.

SIR TO. What, what! Nay then, I must have an ounce or two of this malapert blood from you.　　　　　　[*Draws.*

Enter OLIVIA.

OLI. Hold, Toby! on thy life, I charge thee, hold!

SIR TO. Madam—

OLI. Will it be ever thus? Ungracious wretch!

Fit for the mountains and the barbarous caves,

Where manners ne'er were preach'd. Out of my sight!—

Be not offended, dear Cesario.—

Rudesby, be gone!—I pry'thee, gentle friend,

　　　　[*Exeunt Sir* TOBY, *Sir* ANDREW, *and* FABIAN.

Let thy fair wisdom, not thy passion, sway

In this uncivil and unjust extent

Against thy peace. Go with me to my house;

And hear thou there how many fruitless pranks

This ruffian hath botch'd up, that thou thereby

May'st smile at this: thou shalt not choose but go:

Do not deny. Beshrew his soul for me.

He started one poor heart of mine in thee.

SEB. What relish is in this? how runs the stream?

Or I am mad, or else this is a dream:

Let fancy still my sense in Lethe steep;

If it be thus to dream, still let me sleep!

OLI. Nay, come, I pr'ythee: would thou'dst be rul'd by me!

SEB. Madam, I will.

OLI.　　　　　O, say so, and so be!

　　　　　　　　　　　[*Exeunt.*

SCENE II.—*A Room in* OLIVIA'S *House.*

Enter MARIA *and* Clown.

MAR. Nay, I pr'ythee, put on this gown, and this beard; make him believe thou art Sir Topas, the curate: do it quickly; I'll call Sir Toby the whilst.　[*Exit.*

CLO. Well, I'll put it on, and I will dissemble myself in't; and I would I were the first that ever dissembled in such a gown. I am not tall enough to become the function well; nor lean enough to be thought a good student: but to be said an honest man and a good housekeeper, goes as fairly as to say a careful man and a great scholar. The competitors enter.

Enter Sir TOBY BELCH *and* MARIA.

SIR TO. Jove bless thee, master parson.

CLO. Bonos dies, Sir Toby: for, as the old hermit of Prague, that never saw pen and ink, very wittily said to a niece of king Gorboduc, "That, that is, is;" so I, being master parson, am master parson; for, what is that, but that? and is but is?

SIR TO. To him, Sir Topas.

CLO. What ho! I say,—peace in this prison!

SIR TO. The knave counterfeits well; a good knave.

MAL. [Within.] Who calls there?

CLO. Sir Topas, the curate, who comes to visit Malvolio the lunatic.

MAL. Sir Topas, Sir Topas, good Sir Topas, go to my lady.

CLO. Out hyperbolical fiend! how vexest thou this man! Talkest thou nothing but of ladies?

SIR TO. Well said, master parson.

MAL. [Within.] Sir Topas, never was man thus wronged: good Sir Topas, do not think I am mad: they have laid me here in hideous darkness.

CLO. Fie, thou dishonest Satan! I call thee by the most modest terms; for I am one of those gentle ones, that will use the devil himself with courtesy: say'st thou that house is dark?

MAL. [Within.] As hell, Sir Topas.

CLO. Why, it hath bay-windows transparent as barricadoes, and the clear stories toward the south-north are as lustrous as ebony; and yet complainest thou of obstruction?

MAL. [Within.] I am not mad, Sir Topas: I say to you, this house is dark.

CLO. Madman, thou errest: I say, there is no darkness but ignorance; in which thou art more puzzled than the Egyptians in their fog.

MAL. [Within.] I say, this house is as dark as ignorance, though ignorance were as dark as hell; and I say, there was never man thus abused. I am no more mad than you are: make the trial of it in any constant question.

CLO. What is the opinion of Pythagoras concerning wild-fowl?

MAL. [Within.] That the soul of our grandam might haply inhabit a bird.

CLO. What thinkest thou of his opinion?

MAL. [Within.] I think nobly of the soul, and no way approve his opinion.

CLO. Fare thee well. Remain thou still in darkness: thou shalt hold the opinion of Pythagoras, ere I will allow of thy wits; and fear to kill a wood-cock, lest thou dispossess the soul of thy grandam. Fare thee well.

MAL. [Within.] Sir Topas! Sir Topas!—

SIR TO. My most exquisite Sir Topas!

CLO. Nay, I am for all waters.

MAR. Thou might'st have done this without thy beard, and gown: he sees thee not.

SIR TO. To him in thine own voice, and bring me word how thou findest him: I would we were well rid of this knavery. If he may be conveniently delivered, I would he were; for I am now so far in offence with my niece, that I cannot pursue with any safety this sport to the upshot. Come by and by to my chamber.

[*Exeunt Sir* TOBY *and* MARIA.

CLO. [Singing.] "Hey Robin, jolly Robin, Tell me how thy lady does."

MAL. [Within.] Fool,—

CLO. [Singing.] "My lady is unkind, perdy."

MAL. [Within.] Fool,—

CLO. [Singing.] "Alas, why is she so?"

MAL. [Within.] Fool, I say,—

CLO. [Singing.] "She loves another"— Who calls, ha?

MAL. [Within.] Good fool, as ever thou wilt deserve well at my hand, help me to a candle, and pen, ink, and paper: as I am a gentleman, I will live to be thankful to thee for't.

CLO. Master Malvolio!

MAL. [Within.] Ay, good fool.

CLO. Alas, Sir, how fell you beside your five wits?

MAL. [Within.] Fool, there was never man so notoriously abused: I am as well in my wits, fool, as thou art.

CLO. But as well? then you are mad indeed, if you be no better in your wits than a fool.

MAL. [Within.] They have here propertied me; keep me in darkness, send ministers to me, asses! and do all they can to face me out of my wits.

CLO. Advise you what you say; the minister is here.—[*As Sir Top.*] Malvolio, Malvolio, thy wits the heavens restore! endeavour thyself to sleep, and leave thy vain bibble babble.

MAL. [Within.] Sir Topas,—

CLO. [As Sir Top.] Maintain no words with him, good fellow.—[*As Clo.*] Who, I, Sir? not I, Sir, God b' wi' you, good Sir Topas.—[*As Sir Top.*] Marry, amen.— [*As Clo.*] I will, Sir, I will.

MAL. [Within.] Fool, fool, fool, I say,—

CLO. Alas, Sir, be patient. What say you, Sir? I am shent for speaking to you.

MAL. [Within.] Good fool, help me to some light, and some paper: I tell thee, I am as well in my wits, as any man in Illyria.

CLO. Well-a-day, that you were, Sir!

MAL. [Within.] By this hand, I am. Good fool, some ink, paper, and light; and convey what I will set down to my lady: it shall advantage thee more than ever the bearing of letter did.

CLO. I will help you to't. But tell me true, are you not mad indeed? or do you but counterfeit?

MAL. [Within.] Believe me, I am not; I tell thee true.

CLO. Nay, I'll ne'er believe a madman till I see his brains. I will fetch you light, and paper, and ink.

MAL. [*Within.*] Fool, I'll requite it in the highest degree: I pr'ythee, be gone.

CLO. [*Singing.*]

I am gone, Sir,
    And anon, Sir,
I'll be with you again,
    In a trice,
    Like to the old Vice,
Your need to sustain;

Who, with dagger of lath,
In his rage and his wrath,
    Cries Ah ha! to the devil:
Like a mad lad,
Pare thy nails, dad;
    Adieu, goodman drivel.   [*Exit.*

Scene III.—Olivia's *Garden.*
Enter Sebastian.

SEB. This is the air; that is the glorious sun;

This pearl she gave me, I do feel't and see't:

And though 'tis wonder that enwraps me thus,

Yet 'tis not madness. Where's Antonio, then?

I could not find him at the Elephant:

Yet there he was; and there I found this credit,

That he did range the town to seek me out.

His counsel now might do me golden service:

For though my soul disputes well with my sense,

That this may be some error, but no madness,

Yet doth this accident and flood of fortune

So far exceed all instance, all discourse,

That I am ready to distrust mine eyes,

And wrangle with my reason, that persuades me

To any other trust but that I am mad,—

Or else the lady's mad; yet, if 'twere so,

She could not sway her house, command her followers,

Take and give back affairs, and their despatch,

With such a smooth, discreet, and stable bearing,

As I perceive she does: there's something in't

That is deceivable. But here the lady comes.

Enter Olivia *and a* Priest.

OLI. Blame not this haste of mine. If you mean well,

Now go with me and with this holy man

Into the chantry by: there, before him,

And underneath that consecrated roof,

Plight me the full assurance of your faith;

That my most jealous and too doubtful soul

May live at peace: he shall conceal it,

Whiles you are willing it shall come to note,

What time we will our celebration keep,

According to my birth.—What do you say?

SEB. I'll follow this good man, and go with you;

And, having sworn truth, ever will be true.

OLI. Then lead the way, good father; and heavens so shine,

That they may fairly note this act of mine!

[*Exeunt.*

ACT V.

Scene I.—*Grounds adjoining* Olivia's *House.*

Enter Clown *and* Fabian.

FAB. Now, as thou lovest me, let me see his letter.

CLO. Good master Fabian, grant me another request.

FAB. Any thing.

CLO. Do not desire to see this letter.

FAB. This is, to give a dog, and, in recompense, desire my dog again.

Enter Duke, Viola, *and* Attendants.

DUKE. Belong you to the lady Olivia, friends?

CLO. Ay, Sir; we are some of her trappings.

DUKE. I know thee well: how dost thou, my good fellow?

CLO. Truly, Sir, the better for my foes, and the worse for my friends.

DUKE. Just the contrary; the better for thy friends.

CLO. No, Sir, the worse.

DUKE. How can that be?

CLO. Marry, Sir, they praise me, and make an ass of me; now my foes tell me plainly I am an ass: so that by my foes, Sir, I profit in the knowledge of myself; and by my friends I am abused: so that, conclusions to be as kisses, if your four negatives make your two affirmatives, why then, the worse for my friends, and the better for my foes.

DUKE. Why, this is excellent.

CLO. By my troth, Sir, no; though it pleases you to be one of my friends.

DUKE. Thou shalt not be the worse for me: there's gold.

CLO. But that it would be double-dealing, Sir, I would you could make it another.

DUKE. O, you give me ill counsel.

CLO. Put your grace in your pocket, Sir, for this once, and let your flesh and blood obey it.

DUKE. Well, I will be so much a sinner to be a double-dealer: there's another.

CLO. *Primo, secundo, tertio*, is a good play; and the old saying is, the third pays for all: the *triplex*, Sir, is a good tripping measure; or the bells of St. Bennet, Sir may put you in mind,—One, two, three.

DUKE. You can fool no more money out of me at this throw: if you will let your lady know I am here to speak with her, and bring her along with you, it may awake my bounty farther.

CLO. Marry, Sir, lullaby to your bounty, till I come again. I go, Sir; but I would not have you to think that my desire of having is the sin of covetousness: but, as you say, Sir, let your bounty take a nap, I will awake it anon.   [*Exit.*

VIO. Here comes the man, Sir, that did rescue me.

Enter Officers *with* ANTONIO.

DUKE. That face of his I do remember well;

Yet, when I saw it last, it was besmear'd
As black as Vulcan in the smoke of war:
A bawbling vessel was he captain of,
For shallow draught and bulk unprizable;
With which such scathful grapple did he make
With the most noble bottom of our fleet,
That very envy, and the tongue of loss,
Cried fame and honour on him.—What's the matter?

1 OFF. Orsino, this is that Antonio
That took the Phœnix and her fraught from Candy;
And this is he that did the Tiger board,
When your young nephew Titus lost his leg:
Here in the streets, desperate of shame and state,
In private brabble did we apprehend him.

VIO. He did me kindness, Sir; drew on my side;
But, in conclusion, put strange speech upon me,
I know not what 'twas, but distraction.

DUKE. Notable pirate! thou salt-water thief!
What foolish boldness brought thee to their mercies,
Whom thou, in terms so bloody and so dear,
Hast made thine enemies?

ANT.   Orsino, noble Sir,
Be pleas'd that I shake off these names you give me:
Antonio never yet was thief or pirate,

Though, I confess, on base and ground enough,
Orsino's enemy. A witchcraft drew me hither:
That most ingrateful boy there, by your side,
From the rude sea's enrag'd and foamy mouth
Did I redeem; a wreck past hope he was:
His life I gave him, and did thereto add
My love, without retention or restraint,
All his in dedication; for his sake
Did I expose myself, pure for his love,
Into the danger of this adverse town;
Drew to defend him when he was beset:
Where being apprehended, his false cunning
(Not meaning to partake with me in danger)
Taught him to face me out of his acquaintance,
And grew a twenty-years-removed thing,
While one would wink; denied me mine own purse,
Which I had recommended to his use
Not half an hour before.

VIO.   How can this be?

DUKE. When came he to this town?

ANT. To-day, my lord; and for three months before,
(No interim, not a minute's vacancy,)
Both day and night did we keep company.

DUKE. Here comes the countess: now heaven walks on earth.—
But for thee, fellow,—fellow, thy words are madness:
Three months this youth hath tended upon me;
But more of that anon.—Take him aside.

Enter OLIVIA *and* Attendants.

OLI. What would my lord,—but that he may not have,—
Wherein Olivia may seem serviceable?—
Cesario, you do not keep promise with me.

VIO. Madam!

DUKE. Gracious Olivia,—

OLI. What do you say, Cesario?—Good my lord,—

VIO. My lord would speak; my duty hushes me.

OLI. If it be aught to the old tune, my lord,
It is as fat and fulsome to mine ear,
As howling after music.

DUKE.   Still so cruel?

OLI. Still so constant, lord.

DUKE. What, to perverseness? you uncivil lady,
To whose ingrate and unauspicious altars
My soul the faithfull'st offerings hath breath'd out,

That e'er devotion tender'd! What shall I
do?
OLI. Even what it please my lord, that
shall become him.
DUKE. Why should I not, had I the
heart to do it,
Like to the Egyptian thief at point of
death,
Kill what I love? a savage jealousy,
That sometime savours nobly.—But hear
me this:
Since you to non-regardance cast my faith,
And that I partly know the instrument
That screws me from my true place in
your favour,
Live you, the marble-breasted tyrant, still;
But this your minion, whom I know you
love,
And whom, by heaven I swear, I tender
dearly,
Him will I tear out of that cruel eye,
Where he sits crowned in his master's
spite.—
Come, boy, with me; my thoughts are ripe
in mischief:
I'll sacrifice the lamb that I do love,
To spite a raven's heart within a dove.
                                    [*Going.*
VIO. And I, most jocund, apt, and will-
ingly,
To do you rest, a thousand deaths would
die.   [*Following.*
OLI. Where goes Cesario?
VIO.   After him I love
More than I love these eyes, more than
my life,
More, by all mores, than e'er I shall love
wife.
If I do feign, you witnesses above
Punish my life for tainting of my love!
OLI. Ah me, detested! how am I be-
guil'd!
VIO. Who does beguile you? who does do
you wrong?
OLI. Hast thou forgot thyself? Is it so
long?—
Call forth the holy father.
                      [*Exit an* Attendant.
DUKE. [*To* VIOLA.]   Come away.
OLI. Whither, my lord?—Cesario, hus-
band, stay.
DUKE. Husband!
OLI. Ay, husband: can he that deny?
DUKE. Her husband, sirrah!
VIO.   No, my lord, not I.
OLI. Alas, it is the baseness of thy fear
That makes thee strangle thy propriety:
Fear not, Cesario; take thy fortunes up;
Be that thou know'st thou art, and then
thou art
As great as that thou fear'st.

Re-enter Attendant *with* Priest.
                      O, welcome, father!
Father, I charge thee, by thy reverence,
Here to unfold (though lately we intended
To keep in darkness, what occasion now
Reveals before 'tis ripe) what thou dost
know
Hath newly past between this youth and
me.
PRIEST. A contract of eternal bond of
love,
Confirm'd by mutual joinder of your
hands,
Attested by the holy close of lips,
Strengthen'd by interchangement of your
rings;
And all the ceremony of this compact
Seal'd in my function, by my testimony:
Since when, my watch hath told me,
toward my grave
I have travelled but two hours.
DUKE. O thou dissembling cub! what
wilt thou be
When time hath sow'd a grizzle on thy
case?
Or will not else thy craft so quickly grow,
That thine own trip shall be thine over-
throw?
Farewell, and take her; but direct thy feet
Where thou and I henceforth may never
meet.
VIO. My lord, I do protest,—
OLI.   O, do not swear!
Hold little faith, though thou hast too
much fear.

Enter Sir ANDREW AGUE-CHEEK, *with his
head broken.*
SIR AND. For the love of God, a sur-
geon! send one presently to Sir Toby.
OLI. What's the matter?
SIR AND. He has broke my head across,
and has given Sir Toby a bloody coxcomb
too: for the love of God, your help! I had
rather than forty pound I were at home.
OLI. Who has done this, Sir Andrew?
SIR AND. The count's gentleman, one
Cesario: we took him for a coward, but
he's the very devil incardinate.
DUKE. My gentleman, Cesario?
SIR AND. Od's lifelings, here he is!—
You broke my head for nothing; and that
that I did, I was set on to do't by Sir
Toby.
VIO. Why do you speak to me? I never
hurt you:
You drew your sword upon me, without
cause;
But I bespake you fair, and hurt you not.
SIR AND. If a bloody coxcomb be a hurt,
you have hurt me: I think you set nothing
by a bloody coxcomb.—Here comes Sir

Toby halting,—you shall hear more: but if he had not been in drink, he would have tickled you othergates than he did.

Enter Sir TOBY BELCH, *drunk, led by the* Clown.

DUKE. How now, gentleman! how is't with you?

SIR TO. That's all one: he has hurt me, and there's the end on't.—Sot, did'st see Dick surgeon, sot?

CLO. O, he's drunk, Sir Toby, an hour agone; his eyes were set, at eight i' the morning.

SIR TO. Then he's a rogue, and a passy-measures pavin: I hate a drunken rogue.

OLI. Away with him! Who hath made this havock with them?

SIR AND. I'll help you, Sir Toby, because we'll be dressed together.

SIR TO. Will you help?—An ass-head, and a coxcomb, and a knave! a thin-faced knave, a gull!

OLI. Get him to bed, and let his hurt be look'd to.

[*Exeunt* Clown, *Sir* TOBY, *and Sir* ANDREW.

Enter SEBASTIAN.

SEB. I am sorry, Madam, I have hurt your kinsman;

But, had it been the brother of my blood, I must have done no less with wit and safety.

You throw a strange regard upon me, and by that

I do perceive it hath offended you:

Pardon me, sweet one, even for the vows We made each other but so late ago.

DUKE. One face, one voice, one habit, and two persons,—

A natural perspective, that is, and is not!

SEB. Antonio! O my dear Antonio!

How have the hours rack'd and tortur'd me, Since I have lost thee!

ANT. Sebastian are you?

SEB.   Fear'st thou that, Antonio?

ANT. How have you made division of yourself?—

An apple, cleft in two, is not more twin Than these two creatures. Which is Sebastian?

OLI. Most wonderful!

SEB. Do I stand there? I never had a brother;

Nor can there be that deity in my nature, Of here and every where. I had a sister, Whom the blind waves and surges have devour'd.—

[*To* VIOLA.] Of charity, what kin are you to me?

What countryman? what name? what parentage?

VIO. Of Messaline: Sebastian was my father;

Such a Sebastian was my brother too, So went he suited to his watery tomb: If spirits can assume both form and suit, You come to fright us.

SEB.   A spirit I am indeed;

But am in that dimension grossly clad, Which from the womb I did participate. Were you a woman, as the rest goes even, I should my tears let fall upon your cheek, And say—Thrice welcome, drowned Viola!

VIO. My father had a mole upon his brow,—

SEB. And so had mine.

VIO. And died that day, when Viola from her birth

Had number'd thirteen years.

SEB. O, that record is lively in my soul!

He finished, indeed, his mortal act That day that made my sister thirteen years.

VIO. If nothing lets to make us happy both

But this my masculine usurp'd attire, Do not embrace me till each circumstance Of place, time, fortune, do cohere and jump,

That I am Viola: which to confirm, I'll bring you to a captain in this town, Where lie my maiden weeds; by whose gentle help

I was preserv'd, to serve this noble count. All the occurrence of my fortune since Hath been between this lady, and this lord.

SEB. [*To* OLIVIA.] So comes it, lady, you have been mistook:

But nature to her bias drew in that. You would have been contracted to a maid;

Nor are you therein, by my life, deceiv'd,— You are betroth'd both to a maid and man.

DUKE. Be not amaz'd; right noble is his blood.—

If this be so, as yet the glass seems true, I shall have share in this most happy wreck.—

[*To* VIOLA.] Boy, thou hast said to me a thousand times,

Thou never should'st love woman like to me.

VIO. And all those sayings will I over-swear;

And all those swearings keep as true in soul,

As doth that orbed continent the fire That severs day from night.

DUKE.   Give me thy hand;

And let me see thee in thy woman's weeds.

VIO. The captain, that did bring me first
on shore,
Hath my maid's garments: he, upon some
action,
Is now in durance, at Malvolio's suit,
A gentleman, and follower of my lady's.
OLI. He shall enlarge him:—fetch Mal-
volio hither:—
And yet, alas, now I remember me,
They say, poor gentleman, he's much dis-
tract.

Re-enter Clown, *with a letter.*

A most extracting frenzy of mine own
From my remembrance clearly banish'd
his.—
How does he, sirrah?
CLO. Truly, Madam, he holds Belzebub
at the stave's end, as well as a man in his
case may do: he has here writ a letter to
you; I should have given it you to-day
morning; but as a madman's epistles are
no gospels, so it skills not much when they
are delivered.
OLI. Open it, and read it.
CLO. Look then to be well edified, when
the fool delivers the madman.—[*Reads.*]
"By the Lord, Madam,"—
OLI. How now! art thou mad?
CLO. No, Madam, I do but read madness:
an your ladyship will have it as it ought
to be, you must allow *vox.*
OLI. Pr'ythee, read i' thy right wits.
CLO. So I do, madonna; but to read his
right wits, is to read thus: therefore perpend, my princess, and give ear.
OLI. [*To* FABIAN.] Read it you, sirrah.
FAB. [*Reads.*] "By the Lord, Madam, you
wrong me, and the world shall know it:
though you have put me into darkness, and
given your drunken cousin rule over me,
yet have I the benefit of my senses as well
as your ladyship. I have your own letter
that induced me to the semblance I put
on; with the which I doubt not but to do
myself much right, or you much shame.
Think of me as you please. I leave my
duty a little unthought of, and speak out
of my injury.
The madly-used MALVOLIO."
OLI. Did he write this?
CLO. Ay, Madam.
DUKE. This savours not much of distraction.
OLI. See him deliver'd, Fabian: bring
him hither.   [*Exit* FABIAN.
My lord, so please you, these things farther
thought on,
To think me as well a sister as a wife,
One day shall crown the alliance on't, so
please you,

Here at my house, and at my proper cost.
DUKE. Madam, I am most apt t' embrace
your offer.—
[*To* VIOLA.] Your master quits you; and,
for your service done him,
So much against the mettle of your sex,
So far beneath your soft and tender breed-
ing,
And since you call'd me master for so long,
Here is my hand: you shall from this time
be
Your master's mistress.
OLI.   A sister:—you are she.
Re-enter FABIAN, *with* MALVOLIO.
DUKE. Is this the madman?
OLI.   Ay, my lord, this same.—
How now, Malvolio!
MAL. Madam, you have done me wrong,
Notorious wrong.
OLI.   Have I, Malvolio? no.
MAL. Lady, you have. Pray you, peruse
that letter:
You must not now deny it is your hand,—
Write from it, if you can, in hand, or
phrase;
Or say 'tis not your seal, nor your inven-
tion:
You can say none of this: well, grant it
then,
And tell me, in the modesty of honour,
Why you have given me such clear lights
of favour,
Bade me come smiling and cross-garter'd
to you,
To put on yellow stockings, and to frown
Upon Sir Toby and the lighter people;
And, acting this in an obedient hope,
Why have you suffer'd me to be impris-
on'd,
Kept in a dark house, visited by the priest,
And made the most notorious geck and
gull
That e'er invention play'd on? tell me why.
OLI. Alas, Malvolio, this is not my writ-
ing,
Though, I confess, much like the character:
But, out of question, 'tis Maria's hand.
And now I do bethink me, it was she
First told me thou wast mad; then cam'st
in smiling,
And in such forms which here were pre-
suppos'd
Upon thee in the letter. Pr'ythee, be con-
tent:
This practice hath most shrewdly pass'd
upon thee;
But when we know the grounds and au-
thors of it,
Thou shalt be both the plaintiff and the
judge
Of thine own cause.

FAB.   Good Madam, hear me speak;
And let no quarrel, nor no brawl to come,
Taint the condition of this present hour,
Which I have wonder'd at. In hope it
   shall not,
Most freely I confess, myself and Toby
Set this device against Malvolio here,
Upon some stubborn and uncourteous parts
We had conceiv'd against him: Maria writ
The letter at Sir Toby's great importance:
In recompense whereof, he hath married
   her.
How with a sportful malice it was follow'd,
May rather pluck on laughter than re-
   venge;
If that the injuries be justly weigh'd,
That have on both sides past.
OLI. Alas, poor fool, how have they baf-
fled thee!
CLO. Why, "some are born great, some
achieve greatness, and some have great-
ness thrown upon them." I was one, Sir,
in this interlude,—one Sir Topas, Sir; but
that's all one.—"By the Lord, fool, I am
not mad;"—but do you remember? "Madam, why laugh you at such a barren rascal? an you smile not, he's gagg'd:" and
thus the whirligig of time brings in his revenges.
MAL. I'll be reveng'd on the whole pack
of you.   [*Exit.*
OLI. He has been most notoriously abus'd.
DUKE. Pursue him, and entreat him to
   a peace:—
He hath not told us of the captain yet:
When that is known, and golden time convents,
A solemn combination shall be made

Of our dear souls.—Meantime, sweet sis-
   ter,
We will not part from hence.—Cesario,
   come;
For so you shall be, while you are a man,
But when in other habits you are seen,
Orsino's mistress, and his fancy's queen.
          [*Exeunt all except* Clown.

SONG.

CLO.

When that I was and a little tiny boy,
   With hey, ho, the wind and the rain,
A foolish thing was but a toy,
   For the rain it raineth every day.

But when I came to man's estate,
   With hey, ho, the wind and the rain,
'Gainst knaves and thieves men shut
   their gate,
   For the rain it raineth every day.

But when I came, alas! to wive,
   With hey, ho, the wind and the rain,
By swaggering could I never thrive,
   For the rain it raineth every day.

But when I came unto my bed,
   With hey, ho, the wind and the rain,
With toss-pots still had drunken head,
   For the rain it raineth every day.

A great while ago the world begun,
   With hey, ho, the wind and the rain:
But that's all one, our play is done,
   And we'll strive to please you every
      day.   [*Exit.*

Richard, as King, sounding Buckingham as to the murder of the two children.
Act IV. S. 2.

LIFE AND DEATH OF
KING RICHARD III

DRAMATIS PERSONÆ.

KING EDWARD THE FOURTH.

EDWARD, *Prince of Wales; after-* ⎫
wards KING EDWARD V., ⎬ *Sons to*
RICHARD, *Duke of York,* ⎭ *the* KING.

GEORGE, *Duke of Clarence,* ⎫ *Brothers*
RICHARD, *Duke of Gloster; after-* ⎬ *to the*
wards KING RICHARD III., ⎭ KING.

A young Son of Clarence.

HENRY, *Earl of Richmond; afterwards* KING HENRY VII.

CARDINAL BOUCHIER, *Archbishop of Canterbury.*

THOMAS ROTHERHAM, *Archbishop of York.*

JOHN MORTON, *Bishop of Ely.*

DUKE OF BUCKINGHAM.

DUKE OF NORFOLK. EARL OF SURREY, *his Son.*

EARL RIVERS, *Brother to* KING EDWARD'S *Queen:* MARQUESS OF DORSET, *and* LORD GREY, *her Sons.*

EARL OF OXFORD. LORD HASTINGS.

LORD STANLEY. LORD LOVEL.

SIR THOMAS VAUGHAN. SIR RICHARD RATCLIFF.

SIR WILLIAM CATESBY. SIR JAMES TYRREL.

SIR JAMES BLOUNT. SIR WALTER HERBERT.

SIR ROBERT BRAKENBURY, *Lieutenant of the Tower.*

CHRISTOPHER URSWICK, *a Priest. Another* Priest.

Lord Mayor of London. Sheriff of Wiltshire.

ELIZABETH, *Queen of* KING EDWARD IV.

MARGARET, *Widow of* KING HENRY VI.

DUCHESS OF YORK, *Mother to* KING EDWARD IV., CLARENCE, *and* GLOSTER.

LADY ANNE, *Widow of* EDWARD, *Prince of Wales, Son to* KING HENRY VI; *afterwards married to the* DUKE OF GLOSTER.

LADY MARGARET PLANTAGENET, *a young Daughter of* CLARENCE.

Lords, *and other* Attendants; *two* Gentlemen, *a* Pursuivant, Scrivener, Citizens, Murderers, Messengers, Ghosts, Soldiers, &c.

SCENE,—ENGLAND.

245

ACT I.

SCENE I.—LONDON. *A Street.*

Enter GLOSTER.

GLO. Now is the winter of our discontent
Made glorious summer by this sun of
York;
And all the clouds, that lower'd upon our
house,
In the deep bosom of the ocean buried.
Now are our brows bound with victorious
wreaths;
Our bruised arms hung up for monuments;
Our stern alarums chang'd to merry meet-
ings,
Our dreadful marches to delightful
measures.
Grim-visag'd war hath smooth'd his
wrinkled front;
And now,—instead of mounting barbed
steeds,
To fright the souls of fearful adversaries,—
He capers nimbly in a lady's chamber,
To the lascivious pleasing of a lute.
But I,—that am not shap'd for sportive
tricks,
Nor made to court an amorous looking-
glass;
I, that am rudely stamp'd, and want love's
majesty,
To strut before a wanton ambling nymph;
I, that am curtail'd of this fair proportion,
Cheated of feature by dissembling nature,
Deform'd, unfinish'd, sent before my time
Into this breathing world, scarce half made
up,
And that so lamely and unfashionable,
That dogs bark at me, as I halt by them;—
Why I, in this weak piping time of peace,
Have no delight to pass away the time,
Unless to see my shadow in the sun,
And descant on mine own deformity:
And therefore,—since I cannot prove a
lover,
To entertain these fair well-spoken days,—
I am determined to prove a villain,
And hate the idle pleasures of these days.
Plots have I laid, inductions dangerous,
By drunken prophecies, libels, and dreams,
To set my brother Clarence and the king
In deadly hate the one against the other:
And, if king Edward be as true and just,
As I am subtle, false, and treacherous,
This day should Clarence closely be mew'd
up,
About a prophecy, which says—that G
Of Edward's heirs the murderer shall be.
Dive, thoughts, down to my soul: here
Clarence comes.

Enter CLARENCE, *guarded and* BRAKENBURY.

Brother, good day: what means t
guard,
That waits upon your grace?
CLAR.   His majesty,
Tendering my person's safety, hath ap-
pointed
This conduct to convey me to the Tower.
GLO. Upon what cause?
CLAR.   Because my name is George.
GLO. Alack, my lord, that fault is none of
yours;
He should, for that, commit your god-
fathers:
O, belike his majesty hath some intent
That you should be new christen'd in the
Tower.
But what's the matter, Clarence? may I
know?
CLAR. Yea, Richard, when I know; for
I protest
As yet I do not: but, as I can learn,
He hearkens after prophecies and dreams;
And from the cross-row plucks the letter G,
And says a wizard told him, that by G
His issue disinherited should be;
And, for my name of George begins with
G,
It follows in his thought that I am he.
These, as I learn, and such like toys as
these,
Have mov'd his highness to commit me now.
GLO. Why, this it is, when men are rul'd
by women:
'Tis not the king that sends you to the
Tower;
My lady Grey, his wife, Clarence, 'tis she
That tempers him to this extremity.
Was it not she, and that good man of
worship,
Antony Woodville, her brother there,
That made him send lord Hastings to the
Tower,
From whence this present day he is
deliver'd?
We are not safe, Clarence; we are not safe.
CLAR. By heaven, I think there is no
man secure,
But the queen's kindred, and night-walking
heralds
That trudge betwixt the king and mistress
Shore.
Heard you not, what a humble suppliant
Lord Hastings was to her for his delivery?
GLO. Humbly complaining to her deity
Got my lord chamberlain his liberty.
I'll tell you what,—I think it is our way,
If we will keep in favour with the king,
To be her men, and wear her livery:
The jealous o'er-worn widow and herself,
Since that our brother dubb'd them gentle-
women,

Are mighty gossips in this monarchy.

BRAK. I beseech your graces both to pardon me:

His majesty hath straitly given in charge
That no man shall have private conference,
Of what degree soever, with your brother.

GLO. Even so; an please your worship, Brakenbury,
You may partake of anything we say:
We speak no treason, man;—we say the king
Is wise and virtuous; and his noble queen
Well struck in years, fair, and not jealous;—
We say that Shore's wife hath a pretty foot,
A cherry lip, a bonny eye, a passing pleasing tongue;
And that the queen's kindred are made gentlefolks:
How say you, Sir? can you deny all this?

BRAK. With this, my lord, myself have naught to do.

GLO. Naught to do with mistress Shore!
I tell thee, fellow,
He that doth naught with her, excepting one,
Were best to do it secretly, alone.

BRAK. What one, my lord?

GLO. Her husband, knave: would'st thou betray me?

BRAK. I beseech your grace to pardon me; and withal,
Forbear your conference with the noble duke.

CLAR. We know thy charge, Brackenbury, and will obey.

GLO. We are the queen's abjects, and must obey.—
Brother, farewell: I will unto the king;
And whatsoe'er you will employ me in,—
Were it to call king Edward's widow, sister,—
I will perform it to enfranchise you.
Meantime, this deep disgrace in brotherhood
Touches me deeper than you can imagine.

CLAR. I know it pleaseth neither of us well.

GLO. Well, your imprisonment shall not be long;
I will deliver you, or else lie for you:
Meantime, have patience.

CLAR.   I must perforce: farewell.
[*Exeunt* CLARENCE, BRAKENBURY *and*
               Guard.

GLO. Go, tread the path that thou shalt ne'er return,
Simple, plain Clarence!—I do love thee so,
That I will shortly send thy soul to heaven,

If heaven will take the present at our hands.—
But who comes here? the new-deliver'd Hastings?

Enter HASTINGS.

HAST. Good time of day unto my gracious lord!

GLO. As much unto my good lord chamberlain!
Well are you welcome to this open air.
How hath your lordship brook'd imprisonment?

HAST. With patience, noble lord, as prisoners must:
But I shall live, my lord, to give them thanks,
That were the cause of my imprisonment.

GLO. No doubt, no doubt; and so shall Clarence too;
For they that were your enemies are his,
And have prevail'd as much on him, as you.

HAST. More pity, that the eagles should be mew'd,
While kites and buzzards prey at liberty.

GLO. What news abroad?

HAST. No news so bad abroad, as this at home;—
The king is sickly, weak, and melancholy,
And his physicians fear him mightily.

GLO. Now, by Saint Paul, this news is bad indeed.
O, he hath kept an evil diet long,
And over-much consum'd his royal person:
'Tis very grievous to be thought upon.
What, is he in his bed?

HAST. He is.

GLO. Go you before, and I will follow you.   [*Exit* HASTINGS.
He cannot live, I hope; and must not die,
Till George be pack'd with posthorse up to heaven.
I'll in, to urge his hatred more to Clarence,
With lies well steel'd with weighty arguments,
And, if I fail not in my deep intent,
Clarence hath not another day to live:
Which done, God take king Edward to his mercy,
And leave the world for me to bustle in!
For then I'll marry Warwick's youngest daughter:
What though I kill'd her husband, and her father?
The readiest way to make the wench amends,
Is to become her husband and her father:
The which will I; not all so much for love,
As for another secret close intent,
By marrying her, which I must reach unto.
But yet I run before my horse to market:

Clarence still breathes; Edward still lives
and reigns:
When they are gone, then must I count
my gains. [*Exit.*

SCENE II.—LONDON. *Another Street.*

*Enter the corse of King Henry the Sixth,
borne in an open coffin,* Gentlemen *bearing halberds to guard it; and* LADY
ANNE *as mourner.*

ANNE. Set down, set down, your honourable load,—
If honour may be shrouded in a hearse,—
Whilst I awhile obsequiously lament
Th' untimely fall of virtuous Lancaster.—
Poor key-cold figure of a holy king!
Pale ashes of the house of Lancaster!
Thou bloodless remnant of that royal blood!
Be it lawful that I invocate thy ghost,
To hear the lamentations of poor Anne,
Wife to thy Edward, to thy slaughter'd son,
Stabb'd by the self-same hand that made
these wounds!
Lo, in these windows, that let forth thy life,
I pour the helpless balm of my poor
eyes:—
O, cursed be the hand that made these
holes!
Cursed the heart, that had the heart to
do it!
Cursed the blood, that let this blood from
hence!
More direful hap betide that hated wretch,
That makes us wretched by the death of
thee,
Than I can wish to adders, spiders, toads,
Or any creeping venom'd thing that lives!
If ever he have child, abortive be it,
Prodigious, and untimely brought to light,
Whose ugly and unnatural aspect
May fright the hopeful mother at the view;
And that be heir to his unhappiness!
If ever he have wife, let her be made
More miserable by the death of him,
Than I am made by my young lord, and
thee!—
Come, now toward Chertsey with your holy
load,
Taken from Paul's to be interred there;
And still, as you are weary of the weight,
Rest you, whiles I lament king Henry's
corse.

[*The bearers take up the corse and advance.
Enter* GLOSTER.

GLO. Stay, you that bear the corse, and
set it down.
ANNE. What black magician conjures up
this fiend,
To stop devoted charitable deeds?

GLO. Villains, set down the corse; or, by
Saint Paul,
I'll make a corse of him that disobeys!
1 GENT. My lord, stand back, and let the
coffin pass.
GLO. Unmanner'd dog! stand thou, when
I command:
Advance thy halberd higher than my breast,
Or, by Saint Paul, I'll strike thee to my
foot,
And spurn upon thee, beggar, for thy
boldness.
[*The bearers set down the coffin.*
ANNE. What, do you tremble? are you
all afraid?
Alas, I blame you not; for you are mortal,
And mortal eyes cannot endure the devil.—
Avaunt, thou dreadful minister of hell!
Thou hadst but power over his mortal
body,—
His soul thou canst not have; therefore,
begone.
GLO. Sweet saint, for charity, be not so
curst.
ANNE. Foul devil, for God's sake hence,
and trouble us not;
For thou hast made the happy earth thy
hell,
Fill'd it with cursing cries, and deep
exclaims.
If thou delight to view thy heinous deeds,
Behold this pattern of thy butcheries.—
O, gentlemen, see, see! dead Henry's
wounds
Open their congeal'd mouths, and bleed
afresh!—
Blush, blush, thou lump of foul deformity;
For 'tis thy presence that exhales this blood
From cold and empty veins, where no blood
dwells;
Thy deed, inhuman and unnatural,
Provokes this deluge most unnatural.—
O God, which this blood mad'st, revenge
his death!
O earth, which this blood drink'st, revenge
his death!
Either, heaven, with lightning strike the
murderer dead;
Or, earth, gape open wide, and eat him
quick,
As thou dost swallow up this good king's
blood,
Which his hell-govern'd arm hath butchered!
GLO. Lady, you know no rules of charity,
Which renders good for bad, blessings for
curses.
ANNE. Villain, thou know'st no law of
God nor man:
No beast so fierce but knows some touch
of pity.

GLO. But I know none, and therefore am no beast.

ANNE. O wonderful, when devils tell the truth!

GLO. More wonderful, when angels are so angry.—

Vouchsafe, divine perfection of a woman,
Of these supposed evils, to give me leave,
By circumstance, but to acquit myself.

ANNE. Vouchsafe, diffus'd infection of a man,
For these known evils, but to give me leave,
By circumstance, to curse thy cursed self.

GLO. Fairer than tongue can name thee, let me have
Some patient leisure to excuse myself.

ANNE. Fouler than heart can think thee, thou canst make
No excuse current, but to hang thyself.

GLO. By such despair, I should accuse myself.

ANNE. And, by despairing, shalt thou stand excus'd;
For doing worthy vengeance on thyself,
That didst unworthy slaughter upon others.

GLO. Say, that I slew them not?

ANNE.   Then say they were not slain:
But dead they are, and, devilish slave, by thee.

GLO. I did not kill your husband.

ANNE.   Why, then he is alive.

GLO. Nay, he is dead; and slain by Edward's hand.

ANNE. In thy foul throat thou liest: queen Margaret saw
Thy murderous faulchion smoking in his blood;
The which thou once didst bend against her breast,
But that thy brothers beat aside the point.

GLO. I was provoked by her sland'rous tongue,
That laid their guilt upon my guiltless shoulders.

ANNE. Thou wast provoked by thy bloody mind,
That never dreamt on aught but butcheries:
Didst thou not kill this king?

GLO. I grant ye.

ANNE. Dost grant me, hedge-hog? then, God grant me too,
Thou may'st be damned for that wicked deed!
O, he was gentle, mild, and virtuous!

GLO. The fitter for the King of heaven, that hath him.

ANNE. He is in heaven, where thou shalt never come.

GLO. Let him thank me, that holp to send him thither;
For he was fitter for that place than earth.

ANNE. And thou unfit for any place but hell.

GLO. Yes, one place else, if you will hear me name it.

ANNE. Some dungeon.

GLO. Your bed-chamber.

ANNE. I'll rest betide the chamber where thou liest.

GLO. So will it, Madam, till I lie with

ANNE. I hope so.   [you.

GLO. I know so.—But, gentle lady Anne,—
To leave this keen encounter of our wits,
And fall somewhat into a slower method,—
Is not the causer of the timeless deaths
Of these Plantagenets, Henry and Edward,
As blameful as the executioner?

ANNE. Thou wast the cause, and most accurs'd effect.

GLO. Your beauty was the cause of that effect;
Your beauty, that did haunt me in my sleep,
To undertake the death of all the world,
So I might live one hour in your sweet bosom.

ANNE. If I thought that, I tell thee, homicide,
These nails should rend that beauty from my cheeks.

GLO. These eyes could not endure that beauty's wreck;
You should not blemish it, if I stood by:
As all the world is cheered by the sun,
So I by that; it is my day, my life.

ANNE. Black night o'ershade thy day, and death thy life!

GLO. Curse not thyself, fair creature; thou art both.

ANNE. I would I were, to be reveng'd on thee.

GLO. It is a quarrel most unnatural,
To be reveng'd on him that loveth thee.

ANNE. It is a quarrel just and reasonable,
To be reveng'd on him that kill'd my husband.

GLO. He that bereft thee, lady, of thy husband,
Did it to help thee to a better husband.

ANNE. His better doth not breathe upon the earth.

GLO. He lives that loves thee better than

ANNE. Name him.   [he could.

GLO.   Plantagenet.

ANNE.   Why, that was he.

GLO. The self-same name, but one of better nature.

ANNE. Where is he?

GLO. Here. [She spits at him.] Why dost thou spit at me?

ANNE. 'Would it were mortal poison, for thy sake!

GLO. Never came poison from so sweet a place.

ANNE. Never hung poison on a fouler toad.
Out of my sight! thou dost infect mine eyes.

GLO. Thine eyes, sweet lady, have infected mine.

ANNE. Would they were basilisks, to strike thee dead!

GLO. I would they were, that I might die at once;
For now they kill me with a living death.
Those eyes of thine from mine have drawn salt tears,
Sham'd their aspects with store of childish drops:
These eyes, which never shed remorseful tear,
No, when my father York and Edward wept,
To hear the piteous moan that Rutland made,
When black-fac'd Clifford shook his sword at him;
Nor when thy warlike father, like a child,
Told the sad story of my father's death,
And twenty times made pause, to sob and weep,
That all the standers-by had wet their cheeks,
Like trees bedash'd with rain; in that sad time,
My manly eyes did scorn a humble tear;
And what these sorrows could not thence exhale,
Thy beauty hath, and made them blind with weeping.
I never sued to friend, nor enemy;
My tongue could never learn sweet smoothing word;
But, now thy beauty is propos'd my fee,
My proud heart sues, and prompts my tongue to speak.
                [She looks scornfully at him.
Teach not thy lip such scorn; for it was made
For kissing, lady, not for such contempt.
If thy revengeful heart cannot forgive,
Lo, here I lend thee this sharp-pointed sword;
Which if thou please to hide in this true breast,
And let the soul forth that adoreth thee,
I lay it naked to the deadly stroke,
And humbly beg the death upon my knee.
                [He lays his breast open.
Nay, do not pause; for I did kill king Henry,—
                [She offers at it with his sword.
But 'twas thy beauty that provoked me.

Nay, now despatch; 'twas I that stabbed young Edward,—
                [She again offers at his breast.
But 'twas thy heavenly face that set me on.
                [She lets fall the sword.
Take up the sword again, or take up me.

ANNE. Arise, dissembler: though I wish thy death,
I will not be thy executioner.

GLO. Then bid me kill myself, and I will do it.

ANNE. I have already.

GLO.   That was in thy rage:
Speak it again, and, even with the word,
This hand, which for thy love, did kill thy love,
Shall, for thy love, kill a far truer love:
To both their deaths shalt thou be accessary.

ANNE. I would I knew thy heart.

GLO. 'Tis figur'd in my tongue.

ANNE. I fear me both are false.

GLO. Then never man was true.

ANNE. Well, well, put up your sword.

GLO. Say, then, my peace is made.

ANNE. That shalt thou know hereafter.

GLO. But shall I live in hope?

ANNE. All men, I hope, live so.

GLO. Vouchsafe to wear this ring.

ANNE. To take, is not to give.
                [She puts on the ring.

GLO. Look, how my ring encompasseth thy finger,
Even so thy breast encloseth my poor heart;
Wear both of them, for both of them are thine.
And if thy poor devoted servant may
But beg one favour at thy gracious hand,
Thou dost confirm his happiness for ever.

ANNE. What is it?

GLO. That it may please you leave these sad designs
To him that hath most cause to be a mourner,
And presently repair to Crosby-place;
Where,—after I have solemnly interr'd,
At Chertsey monastery, this noble king,
And wet his grave with my repentant tears,—
I will with all expedient duty see you:
For divers unknown reasons, I beseech you,
Grant me this boon.

ANNE. With all my heart; and much it joys me too,
To see you are become so penitent.—
Tressel, and Berkley, go along with me.

GLO. Bid me farewell.

ANNE.   'Tis more than you deserve;
But since you teach me how to flatter you,
Imagine I have said farewell already.
                [Exeunt LADY ANNE, TRESSEL, and
                        BERKLEY.

RICH. Sirs, take up the corse.
GENT. Towards Chertsey, noble lord?
GLO. No, to White-Friars; there attend
my coming.
            [*Exeunt the rest, with the corse.*
Was ever woman in this humour woo'd?
Was ever woman in this humour won?
I'll have her;—but I will not keep her long.
What! I, that kill'd her husband, and his
father,
To take her in her heart's extremest hate;
With curses in her mouth, tears in her eyes,
The bleeding witness of her hatred by;
Having God, her conscience, and these bars
against me,
And I no friends to back my suit withal,
But the plain devil, and dissembling looks,
And yet to win her,—all the world to
Ha!   [nothing!
Hath she forgot already that brave prince,
Edward, her lord, whom I, some three
months since,
Stabb'd in my angry mood at Tewksbury?
A sweeter and a lovelier gentleman,—
Fram'd in the prodigality of nature,
Young, valiant, wise, and, no doubt, right
royal,—
The spacious world cannot again afford:
And will she yet abase her eyes on me,
That cropp'd the golden prime of this
sweet prince,
And made her widow to a woful bed?
On me, whose all not equals Edward's
moiety?
On me, that halt, and am mis-shapen thus?
My dukedom to a beggarly denier,
I do mistake my person all this while:
Upon my life, she finds, although I cannot,
Myself to be a marvellous proper man.
I'll be at charges for a looking-glass;
And entertain a score or two of tailors,
To study fashions to adorn my body:
Since I am crept in favour with myself,
I will maintain it with some little cost.
But, first, I'll turn yon fellow in his grave;
And then return lamenting to my love.—
Shine out, fair sun, till I have bought a
glass,
That I may see my shadow as I pass.
                              [*Exit.*

SCENE III.—LONDON. *A Room in the*
Palace.

Enter QUEEN ELIZABETH, RIVERS, *and* GREY.
RIV. Have patience, Madam: there's no
doubt, his majesty
Will soon recover his accustom'd health.
GREY. In that you brook it ill, it makes
him worse:

Therefore, for God's sake, entertain good
comfort,
And cheer his grace with quick and merry
words.
Q. ELIZ. If he were dead, what would
betide on me?
GREY. No other harm, but loss of such
a lord.
Q. ELIZ. The loss of such a lord includes
all harms.
GREY. The heavens have bless'd you with
a goodly son,
To be your comforter when he is gone.
Q. ELIZ. Ah, he is young; and his
minority
Is put unto the trust of Richard Gloster,
A man that loves not me, nor none of you.
RIV. Is it concluded he shall be protector?
Q. ELIZ. It is determin'd, not concluded
yet:
But so it must be, if the king miscarry.
GREY. Here come the lords of Bucking-
ham and Stanley.
        Enter BUCKINGHAM *and* STANLEY.
BUCK. Good time of day unto your royal
grace!
STAN. God make your majesty joyful as
you have been!
Q. ELIZ. The countess Richmond, good my
lord of Stanley,
To your good prayer will scarcely say amen.
Yet, Stanley, notwithstanding she's your
wife,
And loves not me, be you, good lord,
assur'd,
I hate not you for her proud arrogance.
STAN. I do beseech you, either not
believe
The envious slanders of her false accusers;
Or, if she be accus'd on true report,
Bear with her weakness, which, I think,
proceeds
From wayward sickness, and no grounded
malice.
Q. ELIZ. Saw you the king to-day, my
lord of Stanley?
STAN. But now, the duke of Buckingham,
and I,
Are come from visiting his majesty.
Q. ELIZ. What likelihood of his amend-
ment, lords?
BUCK. Madam, good hope; his grace
speaks cheerfully.
Q. ELIZ. God grant him health! Did you
confer with him?
BUCK. Ay, Madam: he desires to make
atonement
Between the duke of Gloster and your
brothers,
And between them and my lord chamberlain;

And sent to warn them to his royal presence.

Q. ELIZ. Would all were well!—But that will never be:

I fear our happiness is at the height.

Enter GLOSTER, HASTINGS, *and* DORSET.

GLO. They do me wrong, and I will not endure it:—

Who are they, that complain unto the king,

That I, forsooth, am stern, and love them not?

By holy Paul, they love his grace but lightly,

That fill his ears with such dissentious rumours.

Because I cannot flatter, and speak fair,

Smile in men's faces, smooth, deceive, and cog,

Duck with French nods and apish courtesy,

I must be held a rancorous enemy.

Cannot a plain man live, and think no harm,

But thus his simple truth must be abus'd

By silken, sly, insinuating Jacks?

GREY. To whom in all this presence speaks your grace?

GLO. To thee, that hast nor honesty, nor grace.

When have I injur'd thee? when done thee wrong?—

Or thee?—or thee?—or any of your faction?

A plague upon you all! His royal grace,

(Whom God preserve better than you would wish!)

Cannot be quiet scarce a breathing-while,

But you must trouble him with lewd complaints.

Q. ELIZ. Brother of Gloster, you mistake the matter.

The king, on his own royal disposition,

And not provok'd by any suitor else;

Aiming, belike, at your interior hatred,

That in your outward action shows itself

Against my children, brothers, and myself,

Makes him to send; that thereby he may gather

The ground of your ill-will, and so remove it.

GLO. I cannot tell:—the world is grown so bad,

That wrens make prey where eagles dare not perch:

Since every Jack became a gentleman,

There's many a gentle person made a Jack.

Q. ELIZ. Come, come, we know your meaning, brother Gloster;

You envy my advancement, and my friends':

God grant, we never may have need of you!

GLO. Meantime, God grants that we have need of you:

Our brother is imprison'd by your means,

Myself disgrac'd, and the nobility

Held in contempt; while great promotions

Are daily given, to ennoble those

That scarce, some two days since, were worth a noble.

Q. ELIZ. By Him that rais'd me to this careful height

From that contented hap which I enjoy'd,

I never did incense his majesty

Against the duke of Clarence; but have been

An earnest advocate to plead for him.

My lord, you do me shameful injury,

Falsely to draw me in these vile suspects.

GLO. You may deny that you were not the mean

Of my lord Hastings' late imprisonment.

RIV. She may, my lord; for—

GLO. She may, lord Rivers,—why, who knows not so?

She may do more, Sir, than denying that:

She may help you to many fair preferments;

And then deny her aiding hand therein,

And lay those honours on your high desert.

What may she not? She may,—ay, marry, may she,—

RIV. What, marry, may she?

GLO. What, marry, may she! marry with a king,

A bachelor, a handsome stripling too:

I wis, your grandam had a worser match.

Q. ELIZ. My lord of Gloster, I have too long borne

Your blunt upbraidings, and your bitter scoffs:

By heaven, I will acquaint his majesty

Of those gross taunts that oft I have endur'd.

I had rather be a country servant-maid,

Than a great queen, with this condition,—

To be so baited, scorn'd, and stormed at:

Enter QUEEN MARGARET, *behind.*

Small joy have I in being England's queen.

Q. MAR. [*Apart.*] And lessen'd be that small, God, I beseech him!—

Thy honour, state, and seat, is due to me.

GLO. What! threat you me with telling of the king?

Tell him, and spare not: look, what I have said

I will avouch in presence of the king:

I dare adventure to be sent to the Tower.

'Tis time to speak,—my pains are quite forgot.

Q. MAR. [*Apart.*] Out, devil! I remember them too well:

Thou kill'dst my husband Henry in the Tower,

And Edward, my poor son, at Tewksbury.

GLO. Ere you were queen, ay, or your husband king,
I was a pack-horse in his great affairs;
A weeder-out of his proud adversaries,
A liberal rewarder of his friends:
To royalize his blood, I spilt mine own.
Q. MAR. [*Apart.*] Ay, and much better blood than his, or thine.
GLO. In all which time, you, and your husband Grey,
Were factious for the house of Lancaster;—
And, Rivers, so were you:—was not your husband
In Margaret's battle at Saint Albans slain?
Let me put in your minds, if you forget,
What you have been ere this, and what you are;
Withal, what I have been, and what I am.
Q. MAR. [*Apart.*] A murd'rous villain, and so still thou art.
GLO. Poor Clarence did forsake his father, Warwick;
Ay, and forswore himself,—which Jesu pardon!—
Q. MAR. [*Apart.*] Which God revenge!
GLO. To fight on Edward's party, for the crown;
And for his meed, poor lord, he is mew'd up.
I would to God my heart were flint, like Edward's;
Or Edward's soft and pitiful, like mine:
I am too childish-foolish for this world.
Q. MAR. [*Apart.*] Hie thee to hell for shame, and leave this world,
Thou cacodæmon! there thy kingdom is.
RIV. My lord of Gloster, in those busy days,
Which here you urge to prove us enemies,
We follow'd then our lord, our sovereign king:
So should we you, if you should be our king.
GLO. If I should be!—I had rather be a pedler.
Far be it from my heart, the thought thereof!
Q. ELIZ. As little joy, my lord, as you suppose
You should enjoy, were you this country's king,—
As little joy you may suppose in me,
That I enjoy, being the queen thereof.
Q. MAR. [*Apart.*] As little joy enjoys the queen thereof;
For I am she, and altogether joyless.
I can no longer hold me patient.—
        [*Advancing.*
Hear me, you wrangling pirates, that fall out

In sharing that which you have pill'd from me!
Which of you trembles not, that looks on me?
If not, that, I being queen, you bow like subjects,
Yet that, by you depos'd, you quake like rebels?—
Ah, gentle villain, do not turn away!
GLO. Foul wrinkled witch, what mak'st thou in my sight?
Q. MAR. But repetition of what thou hast marr'd;
That will I make, before I let thee go.
GLO. Wert thou not banished, on pain of death?
Q. MAR. I was; but I do find more pain in banishment,
Than death can yield me here by my abode.
A husband, and a son, thou ow'st to me,—
And thou, a kingdom,—all of you, allegiance:
This sorrow that I have, by right is yours;
And all the pleasures you usurp are mine.
GLO. The curse my noble father laid on thee,
When thou didst crown his warlike brows with paper,
And with thy scorns drew'st rivers from his eyes;
And then, to dry them, gav'st the duke a clout
Steep'd in the faultless blood of pretty Rutland;—
His curses, then from bitterness of soul
Denounc'd against thee, are all fallen upon thee;
And God, not we, hath plagu'd thy bloody deed.
Q. ELIZ. So just is God, to right the innocent.
HAST. O, 'twas the foulest deed to slay that babe,
And the most merciless, that e'er was heard of!
RIV. Tyrants themselves wept when it was reported.
DORS. No man but prophesied revenge for it.
BUCK. Northumberland, then present, wept to see it.
Q. MAR. What, were you snarling all, before I came,
Ready to catch each other by the throat,
And turn you all your hatred now on me?
Did York's dread curse prevail so much with heaven,
That Henry's death, my lovely Edward's death,
Their kingdom's loss, my woful banishment,
Could all but answer for that peevish brat?

Can curses pierce the clouds, and enter
heaven?—
Why, then give way, dull clouds, to my
quick curses!—
Though not by war, by surfeit die your
king,
As ours by murder, to make him a king!
Edward, thy son, that now is prince of
Wales,
For Edward, my son, that was prince of
Wales,
Die in his youth by like untimely violence!
Thyself a queen, for me that was a queen,
Outlive thy glory, like my wretched self!
Long may'st thou live to wail thy children's
loss;
And see another, as I see thee now,
Deck'd in thy rights, as thou art stall'd
in mine!
Long die thy happy days before thy death;
And, after many lengthen'd hours of grief,
Die neither mother, wife, nor England's
queen!—
Rivers, and Dorset, you were standers by,—
And so wast thou, lord Hastings,—when
my son
Was stabb'd with bloody daggers: God, I
pray him,
That none of you may live his natural age,
But by some unlook'd accident cut off!
GLO. Have done thy charm, thou hateful
wither'd hag!
Q. MAR. And leave out thee? stay, dog,
for thou shalt hear me.
If heaven have any grievous plague in store,
Exceeding those that I can wish upon thee,
O, let them keep it till thy sins be ripe,
And then hurl down their indignation
On thee, the troubler of the poor world's
peace!
The worm of conscience still be-gnaw thy
soul!
Thy friends suspect for traitors while thou
liv'st,
And take deep traitors for thy dearest
friends!
No sleep close up that deadly eye of thine,
Unless it be while some tormenting dream
Affrights thee with a hell of ugly devils!
Thou elvish-mark'd, abortive, rooting hog!
Thou that was seal'd in thy nativity
The slave of nature, and the son of hell!
Thou slander of thy mother's heavy womb!
Thou loathed issue of thy father's loins!
Thou rag of honour! thou detested—
GLO. Margaret.
Q. MAR.   Richard!
GLO.   Ha?
Q. MAR.   I call thee not.
GLO. I cry the mercy, then; for I did
think,

That thou hadst call'd me all these bitter
names.
Q. MAR. Why, so I did; but look'd for
no reply.
O, let me make the period to my curse.
GLO. 'Tis done by me, and ends in—
Margaret.
Q. ELIZ. Thus have you breath'd your
curse against yourself.
Q. MAR. Poor painted queen, vain flourish
of my fortune!
Why strew'st thou sugar on that bottled
spider,
Whose deadly web ensnareth thee about?
Fool, fool! thou whet'st a knife to kill
thyself.
The day will come, that thou shalt wish
for me
To help thee curse this pois'nous bunch-
back'd toad.
HAST. False-boding woman, end thy
frantic curse,
Lest to thy harm thou move our patience.
Q. MAR. Foul shame upon you! you have
all mov'd mine.
RIV. Were you well serv'd, you would be
taught your duty.
Q. MAR. To serve me well, you all should
do me duty,
Teach me to be your queen, and you my
subjects:
O, serve me well, and teach yourselves that
duty.
DOR. Dispute not with her, she is lunatic.
Q. MAR. Peace, master marquess! you are
malapert:
Your fire-new stamp of honour is scarce
current:
O, that your young nobility could judge
What 'twere to lose it, and be miserable!
They that stand high have many blasts to
shake them;
And if they fall, they dash themselves to
pieces.
GLO. Good counsel, marry:—learn it, learn
it, marquess.
DOR. It touches you, my lord, as much
as me.
GLO. Ay, and much more: but I was born
so high,
Our aiery buildeth in the cedar's top,
And dallies with the wind, and scorns the
sun.
Q. MAR. And turns the sun to shade;—
alas! alas!—
Witness my son, now in the shade of death;
Whose bright out-shining beams thy cloudy
wrath
Hath in eternal darkness folded up.
Your aiery buildeth in our aiery's nest:—
O God! that seest it, do not suffer it;

As it was won with blood, lost be it so!

BUCK. Peace, peace, for shame, if not
for charity.

Q. MAR. Urge neither charity nor shame
to me:
Uncharitably with me have you dealt,
And shamefully my hopes by you are
butcher'd.
My charity is outrage, life my shame,—
And in that shame still live my sorrow's
rage!

BUCK. Have done, have done.

Q. MAR. O princely Buckingham, I'll kiss
thy hand,
In sign of league and amity with thee:
Now fair befall thee, and thy noble house!
Thy garments are not spotted with our
blood,
Nor thou within the compass of my curse.

BUCK. Nor no one here; for curses never
pass
The lips of those that breathe them in
the air.

Q. MAR. I will not think but they ascend
the sky,
And there awake God's gentle-sleeping
peace.
O Buckingham, take heed of yonder dog!
Look, when he fawns, he bites; and when
he bites,
His venom tooth will rankle to the death:
Have not to do with him, beware of him;
Sin, death, and hell, have set their marks
on him,
And all their ministers attend on him.

GLO. What doth she say, my lord of
Buckingham?

BUCK. Nothing that I respect, my gracious
lord.

Q. MAR. What, dost thou scorn me for my
gentle counsel?
And soothe the devil that I warn thee
from?
O, but remember this another day,
When he shall split thy very heart with
sorrow,
And say, poor Margaret was a prophetess!—
Live each of you the subjects to his hate,
And he to yours, and all of you to God's!
                                        [*Exit.*

HAST. My hair doth stand on end to hear
her curses.

RIV. And so doth mine: I muse why she's
at liberty.

GLO. I cannot blame her: by God's holy
mother,
She hath had too much wrong; and I
repent
My part thereof, that I have done to her.

Q. ELIZ. I never did her any, to my
knowledge.

GLO. Yet you have all the vantage of her
wrong.
I was too hot to do somebody good,
That is too cold in thinking of it now.
Marry, as for Clarence, he is well repaid;
He is frank'd up to fatting for his pains;—
God pardon them that are the cause thereof!

RIV. A virtuous and a Christian-like conclusion,
To pray for them that have done scath
to us.

GLO. [*Aside.*] So do I ever, being well
advis'd;
For had I curs'd now, I had curs'd myself.
                    Enter CATESBY.

CATES. Madam, his majesty doth call for
you,—
And for your grace,—and you, my noble
lords.

Q. ELIZ. Catesby, I come.—Lords, will you
go with me?

RIV. We wait upon your grace.
            [*Exeunt all except* GLOSTER.

GLO. I do the wrong, and first begin to
brawl.
The secret mischiefs that I set abroach,
I lay unto the grievous charge of others.
Clarence,—whom I, indeed, have cast in
darkness,—
I do beweep to many simple gulls;
Namely, to Stanley, Hastings, Buckingham;
And tell them 'tis the queen and her allies,
That stir the king against the duke my
brother.
Now, they believe it; and withal whet me
To be reveng'd on Rivers, Vaughan, Grey:
But then I sigh; and, with a piece of
scripture,   [evil:
Tell them that God bids us do good for
And thus I clothe my naked villany
With odd old ends stol'n forth of holy writ;
And seem a saint, when most I play the
devil.—
But soft! here come my executioners.—
            Enter two Murderers.
How now, my hardy, stout resolved mates!
Are you now going to despatch this thing?

1 *MURD.* We are, my lord; and come to
have the warrant,
That we may be admitted where he is.

GLO. Well thought upon; I have it here
about me.   [*Gives the warrant.*
When you have done, repair to Crosby-
place.
But, Sirs, be sudden in the execution,
Withal obdurate; do not hear him plead;
For Clarence is well-spoken, and perhaps
May move your hearts to pity, if you mark
him.

1 *MURD.* Tut, tut, my lord, we will not
stand to prate;

Talkers are no good doers: be assur'd
We go to use our hands, and not our
    tongues.
GLO. Your eyes drop mill-stones, when
    fools' eyes fall tears:
I like you, lads;—about your business
    straight;
Go, go, despatch.
1 MURD.   We will, my noble lord.
                                  [Exeunt.

               ————

Scene IV.—London. *A Room in the* Tower.
    Enter Clarence *and* Brakenbury.

BRAK. Why looks your grace so heavily
    to-day?
CLAR. O, I have pass'd a miserable night,
So full of fearful dreams, of ugly sights,
That, as I am a Christian faithful man,
I would not spend another such a night,
Though 'twere to buy a world of happy
    days,—
So full of dismal terror was the time!
BRAK. What was your dream, my lord? I
    pray you, tell me.
CLAR. Methought that I had broken from
    the Tower,
And was embark'd to cross to Burgundy;
And, in my company, my brother Gloster;
Who from my cabin tempted me to walk
Upon the hatches: thence we look'd toward
    England,
And cited up a thousand heavy times,
During the wars of York and Lancaster,
That had befall'n us. As we pac'd along
Upon the giddy footing of the hatches,
Methought that Gloster stumbled; and, in
    falling,   [board,
Struck me, that thought to stay him, over-
Into the tumbling billows of the main.
O Lord! methought what pain it was to
    drown!
What dreadful noise of water in mine ears!
What sights of ugly death within mine
    eyes!
Methought I saw a thousand fearful wrecks;
A thousand men that fishes gnaw'd upon;
Wedges of gold, great anchors, heaps of
    pearl,
Inestimable stones, unvalued jewels,
All scatter'd in the bottom of the sea:
Some lay in dead men's skulls; and in
    those holes
Where eyes did once inhabit, there were
    crept
(As 'twere in scorn of eyes) reflecting
    gems,
That woo'd the slimy bottom of the deep,
And mock'd the dead bones that lay scat-
    ter'd by.

BRAK. Had you such leisure in the time
    of death,
To gaze upon these secrets of the deep?
CLAR. Methought I had; and often did I
    strive
To yield the ghost: but still the envious
    flood
Stopt in my soul, and would not let it forth
To find the empty, vast, and wandering
    air;
But smother'd it within my panting bulk,
Which almost burst to belch it in the sea.
BRAK. Awak'd you not with this sore
    agony?
CLAR. No, no, my dream was lengthen'd
    after life;
O, then began the tempest to my soul!
I pass'd, methought, the melancholy flood,
With that grim ferryman which poets write,
Unto the kingdom of perpetual night. [of
The first that there did greet my strange
    soul,   [wick:
Was my great father-in-law, renowned War
Who cried aloud, "What scourge for per
    jury   [Clarence?"
Can this dark monarchy afford false
And so he vanish'd: then came wandering
    by
A shadow like an angel, with bright hair
Dabbled in blood; and he shriek'd out
    aloud,
"Clarence is come,—false, fleeting, perjur'd
    Clarence,—
That stabb'd me in the field by Tewks
    bury;—
Seize on him, Furies! take him to your
    torments!"
With that, methought, a legion of foul
    fiends
Environ'd me, and howled in mine ears
Such hideous cries, that, with the very
    noise,
I trembling wak'd, and, for a season after
Could not believe but that I was in hell,—
Such terrible impression made my dream
BRAK. No marvel, lord, though it af
    frighted you;
I am afraid, methinks, to hear you tell it
CLAR. O Brakenbury, I have done these
    things,
That now give evidence against my soul,
For Edward's sake; and see how he requites
    me!—
O God! if my deep prayers cannot appease
    thee,
But thou wilt be aveng'd on my misdeeds
Yet execute thy wrath on me alone:
O, spare my guiltless wife and my poor
    children!—
I pray thee, gentle keeper, stay by me;
My soul is heavy, and I fain would sleep

BRAK. I will, my lord: God give your grace good rest.— CLARENCE *sleeps.*

Sorrow breaks seasons and reposing hours,
Makes the night morning, and the noon-tide night.
Princes have but their titles for their glories,
An outward honour for an inward toil;
And, for unfelt imaginations,
They often feel a world of restless cares:
So that, between their titles, and low name,
There's nothing differs but the outward fame.

Enter the two Murderers.

MURD. Ho! who's here?

BRAK. What would'st thou, fellow? and how cam'st thou hither?

MURD. I would speak with Clarence, and I came hither on my legs.

BRAK. What, so brief?

MURD. 'Tis better, Sir, than to be tedious.— Let him see our commission; and talk no more.

[*A paper is delivered to* BRAKENBURY, *who reads it.*

BRAK. I am, in this, commanded to deliver The noble duke of Clarence to your hands:— I will not reason what is meant hereby, Because I will be guiltless of the meaning. There lies the duke asleep,—and there the I'll to the king; and signify to him [keys: That thus I have resign'd to you my charge.

MURD. You may, Sir; 'tis a point of wisdom: Fare you well. [*Exit* BRAKENBURY.

MURD. What, shall we stab him as he sleeps?

MURD. No; he'll say 'twas done cowardly, when he wakes.

MURD. When he wakes! why, fool, he shall never wake until the great judgment-day.

MURD. Why, then he'll say, we stabb'd him sleeping.

MURD. The urging of that word, "judgment," hath bred a kind of remorse in me.

MURD. What, art thou afraid?

MURD. Not to kill him, having a warrant for it; but to be damn'd for killing him, from the which no warrant can defend me.

MURD. I thought thou hadst been resolute.

MURD. So I am, to let him live.

MURD. I'll back to the duke of Gloster, and tell him so.

MURD. Nay, I pr'ythee, stay a little: I hope my holy humour will change; it was wont to hold me but while one tells twenty.

MURD. How dost thou feel thyself now?

2 MURD. 'Faith, some certain dregs of conscience are yet within me.

1 MURD. Remember our reward, when the deed's done.

2 MURD. Zounds! he dies: I had forgot the reward.

1 MURD. Where's thy conscience now?

2 MURD. In the duke of Gloster's purse.

1 MURD. So, when he opens his purse to give us our reward, thy conscience flies out.

2 MURD. 'Tis no matter; let it go; there's few or none, will entertain it.

1 MURD. What if it come to thee again?

2 MURD. I'll not meddle with it,—it is a dangerous thing, it makes a man a coward: a man cannot steal, but it accuseth him; a man cannot swear, but it checks him; a man cannot lie with his neighbour's wife, but it detects him: 'tis a blushing shamefaced spirit, that mutinies in a man's bosom; it fills one full of obstacles: it made me once restore a purse of gold, that by chance I found; it beggars any man that keeps it: it is turned out of all towns and cities for a dangerous thing; and every man, that means to live well, endeavours to trust to himself, and live without it.

1 MURD. Zounds! it is even now at my elbow, persuading me not to kill the duke.

2 MURD. Take the devil in thy mind, and believe him not: he would insinuate with thee, but to make thee sigh.

1 MURD. I am strong-fram'd, he cannot prevail with me.

2 MURD. Spoke like a tall fellow that respects his reputation. Come, shall we fall to work?

1 MURD. Take him on the costard with the hilts of thy sword, and then throw him into the malmsey-butt in the next room.

2 MURD. O, excellent device! and make a sop of him.

1 MURD. Soft! he wakes.

2 MURD. Strike!

1 MURD. No, we'll reason with him.

CLAR. [*Waking.*] Where art thou, keeper? give me a cup of wine.

1 MURD. You shall have wine enough, my lord, anon.

CLAR. In God's name, what art thou?

1 MURD. A man, as you are.

CLAR. But not, as I am, royal.

1 MURD. Nor you, as we are, loyal.

CLAR. Thy voice is thunder, but thy looks are humble.

1 MURD. My voice is now the king's, my looks mine own.

CLAR. How darkly, and how deadly dost thou speak!

You eyes do menace me: why look you
pale?   [come?
Who sent you hither? Wherefore do you
BOTH MURD. To, to, to—
CLAR. To murder me?
BOTH MURD. Ay, ay.
CLAR. You scarcely have the hearts to
tell me so,
And therefore cannot have the hearts to do it.
Wherein, my friends, have I offended you?
1 MURD. Offended us you have not, but
the king.
CLAR. I shall be reconcil'd to him again.
2 MURD. Never, my lord; therefore pre-
pare to die.
CLAR. Are you drawn forth among a world
of men
To slay the innocent? What is my offence?
Where is the evidence that doth accuse me?
What lawful quest have given their verdict
up   [nounc'd
Unto the frowning judge? or who pro-
The bitter sentence of poor Clarence's
death?
Before I be convict by course of law,
To threaten me with death is most unlawful.
I charge you, as you hope to have redemp-
tion   [ous sins,
By Christ's dear blood shed for our griev-
That you depart, and lay no hands on me:
The deed you undertake is damnable.
1 MURD. What we will do, we do upon
command.
2 MURD. And he, that hath commanded,
is our king.
CLAR. Erroneous vassals! the great King
of kings
Hath in the table of his law commanded,
That thou shalt do no murder: will you,
then,
Spurn at his edict, and fulfil a man's?
Take heed; for he holds vengeance in his
hand,
To hurl upon their heads that break his law.
2 MURD. And that same vengeance doth
he hurl on thee,
For false forswearing, and for murder too:
Thou didst receive the sacrament, to fight
In quarrel of the house of Lancaster.
1 MURD. And, like a traitor to the name
of God,
Didst break that vow; and, with thy treacherous blade,
Unripp'dst the bowels of thy sovereign's
son.
2 MURD. Whom thou wast sworn to cherish and defend.
1 MURD. How canst thou urge God's
dreadful law to us,
When thou hast broke it in such dear
degree?

CLAR. Alas, for whose sake did I that ill
deed?
For Edward, for my brother, for his sake:
He sends you not to murder me for this;
For in that sin he is as deep as I.
If God will be avenged for the deed,
O, know you yet, he doth it publicly:
Take not the quarrel from his powerful
arm;
He needs no indirect or lawless course,
To cut off those that have offended him.
1 MURD. Who made thee, then, a bloody
minister,
When gallant-springing brave Plantagenet,
That princely novice, was struck dead by
thee?
CLAR. My brother's love, the devil, and
my rage.
1 MURD. Thy brother's love, our duty,
and thy faults,
Provoke us hither now to slaughter thee.
CLAR. If you do love my brother, hate
not me;
I am his brother, and I love him well.
If you are hir'd for meed, go back again,
And I will send you to my brother Gloster:
Who shall reward you better for my life
Than Edward will for tidings of my death.
2 MURD. You are deceiv'd, your brother
Gloster hates you.
CLAR. O, no, he loves me, and he holds
Go you to him from me.   [me dear
BOTH MURD.   Ay, so we will.
CLAR. Tell him, when that our princely
father York
Bless'd his three sons with his victorious
arm   [other
And charg'd us from his soul to love each
He little thought of this divided friendship:
Bid Gloster think on this, and he will weep.
1 MURD. Ay, mill-stones; as he lesson'd
us to weep.   [kind
CLAR. O, do not slander him, for he is
1 MURD. Right; as snow in harvest.—
Come, you deceive yourself:
'Tis he that sends us to destroy you here.
CLAR. It cannot be; for he bewept my
fortune,   [sobs
And hugg'd me in his arms, and swore, with
That he would labour my delivery.
1 MURD. Why, so he doth, when he de-
livers you   [heaven
From this earth's thraldom to the joys of
2 MURD. Make peace with God, for you
must die, my lord.
CLAR. Have you that holy feeling in your
souls,
To counsel me to make my peace with God,
And are you yet to your own souls so blind,
That you will war with God by murdering
me?—

O, Sirs, consider, they that set you on
To do this deed, will hate you for the deed.
2 MURD. What shall we do?
CLAR. 　　　　Relent, and save your souls.
1 MURD. Relent! 'tis cowardly, and wom-
anish. 　　　　　　　　　　[devilish.—
CLAR. Not to relent, is beastly, savage,
Which of you, if you were a prince's son,
Being pent from liberty, as I am now,—
If two such murderers as yourselves came
to you,—
Would not entreat for life?—
My friend, I spy some pity in thy looks;
O, if thine eye be not a flatterer,
Come thou on my side, and entreat for me,
As you would beg, were you in my distress:
A begging prince what beggar pities not?
2 MURD. Look behind you, my lord.
1 MURD. [*Stabs him.*] Take that, and
that: if all this will not do,
I'll drown you in the malmsey-butt within.
　　　　　　　　　[*Exit, with the body.*
2 MURD. A bloody deed, and desperately
despatch'd!
How fain, like Pilate, would I wash my
hands
Of this most grievous guilty murder done!
Re-enter first Murderer.
1 MURD. How now! what mean'st thou,
that thou help'st me not?
By heaven, the duke shall know how slack
you have been.
2 MURD. I would he know that I had
sav'd his brother!
Take thou the fee, and tell him what I say;
For I repent me that the duke is slain.
　　　　　　　　　　　　　　[*Exit.*
1 MURD. So do not I: go, coward as thou
art.—
Well, I'll go hide the body in some hole,
Till that the duke give order for his burial:
And when I have my meed, I will away;
For this will out, and then I must not stay.
　　　　　　　　　　　　　　[*Exit.*

ACT II.

SCENE I.—LONDON. *A Room in the Palace.*

Enter KING EDWARD, *(led in sick.)* QUEEN
ELIZABETH, DORSET, RIVERS, HASTINGS,
BUCKINGHAM, GREY, *and others.*

K. EDW. Why, so;—now have I done a
good day's work:—
You peers, continue this united league:
I every day expect an embassage
From my Redeemer to redeem me hence;
And more in peace my soul shall part to
heaven, 　　　　　　　　　　[earth.
Since I have made my friends at peace on
Rivers and Hastings, take each other's hand;

Dissemble not your hatred, swear your love.
RIV. By heaven, my soul is purg'd from
grudging hate;
And with my hand I seal my true heart's
love.
HAST. So thrive I, as I truly swear the
like!
K. EDW. Take heed, you dally not before
your king;
Lest he, that is the supreme King of kings,
Confound your hidden falsehood, and award
Either of you to be the other's end.
HAST. So prosper I, as I swear perfect
love! 　　　　　　　　　　　[heart!
RIV. And I, as I love Hastings with my
K. EDW. Madam, yourself are not exempt
from this,—
Nor you, son Dorset,—Buckingham, nor
you;—
You have been factious one against the
other. 　　　　　　　　　　　[hand;
Wife, love lord Hastings, let him kiss your
And what you do, do it unfeignedly.
Q. ELIZ. There, Hastings; I will never
more remember
Our former hatred, so thrive I and mine!
K. EDW. Dorset, embrace him;—Hastings,
love lord marquess.
DOR. This interchange of love, I here pro-
Upon my part shall be inviolable. 　[test,
HAST. And so swear I. [*Embraces* DORSET.
K. EDW. Now, princely Buckingham, seal
thou this league
With thy embracements to my wife's allies,
And make me happy in your unity.
BUCK. [*To the* QUEEN.] Whenever Buck-
ingham doth turn his hate
Upon your grace, but with all duteous love
Doth cherish you and yours, God punish me
With hate in those where I expect most
love! 　　　　　　　　　　　[friend,
When I have most need to employ a
And most assured that he is a friend,
Deep, hollow, treacherous, and full of guile,
Be he unto me!—This do I beg of heaven,
When I am cold in love to you or yours.
　　　　　　　　　　[*Embracing* RIVERS, &c.
K. EDW. A pleasing cordial, princely
Buckingham,
Is this thy vow unto my sickly heart.
There wanteth now our brother Gloster
here.
To make the blessed period of this peace.
BUCK. And, in good time, here comes the
noble duke.

Enter GLOSTER

GLO. God-morrow to my sovereign king
and queen;
And, princely peers, a happy time of day!
K. EDW. Happy, indeed, as we have spent
the day.—

Gloster, we have done deeds of charity;
Made peace of enmity, fair love of hate,
Between these swelling wrong-incensed
   peers.   [lord.—
GLO. A blessed labour, my most sovereign
Among this princely heap, if any here,
By false intelligence, or wrong surmise.
Hold me a foe;
If I unwittingly, or in my rage,
Have aught committed that is hardly borne
By any in this presence, I desire
To reconcile me to his friendly peace:
'Tis death to me to be at enmity;
I hate it, and desire all good men's love.—
First, Madam, I entreat true peace of you,
Which I will purchase with my duteous
   service;—
Of you, my noble cousin Buckingham,
If ever any grudge were lodg'd between
   us;—   [set,
Of you, and you, lord Rivers, and of Dor-
That all without desert have frown'd on
   me;   [of you;—
Of you, lord Woodville, and lord Scales,
Dukes, earls, lords, gentlemen;—indeed, of
I do not know that Englishman alive, [all.
With whom my soul is any jot at odds,
More than the infant that is born to-night:
I thank my God for my humility.
Q. ELIZ. A holiday shall this be kept
   hereafter:—
I would to God all strifes were well com-
   pounded.—
My sovereign lord, I do beseech your high-
   ness
To take our brother Clarence to your grace.
GLO. Why, Madam, have I offer'd love for
   this,
To be so flouted in this royal presence?
Who knows not that the gentle duke is
   dead?   [*They all start.*
You do him injury to scorn his corse.
K. EDW. Who knows not he is dead! who
   knows he is?
Q. ELIZ. All-seeing heaven, what a world
   is this!
BUCK. Look I so pale, lord Dorset, as the
   rest?
DOR. Ay, my good lord; and no man in
   the presence
But his red colour hath forsook his cheeks.
K. EDW. Is Clarence dead? the order was
   revers'd.
GLO. But he, poor man, by your first order
   died,
And that a winged Mercury did bear;
Some tardy cripple bore the countermand,
That came too lag to see him buried.
God grant that some, less noble and less
   loyal,   [blood,
Nearer in bloody thoughts, and not in

Deserve not worse than wretched Clarence
And yet go current from suspicion. [did,
       Enter STANLEY.
STAN. [*Kneeling.*] A boon, my sovereign,
   for my service done!
K. EDW. I pr'ythee, peace: my soul is full
   of sorrow.
STAN. I will not rise, unless your high-
   ness hear me.
K. EDW. Then say at once, what is it thou
   request'st.
STAN. The forfeit, sovereign, of my ser-
   vant's life;
Who slew to-day a riotous gentleman,
Lately attendant on the duke of Norfolk.
K. EDW. Have I a tongue to doom my
   brother's death,
And shall that tongue give pardon to a
   slave?   [thought;
My brother kill'd no man,—his fault was
And yet his punishment was bitter death.
Who sued to me for him? who, in my
   wrath,
Kneel'd at my feet, and bade me be advis'd?
Who spoke of brotherhood? who spoke of
   love?
Who told me how the poor soul did forsake
The mighty Warwick, and did fight for me?
Who told me, in the field at Tewksbury,
When Oxford had me down, he rescu'd me,
And said, "Dear brother, live, and be a
   king?"
Who told me, when we both lay in the field,
Frozen almost to death, how he did lap me
Even in his garments, and did give himself,
All thin and naked, to the numb-cold night?
All this from my remembrance brutish wrath
Sinfully pluck'd, and not a man of you
Had so much grace to put it in my mind.
But when your carters, or your waiting-
   vassals,
Have done a drunken slaughter, and defac'd
The precious image of our dear Redeemer,
You straight are on your knees for pardon,
   pardon;
And I, unjustly too, must grant it you:—
But for my brother not a man would
   speak,—
Nor I, ungracious, speak unto myself
For him, poor soul. The proudest of you all
Have been beholden to him in his life;
Yet none of you would once beg for his
   life.
O God, I fear, thy justice will take hold
On me, and you, and mine, and yours, for
   this!—
Come, Hastings, help me to my closet.—
Ah, poor Clarence!
[*Exeunt* KING, QUEEN, HASTINGS, RIVERS,
     DORSET *and* GREY.

GLO. This is the fruit of rashness.—Mark'd
  you not,
How that the guilty kindred of the queen
Look'd pale, when they did hear of Clar-
  ence's death?
O! they did urge it still unto the king:
God will revenge it. Come, lords; will you
  go,
To comfort Edward with our company?
BUCK. We wait upon your grace.
                         [*Exeunt.*

SCENE II.—*Another Room in the Palace.*

Enter the DUCHESS OF YORK, *with a* Son
    and Daughter *of* CLARENCE.

SON. Good grandam, tell us, is our father
  dead?
DUCH. No, boy.
DAUGH. Why do you weep so oft, and
  beat your breast,
And cry—"O Clarence, my unhappy son!"
SON. Why do you look on us, and shake
  your head,
And call us—orphans, wretches, cast-aways,
If that our noble father be alive?
DUCH. My pretty cousins, you mistake me
  both,
I do lament the sickness of the king,
As loath to lose him, not your father's
  death;
It were lost sorrow to wail one that's lost.
SON. Then you conclude, my grandam,
  he is dead.
The king mine uncle is to blame for this:
God will revenge it; whom I will importune
With earnest prayers all to that effect.
DAUGH. And so will I.
DUCH. Peace, children, peace! the king
  doth love you well:
Incapable and shallow innocents,
You cannot guess who caus'd your father's
  death.
SON. Grandam, we can; for my good
  uncle Gloster
Told me, the king, provok'd to it by the
  queen,
Devis'd impeachments to imprison him:
And when my uncle told me so, he wept,
And pitied me, and kindly kiss'd my cheek;
Bade me rely on him, as on my father,
And he would love me dearly as his child.
DUCH. Ah, that deceit should steal such
  gentle shape,
And with a virtuous visor hide deep vice!
He is my son; ay, and therein my shame;
Yet from my dugs he drew not this deceit.
SON. Think you my uncle did dissemble,
  grandam?
DUCH. Ay, boy.
SON. I cannot think it.—Hark! what noise
  is this?

Enter QUEEN ELIZABETH, *distractedly;*
    RIVERS *and* DORSET *following her.*

Q. ELIZ. Ah, who shall hinder me to wail
  and weep,
To chide my fortune, and torment myself?
I'll join with black despair against my soul,
And to myself become an enemy.
DUCH. What means this scene of rude
  impatience?
Q. ELIZ. To make an act of tragic vio-
  lence,—
Edward, my lord, thy son, our king, is dead.
Why grow the branches when the root is
  gone?   [sap?
Why wither not the leaves that want their
If you will live, lament; if die, be brief,
That our swift-winged souls may catch the
  king's;
Or, like obedient subjects, follow him
To his new kingdom of ne'er changing
  night.   [sorrow,
DUCH. Ah, so much interest have I in thy
As I had title in thy noble husband!
I have bewept a worthy husband's death,
And liv'd with looking on his images:
But now two mirrors of his princely sem-
  blance
Are crack'd in pieces by malignant death,
And I for comfort have but one false glass,
That grieves me when I see my shame in
  him.
Thou art a widow; yet thou art a mother,
And hast the comfort of thy children left:
But death hath snatch'd my husband from
  mine arms,   [hands,—
And pluck'd two crutches from my feeble
Clarence and Edward. O, what cause have
(Thine being but a moiety of my moan) [I,
To over-go thy woes, and drown thy cries!
SON. Ah, aunt, you wept not for our
  father's death!
How can we aid you with our kindred
  tears?   [unmoan'd;
DAUGH. Our fatherless distress was left
Your widow-dolour likewise be unwept!
Q. ELIZ. Give me no help in lamentation;
I am not barren to bring forth complaints:
All springs reduce their currents to mine
  eyes,
That I, being govern'd by the watry moon,
May send forth plenteous tears to drown
  the world!   [ward!
Ah, for my husband, for my dear lord, Ed-
CHIL. Ah, for our father, for our dear
  lord Clarence!
DUCH. Alas, for both, both mine, Edward
  and Clarence!
Q. ELIZ. What stay had I but Edward?
  and he's gone.
CHIL. What stay had we but Clarence?
  and he's gone.

DUCH. What stays had I but they? and they are gone.

Q. ELIZ. Was never widow had so dear a loss!

CHIL. Were never orphans had so dear a loss!   [loss!

DUCH. Was never mother had so dear a Alas, I am the mother of these griefs! Their woes are parcell'd, mine are general. She for an Edward weeps, and so do I; I for a Clarence weep, so doth not she: These babes for Clarence weep, and so do I; I for an Edward weep, so do not they:— Alas, you three, on me, threefold distress'd, Pour all your tears! I am your sorrow's nurse, And I will pamper it with lamentation.

DOR. Comfort, dear mother: God is much displeas'd That you take with unthankfulness his doing: [grateful, In common worldly things, 'tis called un- With dull unwillingness to repay a debt, Which with a bounteous hand was kindly lent; Much more to be thus opposite with heaven, For it requires the royal debt it lent you.

RIV. Madam, bethink you, like a careful mother,   [for him; Of the young prince your son: send straight Let him be crown'd; in him your comfort lives: [grave, Drown desperate sorrow in dead Edward's And plant your joys in living Edward's throne.

Enter GLOSTER, BUCKINGHAM, STANLEY, HASTINGS, RATCLIFF, *and others.*

GLO. Sister, have comfort: all of us have cause To wail the dimming of our shining star; But none can cure their harms by wailing them.— Madam, my mother, I do cry you mercy; I did not see vour grace:—humbly on my I crave your blessing.   [knee

DUCH. God bless thee; and put meekness in thy breast, Love, charity, obedience, and true duty!

GLO. Amen; and make me die a good old man!— [*Aside.*] That is the butt-end of a mother's blessing; I marvel that her grace did leave it out.

BUCK. You cloudy princes, and heart-sor- rowing peers, That bear this heavy mutual load of moan, Now cheer each other in each other's love: Though we have spent our harvest of this king, We are to reap the harvest of his son.

The broken rancour of your high-swoln hearts,   [gether, But lately splinter'd, knit, and join'd to- Must gently be preserv'd, cherish'd, and kept: [train, Me seemeth good, that, with some little Forthwith from Ludlow the young prince be fet Hither to London, to be crown'd our king.

RIV. Why with some little train, my lord of Buckingham?

BUCK. Marry, my lord, lest, by a multi- tude,   [break out; The new-heal'd wound of malice should Which would be so much the more dan- gerous,   [ungovern'd; By how much the estate is green and yet Where every horse bears his commanding rein, And may direct his course as please himself, As well the fear of harm, as harm apparent, In my opinion, ought to be prevented.

GLO. I hope the king made peace with all of us; And the compact is firm and true in me.

RIV. And so in me; and so, I think, in all: Yet, since it is but green, it should be put To no apparent likelihood of breach, Which haply by much company might be urg'd: Therefore I say with noble Buckingham, That it is meet so few should fetch the prince.

HAST. And so say I.

GLO. Then be it so; and go we to deter- mine   [to Ludlow. Who they shall be that straight shall post Madam,—and you my mother,—will you go To give your censures in this business?

[*Exeunt all except* BUCKINGHAM *and* GLOSTER.

BUCK. My lord, whoever journey to the prince, For God's sake, let not us two stay at home; For, by the way, I'll sort occasion, As index to the story we late talk'd of, To part the queen's proud kindred from the prince.   [tory.

GLO My other self, my counsel's consis- My oracle, my prophet!—My dear cousin, I, as a child, will go by thy direction. Towards Ludlow then, for we'll not stay behind.   [*Exeunt.*

SCENE III.—LONDON. *A Street.*

Enter two Citizens, *meeting.*

1 *CIT.* Good morrow, neighbour: whither away so fast?

2 *CIT.* I promise you, I scarcely know my- Hear you the news abroad?   [self:

1 *CIT.*   Yes,—that the king is dead.
2 *CIT.* Ill news, by'r lady; seldom comes
the better:
I fear, I fear, 'twill prove a giddy world.
Enter a third Citizen.
3 *CIT.* Neighbours, God speed!
1 *CIT.*   Give you good morrow, Sir.
3 *CIT.* Doth the news hold of good king
Edward's death?
2 *CIT.* Ay, Sir, it is too true; God help,
the while!
3 *CIT.* Then, masters, look to see a trou-
blous world.
1 *CIT.* No, no; by God's good grace, his
son shall reign.
3 *CIT.* Woe to that land that's govern'd
by a child!
2 *CIT.* In him there is a hope of government;
That, in his nonage, council under him,
And, in his full and ripen'd years, himself,
No doubt, shall then, and till then, govern
well.   [Sixth
1 *CIT.* So stood the state, when Henry the
Was crown'd in Paris but at nine months
old.
3 *CIT.* Stood the state so? no, no, good
God wot;   [friends,
For then this land was famously enrich'd
With politic grave counsel; then the king
Had virtuous uncles to protect his grace.
1 *CIT.* Why, so hath this, both by his
father and mother.
3 *CIT.* Better it were they all came by his
father,
Or by his father there were none at all;
For emulation now, who shall be nearest,
Will touch us all too near, if God prevent
not.
O! full of danger is the duke of Gloster!
And the queen's sons and brothers haught
and proud:
And were they to be rul'd, and not to rule,
This sickly land might solace as before.
1 *CIT.* Come, come, we fear the worst; all
will be well.
3 *CIT.* When clouds are seen, wise men
put on their cloaks;
When great leaves fall, then winter is at
hand;   [night?
When the sun sets, who doth not look for
Untimely storms make men expect a dearth.
All may be well; but, if God sort it so,
'Tis more than we deserve, or I expect.
2 *CIT.* Truly, the hearts of men are full of
fear:
You cannot reason almost with a man
That looks not heavily, and full of dread.
3 *CIT.* Before the days of change, still is
it so:

By a divine instinct men's minds mistrust
Ensuing danger; as, by proof, we see
The water swell before a boisterous storm.
But leave it all to God.—Whither away?
2 *CIT.* Marry, we were sent for to the
justices.
3 *CIT.* And so was I: I'll bear you company.   [*Exeunt.*

———

SCENE IV.—LONDON. *A Room in the
Palace.*

Enter the ARCHBISHOP OF YORK, *the young*
DUKE OF YORK, QUEEN ELIZABETH, *and
the* DUCHESS OF YORK.

ARCH. Last night, I hear, they lay at
Northampton;
At Stony-Stratford will they be to-night:
To-morrow, or next day, they will be here.
DUCH. I long with all my heart to see the
prince: [him.
I hope he is much grown since last I saw
Q. ELIZ. But I hear, no; they say my son
of York
Hath almost overta'en him in his growth.
YORK. Ay, mother, but I would not have
it so.
DUCH. Why, my young cousin? it is good
to grow.
YORK. Grandam, one night, as we did sit
at supper,
My uncle Rivers talk'd how I did grow
More than my brother: "Ay," quoth my
uncle Gloster,
Small herbs have grace, great weeds do
grow apace:"
And since, methinks, I would not grow so
fast,
Because sweet flowers are slow, and weeds
make haste.
DUCH. 'Good faith, 'good faith, the say-
ing did not hold
In him that did object the same to thee:
He was the wretched'st thing when he was
young,
So long a growing, and so leisurely,
That, if his rule were true, he should be
gracious.
ARCH. And so, no doubt he is, my gra-
cious Madam.
DUCH. I hope he is; but yet let mothers
doubt.
YORK. Now, by my troth, if I had been
remember'd,
I could have given my uncle's grace a flout,
To touch his growth nearer than he touch'd
mine.
DUCH. How, my young York? I pr'ythee,
let me hear it.
YORK. Marry, they say my uncle grew so
fast,

That he could gnaw a crust at two hours
    old:
'Twas full two years ere I could get a tooth.
Grandam, this would have been a biting
    jest.
DUCH. I pr'ythee, pretty York, who told
YORK. Grandam, his nurse. [thee this?
DUCH. His nurse! why, she was dead ere
    thou wast born.
YORK. If 'twere not she, I cannot tell
    who told me.
Q. ELIZ. A parious boy:—go to, you are
    too shrewd.
ARCH. Good Madam, be not angry with
    the child.
Q. ELIZ. Pitchers have ears.
ARCH. Here comes a messenger.—
            Enter a Messenger.
                        What news?
MESS. Such news, my lord, as grieves me
    to report.
Q. ELIZ. How doth the prince?
MESS.   Well, Madam, and in health.
DUCH. What is thy news?   [to Pomfret,
MESS. Lord Rivers and lord Grey are sent
With them Sir Thomas Vaughan, prisoners.
DUCH. Who hath committed them?
MESS.   The mighty dukes,
Gloster and Buckingham.
Q. ELIZ.   For what offence?
MESS. The sum of all I can, I have dis-
    clos'd;   [ted,
Why or for what the nobles were commit-
Is all unknown to me, my gracious lady.
Q. ELIZ. Ah me, I see the ruin of my
    house!
The tiger now hath seiz'd the gentle hind;
Insulting tyranny begins to jut
Upon the innocent and awless throne:
Welcome, destruction, blood, and massacre!
I see, as in a map, the end of all.
DUCH. Accursed and unquiet wrangling
    days,
How many of you have mine eyes beheld!
My husband lost his life to get the crown;
And often up and down my sons were tost,
For me to joy, and weep, their gain and
    loss:
And being seated, and domestic broils
Clean over-blown, themselves, the con-
    querors,
Make war upon themselves; brother to
    brother,   [posterous
Blood to blood, self again self:—O, pre-
And frantic outrage, end thy damned
    spleen;
Or let me die, to look on death no more!
Q. ELIZ. Come, come, my boy; we will
Madam, farewell.   [to sanctuary.—
DUCH.   Stay, I will go with you.
Q. ELIZ. You have no cause.

ARCH. [To the QUEEN.] My gracious lady,
    go: [goods.
And thither bear your treasure and your
For my part, I'll resign unto your grace
The seal I keep: and so betide to me,
As well I tender you, and all of yours!
Come, I'll conduct you to the sanctuary.
                        [Exeunt.

ACT III.

SCENE I.—LONDON. A Street.

*The trumpets sound. Enter the PRINCE OF
    WALES, GLOSTER, BUCKINGHAM, CATES-
    BY, CARDINAL BOUCHIER, and others.*

BUCK. Welcome, sweet prince, to Lon-
    don, to your chamber.
GLO. Welcome, dear cousin, my thoughts'
    sovereign:
The weary way hath made you melancholy.
PRINCE. No, uncle; but our crosses on
    the way
Have made it tedious, wearisome, and
    heavy:
I want more uncles here to welcome me.
GLO. Sweet prince, the untainted virtue
    of your years
Hath not yet div'd into the world's deceit:
No more can you distinguish of a man,
Than of his outward show; which, God he
    knows,
Seldom or never jumpeth with the heart.
Those uncles which you want were dan-
    gerous;
Your grace attended to their sugar'd words,
But look'd not on the poison of their
    hearts:
God keep you from them, and from such
    false friends!
PRINCE. God keep me from false friends!
    but they were none.
GLO. My lord, the mayor of London comes
    to greet you.
        Enter the Lord Mayor, and his train.
MAY. God bless your grace with health
    and happy days!
PRINCE. I thank you, good my lord;—
    and thank you all.—
                    [Exeunt Mayor, &c.
I thought my mother, and my brother York,
Would long ere this have met us on the
    way: [not
Fie, what a slug is Hastings, that he comes
To tell us whether they will come or no!
BUCK. And in good time here comes the
    sweating lord.
                Enter HASTINGS.
PRINCE. Welcome, my lord: what, will
    our mother come?

HAST. On what occasion, God he knows, not I, [York,
The queen your mother, and your brother
Have taken sanctuary: the tender prince
Would fain have come with me to meet your grace,
But by his mother was perforce withheld.
BUCK. Fie, what an indirect and peevish course [grace
Is this of hers!—Lord cardinal, will your
Persuade the queen to send the duke of York
Unto his princely brother presently?
If she deny,—lord Hastings, go with him,
And from her jealous arms pluck him perforce.
CARD. My lord of Buckingham, if my weak oratory
Can from his mother win the duke of York,
Anon expect him here; but if she be obdurate
To mild entreaties, God in heaven forbid
We should infringe the holy privilege
Of blessed sanctuary! not for all this land
Would I be guilty of so great a sin.
BUCK. You are too senseless-obstinate, my [lord,
Too ceremonious and traditional:
Weigh it but with the grossness of this age,
You break not sanctuary in seizing him.
The benefit thereof is always granted
To those whose dealings have deserv'd the place, [place:
And those who have the wit to claim the
This prince hath neither claim'd it, nor deserv'd it;
And therefore, in mine opinion, cannot have it:
Then, taking him from thence that is not there,
You break no privilege nor charter there.
Oft have I heard of sanctuary men;
But sanctuary children, ne'er till now.
CARD. My lord, you shall o'er-rule my mind for once.—
Come on, lord Hastings, will you go with
HAST. I go, my lord.   [me?
PRINCE. Good lords, make all the speedy haste you may.—
      [*Exeunt* CARDINAL *and* HASTINGS.
Say, uncle Gloster, if our brother come,
Where shall we sojourn till our coronation?
GLO. Where it seems best unto your royal self.
If I may counsel you, some day or two
Your highness shall repose you at the Tower: [most fit
Then where you please, and shall be thought
For your best health and recreation.
PRINCE. I do not like the Tower, of any place.—

Did Julius Cæsar build that place, my lord?   [that place;
BUCK. He did, my gracious lord, begin
Which, since, succeeding ages have re-edified.
PRINCE. Is it upon record, or else reported
Successively from age to age, he built it?
BUCK. Upon record, my gracious lord.
PRINCE. But say, my lord, it were not register'd,
Methinks the truth should live from age to
As 'twere retail'd to all posterity,   [age,
Even to the general all-ending day.
GLO. [*Aside.*] So wise so young, they say, do never live long.
PRINCE. What say you, uncle?
GLO. I say, without characters fame lives long.—   [iquity,
[*Aside.*] Thus, like the formal Vice, In-
I moralize two meanings in one word.
PRINCE. That Julius Cæsar was a famous man;
With what his valour did enrich his wit,
His wit set down to make his valour live:
Death makes no conquest of this conqueror;
For now he lives in fame, though not in life.—
I'll tell you what, my cousin Buckingham,—
BUCK. What, my gracious lord?
PRINCE. An if I live until I be a man,
I'll win our ancient right in France again,
Or die a soldier, as I liv'd a king.
GLO. [*Aside.*] Short summers lightly have a forward spring.
BUCK. Now, in good time, here comes the duke of York.
Enter YORK, HASTINGS, *and the* CARDINAL.
PRINCE. Richard of York! how fares our loving brother?
YORK. Well, my dread lord; so must I call you now.
PRINCE. Ay, brother,—to our grief, as it is yours:
Too late he died that might have kept that title,
Which by his death hath lost much majesty.
GLO. How fares our cousin, noble lord of York?
YORK. I thank you, gentle uncle. O, my lord,
You said that idle weeds are fast in growth:
The prince my brother hath outgrown me far.
GLO. He hath, my lord.   [far.
YORK.   And therefore is he idle?
GLO. O, my fair cousin, I must not say so.
YORK. Then he is more beholden to you than I.
GLO. He may command me as my sovereign;

But you have power in me as in a kinsman.

YORK. I pray you, uncle, give me this dagger.

GLO. My dagger, little cousin? with all my heart.

PRINCE. A beggar, brother?

YORK. Of my kind uncle, that I know will give;
And, being but a toy, which is no grief to give.

GLO. A greater gift than that I'll give my cousin.

YORK. A greater gift! O, that's the sword to it.

GLO. Ay, gentle cousin, were it light enough.

YORK. O, then, I see, you'll part but with light gifts;
In weightier things you'll say a beggar, nay.

GLO. It is too weighty for your grace to wear.

YORK. I weigh it lightly, were it heavier.

GLO. What, would you have my weapon, little lord?

YORK. I would, that I might thank you as

GLO. How?   [you call me.

YORK. Little.

PRINCE. My lord of York will still be cross in talk:—
Uncle, your grace knows how to bear with him.   [with me:—

YORK. You mean, to bear me, not to bear Uncle, my brother mocks both you and me;
Because that I am little, like an ape,
He thinks that you should bear me on your shoulders.

BUCK. [Aside.] With what a sharp provided wit he reasons!
To mitigate the scorn he gives his uncle,
He prettily and aptly taunts himself:
So cunning, and so young, is wonderful.

GLO. My lord, will't please you pass along?
Myself and my good cousin Buckingham
Will to your mother, to entreat of her
To meet you at the Tower, and welcome you.

YORK. What, will you go unto the Tower, my lord?

PRINCE. My lord protector needs will have it so.

YORK. I shall not sleep in quiet at the Tower.

GLO. Why, what should you fear?

YORK. Marry, my uncle Clarence's angry ghost:
My grandam told me he was murder'd there.

PRINCE. I fear no uncles dead.

GLO. Nor none that live, I hope.

PRINCE. An if they live, I hope, I need not fear.

But come, my lord; and, with a heavy heart,
Thinking on them, go I unto the Tower.

[Sennet. Exeunt PRINCE, YORK, HASTINGS, CARDINAL, and Attendants.

BUCK. Think you, my lord, this little prating York
Was not incensed by his subtle mother
To taunt and scorn you thus opprobriously?

GLO. No doubt, no doubt: O, 'tis a parlous boy;
Bold, quick, ingenious, forward, capable:
He's all the mother's, from the top to toe.

BUCK. Well, let them rest.—Come hither, Catesby.
Thou art sworn as deeply to effect what we intend,
As closely to conceal what we impart:
Thou know'st our reasons urg'd upon the way;—   [ter
What think'st thou? is it not an easy mat-
To make William lord Hastings of our mind,
For the instalment of this noble duke
In the seat royal of this famous isle?

CATE. He for his father's sake so loves the prince,
That he will not be won to aught against him.

BUCK. What think'st thou, then, of Stanley? not he?

CATE. He will do all in all as Hastings doth.

BUCK. Well then, no more but this: go, gentle Catesby,
And, as it were far off, sound thou lord Hastings,
How he doth stand affected to our purpose;
And summon him to-morrow to the Tower,
To sit about the coronation.
If thou dost find him tractable to us,
Encourage him, and tell him all our reasons:
If he be leaden, icy, cold, unwilling,
Be thou so too; and so break off the talk,
And give us notice of his inclination:
For we to-morrow hold divided councils,
Wherein thyself shalt highly be employ'd.

GLO. Commend me to lord William: tell him, Catesby,
His ancient knot of dangerous adversaries
To-morrow are let blood at Pomfret castle;
And bid my lord, for joy of this good news,
Give mistress Shore one gentle kiss the more.

BUCK. Good Catesby, go, effect this business soundly.

CATE. My good lords both, with all the heed I can.

GLO. Shall we hear from you, Catesby, ere
    we sleep?
CATE. You shall, my lord.
GLO. At Crosby-place, there shall you find
    us both.   [*Exit* CATESBY.
BUCK. Now, my lord, what shall we do,
    if we perceive
Lord Hastings will not yield to our com-
    plots?
GLO. Chop off his head, man;—somewhat
    we will do:—
And, look, when I am king, claim thou of
    me   [ables
The earldom of Hereford, and all the mov-
Whereof the king, my brother, was pos-
    sess'd.   [grace's hand.
BUCK. I'll claim that promise at your
GLO. And look to have it yielded with all
    kindness.
Come, let us sup betimes, that afterwards
We may digest our complots in some form.
                                [*Exeunt.*

SCENE II.—*Before* LORD HASTINGS' *House.*
           Enter a Messenger.
MESS. [*Knocking.*] My lord! my lord!—
HAST. [*Within.*] Who knocks?
MESS. One from the lord Stanley.
HAST. [*Within.*] What is't o'clock?
MESS. Upon the stroke of four.
           Enter HASTINGS.
HAST. Cannot my lord Stanley sleep these
    tedious nights?
MESS. So it appears by that I have to say.
First, he commends him to your noble self.
HAST. What then?   [this night
MESS. Then certifies your lordship, that
He dreamt the boar had rased off his helm:
Besides, he says there are two councils
    held;
And that may be determin'd at the one,
Which may make you and him to rue at th'
    other.   [pleasure,
Therefore he sends to know your lordship's
If you will presently take horse with him,
And with all speed post with him toward
    the north.
To shun the danger that his soul divines.
HAST. Go, fellow, go, return unto thy
    lord;
Bid him not fear the separated councils:
His honour and myself are at the one,
And at the other is my good friend Catesby;
Where nothing can proceed that toucheth
Whereof I shall not have intelligence. [us,
Tell him his fears are shallow, without
    instance:
And for his dreams—I wonder he's so
    simple
To trust the mockery of unquiet slumbers:

To fly the boar, before the boar pursues,
Were to incense the boar to follow us,
And make pursuit, where he did mean no
    chase.
Go, bid thy master rise and come to me;
And we will both together to the Tower,
Where, he shall see, the boar will use us
    kindly.   [you say.
MESS. I'll go, my lord, and tell him what
                                [*Exit.*
           Enter CATESBY.
CATE. Many good morrows to my noble
    lord!
HAST. Good morrow, Catesby; you are
    early stirring.
What news, what news, in this our totter-
    ing state?   [lord;
CATE. It is a reeling world, indeed, my
And I believe will never stand upright,
Till Richard wear the garland of the realm.
HAST. How! wear the garland! dost thou
    mean the crown?
CATE. Ay, my good lord.
HAST. I'll have this crown of mine cut
    from my shoulders,
Before I'll see the crown so foul misplac'd.
But canst thou guess that he doth aim at it?
CATE. Ay, on my life; and hopes to find
    you forward
Upon his party for the gain thereof:
And thereupon he sends you this good
    news,—
That this same very day your enemies,
The kindred of the queen, must die at
    Pomfret.
HAST. Indeed, I am no mourner for that
    news,
Because they have been still my adversaries:
But, that I'll give my voice on Richard's
    side,
To bar my master's heirs in true descent,
God knows, I will not do it, to the death.
CATE. God keep your lordship in that
    gracious mind!
HAST. But I shall laugh at this a twelve-
    month hence,—
That they which brought me in my master's
I live to look upon their tragedy. [hate,
Well, Catesby, ere a fortnight make me
    older,
I'll send some packing that yet think not
    on't.   [lord,
CATE. 'Tis a vile thing to die, my gracious
When men are unprepar'd, and look not
    for it.   [falls it out
HAST. O monstrous, monstrous! and so
With Rivers, Vaughan, Grey: and so 'twill
    do   [as safe
With some men else, who think themselves
As thou and I; who, as thou know'st, are
    dear

To princely Richard and to Buckingham.
CATE. The princes both make high account of you,—
[Aside.] For they account his head upon
the bridge.
HAST. I know they do, and I have well
deserv'd it.

Enter STANLEY.

Come on, come on; where is your boar-
spear, man?
Fear you the boar, and go so unprovided?
STAN. My lord, good morrow;—good mor-
row, Catesby:—
You may jest on, but by the holy rood,
I do not like these several councils, I.
HAST. My lord, I hold my life as dear as
you do yours;
And never, in my days, I do protest,
Was it so precious to me as 'tis now:
Think you, but that I know our state secure,
I would be so triumphant as I am?
STAN. The lords at Pomfret, when they
rode from London,   [were sure,—
Were jocund, and suppos'd their states
And they, indeed, had no cause to mistrust;
But yet, you see, how soon the day o'er-
cast.
This sudden stab of rancour I misdoubt:
Pray God, I say, I prove a needless coward!
What, shall we toward the Tower? the day
is spent.
HAST. Come, come, have with you.—Wot
you what, my lord?
To-day the lords you talk of are beheaded.
STAN. They, for their truth, might better
wear their heads,
Than some that have accus'd them wear
their hats.—
But come, my lord, let's away.

Enter a Pursuivant.

HAST. Go on before; I'll talk with this
good fellow. [Exeunt STAN. *and* CATESBY.
How now, sirrah! how goes the world with
thee?   [to ask.
PURS. The better, that your lordship please
HAST. I tell thee, man, 'tis better with me
now,   [we meet:
Than when thou met'st me last, where now
Then, was I going prisoner to the Tower,
By the suggestion of the queen's allies;
But now, I tell thee, (keep it to thyself)
This day those enemies are put to death,
And I in better state than ere I was.
PURS. God hold it, to your honour's good
content!
HAST. Gramercy, fellow. There, drink
that for me. [Throwing him his purse.
PURS. I thank your honour.   [Exit.

Enter a Priest.

PR. Well met, my lord; I am glad to see
your honour.

HAST. I thank thee, good Sir John, with
all my heart.
I am in your debt for your last exercise;
Come the next Sabbath, and I will content
you.

Enter BUCKINGHAM.

BUCK. What, talking with a priest, lord
chamberlain!
Your friends at Pomfret, they do need the
priest;
Your honour hath no shriving work in hand.
HAST. 'Good faith, and when I met this
holy man,
The men you talk of came into my mind.—
What, go you toward the Tower?
BUCK. I do, my lord; but long I cannot
stay there:
I shall return before your lordship thence.
HAST. Nay, like enough, for I stay dinner
there.
BUCK. [Aside.] And supper too, although
thou know'st it not.
Come, will you go?
HAST.   I'll wait upon your lordship.
          [Exeunt.

————

SCENE III.—POMFRET. *Before the Castle.*

Enter RATCLIFF, *with a* Guard, *conducting*
RIVERS, GREY, *and* VAUGHAN, *to*
execution.

RIV. Sir Richard Ratcliff, let me tell thee
this,—
To-day shalt thou behold a subject die
For truth, for duty, and for loyalty.
GREY. God bless the prince from all the
pack of you!
A knot you are of damned blood-suckers.
VAUGH. You live, that shall cry woe for
this hereafter.
RAT. Despatch; the limit of your lives is
out.   [prison,
RIV. O Pomfret, Pomfret! O thou bloody
Fatal and ominous to noble peers!
Within the guilty closure of thy walls,
Richard the Second here was hack'd to
death;
And, for more slander to thy dismal seat,
We give thee up our guiltless blood to
drink.
GREY. Now Margaret's curse is fallen
upon our heads,   [me,
When she exclaim'd on Hastings, you, and
For standing by when Richard stabb'd her
son.
RIV. Then curs'd she Richard, then curs'd
she Buckingham,
Then curs'd she Hastings:—O, remember,
God,   [us!
To hear her prayer for them, as now for
And for my sister and her princely sons,

Be satisfied, dear God, with our true blood,
Which, as thou know'st, unjustly must be
    spilt!
RAT. Make haste; the hour of death is
    expiate.
RIV. Come, Grey,—come, Vaughan,—let
    us here embrace:
Farewell, until we meet again in heaven.
                                    [*Exeunt.*

SCENE IV.—LONDON. *A Room in the*
    Tower.

BUCKINGHAM, STANLEY, HASTINGS, *the*
    BISHOP OF ELY, RATCLIFF, LOVEL, *and*
    others, sitting at a table: Officers of the
    Council *attending.*
HAST. Now, noble peers, the cause why
    we are met
Is to determine of the coronation:
In God's name, speak,—when is the royal
    day?
BUCK. Are all things ready for that royal
    time?
STAN. They are; and wants but nomina-
    tion.   [day.
ELY. To-morrow, then, I judge a happy
BUCK. Who knows the lord protector's
    mind herein?
Who is most inward with the noble duke?
ELY. Your grace, we think, should soonest
    know his mind.
BUCK. We know each other's faces; for
    our hearts,
He knows no more of mine, than I of
    yours;
Nor I of his, my lord, than you of mine.—
Lord Hastings, you and he are near in love.
HAST. I thank his grace, I know he loves
    me well;
But, for his purpose in the coronation,
I have not sounded him, nor he deliver'd
His gracious pleasure any way therein:
But you, my honourable lords, may name
    the time;
And in the duke's behalf I'll give my
    voice,
Which, I presume, he'll take in gentle part.
ELY. In happy time, here comes the duke
    himself.
            Enter GLOSTER.
GLO. My noble lords and cousins, all, good
    morrow.
I have been long a sleeper; but, I trust,
My absence doth neglect no great design,
Which by my presence might have been
    concluded.
BUCK. Had you not come upon your cue,
    my lord,   [part,—
William lord Hastings had pronounc'd your

I mean, your voice, for crowning of the
    king.
GLO. Than my lord Hastings, no man
    might be bolder;
His lordship knows me well, and loves me
    well.—
My lord of Ely, when I was last in Holborn,
I saw good strawberries in your garden
    there:
I do beseech you, send for some of them.
ELY. Marry, and will, my lord, with all
    my heart.   [*Exit.*
GLO. Cousin of Buckingham, a word
    with you.   [*Takes him aside.*
Catesby hath sounded Hastings in our
    business,
And finds the testy gentleman so hot,
That he will lose his head ere give consent
His master's child, as worshipfully he
    terms it,
Shall lose the royalty of England's throne.
BUCK. Withdraw yourself awhile; I'll go
    with you.
        [*Exeunt* GLOSTER *and* BUCKINGHAM.
STAN. We have not yet set down this day
    of triumph.
To-morrow, in my judgment, is too sudden;
For I myself am not so well provided
As else I would be, were the day pro-
    long'd.
        Re-enter BISHOP OF ELY.
ELY. Where is my lord, the duke of
    Gloster?
I have sent for these strawberries.
HAST. His grace looks cheerfully and
    smooth this morning;
There's some conceit or other likes him
    well,
When that he bids good morrow with such
    spirit.
I think there's never a man in Christen-
    dom
Can lesser hide his love or hate than he;
For by his face straight shall you know his
    heart.
STAN. What of his heart perceive you in
    his face,
By any livelihood he show'd to-day?
HAST. Marry, that with no man here he
    is offended;
For, were he, he had shown it in his looks.
        Re-enter GLOSTER *and* BUCKINGHAM.
GLO. I pray you all, tell me what they
    deserve,
That do conspire my death with devilish
    plots
Of damned witchcraft, and that have pre-
    vail'd
Upon my body with their hellish charms?
HAST. The tender love I bear your grace,
    my lord,

Makes me most forward in this princely
   presence
To doom th' offenders: whosoe'er they be,
I say, my lord, they have deserved death.
GLO. Then, be your eyes the witness of
   their evil:
Look how I am bewitch'd; behold mine
   arm
Is like a blasted sapling wither'd up:
And this is Edward's wife, that monstrous
   witch,
Consorted with that harlot, strumpet Shore,
That by their witchcraft thus have marked
   me.
HAST. If they have done this deed, my
   noble lord,—
GLO. If! thou protector of this damned
   strumpet,
Talk'st thou to me of "ifs?"—Thou art a
   traitor:—
Off with his head!—now, by Saint Paul
   I swear,
I will not dine until I see the same.—
Lovel, and Ratcliff, look that it be done:—
The rest, that love me, rise, and follow
   me.
     [*Exeunt* Council, *with* GLOSTER *and*
                    BUCKINGHAM.
HAST. Woe, woe, for England; not a
   whit for me;
For I, too fond, might have prevented
   this.
Stanley did dream the boar did rase his
   helm;
And I did scorn it, and disdain'd to fly.
Three times to-day my foot-cloth horse
   did stumble,
And started when he look'd upon the
   Tower,
As loath to bear me to the slaughter-house.
O, now I need the priest that spake to me:
I now repent I told the pursuivant,
As too triumphing, how mine enemies
To-day at Pomfret bloodily were butcher'd,
And I myself secure in grace and favour.
O Margaret, Margaret, now thy heavy curse
Is lighted on poor Hastings' wretched
   head!
RAT. Come, come, despatch; the duke
   would be at dinner:
Make a short shrift; he longs to see your
   head.
HAST. O momentary grace of mortal
   men,
Which we more hunt for than the grace of
   God!
Who builds his hope in air of your good
   looks,
Lives like a drunken sailor on a mast;
Ready, with every nod, to tumble down
Into the fatal bowels of the deep.

LOV. Come, come, despatch; 'tis boot-
   less to exclaim.
HAST. O bloody Richard! —miserable
   England!
I prophesy the fearfull'st time to thee,
That ever wretched age hath look'd upon.
Come, lead me to the block; bear him my
   head:
They smile at me, who shortly shall be
   dead.   [*Exeunt.*

SCENE V.—LONDON. *The Tower Walls.*

Enter GLOSTER *and* BUCKINGHAM, *in rusty
   armour, marvellous ill-favoured.*

GLO. Come, cousin, canst thou quake,
   and change thy colour,
Murder thy breath in middle of a word,
And then again begin, and stop again,
As if thou wert distraught, and mad with
   terror?
BUCK. Tut, I can counterfeit the deep
   tragedian;
Speak and look back, and pry on every
   side,
Tremble and start at wagging of a straw,
Intending deep suspicion: ghastly looks
Are at my service, like enforced smiles;
And both are ready in their offices,
At any time, to grace my stratagems.
But what, is Catesby gone?
GLO. He is; and, see, he brings the mayor
   along.

Enter the Lord Mayor *and* CATESBY.

BUCK. Lord mayor,—
GLO. Look to the drawbridge there!
BUCK.   Hark! a drum.
GLO. Catesby, o'erlook the walls.
BUCK. Lord mayor, the reason we have
   sent,—
GLO. Look back, defend thee,—here are
   enemies.
BUCK. God and our innocency defend and
   guard us!
GLO. Be patient, they are friends,—Rat-
   cliff, and Lovel.

Enter LOVEL *and* RATCLIFF, *with*
          HASTINGS' *head.*

LOV. Here is the head of that ignoble
   traitor,
The dangerous and unsuspected Hastings.
GLO. So dear I lov'd the man, that I
   must weep.
I took him for the plainest harmless crea-
   ture,
That breath'd upon the earth a Christian;
Made him my book, wherein my soul re-
   corded
The history of all her secret thoughts:
So smooth he daub'd his vice with show
   of virtue,

That, his apparent open guilt omitted,—
I mean, his conversation with Shore's
wife,—
He liv'd from all attainder of suspect.
BUCK. Well, well, he was the covert'st
That ever liv'd.— [shelter'd traitor
Would you imagine, or almost believe,
(Were't not that by great preservation
We live to tell it you) the subtle traitor
This day had plotted, in the council-house,
To murder me, and my good lord of Glos-
ter?
MAY. Had he done so?
GLO. What, think you we are Turks or
infidels?
Or that we would, against the form of law,
Proceed thus rashly in the villain's death,
But that the extreme peril of the case,
The peace of England and our person's
safety,
Enforc'd us to this execution?
MAY. Now, fair befall you! he deserv'd
his death;
And your good graces both have well pro-
ceeded,
To warn false traitors from the like at-
tempts.
I never look'd for better at his hands,
After he once fell in with mistress Shore.
BUCK. Yet had we not determin'd he
should die,
Until your lordship came to see his end;
Which now the loving haste of these our
friends,
Something against our meaning, hath pre-
vented:
Because, my lord, we would have had you
heard
The traitor speak, and timorously confess
The manner and the purpose of his trea-
sons;
That you might well have signified the
same
Unto the citizens, who haply may
Misconstrue us in him, and wail his death.
MAY. But, my good lord, your grace's
words shall serve,
As well as I had seen, and heard him
speak:
And do not doubt, right noble princes both,
But I'll acquaint our duteous citizens
With all your just proceedings in this case.
GLO. And to that end we wish'd your
lordship here,
To avoid the censures of the carping world.
BUCK. But since you come too late of our
intent,
Yet witness what you hear we did intend:
And so, my good lord mayor, we bid fare-
well. [*Exit* Lord Mavor.
GLO. Go, after, after, cousin Buckingham.

The mayor towards Guildhall hies him in
all post:—
There, at your meetest vantage of the time,
Infer the bastardy of Edward's children:
Tell them how Edward put to death a citi-
zen,
Only for saying—he would make his son
Heir to the crown; meaning, indeed, his
house,
Which, by the sign thereof, was termed so.
Moreover, urge his hateful luxury,
And bestial appetite in change of lust;
Which stretch'd unto their servants,
daughters, wives,
Even where his raging eye, or savage heart,
Without controul listed to make his prey,
Nay, for a need, thus far come near my
person:—
Tell them, when that my mother went with
child
Of that insatiate Edward, noble York,
My princely father, then had wars in
France;
And, by true computation of the time,
Found that the issue was not his begot;
Which well appeared in his lineaments,
Being nothing like the noble duke my
father:
Yet touch this sparingly, as 'twere far off;
Because, my lord, you know my mother
lives.
BUCK. Doubt not, my lord, I'll play the
orator,
As if the golden fee, for which I plead,
Were for myself: and so, my lord, adieu.
GLO. If you thrive well, bring them to
Baynard's castle;
Where you shall find me well accom-
panied,
With reverend fathers, and well-learned
bishops.
BUCK. I go; and towards three or four
o'clock,
Look for the news that the Guildhall af-
fords. [*Exit.*
GLO. Go, Lovel, with all speed to doctor
Shaw,—
[*To* CATE.] Go thou to friar Penker;—
bid them both
Meet me within this hour at Baynard's
castle. [*Exeunt* LOVEL *and* CATESBY.
Now will I in, to take some privy order,
To draw the brats of Clarence out of sight;
And to give notice, that no manner person
Have any time recourse unto the princes.
————— [*Exit.*

SCENE VI.—LONDON. *A Street.*

Enter a Scrivener.

SCRIV. Here is the indictment of the
good lord Hastings;

Which in a set hand fairly is engross'd,
That it may be to-day read o'er in Paul's:
And mark how well the sequel hangs to-
gether:—
Eleven hours I have spent to write it over,
For yesternight by Catesby was it sent me;
The precedent was full as long a doing:
And yet within these five hours Hastings
liv'd,
Untainted, unexamin'd, free, at liberty.
Here's a good world the while! Who is
so gross,
That cannot see this palpable device?
Yet who so bold, but says he sees it not?
Bad is the world; and all will come to
naught,
When such ill dealing must be seen in
thought.   [*Exit.*

SCENE VII.—LONDON. *The court of*
Baynard's Castle.

Enter GLOSTER *and* BUCKINGHAM, *meeting.*
GLO. How now, how now! what say the
citizens?
BUCK. Now, by the holy mother of our
Lord,
The citizens are mum, say not a word.
GLO. Touch'd you the bastardy of Ed-
ward's children?
BUCK. I did; with his contract with lady
Lucy,
And his contract by deputy in France;
The insatiate greediness of his desires,
And his enforcement of the city wives;
His tyranny for trifles; his own bastardy,—
As being got, your father then in France,
And his resemblance, being not like the
duke:
Withal I did infer your lineaments,—
Being the right idea of your father,
Both in your form and nobleness of mind;
Laid open all your victories in Scotland,
Your discipline in war, wisdom in peace,
Your bounty, virtue, fair humility;
Indeed, left nothing fitting for your pur-
pose
Untouch'd, or slightly handled, in dis-
course:
And when my oratory drew toward end,
I bade them that did love their country's
good,
Cry—"God save Richard, England's royal
king!"
GLO. And did they so?
BUCK. No, so God help me, they spake
not a word;
But, like dumb statuas, or breathing
stones,
Star'd each on other, and look'd deadly
pale.

Which when I saw, I reprehended them;
And ask'd the mayor what meant this
wilful silence:
His answer was,—the people were not us'd
To be spoke to, but by the recorder.
Then he was urg'd to tell my tale again,—
"Thus saith the duke, thus hath the duke
inferr'd;"
But nothing spoke in warrant from himself.
When he had done, some followers of mine
own,
At lower end of the hall, hurl'd up their
caps,
And some ten voices cried, "God save king
Richard!"
And thus I took the vantage of those few,—
"Thanks, gentle citizens and friends,"
quoth I;
"This general applause, and cheerful shout,
Argues your wisdom, and your love to
Richard:"
And even here brake off, and came away.
GLO. What tongueless blocks were they!
would they not speak?
Will not the mayor, then, and his brethren,
come?
BUCK. The mayor is here at hand. In-
tend some fear;
Be not you spoke with, but by mighty suit:
And look you get a prayer-book in your
hand,
And stand between two churchmen, good
my lord;
For on that ground I'll make a holy des-
cant:
And be not easily won to our requests;
Play the maid's part,—still answer nay,
and take it.
GLO. I go; and if you plead as well for
them,
As I can say nay to thee for myself,
No doubt we bring it to a happy issue.
BUCK. Go, go, up to the leads; the lord
mayor knocks.—   [*Exit* GLOSTER.
Enter the Lord Mayor, Aldermen,
and Citizens.
Welcome, my lord: I dance attendance
here;
I think the duke will not be spoke with-
al.—
Enter, from the Castle, CATESBY.
Now, Catesby,—what says your lord to
my request?
CATE. He doth entreat your grace, my
noble lord,
To visit him to-morrow or next day:
He is within, with two right reverend
fathers,
Divinely bent to meditation;
And in no worldly suit would he be mov'd,
To draw him from his holy exercise.

BUCK. Return, good Catesby, to the gracious duke;
Tell him, myself, the mayor and aldermen,
In deep designs, in matter of great moment,
No less importing than our general good,
Are come to have some conference with his grace.
CATE. I'll signify so much unto him straight.   [*Exit.*
BUCK. Ah, ha, my lord, this prince is not an Edward!
He is not lolling on a lewd day-bed,
But on his knees at meditation;
Not dallying with a brace of courtezans,
But meditating with two deep divines;
Not sleeping, to engross his idle body,
But praying, to enrich his watchful soul.
Happy were England, would this virtuous prince
Take on his grace the sovereignty thereof:
But, sure, I fear, we shall not win him to it.
MAY. Marry, God defend his grace should say us nay!
BUCK. I fear he will. Here Catesby comes again.—
            Re-enter CATESBY.
Now, Catesby, what says his grace?
CATE. He wonders to what end you have assembled.
Such troops of citizens to come to him:
His grace not being warn'd thereof before,
He fears, my lord, you mean no good to him.
BUCK. Sorry I am my noble cousin should
Suspect me, that I mean no good to him:
By heaven, we come to him in perfect love;
And so once more return, and tell his grace.   [*Exit* CATESBY.
When holy and devout religious men
Are at their beads, 'tis much to draw them thence,—
So sweet is zealous contemplation.
Enter GLOSTER, *in a gallery above, between two* Bishops.
        CATESBY *returns.*
MAY. See, where his grace stands 'tween two clergymen!
BUCK. Two props of virtue for a Christian prince,
To stay him from the fall of vanity:
And, see, a book of prayer in his hand,—
True ornament to know a holy man.—
Famous Plantagenet, most gracious prince,
Lend favourable ear to our request;
And pardon us the interruption
Of thy devotion, and right christian zeal.
GLO. My lord, there needs no such apology:
I do beseech your grace to pardon me,

Who, earnest in the service of my God,
Deferr'd the visitation of my friends.
But, leaving this, what is your grace's pleasure?
BUCK. Even that, I hope, which pleaseth God above,
And all good men of this ungovern'd isle.
GLO. I do suspect I have done some offence,
That seems disgracious in the city's eye;
And that you come to reprehend my ignorance.
BUCK. You have, my lord: would it might please your grace,
On our entreaties to amend your fault.
GLO. Else wherefore breathe I in a Christian land?
BUCK. Know, then, it is your fault that you resign
The supreme seat, the throne majestical,
The sceptred office of your ancestors,
Your state of fortune and your due of birth,
The lineal glory of your royal house,
To the corruption of a blemish'd stock:
Whiles, in the mildness of your sleepy thoughts,   [good,)
(Which here we waken to our country's
This noble isle doth want her proper limbs;
Her face defac'd with scars of infamy,
Her royal stock graft with ignoble plants,
And almost shoulder'd in the swallowing gulf
Of dark forgetfulness, and deep oblivion.
Which to recure, we heartily solicit
Your gracious self to take on you the charge
And kingly government of this your land;—
Not as protector, steward, substitute,
Or lowly factor for another's gain;
But as successively, from blood to blood,
Your right of birth, your empery, your own.
For this, consorted with the citizens,
Your very worshipful and loving friends,
And by their vehement instigation,
In this just suit come I to move your grace.
GLO. I cannot tell, if to depart in silence,
Or bitterly to speak in your reproof,
Best fitteth my degree, or your condition:
If, not to answer,—you might haply think
Tongue-tied ambition, not replying, yielded
To bear the golden yoke of sovereignty,
Which fondly you would here impose on me:
If to reprove you for this suit of yours,
So season'd with your faithful love to me,
Then, on the other side, I check'd my friends.

Therefore,—to speak, and to avoid the
first,
And then, in speaking, not to incur the
last,—
Definitively thus I answer you.
Your love deserves my thanks; but my de-
sert,
Unmeritable, shuns your high request.
First, if all obstacles were cut away,
And that my path were even to the crown,
As the ripe revenue and due of birth;
Yet so much is my poverty of spirit,
So mighty and so many my defects,
That I would rather hide me from my
greatness,—
Being a bark to brook no mighty sea,—
Than in my greatness covet to be hid,
And in the vapour of my glory smother'd.
But, God be thank'd, there is no need of
me;
(And much I need to help you, were there
need);
The royal tree hath left us royal fruit,
Which, mellow'd by the stealing hours of
time,
Will well become the seat of majesty,
And make, no doubt, us happy by his
reign.
On him I lay that you would lay on me,—
The right and fortune of his happy stars;
Which God defend that I should wring
from him!
BUCK. My lord, this argues conscience
in your grace;
But the respects thereof are nice and triv-
ial,
All circumstances well considered.
You say that Edward is your brother's
son:
So say we too, but not by Edward's wife;
For first was he contract to lady Lucy,—
Your mother lives a witness to his vow,—
And afterward by substitute betroth'd
To Bona, sister to the king of France.
These both put off, a poor petitioner,
A care-craz'd mother to a many sons,
A beauty-waning and distressed widow,
Even in the afternoon of her best days,
Made prize and purchase of his wanton
eye,
Seduc'd the pitch and height of his degree
To base declension and loath'd bigamy:
By her, in his unlawful bed, he got
This Edward, whom our manners call the
prince.
More bitterly could I expostulate,
Save that, for reverence to some alive,
I give a sparing limit to my tongue.
Then, good my lord, take to your royal
self
This proffer'd benefit of dignity;

If not to bless us and the land withal,
Yet to draw forth your noble ancestry
From the corruption of abusing time,
Unto a lineal true-derived course.
MAY. Do, good my lord; your citizens
entreat you.
BUCK. Refuse not, mighty lord, this prof-
fer'd love.
CATE. O, make them joyful, grant their
lawful suit!
GLO. Alas, why would you heap those
cares on me?
I am unfit for state and majesty:—
I do beseech you, take it not amiss;
I cannot, nor I will not, yield to you.
BUCK. If you refuse it,—as, in love and
zeal,
Loath to depose the child, your brother's
son;
As well we know your tenderness of heart,
And gentle, kind, effeminate remorse,
Which we have noted in you to your kin-
dred,
And equally, indeed, to all estates,—
Yet know, whe'r you accept our suit or no,
Your brother's son shall never reign our
king;
But we will plant some other in the throne,
To the disgrace and downfall of your
house:
And, in this resolution, here we leave
you.—
Come, citizens, we will entreat no more.
        [*Exit* BUCKINGHAM; *the* Mayor,
        Aldermen, *and* Citizens, *retiring.*
CATE. Call them again, sweet prince, ac
cept their suit:
If you deny them, all the land will rue it.
GLO. Will you enforce me to a world
of cares?
Call them again.
    [CATESBY *goes to the* Mayor, &c., and
                    then exit
      I am not made of stone,
But penetrable to your kind entreaties,
Albeit against my conscience, and my
soul.—
Re-enter BUCKINGHAM *and* CATESBY; *the*
Mayor, &c, *coming forward.*
Cousin of Buckingham,—and sage, grave
men,—
Since you will buckle fortune on my
back,—
To bear her burden, whe'r I will or no,
I must have patience to endure the load
But if black scandal, or foul-fac'd reproach
Attend the sequel of your imposition,
Your mere enforcement shall acquittance
me
From all the impure blots and stains there
of;

For God he knows, and you may partly see,

How far I am from the desire of this.

MAY. God bless your grace! we see it, and will say it.

GLO. In saying so, you shall but say the truth.

BUCK. Then I salute you with this royal title,—

Long live king Richard, England's worthy king.

ALL. Amen.

BUCK. To-morrow may it please you to be crown'd?

GLO. Even when you please, for you will have it so.

BUCK. To-morrow, then, we will attend your grace:

And so, most joyfully, we take our leave.

GLO. [*To the* Bishops.] Come, let us to our holy work again.—

Farewell, my cousin;—farewell, gentle friends.   [*Exeunt.*

ACT IV.

Scene I.—*Before the* Tower.

Enter, on one side, Queen Elizabeth, Duchess of York, *and* Marquess of Dorset; *on the other,* Anne, *Duchess of Gloster, leading Lady* Margaret Plantagenet, Clarence's *young Daughter.*

DUCH. Who meets us here?—my niece Plantagenet,

Led in the hand of her kind aunt of Gloster?

Now, for my life, she's wand'ring to the Tower,

On pure heart's love, to greet the tender Daughter, well met.   [princes.--

ANNE.   God give your graces both

A happy and a joyful time of day!

Q. ELIZ. As much to you, good sister! whither away?

ANNE. No farther than the Tower; and, as I guess,

Upon the like devotion as yourselves,

To gratulate the gentle princes there.

Q. ELIZ. Kind sister, thanks: we'll enter all together:—

And, in good time, here the lieutenant comes.—

Enter Brakenbury.

Master lieutenant, pray you, by your leave,

How doth the prince, and my young son of York?

BRAK. Right well, dear Madam. By your patience,

I may not suffer you to visit them;

The king hath strictly charg'd the contrary.

Q. ELIZ. The king! who's that?

BRAK.   I mean the lord protector.

Q. ELIZ. The Lord protect him from that kingly title!

Hath he set bounds between their love, and me?

I am their mother; who shall bar me from them?

DUCH. I am their father's mother; I will see them.

ANNE. Their aunt I am in law, in love their mother:

Then bring me to their sights; I'll bear thy blame,

And take thy office from thee, on my peril.

BRAK. No, Madam, no,—I may not leave it so:

I am bound by oath, and therefore pardon me.   [*Exit.*

Enter Stanley.

STAN. Let me but meet you, ladies, one hour hence,

And I'll salute your grace of York as mother,

And reverend looker-on, of two fair queens.—

[*To the Duchess of Gloster.*] Come, Madam, you must straight to Westminster.

There to be crowned Richard's royal queen.

Q. ELIZ. Ah, cut my lace asunder,

That my pent heart may have some scope to beat,

Or else I swoon with this dead-killing news.

ANNE. Despiteful tidings! O, unpleasing news!

DOR. Be of good cheer:—mother, how fares your grace?

Q. ELIZ. O Dorset, speak not to me, get thee gone!

Death and destruction dog thee at the heels:

Thy mother's name is ominous to children.

If thou wilt outstrip death, go cross the seas,

And live with Richmond, from the reach of hell:

Go, hie thee, hie thee, from this slaughter-house,

Lest thou increase the number of the dead;

And make me die the thrall of Margaret's curse,—

Nor mother, wife, nor England's 'counted queen.

STAN. Full of wise care is this your counsel, Madam.—

[*To* Dor.] Take all the swift advantage of the hours;

You shall have letters from me to my son

In your behalf, to meet you on the way:
Be not ta'en tardy by unwise delay.
DUCH. O ill-dispersing wind of misery!—
O my accursed womb, the bed of death!
A cockatrice hast thou hatch'd to the world,
Whose unavoided eye is murderous!
STAN. Come, Madam, come; I in all haste was sent.
ANNE. And I with all unwillingness will go.—
O, would to God that the inclusive verge
Of golden metal, that must round my brow,
Were red-hot steel, to sear me to the brain!
Anointed let me be with deadly venom;
And die, ere men can say—God save the queen!
Q. ELIZ. Go, go, poor soul, I envy not thy glory;
To feed my humour, wish thyself no harm.
ANNE. No! why?—When he, that is my husband now,
Came to me, as I follow'd Henry's corse;
When scarce the blood was well wash'd from his hands,
Which issu'd from my other angel husband,
And that dead saint which then I weeping follow'd;
O, when, I say, I look'd on Richard's face,
This was my wish,—"Be thou," quoth I, "accurs'd,
For making me, so young, so old a widow!
And, when thou wedd'st, let sorrow haunt thy bed;
And be thy wife (if any be so mad)
More miserable by the life of thee,
Than thou hast made me by my dear lord's death!"
Lo, ere I can repeat this curse again,
Within so small a time, my woman's heart
Grossly grew captive to his honey words,
And prov'd the subject of mine own soul's curse,—
Which hitherto hath held mine eyes from rest;
For never yet one hour in his bed
Did I enjoy the golden dew of sleep,
But with his timorous dreams was still awak'd.
Besides, he hates me for my father Warwick;
And will, no doubt, shortly be rid of me.
Q. ELIZ. Poor heart, adieu! I pity thy complaining.
ANNE. No more than with my soul I mourn for yours.
Q. ELIZ. Farewell, thou woful welcomer of glory!
ANNE. Adieu, poor soul, that tak'st thy leave of it!

DUCH. [*To* DORSET.] Go thou to Richmond, and good fortune guide thee!—
[*To* ANNE.] Go thou to Richard, and good angels tend thee!—
[*To* Q. ELIZ.] Go thou to sanctuary, and good thoughts possess thee!—
I to my grave, where peace and rest lie with me!
Eighty odd years of sorrow have I seen,
And each hour's joy wreck'd with a week of teen.
Q. ELIZ. Stay yet, look back with me unto the Tower.—
Pity, you ancient stones, those tender babes,
Whom envy hath immur'd within your walls!
Rough cradle for such little pretty ones!
Rude ragged nurse, old sullen play-fellow
For tender princes, use my babies well!
So foolish sorrow bids your stones farewell.   [*Exeunt.*

SCENE II.—*A Room of State in the Palace.*

Sennet. RICHARD, *as king upon his throne;*
BUCKINGHAM, CATESBY, *a* Page, *and others.*

K. RICH. Stand all apart.—Cousin of Buckingham,—
BUCK. My gracious sovereign?
K. RICH. Give me thy hand. Thus high, by thy advice,
And thy assistance, is king Richard seated:—
But shall we wear these glories for a day?
Or shall they last, and we rejoice in them?
BUCK. Still live they, and for ever let them last!
K. RICH. Ah, Buckingham, now do I play the touch,
To try if thou be current gold indeed:—
Young Edward lives;—think now what I would speak.
BUCK. Say on, my loving lord.
K. RICH. Why, Buckingham, I say, I would be king.
BUCK. Why, so you are, my thrice-renowned liege.
K. RICH. Ha! am I king? 'Tis so:—but Edward lives.
BUCK. True, noble prince.
K. RICH.   O bitter consequence,
That Edward still should live,—"true, noble prince!"
Cousin, thou wast not wont to be so dull:—
Shall I be plain?—I wish the bastards dead;
And I would have it suddenly perform'd.
What say'st thou now? speak suddenly, be brief.
BUCK. Your grace may do your pleasure.

K. RICH. Tut, tut! thou art all ice, thy kindness freezes:
Say, have I thy consent that they shall die?

BUCK. Give me some little breath, some pause, dear lord,
Before I positively speak in this:
I will resolve you herein presently. [*Exit.*

CATE. [*Aside to another.*] The king is angry: see, he gnaws his lip.

K. RICH. [*Descends from his throne.*] I will converse with iron-witted fools,
And unrespective boys: none are for me,
That look into me with considerate eyes:—
High-reaching Buckingham grows circumspect.—
Boy!—   [*spect.—*

PAGE. My lord?

K. RICH. Know'st thou not any, whom corrupting gold
Will tempt unto a close exploit of death?

PAGE. I know a discontented gentleman,
Whose humble means match not his haughty spirit:
Gold were as good as twenty orators,
And will, no doubt, tempt him to any thing.

K. RICH. What is his name?

PAGE.   His name, my lord, is Tyrrel.

K. RICH. I partly know the man: go, call him hither, boy.—   [*Exit Page.*
The deep-revolving witty Buckingham
No more shall be the neighbour to my counsels:
Hath he so long held out with me untir'd,
And stops he now for breath?—well, be it so.

Enter STANLEY.

How now, lord Stanley! what's the news?

STAN. Know, my loving lord,
The marquis Dorset, as I hear, is fled
To Richmond, in the parts where he abides.

K. RICH. Come hither, Catesby:—rumour it abroad,
That Anne, my wife, is very grievous sick;
I will take order for her keeping close:
Enquire me out some mean poor gentleman,
Whom I will marry straight to Clarence's daughter;—
The boy is foolish, and I fear not him.—
Look, how thou dream'st!—I say again, give out
That Anne my queen is sick, and like to die:
About it; for it stands me much upon,
To stop all hopes whose growth may damage me.—   [*Exit* CATESBY.
I must be married to my brother's daughter,
Or else my kingdom stands on brittle glass:—

Murder her brothers, and then marry her!
Uncertain way of gain! But I am in
So far in blood, that sin will pluck on sin:
Tear-falling pity dwells not in this eye.—

Re-enter Page, *with* TYRREL.

Is thy name Tyrrel?

TYR. [*Kneeling.*] James Tyrrel, and your most obedient subject.

K. RICH. Art thou, indeed?

TYR.   Prove me, my gracious lord.

K. RICH. Dar'st thou resolve to kill a friend of mine?

TYR. Please you; but I had rather kill two enemies.

K. RICH. Why, then thou hast it: two deep enemies,
Foes to my rest, and my sweet sleep's disturbers,
Are they that I would have thee deal upon:—
Tyrrel, I mean those bastards in the Tower.

TYR. Let me have open means to come to them,
And soon I'll rid you from the fear of them.

K. RICH. Thou sing'st sweet music.
Hark, come hither, Tyrrel:
Go, by this token.—Rise, and lend thine ear: [*Whispers.*
There is no more but so:—say it is done,
And I will love thee, and prefer thee for

TYR. I will despatch it straight.   [it.
                                             [*Exit.*

Re-enter BUCKINGHAM.

BUCK. My lord, I have consider'd in my mind
The late demand that you did sound me in.

K. RICH. Well, let that rest. Dorset is fled to Richmond.

BUCK. I hear the news, my lord.

K. RICH. Stanley, he is your wife's son:
—well, look to it.

BUCK. My lord, I claim the gift, my due by promise.
For which your honour and your faith is pawn'd;
Th' earldom of Hereford, and the moveables,
Which you have promised I shall possess.

K. RICH. Stanley, look to your wife; if she convey
Letters to Richmond, you shall answer it.

BUCK. What says your highness to my just request?

K. RICH. I do remember me,—Henry the sixth
Did prophesy that Richmond should be king,
When Richmond was a little peevish boy.
A king!—perhaps—

BUCK. My lord,—

K. RICH. How chance, the prophet could not at that time
Have told me, I being by, that I should kill him?

BUCK. My lord, your promise for the earldom,—

K. RICH. Richmond!—When last I was at Exeter,
The mayor in courtesy show'd me the castle,
And call'd it—Rouge-mont: at which name I started,
Because a bard of Ireland told me once,
I should not live long after I saw Rich-

BUCK. My lord,—   [mond.

K. RICH. Ay, what's o'clock?

BUCK. I am thus bold to put your grace in mind
Of what you promis'd me.

K. RICH. Well, but what's o'clock?

BUCK.   Upon the stroke of ten.

K. RICH. Well, let it strike.

BUCK.   Why let it strike?

K. RICH. Because that, like a Jack, thou keep'st the stroke
Betwixt thy begging and my meditation.
I am not in the giving vein to-day.

BUCK. Why, then resolve me whether you will, or no.

K. RICH. Thou troublest me; I am not in the vein.

    [*Exeunt* KING RICHARD *and train.*

BUCK. And is it thus? repays he my deep service
With such contempt? made I him king for this?
O, let me think on Hastings, and be gone
To Brecknock, while my fearful head is on.   [*Exit.*

SCENE III.—*Another Room in the Palace.*
    Enter TYRREL.

TYR. The tyrannous and bloody act is done,—
The most arch deed of piteous massacre
That ever yet this land was guilty of.
Dighton and Forrest, whom I did suborn
To do this piece of ruthless butchery,
Albeit they were flesh'd villains, bloody dogs,
Melting with tenderness and mild compassion,
Wept like to children in their death's sad story.
"O, thus," quoth Dighton, "lay the gentle babes,"—
"Thus, thus," quoth Forrest, "girdling one another
Within their alabaster innocent arms:

Their lips were four red roses on a stalk,
Which in their summer beauty kiss'd each other.
A book of prayers on their pillow lay;
Which once," quoth Forrest, "almost chang'd my mind;
But, O, the devil"—there the villain stopp'd;
When Dighton thus told on,—"We smothered
The most replenished sweet work of nature,
That, from the prime creation, e'er she fram'd."
Hence both are gone with conscience and remorse
They could not speak; and so I left them both,
To bear this tidings to the bloody king:—
And here he comes.—
    Enter KING RICHARD.
        All health, my sovereign lord!

K. RICH. Kind Tyrrel, am I happy in thy news?

TYR. If to have done the thing you gave in charge
Beget your happiness, be happy then,
For it is done.

K. RICH. But didst thou see them dead?

TYR. I did, my lord.

K. RICH.   And buried, gentle Tyrrel?

TYR. The chaplain of the Tower hath buried them;
But where, to say the truth, I do not know.

K. RICH. Come to me, Tyrrel, soon, at after supper,
When thou shalt tell the process of their death.
Meantime, but think how I may do thee good,
And be inheritor of thy desire.
Farewell, till then.

TYR. I humbly take my leave. [*Exit.*

K. RICH. The son of Clarence have I pent up close;
His daughter meanly have I match'd in marriage;
The sons of Edward sleep in Abraham's bosom,
And Anne my wife hath bid the world good night.
Now, for I know the Bretagne Richmond aims
At young Elizabeth, my brother's daughter,
And, by that knot, looks proudly on the crown,
To her go I, a jolly thriving wooer.

CATE. My lord!
    Enter CATESBY.

K. RICH. Good news or bad, that thou com'st in so bluntly?

CATE. Bad news, my lord: Morton is
fled to Richmond;
And Buckingham, back'd with the hardy
Welshmen,
Is in the field, and still his power in-
creaseth.
K. RICH. Ely with Richmond troubles
me more near,
Than Buckingham and his rash-levied
strength.
Come,—I have learn'd that fearful com-
menting
Is leaden servitor to dull delay;
Delay leads impotent and snail-pac'd beg-
gary:
Then fiery expedition be my wing,
Jove's Mercury, and herald for a king!
Go, muster men: my counsel is my shield;
We must be brief, when traitors brave the
field. [*Exeunt.*

Scene IV.—*Before the Palace.*
Enter Queen Margaret.

Q. MAR. So, now prosperity begins to
mellow,
And drop into the rotten mouth of death.
Here in these confines slily have I lurk'd,
To watch the waning of mine enemies.
A dire induction am I witness to,
And will to France; hoping the conse-
quence
Will prove as bitter, black, and tragical.—
Withdraw thee, wretched Margaret: who
comes here? [*Retiring.*
Enter Queen Elizabeth *and the*
Duchess of York.
Q. ELIZ. Ah, my poor princes! ah, my
tender babes!
My unblown flowers, new-appearing sweets!
If yet your gentle souls fly in the air,
And be not fix'd in doom perpetual,
Hover about me with your airy wings,
And hear your mother's lamentation!
Q. MAR. [*Apart.*] Hover about her; say,
that right for right
Hath dimm'd your infant morn to aged
night.
DUCH. So many miseries have craz'd my
voice,
That my woe-wearied tongue is still and
mute.—
Edward Plantagenet, why art thou dead?
Q. MAR. [*Apart.*] Plantagenet doth quit
Plantagenet,
Edward for Edward pays a dying debt.
Q. ELIZ. Wilt thou, O God! fly from
such gentle lambs,
And throw them in the entrails of the
wolf? [was done?
When didst thou sleep, when such a deed

Q. MAR. [*Apart.*] When holy Harry died,
and my sweet son.
DUCH. Dead life, blind sight, poor mortal
living ghost,
Woe's scene, world's shame, grave's due
by life usurp'd,
Brief abstract and record of tedious days,
Rest thy unrest on England's lawful earth,
[*Sitting down.*
Unlawfully made drunk with innocent
blood!
Q. ELIZ. Ah, that thou would'st as soon
afford a grave,
As thou canst yield a melancholy seat!
Then would I hide my bones, not rest
them here.
Ah, who hath any cause to mourn but we?
[*Sitting down by her.*
Q. MAR. [*Coming forward.*] If ancient
sorrow be most reverent,
Give mine the benefit of seniory,
And let my griefs frown on the upper
If sorrow can admit society, [hand.
[*Sitting down with them.*
Tell o'er your woes again by viewing
mine:—
I had an Edward, till a Richard kill'd him;
I had a husband, till a Richard kill'd him:
Thou hadst an Edward, till a Richard
kill'd him;
Thou hadst a Richard, till a Richard kill'd
him.
DUCH. I had a Richard too, and thou
didst kill him;
I had a Rutland too, thou holp'st to kill
him.
Q. MAR. Thou hadst a Clarence too, and
Richard kill'd him.
From forth the kennel of thy womb hath
crept
A hell-hound, that doth hunt us all to
death:
That dog, that had his teeth before his
eyes,
To worry lambs, and lap their gentle
blood;
That foul defacer of God's handy-work;
That excellent grand tyrant of the earth,
That reigns in galled eyes of weeping
souls,—
Thy womb let loose, to chase us to our
graves.—
O, upright, just, and true-disposing God,
How do I thank thee, that this carnal cur
Preys on the issue of his mother's body,
And makes her pew-fellow with other's
moan!
DUCH. O Harry's wife, triumph not in
my woes!
God witness with me, I have wept for
thine.

Q. MAR. Bear with me; I am hungry for revenge,
And now I cloy me with beholding it.
Thy Edward he is dead, that kill'd my Edward;
Thy other Edward dead, to quit my Edward;
Young York he is but boot, because both they
Match not the high perfection of my loss:
Thy Clarence he is dead, that stabb'd my Edward;
And the beholders of this frantic play,
Th' adulterate Hastings, Rivers, Vaughan, Grey,
Untimely smother'd in their dusky graves.
Richard yet lives, hell's black intelligencer;
Only reserv'd their factor, to buy souls,
And send them thither:—but at hand, at hand,
Ensues his piteous and unpitied end:
Earth gapes, hell burns, fiends roar, saints pray,
To have him suddenly convey'd from hence.—
Cancel his bond of life, dear God, I pray,
That I may live to say, the dog is dead!
Q. ELIZ. O, thou didst prophesy the time would come,
That I should wish for thee to help me curse
That bottled spider, that foul bunch-back'd toad!
Q. MAR. I call'd thee then, vain flourish of my fortune;
I call'd thee then, poor shadow, painted queen;
The presentation of but what I was;
The flattering index of a direful pageant;
One heav'd a-high, to be hurl'd down below;
A mother only mock'd with two fair babes;
A dream of what thou wast; a garish flag,
To be the aim of every dangerous shot;
A sign of dignity, a breath, a bubble;
A queen in jest, only to fill the scene.
Where is thy husband now? where be thy brothers?
Where be thy two sons? wherein dost thou joy?
Who sues, and kneels, and says—God save the queen?
Where be the bending peers that flatter'd thee?
Where be the thronging troops that follow'd thee?
Decline all this, and see what now thou art:
For happy wife, a most distressed widow;
For joyful mother, one that wails the name;

For one being sued to, one that humbly sues;
For queen, a very caitiff crown'd with care;
For one that scorn'd at me, now scorn'd of me;
For one being fear'd of all, now fearing one;
For one commanding all, obey'd of none.
Thus hath the course of justice wheel'd about,
And left thee but a very prey to time;
Having no more but thought of what thou wast,
To torture thee the more, being what thou art.
Thou didst usurp my place, and dost thou not
Usurp the just proportion of my sorrow?
Now thy proud neck bears half my burden'd yoke;
From which, even here, I slip my wearied head,
And leave the burden of it all on thee.
Farewell, York's wife, and queen of sad mischance:—
These English woes shall make me smile in France.
Q. ELIZ. O thou, well skill'd in curses, stay a while,
And teach me how to curse mine enemies!
Q. MAR. Forbear to sleep the night, and fast the day;
Compare dead happiness with living woe;
Think that thy babes were fairer than they were,
And he that slew them fouler than he is:
Bettering thy loss makes the bad-causer worse:
Revolving this will teach thee how to curse.
Q. ELIZ. My words are dull; O, quicken them with thine!
Q. MAR. Thy woes will make them sharp and pierce like mine.   [*Exit*
DUCH. Why should calamity be full of words?
Q. ELIZ. Windy attorneys to their client woes,
Airy succeeders of intestate joys,
Poor breathing orators of miseries!
Let them have scope: though what they do impart
Help nothing else, yet do they ease the heart.
DUCH. If so, then be not tongue-tied go with me,
And in the breath of bitter words let's smother
My damned son, that thy two sons smother'd.   [*Drum heard*
I hear his drum:—be copious in exclaims

Enter KING RICHARD, *and his train,
marching.*

K. RICH. Who intercepts me in my expedition?

DUCH. O, she that might have intercepted thee,
By strangling thee in her accursed womb,
From all the slaughters, wretch, that thou hast done!

Q. ELIZ. Hid'st thou that forehead with a golden crown,
Where should be branded, if that right were right,
The slaughter of the prince that ow'd that crown,
And the dire death of my poor sons and brothers?
Tell me, thou villain-slave, where are my children?

DUCH. Thou toad, thou toad, where is thy brother Clarence?
And little Ned Plantagenet, his son?

Q. ELIZ. Where is the gentle Rivers, Vaughan, Grey?

DUCH. Where is kind Hastings?

K. RICH. A flourish, trumpets! strike alarum, drums!
Let not the heavens hear these tell-tale women
Rail on the Lord's anointed: strike, I say!—   [*Flourish. Alarums.*
Either be patient, and entreat me fair,
Or with the clamorous report of war
Thus will I drown your exclamations.

DUCH. Art thou my son?

K. RICH. Ay; I thank God, my father, and yourself.

DUCH. Then patiently hear my impatience.

K. RICH. Madam, I have a touch of your condition,
That cannot brook the accent of reproof.

DUCH. O, let me speak!

K. RICH. Do, then; but I'll not hear.

DUCH. I will be mild and gentle in my words.

K. RICH. And brief, good mother; for I am in haste.

DUCH. Art thou so hasty? I have stay'd for thee,
God knows, in torment and in agony.

K. RICH. And came I not at last to comfort you?

DUCH. No, by the holy rood, thou know'st it well,
Thou cam'st on earth to make the earth my hell.
A grievous burden was thy birth to me;
Tetchy and wayward was thy infancy;
Thy school-days frightful, desperate, wild, and furious;

Thy prime of manhood daring, bold, and venturous:
Thy age confirm'd, proud, subtle, sly, and bloody,
More mild, but yet more harmful, kind in hatred:
What comfortable hour canst thou name,
That ever grac'd me in thy company?

K. RICH. 'Faith, none, but Humphrey Hour, that call'd your grace
To breakfast once forth of my company.
If I be so disgracious in your eye,
Let me march on, and not offend you, Madam.—
Strike up the drum!

DUCH.   I pr'ythee, hear me speak.

K. RICH. You speak too bitterly.

DUCH.   Hear me a word;
For I shall never speak to thee again.

K. RICH. So.

DUCH. Either thou wilt die, by God's just ordinance,
Ere from this war thou turn a conqueror:
Or I with grief and extreme age shall perish,
And never look upon thy face again.
Therefore take with thee my most heavy curse;
Which, in the day of battle, tire thee more
Than all the complete armour that thou wear'st!
My prayers on the adverse party fight:
And there the little souls of Edward's children
Whisper the spirits of thine enemies,
And promise them success and victory.
Bloody thou art, bloody will be thy end;
Shame serves thy life, and doth thy death attend.   [*Exit.*

Q. ELIZ. Though far more cause, yet much less spirit to curse
Abides in me; I say amen to her.   [*Going.*

K. RICH. Stay, Madam; I must talk a word with you.

Q. ELIZ. I have no more sons of the royal blood,
For thee to slaughter: for my daughters, Richard,—
They shall be praying nuns, not weeping queens;
And therefore level not to hit their lives.

K. RICH. You have a daughter call'd Elizabeth,
Virtuous and fair, royal and gracious.

Q. ELIZ. And must she die for this? O, let her live,
And I'll corrupt her manners, stain her beauty;
Slander myself as false to Edward's bed;
Throw over her the veil of infamy:

So she may live unscarr'd of bleeding slaughter,

I will confess she was not Edward's daughter,

K. RICH. Wrong not her birth, she is of royal blood.

Q. ELIZ. To save her life, I'll say she is not so.

K. RICH. Her life is safest only in her birth.

Q. ELIZ. And only in that safety died her brothers.

K. RICH. Lo, at their births good stars were opposite.

Q. ELIZ. No, to their lives bad friends were contrary.

K. RICH. All unavoided is the doom of destiny.

Q. ELIZ. True, when avoided grace makes destiny:

My babes were destin'd to a fairer death,

If grace had bless'd thee with a fairer life.

K. RICH. You speak as if that I had slain my cousins.

Q. ELIZ. Cousins, indeed; and by their uncle cozen'd

Of comfort, kingdom, kindred, freedom, life.

Whose hands soever lanc'd their tender hearts,

Thy head, all indirectly, gave direction:

No doubt the murderous knife was dull and blunt,

Till it was whetted on thy stone-hard heart,

To revel in the entrails of my lambs.

But that still use of grief makes wild grief tame,

My tongue should to thy ears not name my boys,

Till that my nails were anchor'd in thine eyes;

And I, in such a desperate bay of death,

Like a poor bark, of sails and tackling reft,

Rush all to pieces on thy rocky bosom.

K. RICH. Madam, so thrive I in my enterprise,

And dangerous success of bloody wars,

As I intend more good to you and yours,

Than ever you or yours by me were harm'd!

Q. ELIZ. What good is cover'd with the face of heaven,

To be discover'd, that can do me good?

K. RICH. Th' advancement of your children, gentle lady.

Q. ELIZ. Up to some scaffold, there to lose their heads?

K. RICH. No, to the dignity and height of honour,

The high imperial type of this earth's glory.

Q. ELIZ. Flatter my sorrow with report of it;

Tell me what state, what dignity, what honour,

Canst thou demise to any child of mine?

K. RICH. Even all I have; ay, and myself and all,

Will I withal endow a child of thine;

So in the Lethe of thy angry soul

Thou drown the sad remembrance of those wrongs,

Which thou supposest I have done to thee.

Q. ELIZ. Be brief, lest that the process of thy kindness

Last longer telling than thy kindness' date.

K. RICH. Then know, that from my soul I love thy daughter.

Q. ELIZ. My daughter's mother thinks it with her soul.

K. RICH. What do you think?

Q. ELIZ. That thou dost love my daughter from thy soul:

So, from thy soul's love, didst thou love her brothers;

And, from my heart's love, I do thank thee for it.

K. RICH. Be not so hasty to confound my meaning:

I mean, that with my soul I love thy daughter,

And do intend to make her queen of England.

Q. ELIZ. Well then, who dost thou mean shall be her king?

K. RICH. Even he that makes her queen: who else should be?

Q. ELIZ. What, thou?

K. RICH. I, even I: what think you of it, madam?

Q. ELIZ. How canst thou woo her?

K. RICH. That I would learn of you,

As one being best acquainted with her humour.

Q. ELIZ. And wilt thou learn of me?

K. RICH. Madam, with all my heart.

Q. ELIZ. Send to her, by the man that slew her brothers,

A pair of bleeding hearts; thereon engrave

Edward and York; then haply will she weep:

Therefore present to her,—as sometime Margaret

Did to thy father, steep'd in Rutland's blood,—   [drain

A handkerchief; which, say to her, did

The purple sap from her sweet brother's body,

And bid her wipe her weeping eyes withal.

If this inducement move her not to love,

Send her a letter of thy noble deeds;
Tell her thou mad'st away her uncle
Clarence,
Her uncle Rivers; ay, and, for her sake,
Mad'st quick conveyance with her good
aunt Anne.
K. RICH. You mock me, Madam; this is
not the way
To win your daughter.
Q. ELIZ.   There is no other way;
Unless thou couldst put on some other
shape,
And not be Richard that hath done all this.
K. RICH. Say, that I did all this for love
of her?
Q. ELIZ. Nay, then indeed, she cannot
choose but hate thee,
Having bought love with such a bloody
spoil.
K. RICH. Look, what is done cannot be
now amended:
Men shall deal unadvisedly sometimes,
Which after-hours give leisure to repent.
If I did take the kingdom from your sons,
To make amends I'll give it to your daugh-
ter.
If I have kill'd the issue of your womb,
To quicken your increase, I will beget
Mine issue of your blood upon your daugh-
ter:
A grandam's name is little less in love,
Than is the doting title of a mother;
They are as children but one step below,
Even of your mettle, of your very blood;
Of all one pain,—save for a night of
groans   [sorrow.
Endur'd of her, for whom you bid like
Your children were vexation to your youth;
But mine shall be a comfort to your age.
The loss, you have, is but a son being king,
And by that loss, your daughter is made
queen.
I cannot make you what amends I would,
Therefore accept such kindness as I can.
Dorset, your son, that with a fearful soul
Leads discontented steps in foreign soil,
This fair alliance quickly shall call home
To high promotions and great dignity:
The king that calls your beauteous daughter
wife,
Familiarly shall call thy Dorset brother;
Again shall you be mother to a king,
And all the ruins of distressful times
Repair'd with double riches of content.
What! we have many goodly days to see:
The liquid drops of tears that you have
shed,   [pearl,
Shall come again, transform'd to orient
Advantaging their loan with interest
Of ten times double gain of happiness.
Go then, my mother, to thy daughter go;

Make bold her bashful years with your
experience;
Prepare her ears to hear a wooer's tale;
Put in her tender heart th' aspiring flame
Of golden sovereignty; acquaint the prin-
cess   [joys
With the sweet silent hours of marriage
And when this arm of mine hath chastised
The petty rebel, dull-brain'd Buckingham,
Bound with triumphant garlands will I
come,   [bed;
And lead thy daughter to a conqueror's
To whom I will retail my conquest won,
And she shall be sole victress, Cæsar's
Cæsar.
Q. ELIZ. What were I best to say? her
father's brother
Would be her lord? Or shall I say, her
uncle?   [uncles?
Or, he that slew her brothers and her
Under what title shall I woo for thee,
That God, the law, my honour, and her
love,   [years?
Can make seem pleasing to her tender
K. RICH. Infer fair England's peace by
this alliance.
Q. ELIZ. Which she shall purchase with
still lasting war.
K. RICH. Tell her, the king, that may
command, entreats.
Q. ELIZ. That at her hands, which the
king's King forbids.
K. RICH. Say, she shall be a high and
mighty queen.
Q. ELIZ. To wail the title, as her mother
doth.
K. RICH. Say, I will love her everlastingly.
Q. ELIZ. But how long shall that title
"ever" last?
K. RICH. Sweetly in force unto her fair
life's end.
Q. ELIZ. But how long fairly shall her
sweet life last?
K. RICH. As long as heaven, and nature,
lengthen it.
Q. ELIZ. As long as hell, and Richard,
like of it.
K. RICH. Say, I, her sovereign, am her
subject low.
Q. ELIZ. But she, your subject, loathes
such sovereignty.
K. RICH. Be eloquent in my behalf to her.
Q. ELIZ. An honest tale speeds best, be-
ing plainly told.
K. RICH. Then, plainly to her tell my lov-
ing tale.
Q. ELIZ. Plain, and not honest, is too
harsh a style.
K. RICH. Your reasons are too shallow
and too quick.   [and dead;—
Q. ELIZ. O, no, my reasons are too deep

Too deep and dead, poor infants, in their
graves.

K. RICH. Harp not on that string, Madam;
that is past.

Q. ELIZ. Harp on it still shall I, till heart-
strings break.

K. RICH. Now, by my George, my garter,
and my crown,—

Q. ELIZ. Profan'd, dishonour'd, and the
third usurp'd.

K. RICH. I swear—

Q. ELIZ. By nothing; for this is no oath:
Thy George, profan'd, hath lost his holy
honour;
Thy garter, blemish'd, pawn'd his knightly
virtue;
Thy crown, usurp'd, disgrac'd his kingly
glory.
If something thou would'st swear to be
believ'd,
Swear, then, by something that thou hast
not wrong'd.

K. RICH. Now, by the world,—

Q. ELIZ. 'Tis full of thy foul wrongs.

K. RICH. My father's death,—

Q. ELIZ. Thy life hath that dishonour'd.

K. RICH. Then, by myself,—

Q. ELIZ.   Thyself is self misus'd.

K. RICH. Why then, by God,—

Q. ELIZ.   God's wrong is most of all.
If thou hadst fear'd to break an oath by
Him,
The unity, the king thy brother made,
Had not been broken, nor my brother slain:
If thou hadst fear'd to break an oath by
Him,
The imperial metal, circling now thy head,
Had grac'd the tender temples of my child;
And both the princes had been breathing
here,   [dust,
Which now, two tender bed-fellows for
Thy broken faith hath made a prey for
worms.
What canst thou swear by now?

K. RICH.   The time to come.

Q. ELIZ. That thou hast wronged in the
time o'er-past;
For I myself have many tears to wash
Hereafter time, for time past wrong'd by
thee.   [slaughter'd,
The children live, whose parents thou hast
Ungovern'd youth, to wail it in their age;
The parents live, whose children thou hast
butcher'd,
Old barren plants, to wail it with their age.
Swear not by time to come; for that thou
hast
Misus'd ere us'd, by times ill-us'd o'er-
past.

K. RICH. As I intend to prosper and re-
So thrive I in my dangerous attempt [pent,

Of hostile arms! myself myself confound!
Heaven and fortune bar me happy hours!
Day, yield me not thy light, nor, night, thy
rest!
Be opposite all planets of good luck
To my proceeding, if, with pure heart's
love,
Immaculate devotion, holy thoughts, [ter!
I tender not thy beauteous princely daugh-
In her consists my happiness and thine;
Without her, follows to myself and thee,
Herself, the land, and many a Christian
Death, desolation, ruin, and decay: [soul,
It cannot be avoided, but by this;
It will not be avoided, but by this.
Therefore, dear mother, (I must call you
Be the attorney of my love to her: [so)
Plead what I will be, not what I have been;
Not my deserts, but what I will deserve:
Urge the necessity and state of times,
And be not peevish found in great designs.

Q. ELIZ. Shall I be tempted of the devil
thus?

K. RICH. Ay, if the devil tempt thee to do
good.

Q. ELIZ. Shall I forget myself, to be myself?

K. RICH. Ay, if your self's remembrance
wrong yourself.

Q. ELIZ. Yet thou didst kill my children.

K. RICH. But in your daughter's womb
I bury them:
Where, in that nest of spicery, they shall
breed
Selves of themselves, to your recomforture.

Q. ELIZ. Shall I go win my daughter to
thy will?

K. RICH. And be a happy mother by the
deed.

Q. ELIZ. I go.—Write to me very shortly,
And you shall understand from me her
mind.

K. RICH. Bear her my true love's kiss;
and so, farewell.
          [*Kissing her. Exit* Q. ELIZABETH.
Relenting fool, and shallow, changing
woman!
     Enter RATCLIFF; CATESBY *following.*
How now! what news?

RAT. Most mighty sovereign, on the west-
ern coast
Rideth a puissant navy; to the shore
Throng many doubtful hollow-hearted
friends,
Unarm'd, and unresolv'd to beat them back:
'Tis thought that Richmond is their ad-
miral;
And there they hull, expecting but the aid
Of Buckingham to welcome them ashore.

K. RICH. Some light-foot friend post to
the Duke of Norfolk:—

Ratcliff, thyself,—or Catesby; where is he?
CATE. Here, my good lord.
K. RICH.   Catesby, fly to the duke.
CATE. I will, my lord, with all convenient
     haste.
K. RICH. Ratcliff, come hither:—post to
     Salisbury:
When thou com'st thither,—Dull, unmind-
     ful villain,   [*To* CATESBY.
Why stay'st thou here, and go'st not to the
     duke?
CATE. First, mighty liege, tell me your
     highness' pleasure,
What from your grace I shall deliver to
     him.
K. RICH. O, true, good Catesby:—bid him
     levy straight
The greatest strength and power he can
And meet me suddenly at Salisbury. [make,
CATE. I go.   [*Exit.*
RAT. What, may it please you, shall I do
     at Salisbury?
K. RICH. Why, what wouldst thou do
     there, before I go?
RAT. Your highness told me I should post
     before.
           Enter STANLEY.
K. RICH. My mind is chang'd.—Stanley,
     what news with you?
STAN. None good, my liege, to please you
     with the hearing;
Nor none so bad, but well may be reported.
K. RICH. Heyday, a riddle! neither good
     nor bad!
What need'st thou run so many miles
     about,   [way?
When thou may'st tell thy tale the nearest
Once more, what news?
STAN.   Richmond is on the seas.
K. RICH. There let him sink, and be the
     seas on him!
White-liver'd runagate, what doth he there?
STAN. I know not, mighty sovereign, but
     by guess.
K. RICH. Well, as you guess?
STAN. Stirr'd up by Dorset, Buckingham,
     and Morton,
He makes for England, here, to claim the
     crown.
K. RICH. Is the chair empty? is the sword
     unsway'd?
Is the king dead? the empire unpossess'd?
What heir of York is there alive, but we?
And who is England's king, but great
     York's heir?   [seas?
Then, tell me, what makes he upon the
STAN. Unless for that, my liege, I cannot
     guess.
K. RICH. Unless for that he comes to be
     your liege,   [comes.
You cannot guess wherefore the Welshman

Thou wilt revolt, and fly to him, I fear.
STAN. No, mighty liege; therefore, mis-
     trust me not.
K. RICH. Where is thy power, then, to beat
     him back?
Where be thy tenants and thy followers?
Are they not now upon the western shore,
Safe-conducting the rebels from their ships?
STAN. No, my good lord, my friends are
     in the north.
K. RICH. Cold friends to me: What do
     they in the north,
When they should serve their sovereign in
     the west?
STAN. They have not been commanded,
     mighty king:
Pleaseth your majesty to give me leave,
I'll muster up my friends, and meet your
     grace,   [please.
Where and what time your majesty shall
K. RICH. Ay, ay, thou wouldst be gone
     to join with Richmond:
But I'll not trust thee.
STAN.   Most mighty sovereign,
You have no cause to hold my friendship
     doubtful:
I never was, nor never will be false.
K. RICH. Go, then, and muster men. But
     leave behind
Your son, George Stanley: look your heart
     be firm,
Or else his head's assurance is but frail.
STAN. So deal with him, as I prove true
     to you.   [*Exit.*
           Enter a Messenger.
MESS. My gracious sovereign, now in Dev-
     onshire,
As I by friends am well advertised,
Sir Edward Courtney, and the haughty
     prelate,
Bishop of Exeter, his elder brother,
With many more confederates, are in arms.
           Enter a second Messenger.
2 *MESS.* In Kent, my liege, the Guildfords
     are in arms;
And every hour more competitors
Flock to the rebels, and their power grows
     strong.
           Enter a third Messenger.
3 *MESS.* My lord, the army of great Buck-
     ingham—
K. RICH. Out on ye, owls! nothing but
     songs of death?   [*He strikes him.*
There, take thou that, till thou bring better
     news.
3 *MESS.* The news I have to tell your
     majesty
Is, that by sudden floods and fall of waters,
Buckingham's army is dispers'd and scat-
     ter'd;

And he himself wander'd away alone,
No man knows whither.
K. RICH.   I cry thee mercy:
There is my purse, to cure that blow of
thine.
Hath any well-advised friend proclaim'd
Reward to him that brings the traitor in?
3 MESS. Such proclamation hath been
made, my lord.
        Enter a fourth Messenger.
4 MESS. Sir Thomas Lovel, and Lord mar-
quess Dorset,
'Tis said, my liege, in Yorkshire are in
arms: [highness,—
But this good comfort, bring I to your
The Bretagne navy is dispers'd by tempest:
Richmond, in Dorsetshire, sent out a boat
Unto the shore, to ask those on the banks,
If they were his assistants, yea, or no;
Who answer'd him, they came from Buck-
ingham
Upon his party: he, mistrusting them,
Hois'd sail, and made his course again for
Bretagne.
K. RICH. March on, march on, since we
are up in arms;
If not to fight with foreign enemies,
Yet to beat down these rebels here at home.
        Enter CATESBY.
CATE. My liege, the duke of Buckingham
is taken,—
That is the best news: that the earl of
Richmond
Is with a mighty power landed at Milford,
Is colder news, but yet they must be told.
K. RICH. Away towards Salisbury! while
we reason here,
A royal battle might be won and lost:—
Some one take order, Buckingham be
brought
To Salisbury; the rest march on with me.
                        [*Exeunt.*

SCENE V.—*A Room in* LORD STANLEY'S
House.

Enter STANLEY *and* SIR CHRISTOPHER
URSWICK.

STAN. Sir Christopher, tell Richmond this
from me:—
That, in the sty of the most bloody boar,
My son George Stanley is frank'd up in
hold:
If I revolt, off goes young George's head;
The fear of that holds off my present aid.
So, get thee gone: commend me to thy
lord;   [consented
Withal, say that the queen hath heartily
He should espouse Elizabeth her daughter.
But, tell me, where is princely Richmond
now?

CHRIS. At Pembroke, or at Ha'rford-
west, in Wales.
STAN. What men of name resort to him?
CHRIS. Sir Walter Herbert, a renowned
soldier;
Sir Gilbert Talbot, Sir William Stanley;
Oxford, redoubted Pembroke, Sir James
Blunt,
And Rice ap Thomas, with a valiant
crew;
And many other of great name and worth:
And towards London do they bend their
power,
If by the way they be not fought withal.
STAN. Well, hie thee to thy lord; I kiss
his hand:
My letter will resolve him of my mind.
Farewell.   [*Exeunt.*

ACT V.

SCENE I.—SALISBURY. *An open Place.*

Enter the Sheriff *and* Guard, *with* BUCK-
INGHAM, *led to execution.*

BUCK. Will not king Richard let me speak
with him?
SHER. No, my good lord; therefore be
patient.
BUCK. Hastings, and Edward's children,
Grey, and Rivers,
Holy king Henry, and thy fair son Edward,
Vaughan, and all that have miscarried
By underhand corrupted foul injustice,
If that your moody discontented souls
Do through the clouds behold this present
hour,
Even for revenge mock my destruction!—
This is All-Souls' day, fellows, is it not?
SHER. It is, my lord.
BUCK. Why, then All-Souls' day is my
body's dooms-day.
This is the day, which, in king Edward's
time,
I wish'd might fall on me, when I was
found
False to his children, or his wife's allies;
This is the day, wherein I wish'd to fall
By the false faith of him whom most I
trusted;
This, this All-Souls' day to my fearful soul
Is the determin'd respite of my wrongs:
That high All-Seer, which I dallied with,
Hath turn'd my feigned prayer on my head,
And given in earnest what I begg'd in jest.
Thus doth he force the swords of wicked
men
To turn their own points on their masters'
bosoms:
Thus Margaret's curse falls heavy on my
neck,—

"When he," quoth she, "shall split thy
heart with sorrow,
Remember Margaret was a prophetess."—
Come, Sirs, convey me to the block of
shame;
Wrong hath but wrong, and blame the due
of blame.   [*Exeunt.*

SCENE II.—*A Plain near* TAMWORTH.

Enter, with drum and colours, RICHMOND,
OXFORD, SIR JAMES BLUNT, SIR WALTER
HERBERT, *and others, with forces, march-
ing.*

RICHM. Fellows in arms, and my most
loving friends,
Bruis'd underneath the yoke of tyranny,
Thus far into the bowels of the land
Have we march'd on without impediment;
And here receive we from our father
Stanley
Lines of fair comfort and encouragement.
The wretched, bloody, and usurping boar,
That spoil'd your summer fields, and fruit-
ful vines,
Swills your warm blood like wash, and
makes his trough
In your embowell'd bosoms,—this foul swine
Is now even in the centre of this isle,
Near to the town of Leicester, as we learn:
From Tamworth thither is but one day's
march.
In God's name, cheerly on, courageous
friends,
To reap the harvest of perpetual peace
By this one bloody trial of sharp war.
OXF. Every man's conscience is a thousand
swords,
To fight against that bloody homicide.
HERB. I doubt not but his friends will
turn to us.
BLUNT. He hath no friends but what are
friends for fear,
Which in his dearest need will fly from him.
RICHM. All for our vantage. Then, in
God's name, march:
True hope is swift, and flies with swallow's
wings;
Kings it makes gods, and meaner creatures
kings.   [*Exeunt.*

SCENE III.—Bosworth Field.

Enter KING RICHARD *and forces; the* DUKE
OF NORFOLK, EARL OF SURREY, *and others.*
K. RICH. Here pitch our tent, even here
in Bosworth field.—
My lord of Surrey, why look you so sad?
SUR. My heart is ten times lighter than
my looks.
K. RICH. My lord of Norfolk,—

NOR.   Here, most gracious liege.
K. RICH. Norfolk, we must have knocks;
ha! must we not?
NOR. We must both give and take, my
loving lord.
K. RICH. Up with my tent! here will I
lie to-night;
[Soldiers *begin to set up the* KING's *tent.*
But where to-morrow?—Well, all's one for
that.—
Who hath descried the number of the
traitors?
NOR. Six or seven thousand is their ut-
most power.
K. RICH. Why, our battalia trebles that
account!
Besides, the king's name is a tower of
strength,
Which they upon the adverse faction
want.—
Up with the tent!—Come, noble gentlemen,
Let us survey the vantage of the ground;—
Call for some men of sound direction:—
Let's lack no discipline, make no delay;
For, lords, to-morrow is a busy day.
                                 [*Exeunt.*
Enter, on the other side of the field,
RICHMOND, SIR WILLIAM BRANDON, OX-
FORD, *and other Lords. Some of the* Sol-
diers *pitch* RICHMOND's *tent.*
RICHM. The weary sun hath made a gold-
en set,
And, by the bright track of his fiery car,
Gives token of a goodly day to-morrow.—
Sir William Brandon, you shall bear my
standard.—
Give me some ink and paper in my tent:
I'll draw the form and model of our battle,
Limit each leader to his several charge,
And part in just proportion our small
power.—
My lord of Oxford,—you, Sir William Bran-
don,—   [me.—
And you, Sir Walter Herbert,—stay with
The earl of Pembroke keeps his regi-
ment:—   [him.
Good captain Blunt, bear my good night to
And by the second hour in the morning
Desire the earl to see me in my tent:
Yet one thing more, good captain, do for
me,—   [much,
Where is lord Stanley quarter'd, do you
know?
BLUNT. Unless I have mista'en his colours
(Which, well I am assur'd, I have not
done)
His regiment lies half a mile at least
South from the mighty power of the king.
RICHM. If without peril it be possible,
Sweet Blunt, make some good means to
speak with him,

And give him from me this most needful
note,   [take it;
BLUNT. Upon my life, my lord, I'll under-
And so, God give you quiet rest to-night!
RICHM. Good night, good captain Blunt.
—Come, gentlemen,
Let us consult upon to-morrow's business:
In to my tent, the air is raw and cold.
                    [*They withdraw into the tent.*
Enter, to his tent, KING RICHARD, NOR-
    FOLK, RATCLIFF, *and* CATESBY.
K. RICH. What is't o'clock?
CATE. It's supper time, my lord; it's nine
o'clock.
K. RICH. I will not sup to-night.—
Give me some ink and paper.—
What, is my beaver easier than it was?
And all my armour laid into my tent?
CATE. It is, my liege; and all things are
in readiness.
K. RICH. Good Norfolk, hie thee to thy
charge;
Use careful watch, choose trusty sentinels.
NOR. I go, my lord.
K. RICH. Stir with the lark to-morrow,
gentle Norfolk.
NOR. I warrant you, my lord.   [*Exit.*
K. RICH. Ratcliff,—
RAT. My lord?
K. RICH. Send out a pursuivant at arms
To Stanley's regiment; bid him bring his
power
Before sun-rising, lest his son George fall
Into the blind cave of eternal night.—
Fill me a bowl of wine.—Give me a
watch.—
Saddle white Surrey for the field to-mor-
row.—
Look, that my staves be sound, and not too
Ratcliff,—   [heavy.—
RAT. My lord?
K. RICH. Saw'st thou the melancholy
lord Northumberland?
RAT. Thomas the earl of Surrey, and him-
self,   [to troop
Much about cock-shut time, from troop
Went through the army, cheering up the
soldiers.
K. RICH. So, I am satisfied.—Give me a
bowl of wine:
I have not that alacrity of spirit,
Nor cheer of mind, that I was wont to
have.—
Set it down.—Is ink and paper ready?
RAT. It is, my lord.
K. RICH. Bid my guard watch; leave me.
Ratcliff, about the mid of night, come to
my tent
And help to arm me.—Leave me, I say.
        [KING RICHARD *retires into his tent.*
        Exeunt RATCLIFF *and* CATESBY.

RICHMOND'S *tent opens, and discovers him
    and his* Officers, &c.
        Enter STANLEY.
STAN. Fortune and victory sit on thy
helm!
RICHM. All comfort that the dark night
can afford,
Be to thy person, noble father-in-law!
Tell me, how fares our loving mother?
STAN. I, by attorney, bless thee from thy
mother,
Who prays continually for Richmond's
good: [on,
So much for that.—The silent hours steal
And flaky darkness breaks within the east.
In brief,—for so the season bids us be,—
Prepare thy battle early in the morning,
And put thy fortune to the arbitrement
Of bloody strokes, and mortal-staring war.
I, as I may, (that which I would I cannot)
With best advantage will deceive the time,
And aid thee in this doubtful shock of
arms:
But on thy side I may not be too forward,
Lest, being seen, thy brother, tender George,
Be executed in his father's sight.
Farewell: the leisure and the fearful time
Cuts off the ceremonious vows of love,
And ample interchange of sweet discourse,
Which so long sunder'd friends should
dwell upon:
God give us leisure for these rites of love!
Once more, adieu: be valiant, and speed
well!   [regiment:
RICHM. Good lords, conduct him to his
I'll strive, with troubled thoughts, to take
a nap,   [row,
Lest leaden slumber peize me down to-mor-
When I should mount with wings of vic-
tory: [gentlemen.
Once more, good night, kind lords and
        [*Exeunt* Officers, &c. *with* STANLEY.
O Thou, whose captain I account myself,
Look on my forces with a gracious eye;
Put in their hands thy bruising irons of
wrath,
That they may crush down with a heavy
fall
Th' usurping helmets of our adversaries!
Make us thy ministers of chastisement,
That we may praise thee in thy victory!
To thee I do commend my watchful soul,
Ere I let fall the windows of mine eyes:
Sleeping and waking, O, defend me still!
                            [*Sleeps.*
The Ghost of PRINCE EDWARD, *Son to
    Henry the Sixth, rises between the two
    tents.*
GHOST. [*To* KING R.] Let me sit heavy on
thy soul to-morrow!

Think, how thou stab'dst me in my prime
of youth
At Tewksbury: despair, therefore, and
die!—   [souls
Be cheerful, Richmond; for the wronged
Of butcher'd princes fight in thy behalf:
King Henry's issue, Richmond, comforts
thee.
The Ghost of KING HENRY THE SIXTH *rises.*
GHOST. [*To* KING R.] When I was mor-
tal, my anointed body
By thee was punched full of deadly holes:
Think on the Tower, and me: despair and
die,—
Harry the sixth bids thee despair and die!—
[*To* RICHMOND.] Virtuous and holy, be
thou conqueror!
Harry, that prophesied thou should'st be
king,   [ish!
Doth comfort thee in sleep: live, and flour-
The Ghost of CLARENCE *rises.*
GHOST. [*To* KING R.] Let me sit heavy
on thy soul to-morrow!
I, that was wash'd to death with fulsome
wine,   [death!
Poor Clarence, by thy guile betray'd to
To-morrow in the battle think on me,
And fall thy edgeless sword: despair, and
die!
[*To* RICHMOND.] Thou offspring of the
house of Lancaster,
The wronged heirs of York do pray for
thee: [flourish!
Good angels guard thy battle! Live, and
The Ghosts of RIVERS, GREY, *and* VAUGHAN,
rise.
GH. OF RIV. [*To* KING R.] Let me sit
heavy on thy soul to-morrow,
Rivers, that died at Pomfret! Despair, and
die!
GH. OF GREY. [*To* KING R.] Think upon
Grey, and let thy soul despair.
GH. OF VAUGH. [*To* KING R.] Think
upon Vaughan, and with guilty fear
Let fall thy lance: despair, and die!—
ALL THREE. [*To* RICHMOND.] Awake!
and think our wrongs in Richard's bosom
Will conquer him!—Awake, and win the
day!
The Ghost of HASTINGS *rises.*
GHOST. [*To* KING R.] Bloody and guilty,
guiltily awake,
And in a bloody battle end thy days!
Think on lord Hastings: despair, and die!—
[*To* RICHMOND.] Quiet untroubled soul,
awake, awake!
Arm, fight, and conquer, for fair England's
sake.
The Ghosts of the two young PRINCES *rise.*
GHOSTS. Dream on thy cousins smother'd
in the Tower:

Let us be lead within thy bosom, Richard,
And weigh thee down to ruin, shame, and
death!
Thy nephews' souls bid thee despair, and
die!—   [wake in joy;
Sleep, Richmond, sleep in peace, and
Good angels guard thee from the boar's
annoy!
Live, and beget a happy race of kings!
Edward's unhappy sons do bid thee flourish.
The Ghost of QUEEN ANNE *rises.*
GHOST. Richard, thy wife, that wretched
Anne thy wife,
That never slept a quiet hour with thee,
Now fills thy sleep with perturbations:
To-morrow in the battle think on me,
And fall thy edgeless sword: despair, and
die!—
[*To* RICHMOND.] Thou quiet soul, sleep
thou a quiet sleep;
Dream of success and happy victory:
Thy adversary's wife doth pray for thee.
The Ghost of BUCKINGHAM *rises.*
GHOST. [*To* KING R.] The first was I
that help'd thee to the crown;
The last was I that felt thy tyranny:
O, in the battle think on Buckingham,
And die in terror of thy guiltiness!
Dream on, dream on, of bloody deeds and
death: [breath!—
Fainting, despair; despairing, yield thy
[*To* RICHMOND.] I died for hope ere I
could lend thee aid:
But cheer thy heart, and be thou not dis-
may'd:
God and good angels fight on Richmond's
side;
And Richard falls in height of all his pride.
          [*The Ghosts vanish.* KING RICHARD
          starts out of his dream.
K. RICH. Give me another horse!—bind
up my wounds!—
Have mercy, Jesu! — Soft! I did but
dream.—
O coward conscience, how dost thou afflict
me!—   [night.
The lights burn blue.—It is now dead mid-
Cold fearful drops stand on my trembling
flesh.   [by:
What, do I fear myself? there's none else
Richard loves Richard; that is, I am I.
Is there a murderer here? No;—yes, I am:
Then fly. What, from myself? Great rea-
son why,—
Lest I revenge. What, myself upon myself?
Alack, I love myself. Wherefore? for any
good
That I myself have done unto myself?
O, no! alas, I rather hate myself
For hateful deeds committed by myself!
I am a villain: yet I lie, I am not.

Fool, of thyself speak well:—fool, do not flatter.   [tongues,
My conscience hath a thousand several
And every tongue brings in a several tale,
And every tale condemns me for a villain.
Perjury, perjury, in the high'st degree;
Murder, stern murder, in the dir'st degree;
All several sins, all us'd in each degree,
Throng to the bar, crying all,—Guilty! guilty!
I shall despair.—There is no creature loves
And if I die, no soul shall pity me:— [me;
Nay, wherefore should they,—since that I myself
Find in myself no pity to myself?
Methought the souls of all that I had mur-der'd   [threat
Came to my tent; and every one did
To-morrow's vengeance on the head of Richard.

Enter RATCLIFF.

RAT. My lord,—
K. RICH. Who's there?
RAT. Ratcliff, my lord; 'tis I. The early village cock
Hath twice done salutation to the morn;
Your friends are up, and buckle on their armour.
K. RICH. O Ratcliff, I have dream'd a fearful dream!—
What thinkest thou,—will our friends prove all true?
RAT. No doubt, my lord.
K. RICH.   O Ratcliff, I fear, I fear,—
RAT. Nay, good my lord, be not afraid of shadows.
K. RICH. By the apostle Paul, shadows to-night
Have struck more terror to the soul of Richard,   [soldiers,
Than can the substance of ten thousand
Armed in proof, and led by shallow Rich-mond.
It is not yet near day. Come, go with me;
Under our tents I'll play the eaves-dropper,
To hear if any mean to shrink from me.
[*Exeunt* KING RICHARD *and* RATCLIFF.
Enter OXFORD *and others.*
LORDS. Good morrow, Richmond!
RICHM. [*Waking.*] Cry mercy, lords, and watchful gentlemen,
That you have ta'en a tardy sluggard here.
LORDS. How have you slept, my lord?
RICHM. The sweetest sleep, and fairest-boding dreams
That ever enter'd in a drowsy head,
Have I since your departure had, my lords.
Methought their souls, whose bodies Rich-ard murder'd,
Came to my tent, and cried on victory:
I promise you, my heart is very jocund

In the remembrance of so fair a dream.
How far into the morning is it, lords?
LORDS. Upon the stroke of four.
RICHM. Why, then 'tis time to arm, and give direction.—
          [*He advances to the troops.*
More than I have said, loving countrymen,
The leisure and enforcement of the time
Forbids to dwell on: yet remember this,—
God and our good cause fight upon our side;   [souls,
The prayers of holy saints and wronged
Like high-rear'd bulwarks, stand before our faces;
Richard except, those whom we fight against
Had rather have us win, than him they follow: [men,
For what is he they follow? truly, gentle-
A bloody tyrant and a homicide;
One rais'd in blood, and one in blood establish'd;
One that made means to come by what he hath,   [to help him;
And slaughter'd those that were the means
A base foul stone, made precious by the foil
Of England's chair, where he is falsely set;
One that hath ever been God's enemy.
Then, if you fight against God's enemy,
God will, in justice, ward you as his sol-diers;
If you do sweat to put a tyrant down,
You sleep in peace, the tyrant being slain;
If you do fight against your country's foes,
Your country's fat shall pay your pains the hire;
If you do fight in safeguard of your wives,
Your wives shall welcome home the con-querors;
If you do free your children from the sword,
Your children's children quit it in your age.   [rights,
Then, in the name of God and all these
Advance your standards, draw your willing swords.
For me, the ransom of my bold attempt
Shall be this cold corse on the earth's cold face;
But if I thrive, the gain of my attempt
The least of you shall share his part there-of.   [cheerfully;
Sound drums and trumpets boldly and
God and Saint George! Richmond and victory!   [*Exeunt.*
Re-enter KING RICHARD, RATCLIFF, Attend-ants, *and forces.*
K. RICH. What said Northumberland, as touching Richmond?
RAT. That he was never trained up in arms.

K. RICH. He said the truth: and what said
  Surrey then?
RAT. He smil'd, and said, the better for
  our purpose.
K. RICH. He was i' the right; and so,
  indeed, it is.   [*Clock strikes.*
Tell the clock there.—Give me a calen-
Who saw the sun to-day?   [dar.
RAT.   Not I, my lord.
K. RICH. Then he disdains to shine; for
  by the book,   [ago:
He should have brav'd the east an hour
A black day will it be to somebody.—
Ratcliff,—
RAT. My lord?
K. RICH. The sun will not be seen to-day;
The sky doth frown and lower upon our
  army.   [ground.
I would these dewy tears were from the
Not shine to-day! Why, what is that to me,
More than to Richmond? for the self-same
  heaven
That frowns on me, looks sadly upon him.
                Enter NORFOLK.
NOR. Arm, arm, my lord, the foe vaunts
  in the field.
K. RICH. Come, bustle, bustle;—caparison
  my horse;—
Call up lord Stanley, bid him bring his
  power:
I will lead forth my soldiers to the plain,
And thus my battle shall be ordered:—
My foreward shall be drawn out all in
  length,
Consisting equally of horse and foot;
Our archers shall be placed in the midst:
John duke of Norfolk, Thomas earl of
  Surrey,   [horse.
Shall have the leading of this foot and
They thus directed, we will follow
In the main battle; whose puissance on
  either side
Shall be well winged with our chiefest
  horse.
This, and Saint George to boot!—What
  think'st thou, Norfolk?   [eign.—
NOR. A good direction, warlike sover-
This found I on my tent this morning.
                        [*Giving a scroll.*
K. RICH. [*Reads.*] "Jocky of Norfolk, be
  not too bold,
For Dickon thy master is bought and
  sold."
A thing devised by the enemy.—
Go, gentlemen, every man to his charge:
Let not our babbling dreams affright our
  souls;   [use,
Conscience is but a word that cowards
Devis'd at first to keep the strong in awe:
Our strong arms be our conscience, swords
  our law.

March on, join bravely, let us to't pell-mell;
If not to heaven, then hand in hand to
  hell.—
What shall I say more than I have inferr'd?
Remember whom you are to cope withal;—
A sort of vagabonds, rascals, and run-aways,
A scum of Bretagnes, and base lackey
  peasants,
Whom their o'er-cloyed country vomits
  forth   [tion.
To desperate ventures and assur'd destruc-
You sleeping safe, they bring you to unrest;
You having lands, and bless'd with beau-
  teous wives,
They would restrain the one, distain the
  other.   [low,
And who doth lead them, but a paltry fel-
Long kept in Bretagne at our mother's cost?
A milk-sop, one that never in his life
Felt so much cold as over shoes in snow?
Let's whip these stragglers o'er the seas
  again;   [France,
Lash hence these over-weening rags of
These famish'd beggars, weary of their
  lives;
Who, but for dreaming on this fond exploit,
For want of means, poor rats, had hang'd
  themselves:
If we be conquer'd, let men conquer us,
And not these bastard Bretagnes; whom our
  fathers
Have in their own land beaten, bobb'd, and
  thump'd,   [shame.
And, on record, left them the heirs of
Shall these enjoy our lands? lie with our
  wives?
Ravish our daughters?—   [*Drum afar off.*
                Hark! I hear their drum.
Fight, gentlemen of England! fight, bold
  yeomen!   [head!
Draw, archers, draw your arrows to the
Spur your proud horses hard, and ride in
  blood;
Amaze the welkin with your broken staves!
                Enter a Messenger.
What says lord Stanley? will he bring his
  power?
MESS. My lord, he doth deny to come.
K. RICH. Off with his son George's head!
NOR. My lord, the enemy is pass'd the
  marsh:
After the battle let George Stanley die.
K. RICH. A thousand hearts are great
  within my bosom:
Advance our standards, set upon our foes;
Our ancient word of courage, fair Saint
  George,
Inspire us with the spleen of fiery dragons!
Upon them! Victory sits on our helms.
                                  [*Exeunt.*

SCENE IV.—*Another Part of the Field.*

Alarum: Excursions. Enter NORFOLK *and forces; to him* CATESBY.

CATE. Rescue, my lord of Norfolk, rescue, rescue!
The king enacts more wonders than a man,
Daring an opposite to every danger:
His horse is slain, and all on foot he fights,
Seeking for Richmond in the throat of death.
Rescue, fair lord, or else the day is lost!
    Alarum. Enter KING RICHARD.

K. RICH. A horse! a horse! my kingdom for a horse!
CATE. Withdraw, my lord; I'll help you to a horse.
K. RICH. Slave, I have set my life upon a cast,
And I will stand the hazard of the die.
I think there be six Richmonds in the field;
Five have I slain to-day, instead of him.—
A horse! a horse! my kingdom for a horse!
                            [Exeunt.

Alarums. Enter from opposite sides KING RICHARD *and* RICHMOND; *they fight, and exeunt fighting. Retreat and flourish. Then re-enter* RICHMOND, *with* STANLEY *bearing the crown, and divers other Lords, and forces.*

RICHM. God and your arms be prais'd, victorious friends;
The day is ours, the bloody dog is dead.
STAN. Courageous Richmond, well hast thou acquit thee.
Lo, here this long-usurped royalty,
From the dead temples of this bloody wretch
Have I pluck'd off, to grace thy brows withal:
Wear it, enjoy it, and make much of it.
RICHM. Great God of heaven, say amen to all!—
But, tell me, is young George Stanley living?
STAN. He is, my lord, and safe in Leicester town;
Whither, if you please, we may withdraw us.
RICHM. What men of name are slain on either side?
STAN. John duke of Norfolk, Walter lord Ferrers,
Sir Robert Brakenbury, and Sir William Brandon.
RICHM. Inter their bodies as becomes their births:
Proclaim a pardon to the soldiers fled,
That in submission will return to us:
And then, as we have ta'en the sacrament,
We will unite the white rose and the red:—
Smile heaven upon this fair conjunction,
That long hath frown'd upon their enmity!—
What traitor hears me, and says not amen?
England hath long been mad, and scarr'd herself;
The brother blindly shed the brother's blood,
The father rashly slaughter'd his own son,
The son, compell'd, been butcher to the sire:
All this divided York and Lancaster, [sire:
Divided in their dire division,
O, now, let Richmond and Elizabeth,
The true succeeders of each royal house,
By God's fair ordinance conjoin together!
And let their heirs (God, if thy will be so)
Enrich the time to come with smooth-fac'd peace, [days!
With smiling plenty, and fair prosperous
Abate the edge of traitors, gracious Lord,
That would reduce these bloody days again,
And make poor England weep in streams of blood!
Let them not live to taste this land's increase, [land's peace!
That would with treason wound this fair
Now civil wounds are stopp'd, peace lives again:
That she may long live here, God say amen!
                            [Exeunt.

The disgrace of Cardinal Wolsey. Act. III. S. 2.

KING HENRY VIII

DRAMATIS PERSONÆ.

KING HENRY THE EIGHTH.
CARDINAL WOLSEY.
CARDINAL CAMPEIUS.
CAPUCIUS, *Embassador from the Emperor, Charles V.*
CRANMER, *Archbishop of Canterbury.*
DUKE OF NORFOLK.
EARL OF SURREY.
DUKE OF SUFFOLK.
DUKE OF BUCKINGHAM.
LORD CHAMBERLAIN.
LORD CHANCELLOR.
GARDINER, *Bishop of Winchester.*
BISHOP OF LINCOLN. LORD ABERGAVENNY. LORD SANDS.
SIR HENRY GUILDFORD.
SIR THOMAS LOVELL.
SIR ANTHONY DENNY.
SIR NICHOLAS VAUX.
Secretaries *to* WOLSEY.
CROMWELL, *Servant to* WOLSEY.

GRIFFITH, *Gentleman-Usher to* QUEEN KATHARINE.
Three other Gentlemen. Garter, *King at Arms.*
DOCTOR BUTTS, *Physician to the* KING.
Surveyor *to the* DUKE OF BUCKINGHAM.
BRANDON, *and a* Sergeant at Arms.
Door-keeper *of the Council-Chamber.* Porter, *and his* Man.
Page *to* GARDINER. *A* Crier.

QUEEN KATHARINE, *Wife to* KING HENRY; *afterwards divorced.*
ANNE BULLEN, *her Maid of Honour; afterwards* QUEEN.
An Old Lady, *Friend to* ANNE BULLEN.
PATIENCE, *Woman to* QUEEN KATHARINE.

Several Lords *and* Ladies *in the Dumb Shows;* Women *attending upon the* QUEEN, Spirits, *which appear to her;* Scribes, Officers, Guards, *and other* Attendants.

SCENE.—*Chiefly in* LONDON *and* WESTMINSTER; *once, at* KIMBOLTON.

PROLOGUE.

I come no more to make you laugh: things now,
That bear a weighty and a serious brow,
Sad, high, and working, full of state and woe,
Such noble scenes as draw the eye to flow,
We now present. Those that can pity, here
May, if they think it well, let fall a tear;
The subject will deserve it. Such as give
Their money out of hope they may believe,
May here find truth too. Those that come
to see

293

Only a show or two, and so agree
The play may pass, if they be still and
    willing,
I'll undertake may see away their shilling
Richly in two short hours. Only they
That come to hear a merry bawdy play,
A noise of targets, or to see a fellow
In a long motley coat guarded with yellow,
Will be deceiv'd; for, gentle hearers, know,
To rank our chosen truth with such a show
As fool and fight is, beside forfeiting
Our own brains, and the opinion that we
    bring,
To make that only true we now intend,
Will leave us never an understanding
    friend.
Therefore, for goodness' sake, and as you
    are known
The first and happiest hearers of the town,
Be sad, as we would make ye: think, ye
    see
The very persons of our noble story,
As they were living; think, you see them
    great,
And follow'd with the general throng and
    sweat
Of thousand friends; then, in a moment,
    see
How soon this mightiness meets misery:
And, if you can be merry then, I'll say
A man may weep upon his wedding day.

ACT I.

SCENE I.—LONDON. *An Ante-chamber in
    the Palace.*

Enter, on one side, the DUKE OF NORFOLK;
    on the other, the DUKE OF BUCKINGHAM
    and Lord ABERGAVENNY.

BUCK. Good morrow, and well met. How
    have you done,
Since last we saw in France?
NOR.   I thank your grace,
Healthful; and ever since a fresh admirer
Of what I saw there.
BUCK.   An untimely ague
Stay'd me a prisoner in my chamber, when
Those suns of glory, those two lights of
    men,
Met in the vale of Andren.
NOR.   'Twixt Guynes and Arde:
I was then present, saw them salute on
    horseback;
Beheld them, when they lighted, how they
    clung
In their embracement, as they grew to-
    gether;
Which had they, what four thron'd ones
    could have weigh'd
Such a compounded one?

BUCK.   All the whole time
I was my chamber's prisoner.
NOR.   Then you lost
The view of earthly glory: men might say,
Till this time, pomp was single; but now
    married
To one above itself. Each following day
Became the next day's master, till the last
Made former wonders it's: to-day the
    French
All clinquant, all in gold, like heathen
    gods,
Shone down the English; and to-morrow
    they
Made Britain, India: every man that stood
Show'd like a mine. Their dwarfish pages
    were
As cherubins, all gilt: the madams too,
Not us'd to toil, did almost sweat to bear
The pride upon them, that their very
    labour
Was to them as a painting: now this mask
Was cried incomparable; and the ensuing
    night
Made it a fool, and beggar. The two kings,
Equal in lustre, were now best, now worst,
As presence did present them; him in eye,
Still him in praise: and, being present
    both,
'Twas said they saw but one; and no dis-
    cerner
Durst wag his tongue in censure. When
    these suns
(For so they phrase them) by their her-
    alds challeng'd
The noble spirits to arms, they did per-
    form
Beyond thought's compass; that former
    fabulous story,
Being now seen possible enough, got credit,
That Bevis was believ'd.
BUCK.   O, you go far.
NOR. As I belong to worship, and affect
In honour honesty, the tract of every
    thing
Would by a good discourser lose some life,
Which action's self was tongue to. All was
    royal;
To the disposing of it naught rebell'd;
Order gave each thing view; the office did
Distinctly his full function.
BUCK.   Who did guide,
I mean, who set the body and the limbs
Of this great sport together, as you guess?
NOR. One, certes, that promises no ele-
    ment
In such a business.
BUCK. I pray you, who, my lord?
NOR. All this was order'd by the good
    discretion
Of the right reverend cardinal of York.

BUCK. The devil speed him! no man's pie is freed
From his ambitious finger. What had he
To do in these fierce vanities? I wonder
That such a keech can with his very bulk
Take up the rays o' the beneficial sun,
And keep it from the earth.
NOR.   Surely, Sir,
There's in him stuff that puts him to these ends;
For, being not propp'd by ancestry, whose grace
Chalks successors their way; nor call'd upon
For high feats done to the crown; neither allied
To eminent assistants; but, spider-like,
Out of his self-drawing web, he gives us note,
The force of his own merit makes his way;
A gift that heaven gives for him, which buys
A place next to the king.
ABER.   I cannot tell
What heaven hath given him,—let some graver eye
Pierce into that; but I can see his pride
Peep through each part of him: whence has he that?
If not from hell, the devil is a niggard;
Or has given all before, and he begins
A new hell in himself.
BUCK.   Why the devil,
Upon this French going-out, took he upon him,
Without the privity o' the king, to appoint
Who should attend on him? He makes up the file
Of all the gentry; for the most part such
To whom as great a charge as little honour
He meant to lay upon: and his own letter,
The honourable board of council out,
Must fetch him in the papers.
ABER.   I do know
Kinsmen of mine, three at the least, that have
By this so sicken'd their estates, that never
They shall abound as formerly.
BUCK.   O, many
Have broke their backs with laying manors on them
For this great journey. What did this vanity,
But minister communication of
A most poor issue?
NOR.   Grievingly I think,
The peace between the French and us not values
The cost that did conclude it.
BUCK.   Every man,
After the hideous storm that follow'd, was

A thing inspir'd; and, not consulting, broke
Into a general prophecy,—that this tempest,
Dashing the garment of this peace, aboded
The sudden breach on't.
NOR.   Which is budded out;
For France hath flaw'd the league, and hath attach'd
Our merchants' goods at Bourdeaux.
ABER.   Is it therefore
Th' embassador is silenc'd?
NOR.   Marry, is't.
ABER. A proper title of a peace; and purchas'd
At a superfluous rate!
BUCK.   Why, all this business
Our reverend cardinal carried.
NOR.   'Like it your grace,
The state takes notice of the private difference
Betwixt you and the cardinal. I adv'se you,
(And take it from a heart that wishes towards you
Honour and plenteous safety) that you read
The cardinal's malice and his potency
Together; to consider farther, that
What his high hatred would effect, wants not
A minister in his power. You know his nature,
That he's revengeful; and I know his sword
Hath a sharp edge: it's long, and, 't may be said,
It reaches far; and where 'twill not extend,
Thither he darts it. Bosom up my counsel,
You'll find it wholesome.—Lo, where comes that rock
That I advise your shunning.
Enter CARDINAL WOLSEY, *(the Purse borne before him,) certain of the* Guard, *and two* Secretaries *with papers. The* CARDINAL *in his passage fixeth his eye on* BUCKINGHAM, *and* BUCKINGHAM *on him, both full of disdain.*
WOL. The duke of Buckingham's surveyor, ha?
Where's his examination?
1 SECR.   Here, so please you.
WOL. Is he in person ready?
1 SECR.   Ay, please your grace.
WOL. Well, we shall then know more; and Buckingham
Shall lessen this big look.
                    [*Exeunt* WOLSEY *and train.*
BUCK. This butcher's cur is venom-mouth'd, and I
Have not the power to muzzle him; therefore best

Not wake him in his slumber. A beggar's
book
Out-worths a noble's blood.
NOR.   What, are you chaf'd?
Ask God for temperance; that's th' ap-
pliance only,
Which your disease requires.
BUCK.   I read in's looks
Matter against me; and his eye revil'd
Me, as his abject object: at this instant
He bores me with some trick: he's gone t'
the king;
I'll follow, and out-stare him.
NOR.   Stay, my lord,
And let your reason with your choler ques-
tion
What 'tis you go about: to climb steep
hills,
Requires slow pace at first: anger is like
A full-hot horse, who being allow'd his
way,
Self-mettle tires him. Not a man in Eng-
land
Can advise me like you: be to yourself,
As you would to your friend.
BUCK.   I'll to the king;
And from a mouth of honour quite cry
down
This Ipswich fellow's insolence; or pro-
claim
There's difference in no persons.
NOR.   Be advis'd;
Heat not a furnace for your foe so hot
That it do singe yourself: we may outrun,
By violent swiftness, that which we run at,
And lose by over-running. Know you not,
The fire that mounts the liquor till't run
o'er,
In seeming to augment it wastes it? Be
advis'd:
I say again, there is no English soul
More stronger to direct you than yourself,
If with the sap of reason you would quench,
Or but allay, the fire of passion.
BUCK.   Sir,
I am thankful to you; and I'll go along
By your prescription: but this top-proud
fellow,
(Whom from the flow of gall I name not,
but
From sincere motions,) by intelligence,
And proofs as clear as founts in July,
when
We see each grain of gravel, I do know
To be corrupt and treasonous.
NOR.   Say not, treasonous.
BUCK. To the king I'll say't; and make
my vouch as strong
As shore of rock. Attend. This holy fox,
Or wolf, or both, (for he is equal ravenous
As he is subtle, and as prone to mischief

As able to perform't; his mind and place
Infecting one another, yea, reciprocally)
Only to show his pomp as well in France
As here at home, suggests the king our
master
To this last costly treaty, th' interview,
That swallow'd so much treasure, and like
a glass
Did break i' the rinsing.
NOR.   Faith, and so it did.
BUCK. Pray, give me favour, Sir. This
cunning cardinal
The articles o' the combination drew,
As himself pleas'd; and they were ratified,
As he cried, "Thus let be:" to as much
end,
As give a crutch to the dead: but our
count-cardinal
Has done this, and 'tis well; for worthy
Wolsey,
Who cannot err, he did it. Now this fol-
lows,
(Which, as I take it, is a kind of puppy
To the old dam, treason)—Charles the
emperor,
Under pretence to see the queen his aunt,
(For 'twas indeed his colour, but he came
To whisper Wolsey) here makes visitation:
His fears were, that the interview betwixt
England and France, might, through their
amity,
Breed him some prejudice; for from this
league
Peep'd harms that menac'd him: he privily
Deals with our cardinal; and, as I trow,—
Which I do well; for, I am sure, the em-
peror
Paid ere he promis'd; whereby his suit was
granted
Ere it was ask'd;—but when the way was
made,
And pav'd with gold, the emperor thus
desir'd,—
That he would please to alter the king's
course,
And break the foresaid peace. Let the
king know,
(As soon he shall by me) that thus the
cardinal
Does buy and sell his honour as he pleases,
And for his own advantage.
NOR.   I am sorry
To hear this of him; and could wish he
were
Something mistaken in't.
BUCK.   No, not a syllable:
I do pronounce him in that very shape
He shall appear in proof.
Enter BRANDON; *a Sergeant at Arms be-
fore him, and two or three of the Guard.*
BRAN. Your office, sergeant; execute it.

SERG.   Sir,
My lord the duke of Buckingham, and earl
Of Hereford, Stafford, and Northampton, I
Arrest thee of high treason, in the name
Of our most sovereign king.
BUCK.   Lo, you, my lord,
The net has fall'n upon me! I shall perish
Under device and practice.
BRAN.   I am sorry
To see you ta'en from liberty, to look on
The business present: 'tis his highness'
   pleasure,
You shall to the Tower.
BUCK.   It will help me nothing
To plead mine innocence; for that dye is
   on me,
Which makes my whit'st part black. The
   will of heaven
Be done in this and all things!—I obey.—
O my lord Aberga'ny, fare you well!
BRAN. Nay, he must bear you company.
—[*To* ABER.] The king
Is pleas'd you shall to the Tower, till you
   know
How he determines farther.
ABER.   As the duke said,
The will of heaven be done, and the king's
   pleasure
By me obey'd!
BRAN.   Here is a warrant from
The king to attach lord Montacute; and
   the bodies
Of the duke's confessor, John de la Car,
One Gilbert Peck, his chancellor,—
BUCK.   So, so;
These are the limbs o' the plot:—no more,
   I hope.
BRAN. A monk o' the Chartreux.
BUCK.   O, Nicholas Hopkins?
BRAN.   He.
BUCK. My surveyor is false; the o'er-
   great cardinal
Hath show'd him gold; my life is spann'd
   already:
I am the shadow of poor Buckingham,
Whose figures even this instant cloud puts
   on,
By darkening my clear sun.—My lord,
   farewell.   [*Exeunt.*

Scene II.—*The Council-Chamber.*

Cornets. Enter KING HENRY, CARDINAL
WOLSEY, *the* Lords of the Council, SIR
THOMAS LOVELL, Officers, Attendants.
The KING *enters leaning on the* CARDI-
NAL'S *shoulder.*
K. HEN. My life itself, and the best heart
of it,
Thanks you for this great care: I stood i'
   the level

Of a full charg'd confederacy, and give
   thanks
To you that chok'd it.—Let be call'd before us
That gentleman of Buckingham's: in person
I'll hear him his confessions justify:
And point by point the treasons of his
   master
He shall again relate.
   [*The* KING *takes his state. The* Lords
   of the Council take their several
   places. The CARDINAL *places himself*
   under the KING'S *feet, on his right*
   side.
A noise within, crying "Room for the
Queen!" *Enter the* QUEEN, *ushered by
the* DUKES OF NORFOLK *and* SUFFOLK:
she kneels. The KING *riseth from his
state, takes her up, kisses, and placeth
her by him.*
Q. KATH. Nay, we must longer kneel: I
am a suitor.
K. HEN. Arise, and take place by us:—
half your suit
Never name to us; you have half our
power:
The other moiety, ere you ask, is given;
Repeat your will, and take it.
Q. KATH.   Thank your majesty.
That you would love yourself, and in that
   love
Not unconsider'd leave your honour, nor
The dignity of your office, is the point
Of my petition.
K. HEN.   Lady mine, proceed.
Q. KATH. I am solicited, not by a few,
And those of true condition, that your
   subjects
Are in great grievance: there have been
   commissions
Sent down among them, which hath flaw'd
   the heart
Of all their loyalties:—wherein, although,
My good lord cardinal, they vent re-
   proaches
Most bitterly on you, as putter-on
Of these exactions, yet the king our master,
(Whose honour heaven shield from soil!)
   even he escapes not
Language unmannerly; yea, such which
   breaks
The sides of loyalty, and almost appears
In loud rebellion.
NOR.   Not almost appears,—
It doth appear; for, upon these taxations,
The clothiers all, not able to maintain
The many to them 'longing, have put off
The spinsters, carders, fullers, weavers,
   who,
Unfit for other life, compell'd by hunger

And lack of other means, in desperate manner
Daring th' event to the teeth, are all in uproar,
And danger serves among them.
K. HEN.   Taxation!
Wherein? and what taxation?—My lord cardinal,
You that are blam'd for it alike with us,
Know you of this taxation?
WOL.   Please you, Sir,
I know but of a single part, in aught
Pertains to the state; and front but in that file
Where others tell steps with me.
Q. KATH.   No, my lord,
You know no more than others; but you frame
Things that are known alike; which are not wholesome
To those which would not know them, and yet must
Perforce be their acquaintance. These exactions,
Whereof my sovereign would have note, they are
Most pestilent to the hearing; and, to bear them,
The back is sacrifice to the load. They say
They are devis'd by you; or else you suffer
Too hard an exclamation.
K. HEN.   Still exaction!
The nature of it? In what kind, let's know,
Is this exaction?
Q. KATH. I am much too venturous
In tempting of your patience; but am bolden'd
Under your promis'd pardon. The subjects' grief
Comes through commissions, which compel from each
The sixth part of his substance, to be levied
Without delay; and the pretence for this
Is nam'd, your wars in France: this makes bold mouths:
Tongues spit their duties out, and cold hearts freeze
Allegiance in them; their curses now
Live where their prayers did: and it's come to pass,
This tractable obedience is a slave
To each incensed will. I would your highness
Would give it quick consideration, for
There is no primer business.
K. HEN.   By my life,
This is against our pleasure.
WOL.   And for me,
I have no farther gone in this, than by
A single voice; and that not pass'd me but

By learned approbation of the judges. If I am
Traduc'd by ignorant tongues, which neither know
My faculties nor person, yet will be
The chronicles of my doing,—let me say,
'Tis but the fate of place, and the rough brake
That virtue must go through. We must not stint
Our necessary actions, in the fear
To cope malicious censurers; which ever,
As ravenous fishes, do a vessel follow
That is new trimm'd, but benefit no farther
Than vainly longing. What we oft do best,
By sick interpreters, once weak ones, is
Not ours, or not allow'd; what worst, as oft,
Hitting a grosser quality, is cried up
For our best act. If we shall stand still,
In fear our motion will be mock'd or carp'd at,
We should take root here where we sit, or sit
State statues only.
K. HEN.   Things done well,
And with a care, exempt themselves from fear;
Things done without example, in their issue
Are to be fear'd. Have you a precedent
Of this commission? I believe, not any.
We must not rend out subjects from our laws,
And stick them in our will. Sixth part of each?
A trembling contribution! Why, we take
From every tree, lop, bark, and part o' the timber;
And, though we leave it with a root, thus hack'd
The air will drink the sap. To every county
Where this is question'd, send our letters, with
Free pardon to each man that has denied
The force of this commission: pray, look to't;
I put it to your care.
WOL. [To the Secretary.] A word with you.
Let there be letters writ to every shire,
Of the king's grace and pardon. The griev'd commons
Hardly conceive of me; let it be nois'd,
That through our intercession this revokement   [you
And pardon comes: I shall anon advise
Farther in the proceeding.
                              [Exit Secretary.

Enter Surveyor.

Q. KATH. I am sorry that the duke of Buckingham
Is run in your displeasure.

K. HEN.   It grieves many:
The gentleman is learn'd, and a most rare speaker;
To nature none more bound; his training such,
That he may furnish and instruct great teachers,
And never seek for aid out of himself. Yet see,
When these so noble benefits shall prove
Not well dispos'd, the mind growing once corrupt,
They turn to vicious forms, ten times more ugly
Than ever they were fair. This man so complete,
Who was enroll'd 'mongst wonders, and when we,   [find
Almost with ravish'd list'ning, could not
His hour of speech a minute; he, my lady,
Hath into monstrous habits put the graces
That once were his, and is become as black
As if besmear'd in hell. Sit by us; you shall hear
(This was his gentleman in trust) of him
Things to strike honour sad.—Bid him recount
The fore-recited practices; whereof
We cannot feel too little, hear too much.

WOL. Stand forth, and with bold spirit relate what you,
Most like a careful subject, have collected
Out of the duke of Buckingham.

K. HEN.   Speak freely.

SURV. First, it was usual with him, every day
It would infect his speech,—that if the king
Should without issue die, he'd carry it so
To make the sceptre his: these very words
I've heard him utter to his son-in-law,
Lord Aberga'ny; to whom by oath he menac'd
Revenge upon the cardinal.   [menac'd

WOL.   Please your highness, note
This dangerous conception in this point.
Not friended by his wish, to your high person
His will is most malignant; and it stretches
Beyond you, to your friends.

Q. KATH.   My learn'd lord cardinal,
Deliver all with charity.

K. HEN.   Speak on:
How grounded he his title to the crown,
Upon our fail? to this point hast thou heard him
At any time speak aught?

SURV.   He was brought to this
By a vain prophecy of Nicholas Hopkins.

K. HEN. What was that Hopkins?

SURV.   Sir, a Chartreux friar,
His confessor; who fed him every minute
With words of sovereignty.

K. HEN.   How know'st thou this?

SURV. Not long before your highness sped to France,
The duke being at the Rose, within the parish
Saint Lawrence Poultney, did of me demand
What was the speech among the Londoners
Concerning the French journey: I replied,
Men fear'd the French would prove perfidious,
To the king's danger. Presently the duke
Said, 'twas the fear, indeed; and that he doubted
'Twould prove the verity of certain words
Spoke by a holy monk; "that oft," says he,
"Hath sent to me, wishing me to permit
John de la Car, my chaplain, a choice hour
To hear from him a matter of some moment:
Whom after, under the confession's seal,
He solemnly had sworn, that, what he spoke,
My chaplain to no creature living, but
To me, should utter, with demure confidence
This pausingly ensu'd,—Neither the king, nor's heirs,
(Tell you the duke) shall prosper; bid him strive
To gain the love o' the commonalty: the duke
Shall govern England."

Q. KATH.   If I know you well,
You were the duke's surveyor, and lost your office
On the complaint o' the tenants: take good heed
You charge not in your spleen a noble person,
And spoil your nobler soul: I say, take heed;
Yes, heartily beseech you.

K. HEN.   Let him on.—
Go forward.

SURV. On my soul, I'll speak but truth.
I told my lord the duke, by the devil's illusions
The monk might be deceiv'd; and that 'twas dangerous for him
To ruminate on this so far, until
It forg'd him some design, which, being believ'd,
It was much like to do: he answer'd, "Tush!

It can do me no damage;" adding farther,
That, had the king in his last sickness
fail'd,
The cardinal's and Sir Thomas Lovell's
heads
Should have gone off.
K. HEN. Ha! what, so rank? Ah, ha!
There's mischief in this man:—canst thou
SURV. I can, my liege.   [say farther?
K. HEN.   Proceed.
SURV.   Being at Greenwich,
After your highness had reprov'd the duke
About Sir William Blomer,—
K. HEN.   I remember
Of such a time:—being my sworn servant,
The duke retain'd him his.—But on; what
hence?
SURV. "If," quoth he, "I for this had
been committed,
As, to the Tower, I thought,—I would
have play'd
The part my father meant to act upon
Th' usurper Richard; who, being at Salis-
bury,
Made suit to come in's presence; which if
granted,
As he made semblance of his duty, would
Have put his knife into him."
K. HEN.   A giant traitor!
WOL. Now, Madam, may his highness live
in freedom,
And this man out of prison?
Q. KATH.   God mend all!
K. HEN. There's something more would
out of thee; what say'st?
SURV. After "the duke his father," with
"the knife,"
He stretch'd him, and, with one hand on
his dagger,
Another spread on's breast, mounting his
eyes,
He did discharge a horrible oath; whose
tenor
Was,—were he evil us'd, he would out-go
His father, by as much as a performance
Does an irresolute purpose.
K. HEN.   There's his period,
To sheathe his knife in us. He is at-
tach'd;
Call him to present trial: if he may
Find mercy in the law, 'tis his; if none,
Let him not seek't of us. By day and
night,
He's traitor to the height!   [*Exeunt.*

Scene III.—*A Room in the Palace.*
Enter the Lord Chamberlain *and* Lord
Sands.
CHAM. Is't possible the spells of France
should juggle

Men into such strange mysteries?
SANDS.   New customs,
Though they be never so ridiculous,
Nay, let 'em be unmanly, yet are follow'd.
CHAM. As far as I see, all the good our
English
Have got by the late voyage is but merely
A fit or two o' the face; but they are
shrewd ones;
For when they hold 'em, you would swear
directly
Their very noses had been counsellors
To Pepin or Clotharius, they keep state so.
SANDS. They have all new legs, and lame
ones: one would take it,
That never saw them pace before, the
spavin,
Or springhalt reign'd among them.
CHAM.   Death! my Lord,
Their clothes are after such a pagan cut
too,
That, sure, they've worn out christendom.—
        Enter Sir Thomas Lovell.
                    How now!
What news, Sir Thomas Lovell?
LOV.   'Faith, my lord,
I hear of none, but the new proclamation
That's clapp'd upon the court-gate.
CHAM.   What is't for?
LOV. The reformation of our travell'd
gallants,
That fill the court with quarrels, talk, and
tailors.
CHAM. I am glad 'tis there: now I
would pray our monsieurs
To think an English courtier may be wise,
And never see the Louvre.
LOV.   They must either
(For so run the conditions) leave those
remnants
Of food and feather, that they got in
France,
With all their honourable points of igno-
rance
Pertaining thereunto (as fights and fire-
works;
Abusing better men than they can be,
Out of a foreign wisdom); renouncing
clean
The faith they have in tennis, and tall
stockings,
Short blister'd breeches, and those types
of travel,
And understand again like honest men;
Or pack to their old playfellows: there, I
take it,
They may, *cum privilegio*, wear away
The lag end of their lewdness, and be
laugh'd at.

SANDS. 'Tis time to give them physic, their diseases
Are grown so catching.
CHAM. What a loss our ladies
Will have of these trim vanities!
LOV. Ay, marry,
There will be woe indeed, lords: the sly whoresons
Have got a speeding trick to lay down ladies;
A French song, and a fiddle, has no fellow.
SANDS. The devil fiddle them! I am glad they're going:
(For, sure, there's no converting of them) now,
An honest country lord, as I am, beaten
A long time out of play, may bring his plain-song,
And have an hour of hearing; and, by'r lady,
Held current music too.
CHAM. Well said, lord Sands;
Your colt's tooth is not cast yet.
SANDS. No, my lord;
Nor shall not, while I have a stump.
CHAM. Sir Thomas,
Whither were you a-going?
LOV. To the cardinal's:
Your lordship is a guest too.
CHAM. O, 'tis true:
This night he makes a supper, and a great one,
To many lords and ladies; there will be
The beauty of this kingdom, I'll assure you.
LOV. That churchman bears a bounteous mind indeed,
A hand as fruitful as the land that feeds us;
His dews fall every where.
CHAM. No doubt he's noble;
He had a black mouth that said other of him.
SANDS. He may, my lord, he has wherewithal: in him,
Sparing would show a worse sin than ill doctrine:
Men of his way should be most liberal;
They are set here for examples.
CHAM. True, they are so;
But few now give so great ones. My barge stays;
Your lordship shall along.—Come, good Sir Thomas,
We shall be late else; which I would not be,
For I was spoke to, with Sir Henry Guilford,
This night to be comptrollers.
SANDS. I am your lordship's.
[*Exeunt.*

SCENE IV.—*The Presence-Chamber in York-Place.*

Hautboys. A small table under a state for the CARDINAL, *a longer table for the guests. Enter, on one side,* ANNE BULLEN, *and divers* Lords, Ladies, *and* Gentlewomen, *as guests; on the other, enter* SIR HENRY GUILFORD.

GUILD. Ladies, a general welcome from his grace
Salutes ye all; this night he dedicates
To fair content and you: none here, he hopes,
In all this noble bevy, has brought with her
One care abroad; he would have all as merry,
As, first, good company, good wine, good welcome,
Can make good people.—
Enter Lord Chamberlain, LORD SANDS, *and* SIR THOMAS LOVELL.
O, my lord, you're tardy:
The very thought of this fair company
Clapp'd wings to me.
CHAM. You are young, Sir Harry Guildford.
SANDS. Sir Thomas Lovell, had the cardinal
But half my lay-thoughts in him, some of these
Should find a running banquet ere they rested,
I think would better please them: by my life,
They are a sweet society of fair ones.
LOV. O, that your lordship were but now confessor
To one or two of these!
SANDS. I would I were;
They should find easy penance.
LOV. Faith, how easy?
SANDS. As easy as a down-bed would afford it.
CHAM. Sweet ladies, will it please you sit?—Sir Harry,
Place you that side; I'll take the charge of this:
His grace is entering.—Nay, you must not freeze;
Two women plac'd together makes cold weather:—
My lord Sands, you are one will keep them waking;
Pray, sit between these ladies.
SANDS. By my faith,
And thank your lordship.—By your leave, sweet ladies:
[*Seats himself between* ANNE BULLEN *and another* Lady.

If I chance to talk a little wild, forgive
I had it from my father.   [me;
ANNE.   Was he mad, Sir?
SANDS. O, very mad, exceeding mad, in
love too:
But he would bite none; just as I do now,
He would kiss you twenty with a breath.
                              [*Kisses her.*
CHAM.   Well said, my lord.—
So, now you are fairly seated.—Gentlemen,
The penance lies on you, if these fair
ladies
Pass away frowning.
SANDS.   For my little cure,
Let me alone.
Hautboys. Enter CARDINAL WOLSEY, *at-
tended, and takes his state.*
WOL. You're welcome, my fair guests:
that noble lady,
Or gentleman, that is not freely merry,
Is not my friend. This, to confirm my
welcome;
And to you all, good health.   [*Drinks.*
SANDS.   Your grace is noble:—
Let me have such a bowl may hold my
thanks,
And save me so much talking.
WOL.   My lord Sands,
I am beholden to you: cheer your neigh-
bours.—
Ladies, you are not merry:—gentlemen,
Whose fault is this?
SANDS.   The red wine first must rise
In their fair cheeks, my lord; then, we
shall have them
Talk us to silence.
ANNE.   You are a merry gamester,
My lord Sands.
SANDS.   Yes, if I make my play.
Here's to your ladyship: and pledge it,
Madam,
For 'tis to such a thing,—
ANNE.   You cannot show me.
SANDS. I told your grace, they would
talk anon.
     [*Drum and trumpets within; chambers
discharged.*
WOL.   What's that?
CHAM. Look out there, some of you.
                         [*Exit a* Servant.
WOL.   What warlike voice,
And to what end is this?—Nay, ladies, fear
not;
By all the laws of war you're privileg'd.
          Re-enter Servant.
CHAM. How now! what is't?
SERV.   A noble troop of strangers,—
For so they seem: they've left their barge,
and landed;
And hither make, as great embassadors
From foreign princes.

WOL.   Good lord chamberlain,
Go, give them welcome; you can speak the
French tongue;
And, pray, receive them nobly, and conduct
them
Into our presence, where this heaven of
beauty
Shall shine at full upon them.—Some attend
him.—
     [*Exit* Chamberlain. *attended. All arise,
and tables removed.*
You have now a broken banquet; but we'll
mend it.
A good digestion to you all: and, once
more,
I shower a welcome on ye;—welcome all.
Hautboys. Enter the KING, *and others, as
Maskers, habited like shepherds, ushered
by the* Lord Chamberlain. *They pass
directly before the* CARDINAL, *and grace-
fully salute him.*
A noble company! what are their pleas-
ures?
CHAM. Because they speak no English,
thus they pray'd
To tell your grace,—that, having heard by
fame
Of this so noble and so fair assembly
This night to meet here, they could do no
less,
Out of the great respect they bear to beauty,
But leave their flocks; and, under your fair
conduct,
Crave leave to view these ladies, and en-
treat
An hour of revels with them.
WOL.   Say, lord chamberlain,
They have done my poor house grace; for
which I pay them
A thousand thanks, and pray them take
their pleasures.
     [*Ladies chosen for the dance. The*
KING *chooses* ANNE BULLEN.
K. HEN. The fairest hand I ever touch'd.
O beauty,
Till now I never knew thee!
                              [*Music. Dance.*
WOL. My lord,—
CHAM.   Your grace?
WOL. Pray tell them thus much from me.
There should be one amongst them, by his
person,
More worthy this place than myself; to
whom,
If I but knew him, with my love and duty
I would surrender it.
CHAM.   I will, my lord.
     [*Goes to the Maskers, and returns.*
WOL. What say they?
CHAM.   Such a one, they all confess,

There is, indeed; which they would have
    your grace
Find out, and he will take it.
WOL.   Let me see, then.—
                    [*Comes from his state.*
By all your good leaves, gentlemen;—here
    I'll make
My royal choice.
K. HEN. [*Unmasking.*] You have found
    him, cardinal:
You hold a fair assembly; you do well,
    lord:
You are a churchman, or, I'll tell you,
    cardinal,
I should judge now unhappily.
WOL.   I am glad
Your grace is grown so pleasant.
K. HEN.   My lord chamberlain,
Pr'ythee, come hither: what fair lady's
    that?
CHAM. An't please your grace, Sir
    Thomas Bullen's daughter,—
The viscount Rochford,—one of her high-
    ness' women.
K. HEN. By heaven, she is a dainty
    one!—Sweetheart,
I were unmannerly to take you out,
And not to kiss you.—A health, gentlemen!
Let it go round.
WOL. Sir Thomas Lovell, is the banquet
    ready
I' the privy chamber?
LOV.   Yes, my lord.
WOL.   Your grace,
I fear, with dancing is a little heated. .
K. HEN. I fear, too much.
WOL.   There's fresher air, my lord,
In the next chamber.
K. HEN. Lead in your ladies, every
    one:—sweet partner,
I must not yet forsake you:—let's be
    merry:—
Good my lord cardinal, I have half a dozen
    healths
To drink to these fair ladies, and a
    measure
To lead them once again; and then let's
    dream
Who's best in favour.—Let the music
    knock it.   [*Exeunt with trumpets.*

ACT II.

SCENE I.—LONDON. *A Street.*

Enter two Gentlemen, meeting.

1 *GENT.* Whither away so fast?
2 *GENT.*   O,—God save you!
E'en to the hall, to hear what shall become
Of the great duke of Buckingham.
1 *GENT.*   I'll save you

That labour, Sir. All's now done, but the
    ceremony
Of bringing back the prisoner.
2 *GENT.*   Were you there?
1 *GENT.* Yes, indeed, was I.
2 *GENT.* Pray, speak what has happen'd.
1 *GENT.* You may guess quickly what.
2 *GENT.*   Is he found guilty?
1 *GENT.* Yes, truly is he, and condemn'd
2 *GENT.* I am sorry for't.   [upon it.
1 *GENT.*   So, are a number more.
2 *GENT.* But, pray, how pass'd it?
1 *GENT.* I'll tell you a little. The great
    duke
Came to the bar; where, to his accusations
He pleaded still not guilty, and alleg'd
Many sharp reasons to defeat the law.
The king's attorney, on the contrary,
Urg'd on the examinations, proofs, con-
    fessions   [sir'd
Of divers witnesses; which the duke de-
To have brought, *vivâ voce*, to his face:
At which appeared against him, his sur-
    veyor;   [Car,
Sir Gilbert Peck, his chancellor; and John
Confessor to him; with that devil-monk,
Hopkins, that made this mischief.
2 *GENT.*   That was he
That fed him with his prophecies?
1 *GENT.*   The same.
All these accus'd him strongly; which he
    fain
Would have flung from him, but, indeed,
    he could not
And so his peers, upon this evidence,
Have found him guilty of high treason.
Much he spoke, and learnedly, for life;
    but all
Was either pitied in him, or forgotten.
2 *GENT.* After all this, how did he bear
    himself?
1 *GENT.* When he was brought again to
    the bar,—to hear   [stirr'd
His knell rung out, his judgment,—he was
With such an agony, he sweat extremely,
And something spoke in choler, ill, and
    hasty:
But he fell to himself again, and sweetly
In all the rest show'd a most noble patience.
2 *GENT.* I do not think he fears death.
1 *GENT.*   Sure, he does not,—
He was never so womanish; the cause
He may a little grieve at.
2 *GENT.*   Certainly
The cardinal is the end of this.
1 *GENT.*   'Tis likely,
By all conjectures: first, Kildare's attain-
    der,
Then deputy of Ireland; who, remov'd,
Earl Surrey was sent thither, and in haste
Lest he should help his father.   [too,

2 *GENT.*   That trick of state
Was a deep envious one.
1 *GENT.*   At his return,
No doubt he will requite it. This is noted,
And generally,—whoever the king favours,
The cardinal instantly will find employ-
And far enough from court too.   [ment.
2 *GENT.*   All the commons
Hate him perniciously, and, o' my con-
science,   [much
Wish him ten fathom deep: this duke as
They love and dote on; call him bounteous
Buckingham,
The mirror of all courtesy,—
1 *GENT.*   Stay there, Sir,
And see the noble ruin'd man you speak
of.
Enter BUCKINGHAM *from his arraignment;
tipstaves before him; the axe with the
edge towards him; halberds on each
side: with him* SIR THOMAS LOVELL, SIR
NICHOLAS VAUX, SIR WILLIAM SANDS,
and common people.
2 *GENT.* Let's stand close, and behold
him.
BUCK.   All good people,
You that thus far have come to pity me,
Hear what I say, and then go home and
lose me.
I have this day receiv'd a traitor's judg-
ment,   [bear witness,
And by that name must die: yet, heaven
And if I have a conscience let it sink me,
Even as the axe falls, if I be not faithful!
The law I bear no malice for my death;
It has done, upon the premises, but jus-
tice: [Christians:
But those that sought it I could wish more
Be what they will, I heartily forgive them:
Yet let them look they glory not in mis-
chief,   [men,
Nor build their evils on the graves of great
For then my guiltless blood must cry
against them.   [hope,
For farther in life in this world I ne'er
Nor will I sue, although the king have
mercies   [that lov'd me,
More than I dare make faults. You few
And dare be bold to weep for Buckingham,
His noble friends and fellows, whom to
Is only bitter to him, only dying,   [leave
Go with me, like good angels, to my end;
And, as the long divorce of steel falls on
me,
Make of your prayers one sweet sacrifice,
And lift my soul to heaven.—Lead on, o'
God's name.
LOV. I do beseech your grace, for charity,
If ever any malice in your heart
Were hid against me, now to forgive me
frankly.

BUCK. Sir Thomas Lovell, I as free for-
give you,
As I would be forgiven: I forgive all;
There cannot be those numberless offences
'Gainst me, that I can not take peace with:
no black envy   [his grace;
Shall mark my grave. Commend me to
And, if he speak of Buckingham, pray, tell
him   [prayers
You met him half in heaven: my vows and
Yet are the king's; and till my soul for-
sake,
Shall cry for blessings on him: may he live
Longer than I have time to tell his years!
Ever belov'd and loving may his rule be!
And when old time shall lead him to his
end,
Goodness and he fill up one monument!
LOV. To the water side I must conduct
your grace;   [Vaux,
Then give my charge up to Sir Nicholas
Who undertakes you to your end.
VAUX.   Prepare there!
The duke is coming: see, the barge be
ready;
And fit it with such furniture as suits
The greatness of his person.
BUCK.   Nay, Sir Nicholas,
Let it alone; my state now will but mock
me.   [constable,
When I came hither, I was lord high
And duke of Buckingham; now, poor Ed-
ward Bohun:
Yet I am richer than my base accusers,
That never knew what truth meant: I now
seal it;
And with that blood will make them one
day groan for't.
My noble father, Henry of Buckingham,
Who first rais'd head against usurping
Richard,
Flying for succour to his servant Banister,
Being distress'd, was by that wretch be-
tray'd,   [with him!
And without trial fell; God's peace be
Henry the seventh succeeding, truly pitying
My father's loss, like a most royal prince,
Restor'd me to my honours, and, out of
ruins,   [son,
Made my name once more noble. Now his
Henry the eighth, life, honour, name, and
all   [taken
That made me happy, at one stroke has
For ever from the world. I had my trial,
And, must needs say, a noble one; which
makes me
A little happier than my wretched father;
Yet thus far we are one in fortunes,—both
Fell by our servants, by those men we
lov'd most;
A most unnatural and faithless service!

Heaven has an end in all: yet, you that
    hear me,   [tain:—
This from a dying man receive as cer-
Where you are liberal in your loves and
    counsels,
Be sure you be not loose; for those you
    make friends,   [perceive
And give your hearts to, when they once
The least rub in your fortunes, fall away
Like water from ye, never found again
But where they mean to sink ye. All good
    people,   [last hour
Pray for me! I must now forsake ye: the
Of my long weary life is come upon me.
Farewell: [is sad,
And when you would say something that
Speak how I fell.—I have done; and God
    forgive me!
            [Exeunt BUCKINGHAM and train.
1 GENT. O, this is full of pity!—Sir, it
    calls,
I fear, too many curses on their heads
That were the authors.
2 GENT.   If the duke be guiltless,
'Tis full of woe: yet I can give you inkling
Of an ensuing evil, if it fall,
Greater than this.
1 GENT. Good angels keep it from us!
What may it be? You do not doubt my
    faith, Sir?
2 GENT. This secret is so weighty, 'twill
    require
A strong faith to conceal it.
1 GENT.   Let me have it;
I do not talk much.
2 GENT.   I am confident;
You shall, Sir: did you not of late days
    hear
A buzzing of a separation
Between the king and Katharine?
1 GENT.   Yes, but it held not:
For when the king once heard it, out of
    anger   [straight
He sent command to the lord mayor
To stop the rumour, and allay those
    tongues
That durst disperse it.
2 GENT.   But that slander, Sir,
Is found a truth now: for it grows again
Fresher than e'er it was; and held for
    certain   [cardinal,
The king will venture at it. Either the
Or some about him near, have, out of
    malice.   [scruple
To the good queen, possess'd him with a
That will undo her: to confirm this, too,
Cardinal Campeius is arriv'd, and lately;
As all think, for this business.
1 GENT.   'Tis the cardinal;
And merely to revenge him on the emperor,
For not bestowing on him, at his asking,

The archbishopric of Toledo, this ⸺
    pos'd.
2 GENT. I think you have hit the ma⸺
    but is't not cruel
That she should feel the smart of this?
    The cardinal
Will have his will, and she must fall.
1 GENT.   'Tis woful.
We are too open here to argue this;
Let's think in private more.   [Exeunt.

SCENE II.—An Ante-chamber in the Palace.
Enter the Lord Chamberlain, reading a
            letter.
CHAM. "My lord,—The horses your lordship sent for, with all the care I had, I
saw well chosen, ridden, and furnished.
They were young and handsome, and of
the best breed in the north. When they
were ready to set out for London, a man
of my lord cardinal's, by commission and
main power, took them from me; with this
reason,—his master would be served before
a subject, if not before the king; which
stopped our mouths, Sir."
I fear he will indeed:—well, let him have
He will have all, I think.   [them:
    Enter the DUKES OF NORFOLK and
            SUFFOLK.
NOR. Well met, my lord chamberlain.
CHAM. Good day to both your graces.
SUF. How is the king employ'd?
CHAM.   I left him private,
Full of sad thoughts and troubles.
NOR.   What's the cause?
CHAM. It seems, the marriage with his
    brother's wife
Has crept too near his conscience.
SUF.   No, his conscience
Has crept too near another lady.
NOR.   'Tis so:
This is the cardinal's doing, the king-
    cardinal: [fortune,
That blind priest, like the eldest son of
Turns what he list. The king will know
    him one day.
SUF. Pray God he do! he'll never know
    himself else.
NOR. How holily he works in all his
    business!
And with what zeal! for, now he has
    crack'd the league
Between us and the emperor, the queen's
    great nephew,
He dives into the king's soul, and there
    scatters
Dangers, doubts, wringing of the con-
    science,
Fears, and despairs,—and all these for his
    marriage:
And, out of all these, to restore the king,

He counsels a divorce; a loss of her,
That, like a jewel, has hung twenty years
About his neck, yet never lost her lustre:
Of her, that loves him with that excellence
That angels love good men with; even of
    her,   [falls,
That, when the greatest stroke of fortune
Will bless the king: and is not this course
    pious?
CHAM. Heaven keep me from such coun-
sel! 'Tis most true,
These news are every where; every tongue
    speaks them,   [dare
And every true heart weeps for't: all that
Look into these affairs, see this main
    end,—   [day open
The French king's sister. Heaven will one
The king's eyes, that so long have slept
This bold bad man.   [upon
SUF.   And free us from his slavery.
NOR. We had need pray.
And heartily, for our deliverance;
Or this imperious man will work us all
From princes into pages: all men's honours
Lie like one lump before him, to be fash-
    ion'd
Into what pitch he please.
SUF.   For me, my lords,
I love him not, nor fear him; there's my
    creed:
As I am made without him, so I'll stand,
If the king please; his curses and his
    blessings   [lieve in.
Touch me alike, they're breath I not be-
I knew him, and I know him; so I leave
    him
To him that made him proud, the pope.
NOR.   Let's in;
And with some other business put the king
From these sad thoughts, that work too
    much upon him:—
My lord, you'll bear us company?
CHAM.   Excuse me;
The king hath sent me otherwhere: besides,
You'll find a most unfit time to disturb
    him:
Health to your lordships.
NOR. Thanks, my good lord chamberlain.
    [*Exit* Lord Chamberlain.
NORFOLK *opens a folding-door. The* KING
is discovered sitting, and reading pensively.
SUF. How sad he looks! sure, he is much
afflicted.
K. HEN. Who is there, ha?
NOR.   Pray God he be not angry.
K. HEN. Who's there, I say? How dare
    you thrust yourselves
Into my private meditations?
Who am I, ha?
NOR. A gracious king that pardons all
offences

Malice ne'er meant: our breach of duty
    this way
Is business of estate; in which we come
To know your royal pleasure.
K. HEN.   Ye are too bold:
Go to; I'll make ye know your times of
    business:
Is this an hour for temporal affairs, ha?—
    Enter WOLSEY *and* CAMPEIUS.
Who's there? my good lord cardinal?—
    O, my Wolsey,
The quiet of my wounded conscience;
Thou art a cure fit for a king.—[*To*
    CAMPEIUS.] You're welcome,
Most learned reverend Sir, into our king-
    dom:
Use us, and it.—[*To* WOLSEY.] My good
    lord, have great care
I be not found a talker.
WOL.   Sir, you cannot.
I would your grace would give us but an
Of private conference.   [hour
K. HEN. [*To* NORFOLK *and* SUFFOLK.]
    We are busy; go.
NOR. [*Aside* to SUF.] This priest has no
    pride in him.
SUF. [*Aside* to NOR.] Not to speak of;
I would not be so sick though for his
But this cannot continue.   [place:
NOR. [*Aside* to SUF.]   If it do,
I'll venture one have-at-him.
SUF. [*Aside* to NOR.]   I another.
    [*Exeunt* NORFOLK *and* SUFFOLK.
WOL. Your grace has given a precedent
    of wisdom
Above all princes, in committing freely
Your scruple to the voice of Christendom:
Who can be angry now? what envy reach
    you?
The Spaniard, tied by blood and favour to
    her,
Must now confess, if they have any good-
    ness,
The trial just and noble. All the clerks,—
I mean the learned ones,—in Christian
    kingdoms
Have their free voices: Rome, the nurse of
    judgment,
Invited by your noble self, hath sent
One general tongue unto us, this good man,
This just and learned priest, Cardinal
    Campeius,—
Whom once more I present unto your high-
    ness.
K. HEN. And once more in mine arms I
    bid him welcome,
And thank the holy conclave for their
    loves:
They have sent me such a man I would
    have wish'd for.

CAM. Your grace must needs deserve all
  strangers' loves,
You are so noble. To your highness' hand
I tender my commission;—by whose virtue,
(The court of Rome commanding) you,
  my lord
Cardinal of York, are join'd with me, their
  servant,
In the unpartial judging of this business.
K. HEN. Two equal men. The queen shall
  be acquainted
Forthwith for what you come.—Where's
  Gardiner?
WOL. I know your majesty has always
  lov'd her
So dear in heart, not to deny her that
A woman of less place might ask by law,—
Scholars, allow'd freely to argue for her.
K. HEN. Ay, and the best, she shall have;
  and my favour
To him that does best: God forbid else.
  Cardinal,
Pr'ythee, call Gardiner to me, my new
  secretary:
I find him a fit fellow.   [*Exit* WOLSEY.
  Re-enter WOLSEY, *with* GARDINER.
WOL. [*Aside to* GARD.] Give me your
  hand: much joy and favour to you;
You are the king's now.
GARD. [*Aside to* WOL.] But to be com-
  manded
For ever by your grace, whose hand has
  rais'd me.
K. HEN. Come hither, Gardiner.
                    [*They converse apart.*
CAM. My lord of York, was not one
  doctor Pace
In this man's place before him?
WOL.   Yes, he was.
CAM. Was he not held a learned man?
WOL.   Yes, surely.
CAM. Believe me, there's an ill opinion
  spread, then
Even of yourself, lord cardinal.
WOL.   How! of me?
CAM. They will not stick to say, you
  envied him;
And fearing he would rise, he was so
  virtuous,
Kept him a foreign man still; which so
  griev'd him,
That he ran mad and died.
WOL.   Heaven's peace be with him!
That's Christian care enough: for living
  murmurers
There's places of rebuke. He was a fool;
For he would needs be virtuous: that good
  fellow,
If I command him, follows my appoint-
  ment:

I will have none so near else. Learn this,
  brother,
We live not to be grip'd by meaner per-
  sons.
K. HEN. Deliver this with modesty to the
  queen.   [*Exit* GARDINER.
The most convenient place that I can think
  of,   [*Friars*;
For such receipt of learning, is Black-
There ye shall meet about this weighty
  business:—
My Wolsey, see it furnish'd.—O my lord,
Would it not grieve an able man to leave
So sweet a bedfellow? But, conscience,
  conscience,—
O, 'tis a tender place! and I must leave
  her.   [*Exeunt.*

———

SCENE III.—*An Ante-chamber in the*
  QUEEN'S *Apartments.*

Enter ANNE BULLEN *and an* OLD LADY.

ANNE. Not for that neither: here's the
  pang that pinches:—
His highness having liv'd so long with her,
  and she
So good a lady, that no tongue could ever
Pronounce dishonour of her,—by my life,
She never knew harm-doing;—O, now,
  after
So many courses of the sun enthron'd,
Still growing in a majesty and pomp,—the
  which
To leave, a thousand-fold more bitter than
'Tis sweet at first t' acquire,—after this
  process,
To give her the avaunt! it is a pity
Would move a monster.
OLD L.   Hearts of most hard temper
Melt and lament for her.
ANNE.   O, God's will! much better
She ne'er had known pomp: though it be
  temporal,
Yet, if that quarrel, fortune, do divorce
It from the bearer, 'tis a sufferance pang-
As soul and body's severing.   [*ing
OLD. L.   Alas, poor lady!
She's a stranger now again.
ANNE.   So much the more
Must pity drop upon her. Verily,
I swear, 'tis better to be lowly born,
And range with humble livers in content,
Than to be perk'd up in a glistering grief,
And wear a golden sorrow.
OLD L.   Our content
Is our best having.
ANNE.   By my troth and maidenhead,
I would not be a queen.
OLD. L.   Beshrew me, I would,
And venture maidenhead for't; and so
  would you,

For all this spice of your hypocrisy:
You, that have so fair parts of woman on
you,
Have too a woman's heart; which ever yet
Affected eminence, wealth, sovereignty;
Which, to say sooth, are blessings; and
which gifts
(Saving your mincing) the capacity
Of your soft cheveril conscience would
receive,
If you might please to stretch it.
ANNE.   Nay, good troth,—
OLD L. Yes, troth, and troth;—you would
not be a queen?
ANNE. No, not for all the riches under
heaven.
OLD L. 'Tis strange: a three-pence bowed
would hire me,
Old as I am, to queen it: but, I pray you,
What think you of a duchess? have you
To bear that load of title?   [limbs
ANNE.   No, in truth.
OLD L. Then you are weakly made: pluck
off a little;
I would not be a young count in your way,
For more than blushing comes to: if your
back
Cannot vouchsafe this burden, 'tis too weak
Ever to get a boy.
ANNE.   How you do talk!
I swear again, I would not be a queen
For all the world.
OLD L.   In faith, for little England
You'd venture an emballing: I myself
Would for Carnarvonshire, although there
'long'd
No more to the crown but that.—Lo, who
comes here?
            Enter the Lord Chamberlain.
CHAM. Good morrow, ladies. What were't
worth to know
The secret of your conference?
ANNE.   My good lord,
Not your demand; it values not your ask-
ing:
Our mistress' sorrows we were pitying.
CHAM. It was a gentle business, and
becoming
The action of good women: there is hope
All will be well.
ANNE.   Now, I pray God, amen!
CHAM. You bear a gentle mind, and
heavenly blessings
Follow such creatures. That you may, fair
lady,
Perceive I speak sincerely, and high note's
Ta'en of your many virtues, the king's
majesty
Commends his good opinion of you to you,
and
Does purpose honour to you no less flowing

Than marchioness of Pembroke; to which
title
A thousand pound a-year, annual support,
Out of his grace he adds.
ANNE.   I do not know
What kind of my obedience I should
tender;
More than my all is nothing: nor my pray-
ers
Are not words duly hallow'd, nor my
wishes
More worth than empty vanities: yet
prayers and wishes
Are all I can return. Beseech your lord-
ship,
Vouchsafe to speak my thanks and my
obedience,
As from a blushing handmaid, to his high-
ness;
Whose health and royalty I pray for.
CHAM.   Lady,
I shall not fail to approve the fair conceit
The king hath of you.—[Aside.] I have
perus'd her well;
Beauty and honour in her are so mingled,
That they have caught the king: and who
knows yet,
But from this lady may proceed a gem
To lighten all this isle?—[To her.] I'll to
the king,
And say, I spoke with you.
ANNE.   My honour'd lord,
                    [Exit Lord Chamberlain.
OLD L. Why, this it is; see, see!
I have been begging sixteen years in court,
(Am yet a courtier beggarly) nor could
Come pat betwixt too early and too late,
For any suit of pounds; and you, O fate!
A very fresh-fish here, (fie, fie, fie upon
This compell'd fortune!) have your mouth
Before you open it.   [fill'd up,
ANNE.   This is strange to me.
OLD L. How tastes it? is it bitter? forty
pence, no.
There was a lady once, ('tis an old story)
That would not be a queen, that would
she not,
For all the mud in Egypt:—have you
heard it?
ANNE. Come, you are pleasant.
OLD L.   With your theme, I could
O'ermount the lark. The marchioness of
Pembroke!
A thousand pounds a-year, for pure re-
spect!
No other obligation By my life,
That promises more thousands: honour's
train
Is longer than his foreskirt. By this time,
I know, your back will bear a duchess:—
say,

Are you not stronger than you were?
ANNE.   Good lady,
Make yourself mirth with your particular
      fancy,
And leave me out on't. Would I had no
      being,
If this salute my blood a jot: it faints me,
To think what follows.
The queen is comfortless, and we forgetful
In our long absence: pray, do not deliver
What here you've heard, to her.
OLD L.   What do you think me?
                                    [Exeunt.

SCENE IV.—*A Hall in* Black-Friars.

Trumpets, sennet, and cornets. Enter two
Vergers, *with short silver wands; next*
them, two Scribes, *in the habit of*
doctors; after them, the ARCHBISHOP OF
CANTERBURY, *alone; after him, the*
BISHOPS OF LINCOLN, ELY, ROCHESTER,
and SAINT ASAPH; *next them, with some*
small distance, follows a Gentleman *bear-*
ing the Purse, with the Great Seal, and a
cardinal's hat; then two Priests, *bearing*
each a silver cross; then a Gentleman-
Usher *bare-headed, accompanied with a*
Sergeant at Arms, *bearing a silver mace;*
then two Gentlemen, *bearing two great*
silver pillars; after them, side by side,
the two CARDINALS WOLSEY *and* CAM-
PEIUS; *two* Noblemen *with the sword*
and mace. Then enter the KING *and*
QUEEN, *and their trains. The* KING *takes*
place under the cloth of state; the two
CARDINALS *sit under him as judges. The*
QUEEN *takes place at some distance from*
the KING. *The* BISHOPS *place themselves*
on each side the court, in manner of a
consistory; below them, the Scribes. *The*
Lords *sit next the* BISHOPS. *The* Crier
and the rest of the Attendants *stand in*
convenient order about the Hall.

WOL. Whilst our commission from Rome
      is read,
Let silence be commanded.
K. HEN.   What's the need?
It hath already publicly been read,
And on all sides th' authority allow'd;
You may, then, spare that time.
WOL.   Be't so.—Proceed.
SCRIBE. Say, Henry king of England,
      come into the court.
CRIER. Henry king of England, &c.
K. HEN. Here.
SCRIBE. Say, Katharine queen of Eng-
      land, come into the court.
CRIER. Katharine, queen of England, &c.
      [*The* QUEEN *makes no answer, rises out*

of her chair, goes about the court,
comes to the KING, *and kneels at his*
feet; then speaks.
Q. KATH. Sir, I desire you do me right
      and justice;
And to bestow your pity on me: for
I am a most poor woman, and a stranger,
Born out of your dominions; having here
No judge indifferent, nor no more assur-
      ance
Of equal friendship and proceeding. Alas,
      Sir,
In what have I offended you? what cause
Hath my behaviour given to your dis-
      pleasure,   [off.
That thus you should proceed to put me
And take your good grace from me?
      Heaven witness,
I have been to you a true and humble wife,
At all times to your will conformable;
Ever in fear to kindle your dislike,
Yea, subject to your countenance,—glad
      or sorry
As I saw it inclin'd. When was the hour
I ever contradicted your desire,
Or made it not mine too? Or which of
      your friends
Have I not strove to love, although I knew
He were mine enemy? what friend of mine
That had to him deriv'd your anger, did I
Continue in my liking? nay, gave notice
He was from thence discharg'd. Sir, call
      to mind
That I have been your wife, in this obe-
      dience,
Upward of twenty years, and have been
      blest
With many children by you: if, in the
      course
And process of this time, you can report,
And prove it too, against mine honour
      aught,
My bond to wedlock, or my love and duty,
Against your sacred person, in God's name,
Turn me away; and let the foul'st con-
      tempt
Shut door upon me, and so give me up
To the sharp'st kind of justice. Please you,
      Sir,
The king, your father, was reputed for
A prince most prudent, of an excellent
An unmatch'd wit and judgment: Ferdi-
      nand,
My father, king of Spain, was reckon'd one
The wisest prince that there had reign'd by
      many
A year before: it is not to be question'd
That they had gather'd a wise council to
      them
Of every realm, that did debate this busi-
      ness,

Who deem'd our marriage lawful: where-
fore I humbly
Beseech you, Sir, to spare me, till I may
Be by my friends in Spain advis'd; whose
counsel
I will implore: if not, i' the name of God,
Your pleasure be fulfill'd!
WOL.   You have here, lady,
(And of your choice) these reverend
fathers; men
Of singular integrity and learning,
Yea, the elect o' the land, who are assem-
bled   [bootless
To plead your cause: it shall be therefore
That longer you desire the court; as well
For your own quiet, as to rectify
What is unsettled in the king.
CAM.   His grace
Hath spoken well and justly: therefore,
Madam,
It's fit this royal session do proceed;
And that, without delay, their arguments
Be now produc'd and heard.
Q. KATH.   Lord cardinal,—
To you I speak.
WOL.   Your pleasure, Madam?
Q. KATH.   Sir,
I am about to weep; but, thinking that
We are a queen, (or long have dream'd
so) certain
The daughter of a king, my drops of tears
I'll turn to sparks of fire.
WOL.   Be patient yet.
Q. KATH. I will, when you are humble;
nay, before,
Or God will punish me. I do believe,
Induc'd by potent circumstances, that
You are mine enemy; and make my chal-
lenge
You shall not be my judge: for it is you
Have blown this coal betwixt my lord and
me,—   [say again,
Which God's dew quench!—Therefore I
I utterly abhor, yea, from my soul
Refuse you for my judge; whom, yet once
more,
I hold my most malicious foe, and think not
At all a friend to truth.
WOL.   I do profess
You speak not like yourself; who ever yet
Have stood to charity, and display'd th'
effects
Of disposition gentle, and of wisdom
O'ertopping woman's power. Madam, you
do me wrong;
I have no spleen against you; nor injustice
For you, or any: how far I have proceeded,
Or how far farther shall, is warranted
By a commission from the consistory,—
Yea, the whole consistory of Rome. You
charge me

That I have blown this coal: I do deny it:
The king is present: if it be known to him
That I gainsay my deed, how may he
wound,
And worthily, my falsehood! yea, as much
As you have done my truth. If he know
That I am free of your report, he knows
I am not of your wrong. Therefore in him
It lies to cure me and the cure is, to
Remove these thoughts from you: the
which before
His highness shall speak in, I do beseech
You, gracious Madam, to unthink your
And to say so no more.   [speaking,
Q. KATH.   My lord, my lord,
I am a simple woman, much too weak
To oppose your cunning. You're meek and
humble-mouth'd;
You sign your place and calling, in full
seeming,
With meekness and humility; but your
heart
Is cramm'd with arrogancy, spleen, and
pride.
You have, by fortune and his highness'
favours,
Gone slightly o'er low steps, and now are
mounted
Where powers are your retainers; and your
words,
Domestics to you, serve your will as't
please
Yourself pronounce their office. I must tell
you,
You tender more your person's honour than
Your high profession spiritual: that again
I do refuse you for my judge; and here,
Before you all, appeal unto the pope,
To bring my whole cause 'fore his holiness,
And to be judg'd by him.
    [*She courtsies to the* KING, *and offers
                    to depart.*
CAM.   The queen is obstinate,
Stubborn to justice, apt to accuse it, and
Disdainful to be tried by't: 'tis not well.
She's going away.
K. HEN. Call her again.
CRIER. Katharine, queen of England,
come into the court.
GRIF. Madam, you are call'd back.
Q. KATH. What need you note it? pray
you, keep your way;
When you are call'd, return.—Now, the
Lord help!
They vex me past my patience!—Pray you,
pass on:
I will not tarry; no, nor ever more
Upon this business my appearance make
In any of their courts.
        [*Exeunt* QUEEN, GRIFFITH, *and her
                other* Attendants.

K. HEN.　　　　　Go thy ways, Kate:
That man i' the world who shall report he has
A better wife, let him in naught be trusted,
For speaking false in that: thou art, alone,
(If thy rare qualities, sweet gentleness,
Thy meekness saint-like, wife-like government,—
Obeying in commanding,—and thy parts
Sovereign and pious else, could speak thee out)
The queen of earthly queens:—she's noble born;
And, like her true nobility, she has
Carried herself towards me.

WOL.　　　　　Most gracious, Sir,
In humblest manner I require your highness,
That it shall please you to declare, in hearing
Of all these ears, (for where I am robb'd and bound,
There must I be unloos'd; and although not there
At once, and fully satisfied) whether ever I
Did broach this business to your highness; or
Laid any scruple in your way, which might
Induce you to the question on't? or ever
Have to you,—but with thanks to God for such
A royal lady,—spake one the least word that might
Be to the prejudice of her present state,
Or touch of her good person?

K. HEN.　　　　　My lord cardinal,
I do excuse you; yea, upon mine honour,
I free you from't. You are not to be taught
That you have many enemies, that know not
Why they are so, but, like to village curs,
Bark when their fellows do: by some of these
The queen is put in anger. You're excus'd:
But will you be more justified? you ever
Have wish'd the sleeping of this business; never
Desir'd it to be stirr'd; but oft have hinder'd, oft,
The passages made toward it:—on my honour,
I speak my good lord cardinal to this point.
And thus far clear him. Now, what mov'd me to't, 　　　　　[tion:—
I will be bold with time, and your atten-
Then mark th' inducement. Thus it came;
—give heed to't—
My conscience first receiv'd a tenderness,
Scruple, and prick, on certain speeches utter'd

By the bishop of Bayonne, then French embassador;
Who had been hither sent on the debating
A marriage 'twixt the duke of Orleans and
Our daughter Mary: i' the progress of this business,
Ere a determinate resolution, he
(I mean the bishop) did require a respite;
Wherein he might the king his lord advertise
Whether our daughter were legitimate,
Respecting this our marriage with the dowager,
Sometime our brother's wife. This respite shook
The bosom of my conscience, enter'd me,
Yea, with a splitting power, and made to tremble
The region of my breast; which forc'd such way,
That many maz'd considering did throng,
And press'd in with this caution. First, methought
I stood not in the smile of Heaven; who had
Commanded nature, that my lady's womb,
If it conceiv'd a male child by me, should
Do no more offices of life to't, than
The grave does to the dead; for her male issue
Or died where they were made, or shortly after
This world had air'd them: hence I took a thought,
This was a judgment on me; that my kingdom,
Well worthy the best heir o' the world, should not
Be gladded in't by me: then follows, that
I weigh'd the danger which my realms stood in
By this my issues' fail; and that gave to me
Many a groaning throe. Thus hulling in
The wild sea of my conscience, I did steer
Toward this remedy, whereupon we are
Now present here together; that's to say,
I meant to rectify my conscience,—which
I then did feel full sick, and yet not well,—
By all the reverend fathers of the land,
And doctors learn'd:—first I began in private
With you, my lord of Lincoln; you remember
How under my oppression I did reek,
When I first mov'd you.

LIN.　　　　　Very well, my liege.

K. HEN. I have spoke long: be pleas'd yourself to say
How far you satisfied me.

LIN.　　　　　So please your highness,

The question did at first so stagger me,—
Bearing a state of mighty moment in't,
And consequence of dread,—that I committed
The daring'st counsel which I had to doubt;
And did entreat your highness to this course
Which you are running here.

K. HEN.   I then mov'd you,
My lord of Canterbury; and got your leave
To make this present summons:—unsolicited
I left no reverend person in this court;
But by particular consent proceeded
Under your hands and seals: therefore, go on;
For no dislike i' the world against the person
Of the good queen, but the sharp thorny points
Of my alleged reasons, drive this forward:
Prove but our marriage lawful, by my life
And kingly dignity, we are contented
To wear our mortal state to come with her,
Katharine our queen, before the primest creature
That's paragon'd o' the world.

CAM.   So please your highness,
The queen being absent, 'tis a needful fitness
That we adjourn this court till farther day:
Meanwhile must be an earnest motion
Made to the queen, to call back her appeal
She intends unto his holiness.
                    [They rise to depart.

K. HEN. [Aside.]   I may perceive,
These cardinals trifle with me: I abhor
This dilatory sloth and tricks of Rome.
My learn'd and well-beloved servant, Cranmer,
Pr'ythee, return! with thy approach, I know,
My comfort comes along.—Break up the court
I say, set on.
          [Exeunt, in manner as they entered.

ACT III.

SCENE I.—LONDON. The Palace at Bridewell. A Room in the QUEEN's Apartment.

The QUEEN, and some of her women, at work.

Q. KATH. Take thy lute, wench: my soul grows sad with troubles;
Sing, and disperse them, if thou canst: leave working.

SONG.

Orpheus with his lute made trees,
And the mountain-tops that freeze,
  Bow themselves, when he did sing:
To his music, plants and flowers

Ever sprung; as sun and showers
  There had made a lasting spring.

Every thing that heard him play,
Even in the billows of the sea,
  Hung their heads, and then lay by.
In sweet music is such art,
Killing care and grief of heart
  Fall asleep, or hearing, die.

Enter a Gentleman.

Q. KATH. How now!
GENT. An't please your grace, the two great cardinals
Wait in the presence.
Q. KATH.   Would they speak with me?
GENT. They will'd me to say so, Madam.
Q. KATH.   Pray their graces
To come near. [Exit Gent.] What can be their business
With me, a poor weak woman, fallen from favour?
I do not like their coming, now I think on't.
They should be good men; their affairs as righteous;
But all hoods make not monks.

Enter WOLSEY and CAMPEIUS.

WOL.   Peace to your highness!
Q. KATH. Your graces find me here part of a housewife;
I would be all, against the worst may happen.
What are your pleasures with me, reverend lords?
WOL. May it please you, noble Madam, to withdraw
Into your private chamber, we shall give you
The full cause of our coming.
Q. KATH.   Speak it here;
There's nothing I have done yet, o' my conscience,
Deserves a corner: would all other women
Could speak this with as free a soul as I do!
My lords, I care not, (so much I am happy
Above a number) if my actions
Were tried by every tongue, every eye saw them,
Envy and base opinion set against them,
I know my life so even. If your business
Seek me out, and that way I am wife in,
Out with it boldly: truth loves open dealing.
WOL. Tanta est erga te mentis integritas, regina serenissima,—
Q. KATH. O, good my lord, no Latin;
I am not such a truant since my coming,
As not to know the language I have liv'd in:

A strange tongue makes my cause more
　strange, suspicious;
Pray, speak in English: here are some will
　thank you,
If you speak truth, for their poor mistress'
　sake,—
Believe me, she has had much wrong: lord
　cardinal,
The willing'st sin I ever yet committed
May be absolv'd in English.

WOL.　　　　　　　Noble lady,
I am sorry my integrity should breed
(And service to his majesty and you)
So deep suspicion, where all faith was
　meant.
We come not by the way of accusation,
To taint that honour every good tongue
　blesses,
Nor to betray you any way to sorrow,—
You have too much, good lady; but to
　know
How you stand minded in the weighty
　difference
Between the king and you; and to deliver,
Like free and honest men, our just opin-
　ions,
And comforts to your cause.

CAM.　　　　　　Most honour'd Madam,
My lord of York,—out of his noble nature,
Zeal and obedience he still bore your
　grace,—
Forgetting, like a good man, your late
　censure
Both of his truth and him, (which was
　too far)—
Offers, as I do, in a sign of peace,
His service and his counsel.

Q. KATH. [*Aside.*]　　To betray me.—
My lords, I thank you both for your good
　wills;
Ye speak like honest men: (pray God, ye
　prove so!)
But how to make ye suddenly an answer,
In such a point of weight, so near mine
　honour,
More near my life, I fear) with my weak
　wit,
And to such men of gravity and learning,
In truth, I know not. I was set at work
Among my maids; full little, God knows,
　looking
Either for such men, or such business.
For her sake that I have been, (for I feel
The last fit of my greatness,) good your
　graces,
Let me have time and counsel for my
　cause:
Alas, I am a woman, friendless, hopeless!

WOL. Madam, you wrong the king's love
　with these fears:
Your hopes and friends are infinite.

Q. KATH.　　　　　　In England
But little for my profit: can you think,
　lords,
That any Englishman dare give me counsel?
Or be a known friend, 'gainst his highness'
　pleasure,
(Though he be grown so desperate to be
　honest)
And live a subject? Nay, forsooth, my
　friends,
They that must weigh out my afflictions,
They that my trust must grow to, live not
　here:
They are, as all my other comforts, far
　hence,
In mine own country, lords.

CAM.　　　　I would your grace
Would leave your griefs, and take my
　counsel.

Q. KATH.　　　　　　How, Sir?

CAM. Put your main cause into the king's
　protection;
He's loving, and most gracious: 'twill be
　much
Both for your honour better, and your
　cause;
For if the trial of the law o'ertake you,
You'll part away disgrac'd.

WOL.　　　　　He tells you rightly.

Q. KATH. Ye tell me what ye wish for
　both,—my ruin:
Is this your Christian counsel? out upon
　ye!
Heaven is above all yet; there sits a Judge
That no king can corrupt.

CAM.　　　　Your rage mistakes us.

Q. KATH. The more shame for ye! holy
　men I thought ye,
Upon my soul, two reverend cardinal vir-
　tues;
But cardinal sins, and hollow hearts, I
　fear ye:
Mend them, for shame, my lords. Is this
　your comfort?
The cordial that ye bring a wretched
　lady,—
A woman lost among ye, laugh'd at,
　scorn'd?
I will not wish ye half my miseries;
I have more charity: but say, I warn'd ye,
Take heed, for heaven's sake, take heed,
　lest at once
The burden of my sorrows fall upon ye.

WOL. Madam, this is a mere distraction;
You turn the good we offer into envy.

Q. KATH. Ye turn me into nothing: woe
　upon ye,
And all such false professors! Would ye
　have me
(If ye have any justice, any pity;
If ye be any thing but churchmen's habits)

Put my sick cause into hands that hates
    me?
Alas, he has banish'd me his bed already,—
His love, too long ago! I am old, my
    lords,
And all the fellowship I hold now with him
Is only my obedience. What can happen
To me above this wretchedness? all your
    studies
Make me a curse like this.
CAM.   Your fears are worse.
Q. KATH. Have I liv'd thus long—(let me
    speak myself,
Since virtue finds no friends,)—a wife, a
    true one?
A woman (I dare say without vain-glory)
Never yet branded with suspicion?
Have I with all my full affections
Still met the king? lov'd him next heaven?
    obey'd him?
Been, out of fondness, superstitious to him?
Almost forgot my prayers to content him?
And am I thus rewarded? 'tis not well,
    lords.
Bring me a constant woman to her hus-
    band,
One that ne'er dream'd a joy beyond his
    pleasure;
And to that woman, when she has done
    most,
Yet will I add an honour,—a great pa-
    tience.
WOL. Madam, you wander from the good
    we aim at.
Q. KATH. My lord, I dare not make my-
    self so guilty,
To give up willingly that noble title
Your master wed me to: nothing but death
Shall e'er divorce my dignities.
WOL.   Pray, hear me.
Q. KATH. Would I had never trod this
    English earth,
Or felt the flatteries that grow upon it!
Ye have angels' faces, but heaven knows
    your hearts.
What will become of me now, wretched
    lady!
I am the most unhappy woman living.—
[To her women.] Alas, poor wenches,
    where are now your fortunes!
Shipwreck'd upon a kingdom, where no
    pity,
No friends, no hope; no kindred weep for
    me;
Almost no grave allow'd me:—like the lily,
That once was mistress of the field and
    flourish'd,
I'll hang my head and perish.
WOL.   If your grace
Could but be brought to know our ends
    are honest,

You'd feel more comfort: why should we,
    good lady,
Upon what cause, wrong you? alas, our
    places,
The way of our profession is against it:
We are to cure such sorrows, not to sow
    them.
For goodness' sake, consider what you do;
How you may hurt yourself, ay, utterly
Grow from the king's acquaintance, by this
    carriage.
The hearts of princes kiss obedience,
So much they love it; but to stubborn
    spirits
They swell, and grow as terrible as storms.
I know you have a gentle, noble temper,
A soul as even as a calm: pray, think us
Those we profess, peace-makers, friends,
    and servants.
CAM. Madam, you'll find it so. You wrong
    your virtues
With these weak women's fears: a noble
    spirit,
As yours was put into you, ever casts
Such doubts, as false coin, from it. The
    king loves you;
Beware you lose it not: for us, if you
    please
To trust us in your business, we are ready
To use our utmost studies in your service.
Q. KATH. Do what ye will, my lords: and
    pray, forgive me,
If I have us'd myself unmannerly;
You know I am a woman, lacking wit
To make a seemly answer to such persons.
Pray, do my service to his majesty:
He has my heart yet; and shall have my
    prayers
While I shall have my life. Come, reverend
    fathers,
Bestow your counsels on me: she now begs,
That little thought when she set footing
    here,
She should have bought her dignities so
    dear.   [Exeunt.

SCENE II.—Ante-chamber to the KING'S
    Apartment.

Enter the DUKE OF NORFOLK, the DUKE OF
    SUFFOLK, the EARL OF SURREY, and the
    Lord Chamberlain.

NOR. If you will now unite in your com-
    plaints,
And force them with a constancy, the car-
    dinal
Cannot stand under them: if you omit
The offer of this time, I cannot promise
But that you shall sustain more new dis-
    graces
With these you bear already.

SUR.   I am joyful
To meet the least occasion that may give me
Remembrance of my father-in-law, the duke,
To be reveng'd on him.
SUF.   Which of the peers
Have uncontemn'd gone by him, or at least
Strangely neglected? when did he regard
The stamp of nobleness in any person,
Out of himself?
CHAM. My lords, you speak your pleasures:
What he deserves of you and me, I know;
What we can do to him, (though now the time
Gives way to us) I much fear. If you cannot
Bar his access to the king, never attempt
Any thing on him; for he hath a witchcraft
Over the king in's tongue.
NOR.   O, fear him not;
His spell in that is out: the king hath found
Matter against him, that for ever mars
The honey of his language. No, he's settled,
Not to come off, in his displeasure.
SUR.   Sir,
should be glad to hear such news as this
Once every hour.
NOR.   Believe it, this is true:
In the divorce his contrary proceedings
Are all unfolded; wherein he appears,
As I would wish mine enemy.
SUR.   How came
His practices to light?
SUF.   Most strangely.
SUR.   O, how, how?
SUF. The cardinal's letter to the pope miscarried,
And came to the eye o' the king: wherein
was read,
How that the cardinal did entreat his holiness
To stay the judgment o' the divorce; for if it
did take place, "I do," quoth he, "perceive
My king is tangled in affection to
A creature of the queen's, lady Anne
Bullen."
SUR. Has the king this?
SUF.   Believe it.
SUR.   Will this work?
CHAM. The king in this perceives him,
how he coasts
And hedges his own way. But in this point
All his tricks founder, and he brings his
physic

After his patient's death: the king already
Hath married the fair lady.
SUR.   Would he had!
SUF. May you be happy in your wish, my
lord!
For, I profess, you have it.
SUR.   Now, all my joy
Trace the conjunction!
SUF.   My amen to't!
NOR.   All men's!
SUF. There's order given for her coronation:
Marry, this is yet but young, and may be left
To some ears unrecounted.—But, my lords,
She is a gallant creature, and complete
In mind and feature: I persuade me, from her
Will fall some blessing to this land, which shall
In it be memoriz'd.
SUR.   But, will the king
Digest this letter of the cardinal's?
The Lord forbid!
NOR.   Marry, amen!
SUF.   No, no;
There be more wasps that buz about his nose,
Will make this sting the sooner. Cardinal
Campeius
Is stolen away to Rome; hath ta'en no
leave;
Has left the cause o' the king unhandled;
and
Is posted, as the agent of our cardinal,
To second all his plot. I do assure you
The king cried, ha! at this.
CHAM.   Now, God incense him,
And let him cry ha! louder!
NOR.   But, my lord,
When returns Cranmer?
SUF. He is return'd, in his opinions; which
Have satisfied the king for his divorce,
Together with all famous colleges
Almost in Christendom: shortly, I believe,
His second marriage shall be publish'd,
and
Her coronation. Katharine no more
Shall be call'd queen, but princess dowager,
And widow to prince Arthur.
NOR.   This same Cranmer's
A worthy fellow, and hath ta'en much pain
In the king's business.
SUF.   He has; and we shall see him
For it an archbishop.
NOR.   So I hear.
SUF.   'Tis so.—
The cardinal!   [*They stand aside.*
      Enter WOLSEY and CROMWELL.

NOR. Observe, observe, he's moody.

WOL. The packet, Cromwell, gave it you the king?

CROM. To his own hand, in his bed-chamber.

WOL. Look'd he o' th' inside of the paper?

CROM.   Presently
He did unseal them: and the first he view'd,
He did it with a serious mind; a heed
Was in his countenance. You he bade
Attend him here this morning.

WOL.   Is he ready
To come abroad?

CROM.   I think, by this he is.

WOL. Leave me awhile.—
                          [*Exit* CROMWELL.
It shall be to the duchess of Alençon
The French king's sister: he shall marry her.—
Anne Bullen? No, I'll no Anne Bullens for him:
There's more in't than fair visage.—Bullen!
No, we'll no Bullens.—Speedily I wish
To hear from Rome.—The marchioness of Pembroke!

NOR. He's discontented.

SUF.   May be, he hears the king
Does whet his anger to him.

SUR.   Sharp enough,
Lord, for thy justice!

WOL. The late queen's gentlewoman, a knight's daughter,
To be her mistress' mistress! the queen's queen!—
This candle burns not clear: 'tis I must snuff it;
Then, out it goes.—What though I know her virtuous
And well deserving? yet I know her for
A spleeny Lutheran; and not wholesome to
Our cause, that she should lie i' the bosom of
Our hard-rul'd king. Again, there is sprung up
A heretic, an arch one, Cranmer; one
Hath crawl'd into the favour of the king,
And is his oracle.
                  [*Remains aloof, meditating.*

NOR.   He is vex'd at something.

SUF. I would 'twere something that would fret the string,
The master-cord on's heart!

SUF.   The king, the king!
Enter the KING, *reading a schedule; and* LOVELL.

K. HEN. What piles of wealth hath he accumulated
To his own portion! and what expence by the hour
Seems to flow from him! How, i' the name of thrift,

Does he rake this together?—Now, my lords,
Saw you the cardinal?

NOR. [*Advancing.*] My lord, we have
Stood here observing him: some strange commotion
Is in his brain: he bites his lip, and starts;
Stops on a sudden, looks upon the ground,
Then lays his finger on his temple; straight
Springs out into fast gait; then stops again,
Strikes his breast hard; and anon he casts
His eye against the moon: in most strange postures
We have seen him set himself.

K. HEN.   It may be well;
There is a mutiny in's mind. This morning
Papers of state he sent me to peruse,
As I requir'd: and wot you what I found
There, on my conscience, put unwittingly?
Forsooth, an inventory, thus importing,—
The several parcels of his plate, his treasure,
Rich stuffs, and ornaments of household; which
I find at such proud rate, that it out-speaks
Possession of a subject.

NOR.   It's heaven's will:
Some spirit put this paper in the packet,
To bless your eye withal.

K. HEN.   If we did think
His contemplation were above the earth,
And fix'd on spiritual object, he should still
Dwell in his musings: but I am afraid
His thinkings are below the moon, not worth
His serious considering.
    [*He takes his seat, and whispers* LOVELL,
                          who goes to WOLSEY.

WOL.   Heaven forgive me!—
Ever God bless your highness.

K. HEN.   Good my lord,
You are full of heavenly stuff, and bear the inventory
Of your best graces in your mind; the which
You were now running o'er: you have scarce time
To steal from spiritual leisure a brief span,
To keep your earthly audit: sure, in that
I deem you an ill husband, and am glad
To have you therein my companion.

WOL.   Sir,
For holy offices I have a time; a time
To think upon the part of business which
I bear i' the state; and nature does require
Her times of preservation, which perforce
I, her frail son, amongst my brethren mortal,
Must give my tendance to.

K. HEN.   You have said well,

WOL. And ever may your highness yoke together,
As I will lend you cause, my doing well
With my well saying!
K. HEN.   'Tis well said again;
And 'tis a kind of good deed to say well:
And yet words are no deeds. My father lov'd you:
He said he did; and with his deed did crown
His word upon you. Since I had my office,
I have kept you next my heart; have not alone
Employ'd you where high profits might come home,
But par'd my present havings, to bestow
My bounties upon you.
WOL. [*Aside.*]   What should this mean?
SUR. [*Aside to the others.*] The Lord increase this business!
K. HEN.   Have I not made you
The prime man of the state? I pray you, tell me,
If what I now pronounce you have found true:
And, if you may confess it, say withal,
If you are bound to us, or no. What say you?
WOL. My sovereign, I confess, your royal graces,
Shower'd on me daily, have been more than could
My studied purposes requite; which went
Beyond all man's endeavours:—my endeavours
Have ever come too short of my desires,
Yet fil'd with my abilities: mine own ends
Have been mine so, that evermore they pointed
To the good of your most sacred person, and
The profit of the state. For your great graces
Heap'd upon me, poor undeserver, I
Can nothing render but allegiant thanks;
My prayers to heaven for you; my loyalty,
Which ever has and ever shall be growing,
Till death, that winter, kill it.
K. HEN.   Fairly answer'd;
A loyal and obedient subject is
Therein illustrated: the honour of it
Does pay the act of it; as, i' the contrary,
The foulness is the punishment. I presume,
That as my hand has open'd bounty to you,
My heart dropp'd love, my power rain'd honour, more
On you than any; so your hand and heart,
Your brain, and every function of your power,
Should, notwithstanding that your bond of duty,

As 'twere in love's particular, be more
To me, your friend, than any.
WOL.   I do profess,
That for your highness' good I ever labour'd
More than mine own; that am, have, and will be,
Though all the world should crack their duty to you,
And throw it from their soul; though perils did
Abound, as thick as thought could make them, and
Appear in forms more horrid, yet my duty,
As doth a rock against the chiding flood,
Should the approach of this wild river break,
And stand unshaken yours.
K. HEN.   'Tis nobly spoken:—
Take notice, lords, he has a loyal breast,
For you have seen him open't.—Read o'er this;   [*Giving him papers.*
And after, this: and then to breakfast, with
What appetite you have.

[*Exit, frowning upon* CARDINAL WOLSEY:
the Nobles *throng after him, smiling,
and whispering.*
WOL.   What should this mean?
What sudden anger's this? how have I reap'd it?
He parted frowning from me, as if ruin
Leap'd from his eyes: so looks the chafed lion
Upon the daring huntsman that has gall'd him;
Then makes him nothing. I must read this paper;
I fear, the story of his anger.—'Tis so;
This paper has undone me:—'Tis th' account
Of all that world of wealth I have drawn together
For mine own ends; indeed, to gain the popedom,
And fee my friends in Rome. O negligence,
Fit for a fool to fall by! What cross devil
Made me put this main secret in the packet
I sent the king?—Is there no way to cure this?
No new device to beat this from his brains?
I know 'twill stir him strongly; yet I know
A way, if it takes right, in spite of fortune
Will bring me off again.—What's this—
"To the Pope?"
The letter, as I live, with all the business
I writ to his holiness. Nay then, farewell!
I have touch'd the highest point of all my greatness;
And, from that full meridian of my glory,
I haste now to my setting: I shall fall

Like a bright exhalation in the evening,
And no man see me more.

Re-enter the DUKES OF NORFOLK *and* SUF-
FOLK, *the* EARL OF SURREY, *and the* Lord
Chamberlain.

NOR. Hear the king's pleasure, cardinal:
who commands you
To render up the great seal presently
Into our hands; and to confine yourself
To Asher-house, my lord of Winchester's,
Till you hear farther from his highness.

WOL. Stay,—
Where's your commission, lords? words
cannot carry
Authority so weighty.

SUF. Who dare cross them,
Bearing the king's will from his mouth
expressly?

WOL. Till I find more than will or words
to do it,
(I mean your malice) know, officious lords,
I dare and must deny it. Now I feel
Of what coarse metal ye are moulded,—
envy:
How eagerly ye fellow my disgraces,
As if it fed ye! and how sleek and wanton
Ye appear in every thing may bring my
ruin!
Follow your envious courses, men of
malice;
You have Christian warrant for them, and,
no doubt,
In time will find their fit rewards. That
seal,
You ask with such a violence, the king
(Mine and your master) with his own
hand gave me;
Bade me enjoy it, with the place and
honours,
During my life; and to confirm his good-
ness,
Tied it by letters patent:—now, who'll
take it?

SUR. The king, that gave it.

WOL. It must be himself, then.

SUR. Thou art a proud traitor, priest.

WOL. Proud lord, thou liest:
Within these forty hours Surrey durst
better
Have burnt that tongue than said so.

SUR. Thy ambition,
Thou scarlet sin, robb'd this bewailing land
Of noble Buckingham, my father-in-law:
The heads of all thy brother cardinals
(With thee and all thy best parts bound
together)
Weigh'd not a hair of his. Plague of your
policy!
You sent me deputy for Ireland;
Far from his succour, from the king, from
all

That might have mercy on the fault thou
gav'st him;
Whilst your great goodness, out of holy
pity,
Absolv'd him with an axe.

WOL. This, and all else
This talking lord can lay upon my credit,
I answer is most false. The duke by law
Found his deserts: how innocent I was
From any private malice in his end,
His noble jury and foul cause can witness.
If I lov'd many words, lord, I should tell
you,
You have as little honesty as honour;
That I, in the way of loyalty and truth
Toward the king, my ever royal master,
Dare mate a sounder man than Surrey can
be,
And all that love his follies.

SUR. By my soul,
Your long coat, priest, protects you; thou
shouldst feel [My lords,
My sword i' the life-blood of thee else.—
Can ye endure to hear this arrogance?
And from this fellow? If we live thus
tamely,
To be just jaded by a piece of scarlet,
Farewell nobility; let his grace go for-
ward,
And dare us with his cap, like larks.

WOL. All goodness
Is poison to thy stomach.

SUR. Yes, that goodness
Of gleaning all the land's wealth into one,
Into your own hands, cardinal, by extor-
tion;
The goodness of your intercepted packets,
You writ to the pope, against the king:
your goodness, [torious.—
Since you provoke me, shall be most no-
My lord of Norfolk,—as you are truly
noble,
As you respect the common good, the state
Of our despis'd nobility, our issues,
Who, if he live, will scarce be gentle-
men)—
Produce the grand sum of his sins, the
articles
Collected from his life:—I'll startle you
Worse than the sacring bell, when the
brown wench
Lay kissing in your arms, lord cardinal.

WOL. How much, methinks, I could de
spise this man,
But that I am bound in charity against it

NOR. Those articles, my lord, are in the
king's hand:
But, thus much, they are foul ones.

WOL. So much fairer
And spotless shall mine innocence arise,
When the king knows my truth.

SUR.   This cannot save you:
I thank my memory, I yet remember
Some of these articles; and out they shall.
Now, if you can blush, and cry guilty,
     cardinal,
You'll show a little honesty.
WOL.   Speak on, Sir;
I dare your worst objections: if I blush,
It is to see a nobleman want manners.
SUR. I had rather want those, than my
     head.—Have at you!
First, that, without the king's assent or
     knowledge,   [power
You wrought to be a legate; by which
You maim'd the jurisdiction of all bishops.
NOR. Then, that in all you writ to Rome,
     or else
To foreign princes, *Ego et Rex meus*
Was still inscrib'd; in which you brought
     the king
To be your servant.
SUF. Then, that, without the knowledge
Either of king or council, when you went
Embassador to the emperor, you made
     bold
To carry into Flanders the great seal.
SUR. Item, you sent a large commission
To Gregory de Cassalis, to conclude,
Without the king's will or the state's allow-
     ance,
A league between his highness and Ferrara.
SUF. That, out of mere ambition, you
     have caus'd   [coin.
Your holy hat to be stamp'd on the king's
SUR. Then, that you have sent innumer-
     able substance,
(By what means got, I leave to your own
     conscience)
To furnish Rome, and to prepare the ways
You have for dignities; to the mere un-
     doing
Of all the kingdom. Many more there are;
Which, since they are of you, and odious,
I will not taint my mouth with.
CHAM.   O my lord,
Press not a falling man too far! 'tis virtue:
His faults lie open to the laws; let them,
Not you, correct him. My heart weeps to
     see him
So little of his great self.
SUR.   I forgive him.
SUF. Lord cardinal, the king's farther
     pleasure is,—
Because all those things you have done of
     late,   [dom,
By your power legatine, within this king-
Fall into the compass of a *præmunire*,—
That therefore such a writ be sued against
     you;
To forfeit all your goods, lands, tenements,
Chattels, and whatsoever, and to be

Out of the king's protection:—this is my
     charge.
NOR. And so we'll leave you to your
     meditations   [answer
How to live better. For your stubborn
About the giving back the great seal to us,
The king shall know it, and, no doubt,
     shall thank you.
So fare you well, my little good lord car-
     dinal.   [*Exeunt all except* WOLSEY.
WOL. So, farewell to the little good you
     bear me.
Farewell, a long farewell, to all my great-
     ness!
This is the state of man: to-day he puts
     forth
The tender leaves of hope; to-morrow blos-
     soms,
And bears his blushing honours thick upon
     him:
The third day comes a frost, a killing
     frost;
And,—when he thinks, good easy man, full
     surely
His greatness is a ripening,—nips his root,
And then he falls, as I do. I have ven-
     tur'd,
Like little wanton boys that swim on blad-
     ders,
This many summers in a sea of glory;
But far beyond my depth: my high blown
     pride
At length broke under me; and now has
     left me,
Weary and old with service, to the mercy
Of a rude stream, that must for ever hide
     me.
Vain pomp and glory of this world, I hate ye:
I feel my heart new open'd. O, how
     wretched
Is that poor man that hangs on princes'
     favours!
There is, betwixt that smile we would as-
     pire to,
That sweet aspect of princes, and their
     ruin,
More pangs and fears than wars or women
     have:
And when he falls, he falls like Lucifer,
Never to hope again.—
          Enter CROMWELL, *amazedly.*
               Why, how now, Cromwell!
CROM. I have no power to speak, Sir.
WOL.   What, amaz'd
At my misfortunes? can thy spirit wonder
A great man should decline? Nay, an you
     weep,
I am fallen indeed.
CROM.   How does your grace?
WOL.   Why, well;
Never so truly happy, my good Cromwell.

I know myself now; and I feel within me
A peace above all earthly dignities,
A still and quiet conscience. The king has
cur'd me,   [shoulders,
* I humbly thank his grace; and from these
These ruin'd pillars, out of pity, taken
A load would sink a navy,—too much
honour:
O, 'tis a burden, Cromwell, 'tis a burden
Too heavy for a man that hopes for heaven!
CROM. I am glad your grace has made
that right use of it.
WOL. I hope I have: I am able now, me-
thinks,
(Out of a fortitude of soul I feel)
To endure more miseries, and greater far,
Than my weak-hearted enemies dare of-
fer.—
What news abroad?
CROM.   The heaviest, and the worst,
Is your displeasure with the king.
WOL.   God bless him!
CROM. The next is, that Sir Thomas
More is chosen
Lord Chancellor in your place.
WOL.   That's somewhat sudden:
But he's a learned man. May he continue
Long in his highness' favour, and do justice
For truth's sake, and his conscience; that
his bones,   [blessings,
When he has run his course and sleeps in
May have a tomb of orphans' tears wept on
them!
What more?
CROM. That Cranmer is returned with
welcome,
Install'd lord archbishop of Canterbury.
WOL. That's news indeed!
CROM.   Last, that the lady Anne,
Whom the king hath in secrecy long mar-
ried,
This day was view'd in open, as his queen,
Going to chapel; and the voice is now
Only about her coronation.
WOL. There was the weight that pulled
me down.
          O Cromwell,
The king has gone beyond me: all my
glories
In that one woman I have lost for ever:
No sun shall ever usher forth mine honours,
Or gild again the noble troops that waited
Upon my smiles. Go, get thee from me,
Cromwell;
I am a poor fallen man, unworthy now
To be thy lord and master: seek the king;
(That sun, I pray, may never set!) I have
told him   [vance thee;
What, and how true thou art: he will ad-
Some little memory of me will stir him,
(I know his noble nature) not to let

Thy hopeful service perish too: good
Cromwell
Neglect him not; make use now, and pro-
vide
For thine own future safety.
CROM.   O my lord,
Must I, then, leave you? must I needs
forego
So good, so noble, and so true a master?
Bear witness, all that have not hearts of
iron,   [lord.
With what a sorrow Cromwell leaves his
The king shall have my service; but my
prayers,
For ever and for ever, shall be yours.
WOL. Cromwell, I did not think to shed
a tear
In all my miseries; but thou hast forc'd me,
Out of thy honest truth, to play the woman.
Let's dry our eyes: and thus far hear me,
Cromwell;
And,—when I am forgotten, as I shall be,
And sleep in dull cold marble, where no
mention
Of me more must be heard of,—say, I
taught thee,
Say, Wolsey,—that once trod the ways of
glory,
And sounded all the depths and shoals of
honour,—
Found thee a way, out of his wreck, to
rise in;
A sure and safe one, though thy master
miss'd it.
Mark but my fall, and that that ruin'd me.
Cromwell, I charge thee, fling away ambi-
tion:
By that sin fell the angels; how can man,
then,
The image of his Maker, hope to win by't?
Love thyself last: cherish those hearts that
hate thee:
Corruption wins not more than honesty.
Still in thy right hand carry gentle peace,
To silence envious tongues. Be just, and
fear not:
Let all the ends thou aim'st at be thy
country's,
Thy God's, and truth's; then if thou fall'st,
O Cromwell,
Thou fall'st a blessed martyr!
Serve the king; and,—pr'ythee, lead me in:
There take an inventory of all I have,
To the last penny; 'tis the king's: my robe,
And my integrity to heaven, is all
I dare now call mine own. O Cromwell,
Cromwell!
Had I but serv'd my God with half the
zeal
I serv'd my king, he would not in mine age
Have left me naked to mine enemies.

CROM. Good Sir, have patience.
WOL.   So I have. Farewell
The hopes of court! my hopes in heaven do
    dwell.   [Exeunt.

___

ACT IV.

SCENE I.—*A Street in* Westminster.

Enter two Gentlemen, *meeting.*
1 GENT. You're well met once again.
2 GENT. So are you.
1 GENT. You come to take your stand
here, and behold
The lady Anne pass from her coronation?
2 GENT. 'Tis all my business. At our
    last encounter,   [trial,
The duke of Buckingham came from his
1 GENT. 'Tis very true: but that time offer'd sorrow,
This, general joy.
2 GENT. 'Tis well: the citizens,
I am sure, have shown at full their royal
    minds;   [forward
As, let 'em have their rights, they are ever
In celebration of this day with shows,
Pageants, and sights of honour.
1 GENT.   Never greater;
Nor, I'll assure you, better taken, Sir.
2 GENT. May I be bold to ask what that
    contains,
That paper in your hand?
1 GENT.   Yes; 'tis the list
Of those that claim their offices this day,
By custom of the coronation.
The duke of Suffolk is the first, and claims
To be high steward; next, the duke of Nor-
folk,
He to be earl marshal: you may read the
    rest.
2 GENT. I thank you, Sir: had I not
    known those customs,
I should have been beholden to your paper.
But, I beseech you, what's become of
Katharine,
The princess dowager? how goes her busi-
    ness?
1 GENT. That I can tell you too. The
    archbishop
Of Canterbury, accompanied with other
Learned and reverend fathers of his order,
Held a late court at Dunstable, six miles
    off
From Ampthill, where the princess lay; to
    which
She was often cited by them, but appear'd
    not:
And, to be short, for not appearance, and
The king's late scruple, by the main assent
Of all these learned men she was divorc'd,
And the late marriage made of none effect:

Since which she was removed to Kim-
    bolton,
Where she remains now, sick.
2 GENT.   Alas, good lady!—
                              [Trumpets.
The trumpets sound: stand close, the
    queen is coming.

THE ORDER OF THE PROCESSION.
A lively flourish of trumpets.
1. *Two* Judges.
2. LORD CHANCELLOR, *with the purse and
    mace before him.*
3. Choristers *singing.*   [Music.
4. Mayor of London, *bearing the mace.
    Then* Garter, *in his coat of arms, and
    on his head a gilt copper crown.*
5. MARQUESS DORSET, *bearing a sceptre of
    gold, on his head a demi-coronal of
    gold. With him, the* EARL OF SURREY,
    *bearing the rod of silver with the
    dove, crowned with an earl's coronet.
    Collars of SS.*
6. DUKE OF SUFFOLK, *in his robe of estate,
    his coronet on his head, bearing a
    long white wand, as high-steward.
    With him, the* DUKE OF NORFOLK,
    *with the rod of marshalship, a coronet
    on his head. Collars of SS.*
7. *A canopy borne by four of the Cinque-
    ports; under it the* QUEEN *in her
    robe: in her hair, richly adorned with
    pearl, crowned. On each side of her,
    the* BISHOPS OF LONDON *and* WIN-
    CHESTER.
8. *The old* DUCHESS OF NORFOLK, *in a cor-
    onal of gold, wrought with flowers,
    bearing the* QUEEN'S *train.*
9. *Certain* Ladies *or* Countesses, *with plain
    circlets of gold without flowers.*
2 GENT. A royal train, believe me.—These
    I know:—
Who's that that bears the sceptre?
1 GENT.   Marquess Dorset:
And that the earl of Surrey, with the rod.
2 GENT. A bold brave gentleman. That
    should be
The duke of Suffolk?
1 GENT.   'Tis the same,—high-steward.
2 GENT. And that my lord of Norfolk?
1 GENT.   Yes.
2 GENT [*Looking on the* QUEEN.] Heaven
    bless thee!
Thou hast the sweetest face I ever look'd
    on.—
Sir, as I have a soul, she is an angel:
Our king has all the Indies in his arms,
And more and richer, when he strains that
    lady:
I cannot blame his conscience.
1 GENT.   They that bear

The cloth of honour over her, are four barons
Of the cinque-ports.

2 *GENT.* Those men are happy; and so are all, are near her.

I take it, she that carries up the train
Is that old noble lady, duchess of Norfolk.

1 *GENT.* It is; and all the rest are countesses.

2. *GENT.* Their coronets say so. These are stars indeed;
And sometimes falling ones.

1 *GENT.*   No more of that.

[*Exit Procession, with a great flourish of trumpets.*

Enter a third Gentleman.

God save you, Sir! Where have you been broiling?

3 *GENT.* Among the crowd i' the abbey; where a finger
Could not be wedg'd in more: I am stifled
With the mere rankness of their joy.

2 *GENT.* You saw the ceremony?

3 *GENT.* That I did.

1 *GENT.* How was it?

3 *GENT.* Well worth the seeing.

2 *GENT.* Good Sir, speak it to us.

3 *GENT.* As well as I am able. The rich stream
Of lords and ladies, having brought the queen
To a prepar'd place in the choir, fell off
A distance from her; while her grace sat down
To rest a while, some half an hour or so,
In a rich chair of state, opposing freely
The beauty of her person to the people:
Believe me, Sir, she is the goodliest woman
That ever lay by man: which when the people
Had the full view of, such a noise arose
As the shrouds make at sea in a stiff tempest,
As loud, and to as many tunes: hats, cloaks,
(Doublets, I think) flew up; and had their faces
Been loose, this day they had been lost. Such joy
I never saw before. Great-bellied women,
That had not half a week to go, like rams
In the old time of war, would shake the press,
And make them reel before them. No man living
Could say, "This is my wife," there; all were women
So strangely in one piece.

2 *GENT.* But, what follow'd?

3 *GENT.* At length her grace rose, and with modest paces

Came to the altar; where she kneel'd, and, saint-like,
Cast her fair eyes to heaven, and pray'd devoutly.
Then rose again, and bow'd her to the people:
When by the archbishop of Canterbury
She had all the royal makings of a queen;
As holy oil, Edward Confessor's crown,
The rod, and bird of peace, and all such emblems
Laid nobly on her: which perform'd, the choir,
With all the choicest music of the kingdom,
Together sung *Te Deum.* So she parted,
And with the same full state pac'd back again
To York-place, where the feast is held.

1 *GENT.*   Sir,
You must no more call it York-place, that's past;
For, since the cardinal fell, that title's lost:
'Tis now the king's, and call'd—Whitehall.

3 *GENT.*   I know it;
But 'tis so lately alter'd, that the old name
Is fresh about me.

2 *GENT.*   What two reverend bishops
Were those that went on each side of the queen?

3 *GENT.* Stokesly and Gardiner; the one of Winchester,
(Newly preferr'd from the king's secretary;)
The other, London.   [tary;)

2 *GENT.*   He of Winchester
Is held no great good lover of the archbishop's,
The virtuous Cranmer.

3 *GENT.*   All the land knows that:
However, yet there's no great breach; when it comes,
Cranmer will find a friend will not shrink from him.

2 *GENT.* Who may that be, I pray you?

3 *GENT.*   Thomas Cromwell;
A man in much esteem with the king, and truly
A worthy friend. The king
Has made him master o' the jewel-house,
And one, already, of the privy-council.

2 *GENT.* He will deserve more.

3 *GENT.*   Yes, without all doubt.—
Come, gentlemen, ye shall go my way, which
Is to the court, and there ye shall be my guests:
Something I can command. As I walk thither,
I'll tell ye more.

BOTH. You may command us, Sir.

[*Exeunt.*

SCENE II.—KIMBOLTON.

Enter KATHARINE, *Dowager, sick; led between* GRIFFITH *and* PATIENCE.

GRIF. How does your grace?

KATH.   O Griffith, sick to death!
My legs, like loaden branches, bow to the earth,
Willing to leave their burden. Reach a chair:—
So,—now, methinks, I feel a little ease.
Didst thou not tell me, Griffith, as thou led'st me,
That the great child of honour cardinal Wolsey,
Was dead?

GRIF.   Yes, Madam; but I think your grace,
Out of the pain you suffer'd, gave no ear to't.

KATH. Pr'ythee, good Griffith, tell me how he died:
If well, he stepp'd before me, happily,
For my example.

GRIF.   Well, the voice goes, Madam:
For after the stout earl Northumberland
Arrested him at York, and brought him forward
(As a man sorely tainted) to his answer,
He fell sick suddenly, and grew so ill,
He could not sit his mule.

KATH.   Alas, poor man!

GRIF. At last, with easy roads, he came to Leicester;
Lodg'd in the abbey; where the reverend abbot,
With all his convent, honourably receiv'd him;
To whom he gave these words,—"O father abbot,
An old man, broken with the storms of state,
Is come to lay his weary bones among ye;
Give him a little earth for charity!"
So went to bed; where eagerly his sickness
Pursu'd him still: and, three nights after this,
About the hour of eight, (which he himself
Foretold should be his last) full of repentance,
Continued meditations, tears, and sorrows,
He gave his honours to the world again,
His blessed part to heaven, and slept in peace.

KATH. So may he rest; his faults lie gently on him!
Yet thus far, Griffith, give me leave to speak him,
And yet with charity. He was a man
Of an unbounded stomach, ever ranking

Himself with princes; one, that, by suggestion,
Tied all the kingdom: simony was fair play;
His own opinion was his law: i' the presence
He would say untruths; and be ever double,
Both in his words and meaning. He was never,
But where he meant to ruin, pitiful:
His promises were, as he then was, mighty;
But his performance, as he is now, nothing.
Of his own body he was ill, and gave
The clergy ill example.

GRIF.   Noble Madam,
Men's evil manners live in brass; their virtues
We write in water. May it please your highness
To hear me speak his good now?

KATH.   Yes, good Griffith:
I were malicious else.

GRIF.   This cardinal,
Though from a humble stock, undoubtedly
Was fashion'd to much honour from his cradle.
He was a scholar, and a ripe and good one;
Exceeding wise, fair spoken, and persuading:
Lofty and sour to them that lov'd him not;
But, to those men that sought him, sweet as summer.
And though he were unsatisfied in getting,
(Which was a sin) yet in bestowing, Madam,
He was most princely: ever witness for him [him
Those twins of learning, that he rais'd in you,
Ipswich, and Oxford! one of which fell with him,
Unwilling to outlive the good that did it;
The other, though unfinish'd, yet so famous,
So excellent in art, and still so rising,
That Christendom shall ever speak his virtue.
His overthrow heap'd happiness upon him;
For then, and not till then, he felt himself,
And found the blessedness of being little:
And, to add greater honours to his age
Than man could give him, he died fearing God.

KATH. After my death I wish no other herald,
No other speaker of my living actions,
To keep mine honour from corruption,
But such an honest chronicler as Griffith.
Whom I most hated living, thou hast made me,
With thy religious truth and modesty,
Now in his ashes honour: peace be with him!—

Patience, be near me still; and set me
lower:
I have not long to trouble thee.—Good
Griffith,
Cause the musicians play me that sad note
I nam'd my knell, whilst I sit meditating
On that celestial harmony I go to.
                              [*Sad and solemn music.*
GRIF. She is asleep: good wench, let's sit
down quiet,
For fear we wake her:—softly, gentle
Patience.

*The Vision. Enter, solemnly tripping one
after another, six Personages, clad in
white robes, wearing on their heads garlands of bays, and golden vizards on
their faces; branches of bays, or palm, in
their hands. They first congee unto her,
then dance; and, at certain changes, the
first two hold a spare garland over her
head; at which, the other four make
reverend court'sies: then, the two that
held the garland deliver the same to the
other next two, who observe the same
order in their changes, and holding the
garland over her head: which done, they
deliver the same garland to the last two,
who likewise observe the same order: at
which, (as it were by inspiration) she
makes in her sleep signs of rejoicing,
and holdeth up her hands to heaven:
and so in their dancing they vanish, carrying the garland with them. The music
continues.*

KATH. Spirits of peace, where are ye?
Are ye all gone,
And leave me here in wretchedness be-
hind ye?
GRIF. Madam, we are here.
KATH.   It is not you I call for:
Saw ye none enter, since I slept?
GRIF.   None, Madam.
KATH. No? Saw you not, even now, a
blessed troop
Invite me to a banquet; whose bright faces
Cast thousand beams upon me, like the
sun?
They promis'd me eternal happiness;
And brought me garlands, Griffith, which
I feel
I am not worthy yet to wear: I shall, as-
suredly.
GRIF. I am most joyful, Madam, such
Possess your fancy.   [good dreams
KATH.   Bid the music leave,
They are harsh and heavy to me.
                              [*Music ceases.*
PAT. [*Aside to* GRIF.] Do you note
How much her grace is alter'd on the
sudden?

How long her face is drawn? How pale
she looks,
And of an earthy cold? Mark her eyes!
GRIF. [*Aside to* PAT.] She is going, wench:
pray, pray.
PAT. [*Aside to* GRIF.] Heaven comfort
her!
                              Enter a Messenger.
MESS. An't like your grace,—
KATH.   You are a saucy fellow:
Deserve we no more reverence?
GRIF.   You are to blame,
Knowing she will not lose her wonted
greatness,
To use so rude behaviour; go to, kneel.
MESS. I humbly do entreat your highness'
pardon;
My haste made me unmannerly. There is
staying
A gentleman, sent from the king, to see
you.
KATH. Admit him entrance, Griffith: but
this fellow
Let me ne'er see again.
                    [*Exeunt* GRIFFITH *and* Messenger.
              Re-enter GRIFFITH, *with* CAPUCIUS.
                          If my sight fail not,
You should be lord embassador from the
emperor,
My royal nephew, and your name Capucius.
CAP. Madam, the same,—your servant.
KATH.   O my lord,
The times and titles now are alter'd
strangely
With me, since first you knew me. But,
I pray you,
What is your pleasure with me?
CAP.   Noble lady,
First, mine own service to your grace; the
next,
The king's request that I would visit you;
Who grieves much for your weakness, and
by me
Sends you his princely commendations,
And heartily entreats you take good com-
fort.
KATH. O, my good lord, that comfort
comes too late;
'Tis like a pardon after execution:
That gentle physic, given in time, had
cur'd me;
But now I am past all comforts here, but
prayers.
How does his highness?
CAP.   Madam, in good health.
KATH. So may he ever do! and ever
flourish,
When I shall dwell with worms, and my
poor name
Banish'd the kingdom!—Patience, is that
letter,

I caus'd you write, yet sent away?
PAT.   No, Madam.
     [*Giving it to* KATHARINE.
KATH. Sir, I most humbly pray you to
This to my lord the king.   [deliver
CAP.   Most willing, Madam.
KATH. In which I have commended to
his goodness
The model of our chaste loves, his young
daughter,—
The dews of heaven fall thick in blessings
on her!—
Beseeching him to give her virtuous breed-
ing;
(She is young, and of a noble modest
nature,—
I hope, she will deserve well) and a little
To love her for her mother's sake, that
lov'd him,
Heaven knows how dearly. My next poor
petition
Is, that his noble grace would have some
pity
Upon my wretched women, that so long
Have follow'd both my fortunes faithfully:
Of which there is not one, I dare avow,
(And now I should not lie) but will de-
serve,
For virtue and true beauty of the soul,
For honesty and decent carriage,
A right good husband, let him be a noble;
And, sure, those men are happy that shall
have them.
The last is, for my men;—they are the
poorest,
But poverty could never draw them from
me;—
That they may have their wages duly paid
them,
And something over to remember me by:
If heaven had pleas'd to have given me
longer life,
And able means, we had not parted thus.
These are the whole contents:—and, good
my lord,
By that you love the dearest in this world,
As you wish Christian peace to souls de-
parted,
Stand these poor people's friend, and urge
the king
To do me this last right.
CAP.   By heaven, I will,
Or let me lose the fashion of a man!
KATH. I thank you, honest lord. Remem-
ber me
In all humility unto his highness:
Say, his long trouble now is passing;
Out of this world; tell him, in death I
bless'd him,
For so I will.—Mine eyes grow dim.—
Farewell;

My lord.—Griffith, farewell.—Nay, Pa-
tience,
You must not leave me yet: I must to bed;
Call in more women.—When I am dead,
good wench,
Let me be us'd with honour: strew me
over
With maiden flowers, that all the world
may know
I was a chaste wife to my grave: embalm
me,
Then lay me forth: although unqueen'd,
yet like
A queen, and daughter to a king, inter me.
I can no more.
     [*Exeunt, leading* KATHARINE.

ACT V.

SCENE I.—LONDON. *A Gallery in the
Palace.*

Enter GARDINER, *Bishop of Winchester,
a* Page *with a torch before him.*
GAR. It's one o'clock, boy, is't not?
BOY.   It hath struck.
GAR. These should be hours for necessi-
ties,
Not for delights; times to repair our nature
With comforting repose, and not for us
To waste these times.—
     Enter SIR THOMAS LOVELL.
     Good hour of night, Sir Thomas!
Whither so late?
LOV. Came you from the king, my lord?
GAR. I did, Sir Thomas; and left him at
primero
With the duke of Suffolk.
LOV.   I must to him too,
Before he go to bed. I'll take my leave.
GAR. Not yet, Sir Thomas Lovell. What's
the matter?
It seems you are in haste: an if there be
No great offence belongs to't, give your
friend
Some touch of your late business: affairs,
that walk
(As they say spirits do) at midnight, have
In them a wilder nature, than the business
That seeks despatch by day.
LOV.   My lord, I love you;
And durst commend a secret to your ear
Much weightier than this work. The
queen's in labour,
They say, in great extremity; and fear'd,
She'll with the labour end.
GAR.   The fruit she goes with
I pray for heartily, that it may find
Good time, and live: but for the stock, Sir
Thomas,
I wish it grubb'd up now.
LOV.   Methinks I could
Cry the amen; and yet my conscience says

She's a good creature, and, sweet lady,
Deserve our better wishes.   [does
GAR.   But, Sir, Sir,—
Hear me, Sir Thomas: you're a gentleman
Of mine own way; I know you wise,
  religious;
And, let me tell you, it will ne'er be well,—
'Twill not, Sir Thomas Lovell, take't of
  me,—
Till Cranmer, Cromwell, her two hands,
Sleep in their graves.   [and she,
LOV.   Now, Sir, you speak of two
The most remark'd i' the kingdom. As for
  Cromwell,—   [master
Beside that of the jewel-house, he's made
O' the rolls, and the king's secretary;
  farther, Sir,   [ments,
Stands in the gap and trade of more prefer-
With which the time will load him. Th'
  archbishop   [dare speak
Is the king's hand and tongue; and who
One syllable against him?
GAR.   Yes, yes, Sir Thomas,
There are that dare; and I myself have
  ventur'd
To speak my mind of him: and indeed this
  day,
Sir, (I may tell it you) I think I have
Incens'd the lords o' the council, that he is
(For so I know he is, they know he is)
A most arch heretic, a pestilence
That does infect the land: with which
  they moved,   [far
Have broken with the king; who hath so
Given ear to our complaint, (of his great
  grace   [mischiefs
And princely care, foreseeing those fell
Our reasons laid before him) hath com-
  manded
To-morrow morning to the council-board
He be convented. He's a rank weed, Sir
  Thomas,
And we must root him out. From your
  affairs
I hinder you too long: good night, Sir
  Thomas,
LOV. Many good nights, my lord: I rest
  your servant.
            [Exeunt GARDINER and Page.
As LOVELL is going out, enter the KING and
      the DUKE OF SUFFOLK.
K. HEN. Charles, I will play no more to-
  night;   [me.
My mind's not on't; you are too hard for
SUF. Sir, I did never win of you before.
K. HEN. But little, Charles;
Nor shall not, when my fancy's on my
  play.—   [news?
Now, Lovell, from the queen what is the
LOV. I could not personally deliver to her
What you commanded me, but by her
  woman   [thanks
I sent your message; who return'd her
In the greatest humbleness, and desir'd
  your highness
Most heartily to pray for her.
K. HEN.   What say'st thou, ha?
To pray for her? what, is she crying out?
LOV. So said her woman; and that her
  sufferance made
Almost each pang a death.
K. HEN.   Alas, good lady!
SUF. God safely quit her of her burden,
  and
With gentle travail, to the gladding of
Your highness with an heir!
K. HEN.   'Tis midnight, Charles;
Pr'ythee, to bed; and in thy prayers re-
  member
Th' estate of my poor queen. Leave me
  alone;
For I must think of that, which company
Would not be friendly to.
SUF.   I wish your highness
A quiet night; and my good mistress will
Remember in my prayers.
K. HEN.   Charles, good night.—
                        [Exit SUFFOLK.
      Enter SIR ANTHONY DENNY.
Well, Sir, what follows?
DEN. Sir, I have brought my lord the
As you commanded me.   [archbishop,
K. HEN.   Ha! Canterbury?
DEN. Ay, my good lord.
K. HEN. 'Tis true: where is he, Denny?
DEN. He attends your highness' pleasure.
K. HEN.   Bring him to us.
                        [Exit DENNY.
LOV. [Aside.] This is about that which
  the bishop spake:
I am happily come hither.
      Re-enter DENNY, with CRANMER.
K. HEN.   Avoid the gallery.
                  [LOVELL seems to stay.
Ha!—I have said.—Be gone.
What!—   [Exeunt LOVELL and DENNY.
CRAN. [Aside.] I am fearful:—wherefore
  frowns he thus?
'Tis his aspect of terror. All's not well.
K. HEN. How now, my lord! You do
  desire to know
Wherefore I sent for you.
CRAN. [Kneeling.]   It is my duty
T' attend your highness' pleasure.
K. HEN.   Pray you, arise,
My good and gracious lord of Canterbury.
Come, you and I must walk a turn to-
  gether;
I have news to tell you: come, come, give
  me your hand.
Ah, my good lord, I grieve at what I
  speak,

And am right sorry to repeat what follows:
I have, and most unwillingly, of late
Heard many grievous, I do say, my lord,
Grievous complaints of you; which, being
consider'd,   [shall
Have mov'd us and our council, that you
This morning come before us; where, I
know,   [self,
You cannot with such freedom purge your-
But that, till farther trial in those charges
Which will require your answer, you must
take   [tented
Your patience to you, and be well con-
To make your house our Tower: you a
brother of us,
It fits we thus proceed, or else no witness
Would come against you.
CRAN.   I humbly thank your highness;
And am right glad to catch this good
occasion   [chaff
Most throughly to be winnow'd, where my
And corn shall fly asunder: for, I know,
There's none stands under more calum-
nious tongues,
Than I myself, poor man.
K. HEN.   Stand up, good Canterbury:
Thy truth, and thy integrity, is rooted
In us, thy friend. Give me thy hand, stand
up: [dame,
Pr'ythee, let's walk. Now, by my holy-
What manner of man are you? My lord,
I look'd   [that
You would have given me your petition,
I should have ta'en some pains to bring
together
Yourself and your accusers; and to have
heard you,
Without indurance, farther.
CRAN.   Most dread liege,
The good I stand on is my truth and
honesty:
If they shall fail, I, with mine enemies,
Will triumph o'er my person; which I
weigh not,
Being of those virtues vacant. I fear
What can be said against me.   [nothing
K. HEN.   Know you not
How your state stands i' the world, with
the whole world?
Your enemies are many, and not small;
their practices   [ever
Must bear the same proportion; and not
The justice and the truth o' the question
carries
The due o' the verdict with it: at what ease
Might corrupt minds procure knaves as
corrupt   [been done.
To swear against you? such things have
You are potently oppos'd; and with a
malice

Of as great size. Ween you of better luck,
I mean in perjur'd witness, than your Mas-
ter,   [liv'd
Whose minister you are, whiles here he
Upon this naughty earth? Go to, go to;
You take a precipice for no leap of danger,
And woo your own destruction.
CRAN.   God and your majesty
Protect mine innocence, or I fall into
The trap is laid for me!
K. HEN.   Be of good cheer;
They shall no more prevail, than we give
way to.   [see
Keep comfort to you; and this morning,
You do appear before them: if they shall
chance,   [you,
In charging you with matters, to commit
The best persuasions to the contrary
Fail not to use, and with what vehemency
The occasion shall instruct you: if en-
treaties
Will render you no remedy, this ring
Deliver them, and your appeal to us
There make before them.—Look, the good
man weeps!
He's honest, on mine honour. God's blest
mother!
I swear, he is true-hearted; and a soul
None better in my kingdom.—Get you
gone,
And do as I have bid you.—[Exit CRAN-
MER.] He has strangled
His language in his tears.
            Enter Old Lady.
GENT.   [Within.] Come back: what mean
you?
OLD L.   I'll not come back; the tidings
that I bring   [good angels
Will make my boldness manners.—Now,
Fly o'er thy royal head, and shade thy
person
Under their blessed wings!
K. HEN.   Now, by thy looks
I guess thy message. Is the queen de-
Say, ay; and of a boy.   [liver'd?
OLD L.   Ay, ay, my liege;
And of a lovely boy: the God of heaven
Both now and ever bless her! 'tis a girl,—
Promises boys hereafter. Sir, your queen
Desires your visitation, and to be
Acquainted with this stranger: 'tis as like
As cherry is to cherry.   [you
K. HEN.   Lovell,—
            Re-enter LOVELL.
LOV.   Sir?
K. HEN.   Give her a hundred marks. I'll
to the queen.   [Exit.
OLD L.   A hundred marks! By this light,
I'll ha' more.
An ordinary groom is for such payment.
I will have more, or scold it out of him.

Said I for this, the girl was like to him?
I will have more, or else unsay't; and now,
While it is hot, I'll put it to the issue.

[*Exeunt.*

SCENE II.—*The Lobby before the* Council-
Chamber.

Enter CRANMER; *Servants, Door-Keeper,
&c., attending.*

CRAN. I hope I am not too late; and yet
the gentleman,
That was sent to me from the council,
pray'd me
To make great haste.—All fast? what
means this?—Ho!
Who waits there?—Sure, you know me?
D. KEEP.   Yes, my lord;
But yet I cannot help you.
CRAN.   Why?
D. KEEP. Your grace must wait till you
be call'd for.
Enter DOCTOR BUTTS.
CRAN.   So.
BUTTS. [*Aside.*] This is a piece of
malice. I am glad
I came this way so happily: the king
Shall understand it presently.   [*Exit.*
CRAN. [*Aside.*]   'Tis Butts,
The king's physician: as he past along,
How earnestly he cast his eyes upon me!
Pray heaven, he sound not my disgrace!
For certain,   [me,
This is of purpose laid by some that hate
(God turn their hearts! I never sought
their malice)   [to make me
To quench mine honour: they would shame
Wait else at door, a fellow counsellor,
'Mong boys, grooms, and lackeys. But
their pleasures   [tience.
Must be fulfill'd, and I attend with pa-
Enter the KING *and* BUTTS, *at a window
above.*
BUTTS. I'll show your grace the strangest
sight,—
K. HEN.   What's that, Butts?
BUTTS. I think your highness saw this
many a day.
K. HEN. Body o' me, where is it?
BUTTS.   There, my lord:
The high promotion of his grace of Canter-
bury;
Who holds his state at door, 'mongst pur-
Pages, and footboys.   [suivants,
K. HEN. Ha! 'Tis he, indeed:
Is this the honour they do one another?
'Tis well there's one above them yet. I
had thought,   [them,
They had parted so much honesty among
(At least, good manners) as not thus to
suffer

A man of his place, and so near our favour,
To dance attendance on their lordships'
pleasures,   [packets.
And at the door too, like a post with
By holy Mary, Butts, there's knavery:
Let them alone, and draw the curtain
We shall hear more anon.—   [close;
[*Exeunt above.*

THE COUNCIL-CHAMBER.

Enter the LORD CHANCELLOR, *the* DUKE OF
SUFFOLK, *the* DUKE OF NORFOLK, EARL
OF SURREY, *Lord Chamberlain,* GARDINER,
and CROMWELL. *The* CHANCELLOR *places
himself at the upper end of the table on
the left hand; a seat being left void
above him, as for the* ARCHBISHOP OF
CANTERBURY. *The rest seat themselves
in order on each side.* CROMWELL *at the
lower end, as secretary.*

CHAN. Speak to the business, master
Why are we met in council?   [secretary:
CROM.   Please your honours,
The chief cause concerns his grace of
Canterbury.
GAR. Has he had knowledge of it?
CROM.   Yes.
NOR.   Who waits there?
D. KEEP. Without, my noble lords?
GAR.   Yes.
D. KEEP.   My lord archbishop;
And has done half an hour, to know your
CHAN. Let him come in.   [pleasures
D. KEEP.   Your grace may enter now.
[CRANMER *approaches the Council-
table.*
CHAN. My good lord archbishop, I am
very sorry
To sit here at this present, and behold
That chair stand empty: but we all are
men,
In our own natures frail, and capable
Of our flesh; few are angels: out of which
frailty,   [teach us,
And want of wisdom, you, that best should
Have misdemean'd yourself, and not a
little,   [ing
Toward the king first, then his laws, in fill-
The whole realm, by your teaching and
your chaplains,
(For so we are inform'd) with new opin-
ions,
Divers and dangerous; which are heresies,
And, not reform'd, may prove pernicious.
GAR. Which reformation must be sudden
too,   [horses
My noble lords; for those that tame wild
Pace them not in their hands to make
them gentle,
But stop their mouths with stubborn bits,
and spur them,

Till they obey the manage. If we suffer
(Out of our easiness and childish pity
To one man's honour) this contagious sick-
ness,   [then?
Farewell all physic: and what follows
Commotions, uproars, with a general taint
Of the whole state: as, of late days, our
neighbours,
The upper Germany, can dearly witness,
Yet freshly pitied in our memories.
CRAN. My good lords, hitherto, in all
the progress
Both of my life and office, I have labour'd,
And with no little study, that my teaching,
And the strong course of my authority,
Might go one way, and safely; and the end
Was ever, to do well: nor is there living
(I speak it with a single heart, my lords,)
A man that more detests, more stirs
against,   [place,
Both in his private conscience and his
Defacers of a public peace, than I do.
Pray heaven, the king may never find a
heart
With less allegiance in it! Men, that make
Envy and crooked malice nourishment,
Dare bite the best. I do beseech your
lordships,
That, in this case of justice, my accusers,
Be what they will, may stand forth face
And freely urge against me.   [to face,
SUF.   Nay, my lord,
That cannot be: you are a counsellor,
And, by that virtue, no man dare accuse
you.
GAR. My lord, because we have business
of more moment,
We will be short with you. 'Tis his high-
ness' pleasure,
And our consent, for better trial of you,
From hence, you be committed to the
Tower;
Where, being but a private man again,
You shall know many dare accuse you
boldly,
More than, I fear, you are provided for.
CRAN. Ah, my good lord of Winchester,
I thank you;   [will pass,
You are always my good friend; if your
I shall both find your lordship judge and
juror,
You are so merciful: I see your end,—
'Tis my undoing: love and meekness, lord,
Become a churchman better than ambition:
Win straying souls with modesty again,
Cast none away. That I shall clear myself,
Lay all the weight ye can upon my pa-
tience,   [science,
I make as little doubt, as you do con-
In doing daily wrongs. I could say more,

But reverence to your calling makes me
modest.
GAR. My lord, my lord, you are a sec-
tary;   [discovers,
That's the plain truth: your painted gloss
To men that understand you, words and
weakness.
CROM. My lord of Winchester, you are
a little,   [noble,
By your good favour, too sharp; men so
However faulty, yet should find respect
For what they have been: 'tis a cruelty
To load a falling man.
GAR.   Good master secretary,
I cry your honour mercy; you may, worst
Of all this table, say so.
CROM.   Why, my lord?
GAR. Do not I know you for a favourer
Of this new sect? ye are not sound.
CROM.   Not sound?
GAR. Not sound, I say.
CROM.   Would you were half so honest!
Men's prayers then would seek you, not
their fears.
GAR. I shall remember this bold language.
CROM.   Do.
Remember your bold life too.
CHAN.   This is too much;
Forbear, for shame, my lords.
GAR.   I have done.
CROM.   And I.
CRAN. Then thus for you, my lord:—it
stands agreed,
I take it, by all voices, that forthwith
You be convey'd to the Tower a prisoner;
There to remain, till the king's farther
pleasure   [lords?
Be known unto us:—are you all agreed,
ALL. We are.
CRAN. Is there no other way of mercy,
But I must needs to the Tower, my lords?
GAR.   What other
Would you expect? You are strangely
troublesome.—
Let some o' the guard be ready there.
                  Enter Guard.
CRAN.   For me?
Must I go like a traitor thither?
GAR.   Receive him,
And see him safe i' the Tower.
CRAN.   Stay, good my lords,
I have a little yet to say. Look there, my
lords;
By virtue of that ring, I take my cause
Out of the gripes of cruel men, and give it
To a most noble judge, the king my master.
CHAN. This is the king's ring.
SUR.   'Tis no counterfeit.
SUF. 'Tis the right ring, by heaven: I
told ye all,   [rolling,
When we first put this dangerous stone a

'Twould fall upon ourselves.

NOR.   Do you think, my lords,
The king will suffer but the little finger
Of this man to be vex'd?

CHAN.   'Tis now too certain:
How much more is his life in value with
Would I were fairly out on't.   [him!

CROM.   My mind gave me,
In seeking tales and informations
Against this man, (whose honesty the devil
And his disciples only envy at)
Ye blew the fire that burns ye.—Now have
     at ye!

Enter the KING, *frowning on them; he*
takes his seat.

GAR. Dread sovereign, how much are we
     bound to heaven   [prince;
In daily thanks, that gave us such a
Not only good and wise, but most reli-
     gious: [church
One that, in all obedience, makes the
The chief aim of his honour; and, to
     strengthen
That holy duty, out of dear respect,
His royal self in judgment comes to hear
The cause betwixt her and this great of-
     fender.

K. HEN. You were ever good at sudden
     commendations,   [not
Bishop of Winchester. But know, I come
To hear such flattery now, and in my
     presence;
They are too thin and base to hide offences.
To me you cannot reach: you play the
     spaniel,   [win me:
And think with wagging of your tongue to
But, whatsoe'er thou tak'st me for, I'm
     sure
Thou hast a cruel nature and a bloody.—
[*To* CRANMER.] Good man, sit down. Now
     let me see the proudest,
He that dares most, but wag his finger at
     thee:
By all that's holy, he had better starve,
Than but once think this place becomes
     thee not.

SUR. May it please your grace,—

K. HEN.   No, Sir, it does not please me.
I had thought, I had had men of some
     understanding
And wisdom of my council; but I find
     none.
Was it discretion, lords, to let this man,
This good man, (few of you deserve that
     title)
This honest man, wait like a lousy footboy
At chamber door? and one as great as you
     are?   [mission
Why, what a shame was this! Did my com-
Bid ye so far forget yourselves? I gave ye
Power, as he was a counsellor to try him,

Not as a groom: there's some of ye, I see,
More out of malice than integrity,
Would try him to the utmost, had ye mean;
Which ye shall never have while I live.

CHAN.   Thus far,
My most dread sovereign, may it like your
     grace,
To let my tongue excuse all. What was
     purpos'd
Concerning his imprisonment, was rather
(If there be faith in men) meant for his
     trial,
And fair purgation to the world, than
I'm sure, in me.   [malice,—

K. HEN. Well, well, my lords, respect
     him;
Take him, and use him well, he's worthy
     of it.
I will say thus much for him,—if a prince
May be beholden to a subject, I
Am, for his love and service, so to him.
Make me no more ado, but all embrace
     him:
Be friends, for shame, my lords!—My
     lord of Canterbury,
I have a suit which you must not deny me;
That is, a fair young maid that yet wants
     baptism,
You must be godfather, and answer for
     her.

CRAN. The greatest monarch now alive
     may glory
In such an honour: how may I deserve it,
That am a poor and humble subject to
     you?

K. HEN. Come, come, my lord, you'd
     spare your spoons: [you;
You shall have two noble partners with
The old duchess of Norfolk, and lady
     marquess Dorset:
Will these please you?—
Once more, my lord of Winchester, I
     charge you,
Embrace and love this man.

GAR.   With a true heart
And brother-love I do it.

CRAN.   And let heaven
Witness, how dear I hold this confirmation.

K. HEN. Good man, those joyful tears
     show thy true heart:
The common voice, I see, is verified
Of thee, which says thus, "Do my lord of
     Canterbury   [ever."—
A shrewd turn, and he is your friend for
Come, lords, we trifle time away; I long
To have this young one made a Christian.
As I made ye one, lords, one remain;
So I grow stronger, you more honour gain.
     [*Exeunt.*

SCENE III.—*The Palace-Yard.*

Noise and tumult within. Enter Porter *and his* Man.

PORT. You'll leave your noise anon, ye rascals: do you take the court for Paris-garden? ye rude slaves, leave your gaping. [*Within*] Good master porter, I belong to the larder.

PORT. Belong to the gallows, and be hanged, you rogue! Is this a place to roar in?—Fetch me a dozen crab-tree staves, and strong ones: these are but switches to 'em.—I'll scratch your heads: you must be seeing christenings? Do you look for ale and cakes here, you rude rascals?

MAN. Pray, Sir, be patient: 'tis as much impossible   [cannons] (Unless we sweep 'em from the door with To scatter 'em, as 'tis to make 'em sleep On May-day morning; which will never be: We may as well push against Paul's, as stir 'em.

PORT. How got they in, and be hang'd?

MAN. Alas, I know not; how gets the tide in? As much as one sound cudgel of four foot (You see the poor remainder) could dis- I made no spare, Sir.   [tribute,

PORT.   You did nothing, Sir.

MAN. I am not Samson, nor Sir Guy, nor Colbrand. To mow 'em down before me: but if I spared any   [old, That had a head to hit, either young or He or she, cuckold or cuckold-maker, Let me ne'er hope to see a chine again; And that I would not for a cow, God save her!

[*Within.*] Do you hear, master porter?

PORT. I shall be with you presently, good master puppy.—Keep the door close, sirrah.

MAN. What would you have me do?

PORT. What should you do, but knock 'em down by the dozens? Is this Moor-fields to muster in? or have we some strange Indian with the great tool come to court, the women so besiege us? Bless me, what a fry of fornication is at door! On my Christian conscience, this one chris-tening will beget a thousand; here will be father, godfather, and all together.

MAN. The spoons will be the bigger, Sir. There is a fellow somewhat near the door, he should be a brazier by his face; for, o' my conscience, twenty of the dog-days now reign in's nose: all that stand about him are under the line, they need no other penance. That fire-drake did I hit three times on the head, and three times was

his nose discharged against me: he stands there, like a mortar-piece, to blow us. There was a haberdasher's wife of small wit near him, that railed upon me till her pink'd porringer fell off her head, for kindling such a combustion in the state. I miss'd the meteor once, and hit that woman, who cried out, "Clubs!" when I might see from far some forty truncheoners draw to her succour, which were the hope o' the Strand, where she was quartered. They fell on; I made good my place: at length they came to the broom-staff with me; I defied 'em still: when suddenly a file of boys behind 'em, loose shot, de-livered such a shower of pebbles, that I was fain to draw mine honour in, and let 'em win the work. The devil was amongst 'em, I think, surely.

PORT. These are the youths that thunder at a play-house, and fight for bitten apples; that no audience, but the Tribulation of Tower-hill, or the Limbs of Limehouse, their dear brothers, are able to endure. I have some of 'em in *Limbo Patrum*, and there they are like to dance these three days; besides the running banquet of two beadles, that is to come.

Enter the Lord Chamberlain.

CHAM. Mercy o' me, what a multitude are here! They grow still too; from all parts they are coming,   [porters, As if we kept a fair here! Where are these These lazy knaves?—Ye have made a fine hand, fellows: There's a trim rabble let in: are all these Your faithful friends o' the suburbs? We shall have   [ladies, Great store of room, no doubt, left for the When they pass back from the christening.

PORT.   An't please your honour, We are but men; and what so many may do, Not being torn a pieces, we have done: An army cannot rule 'em.

CHAM.   As I live, If the king blame me for't, I'll lay ye all By the heels, and suddenly; and on your heads   [knaves; Clap round fines for neglect: you're lazy And here ye lie baiting of bombards, when Ye should do service. Hark! the trumpets sound; They're come already from the christening: Go, break among the press, and find a way out To let the troop pass fairly; or I'll find A Marshalsea shall hold ye play these two months.

PORT. Make way there for the princess.

MAN. You great fellow,
Stand close up, or I'll make your head
ache.
PORT. You i' the camblet, get up o' the
rail;
I'll pick you o'er the pales else.
                                        [*Exeunt.*

SCENE IV.—*The Palace.*

Enter trumpets, sounding; then two Aldermen, Lord Mayor, Garter, CRANMER,
DUKE OF NORFOLK, *with his marshal's
staff,* DUKE OF SUFFOLK, *two* Noblemen,
*bearing great standing bowls for the
christening gifts; then, four* Noblemen
bearing a canopy, under which the
DUCHESS OF NORFOLK, *godmother, bearing the child richly habited in a mantle,*
&c. *Train borne by a* Lady; *then follows
the* MARCHIONESS OF DORSET, *the other
godmother, and* Ladies. *The troop pass
once about the stage, and* Garter *speaks.*
GART. Heaven, from thy endless goodness, send prosperous life, long, and ever
happy, to the high and mighty princess of
England, Elizabeth!
      Flourish. Enter KING *and train.*
CRAN. [*Kneeling.*] And to your royal
grace, and the good queen,
My noble partners, and myself, thus
pray;—
All comfort, joy, in this most gracious lady,
Heaven ever laid up to make parents
May hourly fall upon ye!   [happy,
K. HEN. Thank you, good lord arch-
What is her name?   [bishop:
CRAN.   Elizabeth.
K. HEN.   Stand up, lord.—
          [*The* KING *kisses the child.*
With this kiss take my blessing: God
protect thee!
Into whose hand I give thy life.
CRAN.   Amen.
K. HEN. My noble gossips, ye have been
too prodigal:
I thank ye heartily; so shall this lady,
When she has so much English.
CRAN.   Let me speak, Sir.
For Heaven now bids me; and the words
I utter   [them truth.
Let none think flattery, for they'll find
This royal infant, (heaven still move about
her!)
Though in her cradle, yet now promises
Upon this land a thousand thousand bless-
ings,   [shall be
Which time shall bring to ripeness: she
(But few now living can behold that
goodness)
A pattern to all princes living with her,

And all that shall succeed: Saba was
never
More covetous of wisdom, and fair virtue,
Than this pure soul shall be: all princely
graces,
That mould up such a mighty piece as this
is,
With all the virtues that attend the good,
Shall still be doubled on her: truth shall
nurse her,   [her:
Holy and heavenly thoughts still counsel
She shall be lov'd and fear'd: her own
shall bless her;
Her foes shake like a field of beaten corn,
And hang their heads with sorrow: good
grows with her:
In her days every man shall eat in safety,
Under his own vine, what he plants; and
sing   [bours:
The merry songs of peace to all his neigh-
God shall be truly known; and those about
her   [honour,
From her shall read the perfect ways of
And by those claim their greatness, not by
blood.
Nor shall this peace sleep with her: but
as when
The bird of wonder dies, the maiden
phœnix,
Her ashes new create another heir,
As great in admiration as herself;
So shall she leave her blessedness to one,
(When heaven shall call her from this
cloud of darkness)
Who, from the sacred ashes of her honour,
Shall star-like rise, as great in fame as
she was,   [truth, terror,
And so stand fix'd: peace, plenty, love,
That were the servants to this chosen
infant,   [him:
Shall then be his, and like a vine grow to
Wherever the bright sun of heaven shall
shine,
His honour and the greatness of his name
Shall be, and make new nations: he shall
flourish,   [branches
And, like a mountain cedar, reach his
To all the plains about him:—our child-
ren's children
Shall see this, and bless heaven.
K. HEN.   Thou speakest wonders.
CRAN. She shall be, to the happiness of
England,
An aged princess; many days shall see her,
And yet no day without a deed to crown it.
Would I had known no more! but she
must die,—   [virgin;
She must, the saints must have her,—yet a
A most unspotted lily shall she pass
To the ground, and all the world shall
mourn her.

K. HEN. O lord archbishop,
Thou hast made me now a man! never,
　　before
This happy child, did I get any thing:
This oracle of comfort has so pleased me,
That when I am in heaven I shall desire
To see what this child does, and praise my
　　Maker.—　　　　　　　　　[mayor,
I thank ye all.—To you, my good lord
And your good brethren, I am much be-
　　holden;　　　　　　　　　[ence,
I have received much honour by your pres-
And ye shall find me thankful.—Lead the
　　way, lords:—
Ye must all see the queen, and she must
　　thank ye;　　　　　　　　　[think
She will be sick else. This day, no man
He has business at his house; for all shall
　　stay:
This little one shall make it holiday.
　　　　　　　　　　　　　[*Exeunt.*

EPILOGUE.

'Tis ten to one, this play can never please
All that are here: some come to take their
　　ease,　　　　　　　　　　　[fear,
And sleep an act or two; but those, we
We've frighted with our trumpets; so, 'tis
　　clear,　　　　　　　　　　　[city
They'll say 'tis naught: others, to hear the
Abus'd extremely, and to cry,—"that's
　　witty!"
Which we have not done neither: that, I
　　fear,
All the expected good we're like to hear
For this play at this time, is only in
The merciful construction of good women;
For such a one we show'd them: if they
　　smile,
And say 'twill do, I know, within a while
All the best men are ours; for 'tis ill hap,
If they hold, when their ladies bid them
　　clap.

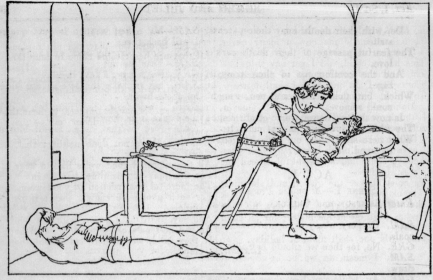

Romeo in the tomb, having brought down the body of Paris. Juliet on the bier.
Act IV. S. 1.

ROMEO AND JULIET

DRAMATIS PERSONÆ.

ESCALUS, *Prince of Verona.*
PARIS, *a young Nobleman, Kinsman to the*
   Prince.
MONTAGUE, ⎱ *Heads of two Houses at vari-*
CAPULET, ⎰   *ance with each other.*
An Old Man, *Kinsman to* CAPULET.
ROMEO, *Son to* MONTAGUE.
MERCUTIO, *Kinsman to the Prince, and*
   Friend to ROMEO.
BENVOLIO, *Nephew to* MONTAGUE, *and*
   Friend to ROMEO.
TYBALT, *Nephew to* LADY CAPULET.
FRIAR LAURENCE, *a Franciscan.*
FRIAR JOHN, *of the same Order.*
BALTHASAR, *Servant to* ROMEO.
SAMPSON, ⎱ *Servants to* CAPULET.
GREGORY, ⎰

PETER, *another Servant to* CAPULET.
ABRAM, *servant to* MONTAGUE.
An Apothecary.
Three Musicians.
CHORUS. Page *to* MERCUTIO; Page *to*
   PARIS; *an* Officer.

LADY MONTAGUE, *Wife to* MONTAGUE.
LADY CAPULET, *Wife to* CAPULET.
JULIET, *Daughter to* CAPULET.
Nurse *to* JULIET.

Citizens *of* Verona; male and female Relations to both Houses; Maskers, Guards,
   Watchmen, *and* Attendants.

SCENE,—*During the greater Part of the Play, in* VERONA: *once, (in the fifth Act,) at*
   MANTUA.

PROLOGUE.
Chorus.

Two households, both alike in dignity,
  In fair Verona, where we lay our scene,
From ancient grudge break to new mutiny,

Where civil blood makes civil hands
  unclean.
From forth the fatal loins of these two foes
  A pair of star-cross'd lovers take their
  life;
Whose misadventur'd piteous overthrows

Do, with their death, bury their parents'
 strife.
The fearful passage of their death-mark'd
 love,
And the continuance of their parents'
 rage,
Which, but their children's end, naught
 could remove,
Is now the two hours' traffic of our stage;
The which if you with patient ears attend,
What here shall miss, our toil shall strive
 to mend.

ACT I.

Scene I.—*A public Place.*

Enter Sampson *and* Gregory, *armed with
swords and bucklers.*

SAM. Gregory, o' my word, we'll not carry
coals.

GRE. No, for then we should be colliers.

SAM. I mean, an we be in choler, we'll
draw.

GRE. Ay, while you live, draw your neck
out of the collar.

SAM. I strike quickly, being moved.

GRE. But thou art not quickly moved to
strike.

SAM. A dog of the house of Montague
moves me.

GRE. To move is to stir; and to be valiant
is to stand: therefore, if thou are moved,
thou run'st away.

SAM. A dog of that house shall move me
to stand: I will take the wall of any man
or maid of Montague's.

GRE. That shows thee a weak slave; for
the weakest goes to the wall.

SAM. True; and therefore women, being
the weaker vessels, are ever thrust to the
wall:—therefore, I will push Montague's
men from the wall, and thrust his maids
to the wall.

GRE. The quarrel is between our masters,
and us their men.

SAM. 'Tis all one, I will show myself a
tyrant: when I have fought with the men,
I will be cruel with the maids, I will cut
off their heads.

GRE. The heads of the maids?

SAM. Ay, the heads of the maids, or their
maidenheads; take it in what sense thou
wilt.   [it.

GRE. They must take it in sense, that feel

SAM. Me they shall feel, while I am able
to stand: and 'tis known I am a pretty
piece of flesh.

GRE. 'Tis well thou art not fish; if thou
hadst, thou hadst been poor John.—Draw
thy tool; here comes two of the house of
the Montagues.

SAM. My naked weapon is out: quarrel,
I will back thee.

GRE. How! turn thy back, and run?

SAM. Fear me not.

GRE. No, marry; I fear thee!

SAM. Let us take the law of our sides;
let them begin.

GRE. I will frown as I pass by; and let
them take it as they list.

SAM. Nay, as they dare. I will bite my
thumb at them; which is a disgrace to
them, if they bear it.

Enter Abram *and* Balthasar.

ABR. Do you bite your thumb at us, Sir?

SAM. I do bite my thumb, Sir.

ABR. Do you bite your thumb at us, Sir?

SAM. Is the law of our side, if I say—

GRE. No.   [ay?

SAM. No, Sir, I do not bite my thumb at
you, Sir; but I bite my thumb, Sir.

GRE. Do you quarrel, Sir?

ABR. Quarrel, Sir? no, Sir.

SAM. If you do, Sir, I am for you: I
serve as good a man as you.

ABR. No better.

SAM. Well, Sir.

GRE. Say—better; here comes one of my
master's kinsmen.

SAM. Yes, better, Sir.

ABR. You lie.

SAM. Draw, if you be men.—Gregory,
remember thy swashing blow. [*They fight.*

Enter Benvolio.

BEN. Part, fools! put up your swords;
you know not what you do.

    [*Beats down their swords.*

Enter Tybalt.

TYB. What, art thou drawn among these
 heartless hinds?
Turn thee, Benvolio; look upon thy death.

BEN. I do but keep the peace: put up thy
 sword,
Or manage it to part these men with me.

TYB. What, drawn, and talk of peace! I
 hate the word,
As I hate hell, all Montagues, and thee:
Have at thee, coward! [*They fight.*

*Enter several persons of both Houses, who
join the fray; then enter* Citizens, *with
clubs and partisans.*

CITIZENS. Clubs, bills, and partisans!
strike! beat them down!
Down with the Capulets! down with the
Montagues!

Enter Capulet, *in his gown; and*
Lady Capulet.

CAP. What noise is this? Give me my
long sword, ho!

LA. CAP. A crutch, a crutch! Why call
you for a sword?

CAP. My sword, I say! Old Montague is come,
And flourishes his blade in spite of me.
   Enter MONTAGUE *and* LADY MONTAGUE.
MON. Thou villain Capulet!—Hold me not, let me go.
LA. MON. Thou shalt not stir one foot to seek a foe.
   Enter PRINCE, *with* Attendants.
PRIN. Rebellious subjects, enemies to peace,
Profaners of this neighbour-stained steel,—
Will they not hear?—what ho! you men, you beasts,
That quench the fire of your pernicious rage
With purple fountains issuing from your veins,—
On pain of torture, from those bloody hands
Throw your mis-temper'd weapons to the ground,
And hear the sentence of your moved prince.—
Three civil brawls, bred of an airy word,
By thee, old Capulet, and Montague,
Have thrice disturb'd the quiet of our streets;
And made Verona's ancient citizens
Cast by their grave beseeming ornaments,
To wield old partisans, in hands as old,
Canker'd with peace, to part your canker'd hate:
If ever you disturb our streets again,
Your lives shall pay the forfeit of the peace.
For this time, all the rest depart away:—
You, Capulet, shall go along with me;—
And, Montague, come you this afternoon,
To know our farther pleasure in this case,
To old Free-town, our common judgment-place.—
Once more, on pain of death, all men depart.
   [*Exeunt* PRINCE *and* Attendants; CAPULET, LADY CAPULET, TYBALT, Citizens, *and* Servants.
MON. Who set this ancient quarrel new abroach?—
Speak, nephew, were you by when it began?
BEN. Here were the servants of your adversary,
And yours, close fighting ere I did approach:
I drew to part them: in the instant came
The fiery Tybalt, with his sword prepar'd;
Which, as he breath'd defiance to my ears,
He swung about his head, and cut the winds,   [scorn:
Who, nothing hurt withal, hiss'd him in

While we were interchanging thrusts and blows,   [and part,
Came more and more, and fought on part
Till the prince came, who parted either part.
LA. MON. O, where is Romeo?—saw you him to-day?—
Right glad I am he was not at this fray.
BEN. Madam, an hour before the worshipp'd sun
Peer'd forth the golden window of the east,
A troubled mind drave me to walk abroad;
Where,—underneath the grove of sycamore
That westward rooteth from the city's side,—
So early walking did I see your son:
Towards him I made; but he was 'ware of me,
And stole into the covert of the wood:
I, measuring his affections by my own,—
That most are busied when they're most alone,—
Pursu'd my humour, not pursuing his,
And gladly shunn'd who gladly fled from me.
MON. Many a morning hath he there been seen,
With tears augmenting the fresh morning's dew,   [sighs:
Adding to clouds more clouds with his deep
But all so soon as the all-cheering sun
Should in the farthest east begin to draw
The shady curtains from Aurora's bed,
Away from light steals home my heavy son,
And private in his chamber pens himself;
Shuts up his windows, locks fair daylight out,
And makes himself an artificial night:
Black and portentous must this humour prove,
Unless good counsel may the cause remove.
BEN. My noble uncle, do you know the cause?
MON. I neither know it, nor can learn of him.
BEN. Have you importun'd him by any means?
MON. Both by myself, and many other friends:
But he, his own affections' counsellor,
Is to himself,—I will not say how true,—
But to himself so secret and so close,
So far from sounding and discovery,
As is the bud bit with an envious worm,
Ere he can spread his sweet leaves to the air,
Or dedicate his beauty to the sun.   [air,
Could we but learn from whence his sorrows grow,

We would as willingly give cure, as know.

BEN. See, where he comes: so please you, step aside;

I'll know his grievance, or be much denied.

MON. I would, thou wert so happy by thy stay,

To hear true shrift.—Come, Madam, let's away.   [*Exeunt* MONTAGUE *and* LADY.

Enter ROMEO.

BEN. Good morrow, cousin.

ROM.   Is the day so young?

BEN. But new struck nine.

ROM.   Ah me! sad hours seem long.

Was that my father that went hence so fast?

BEN. It was.—What sadness lengthens Romeo's hours?

ROM. Not having that, which, having, makes them short.

BEN. In love?

ROM. Out—

BEN. Of love?

ROM. Out of her favour, where I am in love.

BEN. Alas, that love, so gentle in his view,   [proof!

Should be so tyrannous and rough in

ROM. Alas, that love, whose view is muffled still,

Should, without eyes, see pathways to his will!—

Where shall we dine?—O me!—What fray was here?

Yet tell me not, for I have heard it all.

Here's much to do with hate, but more with love:—

Why, then, O brawling love! O loving hate!

O any thing, of nothing first create!

O heavy lightness! serious vanity!

Mis-shapen chaos of well-seeming forms!

Feather of lead, bright smoke, cold fire, sick health!

Still-waking sleep, that is not what it is!—

This love feel I, that feel no love in this.

Dost thou not laugh?

BEN.   No, coz, I rather weep.

ROM. Good heart, at what?

BEN.   At thy good heart's oppression.

ROM. Why, such is love's transgression.—

Griefs of mine own lie heavy in my breast;

Which thou wilt propagate, to have it press'd

With more of thine: this love, that thou hast shown,

Doth add more grief to too much of mine own.

Love is a smoke rais'd with the fume of sighs;

Being purg'd, a fire sparkling in lovers' eyes;

Being vex'd, a sea nourish'd with lovers' tears:

What is it else? a madness most discreet,

A choking gall, and a preserving sweet.—

Farewell, my coz.   [*Going.*

BEN.   Soft! I will go along:

An if you leave me so, you do me wrong.

ROM. Tut, I have lost myself; I am not here;

This is not Romeo, he's some other where.

BEN. Tell me in sadness, who is that you love.

ROM. What, shall I groan, and tell thee?

BEN.   Groan! why, no;

But sadly tell me who.

ROM. Bid a sick man in sadness make his will,—

Ah, word ill urg'd to one that is so ill!—

In sadness, cousin, I do love a woman.

BEN. I aim'd so near, when I suppos'd you lov'd.

ROM. A right good mark-man!—And she's fair I love.

BEN. A right fair mark, fair coz, is soonest hit.

ROM. Well, in that hit, you miss: she'll not be hit

With Cupid's arrow,—she hath Dian's wit;

And, in strong proof of chastity well arm'd,

From love's weak childish bow she lives unharm'd.

She will not stay the siege of loving terms,

Nor bide th' encounter of assailing eyes,

Nor ope her lap to saint-seducing gold:

O, she is rich in beauty; only poor,

That, when she dies, with beauty dies her store.

BEN. Then she hath sworn that she will still live chaste?

ROM. She hath, and in that sparing makes huge waste;

For beauty, starv'd with her severity,

Cuts beauty off from all posterity.

She is too fair, too wise; wisely too fair,

To merit bliss by making me despair:

She hath forsworn to love; and in that vow

Do I live dead, that live to tell it now.

BEN. Be rul'd by me, forget to think of her.

ROM. O, teach me how I should forget to think.

BEN. By giving liberty unto thine eyes;

Examine other beauties.

ROM.   'Tis the way

To call her's, exquisite, in question more:

These happy masks, that kiss fair ladies' brows,

Being black, put us in mind they hide the fair;

He, that is strucken blind, cannot forget
The precious treasure of his eyesight lost:
Show me a mistress that is passing fair,
What doth her beauty serve, but as a note
Where I may read who pass'd that pass-
   ing fair?
Farewell: thou canst not teach me to for-
   get.
BEN. I'll pay that doctrine, or else die in
   debt.   *[Exeunt.*

Scene II.—*A Street.*

Enter Capulet, Paris, *and* Servant.

CAP. But Montague is bound as well as I,
In penalty alike; and 'tis not hard, I think,
For men so old as we to keep the peace.
PAR. Of honourable reckoning are you
   both;
And pity 'tis you liv'd at odds so long.
But now, my lord, what say you to my
   suit?
CAP. But saying o'er what I have said
   before:
My child is yet a stranger in the world,
She hath not seen the change of fourteen
   years;
Let two more summers wither in their
   pride,
Ere we may think her ripe to be a bride.
PAR. Younger than she are happy moth-
   ers made.
CAP. And too soon marr'd are those so
   early made.
Earth hath swallow'd all my hopes but
   she,
She is the hopeful lady of my earth:
But woo her, gentle Paris, get her heart,
My will to her consent is but a part;
An she agree, within her scope of choice
Lies my consent and fair according voice.
This night I hold an old accustom'd feast,
Whereto I have invited many a guest,
Such as I love; and you, among the store,
One more, most welcome, makes my num-
   ber more.
At my poor house look to behold this night
Earth-treading stars, that make dark heav-
   en light:
Such comfort as do lusty young men feel,
When well-apparel'd April on the heel
Of limping winter treads, even such delight
Among fresh female buds shall you this
   night
Inherit at my house; hear all, all see,
And like her most, whose merit most shall
   be: [one,
Such, amongst view of many, mine being
May stand in number, though in reckoning
   none.   [about
Come, go with me.—Go, sirrah, trudge

Through fair Verona; find those persons
   out,
Whose names are written there, [*Giving a
   paper.*] and to them say,
My house and welcome on their pleasure
   stay.   *[Exeunt* Capulet *and* Paris.
SERV. Find them out, whose names are
written here! It is written, that the shoe-
maker should meddle with his yard, and
the tailor with his last, the fisher with his
pencil, and the painter with his nets; but
I am sent to find those persons, whose
names are here writ, and can never find
what names the writing person hath here
writ. I must to the learned:—in good time.
   Enter Benvolio *and* Romeo.
BEN. Tut, man, one fire burns out an-
   other's burning,
One pain is lessen'd by another's an-
   guish;
Turn giddy, and be holp by backward
   turning;
One desperate grief cures with another's
   languish:
Take thou some new infection to thy eye,
And the rank poison of the old will die.
ROM. Your plaintain leaf is excellent for
   that.
BEN. For what, I pray thee?
ROM.   For your broken shin.
BEN. Why, Romeo, art thou mad?
ROM. Not mad, but bound more than a
   madman is;
Shut up in prison, kept without my food,
Whipp'd, and tormented, and—Good-den,
   good fellow.
SERV. God gi' good den.—I pray, Sir,
   can you read?   [misery.
ROM. Ay, mine own fortune in my
SERV. Perhaps you have learn'd it with-
out book: but, I pray, can you read any
thing you see?
ROM. Ay, if I know the letters, and the
language.
SERV. Ye say honestly: rest you merry!
                    [*Going.*
ROM. Stay, fellow; I can read.   [*Reads.*
"Signior Martino, and his wife, and daugh-
ters; County Anselme, and his beauteous
sisters; the lady widow of Vitruvio; Signior
Placentio, and his lovely nieces; Mercutio,
and his brother Valentine; mine uncle
Capulet, his wife, and daughters; my fair
niece Rosaline; Livia; Signior Valentio,
and his cousin Tybalt; Lucio, and the
lively Helena."
A fair assembly: [*Gives back the paper.*]
   whither should they come?
SERV. Up.
ROM. Whither?
SERV. To supper; to our house.

ROM. Whose house?

SERV. My master's.

ROM. Indeed, I should have asked you that before.

SERV. Now I'll tell you without asking: my master is the great rich Capulet; and if you be not of the house of Montagues, I pray, come and crush a cup of wine. Rest you merry!　　　　　　　[*Exit.*

BEN. At this same ancient feast of Capulet's

Sups the fair Rosaline, whom thou so lov'st;

With all the admired beauties of Verona:

Go thither; and, with unattainted eye,

Compare her face with some that I shall show,

And I will make thee think thy swan a crow.

ROM. When the devout religion of mine eye

Maintains such falsehood, then turn tears to fires;

And these,—who, often drown'd, could never die,—

Transparent heretics, be burnt for liars!

One fairer than my love! the all-seeing sun

Ne'er saw her match, since first the world begun.

BEN. Tut, you saw her fair, none else being by,

Herself pois'd with herself in either eye:

But in that crystal scales, let there be weigh'd

Your lady's love against some other maid,

That I will show you shining at this feast,

And she shall scant show well, that now shows best.

ROM. I'll go along, no such sight to be shown,

But to rejoice in splendour of mine own.

　　　　　　　　　　　　　[*Exeunt.*

SCENE III.—*A Room in* CAPULET'S *House.*

Enter LADY CAPULET *and* Nurse.

LA. CAP. Nurse, where's my daughter? call her forth to me.

NURSE. Now, by my maidenhead,—at twelve year old,—

I bade her come.—What, lamb! what, ladybird!—

God forbid!—where's this girl?—what, Juliet!

Enter JULIET.

JUL. How now! who calls?

NURSE.　　　　　Your mother.

JUL.　　　　　　Madam, I am here. What is your will?

LA. CAP. This is the matter,—Nurse, give leave awhile,

We must talk in secret:—Nurse, come back again;

I have remember'd me, thou shalt hear our counsel.

Thou know'st my daughter's of a pretty age.

NURSE. 'Faith, I can tell her age unto an hour.

LA. CAP. She's not fourteen.

NURSE.　　I'll lay fourteen of my teeth,—

And yet to my teen be it spoken I have but four,—

She is not fourteen. How long is it now To Lammas-tide?

LA. CAP.　　　A fortnight, and odd days.

NURSE. Even or odd, of all days in the year,

Come Lammas-eve at night, shall she be fourteen.

Susan and she,—God rest all Christian souls!—

Were of an age: well, Susan is with God;

She was too good for me:—but, as I said,

On Lammas-eve at night shall she be fourteen;

That shall she, marry; I remember it well.

'Tis since the earthquake now eleven years;

And she was wean'd,—I never shall forget it,—

Of all the days of the year, upon that day:

For I had then laid wormwood to my dug,

Sitting in the sun under the dove-house wall;

My lord and you were then at Mantua:—

Nay, I do bear a brain:—but, as I said,

When it did taste the wormwood on the nipple

Of my dug, and felt it bitter, pretty fool,

To see it tetchy, and fall out with the dug!

Shake, quoth the dove-house: 'twas no need, I trow,

To bid me trudge.

And since that time it is eleven years;

For then she could stand alone; nay, by the rood,

She could have run and waddled all about;

For even the day before she broke her brow:

And then my husband,—God be with his soul!

'A was a merry man,—took up the child:

"Yea," quoth he, "dost thou fall upon thy face?

Thou wilt fall backward, when thou hast more wit,

Wilt thou not, Jule?" and, by my holydame,

The pretty wretch left crying, and said—"Ay:"

To see, now, how a jest shall come about!

I warrant, an I should live a thousand years,
I never should forget it: "Wilt thou not, Jule?" quoth he;
And, pretty fool, it stinted, and said—"Ay."
LA. CAP. Enough of this; I pray thee, hold thy peace.
NURSE. Yes, Madam;—yet I cannot choose but laugh,
To think it should leave crying, and say—"Ay:"
And yet, I warrant, it had upon its brow
A bump as big as a young cockrel's stone;
A parlous knock; and it cried bitterly:
"Yea," quoth my husband, "fall'st upon thy face?
Thou wilt fall backward, when thou com'st to age;
Wilt thou not, Jule?" it stinted, and said—"Ay."
JUL. And stint thou too, I pray thee, nurse, say I.
NURSE. Peace, I have done. God mark thee to his grace!
Thou wast the prettiest babe that e'er I nurs'd;
An I might live to see thee married once, I have my wish.
LA. CAP. Marry, that marry is the very theme
I came to talk of:—tell me, daughter Juliet,
How stands your disposition to be married?
JUL. It is an honour that I dream not of.
NURSE. An honour! were not I thine only nurse,
I would say thou hadst suck'd wisdom from thy teat.
LA. CAP. Well, think of marriage now; younger than you,
Here in Verona, ladies of esteem,
Are made already mothers: by my count,
I was your mother, much upon these years
That you are now a maid. Thus, then, in brief;—
The valiant Paris seeks you for his love.
NURSE. A man, young lady! lady, such a man,
As all the world—Why, he's a man of wax.
LA. CAP. Verona's summer hath not such a flower.
NURSE. Nay, he's a flower; in faith, a very flower.
LA. CAP. What say you? can you love the gentleman?
This night you shall behold him at our feast;
Read o'er the volume of young Paris' face,

And find delight writ there with beauty's pen;
Examine every married lineament,
And see how one an other lends content;
And what obscur'd in this fair volume lies,
Find written in the margin of his eyes.
This precious book of love, this unbound lover,
To beautify him, only lacks a cover:
The fish lives in the sea; and 'tis much pride,
For fair without the fair within to hide.
That book in many's eyes doth share the glory,
That in gold clasps locks in the golden story;
So shall you share all that he doth possess,
By having him, making yourself no less.
NURSE. No less? nay, bigger; women grow by men.
LA. CAP. Speak briefly, can you like of Paris' love?
JUL. I'll look to like it, if looking liking move:
But no more deep will I endart mine eye,
Than your consent gives strength to make it fly.

                    Enter a Servant.

SERV. Madam, the guests are come, supper served up, you called, my young lady asked for, the nurse cursed in the pantry, and every thing in extremity. I must hence to wait; I beseech you, follow straight.
LA. CAP. We follow thee.—[*Exit* Serv.]
Juliet, the county stays.
NURSE. Go, girl, seek happy nights to happy days.   [*Exeunt.*

                    ———

          SCENE IV.—*A Street.*

Enter ROMEO, MERCUTIO, BENVOLIO, *with five or six Maskers, Torch-Bearers, and others.*

ROM. What, shall this speech be spoke for our excuse,
Or shall we on without apology?
BEN. The date is out of such prolixity:
We'll have no Cupid hood-wink'd with a scarf,
Bearing a Tartar's painted bow of lath,
Scaring the ladies like a crow-keeper;
Nor no without-book prologue, faintly spoke
After the prompter, for our entrance:
But, let them measure us by what they will,
We'll measure them a measure, and be gone.
ROM. Give me a torch,—I am not for this ambling;
Being but heavy, I will bear the light.

MER. Nay, gentle Romeo, we must have
you dance.

ROM. Not I, believe me: you have danc-
ing shoes
With nimble soles; I have a soul of lead,
So stakes me to the ground, I cannot move.

MER. You are a lover; borrow Cupid's
wings,
And soar with them above a common
bound.

ROM. I am too sore enpierced with his
shaft,
To soar with his light feathers; and so
bound,
I cannot bound a pitch above dull woe:
Under love's heavy burden do I sink.

MER. And, to sink in it, should you burden love;
Too great oppression for a tender thing.

ROM. Is love a tender thing? it is too
rough,
Too rude, too boisterous; and it pricks like
thorn.

MER. If love be rough with you, be rough
with love;
Prick love for pricking, and you beat love
down.—
Give me a case to put my visage in:
                    [*Putting on a mask.*
A visor for a visor!—what care I,
What curious eye doth quote deformities?
Here are the beetle-brows shall blush for
me.

BEN. Come, knock, and enter; and no
sooner in,
But every man betake him to his legs.

ROM. A torch for me: let wantons, light
of heart,
Tickle the senseless rushes with their
heels;
For I am proverb'd with a grandsire
phrase,—
I'll be a candle-holder, and look on,—
The game was ne'er so fair, and I am
done.

MER. Tut, dun's the mouse, the constable's own word:
If thou art dun, we'll draw thee from the
mire
Of this (save reverence) love, wherein
thou stick'st
Up to the ears.—Come, we burn day-light,
ho.

ROM. Nay, that's not so.

MER.   I mean, Sir, in delay
We waste our lights in vain, like lamps
by day.
Take our good meaning, for our judgment
sits
Five times in that, ere once in our five
wits.

ROM. And we mean well, in going to this
mask;
But 'tis no wit to go.

MER.   Why, may one ask?

ROM. I dreamt a dream to-night.

MER.   And so did I.

ROM. Well, what was yours?

MER.   That dreamers often lie.

ROM. In bed asleep, while they do dream
things true.

MER. O then, I see, queen Mab hath been
with you.
She is the fairies' midwife; and she comes
In shape no bigger than an agate-stone
On the fore-finger of an alderman,
Drawn with a team of little atomies
Athwart men's noses as they lie asleep:
Her waggon-spoke made of long spinners'
legs;
The cover, of the wings of grasshoppers;
The traces, of the smallest spider's web;
The collars, of the moonshine's watery
beams;
Her whip, of cricket's bone; the lash, of
film;
Her waggoner, a small grey-coated gnat,
Not half so big as a round little worm
Prick'd from the lazy finger of a maid:
Her chariot is an empty hazel-nut,
Made by the joiner squirrel, or old grub,
Time out of mind the fairies' coach-makers.
And in this state she gallops night by night
Through lovers' brains, and then they
dream of love;
O'er courtiers' knees, that dream on
court'sies straight;
O'er lawyers' fingers, who straight dream
on fees;
O'er ladies' lips, who straight on kisses
dream,—
Which oft the angry Mab with blisters
plagues,
Because their breaths with sweet-meats
tainted are:
Sometime she gallops o'er a courtier's
nose;
And then dreams he of smelling out a
suit;
And sometime comes she with a tithe-
pig's tail,
Tickling a parson's nose as 'a lies asleep,
Then dreams he of another benefice:
Sometime she driveth o'er a soldier's neck,
And then dreams he of cutting foreign
throats,
Of breaches, ambuscadoes, Spanish blades,
Of healths five fathom deep; and then
anon
Drums in his ear, at which he starts, and
wakes;

And, being thus frighted, swears a prayer
or two,
And sleeps again. This is that very Mab,
That plats the manes of horses in the
night;
And bakes the elf-locks in foul sluttish
hairs,
Which, once untangled, much misfortune
bodes:
This is the hag, when maids lie on their
backs,
That presses them, and learns them first
to bear,
Making them women of good carriage:
This is she—
ROM.   Peace, peace, Mercutio, peace!
Thou talk'st of nothing.
MER.   True, I talk of dreams;
Which are the children of an idle brain,
Begot of nothing but vain fantasy;
Which is as thin of substance as the air;
And more inconstant than the wind, who
wooes
Even now the frozen bosom of the north,
And, being anger'd, puffs away from
thence,
Turning his face to the dew-dropping south.
BEN. This wind, you talk of, blows us
from ourselves;
Supper is done, and we shall come too
late.
ROM. I fear, too early: for my mind mis-
gives,
Some consequence, yet hanging in the
stars,
Shall bitterly begin his fearful date
With this night's revels; and expire the
term
Of a despised life, clos'd in my breast,
By some vile forfeit of untimely death:
But He, that hath the steerage of my
course,
Direct my sail!—On, lusty gentlemen.
BEN. Strike, drum.   [*Exeunt.*

SCENE V.—*A Hall in* CAPULET'S *House.*
Musicians *waiting. Enter* Servants.

1 *SERV.* Where's Potpan, that he helps
not to take away? he shift a trencher! he
scrape a trencher!
2 *SERV.* When good manners shall lie
all in one or two men's hands, and they
unwashed too, 'tis a foul thing.
1 *SERV.* Away with the joint-stools, remove the court-cupboard, look to the plate:
—good thou, save me a piece of march-
pane; and, as thou lovest me, let the porter
let in Susan Grindstone, and Nell.—Antony! and Potpan!

Enter third and fourth Servant.
3 & 4 *SERV.* Ay, boy; ready.
1 *SERV.* You are looked for, and called
for, asked for, and sought for, in the great
chamber.
3 & 4 *SERV.* We cannot be here and
there too.
2 *SERV.* Cheerly, boys: be brisk awhile,
and the longer liver take all.
          [*They retire behind.*
Enter CAPULET, &c. *with the Guests
and the Maskers.*

CAP. Welcome, gentlemen! ladies, that
have their toes
Unplagu'd with corns, will have a bout
with you:—
Ah ha, my mistresses! which of you all
Will now deny to dance? she that makes
dainty, she,
I'll swear, hath corns; am I come near
you now?—
Welcome, gentlemen! I have seen the
day,
That I have worn a visor; and could tell
A whispering tale in a fair lady's ear,
Such as would please;—'tis gone, 'tis gone,
'tis gone:
You are welcome, gentlemen!—Come, mu-
sicians, play.—
A hall, a hall! give room! and foot it,
girls.   [*Music plays, and they dance.*
More light, ye knaves; and turn the tables
up,
And quench the fire, the room is grown
too hot.—
Ah, sirrah, this unlook'd-for sport comes
well.
Nay, sit, nay, sit, good cousin Capulet;
For you and I are past our dancing days:
How long is't now, since last yourself and
Were in a mask?   [I
2 *CAP.*   By'r lady, thirty years.
CAP. What, man! 'tis not so much, 'tis
not so much.
'Tis since the nuptial of Lucentio,
Come pentecost as quickly as it will.
Some five and twenty years; and then we
mask'd.
2 *CAP.* 'Tis more, 'tis more: his son is
His son is thirty.   [elder, Sir;
CAP.   Will you tell me that?
His son was but a ward two years ago.
ROM. What lady is that, which doth en-
Of yonder knight?   [rich the hand
SERV. I know not, Sir.
ROM. O, she doth teach the torches to
burn bright!
It seems she hangs upon the cheek of
night
Like a rich jewel in an Æthiop's ear;

Beauty too rich for use, for earth too dear!
So shows a snowy dove trooping with
      crows,
As yonder lady o'er her fellows shows.
The measure done, I'll watch her place of
      stand,
And, touching hers, make blessed my rude
      hand.
Did my heart love till now? forswear it,
      sight!
For I ne'er saw true beauty till this night.
TYB. This, by his voice, should be a
      Montague:—
Fetch me my rapier, boy:—What, dares
      the slave
Come hither, cover'd with an antick face,
To fleer and scorn at our solemnity?
Now, by the stock and honour of my kin,
To strike him dead I hold it not a sin.
CAP. Why, how now, kinsman! where-
      fore storm you so?
TYB. Uncle, this is a Montague, our foe;
A villain, that is hither come in spite,
To scorn at our solemnity this night.
CAP. Young Romeo is it?
TYB.   'Tis he, that villain Romeo.
CAP. Content thee, gentle coz, let him
      alone,
He bears him like a portly gentleman;
And, to say truth, Verona brags of him
To be a virtuous and well-govern'd youth:
I would not for the wealth of all this town,
Here in my house, do him disparagement:
Therefore be patient, take no note of
      him,—
It is my will; the which if thou respect,
Show a fair presence, and put off these
      frowns,
An ill-beseeming semblance for a feast.
TYB. It fits, when such a villain is a
      'll not endure him.   [guest:
CAP.   He shall be endur'd:
What, goodman boy!—I say, he shall;—
      go to;
Am I the master here, or you? go to.
You'll not endure him!—God shall mend
      my soul,
You'll make a mutiny among my guests!
You will set cock-a-hoop! you'll be the
      man!
TYB. Why, uncle, 'tis a shame.
CAP.   Go to, go to;
You are a saucy boy:—is't so, indeed?—
This trick may chance to scath you,—I
      know what:
You must contrary me! marry, 'tis time.—
Well said, my hearts!—You are a princox;
      go:
Be quiet, or—More light, more light!—
      For shame!

I'll make you quiet.—What, cheerly, my
      hearts!
TYB. Patience perforce with wilful choler
      meeting,
Makes my flesh tremble in their different
      greeting.
I will withdraw: but this intrusion shall,
Now seeming sweet, convert to bitter gall.
                                    [*Exit.*
ROM. [*To* JULIET.] If I profane with my
      unworthiest hand
This holy shrine, the gentle fine is this,—
My lips, two blushing pilgrims, ready stand
To smooth that rough touch with a ten-
      der kiss.
JUL. Good pilgrim, you do wrong your
      hand too much,
Which mannerly devotion shows in this;
For saints have hands that pilgrims' hands
      do touch,
And palm to palm is holy palmers' kiss.
ROM. Have not saints lips, and holy palm-
      ers too?
JUL. Ay, pilgrim, lips that they must use
      in prayer.
ROM. O, then, dear saint, let lips do what
      hands do;
They pray, grant thou, lest faith turn
      to despair.
JUL. Saints do not move, though grant
      for prayers' sake.
ROM. Then move not, while my prayer's
      effect I take.
Thus from my lips, by yours, my sin is
      purg'd.   [*Kissing her.*
JUL. Then have my lips the sin that they
      have took.
ROM. Sin from my lips? O trespass
      sweetly urg'd!
Give me my sin again.
JUL.   You kiss by the book.
NURSE. Madam, your mother craves a
      word with you.
ROM. What is her mother?
NURSE.   Marry, bachelor,
Her mother is the lady of the house,
And a good lady, and a wise, and virtuous:
I nurs'd her daughter, that you talk'd
      withal;
I tell you,—he that can lay hold of her
Shall have the chinks.
ROM.   Is she a Capulet?
O dear account! my life is my foe's debt.
BEN. Away, be gone; the sport is at the
      best.
ROM. Ay, so I fear; the more is my un-
      rest.
CAP. Nay, gentlemen, prepare not to be
      gone;
We have a trifling foolish banquet
      towards.—

Is it e'en so? Why then, I thank you all;
I thank you, honest gentlemen; good
night.—
More torches here!—Come on, then, let's
to bed.
[*To* 2 CAP.] Ah, sirrah, by my fay, it
I'll to my rest. [*waxes late*:
[*Exeunt all except* JULIET *and* Nurse.
JUL. Come hither, nurse. What is yond'
gentleman?
NURSE. The son and heir of old Tiberio.
JUL. What's he, that now is going out of
door?
NURSE. Marry, that, I think, be young
Petruchio.
JUL. What's he, that follows there, that
would not dance?
NURSE. I know not.
JUL. Go, ask his name:—if he be married,
My grave is like to be my wedding bed.
NURSE. His name is Romeo, and a
Montague;
The only son of your great enemy.
JUL. My only love sprung from my only
hate!
Too early seen unknown, and known too
late!
Prodigious birth of love it is to me,
That I must love a loathed enemy.
NURSE. What's this? what's this?
JUL. A rhyme I learn'd even now
Of one I danc'd withal. [*One calls within*,
"*Juliet!*"
NURSE. Anon, anon!—
Come, let's away; the strangers all are
gone. [*Exeunt.*

Enter CHORUS.

Now old desire doth in his death-bed lie,
And young affection gapes to be his heir;
That fair, for which love groan'd for, and
would die,
With tender Juliet match'd, is now not
fair.
Now Romeo is belov'd, and loves again,
Alike bewitched by the charm of looks;
But to his foe suppos'd he must complain,
And she steal love's sweet bait from fear-
ful hooks:
Being held a foe, he may not have access
To breathe such vows as lovers use to
swear;
And she as much in love, her means much
less,
To meet her new-beloved any where:
But passion lends them power, time means,
to meet,
Tempering extremities with extreme sweet.
[*Exit.*

ACT II.

SCENE I.—*An open Place, adjoining*
CAPULET'S *Garden.*
Enter ROMEO.

ROM. Can I go forward, when my heart
is here?
Turn back, dull earth, and find thy centre
out.
[*He climbs the wall, and leaps down
within it.*

Enter BENVOLIO *and* MERCUTIO.

BEN. Romeo! my cousin Romeo!
MER. He is wise;
And, on my life, hath stolen him home to
bed.
BEN. He ran this way, and leap'd this
orchard wall:
Call, good Mercutio.
MER. Nay, I'll conjure too.—
Romeo! humours! madman! passion!
lover!
Appear thou in the likeness of a sigh:
Speak but one rhyme, and I am satisfied;
Cry but—Ah me! pronounce but—love and
dove;
Speak to my gossip Venus one fair word,
One nick-name for her purblind son and
heir,
Young Adam Cupid, he that shot so trim,
When king Cophetua lov'd the beggar-
maid!—
He heareth not, he stirreth not, he moveth
not;
The ape is dead, and I must conjure him.—
I conjure thee by Rosaline's bright eyes,
By her high forehead, and her scarlet lip,
By her fine foot, straight leg, and quiver-
ing thigh,
And the demesnes that there adjacent lie,
That in thy likeness thou appear to us!
BEN. An if he hear thee, thou wilt anger
him.
MER. This cannot anger him: 'twould an-
ger him
To raise a spirit in his mistress' circle
Of some strange nature, letting it there
stand
Till she had laid it, and conjur'd it down;
That were some spite: my invocation
Is fair and honest, and, in his mistress
name,
I conjure only but to raise up him.
BEN. Come, he hath hid himself among
these trees,
To be consorted with the humorous night
Blind is his love, and best befits the dark
MER. If love be blind, love cannot hit the
mark.
Now will he sit under a medlar tree,

And wish his mistress were that kind of
  fruit,
As maids call medlars when they laugh
  alone.—
O Romeo, that she were, O, that she were
An open *et cætera*, thou a poprin pear!
Romeo, good night:—I'll to my truckle-
  bed;
This field-bed is too cold for me to sleep:
Come, shall we go?
BEN.   Go, then; for 'tis in vain
To seek him here, that means not to be
  found.   [*Exeunt.*

Scene II.—Capulet's *Garden.*

Enter Romeo.
ROM. He jests at scars, that never felt a
  wound.—
      [Juliet *appears above, at a window.*
But, soft! what light through yonder win-
  dow breaks?
It is the east, and Juliet is the sun!—
Arise, fair sun, and kill the envious moon,
Who is already sick and pale with grief,
That thou, her maid, art far more fair than
  she:
Be not her maid, since she is envious;
Her vestal livery is but sick and green,
And none but fools do wear it; cast it
  off.—
It is my lady; O, it is my love!
O, that she knew she were!—
She speaks, yet she says nothing: what of
  that?
Her eye discourses, I will answer it.—
I am too bold, 'tis not to me she speaks:
Two of the fairest stars in all the heaven,
Having some business, do entreat her eyes
To twinkle in their spheres till they return.
What if her eyes were there, they in her
  head?
The brightness of her cheek would shame
  those stars,
As daylight doth a lamp; her eyes in
  heaven
Would through the airy region stream so
  bright,
That birds would sing, and think it were
  not night.—
See, how she leans her cheek upon her
  hand!
O, that I were a glove upon that hand,
That I might touch that cheek!
JUL.   Ah me!
ROM.   She speaks:—
O, speak again, bright angel! for thou art
As glorious to this night, being o'er my
  head,
As is a winged messenger of heaven
Unto the white-upturned wond'ring eyes

Of mortals, that fall back to gaze on him,
When he bestrides the lazy-pacing clouds,
And sails upon the bosom of the air.
JUL. O Romeo, Romeo! wherefore art
  thou Romeo?
Deny thy father, and refuse thy name;
Or, if thou wilt not, be but sworn my love,
And I'll no longer be a Capulet.
ROM. [*Aside.*] Shall I hear more, or shall
  I speak at this?
JUL. 'Tis but thy name, that is my ene-
  my;—
Thou art thyself though, not a Montague.
What's Montague? it is nor hand, nor foot,
Nor arm, nor face, nor any other part
Belonging to a man. O, be some other
  name!
What's in a name? that which we call a
  rose,
By any other name would smell as sweet;
So Romeo would, were he not Romeo
  call'd,
Retain that dear perfection which he owes,
Without that title:—Romeo, doff thy name;
And for that name, which is no part of
  thee,   [thee,
Take all myself.
ROM.   I take thee at thy word:
Call me but love, and I'll be new baptiz'd;
Henceforth I never will be Romeo.
JUL. What man art thou, that, thus be-
  screen'd in night,
So stumblest on my counsel?
ROM.   By a name
I know not how to tell thee who I am:
My name, dear saint, is hateful to myself,
Because it is an enemy to thee;
Had I it written, I would tear the word.
JUL. My ears have not yet drunk a hun-
  dred words
Of that tongue's utterance, yet I know the
  sound:
Art thou not Romeo, and a Montague?
ROM. Neither, fair saint, if either thee
  dislike.
JUL. How cam'st thou hither, tell me,
  and wherefore?
The orchard walls are high, and hard to
  climb;
And the place death, considering who thou
  art,
If any of my kinsmen find thee here.
ROM. With love's light wings did I o'er-
  perch these walls;
For stony limits cannot hold love out:
And what love can do, that dares love at-
  tempt;
Therefore, thy kinsmen are no let to me.
JUL. If they do see thee, they will mur-
  der thee.
ROM. Alack, there lies more peril in thine
  eye,

Than twenty of their swords: look thou but
sweet,
And I am proof against their enmity.
JUL. I would not for the world they saw
thee here.
ROM. I have night's cloak to hide me
from their sight;
And but thou love me, let them find me
here;
My life were better ended by their hate,
Than death prorogued, wanting of thy
love.
JUL. By whose direction found'st thou out
this place?
ROM. By Love, who first did prompt me
to enquire;
He lent me counsel, and I lent him eyes.
I am no pilot; yet, wert thou as far
As that vast shore, wash'd with the far-
thest sea,
I would adventure for such merchandise.
JUL. Thou know'st the mask of night is
on my face;
Else would a maiden blush bepaint my
cheek,
For that which thou hast heard me speak
to-night.
Fain would I dwell on form, fain, fain
deny
What I have spoke: but farewell compli-
ment!
Dost thou love me? I know thou wilt say
—Ay;
And I will take thy word: yet, if thou
swear'st,
Thou may'st prove false; at lovers' per-
juries,
They say, Jove laughs. O gentle Romeo,
If thou dost love, pronounce it faithfully:
Or if thou think'st I am too quickly won,
I'll frown, and be perverse, and say thee
nay,
So thou wilt woo; but else, not for the
world.
In truth, fair Montague, I am too fond;
And therefore thou may'st think my 'havi-
our light:
But trust me, gentleman, I'll prove more
true
Than those that have more cunning to be
strange.
I should have been more strange, I must
confess,
But that thou over-heard'st, ere I was 'ware,
My true love's passion: therefore, pardon
me;
And not impute this yielding to light love,
Which the dark night hath so discovered.
ROM. Lady, by yonder blessed moon I
swear,

That tips with silver all these fruit-tree
tops,—
JUL. O, swear not by the moon, th' in-
constant moon,
That monthly changes in her circled orb,
Lest that thy love prove likewise variable.
ROM. What shall I swear by?
JUL.   Do not swear at all;
Or, if thou wilt, swear by thy gracious self,
Which is the god of my idolatry,
And I'll believe thee.
ROM.   If my heart's dear love—
JUL. Well, do not swear: although I joy
in thee,
I have no joy of this contract to-night:
It is too rash, too unadvis'd, too sudden;
Too like the lightning, which doth cease
to be,
Ere one can say, It lightens. Sweet, good
night!
This bud of love, by summer's ripening
breath,
May prove a beauteous flower when next
we meet.
Good night, good night! as sweet repose
and rest
Come to thy heart, as that within my
breast!
ROM. O, wilt thou leave me so unsatis-
fied?
JUL. What satisfaction canst thou have
to-night?
ROM. Th' exchange of thy love's faithful
vow for mine.
JUL. I gave thee mine before thou didst
request it:
And yet I would it were to give again.
ROM. Would'st thou withdraw it? for
what purpose, love?
JUL. But to be frank, and give it thee
again.
And yet I wish but for the thing I have:
My bounty is as boundless as the sea,
My love as deep; the more I give to thee,
The more I have, for both are infinite.
          [Nurse calls within.
I hear some noise within; dear love,
adieu!—
Anon, good nurse!—Sweet Montague, be
true.
Stay but a little, I will come again.
          [Exit above.
ROM. O blessed, blessed night! I am
afeard,
Being in night, all this is but a dream,
Too flattering-sweet to be substantial.
          Re-enter JULIET, above.
JUL. Three words, dear Romeo, and good
night indeed.
If that thy bent of love be honourable,

Thy purpose marriage, send me word to-
    morrow,
By one that I'll procure to come to thee,
Where, and what time, thou wilt perform
    the rite;
And all my fortunes at thy foot I'll lay,
And follow thee my lord throughout the
    world.
NURSE. [*Within.*] Madam!
JUL. I come, anon:—but if thou mean'st
    do beseech thee,—   [not well,
NURSE. [*Within.*] Madam!
JUL.   By and by; I come:—
To cease thy suit, and leave me to my
To-morrow will I send.   [grief:
ROM.   So thrive my soul,—
JUL. A thousand times good night!
                                [*Exit above.*
ROM. A thousand times the worse, to
    want thy light.—
Love goes toward love, as school-boys from
    their books;
But love from love, toward school with
    heavy looks.   [*Retiring.*
        Re-enter JULIET, *above.*
JUL. Hist! Romeo, hist!—O, for a fal-
    coner's voice,
To lure this tassel-gentle back again!
Bondage is hoarse, and may not speak
    aloud;
Else would I tear the cave where Echo
    lies,
And make her airy tongue more hoarse
    than mine,
With repetition of my Romeo's name.
ROM. It is my soul, that calls upon my
    name:
How silver-sweet sound lovers' tongues by
    night,
Like softest music to attending ears!
JUL. Romeo!
ROM.   My dear?
JUL.   At what o'clock to-morrow
hall I send to thee?
ROM.   At the hour of nine.
JUL. I will not fail: 'tis twenty years till
    then.
I have forgot why I did call thee back.
ROM. Let me stand here till thou remem-
    ber it.
JUL. I shall forget, to have thee still stand
    there,
Remembering how I love thy company.
ROM. And I'll still stay, to have thee still
    forget,
Forgetting any other home but this.
JUL. 'Tis almost morning; I would have
    thee gone;
And yet no farther than a wanton's bird;
Who lets it hop a little from her hand,
Like a poor prisoner in his twisted gyves,

And with a silk thread plucks it back
    again,
So loving-jealous of his liberty.
ROM. I would I were thy bird.
JUL.   Sweet, so would I:
Yet I should kill thee with much cherish-
    ing.
Good night, good night! parting is such
    sweet sorrow,
That I shall say good night, till it be mor-
    row.   [*Exit above.*
ROM. Sleep dwell upon thine eyes, peace
    in thy breast!—
Would I were sleep and peace, so sweet
    to rest!
Hence will I to my ghostly father's cell,
His help to crave, and my dear hap to
    tell.   [*Exit.*

————

SCENE III.—FRIAR LAURENCE'S *Cell.*

Enter FRIAR LAURENCE, *with a basket.*

FRI. L. The grey-ey'd morn smiles on the
    frowning night,
Checkering the eastern clouds with streaks
    of light;
And fleckèd darkness like a drunkard reels
From forth day's path and Titan's fiery
    wheels:
Now, ere the sun advance his burning eye,
The day to cheer, and night's dank dew
    to dry,
I must up-fill this osier cage of ours,
With baleful weeds, and precious-juicèd
    flowers.
The earth, that's nature's mother, is her
    tomb;
What is her burying grave, that is her
    womb:
And from her womb children of divers kind
We sucking on her natural bosom find;
Many for many virtues excellent,
None but for some, and yet all different.
O, mickle is the powerful grace that lies
In herbs, plants, stones, and their true
    qualities:
For naught so vile that on the earth doth
    live,
But to the earth some special good doth
    give;
Nor aught so good, but, strain'd from that
    fair use,
Revolts from true birth, stumbling on
    abuse:
Virtue itself turns vice, being misapplied;
And vice sometime's by action dignified.
Within the infant rind of this small flower
Poison hath residence, and medicine
    power:
For this, being smelt, with that part cheers
    each part;

Being tasted, slays all senses with the
 heart.
Two such opposed kings encamp them still
In man as well as herbs,—grace, and rude
 will;
And where the worser is predominant,
Full soon the canker death eats up that
 plant.

Enter ROMEO.

ROM. Good morrow, father!
FRI. L.   *Benedicite!*
What early tongue so sweet saluteth me?—
Young son, it argues a distemper'd head,
So soon to bid good morrow to thy bed:
Care keeps his watch in every old man's
 eye,
And where care lodges, sleep will never
 lie;
But where unbruised youth, with unstuff'd
 brain,
Doth couch his limbs, there golden sleep
 doth reign:
Therefore thy earliness doth me assure,
Thou art up-rous'd by some distempera-
 ture:
Or if not so, then here I hit it right,—
Our Romeo hath not been in bed to-night.
ROM. That last is true; the sweeter rest
 was mine.
FRI. L. God pardon sin! wast thou with
 Rosaline?
ROM. With Rosaline, my ghostly father?
 no;
I have forgot that name, and that name's
 woe.
FRI. L. That's my good son: but where
 hast thou been, then?
ROM. I'll tell thee, ere thou ask it me
 again.
I have been feasting with mine enemy;
Where, on a sudden, one hath wounded
 me,
That's by me wounded: both our remedies
Within thy help and holy physic lies:
I bear no hatred, blessed man; for, lo,
My intercession likewise steads my foe.
FRI. L. Be plain, good son, and homely
 in thy drift;
Riddling confession finds but riddling
 shrift.
ROM. Then plainly know, my heart's dear
 love is set
On the fair daughter of rich Capulet:
As mine on hers, so hers is set on mine;
And all combin'd, save what thou must
 combine
By holy marriage: when, and where, and
 how,
We met, we woo'd, and made exchange of
 vow,
I'll tell thee as we pass; but this I pray,

That thou consent to marry us to-day.
FRI. L. Holy Saint Francis! what a
 change is here!
Is Rosaline, whom thou didst love so dear,
So soon forsaken? young men's love, then,
 lies
Not truly in their hearts, but in their eyes.
Jesu Maria! what a deal of brine
Hath wash'd thy sallow cheeks for Rosa-
 line!
How much salt water thrown away in
 waste,
To season love, that of it doth not taste!
The sun not yet thy sighs from heaven
 clears,
Thy old groans ring yet in my ancient
 ears;
Lo, here upon thy cheek the stain doth sit
Of an old tear that is not wash'd off yet:
If e'er thou wast thyself, and these woes
 thine,
Thou and these woes were all for Rosaline:
And art thou chang'd? pronounce this sen-
 tence, then,—
Women may fall, when there's no strength
 in men.
ROM. Thou chidd'st me oft for loving
 Rosaline.
FRI. L. For doting, not for loving, pupil
 mine.
ROM. And bad'st me bury love.
FRI. L.   Not in a grave,
To lay one in, another out to have.
ROM. I pray thee, chide not: she, whom
 I love now,
Doth grace for grace, and love for love
 allow;
The other did not so.
FRI. L.   O, she knew well,
Thy love did read by rote, and could not
 spell.
But come, young waverer, come, go with
 me,
In one respect I'll thy assistant be;
For this alliance may so happy prove,
To turn your households' rancour to pure
 love.
ROM. O, let us hence; I stand on sud-
 den haste.
FRI. L. Wisely, and slow; they stumble
 that run fast.   [*Exeunt.*

SCENE IV.—*A Street.*

Enter BENVOLIO *and* MERCUTIO.

MER. Where the devil should this Romeo
 be?—
Came he not home to-night?
BEN. Not to his father's; I spoke with
 his man.

MER. Ah, that same pale hard-hearted wench, that Rosaline,
Torments him so, that he will sure run mad.

BEN. Tybalt, the kinsman of old Capulet, Hath sent a letter to his father's house.

MER. A challenge, on my life.

BEN. Romeo will answer it.

MER. Any man, that can write, may answer a letter.

BEN. Nay, he will answer the letter's master, how he dares, being dared.

MER. Alas, poor Romeo, he is already dead! stabbed with a white wench's black eye; shot thorough the ear with a love-song; the very pin of his heart cleft with the blind bow-boy's butt-shaft: and is he a man to encounter Tybalt?

BEN. Why, what is Tybalt?

MER. More than prince of cats, I can tell you. O, he is the courageous captain of compliments. He fights as you sing prick-song, keeps time, distance, and proportion; rests me his minim rest, one, two, and the third in your bosom: the very butcher of a silk button, a duellist, a duellist; a gentleman of the very first house,—of the first and second cause: ah, the immortal passado! the punto reverso! the hay!—

BEN. The what?

MER. The pox of such antick, lisping, affecting fantasticoes, these new tuners of accents!—"By jesu, a very good blade!—a very tall man!—a very good whore!"—Why, is not this a lamentable thing, grandsire, that we should be thus afflicted with these strange flies, these fashion-mongers, these *pardonnez-mois*, who stand so much on the new form, that they cannot sit at ease on the old bench? O, their *bons*, their *bons!*

BEN. Here comes Romeo, here comes Romeo.

MER. Without his roe, like a dried herring:—O flesh, flesh, how art thou fishified!—Now is he for the numbers that Petrarch flowed in: Laura, to his lady, was but a kitchen-wench,—marry, she had a better love to be-rhyme her; Dido, a dowdy; Cleopatra, a gipsy; Helen and Hero, hildings and harlots; Thisbe, a grey eye or so, but not to the purpose.—

Enter ROMEO.

Signior Romeo, *bon jour!* there's a French salutation to your French slop. You gave us the counterfeit fairly last night.

ROM. Good morrow to you both. What counterfeit did I give you?

MER. The slip, Sir, the slip; can you not conceive?

ROM. Pardon, good Mercutio, my business was great; and in such a case as mine, a man may strain courtesy.

MER. That's as much as to say—Such a case as yours constrains a man to bow in the hams.

ROM. Meaning—to court'sy.

MER. Thou hast most kindly hit it.

ROM. A most courteous exposition.

MER. Nay, I am the very pink of courtesy.

ROM. Pink for flower.

MER. Right.

ROM. Why, then is my pump well flowered.

MER. Well said: follow me this jest now, till thou hast worn out thy pump; that, when the single sole of it is worn, the jest may remain, after the wearing, solely singular.

ROM. O single-soled jest, solely singular for the singleness!

MER. Come between us, good Benvolio; my wits fail.

ROM. Switch and spurs, switch and spurs; or I'll cry a match.

MER. Nay, if thy wits run the wild-goose chase, I have done; for thou hast more of the wild-goose in one of thy wits, than, I am sure, I have in my whole five: was I with you there for the goose?

ROM. Thou wast never with me for any thing, when thou wast not there for the goose.

MER. I will bite thee by the ear for that jest.

ROM. Nay, good goose, bite not.

MER. Thy wit is a very bitter sweeting; it is a most sharp sauce.

ROM. And is it not well served in to a sweet goose?

MER. O, here's a wit of cheveril, that stretches from an inch narrow to an ell broad!

ROM. I stretch it out for that word—broad; which added to the goose, proves thee far and wide a broad goose.

MER. Why, is not this better now than groaning for love? now art thou sociable, now art thou Romeo; now art thou what thou art, by art as well as by nature: for this driveling love is like a great natural, that runs lolling up and down to hide his bauble in a hole.

BEN. Stop there, stop there.

MER. Thou desirest me to stop in my tale against the hair.

BEN. Thou would'st else have made thy tale large.

MER. O, thou art deceived; I would have made it short: for I was come to the whole depth of my tale; and meant, indeed, to occupy the argument no longer.

ROM. Here's goodly gear!

Enter Nurse *and* PETER.

MER. A sail, a sail, a sail!

BEN. Two, two; a shirt, and a smock.

NURSE. Peter!

PETER. Anon?

NURSE. My fan, Peter.

MER. Good Peter, to hide her face; for her fan's the fairer face.

NURSE. God ye good morrow, gentlemen.

MER. God ye good den, fair gentlewoman.

NURSE. Is it good den?

MER. 'Tis no less, I tell you; for the bawdy hand of the dial is now upon the prick of noon.

NURSE. Out upon you! what a man are you.

ROM. One, gentlewoman, that God hath made, for himself to mar.

NURSE. By my troth, it is well said;—for himself to mar, quoth'a?—Gentlemen, can any of you tell me where I may find the young Romeo?

ROM. I can tell you; but young Romeo will be older when you have found him, than he was when you sought him: I am the youngest of that name, for fault of a worse.

NURSE. You say well.

MER. Yea, is the worst well? very well took, i' faith; wisely, wisely.

NURSE. If you be he, Sir, I desire some confidence with you.

BEN. She will indite him to some supper.

MER. A bawd, a bawd, a bawd! So ho!

ROM. What hast thou found?

MER. No hare, Sir; unless a hare, Sir, in a lenten pie, that is something stale and hoar ere it be spent.

[*Sings.*]

"An old hare hoar,
   And an old hare hoar,
Is very good meat in lent:
But a hare that is hoar,
   Is too much for a score,
When it hoars ere it be spent."—

Romeo, will you come to your father's? we'll to dinner thither.

ROM. I will follow you.

MER. Farewell, ancient lady; farewell,—[*singing.*] "lady, lady, lady."

[*Exeunt* MERCUTIO *and* BENVOLIO.

NURSE. Marry, farewell!—I pray you, Sir, what saucy merchant was this, that was so full of his ropery?

ROM. A gentleman, nurse, that loves to hear himself talk; and will speak more in a minute, than he will stand to in a month.

NURSE. An 'a speak any thing against me, I'll take him down, an 'a were lustier than he is, and twenty such Jacks; and if I cannot, I'll find those that shall. Scurvy knave! I am none of his flirt-gills; I am none of his skains-mates.—And thou must stand by, too, and suffer every knave to use me at his pleasure!

PET. I saw no man use you at his pleasure; if I had, my weapon should quickly have been out, I warrant you: I dare draw as soon as another man, if I see occasion in a good quarrel, and the law on my side.

NURSE. Now, afore God, I am so vexed, that every part about me quivers. Scurvy knave!—Pray you, Sir, a word: and as I told you, my young lady bade me enquire you out; what she bid me say, I will keep to myself: but first let me tell ye, if ye should lead her into a fool's paradise, as they say, it were a very gross kind of behaviour, as they say: for the gentlewoman is young; and, therefore, if you should deal double with her, truly, it were an ill thing to be offered to any gentlewoman, and very weak dealing.

ROM. Nurse, commend me to thy lady and mistress. I protest unto thee,—

NURSE. Good heart! and, i' faith, I will tell her as much. Lord, lord! she will be a joyful woman.

ROM. What wilt thou tell her, nurse? thou dost not mark me.

NURSE. I will tell her, Sir,—that you do protest; which, as I take it, is a gentlemanlike offer.

ROM. Bid her devise some means to come This afternoon;   [to shrift
And there she shall at friar Laurence's cell
Be shriv'd, and married. Here is for thy pains.

NURSE. No, truly, Sir; not a penny.

ROM. Go to; I say, you shall.

NURSE. This afternoon, Sir? well, she shall be there.

ROM. And stay, good nurse, behind the abbey-wall:
Within this hour my man shall be with thee,
And bring thee cords made like a tackled stair;
Which to the high top-gallant of my joy
Must be my convoy in the secret night.
Farewell: be trusty, and I'll quit thy pains:
Farewell; commend me to thy mistress.

NURSE. Now, God in heaven bless thee!
—Hark you, Sir.

ROM. What say'st thou, my dear nurse?

NURSE. Is your man secret? Did you ne'er hear say,

Two may keep counsel, putting one away?

ROM. I warrant thee, my man's as true as steel.

NURSE. Well, Sir; my mistress is the sweetest lady—Lord, lord!—when 'twas a little prating thing,—O,—there's a nobleman in town, one Paris, that would fain lay knife aboard; but she, good soul, had as lief see a toad, a very toad, as see him. I anger her sometimes, and tell her that Paris is the properer man; but, I'll warrant you, when I say so, she looks as pale as any clout in the varsal world. Doth not rosemary and Romeo begin both with a letter?

ROM. Ay, nurse; What of that? both with an R.

NURSE. Ah, mocker! that's the dog's name; R is for the dog. No; I know it begins with some other letter:—and she hath the prettiest sententious of it, of you and rosemary, that it would do you good to hear it.

ROM. Commend me to thy lady.

NURSE. Ay, a thousand times.—[*Exit* ROMEO.] Peter!

PET. Anon?

NURSE. Peter, take my fan, and go before.   [*Exeunt.*

SCENE V.—CAPULET'S *Garden.*

Enter JULIET.

JUL. The clock struck nine, when I did send the nurse;

In half an hour she promis'd to return.

Perchance, she cannot meet him:—that's not so.—

O, she is lame! love's heralds should be thoughts,

Which ten times faster glide than the sun's beams,

Driving back shadows over lowering hills:

Therefore do nimble-pinioned doves draw love,   [wings.

And therefore hath the wind-swift Cupid

Now is the sun upon the highmost hill

Of this day's journey; and from nine till twelve

Is three long hours,—yet she is not come.

Had she affections, and warm youthful blood,

She'd be as swift in motion as a ball;

My words would bandy her to my sweet

And his to me: [love,

But old folks, many feign as they were dead;

Unwieldy, slow, heavy and pale as lead.

O God, she comes!—

Enter Nurse *and* PETER.

      O honey nurse! what news?

Hast thou met with him? Send thy man away.

NURSE. Peter, stay at the gate.

      [*Exit* PETER.

JUL. Now, good sweet nurse,—O lord! why look'st thou sad?

Though news be sad, yet tell them merrily;

If good, thou sham'st the music of sweet news

By playing it to me with so sour a face.

NURSE. I am aweary, give me leave awhile:—   [have I had!

Fie, how my bones ache! What a jaunt

JUL. I would thou hadst my bones, and I thy news:

Nay, come, I pray thee, speak;—good, good nurse, speak.

NURSE. Jesu, what haste? can you not stay awhile?

Do you not see that I am out of breath?

JUL. How art thou out of breath, when thou hast breath

To say to me—that thou art out of breath?

The excuse that thou dost make in this delay

Is longer than the tale thou dost excuse.

Is thy news good, or bad? answer to that;

Say either, and I'll stay the circumstance:

Let me be satisfied, is't good or bad?

NURSE. Well, you have made a simple choice; you know not how to choose a man: Romeo? no, not he; though his face be better than any man's, yet his leg excels all men's; and for a hand, and a foot, and a body,—though they be not to be talked on, yet they are past compare: he is not the flower of courtesy,—but, I'll warrant him, as gentle as a lamb.—Go thy ways, wench; serve God.—What, have you dined at home?

JUL. No, no: but all this did I know before.   [that?

What says he of our marriage? what of

NURSE. Lord, how my head aches! what a head have I!

It beats as it would fall in twenty pieces.

My back! o' t'other side:—O, my back, my back!—

Beshrew your heart for sending me about,

To catch my death with jaunting up and down.   [not well.

JUL. I' faith, I am sorry that thou art

Sweet, sweet, sweet nurse, tell me, what says my love?

NURSE. Your love says, like an honest gentleman,

And a courteous, and a kind, and a hand-
some, [mother?
And, I warrant, a virtuous,—Where is your
JUL. Where is my mother!—why, she is
within; [reply'st!
Where should she be? How oddly thou
"Your love says, like an honest gentle-
Where is your mother?" [man,
NURSE. O, God's lady dear!
Are you so hot? Marry, come up, I trow;
Is this the poultice for my aching bones?
Henceforward do your messages yourself.
JUL. Here's such a coil!—Come, what says
Romeo? [to-day?
NURSE. Have you got leave to go to shrift
JUL. I have.
NURSE. Then hie you hence to friar
Laurence' cell,
There stays a husband to make you a wife:
Now comes the wanton blood up in your
cheeks,
They'll be in scarlet straight at any news.
Hie you to church; I must another way,
To fetch a ladder, by the which your love
Must climb a bird's nest soon, when it is
dark:
I am the drudge, and toil in your delight;
But you shall bear the burden soon at
night.
Go; I'll to dinner; hie you to the cell.
JUL. Hie to high fortune!—honest nurse,
farewell. [Exeunt.

SCENE VI.—FRIAR LAURENCE'S Cell.
Enter FRIAR LAURENCE and ROMEO.

FRI. L. So smile the heavens upon this
holy act,
That after-hours with sorrow chide us not!
ROM. Amen, amen! but come what sorrow
can,
It cannot countervail the exchange of joy
That one short minute gives me in her
sight: [words,
Do thou but close our hands with holy
Then love-devouring death do what he
dare,—
It is enough I may but call her mine.
FRI. L. These violent delights have violent
ends, [powder,
And in their triumph die; like fire and
Which, as they kiss, consume: the sweetest
honey
Is loathsome in his own deliciousness,
And in the taste confounds the appetite:
Therefore, love moderately; long love doth
so;
Too swift arrives as tardy as too slow.—
Here comes the lady:—O, so light a foot
Will ne'er wear out the everlasting flint:
A lover may bestride the gossamer

That idles in the wanton summer air,
And yet not fall; so light is vanity.
Enter JULIET.
JUL. Good even to my ghostly confessor.
FRI. L. Romeo shall thank thee, daughter,
for us both.
JUL. As much to him, else are his thanks
too much.
ROM. Ah, Juliet, if the measure of thy
joy [be more
Be heap'd like mine, and that thy skill
To blazon it, then sweeten with thy breath
This neighbour air, and let rich music's
tongue
Unfold the imagin'd happiness, that both
Receive in either by this dear encounter.
JUL. Conceit, more rich in matter than in
words,
Brags of his substance, not of ornament:
They are but beggars that can count their
worth;
But my true love is grown to such excess,
I cannot sum up half my sum of wealth.
FRI. L. Come, come with me, and we will
make short work;
For, by your leaves, you shall not stay
alone,
Till holy church incorporate two in one.
[Exeunt.

ACT III.

SCENE I.—A public Place.

Enter MERCUTIO, BENVOLIO, Page, and
Servants.

BEN. I pray thee, good Mercutio, let's
retire:
The day is hot, the Capulets abroad,
And, if we meet, we shall not 'scape a
brawl; [stirring.
For now, these hot days, is the mad blood
MER. Thou art like one of those fellows
that, when he enters the confines of a
tavern, claps me his sword upon the table,
and says, "God send me no need of thee!"
and, by the operation of the second cup,
draws it on the drawer, when, indeed, there
is no need.
BEN. Am I like such a fellow?
MER. Come, come, thou art as hot a Jack
in thy mood, as any in Italy; and as soon
moved to be moody, and as soon moody
to be moved.
BEN. And what to?
MER. Nay, an there were two such, we
should have none shortly, for one would kill
the other. Thou! why, thou wilt quarrel
with a man that hath a hair more, or a
hair less, in his beard, than thou hast: thou
wilt quarrel with a man for cracking nuts
having no other reason, but because thou

hast hazel eyes; what eye, but such an eye, would spy out such a quarrel? Thy head is as full of quarrels, as an egg is full of meat; and yet thy head hath been beaten as addle as an egg, for quarrelling. Thou hast quarrelled with a man for coughing in the street, because he hath wakened thy dog that hath lain asleep in the sun: didst thou not fall out with a tailor for wearing his new doublet before Easter? with another, for tying his new shoes with old riband? and yet thou wilt tutor me from quarrelling!

BEN. An I were so apt to quarrel as thou art, any man should buy the fee-simple of my life for an hour and a quarter.

MER. The fee-simple! O simple!

BEN. By my head, here come the Capulets.

MER. By my heel, I care not.

Enter TYBALT and others.

TYB. Follow me close, for I will speak to them.—Gentlemen, good den: a word with one of you.

MER. And but one word with one of us? Couple it with something; make it a word and a blow.

TYB. You shall find me apt enough to that, Sir, if you will give me occasion.

MER. Could you not take some occasion without giving?

TYB. Mercutio, thou consort'st with Romeo,—

MER. Consort! what, dost thou make us minstrels? an thou make minstrels of us, look to hear nothing but discords: here's my fiddlestick; here's that shall make you dance. 'Zounds, consort!

BEN. We talk here in the public haunt of men:

Either withdraw unto some private place, And reason coldly of your grievances, Or else depart; here all eyes gaze on us.

MER. Men's eyes were made to look, and let them gaze;

I will not budge for no man's pleasure, I.

TYB. Well, peace be with you, Sir: here comes my man.

Enter ROMEO.

MER. But I'll be hang'd, Sir, if he wear your livery:

Marry, go before to field, he'll be your follower; [man.

Your worship, in that sense, may call him—

TYB. Romeo, the hate I bear thee, can afford [lain.

No better term than this,—thou art a vil-

ROM. Tybalt, the reason that I have to love thee

Doth much excuse the appertaining rage To such a greeting:—villain am I none;

Therefore farewell; I see thou know'st me not.

TYB. Boy, this shall not excuse the injuries That thou hast done me; therefore turn, and draw.

ROM. I do protest, I never injur'd thee; But love thee better than thou canst devise, Till thou shalt know the reason of my love: And so, good Capulet,—which name I tender

As dearly as my own,—be satisfied. [der

MER. O calm, dishonourable, vile submission!

A la stoccata carries it away.— [*Draws.*

Tybalt, you rat-catcher, will you walk?

TYB. What would'st thou have with me?

MER. Good king of cats, nothing but one of your nine lives; that I mean to make bold withal, and, as you shall use me hereafter, dry-beat the rest of the eight. Will you pluck your sword out of his pilcher by the ears? make haste, lest mine be about your ears ere it be out.

TYB. [*Drawing.*] I am for you.

ROM. Gentle Mercutio, put thy rapier up.

MER. Come, Sir, your passado. [*They fight.*

ROM. Draw, Benvolio; beat down their weapons.—

Gentlemen, for shame, forbear this outrage! Tybalt,—Mercutio,—the prince expressly hath

Forbidden bandying in Verona streets:— Hold, Tybalt!—good Mercutio,—

[*Exeunt* TYBALT *and his partisans.*

MER. I am hurt;—

A plague o' both the houses!—I am sped:— Is he gone, and hath nothing?

BEN. What, art thou hurt?

MER. Ay, ay, a scratch, a scratch; marry, 'tis enough.—

Where is my page?—go, villain, fetch a surgeon. [*Exit* Page.

ROM. Courage, man; the hurt cannot be much.

MER. No, 'tis not so deep as a well, nor so wide as a church door; but 'tis enough, 'twill serve: ask for me to-morrow, and you shall find me a grave man. I am peppered, I warrant, for this world:—a plague o' both your houses!—'Zounds, a dog, a rat, a mouse, a cat, to scratch a man to death! a braggart, a rogue, a villain, that fights by the book of arithmetic!—Why, the devil, came you between us? I was hurt under your arm.

ROM. I thought all for the best.

MER. Help me into some house, Benvolio, Or I shall faint.—A plague o' both your houses!

They have made worms' meat of me: I have it, and soundly too:—your houses!

[*Exeunt* MERCUTIO *and* BENVOLIO.

ROM. This gentleman, the prince's near
ally,
My very friend, hath got his mortal hurt
In my behalf; my reputation stain'd
With Tybalt's slander,—Tybalt, that an
hour
Hath been my kinsman;—O sweet Juliet,
Thy beauty hath made me effeminate,
And in my temper soften'd valour's steel!

Re-enter BENVOLIO.

BEN. O Romeo, Romeo, brave Mercutio's
dead!
That gallant spirit hath aspir'd the clouds,
Which too untimely here did scorn the
earth.
ROM. This day's black fate on more days
doth depend;
This but begins the woe, others must end.
BEN. Here comes the furious Tybalt back
again.   [slain!
ROM. Alive, in triumph! and Mercutio
Away to heaven, respective lenity,
And fire-ey'd fury be my conduct now!—

Re-enter TYBALT.

Now, Tybalt, take the villain back again,
That late thou gav'st me; for Mercutio's
soul
Is but a little way above our heads,
Staying for thine to keep him company:
Either thou, or I, or both, must go with him.
TYB. Thou, wretched boy, that didst con-
sort him here,
Shalt with him hence.
ROM.   This shall determine that.
                    [*They fight*; TYBALT *falls.*
BEN. Romeo, away, be gone!
The citizens are up, and Tybalt slain:—
Stand not amaz'd:—the prince will doom
thee death,
If thou art taken:—hence, be gone, away!
ROM. O, I am fortune's fool!
BEN.   Why dost thou stay?
                              [*Exit* ROMEO.

Enter Citizens, &c.

1 *CIT.* Which way ran he, that kill'd
Mercutio?
Tybalt, that murderer, which way ran he?
BEN. There lies that Tybalt.
1 *CIT.*   Up, Sir, go with me;
I charge thee in the prince's name, obey.

Enter PRINCE, *attended*; MONTAGUE, CAPU-
LET, *their wives, and others.*

PRIN. Where are the vile beginners of this
fray?
BEN. O noble prince, I can discover all
The unlucky manage of this fatal brawl:
There lies the man, slain by young Romeo,
That slew thy kinsman, brave Mercutio.
LA. CAP. Tybalt, my cousin! O my broth-
er's child!—

O prince!—O husband!—O, the blood is
spill'd   [art true,
Of my dear kinsman!—Prince, as thou
For blood of ours, shed blood of Mon-
O cousin, cousin!   [tague.—
PRIN. Benvolio, who began this bloody
fray?
BEN. Tybalt, here slain, whom Romeo's
hand did slay;
Romeo, that spoke him fair, bade him be-
think
How nice the quarrel was, and urg'd withal
Your high displeasure:—all this,—uttered
With gentle breath, calm look, knees hum-
bly bow'd,—
Could not take truce with the unruly
spleen
Of Tybalt, deaf to peace, but that he tilts
With piercing steel at bold Mercutio's
breast;
Who, all as hot, turns deadly point to point,
And, with a martial scorn, with one hand
beats
Cold death aside, and with the other sends
It back to Tybalt, whose dexterity
Retorts it: Romeo he cries aloud,
"Hold, friends! friends, part!" and, swifter
than his tongue,
His agile arm beats down their fatal points,
And 'twixt them rushes; underneath whose
arm,
An envious thrust from Tybalt hit the life
Of stout Mercutio, and then Tybalt fled:
But by and by comes back to Romeo,
Who had but newly entertain'd revenge,
And to't they go like lightning; for, ere I
Could draw to part them, was stout Tybalt
slain;
And, as he fell, did Romeo turn and fly:—
This is the truth, or let Benvolio die.
LA. CAP. He is a kinsman to the Mon-
tague;   [true:
Affection makes him false, he speaks not
Some twenty of them fought in this black
strife,
And all those twenty could but kill one life.
I beg for justice, which thou, prince, must
give;
Romeo slew Tybalt, Romeo must not live.
PRIN. Romeo slew him, he slew Mercutio;
Who now the price of his dear blood doth
owe?   [cutio's friend;
MON. Not Romeo, prince, he was Mer-
His fault concludes but what the law
The life of Tybalt.   [should end,
PRIN.   And for that offence,
Immediately we do exile him hence:
I have an interest in your hate's proceeding,
My blood for your rude brawls doth lie a
bleeding;
But I'll amerce you with so strong a fine,

That you shall all repent the loss of mine:
I will be deaf to pleading and excuses;
Nor tears, nor prayers, shall purchase out
  abuses,—
Therefore use none: let Romeo hence in
  haste,
Else, when he's found, that hour is his last.
Bear hence this body, and attend our will:
Mercy but murders, pardoning those that
  kill.   [*Exeunt.*

SCENE II.—*A Room in* CAPULET'S *House.*
Enter JULIET.

JUL. Gallop apace, you fiery-footed steeds,
Towards Phœbus' mansion: such a wag-
  goner
As Phaeton would whip you to the west,
And bring in cloudy night immediately.—
Spread thy close curtain, love-performing
  night,
That runaways' eyes may wink, and Romeo
Leap to these arms, untalk'd of and un-
  seen.—
Lovers can see to do their amorous rites
By their own beauties; or, if love be blind,
It best agrees with night.—Come, civil
  night,
Thou sober-suited matron, all in black,
And learn me how to lose a winning match,
Play'd for a pair of stainless maidenhoods:
Hood my unmann'd blood, bating in my
  cheeks,   [grown bold,
With thy black mantle; till strange love,
Think true love acted simple modesty.
Come, night; come, Romeo,—come, thou
  day in night;
For thou wilt lie upon the wings of night
Whiter than new snow upon a raven's
  back.—
Come, gentle night,—come, loving, black-
  brow'd night,
Give me my Romeo; and, when he shall die,
Take him and cut him out in little stars,
And he will make the face of heaven so
  fine,   [night,
That all the world will be in love with
And pay no worship to the garish sun.—
O, I have bought the mansion of a love,
But not possess'd it; and, though I am
  sold,
Not yet enjoy'd: so tedious is this day,
As is the night before some festival
To an impatient child, that hath new robes,
And may not wear them.—O, here comes
  my nurse,   [that speaks
And she brings news; and every tongue,
But Romeo's name, speaks heavenly elo-
  quence.—

Enter Nurse, *with cords.*

Now, nurse, what news? What hast thou
  there? the cords
That Romeo bade thee fetch?
NURSE.   Ay, ay, the cords.
                          [*Throws them down.*
JUL. Ah me! what news? why dost thou
  wring thy hands?
NURSE. Ah well-a-day! he's dead, he's
  dead, he's dead!
We are undone, lady, we are undone!—
Alack the day!—he's gone, he's kill'd, he's
  dead!
JUL. Can heaven be so envious?
NURSE.   Romeo can,
Though heaven cannot:—O Romeo,
  Romeo!
Who ever would have thought it?—
  Romeo!
JUL. What devil art thou, that dost tor-
  ment me thus?
This torture should be roar'd in dismal hell.
Hath Romeo slain himself? say thou but *I*,
And that bare vowel, *I*, shall poison more
Than the death-darting eye of cockatrice:
I am not I, if there be such an *I*;
Or those eyes shut, that make the answer,
If he be slain, say—I; or if not—No: [*I.*
Brief sounds determine of my weal or woe.
NURSE. I saw the wound, I saw it with
  mine eyes,—
God save the mark!—here on his manly
  breast:
A piteous corse, a bloody piteous corse;
Pale, pale as ashes, all bedaub'd in blood,
All in gore blood;—I swoonded at the
  sight.
JUL. O break, my heart!—poor bankrupt,
  break at once!
To prison, eyes, ne'er look on liberty!
Vile earth, to earth resign; end motion
  here;   [bier!
And thou, and Romeo, press one heavy
NURSE. O Tybalt, Tybalt, the best friend
  I had!
O courteous Tybalt! honest gentleman!
That ever I should live to see thee dead!
JUL. What storm is this that blows so
  contrary?
Is Romeo slaughter'd, and is Tybalt dead?
My dear-lov'd cousin, and my dearer
  lord?—
Then, dreadful trumpet, sound the general
  doom!
For who is living, if those two are gone?
NURSE. Tybalt is gone, and Romeo ban-
  ished;
Romeo, that kill'd him, he is banished.
JUI. O God—did Romeo's hand shed
  Tybalt's blood?
NURSE. It did, it did; alas the day, it did!

JUL. O serpent heart, hid with a flowering
  face!
Did ever dragon keep so fair a cave?
Beautiful tyrant! fiend angelical!
Dove-feather'd   raven!   wolfish-ravening
  lamb!
Despised substance of divinest show!
Just opposite to what thou justly seem'st,
A damned saint, an honourable villain!—
O, nature! what hadst thou to do in hell,
When thou didst bower the spirit of a fiend
In mortal paradise of such sweet flesh?—
Was ever book containing such vile matter,
So fairly bound? O, that deceit should
In such a gorgeous palace!   [dwell
NURSE.   There's no trust,
No faith, no honesty in men; all perjur'd,
All forsworn, all naught, all dissemblers.—
Ah, where's my man? give me some *aqua
  vitæ:*—   [make me old.
These griefs, these woes, these sorrows
Shame come to Romeo!
JUL.   Blister'd be thy tongue,
For such a wish! he was not born to shame:
Upon his brow shame is asham'd to sit;
For 'tis a throne where honour may be
  crown'd
Sole monarch of the universal earth.
O, what a beast was I to chide at him!
NURSE. Will you speak well of him that
  kill'd your cousin?
JUL. Shall I speak ill of him that is my
  husband?
Ah, poor my lord, what tongue shall smooth
  thy name,
When I, thy three-hours wife, have man-
  gled it?—   [cousin?
But, wherefore, villain, didst thou kill my
That villain cousin would have kill'd my
  husband: [spring;
Back, foolish tears, back to your native
Your tributary drops belong to woe,
Which you, mistaking, offer up to joy.
My husband lives, that Tybalt would have
  slain;
And Tybalt's dead, that would have slain
  my husband:
All this is comfort; wherefore weep I,
  then?   [death,
Some word there was, worser than Tybalt's
That murder'd me: I would forget it fain;
But, O, it presses to my memory,
Like damned guilty deeds to sinners' minds:
"Tybalt is dead, and Romeo—banished;"
That—"banished," that one word—"ban-
  ished,"   [death
Hath slain ten thousand Tybalts. Tybalt's
Was woe enough, if it had ended there:
Or,—if sour woe delights in fellowship,
And needly will be rank'd with other
  griefs,—

Why follow'd not, when she said—Tybalt's
  dead,
Thy father, or thy mother, nay, or both,
Which modern lamentation might have
  mov'd?   [death,
But, with a rear-ward following Tybalt's
"Romeo is banished,"—to speak that word,
Is father, mother, Tybalt, Romeo, Juliet,
All slain, all dead:—"Romeo is banished,"—
There is no end, no limit, measure, bound,
In that word's death; no words can that
  woe sound.—
Where is my father, and my mother, nurse?
NURSE. Weeping and wailing over Tybalt's
  corse: [thither.
Will you go to them? I will bring you
JUL. Wash they his wounds with tears:
  mine shall be spent,
When theirs are dry, for Romeo's banish-
  ment.   [beguil'd,
Take up those cords:—poor ropes, you are
Both you and I; for Romeo is exil'd:
He made you for a highway to my bed;
But I, a maid, die maiden-widowed.
Come, cords; come, nurse; I'll to my wed-
  ding bed;
And death, not Romeo, take my maiden-
  head!
NURSE. Hie to your chamber: I'll find
  Romeo
To comfort you:—I wot well where he is.
Hark ye, your Romeo will be here at night:
I'll to him; he is hid at Laurence' cell.
JUL. O, find him! give this ring to my
  true knight,
And bid him come to take his last farewell.
         [Exeunt.

SCENE III.—FRIAR LAURENCE'S *Cell.*
    Enter FRIAR LAURENCE.
FRI. L. Romeo, come forth, thou fearful
  man:
Affliction is enamour'd of thy parts,
And thou art wedded to calamity.
    Enter ROMEO.
ROM. Father, what news? what is the
  prince's doom?
What sorrow craves acquaintance at my
  That I yet know not?   [hand,
FRI. L.   Too familiar
Is my dear son with such sour company:
I bring thee tidings of the prince's doom.
ROM. What less than dooms-day is the
  prince's doom?
FRI. L. A gentler judgment vanish'd from
  his lips,—
Not body's death, but body's banishment.
ROM. Ha! banishment? be merciful, say
  —death;
For exile hath more terror in his look,

Much more than death: do not say—ban-
    ishment.   [ished:
FRI. L. Hence from Verona art thou ban-
Be patient, for the world is broad and wide.
ROM. There is no world without Verona
But purgatory, torture, hell itself.   [walls,
Hence banished is banish'd from the world,
And world's exile is death:—then, ban-
    ished,   [ment,
Is death mis-term'd: calling death—banish-
Thou cut'st my head off with a golden axe,
And smil'st upon the stroke that murders
    me.   [ness!
FRI. L. O deadly sin! O rude unthankful-
Thy fault our law calls death; but the kind
    prince,
Taking thy part, hath rush'd aside the law,
And turn'd that black word death to ban-
    ishment:
This is dear mercy, and thou seest it not.
ROM. 'Tis torture, and not mercy: heaven
    is here,
Where Juliet lives; and every cat, and dog,
And little mouse, every unworthy thing,
Live here in heaven, and may look on her;
But Romeo may not:—more validity,
More honourable state, more courtship lives
In carrion flies, than Romeo: they may
    seize
On the white wonder of dear Juliet's hand,
And steal immortal blessing from her lips;
Who, even in pure and vestal modesty,
Still blush, as thinking their own kisses
    sin;   [fly:—
This may flies do, when I from this must
But Romeo may not,—he is banished:
And say'st thou yet, that exile is not
    death?
Hadst thou no poison mix'd, no sharp-
    ground knife,
No sudden mean of death, though ne'er so
    mean,
But—"banished"—to kill me,—"banished?"
O friar, the damned use that word in hell;
Howlings attend it; how hast thou the
Being a divine, a ghostly confessor, [heart,
A sin-absolver, and my friend profess'd,
To mangle me with that word—"banished?"
FRI. L. Thou fond mad man, hear me but
    speak a word.
ROM. O, thou wilt speak again of banish-
    ment.
FRI. L. I'll give thee armour to keep off
    that word:
Adversity's sweet milk, philosophy,
To comfort thee, though thou art banished.
ROM. Yet "banished?"—Hang up philoso-
Unless philosophy can make a Juliet, [phy!
Displant a town, reverse a prince's doom,
It helps not, it prevails not: talk no more.

FRI. L. O then I see that madmen have
    no ears.
ROM. How should they, when that wise
    men have no eyes?
FRI. L. Let me dispute with thee of thy
    estate.
ROM. Thou canst not speak of that thou
    dost not feel:
Wert thou as young as I, Juliet thy love,
An hour but married, Tybalt murdered,
Doting like me, and like me banished,
Then might'st thou speak, then might'st
    thou tear thy hair,
And fall upon the ground, as I do now,
Taking the measure of an unmade grave.
                        [*Knocking within.*
FRI. L. Arise; one knocks; good Romeo,
    hide thyself.
ROM. Not I; unless the breath of heart-
    sick groans,
Mist-like, infold me from the search of
    eyes.   [*Knocking.*
FRI. L. Hark, how they knock!—Who's
    there?—Romeo, arise;
Thou wilt be taken.—Stay a while!—Stand
    up;   [*Knocking.*
Run to my study.—By and by!—God's
    will,
What wilfulness is this!—I come, I come!
                             [*Knocking.*
Who knocks so hard? whence come you?
    what's your will?
NURSE. [*Within.*] Let me come in, and
    you shall know my errand;
I come from lady Juliet.
FRI. L.   Welcome, then.
                        Enter Nurse.
NURSE. O holy friar, O, tell me, holy
    friar,
Where is my lady's lord, where's Romeo?
FRI. L. There on the ground, with his own
    tears made drunk.
NURSE. O, he is even in my mistress'
Just in her case!   case,
FRI. L.   O woful sympathy!
Piteous predicament!
NURSE.   Even so lies she,
Blubbering and weeping, weeping and blub-
    bering.—   [man:
Stand up, stand up; stand, an you be a
For Juliet's sake, for her sake, rise and
    stand:
Why should you fall into so deep an O?
ROM. Nurse!
NURSE. Ah Sir! ah Sir!—Well, death's
    the end of all.
ROM. Spak'st thou of Juliet? how is it
    with her?
Doth she not think me an old murderer,
Now I have stain'd the childhood of our joy

With blood remov'd but little from her
own?   [what says
Where is she? and how doth she? and
My conceal'd lady to our cancell'd love?
NURSE. O, she says nothing, Sir, but
weeps and weeps;   [up,
And now falls on her bed; and then starts
And Tybalt calls; and then on Romeo cries,
And then down falls again.
ROM.   As if that name,
Shot from the deadly level of a gun,
Did murder her; as that name's cursed
hand
Murder'd her kinsman.—O tell me, friar,
In what vile part of this anatomy [tell me,
Doth my name lodge? tell me, that I may
sack
The hateful mansion. [*Drawing his sword.*
FRI. L.   Hold thy desperate hand:
Art thou a man? thy form cries out, thou
art:
Thy tears are womanish; thy wild acts
The unreasonable fury of a beast: [denote
Unseemly woman, in a seeming man;
Or ill-beseeming beast, in seeming both!
Thou hast amaz'd me: by my holy order,
I thought thy disposition better temper'd.
Hast thou slain Tybalt? wilt thou slay thy-
self?
And slay thy lady too that lives in thee,
By doing damned hate upon thyself?
Why rail'st thou on thy birth, the heaven,
and earth?
Since birth, and heaven, and earth, all three
do meet
In thee at once; which thou at once
would'st lose.
Fie, fie, thou sham'st thy shape, thy love,
thy wit;
Which, like a usurer, abound'st in all,
And usest none in that true use indeed
Which should bedeck thy shape, thy love,
thy wit:
Thy noble shape is but a form of wax,
Digressing from the valour of a man;
Thy dear love, sworn, but hollow perjury,
Killing that love which thou hast vow'd
to cherish;
Thy wit, that ornament to shape and love,
Mis-shapen in the conduct of them both,
Like powder in a skill-less soldier's flask,
Is set afire by thine own ignorance,
And thou dismembered with thine own
defence.
What, rouse thee, man! thy Juliet is alive,
For whose dear sake thou wast but lately
dead;   [thee,
There art thou happy: Tybalt would kill
But thou slew'st Tybalt; there art thou
happy too: [friend,
The law, that threaten'd death, becomes thy

And turns it to exile; there art thou happy:
A pack of blessings lights upon thy back:
Happiness courts thee in her best array;
But, like a mis-behav'd and sullen wench,
Thou pout'st upon thy fortune and thy
love: [able.
Take heed, take heed, for such die miser-
Go, get thee to thy love, as was decreed,
Ascend her chamber, hence and comfort
her:
But look thou stay not till the watch be set,
For then thou canst not pass to Mantua;
Where thou shalt live, till we can find a
time   [friends,
To blaze your marriage, reconcile your
Beg pardon of the prince, and call thee
back
With twenty hundred thousand times more
joy
Than thou went'st forth in lamentation.—
Go before, nurse: commend me to thy
lady;
And bid her hasten all the house to bed,
Which heavy sorrow makes them apt unto:
Romeo is coming.
NURSE. O Lord, I could have stay'd here
all the night,
To hear good counsel: O, what learning
is!—
My lord, I'll tell my lady you will come.
ROM. Do so, and bid my sweet prepare
to chide.
NURSE. Here, Sir, a ring she bid me give
you, Sir.
Hie you, make haste, for it grows very
late.   [*Exit.*
ROM. How well my comfort is reviv'd by
this!
FRI. L. Go hence; good night; and here
stands all your state:—
Either be gone before the watch be set,
Or by the break of day disguis'd from
hence:
Sojourn in Mantua; I'll find out your man,
And he shall signify from time to time
Every good hap to you, that chances here:
Give me thy hand; 'tis late: farewell; good
night.
ROM. But that a joy past joy calls out on
me,
It were a grief, so brief to part with thee:
Farewell.   [*Exeunt.*

SCENE IV.—*A Room in* CAPULET'S *House.*

Enter CAPULET, LADY CAPULET, *and* PARIS.
CAP. Things have fallen out, Sir, so un-
luckily,   [daughter:
That we have had no time to move our
Look you, she lov'd her kinsman Tybalt
dearly,

And so did I;—well, we were born to die.—
'Tis very late, she'll not come down to-
night:
I promise you, but for your company,
I would have been a-bed an hour ago.
PAR. These times of woe afford no time
to woo.—
Madam, good night: commend me to your
daughter.
LA. CAP. I will, and know her mind early
to-morrow;
To-night she's mew'd up to her heaviness.
CAP. Sir Paris, I will make a desperate
tender
Of my child's love: I think she will be
rul'd   [it not.
In all respects by me; nay, more, I doubt
Wife, go you to her ere you go to bed;
Acquaint her here of my son Paris' love;
And bid her, mark you me, on Wednesday
But, soft! What day is this   [next—
PAR.   Monday, my lord.
CAP. Monday! ha, ha! Well, Wednesday
is too soon;
O' Thursday let it be:—o' Thursday, tell
her,
She shall be married to this noble earl.—
Will you be ready? do you like this haste?
We'll keep no great ado,—a friend or two;
For, hark you, Tybalt being slain so late,
It may be thought we held him carelessly,
Being our kinsman, if we revel much:
Therefore we'll have some half a dozen
friends,   [Thursday?
And there an end. But what say you to
PAR. My lord, I would that Thursday were
to-morrow.
CAP. Well, get you gone:—o' Thursday be
it, then.—
Go you to Juliet ere you go to bed,
Prepare her, wife, against this wedding-
day.—
Farewell, my lord.—Light to my chamber,
Afore me, it is so very late, that we   [ho!
May call it early by and by:—good night.
                                    [*Exeunt.*

———

SCENE V.—JULIET'S *Chamber.*

Enter ROMEO *and* JULIET.

JUL. Wilt thou be gone? it is not yet near
day:
It was the nightingale, and not the lark,
That pierc'd the fearful hollow of thine
ear;   [tree;
Nightly she sings on yon pomegranate
Believe me, love, it was the nightingale.
ROM. It was the lark, the herald of the
morn,
No nightingale: look, love, what envious
streaks

Do lace the severing clouds in yonder east:
Night's candles are burnt out, and jocund
day
Stands tiptoe on the misty mountain tops.
I must be gone and live, or stay and die.
JUL. Yon light is not day-light, I know
it, I:
It is some meteor that the sun exhales,
To be to thee this night a torch-bearer,
And light thee on thy way to Mantua:
Therefore stay yet,—thou need'st not to be
gone.
ROM. Let me be ta'en, let me be put to
death;
I am content, so thou wilt have it so.
I'll say yon grey is not the morning's eye,
'Tis but the pale reflex of Cynthia's
brow;   [beat;
Nor that is not the lark, whose notes do
The vaulty heaven so high above our heads:
I have more care to stay, than will to go:—
Come, death, and welcome! Juliet wills
it so.—
How is't, my soul? let's talk,—it is not day.
JUL. It is, it is,—hie hence, be gone,
away!
It is the lark that sings so out of tune,
Straining harsh discords, and unpleasing
sharps.
Some say, the lark makes sweet division;
This doth not so, for she divideth us:
Some say, the lark and loathed toad change
eyes;
O, now I would they had chang'd voices
too!
Since arm from arm that voice doth us
affray,
Hunting thee hence with hunts-up to the
day.   [grows.
O, now be gone; more light and light it
ROM. More light and light,—more dark
and dark our woes.

Enter Nurse.

NURSE. Madam!
JUL. Nurse?
NURSE. Your ladys' mother's coming to
your chamber:
The day is broke; be wary, look about.
                                     [*Exit.*
JUL. Then, window, let day in, and let
life out.
ROM. Farewell, farewell! one kiss, and
I'll descend.   [*Descends.*
JUL. Art thou gone so? my love! my lord!
my friend!
I must hear from thee every day in the
hour,
For in a minute there are many days:
O! by this count I shall be much in years
Ere I again behold my Romeo.

ROM. Farewell! I will omit no oppor-
tunity [thee.
That may convey my greetings, love, to
JUL. O, think'st thou we shall ever meet
again?
ROM. I doubt it not; and all these woes
shall serve
For sweet discourses in our time to come.
JUL. O God, I have an ill-divining soul!
Methinks I see thee, now thou art below,
As one dead in the bottom of a tomb:
Either my eyesight fails, or thou look'st
pale. [do you:
ROM. And trust me, love, in my eye so
Dry sorrow drinks our blood. Adieu!
adieu! [*Exit.*
JUL. O fortune, fortune! all men call thee
fickle:
If thou art fickle, what dost thou with him
That is renown'd for faith? Be fickle, for-
tune;
For then, I hope, thou wilt not keep him
But send him back. [long,
LA. CAP. [*Within.*] Ho, daughter! are you
up? [mother?
JUL. Who is't that calls? is it my lady
Is she not down so late, or up so early?
What unaccustom'd cause procures her
hither?

Enter LADY CAPULET.

LA. CAP. Why, how now, Juliet!
JUL. Madam, I am not well.
LA. CAP. Evermore weeping for your cous-
in's death?
What, wilt thou wash him from his grave
with tears? [him live;
An if thou could'st, thou could'st not make
Therefore, have done: some grief shows
much of love;
But much of grief shows still some want of
wit.
JUL. Yet let me weep for such a feeling
loss.
LA. CAP. So shall you feel the loss, but
not the friend
Which you weep for.
JUL. Feeling so the loss,
I cannot choose but ever weep the friend.
LA. CAP. Well, girl, thou weep'st not so
much for his death,
As that the villain lives which slaughter'd
JUL. What villain, Madam? [him.
LA. CAP. That same villain, Romeo.
JUL. Villain and he be many miles
asunder.
God pardon him! I do, with all my heart;
And yet no man, like he, doth grieve my
heart.

LA. CAP. That is, because the traitor mur-
derer lives.
JUL. Ay, Madam, from the reach of these
my hands:—
Would none but I might venge my cousin's
death!
LA. CAP. We will have vengeance for it,
fear thou not:
Then weep no more. I'll send to one in
Mantua,—
Where that same banish'd runagate doth
live,—
Shall give him such an unaccustom'd
dram,
That he shall soon keep Tybalt company:
And then, I hope, thou wilt be satisfied.
JUL. Indeed, I never shall be satisfied
With Romeo, till I behold him—dead—
Is my poor heart so for a kinsman vex'd:
Madam, if you could find out but a man
To bear a poison, I would temper it;
That Romeo should, upon receipt thereof,
Soon sleep in quiet. O, how my heart
abhors
To hear him nam'd,—and cannot come to
him,
To wreak the love I bore my cousin Tybalt
Upon his body that hath slaughter'd him!
LA. CAP. Find thou the means, and I'll
find such a man.
But now I'll tell thee joyful tidings, girl.
JUL. And joy comes well in such a needy
time:
What are they, I beseech your ladyship?
LA. CAP. Well, well, thou hast a careful
father, child;
One who, to put thee from thy heaviness,
Hath sorted out a sudden day of joy,
That thou expect'st not, nor I look'd not
for. [that?
JUL. Madam, in happy time, what day is
LA. CAP. Marry, my child, early next
Thursday morn,
The gallant, young, and noble gentleman,
The county Paris, at Saint Peter's church,
Shall happily make thee there a joyful
bride. [Peter too,
JUL. Now, by Saint Peter's church, and
He shall not make me there a joyful bride.
I wonder at this haste; that I must wed
Ere he, that should be husband, comes to
woo:
I pray you, tell my lord and father, Madam,
I will not marry yet; and, when I do, I
swear,
It shall be Romeo, whom you know I hate,
Rather than Paris:—these are news indeed!
LA CAP. Here comes your father; tell him
so yourself,
And see how he will take it at your hands.

Enter CAPULET *and Nurse.*

CAP. When the sun sets, the air doth
　　drizzle dew;
But for the sunset of my brother's son,
It rains downright.—
How now! a conduit, girl? what, still in
　　tears?
Evermore showering? In one little body
Thou counterfeit'st a bark, a sea, a wind:
For still thy eyes, which I may call the sea,
Do ebb and flow with tears; the bark thy
　　body is,　　　　　　　　　　[sighs;
Sailing in this salt flood; the winds, thy
Who,—raging with thy tears, and they with
　　them,—
Without a sudden calm, will overset
Thy tempest-tossed body.—How now, wife!
Have you deliver'd to her our decree?
LA. CAP. Ay, Sir; but she will none, she
　　gives you thanks.
I would the fool were married to her grave!
CAP. Soft! take me with you, take me
　　with you, wife.
How! will she none? doth she not give us
　　thanks?
Is she not proud? doth she not count her
　　bless'd,
Unworthy as she is, that we have wrought
So worthy a gentleman to be her bride-
　　groom?
JUL. Not proud, you have; but thankful,
　　that you have:
Proud can I never be of what I hate;
But thankful even for hate, that is meant
　　love.
CAP. How now, how now, chop-logic!
　　What is this?
Proud,—and, I thank you,—and, I thank
　　you not;—
And yet not proud:—mistress minion, you,
Thank me no thankings, nor proud me no
　　prouds,　　　　　　　　　　[next,
But fettle your fine joints 'gainst Thursday
To go with Paris to Saint Peter's church,
Or I will drag thee on a hurdle thither.
Out, you green-sickness carrion! out, you
You tallow face!　　　　　　[baggage!
LA. CAP. Fie, fie! what, are you mad?
JUL. Good father, I beseech you on my
　　knees,
Hear me with patience but to speak a word.
CAP. Hang thee, young baggage! disobe-
　　dient wretch!　　　　　　　[Thursday,
I tell thee what,—get thee to church o'
Or never after look me in the face:
Speak not, reply not, do not answer me;
My fingers itch.—Wife, we scarce thought
　　us bless'd,
That God had lent us but this only child;
But now I see this one is one too much,
And that we have a curse in having her:

Out on her, hilding!
NURSE.　　　God in heaven bless her!—
You are to blame, my lord, to rate her so.
CAP. And why, my lady wisdom? hold
　　your tongue,
Good prudence; smatter with your gossips,
NURSE. I speak no treason.　　　　[go.
CAP.　　　　O, God ye good den.
NURSE. May not one speak?
CAP.　　　　Peace, you mumbling fool!
Utter your gravity o'er a gossip's bowl;
For here we need it not.
LA. CAP.　　　　You are too hot.
CAP. God's bread! it makes me mad:
Day, night, hour, tide, time, work, play,
Alone, in company, still my care hath been
To have her match'd: and having now pro-
A gentleman of noble parentage,　　[vided
Of fair demesnes, youthful, and nobly
　　train'd,
Stuff'd (as they say) with honourable parts,
Proportion'd as one's thought would wish a
　　man,—
And then to have a wretched puling fool,
A whining mammet, in her fortune's tender,
To answer—"I'll not wed,"—"I cannot
　　love,"　　　　　　　　　　[me;"—
"I am too young,"—"I pray you, pardon
But, an you will not wed, I'll pardon you:
Graze where you will, you shall not house
　　with me.
Look to't, think on't, I do not use to jest.
Thursday is near; lay hand on heart,
　　advise:
An you be mine, I'll give you to my friend;
An you be not, hang, beg, starve, die i'
　　the streets,
For, by my soul, I'll ne'er acknowledge
　　thee,　　　　　　　　　　[good:
Nor what is mine shall never do thee
Trust to't, bethink you; I'll not be for-
　　sworn.　　　　　　　　　　[*Exit.*
JUL. Is there no pity sitting in the clouds,
That sees into the bottom of my grief?—
O, sweet my mother, cast me not away!
Delay this marriage for a month, a week;
Or, if you do not, make the bridal bed
In that dim monument where Tybalt lies.
LA. CAP. Talk not to me, for I'll not
　　speak a word:
Do as thou wilt, for I have done with thee.
　　　　　　　　　　　　　　[*Exit.*
JUL. O God!—O nurse, how shall this be
　　prevented?　　　　　　　　[en;
My husband is on earth, my faith in heav-
How shall that faith return again to earth,
Unless that husband send it me from heaven
By leaving earth?—comfort me, counsel
　　me.—　　　　　　　　　[stratagems
Alack, alack, that heaven should practise
Upon so soft a subject as myself!—

What say'st thou? hast thou not a word of
Some comfort, nurse?   [joy?
NURSE.   Faith, here it is. Romeo
Is banished; and all the world to nothing,
That he dares ne'er come back to challenge
    you;
Or, if he do, it needs must be by stealth.
Then, since the case so stands as now it
    doth,
I think it best you married with the county.
O, he's a lovely gentleman!
Romeo's a dishclout to him: an eagle,
    Madam,
Hath not so green, so quick, so fair an eye,
As Paris hath. Beshrew my very heart,
I think you are happy in this second match,
For it excels your first: or if it did not,
Your first is dead; or 'twere as good he
    were,
As living here and you no use of him.
JUL. Speakest thou from thy heart?
NURSE.   And from my soul too;
Or else beshrew them both.
JUL.   Amen!
NURSE.   What?
JUL. Well, thou hast comforted me mar-
    vellous much.
Go in; and tell my lady I am gone,
Having displeas'd my father, to Laurence'
    cell,
To make confession, and to be absolv'd.
NURSE. Marry, I will; and this is wisely
    done.   [*Exit.*
JUL. Ancient damnation! O most wicked
    fiend!
Is it more sin to wish me thus forsworn,
Or to dispraise my lord with that same
    tongue   [compare
Which she hath praised him with above
So many thousand times?—Go, counsellor;
Thou and my bosom henceforth shall be
    twain.—
I'll to the friar, to know his remedy:
If all else fail, myself have power to die.
                            [*Exit.*

ACT IV.

SCENE I.—FRIAR LAURENCE'S *Cell.*
Enter FRIAR LAURENCE *and* PARIS.
FRI. L. On Thursday, Sir? the time is
    very short.
PAR. My father Capulet will have it so;
And I am nothing slow, to slack his haste.
FRI. L. You say you do not know the
    lady's mind:
Uneven is the course, I like it not.
PAR. Immoderately she weeps for Tybalt's
    death,
And therefore have I little talk'd of love;
For Venus smiles not in a house of tears.

Now, Sir, her father counts it dangerous,
That she doth give her sorrow so much
    sway;
And, in his wisdom, hastes our marriage,
To stop the inundation of her tears;
Which, too much minded by herself alone,
May be put from her by society:
Now do you know the reason of this haste.
FRI. L. [*Aside.*] I would I knew not why
    it should be slow'd.—
Look, Sir, here comes the lady towards my
    cell.

Enter JULIET.

PAR. Happily met, my lady, and my wife!
JUL. That may be, Sir, when I may be a
    wife.   [Thursday next.
PAR. That may be, must be, love, on
JUL. What must be, shall be.
FRI. L.   That's a certain text.
PAR. Come you to make confession to this
    father?
JUL. To answer that, I should confess to
    you.   [me.
PAR. Do not deny to him, that you love
JUL. I will confess to you, that I love him.
PAR. So will you, I am sure, that you
    love me.
JUL. If I do so, it will be of more price,
Being spoke behind your back, than to your
    face.   [with tears.
PAR. Poor soul, thy face is much abus'd
JUL. The tears have got small victory by
    that;
For it was bad enough before their spite.
PAR. Thou wrong'st it, more than tears,
    with that report.   [truth;
JUL. That is no slander, Sir, which is a
And what I spake, I spake it to my face.
PAR. Thy face is mine, and thou hast
    slander'd it.
JUL. It may be so, for it is not mine own.—
Are you at leisure, holy father, now;
Or shall I come to you at evening mass?
FRI. L. My leisure serves me, pensive
    daughter, now.—
My lord, we must entreat the time alone.
PAR. God shield, I should disturb devo-
    tion!—
Juliet, on Thursday early will I rouse you:
Till then, adieu; and keep this holy kiss.
                            [*Exit.*
JUL. O, shut the door! and when thou
    hast done so,   [past help!
Come weep with me; past hope, past cure,
FRI. L. Ah, Juliet, I already know thy
    grief;
It strains me past the compass of my wits:
I hear thou must, and nothing may pro-
    rogue it,
On Thursday next be married to this county.

JUL. Tell me not, friar, that thou hear'st of this,
Unless thou tell me how I may prevent it:
If, in thy wisdom, thou canst give no help,
Do thou but call my resolution wise,
And with this knife I'll help it presently.
God join'd my heart and Romeo's, thou our hands;
And ere this hand, by thee to Romeo seal'd,
Shall be the label to another deed,
Or my true heart with treacherous revolt
Turn to another, this shall slay them both:
Therefore, out of thy long-experienc'd time,
Give me some present counsel; or, behold,
'Twixt my extremes and me this bloody knife
Shall play the umpire; arbitrating that
Which the commission of thy years and art
Could to no issue of true honour bring.
Be not so long to speak; I long to die,
If what thou speak'st speak not of remedy.
FRI. L. Hold, daughter: I do spy a kind of hope,
Which craves as desperate an execution
As that is desperate which we would prevent.
If, rather than to marry county Paris,
Thou hast the strength of will to slay thyself,
Then is it likely thou wilt undertake
A thing like death to chide away this shame,
That cop'st with death himself to scape from it;
And, if thou dar'st, I'll give thee remedy.
JUL. O, bid me leap, rather than marry Paris,
From off the battlements of yonder tower;
Or walk in thievish ways; or bid me lurk
Where serpents are; chain me with roaring bears;
Or shut me nightly in a charnel-house,
O'er-cover'd quite with dead men's rattling bones,
With reeky shanks, and yellow chapless sculls;
Or bid me go into a new-made grave,
And hide me with a dead man in his shroud;
Things that, to hear them told, have made me tremble;
And I will do it without fear or doubt,
To live an unstain'd wife to my sweet love.
FRI. L. Hold, then; go home, be merry, give consent
To marry Paris: Wednesday is to-morrow;
To-morrow night look that thou lie alone,
Let not thy nurse lie with thee in thy chamber:
Take thou this phial, being then in bed,
And this distilled liquor drink thou off:

When, presently, through all thy veins shall run
A cold and drowsy humour; for no pulse
Shall keep his native progress, but surcease:
No warmth, no breath, shall testify thou liv'st;
The roses in thy lips and cheeks shall fade
To paly ashes; thy eyes' windows fall,
Like death, when he shuts up the day of life:
Each part, depriv'd of supple government,
Shall, stiff and stark and cold, appear like death:
And in this borrow'd likeness of shrunk death
Thou shalt continue two and forty hours,
And then awake as from a pleasant sleep.
Now, when the bridegroom in the morning comes
To rouse thee from thy bed, there art thou dead:
Then (as the manner of our country is)
In thy best robes uncover'd on the bier,
Thou shalt be borne to that same ancient vault,
Where all the kindred of the Capulets lie.
In the mean time, against thou shalt awake,
Shall Romeo by my letters know our drift;
And hither shall he come: and he and I
Will watch thy waking, and that very night
Shall Romeo bear thee hence to Mantua.
And this shall free thee from this present shame;
If no unconstant toy, nor womanish fear,
Abate thy valour in the acting it.
JUL. Give me, give me! O, tell me not of fear!
FRI. L. Hold; get you gone, be strong and prosperous
In this resolve: I'll send a friar with speed
To Mantua, with my letters to thy lord.
JUL. Love, give me strength! and strength shall help afford.
Farewell, dear father!　　　　　[*Exeunt.*

SCENE II.—*Hall in* CAPULET'S *House.*

Enter CAPULET, LADY CAPULET, NURSE, *and* Servants.

CAP. So many guests invite as here are writ.——　　　　　[*Exit* 1 Servant.
Sirrah, go hire me twenty cunning cooks.
2 SERV. You shall have none ill, Sir; for I'll try if they can lick their fingers.
CAP. How canst thou try them so?
2 SERV. Marry, Sir, 'tis an ill cook that cannot lick his own fingers: therefore he that cannot lick his fingers, goes not with me.

CAP. Go, be gone.— [*Exit* 2 Servant.
We shall be much unfurnish'd for this
time.—
What, is my daughter gone to Friar Lau-
rence?
NURSE. Ay, forsooth.
CAP. Well, he may chance to do some
good on her:
A peevish self-will'd harlotry it is.
NURSE. See, where she comes from shrift
with merry look.

Enter JULIET.

CAP. How now, my headstrong! where
have you been gadding?
JUL. Where I have learn'd me to repent
Of disobedient opposition   [the sin
To you, and your behests; and am enjoin'd
By holy Laurence to fall prostrate here,
And beg your pardon:—pardon, I beseech
you!
Henceforward I am ever rul'd by you.
CAP. Send for the county; go tell him
of this:
I'll have this knot knit up to-morrow morn-
ing.   [cell;
JUL. I met the youthful lord at Laurence'
And gave him what becomed love I might,
Not stepping o'er the bounds of modesty.
CAP. Why, I am glad on't; this is well,
—stand up,—
This is as't should be.—Let me see the
county;
Ay, marry, go, I say, and fetch him
hither.—
Now, afore God, this reverend holy friar,
All our whole city is much bound to him.
JUL. Nurse, will you go with me into my
closet,
To help me sort such needful ornaments
As you think fit to furnish me to-morrow?
LA. CAP. No, not till Thursday; there is
time enough.
CAP. Go, nurse, go with her:—we'll to
church to-morrow.
            [*Exeunt* JULIET *and* Nurse.
LA. CAP. We shall be short in our provi-
'Tis now near night.   [sion:
CAP.   Tush, I will stir about,
And all things shall be well, I warrant thee,
wife:
Go thou to Juliet, help to deck up her;
I'll not to bed to-night;—let me alone;
I'll play the housewife for this once.—
What, ho!—
They are all forth: well, I will walk myself
To county Paris, to prepare him up
Against to-morrow: my heart is wond'rous
light,
Since this same wayward girl is so re-
claim'd.   [*Exeunt.*

SCENE III.—JULIET'S *Chamber.*
Enter JULIET *and* Nurse.

JUL. Ay, those attires are best:—but, gen-
tle nurse,
I pray thee, leave me to myself to-night;
For I have need of many orisons
To move the heavens to smile upon my
state,   [of sin.
Which, well thou know'st, is cross and full

Enter LADY CAPULET.

LA. CAP. What, are you busy, ho? need
you my help?
JUL. No, Madam; we have cull'd such
necessaries
As are behoveful for our state to-morrow:
So please you, let me now be left alone,
And let the nurse this night sit up with
you,   [all,
For, I am sure, you have your hands full
In this so sudden business.
LA. CAP.   Good night:
Get thee to bed, and rest; for thou hast
need. [*Exeunt* LADY CAPULET *and* Nurse.
JUL. Farewell!—God knows when we shall
meet again.
I have a faint cold fear thrills through my
veins,
That almost freezes up the heat of life:
I'll call them back again to comfort me;—
Nurse!—What should she do here?
My dismal scene I needs must act alone.—
Come, phial.—
What if this mixture do not work at all?
Shall I be married, then, to-morrow morn-
ing?—   [there.
No, no;—this shall forbid it:—lie thou
                 [*Laying down a dagger.*
What if it be a poison, which the friar
Subtly hath minister'd to have me dead,
Lest in this marriage he should be dis-
honour'd,
Because he married me before to Romeo?
I fear it is; and yet, methinks, it should
not,
For he hath still been tried a holy man:
I will not entertain so bad a thought.—
How if, when I am laid into the tomb,
I wake before the time that Romeo
Come to redeem me? there's a fearful
point!
Shall I not, then, be stifled in the vault,
To whose foul mouth no healthsome air
breathes in,
And there die strangled ere my Romeo
comes?
Or, if I live, is it not very like,
The horrible conceit of death and night,
Together with the terror of the place,—
As in a vault, an ancient receptacle,

Where, for these many hundred years, the
　　bones
Of all my buried ancestors are pack'd;
Where bloody Tybalt, yet but green in
　　earth,
Lies festering in his shroud; where, as
　　they say,
At some hours in the night spirits resort;—
Alack, alack, is it not like, that I,
So early waking,—what with loathsome
　　smells,
And shrieks like mandrakes' torn out of the
　　earth,
That living mortals, hearing them, run
　　mad;—
O, if I wake, shall I not be distraught,
Environed with all these hideous fears?
And madly play with my forefathers'
　　joints?
And pluck the mangled Tybalt from his
　　shroud?
And, in this rage, with some great kins-
　　man's bone,
As with a club, dash out my desperate
　　brains?—
O, look! methinks I see my cousin's ghost
Seeking out Romeo, that did spit his body
Upon a rapier's point:—stay, Tybalt,
　　stay!—
Romeo, I come! this do I drink to thee.
　　　　　　　　[Throws herself on the bed.

SCENE IV.—Hall in CAPULET's House.

Enter LADY CAPULET and Nurse.

LA. CAP. Hold, take these keys, and
　　fetch more spices, nurse.
NURSE. They call for dates and quinces
　　in the pastry.

Enter CAPULET.

CAP. Come, stir, stir, stir! the second
　　cock hath crow'd,
The curfew bell hath rung, 'tis three
　　o'clock:—
Look to the bak'd meats, good Angelica:
Spare not for cost.
NURSE. 　　　　Go, go, you cot-quean, go;
Get you to bed: 'faith, you'll be sick to-
For this night's watching. 　　　[morrow
CAP. No, not a whit: what! I have
　　watch'd ere now
All night for lesser cause, and ne'er been
　　sick.
LA. CAP. Ay, you have been a mouse-
　　hunt in your time;
But I will watch you from such watching
　　now. [Exeunt LADY CAPULET and Nurse.
CAP. A jealous-hood, a jealous-hood!—
Now, fellow,

Enter Servants, with spits, logs, and
　　　　baskets.

What's there?
1 SERV. Things for the cook, Sir; but
　　I know not what.
CAP. Make haste, make haste.—[Exit 1
Sirrah, fetch drier logs: 　　　　　[Serv.
Call Peter, he will show thee where they
　　are.
2 SERV. I have a head, Sir, that will find
　　out logs,
And never trouble Peter for the matter.
　　　　　　　　　　　　　　　　[Exit.
CAP. 'Mass, and well said; a merry whore-
　　son, ha!
Thou shalt be logger-head.—Good faith,
　　'tis day:
The county will be here with music straight,
　　　　　　　　　　　　　　[Music within.
For so he said he would:—I hear him
　　near.—
Nurse!—Wife!—what, ho!—what, nurse, I
　　say!

Re-enter Nurse.

Go waken Juliet, go and trim her up;
I'll go and chat with Paris:—hie, make
　　haste,
Make haste; the bridegroom he is come al-
Make haste, I say. 　　　　　　　[ready:
　　　　　　　　　　　　　　　　　[Exeunt.
SCENE V.—JULIET's Chamber; JULIET on
　　　　the bed.

Enter Nurse.

NURSE. Mistress!—what, mistress!—Ju-
　　liet!—fast, I warrant her, she:—
Why, lamb!—why, lady!—fie, you slug-a-
　　bed!—
Why, love, I say!—madam! sweet-heart!—
　　why, bride!—
What, not a word?—you take your penny-
　　worths now;
Sleep for a week; for the next night, I
　　warrant,
The county Paris hath set up his rest,
That you shall rest but little.—God for-
　　give me,
Marry, and amen, how sound is she asleep!
I needs must wake her.—Madam, madam,
　　madam!—
Ay, let the county take you in your bed;
He'll fright you up, i' faith.—Will it not
　　be? 　　　　　　　　　　[down again!
What, dress'd! and in your clothes! and
I must needs wake you:—lady! lady!
　　lady!— 　　　　　　　　　　[dead!—
Alas! alas!—Help! help! my lady's
O, well-a-day, that ever I was born!—
Some aqua-vitæ, ho!—my lord! my lady!

Enter LADY CAPULET.

LA. CAP. What noise is here?

NURSE.　　　　　　　O lamentable day!

LA. CAP. What is the matter?

NURSE.　　　　Look, look! O heavy day!

LA. CAP. O me, O me!—my child, my
　only life,

Revive, look up, or I will die with thee!—

Help, help!—call help.

Enter CAPULET.

CAP. For shame! bring Juliet forth; her
　lord is come.

NURSE. She's dead, deceas'd, she's dead;
　alack the day!

LA. CAP. Alack the day! she's dead, she's
　dead, she's dead!

CAP. Ha! let me see her:—out, alas!
　she's cold;

Her blood is settled, and her joints are
　stiff;　　　　　　　　　　　[rated:

Life and these lips have long been sepa-

Death lies on her, like an untimely frost

Upon the sweetest flower of all the field.

NURSE. O lamentable day!

LA. CAP.　　　　　　O woful time!

CAP. Death, that hath ta'en her hence
　to make me wail,

Ties up my tongue, and will not let me
　speak.

Enter FRIAR LAURENCE, and PARIS,
with Musicians.

FRI. L. Come, is the bride ready to go
　to church?

CAP. Ready to go, but never to return:—

O son, the night before thy wedding-day

Hath death lain with thy wife:—there she
　lies,

Flower as she was, deflowered by him.

Death is my son-in-law, death is my heir;

My daughter he hath wedded: I will die,

And leave him all; life, living, all is
　death's.

PAR. Have I thought long to see this
　morning's face,

And doth it give me such a sight as this?

LA. CAP. Accurs'd, unhappy, wretched,
　hateful day!

Most miserable hour, that e'er time saw

In lasting labour of his pilgrimage!

But one, poor one, one poor and loving
　child,

But one thing to rejoice and solace in,

And cruel death hath catch'd it from my
　sight.

NURSE. O woe! O woful, woful, woful
　day!

Most lamentable day, most woful day,

That ever, ever, I did yet behold!

O day! O day! O day! O hateful day!

Never was seen so black a day as this:

O woful day, O woful day!

PAR. Beguil'd, divorced, wronged, spited,
　slain!

Most detestable death, by thee beguil'd,

By cruel cruel thee quite overthrown!—

O love! O life!—not life, but love in death!

CAP. Despis'd, distressed, hated, martyr'd,
　kill'd!—

Uncomfortable time, why cam'st thou now

To murder, murder our solemnity?—

O child! O child!—my soul, and not my
　child!—

Dead art thou!—alack, my child is dead;

And with my child my joys are buried!

FRI. L. Peace, ho, for shame! confusion's
　cure lives not

In these confusions. Heaven and yourself

Had part in this fair maid; now heaven
　hath all,

And all the better is it for the maid:

Your part in her you could not keep from
　death;

But heaven keeps his part in eternal life.

The most you sought was her promotion;

For 'twas your heaven she should be ad-
　vanc'd:

And weep ye now, seeing she is advanc'd

Above the clouds, as high as heaven itself?

O, in this love, you love your child so ill,

That you run mad, seeing that she is well:

She's not well married that lives married
　long;

But she's best married that dies married
　young.

Dry up your tears, and stick your rosemary

On this fair corse; and, as the custom is,

In all her best array bear her to church:

For though fond nature bids us all lament,

Yet nature's tears are reason's merriment.

CAP. All things that we ordained festival,

Turn from their office to black funeral:

Our instruments, to melancholy bells;

Our wedding cheer, to a sad burial feast;

Our solemn hymns to sullen dirges change;

Our bridal flowers serve for a buried corse,

And all things change them to the con-
　trary.

FRI. L. Sir, go you in,—and, Madam, go
　with him;—

And go, Sir Paris;—every one prepare

To follow this fair corse unto her grave:

The heavens do lower upon you, for some
　ill:

Move them no more, by crossing their
　high will.

　　　　[*Exeunt* CAPULET, LADY CAPULET,
　　　　　　　　　　　　PARIS, *and* FRIAR.

1 MUS. 'Faith, we may put up our pipes,
　and be gone.

NURSE. Honest good fellows, ah, put up,
　put up; for, well you know, this is a piti-
　ful case.　　　　　　　　　　　[*Exit.*

1 MUS. Ay, by my troth, the case may be
　amended.

Enter PETER.

PET. Musicians, O, musicians, "Heart's ease, Hearts ease:" O, an you will have me live, play "Heart's ease."

1 MUS. Why "Heart's ease?"

PET. O, musicians, because my heart itself plays "My heart is full of woe:" O, play me some merry dump, to comfort me.

2 MUS. Not a dump we; 'tis no time to play now.

PET. You will not, then?

MUSICIANS. No.

PET. I will, then, give it you soundly.

1 MUS. What will you give us?

PET. No money, on my faith; but the gleek,—I will give you the minstrel.

1 MUS. Then will I give you the serving-creature.

PET. Then will I lay the serving-creature's dagger on your pate. I will carry no crotchets: I'll *re* you, I'll *fa* you; do you note me?

1 MUS. An you *re* us, and *fa* us, you note us.

2 MUS. Pray you, put up your dagger, and put out your wit.

PET. Then have at you with my wit! I will dry-beat you with an iron wit, and put up my iron dagger.—Answer me like men:

"When griping grief the heart doth
          wound,
      And doleful dumps the mind oppress,
    Then music, with her silver sound—"

Why, "silver sound?" why, "music with her silver sound?"—What say you, Simon Catling?

1 MUS. Marry, Sir, because silver hath a sweet sound.

PET. Pretty!—What say you, Hugh Rebeck?

2 MUS. I say, "silver sound," because musicians sound for silver.

PET. Pretty too!—What say you, James Soundpost?

3 MUS. 'Faith, I know not what to say.

PET. O, I cry you mercy; you are the singer: I will say for you. It is, "music with her silver sound," because musicians have seldom gold for sounding:—

"Then music with her silver sound,
    With speedy help doth lend redress."
                                    [*Exit.*

1 MUS. What a pestilent knave is this same!

2 MUS. Hang him, Jack!—Come, we'll in here; tarry for the mourners, and stay dinner.   [*Exeunt.*

ACT V.

SCENE I.—MANTUA. *A Street.*

Enter ROMEO.

ROM. If I may trust the flattering truth of sleep,
My dreams presage some joyful news at hand:
My bosom's lord sits lightly in his throne;
And all this day an unaccustom'd spirit
Lifts me above the ground with cheerful thoughts.
I dreamt, my lady came and found me dead,
(Strange dream! that gives a dead man leave to think)
And breath'd such life with kisses in my lips,
That I reviv'd, and was an emperor.
Ah me! how sweet is love itself possess'd,
When but love's shadows are so rich in joy!

Enter BALTHASAR.

News from Verona!—How now, Balthasar!
Dost thou not bring me letters from the friar?
How doth my lady? Is my father well?
How fares my Juliet? That I ask again;
For nothing can be ill, if she be well.

BAL. Then she is well, and nothing can be ill:
Her body sleeps in Capels' monument,
And her immortal part with angels lives.
I saw her laid low in her kindred's vault,
And presently took post to tell it you:—
O, pardon me for bringing these ill news,
Since you did leave it for my office, Sir.

ROM. Is it even so? then I defy you, stars!—
Thou know'st my lodging: get me ink and paper,
And hire post-horses; I will hence to-night.

BAL. I do beseech you, Sir, have patience:
Your looks are pale and wild, and do import
Some misadventure.   [port

ROM.   Tush, thou art deceiv'd:
Leave me, and do the thing I bid thee do.
Hast thou no letters to me from the friar?

BAL. No, my good lord.

ROM.   No matter: get thee gone,
And hire those horses; I'll be with thee straight.   [*Exit* BALTHASAR.

Well, Juliet, I will lie with thee to-night.
Let's see for means:—O mischief, thou art swift
To enter in the thoughts of desperate men!
I do remember an apothecary,—
And hereabouts he dwells,—which late I noted
In tatter'd weeds, with overwhelming brows,
Culling of simples; meagre were his looks,

Sharp misery had worn him to the bones:
And in his needy shop a tortoise hung,
An alligator stuff'd, and other skins
Of ill-shap'd fishes; and about his shelves
A beggarly account of empty boxes,
Green earthen pots, bladders, and musty
   seeds,
Remnants of packthread, and old cakes of
   roses,
Were thinly scatter'd, to make up a show.
Noting this penury, to myself I said—
An if a man did need a poison now,
Whose sale is present death in Mantua,
Here lives a caitiff wretch would sell it him.
O, this same thought did but fore-run my
   need;
And this same needy man must sell it me.
As I remember, this should be the house:
Being holiday, the beggar's shop is shut.—
What, ho! apothecary!

      Enter Apothecary.

AP.   Who calls so loud?
ROM. Come hither, man.—I see that thou
   art poor;
Hold, there is forty ducats: let me have
A dram of poison; such soon-speeding gear
As will disperse itself through all the
   veins,
That the life-weary taker may fall dead;
And that the trunk may be discharg'd of
   breath
As violently, as hasty powder fir'd
Doth hurry from the fatal cannon's womb.
AP. Such mortal drugs I have; but Man-
   tua's law
Is death to any he that utters them.
ROM. Art thou so bare and full of wretch-
   edness,
And fear'st to die? famine is in thy cheeks,
Need and oppression starveth in thine eyes,
Contempt and beggary hang upon thy back,
The world is not thy friend, nor the
   world's law:
The world affords no law to make thee
   rich;
Then be not poor, but break it, and take
   this.
AP. My poverty, but not my will, con-
   sents.
ROM. I pay thy poverty, and not thy will.
AP. Put this in any liquid thing you will,
And drink it off; and, if you had the
   strength
Of twenty men, it would despatch you
   straight.
ROM. There is thy gold; worse poison to
   men's souls,
Doing more murders in this loathsome
   world,
Than these poor compounds that thou
   may'st not sell:

I sell thee poison, thou hast sold me none.
Farewell: buy food, and get thyself in
   flesh.—
Come, cordial, and not poison, go with me
To Juliet's grave; for there must I use thee.
                    [*Exeunt.*

    SCENE II.—FRIAR LAURENCE'S *Cell.*
         Enter FRIAR JOHN.
FRI. J. Holy Franciscan friar! brother,
   ho!

     Enter FRIAR LAURENCE.
FRI. L. This same should be the voice of
   friar John.—
Welcome from Mantua: what says Romeo?
Or, if his mind be writ, give me his letter.
FRI. J. Going to find a bare-foot brother
   out,
One of our order, to associate me,
Here in this city visiting the sick,
And finding him, the searchers of the town,
Suspecting that we both were in a house
Where the infectious pestilence did reign,
Seal'd up the doors, and would not let us
   forth;
So that my speed to Mantua there was
   stay'd.
FRI. L. Who bare my letter, then, to
   Romeo?
FRI. J. I could not send it,—here it is
   again,—
Nor get a messenger to bring it thee,
So fearful were they of infection.
FRI. L. Unhappy fortune! by my brother-
   hood,
The letter was not nice, but full of charge,
Of dear import; and the neglecting it
May do much danger. Friar John, go
   hence;
Get me an iron crow, and bring it straight
Unto my cell.
FRI. J. Brother, I'll go and bring it thee.
                      [*Exit.*
FRI. L. Now must I to the monument
   alone;
Within this three hours will fair Juliet
   wake:
She will beshrew me much, that Romeo
Hath had no notice of these accidents;
But I will write again to Mantua,
And keep her at my cell till Romeo
   come:—
Poor living corse, clos'd in a dead man's
   tomb!   [*Exit.*

SCENE III.—*A Church-Yard; in it a Monu-*
   ment belonging to the CAPULETS.

Enter PARIS, *and his* Page, *bearing flowers*
          and a torch.
PAR. Give me thy torch, boy; hence, and
   stand aloof;—

Yet put it out, for I would not be seen.
Under yond' yew-trees lay thee all along,
Holding thine ear close to the hollow
    ground;
So shall no foot upon the church-yard
    tread,
(Being loose, unfirm, with digging up of
    graves)
But thou shalt hear it: whistle then to me,
As signal that thou hear'st something ap-
    proach.
Give me those flowers. Do as I bid thee, go.
PAGE. [*Aside.*] I am almost afraid to
    stand alone
Here in the church-yard; yet I will adven-
    ture.   [*Retires.*
PAR. Sweet flower, with flowers thy bridal
    bed I strew,—
(O woe, thy canopy is dust and stones!)
Which with sweet water nightly I will dew;
Or, wanting that, with tears distill'd by
    moans:
The obsequies, that I for thee will keep,
Nightly shall be, to strew thy grave and
    weep.   [*The* Page *whistles.*
The boy gives warning something doth ap-
    proach.
What cursed foot wanders this way to-
    night,
To cross my obsequies, and true love's
    rite?
What, with a torch?—muffle me, night,
    awhile.   [*Retires.*
Enter ROMEO *and* BALTHASAR, *with a
    torch, mattock, &c.*
ROM. Give me that mattock, and the
    wrenching iron.
Hold, take this letter; early in the morning
See thou deliver it to my lord and father.
Give me the light: upon thy life, I charge
    thee,
Whate'er thou hear'st or seest, stand all
    aloof,
And do not interrupt me in my course.
Why I descend into this bed of death,
Is, partly, to behold my lady's face;
But, chiefly, to take thence from her dead
    finger
A precious ring,—a ring that I must use
In dear employment: therefore hence, be
    gone:—
But if thou, jealous, dost return to pry
In what I farther shall intend to do,
By heaven, I will tear thee joint by joint,
And strew this hungry church-yard with
    thy limbs
The time and my intents are savage-wild;
More fierce, and more inexorable far,
Than empty tigers, or the roaring sea.
BAL. I will be gone, Sir, and not trouble
    you.

ROM. So shalt thou show me friendship.
    —Take thou that:
Live, and be prosperous: and farewell,
    good fellow.
BAL. [*Aside.*] For all this same, I'll hide
    me here about:
His looks I fear, and his intents I doubt.
                                     [*Retires.*
ROM. Thou detestable maw, thou womb
    of death,
Gorg'd with the dearest morsel of the earth,
Thus I enforce thy rotten jaws to open,
[*Breaking open the door of the monument.*
And, in despite, I'll cram thee with more
    food!
PAR. This is that banish'd haughty Mon-
    tague,
That murder'd my love's cousin,—with
    which grief,
It is supposed, the fair creature died,—
And here is come to do some villanous
    shame
To the dead bodies: I will apprehend
    him.   [*Advancing.*
Stop thy unhallow'd toil, vile Montague!
Can vengeance be pursu'd farther than
    death?
Condemned villain, I do apprehend thee:
Obey, and go with me; for thou must die.
ROM. I must, indeed; and therefore came
    I hither.—
Good gentle youth, tempt not a desperate
    man;
Fly hence, and leave me:—think upon
    these gone;
Let them affright thee.—I beseech thee,
    youth,
Put not another sin upon my head,
By urging me to fury:—O, be gone!
By heaven, I love thee better than myself,
For I come hither arm'd against myself:
Stay not, be gone;—live, and hereafter
    say—
A madman's mercy bade thee run away.
PAR. I do defy thy conjurations,
And apprehend thee for a felon here.
ROM. Wilt thou provoke me? then have
    at thee, boy!   [*They fight.*
PAGE. O Lord, they fight! I will go call
    the watch.   [*Exit.*
PAR. [*Falls.*] O, I am slain!—If thou be
    merciful,
Open the tomb, lay me with Juliet. [*Dies.*
ROM. In faith, I will.—Let me peruse
    this face:—
Mercutio's kinsman, noble county Paris!—
What said my man, when my betossed soul
Did not attend him as we rode? I think
He told me, Paris should have married
    Juliet:

Said he not so? or did I dream it so?
Or am I mad, hearing him talk of Juliet,
To think it was so?—O, give me thy hand,
One writ with me in sour misfortune's
    book!
I'll bury thee in a triumphant grave,—
A grave? O, no, a lantern, slaughter'd
    youth;
For here lies Juliet, and her beauty makes
This vault a feasting presence full of light.
Death, lie thou there, by a dead man in-
    terr'd.   [Laying Paris in the monument.
How oft, when men are at the point of
    death,
Have they been merry! which their keep-
    ers call
A lightning before death: O, how may I
Call this a lightning?—O my love! my
    wife!   [breath,
Death, that hath suck'd the honey of thy
Hath had no power yet upon thy beauty:
Thou art not conquer'd; beauty's ensign
    yet
Is crimson in thy lips, and in thy cheeks,
And death's pale flag is not advanced
    there.—
Tybalt, liest thou there in thy bloody sheet?
O, what more favour can I do to thee,
Than with that hand that cut thy youth in
    twain,
To sunder his that was thine enemy?
Forgive me, cousin!—Ah, dear Juliet,
Why art thou yet so fair? Shall I believe
That unsubstantial death is amorous;
And that the lean abhorred monster keeps
Thee here in dark to be his paramour?
For fear of that, I still will stay with thee;
And never from this palace of dim night
Depart again: here, here will I remain
With worms that are thy chamber-maids;
    O, here
Will I set up my everlasting rest;
And shake the yoke of inauspicious stars
From this world-wearied flesh.—Eyes, look
    your last!
Arms, take your last embrace! and, lips,
    O you
The doors of breath, seal with a righteous
    kiss
A dateless bargain to engrossing death!—
Come, bitter conduct, come, unsavoury
    guide!
Thou desperate pilot, now at once run on
The dashing rocks thy sea-sick weary bark!
Here's to my love!—[Drinks.] O true
    apothecary!
Thy drugs are quick.—Thus with a kiss I
    die.   [Dies.
Enter, at the other end of the Church-yard,
    Friar Laurence, with a lantern,
        crow, and spade.

FRI. L. Saint Francis be my speed! how
    oft to-night
Have my old feet stumbled at graves!—
    Who's there?
BAL. [Advancing.] Here's one, a friend,
    and one that knows you well.
FRI. L. Bliss be upon you! Tell me, good
    my friend,
What torch is yond', that vainly lends his
    light
To grubs and eyeless sculls? as I discern,
It burneth in the Capels' monument.
BAL. It doth so, holy Sir; and there's my
One that you love.   [master,
FRI. L.   Who is it?
BAL.   Romeo.
FRI. L. How long hath he been there?
BAL.   Full half an hour.
FRI. L. Go with me to the vault.
BAL.   I dare not, Sir:
My master knows not, but I am gone
    hence;
And fearfully did menace me with death,
If I did stay to look on his intents.
FRI. L. Stay, then, I'll go alone.—Fear
    comes upon me;
O! much I fear some ill unlucky thing.
BAL. As I did sleep under this yew-tree
    here,
I dreamt my master and another fought,
And that my master slew him.
FRI. L. [Approaching the monument.]
    Romeo!—
Alack, alack; what blood is this, which
    stains
The stony entrance of this sepulchre?—
What mean these masterless and gory
    swords
To lie discolour'd by this place of peace?
                    [Enters the monument.
Romeo! O, pale!—Who else? what, Paris
    too?
And steep'd in blood?—Ah, what an un-
    kind hour
Is guilty of this lamentable chance!—
The lady stirs.   [Juliet wakes.
JUL. O, comfortable friar! where is my
    lord?—
I do remember well where I should be,
And there I am:—where is my Romeo?
                        [Noise within.
FRI. L. I hear some noise.—Lady, come
    from that nest
Of death, contagion, and unnatural sleep:
A greater Power than we can contradict
Hath thwarted our intents:—come, come
    away:
Thy husband in thy bosom there lies dead;
And Paris too—come, I'll dispose of thee
Among a sisterhood of holy nuns:

Stay not to question, for the watch is
coming;
Come, go, good Juliet.—[*Noise again.*] I
dare no longer stay.
JUL. Go, get thee hence, for I will not
away.—   [*Exit* Fri. L.
What's here? a cup, clos'd in my true
love's hand?
Poison, I see, hath been his timeless
end:—
O churl! drink all, and leave no friendly
drop,
To help me after?—I will kiss thy lips;
Haply, some poison yet doth hang on them,
To make me die with a restorative.
Thy lips are warm!   [*Kisses him.*
1 *WATCH.* [*Within.*] Lead, boy:—which
way?
JUL. Yea, noise?—then I'll be brief.—
O happy dagger!
                [*Snatching* Romeo's *dagger.*
This is thy sheath; [*Stabs herself.*] there
rest, and let me die.
          [*Falls on* Romeo's *body, and dies.*
Enter Watch, *with the* Page *of* Paris.
PAGE. This is the place; there, where the
torch doth burn.
1 *WATCH.* The ground is bloody; search
about the church-yard:
Go, some of you; whoe'er you find, attach.
                [*Exeunt some of the* Watch.
Pitiful sight! here lies the county slain;—
And Juliet bleeding; warm, and newly
dead,
Who here hath lain these two days bur-
ied.—
Go, tell the Prince,—run to the Capulets,—
Raise up the Montagues,—some others
search:—   [*Exeunt other of the* Watch.
We see the ground whereon these woes do
lie;
But the true ground of all these piteous
woes,
We cannot without circumstance descry.
    Re-enter some of the Watch, *with*
                BALTHASAR.
2 *WATCH.* Here's Romeo's man; we
found him in the church-yard.
1 *WATCH.* Hold him in safety, till the
Prince come hither.
    Re-enter other of the Watch, *with*
                FRIAR LAURENCE.
3 *WATCH.* Here is a friar, that trembles,
sighs, and weeps:
We took this mattock and this spade from
him,
As he was coming from this church-yard
side.
1 *WATCH.* A great suspicion: stay the
friar too.

Enter the PRINCE *and* Attendants.
PRINCE. What misadventure is so early
up,   [rest?
That calls our person from our morning's
Enter CAPULET, LADY CAPULET, *and others.*
CAP. What should it be, that they so
shriek abroad?
LA. CAP. The people in the street cry
Romeo,
Some Juliet, and some Paris; and all run,
With open outcry, toward our monument.
PRINCE. What fear is this, which startles
in our ears?
1 *WATCH.* Sovereign, here lies the coun-
ty Paris slain;
And Romeo dead; and Juliet, dead before,
Warm and new kill'd.
PRINCE. Search, seek, and know how
this foul murder comes.
1 *WATCH.* Here is a friar, and slaugh-
ter'd Romeo's man;
With instruments upon them, fit to open
These dead men's tombs.
CAP. O, heaven!—O wife, look how our
daughter bleeds!
This dagger hath mista'en,—for, lo, his
house
Is empty on the back of Montague,—
And is mis-sheathed in my daughter's
bosom.
LA. CAP. O me! this sight of death is
as a bell,
That warns my old age to a sepulchre.
          Enter MONTAGUE *and others.*
PRINCE. Come, Montague; for thou art
early up,
To see thy son and heir more early down.
MON. Alas, my liege, my wife is dead
to-night:
Grief of my son's exile hath stopp'd her
breath:
What farther woe conspires against mine
age?
PRINCE. Look, and thou shalt see.
MON. O thou untaught! what manners is
in this,
To press before thy father to a grave?
PRINCE. Seal up the mouth of outrage
for a while,
Till we can clear these ambiguities,
And know their spring, their head, their
true descent;
And then will I be general of your woes,
And lead you even to death: meantime
forbear,
And let mischance be slave to patience.—
Bring forth the parties of suspicion.
FRI. L. I am the greatest, able to do least,
Yet most suspected, as the time and place
Doth make against me, of this direful mur-
der;

And here I stand, both to impeach and
purge
Myself condemned, and myself excus'd.
PRINCE. Then say at once what thou
dost know in this.
FRI. L. I will be brief, for my short date
of breath
Is not so long as is a tedious tale.
Romeo, there dead, was husband to that
Juliet;   [ful wife:
And she, there dead, that Romeo's faith-
I married them; and their stolen marriage-
day   [death
Was Tybalt's dooms-day, whose untimely
Banish'd the new-made bridegroom from
this city;
For whom, and not for Tybalt, Juliet pin'd.
You, to remove that siege of grief from her,
Betroth'd, and would have married her
perforce,
To county Paris:—then comes she to me;
And, with wild looks, bid me devise some
means
To rid her from this second marriage,
Or in my cell there would she kill herself.
Then gave I her, (so tutor'd by my art)
A sleeping potion; which so took effect
As I intended, for it wrought on her
The form of death: meantime I writ to
Romeo,   [night,
That he should hither come, as this dire
To help to take her from her borrow'd
grave,   [cease.
Being the time the potion's force should
But he which bore my letter, friar John,
Was stay'd by accident; and yesternight
Return'd my letter back. Then, all alone,
At the prefixed hour of her waking,
Came I to take her from her kindred's
vault;
Meaning to keep her closely at my cell,
Till I conveniently could send to Romeo:
But, when I came, (some minute ere the
time
Of her awakening) here untimely lay
The noble Paris, and true Romeo, dead.
She wakes; and I entreated her come forth,
And bear this work of heaven with pa-
tience: [tomb;
But then a noise did scare me from the
And she, too desperate, would not go with
me,
But (as it seems) did violence on herself.
All this I know; and to the marriage
Her nurse is privy: and, if aught in this
Miscarried by my fault, let my old life
Be sacrific'd, some hour before his time,
Unto the rigour of severest law.
PRINCE. We still have known thee for a
holy man.—   [in this?
Where's Romeo's man? what can he say

BAL. I brought my master news of Ju-
liet's death;
And then in post he came from Mantua,
To this same place, to this same monu-
ment.
This letter he early bid me give his father;
And threaten'd me with death, going in the
vault,
If I departed not, and left him there.
PRINCE. Give me the letter,—I will look
on it.—
Where is the county's page, that rais'd the
watch?—
Sirrah, what made your master in this
place?
PAGE. He came with flowers to strew his
lady's grave;
And bid me stand aloof, and so I did:
Anon, comes one with light to ope the
tomb;
And, by and by, my master drew on him;
And then I ran away to call the watch.
PRINCE. This letter doth make good the
friar's words,
Their course of love, the tidings of her
death:
And here he writes, that he did buy a
poison
Of a poor 'pothecary; and therewithal
Came to this vault to die, and lie with
Juliet.—   [tague,—
Where be these enemies?—Capulet,—Mon-
See, what a scourge is laid upon your hate,
That heaven finds means to kill your joys
with love!
And I, for winking at your discords too,
Have lost a brace of kinsmen:—all are
punish'd.
CAP. O brother Montague, give me thy
hand:
This is my daughter's jointure, for no more
Can I demand.
MON.   But I can give thee more:
For I will raise her statue in pure gold;
That, while Verona by that name is known,
There shall no figure at such rate be set,
As that of true and faithful Juliet,
CAP. As rich shall Romeo by his lady
Poor sacrifices of our enmity!   [lie;
PRINCE. A glooming peace this morning
with it brings;
The sun, for sorrow, will not show his
head:
Go hence, to have more talk of these sad
things;
Some shall be pardon'd, and some pun-
ished:
For never was a story of more woe,
Than this of Juliet and her Romeo.
                                        [*Exeunt.*

The death of Cæsar. Act III. S. 1.

JULIUS CAESAR

DRAMATIS PERSONÆ.

JULIUS CÆSAR.
OCTAVIUS CÆSAR, }
MARCUS ANTONIUS, } *Triumvirs, after the*
M. ÆMIL. LEPIDUS, } *Death of*
} JULIUS CÆSAR.
CICERO, PUBLIUS, } *Senators.*
POPILIUS LENA, }
MARCUS BRUTUS, ⎫
CASSIUS, ⎪
CASCA, ⎪
TREBONIUS, ⎬ *Conspirators against*
LIGARIUS, ⎪ JULIUS
DECIUS BRUTUS, ⎪ CÆSAR.
METELLUS CIMBER, ⎪
CINNA, ⎭

FLAVIUS *and* MARULLUS, *Tribunes.*
ARTEMIDORUS, *a Sophist of* Cnidos.
A Soothsayer.
CINNA, *a Poet. Another* Poet.
LUCILIUS, TITINIUS, MESSALA, *Young* CATO,
    and VOLUMNIUS; *Friends to* BRUTUS *and*
    CASSIUS.
VARRO, CLITUS, CLAUDIUS, STRATO, LUCIUS,
    DARDANIUS; *Servants to* BRUTUS.
PINDARUS, *Servant to* CASSIUS.

CALPHURNIA, *Wife to* CÆSAR.
PORTIA, *Wife to* BRUTUS.

Senators, Citizens, Guards, Attendants, &c.

SCENE,—*During a great part of the Play,* at ROME: *afterwards at* SARDIS *and near*
    PHILIPPI.

ACT I.

SCENE I.—ROME. *A Street.*

Enter FLAVIUS, MARULLUS, *and a throng of*
    Citizens.

FLA. Hence! home, you idle creatures,
    get you home:
Is this a holiday? What! know you not,
Being mechanical, you ought not walk
Upon a labouring day without the sign

Of your profession?—Speak, what trade
    art thou?
1 *CIT.* Why, Sir, a carpenter.
MAR. Where is thy leather apron, and
    thy rule?
What dost thou with thy best apparel
You, Sir, what trade are you?   [on?—
2 *CIT.* Truly, Sir, in respect of a fine
    workman, I am but, as you would say, a
    cobbler.

373

MAR. But what trade art thou? Answer me directly.

2 CIT. A trade Sir, that, I hope, I may use with a safe conscience; which is, indeed, Sir, a mender of bad soles.

MAR. What trade, thou knave? thou naughty knave, what trade?

2 CIT. Nay, I beseech you, Sir, be not out with me: yet, if you be out, Sir, I can mend you.

MAR. What meanest thou by that? Mend me, thou saucy fellow!

2 CIT. Why, Sir, cobble you.

FLAV. Thou art a cobbler, art thou?

2 CIT. Truly, Sir, all that I live by is, with the awl: I meddle with no tradesman's matters, nor women's matters, but with awl. I am, indeed, Sir, a surgeon to old shoes; when they are in great danger, I recover them. As proper men as ever trod upon neats-leather have gone upon my handywork.

FLAV. But wherefore art not in thy shop to-day?
Why dost thou lead these men about the streets?

2 CIT. Truly, Sir, to wear out their shoes, to get myself into more work. But, indeed, Sir, we make holiday to see Cæsar, and to rejoice in his triumph.

MAR. Wherefore rejoice? What conquest brings he home?
What tributaries follow him to Rome,
To grace in captive bonds his chariot wheels?
You blocks, you stones, you worse than senseless things!
O you hard hearts, you cruel men of Rome,
Knew you not Pompey? Many a time and oft
Have you climb'd up to walls and battlements,
To towers and windows, yea, to chimneytops,
Your infants in your arms, and there have sat
The live-long day, with patient expectation,
To see great Pompey pass the streets of Rome:
And when you saw his chariot but appear,
Have you not made a universal shout,
That Tiber trembled underneath her banks,
To hear the replication of your sounds
Made in her concave shores?
And do you now put on your best attire?
And do you now cull out a holiday?
And do you now strew flowers in his way,
That comes in triumph over Pompey's blood?
Be gone!
Run to your houses, fall upon your knees,

Pray to the gods to intermit the plague
That needs must light on this ingratitude.

FLAV. Go, go, good countrymen, and, for this fault,
Assemble all the poor men of your sort;
Draw them to Tiber banks, and weep your tears
Into the channel, till the lowest stream
Do kiss the most exalted shores of all.—
           [*Exeunt* Citizens.
See, whe'r their basest metal be not mov'd;
They vanish tongue-tied in their guiltiness.
Go you down that way towards the Capitol;
This way will I: disrobe the images,
If you do find them deck'd with ceremonies.

MAR. May we do so?
You know it is the feast of Lupercal.

FLAV. It is no matter; let no images
Be hung with Cæsar's trophies. I'll about,
And drive away the vulgar from the streets:
So do you too, where you perceive them thick.
These growing feathers pluck'd from Cæsar's wing,
Will make him fly an ordinary pitch;
Who else would soar above the view of men,
And keep us all in servile fearfulness.
           [*Exeunt.*

SCENE II.—ROME. *A public Place.*

Enter, in procession, with music, CÆSAR; ANTONY, *for the course;* CALPHURNIA, PORTIA, DECIUS, CICERO, BRUTUS, CASSIUS, *and* CASCA; *a great crowd following, among them a* Soothsayer.

CÆS. Calphurnia,—

CASCA.   Peace, ho! Cæsar speaks.
           [*Music ceases.*

CÆS.   Calphurnia,—

CAL. Here, my lord.

CÆS. Stand you directly in Antonius' way,
When he doth run his course.—Antonius.

ANT. Cæsar, my lord?

CÆS. Forget not, in your speed, Antonius,
To touch Calphurnia; for our elders say,
The barren, touched in this holy chase,
Shake off their sterile curse.

ANT.   I shall remember:
When Cæsar says, "Do this," it is perform'd.

CÆS. Set on; and leave no ceremony out.
           [*Music.*

SOOTH. Cæsar!

CÆS. Ha! Who calls?

CASCA. Bid every noise be still:—peace yet again!   [*Music ceases.*

CÆS. Who is it in the press that calls on me?
I hear a tongue, shriller than all the music,

Cry, "Cæsar." Speak; Cæsar is turn'd to
  hear.
SOOTH. Beware the ides of March.
CÆS.   What man is that?
BRU. A soothsayer bids you beware the
  ides of March.
CÆS. Set him before me; let me see his
  face.
CAS. Fellow, come from the throng; look
  upon Cæsar.
CÆS. What say'st thou to me now? Speak
  once again.
SOOTH. Beware the ides of March.
CÆS. He is a dreamer; let us leave him:
  —pass.
  [*Sennet. Exeunt all except* BRU. *and* CAS.
CAS. Will you go see the order of the
  course?
BRU. Not I.
CAS. I pray you, do.
BRU. I am not gamesome: I do lack some
  part
Of that quick spirit that is in Antony.
Let me not hinder, Cassius, your desires;
I'll leave you.
CAS. Brutus, I do observe you now of
  late:
I have not from your eyes that gentleness,
And show of love, as I was wont to have:
You bear too stubborn and too strange a
  hand
Over your friend that loves you.
BRU.   Cassius,
Be not deceiv'd: if I have veil'd my look,
I turn the trouble of my countenance
Merely upon myself. Vexed I am,
Of late, with passions of some difference,
Conceptions only proper to myself,
Which give some soil, perhaps, to my be-
  haviours;
But let not therefore my good friends be
  griev'd,
(Among which number, Cassius, be you
  one)
Nor construe any farther my neglect,
Than that poor Brutus, with himself at
  war,
Forgets the shows of love to other men.
CAS. Then, Brutus, I have much mistook
  your passion;
By means whereof, this breast of mine hath
  buried
Thoughts of great value, worthy cogitations.
Tell me, good Brutus, can you see your
  face?
BRU. No, Cassius; for the eye sees not
  itself,
But by reflection, by some other things.
CAS. 'Tis just:
And it is very much lamented, Brutus,
That you have no such mirrors as will turn

Your hidden worthiness into your eye,
That you might see your shadow. I have
  heard,
Where many of the best respect in Rome,
(Except immortal Cæsar) speaking of
  Brutus,
And groaning underneath this age's yoke,
Have wish'd that noble Brutus had his eyes.
BRU. Into what dangers would you lead
  me, Cassius,
That you would have me seek into myself
For that which is not in me?
CAS. Therefore, good Brutus, be prepar'd
  to hear:
And, since you know you cannot see your-
  self
So well as by reflection, I, your glass,
Will modestly discover to yourself
That of yourself which you yet know not of.
And be not jealous on me, gentle Brutus:
Were I a common laugher, or did use
To stale with ordinary oaths my love
To every new protester; if you know
That I do fawn on men, and hug them
  hard,
And after scandal them; or if you know
That I profess myself, in banqueting,
To all the rout, then hold me dangerous.
                         [*Flourish, and shout.*
BRU. What means this shouting? I do
  fear, the people
Choose Cæsar for their king.
CAS.   Ay, do you fear it?
Then must I think you would not have it so.
BRU. I would not, Cassius; yet I love him
  well.—
But wherefore do you hold me here so long?
What is it that you would impart to me?
If it be aught toward the general good,
Set honour in one eye, and death i' the
  other,
And I will look on both indifferently;
For, let the gods so speed me, as I love
The name of honour more than I fear death.
CAS. I know that virtue to be in you,
  Brutus,
As well as I do know your outward favour.
Well, honour is the subject of my story.—
I cannot tell what you and other men
Think of this life; but, for my single self,
I had as lief not be, as live to be
In awe of such a thing as I myself.
I was born free as Cæsar; so were you:
We both have fed as well; and we can both
Endure the winter's cold as well as he:
For once, upon a raw and gusty day,
The troubled Tiber chafing with her shores,
Cæsar said to me, "Dar'st thou, Cassius, now
Leap in with me into this angry flood,
And swim to yonder point?" Upon the
  word,

Accoutred as I was, I plunged in,
And bade him follow: so, indeed, he did.
The torrent roar'd; and we did buffet it
With lusty sinews, throwing it aside,
And stemming it, with hearts of contro-
  versy:
But ere we could arrive the point propos'd,
Cæsar cried, "Help me, Cassius, or I sink!"
I, as Æneas, our great ancestor,
Did from the flames of Troy upon his
  shoulder
The old Anchises bear, so from the waves
  of Tiber
Did I the tired Cæsar: and this man
Is now become a god; and Cassius is
A wretched creature, and must bend his
  body,
If Cæsar carelessly but nod on him.
He had a fever when he was in Spain,
And, when the fit was on him, I did mark
How he did shake: 'tis true, this god did
  shake:
His coward lips did from their colour fly;
And that same eye, whose bend doth awe
  the world,
Did lose his lustre: I did hear him groan:
Ay, and that tongue of his, that bade the
  Romans
Mark him, and write his speeches in their
  books,
Alas, it cried, "Give me some drink,
  Titinius,"
As a sick girl. Ye gods, it doth amaze me,
A man of such a feeble temper should
So get the start of the majestic world,
And bear the palm alone.
                    [*Flourish, and shout.*
BRU.   Another general shout!
I do believe that these applauses are
For some new honours that are heap'd on
  Cæsar.
CAS. Why, man, he doth bestride the nar-
  row world,
Like a Colossus; and we petty men
Walk under his huge legs, and peep about
To find ourselves dishonourable graves.
Men at some time are masters of their fates:
The fault, dear Brutus, is not in our stars,
But in ourselves, that we are underlings.
Brutus, and Cæsar: what should be in that
  Cæsar?
Why should that name be sounded more
  than yours?
Write them together, yours is as fair a
  name;
Sound them, it doth become the mouth as
  well;
Weigh them, it is as heavy; conjure with
  them,
Brutus will start a spirit as soon as Cæsar.
Now, in the names of all the gods at once,

Upon what meat doth this our Cæsar feed,
That he is grown so great? Age, thou art
  sham'd!
Rome, thou hast lost the breed of noble
  bloods!
When went there by an age, since the great
  flood,
But it was fam'd with more than with one
  man?
When could they say, till now, that talk'd
  of Rome,
That her wide walls encompass'd but one
  man?
Now is it Rome indeed, and room enough,
When there is in it but one only man.
O, you and I have heard our fathers say,
There was a Brutus once, that would have
  brook'd
Th' eternal devil to keep his state in Rome,
As easily as a king.
BRU. That you do love me, I am nothing
  jealous;
What you would work me to, I have some
  aim:
How I have thought of this, and of these
  times,
I shall recount hereafter; for this present,
I would not, so with love I might entreat
  you,
Be any farther mov'd. What you have said,
I will consider; what you have to say,
I will with patience hear; and find a time
Both meet to hear, and answer, such high
  things.
Till then, my noble friend, chew upon this;
Brutus had rather be a villager,
Than to repute himself a son of Rome
Under these hard conditions, as this time
Is like to lay upon us.
CAS.   I am glad that my weak words
Have struck but thus much show of fire
  from Brutus.
BRU. The games are done, and Cæsar is
  returning.   [*sleeve,*
CAS. As they pass by, pluck Casca by the
And he will, after his sour fashion, tell you
What hath proceeded, worthy note, to-day.

          Re-enter CÆSAR *and his train.*

BRU. I will do so:—but, look you, Cassius,
The angry spot doth glow on Cæsar's brow,
And all the rest look like a chidden train:
Calphurnia's cheek is pale; and Cicero
Looks with such ferret and such fiery eyes,
As we have seen him in the Capitol,
Being cross'd in conference by some sen-
  ators.
CAS. Casca will tell us what the matter is.
CÆS. Antonius,—
ANT. Cæsar?   [fat;
CÆS. Let me have men about me that are

Sleek-headed men, and such as sleep o'
nights:
Yond' Cassius has a lean and hungry look;
He thinks too much: such men are danger-
ous;   [gerous;
ANT. Fear him not, Cæsar; he's not dan-
He is a noble Roman, and well given.
CÆS. 'Would he were fatter! but I fear
him not:
Yet if my name were liable to fear,
I do not know the man I should avoid
So soon as that spare Cassius. He reads
much;
He is a great observer, and he looks
Quite through the deeds of men: he loves no
plays,
As thou dost, Antony; he hears no music:
Seldom he smiles; and smiles in such a sort,
As if he mock'd himself, and scorn'd his
spirit
That could be mov'd to smile at any thing.
Such men as he be never at heart's ease,
Whiles they behold a greater than them-
selves;
And therefore are they very dangerous.
I rather tell thee what is to be fear'd,
Than what I fear,—for always I am Cæsar.
Come on my right hand, for this ear is deaf,
And tell me truly what thou think'st of him.
 [Exeunt Cæsar and his train. Casca
  stays behind.
CASCA. You pull'd me by the cloak;
would you speak with me?
BRU. Ay, Casca; tell us what hath chanc'd
That Cæsar looks so sad.   [today,
CASCA. Why, you were with him, were
you not?
BRU. I should not, then, ask Casca what
had chanc'd.
CASCA. Why, there was a crown offered
him: and, being offered him, he put it by
with the back of his hand, thus; and then
the people fell a shouting.
BRU. What was the second noise for?
CASCA. Why, for that too.
CAS. They shouted thrice: what was the
last cry for?
CASCA. Why, for that too.
BRU. Was the crown offer'd him thrice?
CASCA. Ay, marry, was't, and he put it
by thrice, every time gentler than other;
and at every putting by mine honest neigh-
bours shouted.
CAS. Who offered him the crown?
CASCA. Why, Antony.
BRU. Tell us the manner of it, gentle
Casca.
CASCA. I can as well be hanged, as tell
the manner of it: it was mere foolery; I
did not mark it. I saw Mark Antony offer
him a crown;—yet 'twas not a crown

neither, 'twas one of these coronets;—and,
as I told you, he put it by once: but, for
all that, to my thinking, he would fain have
had it. Then he offered it to him again;
then he put it by again: but, to my thinking,
he was very loath to lay his fingers off it.
And then he offered it the third time: he
put it the third time by; and still as he
refused it, the rabblement hooted, and
clapped their chopped hands, and threw up
their sweaty nightcaps, and uttered such a
deal of stinking breath, because Cæsar refused the crown, that it had almost choked
Cæsar; for he swooned, and fell down at
it: and for mine own part, I durst not
laugh, for fear of opening my lips, and receiving the bad air.
CAS. But, soft, I pray you: what, did
Cæsar swoon?
CASCA. He fell down in the market-place,
and foamed at mouth, and was speechless.
BRU. 'Tis very like,—he hath the falling-
sickness.
CAS. No, Cæsar hath it not; but you, and I,
And honest Casca, we have the falling-
sickness.
CASCA. I know not what you mean by
that; but, I am sure, Cæsar fell down. If
the tag-rag people did not clap him and
hiss him, according as he pleased and dis-
pleased them, as they use to do the players
in the theatre, I am no true man.
BRU. What said he, when he came unto
himself?
CASCA. Marry, before he fell down, when
he perceiv'd the common herd was glad he
refused the crown, he plucked me ope his
doublet, and offered them his throat to cut:
—an I had been a man of any occupation,
if I would not have taken him at a word,
I would I might go to hell among the
rogues:—and so he fell. When he came to
himself again, he said, if he had done or
said any thing amiss, he desired their worships to think it was his infirmity. Three
or four wenches, where I stood, cried,
"Alas, good soul!" and forgave him with
all their hearts; but there's no heed to be
taken of them; if Cæsar had stabbed their
mothers, they would have done no less.
BRU. And after that, he came, thus sad,
away?
CASCA. Ay.
CAS. Did Cicero say any thing?
CASCA. Ay, he spoke Greek.
CAS. To what effect?
CASCA. Nay, an I tell you that, I'll ne'er
look you i' the face again: but those that
understood him smiled at one another, and
shook their heads; but, for mine own part,
it was Greek to me. I could tell you more

news, too: Marullus and Flavius, for pulling
scarfs off Cæsar's images, are put to silence.
Fare you well. There was more foolery yet,
if I could remember it.

CAS. Will you sup with me to-night, Casca?

CASCA. No, I am promised forth.

CAS. Will you dine with me to-morrow?

CASCA. Ay, if I be alive, and your mind
hold, and your dinner worth the eating.

CAS. Good; I will expect you.

CASCA. Do so: farewell, both.   [*Exit.*

BRU. What a blunt fellow is this grown
to be!
He was quick mettle when he went to school.

CAS. So is he now, in execution
Of any bold or noble enterprise,
However he puts on this tardy form.
This rudeness is a sauce to his good wit,
Which gives men stomach to digest his
words
With better appetite.

BRU. And so it is. For this time I will
leave you:
To-morrow, if you please to speak with me,
I will come home to you; or, if you will,
Come home to me, and I will wait for you.

CAS. I will do so:—till then, think of the
world.   [*Exit* BRUTUS.
Well, Brutus, thou art noble; yet, I see,
Thy honourable metal may be wrought
From that it is dispos'd: therefore 'tis meet
That noble minds keep ever with their likes;
For who so firm that cannot be seduc'd?
Cæsar doth bear me hard; but he loves
Brutus:
If I were Brutus now, and he were Cassius,
He should not humour me. I will this night,
In several hands, in at his windows throw,
As if they came from several citizens,
Writings, all tending to the great opinion
That Rome holds of his name; wherein
obscurely
Cæsar's ambition shall be glanced at:
And, after this, let Cæsar seat him sure;
For we will shake him, or worse days en-
dure.   [*Exit.*

Scene III.—Rome. *A Street.*

*Thunder and lightning. Enter, from oppo-
site sides,* Casca, *with his sword drawn,
and* Cicero.

CIC. Good even, Casca: brought you
Cæsar home?   [so?

Why are you breathless? and why stare you

CASCA. Are not you mov'd, when all the
sway of earth
Shakes like a thing unfirm? O Cicero,
I have seen tempests, when the scolding
winds
Have riv'd the knotty oaks; and I have seen

The ambitious ocean swell, and rage, and
foam,
To be exalted with the threatening clouds:
But never till to-night, never till now,
Did I go through a tempest dropping fire.
Either there is a civil strife in heaven;
Or else the world, too saucy with the gods,
Incenses them to send destruction.

CIC. Why, saw you any thing more wonderful?

CASCA. A common slave (you know him
well by sight)
Held up his left hand, which did flame and
burn
Like twenty torches join'd; and yet his hand,
Not sensible of fire, remain'd unscorch'd.
Besides, (I have not since put up my sword)
Against the Capitol I met a lion,
Who glar'd upon me, and went surly by,
Without annoying me: and there were
drawn
Upon a heap a hundred ghastly women,
Transformed with their fear; who swore
they saw
Men, all in fire, walk up and down the
streets.
And yesterday the bird of night did sit,
Even at noon-day, upon the market-place,
Hooting and shrieking. When these prod-
igies
Do so conjointly meet, let not men say,
"These are their reasons,—they are nat-
ural;"
For, I believe, they are portentous things
Upon the climate that they point upon.

CIC. Indeed, it is a strange-disposed time:
But men may construe things after their
fashion,
Clean from the purpose of the things them-
selves.
Comes Cæsar to the Capitol to-morrow?

CASCA. He doth; for he did bid Antonius
Send word to you, he would be there to-
morrow.

CIC. Good night, then, Casca: this dis-
turbed sky
Is not to walk in.

CASCA.   Farewell, Cicero. [*Exit* CICERO.
          Enter Cassius.

CAS. Who's there?

CASCA.   A Roman.

CAS.   Casca, by your voice.

CASCA. Your ear is good. Cassius, what
night is this?

CAS. A very pleasing night to honest men.

CASCA. Who ever knew the heavens menace so?

CAS. Those that have known the earth so
full of faults.
For my part, I have walk'd about the streets,
Submitting me unto the perilous night;

And, thus unbraced, Casca, as you see,
Have bar'd my bosom to the thunder-stone:
And, when the cross blue lightning seem'd
    to open
The breast of heaven, I did present myself
Even in the aim and very flash of it.
CASCA. But wherefore did you so much
    tempt the heavens?
It is the part of men to fear and tremble,
When the most mighty gods, by tokens, send
Such dreadful heralds to astonish us.
CAS. You are dull, Casca; and those sparks
    of life
That should be in a Roman you do want,
Or else you use not. You look pale, and
    gaze,   [der,
And put on fear, and cast yourself in won-
To see the strange impatience of the
    heavens:
But if you would consider the true cause
Why all these fires, why all these gliding
    ghosts,   [kind,
Why birds and beasts, from quality and
Why old men, fools, and children calculate;
Why all these things change, from their
    ordinance,
Their natures, and pre-formed faculties,
To monstrous quality;—why, you shall find
That heaven hath infus'd them with these
    spirits,   [warning
To make them instruments of fear and
Unto some monstrous state.
Now could I, Casca, name to thee a man
Most like this dreadful night;
That thunders, lightens, opens graves and
    roars
As doth the lion in the Capitol,—
A man no mightier than thyself, or me,
In personal action; yet prodigious grown,
And fearful, as these strange eruptions are.
CASCA. 'Tis Cæsar that you mean; is it
    not, Cassius?
CAS. Let it be who it is: for Romans now
Have thewes and limbs like to their an-
    cestors;   [dead,
But, woe the while! our fathers' minds are
And we are govern'd with our mothers'
    spirits;   [ish.
Our yoke and sufferance show us woman-
CASCA. Indeed, they say, the senators to-
    morrow
Mean to establish Cæsar as a king;
And he shall wear his crown by sea and
    land,
In every place, save here in Italy.
CAS. I know where I will wear this dagger,
    then;
Cassius from bondage will deliver Cassius:
Therein, ye gods, you make the weak most
    strong;
Therein, ye gods, you tyrants do defeat:

Nor stony tower, nor walls of beaten brass,
Nor airless dungeon, nor strong links of
    iron,
Can be retentive to the strength of spirit;
But life, being weary of these worldly bars,
Never lacks power to dismiss itself.
If I know this, know all the world besides,
That part of tyranny, that I do bear,
I can shake off at pleasure. [Thunder still.
CASCA.   So can I:
So every bondman in his own hand bears
The power to cancel his captivity.
CAS. And why should Cæsar be a tyrant,
    then?
Poor man! I know he would not be a wolf,
But that he sees the Romans are but sheep:
He were no lion, were not Romans hinds.
Those that with haste will make a mighty
    fire,   [Rome,
Begin it with weak straws: what trash is
What rubbish, and what offal, when it serves
For the base matter to illuminate
So vile a thing as Cæsar! But, O grief,
Where hast thou led me? I, perhaps, speak
    this
Before a willing bondman; then I know
My answer must be made: but I am arm'd,
And dangers are to me indifferent.
CASCA. You speak to Casca; and to such
    a man
That is no fleering tell-tale. Hold, my hand:
Be factious for redress of all these griefs;
And I will set this foot of mine as far
As who goes farthest.
CAS.   There's a bargain made.
Now know you, Casca, I have mov'd already
Some certain of the noblest-minded Romans,
To undergo with me an enterprise
Of honourable-dangerous consequence;
And I do know, by this, they stay for me
In Pompey's porch: for now, this fearful
    night,
There is no stir, or walking in the streets;
And the complexion of the element
In favour's like the work we have in hand,
Most bloody, fiery, and most terrible.
CASCA. Stand close awhile, for here comes
    one in haste.
CAS. 'Tis Cinna,—I do know him by his
    gait;
He is a friend.—
                Enter CINNA.
    Cinna, where haste you so?
CIN. To find out you. Who's that? Metel-
    lus Cimber?
CAS. No, it is Casca; one incorporate
To our attempts. Am I not stay'd for, Cinna?
CIN. I am glad on't. What a fearful night
    is this!   [sights.
There's two or three of us have seen strange
CAS. Am I not stay'd for? Tell me.

CIN.   Yes, you are.
O Cassius, if you could but win the noble
    Brutus
To our party—
CAS. Be you content: good Cinna, take
    this paper,
And look you lay it in the prætors chair,
Where Brutus may but find it; and throw
    this
In at his window; set this up with wax
Upon old Brutus' statue: all this done,
Repair to Pompey's porch, where you shall
    find us.
Is Decius Brutus, and Trebonius, there?
CIN. All but Metellus Cimber; and he's
    gone
To seek you at your house. Well, I will hie,
And so bestow these papers as you bade me.
CAS. That done, repair to Pompey's the-
    atre.   [*Exit* CINNA.
Come, Casca, you and I will, yet, ere day,
See Brutus at his house: three parts of him
Is ours already; and the man entire,
Upon the next encounter, yields him ours.
CASCA. O, he sits high in all the people's
    hearts:
And that which would appear offence in us,
His countenance, like richest alchemy,
Will change to virtue and to worthiness.
CAS. Him, and his worth, and our great
    need of him,
You have right well conceited. Let us go,
For it is after midnight; and, ere day,
We will awake him, and be sure of him.
                                    [*Exeunt.*

ACT II.

SCENE I.—ROME. BRUTUS' *Orchard.*

Enter BRUTUS.

BRU. What, Lucius, ho!—
I cannot, by the progress of the stars,
Give guess how near to day.—Lucius, I
    say!—   [ly.
I would it were my fault to sleep so sound-
When, Lucius, when? Awake, I say! what,
    Lucius!

Enter LUCIUS.

LUC. Call'd you, my lord?
BRU. Get me a taper in my study, Lucius:
When it is lighted, come and call me here.
LUC. I will, my lord.   [*Exit.*
BRU. It must be by his death: and, for my
    part,
I know no personal cause to spurn at him,
But for the general. He would be crown'd:—
How that might change his nature, there's
    the question:

It is the bright day that brings forth the
    adder;
And that craves wary walking. Crown him?
    —that;—
And then, I grant, we put a sting in him,
That at his will he may do danger with.
Th' abuse of greatness is, when it disjoins
Remorse from power: and, to speak truth of
    Cæsar,
I have not known when his affections
    sway'd
More than his reason. But 'tis a common
    proof,
That lowliness is young ambition's ladder,
Whereto the climber-upward turns his face;
But when he once attains the upmost round,
He then unto the latter turns his back,
Looks in the clouds, scorning the base de-
    grees
By which he did ascend: so Cæsar may;
Then, lest he may, prevent. And, since the
    quarrel
Will bear no colour for the thing he is,
Fashion it thus; that what he is, augmented,
Would run to these and these extremities:
And therefore think him as a serpent's egg,
Which, hatch'd, would, as his kind, grow
    mischievous;
And kill him in the shell.

Re-enter LUCIUS.

LUC. The taper burneth in your closet, Sir.
Searching the window for a flint, I found
              [*Giving him a letter.*
This paper, thus seal'd up; and, I am sure,
It did not lie there when I went to bed.
BRU. Get you to bed again; it is not day.
Is not to-morrow, boy, the ides of March?
LUC. I know not, Sir.
BRU. Look in the calendar, and bring me
    word.
LUC. I will, sir.   [*Exit.*
BRU. The exhalations, whizzing in the air,
Give so much light, that I may read by
    them.   [*Opens the letter, and reads.*
"Brutus, thou sleep'st: awake, and see thy-
    self.
Shall Rome, &c. Speak, strike, redress!
Brutus, thou sleep'st: awake!"—
Such instigations have been often dropp'd
Where I have took them up.
"Shall Rome, &c." Thus must I piece it
    out;
Shall Rome stand under one man's awe?
    What, Rome?
My ancestors did from the streets of Rome
The Tarquin drive, when he was call'd a
    king.
"Speak, strike, redress!"—Am I entreated
To speak, and strike? O Rome, I make thee
    promise,

If the redress will follow, thou receiv'st
Thy full petition at the hand of Brutus!
Re-enter LUCIUS.
LUC. Sir, March is wasted fourteen days.
                        [*Knocking within.*
BRU. 'Tis good. Go to the gate; some-
  body knocks.   [*Exit* LUCIUS.
Since Cassius first did whet me against
  Cæsar,
I have not slept.
Between the acting of a dreadful thing
And the first motion, all the interim is
Like a phantasma, or a hideous dream:
The Genius, and the mortal instruments,
Are then in council; and the state of man,
Like to a little kingdom, suffers then
The nature of an insurrection.
Re-enter LUCIUS.
LUC. Sir, 'tis your brother Cassius at the
  door,
Who doth desire to see you.
BRU.   Is he alone?
LUC. No, Sir, there are more with him.
BRU.   Do you know them?
LUC. No, Sir; their hats are pluck'd about
  their ears,
And half their faces buried in their cloaks,
That by no means I may discover them
By any mark of favour.
BRU.   Let them enter.
                        [*Exit* LUCIUS.
They are the faction. O conspiracy,
Sham'st thou to show thy dangerous brow
  by night,
When evils are most free? O, then, by day
Where wilt thou find a cavern dark enough
To mask thy monstrous visage? Seek none,
  conspiracy;
Hide it in smiles and affability:
For if thou path, thy native semblance on,
Not Erebus itself were dim enough
To hide thee from prevention.
Enter CASSIUS, CASCA, DECIUS, CINNA,
  METELLUS CIMBER, *and* TREBONIUS.
CAS. I think we are too bold upon your
  rest:
Good morrow, Brutus; do we trouble you?
BRU. I have been up this hour; awake, all
  night.   [you?
Know I these men that come along with
CAS. Yes, every man of them; and no man
  here,
But honours you; and every one doth wish
You had but that opinion of yourself,
Which every noble Roman bears of you.
This is Trebonius.
BRU.   He is welcome hither.
CAS. This, Decius Brutus.
BRU.   He is welcome too.
CAS. This, Casca; this, Cinna;

And this, Metellus Cimber.
BRU.   They are all welcome.
What watchful cares do interpose them-
  selves
Betwixt your eyes and night?
CAS. Shall I entreat a word?
            [BRUTUS *and* CASSIUS *whisper.*
DEC. Here lies the east: doth not the day
  break here?
CASCA. No.
CIN. O, pardon, Sir, it doth; and yon grey
  lines
That fret the clouds, are messengers of day.
CASCA. You shall confess that you are
  both deceiv'd.
Here, as I point my sword, the sun arises;
Which is a great way growing on the south,
Weighing the youthful season of the year.
Some two months hence, up higher toward
  the north
He first presents his fire; and the high east
Stands, as the Capitol, directly here.
BRU. Give me your hands all over, one by
  one.
CAS. And let us swear our resolution.
BRU. No, not an oath: if not the face of
  men,   [abuse,—
The sufferance of our souls, the time's
If these be motives weak, break off betimes,
And every man hence to his idle bed;
So let high-sighted tyranny range on,
Till each man drop by lottery. But if these,
As I am sure they do, bear fire enough
To kindle cowards, and to steel with valour
The melting spirits of women; then, coun-
  trymen,
What need we any spur, but our own cause,
To prick us to redress? what other bond,
Then secret Romans, that have spoke the
  word,
And will not palter? and what other oath,
Than honesty to honesty engag'd,
That this shall be, or we will fall for it?
Swear priests, and cowards, and men cau-
  telous,
Old feeble carrions, and such suffering souls
That welcome wrongs; unto bad causes
  swear   [stain
Such creatures as men doubt: but do not
The even virtue of our enterprise,
Nor th' insuppressive mettle of our spirits,
To think that or our cause or our perform-
  ance   [blood,
Did need an oath; when every drop of
That every Roman bears, and nobly bears,
Is guilty of a several bastardy,
If he do break the smallest particle
Of any promise that hath pass'd from him.
CAS. But what of Cicero? Shall we sound
  him?

I think he will stand very strong with us.
CASCA. Let us not leave him out.
CIN.   No, by no means.
MET. O, let us have him: for his silver
  hairs
Will purchase us a good opinion,
And buy men's voices to commend our
  deeds: [hands;
It shall be said, his judgment rul'd our
Our youths and wildness shall no whit
  appear,
But all be buried in his gravity.
BRU. O, name him not: let us not break
  with him;
For he will never follow any thing
That other men begin.
CAS.   Then leave him out.
CASCA. Indeed he is not fit.
DEC. Shall no man else be touch'd but
  only Cæsar?   [meet,
CAS. Decius, well urg'd:—I think it is not
Mark Antony, so well belov'd of Cæsar,
Should outlive Cæsar: we shall find of him
A shrewd contriver; and, you know, his
  means,
If he improve them, may well stretch so far
As to annoy us all: which to prevent,
Let Antony and Cæsar fall together.
BRU. Our course will seem too bloody,
  Caius Cassius,
To cut the head off, and then hack the
  limbs,—
Like wrath in death, and envy afterwards;
For Antony is but a limb of Cæsar:
Let us be sacrificers, but not butchers,
  Caius.
We all stand up against the spirit of Cæsar;
And in the spirit of men there is no blood:
O, that we then could come by Cæsar's
  spirit,
And not dismember Cæsar! But, alas,
Cæsar must bleed for it! And, gentle
  friends,
Let's kill him boldly, but not wrathfully;
Let's carve him as a dish fit for the gods,
Not hew him as a carcass fit for hounds:
And let our hearts, as subtle masters do,
Stir up their servants to an act of rage,
And after seem to chide them. This shall
  make
Our purpose necessary, and not envious:
Which so appearing to the common eyes,
We shall be call'd purgers, not murderers.
And, for Mark Antony, think not of him;
For he can do no more than Cæsar's arm,
When Cæsar's head is off.
CAS.   Yet I fear him;
For in the ingrafted love he bears to
  Cæsar,—
BRU. Alas, good Cassius, do not think of
  him:

If he love Cæsar, all that he can do
Is to himself,—take thought, and die for
  Cæsar: [given
And that were much he should; for he is
To sports, to wildness, and much company.
TREB. There is no fear in him; let him
  not die;
For he will live, and laugh at this hereafter.
                            [*Clock strikes.*
BRU. Peace! count the clock.
CAS.   The clock hath stricken three.
TREB. 'Tis time to part.
CAS.   But it is doubtful yet,
Whether Cæsar will come forth to-day, or
  no;
For he is superstitious grown of late;
Quite from the main opinion he held once
Of fantasy, of dreams, and ceremonies:
It may be, these apparent prodigies,
The unaccustom'd terror of this night,
And the persuasion of his augurers,
May hold him from the Capitol to-day.
DEC. Never fear that: if he be so resolv'd,
I can o'ersway him; for he loves to hear
That unicorns may be betrayed with trees,
And bears with glasses, elephants with
  holes,
Lions with toils, and men with flatterers:
But when I tell him he hates flatterers,
He says he does,—being then most flattered.
Let me work;
For I can give his humour the true bent,
And I will bring him to the Capitol.
CAS. Nay, we will all of us be there to
  fetch him.   [most?
BRU. By the eighth hour: is that the utter-
CIN. Be that the uttermost, and fail not
  then.
MET. Caius Ligarius doth bear Cæsar hard,
Who rated him for speaking well of Pom-
  pey:
I wonder none of you have thought of him.
BRU. Now, good Metellus, go along by
  him;   [reasons;
He loves me well, and I have given him
Send him but hither, and I'll fashion him.
CAS. The morning comes upon us: we'll
  leave you, Brutus:—
And, friends, disperse yourselves: but all
  remember   [true Romans.
What you have said, and show yourselves
BRU. Good gentleman, look fresh and
  merrily;
Let not our looks put on our purposes;
But bear it as our Roman actors do,
With untir'd spirits and formal constancy:
And so, good-morrow to you every one.—
                  [*Exeunt all except* BRUTUS.
Boy! Lucius!—Fast asleep? It is no matter;
Enjoy the heavy honey-dew of slumber:
Thou hast no figures, nor no fantasies,

Which busy care draws in the brains of
men;
Therefore thou sleep'st so sound.

Enter PORTIA.

POR.   Brutus, my lord!
BRU. Portia, what mean you? Wherefore
rise you now?
It is not for your health thus to commit
Your weak condition to the raw-cold morn-
ing.
POR. Nor for yours neither. You've un-
gently, Brutus,
Stole from my bed: and yesternight, at
supper,
You suddenly arose, and walk'd about,
Musing and sighing, with your arms across;
And when I ask'd you what the matter was,
You star'd upon me with ungentle looks:
I urg'd you farther; then you scratch'd your
head,
And too impatiently stamp'd with your foot:
Yet I insisted, yet you answer'd not;
But, with an angry wafture of your hand,
Give sign for me to leave you: so I did;
Fearing to strengthen that impatience,
Which seem'd too much enkindled; and,
withal,
Hoping it was but an effect of humour,
Which sometime hath his hour with every
man.
It will not let you eat, nor talk, nor sleep;
And, could it work so much upon your
shape,
As it hath much prevail'd on your condition,
I should not know you, Brutus. Dear my
lord,   [grief.
Make me acquainted with your cause of
BRU. I am not well in health, and that is
all.
POR. Brutus is wise, and were he not in
health,
He would embrace the means to come by it.
BRU. Why, so I do:—good Portia, go to
bed.
POR. Is Brutus sick,—and is it physical
To walk unbraced, and suck up the hu-
mours   [sick,—
Of the dank morning? What, is Brutus
And will he steal out of his wholesome bed,
To dare the vile contagion of the night,
And tempt the rheumy and unpurged air
To add unto his sickness? No, my Brutus;
You have some sick offence within your
mind,
Which, by the right and virtue of my place,
I ought to know of: and, upon my knees,
I charm you, by my once commended beauty,
By all your vows of love, and that great vow
Which did incorporate and make us one,
That you unfold to me, yourself, your half,
Why you are heavy; and what men to-night

Have had resort to you,—for here have been
Some six or seven, who did hide their faces
Even from darkness.
BRU.   Kneel not, gentle Portia.
POR. I should not need, if you were gentle
Brutus.
Within the bond of marriage, tell me,
Brutus,
Is it excepted, I should know no secrets
That appertain to you? Am I yourself
But, as it were, in sort or limitation,—
To keep with you at meals, comfort your
bed,
And talk to you sometimes? Dwell I but
in the suburbs
Of your good pleasure? If it be no more,
Portia is Brutus' harlot, not his wife.
BRU. You are my true and honourable
wife;
As dear to me, as are the ruddy drops
That visit my sad heart.
POR. If this were true, then should I know
this secret.
I grant, I am a woman; but, withal,
A woman that lord Brutus took to wife.
I grant, I am a woman; but, withal,
A woman well-reputed,—Cato's daughter.
Think you, I am no stronger than my sex,
Being so father'd, and so husbanded?
Tell me your counsels, I will not disclose
them:
I have made strong proof of my constancy,
Giving myself a voluntary wound
Here, in the thigh: can I bear that with
patience,
And not my husband's secrets?
BRU.   O ye gods,
Render me worthy of this noble wife!
                              [*Knocking within.*
Hark, hark! one knocks: Portia, go in a
while;
And by and by thy bosom shall partake
The secrets of my heart:
All my engagements I will construe to thee,
All the charactery of my sad brows:—
Leave me with haste.—   [*Exit* PORTIA.
           Lucius, who's that, knocks?

Enter LUCIUS *and* LIGARIUS.

LUC. Here is a sick man, that would speak
with you.
BRU. [*Aside.*] Caius Ligarius, that Metellus
spake of.—
Boy, stand aside.—[*Exit* LUCIUS.] Caius Ligarius,—how!
LIG. Vouchsafe good morrow from a feeble
tongue.
BRU. O, what a time have you chose out,
brave Caius,
To wear a kerchief! Would you were not
sick!

LIG. I am not sick, if Brutus have in hand
Any exploit worthy the name of honour.
BRU. Such an exploit have I in hand, Ligarius,
Had you a healthful ear to hear of it.
LIG. By all the gods that Romans bow before,
I here discard my sickness! Soul of Rome!
Brave son, deriv'd from honourable loins!
Thou, like an exorcist, hast conjur'd up
My mortified spirit. Now bid me run,
And I will strive with things impossible;
Yea, get the better of them. What's to do?
BRU. A piece of work that will make sick men whole.
LIG. But are not some whole that we must make sick?
BRU. That must we also. What it is, my Caius,
I shall unfold to thee, as we are going
To whom it must be done.
LIG.   Set on your foot;
And, with a heart new-fir'd, I follow you,
To do I know not what: but it sufficeth,
That Brutus leads me on.
BRU.   Follow me, then.

SCENE II.—ROME. *A Hall in* CÆSAR'S
Palace.

Thunder and lightning. Enter CÆSAR, *in
his night-gown.*

CÆS. Nor heaven nor earth have been at peace to-night:
Thrice hath Calphurnia in her sleep cried out,
"Help, ho! They murder Cæsar!"—Who's within?

Enter a Servant.

SERV. My lord?
CÆS. Go bid the priests do present sacrifice,
And bring me their opinions of success.
SERV. I will, my lord.   [*Exit.*

Enter CALPHURNIA.

CAL. What mean you, Cæsar? Think you to walk forth?
You shall not stir out of your house to-day.
CÆS. Cæsar shall forth: the things that threaten'd me,   [shall see
Ne'er look'd but on my back; when they
The face of Cæsar, they are vanished.
CAL. Cæsar, I never stood on ceremonies,
Yet now they fright me. There is one within,   [seen,
Besides the things that we have heard and
Recounts most horrid sights seen by the watch.
A lioness hath whelped in the streets;

And graves have yawn'd, and yielded up their dead;
Fierce fiery warriors fight upon the clouds,
In ranks, and squadrons, and right form of war,
Which drizzled blood upon the Capitol;
The noise of battle hurtled in the air,
Horses did neigh, and dying men did groan;
And ghosts did shriek and squeal about the streets.
O Cæsar! these things are beyond all use,
And I do fear them.
CÆS.   What can be avoided,
Whose end is purpos'd by the mighty gods?   [dictions
Yet Cæsar shall go forth; for these pre-
Are to the world in general, as to Cæsar.
CAL. When beggars die, there are no comets seen;
The heavens themselves blaze forth the death of princes.
CÆS. Cowards die many times before their deaths;
The valiant never taste of death but once.
Of all the wonders that I yet have heard,
It seems to me most strange that men should fear;
Seeing that death, a necessary end,
Will come when it will come.
Re-enter Servant.
                               What say the augurers?
SERV. They would not have you to stir forth to-day.
Plucking the entrails of an offering forth,
They could not find a heart within the beast.
CÆS. The gods do this in shame of cowardice:
Cæsar should be a beast without a heart,
If he should stay at home to-day for fear.
No, Cæsar shall not: Danger knows full well
That Cæsar is more dangerous than he:
We are two lions litter'd in one day,
And I the elder and more terrible:—
And Cæsar shall go forth.
CAL.   Alas, my lord,
Your wisdom is consum'd in confidence.
Do not go forth to-day: call it my fear
That keeps you in the house, and not your own.   [house;
We'll send Mark Antony to the senate-
And he shall say you are not well to-day:
Let me, upon my knee, prevail in this.
CÆS. Mark Antony shall say I am not well;
And, for thy humour, I will stay at home.
Enter DECIUS.
Here's Decius Brutus, he shall tell them so.

DEC. Cæsar, all hail! Good morrow,
    worthy Cæsar:
I come to fetch you to the senate-house.
CÆS. And you are come in very happy
    time
To bear my greeting to the senators,
And tell them that I will not come to-day:
Cannot is false; and that I dare not, falser:
I will not come to-day,—tell them so,
    Decius.
CAL. Say he is sick.
CÆS.   Shall Cæsar send a lie?
Have I in conquest stretch'd mine arm so
    far,
To be afeard to tell grey-beards the truth?
Decius, go tell them Cæsar will not come.
DEC. Most mighty Cæsar, let me know
    some cause,
Lest I be laugh'd at when I tell them so.
CÆS. The cause is in my will,—I will
    not come;
That is enough to satisfy the senate.
But, for your private satisfaction,
Because I love you, I will let you know.
Calphurnia here, my wife, stays me at
    home:
She dreamt to-night she saw my statua,
Which, like a fountain with a hundred
    spouts,
Did run pure blood; and many lusty
    Romans
Came smiling, and did bathe their hands
    in it: [and portents,
And these does she apply for warnings,
And evils imminent; and on her knee
Hath begg'd that I will stay at home to-
    day.
DEC. This dream is all amiss interpreted;
It was a vision fair and fortunate:
Your statue spouting blood in many pipes,
In which so many smiling Romans bath'd,
Signifies that from you great Rome shall
    suck   [press
Reviving blood; and that great men shall
For tinctures, stains, relics, and cognizance.
This by Calphurnia's dream is signified.
CÆS. And this way have you well ex-
    pounded it.
DEC. I have, when you have heard what
    I can say:
And know it now: the senate have con-
    cluded
To give this day a crown to mighty Cæsar.
If you shall send them word, you will not
    come,   [a mock
Their minds may change. Besides, it were
Apt to be render'd, for some one to say,
"Break up the senate till another time,
When Cæsar's wife shall meet with better
    dreams."

If Cæsar hide himself, shall they not whis-
"Lo, Cæsar is afraid?"   [per,
Pardon me, Cæsar; for my dear dear love
To your proceeding bids me tell you this;
And reason to my love is liable.
CÆS. How foolish do your fears seem
    now, Calphurnia!
I am ashamed I did yield to them.—
Give me my robe, for I will go:—
Enter PUBLIUS, BRUTUS, LIGARIUS, METEL-
    LUS, CASCA, TREBONIUS, *and* CINNA.
And look where Publius is come to fetch
    me.
PUB. Good morrow, Cæsar.
CÆS.   Welcome, Publius.—
What, Brutus, are you stirr'd so early
    too?—
Good morrow, Casca.—Caius Ligarius,
Cæsar was ne'er so much your enemy
As that same ague which hath made you
What is't o'clock?   [lean.—
BRU.   Cæsar, 'tis strucken eight.
CÆS. I thank you for your pains and
    courtesy.

        Enter ANTONY.
See! Antony, that revels long o' nights,
Is notwithstanding up.—Good morrow,
    Antony.
ANT. So to most noble Cæsar.
CÆS.   Bid them prepare within:—
I am to blame to be thus waited for.—
Now, Cinna:—Now, Metellus:—What,
    Trebonius!
I have an hour's talk in store for you;
Remember that you call on me to-day:
Be near me, that I may remember you.
TREB. Cæsar, I will:—[*Aside.*] and so
    near will I be,
That your best friends shall wish I had
    been farther.
CÆS. Good friends, go in, and taste some
    wine with me;
And we, like friends, will straightway go
    together.
BRU. [*Aside.*] That every like is not the
    same, O Cæsar,
The heart of Brutus yearns to think upon.
                              [*Exeunt.*

        SCENE III.—ROME. *A Street near the
                Capitol.*

Enter ARTEMIDORUS, *reading a paper.*
ART. "Cæsar, beware of Brutus; take
heed of Cassius; come not near Casca;
have an eye to Cinna; trust not Trebonius;
mark well Metellus Cimber; Decius Brutus
loves thee not; thou hast wronged Caius
Ligarius. There is but one mind in all
these men, and it is bent against Cæsar.
If thou be'st not immortal, look about you:

security gives way to conspiracy. The
mighty gods defend thee! Thy lover,
                        ARTEMIDORUS."
Here will I stand till Cæsar pass along,
And as a suitor will I give him this.
My heart laments that virtue cannot live
Out of the teeth of emulation.
If thou read this, O Cæsar, thou may'st
live;
If not, the fates with traitors do contrive.
                              [*Exit.*

SCENE IV.—ROME. *Another Part of the
same Street, before the House of* BRUTUS.

Enter PORTIA *and* LUCIUS.

POR. I pr'ythee, boy, run to the senate-
house;
Stay not to answer me, but get thee gone.
Why dost thou stay?
LUC.   To know my errand, Madam.
POR. I would have had thee there, and
here again,   [there.—
Ere I can tell thee what thou should'st do
O constancy, be strong upon my side!
Set a huge mountain 'tween my heart and
tongue!
I have a man's mind, but a woman's might.
How hard it is for women to keep coun-
Art thou here yet?   [sel!—
LUC.   Madam, what should I do?
Run to the Capitol, and nothing else?
And so return to you, and nothing else?
POR. Yes, bring me word, boy, if thy lord
look well,   [note
For he went sickly forth: and take good
What Cæsar doth, what suitors press to
him.
Hark, boy! what noise is that?
LUC. I hear none, Madam.
POR.   Pr'ythee, listen well!
I heard a bustling rumour, like a fray,
And the wind brings it from the Capitol.
LUC. Sooth, Madam, I hear nothing.

Enter ARTEMIDORUS.

POR.   Come hither, fellow.
Which way hast thou been?
ART.   At mine own house, good lady.
POR. What is't o'clock?
ART.   About the ninth hour, lady.
POR. Is Cæsar yet gone to the Capitol?
ART. Madam, not yet: I go to take my
stand,
To see him pass on to the Capitol.
POR. Thou hast some suit to Cæsar, hast
thou not?
ART. That I have, lady: if it will please
Cæsar
To be so good to Cæsar as to hear me,
I shall beseech him to befriend himself.

POR. Why, know'st thou any harm's in-
tended towards him?
ART. None that I know will be, much
that I fear may chance.
Good morrow to you. Here the street is
narrow:
The throng that follows Cæsar at the heels,
Of senators, of prætors, common suitors,
Will crowd a feeble man almost to death:
I'll get me to a place more void, and there
Speak to great Cæsar as he comes along.
                              [*Exit.*
POR. I must go in.—Ah me, how weak a
thing
The heart of woman is! O Brutus,
The heavens speed thee in thine enter-
prise!—   [suit
Sure, the boy heard me:—Brutus hath a
That Cæsar will not grant.—O, I grow
faint.
Run, Lucius, and commend me to my lord;
Say I am merry: come to me again,
And bring me word what he doth say to
thee.   [*Exeunt severally.*

ACT III.

SCENE I.—ROME. *The* Capitol; *the Senate
sitting.*

*A crowd of people in the street leading to
the Capitol; among them* ARTEMIDORUS
and the Soothsayer. *Flourish. Enter*
CÆSAR, BRUTUS, CASSIUS, CASCA, DECIUS,
METELLUS, TREBONIUS, CINNA, ANTONY,
LEPIDUS, POPILIUS, PUBLIUS, *and others.*

CÆS. The ides of March are come.
SOOTH. Ay, Cæsar; but not gone.
ART. Hail, Cæsar! Read this schedule.
DEC. Trebonius doth desire you to o'er-
read,
At your best leisure, this his humble suit.
ART. O Cæsar, read mine first; for mine's
a suit   [Cæsar.
That touches Cæsar nearer: read it, great
CÆS. What touches us ourself shall be
last serv'd.
ART. Delay not, Cæsar; read it instantly.
CÆS. What, is the fellow mad?
PUB.   Sirrah, give place.
CAS. What, urge you your petitions in
the street?
Come to the Capitol.
CÆSAR *enters the Capitol, the rest follow-
ing. All the* Senators *rise.*
POP. I wish your enterprise to-day may
thrive.
CAS. What enterprise, Popilius?
POP.   Fare you well.
                    [*Advances to* CÆSAR.
BRU. What said Popilius Lena?

CAS. He wish'd to-day our enterprise might thrive.

I fear our purpose is discovered.

BRU. Look, how he makes to Cæsar: mark him.

CAS. Casca, be sudden, for we fear prevention.—

Brutus, what shall be done? If this be known,

Cassius or Cæsar never shall turn back,

For I will slay myself.

BRU. Cassius, be constant:

Popilius Lena speaks not of our purposes;

For, look, he smiles, and Cæsar doth not change.

CAS. Trebonius knows his time; for, look you, Brutus,

He draws Mark Antony out of the way.

[*Exeunt* ANTONY *and* TREBONIUS. CÆSAR *and the* Senators *take their seats.*

DEC. Where is Metellus Cimber? Let him go,

And presently prefer his suit to Cæsar.

BRU. He is address'd: press near and second him.

CIN. Casca, you are the first that rears your hand.

CASCA. Are we all ready?

CÆS.　　　　　What is now amiss,

That Cæsar and his senate must redress?

MET. Most high, most mighty, and most puissant Cæsar,

Metellus Cimber throws before thy seat

A humble heart,—　　　　　　[*Kneeling.*

CÆS.　　　I must prevent thee, Cimber.

These couchings and these lowly courtesies

Might fire the blood of ordinary men,

And turn pre-ordinance and first decree

Into the law of children. Be not fond,

To think that Cæsar bears such rebel blood,

That will be thaw'd from the true quality

With that which melteth fools; I mean, sweet words,

Low-crooked court'sies, and base spaniel fawning.

Thy brother by decree is banished:

If thou dost bend, and pray, and fawn for him,

I spurn thee like a cur out of my way.

Know, Cæsar doth not wrong; nor without cause

Will he be satisfied.　　　　　[*cause

MET. Is there no voice more worthy than my own,　　　　　　[*ear,*

To sound more sweetly in great Cæsar's

For the repealing of my banish'd brother?

BRU. I kiss thy hand, but not in flattery, Cæsar;

Desiring thee, that Publius Cimber may

Have an immediate freedom of repeal.

CÆS. What, Brutus!

CAS.　　　Pardon, Cæsar; Cæsar, pardon:

As low as to thy foot doth Cassius fall,

To beg enfranchisement for Publius Cimber.

CÆS. I could be well mov'd, if I were as you;　　　　　　[move me:

If I could pray to move, prayers would move me:

But I am constant as the northern star,

Of whose true-fix'd and resting quality

There is no fellow in the firmament.

The skies are painted with unnumber'd sparks,

They are all fire, and every one doth shine;

But there's but one in all doth hold his place:　　　　　　[men,

So, in the world,—'tis furnish'd well with men,

And men are flesh and blood, and apprehensive;

Yet in the number I do know but one

That unassailable holds on his rank,

Unshak'd of motion: and that I am he,

Let me a little show it, even in this,—

That I was constant Cimber should be banish'd,

And constant do remain to keep him so.

CIN. O Cæsar,—

CÆS. Hence! Wilt thou lift up Olympus?

DEC. Great Cæsar,—

CÆS.　　　Doth not Brutus bootless kneel?

CASCA. Speak, hands, for me!

[CASCA *stabs* CÆSAR *in the neck.* CÆSAR *catches hold of his arm. He is then stabbed by several other conspirators, and last by* MARCUS BRUTUS.

CÆS. Et tu, Brute?—Then fall, Cæsar!

[*Dies. The* Senators *and people retire in confusion.*

CIN. Liberty! Freedom! Tyranny is dead!—

Run hence, proclaim, cry it about the streets.

CAS. Some to the common pulpits, and cry out,

"Liberty, freedom, and enfranchisement!"

BRU. People, and senators, be not affrighted.　　　　　　[paid.

Fly not; stand still:—ambition's debt is paid.

CASCA. Go to the pulpit, Brutus.

DEC.　　　　　　And Cassius too.

BRU. Where's Publius?

CIN. Here, quite confounded with this mutiny.

MET. Stand fast together, lest some friend Should chance—　　　　[of Cæsar's

BRU. Talk not of standing.—Publius, good cheer;

There is no harm intended to your person,

Nor to no Roman else: so tell them, Publius.

CAS. And leave us, Publius: lest that the people,   [mischief.
Rushing on us, should do your age some
BRU. Do so:—and let no man abide this
But we, the doers.   [deed.

Re-enter TREBONIUS.

CAS. Where's Antony?
TRE.   Fled to his house amaz'd.
Men, wives, and children, stare, cry out,
As it were doomsday.   [and run,
BRU.   Fates, we will know your pleasures:—
That we shall die, we know; 'tis but the time,
And drawing days out, that men stand upon.
CASCA. Why, he that cuts off twenty years of life,
Cuts off so many years of fearing death.
BRU. Grant that, and then is death a benefit:
So are we Cæsar's friends, that have abridg'd
His time of fearing death.—Stoop, Romans, stoop,   [blood
And let us bathe our hands in Cæsar's
Up to the elbows, and besmear our swords:
Then walk we forth, even to the market-place,
And, waving our red weapons o'er our heads,
Let's all cry, "Peace, freedom, and liberty!"
CAS. Stoop, then, and wash.—How many ages hence,
Shall this our lofty scene be acted over
In states unborn and accents yet unknown!
BRU. How many times shall Cæsar bleed in sport
That now on Pompey's basis lies along,
No worthier than the dust!
CAS.   So oft as that shall be,
So often shall the knot of us be call'd
The men that gave their country liberty.
DEC. What, shall we forth?
CAS.   Ay, every man away:
Brutus shall lead; and we will grace his heels   [Rome.
With the most boldest and best hearts of
BRU. Soft! who comes here?

Enter a Servant.

A friend of Antony's.
SERV. Thus, Brutus, did my master bid me kneel;
Thus did Mark Antony bid me fall down;
And, being prostrate, thus he bade me say:—
Brutus is noble, wise, valiant, and honest;
Cæsar was mighty, bold, royal, and loving:
Say, I love Brutus and I honour him;
Say, I fear'd Cæsar, honour'd him, and lov'd him.

If Brutus will vouchsafe that Antony
May safely come to him, and be resolv'd
How Cæsar hath deserv'd to lie in death,
Mark Antony shall not love Cæsar dead
So well as Brutus living; but will follow
The fortunes and affairs of noble Brutus,
Thorough the hazards of this untrod state,
With all true faith. So says my master Antony.
BRU. Thy master is a wise and valiant Roman;
I never thought him worse.
Tell him, so please him come unto this place,
He shall be satisfied; and, by my honour,
Depart untouch'd.
SERV. I'll fetch him presently.   [Exit.
BRU. I know that we shall have him well to friend.
CAS. I wish we may: but yet have I a mind   [still
That fears him much; and my misgiving
Falls shrewdly to the purpose.
BRU. But here comes Antony.—

Re-enter ANTONY.

                    Welcome, Mark Antony.
ANT. O mighty Cæsar! dost thou lie so low?   [spoils,
Are all thy conquests, glories, triumphs,
Shrunk to this little measure?—Fare thee well.—
I know not, gentlemen, what you intend,
Who else must be let blood, who else is rank:
If I myself, there is no hour so fit
As Cæsar's death's hour: nor no instrument
Of half that worth as those your swords, made rich
With the most noble blood of all this world.
I do beseech ye, if you bear me hard,
Now, whilst your purpled hands do reek and smoke,
Fulfil your pleasure. Live a thousand years,
I shall not find myself so apt to die:
No place will please me so, no mean of death,
As here by Cæsar, and by you cut off,
The choice and master spirits of this age.
BRU. O Antony, beg not your death of us.
Though now we must appear bloody and cruel,
As, by our hands, and this our present act,
You see we do; yet see you but our hands,
And this the bleeding business they have done:
Our hearts you see not,—they are pitiful;
And pity to the general wrong of Rome
(As fire drives out fire, so pity, pity)
Hath done this deed on Cæsar. For your part,

To you our swords have leaden points, Mark
    Antony;   [hearts,
Our arms no strength of malice; and our
Of brothers' temper, do receive you in
With all kind love, good thoughts, and rev-
    erence,   [man's,
CAS. Your voice shall be as strong as any
In the disposing of new dignities.
BRU. Only be patient till we have appeas'd
The multitude, beside themselves with fear,
And then we will deliver you the cause,
Why I, that did love Cæsar when I struck
    him,
Have thus proceeded.
ANT.   I doubt not of your wisdom.
Let each man render me his bloody hand:
First, Marcus Brutus, will I shake with
    you;—
Next, Caius Cassius, do I take your hand;—
Now, Decius Brutus, yours;—now yours,
    Metellus;—   [yours;—
Yours, Cinna;—and, my valiant Casca,
Though last, not least in love, yours, good
    Trebonius.
Gentlemen all,—alas, what shall I say?
My credit now stands on such slippery
    ground,   [ceit me,
That one of two bad ways you must con-
Either a coward or a flatterer.—
That I did love thee, Cæsar, O, 'tis true:
If, then, thy spirit look upon us now,
Shall it not grieve thee dearer than thy
    death,
To see thy Antony making his peace,
Shaking the bloody fingers of thy foes,
Most noble! in the presence of thy corse?
Had I as many eyes as thou hast wounds,
Weeping as fast as they stream forth thy
    blood,
It would become me better, than to close
In terms of friendship with thine enemies.
Pardon me, Julius! Here wast thou bay'd,
    brave hart;   [stand,
Here didst thou fall; and here thy hunters
Sign'd, in thy spoil, and crimson'd in thy
    lethe.
O world, thou wast the forest to this hart;
And this, indeed, O world, the heart of
    thee.—
How like a deer, stricken by many princes,
Dost thou here lie!
CAS. Mark Antony,—
ANT.   Pardon me, Caius Cassius:
The enemies of Cæsar shall say this;
Then, in a friend, it is cold modesty.
CAS. I blame you not for praising Cæsar
    so;   [lus?
But what compact mean you to have with
Will you be prick'd in number of our
    friends;
Or shall we on, and not depend on you?

ANT. Therefore I took your hands; but
    was, indeed,   [Cæsar.
Sway'd from the point, by looking down on
Friends am I with you all, and love you all;
Upon this hope, that you shall give me
    reasons
Why and wherein Cæsar was dangerous.
BRU. Or else were this a savage spectacle.
Our reasons are so full of good regard,
That were you, Antony, the son of Cæsar,
You should be satisfied.
ANT.   That's all I seek:
And am moreover suitor that I may
Produce his body to the market-place;
And in the pulpit, as becomes a friend,
Speak in the order of his funeral.
BRU. You shall, Mark Antony.
CAS.   Brutus, a word with you.—
[*Aside to* BRU.] You know not what you
    do: do not consent
That Antony speak in his funeral:
Know you how much the people may be
    mov'd
By that which he will utter?
BRU. [*Aside to* CAS.]   By your pardon;—
I will myself into the pulpit first,
And show the reason of our Cæsar's death:
What Antony shall speak, I will protest
He speaks by leave and by permission;
And that we are contented Cæsar shall
Have all true rites and lawful ceremonies.
It shall advantage more than do us wrong.
CAS. [*Aside to* BRU.] I know not what may
    fall; I like it not.
BRU. Mark Antony, here, take you Cæsar's
    body.
You shall not in your funeral speech blame
    us,
But speak all good you can devise of Cæsar
And say you do't by our permission;
Else shall you not have any hand at all
About his funeral: and you shall speak
In the same pulpit whereto I am going,
After my speech is ended.
ANT.   Be it so;
I do desire no more.
BRU. Prepare the body, then, and follow
    us.   [*Exeunt all except* ANTONY.
ANT. O, pardon me, thou bleeding piece
    of earth,   [butchers!
That I am meek and gentle with these
Thou art the ruins of the noblest man
That ever lived in the tide of times.
Woe to the hand that shed this costly
    blood!
Over thy wounds now do I prophesy,—
Which, like dumb mouths, do ope their
    ruby lips,   [tongue,—
To beg the voice and utterance of my
A curse shall light upon the limbs of men;
Domestic fury, and fierce civil strife,

Shall cumber all the parts of Italy;
Blood and destruction shall be so in use,
And dreadful objects so familiar,
That mothers shall but smile when they
behold
Their infants quarter'd with the hands of
war;
All pity chok'd with custom of fell deeds:
And Cæsar's spirit, ranging for revenge,
With Até by his side, come hot from hell,
Shall in these confines, with a monarch's
voice,
Cry "Havock!" and let slip the dogs of war;
That this foul deed shall smell above the
earth
With carrion men, groaning for burial.

Enter a Servant.

You serve Octavius Cæsar, do you not?
SERV. I do, Mark Antony.
ANT. Cæsar did write for him to come to
Rome.   [coming;
SERV. He did receive his letters, and is
And bid me say to you by word of mouth,—
                              [*Seeing the body.*
O Cæsar!—
ANT. Thy heart is big, get thee apart and
weep.
Passion, I see, is catching; for mine eyes,
Seeing those beads of sorrow stand in thine,
Began to water. Is thy master coming?
SERV. He lies to-night within seven
leagues of Rome.
ANT. Post back with speed, and tell him
what hath chanc'd:
Here is a mourning Rome, a dangerous
Rome,
No Rome of safety for Octavius yet;
Hie hence, and tell him so. Yet, stay a
while;   [corse
Thou shalt not back, till I have borne this
Into the market-place: there shall I try,
In my oration, how the people take
The cruel issue of these bloody men;
According to the which, thou shalt discourse
To young Octavius of the state of things.
Lend me your hand.
                    [*Exeunt, with* CÆSAR'S *body.*

SCENE II.—ROME. *The* Forum.

Enter BRUTUS *and* CASSIUS, *and a throng of*
Citizens.

CITIZENS. We will be satisfied; let us be
satisfied.
BRU. Then follow me, and give me au-
dience, friends.—
Cassius, go you into the other street,
And part the numbers.—
Those that will hear me speak, let them
stay here;
Those that will follow Cassius, go with him;

And public reasons shall be rendered
Of Cæsar's death.
1 CIT.   I will hear Brutus speak.
2 CIT. I will hear Cassius; and compare
their reasons,
When severally we hear them rendered.
    [*Exit* CASSIUS, *with some of the* Citizens.
    BRUTUS *goes into the rostrum.*
3 CIT. The noble Brutus is ascended:
silence!
BRU. Be patient till the last.
Romans, countrymen, and lovers! hear me
for my cause; and be silent, that you may
hear: believe me for mine honour; and
have respect to mine honour, that you may
believe: censure me in your wisdom; and
awake your senses, that you may the better
judge. If there be any in this assembly,
any dear friend of Cæsar's, to him I say,
that Brutus' love to Cæsar was no less than
his. If, then, that friend demand why
Brutus rose against Cæsar, this is my answer,—not that I loved Cæsar less, but that
I loved Rome more. Had you rather
Cæsar were living, and die all slaves; than
that Cæsar were dead, to live all free men?
As Cæsar loved me, I weep for him; as he
was fortunate, I rejoice at it; as he was
valiant, I honour him: but, as he was ambitious, I slew him: there is tears for his
love; joy for his fortune; honour for his
valour; and death for his ambition. Who is
here so base, that would be a bondman?
If any, speak; for him have I offended. Who
is here so rude, that would not be a Roman?
If any, speak; for him have I offended.
Who is here so vile, that will not love his
country? If any, speak; for him have I
offended. I pause for a reply.
CITIZENS. None, Brutus, none.
BRU. Then none have I offended. I have
done no more to Cæsar, than you shall do to
Brutus. The question of his death is en-
rolled in the Capitol; his glory not ex-
tenuated, wherein he was worthy; nor his
offences enforced, for which he suffered
death. Here comes his body; mourned by
Mark Antony:
Enter ANTONY *and others, with* CÆSAR'S
                              body.
who, though he had no hand in his death,
shall receive the benefit of his dying, a place
in the commonwealth; as which of you shall
not? With this I depart,—that, as I slew
my best lover for the good of Rome, I
have the same dagger for myself, when it
shall please my country to need my death.
CITIZENS. Live, Brutus! live, live!
1 CIT. Bring him with triumph home unto
his house.   [tors.
2 CIT. Give him a statue with his ances-

3 *CIT.* Let him be Cæsar.
4 *CIT.*   Cæsar's better parts
Shall be crown'd in Brutus.
1 *CIT.* We'll bring him to his house with
shouts and clamours.
BRU. My countrymen,—
2 *CIT.*   Peace, silence! Brutus speaks.
1 *CIT.* Peace, ho!
BRU. Good countrymen, let me depart
alone,
And, for my sake, stay here with Antony:
Do grace to Cæsar's corse, and grace his
speech   [Antony,
Tending to Cæsar's glories, which Mark
By our permission, is allow'd to make.
I do entreat you, not a man depart,
Save I alone, till Antony have spoke. [*Exit.*
1 *CIT.* Stay, ho! and let us hear Mark
[Antony.
3 *CIT.* Let him go up into the public
chair;
We'll hear him.—Noble Antony, go up.
ANT. For Brutus' sake, I am beholden to
you.   [*Goes up.*
4 *CIT.* What does he say of Brutus?
3 *CIT.*   He says, for Brutus' sake,
He finds himself beholden to us all.
4 *CIT.* 'Twere best he speak no harm of
Brutus here.
1 *CIT.* This Cæsar was a tyrant.
3 *CIT.*   Nay, that's certain:
We are bless'd that Rome is rid of him.
2 *CIT.* Peace! let us hear what Antony
can say.
ANT. You gentle Romans,—
CITIZENS. Peace, ho! let us hear him.
ANT. Friends, Romans, countrymen, lend
me your ears;
I come to bury Cæsar, not to praise him.
The evil that men do lives after them;
The good is oft interred with their bones;
So let it be with Cæsar. The noble Brutus
Hath told you Cæsar was ambitious:
If it were so, it was a grievous fault;
And grievously hath Cæsar answer'd it.
Here, under leave of Brutus and the rest,
(For Brutus is an honourable man;
So are they all, all honourable men)
Come I to speak in Cæsar's funeral.
He was my friend, faithful and just to me:
But Brutus says he was ambitious;
And Brutus is an honourable man.
He hath brought many captives home to
Rome,
Whose ransoms did the general coffers fill:
Did this in Cæsar seem ambitious?
When that the poor have cried, Cæsar hath
wept:
Ambition should be made of sterner stuff:
Yet Brutus says he was ambitious;

And Brutus is an honourable man.
You all did see that on the Lupercal
I thrice presented him a kingly crown,
Which he did thrice refuse: was this ambi-
tion?
Yet Brutus says he was ambitious;
And, sure, he is an honourable man.
I speak not to disprove what Brutus spoke,
But here I am to speak what I do know.
You all did love him once,—not without
cause: [for him?
What cause withholds you, then, to mourn
O judgment, thou art fled to brutish beasts,
And men have lost their reason!—Bear with
me;
My heart is in the coffin there with Cæsar,
And I must pause till it come back to me.
1 *CIT.* Methinks there is much reason in
his sayings.   [ter,
2 *CIT.* If thou consider rightly of the mat-
Cæsar has had great wrong.
3 *CIT.*   Has he, masters?
I fear there will a worse come in his place.
4 *CIT.* Mark'd ye his words? He would
not take the crown;
Therefore 'tis certain he was not ambitious.
1 *CIT.* If it be found so, some will dear
abide it.   [with weeping.
2 *CIT.* Poor soul! his eyes are red as fire.
3 *CIT.* There's not a nobler man in Rome
than Antony.   [speak.
4 *CIT.* Now mark him, he begins again to
ANT. But yesterday, the word of Cæsar
might   [there,
Have stood against the world: now, lies he
And none so poor to do him reverence.
O masters! if I were dispos'd to stir
Your hearts and minds to mutiny and rage,
I should do Brutus wrong, and Cassius
wrong,
Who, you all know, are honourable men:
I will not do them wrong; I rather choose
To wrong the dead, to wrong myself, and
you,
Than I will wrong such honourable men.
But here's a parchment with the seal of
Cæsar,—
I found it in his closet,—'tis his will:
Let but the commons hear this testament,
(Which, pardon me, I do not mean to read)
And they would go and kiss dead Cæsar's
wounds,
And dip their napkins in his sacred blood;
Yea, beg a hair of him for memory,
And, dying, mention it within their wills,
Bequeathing it, as a rich legacy,
Unto their issue.
4 *CIT.* We'll hear the will: read it, Mark
Antony.   [Cæsar's will.
CITIZENS. The will, the will! we will hear

ANT. Have patience, gentle friends, I must
not read it;
It is not meet you know how Cæsar lov'd you.
You are not wood, you are not stone, but
men;
And, being men, hearing the will of Cæsar,
It will inflame you, it will make you mad:
'Tis good you know not that you are his
heirs;
For if you should, O, what would come of it!
4 CIT. Read the will; we'll hear it,
Antony;
You shall read us the will,—Cæsar's will.
ANT. Will you be patient? Will you stay
a while?
I have o'ershot myself to tell you of it:
I fear I wrong the honourable men,
Whose daggers have stabb'd Cæsar; I do
fear it.   [men!
4 CIT. They were traitors: honourable
CITIZENS. The will! the testament!
2 CIT. They were villains, murderers: the
will! read the will.
ANT. You will compel me, then, to read
the will?
Then make a ring about the corse of Cæsar,
And let me show you him that made the
will.   [leave?
Shall I descend? and will you give me
CITIZENS. Come down.
2 CIT. Descend.   [ANTONY *comes down.*
3 CIT. You shall have leave.
4 CIT. A ring; stand round.   the body.
1 CIT. Stand from the hearse, stand from
2 CIT. Room for Antony, most noble
Antony!   [far off.
ANT. Nay, press not so upon me; stand
CITIZENS. Stand back; room; bear back.
ANT. If you have tears, prepare to shed
them now.
You all do know this mantle: I remember
The first time ever Cæsar put it on;
'Twas on a summer's evening, in his tent,
That day he overcame the Nervii:—
Look, in this place, ran Cassius' dagger
through:
See what a rent the envious Casca made:
Through this the well-beloved Brutus
stabb'd;
And, as he pluck'd his cursed steel away,
Mark how the blood of Cæsar follow'd it,
As rushing out of doors, to be resolv'd
If Brutus so unkindly knock'd, or no;
For Brutus, as you know, was Cæsar's angel:
Judge, O you gods, how dearly Cæsar lov'd
him!
This was the most unkindest cut of all;
For when the noble Cæsar saw him stab,
Ingratitude, more strong than traitors'
arms,   [heart;
Quite vanquish'd him: then burst his mighty

And, in his mantle muffling up his face,
Even at the base of Pompey's statua,
Which all the while ran blood, great Cæsar
fell.
O, what a fall was there, my countrymen!
Then I, and you, and all of us fell down,
Whilst bloody treason flourish'd over us.
O, now you weep; and, I perceive, you feel
The dint of pity: these are gracious drops.
Kind souls, what, weep you when you but
behold
Our Cæsar's vesture wounded? Look you
here,   [traitors.
Here is himself, marr'd, as you see, with
1 CIT. O piteous spectacle!
2 CIT. O noble Cæsar!
3 CIT. O woful day!
4 CIT. O traitors, villains!
1 CIT. O most bloody sight!
2 CIT. We will be revenged: revenge,—
about,—seek,—burn,—fire,—kill,— slay,—
let not a traitor live!
ANT. Stay, countrymen.
1 CIT. Peace there! hear the noble Antony.
2 CIT. We'll hear him, we'll follow him,
we'll die with him.
ANT. Good friends, sweet friends, let me
not stir you up
To such a sudden flood of mutiny.
They that have done this deed are honourable;—   [not,
What private griefs they have, alas, I know
That made them do it;—they are wise and
honourable,   [you.
And will, no doubt, with reasons answer
I come not, friends, to steal away your
hearts:
I am no orator, as Brutus is;
But, as you know me all, a plain blunt man,
That love my friend; and that they know
full well
That gave me public leave to speak of him:
For I have neither wit, nor words, nor
worth,
Action, nor utterance, nor the power of
speech,
To stir men's blood: I only speak right on;
I tell you that which you yourselves do
know;
Show you sweet Cæsar's wounds, poor,
poor dumb mouths,
And bid them speak for me: but were I
Brutus,
And Brutus Antony, there were an Antony
Would ruffle up your spirits, and put a
tongue
In every wound of Cæsar, that should move
The stones of Rome to rise and mutiny.
CITIZENS. We'll mutiny.

1 CIT. We'll burn the house of Brutus.
3 CIT. Away, then! come, seek the conspirators.
ANT. Yet hear me, countrymen; yet hear me speak.   [noble Antony.
CITIZENS. Peace, ho! Hear Antony, most
ANT. Why, friends, you go to do you know not what:
Wherein hath Cæsar thus deserv'd your loves?
Alas, you know not,—I must tell you, then:—
You have forgot the will I told you of.
CITIZENS. Most true;—the will:—let's stay and hear the will.
ANT. Here is the will, and under Cæsar's seal:—
To every Roman citizen he gives,
To every several man, seventy-five drachmas.
2 CIT. Most noble Cæsar!—we'll revenge his death.
3 CIT. O royal Cæsar!
ANT. Hear me with patience.
CITIZENS. Peace, ho!
ANT. Moreover, he hath left you all his walks,   [orchards,
His private arbours, and new-planted
On this side Tiber; he hath left them you,
And to your heirs for ever,—common pleasures,
To walk abroad, and recreate yourselves.
Here was a Cæsar! when comes such another?
1 CIT. Never, never!—Come, away, away!
We'll burn his body in the holy place,
And with the brands fire the traitors' houses.
Take up the body.
2 CIT. Go fetch fire.
3 CIT. Pluck down benches.
4 CIT. Pluck down forms, windows, any thing.   [Exeunt Citizens, with the body.
ANT. Now let it work:—mischief, thou art afoot,
Take thou what course thou wilt!—
                Enter a Servant.
                How now, fellow!
SERV. Sir, Octavius is already come to Rome.
ANT. Where is he?
SERV. He and Lepidus are at Cæsar's house.
ANT. And thither will I straight to visit him:
He comes upon a wish. Fortune is merry,
And in this mood will give us any thing.
SERV. I heard him say, Brutus and Cassius
Are rid like madmen through the gates of Rome.
ANT. Belike they had some notice of the people,

How I had mov'd them. Bring me to Octavius.   [Exeunt.

SCENE III.—ROME. *A Street.*

Enter CINNA, *the poet.*

CIN. I dreamt to-night that I did feast with Cæsar,
And things unlucky charge my fantasy:
I have no will to wander forth of doors,
Yet something leads me forth.
                Enter Citizens.
1 CIT. What is your name?
2 CIT. Whither are you going?
3 CIT. Where do you dwell?
4 CIT. Are you a married man, or a bachelor?
2 CIT. Answer every man directly.
1 CIT. Ay, and briefly.
4 CIT. Ay, and wisely.
3 CIT. Ay, and truly; you were best.
CIN. What is my name? Whither am I going? Where do I dwell? Am I a married man, or a bachelor? Then, to answer every man directly and briefly, wisely and truly:
—wisely I say, I am a bachelor.
2 CIT. That's as much as to say, they are fools that marry:—you'll bear me a bang for that, I fear. Proceed; directly.
CIN. Directly, I am going to Cæsar's funeral.
1 CIT. As a friend, or an enemy?
CIN. As a friend.
2 CIT. That matter is answered directly.
4 CIT. For your dwelling,—briefly.
CIN. Briefly, I dwell by the Capitol.
3 CIT. Your name, Sir, truly.
CIN. Truly, my name is Cinna.
1 CIT. Tear him to pieces; he's a conspirator.
CIN. I am Cinna the poet, I am Cinna the poet.
4 CIT. Tear him for his bad verses, tear him for his bad verses.
CIN. I am not Cinna the conspirator.
2 CIT. It is no matter, his name's Cinna; pluck but his name out of his heart, and turn him going.
3 CIT. Tear him, tear him! Come, brands, ho! fire-brands! To Brutus, to Cassius; burn all: some to Decius' house, and some to Casca's; some to Ligarius': away, go!
                [Exeunt.

ACT IV.

SCENE I.—ROME. *A Room in* ANTONY'S *House.*

ANTONY, OCTAVIUS, *and* LEPIDUS, *seated at a table.*

ANT. These many, then, shall die; their
names are prick'd.
OCT. Your brother too must die; consent
you, Lepidus?
LEP. I do consent,—
OCT.   Prick him down, Antony.
LEP. Upon condition Publius shall not
live,
Who is your sister's son, Mark Antony.
ANT. He shall not live; look, with a spot
I damn him.
But, Lepidus, go you to Cæsar's house;
Fetch the will hither, and we shall
determine
How to cut off some charge in legacies.
LEP. What, shall I find you here?
OCT. Or here, or at the Capitol.
          [*Exit* LEPIDUS.
ANT. This is a slight unmeritable man,
Meet to be sent on errands: is it fit, [stand
The threefold world divided, he should
One of the three to share it?
OCT.   So you thought him,
And took his voice who should be prick'd
to die,
In our black sentence and proscription.
ANT. Octavius, I have seen more days
than you:
And though we lay these honours on this
man,
To ease ourselves of divers slanderous loads,
He shall but bear them as the ass bears
gold,
To groan and sweat under the business,
Either led or driven, as we point the way;
And having brought our treasure where
we will,
Then take we down his load, and turn him
off,
Like to the empty ass, to shake his ears,
And graze in commons.
OCT.   You may do your will:
But he's a tried and valiant soldier.
ANT. So is my horse, Octavius; and for
that
I do appoint him store of provender:
It is a creature that I teach to fight,
To wind, to stop, to run directly on,—
His corporal motion govern'd by my spirit.
And, in some taste, is Lepidus but so;
He must be taught, and train'd, and bid go
forth;—
A barren-spirited fellow; one that feeds
On objects, arts, and imitations,
Which, out of use and stal'd by other men,
Begin his fashion: do not talk of him,
But as a property. And now, Octavius,
Listen great things:—Brutus and Cassius
Are levying powers: we must straight make
head:
Therefore let our alliance be combin'd,

Our best friends made, and our best means
stretch'd out;
And let us presently go sit in council,
How covert matters may be best disclos'd,
And open perils surest answered.
OCT. Let us do so: for we are at the stake,
And bay'd about with many enemies;
And some, that smile, have in their hearts, I
Millions of mischiefs.   [fear,
          [*Exeunt.*

SCENE II.—*Before* BRUTUS' *Tent, in the
Camp near* SARDIS.

Drum. Enter BRUTUS, LUCILIUS, LUCIUS, *and*
Soldiers: TITINIUS *and* PINDARUS *meeting
them.*

BRU. Stand, ho!
LUCIL. Give the word, ho! and stand.
BRU. What now, Lucilius! Is Cassius
near?
LUCIL. He is at hand; and Pindarus is
come
To do you salutation from his master.
          [PINDARUS *gives a letter to* BRUTUS.
BRU. He greets me well.—Your master,
Pindarus,
In his own change, or by ill officers,
Hath given me some worthy cause to wish
Things done, undone: but, if he be at hand
I shall be satisfied.
PIN.   I do not doubt
But that my noble master will appear
Such as he is, full of regard and honour.
BRU. He is not doubted.—A word, Lu-
cilius;
How he receiv'd you, let me be resolv'd.
LUCIL. With courtesy, and with respect
enough;
But not with such familiar instances,
Nor with such free and friendly confer-
As he hath used of old.   [ence,
BRU.   Thou hast describ'd
A hot friend cooling: ever note, Lucilius,
When love begins to sicken and decay,
It useth an enforced ceremony.
There are no tricks in plain and simple
faith:
But hollow men, like horses hot at hand,
Make gallant show and promise of their
mettle;
But when they should endure the bloody
spur,
They fall their crests, and, like deceitful
jades,
Sink in the trial. Comes his army on?
LUCIL. They mean this night in Sardis to
be quarter'd;
The greater part, the horse in general,
Are come with Cassius.   [*March within.*
BRU.   Hark! he is arriv'd.—

March gently on to meet him.
> *Enter* CASSIUS *and* Soldiers.

CAS. Stand, ho!
BRU. Stand, ho! Speak the word along.
WITHIN. Stand!
WITHIN. Stand!
WITHIN. Stand!
CAS. Most noble brother, you have done me wrong.
BRU. Judge me, you gods! Wrong I mine enemies?
And, if not so, how should I wrong a brother?
CAS. Brutus, this sober form of yours hides
And when you do them—   [wrongs;
BRU.   Cassius, be content;
Speak your griefs softly,—I do know you well:—
Before the eyes of both our armies here,
Which should perceive nothing but love from us,
Let us not wrangle: bid them move away;
Then in my tent, Cassius, enlarge your griefs,
And I will give you audience.
CAS.   Pindarus,
Bid our commanders lead their charges off
A little from this ground.
BRU. Lucilius, do you the like; and let no man
Come to our tent, till we have done our conference.
Let Lucius and Titinius guard our door.
> [*Exeunt.*

SCENE III.—*Within the Tent of* BRUTUS.

> *Enter* BRUTUS *and* CASSIUS.

CAS. That you have wrong'd me doth appear in this,—
You have condemn'd and noted Lucius Pella
For taking bribes here of the Sardians;
Wherein my letters, praying on his side,
Because I knew the man, were slighted off.
BRU. You wrong'd yourself to write in such a case.
CAS. In such a time as this, it is not meet
That every nice offence should bear his comment.
BRU. Let me tell you, Cassius, you yourself
Are much condemn'd to have an itching palm;
To sell and mart your offices for gold
To undeservers.
CAS.   I an itching palm!
You know that you are Brutus that speak this,
Or, by the gods, this speech were else your last.

BRU. The name of Cassius honours this corruption,
And chastisement doth therefore hide his head.
CAS. Chastisement!
BRU. Remember March, the ides of March remember:
Did not great Julius bleed for justice' sake?
What villain touch'd his body, that did stab,
And not for justice? What, shall one of us,
That struck the foremost man of all this world,
But for supporting robbers, shall we now
Contaminate our fingers with base bribes,
And sell the mighty space of our large honours,
For so much trash as may be grasped thus?
I had rather be a dog, and bay the moon,
Than such a Roman.
CAS.   Brutus, bay not me,—
I'll not endure it: you forget yourself,
To hedge me in; I am a soldier, I,
Older in practice, abler than yourself
To make conditions.
BRU.   Go to; you are not, Cassius.
CAS. I am.
BRU. I say, you are not.
CAS. Urge me no more, I shall forget myself;
Have mind upon your health, tempt me no farther.
BRU. Away, slight man!
CAS. Is't possible?
BRU.   Hear me, for I will speak.
Must I give way and room to your rash choler?
Shall I be frighted, when a madman stares?
CAS. O ye gods, ye gods! Must I endure all this?
BRU. All this! ay, more: fret till your proud heart breaks;
Go show your slaves how choleric you are,
And make your bondmen tremble. Must I budge?
Must I observe you? Must I stand and crouch
Under your testy humour? By the gods,
You shall digest the venom of your spleen,
Though it do split you; for, from this day forth,
I'll use you for my mirth, yea, for my laughter,
When you are waspish.
CAS.   Is it come to this?
BRU. You say you are a better soldier:
Let it appear so; make your vaunting true,
And it shall please me well: for mine own part,
I shall be glad to learn of noble men.
CAS. You wrong me every way; you wrong me, Brutus;

I said an elder soldier, not a better:
Did I say, better?

BRU. If you did, I care not.

CAS. When Cæsar liv'd, he durst not thus
have mov'd me.

BRU. Peace, peace! you durst not so have
tempted him.

CAS. I durst not!

BRU. No.

CAS. What, durst not tempt him?

BRU. For your life you durst not.

CAS. Do not presume too much upon my
love;
I may do that I shall be sorry for.

BRU. You have done that you should be
sorry for.
There is no terror, Cassius, in your threats;
For I am arm'd so strong in honesty,
That they pass by me as the idle wind,
Which I respect not. I did send to you
For certain sums of gold, which you denied
me;—
For I can raise no money by vile means:
By heaven, I had rather coin my heart,
And drop my blood for drachmas, than to
wring
From the hard hands of peasants, their vile
trash
By any indirection;—I did send
To you for gold to pay my legions,
Which you denied me: was that done like
Cassius?
Should I have answer'd Caius Cassius so?
When Marcus Brutus grows so covetous,
To lock such rascal counters from his
friends,
Be ready, gods, with all your thunderbolts,
Dash him to pieces!

CAS. I denied you not.

BRU. You did.

CAS. I did not: he was but a fool
That brought my answer back.—Brutus hath
riv'd my heart:
A friend should bear his friend's infirmities,
But Brutus makes mine greater than they
are.

BRU. I do not, till you practise them on
me.

CAS. You love me not. [me.

BRU. I do not like your faults.

CAS. A friendly eye could never see such
faults.

BRU. A flatterer's would not, though they
do appear
As huge as high Olympus.

CAS. Come, Antony, and young Octavius,
come,
Revenge yourselves alone on Cassius,
For Cassius is aweary of the world;
Hated by one he loves: brav'd by his
brother;

Check'd like a bondman; all his faults
observ'd,
Set in a note-book, learn'd, and conn'd by
rote,
To cast into my teeth. O, I could weep
My spirit from mine eyes!—There is my
dagger,
And here my naked breast; within, a heart
Dearer than Plutus' mine, richer than gold:
If that thou be'st a Roman, take it forth;
I, that denied thee gold, will give my heart:
Strike, as thou didst at Caesar; for, I know,
When thou didst hate him worst, thou
lov'dst him better
Than ever thou lov'dst Cassius.

BRU. Sheathe your dagger:
Be angry when you will, it shall have scope;
Do what you will, dishonour shall be
humour.
O Cassius, you are yoked with a lamb
That carries anger as the flint bears fire;
Who, much enforced, shows a hasty spark,
And straight is cold again.

CAS. Hath Cassius liv'd
To be but mirth and laughter to his Brutus,
When grief, and blood ill-temper'd, vexeth
him?

BRU. When I spoke that, I was ill-temper'd
too.

CAS. Do you confess so much? Give me
your hand.

BRU. And my heart too.

CAS. O Brutus,—

BRU. What's the matter?

CAS. Have you not love enough to bear
with me,
When that rash humour which my mother
Makes me forgetful? [gave me

BRU. Yes, Cassius; and, from henceforth,
When you are over-earnest with your Brutus,
He'll think your mother chides, and leave
you so. [*Noise within.*

POET. [*Within.*] Let me go in to see the
generals;
There is some grudge between them, 'tis not
They be alone. [meet

LUCIL. [*Within.*] You shall not come to
them.

POET. [*Within.*] Nothing but death shall
stay me.

Enter Poet, *followed by* LUCILIUS *and*
TITINIUS.

CAS. How now! What's the matter?

POET. For shame, you generals! What do
you mean?
Love, and be friends, as two such men
should be;
For I have seen more years, I am sure, than
ye.

CAS. Ha, ha! how vilely doth this cynic
rhyme.

BRU. Get you hence, sirrah: saucy fellow, hence!

CAS. Bear with him, Brutus; 'tis his fashion.

BRU. I'll know his humour, when he knows his time:
What should the wars do with these jigging Companion, hence!   [fools?—

CAS.   Away, away, be gone!
                    [*Exit* Poet.

BRU. Lucilius and Titinius, bid the commanders
Prepare to lodge their companies to-night.

CAS. And come yourselves, and bring Messala with you,
Immediately to us.

                [*Exeunt* LUCILIUS *and* TITINIUS.

BRU.   Lucius, a bowl of wine!

CAS. I did not think you could have been so angry.

BRU. O Cassius, I am sick of many griefs.

CAS. Of your philosophy you make no use,
If you give place to accidental evils.

BRU. No man bears sorrow better.—Portia is dead.

CAS. Ha! Portia!

BRU. She is dead.

CAS. How scap'd I killing when I cross'd you so?—
O insupportable and touching loss!—
Upon what sickness?

BRU.   Impatient of my absence,
And grief that young Octavius with Mark Antony
Have made themselves so strong;—for with her death
That tidings came:—with this she fell distract,
And, her attendants absent, swallow'd fire.

CAS. And died so?

BRU. Even so.

CAS. O ye immortal gods!
    Enter LUCIUS, *with wine and tapers.*

BRU. Speak no more of her.—Give me a bowl of wine.—
In this I bury all unkindness, Cassius.
                        [*Drinks.*

CAS. My heart is thirsty for that noble pledge.—
Fill, Lucius, till the wine o'erswell the cup;
I cannot drink too much of Brutus' love.
                        [*Drinks.*

BRU. Come in, Titinius!—
    Re-enter TITINIUS, *with* MESSALA.
                Welcome, good Messala.—
Now sit we close about this taper here,
And call in question our necessities.

CAS. Portia, art thou gone?

BRU.   No more, I pray you.—
Messala, I have here received letters,
That young Octavius and Mark Antony

Come down upon us with a mighty power,
Bending their expedition toward Philippi.

MES. Myself have letters of the self-same tenor.

BRU. With what addition?

MES. That by proscription, and bills of outlawry,
Octavius, Antony, and Lepidus,
Have put to death a hundred senators.

BRU. Therein our letters do not well agree;
Mine speak of seventy senators that died
By their proscriptions, Cicero being one.

CAS. Cicero one!

MES. Cicero is dead,
And by that order of proscription.—
Had you your letters from your wife, my lord?

BRU. No, Messala.

MES. Nor nothing in your letters writ of her?

BRU. Nothing, Messala.

MES.   That, methinks, is strange.

BRU. Why ask you? Hear you aught of her in yours?

MES. No, my lord.

BRU. Now, as you are a Roman, tell me true.

MES. Then like a Roman bear the truth I tell:
For certain she is dead, and by strange manner.

BRU. Why, farewell, Portia.—We must die, Messala:
With meditating that she must die once,
I have the patience to endure it now.

MES. Even so great men great losses should endure.

CAS. I have as much of this in art as you,
But yet my nature could not bear it so.

BRU. Well, to our work alive.—What do you think
Of marching to Philippi presently?

CAS. I do not think it good.

BRU.   Your reason?

CAS.   This it is:—
'Tis better, that the enemy seek us:
So shall he waste his means, weary his soldiers,
Doing himself offence; whilst we, lying still,
Are full of rest, defence, and nimbleness.

BRU. Good reasons must, of force, give place to better.
The people 'twixt Philippi and this ground
Do stand but in a forc'd affection;
For they have grudg'd us contribution:
The enemy, marching along by them,
By them shall make a fuller number up,
Come on refresh'd, new-added, and encourag'd;
From which advantage shall we cut him off,
If at Philippi we do face him there,

These people at our back.
CAS.   Hear me, good brother.—
BRU. Under your pardon.—You must note
beside,
That we have tried the utmost of our friends,
Our legions are brim-full, our cause is ripe:
The enemy increaseth every day;
We, at the height, are ready to decline.
There is a tide in the affairs of men,
Which, taken at the flood, leads on to
fortune;
Omitted, all the voyage of their life
Is bound in shallows, and in miseries.
On such a full sea are we now afloat;
And we must take the current when it
serves,
Or lose our ventures.   [serves,
CAS.   Then, with your will, go on;
We'll along ourselves, and meet them at
Philippi.
BRU. The deep of night is crept upon our
talk,
And nature must obey necessity;
Which we will niggard with a little rest,
There is no more to say?
CAS.   No more. Good night:
Early to-morrow will we rise, and hence.
BRU. Lucius, my gown.—[*Exit* LUCIUS.]
Farewell, good Messala:—
Good night, Titinius:—noble, noble Cassius,
Good night, and good repose.
CAS.   O my dear brother!
This was an ill beginning of the night:
Never come such division 'tween our souls!
Let it not, Brutus.
BRU.   Every thing is well.
CAS. Good night, my lord.
BRU.   Good night, good brother.
TIT. MES. Good night, lord Brutus.
BRU.   Farewell, every one.
            [*Exeunt* CAS., TIT., *and* MES.
Re-enter LUCIUS, *with the gown.*

Give me the gown. Where is thy instrument?
LUC. Here in the tent.
BRU.   What, thou speak'st drowsily?
Poor knave, I blame thee not; thou art
o'erwatch'd.
Call Claudius, and some other of my men;
I'll have them sleep on cushions in my tent.
LUC. Varro and Claudius!

Enter VARRO *and* CLAUDIUS.

VAR. Calls my lord?
BRU. I pray you, Sirs, lie in my tent, and
sleep;
It may be I shall raise you by and by
On business to my brother Cassius.
VAR. So please you, we will stand, and
watch your pleasure.
BRU. I will not have it so: lie down, good
Sirs;
It may be I shall otherwise bethink me.—

Look, Lucius, here's the book I sought for
so;
I put it in the pocket of my gown.
            [VAR. *and* CLAU. *lie down.*
LUC. I was sure your lordship did not give
it me.
BRU. Bear with me, good boy, I am much
forgetful.
Canst thou hold up thy heavy eyes awhile,
And touch thy instrument a strain or two?
LUC. Ay, my lord, an't please you.
BRU.   It does, my boy:
I trouble thee too much, but thou art will-
LUC. It is my duty, Sir.   [ing.
BRU. I should not urge thy duty past thy
might;
I know young bloods look for a time of rest.
LUC. I have slept, my lord, already.
BRU. It was well done; and thou shalt
sleep again;
I will not hold thee long: if I do live,
I will be good to thee.   [*Music, and a song.*
This is a sleepy tune:—O murderous
slumber,
Lay'st thou thy leaden mace upon my boy,
That plays thee music?—Gentle knave, good
night;
I will not do thee so much wrong to wake
thee:
If thou dost nod, thou break'st thy instru-
ment;
I'll take it from thee; and, good boy, good
night.—
Let me see, let me see;—is not the leaf
turn'd down,
Where I left reading? Here it is, I think.
            [*Sits down.*
            The Ghost of CÆSAR *appears.*
How ill this taper burns!—Ha! who comes
here?
I think it is the weakness of mine eyes
That shapes this monstrous apparition.
It comes upon me.—Art thou any thing?
Art thou some god, some angel, or some
devil,
That mak'st my blood cold, and my hair to
Speak to me what thou art.   [stare?
GHOST. Thy evil spirit, Brutus.
BRU.   Why com'st thou?
GHOST. To tell thee thou shalt see me at
Philippi.
BRU. Well; then I shall see thee again?
GHOST.   Ay, at Philippi.
BRU. Why, I will see thee at Philippi,
then.—   [*Ghost vanishes.*
Now I have taken heart thou vanishest:
Ill spirit, I would hold more talk with
thee.   [awake!—
Boy, Lucius!—Varro! Claudius! Sirs,
Claudius!
LUC. The strings, my lord, are false.

BRU. He thinks he still is at his instru-
Lucius, awake!   [ment.—
LUC. My lord?
BRU. Didst thou dream, Lucius, that thou
so criedst out?
LUC. My lord, I do not know that I did
cry.
BRU. Yes, that thou didst: didst thou see
any thing?
LUC. Nothing, my lord.
BRU. Sleep again, Lucius.—Sirrah Clau-
Fellow thou, awake!   [dius!
VAR. My lord?
CLAU. My lord?
BRU. Why did you so cry out, Sirs, in your
sleep?
VAR. CLAU. Did we, my lord?
BRU.   Ay: saw you any thing?
VAR. No, my lord, I saw nothing.
CLAU.   Nor I, my lord.
BRU. Go and commend me to my brother
Cassius;
Bid him set on his powers betimes before,
And we will follow.
VAR. CLAU.   It shall be done, my lord.
                                       [*Exeunt.*

ACT V.

Scene I.—*The Plains of* PHILIPPI.

Enter OCTAVIUS, ANTONY, *and their army.*

OCT. Now, Antony, our hopes are an-
swered:
You said the enemy would not come down,
But keep the hills and upper regions;
It proves not so: their battles are at hand;
They mean to warn us at Philippi here,
Answering before we do demand of them.
ANT. Tut, I am in their bosoms, and I
know
Wherefore they do it: they could be con-
tent
To visit other places; and come down
With fearful bravery, thinking by this face
To fasten in our thoughts that they have
But 'tis not so.   [courage;
            Enter a Messenger.
MESS. Prepare you, generals:
The enemy comes on in gallant show;
Their bloody sign of battle is hung out,
And something to be done immediately.
ANT. Octavius, lead your battle softly on,
Upon the left hand of the even field.
OCT. Upon the right hand I; keep thou
the left.
ANT. Why do you cross me in this exigent?
OCT. I do not cross you: but I will do so.
                                        [*March.*
Drum. Enter BRUTUS, CASSIUS, *and their
army;* LUCILIUS, TITINIUS, MESSALA,
and others.

BRU. They stand, and would have parley.
CAS. Stand fast, Titinius: we must out and
talk.
OCT. Mark Antony, shall we give sign of
battle?
ANT. No, Cæsar, we will answer on their
charge.
Make forth; the generals would have some
words.
OCT. Stir not until the signal.
BRU. Words before blows:—is it so, coun-
trymen?
OCT. Not that we love words better, as
you do.
BRU. Good words are better than bad
strokes, Octavius.
ANT. In your bad strokes, Brutus, you give
good words:
Witness the hole you made in Cæsar's heart,
Crying, "Long live! hail, Cæsar!"
CAS.   Antony,
The posture of your blows are yet unknown;
But for your words, they rob the Hybla
And leave them honeyless.   [bees,
ANT.   Not stingless too.
BRU. O, yes, and soundless too;
For you have stol'n their buzzing, Antony,
And very wisely threat before you sting.
ANT. Villains, you did not so when your
vile daggers
Hack'd one another in the sides of Cæsar:
You show'd your teeth like apes, and fawn'd
like hounds,
And bow'd like bondmen, kissing Cæsar's
feet;
Whilst damned Casca, like a cur, behind
Struck Cæsar on the neck. O you flatterers!
CAS. Flatterers!—Now Brutus, thank your-
self:
This tongue had not offended so to-day,
If Cassius might have rul'd.
OCT. Come, come, the cause: if arguing
make us sweat,
The proof of it will turn to redder drops.
Look,—I draw a sword against conspirators;
When think you that the sword goes up
again?—
Never, till Cæsar's three and thirty wounds
Be well aveng'd; or till another Cæsar
Have added slaughter to the sword of
traitors.
BRU. Cæsar, thou canst not die by traitors'
hands,
Unless thou bring'st them with thee.
OCT.   So I hope;
I was not born to die on Brutus' sword.
BRU. O, if thou wert the noblest of thy
strain,
Young man, thou could'st not die more
honourable.

CAS. A peevish school-boy, worthless of such honour,
Join'd with a masker and a reveller!
ANT. Old Cassius still!
OCT. Come, Antony; away!—
Defiance, traitors, hurl we in your teeth:
If you dare fight to-day, come to the field;
If not, when you have stomachs.

[*Exeunt* OCTAVIUS, ANTONY, *and their
army.*

CAS. Why, now, blow wind, swell billow, and swim bark!
The storm is up, and all is on the hazard.
BRU. Ho, Lucilius! hark, a word with you.
LUCIL. My lord?

[BRUTUS *and* LUCILIUS *talk apart.*

CAS. Messala.—
MES. What says my general?
CAS. Messala,
This is my birth-day; as this very day
Was Cassius born. Give me thy hand, Messala:
Be thou my witness, that, against my will,
As Pompey was, am I compell'd to set
Upon one battle all our liberties.
You know that I held Epicurus strong,
And his opinion: now I change my mind,
And partly credit things that do presage.
Coming from Sardis, on our former ensign
Two mighty eagles fell; and there they perch'd,
Gorging and feeding from our soldiers' hands;
Who to Philippi here consorted us:
This morning are they fled away and gone;
And in their steads do ravens, crows, and kites,
Fly o'er our heads, and downward look on us,
As we were sickly prey: their shadows seem
A canopy most fatal, under which
Our army lies, ready to give up the ghost.
MES. Believe not so.
CAS. I but believe it partly;
For I am fresh of spirit, and resolv'd
To meet all perils very constantly.
BRU. Even so, Lucilius.
CAS. Now, most noble Brutus,
The gods to-day stand friendly, that we may,
Lovers in peace lead on our days to age!
But, since the affairs of men rest still in-certain,
Let's reason with the worst that may befall.
If we do lose this battle, then is this
The very last time we shall speak together:
What are you, then, determined to do?
BRU. Even by the rule of that philosophy,
By which I did blame Cato for the death
Which he did give himself:—I know not how,
But I do find it cowardly and vile,

For fear of what might fall, so to prevent
The time of life:—arming myself with pa-tience,
To stay the providence of some high powers
That govern us below.
CAS. Then, if we lose this battle,
You are contented to be led in triumph
Thorough the streets of Rome?
BRU. No, Cassius, no: think not, thou noble Roman,
That ever Brutus will go bound to Rome;
He bears too great a mind. But this same day
Must end that work the ides of March begun;
And whether we shall meet again, I know not.
Therefore, our everlasting farewell take:—
For ever, and for ever, farewell, Cassius!
If we do meet again, why, we shall smile;
If not, why, then, this parting was well made.
CAS. For ever, and for ever, farewell, Brutus!
If we do meet again, we'll smile indeed;
If not, 'tis true, this parting was well made.
BRU. Why, then, lead on.—O, that a man might know
The end of this day's business, ere it come!
But it sufficeth, that the day will end,
And then the end is known.—Come, ho! away! [*Exeunt.*

SCENE II.—PHILIPPI. *The Field of Battle.*

Alarum. Enter BRUTUS *and* MESSALA.

BRU. Ride, ride, Messala, ride, and give these bills
Unto the legions on the other side:

[*Loud alarum.*

Let them set on at once; for I perceive
But cold demeanour in Octavius' wing,
And sudden push gives them the overthrow.
Ride, ride, Messala: let them all come down.

[*Exeunt.*

SCENE III.—*Another Part of the Field.*

Alarum. Enter CASSIUS *and* TITINIUS.

CAS. O, look, Titinius, look, the villains fly!
Myself have to mine own turn'd enemy:
This ensign here of mine was turning back;
I slew the coward, and did take it from him.
TIT. O Cassius, Brutus gave the word too early;
Who, having some advantage on Octavius,
Took it too eagerly: his soldiers fell to spoil,
Whilst we by Antony are all enclos'd.

Enter PINDARUS.

PIN. Fly farther off, my lord, fly farther
   off;
Mark Antony is in your tents, my lord:
Fly, therefore, noble Cassius, fly far off.
CAS. This hill is far enough.—Look, look,
   Titinius;
Are those my tents where I perceive the
   fire?
TIT. They are, my lord.
CAS.   Titinius, if thou lov'st me,
Mount thou my horse, and hide thy spurs
   in him,
Till he have brought thee up to yonder
   troops,
And here again; that I may rest assur'd
Whether yond' troops are friend or enemy.
TIT. I will be here again, even with a
   thought.   [*Exit.*
CAS. Go, Pindarus, get higher on that hill;
My sight was ever thick; regard Titinius,
And tell me what thou not'st about the
   field.—   [PINDARUS *goes up.*
This day I breathed first: time is come
   round,
And where I did begin, there shall I end;
My life is run his compass—Sirrah, what
   news?
PIN. [*Above.*] O my lord!
CAS. What news?
PIN. [*Above.*] Titinius is enclosed round
   about
With horsemen, that make to him on the
   spur;—
Yet he spurs on:—now they are almost on
   him;—
Now, Titinius!—now some 'light;—O, he
   'lights too:—
He's ta'en;—[*Shout.*] and, hark! they shout
   for joy.
CAS. Come down; behold no more.—
O, coward that I am. to live so long,
To see my best friend ta'en before my face!
          [PINDARUS *descends.*
Come hither, sirrah:
In Parthia did I take thee prisoner;
And then I swore thee, saving of thy life,
That whatsoever I did bid thee do,
Thou should'st attempt it. Come now, keep
   thine oath;
Now be a freeman; and, with this good
   sword,
That ran through Cæsar's bowels, search this
   bosom.
Stand not to answer: here, take thou the
   hilts;
And, when my face is cover'd, as 'tis now,
Guide thou the sword.—Cæsar, thou art
   reveng'd,
Even with the sword that kill'd thee.
          [*Dies.*

PIN. So, I am free: yet would not so have
   been,
Durst I have done my will. O Cassius!
Far from this country Pindarus shall run,
Where never Roman shall take note of him.
          [*Exit.*
Re-enter TITINIUS *with* MESSALA.

MES. It is but change, Titinius; for Oc-
   tavius
Is overthrown by noble Brutus' power,
As Cassius' legions are by Antony.
TIT. These tidings will well comfort Cas-
MES. Where did you leave him?   [sius.
TIT.   All disconsolate,
With Pindarus his bondman, on this hill.
MES. Is not that he that lies upon the
   ground?
TIT. He lies not like the living. O my
MES. Is not that he?   [heart!
TIT.   No, this was he, Messala,
But Cassius is no more.—O setting sun,
As in thy red rays thou dost sink to-night,
So in his red blood Cassius' day is set,—
The sun of Rome is set! Our day is gone;
Clouds, dews, and dangers come; our deeds
   are done!
Mistrust of my success hath done this deed.
MES. Mistrust of good success hath done
   this deed.
O hateful error, melancholy's child,
Why dost thou show to the apt thoughts of
   men
The things that are not? O error, soon con-
   ceiv'd,
Thou never com'st unto a happy birth,
But kill'st the mother that engender'd thee!
TIT. What, Pindarus! Where art thou,
   Pindarus?
MES. Seek him, Titinius, whilst I go to
   meet
The noble Brutus, thrusting this report
Into his ears: I may say, thrusting it;
For piercing steel, and darts envenomed,
Shall be as welcome to the ears of Brutus,
As tidings of this sight.
TIT.   Hie you, Messala,
And I will seek for Pindarus the while.
          [*Exit* MESSALA.
Why didst thou send me forth, brave
   Cassius?
Did I not meet thy friends? and did not
   they
Put on my brows this wreath of victory,
And bid me give it thee? Didst thou not
   hear their shouts?
Alas, thou hast misconstrued every thing!
But, hold thee, take this garland on thy
   brow;
Thy Brutus bid me give it thee, and I
Will do his bidding.—Brutus, come apace,
And see how I regarded Caius Cassius.—

By your leave, gods:—this is a Roman's
    part:
Come, Cassius' sword, and find Titinius'
    heart.   [*Dies.*
Alarum. Re-enter MESSALA, *with* BRUTUS,
    Young CATO, STRATO, VOLUMNIUS,
        and LUCILIUS.
BRU. Where, where, Messala, doth his
    body lie?
MES. Lo, yonder; and Titinius mourning
BRU. Titinius' face is upward.   [*it.*
CATO.   He is slain.
BRU. O Julius Cæsar, thou art mighty yet!
Thy spirit walks abroad, and turns our
In our own proper entrails.   [*swords*
                            [*Low alarums.*
CATO.   Brave Titinius!
Look, whe'r he have not crown'd dead
    Cassius!
BRU. Are yet two Romans living such as
    these?—
The last of all the Romans, fare thee well!
It is impossible that ever Rome
Should breed thy fellow.—Friends, I owe
    more tears
To this dead man, than you shall see me
    pay.—
I shall find time, Cassius, I shall find time.—
Come, therefore, and to Thassos send his
    body:
His funerals shall not be in our camp,
Lest it discomfort us.—Lucilius, come;—
And come, young Cato;—let us to the
    field.—
Labeo and Flavius, set our battles on:—
'Tis three o'clock; and, Romans, yet ere
    night
We shall try fortune in a second fight.
                                    [*Exeunt.*

SCENE IV.—*Another Part of the Field.*

Alarum. Enter, fighting, Soldiers *of both
    armies; then* BRUTUS, *Young* CATO,
        LUCILIUS, *and others.*

BRU. Yet, countrymen, O, yet hold up
    your heads!
CATO. What bastard doth not? Who will
    go with me?
I will proclaim my name about the field:—
I am the son of Marcus Cato, ho!
A foe to tyrants, and my country's friend;
I am the son of Marcus Cato, ho!
                        [*Charges the enemy.*
BRU. And I am Brutus, Marcus Brutus, I;
Brutus, my country's friend; know me for
    Brutus!
[*Exit charging the enemy. Young* CATO *is
    overpowered, and falls.*
LUCIL. O young and noble Cato, art thou
    down?

Why, now thou diest as bravely as Titinius;
And may'st be honour'd being Cato's son.
1 SOLD. Yield, or thou diest.
LUCIL.   Only I yield to die:
There is so much that thou wilt kill me
    straight.   [*Offering money.*
Kill Brutus, and be honour'd in his death.
1 SOLD. We must not.—A noble prisoner!
2 SOLD. Room, ho! Tell Antony, Brutus is
    ta'en.
1 SOLD. I'll tell the news:—here comes
    the general.—

Enter ANTONY.

Brutus is ta'en, Brutus is ta'en, my lord.
ANT. Where is he?
LUCIL. Safe, Antony; Brutus is safe
    enough:
I dare assure thee, that no enemy
Shall ever take alive the noble Brutus:
The gods defend him from so great a shame!
When you do find him, or alive, or dead,
He will be found like Brutus, like himself.
ANT. This is not Brutus, friend; but, I
    assure you,
A prize no less in worth: keep this man
    safe,
Give him all kindness: I had rather have
Such men my friends, than enemies. Go on,
And see whe'r Brutus be alive, or dead;
And bring us word, unto Octavius' tent,
How every thing is chanc'd.   [*Exeunt.*

SCENE V.—*Another Part of the Field.*

Enter BRUTUS, DARDANIUS, CLITUS, STRATO,
        and VOLUMNIUS.

BRU. Come, poor remains of friends, rest
    on this rock.
CLI. Statilius show'd the torch-light; but,
    my lord,
He came not back: he is or ta'en, or slain.
BRU. Sit thee down, Clitus: slaying is the
    word;
It is a deed in fashion. Hark thee, Clitus.
                            [*Whispering him.*
CLI. What, I, my lord? No, not for all the
    world.
BRU. Peace, then, no words.
CLI.   I'll rather kill myself.
BRU. Hark thee, Dardanius.
                            [*Whispers him.*
DAR.   Shall I do such a deed?
CLI. O, Dardanius!
DAR. O, Clitus!
CLI. What ill request did Brutus make to
    thee?
DAR. To kill him, Clitus. Look, he medi-
    tates.
CLI. Now is that noble vessel full of grief,
That it runs over even at his eyes.

BRU. Come hither, good Volumnius; list
a word.
VOL. What says my lord?
BRU.   Why, this, Volumnius:
The ghost of Cæsar hath appear'd to me
Two several times by night,—at Sardis once,
And, this last night, here in Philippi fields:
I know my hour is come.
VOL.   Not so, my lord.
BRU. Nay, I am sure it is, Volumnius.
Thou seest the world, Volumnius, how it
goes;
Our enemies have beat us to the pit:
                            [*Low alarums.*
It is more worthy to leap in ourselves,
Than tarry till they push us. Good Volum-
nius,
Thou know'st that we two went to school
together:
Even for that our love of old, I pray thee,
Hold thou my sword-hilts, whilst I run on it.
VOL. That's not an office for a friend, my
lord.   [*Alarum still.*
CLI. Fly, fly, my lord; there is no tarrying
here.
BRU. Farewell to you;—and you;—and
you, Volumnius.—
Strato, thou hast been all this while asleep;
Farewell to thee too, Strato.—Countrymen,
My heart doth joy, that yet, in all my life,
I found no man but he was true to me.
I shall have glory by this losing day,
More than Octavius and Mark Antony
By this vile conquest shall attain unto.
So, fare you well at once; for Brutus'
tongue
Hath almost ended his life's history:
Night hangs upon mine eyes; my bones
would rest,
That have but labour'd to attain this hour.
            [*Alarum. Cry within,* "Fly, fly, fly!"
CLI. Fly, my lord, fly.
BRU.   Hence! I will follow.
        [*Exeunt* CLITUS, DARDANIUS, *and*
                VOLUMNIUS.
I pr'ythee Strato, stay thou by thy lord:
Thou art a fellow of a good respect;
Thy life hath had some smatch of honour
in it:
Hold, then my sword, and turn away thy
face,

While I do run upon it. Wilt thou, Strato?
STRA. Give me your hand first: fare you
well, my lord.
BRU. Farewell, good Strato.—Cæsar, now
be still:
I kill'd not thee with half so good a will.
            [*He runs on his sword, and dies.*
Alarum. Retreat. Enter OCTAVIUS, ANTONY,
            MESSALA, LUCILIUS, *and army.*
OCT. What man is that?
MES. My master's man.—Strato, where is
thy master?
STRA. Free from the bondage you are in,
Messala:
The conquerors can but make a fire of him;
For Brutus only overcame himself,
And no man else hath honour by his death.
LUCIL. So Brutus should be found.—I
thank thee, Brutus,
That thou hast prov'd Lucilius' saying true.
OCT. All that serv'd Brutus, I will enter-
tain them.—
Fellow, wilt thou bestow thy time with me?
STRA. Ay, if Messala will prefer me to
you.
OCT. Do so, good Messala.   [you.
MES. How died my master, Strato?
STRA. I held the sword, and he did run
on it.
MES. Octavius, then take him to follow
thee,
That did the latest service to my master.
ANT. This was the noblest Roman of
them all:
All the conspirators, save only he,
Did that they did in envy of great Cæsar;
He, only, in a general honest thought,
And common good to all, made one of
them.
His life was gentle; and the elements
So mix'd in him, that Nature might stand
up,   [man!"
And say to all the world, "This was a
OCT. According to his virtue let us use
him,
With all respect and rites of burial.
Within my tent his bones to-night shall lie.
Most like a soldier, order'd honourably.—
So, call the field to rest: and let's away,
To part the glories of this happy day.
                            [*Exeunt.*

Macbeth about to murder Duncan. Act II. S.2.

MACBETH

DRAMATIS PERSONÆ.

DUNCAN, *King of Scotland.*
MALCOLM, } *his Sons.*
DONALBAIN,
MACBETH, } *Generals of the King's Army.*
BANQUO,
MACDUFF,
LENOX,
ROSSE, } *Noblemen of Scotland.*
MENTETH,
ANGUS,
CATHNESS,
FLEANCE, *Son to* BANQUO.
SIWARD, *Earl of Northumberland, General of the English Forces.*
Young SIWARD, *his Son.*

SEYTON, *an Officer attending* MACBETH.
Boy, *Son to* MACDUFF.
An English Doctor.
A Scotch Doctor.
A Soldier. *A* Porter. *An* Old Man.

LADY MACBETH.
LADY MACDUFF.
Gentlewoman *attending on* LADY MACBETH.
HECATE, *and three* Witches.

Lords, Gentlemen, Officers, Soldiers, Murderers, Attendants, *and* Messengers. *The Ghost of* BANQUO, *and other* Apparitions.

SCENE.—*In the end of the fourth Act, in* ENGLAND; *through the rest of the Play, in* SCOTLAND.

ACT I.

SCENE I.—*An open Place.*

Thunder and lightning. Enter three Witches.

1 *WITCH.* When shall we three meet again
In thunder, lightning, or in rain?
2 *WITCH.* When the hurlyburly's done,
When the battle's lost and won.

3 *WITCH.* That will be ere the set of sun.
1 *WITCH.* Where the place?
2 *WITCH.*   Upon the heath.
3 *WITCH.* There to meet with Macbeth.
1 *WITCH.* I come, Graymalkin!
ALL. Paddock calls:—Anon!—
Fair is foul, and foul is fair:
Hover through the fog and filthy air.
                    [*Witches vanish.*

SCENE II.—*A Camp near* FORES.

Alarum within. Enter KING DUNCAN, MAL-
COLM, DONALBAIN, LENOX, *with* Attendants, *meeting a bleeding* Soldier.

DUN. What bloody man is that? He can
report,
As seemeth by his plight, of the revolt
The newest state.
MAL.   This is the sergeant,
Who, like a good and hardy soldier, fought
'Gainst my captivity.—Hail, brave friend!
Say to the king the knowledge of the broil,
As thou didst leave it.
SOLD.   Doubtful it stood;
As two spent swimmers, that do cling to-
gether
And choke their art. The merciless Mac-
donwald
(Worthy to be a rebel,—for, to that,
The multiplying villanies of nature
Do swarm upon him) from the western
isles
Of Kernes and Gallowglasses is supplied;
And fortune, on his damned quarry smiling,
Show'd like a rebel's whore: but all's too
weak: [name)
For brave Macbeth, (well he deserves that
Disdaining fortune, with his brandish'd
steel,
Which smok'd with bloody execution,
Like valour's minion,   [slave;
Carv'd out his passage till he fac'd the
Which ne'er shook hands, nor bade fare-
well to him,
Till he unseam'd him from the nave to
the chops,
And fix'd his head upon our battlements.
DUN. O valiant cousin! worthy gentleman!
SOLD. As whence the sun 'gins his re-
flection   [break;
Shipwrecking storms and direful thunders
So from that spring, whence comfort
seem'd to come,
Discomfort swells. Mark, king of Scotland,
mark:
No sooner justice had, with valour arm'd,
Compell'd these skipping Kernes to trust
their heels,
But the Norweyan lord, surveying vantage,
With furbish'd arms, and new supplies of
Began a fresh assault.   [men,
DUN.   Dismay'd not this
Our captains, Macbeth and Banquo?
SOLD.   Yes;
As sparrows eagles, or the hare the lion.
If I say sooth, I must report they were
As cannons overcharg'd with double
cracks;   [the foe:
So they doubly redoubled strokes upon

Except they meant to bathe in reeking
wounds,
Or memorize another Golgotha,
I cannot tell:—
But I am faint, my gashes cry for help.
DUN. So well thy words become thee as
thy wounds:
They smack of honour both.—Go, get him
surgeons.   [*Exit* Soldier, *attended.*
Who comes here?
MAL.   The worthy thane of Rosse.
LEN. What a haste looks through his eyes!
So should he look, that seems to speak
things strange.

Enter ROSSE.

ROSSE. God save the king!
DUN. Whence cam'st thou, worthy thane?
ROSSE. From Fife, great king;
Where the Norweyan banners flout the sky
And fan our people cold.
Norway himself, with terrible numbers,
Assisted by that most disloyal traitor,
The thane of Cawdor, began a dismal con-
flict;   [proof,
Till that Bellona's bridegroom, lapp'd in
Confronted him with self-comparisons,
Point against point rebellious, arm 'gainst
arm,
Curbing his lavish spirit: and, to conclude,
The victory fell on us;—
DUN.   Great happiness!
ROSSE. That now
Sweno, the Norways' king, craves composi-
tion;
Nor would we deign him burial of his men
Till he disbursed, at Saint Colmes' Inch,
Ten thousand dollars to our general use.
DUN. No more that thane of Cawdor shall
deceive
Our bosom interest:—go, pronounce his
present death,
And with his former title greet Macbeth.
ROSSE. I'll see it done.
DUN. What he hath lost, noble Macbeth
hath won.   [*Exeunt.*

SCENE III.—*A Heath.*

Thunder. Enter the three Witches.

1 *WITCH.* Where hast thou been, sister?
2 *WITCH.* Killing swine.
3 *WITCH.* Sister, where thou?
1 *WITCH.* A sailor's wife had chesnuts in
her lap,
And mounch'd, and mounch'd, and
mounch'd:—
"Give me," quoth I:—
"Aroint thee, witch!" the rump-fed ronyon
cries.   [Tiger:
Her husband's to Aleppo gone, master o' the
But in a sieve I'll thither sail,

And, like a rat without a tail,
I'll do, I'll do, and I'll do.
2 *WITCH.* I'll give thee a wind.
1 *WITCH.* Thou art kind.
3 *WITCH.* And I another.
1 *WITCH.* I myself have all the other;
And the very ports they blow,
All the quarters that they know
I' the shipman's card.
I'll drain him dry as hay:
Sleep shall neither night nor day
Hang upon his pent-house lid;
He shall live a man forbid:
Weary sev'n-nights, nine times nine,
Shall he dwindle, peak, and pine:
Though his bark cannot be lost,
Yet it shall be tempest-toss'd.—
Look what I have.
2 *WITCH.* Show me, show me.
1 *WITCH.* Here I have a pilot's thumb,
Wreck'd as homeward he did come.
                           [*Drum within.*
3 *WITCH.* A drum, a drum!
Macbeth doth come.
ALL. The weird sisters, hand in hand,
Posters of the sea and land,
Thus do go about, about:
Thrice to thine, and thrice to mine,
And thrice again, to make up nine:—
Peace!—the charm's wound up.
          Enter MACBETH *and* BANQUO.
MACB. So foul and fair a day I have not
  seen.
BAN. How far is't call'd to Fores?—What
  are these,
So wither'd, and so wild in their attire,
That look not like th' inhabitants o' the
  earth,   [aught
And yet are on't?—Live you? or are you
That man may question? You seem to
  understand me,
By each at once her choppy finger laying
Upon her skinny lips:—You should be
  women,
And yet your beards forbid me to interpret
That you are so.
MACB. Speak, if you can;—what are you?
1 *WITCH.* All hail, Macbeth! hail to thee,
  thane of Glamis!
2 *WITCH.* All hail, Macbeth! hail to thee,
  thane of Cawdor!
3 *WITCH.* All hail, Macbeth! that shalt
  be king hereafter.
BAN. Good Sir, why do you start; and
  seem to fear
Things that do sound so fair?—I' the name
  of truth,
Are ye fantastical, or that indeed
Which outwardly ye show? My noble
  partner

You greet with present grace, and great
  prediction
Of noble having, and of royal hope,
That he seems rapt withal:—to me you
  speak not:
If you can look into the seeds of time,
And say which grain will grow, and which
  will not,
Speak then to me, who neither beg, nor
Your favours, nor your hate.   [fear,
1 *WITCH.* Hail!
2 *WITCH.* Hail!
3 *WITCH.* Hail!
1 *WITCH.* Lesser than Macbeth, and
  greater.
2 *WITCH.* Not so happy, yet much hap-
  pier.
3 *WITCH.* Thou shalt get kings, though
  thou be none:
So, all hail, Macbeth and Banquo!
1 *WITCH.* Banquo and Macbeth, all hail!
MACB. Stay, you imperfect speakers, tell
  me more:
By Sinel's death, I know, I am thane of
  Glamis;
But how of Cawdor? the thane of Cawdor
  lives,
A prosperous gentleman; and to be king
Stands not within the prospect of belief,
No more than to be Cawdor. Say, from
  whence
You owe this strange intelligence; or why
Upon this blasted heath you stop our way
With such prophetic greeting:—speak, I
  charge you.   [*Witches vanish.*
BAN. The earth hath bubbles, as the water
  has,
And these are of them:—whither are they
  vanish'd?
MACB. Into the air; and what seem'd
  corporal, melted
As breath into the wind.—'Would they
  had stay'd!
BAN. Were such things here as we do
  speak about?
Or have we eaten on the insane root,
That takes the reason prisoner?
MACB. Your children shall be kings.
BAN.   You shall be king.
MACB. And thane of Cawdor too,—went
  it not so?
BAN. To the self-same tune and words.
  Who's here?
          Enter ROSSE *and* ANGUS.
ROSSE. The king hath happily receiv'd,
  Macbeth,
The news of thy success: and when he reads
Thy personal venture in the rebels' fight,
His wonders and his praises do contend,
Which should be thine, or his: silenc'd with
  that,

In viewing o'er the rest o' the self-same day,
He finds thee in the stout Norweyan ranks,
Nothing afeard of what thyself didst make,
Strange images of death. As thick as tale,
Came post with post; and every one did
  bear
Thy praises in his kingdom's great defence,
And pour'd them down before him.
ANG.   We are sent
To give thee, from our royal master,
  thanks;
Only to herald thee into his sight,
Not pay thee.
ROSSE. And, for an earnest of a greater
  honour,
He bade me, from him, call thee thane of
  Cawdor:
In which addition, hail, most worthy thane!
For it is thine.
BAN.   What, can the devil speak true?
MACB. The thane of Cawdor lives: why
  do you dress me
In borrow'd robes?
ANG.   Who was the thane, lives yet;
But under heavy judgment bears that life
Which he deserves to lose. Whether he was
  combin'd
With those of Norway, or did line the rebel
With hidden help and vantage, or that
  with both
He labour'd in his country's wreck, I know
  not;
But treasons capital, confess'd, and prov'd,
Have overthrown him.
MACB. [*Aside.*] Glamis, and thane of
  Cawdor:
The greatest is behind.—[*Aloud.*] Thanks
  for your pains.—
Do you not hope your children shall be
  kings,
When those that gave the thane of Cawdor
Promis'd no less to them?   [to me,
BAN.   That, trusted home,
Might yet enkindle you unto the crown,
Besides the thane of Cawdor. But 'tis
  strange:
And oftentimes, to win us to our harm,
The instruments of darkness tell us truths;
Win us with honest trifles, to betray us
In deepest consequence.—
Cousins, a word, I pray you.
MACB. [*Aside.*]   Two truths are told,
As happy prologues to the swelling act
Of the imperial theme.—[*Aloud.*] I thank
  you, gentlemen.
[*Aside.*] This supernatural soliciting
Cannot be ill; cannot be good:—if ill,
Why hath it given me earnest of success,
Commencing in a truth? I am thane of
  Cawdor:

If good, why do I yield to that suggestion
Whose horrid image doth unfix my hair,
And make my seated heart knock at my
  ribs,
Against the use of nature? Present fears
Are less than horrible imaginings:
My thought, whose murder yet is but
  fantastical,
Shakes so my single state of man, that
  function
Is smother'd in surmise; and nothing is,
But what is not.
BAN.   Look, how our partner's rapt.
MACB. [*Aside.*] If chance will have me
  king, why, chance may crown me,
Without my stir.
BAN.   New honours come upon him,
Like our strange garments,—cleave not to
  their mould,
But with the aid of use.
MACB. [*Aside.*]   Come what come may,
Time and the hour runs through the rough-
  est day.
BAN. Worthy Macbeth, we stay upon your
  leisure.
MACB. Give me your favour: my dull
  brain was wrought
With things forgotten.—Kind gentlemen
  your pains
Are register'd where every day I turn
The leaf to read them.—Let us toward the
  king.—
Think upon what hath chanc'd; and, at
  more time,
The interim having weigh'd it, let us speak
Our free hearts each to other.
BAN.   Very gladly.
MACB. Till then, enough.—Come, friends.
                    [*Exeunt.*

SCENE IV.—FORES. *A Room in the Palace.*
  Flourish. Enter DUNCAN, MALCOLM,
  DONALBAIN, LENOX, *and* Attendants.

DUN. Is execution done on Cawdor? Are
Those in commission yet return'd?   [not
MAL.   My liege,
They are not yet come back. But I have
  spoke
With one that saw him die: who did report,
That very frankly he confess'd his treasons;
Implor'd your highness' pardon; and set
  forth
A deep repentance: nothing in his life
Became him like the leaving it; he died
As one that had been studied in his death,
To throw away the dearest thing he ow'd,
As 'twere a careless trifle.
DUN.   There's no art

To find the mind's construction in the face:
He was a gentleman on whom I built
An absolute trust.—

     Enter MACBETH, BANQUO, ROSSE,
         and ANGUS.

           O worthiest cousin!
The sin of my ingratitude even now
Was heavy on me: thou art so far before,
That swiftest wing of recompense is slow
To overtake thee. Would thou hadst less
   deserv'd;
That the proportion both of thanks and
   payment
Might have been mine! only I have left
   to say,
More is thy due than more than all can
   pay.
MACB. The service and the loyalty I owe,
In doing it, pays itself. Your highness' part
Is to receive our duties: and our duties
Are to your throne and state, children and
   servants;
Which do but what they should, by doing
   every thing
Safe toward your love and honour.
DUN.   Welcome hither:
I have begun to plant thee, and will labour
To make thee full of growing.—Noble
   Banquo,
Thou hast no less deserv'd, nor must be
   known
No less to have done so; let me infold thee,
And hold thee to my heart.
BAN.   There if I grow,
The harvest is your own.
DUN.   My plenteous joys
Wanton in fulness, seek to hide themselves
In drops of sorrow.—Sons, kinsmen, thanes,
And you whose places are the nearest,
   know,
We will establish our estate upon
Our eldest, Malcolm; whom we name here-
   after,
The prince of Cumberland: which honour
   must
Not, unaccompanied, invest him only;
But signs of nobleness, like stars, shall
   shine
On all deservers.—From hence to Inverness,
And bind us farther to you.
MACB. The rest is labour, which is not
   us'd for you:
I'll be myself the harbinger, and make
   joyful
The hearing of my wife with your ap-
So, humbly take my leave.   [proach;
DUN.   My worthy Cawdor!
MACB. [*Aside.*] The prince of Cumber-
   land! that is a step,
On which I must fall down, or else o'er-
   leap,

For in my way it lies. Stars, hide your
   fires!
Let not light see my black and deep
   desires:
The eye wink at the hand; yet let that be,
Which the eye fears, when it is done, to
   see!   [*Exit.*
DUN. True, worthy Banquo,—he is full so
   valiant;
And in his commendations I am fed,—
It is a banquet to me. Let us after him,
Whose care is gone before to bid us
   welcome:
It is a peerless kinsman.
                         [*Flourish. Exeunt.*

SCENE V.—INVERNESS. *A Room in* MACBETH'S *Castle.*

Enter LADY MACBETH, *reading a letter.*

LADY M. "They met me in the day of success; and I have learned by the perfectest
report, they have more in them than mortal
knowledge. When I burned in desire to
question them farther, they made themselves air, into which they vanished. Whiles
I stood rapt in the wonder of it, came missives from the king, who all hailed me,
'Thane of Cawdor;' by which title, before,
these weird sisters saluted me, and referred
me to the coming on of time, with, 'Hail,
king that shalt be!' This have I thought
good to deliver thee, my dearest partner of
greatness, that thou mightest not lose the
dues of rejoicing, by being ignorant of what
greatness is promised thee. Lay it to thy
heart and farewell."
Glamis thou art, and Cawdor; and shalt be
What thou art promis'd:—yet do I fear
   thy nature;
It is too full o' the milk of human kindness,
To catch the nearest way: thou wouldst
   be great;
Art not without ambition; but without
The illness should attend it: what thou
   wouldst highly,
That wouldst thou holily; wouldst not play
   false,
And yet wouldst wrongly win: thou'dst
   have, great Glamis,
That which cries, "Thus thou must do, if
   thou have it;
And that which rather thou dost fear to do,
Than wishest should be undone." Hie thee
   hither,
That I may pour my spirits in thine ear;
And chastise with the valour of my tongue
All that impedes thee from the golden
   round,
Which fate and metaphysical aid doth seem
To have thee crown'd withal.—

Enter an Attendant.
　　　　　　What is your tidings?
ATTEN. The king comes here to-night.
LADY M. 　　　　　Thou'rt mad to say it:
Is not thy master with him? who, wer't so,
Would have inform'd for preparation.
ATTEN. So please you, it is true:—our
　　thane is coming:
One of my fellows had the speed of him;
Who, almost dead for breath, had scarcely
　　more
Than would make up his message.
LADY M. 　　　　　Give him tending;
He brings great news. [*Exit* Attendant.]
　　The raven himself is hoarse
That croaks the fatal entrance of Duncan
Under my battlements. Come, you spirits
That tend on mortal thoughts, unsex me
　　here;
And fill me, from the crown to the toe,
　　top-full
Of direst cruelty! make thick my blood,
Stop up th' access and passage to remorse;
That no compunctious visitings of nature
Shake my fell purpose, nor keep peace
　　between
Th' effect and it! Come to my woman's
　　breasts,
And take my milk for gall, you murdering
　　ministers,
Wherever in your sightless substances
You wait on nature's mischief! Come, thick
　　night,
And pall thee in the dunnest smoke of hell,
That my keen knife see not the wound it
　　makes,
Nor heaven peep through the blanket of
To cry, "Hold, hold!"—　　[the dark,
　　　Enter MACBETH.
　　　Great Glamis! worthy Cawdor!
Greater than both, by the all-hail hereafter!
Thy letters have transported me beyond
This ignorant present, and I feel now
The future in the instant.
MACB. 　　　　　My dearest love,
Duncan comes here to-night.
LADY M. 　　　And when goes hence?
MACB. Tomorrow, as he purposes.
LADY M. 　　　　　　O, never
Shall sun that morrow see!
Your face, my thane, is as a book where
　　men
May read strange matters:—to beguile the
　　time,
Look like the time; bear welcome in your
　　eye,
Your hand, your tongue: look like the
　　innocent flower,
But be the serpent under it. He that's
　　coming

Must be provided for: and you shall put
This night's great business into my
　　despatch;
Which shall to all our nights and days to
　　come
Give solely sovereign sway and masterdom.
MACB. We will speak farther.
LADY M. 　　　　Only look up clear;
To alter favour ever is to fear:
Leave all the rest to me. 　　[*Exeunt.*

SCENE VI.—INVERNESS. *Before the Castle.*
Hautboys. Servants *of* MACBETH *attending.*
　　Enter DUNCAN, MALCOLM, DONALBAIN,
　　BANQUO, LENOX, MACDUFF, ROSSE,
　　ANGUS, *and* Attendants.
DUN. This castle hath a pleasant seat;
　　the air
Nimbly and sweetly recommends itself
Unto our gentle senses.
BAN. 　　　　This guest of summer,
The temple-haunting martlet, does approve,
By his lov'd mansionry, that the heaven's
　　breath
Smells wooingly here: no jutty, frieze,
Buttress, nor coigne of vantage, but this
　　bird
Hath made his pendent bed, and procreant
　　cradle:
Where they most breed and haunt, I have
The air is delicate. 　　[observ'd,
　　　Enter LADY MACBETH.
DUN. See, see, our honour'd hostess!—
The love that follows us sometime is our
　　trouble,
Which still we thank as love. Herein I
　　teach you,
How you shall bid God yield us for your
And thank us for your trouble. 　[pains,
LADY M. 　　　　　All our service,
In every point twice done, and then done
　　double,
Were poor and single business to contend
Against those honours deep and broad,
　　wherewith
Your majesty loads our house: for those
　　of old,
And the late dignities heap'd up to them,
We rest your hermits.
DUN. 　　Where's the thane of Cawdor?
We cours'd him at the heels, and had a
　　purpose
To be his purveyor: but he rides well;
And his great love, sharp as his spur,
　　hath holp him
To his home before us. Fair and noble
We are your guest to-night. 　[hostess,
LADY M. 　　　Your servants ever
Have theirs, themselves, and what is theirs,
　　in compt,

To make their audit at your highness'
Still to return your own.   [pleasure,
DUN.   Give me your hand;
Conduct me to mine host: we love him
  highly,
And shall continue our graces towards him.
By your leave, hostess.   [*Exeunt.*

———

SCENE VII.—INVERNESS. *A Passage-room in
            the Castle.*

*Hautboys and torches. Enter, and pass, a
  Sewer, and divers Servants with dishes
  and service. Then, enter* MACBETH.

MACB. If it were done, when 'tis done,
  then 'twere well
It were done quickly: if the assassination
Could trammel up the consequence, and
  catch,
With his surcease, success; that but this
  blow
Might be the be-all and the end-all here,
But here, upon this bank and shoal of
  time,—
We'd jump the life to come. But in these
  cases,
We still have judgment here; that we but
  teach
Bloody instructions, which, being taught,
  return
To plague th' inventor: this even-handed
  justice
Commends th' ingredients of our poison'd
  chalice
To our own lips. He's here in double trust:
First, as I am his kinsman and his subject,
Strong both against the deed; then, as his
  host,
Who should against his murderer shut the
  door,
Not bear the knife myself. Besides, this
  Duncan
Hath borne his faculties so meek, hath been
So clear in his great office, that his virtues
Will plead like angels, trumpet-tongued,
  against
The deep damnation of his taking-off;
And pity, like a naked new-born babe,
Striding the blast, or heaven's cherubin,
  hors'd
Upon the sightless couriers of the air,
Shall blow the horrid deed in every eye,
That tears shall drown the wind.—I have
  no spur
To prick the sides of my intent, but only
Vaulting ambition, which o'er-leaps itself,
And falls on the other.
            Enter LADY MACBETH.
                How now! what news?
LADY M. He has almost supp'd: why
have you left the chamber?

MACB. Hath he ask'd for me?
LADY M.   Know you not he has?
MACB. We will proceed no farther in this
  business:
He hath honour'd me of late; and I have
  bought
Golden opinions from all sorts of people,
Which would be worn now in their newest
  gloss,
Not cast aside so soon.   [gloss,
LADY M.   Was the hope drunk,
Wherein you dress'd yourself? hath it slept
  since?
And wakes it now, to look so green and
  pale
At what it did so freely? From this time,
Such I account thy love. Art thou afeard
To be the same in thine own act and valour,
As thou art in desire? Would'st thou have
  that
Which thou esteem'st the ornament of life,
And live a coward in thine own esteem,
Letting "I dare not" wait upon "I would,"
Like the poor cat i' the adage?
MACB.   Pr'ythee, peace:
I dare do all that may become a man;
Who dares do more is none.
LADY M.   What beast was't, then,
That made you break this enterprise to
  me?
When you durst do it, then you were a
  man;
And, to be more than what you were, you
  would
Be so much more the man. Nor time, nor
  place,
Did then adhere, and yet you would make
  both:
They have made themselves, and that their
  fitness now
Does unmake you. I have given suck, and
  know
How tender 'tis to love the babe that
  milks me:
I would, while it was smiling in my face,
Have pluck'd my nipple from his boneless
  gums,
And dash'd the brains out, had I so sworn
Have done to this.   [as you
MACB.   If we should fail?
LADY M.   We fail!
But screw your courage to the sticking-
  place,
And we'll not fail. When Duncan is asleep
(Whereto the rather shall his day's hard
  journey
Soundly invite him) his two chamberlains
Will I with wine and wassail so convince,
That memory, the warder of the brain,
Shall be a fume, and the receipt of reason
A limbeck only: when in swinish sleep

Their drenched natures lie, as in a death,
What cannot you and I perform upon
Th' unguarded Duncan? what not put upon
His spungy officers, who shall bear the guilt
Of our great quell?

MACB.   Bring forth men-children only;
For thy undaunted mettle should compose
Nothing but males. Will it not be receiv'd,
When we have mark'd with blood those
        sleepy two
Of his own chamber, and us'd their very
        daggers,
That they have done't?

LADY M.   Who dares receive it other,
As we shall make our griefs and clamour
Upon his death?   [roar

MACB.   I am settled, and bend up
Each corporal agent to this terrible feat.
Away, and mock the time with fairest
        show:
False face must hide what the false heart
        doth know.   [*Exeunt.*

ACT II.

SCENE I.—INVERNESS. *Court within*
        MACBETH'S *Castle.*

Enter BANQUO, *preceded by* FLEANCE, *with
        a torch.*

BAN. How goes the night, boy?

FLE. The moon is down; I have not heard
        the clock.

BAN. And she goes down at twelve.

FLE.   I take't, 'tis later, Sir.

BAN. Hold, take my sword:—there's hus-
        bandry in heaven,
Their candles are all out:—take thee that
        too.—
A heavy summons lies like lead upon me,
And yet I would not sleep:—merciful
        powers,
Restrain in me the cursed thoughts that
        nature
Gives way to in repose!—Give me my
Who's there?   [sword.—

Enter MACBETH, *and a* Servant *with a torch.*

MACB. A friend.

BAN. What, Sir, not yet at rest? The
        king's a-bed:
He hath been in unusual pleasure, and
Sent forth great largess to your offices:
This diamond he greets your wife withal,
By the name of most kind hostess; and
In measureless content.   [shut up

MACB.   Being unprepar'd,
Our will became the servant to defect;
Which else should free have wrought.

BAN.   All's well.—
I dreamt last night of the three weird
        sisters:
To you they have show'd some truth.

MACB.   I think not of them:
Yet, when we can entreat an hour to serve,
We would spend it in some words upon that
        business,
If you would grant the time.

BAN.   At your kind'st leisure.

MACB. If you shall cleave to my consent,
        —when 'tis,
It shall make honour for you.

BAN.   So I lose none
In seeking to augment it, but still keep
My bosom franchis'd, and allegiance clear,
I shall be counsell'd.

MACB.   Good repose the while!

BAN. Thanks, Sir: the like to you!
        [*Exeunt* BANQUO *and* FLEANCE.

MACB. Go bid thy mistress, when my
        drink is ready,
She strike upon the bell. Get thee to bed.—
        [*Exit* Servant.
Is this a dagger which I see before me,
The handle toward my hand? Come, let
        me clutch thee:—
I have thee not, and yet I see thee still.
Art thou not, fatal vision, sensible
To feeling as to sight? or art thou but
A dagger of the mind, a false creation,
Proceeding from the heat-oppressed brain?
I see thee yet, in form as palpable
As this which now I draw.
Thou marshall'st me the way that I was
        going;
And such an instrument I was to use.
Mine eyes are made the fools o' the other
        senses,
Or else worth all the rest: I see thee still;
And on thy blade and dudgeon gouts of
        blood,
Which was not so before.—There's no such
        thing:
It is the bloody business, which informs
Thus to mine eyes.—Now o'er the one half
        world
Nature seems dead, and wicked dreams
        abuse
The curtain'd sleep; witchcraft celebrates
Pale Hecate's offerings; and wither'd
        murder,
Alarum'd by his sentinel, the wolf,
Whose howl's his watch, thus with his
        stealthy pace,
With Tarquin's ravishing strides, towards
        his design
Moves like a ghost.—Thou sure and firm-
        set earth,
Hear not my steps, which way they walk,
        for fear
Thy very stones prate of my whereabout,
And take the present horror from the time,
Which now suits with it.—Whiles I threat,
        he lives:

Words to the heat of deeds too cold
  breath gives.   [*A bell rings.*
I go, and it is done; the bell invites me.
Hear it not, Duncan; for it is a knell
That summons thee to heaven or to hell.
                                [*Exit.*

———

SCENE II.—*The Same.*
Enter LADY MACBETH.

LADY M. That which hath made them
  drunk hath made me bold;
What hath quench'd them hath given me
  fire.—Hark!—Peace!
It was the owl that shriek'd, the fatal bell-
  man,
Which gives the stern'st good-night.—He is
  about it:
The doors are open; and the surfeited
  grooms
Do mock their charge with snores: I have
  drugg'd their possets,
That death and nature do contend about
Whether they live, or die.   [*them,*
MACB. [*Within.*] Who's there? what, ho!
LADY M. Alack, I am afraid they have
  awak'd,
And 'tis not done:—the attempt, and not
  the deed,
Confounds us.—Hark!—I laid their daggers
  ready;
He could not miss them.—Had he not
  resembled
My father as he slept, I had done't.—My
  husband!
            Enter MACBETH.
MACB. I have done the deed.—Didst thou
  not hear a noise?
LADY M. I heard the owl scream, and the
  crickets cry.
Did not you speak?
MACB.   When?
LADY M.   Now.
MACB.   As I descended?
LADY M. Ay.
MACB. Hark!—
Who lies i' the second chamber?
LADY M.   Donalbain.
MACB. [*Looking on his hands.*] This is
  a sorry sight.
LADY M. A foolish thought, to say a
  sorry sight.
MACB. There's one did laugh in's sleep,
  and one cried, "murder!"
That they did wake each other: I stood
  and heard them:
But they did say their prayers, and ad-
Again to sleep.   [*dress'd them*
LADY M. There are two lodg'd together.
MACB. One cried, "God bless us!" and,
  "Amen," the other;

As they had seen me with these hangman's
  hands.
Listening their fear, I could not say
  "Amen,"
When they did say, "God bless us."
LADY M.   Consider it not so deeply.
MACB. But wherefore could not I pro-
  nounce "Amen?"
I had most need of blessing, and "Amen"
Stuck in my throat.
LADY M. These deeds must not be thought
After these ways; so, it will make us mad.
MACB. Methought I heard a voice cry,
  "Sleep no more!
Macbeth does murder sleep,"—the innocent
  sleep,
Sleep that knits up the ravell'd sleave of
  care,
The death of each day's life, sore labour's
  bath,
Balm of hurt minds, great nature's second
  course,
Chief nourisher in life's feast,—
LADY M.   What do you mean?
MACB. Still it cried, "Sleep no more!" to
  all the house:
"Glamis hath murder'd sleep, and therefore
  Cawdor
Shall sleep no more,—Macbeth shall sleep
  no more!"
LADY M. Who was it that thus cried?
  Why, worthy thane,
You do unbend your noble strength, to
  think
So brainsickly of things.—Go get some
  water,
And wash this filthy witness from your
  hand.—
Why did you bring these daggers from
  the place?
They must lie there: go carry them; and
The sleepy grooms with blood.   [*smear*
MACB.   I'll go no more:
I am afraid to think what I have done;
Look on't again, I dare not.
LADY M.   Infirm of purpose!
Give me the daggers: the sleeping, and the
  dead,
Are but as pictures: 'tis the eye of child-
  hood
That fears a painted devil. If he do bleed,
I'll gild the faces of the grooms withal;
For it must seem their guilt.
            [*Exit. Knocking heard.*
MACB.   Whence is that knocking?
How is't with me, when every noise appals
  me?
What hands are here! Ha! they pluck out
  mine eyes!
Will all great Neptune's ocean wash this
  blood

Clean from my hand? No; this my hand
will rather
The multitudinous seas incarnardine,
Making the green—one red.
Re-enter LADY MACBETH.
LADY M. My hands are of your colour;
but I shame
To wear a heart so white. [*Knocking.*] I
hear a knocking
At the south entry:—retire we to our
chamber:
A little water clears us of this deed:
How easy is it, then! Your constancy
Hath left you unattended.—[*Knocking.*]
Hark! more knocking:
Get on your night-gown, lest occasion call
us,
And show us to be watchers:—be not lost
So poorly in your thoughts.
MACB. To know my deed, 'twere best not
know myself.   [*Knocking.*
Wake Duncan with thy knocking! I would
thou couldst!   [*Exeunt.*

SCENE III.—*The Same.*
Knocking heard. Enter a Porter.
PORT. Here's a knocking, indeed! If a
man were porter of hell-gate, he should
have old turning of the key. [*Knocking.*]
Knock, knock, knock! Who's there, i' the
name of Beelzebub? Here's a farmer, that
hanged himself on the expectation of
plenty: come in time; have napkins enough
about you; here you'll sweat for't. [*Knocking.*] Knock, knock! Who's there, in the
other devil's name?—'Faith, here's an
equivocator, that could swear in both the
scales against either scale; who committed
treason enough for God's sake, yet could
not equivocate to heaven: O, come in,
equivocator. [*Knocking.*] Knock, knock,
knock! Who's there?—'Faith, here's an
English tailor come hither, for stealing out
of a French hose: come in, tailor; here
you may roast your goose. [*Knocking.*]
Knock, knock; never at quiet! What are
you?—But this place is too cold for hell.
I'll devil-porter it no farther: I had thought
to have let in some of all professions, that
go the primrose way to the everlasting bon-
fire. [*Knocking.*] Anon, anon! I pray you,
remember the porter.   [*Opens the gate.*
Enter MACDUFF *and* LENOX.
MACD. Was it so late, friend, ere you
went to bed,
That you do lie so late?
PORT. 'Faith, Sir, we were carousing till
the second cock: and drink, Sir, is a great
provoker of three things.

MACD. What three things does drink
especially provoke?
PORT. Marry, Sir, nose-painting, sleep,
and urine. Lechery, Sir, it provokes, and
unprovokes; it provokes the desire, but it
takes away the performance: therefore,
much drink may be said to be an equivocator with lechery: it makes him, and it
mars him; it sets him on, and it takes him
off; it persuades him, and disheartens him;
makes him stand to, and not stand to; in
conclusion, equivocates him in a sleep, and,
giving him the lie, leaves him.
MACD. I believe, drink gave thee the lie
last night.
PORT. That it did, Sir, i' the very throat
on me: but I requited him for his lie; and,
think, being too strong for him, though he
took up my legs sometime, yet I made a
shift to cast him.
MACD. Is thy master stirring?—
Our knocking has awak'd him; here he
comes.
Enter MACBETH.
LEN. Good morrow, noble Sir.
MACB.   Good morrow, both.
MACD. Is the king stirring, worthy thane?
MACB.   Not yet.
MACD. He did command me to call time-
ly on him:
I have almost slipp'd the hour.
MACB.   I'll bring you to him.
MACD. I know this is a joyful trouble
But yet 'tis one.   [to you;
MACB. The labour we delight in physics
This is the door.   [pain.
MACD.   I'll make so bold to call,
For 'tis my limited service.   [*Exit.*
LEN. Goes the king hence to-day?
MACB.   He does:—he did appoint so.
LEN. The night has been unruly: where
we lay,
Our chimneys were blown down; and, as
they say,
Lamentings heard i' the air; strange
screams of death;
And prophesying, with accents terrible,
Of dire combustion, and confus'd events,
New hatch'd to the woful time: the obscure
bird
Clamour'd the livelong night: some say,
the earth
Was feverous, and did shake.
MACB.   'Twas a rough night.
LEN. My young remembrance cannot
A fellow to it.   [parallel
Re-enter MACDUFF.
MACD. O horror! horror! horror! Tongue
nor heart
Cannot conceive, nor name thee!

MACB. LEN.   What's the matter?
MACD. Confusion now hath made his
master-piece!
Most sacrilegious murder hath broke ope
The Lord's anointed temple, and stole
The life o' the building!   [thence
MACB. What is't you say? the life?
LEN. Mean you his majesty?
MACD. Approach the chamber, and
destroy your sight
With a new Gorgon:—do not bid me speak;
See, and then speak yourselves.—
            [*Exeunt* Macbeth *and* Lenox.
                Awake, awake!—
Ring the alarum-bell:—murder and trea-
son!—
Banquo and Donalbain! Malcolm! awake!
Shake off this downy sleep, death's counter-
feit,
And look on death itself! up, up, and see
The great doom's image! Malcolm!
Banquo!
As from your graves rise up, and walk
like sprites
To countenance this horror! Ring the bell.
            [*Alarum-bell rings.*
        Enter Lady Macbeth.
LADY M. What's the business,
That such a hideous trumpet calls to parley
The sleepers of the house? speak, speak!
MACD.   O gentle lady,
'Tis not for you to hear what I can speak:
The repetition, in a woman's ear,
Would murder as it fell.—
        Enter Banquo.
                O Banquo, Banquo,
Our royal master's murder'd!
LADY M.   Woe, alas!
What, in our house?
BAN.   Too cruel, anywhere.—
Dear Duff, I pr'ythee, contradict thyself,
And say it is not so.
        Re-enter Macbeth *and* Lenox.
MACB. Had I but died an hour before
    this chance,
I had liv'd a blessed time; for, from this
    instant,
There's nothing serious in mortality:
All is but toys: renown and grace is dead;
The wine of life is drawn, and the mere
Is left this vault to brag of.   [lees
        Enter Malcolm *and* Donalbain.
DON. What is amiss?
MACB.   You are, and do not know't:
The spring, the head, the fountain of your
    blood
Is stopp'd,—the very source of it is stopp'd.
MACD. Your royal father's murder'd.
MAL.   O, by whom?
LEN. Those of his chamber, as it seem'd,
    had done't:

Their hands and faces were all badg'd
    with blood;
So were their daggers, which, unwip'd, we
    found
Upon their pillows: they star'd, and were
    distracted;
No man's life was to be trusted with them.
MACB. O, yet I do repent me of my fury,
That I did kill them.
MACD.   Wherefore did you so?
MACB. Who can be wise, amaz'd, temper-
    ate and furious,
Loyal and neutral, in a moment? No man:
The expedition of my violent love
Outran the pauser reason. Here lay Duncan,
His silver skin lac'd with his golden blood;
And his gash'd stabs look'd like a breach
    in nature,
For ruin's wasteful entrance: there, the
    murderers,
Steep'd in the colours of their trade, their
    daggers
Unmannerly breech'd with gore: who could
    refrain,
That had a heart to love, and in that heart
Courage to make his love known?
LADY M.   Help me hence, ho!
MACD. Look to the lady.
MAL. [*Aside to* Don.] Why do we hold
    our tongues,
That most may claim this argument for
    ours?
DON. [*Aside to* Mal.] What should be
    spoken
Here, where our fate, hid in an auger-hole,
May rush, and seize us? Let's away: our
Are not yet brew'd.   [tears
MAL. [*Aside to* Don.] Nor our strong
Upon the foot of motion.   [sorrow
BAN.   Look to the lady:—
        [Lady Macbeth *is carried out.*
And when we have our naked frailties hid,
That suffer in exposure, let us meet,
And question this most bloody piece of
    work,
To know it farther. Fears and scruples
    shake us:
In the great hand of God I stand; and
    thence,
Against the undivulg'd pretence I fight
Of treasonous malice.
MACD.   And so do I.
ALL.   So all.
MACB. Let's briefly put on manly readi-
And meet i' the hall together.   [ness,
ALL.   Well contented.
        [*Exeunt all but* Mal. *and* Don.
MAL. What will you do? Let's not consort
    with them:
To show an unfelt sorrow is an office

Which the false man does easy. I'll to
England.
DON. To Ireland, I; our separated fortune
Shall keep us both the safer: where we are,
There's daggers in men's smiles: the near
The nearer bloody. [in blood,
MAL. This murderous shaft that's shot
Hath not yet lighted; and our safest way
Is to avoid the aim. Therefore, to horse;
And let us not be dainty of leave-taking,
But shift away: there's warrant in that
theft
Which steals itself, when there's no mercy
left. [Exeunt.

SCENE IV.—INVERNESS. *Without the Castle.*
Enter ROSSE *and an* OLD MAN.

OLD M. Threescore and ten I can remem-
ber well:
Within the volume of which time I have
seen
Hours dreadful, and things strange; but
this sore night
Hath trifled former knowings.
ROSSE. Ah, good father,
Thou seest, the heavens, as troubled with
man's act,
Threaten his bloody stage: by the clock,
'tis day,
And yet dark night strangles the travelling
lamp:
Is't night's predominance, or the day's
shame,
That darkness does the face of earth
entomb,
When living light should kiss it?
OLD M. 'Tis unnatural,
Even like the deed that's done. On Tuesday
last,
A falcon, towering in her pride of place,
Was by a mousing owl hawk'd at, and
kill'd.
ROSSE. And Duncan's horses, (a thing
most strange and certain)
Beauteous and swift, the minions of their
race,
Turn'd wild in nature, broke their stalls,
flung out,
Contending 'gainst obedience, as they
Make war with mankind. [would
OLD M. 'Tis said, they eat each other.
ROSSE. They did so,—to th' amazement
of mine eyes,
That look'd upon't.—Here comes the good
Macduff.—
Enter MACDUFF.
How goes the world, Sir, now?
MACD. Why, see you not?
ROSSE. Is't known who did this more than
bloody deed?

MACD. Those that Macbeth hath slain.
ROSSE. Alas, the day!
What good could they pretend?
MACD. They were suborn'd:
Malcolm and Donalbain, the king's two
sons,
Are stol'n away and fled; which puts upon
Suspicion of the deed. [them
ROSSE. 'Gainst nature still:
Thriftless ambition, that wilt ravin up
Thine own life's means!—Then, 'tis most
like,
The sovereignty will fall upon Macbeth.
MACD. He is already nam'd; and gone
To be invested. [to Scone
ROSSE. Where is Duncan's body?
MACD. Carried to Colme-kill.
The sacred store-house of his predecessors,
And guardian of their bones.
ROSSE. Will you to Scone?
MACD. No, cousin, I'll to Fife.
ROSSE. Well, I will thither.
MACD. Well, may you see things well
done there,—adieu,—
Lest our old robes sit easier than our new!
ROSSE. Farewell, father.
OLD M. God's benison go with you; and
with those
That would make good of bad, and friends
of foes! [Exeunt.

ACT III.

SCENE I.—FORES. *A Room in the Palace.*
Enter BANQUO.

BAN. Thou hast it now,—King, Cawdor,
Glamis, all,
As the weird women promis'd; and, I fear,
Thou play'd'st most foully for't: yet it was
said,
It should not stand in thy posterity;
But that myself should be the root and
father
Of many kings. If there come truth from
them,
(As upon thee, Macbeth, their speeches
shine)
Why, by the verities on thee made good,
May they not be my oracles as well,
And set me up in hope? But, hush; no
more.
Sennet sounded. Enter MACBETH, *as King;*
LADY MACBETH, *as Queen;* LENOX, ROSSE,
Lords, Ladies, *and* Attendants.
MACB. Here's our chief guest.
LADY M. If he had been forgotten,
It had been as a gap in our great feast,
And all-thing unbecoming.
MACB. To-night we hold a solemn supper,
And I'll request your presence. [Sir,

BAN.   Let your highness
Command upon me; to the which my duties
Are with a most indissoluble tie
For ever knit.
MACB. Ride you this afternoon?
BAN. Ay, my good lord.
MACB. We should have else desir'd your
good advice
(Which still hath been both grave and
prosperous)
In this day's council; but we'll take to-
Is't far you ride?   [morrow.
BAN. As far, my lord, as will fill up the
time
'Twixt this and supper: go not my horse
the better,
I must become a borrower of the night
For a dark hour, or twain.
MACB.   Fail not our feast.
BAN. My lord, I will not.
MACB. We hear, our bloody cousins are
bestow'd
In England, and in Ireland; not confess-
ing
Their cruel parricide, filling their hearers
With strange invention: but of that to-
morrow;
When, therewithal, we shall have cause of
state
Craving us jointly. Hie you to horse: adieu,
Till you return at night. Goes Fleance
with you?
BAN. Ay, my good lord: our time does
call upon us.
MACB. I wish your horses swift, and sure
of foot;
And so I do commend you to their backs.
Farewell.—   [*Exit* BANQUO.
Let every man be master of his time
Till seven at night: to make society
The sweeter welcome, we will keep ourself
Till supper-time alone: while then, God
be with you!
[*Exeunt* LADY MACBETH, Lords, Ladies, &c.
Sirrah, a word with you: attend those men
Our pleasure?
ATTEN. They are, my lord, without the
palace gate.
MACB. Bring them before us.—[*Exit* At-
ten.] To be thus is nothing;
But to be safely thus:—our fears in Banquo
Stick deep; and in his royalty of nature
Reigns that which would be fear'd: 'tis
much he dares;
And, to that dauntless temper of his mind,
He hath a wisdom that doth guide his
valour
To act in safety. There is none but he
Whose being I do fear: and, under him,
My Genius is rebuk'd; as, it is said,

Mark Antony's was by Cæsar. He chid
the sisters,
When first they put the name of King upon
me,
And bade them speak to him; then,
prophet-like,
They hail'd him father to a line of kings:
Upon my head they plac'd a fruitless
crown,
And put a barren sceptre in my gripe,
Thence to be wrench'd with an unlineal
hand,
No son of mine succeeding. If't be so,
For Banquo's issue have I fil'd my mind;
For them the gracious Duncan have I mur-
der'd;
Put rancours in the vessel of my peace
Only for them; and mine eternal jewel
Given to the common enemy of man,
To make them kings, the seed of Banquo
kings!
Rather than so, come, fate, into the list,
And champion me to the utterance!—Who's
there?
Re-enter Attendant, *with two* Murderers.
Now go to the door, and stay there till
we call.   [*Exit* Attendant.
Was it not yesterday we spoke together?
1 *MUR.* It was, so please your highness.
MACB.   Well then, now
Have you consider'd of my speeches? Know,
That it was he, in the times past, which
held you
So under fortune; which you thought had
been
Our innocent self: this I made good to you
In our last conference, pass'd in probation
with you,
How you were borne in hand, how cross'd,
the instruments
Who wrought with them, and all things
else that might,
To half a soul, and to a notion craz'd,
Say, "Thus did Banquo."
1 *MUR.*   You made it known to us.
MACB. I did so; and went farther, which
is now
Our point of second meeting. Do you find
Your patience so predominant in your
nature,
That you can let this go? Are you so
gospell'd,
To pray for this good man, and for his
issue,
Whose heavy hand hath bow'd you to the
And beggar'd yours for ever?   [grave,
1 *MUR.*   We are men, my liege.
MACB. Ay, in the catalogue ye go for men,
As hounds, and grey-hounds, mongrels,
spaniels, curs,

Shoughs, water-rugs, and demi-wolves, are
    cleped
All by the name of dogs: the valued file
Distinguishes the swift, the slow, the subtle,
The house-keeper, the hunter, every one
According to the gift which bounteous
    nature
Hath in him clos'd; whereby he does
    receive
Particular addition, from the bill
That writes them all alike: and so of men.
Now, if you have a station in the file,
Not i' the worst rank of manhood, say it;
And I will put that business in your
    bosoms,
Whose execution takes your enemy off;
Grapples you to the heart and love of us,
Who wear our health but sickly in his life,
Which in his death were perfect.
2 MUR.   I am one, my liege,
Whom the vile blows and buffets of the
    world
Have so incens'd, that I am reckless what
I do to spite the world.
1 MUR.   And I another,
So weary with disasters, tugg'd with
    fortune,
That I would set my life on any chance,
To mend it, or be rid on't.
MACB.   Both of you
Know Banquo was your enemy.
2 MUR.   True, my lord.
MACB. So is he mine; and in such bloody
    distance,
That every minute of his being thrusts
Against my near'st of life: and though I
    could
With bare-fac'd power sweep him from my
    sight,
And bid my will avouch it, yet I must not,
For certain friends that are both his and
    mine,
Whose loves I may not drop, but wail his
    fall
Whom I myself struck down: and thence
    it is,
That I to your assistance do make love;
Masking the business from the common eye
For sundry weighty reasons.
2 MUR.   We shall, my lord,
Perform what you command us.
1 MUR.   Though our lives—
MACB. Your spirits shine through you.
Within this hour, at most,
I will advise you where to plant yourselves;
Acquaint you with the perfect spy o' the
    time,   [night,
The moment on't; for't must be done to-
And something from the palace; always
    thought,

That I require a clearness: and with him,
(To leave no rubs nor botches in the work)
Fleance his son, that keeps him company,
Whose absence is no less material to me
Than is his father's, must embrace the fate
Of that dark hour. Resolve yourselves
I'll come to you anon.   [apart:
2 MUR.   We are resolv'd, my lord.
MACB. I'll call upon you straight: abide
    within.   [Exeunt Murderers.
It is concluded:—Banquo, thy soul's flight,
If it find heaven, must find it out to-night.
                                      [Exit.

SCENE II.—FORES. *Another Room in the
                Palace.*

    Enter LADY MACBETH *and a* Servant.

LADY M. Is Banquo gone from court?
SERV. Ay, Madam, but returns again to-
    night.   [his leisure
LADY M. Say to the king, I would attend
For a few words.
SERV.   Madam, I will.   [Exit.
LADY M. Naught's had, all's spent,
Where our desire is got without content:
'Tis safer to be that which we destroy,
Than, by destruction, dwell in doubtful joy.
                Enter MACBETH.
How now, my lord! why do you keep alone,
Of sorriest fancies your companions mak-
    ing;   [have died
Using those thoughts, which should indeed
With them they think on? Things without
    all remedy,
Should be without regard: what's done, is
    done.
MACB. We have scotch'd the snake, not
    kill'd it: [poor malice
She'll close, and be herself; whilst our
Remains in danger of her former tooth.
But let the frame of things disjoint,
Both the worlds suffer,
Ere we will eat our meal in fear, and sleep
In the affliction of these terrible dreams,
That shake us nightly: better be with the
    dead,   [peace,
Whom we, to gain our peace, have sent to
Than on the torture of the mind to lie
In restless ecstasy. Duncan is in his grave;
After life's fitful fever, he sleeps well;
Treason has done his worst: nor steel, nor
    poison,
Malice domestic, foreign levy, nothing,
Can touch him farther.
    LADY M.   Come on;
Gentle my lord, sleek o'er your rugged
    looks;   [to-night.
Be bright and jovial among your guests
MACB. So shall I, love; and so, I pray, be
    you;

Let your remembrance apply to Banquo;
Present him eminence, both with eye and
Unsafe the while, that we   [tongue:
Must lave our honours in these flattering
    streams;
And make our faces vizards to our hearts,
Disguising what they are.
LADY M.   You must leave this.
MACB. O, full of scorpions is my mind,
    dear wife!
Thou know'st that Banquo, and his Fleance,
    live.
LADY M. But in them nature's copy's not
    eterne.   [able;
MACB. There's comfort yet; they are assail-
Then be thou jocund: ere the bat hath
    flown   [summons,
His cloister'd flight; ere, to black Hecate's
The shard-borne beetle, with his drowsy
    hums,
Hath rung night's yawning peal, there shall
A deed of dreadful note.   [be done
LADY M.   What's to be done?
MACB. Be innocent of the knowledge,
    dearest chuck,
Till thou applaud the deed.—Come, seeling
    night,
Scarf up the tender eye of pitiful day;
And with thy bloody and invisible hand,
Cancel, and tear to pieces that great bond
Which keeps me pale!—Light thickens;
    and the crow
Makes wing to the rooky wood:
Good things of day begin to droop and
    drowse;
Whiles night's black agents to their preys
    do rouse.—
Thou marvell'st at my words: but hold
    thee still;
Things, bad begun, make strong themselves
    by ill:
So, pr'ythee, go with me.   [Exeunt.

SCENE III.—FORES. A Park, with a path
    leading to the Palace gate.
        Enter three Murderers.
1 MUR. But who did bid thee join with
    us?
3 MUR.   Macbeth.
2 MUR. He needs not our mistrust; since
    he delivers
Our offices, and what we have to do,
To the direction just.
1 MUR.   Then stand with us.
The west yet glimmers with some streaks of
    day:
Now spurs the lated traveller apace,
To gain the timely inn; and near ap-
The subject of our watch.   [proaches

3 MUR.   Hark! I hear horses.
BAN. [Within.] Give us a light there, ho!
2 MUR.   Then, 'tis he: the rest
That are within the note of expectation
Already are i' the court.
1 MUR.   His horses go about.
3 MUR. Almost a mile: but he does usu-
    ally,
So all men do, from hence to the palace
Make it their walk.   [gate
2 MUR.   A light, a light!
3 MUR.   'Tis he.
1 MUR. Stand to't.
    Enter BANQUO and FLEANCE, with a torch.
BAN. It will be rain to-night.
1 MUR.   Let it come down.
        [Assaults BANQUO.
BAN. O, treachery!—Fly, good Fleance,
    fly, fly, fly!
Thou may'st revenge.—O slave!
        [Dies. FLEANCE escapes.
3 MUR. Who did strike out the light?
1 MUR.   Was't not the way?
3 MUR. There's but one down; the son is
    fled.
2 MUR. We have lost best half of our
    affair.
1 MUR. Well, let's away, and say how
    much is done.   [Exeunt.

SCENE IV.—FORES. A Room of State in
    the Palace.

A banquet prepared. Enter MACBETH,
    LADY MACBETH, ROSSE, LENOX, Lords,
    and Attendants.
MACB. You know your own degrees, sit
    down: at first
And last, the hearty welcome.
LORDS.   Thanks to your majesty.
MACB. Ourself will mingle with society,
And play the humble host.
Our hostess keeps her state; but, in best
We will require her welcome.   [time,
LADY M. Pronounce it for me, Sir, to all
    our friends;
For my heart speaks, they are welcome.
MACB. See, they encounter thee with their
    hearts' thanks.—
Both sides are even: here I'll sit i' the
    midst:
    Enter first Murderer, to the door.
Be large in mirth; anon, we'll drink a
    measure
The table round.—There's blood upon thy
MUR. 'Tis Banquo's then.   [face.
MACB. 'Tis better thee without, than he
    within.
Is he despatch'd?
MUR. My lord, his throat is cut; that I
    did for him.

MACB. Thou art the best o' the cut-throats: yet he's good
That did the like for Fleance: if thou didst it,
Thou art the nonpareil.
MUR.   Most royal Sir,
Fleance is 'scap'd.
MACB. Then comes my fit again: I had else been perfect;
Whole as the marble, founded as the rock;
As broad and general as the casing air:
But now, I am cabin'd, cribb'd, confin'd, bound in
To saucy doubts and fears.—But Banquo's safe?
MUR. Ay, my good lord: safe in a ditch he bides,
With twenty trenched gashes on his head;
The least a death to nature.
MACB.   Thanks for that.—
There the grown serpent lies: the worm, that's fled,
Hath nature that in time will venom breed,
No teeth for the present.—Get thee gone; to-morrow
We'll hear, ourselves, again.
          [*Exit* Murderer.
LADY M.   My royal lord,
You do not give the cheer: the feast is sold
That is not often vouch'd, while 'tis a making,
'Tis given with welcome. To feed, were best at home;
From thence, the sauce to meat is cere-mony,—
Meeting were bare without it.
MACB.   Sweet remembrancer!—
Now, good digestion wait on appetite,
And health on both!
LEN.   May it please your highness sit?
[*The Ghost of* BANQUO *appears, and sits in* MACBETH's *place.*
MACB. Here had we now our country's honour roof'd,
Were the grac'd person of our Banquo present;   [ness,
Whom may I rather challenge for unkind-Than pity for mischance!
ROSSE.   His absence, Sir,
Lays blame upon his promise. Please it your highness
To grace us with your royal company?
MACB. The table's full.
LEN.   Here is a place reserv'd, Sir.
MACB. Where?
LEN. Here, my good lord. What is't that moves your highness?
MACB. Which of you have done this?
LORDS.   What, my good lord?
MACB. Thou canst not say I did it: never Thy gory locks at me.   [shake

ROSSE. Gentlemen, rise; his highness is not well.
LADY M. Sit, worthy friends:—my lord is often thus,
And hath been from his youth: pray you, keep seat;
The fit is momentary; upon a thought
He will again be well: if much you note him,   [sion:
You shall offend him, and extend his pas-Feed, and regard him not.—Are you a man?
MACB. Ay, and a bold one, that dare look on that
Which might appal the devil.
LADY M.   O proper stuff!
This is the very painting of your fear:
This is the air-drawn dagger, which, you said,   [starts
Led you to Duncan. O, these flaws and (Impostors to true fear) would well become
A woman's story at a winter's fire,
Authoriz'd by her grandam. Shame itself!
Why do you make such faces? When all's done,   [done,
You look but on a stool.
MACB. Pr'ythee, see there! behold! look! lo! how say you?—
Why, what care I? If thou canst nod, speak too.—
If charnel-houses, and our graves, must send
Those that we bury back, our monuments
Shall be the maws of kites.
          [*Ghost disappears.*
LADY M. What, quite unmann'd in folly?
MACB. If I stand here, I saw him.
LADY M.   Fie, for shame!
MACB. Blood hath been shed ere now, i' th' olden time,
Ere human statute purg'd the gentle weal;
Ay, and since too, murders have been per-form'd   [been,
Too terrible for the ear: the times have
That, when the brains were out, the man would die,
And there an end; but now, they rise again,
With twenty mortal murders on their crowns,
And push us from our stools: this is more
Than such a murder is.   [strange
LADY M.   My worthy lord,
Your noble friends do lack you.
MACB.   I do forget:—
Do not muse at me, my most worthy friends;
I have a strange infirmity, which is nothing
To those that know me. Come, love and health to all;
Then, I'll sit down.—Give me some wine, fill full.—

I drink to the general joy of the whole
table,   [miss;
And to our dear friend Banquo, whom we
Would he were here! to all, and him, we
And all to all.   [thirst,
LORDS.   Our duties, and the pledge.
                Ghost re-appears.
MACB. Avaunt! and quit my sight! Let
the earth hide thee!
Thy bones are marrowless, thy blood is
cold;
Thou hast no speculation in those eyes
Which thou dost glare with.
LADY M.   Think of this, good peers,
But as a thing of custom: 'tis no other;
Only it spoils the pleasure of the time.
MACB. What man dare, I dare:
Approach thou like the rugged Russian
bear,
The arm'd rhinoceros, or the Hyrcan tiger;
Take any shape but that, and my firm
nerves
Shall never tremble: or be alive again,
And dare me to the desert with thy sword;
If trembling I inhabit then, protest me
The baby of a girl. Hence, horrible shadow!
Unreal mockery, hence!—
                    [*Ghost disappears.*
                Why, so;—being gone,
I am a man again.—Pray you, sit still.
LADY M. You have displac'd the mirth,
broke the good meeting,
With most admir'd disorder.
MACB.   Can such things be,
And overcome us like a summer's cloud,
Without our special wonder? You make
me strange
Even to the disposition that I owe,
When now I think you can behold such
sights,
And keep the natural ruby of your cheeks,
When mine are blanch'd with fear.
ROSSE.   What sights, my lord?
LADY M. I pray you, speak not; he grows
worse and worse;
Question enrages him: at once, good
night:—
Stand not upon the order of your going,
But go at once.
LEN.   Good night; and better health
Attend his majesty!
LADY M.   A kind good night to all!
        [*Exeunt all except* MACBETH *and*
                LADY MACBETH.
MACB. It will have blood; they say, blood
will have blood:
Stones have been known to move, and trees
to speak;
Augurs, and understood relations, have
By magot-pies, and choughs, and rooks,
brought forth

The secret'st man of blood.—What is the
night?
LADY M. Almost at odds with morning,
which is which.
MACB. How say'st thou, that Macduff de-
nies his person
At our great bidding?
LADY M. Did you send to him, Sir?
MACB. I hear it by the way; but I will
send:
There's not a one of them, but in his house
I keep a servant fee'd. I will to-morrow
(And betimes I will) to the weird sisters:
More shall they speak; for now I am bent
to know,
By the worst means, the worst. For mine
own good,
All causes shall give way: I am in blood
Stept in so far, that, should I wade no more,
Returning were as tedious as go o'er:
Strange things I have in head, that will to
hand;
Which must be acted ere they may be
scann'd.
LADY M. You lack the season of all na-
tures, sleep.
MACB. Come, we'll to sleep. My strange
and self-abuse
Is the initiate fear, that wants hard use:—
We are yet but young in deed.   [*Exeunt.*

SCENE V.—*The Heath.*

Thunder. Enter the three Witches,
meeting HECATE.

1 WITCH. Why, how now, Hecate! you
look angerly.
HEC. Have I not reason, beldams as you
are,
Saucy and overbold? How did you dare
To trade and traffic with Macbeth,
In riddles, and affairs of death;
And I, the mistress of your charms,
The close contriver of all harms,
Was never call'd to bear my part,
Or show the glory of our art?
And, which is worse, all you have done
Hath been but for a wayward son,
Spiteful and wrathful; who, as others do,
Loves for his own ends, not for you.
But make amends now: get you gone,
And at the pit of Acheron
Meet me i' the morning: thither he
Will come to know his destiny:
Your vessels and your spells provide,
Your charms, and every thing beside.
I am for the air; this night I'll spend
Unto a dismal and a fatal end:
Great business must be wrought ere noon:
Upon the corner of the moon

There hangs a vaporous drop profound;
I'll catch it ere it come to ground:
And that, distill'd by magic sleights,
Shall raise such artificial sprites,
As, by the strength of their illusion,
Shall draw him on to his confusion:
He shall spurn fate, scorn death, and bear
His hopes 'bove wisdom, grace and fear:
And, you all know, security
Is mortals' chiefest enemy.

    [*Song within,* "Come away, come
       away," &c.
Hark! I am call'd; my little spirit, see,
Sits in a foggy cloud, and stays for me.
                    [*Exit.*

1 *WITCH.* Come, let's make haste; she'll
soon be back again.   [*Exeunt.*

SCENE VI.—FORES. *A Room in the Palace.*
    Enter LENOX *and another* Lord.

LEN. My former speeches have but hit
your thoughts,
Which can interpret farther: only, I say,
Things have been strangely borne. The
gracious Duncan
Was pitied of Macbeth:—marry, he was
dead:—
And the right-valiant Banquo walk'd too
late;
Whom, you may say, if't please you, Fle-
ance kill'd,
For Fleance fled: men must not walk too
late.
Who cannot want the thought, how mon-
strous
It was for Malcolm and for Donalbain
To kill their gracious father? damned fact!
How it did grieve Macbeth! did he not
straight,
In pious rage, the two delinquents tear,
That were the slaves of drink, and thralls
of sleep?
Was not that nobly done? Ay, and wisely
too;
For 'twould have anger'd any heart alive,
To hear the men deny't. So that, I say,
He has borne all things well: and I do
think,
That, had he Duncan's sons under his key,
(As, an't please heaven, he shall not) they
should find
What 'twere to kill a father; so should
Fleance.
But, peace!—for from broad words, and
'cause he fail'd
His presence at the tyrant's feast, I hear,
Macduff lives in disgrace: Sir, can you tell
Where he bestows himself?
LORD.   The son of Duncan,

From whom this tyrant holds the due of
birth,
Lives in the English court; and is receiv'd
Of the most pious Edward with such grace,
That the malevolence of fortune nothing
Takes from his high respect: thither Mac-
duff   [aid
Is gone to pray the holy king, upon his
To wake Northumberland and warlike
Siward:
That, by the help of these, (with Him
above
To ratify the work) we may again
Give to our tables meat, sleep to our
nights;
Free from our feasts and banquets bloody
knives;
Do faithful homage, and receive free hon-
ours;—
All which we pine for now: and this report
Hath so exasperate the king, that he
Prepares for some attempt of war.
LEN.   Sent he to Macduff?
LORD. He did: and with an absolute,
"Sir, not I,"
The cloudy messenger turns me his back,
And hums, as who should say, "You'll rue
the time
That clogs me with this answer."
LEN.   And that well might
Advise him to a caution, to hold what dis-
tance
His wisdom can provide. Some holy angel
Fly to the court of England, and unfold
His message ere he come; that a swift
blessing
May soon return to this our suffering coun-
try
Under a hand accurs'd!   [try
LORD.   I'll send my prayers with him!
                    [*Exeunt.*

ACT IV.

SCENE I.—*A dark Cave. In the middle, a
cauldron boiling.*

    Thunder. Enter the three Witches.

1 *WITCH.* Thrice the brinded cat hath
mew'd.
2 *WITCH.* Thrice; and once the hedge-pig
whin'd.
3 *WITCH.* Harper cries:—'tis time, 'tis
time.
1 *WITCH.* Round about the cauldron go;
    In the poison'd entrails throw.—
Toad, that under cold stone,
Days and nights has thirty-one
Swelter'd venom sleeping got,
Boil thou first i' the charmed pot.
ALL. Double, double toil and trouble;
    Fire, burn; and, cauldron, bubble.

2 *WITCH.* Fillet of a fenny snake,
  In the cauldron boil and bake;
  Eye of newt, and toe of frog,
  Wool of bat, and tongue of dog,
  Adder's fork, and blind-worm's sting,
  Lizard's leg, and owlet's wing,—
  For a charm of powerful trouble,
  Like a hell-broth boil and bubble.
ALL. Double, double toil and trouble;
  Fire, burn; and, cauldron, bubble.
3 *WITCH.* Scale of dragon; tooth of wolf;
  Witches' mummy; maw and gulf
  Of the ravin'd salt-sea shark;
  Root of hemlock, digg'd i' the dark;
  Liver of blaspheming Jew;
  Gall of goat; and slips of yew,
  Sliver'd in the moon's eclipse;
  Nose of Turk, and Tartar's lips;
  Finger of birth-strangled babe,
  Ditch-deliver'd by a drab,—
  Make the gruel thick and slab:
  Add thereto a tiger's chaudron,
  For the ingredients of our cauldron.
ALL. Double, double toil and trouble;
  Fire, burn; and, cauldron, bubble.
2 *WITCH.* Cool it with a baboon's blood;
  Then the charm is firm and good.

      Enter HECATE.

HEC. O, well done! I commend your
  pains,
And every one shall share i' the gains.
  And now about the cauldron sing,
  Like elves and fairies in a ring,
  Enchanting all that you put in.
  [*Music and a song,* "Black spirits," &c.
      Exit HECATE.

2 *WITCH.* By the pricking of my thumbs,
Something wicked this way comes:—
Open, locks, whoever knocks.

      Enter MACBETH.

MACB. How now, you secret, black, and
  midnight hags!
What is't you do?
ALL.   A deed without a name.
MACB. I conjure you, by that which you
  profess,
(Howe'er you come to know it) answer me:
Though you untie the winds, and let them
  fight   [waves
Against the churches; though the yesty
Confound and swallow navigation up;
Though bladed corn be lodg'd, and trees
  blown down;
Though castles topple on their warders'
  heads;
Though palaces and pyramids do slope
Their heads to their foundations; though
  the treasure
Of nature's germins tumble all together,
Even till destruction sicken,—answer me
To what I ask you.

1 *WITCH.*   Speak.
2 *WITCH.*   Demand.
3 *WITCH.*   We'll answer.
1 *WITCH.* Say, if thou'dst rather hear it
  from our mouths,
Or from our masters'?
MACB.   Call them: let me see them.
1 *WITCH.* Pour in sow's blood, that hath
  eaten
Her nine farrow; grease, that's sweaten
From the murderer's gibbet, throw
Into the flame.
ALL.   Come, high or low;
Thyself and office deftly show.

  Thunder. An Apparition *of an armed*
      head rises.

MACB. Tell me, thou unknown power,—
1 *WITCH.*   He knows thy thought:
Hear his speech, but say thou naught.
APP. Macbeth! Macbeth! Macbeth! beware Macduff;
Beware the thane of Fife.—Dismiss me:—
  enough.   [*Descends.*
MACB. Whate'er thou art, for thy good
  caution thanks;
Thou hast harp'd my fear aright:—but one
  word more,—
1 *WITCH.* He will not be commanded:
  here's another,
More potent than the first.

  Thunder. An Apparition *of a bloody*
      child rises.

APP.   Macbeth! Macbeth! Macbeth!—
MACB. Had I three ears, I'd hear thee.
APP. Be bloody, bold, and resolute; laugh
  to scorn
The power of man, for none of woman born
Shall harm Macbeth.   [*Descends.*
MACB. Then live, Macduff: what need I
  fear of thee?
But yet I'll make assurance double sure,
And take a bond of fate: thou shalt not
  live;
That I may tell pale-hearted fear it lies,
And sleep in spite of thunder.—What is
  this,

  Thunder. An Apparition *of a child*
     crowned, with a tree in his
      hand, rises.

That rises like the issue of a king,
And wears upon his baby brow the round
And top of sovereignty?
ALL.   Listen, but speak not to't.
APP. Be lion-mettled, proud; and take
  no care
Who chafes, who frets, or where conspirers
  are:
Macbeth shall never vanquish'd be, until
Great Birnam wood to high Dunsinane hill
Shall come against him.   [*Descends.*

MACB.   That will never be:
Who can impress the forest; bid the tree
Unfix his earth-bound root? sweet bodements! good!
Rebellious head, rise never, till the wood
Of Birnam rise, and our high-plac'd Macbeth
Shall live the lease of nature, pay his breath   [heart
To time and mortal custom.—Yet my
Throbs to know one thing: tell me, (if your art
Can tell so much) shall Banquo's issue ever
Reign in this kingdom?
ALL.   Seek to know no more.
MACB. I will be satisfied: deny me this,
And an eternal curse fall on you! Let me know:—
Why sinks that cauldron? [*Hautboys.*] and what noise is this?
1 WITCH. Show!
2 WITCH. Show!
3 WITCH. Show!
ALL. Show his eyes, and grieve his heart;
Come like shadows, so depart.
Eight Kings appear, and pass in order; the last with a glass in his hand:
      Banquo *following.*
MACB. Thou art too like the spirit of
Banquo; down!
Thy crown does sear mine eyeballs:—and thy hair,
Thou other gold-bound brow, is like the first:—
A third is like the former.—Filthy hags!
Why do you show me this?—A fourth?—Start, eyes!—
What, will the line stretch out to the crack of doom?—
Another yet?—A seventh?—I'll see no more:—
And yet the eighth appears, who bears a glass,   [I see,
Which shows me many more; and some
That two-fold balls and treble sceptres carry;
Horrible sight!—Now, I see, 'tis true;
For the blood-bolter'd Banquo smiles upon me,   [so?
And points at them for his.—What, is this
1 WITCH. Ay, Sir, all this is so:—but why
Stands Macbeth thus amazedly?—
Come, sisters, cheer we up his sprites,
And show the best of our delights:
I'll charm the air to give a sound,
While you perform your antic round;
That this great king may kindly say,
Our duties did his welcome pay.
      [*Music. The* Witches *dance, and then vanish.*

MACB. Where are they? Gone?—Let this pernicious hour
Stand aye accursed in the calendar!—
Come in! without there!
      Enter Lenox.
LEN.   What's your grace's will?
MACB. Saw you the weird sisters?
LEN.   No, my lord.
MACB. Came they not by you?
LEN.   No, indeed, my lord.
MACB. Infected be the air whereon they ride;
And damn'd all those that trust them!—
I did hear
The galloping of horse: who was't came by?
LEN. 'Tis two or three, my lord, that bring you word,
Macduff is fled to England.
MACB.   Fled to England!
LEN. Ay, my good lord.
MACB. Time, thou anticipat'st my dread exploits:
The flighty purpose never is o'ertook,
Unless the deed go with it: from this moment,
The very firstlings of my heart shall be
The firstlings of my hand. And even now,
To crown my thoughts with acts, be it thought and done:
The castle of Macduff I will surprise;
Seize upon Fife; give to the edge o' the sword   [souls
His wife, his babes, and all unfortunate
That trace him in his line. No boasting like a fool;
This deed I'll do, before this purpose cool:
But no more sights!—Where are these gentlemen?
Come, bring me where they are.
      [*Exeunt.*

Scene II.—Fife. *A Room in* Macduff's *Castle.*

Enter Lady Macduff, *her Son, and* Rosse.
L. MACD. What had he done to make him fly the land?
ROSSE. You must have patience, Madam.
L. MACD.   He had none:
His flight was madness: when our actions
Our fears do make us traitors.   [do not,
ROSSE.   You know not
Whether it was his wisdom, or his fear.
L. MACD. Wisdom! to leave his wife, to leave his babes,
His mansion, and his titles, in a place
From whence himself does fly? He loves us not;
He wants the natural touch: for the poor wren,

The most diminutive of birds, will fight,
Her young ones in her nest, against the owl.
All is the fear, and nothing is the love;
As little is the wisdom, where the flight
So runs against all reason.
ROSSE.   My dearest coz',
I pray you, school yourself: but, for your
    husband,
He is noble, wise, judicious, and best knows
The fits o' the season. I dare not speak
    much farther:
But cruel are the times, when we are
    traitors,
And do not know ourselves; when we hold
    rumour
From what we fear, yet know not what we
    fear,
But float upon a wild and violent sea,
Each way and move.—I take my leave of
    you:
Shall not be long but I'll be here again:
Things at the worst will cease, or else climb
    upward   [in,
To what they were before.—My pretty cous-
Blessing upon you!
L. MACD. Father'd he is, and yet he's
    fatherless.
ROSSE. I am so much a fool, should I
    stay longer,   [comfort.
It would be my disgrace, and your dis-
I take my leave at once.   [*Exit.*
L. MACD.   Sirrah, your father's dead:
And what will you do now? How will you
SON. As birds do, mother.   [live?
L. MACD. What, with worms and flies?
SON. With what I get, I mean; and so
    do they.
L. MACD. Poor bird! thou'dst never fear
    the net, nor lime,
The pit-fall, nor the gin.
SON. Why should I, mother? Poor birds
    they are not set for.
My father is not dead, for all your saying.
L. MACD. Yes, he is dead: how wilt
    thou do for a father?
SON. Nay, how will you do for a hus-
    band?
L. MACD. Why, I can buy me twenty at
    any market.
SON. Then you'll buy 'em to sell again.
L. MACD. Thou speak'st with all thy wit;
And yet, i' faith, with wit enough for thee.
SON. Was my father a traitor, mother?
L. MACD. Ay, that he was.
SON. What is a traitor?
L. MACD. Why, one that swears and lies.
SON. And be all traitors that do so?
L. MACD. Every one that does so is a
    traitor, and must be hanged.

SON. And must they all be hanged, that
swear and lie?
L. MACD. Every one.
SON. Who must hang them?
L. MACD. Why, the honest men.
SON. Then the liars and swearers are
fools; for there are liars and swearers
enough to beat the honest men, and hang
up them.
L. MACD. Now God help thee, poor mon-
key! But how wilt thou do for a father?
SON. If he were dead, you'd weep for
him: if you would not, it were a good sign
that I should quickly have a new father.
L. MACD. Poor prattler, how thou talk'st!
              Enter a Messenger.
MESS. Bless you, fair dame! I am not to
    you known,
Though in your state of honour I am per-
    fect.   [nearly:
I doubt some danger does approach you
If you will take a homely man's advice,
Be not found here; hence, with your little
    ones.   [savage;
To fright you thus, methinks, I am too
To do worse to you were fell cruelty,
Which is too nigh your person. Heaven
    preserve you!
I dare abide no longer.   [*Exit.*
L. MACD.   Whither should I fly?
I have done no harm: but I remember now
I am in this earthly world; where, to do
    harm
Is often laudable; to do good, sometime
Accounted dangerous folly: why then, alas,
Do I put up that womanly defence,
To say I have done no harm?—What are
    these faces?
              Enter Murderers.
MUR. Where is your husband?
L. MACD. I hope, in no place so unsanc-
    tified,
Where such as thou may'st find him.
MUR.   He's a traitor.
SON. Thou liest, thou shag-hair'd villain.
MUR.   What, you egg!
                              [*Stabbing him.*
Young fry of treachery!
SON.   He has killed me, mother:
Run away, I pray you!   [*Dies.*
[*Exit* LADY MACDUFF, *crying* "Murder!"
    and pursued by the Murderers.

────────

SCENE III.—ENGLAND. *Before the King's
              Palace.*

      Enter MALCOLM *and* MACDUFF.
MAL. Let us seek out some desolate shade,
    and there
Weep our sad bosoms empty.

MACD.   Let us rather
Hold fast the mortal sword; and, like good
men,
Bestride our down-fall'n birthdom: each
new morn,
New widows howl, new orphans cry; new
sorrows
Strike heaven on the face, that it resounds
As if it felt with Scotland, and yell'd out
Like syllable of dolour.
MAL.   What I believe, I'll wail;
What know, believe; and what I can
redress,
As I shall find the time to friend, I will.
What you have spoke, it may be so per-
chance.
This tyrant, whose sole name blisters our
tongues,
Was once thought honest: you have lov'd
him well;
He hath not touch'd you yet. I am young:
but something
You may discern of him through me; and
wisdom
To offer up a weak, poor, innocent lamb
To appease an angry god.
MACD. I am not treacherous.
MAL.   But Macbeth is.
A good and virtuous nature may recoil,
In an imperial charge. But I shall crave
your pardon;
That which you are, my thoughts cannot
transpose:
Angels are bright still, though the bright-
est fell: [brows of grace,
Though all things foul would wear the
Yet grace must still look so.
MACD.   I have lost my hopes.
MAL. Perchance, even there, where I did
find my doubts.
Why in that rawness left you wife and child
(Those precious motives, those strong knots
of love)
Without leave-taking?—I pray you,
Let not my jealousies be your dishonours,
But mine own safeties:—you may be right-
Whatever I shall think.   [ly just,
MACD.   Bleed, bleed, poor country!
Great tyranny, lay thou thy basis sure,
For goodness dares not check thee! wear
thou thy wrongs,
The title is affeer'd!—Fare thee well, lord:
I would not be the villain that thou
think'st,
For the whole space that's in the tyrant's
And the rich East to boot.   [grasp,
MAL.   Be not offended:
I speak not as in absolute fear of you.
I think our country sinks beneath the yoke;
It weeps, it bleeds; and each new day a
gash

Is added to her wounds: I think, withal,
There would be hands uplifted in my right;
And here, from gracious England, have I
offer
Of goodly thousands: but, for all this,
When I shall tread upon the tyrant's head,
Or wear it on my sword, yet my poor country
Shall have more vices than it had before;
More suffer, and more sundry ways than
By him that shall succeed.   [ever,
MACD.   What should he be?
MAL. It is myself I mean: in whom I
know
All the particulars of vice so grafted,
That, when they shall be open'd, black
Macbeth
Will seem as pure as snow; and the poor
state
Esteem him as a lamb, being compar'd
With my confineless harms.
MACD.   Not in the legions
Of horrid hell can come a devil more
In evils to top Macbeth.   [damn'd
MAL.   I grant him bloody,
Luxurious, avaricious, false, deceitful,
Sudden, malicious, smacking of every sin
That has a name: but there's no bottom,
none,   [daughters,
In my voluptuousness: your wives, your
Your matrons, and your maids, could not
fill up
The cistern of my lust; and my desire
All continent impediments would o'erbear,
That did oppose my will: better Macbeth,
Than such a one to reign.
MACD.   Boundless intemperance
In nature is a tyranny; it hath been
Th' untimely emptying of the happy throne,
And fall of many kings. But fear not yet
To take upon you what is yours: you may
Convey your pleasures in a spacious plenty,
And yet seem cold, the time you may so
hoodwink.
We have willing dames enough; there can-
not be
That vulture in you, to devour so many
As will to greatness dedicate themselves,
Finding it so inclin'd.
MAL.   With this, there grows,
In my most ill-compos'd affection, such
A stanchless avarice, that, were I king,
I should cut off the nobles for their lands;
Desire his jewels, and this other's house:
And my more-having would be as a sauce
To make me hunger more; that I should
forge
Quarrels unjust against the good and loyal,
Destroying them for wealth.
MACD.   This avarice
Sticks deeper; grows with more pernicious
root

Than summer-seeming lust; and it hath
been
The sword of our slain kings: yet do not
fear;
Scotland hath foisons to fill up your will,
Of your mere own: all these are portable,
With other graces weigh'd.
MAL. But I have none: the king-becom-
ing graces,
As justice, verity, temperance, stableness,
Bounty, perseverance, mercy, lowliness,
Devotion, patience, courage, fortitude,
I have no relish of them; but abound
In the division of each several crime,
Acting it many ways. Nay, had I power, I
should
Pour the sweet milk of concord into hell,
Uproar the universal peace, confound
All unity on earth.
MACD.   O Scotland, Scotland!
MAL. If such a one be fit to govern,
I am as I have spoken.   [speak:
MACD.   Fit to govern!
No, not to live.—O nation miserable!
With an untitled tyrant, bloody-scepter'd,
When shalt thou see thy wholesome days
again,
Since that the truest issue of thy throne
By his own interdiction stands accurs'd,
And does blaspheme his breed?—Thy royal
father
Was a most sainted king: the queen that
bore thee,
Oft'ner upon her knees than on her feet,
Died every day she liv'd. Fare thee well.
These evils thou repeat'st upon thyself
Have banish'd me from Scotland.—O my
Thy hope ends here!   [breast,
MAL.   Macduff, this noble passion,
Child of integrity, hath from my soul
Wip'd the black scruples, reconcil'd my
thoughts
To thy good truth and honour. Devilish
Macbeth
By many of these trains hath sought to win
me   [me
Into his power; and modest wisdom plucks
From over-credulous haste: but God above
Deal between thee and me! for even now
I put myself to thy direction, and
Unspeak mine own detraction; here abjure
The taints and blames I laid upon myself,
For strangers to my nature. I am yet
Unknown to woman; never was forsworn;
Scarcely have coveted what was mine own;
At no time broke my faith; would not
betray
The devil to his fellow; and delight
No less in truth than life: my first false
speaking
Was this upon myself:—what I am truly,

Is thine, and my poor country's, to com-
mand:
Whither, indeed, before thy here-approach,
Old Siward, with ten thousand warlike
men,
Already at a point, was setting forth:
Now we'll together; and the chance of
goodness
Be like our warranted quarrel! Why are
you silent?
MACD. Such welcome and unwelcome
things at once,
'Tis hard to reconcile.
           Enter a Doctor.
MAL. Well; more anon.—Comes the king
forth, I pray you?
DOCT. Ay, Sir; there are a crew of
wretched souls,
That stay his cure: their malady convinces
The great assay of art; but, at his touch,
Such sanctity hath heaven given his hand,
They presently amend.
MAL.   I thank you, doctor.
                         [*Exit* Doctor.
MACD. What's the disease he means?
MAL.   'Tis call'd the evil:
A most miraculous work in this good king;
Which often, since my here remain in
England,
I have seen him do. How he solicits heaven,
Himself best knows: but strangely-visited
people,
All swoln and ulcerous, pitiful to the eye,
The mere despair of surgery, he cures;
Hanging a golden stamp about their necks,
Put on with holy prayers: and 'tis spoken,
To the succeeding royalty he leaves
The healing benediction. With this strange
virtue,
He hath a heavenly gift of prophecy;
And sundry blessings hang about his
throne,
That speak him full of grace.
MACD.   See, who comes here?
MAL. My countryman; but yet I know
him not.
           Enter ROSSE.
MACD. My ever-gentle cousin, welcome
hither.
MAL. I know him now:—good God, be-
times remove
The means that make us strangers!
ROSSE.   Sir, amen.
MACD. Stands Scotland where it did?
ROSSE.   Alas, poor country,—
Almost afraid to know itself! It cannot
Be call'd our mother, but our grave: where
nothing,
But who knows nothing, is once seen to
smile;

Where sighs, and groans, and shrieks that
   rent the air,
Are made, not mark'd; where violent sor-
   row seems
A modern ecstasy: the dead man's knell
Is there scarce ask'd, for whom; and good
   men's lives
Expire before the flowers in their caps,
Dying or ere they sicken.
MACD.   O, relation
Too nice, and yet too true!
MAL.   What is the newest grief?
ROSSE. That of an hour's age doth hiss
   the speaker;
Each minute teems a new one.
MACD.   How does my wife?
ROSSE. Why, well.
MACD.   And all my children?
ROSSE.   Well too.
MACD. The tyrant has not batter'd at
   their peace?
ROSSE. No; they were well at peace,
   when I did leave them.
MACD. Be not a niggard of your speech:
   how goes it?
ROSSE. When I came hither to transport
   the tidings,
Which I have heavily borne, there ran a
   rumour
Of many worthy fellows that were out;
Which was to my belief witness'd the
   rather,
For that I saw the tyrant's power a-foot:
Now is the time of help; your eye in
   Scotland
Would create soldiers, make our women
To doff their dire distresses.   [fight,
MAL.   Be it their comfort,
We are coming thither: gracious England
   hath
Lent us good Siward, and ten thousand
   men;
An older, and a better soldier, none
That Christendom gives out.
ROSSE.   Would I could answer
This comfort with the like! But I have
   words,
That would be howl'd out in the desert air,
Where hearing should not latch them.
MACD.   What concern they?
The general cause? or is it a fee-grief,
Due to some single breast?
ROSSE.   No mind that's honest
But in it shares some woe; though the
   main part
Pertains to you alone.
MACD.   If it be mine,
Keep it not from me, quickly let me have it.
ROSSE. Let not your ears despise my
   tongue for ever,   [sound
Which shall possess them with the heaviest

That ever yet they heard.
MACD.   Hm! I guess at it.
ROSSE. Your castle is surpris'd; your
   wife and babes
Savagely slaughter'd: to relate the manner,
Were, on the quarry of these murder'd
   deer,
To add the death of you.
MAL.   Merciful heaven!—
What, man! ne'er pull your hat upon your
   brows;   [speak,
Give sorrow words: the grief, that does not
Whispers the o'er-fraught heart, and bids
   it break.
MACD. My children too?
ROSSE.   Wife, children, servants, all
That could be found.
MACD.   And I must be from thence!—
My wife kill'd too?
ROSSE.   I have said.
MAL.   Be comforted:
Let's make us medicines of our great re-
To cure this deadly grief.   [venge,
MACD. He has no children.—All my pretty
   ones?
Did you say, all?—O hell-kite!—All?
What, all my pretty chickens, and their
At one fell swoop?   [dam,
MAL.   Dispute it like a man.
MACD.   I shall do so;
But I must also feel it as a man:
I cannot but remember such things were,
That were most precious to me.—Did
   heaven look on,   [Macduff,
And would not take their part? Sinful
They were all struck for thee! Naught
   that I am,
Not for their own demerits, but for mine,
Fell slaughter on their souls: Heaven rest
   them now!
MAL. Be this the whetstone of your
   sword: let grief
Convert to anger; blunt not the heart,
   enrage it.   [mine eyes,
MACD. O, I could play the woman with
And braggart with my tongue!—But, gentle
   Heavens,
Cut short all intermission; front to front,
Bring thou this fiend of Scotland, and
   myself;   ['scape,
Within my sword's length set him; if he
Heaven forgive him too!
MAL.   This tune goes manly.
Come, go we to the king; our power is
   ready;
Our lack is nothing but our leave: Macbeth
Is ripe for shaking, and the powers above
Put on their instruments. Receive what
   cheer you may;
The night is long that never finds the day.
                   [Exeunt.

ACT V.

SCENE I.—DUNSINANE. *A Room in the Castle.*

Enter a Doctor of Physic *and a waiting* Gentlewoman.

DOCT. I have two nights watched with you, but can perceive no truth in your report. When was it she last walked?

GENT. Since his majesty went into the field, I have seen her rise from her bed, throw her night-gown upon her, unlock her closet, take forth paper, fold it, write upon it, read it, afterwards seal it, and again return to bed; yet all this while in a most fast sleep.

DOCT. A great perturbation in nature,—to receive at once the benefit of sleep, and do the effects of watching!—In this slumbery agitation, besides her walking and other actual performances, what, at any time, have you heard her say?

GENT. That, Sir, which I will not report after her.

DOCT. You may, to me; and 'tis most meet you should.

GENT. Neither to you, nor any one; having no witness to confirm my speech.—Lo you, here she comes! [*Enter* LADY MACBETH, *with a lighted taper.*] This is her very guise; and, upon my life, fast asleep. Observe her; stand close.

DOCT. How came she by that light?

GENT. Why, it stood by her: she has light by her continually; 'tis her command.

DOCT. You see, her eyes are open.

GENT. Ay, but their sense is shut.

DOCT. What is it she does now? Look, how she rubs her hands.

GENT. It is an accustomed action with her, to seem thus washing her hands: I have known her continue in this a quarter of an hour.

LADY M. Yet here's a spot.

DOCT. Hark! she speaks: I will set down what comes from her, to satisfy my remembrance the more strongly.

LADY M. Out, damned spot! out, I say! —One, two; why, then 'tis time to do't.— Hell is murky!—Fie, my lord, fie! a soldier, and afeard? What need we fear who knows it, when none can call our power to account?—Yet who would have thought the old man to have had so much blood in him?

DOCT. Do you mark that?

LADY M. The thane of Fife had a wife; where is she now?—What, will these hands ne'er be clean?—No more o' that, my lord, no more o' that: you mar all with this starting.

DOCT. Go to, go to; you have known what you should not.

GENT. She has spoke what she should not, I am sure of that: Heaven knows what she has known.

LADY M. Here's the smell of the blood still: all the perfumes of Arabia will not sweeten this little hand. Oh, oh, oh!

DOCT. What a sigh is there! The heart is sorely charged.

GENT. I would not have such a heart in my bosom, for the dignity of the whole body.

DOCT. Well, well, well,—

GENT. Pray God, it be, Sir.

DOCT. This disease is beyond my practice: yet I have known those which have walked in their sleep, who have died holily in their beds.

LADY M. Wash your hands, put on your night-gown; look not so pale:—I tell you yet again, Banquo's buried; he cannot come out on's grave.

DOCT. Even so?

LADY M. To bed, to bed; there's knocking at the gate: come, come, come, come, give me your hand: what's done, cannot be undone: to bed, to bed, to bed.

[*Exit.*

DOCT. Will she go now to bed?

GENT. Directly.

DOCT. Foul whisperings are abroad: unnatural deeds
Do breed unnatural troubles: infected minds   [secrets:
To their deaf pillows will discharge their
More needs she the divine, than the physician:—
God, God, forgive us all! Look after her;
Remove from her the means of all annoyance,
And still keep eyes upon her:—so, good night: [sight:
My mind she has mated, and amaz'd my
I think, but dare not speak.

GENT.   Good night, good doctor.

[*Exeunt.*

SCENE II.—*The Country near* DUNSINANE.

Enter, with drum and colours, MENTETH, CATHNESS, ANGUS, LENOX, *and* Soldiers.

MENT. The English power is near, led on by Malcolm,
His uncle Siward, and the good Macduff:
Revenges burn in them; for their dear causes
Would, to the bleeding, and the grim alarm,
Excite the mortified man.

ANG.   Near Birnam wood

Shall we well meet them; that way are
they coming.
CATH. Who knows if Donalbain be with
his brother?
LEN. For certain, Sir, he is not: I have
a file
Of all the gentry: there is Siward's son,
And many unrough youths, that even now
Protest their first of manhood.
MENT.   What does the tyrant?
CATH. Great Dunsinane he strongly for-
tifies: [hate him,
Some say, he's mad: others, that lesser
Do call it valiant fury; but, for certain,
He cannot buckle his distemper'd cause
Within the belt of rule.
ANG.   Now does he feel
His secret murders sticking on his hands;
Now minutely revolts upbraid his faith-
breach;
Those he commands move only in com-
mand,
Nothing in love: now does he feel his title
Hang loose about him, like a giant's robe
Upon a dwarfish thief.
MENT.   Who, then, shall blame
His pester'd senses to recoil and start,
When all that is within him does condemn
Itself for being there?
CATH.   Well, march we on,
To give obedience where 'tis truly ow'd:
Meet we the medicine of the sickly weal;
And with him pour we, in our country's
Each drop of us.   [purge,
LEN.   Or so much as it needs,
To dew the sovereign flower, and drown
the weeds.
Make we our march towards Birnam.
                          [*Exeunt, marching.*

SCENE III.—DUNSINANE. *A Room in the
Castle.*

Enter MACBETH, Doctor, *and* Attendants.

MACB. Bring me no more reports; let
them fly all:
Till Birnam wood remove to Dunsinane,
I cannot taint with fear. What's the boy
Malcolm?
Was he not born of woman? The spirits
that know   [me thus,—
All mortal consequences have pronounc'd
"Fear not, Macbeth; no man that's born of
woman
Shall e'er have power upon thee."—Then
fly, false thanes,
And mingle with the English epicures:
The mind I sway by, and the heart I bear,
Shall never sag with doubt, nor shake with
fear.

Enter a Servant.

The devil damn thee black, thou cream-
fac'd loon!
Where got'st thou that goose look?
SERV. There is ten thousand—
MACB.   Geese, villain?
SERV.   Soldiers, Sir.
MACB. Go prick thy face, and over-red
thy fear,
Thou lily-liver'd boy. What soldiers, patch?
Death of thy soul! those linen cheeks of
thine
Are counsellors to fear. What soldiers,
whey-face?
SERV. The English force, so please you.
MACB. Take thy face hence.—
                          [*Exit Serv.*
          Seyton!—I am sick at heart,
When I behold—Seyton, I say!—This push
Will cheer me ever, or disseat me now
I have liv'd long enough: my way of life
Is fall'n into the sear, the yellow leaf;
And that which should accompany old age,
As honour, love, obedience, troops of
friends,
I must not look to have; but, in their stead,
Curses, not loud, but deep, mouth-honour,
breath,
Which the poor heart would fain deny, and
Seyton!   [dare not.—

Enter SEYTON.

SEY. What is your gracious pleasure?
MACB.   What news more?
SEY. All is confirm'd, my lord, which was
reported.
MACB. I'll fight, till from my bones my
flesh be hack'd.
Give me my armour.
SEY.   'Tis not needed yet.
MACB. I'll put it on.—
Send out more horses, skirr the country
round;
Hang those that talk of fear.—Give me
mine armour.—
How does your patient, doctor?
DOCT.   Not so sick, my lord,
As she is troubled with thick-coming
fancies,
That keep her from her rest.
MACB.   Cure her of that:
Canst thou not minister to a mind diseas'd;
Pluck from the memory a rooted sorrow;
Raze out the written troubles of the brain;
And, with some sweet oblivious antidote,
Cleanse the stuff'd bosom of that perilous
stuff,
Which weighs upon the heart?
DOCT.   Therein the patient
Must minister to himself.
MACB. Throw physic to the dogs,—I'll
none of it.—

Come, put mine armour on; give me my
staff:—   [from me.—
Seyton, send out.—Doctor, the thanes fly
Come, Sir, despatch.—If thou could'st,
doctor, cast
The water of my land, find her disease,
And purge it to a sound and pristine health,
I would applaud thee to the very echo,
That should applaud again.—Pull't off, I
say.—   [drug,
What rhubarb, senna, or what purgative
Would scour these English hence? Hear'st
thou of them?
DOCT. Ay, my good lord; your royal
preparation
Makes us hear something.
MACB.   Bring it after me.—
I will not be afraid of death and bane,
Till Birnam forest come to Dunsinane.
                    [*Exeunt all except* Doctor.
DOCT. Were I from Dunsinane away and
clear,
Profit again should hardly draw me here.
                                      [*Exit.*

SCENE IV.—*Country near* DUNSINANE: *a
Wood in view.*

Enter, with drum and colours, MALCOLM,
Old SIWARD *and his* Son, MACDUFF, MEN-
TETH, CATHNESS, ANGUS, LENOX, ROSSE,
and Soldiers *marching.*

MAL. Cousins, I hope the days are near
at hand
That chambers will be safe.
MENT.   We doubt it nothing.
SIW. What wood is this before us?
MENT.   The wood of Birnam.
MAL. Let every soldier hew him down a
bough,   [shadow
And bear't before him: thereby shall we
The numbers of our host, and make dis-
covery
Err in report of us.
SOLD.   It shall be done.
SIW. We learn no other but the confident
tyrant
Keeps still in Dunsinane, and will endure
Our setting down before't.
MAL.   'Tis his main hope:
For where there is advantage to be given,
Both more and less have given him the
revolt;   [things,
And none serve with him but constrained
Whose hearts are absent too.
MACD.   Let our just censures
Attend the true event, and put we on
Industrious soldiership.
SIW.   The time approaches,
That will with due decision make us know

What we shall say we have, and what we
owe.   [relate;
Thoughts speculative their unsure hopes
But certain issue strokes must arbitrate:
Towards which, advance the war.
                              [*Exeunt, marching.*

SCENE V.—DUNSINANE. *Within the Castle.*
Enter, with drum and colours, MACBETH,
SEYTON, *and* Soldiers.

MACB. Hang out our banners on the out-
ward walls;   [strength
The cry is still, "They come:" our castle's
Will laugh a siege to scorn: here let them
lie,
Till famine and the ague eat them up:
Were they not forc'd with those that should
be ours,   [beard,
We might have met them dareful, beard to
And beat them backward home.—
                          [*A cry within of women.*
What is that noise?
SEY. It is the cry of women, my good
lord.   [*Exit.*
MACB. I have almost forgot the taste of
fears: [cool'd
The time has been, my senses would have
To hear a night-shriek; and my fell of hair
Would at a dismal treatise rouse, and stir,
As life were in't: I have supp'd full with
horrors;   [thoughts,
Direness, familiar to my slaughterous
Cannot once start me.—
                        Re-enter SEYTON.
                    Wherefore was that cry?
SEY. The queen, my lord, is dead.
MACB. She should have died hereafter;
There would have been a time for such a
word.—
To-morrow, and to-morrow, and to-morrow,
Creeps in this petty pace from day to day,
To the last syllable of recorded time;
And all our yesterdays have lighted fools
The way to dusty death. Out, out, brief
candle!
Life's but a walking shadow; a poor player,
That struts and frets his hour upon the
stage,
And then is heard no more: it is a tale
Told by an idiot, full of sound and fury,
Signifying nothing.
                    Enter a Messenger.
Thou com'st to use thy tongue; thy story,
quickly,
MESS. Gracious my lord,
I should report that which I say I saw,
But know not how to do it.
MACB.   Well, say, Sir.

MESS. As I did stand my watch upon the hill,   [thought,
I look'd toward Birnam, and anon, me-
The wood began to move.
MACB.   Liar and slave!
MESS. Let me endure your wrath, if't be not so: [ing;
Within this three mile may you see it com-
I say, a moving grove.
MACB.   If thou speak'st false,
Upon the next tree shalt thou hang alive,
Till famine cling thee: if thy speech be sooth,
I care not if thou dost for me as much.—
I pull in resolution; and begin
To doubt th' equivocation of the fiend,
That lies like truth: "Fear not, till Birnam wood
Do come to Dunsinane;"—and now a wood
Comes toward Dunsinane.—Arm, arm, and out!—
If this which he avouches does appear,
There is nor flying hence, nor tarrying here.
I 'gin to be a-weary of the sun,
And wish th' estate o' the world were now undone.—   [wrack!
Ring the alarum bell!—Blow, wind! come,
At least we'll die with harness on our back.
                                        [*Exeunt.*

SCENE VI.—DUNSINANE. *A Plain before the Castle.*

Enter, with drum and colours, MALCOLM, *Old* SIWARD, MACDUFF, *&c., and their army with boughs.*

MAL. Now near enough; your leafy screens throw down,
And show like those you are.—You, worthy uncle,
Shall, with my cousin, your right-noble son,
Lead our first battle: worthy Macduff, and we,
Shall take upon us what else remains to do,
According to our order.
SIW.   Fare you well.—
Do we but find the tyrant's power to-night,
Let us be beaten, if we cannot fight.
MACD. Make all our trumpets speak; give them all breath,   [death.
Those clamorous harbingers of blood and
                                [*Exeunt. Alarums.*

SCENE VII.—*Another Part of the Plain.*
Alarums. Enter MACBETH.

MACB. They have tied me to a stake; I cannot fly,   [What's he
But, bear-like, I must fight the course.—
That was not born of woman? Such a one
Am I to fear, or none.

Enter Young SIWARD.
YO. SIW. What is thy name?
MACB.   Thou'lt be afraid to hear it.
YO. SIW. No; though thou call'st thyself a hotter name,
Than any is in hell.
MACB.   My name's Macbeth.
YO. SIW. The devil himself could not pro-
nounce a title
More hateful to mine ear.
MACB.   No, nor more fearful.
YO. SIW. Thou liest, abhorred tyrant; with my sword
I'll prove the lie thou speak'st.
            [*They fight, and Young* SIWARD *is slain.*
MACB.   Thou wast born of woman:—
But swords I smile at, weapons laugh to scorn,
Brandish'd by man that's of a woman born.
                                        [*Exit.*

Alarums. Enter MACDUFF.
MACD. That way the noise is.—Tyrant, show thy face!
If thou be'st slain, and with no stroke of mine,   [me still.
My wife and children's ghosts will haunt
I cannot strike at wretched kernes, whose arms   [Macbeth,
Are hir'd to bear their staves; either thou,
Or else my sword, with an unbatter'd edge,
I sheathe again undeeded. There thou should'st be;
By this great clatter, one of greatest note
Seems bruited:—let me find him, fortune!
And more I beg not.   [*Exit. Alarum.*
Enter MALCOLM *and Old* SIWARD.
SIW. This way, my lord;—The castle's gently render'd:
The tyrant's people on both sides do fight;
The noble thanes do bravely in the war;
The day almost itself professes yours,
And little is to do.
MAL.   We have met with foes
That strike beside us.
SIW.   Enter, Sir, the castle.
                                [*Exeunt. Alarum.*
Re-enter MACBETH.
MACB. Why should I play the Roman fool, and die
On mine own sword? whiles I see lives, the gashes
Do better upon them.
Re-enter MACDUFF.
MACD.   Turn, hell-hound, turn!
MACB. Of all men else I have avoided thee;   [charg'd
But get thee back; my soul is too much
With blood of thine already.
MACD.   I have no words,—

My voice is in my sword; thou bloodier
villain
Than terms can give thee out!
                              [*They fight.*
MACB.   Thou losest labour:
As easy may'st thou the intrenchant air
With thy keen sword impress, as make me
bleed:
Let fall thy blade on vulnerable crests;
I bear a charmed life, which must not yield
To one of woman born.
MACD.   Despair thy charm;
And let the angel whom thou still hast
serv'd   [womb
Tell thee, Macduff was from his mother's
Untimely ripp'd.
MACB. Accursed be that tongue that tells
me so,
For it hath cow'd my better part of man!
And be these juggling fiends no more be-
liev'd,
That palter with us in a double sense;
That keep the word of promise to our ear,
And break it to our hope.—I'll not fight
with thee.
MACD. Then yield thee, coward,
And live to be the show and gaze o' the
time:
We'll have thee, as our rarer monsters are,
Painted upon a pole, and underwrit,
"Here may you see the tyrant."
MACB.   I will not yield,
To kiss the ground before young Mal-
colm's feet,
And to be baited with the rabble's curse.
Though Birnam wood be come to Dun-
sinane,   [born,
And thou oppos'd, being of no woman
Yet I will try the last:—before my body
I throw my warlike shield: lay on, Macduff;
And damn'd be he that first cries, "Hold,
enough!"   [*Exeunt, fighting.*
*Retreat. Flourish. Re-enter, with drums
and colours,* MALCOLM, *Old* SIWARD,
ROSSE, *Thanes, and* Soldiers.
MAL. I would the friends we miss were
safe arriv'd.
SIW. Some must go off: and yet, by these
I see,
So great a day as this is cheaply bought.
MAL. Macduff is missing, and your noble
son.
ROSSE. Your son, my lord, has paid a
soldier's debt:
He only liv'd but till he was a man;
The which no sooner had his prowess con-
firm'd

In the unshrinking station where he fought,
But like a man he died.
SIW.   Then he is dead?
ROSSE. Ay, and brought off the field:
your cause of sorrow
Must not be measur'd by his worth, for then
It hath no end.
SIW.   Had he his hurts before?
ROSSE. Ay, on the front.
SIW.   Why then, God's soldier be he!
Had I as many sons as I have hairs,
I would not wish them to a fairer death:
And so, his knell is knoll'd.
MAL.   He's worth more sorrow,
And that I'll spend for him.
SIW.   He's worth no more:
They say he parted well, and paid his
score:
And so, God be with him!—Here comes
newer comfort.
Re-enter MACDUFF, *with* MACBETH'S *head.*
MACD. Hail, king! for so thou art: be-
hold, where stands
The usurper's cursed head: the time is free:
I see thee compass'd with thy kingdom's
pearl,
That speak my salutation in their minds;
Whose voices I desire aloud with mine,—
Hail, king of Scotland!
ALL.   Hail, king of Scotland!
                              [*Flourish.*
MAL. We shall not spend a large expense
of time,
Before we reckon with your several loves,
And make us even with you. My thanes
and kinsmen,
Henceforth be earls,—the first that ever
Scotland
In such an honour nam'd. What's more to
do,   [time,—
Which would be planted newly with the
As calling home our exil'd friends abroad,
That fled the snares of watchful tyranny;
Producing forth the cruel ministers
Of this dead butcher, and his fiend-like
queen,—   [hands
Who, as 'tis thought, by self and violent
Took off her life;—this, and what needful
else
That calls upon us, by the grace of Grace,
We will perform in measure, time, and
place:
So, thanks to all at once, and to each one,
Whom we invite to see us crown'd at
Scone.
                              [*Flourish. Exeunt.*

Hamlet stabbing the King. Act V. S. 2.

HAMLET, PRINCE OF DENMARK

DRAMATIS PERSONÆ

CLAUDIUS, *King of Denmark.*
HAMLET, *Son to the former, and Nephew to the present King.*
HORATIO, *Friend to* HAMLET.
POLONIUS, *Lord Chamberlain.*
LAERTES, *his Son.*
VOLTIMAND,
CORNELIUS,
ROSENCRANTZ,
GUILDENSTERN, } *Courtiers.*
OSRICK,
A Gentleman,
A Priest.

MARCELLUS, } *Officers.*
BERNARDO, }
FRANCISCO, *a Soldier.*
REYNALDO, *Servant to* POLONIUS.
A Captain. Embassadors.
Ghost *of* HAMLET's *Father.*
FORTINBRAS, *Prince of Norway.*
Two Clowns, *Grave-diggers.*

GERTRUDE, *Queen of Denmark, and Mother to* HAMLET.
OPHELIA, *Daughter to* POLONIUS.

Lords, Ladies, Officers, Soldiers, Players, Sailors, Messengers, *and* Attendants.

SCENE,—ELSINORE.

ACT I.

SCENE I.—ELSINORE. *A Platform before the Castle.*

FRANCISCO *on his post. Enter to him* BERNARDO.

BER. Who's there?
FRAN. Nay, answer me: stand, and unfold yourself.
BER. Long live the king!

FRAN. Bernardo?
BER. He.
FRAN. You come most carefully upon your hour.
BER. 'Tis now struck twelve; get thee to bed, Francisco.
FRAN. For this relief much thanks: 'tis bitter cold,
And I am sick at heart.
BER. Have you had quiet guard?

433

FRAN.   Not a mouse stirring.
BER. Well, good night.
If you do meet Horatio and Marcellus,
The rivals of my watch, bid them make
   haste.
FRAN. I think I hear them.—Stand, ho!
   Who is there?
        Enter HORATIO *and* MARCELLUS.
HOR. Friends to this ground.
MAR.   And liegemen to the Dane.
FRAN. Give you good night.
MAR.   O! Farewell, honest soldier:
Who hath reliev'd you?
FRAN.   Bernardo has my place.
Give you good night.   [*Exit.*
MAR.   Holla! Bernardo!
BER.   Say.
What, is Horatio there?
HOR.   A piece of him.
BER. Welcome, Horatio:—welcome, good
   Marcellus.
MAR. What, has this thing appear'd again
   to-night?
BER. I have seen nothing.
MAR. Horatio says, 'tis but our fantasy,
And will not let belief take hold of him,
Touching this dreaded sight, twice seen
   of us:
Therefore I have entreated him along
With us to watch the minutes of this
   night;
That, if again this apparition come,
He may approve our eyes, and speak to it.
HOR. Tush, tush, 'twill not appear.
BER.   Sit down awhile;
And let us once again assail your ears,
That are so fortified against our story,
What we two nights have seen.
HOR.   Well, sit we down,
And let us hear Bernardo speak of this.
BER. Last night of all,
When yon same star, that's westward from
   the pole,
Had made his course to illume that part
   of heaven
Where now it burns, Marcellus and myself,
The bell then beating one,—
MAR. Peace! break thee off; look, where
   it comes again!
        Enter Ghost.
BER. In the same figure, like the king
   that's dead.
MAR. Thou art a scholar; speak to it,
   Horatio.
BER. Looks it not like the king? mark it,
   Horatio.
HOR. Most like:—it harrows me with fear
   and wonder.
BER. It would be spoke to.
MAR.   Question it, Horatio.

HOR. What art thou, that usurp'st this
   time of night,
Together with that fair and warlike form,
In which the majesty of buried Denmark
Did sometimes march? by heaven I charge
   thee, speak!
MAR. It is offended.
BER.   See, it stalks away.
HOR. Stay! speak, speak! I charge thee,
   speak!   [*Exit* Ghost.
MAR. 'Tis gone, and will not answer.
BER. How now, Horatio! you tremble,
   and look pale:
Is not this something more than fantasy?
What think you on't?   [believe,
HOR. Before my God, I might not this
Without the sensible and true avouch
Of mine own eyes.
MAR.   Is it not like the king?
HOR. As thou art to thyself:
Such was the very armour he had on,
When he th' ambitious Norway combated;
So frown'd he once, when, in an angry
   parle,
He smote the sledded Polack on the ice.
'Tis strange.
MAR. Thus, twice before, and just at this
   dead hour,
With martial stalk hath he gone by our
   watch.
HOR. In what particular thought to work,
   I know not;
But, in the gross and scope of my opinion,
This bodes some strange eruption to our
   state.
MAR. Good now, sit down, and tell me,
   he that knows,
Why this same strict and most observant
   watch
So nightly toils the subject of the land;
And why such daily cast of brazen cannon,
And foreign mart for implements of war;
Why such impress of shipwrights, whose
   sore task
Does not divide the Sunday from the
   week;
What might be toward, that this sweaty
   haste
Doth make the night joint labourer with
   the day:
Who is't that can inform me?
HOR.   That can I;
At least, the whisper goes so. Our last
   king,
Whose image even but now appear'd to us,
Was, as you know, by Fortinbras of Nor-
   way,
Thereto prick'd on by a most emulate
   pride,
Dar'd to the combat; in which our valiant
   Hamlet

(For so this side of our known world
　esteem'd him)
Did slay this Fortinbras; who, by a seal'd
　compact,
Well ratified by law and heraldry,
Did forfeit, with his life, all those his
　lands
Which he stood seiz'd of, to the conqueror:
Against the which, a moiety competent
Was gaged by our king; which had re-
　turn'd
To the inheritance of Fortinbras,
Had he been vanquisher; as, by the same
　co-mart,
And carriage of the article design'd,
His fell to Hamlet. Now, Sir, young For-
　tinbras,
Of unimproved mettle hot and full,
Hath in the skirts of Norway, here and
　there,
Shark'd up a list of landless resolutes,
For food and diet, to some enterprise
That hath a stomach in't: which is no
　other
(As it doth well appear unto our state)
But to recover of us, by strong hand
And terms compulsative, those 'foresaid
　lands
So by his father lost: and this, I take it,
Is the main motive of our preparations,
The source of this our watch, and the chief
　head
Of this post-haste and romage in the land.
BER. I think it be no other, but e'en so:
Well may it sort, that this portentous
　figure
Comes armed through our watch; so like
　the king
That was, and is, the question of these
　wars.
HOR. A mote it is to trouble the mind's
　eye.
In the most high and palmy state of Rome,
A little ere the mightiest Julius fell,
The graves stood tenantless, and the
　sheeted dead
Did squeak and gibber in the Roman
　streets:
As, stars with trains of fire, and dews of
　blood,
Disasters in the sun; and the moist star,
Upon whose influence Neptune's empire
　stands,
Was sick almost to dooms-day with eclipse:
And even the like precurse of fierce
　events,—
As harbingers preceding still the fates,
And prologue to the omen coming on,—
Have heaven and earth together demon-
　strated
Unto our climatures and countrymen.—

But, soft, behold! lo, where it comes
　again!

　　　　　Re-enter Ghost.

I'll cross it, though it blast me.—Stay,
　illusion!
If thou hast any sound, or use of voice,
Speak to me:
If there be any good thing to be done,
That may to thee do ease, and grace to
Speak to me:　　　　　　　　　[me,
If thou art privy to thy country's fate,
Which, happily, foreknowing may avoid,
O, speak!
Or if thou hast uphoarded in thy life
Extorted treasure in the womb of earth,
For which, they say, you spirits oft walk in
　death,　　　　　　　　　[*Cock crows.*
Speak of it: stay and speak!—Stop it,
　Marcellus.
MAR. Shall I strike at it with my par-
HOR. Do, if it will not stand. [tisan?
BER. 　　　　　　　　'Tis here!
HOR. 　　　'Tis here! 　　　[*Exit* Ghost.
MAR. 'Tis gone!
We do it wrong, being so majestical,
To offer it the show of violence;
For it is, as the air, invulnerable,
And our vain blows malicious mockery.
BER. It was about to speak, when the
　cock crew.
HOR. And then it started, like a guilty
　thing
Upon a fearful summons. I have heard,
The cock, that is the trumpet to the morn,
Doth with his lofty and shrill-sounding
　throat
Awake the god of day; and at his warning,
Whether in sea or fire, in earth or air,
Th' extravagant and erring spirit hies
To his confine: and of the truth herein
This present object made probation.
MAR. It faded on the crowing of the
　cock.
Some say, that ever 'gainst that season
　comes
Wherein our Saviour's birth is celebrated,
This bird of dawning singeth all night
　long:
And then, they say, no spirit can walk
　abroad;
The nights are wholesome; then no
　planets strike,
No fairy takes, nor witch hath power to
　charm;
So hallow'd and so gracious is the time.
HOR. So have I heard, and do in part
　believe it.
But, look, the morn, in russet mantle clad,
Walks o'er the dew of yon high eastern
　hill.

Break we our watch up: and, by my
    advice,
Let us impart what we have seen to-night
Unto young Hamlet; for, upon my life,
This spirit, dumb to us, will speak to him.
Do you consent we shall acquaint him with
    it,
As needful in our loves, fitting our duty?
MAR. Let's do't, I pray; and I this morn-
    ing know
Where we shall find him most conveniently.
                                    [*Exeunt.*]

SCENE II.—*A Room of State in the Castle.*

Enter the KING, QUEEN, HAMLET, POLONIUS,
    LAERTES, VOLTIMAND, CORNELIUS, Lords
            and Attendants.

KING. Though yet of Hamlet our dear
    brother's death
The memory be green; and that it us be-
    fitted
To bear our hearts in grief, and our whole
    kingdom
To be contracted in one brow of woe;
Yet so far hath discretion fought with
    nature,
That we with wisest sorrow think on him,
Together with remembrance of ourselves.
Therefore, our sometime sister, now our
    queen,
Th' imperial jointress of this warlike state,
Have we, as 'twere with a defeated joy,—
With one auspicious, and one dropping
    eye,
With mirth in funeral, and with dirge in
    marriage,
In equal scale weighing delight and dole,—
Taken to wife: nor have we herein barr'd
Your better wisdoms, which have freely
    gone
With this affair along:—for all, our thanks.
Now follows, that you know, young Fortin-
    bras,
Holding a weak supposal of our worth,
Or thinking, by our late dear brother's
    death,
Our state to be disjoint and out of frame,
Colleagued with the dream of his advan-
    tage,—
He hath not fail'd to pester us with mes-
    sage,
Importing the surrender of those lands
Lost by his father, with all bands of law,
To our most valiant brother. So much for
    him.—
Now for ourself, and for this time of meet-
    ing:
Thus much the business is:—we have here
    writ
To Norway, uncle of young Fortinbras,—

Who, impotent and bed-rid, scarcely hears
Of this his nephew's purpose,—to suppress
His farther gait herein; in that the levies,
The lists, and full proportions, are all
    made
Out of his subject:—and we here despatch
You, good Cornelius, and you, Voltimand,
For bearers of this greeting to old Norway;
Giving to you no farther personal power
To business with the king, more than the
    scope
Of these dilated articles allow.
Farewell; and let your haste commend your
    duty.
COR. VOL. In that, and all things, will
    we show our duty.
KING. We doubt it nothing: heartily fare-
    well.
            [*Exeunt* VOLTIMAND *and* CORNELIUS.
And now, Laertes, what's the news with
    you?
You told us of some suit; what is't
    Laertes?
You cannot speak of reason to the Dane,
And lose your voice: what would'st thou
    beg, Laertes,
That shall not be my offer, not thy asking?
The head is not more native to the heart,
The hand more instrumental to the mouth,
Than is the throne of Denmark to thy
    father.
What would'st thou have, Laertes?
LAER.   My dread lord,
Your leave and favour to return to France;
From whence though willingly I came to
    Denmark,
To show my duty in your coronation;
Yet now, I must confess, that duty done,
My thoughts and wishes bend again toward
    France,
And bow them to your gracious leave and
    pardon.
KING. Have you your father's leave?
    What says Polonius?
POL. He hath, my lord, wrung from me
    my slow leave,
By laboursome petition; and, at last,
Upon his will I seal'd my hard consent:
I do beseech you, give him leave to go.
KING. Take thy fair hour, Laertes; time
    be thine,
And thy best graces spend it at thy will!—
But now, my cousin Hamlet, and my son,—
HAM. [*Aside.*] A little more than kin,
    and less than kind.
KING. How is it that the clouds still
    hang on you?
HAM. Not so, my lord; I am too much i'
    the sun.
QUEEN. Good Hamlet, cast thy nighted
    colour off,

And let thine eye look like a friend on
Denmark.
Do not, for ever, with thy vailed lids
Seek for thy noble father in the dust:
Thou know'st 'tis common,—all that live
must die,
Passing through nature to eternity.

HAM. Ay, Madam, it is common.

QUEEN.　　　　　　　　　If it be,
Why seems it so particular with thee?

HAM. Seems, Madam! nay, it is; I know
not seems.
'Tis not alone my inky cloak, good mother,
Nor customary suits of solemn black,
Nor windy suspiration of forc'd breath,
No, nor the fruitful river in the eye,
Nor the dejected haviour of the visage,
Together with all forms, modes, shows of
grief,
That can denote me truly: these, indeed,
seem,
For they are actions that a man might
play:
But I have that within, which passeth
show;
These, but the trappings and the suits of
woe.

KING. 'Tis sweet and commendable in
your nature, Hamlet,
To give these mourning duties to your
father:
But, you must know, your father lost a
father;
That father lost, lost his; and the survivor
bound,
In filial obligation, for some term
To do obsequious sorrow: but to persever
In obstinate condolement, is a course
Of impious stubbornness; 'tis unmanly
grief:
It shows a will most incorrect to heaven;
A heart unfortified, a mind impatient;
And understanding simple and unschool'd:
For what we know must be, and is as
common
As any the most vulgar thing to sense,
Why should we, in our peevish opposition,
Take it to heart? Fie! 'tis a fault to
heaven,
A fault against the dead, a fault to nature,
To reason most absurd; whose common
theme
Is death of fathers, and who still hath
cried,
From the first corse till he that died to-day,
"This must be so." We pray you, throw to
earth
This unprevailing woe; and think of us
As of a father: for let the world take note,
You are the most immediate to our throne;

And, with no less nobility of love
Than that which dearest father bears his
son,
Do I impart toward you. For your intent
In going back to school in Wittenberg,
It is most retrograde to our desire:
And we beseech you, bend you to remain
Here, in the cheer and comfort of our eye,
Our chiefest courtier, cousin, and our son.

QUEEN. Let not thy mother lose her
prayers, Hamlet:
I pray thee, stay with us; go not to Wittenberg.

HAM. I shall in all my best obey you,
Madam.

KING. Why, 'tis a loving and a fair reply:
Be as ourself in Denmark.—Madam, come;
This gentle and unforc'd accord of Hamlet
Sits smiling to my heart: in grace whereof,
No jocund health that Denmark drinks to-
day,
But the great cannon to the clouds shall
tell;
And the king's rouse the heaven shall
bruit again,
Re-speaking earthly thunder. Come away.
　　　　　[*Exeunt all except* HAMLET.

HAM. O, that this too too solid flesh
would melt,
Thaw, and resolve itself into a dew!
Or that the Everlasting had not fix'd
His canon 'gainst self-slaughter! O God!
O God!
How weary, stale, flat, and unprofitable
Seem to me all the uses of this world!
Fie on't! O fie! 'tis an unweeded garden,
That grows to seed; things rank and gross
in nature
Possess it merely. That it should come
to this!
But two months dead!—nay, not so much,
not two:
So excellent a king; that was, to this,
Hyperion to a satyr: so loving to my
mother,
That he might not beteem the winds of
heaven
Visit her face too roughly. Heaven and
earth!
Must I remember? why, she would hang on
him,
As if increase of appetite had grown
By what it fed on: and yet, within a
month,—
Let me not think on't,—Frailty, thy name
is woman!—
A little month; or ere those shoes were
old,
With which she follow'd my poor father's
body,

Like Niobe, all tears;—why she, even
she,—
O God! a beast, that wants discourse of
reason,
Would have mourn'd longer,—married with
mine uncle,
My father's brother; but no more like my
father,
Than I to Hercules: within a month;
Ere yet the salt of most unrighteous tears
Had left the flushing in her galled eyes,
She married:—O, most wicked speed, to
post
With such dexterity to incestuous sheets!
It is not, nor it cannot come to, good:
But break, my heart,—for I must hold my
tongue!

Enter HORATIO, MARCELLUS, *and* BERNARDO.

HOR. Hail to your lordship!
HAM.   I am glad to see you well:
Horatio,—or I do forget myself.
HOR. The same, my lord, and your poor
servant ever.
HAM. Sir, my good friend; I'll change
that name with you:
And what make you from Wittenberg,
Horatio?—
Marcellus?
MAR. My good lord,—
HAM. I am very glad to see you.—Good
even, Sir.—
But what, in faith, make you from Wittenberg?
HOR. A truant disposition, good my lord.
HAM. I would not hear your enemy say
so;
Nor shall you do mine ear that violence,
To make it truster of your own report
Against yourself: I know you are no truant.
But what is your affair in Elsinore?
We'll teach you to drink deep ere you
depart.
HOR. My lord, I came to see your father's
funeral.
HAM. I pray thee, do not mock me, fellow-student;
I think it was to see my mother's wedding.
HOR. Indeed, my lord, it follow'd hard
upon.
HAM. Thrift, thrift, Horatio! the funeral
bak'd meats
Did coldly furnish forth the marriage
tables.
Would I had met my dearest foe in heaven
Ere I had ever seen that day, Horatio!—
My father,—methinks I see my father.
HOR. O, where, my lord?
HAM. In my mind's eye, Horatio.
HOR. I saw him once; he was a goodly
king.

HAM. He was a man, take him for all in
all,
I shall not look upon his like again.
HOR. My lord, I think I saw him yester
HAM. Saw who?   [nigh
HOR. My lord, the king your father.
HAM.   The king my father
HOR. Season your admiration for a whil
With an attent ear; till I may deliver,
Upon the witness of these gentlemen,
This marvel to you.
HAM.   For God's love, let me hear
HOR. Two nights together, had thes
gentlemen,
Marcellus and Bernardo, on their watch,
In the dead vast and middle of the night
Been thus encounter'd. A figure like you
father,
Armed at all points exactly, cap-à-pé,
Appears before them, and with solemn
march
Goes slow and stately by them: thrice he
walk'd
By their oppress'd and fear-surprised eyes
Within his truncheon's length; whilst they,
distill'd
Almost to jelly with the act of fear,
Stand dumb, and speak not to him. This
to me
In dreadful secrecy impart they did;
And I with them the third night kept the
watch:
Where, as they had deliver'd, both in time,
Form of the thing, each word made true
and good,
The apparition comes: I knew your father;
These hands are not more like.
HAM.   But where was this?
MAR. My lord, upon the platform where
we watch'd.
HAM. Did you not speak to it?
HOR.   My lord, I did;
But answer made it none: yet once, methought,
It lifted up its head, and did address
Itself to motion, like as it would speak:
But, even then, the morning cock crew
loud;
And at the sound it shrunk in haste away,
And vanish'd from our sight.
HAM.   'Tis very strange.
HOR. As I do live, my honour'd lord, 'tis
true;
And we did think it writ down in our duty,
To let you know of it.
HAM. Indeed, indeed, Sirs, but this
troubles me.
Hold you the watch to-night?
MAR. BER.   We do, my lord.
HAM. Arm'd, say you?

MAR. BER.   Arm'd, my lord.
HAM.   From top to toe?
MAR. BER. My lord, from head to foot.
HAM. Then, saw you not his face?
HOR. O, yes, my lord; he wore his beaver
up.
HAM. What, look'd he frowningly?
HOR.   A countenance more
in sorrow than in anger,
HAM.   Pale, or red?
HOR. Nay, very pale.
HAM.   And fix'd his eyes upon you?
HOR. Most constantly.
HAM.   I would I had been there.
HOR. It would have much amaz'd you.
HAM.   Very like,
Very like. Stay'd it long?
HOR. While one with moderate haste
might tell a hundred.
MAR. BER. Longer, longer.
HOR. Not when I saw it.
HAM. His beard was grizzled,—no?
HOR. It was, as I have seen it in his life,
A sable silver'd.
HAM.   I will watch to-night;
Perchance 'twill walk again.
HOR.   I warrant it will.
HAM. If it assume my noble father's
person,
I'll speak to it, though hell itself should
gape,
And bid me hold my peace. I pray you all,
If you have hitherto conceal'd this sight,
Let it be tenable in your silence still;
And whatsoever else shall hap to-night,
Give it an understanding, but no tongue:
I will requite your loves. So, fare you well:
Upon the platform, 'twixt eleven and
twelve,
I'll visit you.
ALL.   Our duty to your honour.
HAM. Your loves, as mine to you: fare-
well.
   [*Exeunt* HORATIO, MARCELLUS, *and*
BERNARDO.
My father's spirit in arms! all is not well;
I doubt some foul play: would the night
were come!
Till then sit still, my <u>soul</u>: foul deeds
will rise,
Though all the earth o'erwhelm them, to
men's eyes.   [*Exit.*

———

SCENE III.—*A Room in* POLONIUS' *House.*

Enter LAERTES *and* OPHELIA.

LAER. My necessaries are embark'd: fare-
well:
And, sister, as the winds give benefit,
And convoy is assistant, do not sleep,
But let me hear from you.

OPH.   Do you doubt that?
LAER. For Hamlet, and the trifling of his
favour,
Hold it a fashion, and a toy in blood;
A violet in the youth of primy nature,
Forward, not permanent, sweet, not lasting,
The perfume and suppliance of a minute;
No more.
OPH. No more but so?
LAER.   Think it no more:
For nature, crescent, does not grow alone
In thewes and bulk; but, as this temple
waxes,
The inward service of the mind and soul
Grows wide withal. Perhaps he loves you
now;
And now no soil, nor cautel, doth besmirch
The virtue of his will: but you must fear,
His greatness weigh'd, his will is not his
own;
For he himself is subject to his birth:
He may not, as unvalued persons do,
Carve for himself; for on his choice de-
pends
The safety and the health of the whole
state;
And therefore must his choice be circum-
scrib'd
Unto the voice and yielding of that body,
Whereof he is the head. Then, if he says
he loves you,
It fits your wisdom so far to believe it,
As he in his particular act and place
May give his saying deed; which is no
farther
Than the main voice of Denmark goes
withal.
Then weigh what loss your honour may
sustain,
If with too credent ear you list his songs;
Or lose your heart; or your chaste treas-
ure open
To his unmaster'd importunity.
Fear it, Ophelia, fear it, my dear sister;
And keep you in the rear of your affection,
Out of the shot and danger of desire.
The chariest maid is prodigal enough,
If she unmask her beauty to the moon:
Virtue itself scapes not calumnious strokes:
The canker galls the infants of the spring,
Too oft before their buttons be disclos'd;
And in the morn and liquid dew of youth
Contagious blastments are most imminent.
Be wary, then; best safety lies in fear:
Youth to itself rebels, though none else
near.
OPH. I shall th' effect of this good les-
son keep,
As watchman to my heart. But, good my
brother,
Do not, as some ungracious pastors do,

Show me the steep and thorny way to heaven;
Whilst, like a puff'd and reckless libertine,
Himself the primrose path of dalliance treads,
And recks not his own read.

LAER.   O, fear me not.
I stay too long:—but here my father comes.
            Enter POLONIUS.
A double blessing is a double grace;
Occasion smiles upon a second leave.

POL. Yet here, Laertes! aboard, aboard, for shame!
The wind sits in the shoulder of your sail,
And you are stay'd for. There,—my blessing with you!
            [*Laying his hand on* LAERTES' *head.*
And these few precepts in thy memory
Look thou character. Give thy thoughts no tongue,
Nor any unproportion'd thought his act.
Be thou familiar, but by no means vulgar.
The friends thou hast, and their adoption tried,
Grapple them to thy soul with hooks of steel;
But do not dull thy palm with entertainment
Of each new-hatch'd, unfledg'd comrade. Beware
Of entrance to a quarrel; but, being in,
Bear't, that th' opposed may beware of thee.
Give every man thine ear, but few thy voice:
Take each man's censure, but reserve thy judgment.
Costly thy habit as thy purse can buy,
But not express'd in fancy; rich, not gaudy:
For the apparel oft proclaims the man;
And they in France, of the best rank and station,
Are most select and generous, chief in that.
Neither a borrower, nor a lender be:
For loan oft loses both itself and friend;
And borrowing dulls the edge of husbandry.
This above all,—to thine ownself be true;
And it must follow, as the night the day,
Thou canst not then be false to any man.
Farewell: my blessing season this in thee!

LAER. Most humbly do I take my leave, my lord.

POL. The time invites you; go, your servants tend.

LAER. Farewell, Ophelia; and remember well
What I have said to you.   [well

OPH.   'Tis in my memory lock'd,
And you yourself shall keep the key of it.

LAER. Farewell.   [*Exit.*

POL. What is't, Ophelia, he hath said to you?

OPH. So please you, something touching the lord Hamlet.

POL. Marry, well bethought:
'Tis told me, he hath very oft of late
Given private time to you; and you yourself
Have of your audience been most free and bounteous:
If it be so, (as so 'tis put on me,
And that in way of caution) I must tell you,
You do not understand yourself so clearly,
As it behoves my daughter, and your honour.
What is between you? give me up the truth.

OPH. He hath, my lord, of late made many tenders
Of his affection to me.

POL. Affection! pooh! you speak like a green girl,
Unsifted in such perilous circumstance.
Do you believe his tenders, as you call them?

OPH. I do not know, my lord, what I should think.

POL. Marry, I'll teach you: think yourself a baby;
That you have ta'en these tenders for true pay,
Which are not sterling. Tender yourself more dearly;
Or,—not to crack the wind of the poor phrase,
Wronging it thus,—you'll tender me a fool.

OPH. My lord, he hath importun'd me
In honourable fashion.   [with love,

POL. Ay, fashion you may call it; go to, go to.

OPH. And hath given countenance to his speech, my lord,
With almost all the holy vows of heaven.

POL. Ay, springes to catch woodcocks. I do know,
When the blood burns, how prodigal the soul
Lends the tongue vows: these blazes, daughter,
Giving more light than heat,—extinct in both,
Even in their promise, as it is a making,—
You must not take for fire. From this time,
Be somewhat scanter of your maiden presence;
Set your entreatments at a higher rate,
Than a command to parley. For lord Hamlet,

Believe so much in him, that he is young;
And with a larger tether may he walk,
Than may be given you: in few, Ophelia,
Do not believe his vows; for they are
  brokers,—
Not of that dye which their investments
  show,
But mere implorators of unholy suits,
Breathing like sanctified and pious bonds,
The better to beguile. This is for all,—
I would not, in plain terms, from this time
  forth,
Have you so slander any moment's leisure,
As to give words or talk with the lord
  Hamlet.
Look to't, I charge you: come your ways.
OPH. I shall obey, my lord.   [*Exeunt.*

SCENE IV.—*The Platform.*

Enter HAMLET, HORATIO, *and* MARCELLUS.

HAM. The air bites shrewdly; it is very
  cold.
HOR. It is a nipping and an eager air.
HAM. What hour now?
HOR.   I think it lacks of twelve.
MAR. No, it is struck.
HOR. Indeed? I heard it not: then it
  draws near the season,
Wherein the spirit held his wont to walk.
[*A flourish of trumpets, and ordnance shot
  off, within.*
What does this mean, my lord?
HAM. The king doth wake to-night, and
  takes his rouse,
Keeps wassail, and the swaggering up-
  spring reels;
And, as he drains his draughts of Rhenish
  down,
The kettle-drum and trumpet thus bray out
The triumph of his pledge.
HOR.   Is it a custom?
HAM. Ay, marry, is't:
But to my mind,—though I am native here,
And to the manner born,—it is a custom
More honour'd in the breach, than the
  observance.
This heavy-headed revel, east and west
Makes us traduc'd and tax'd of other
  nations:
They clepe us drunkards, and with swinish
  phrase
Soil our addition; and, indeed, it takes
From our achievements, though perform'd
  at height,
The pith and marrow of our attribute.
So, oft it chances in particular men,
That, for some vicious mole of nature in
  them,
As, in their birth (wherein they are not
  guilty,

Since nature cannot choose his origin)
By the o'ergrowth of some complexion,
Oft breaking down the pales and forts of
  reason;
Or by some habit, that too much o'er-
  leavens
The form of plausive manners;—that these
  men,—
Carrying, I say, the stamp of one defect,
Being nature's livery, or fortune's star,—
Their virtues else (be they as pure as
  grace,
As infinite as man may undergo)
Shall in the general censure take corrup-
  tion
From that particular fault: the dram of
  base
Doth all the noble substance often dout,
To his own scandal.
HOR.   Look, my lord! it comes.
                Enter Ghost.
HAM. Angels and ministers of grace de-
  fend us!—
Be thou a spirit of health, or goblin
  damn'd,
Bring with thee airs from heaven, or blasts
  from hell,
Be thy intents wicked, or charitable,
Thou com'st in such a questionable shape,
That I will speak to thee: I'll call thee,
  Hamlet,
King, Father, Royal Dane: O, answer me!
Let me not burst in ignorance; but tell
Why thy canoniz'd bones, hearsed in death,
Have burst their cerements; why the sep-
  ulchre,
Wherein we saw thee quietly in-urn'd,
Hath op'd his ponderous and marble jaws,
To cast thee up again! What may this
  mean,
That thou, dead corse, again, in complete
  steel,
Revisit'st thus the glimpses of the moon,
Making night hideous; and we fools of
  nature,
So horridly to shake our disposition,
With thoughts beyond the reaches of our
  souls?
Say, why is this? wherefore? what should
  we do?   [*The* Ghost *beckons* HAMLET.
HOR. It beckons you to go away with it,
As if it some impartment did desire
To you alone.
MAR.   Look, with what courteous action
It waves you to a more removed ground:
But do not go with it.
HOR.   No, by no means.
HAM. It will not speak; then, will I follow
  it.
HOR. Do not, my lord.

HAM.   Why, what should be the fear?
I do not set my life at a pin's fee;
And, for my soul, what can it do to that,
Being a thing immortal as itself?
It waves me forth again:—I'll follow it.
HOR. What if it tempt you toward the
    flood, my lord,
Or to the dreadful summit of the cliff,
That beetles o'er his base into the sea,
And there assume some other horrible
    form,
Which might deprive your sovereignty of
    reason,
And draw you into madness? think of it:
The very place puts toys of desperation,
Without more motive, into every brain,
That looks so many fathoms to the sea,
And hears it roar beneath.
HAM. It waves me still.—Go on: I'll fol-
    low thee.
MAR. You shall not go, my lord.
HAM.   Hold off your hands.
HOR. Be rul'd; you shall not go.
HAM.   My fate cries out,
And makes each petty artery in this body
As hardy as the Nemean lion's nerve.—
                    [Ghost beckons.
Still am I call'd:—unhand me, gentle-
    men;—   [Breaking from them.
By heaven, I'll make a ghost of him that
    lets me:—
I say, away!—Go on; I'll follow thee.
        [Exeunt Ghost and HAMLET.
HOR. He waxes desperate with imagina-
    tion.
MAR. Let's follow; 'tis not fit thus to
    obey him.
HOR. Have after.—To what issue will this
    come?
MAR. Something is rotten in the state of
    Denmark.
HOR. Heaven will direct it.
MAR.   Nay, let's follow him.
                         [Exeunt.

———

SCENE V.—A more remote Part of the
            Platform.

        Enter Ghost and HAMLET.

HAM. Whither wilt thou lead me? speak;
    I'll go no farther.
GHOST. Mark me.
HAM.   I will.
GHOST.   My hour is almost come,
When I to sulphurous and tormenting
    flames
Must render up myself.
HAM.   Alas, poor ghost!
GHOST. Pity me not; but lend thy seri-
    ous hearing
To what I shall unfold.

HAM.   Speak; I am bound to hear.
GHOST. So art thou to revenge, when
    thou shalt hear.
HAM. What?
GHOST. I am thy father's spirit;
Doom'd for a certain term to walk the
    night,
And, for the day, confin'd to fast in fires,
Till the foul crimes, done in my days of
    nature,
Are burnt and purg'd away. But that I
    am forbid
To tell the secrets of my prison-house,
I could a tale unfold, whose lightest word
Would harrow up thy soul; freeze thy
    young blood;
Make thy two eyes, like stars, start from
    their spheres;
Thy knotted and combined locks to part,
And each particular hair to stand on end,
Like quills upon the fretful porcupine:
But this eternal blazon must not be
To ears of flesh and blood.—List, list, O,
    list!—
If thou didst ever thy dear father love,—
HAM. O God!
GHOST. Revenge his foul and most un-
    natural murder.
HAM. Murder!
GHOST. Murder most foul, as in the best
    it is;
But this most foul, strange, and unnatural.
HAM. Haste me to know it, that I, with
    wings as swift
As meditation, or the thoughts of love,
May sweep to my revenge.
GHOST.   I find thee apt;
And duller should'st thou be than the fat
    weed
That rots itself in ease on Lethe wharf,
Would'st thou not stir in this. Now, Ham-
    let, hear;
'Tis given out, that, sleeping in mine or-
    chard,
A serpent stung me; so the whole ear of
    Denmark
Is by a forged process of my death
Rankly abus'd: but know, thou noble
    youth,
The serpent that did sting thy father's life
Now wears his crown.
HAM. O my prophetic soul! my uncle!
GHOST. Ay, that incestuous, that adulter-
    ate beast,
With witchcraft of his wit, with traitorous
    gifts,
(O wicked wit, and gifts, that have the
    power
So to seduce!) won to his shameful lust
The will of my most seeming-virtuous
    queen:

O Hamlet, what a falling-off was there!
From me, whose love was of that dignity,
That it went hand in hand even with the
    vow
I made to her in marriage; and to decline
Upon a wretch, whose natural gifts were
    poor
To those of mine!
But virtue, as it never will be mov'd,
Though lewdness court it in a shape of
    heaven;
So lust, though to a radiant angel link'd,
Will sate itself in a celestial bed,
And prey on garbage.
But, soft! methinks I scent the morning
    air;
Brief let me be.—Sleeping within mine
    orchard,
My custom always in the afternoon,
Upon my secure hour thy uncle stole,
With juice of cursed hebenon in a vial,
And in the porches of mine ears did pour
The leperous distilment; whose effect
Holds such an enmity with blood of man,
That, swift as quicksilver, it courses
    through
The natural gates and alleys of the body;
And, with a sudden vigour, it doth posset
And curd, like eager droppings into milk,
The thin and wholesome blood: so did it
    mine;
And a most instant tetter bark'd about,
Most lazar-like, with vile and loathsome
    crust,
All my smooth body.
Thus was I, sleeping, by a brother's hand,
Of life, of crown, of queen, at once des-
    patch'd:
Cut off even in the blossoms of my sin,
Unhousel'd, disappointed, unanel'd;
No reckoning made, but sent to my ac-
    count
With all my imperfections on my head:
O, horrible! O, horrible! most horrible!
If thou hast nature in thee, bear it not;
Let not the royal bed of Denmark be
A couch for luxury and damned incest.
But, howsoever thou pursu'st this act,
Taint not thy mind, nor let thy soul con-
    trive
Against thy mother aught: leave her to
    heaven,
And to those thorns that in her bosom
    lodge,
To prick and sting her. Fare thee well at
    once!
The glow-worm shows the matin to be
    near,
And 'gins to pale his uneffectual fire:
Adieu, adieu! Hamlet, remember me.
                                    [*Exit.*

HAM. O all you host of heaven! O earth!
    What else?
And shall I couple hell?—O fie!—Hold,
    hold, my heart!
And you, my sinews, grow not instant old,
But bear me stiffly up!—Remember thee!
Ay, thou poor ghost, while memory holds
    a seat
In this distracted globe. Remember thee!
Yea, from the table of my memory
I'll wipe away all trivial fond records,
All saws of books, all forms, all pressures
    past,
That youth and observation copied there;
And thy commandment all alone shall live
Within the book and volume of my brain,
Unmix'd with baser matter: yes, by
    [heaven.—
O most pernicious woman!
O villain, villain, smiling, damned villain!
My tables,—meet it is I set it down,
That one may smile, and smile, and be a
    villain;
At least I'm sure it may be so in Den-
    mark: [*Writing.*
So, uncle, there you are. Now to my word;
It is, "Adieu, adieu! remember me:"
I have sworn't.
HOR. [*Within.*] My lord! my lord!
MAR. [*Within.*] Lord Hamlet!
HOR. [*Within.*]   Heaven secure him!
MAR. [*Within.*] So be it!
HOR. [*Within.*] Illo, ho, ho, my lord!
HAM. Hillo, ho, ho, boy! come, bird, come.
          Enter HORATIO *and* MARCELLUS.
MAR. How is't, my noble lord?
HOR.   What news, my lord?
HAM. O, wonderful!
HOR.   Good my lord, tell it.
HAM.   No;
You'll reveal it.
HOR. Not I, my lord, by heaven.
MAR.   Nor I, my lord.
HAM. How say you, then; would heart of
    man once think it?—
But you'll be secret.
HOR. MAR.   Ay, by heaven, my lord.
HAM. There's ne'er a villain dwelling in
    all Denmark,
But he's an arrant knave.
HOR. There needs no ghost, my lord, come
    from the grave
To tell us this.
HAM.   Why, right; you are i' the right;
And so, without more circumstance at all,
I hold it fit that we shake hands and part:
You, as your business and desire shall
    point you,—
For every man hath business and desire,
Such as it is;—and, for mine own poor
    part,
Look you, I'll go pray.

HOR. These are but wild and whirling words, my lord.

HAM. I am sorry they offend you, heart-'Faith, heartily.   [ily; yes,

HOR.   There's no offence, my lord.

HAM. Yes, by Saint Patrick, but there is, Horatio,
And much offence too. Touching this vision here,—
It is an honest ghost, that let me tell you:
For your desire to know what is between us,   [friends,
O'ermaster it as you may. And now, good
As you are friends, scholars, and, soldiers,
Give me one poor request.

HOR. What is't, my lord? we will.

HAM. Never make known what you have seen to-night.

HOR. MAR. My lord, we will not.

HAM.   Nay, but swear't.

HOR.   In faith,
My lord, not I.

MAR.   Nor I, my lord, in faith.

HAM. Upon my sword.

MAR.   We have sworn, my lord, already.

HAM. Indeed, upon my sword, indeed.

GHOST. [*Beneath.*] Swear.

HAM. Ah, ha, boy! say'st thou so? art thou there, truepenny?—
Come on,—you hear this fellow in the consent to swear.   [cellarage,—

HOR.   Propose the oath, my lord.

HAM. Never to speak of this that you have Swear by my sword.   [seen,

GHOST. [*Beneath.*] Swear.

HAM. Hic et ubique? then we'll shift our Come hither, gentlemen,   [ground.—
And lay your hands again upon my sword:
Never to speak of this that you have heard,
Swear by my sword.

GHOST. [*Beneath.*] Swear.

HAM. Well said, old mole! can'st work i' the earth so fast?
A worthy pioneer!—Once more remove, good friends.

HOR. O day and night, but this is wondrous strange!

HAM. And therefore as a stranger give it welcome.
There are more things in heaven and earth, Horatio,
Than are dreamt of in your philosophy.
But come;—
Here, as before, never, so help you mercy,
How strange or odd soe'er I bear myself,—
As I, perchance, hereafter shall think meet
To put an antick disposition on,—
That you, at such times seeing me, never shall,   [shake,
With arms encumber'd thus, or this head-

Or by pronouncing of some doubtful phrase,
As, "Well, well, we know;"—or, "We could, an if we would;"—
Or, "If we list to speak;"—or, "There be, an if they might;"—
Or such ambiguous giving out, to note
That you know aught of me:—this not to do,
So grace and mercy at your most need Swear.   [help you,

GHOST. [*Beneath.*] Swear.

HAM. Rest, rest, perturbed spirit!—So, gentlemen,
With all my love I do commend me to you:
And what so poor a man as Hamlet is
May do, to express his love and friending to you,   [together;
God willing, shall not lack. Let us go in
And still your fingers on your lips, I pray.
The time is out of joint:—O cursed spite,
That ever I was born to set it right!—
Nay, come, let's go together.   [*Exeunt.*

ACT II.

SCENE I.—*A Room in* POLONIUS' *House.*

Enter POLONIUS *and* REYNALDO.

POL. Give him this money, and these notes, Reynaldo.

REY. I will, my lord.

POL. You shall do marv'lous wisely, good Reynaldo,
Before you visit him, to make enquiry
Of his behaviour.

REY.   My lord, I did intend it.

POL. Marry, well said; very well said.
Look you, Sir,
Enquire me first what Danskers are in Paris;
And how, and who, what means, and where they keep,
What company, at what expense; and finding,
By this encompassment and drift of question,
That they do know my son, come you more nearer
Than your particular demands will touch it: [edge of him;
Take you, as 'twere, some distant knowl-
As thus, "I know his father, and his friends,
And, in part, him;"—do you mark this, Reynaldo?

REY. Ay, very well, my lord.

POL. "And, in part, him;—but," you may say, "not well:
But if't be he I mean, he's very wild;
Addicted so and so;"—and there put on him

What forgeries you please; marry, none so
  rank
As may dishonour him; take heed of that;
But, Sir, such wanton, wild, and usual
  slips,
As are companions noted and most known
To youth and liberty.
REY.   As gaming, my lord.
POL. Ay, or drinking, fencing, swearing,
  quarrelling,
Drabbing:—you may go so far.
REY. My lord, that would dishonour him.
POL. 'Faith, no; as you may season it in
  the charge.
You must not put another scandal on him,
That he is open to incontinency;
That's not my meaning: but breathe his
  faults so quaintly,
That they may seem the taints of liberty,
The flash and out-break of a fiery mind;
A savageness in unreclaimed blood,
Of general assault.
REY.   But, my good lord,—
POL. Wherefore should you do this?
REY.   Ay, my lord,
I would know that.
POL.   Marry, Sir, here's my drift;
And, I believe, it is a fetch of warrant:
You laying these slight sullies on my son,
As 'twere a thing a little soil'd i' the
Mark you,   [working,
Your party in converse, him you would
  sound,
Having ever seen in the prenominate crimes
The youth you breathe of guilty, be assur'd,
He closes with you in this consequence;
"Good Sir," or so; or "friend," or "gentle-
  man,"—
According to the phrase, or the addition,
Of man, and country.
REY.   Very good, my lord.
POL. And then, Sir, does he this,—he
  does—   [I was
What was I about to say?—By the mass,
About to say something:—where did I
  leave?
REY. At "closes in the consequence,"
At "friend or so," and "gentleman."
POL. At, closes in the consequence,—ay,
  marry;
He closes with you thus:—"I know the gen-
  tleman;
I saw him yesterday, or t'other day,
Or then, or then; with such, or such; and,
  as you say,
There was he gaming; there o'ertook in's
  rouse;
There falling out at tennis:" or perchance,
"I saw him enter such a house of sale,"—
Videlicet, a brothel,—or so-forth.—
See you now;

Your bait of falsehood takes this carp of
  truth:
And thus do we of wisdom and of reach,
With windlaces, and with assays of bias,
By indirections find directions out:
So, by my former lecture and advice,
Shall you my son. You have me, have you
REY. My lord, I have.   [not?
POL.   God be wi' you; fare you well.
REY. Good my lord!
POL. Observe his inclination in yourself.
REY. I shall, my lord.
POL. And let him ply his music.
REY.   Well, my lord.
POL. Farewell!—   [Exit REYNALDO.
          Enter OPHELIA.
     How now, Ophelia! what's the matter?
OPH. Alas, my lord, I have been so
  affrighted!
POL. With what, in the name of God?
OPH. My lord, as I was sewing in my
  chamber,
Lord Hamlet,—with his doublet all un-
  brac'd;
No hat upon his head; his stockings foul'd,
Ungarter'd, and down-gyved to his ancle;
Pale as his shirt; his knees knocking each
  other;
And with a look so piteous in purport,
As if he had been loosed out of hell
To speak of horrors,—he comes before me.
POL. Mad for thy love?
OPH.   My lord, I do not know,
But, truly, I do fear it.
POL.   What said he?
OPH. He took me by the wrist, and held
  me hard;
Then goes he to the length of all his arm;
And, with his other hand thus o'er his
  brow,
He falls to such perusal of my face,
As he would draw it. Long stay'd he so;
At last,—a little shaking of mine arm,
And thrice his head thus waving up and
  down,—
He rais'd a sigh so piteous and profound,
That it did seem to shatter all his bulk,
And end his being: that done, he lets me
  go:
And, with his head over his shoulder turn'd,
He seem'd to find his way without his
  eyes;
For out o' doors he went without their help,
And, to the last, bended their light on me.
POL. Come, go with me: I will go seek
  the king.
This is the very ecstasy of love;
Whose violent property fordoes itself,
And leads the will to desperate undertak-
As oft as any passion under heaven, [ings,
That does afflict our natures. I am sorry,—

What, have you given him any hard words
of late?
OPH. No, my good lord; but, as you did
command,
I did repel his letters, and denied
His access to me.
POL. That hath made him mad.
I am sorry that with better heed and judg-
ment [but trifle,
I had not quoted him: I fear'd he did
And meant to wreck thee; but, beshrew
my jealousy!
It seems, it is as proper to our age
To cast beyond ourselves in our opinions,
As it is common for the younger sort
To lack discretion. Come, go we to the
king:
This must be known; which, being kept
close, might move
More grief to hide, than hate to utter love.
[*Exeunt.*

SCENE II.—*A Room in the Castle.*

Enter KING, QUEEN, ROSENCRANTZ, GUIL-
DENSTERN, *and* Attendants.

KING. Welcome, dear Rosencrantz, and
Guildenstern!
Moreover that we much did long to see you,
The need we have to use you, did provoke
Our hasty sending. Something have you
heard
Of Hamlet's transformation; so I call it,
Since nor th' exterior nor the inward man
Resembles that it was. What it should be,
More than his father's death, that thus hath
put him
So much from the understanding of himself,
I cannot dream of: I entreat you both,
That, being of so young days brought up
with him,
And since so neighbour'd to his youth and
humour,
That you vouchsafe your rest here in our
court
Some little time: so by your companies
To draw him on to pleasures, and to gather,
So much as from occasion you may glean,
Whether aught, to us unknown, afflicts him
thus,
That, open'd, lies within our remedy.
QUEEN. Good gentlemen, he hath much
talk'd of you;
And, sure I am, two men there are not
living, [you
To whom he more adheres. If it will please
To show us so much gentry, and good will,
As to expend your time with us a while,
For the supply and profit of our hope,
Your visitation shall receive such thanks
As fits a king's remembrance.

ROS. Both your majesties
Might, by the sovereign power you have
of us,
Put your dread pleasures more into com-
Than to entreaty. [mand
GUIL. But we both obey,
And here give up ourselves, in the full bent,
To lay our service freely at your feet,
To be commanded.
KING. Thanks, Rosencrantz and gentle
Guildenstern.
QUEEN. Thanks, Guildenstern and gentle
Rosencrantz:
And I beseech you instantly to visit
My too much changed son.—Go, some of
you, [is.
And bring these gentlemen where Hamlet
GUIL. Heavens make our presence, and
our practices,
Pleasant and helpful to him!
QUEEN. Ay, amen!
[*Exeunt* ROSENCRANTZ, GUILDENSTERN,
and some Attendants.
Enter POLONIUS.

POL. Th' embassadors from Norway, my
Are joyfully return'd. [good lord,
KING. Thou still hast been the father of
good news.
POL. Have I, my lord? Assure you, my
good liege,
I hold my duty, as I hold my soul,
Both to my God, and to my gracious king:
And I do think, (or else this brain of mine
Hunts not the trail of policy so sure
As it hath us'd to do) that I have found
The very cause of Hamlet's lunacy.
KING. O, speak of that; that do I long
to hear.
POL. Give first admittance to th' embassa-
dors;
My news shall be the fruit to that great
feast.
KING. Thyself do grace to them, and bring
them in. [*Exit* POLONIUS.
He tells me, my dear Gertrude, he hath
found
The head and source of all your son's dis-
temper.
QUEEN. I doubt, it is no other but the
main,— [riage.
His father's death, and our o'erhasty mar-
KING. Well, we shall sift him.—
Re-enter POLONIUS, *with* VOLTIMAND
and CORNELIUS.
Welcome, my good friends!
Say, Voltimand, what from our brother
Norway?
VOLT. Most fair return of greetings, and
desires:

Upon our first, he sent out to suppress
His nephew's levies; which to him appear'd
To be a preparation 'gainst the Polack;
But, better look'd into, he truly found
It was against your highness: whereat
  griev'd,—
That so his sickness, age, and impotence,
Was falsely borne in hand,—sends out
  arrests
On Fortinbras; which he, in brief, obeys;
Receives rebuke from Norway; and, in fine,
Makes vow before his uncle, never more
To give th' assay of arms against your
  majesty.
Whereon old Norway, overcome with joy,
Gives him three thousand crowns in annual
  fee;   [diers,
And his commission to employ those sol-
So levied as before, against the Polack:
With an entreaty, herein farther shown,
                              [*Giving a paper.*
That it might please you to give quiet pass
Through your dominions for this enterprise,
On such regards of safety, and allowance,
As therein are set down.
KING.   It likes us well;
And, at our more consider'd time, we'll read,
Answer, and think upon this business.
Meantime, we thank you for your well-
took labour:
Go to your rest; at night we'll feast to-
Most welcome home.   [gether:
        [*Exeunt* VOLTIMAND *and* CORNELIUS.
POL.   This business is well ended.—
My liege, and madam,—to expostulate
What majesty should be, what duty is,
Why day is day, night night, and time is
  time,   [and time.
Were nothing but to waste night, day,
Therefore, since brevity is the soul of wit,
And tediousness the limbs and outward
  flourishes,
I will be brief:—your noble son is mad:
Mad call I it; for, to define true madness,
What is't, but to be nothing else but mad?
But let that go.
QUEEN.   More matter, with less art.
POL. Madam, I swear, I use no art at all.
That he is mad, 'tis true: 'tis true 'tis
  pity;
And pity 'tis 'tis true: a foolish figure;
But farewell it, for I will use no art.
Mad let us grant him, then: and now
  remains,
That we find out the cause of this effect,—
Or rather say, the cause of this defect,
For this effect defective comes by cause:
Thus it remains, and the remainder thus.
Perpend.
I have a daughter,—have, while she is
  mine,—

Who, in her duty and obedience, mark,
Hath given me this: now gather, and sur-
  mise.
[*Reads.*] "To the celestial, and my soul's
  idol, the most beautified Ophelia,"—
That's an ill phrase, a vile phrase,—"beau-
tified" is a vile phrase: but you shall hear.
Thus:
[*Reads.*] "In her excellent white bosom,
  these," &c.—
QUEEN. Came this from Hamlet to her?
POL. Good Madam, stay awhile; I will
be faithful.
[*Reads.*] "Doubt thou the stars are fire;
          Doubt that the sun doth move;
          Doubt truth to be a liar;
          But never doubt I love.
"O dear Ophelia, I am ill at these num-
bers; I have not art to reckon my groans:
but that I love thee best, O most best, be-
lieve it. Adieu.
"Thine evermore, most dear lady, whilst
  this machine is to him, Hamlet."
This, in obedience, hath my daughter
  shown me:
And more above, hath his solicitings,
As they fell out by time, by means, and
All given to mine ear.   [place,
KING.   But how hath she
Receiv'd his love?
POL.   What do you think of me?
KING. As of a man faithful and honour-
able.
POL. I would fain prove so. But what
  might you think,
When I had seen this hot love on the
  wing,—
(As I perceiv'd it, I must tell you that,
Before my daughter told me) what might
  you,   [think,
Or my dear majesty, your queen here,
If I had play'd the desk, or table-book,
Or given my heart a winking, mute and
  dumb;
Or look'd upon this love with idle sight;—
What might you think? No, I went round
  to work,
And my young mistress thus I did bespeak:
"Lord Hamlet is a prince, out of thy
  star;
This must not be:" and then I precepts
gave her,
That she should lock herself from his
  resort,
Admit no messengers, receive no tokens.
Which done, she took the fruits of my
  advice;
And he, repulsed, (a short tale to make)
Fell into a sadness; then into a fast;
Thence to a watch; thence into a weakness;

Thence to a lightness; and, by this declension,
Into the madness wherein now he raves,
And all we wail for.
KING.   Do you think 'tis this?
QUEEN. It may be, very likely.
POL. Hath there been such a time, (I'd
fain know that)
That I have positively said, " 'Tis so,"
When it prov'd otherwise?
KING.   Not that I know.
POL. Take this from this, if this be otherwise:
          [Pointing to his head and shoulder.
If circumstances lead me, I will find
Where truth is hid, though it were hid
Within the centre.   [indeed
KING.   How may we try it farther?
POL. You know, sometimes he walks four
hours together,
Here in the lobby.
QUEEN.   So he does, indeed.
POL. At such a time I'll loose my daughter
to him:
Be you and I behind an arras then;
Mark the encounter: if he love her not,
And be not from his reason fallen thereon,
Let me be no assistant for a state,
But keep a farm, and carters.
KING.   We will try it.
QUEEN. But, look, where sadly the poor
wretch comes reading.
POL. Away, I do beseech you, both away:
I'll board him presently:—O, give me
leave.—
          [Exeunt KING, QUEEN, and Attendants.
               Enter HAMLET, reading.
How does my good lord Hamlet?
HAM. Well, God-a-mercy.
POL. Do you know me, my lord?
HAM. Excellent well; you are a fishmonger.
POL. Not I, my lord.
HAM. Then I would you were so honest
a man.
POL. Honest, my lord!
HAM. Ay, Sir; to be honest, as this world
goes, is to be one man picked out of ten
thousand.
POL. That's very true, my lord.
HAM. For if the sun breed maggots in a
dead dog, being a god kissing carrion,—
Have you a daughter?
POL. I have, my lord.
HAM. Let her not walk i' the sun: conception is a blessing; but not as your
daughter may conceive:—friend, look to't.
POL. How say you by that?—[Aside.]
Still harping on my daughter:—yet he knew
me not at first; he said I was a fishmonger:

he is far gone, far gone: and truly in my
youth I suffered much extremity for love;
very near this. I'll speak to him again.—
What do you read, my lord?
HAM. Words, words, words.
POL. What is the matter, my lord?
HAM. Between whom?
POL. I mean, the matter that you read,
my lord.
HAM. Slanders, Sir: for the satirical rogue
says here, that old men have grey beards;
that their faces are wrinkled; their eyes
purging thick amber and plum-tree gum;
and that they have a plentiful lack of wit,
together with most weak hams: all which,
Sir, though I most powerfully and potently
believe, yet I hold it not honesty to have
it thus set down; for you yourself, Sir,
should be old as I am, if like a crab, you
could go backward.
POL. [Aside.] Though this be madness, yet
there is method in't.—Will you walk out of
the air, my lord?
HAM. Into my grave?
POL. Indeed, that is out o' the air.—
[Aside.] How pregnant sometimes his replies are! a happiness that often madness
hits on, which reason and sanity could not
so prosperously be delivered of. I will leave
him, and suddenly contrive the means of
meeting between him and my daughter.—
My honourable lord, I will most humbly
take my leave of you.
HAM. You cannot, Sir, take from me any
thing that I will more willingly part withal,
—except my life, except my life, except my
life.
POL. Fare you well, my lord.   [Going.
HAM. These tedious old fools!
     Enter ROSENCRANTZ and GUILDENSTERN.
POL. You go to seek the lord Hamlet;
there he is.
ROS. [To POLONIUS.] God save you, Sir!
          [Exit POLONIUS.
GUIL. Mine honour'd lord!
ROS. My most dear lord!
HAM. My excellent good friends! How
dost thou, Guildenstern? Ah, Rosencrantz!
Good lads, how do ye both?
ROS. As the indifferent children of the
earth.
GUIL. Happy, in that we are not overhappy;
On fortune's cap we are not the very
button.
HAM. Nor the soles of her shoe?
ROS. Neither, my lord.
HAM. Then you live about her waist, or
in the middle of her favours?
GUIL. 'Faith, her privates we.

HAM. In the secret parts of fortune? O, most true; she is a strumpet. What news?

ROS. None, my lord, but that the world's grown honest.

HAM. Then is dooms-day near: but your news is not true. Let me question more in particular: what have you, my good friends, deserved at the hands of fortune, that she sends you to prison hither?

GUIL. Prison, my lord!

HAM. Denmark's a prison.

ROS. Then is the world one.

HAM. A goodly one; in which there are many confines, wards, and dungeons, Denmark being one of the worst.

ROS. We think not so, my lord.

HAM. Why, then, 'tis none to you; for there is nothing either good or bad, but thinking makes it so; to me it is a prison.

ROS. Why, then, your ambition makes it one; 'tis too narrow for your mind.

HAM. O God! I could be bounded in a nut-shell, and count myself a king of infinite space, were it not that I have bad dreams.

GUIL. Which dreams, indeed, are ambition; for the very substance of the ambitious is merely the shadow of a dream.

HAM. A dream itself is but a shadow.

ROS. Truly, and I hold ambition of so airy and light a quality, that it is but a shadow's shadow.

HAM. Then are our beggars bodies, and our monarchs and outstretched heroes the beggars' shadows. Shall we to the court? for, by my fay, I cannot reason.

ROS. GUIL. We'll wait upon you.

HAM. No such matter: I will not sort you with the rest of my servants; for, to speak to you like an honest man, I am most dreadfully attended. But, in the beaten way of friendship, what make you at Elsinore?

ROS. To visit you, my lord; no other occasion.

HAM. Beggar that I am, I am even poor in thanks; but I thank you: and sure, dear friends, my thanks are too dear, a halfpenny. Were you not sent for? Is it your own inclining? Is it a free visitation? Come, deal justly with me: come, come; nay, speak.

GUIL. What should we say, my lord?

HAM. Why, anything,—but to the purpose. You were sent for; and there is a kind of confession in your looks, which your modesties have not craft enough to colour: I know the good king and queen have sent for you.

ROS. To what end, my lord?

HAM. That you must teach me. But let me conjure you, by the rights of our fellowship, by the consonancy of our youth, by the obligation of our ever-preserved love, and by what more dear a better proposer could charge you withal, be even and direct with me, whether you were sent for, or no?

ROS. [*To* GUILDENSTERN.] What say you?

HAM. [*Aside.*] Nay, then, I have an eye of you.—If you love me, hold not off.

GUIL. My lord, we were sent for.

HAM. I will tell you why; so shall my anticipation prevent your discovery, and your secresy to the king and queen moult no feather. I have of late (but wherefore I know not) lost all my mirth, foregone all custom of exercises; and, indeed, it goes so heavily with my disposition, that this goodly frame, the earth, seems to me a sterile promontory; this most excellent canopy, the air, look you, this brave o'erhanging firmament, this majestical roof fretted with golden fire,—why, it appears no other thing to me, but a foul and pestilent congregation of vapours. What a piece of work is a man! How noble in reason! how infinite in faculty! in form, and moving, how express and admirable! in action, how like an angel! in apprehension, how like a god! the beauty of the world! the paragon of animals! And yet, to me, what is this quintessence of dust? man delights not me; no, nor woman neither, though, by your smiling, you seem to say so.

ROS. My lord, there was no such stuff in my thoughts.

HAM. Why did you laugh, then, when I said, man delights not me?

ROS. To think, my lord, if you delight not in man, what lenten entertainment the players shall receive from you: we coted them on the way; and hither are they coming, to offer you service.

HAM. He that plays the king, shall be welcome,—his majesty shall have tribute of me; the adventurous knight shall use his foil and target; the lover shall not sigh gratis; the humorous man shall end his part in peace; the clown shall make those laugh, whose lungs are tickled o' the sere; and the lady shall say her mind freely, or the blank verse shall halt for't.—What players are they?

ROS. Even those you were wont to take delight in, the tragedians of the city.

HAM. How chances it, they travel? their residence, both in reputation and profit, was better both ways.

ROS. I think, their inhibition comes by the means of the late innovation.

HAM. Do they hold the same estimation they did when I was in the city? Are they so followed?

ROS. No, indeed, they are not.

HAM. How comes it? Do they grow rusty?

ROS. Nay, their endeavour keeps in the wonted pace: but there is, Sir, an aiery of children, little eyases, that cry out on the top of question, and are most tyrannically clapped for't: these are now the fashion; and so berattle the common stages, (so they call them) that many, wearing rapiers, are afraid of goose quills, and dare scarce come thither.

HAM. What, are they children? who maintains them? how are they escoted? Will they pursue the quality no longer than they can sing? will they not say afterwards, if they should grow themselves to common players, (as it is most like, if their means are no better) their writers do them wrong, to make them exclaim against their own succession?

ROS. 'Faith, there has been much to do on both sides; and the nation holds it no sin, to tarre them to controversy: there was, for a while, no money bid for argument, unless the poet and the player went to cuffs in the question.

HAM. Is it possible?

GUIL. O, there has been much throwing about of brains.

HAM. Do the boys carry it away?

ROS. Ay, that they do, my lord; Hercules, and his load too.

HAM. It is not strange; for my uncle is king of Denmark, and those that would make mows at him while my father lived, give twenty, forty, fifty, a hundred ducats a-piece, for his picture in little. 'Sblood, there is something in this more than natural, if philosophy could find it out.

[Flourish of trumpets within.

GUIL. There are the players.

HAM. Gentlemen, you are welcome to Elsinore. Your hands,—come: the appurtenance of welcome is fashion and ceremony: let me comply with you in this garb; lest my extent to the players, (which, I tell you, must show fairly outward) should more appear like entertainment than yours. You are welcome: but my uncle-father and aunt-mother are deceived.

GUIL. In what, my dear lord?

HAM. I am but mad north-north-west: when the wind is southerly, I know a hawk from a handsaw.

Enter POLONIUS.

POL. Well be with you, gentlemen!

HAM. Hark you, Guildenstern;—and you too;—at each ear a hearer: that great baby, you see there, is not yet out of his swathing-clouts.

ROS. Haply, he's the second time come to them; for, they say, an old man is twice a child.

HAM. I will prophesy, he comes to tell me of the players; mark it.—You say right, Sir: o' Monday morning; 'twas so, indeed.

POL. My lord, I have news to tell you.

HAM. My lord, I have news to tell you. When Roscius was an actor in Rome,—

POL. The actors are come hither, my lord.

HAM. Buz, buz!

POL. Upon my honour,—

HAM. Then came each actor on his ass,—

POL. The best actors in the world, either for tragedy, comedy, history, pastoral, pastoral-comical, historical-pastoral, tragical-historical, tragical-comical-historical-pastoral, scene individable, or poem unlimited: Seneca cannot be too heavy, nor Plautus too light. For the law of writ, and the liberty, these are the only men.

HAM. O Jephthah, Judge of Israel, what a treasure hadst thou!

POL. What a treasure had he, my lord?

HAM. Why

"One fair daughter, and no more,
　　The which he loved passing well."

POL. [*Aside.*] Still on my daughter.

HAM. Am I not i' the right, old Jephthah?

POL. If you call me Jephthah, my lord, I have a daughter that I love passing well.

HAM. Nay, that follows not.

POL. What follows, then, my lord?

HAM. Why,

"As by lot, God wot,"

And then, you know,

"It came to pass, as most like it was,"—

The first row of the pious chanson will show you more; for look, where my abridgment comes.

Enter four or five Players.

You are welcome, masters; welcome, all: —I am glad to see thee well:—welcome, good friends.—O, my old friend! Thy face is valanced since I saw thee last: com'st thou to beard me in Denmark?—What, my young lady and mistress! By'r lady, your ladyship is nearer heaven, than when I saw you last, by the altitude of a chopine. Pray God, your voice, like a piece of uncurrent gold, be not cracked within the ring. —Masters, you are all welcome. We'll e'en to't like French falconers, fly at any thing we see: we'll have a speech straight: come, give us a taste of your quality; come, a passionate speech.

1 PLAY. What speech, my lord?

HAM. I heard thee speak me a speech once,—but it was never acted; or, if it was, not above once; for the play, I remember, pleased not the million; 'twas caviare to the general: but it was (as I received it, and others, whose judgments in such matters cried in the top of mine) an excellent play; well digested in the scenes, set down with as much modesty as cunning. I remember, one said, there were no sallets in the lines to make the matter savoury, nor no matter in the phrase that might indict the author of affectation; but called it an honest method, as wholesome as sweet, and by very much more handsome than fine. One speech in it I chiefly loved: 'twas Æneas' tale to Dido; and thereabout of it especially, where he speaks of Priam's slaughter. If it live in your memory, begin at this line;—let me see, let me see;—

"The rugged Pyrrhus, like the Hyrcanian beast,"

—'tis not so:—it begins with Pyrrhus:—
"The rugged Pyrrhus,—he, whose sable arms,
"Black as his purpose, did the night resemble   [horse,—
"When he lay couched in the ominous
"Hath now this dread and black complexion smear'd
"With heraldry more dismal; head to foot
"Now is he total gules; horridly trick'd
"With blood of fathers, mothers, daughters, sons;
"Bak'd and impasted with the parching streets,
"That lend a tyrannous and damned light
"To their vile murders: Roasted in wrath and fire,
"And thus o'er-sized with coagulate gore,
"With eyes like carbuncles, the hellish Pyrrhus
"Old grandsire Priam seeks."—

So, proceed you.

POL. 'Fore God, my lord, well spoken; with good accent, and good discretion.

1 *PLAY.*   "Anon he finds him
"Striking too short at Greeks; his antique sword,
"Rebellious to his arm, lies where it falls,
"Repugnant to command: unequal match'd,
"Pyrrhus at Priam drives; in rage, strikes wide: [sword
"But with the whiff and wind of his fell
"The unnerved father falls. Then senseless Ilium,
"Seeming to feel this blow, with flaming top
"Stoops to his base; and with a hideous crash

"Takes prisoner Pyrrhus' ear: for, lo! his sword,
"Which was declining on the milky head
"Of reverend Priam, seem'd i' the air to stick:
"So, as a painted tyrant, Pyrrhus stood;
"And, like a neutral to his will and matter,
"Did nothing.
"But, as we often see, against some storm,
"A silence in the heavens, the rack stand still,   [below
"The bold winds speechless, and the orb
"As hush as death, anon the dreadful thunder
"Doth rend the region; so, after Pyrrhus' pause,
"Aroused vengeance sets him new a-work;
"And never did the Cyclops' hammers fall
"On Mars's armour, forg'd for proof eterne,
"With less remorse than Pyrrhus' bleeding
"Now falls on Priam.—   [sword
"Out, out, thou strumpet, Fortune! All you gods,
"In general synod, take away her power;
"Break all the spokes and fellies from her wheel,
"And bowl the round nave down the hill
"As low as to the fiends!"   [of heaven,

POL. This is too long.

HAM.—Pr'ythee, say on:—he's for a jig, or a tale of bawdry, or he sleeps:—say on;—come to Hecuba.

1 *PLAY.* "But who, O, who had seen the mobled queen"—

HAM. The mobled queen?

POL. That's good; mobled queen is good.

1 *PLAY.* "Run barefoot up and down, threat'ning the flames
"With bisson rheum; a clout upon that head,
"Where late the diadem stood; and, for a robe,
"About her lank and all o'erteemed loins,
"A blanket, in th' alarm of fear caught up;—
"Who this had seen, with tongue in venom steep'd,
" 'Gainst fortune's state would treason have pronounc'd:
"But if the gods themselves did see her then,   [sport
"When she saw Pyrrhus make malicious
"In mincing with his sword her husband's limbs,   [made,
"The instant burst of clamour that she
"(Unless things mortal move them not at all)
"Would have made milch the burning eyes of heaven,
"And passion in the gods."

POL. Look, whether he has not turned his colour, and has tears in's eyes!—Pr'ythee, no more.

HAM. 'Tis well; I'll have thee speak out the rest soon.—Good my lord, will you see the players well bestowed? Do you hear, let them be well used; for they are the abstracts, and brief chronicles, of the time: after your death you were better have a bad epitaph, than their ill report while you live.

POL. My lord, I will use them according to their desert.

HAM. God's bodikins, man, much better: use every man after his desert, and who should 'scape whipping? Use them after your own honour and dignity: the less they deserve, the more merit is in your bounty. Take them in.

POL. Come, Sirs.

HAM. Follow him, friends: we'll hear a play to-morrow.—[*Exit* POLONIUS, *with all the* Players *except the first.*] Dost thou hear me, old friend; can you play the murder of Gonzago?

1 PLAY. Ay, my lord.

HAM. We'll have it to-morrow night. You could, for a need, study a speech of some dozen or sixteen lines, which I would set down and insert in't, could you not?

1 PLAY. Ay, my lord.

HAM. Very well.—Follow that lord; and look you mock him not. [*Exit* 1 Player.] [*To* ROS. *and* GUIL.] My good friends, I'll leave you till night: you are welcome to Elsinore.

ROS. Good my lord!

[*Exeunt* ROSENCRANTZ *and* GUILDENSTERN.

HAM. Ay, so, God be wi' you!—Now I am alone.

O, what a rogue and peasant slave am I!
Is it not monstrous, that this player here,
But in a fiction, in a dream of passion,
Could force his soul so to his own conceit,
That, from her working, all his visage wann'd;
Tears in his eyes, distraction in's aspect,
A broken voice, and his whole function suiting   [ing!
With forms to his conceit? and all for noth-
For Hecuba!
What's Hecuba to him, or he to Hecuba,
That he should weep for her? What would he do,
Had he the motive and the cue for passion,
That I have? He would drown the stage with tears,
And cleave the general ear with horrid speech;

Make mad the guilty, and appal the free,
Confound the ignorant; and amaze, indeed,
The very faculties of eyes and ears.
Yet I,
A dull and muddy-mettled rascal, peak,
Like John-a-dreams, unpregnant of my cause,
And can say nothing; no, not for a king,
Upon whose property, and most dear life,
A damn'd defeat was made. Am I a coward?
Who calls me villain? breaks my pate across?
Plucks off my beard, and blows it in my face?
Tweaks me by the nose? gives me the lie i' the throat,
As deep as to the lungs? Who does me this, ha?
Why, I should take it: for it cannot be,
But I am pigeon-liver'd and lack gall
To make oppression bitter; or, ere this,
I should have fatted all the region kites
With this slave's offal: bloody, bawdy villain!
Remorseless, treacherous, lecherous, kind-
O, vengeance!   [less villain!
Why, what an ass am I! This is most brave,
That I, the son of a dear father murder'd,
Prompted to my revenge by heaven and hell,   [words,
Must, like a whore, unpack my heart with
And fall a cursing, like a very drab,
A scullion!
Fie upon't! foh!—About, my brain! I have heard,
That guilty creatures, sitting at a play,
Have by the very cunning of the scene
Been struck so to the soul, that presently
They have proclaim'd their malefactions;
For murder, though it have no tongue, will speak
With most miraculous organ. I'll have these players
Play something like the murder of my father,
Before mine uncle: I'll observe his looks;
I'll tent him to the quick: if he but blench,
I know my course. The spirit that I have seen
May be the devil: and the devil hath power
T' assume a pleasing shape; yea, and perhaps
Out of my weakness, and my melancholy,
(As he is very potent with such spirits)
Abuses me to damn me: I'll have grounds
More relative than this:—the play's the thing
Wherein I'll catch the conscience of the king.   [*Exit.*

ACT III.

Scene I.—*A Room in the Castle.*

Enter King, Queen, Polonius, Ophelia, Rosencrantz, *and* Guildenstern.

KING. And can you, by no drift of circumstance,
Get from him why he puts on this confusion,
Grating so harshly all his days of quiet
With turbulent and dangerous lunacy?

ROS. He does confess he feels himself distracted;
But from what cause, he will by no means speak.

GUIL. Nor do we find him forward to be sounded;
But, with a crafty madness, keeps aloof,
When we would bring him on to some confession
Of his true state.   [confession

QUEEN.   Did he receive you well?

ROS. Most like a gentleman.

GUIL. But with much forcing of his disposition.

ROS. Niggard of question; but, of our demands,
Most free in his reply.

QUEEN.   Did you assay him
To any pastime?

ROS. Madam, it so fell out, that certain players
We o'er-raught on the way: of these we told him;
And there did seem in him a kind of joy
To hear of it: they are about the court;
And, as I think, they have already order
This night to play before him.

POL.   'Tis most true:
And he beseech'd me to entreat your majesties,
To hear and see the matter.   [ties,

KING. With all my heart; and it doth much content me
To hear him so inclin'd.—
Good gentlemen, give him a farther edge,
And drive his purpose on to these delights.

ROS. We shall, my lord.

[*Exeunt* Rosencrantz *and* Guildenstern.

KING.   Sweet Gertrude, leave us too;
For we have closely sent for Hamlet hither,
That he, as 'twere by accident, may here
Affront Ophelia:
Her father and myself,—lawful espials,—
Will so bestow ourselves, that, seeing, unseen,
We may of their encounter frankly judge;
And gather by him, as he is behav'd,
If 't be th' affliction of his love, or no,
That thus he suffers for.

QUEEN.   I shall obey you.—
And for your part, Ophelia, I do wish
That your good beauties be the happy cause
Of Hamlet's wildness: so shall I hope your virtues
Will bring him to his wonted way again,
To both your honours.

OPH.   Madam, I wish it may.

[*Exit* Queen.

POL. Ophelia, walk you here.—Gracious, so please you,
We will bestow ourselves.—[*To* Ophelia.]
Read on this book;
That show of such an exercise may colour
Your loneliness.—We are oft to blame in this,—
'Tis too much prov'd,—that, with devotion's visage,
And pious action, we do sugar o'er
The devil himself.

KING. [*Aside.*] O, 'tis too true! how smart
A lash that speech doth give my conscience!
The harlot's cheek, beautied with plastering art,
Is not more ugly to the thing that helps it,
Than is my deed to my most painted word:
O heavy burden!

POL. I hear him coming: let's withdraw, my lord. [*Exeunt* King *and* Polonius.

Enter Hamlet.

HAM. To be, or not to be,—that is the question:—
Whether 'tis nobler in the mind to suffer
The slings and arrows of outrageous fortune,
Or to take arms against a sea of troubles,
And by opposing end them?—To die,—to sleep;—
No more; and, by a sleep, to say we end
The heart-ache, and the thousand natural shocks
That flesh is heir to,—'tis a consummation
Devoutly to be wish'd. To die,—to sleep;—
To sleep! perchance to dream:—ay, there's the rub:
For in that sleep of death what dreams may come,
When we have shuffled off this mortal coil,
Must give us pause: there's the respect
That makes calamity of so long life;
For who would bear the whips and scorns of time,
The oppressor's wrong, the proud man's contumely,
The pangs of despis'd love, the law's delay,
The insolence of office, and the spurns
That patient merit of the unworthy takes,
When he himself might his quietus make
With a bare bodkin? who would fardels bear,

To grunt and sweat under a weary life,
But that the dread of something after
death,—
The undiscover'd country, from whose
bourn
No traveller returns,—puzzles the will,
And makes us rather bear those ills we
have,
Than fly to others that we know not of?
Thus conscience does make cowards of us
all;
And thus the native hue of resolution
Is sicklied o'er with the pale cast of
thought;
And enterprises of great pith and moment,
With this regard, their currents turn awry,
And lose the name of action.—Soft you
now!
The fair Ophelia.—Nymph, in thy orisons
Be all my sins remember'd.

OPH. Good my lord,
How does your honour for this many a
day?

HAM. I humbly thank you; well, well,
well.

OPH. My lord, I have remembrances of
yours,
That I have longed long to re-deliver;
I pray you, now receive them.

HAM. No, not I;
I never gave you aught.

OPH. My honour'd lord, I know right well
you did;
And with them, words of so sweet breath
compos'd,
As made the things more rich: their per-
fume lost,
Take these again; for to the noble mind,
Rich gifts wax poor when givers prove
There, my lord. [unkind.

HAM. Ha, ha! are you honest?

OPH. My lord!

HAM. Are you fair?

OPH. What means your lordship?

HAM. That if you be honest, and fair,
your honesty should admit no discourse to
your beauty.

OPH. Could beauty, my lord, have better
commerce than with honesty?

HAM. Ay, truly; for the power of beauty
will sooner transform honesty from what it
is to a bawd, than the force of honesty
can translate beauty into his likeness: this
was sometime a paradox, but now the time
gives it proof. I did love you once.

OPH. Indeed, my lord, you made me believe so.

HAM. You should not have believed me;
for virtue cannot so inoculate our old stock,
but we shall relish of it: I loved you not.

OPH. I was the more deceived.

HAM. Get thee to a nunnery: why would'st
thou be a breeder of sinners? I am myself
indifferent honest; but yet I could accuse
me of such things, that it were better my
mother had not borne me: I am very proud,
revengeful, ambitious; with more offences
at my beck, than I have thoughts to put
them in, imagination to give them shape,
or time to act them in. What should such
fellows as I do crawling between heaven
and earth? We are arrant knaves, all; believe none of us. Go thy ways to a nunnery. Where's your father?

OPH. At home, my lord.

HAM. Let the doors be shut upon him,
that he may play the fool no where but in's
own house. Farewell.

OPH. O, help him, you sweet heavens!

HAM. If thou dost marry, I'll give thee
this plague for thy dowry,—be thou as
chaste as ice, as pure as snow, thou shalt
not escape calumny. Get thee to a nunnery, go: farewell. Or, if thou wilt needs
marry, marry a fool; for wise men know
well enough what monsters you make of
them. To a nunnery, go; and quickly too.
Farewell.

OPH. O heavenly powers, restore him!

HAM. I have heard of your paintings too,
well enough; God hath given you one face,
and you make yourselves another. You jig,
you amble, and you lisp, and nickname
God's creatures, and make your wantonness
your ignorance. Go to, I'll no more on't;
it hath made me mad. I say, we will have
no more marriages: those that are married
already, all but one, shall live; the rest
shall keep as they are. To a nunnery, go.
[*Exit.*

OPH. O, what a noble mind is here o'er-
thrown!
The courtier's, soldier's, scholar's, eye,
tongue, sword:
Th' expectancy and rose of the fair state,
The glass of fashion, and the mould of
form,
Th' observ'd of all observers,—quite, quite
down!
And I, of ladies most deject and wretched,
That suck'd the honey of his music vows,
Now see that noble and most sovereign
reason,
Like sweet bells jangled, out of tune and
harsh,
That unmatch'd form and feature of blown
youth,
Blasted with ecstasy. O, woe is me!
To have seen what I have seen, see what
I see!

Re-enter KING *and* POLONIUS.

KING. Love! his affections do not that
   way tend;
Nor what he spake, though it lack'd form
   a little,
Was not like madness. There's something
   in his soul,
O'er which his melancholy sits on brood;
And, I do doubt, the hatch, and the dis-
   close,
Will be some danger: which, for to prevent,
I have, in quick determination,
Thus set it down:—he shall with speed to
   England,
For the demand of our neglected tribute:
Haply, the seas, and countries different,
With variable objects, shall expel
This something-settled matter in his heart;
Whereon his brains still beating, puts him
   thus   [on't?
From fashion of himself. What think you
POL. It shall do well: but yet do I
   believe,
The origin and commencement of his grief
Sprung from neglected love.—How now,
   Ophelia!
You need not tell us what lord Hamlet
   said;   [please;
We heard it all.—My lord, do as you
But, if you hold it fit, after the play,
Let his queen mother all alone entreat him
To show his grief: let her be round with
   him;
And I'll be plac'd, so please you, in the ear
Of all their conference. If she find him
   not,   [where
To England send him; or confine him
Your wisdom best shall think.
KING.   It shall be so:
Madness in great ones must not unwatch'd
   go.   [*Exeunt.*

SCENE II.—*A Hall in the Castle.*

Enter HAMLET *and certain* Players.

HAM. Speak the speech, I pray you, as I
pronounced it to you, trippingly on the
tongue: but if you mouth it, as many of
your players do, I had as lief the town-crier
spoke my lines. Nor do not saw the air
too much with your hand, thus; but use all
gently: for in the very torrent, tempest, and
(as I may say) whirlwind of passion, you
must acquire and beget a temperance, that
may give it smoothness. O, it offends me
to the soul, to hear a robustious periwig-
pated fellow tear a passion to tatters, to
very rags, to split the ears of the groundlings; who, for the most part, are capable
of nothing but inexplicable dumb shows,
and noise: I would have such a fellow

whipped for o'er-doing Termagant; it out-
herods Herod: pray you, avoid it.
1 PLAY. I warrant your honour.
HAM. Be not too tame neither, but let
your own discretion be your tutor: suit the
action to the word, the word to the action;
with this special observance, that you o'er-
step not the modesty of nature: for any
thing so overdone is from the purpose of
playing; whose end, both at the first, and
now, was, and is, to hold, as 'twere, the
mirror up to nature; to show virtue her
own feature, scorn her own image, and the
very age and body of the time, his form
and pressure. Now, this overdone, or come
tardy off, though it make the unskilful
laugh, cannot but make the judicious
grieve; the censure of which one, must,
in your allowance, o'er-weigh a whole theatre of others. O, there be players, that I
have seen play,—and heard others praise,
and that highly,—not to speak it profanely,
that, neither having the accent of Christians, nor the gait of Christian, pagan, nor
man, have so strutted and bellowed, that I
have thought some of nature's journeymen
had made men, and not made them well,
they imitated humanity so abominably.
1 PLAY. I hope we have reformed that
indifferently with us, Sir.
HAM. O, reform it altogether. And let
those that play your clowns, speak no more
than is set down for them: for there be of
them that will themselves laugh, to set on
some quantity of barren spectators to laugh
too; though, in the mean time, some necessary question of the play be then to be
considered: that's villanous, and shows a
most pitiful ambition in the fool that uses
it. Go, make you ready.—
              [*Exeunt* Players.
Enter POLONIUS, ROSENCRANTZ, *and*
             GUILDENSTERN.
How now, my lord! will the king hear this
piece of work?
POL. And the queen too, and that pres-
ently.
HAM. Bid the players make haste.—
              [*Exit* POLONIUS.
Will you two help to hasten them?
ROS. GUIL. We will, my lord.
  [*Exeunt* ROSENCRANTZ *and* GUILDENSTERN.
HAM. What, ho, Horatio!
        Enter HORATIO.
HOR. Here, sweet lord, at your service.
HAM. Horatio, thou art e'en as just a man
As e'er my conversation cop'd withal.
HOR. O, my dear lord,—
HAM.   Nay, do not think I flatter;
For what advancement may I hope from
   thee,

That no revenue hast, but thy good spirits,
To feed and clothe thee? Why should the
poor be flatter'd?
No, let the candied tongue lick absurd
pomp;
And crook the pregnant hinges of the knee,
Where thrift may follow fawning. Dost
thou hear?
Since my dear soul was mistress of her
choice,
And could of men distinguish, her election
Hath seal'd thee for herself: for thou hast
been   [ing;
As one, in suffering all, that suffers noth-
A man, that fortune's buffets and rewards
Hast ta'en with equal thanks: and bless'd
are those,
Whose blood and judgment are so well co-
mingled,
That they are not a pipe for fortune's
finger
To sound what stop she please. Give me
that man
That is not passion's slave, and I will
wear him
In my heart's core, ay, in my heart of
heart,   [this.—
As I do thee.—Something too much of
There is a play to-night before the king;
One scene of it comes near the circum-
stance,
Which I have told thee, of my father's
death:
I pr'ythee, when thou seest that act a-foot,
Even with the very comment of thy soul
Observe mine uncle: if his occulted guilt
Do not itself unkennel in one speech
It is a damned ghost that we have seen;
And my imaginations are as foul
As Vulcan's stithy. Give him heedful note:
For I mine eyes will rivet to his face;
And, after, we will both our judgments join
In censure of his seeming.
HOR.   Well, my lord:
If he steal aught the whilst this play is
playing,
And 'scape detecting, I will pay the theft.
HAM. They are coming to the play; I
must be idle:
Get you a place.
Danish march. A flourish. Enter KING,
QUEEN, POLONIUS, OPHELIA, ROSEN-
CRANTZ, GUILDENSTERN, and others.
KING. How fares our cousin Hamlet?
HAM. Excellent, i' faith; of the camelion's
dish: I eat the air, promise-crammed: you
cannot feed capons so.
KING. I have nothing with this answer,
Hamlet: these words are not mine.

HAM. No, nor mine now.—[To POLON-
IUS.] My lord, you played once in the uni-
versity, you say?
POL. That did I, my lord; and was ac-
counted a good actor.
HAM. And what did you enact?
POL. I did enact Julius Cæsar: I was
killed i' the Capitol; Brutus killed me.
HAM. It was a brute part of him to kill
so capital a calf there.—Be the players
ready?
ROS. Ay, my lord; they stay upon your
patience.
QUEEN. Come hither, my dear Hamlet, sit
by me.
HAM. No, good mother, here's metal more
attractive.
POL. [To the KING.] O ho! do you mark
that?
HAM. Lady, shall I lie in your lap?
          [Lying down at OPHELIA'S feet.
OPH. No, my lord.
HAM. I mean, my head upon your lap?
OPH. Ay, my lord.
HAM. Do you think, I meant country mat-
ters?
OPH. I think nothing, my lord.
HAM. That's a fair thought to lie between
maids' legs.
OPH. What is, my lord?
HAM. Nothing.
OPH. You are merry, my lord.
HAM. Who, I?
OPH. Ay, my lord.
HAM. O God! your only jig-maker. What
should a man do, but be merry? for, look
you, how cheerfully my mother looks, and
my father died within these two hours.
OPH. Nay, 'tis twice two months, my lord.
HAM. So long? Nay, then let the devil
wear black, for I'll have a suit of sables.
O heavens! die two months ago, and not
forgotten yet? Then there's hope a great
man's memory may outlive his life half a
year: but, by'r lady, he must build churches, then; or else shall he suffer not thinking on, with the hobby-horse, whose epitaph
is, "For, O, for, O, the hobby-horse is forgot."

Trumpets sound. The dumb show enters.
*Enter a King and a Queen, very lovingly;
the Queen embracing him, and he her.
She kneels, and makes show of protesta-
tion unto him. He takes her up, and
declines his head upon her neck: lays
him down upon a bank of flowers: she,
seeing him asleep, leaves him. Anon
comes in a fellow, takes off his crown,
kisses it, and pours poison in the King's
ears, and exit. The Queen returns, finds
the King dead, and makes passionate*

action. The poisoner, with some two or three mutes, comes in again, seeming to lament with her. The dead body is carried away. The poisoner wooes the Queen with gifts: she seems loath and unwilling awhile; but in the end accepts his love. 　　　　　　　　　[*Exeunt.*

OPH. What means this, my lord?

HAM. Marry, this is miching mallecho; it means mischief.

OPH. Belike, this show imports the argument of the play.

Enter Prologue.

HAM. We shall know by this fellow: the players cannot keep counsel; they'll tell all.

OPH. Will he tell us what this show meant?

HAM. Ay, or any show that you will show him: be not you ashamed to show, he'll not shame to tell you what it means.

OPH. You are naught, you are naught: I'll mark the play.

PRO. "For us, and for our tragedy,
Here stooping to your clemency,
We beg your hearing patiently."

HAM. Is this a prologue, or the posy of a ring?

OPH. 'Tis brief, my lord.

HAM. As woman's love.

Enter a King *and a* Queen.

P. KING. Full thirty times hath Phœbus' cart gone round
Neptune's salt wash, and Tellus' orbed ground;
And thirty dozen moons, with borrow'd sheen, 　　　　　　　　[been;
About the world have times twelve thirties
Since love our hearts, and Hymen did our hands,
Unite commutual in most sacred bands.

P. QUEEN. So many journeys may the sun and moon
Make us again count o'er, ere love be done!
But, woe is me, you are so sick of late,
So far from cheer, and from your former state,
That I distrust you. Yet, though I distrust,
Discomfort you, my lord, it nothing must:
For women's fear and love hold quantity;
In neither aught, or in extremity.
Now, what my love is, proof hath made you know;
And as my love is siz'd, my fear is so:
Where love is great, the littlest doubts are fear;
Where little fears grow great, great love grows there.

P. KING. 'Faith, I must leave thee, love, and shortly too;
My operant powers their functions leave to do:

And thou shalt live in this fair world behind,
Honour'd, belov'd; and, haply, one as
For husband shalt thou— 　　　　　　[kind
P. QUEEN. 　　　　　O, confound the rest!
Such love must needs be treason in my breast:
In second husband let me be accurst!
None wed the second, but who kill'd the first.

HAM. [*Aside.*] Wormwood, wormwood.

P. QUEEN. The instances, that second marriage move,
Are base respects of thrift, but none of love:
A second time I kill my husband dead,
When second husband kisses me in bed.

P. KING. I do believe you think what now you speak;
But what we do determine, oft we break.
Purpose is but the slave to memory;
Of violent birth, but poor validity:
Which now, like fruit unripe, sticks on the tree;
But fall, unshaken, when they mellow be.
Most necessary 'tis, that we forget
To pay ourselves what to ourselves is debt:
What to ourselves in passion we propose,
The passion ending, doth the purpose lose.
The violence of either grief or joy
Their own enactures with themselves destroy: 　　　　　　　　　[lament.
Where joy most revels, grief doth most
Grief joys, joy grieves, on slender accident.
This world is not for aye; nor 'tis not strange,
That even our loves should with our fortunes change;
For 'tis a question left us yet to prove,
Whether love lead fortune, or else fortune love 　　　　　　　　[ite flies;
The great man down, you mark his favour-
The poor advanc'd makes friends of enemies.
And hitherto doth love on fortune tend:
For who not needs, shall never lack a friend;
And who in want a hollow friend doth try,
Directly seasons him his enemy.
But, orderly to end where I begun,—
Our wills and fates do so contrary run,
That our devices still are overthrown;
Our thoughts are ours, their ends none of our own:
So think thou wilt no second husband wed;
But die thy thoughts, when thy first lord is dead.

P. QUEEN. Nor earth to me give food, nor heaven light!
Sport and repose lock from me, day and night!

To desperation turn my trust and hope!
An anchor's cheer in prison be my scope!
Each opposite that blanks the face of joy,
Meet what I would have well, and it destroy   [strife,
Both here and hence, pursue me lasting
If, once a widow, ever I be wife!
HAM. If she should break it now!
P. KING. 'Tis deeply sworn. Sweet, leave
    me here a while;
My spirits grow dull, and fain I would
    beguile
The tedious day with sleep.   [*Sleeps.*
P. QUEEN.   Sleep rock thy brain;
And never come mischance between us
    twain!   [*Exit.*
HAM. Madam, how like you this play?
QUEEN. The lady doth protest too much,
methinks.
HAM. O, but she'll keep her word.
KING. Have you heard the argument? Is
there no offence in't?
HAM. No, no, they do but jest, poison in
jest; no offence i' the world.
KING. What do you call the play?
HAM. The mouse-trap. Marry, how? Tropically. This play is the image of a murder
done in Vienna: Gonzago is the duke's
name; his wife, Baptista: you shall see
anon; 'tis a knavish piece of work: but
what of that? your majesty, and we that
have free souls, it touches us not: let the
galled jade wince, our withers are unwrung.

Enter LUCIANUS.

This is one Lucianus, nephew to the king.
OPH. You are as good as a chorus, my
lord.
HAM. I could interpret between you and
your love, if I could see the puppets dallying.
OPH. You are keen, my lord, you are keen.
HAM. It would cost you a groaning to
take off my edge.
OPH. Still better, and worse.
HAM. So you must take your husbands.—
Begin, murderer; leave thy damnable faces,
and begin. Come:—The croaking raven
doth bellow for revenge.
LUC. Thoughts black, hands apt, drugs fit,
    and time agreeing;
Confederate season, else no creature seeing;   [lected,
Thou mixture rank, of midnight weeds colWith Hecate's ban thrice blasted, thrice
    infected,
Thy natural magic and dire property,
On wholesome life usurp immediately.
    [*Pours the poison into the sleeper's ears.*

HAM. He poisons him i' the garden for
his estate. His name's Gonzago: the story
is extant, and written in very choice
Italian. You shall see anon, how the murderer gets the love of Gonzago's wife.
OPH. The king rises.
HAM. What, frighted with false fire!
QUEEN. How fares my lord?
POL. Give o'er the play.
KING. Give me some light:—away!
ALL. Lights, lights, lights!
          [*Exeunt all except* HAMLET *and*
              HORATIO.
HAM. Why, let the strucken deer go weep,
    The hart ungalled play;
For some must watch, while some
        must sleep:
So runs the world away.—
Would not this, Sir, and a forest of feathers, (if the rest of my fortunes turn Turk
with me) with two Provincial roses on
my razed shoes, get me a fellowship in a
cry of players, Sir?
HOR. Half a share.
HAM. A whole one, I.
For thou dost know, O Damon dear,
    This realm dismantled was
Of Jove himself; and now reigns
    A very, very—peacock.   [here
HOR. You might have rhymed.
HAM. O good Horatio, I'll take the ghost's
word for a thousand pound. Didst perceive?
HOR. Very well, my lord.
HAM. Upon the talk of the poisoning,—
HOR. I did very well note him.
HAM. Ah, ha!—Come, some music! come,
the recorders!—
For if the king like not the comedy,
Why, then, belike,—he likes it not,
Come, some music!   [perdy.—
Re-enter ROSENCRANTZ *and* GUILDENSTERN.
GUIL. Good my lord, vouchsafe me a word
with you.
HAM. Sir, a whole history.
GUIL. The king, Sir,—
HAM. Ay, Sir, what of him?
GUIL. Is, in his retirement, marvellous distempered.
HAM. With drink, Sir?
GUIL. No, my lord, rather with choler.
HAM. Your wisdom should show itself
more richer, to signify this to his doctor;
for, for me to put him to his purgation
would, perhaps, plunge him into more
choler.
GUIL. Good my lord, put your discourse
into some frame, and start not so wildly
from my affair.
HAM. I am tame, Sir:—pronounce.

GUIL. The queen, your mother, in most great affliction of spirit, hath sent me to you.

HAM. You are welcome.

GUIL. Nay, good my lord, this courtesy is not of the right breed. If it shall please you to make me a wholesome answer, I will do your mother's commandment: if not, your pardon and my return shall be the end of my business.

HAM. Sir, I cannot.

GUIL. What, my lord?

HAM. Make you a wholesome answer; my wit's diseased: but, Sir, such answer as I can make, you shall command; or, rather, as you say, my mother: therefore no more, but to the matter: my mother, you say,—

ROS. Then, thus she says: your behaviour hath struck her into amazement and admiration.

HAM. O wonderful son, that can so astonish a mother!—But is there no sequel at the heels of this mother's admiration? impart.

ROS. She desires to speak with you in her closet, ere you go to bed.

HAM. We shall obey, were she ten times our mother. Have you any farther trade with us?

ROS. My lord, you once did love me.

HAM. So I do still, by these pickers and stealers.

ROS. Good my lord, what is your cause of distemper? you do, surely, bar the door upon your own liberty, if you deny your griefs to your friend.

HAM. Sir, I lack advancement.

ROS. How can that be, when you have the voice of the king himself for your succession in Denmark?

HAM. Ay, Sir, but "while the grass grows,"—the proverb is something musty.

Enter the Players, *with recorders.*

O, the recorders:—let me see one.—To withdraw with you:—why do you go about to recover the wind of me, as if you would drive me into a toil?

GUIL. O, my lord, if my duty be too bold, my love is too unmannerly.

HAM. I do not well understand that. Will you play upon this pipe?

GUIL. My lord, I cannot.

HAM. I pray you.

GUIL. Believe me, I cannot.

HAM. I do beseech you.

GUIL. I know no touch of it, my lord.

HAM. 'Tis as easy as lying: govern these ventages with your fingers and thumb, give it breath with your mouth, and it will discourse most eloquent music. Look you, these are the stops.

GUIL. But these cannot I command to any utterance of harmony; I have not the skill.

HAM. Why, look you now, how unworthy a thing you make of me! You would play upon me; you would seem to know my stops; you would pluck out the heart of my mystery; you would sound me from my lowest note to the top of my compass: and there is much music, excellent voice, in this little organ; yet cannot you make it speak. 'Sblood, do you think I am easier to be played on than a pipe? Call me what instrument you will, though you can fret me, you cannot play upon me.—

Re-enter POLONIUS.

God bless you, Sir!

POL. My lord, the queen would speak with you, and presently.

HAM. Do you see yonder cloud, that's almost in shape of a camel?

POL. By the mass, and 'tis like a camel, indeed.

HAM. Methinks it is like a weasel.

POL. It is backed like a weasel.

HAM. Or, like a whale?

POL. Very like a whale.

HAM. Then will I come to my mother by and by.—They fool me to the top of my bent.—I will come by and by.

POL. I will say so.   [*Exit.*

HAM. By and by is easily said.—Leave me, friends.—

[*Exeunt* Ros. Guil. Hor. *and* Players.

'Tis now the very witching time of night,
When churchyards yawn, and hell itself breathes out
Contagion to this world: now could I drink hot blood,
And do such bitter business as the day
Would quake to look on. Soft! now to my mother.—
O heart, lose not thy nature; let not ever
The soul of Nero enter this firm bosom:
Let me be cruel, not unnatural:
I will speak daggers to her, but use none;
My tongue and soul in this be hypocrites,—
How in my words soever she be shent,
To give them seals never, my soul, consent!   [*Exit.*

SCENE III.—*A Room in the Castle.*

Enter KING, ROSENCRANTZ, *and* GUILDENSTERN.

KING. I like him not; nor stands it safe with us,
To let his madness range. Therefore prepare you;
I your commission will forthwith despatch,
And he to England shall along with you:

The terms of our estate may not endure
Hazard so dangerous, as doth hourly grow
Out of his lunacies.
GUIL.   We will ourselves provide:
Most holy and religious fear it is,
To keep those many many bodies safe,
That live, and feed, upon your majesty.
ROS. The single and peculiar life is bound,
With all the strength and armour of the
      mind,   [more
To keep itself from 'noyance; but much
That spirit, upon whose weal depend and
      rest
The lives of many. The cease of majesty
Dies not alone; but, like a gulf, doth draw
What's near it with it: it is a massy wheel,
Fix'd on the summit of the highest mount,
To whose huge spokes ten thousand lesser
      things   [falls,
Are mortis'd and adjoin'd; which, when it
Each small annexment, petty consequence,
Attends the boisterous ruin. Never alone
Did the king sigh, but with a general
      groan.
KING. Arm you, I pray you, to this speedy
      voyage;
For we will fetters put upon this fear,
Which now goes too free-footed.
ROS. GUIL.   We will haste us.
[Exeunt ROSENCRANTZ and GUILDENSTERN.
      Enter POLONIUS.
POL. My lord, he's going to his mother's
      closet:
Behind the arras I'll convey myself,
To hear the process; I'll warrant, she'll
      tax him home:
And, as you said, and wisely was it said,
'Tis meet that some more audience than a
      mother,   [o'erhear
Since nature makes them partial, should
The speech, of vantage. Fare you well,
      my liege:
I'll call upon you ere you go to bed,
And tell you what I know.
KING.   Thanks, dear my lord.
                              [Exit POLONIUS.
O, my offence is rank, it smells to heaven;
It hath the primal eldest curse upon't,—
A brother's murder!—Pray can I not,
Though inclination be as sharp as will:
My stronger guilt defeats my strong intent;
And, like a man to double business bound,
I stand in pause where I shall first begin,
And both neglect. What if this cursed hand
Were thicker than itself with brother's
      blood,—   [heavens,
Is there not rain enough in the sweet
To wash it white as snow? Whereto serves
      mercy,
But to confront the visage of offence?

And what's in prayer, but this two-fold
      force,—
To be forestalled, ere we come to fall,
Or pardon'd, being down? Then, I'll look
      up;   [prayer
My fault is past. But, O, what form of
Can serve my turn? Forgive me my foul
      murder!—
That cannot be; since I am still possess'd
Of those effects for which I did the mur-
      der,—   [queen.
My crown, mine own ambition, and my
May one be pardon'd, and retain th' of-
      fence?
In the corrupted currents of this world,
Offence's gilded hand may shove by jus-
      tice;
And oft 'tis seen, the wicked prize itself
Buys out the law: but 'tis not so above;
There is no shuffling,—there the action lies
In his true nature; and we ourselves com-
      pell'd,   [faults,
Even to the teeth and forehead of our
To give in evidence. What then? what
      rests?
Try what repentance can: what can it not?
Yet what can it, when one can not repent?
O wretched state! O bosom, black as
      death!
O limed soul, that, struggling to be free,
Art more engaged! Help, angels! make
      assay!
Bow, stubborn knees; and, heart, with
      strings of steel,
Be soft as sinews of the new-born babe!
All may be well.   [Retires and kneels.
            Enter HAMLET.
HAM. Now might I do it, pat, now he is
      praying;   [en;
And now I'll do't:—and so he goes to heav-
And so am I reveng'd:—that would be
      scann'd:—
A villain kills my father; and, for that,
I, his sole son, do this same villain send
To heaven.
Why, this is hire and salary, not revenge.
He took my father grossly, full of bread;
With all his crimes broad blown, as flush
      as May;   [heaven?
And how his audit stands, who knows, save
But, in our circumstance and course of
      thought,   [reveng'd,
'Tis heavy with him: and am I, then,
To take him in the purging of his soul,
When he is fit and season'd for his pas-
No.   [sage?
Up, sword; and know thou a more horrid
      hent:
When he is drunk, asleep, or in his rage:
Or in th' incestuous pleasure of his bed;

At gaming, swearing; or about some act
That has no relish of salvation in't;—
Then trip him, that his heels may kick at
heaven;   [black
And that his soul may be as damn'd and
As hell, whereto it goes. My mother stays:
This physic but prolongs thy sickly days.
                                   [Exit.

The KING *rises and advances.*

KING. My words fly up, my thoughts remain below:
Words without thoughts never to heaven
go.   [Exit.

SCENE IV.—*The* QUEEN'S *private Apartment in the Castle.*

Enter QUEEN *and* POLONIUS.

POL. He will come straight. Look, you
lay home to him:
Tell him his pranks have been too broad
to bear with,
And that your grace hath screen'd and
stood between
Much heat and him. I'll silence me e'en
Pray you, be round with him.   [here.
HAM. [*Within.*] Mother, mother, mother!
QUEEN.   I'll warrant you;
Fear me not:—withdraw, I hear him com-
ing.

[POLONIUS *conceals himself behind
the arras.*
Enter HAMLET.

HAM. Now, mother, what's the matter?
QUEEN. Hamlet, thou hast thy father
much offended.
HAM. Mother, you have my father much
offended.
QUEEN. Come, come, you answer with an
idle tongue.
HAM. Go, go, you question with a wicked
tongue.
QUEEN. Why, how now, Hamlet!
HAM.   What's the matter now?
QUEEN. Have you forgot me?
HAM.   No, by the rood, not so:
You are the queen, your husband's broth-
er's wife;
And,—would it were not so!—you are my
mother.
QUEEN. Nay, then, I'll set those to you
that can speak.
HAM. Come, come, and sit you down;
you shall not budge;
You go not, till I set you up a glass
Where you may see the inmost part of you.
QUEEN. What wilt thou do? thou wilt not
murder me?—
Help, help, ho!
POL. [*Behind.*] What, ho! help! help!
help!

HAM. How now! a rat? [*Draws.*] Dead,
for a ducat, dead!
            [*Makes a pass through the arras.*
POL. [*Behind.*] O, I am slain!
                        [*Falls and dies.*
QUEEN.   O me, what hast thou done?
HAM.   Nay, I know not:
Is it the king?
            [*Lifts up the arras, and draws
            forth* POLONIUS.
QUEEN. O, what a rash and bloody deed
is this!
HAM. A bloody deed!—almost as bad,
good mother,
As kill a king, and marry with his brother.
QUEEN. As kill a king!
HAM.   Ay, lady, 'twas my word.—
[*To* POL.] Thou wretched, rash, intrud-
ing fool, farewell!
I took thee for thy better: take thy for-
tune;   [ger.—
Thou find'st to be too busy is some dan-
Leave wringing of your hands: peace! sit
you down,
And let me wring your heart: for so I
shall,
If it be made of penetrable stuff;
If damned custom have not braz'd it so,
That it is proof and bulwark against sense.
QUEEN. What have I done, that thou
dar'st wag thy tongue
In noise so rude against me?
HAM.   Such an act,
That blurs the grace and blush of modesty;
Calls virtue, hypocrite; takes off the rose
From the fair forehead of an innocent love,
And sets a blister there; makes marriage
vows
As false as dicers' oaths: O, such a deed,
As from the body of contraction plucks
The very soul; and sweet religion makes
A rhapsody of words: Heaven's face doth
glow;
Yea, this solidity and compound mass,
With tristful visage, as against the doom,
Is thought-sick at the act.
QUEEN.   Ah me, what act,
That roars so loud, and thunders in the
index?
HAM. Look here, upon this picture, and
on this,—
The counterfeit presentment of two broth-
ers.
See, what a grace was seated on this brow;
Hyperion's curls; the front of Jove himself;
An eye like Mars, to threaten and com-
mand;
A station like the herald Mercury,
New-lighted on a heaven-kissing hill;
A combination, and a form, indeed,

Where every god did seem to set his seal,
To give the world assurance of a man:
This was your husband. Look you now,
    what follows:
Here is your husband; like a mildew'd ear,
Blasting his wholesome brother. Have you
    eyes?   [feed,
Could you on this fair mountain leave to
And batten on this moor? Ha! have you
    eyes?
You cannot call it love; for, at your age,
The hey-day in the blood is tame, it's
    humble,   [judgment
And waits upon the judgment: and what
Would step from this to this? Sense, sure,
    you have,
Else, could you not have motion: but, sure,
    that sense
Is apoplex'd: for madness would not err;
Nor sense to ecstasy was ne'er so thrall'd
But it reserv'd some quantity of choice,
To serve in such a difference. What devil
    was't,   [blind?
That thus hath cozen'd you at hoodman-
Eyes without feeling, feeling without sight,
Ears without hands or eyes, smelling sans
    all,
Or but a sickly part of one true sense
Could not so mope.
O shame! where is thy blush? Rebellious
    hell,
If thou canst mutine in a matron's bones,
To flaming youth let virtue be as wax,
And melt in her own fire: proclaim no
    shame   [charge,
When the compulsive ardour gives the
Since frost itself as actively doth burn,
And reason panders will.
QUEEN.   O Hamlet, speak no more!
Thou turn'st mine eyes into my very soul;
And there I see such black and grained
As will not leave their tinct.   [spots,
HAM.   Nay, but to live
In the rank sweat of an enseamed bed,
Stew'd in corruption, honeying and mak-
Over the nasty sty,—   [ing love
QUEEN.   O, speak to me no more;
These words, like daggers, enter in mine
No more, sweet Hamlet!   [ears:
HAM.   A murderer, and a villain;
A slave, that is not twentieth part the tithe
Of your precedent lord; a vice of kings;
A cutpurse of the empire and the rule,
That from a shelf the precious diadem
And put it in his pocket!   [stole,
QUEEN.   No more!
HAM. A king of shreds and patches,—
            Enter Ghost.
Save me, and hover o'er me with your
    wings,

You heavenly guards!—What would your
    gracious figure?
QUEEN. Alas, he's mad!
HAM. Do you not come your tardy son to
    chide,   [by
That, laps'd in time and passion, lets go
Th' important acting of your dread com-
O, say!   [mand?
GHOST. Do not forget: this visitation
Is but to whet thy almost blunted purpose.
But, look, amazement on thy mother sits:
O, step between her and her fighting
    soul,—
Conceit in weakest bodies strongest
Speak to her, Hamlet.   [works,—
HAM.   How is it with you, lady?
QUEEN. Alas, how is't with you,
That you do bend your eye on vacancy,
And with th' incorporal air do hold dis-
    course?   [peep;
Forth at your eyes your spirits wildly
And, as the sleeping soldiers in th' alarm,
Your bedded hair, like life in excrements,
Starts up, and stands on end. O gentle son,
Upon the heat and flame of thy distemper
Sprinkle cool patience. Whereon do you
    look?
HAM. On him, on him! Look you, how
    pale he glares!
His form and cause conjoin'd, preaching
    to stones,
Would make them capable.—Do not look
    upon me;
Lest with this piteous action you convert
My stern effects: then, what I have to do
Will want true colour; tears, perchance,
    for blood.
QUEEN. To whom do you speak this?
HAM.   Do you see nothing there?
QUEEN. Nothing at all; yet all, that is,
    I see.
HAM. Nor did you nothing hear?
QUEEN.   No, nothing but ourselves.
HAM. Why, look you there! look, how
    it steals away!
My father, in his habit as he liv'd!
Look, where he goes, even now, out at the
    portal!   [Exit Ghost.
QUEEN. This is the very coinage of your
This bodiless creation ecstasy.   [brain:
Is very cunning in.
HAM. Ecstasy!
My pulse, as yours, doth temperately keep
    time,   [madness
And makes as healthful music: it is not
That I have utter'd: bring me to the test,
And I the matter will re-word; which mad-
    ness   [grace,
Would gambol from. Mother, for love of
Lay not that flattering unction to your soul,

That not your trespass, but my madness speaks: [place,
It will but skin and film the ulcerous
Whilst rank corruption, mining all within,
Infects unseen. Confess yourself to heaven;
Repent what's past; avoid what is to come;
And do not spread the compost on the weeds,   [my virtue;
To make them ranker. Forgive me this
For in the fatness of these pursy times,
Virtue itself of vice must pardon beg,
Yea, curb and woo, for leave to do him good.
QUEEN. O Hamlet, thou hast cleft my heart in twain.
HAM. O, throw away the worser part of it,
And live the purer with the other half.
Good night: but go not to mine uncle's bed;
Assume a virtue, if you have it not.
That monster, custom, who all sense doth eat,
Of habits devil, is angel yet in this,—
That to the use of actions fair and good
He likewise gives a frock, or livery,
That aptly is put on. Refrain to-night;
And that shall lend a kind of easiness
To the next abstinence: the next more easy;
For use almost can change the stamp of nature,
And master the devil, or throw him out
With wondrous potency. Once more, good night:
And when you are desirous to be bless'd,
I'll blessing beg of you.—For this same lord,   [*Pointing to* POLONIUS.
I do repent: but heaven hath pleas'd it so,—
To punish me with this, and this with me,
That I must be their scourge and minister.
I will bestow him, and will answer well
The death I gave him. So, again, good night.—
I must be cruel, only to be kind:
Thus bad begins, and worse remains behind.—   [hind.—
QUEEN.   What shall I do?
HAM. Not this, by no means, that I bid you do:
Let the bloat king tempt you again to bed;
Pinch wanton on your cheek; call you his mouse;
And let him, for a pair of reechy kisses,
Or paddling in your neck with his damn'd fingers,
Make you to ravel all this matter out,
That I essentially am not in madness,
But mad in craft. 'Twere good, you let him know;   [wise,
For who, that's but a queen, fair, sober,

Would from a paddock, from a bat, a gib,
Such dear concernings hide? who would do so?
No, in despite of sense and secrecy,
Unpeg the basket on the house's top,
Let the birds fly, and, like the famous ape,
To try conclusions, in the basket creep,
And break your own neck down.
QUEEN. Be thou assur'd, if words be made of breath,
And breath of life, I have no life to breathe
What thou hast said to me.
HAM. I must to England; you know that?
QUEEN.   Alack,
I had forgot: 'tis so concluded on.
HAM. There's letters seal'd: and my two schoolfellows,—
Whom I will trust as I will adders fang'd,—
They bear the mandate; they must sweep my way,
And marshal me to knavery. Let it work;
For 'tis the sport, to have the engineer
Hoist with his own petar: and it shall go hard,
But I will delve one yard below their mines,
And blow them at the moon: O, 'tis most sweet,   [meet.—
When in one line two crafts directly
This man shall set me packing:
I'll lug the guts into the neighbour room.—
Mother, good night.—Indeed, this counsellor   [grave,
Is now most still, most secret, and most
Who was in life a foolish prating knave.
Come, Sir, to draw toward an end with you.—
Good night, mother.   [you.—
        [*Exeunt severally;* HAMLET *dragging away the body of* POLONIUS.

ACT IV.

SCENE I.—*The Same.*

Enter KING, QUEEN, ROSENCRANTZ, *and* GUILDENSTERN.

KING. There's matter in these sighs, these profound heaves:
You must translate: 'tis fit we understand
Where is your son?   [them.
QUEEN. [*To* ROS. *and* GUIL.] Bestow this place on us a little while.—
        [*Exeunt* ROSENCRANTZ *and* GUILDENSTERN.
Ah, my good lord, what have I seen to-night!
KING. What, Gertrude? How does Hamlet?
QUEEN. Mad as the sea and wind, when both contend
Which is the mightier: in his lawless fit,
Behind the arras hearing something stir,

He whips his rapier out, and cries, "A rat,
a rat!"
And, in his brainish apprehension, kills
The unseen good old man.
KING. O heavy deed!
It had been so with us, had we been there:
His liberty is full of threats to all;
To you yourself, to us, to every one.
Alas, how shall this bloody deed be an-
swered?
It will be laid to us, whose providence
Should have kept short, restrain'd, and out
of haunt,
This mad young man: but so much was
our love,
We would not understand what was most
fit;
But, like the owner of a foul disease,
To keep it from divulging, let it feed
Even on the pith of life. Where is he gone?
QUEEN. To draw apart the body he hath
kill'd:
O'er whom his very madness, like some ore
Among a mineral of metals base,
Shows itself pure; he weeps for what is
done.
KING. O Gertrude, come away!
The sun no sooner shall the mountains
touch,   [deed
But we will ship him hence: and this vile
We must, with all our majesty and skill,
Both countenance and excuse.—Ho, Guil-
denstern!
Re-enter ROSENCRANTZ *and* GUILDENSTERN.
Friends both, go join you with some far-
ther aid:
Hamlet in madness hath Polonius slain,
And from his mother's closet hath he
dragg'd him:
Go seek him out: speak fair, and bring
the body
Into the chapel. I pray you, haste in this.
                    [*Exeunt* ROS. *and* GUIL.
Come, Gertrude, we'll call up our wisest
friends;   [to do,
And let them know, both what we mean
And what's untimely done: so, haply, slan-
der,—
Whose whisper o'er the world's diameter,
As level as the cannon to his blank,
Transports his poison'd shot,—may miss
our name,
And hit the woundless air.—O, come away!
My soul is full of discord and dismay.
                                        [*Exeunt.*

SCENE II.—*Another Room in the Castle.*

Enter HAMLET.

HAM. Safely stowed.
ROS. GUIL. [*Within.*] Hamlet! Lord
Hamlet!

HAM. What noise? who calls on Hamlet?
O! here they come.
Enter ROSENCRANTZ *and* GUILDENSTERN.
ROS. What have you done, my lord, with
the dead body?
HAM. Compounded it with dust, whereto
'tis kin.
ROS. Tell us where 'tis; that we may take
it thence,
And bear it to the chapel.
HAM. Do not believe it.
ROS. Believe what?
HAM. That I can keep your counsel, and
not mine own. Besides, to be demanded
of a spunge!—what replication should be
made by the son of a king?
ROS. Take you me for a spunge, my lord?
HAM. Ay, Sir; that soaks up the king's
countenance, his rewards, his authorities.
But such offices do the king best service
in the end: he keeps them, like an ape, in
the corner of his jaw; first mouthed, to be
last swallowed: when he needs what you
have gleaned, it is but squeezing you, and,
spunge, you shall be dry again.
ROS. I understand you not, my lord.
HAM. I am glad of it: a knavish speech
sleeps in a foolish ear.
ROS. My lord, you must tell us where the
body is, and go with us to the king.
HAM. The body is with the king, but
the king is not with the body. The king
is a thing—
GUIL. A thing, my lord!
HAM. Of nothing: bring me to him. Hide
fox, and all after.   [*Exeunt.*

SCENE III.—*Another Room in the Castle.*

Enter KING, *attended.*

KING. I have sent to seek him, and to
find the body.
How dangerous is it, that this man goes
loose!   [him.
Yet must not we put the strong law on
He's lov'd of the distracted multitude.
Who like not in their judgment, but their
eyes;   [weigh'd,
And where 'tis so, th' offender's scourge is
But never the offence. To bear all smooth
and even,
This sudden sending him away must seem
Deliberate pause: diseases, desperate grown,
By desperate appliance are reliev'd,
Or not at all.—

Enter ROSENCRANTZ.

How now! what hath befallen?
ROS. Where the dead body is bestow'd,
We cannot get from him.   [my lord,
KING. But where is he?

ROS. Without, my lord; guarded, to know your pleasure.

KING. Bring him before us.

ROS. Ho, Guildenstern! bring in my lord.

Enter HAMLET *and* GUILDENSTERN.

KING. Now, Hamlet, where's Polonius?

HAM. At supper.

KING. At supper! Where?

HAM. Not where he eats, but where he is eaten: a certain convocation of politic worms are e'en at him. Your worm 'is your only emperor for diet: we fat all creatures else to fat us, and we fat ourselves for maggots: your fat king, and your lean beggar, is but variable service; two dishes, but to one table: that's the end.

KING. Alas, alas!

HAM. A man may fish with the worm that hath eat of a king, and eat of the fish that hath fed of that worm.

KING. What dost thou mean by this?

HAM. Nothing, but to show you how a king may go a progress through the guts of a beggar.

KING. Where is Polonius?

HAM. In heaven; send thither to see: if your messenger find him not there, seek him i' the other place yourself. But, indeed, if you find him not within this month, you shall nose him as you go up the stairs into the lobby.

KING. [*To some* Attendants.] Go seek him there.

HAM. He will stay till you come.

[*Exeunt* Attendants.

KING. Hamlet, this deed, for thine especial safety,—
Which we do tender, as we dearly grieve
For that which thou hast done,—must send thee hence
With fiery quickness: therefore prepare thyself;
The bark is ready, and the wind at help,
Th' associates tend, and every thing is bent
For England.

HAM.   For England!

KING.   Ay, Hamlet.

HAM.   Good.

KING. So is it, if thou knew'st our purposes.

HAM. I see a cherub that sees them.— But, come; for England!—Farewell, dear mother.

KING. Thy loving father, Hamlet.

HAM. My mother: father and mother is man and wife; man and wife is one flesh; and so, my mother.—Come, for England!

[*Exit.*

KING. Follow him at foot; tempt him with speed aboard;

Delay it not; I'll have him hence to-night:
Away! for every thing is seal'd and done,
That else leans on th' affair: pray you, make haste.   [*Exeunt* ROS. *and* GUIL.
And, England, if my love thou hold'st at aught,   [sense,
(As my great power thereof may give thee
Since yet thy cicatrice looks raw and red
After the Danish sword, and thy free awe
Pays homage to us) thou may'st not coldly set   [full,
Our sovereign process; which imports at
By letters conjuring to that effect,
The present death of Hamlet. Do it, England;
For like the hectic in my blood he rages,
And thou must cure me: till I know 'tis done,   [gun.
Howe'er my haps, my joys were ne'er be-   [*Exit.*

SCENE IV.—*A Plain in* DENMARK.

Enter FORTINBRAS *and forces, marching.*

FOR. Go, captain, from me greet the Danish king;
Tell him, that, by his licence, Fortinbras
Claims the conveyance of a promis'd march
Over his kingdom. You know the rendezvous.
If that his majesty would aught with us,
We shall express our duty in his eye;
And let him know so.

CAP.   I will do't, my lord.

FOR. Go softly on.

[*Exeunt* FORTINBRAS *and forces.*

Enter HAMLET, ROSENCRANTZ, GUILDENSTERN, &c.

HAM. Good Sir, whose powers are these?

CAP. They are of Norway, Sir.

HAM.   How purpos'd, Sir,
I pray you?

CAP. Against some part of Poland.

HAM.   Who
Commands them, Sir?

CAP. The nephew to old Norway, Fortinbras.   [Sir,

HAM. Goes it against the main of Poland,
Or for some frontier?

CAP. Truly to speak, and with no addition,
We go to gain a little patch of ground,
That hath in it no profit but the name.
To pay five ducats, five, I would not farm it;
Nor will it yield to Norway, or the Pole,
A ranker rate, should it be sold in fee.

HAM. Why, then the Polack never will defend it.

CAP. Yes, 'tis already garrison'd.

HAM. Two thousand souls, and twenty
thousand ducats,
Will not debate the question of this straw:
This is th' imposthume of much wealth
and peace,
That inward breaks, and shows no cause
without   [*Sir.*
Why the man dies.—I humbly thank you,
CAP. God be wi' you, Sir.   [*Exit.*
ROS.   Will't please you go, my lord?
HAM. I'll be with you straight. Go a
little before.—
                [*Exeunt all except* HAMLET.
How all occasion do inform against me,
And spur my dull revenge! What is a man,
If his chief good, and market of his time,
Be but to sleep, and feed? a beast, no
more.   [*discourse,*
Sure, He, that made us with such large
Looking before and after, gave us not
That capability and godlike reason,
To fust in us unus'd. Now, whether it be
Bestial oblivion, or some craven scruple
Of thinking too precisely on th' event,—
A thought, which, quarter'd, hath but one
part wisdom,
And ever three parts coward,—I do not
know   [*do;*"
Why yet I live to say, "This thing's to
Sith I have cause, and will, and strength,
and means,
To do't. Examples, gross as earth, exhort
me:
Witness this army, of such mass and
charge,
Led by a delicate and tender prince;
Whose spirit, with divine ambition puff'd,
Makes mouths at the invisible event;
Exposing what is mortal, and unsure,
To all that fortune, death, and danger,
dare,   [*great,*
Even for an egg-shell. Rightly to be
Is not to stir without great argument,
But greatly to find quarrel in a straw,
When honour's at the stake. How stand
I, then,
That have a father kill'd, a mother stain'd,
Excitements of my reason, and my blood,
And let all sleep? while, to my shame, I
see   [*men,*
The imminent death of twenty thousand
That, for a fantasy and trick of fame,
Go to their graves like beds; fight for a
plot
Whereon the numbers cannot try the cause,
Which is not tomb enough, and continent,
To hide the slain?—O, from this time
forth,
My thoughts be bloody, or be nothing
worth!   [*Exit.*

SCENE V.—ELSINORE. *A Room in the Castle.*
        Enter QUEEN *and* HORATIO.
QUEEN. I will not speak with her.
HOR. She is importunate; indeed, dis-
Her mood will needs be pitied.   [*tract:*
QUEEN.   What would she have?
HOR. She speaks much of her father; says
she hears
There's tricks i' the world; and hems, and
beats her heart;
Spurns enviously at straws; speaks things
in doubt,
That carry but half sense: her speech is
nothing,
Yet the unshaped use of it doth move
The hearers to collection; they aim at it,
And botch the words up fit to their own
thoughts;
Which, as her winks, and nods, and ges-
tures yield them,
Indeed would make one think, there might
be thought,
Though nothing sure, yet much unhappily.
'Twere good she were spoken with, for
she may strew
Dangerous conjectures in ill-breeding
QUEEN. Let her come in.—   [*minds.*
                        [*Exit* HORATIO.
To my sick soul, as sin's true nature is,
Each toy seems prologue to some great
amiss:
So full of artless jealousy is guilt,
It spills itself in fearing to be spilt.
        Re-enter HORATIO, *with* OPHELIA.
OPH. Where is the beauteous majesty of
Denmark?
QUEEN. How now, Ophelia!
OPH. [*Singing.*]
        How should I your true love know
            From another one?
        By his cockle hat and staff,
            And his sandal shoon.
QUEEN. Alas, sweet lady, what imports
this song?
OPH. Say you? nay, pray you, mark.
[*Singing.*]
        He is dead and gone, lady,
            He is dead and gone;
        At his head a grass-green turf,
            At his heels a stone.
O, ho!
QUEEN.   Nay, but Ophelia,—
OPH.   Pray you, mark.
[*Singing.*]
        White his shroud as the mountain snow,
                Enter KING.
QUEEN. Alas, look here, my lord.
OPH. [*Singing.*]
        Larded with sweet flowers;
        Which bewept to the grave did go,
            With true-love showers.

KING. How do you, pretty lady?

OPH. Well, God 'ield you! They say, the owl was a baker's daughter. Lord! we know what we are, but know not what we may be. God be at your table!

KING. Conceit upon her father.

OPH. Pray you, let's have no words of this; but when they ask you what it means, say you this:

Singing.]
　To-morrow is Saint Valentine's day,
　　All in the morning betime,
　And I a maid at your window,
　　To be your Valentine.
　Then up he rose, and donn'd his
　　　clothes,
　　And dupp'd the chamber door;
　Let in the maid, that out a maid
　　Never departed more.

KING. Pretty Ophelia!

OPH. Indeed, la, without an oath, I'll make an end on't:

Singing.]
　By Gis, and by Saint Charity,
　　Alack, and fie for shame!
　Young men will do't, if they come to't;
　　By cock, they are to blame.
　Quoth she, before you tumbled me,
　　You promis'd me to wed.
　So would I ha' done, by yonder sun,
　　An thou hadst not come to my bed.

KING. How long hath she been thus?

OPH. I hope, all will be well. We must be patient: but I cannot choose but weep, to think they should lay him i' the cold ground. My brother shall know of it: and so I thank you for your good counsel.—Come, my coach! Good night, ladies; good night, sweet ladies; good night, good night.　　　　　　　　　　*[Exit.*

KING. Follow her close; give her good watch, I pray you.　*[Exit* HORATIO.
O, this is the poison of deep grief; it springs　　　　　　　　　*[Gertrude,*
All from her father's death. O Gertrude,
When sorrows come, they come not single spies,
But in battalions. First, her father slain:
Next, your son gone; and he most violent author
Of his own just remove: the people muddied,
Thick and unwholesome in their thoughts and whispers,
For good Polonius' death; and we have done but greenly,
In hugger-mugger to inter him: poor Ophelia
Divided from herself and her fair judgment,

Without the which we are pictures, or mere beasts:
Last, and as much containing as all these,
Her brother is in secret come from France;
Feeds on his wonder, keeps himself in clouds,
And wants not buzzers to infect his ear
With pestilent speeches of his father's death;
Wherein necessity, of matter beggar'd,
Will nothing stick our person to arraign
In ear and ear. O my dear Gertrude, this,
Like to a murdering-piece, in many places
Gives me superfluous death.
　　　　　　　　[A noise within.

QUEEN. 　　　Alack, what noise is this?

KING. Where are my Switzers? Let them guard the door.
　　　　Enter a Gentleman.
What is the matter?

GENT. 　　　Save yourself, my lord:
The ocean, overpeering his list,
Eats not the flats with more impetuous haste,
Than young Laertes, in a riotous head,
O'erbears your officers. The rabble call him lord;
And, as the world were now but to begin,
Antiquity forgot, custom not known,
The ratifiers and props of every word,
They cry, "Choose we; Laertes shall be king!"　　　　　　　　　　　*[clouds,*
Caps, hands, and tongues, applaud it to the "Laertes shall be king, Laertes king!"

QUEEN. How cheerfully on the false trail they cry!
O, this is counter, you false Danish dogs!

KING. The doors are broke.
　　　　　　　　[Noise within.
Enter LAERTES, *armed;* Danes *following.*

LAER. Where is this king?—Sirs, stand you all without.

DANES. No, let's come in.

LAER. 　　　I pray you, give me leave.

DANES. We will, we will.
　　[They retire without the door.

LAER. I thank you:—keep the door.—
O thou vile king,
Give me my father!

QUEEN. 　　　Calmly, good Laertes.

LAER. That drop of blood that's calm proclaims me bastard;
Cries cuckold to my father; brands the harlot
Even here, between the chaste unsmirched
Of my true mother.　　　　　　*[brow*

KING. 　　　What is the cause, Laertes,
That thy rebellion looks so giant-like?—
Let him go, Gertrude; do not fear our person:

There's such divinity doth hedge a king,
That treason can but peep to what it
  would,
Acts little of his will.—Tell me, Laertes,
Why thou are thus incens'd:—let him go,
Speak, man.   [Gertrude:—
LAER. Where is my father?
KING.   Dead.
QUEEN.   But not by him.
KING. Let him demand his fill.
LAER. How came he dead? I'll not be
  juggled with:
To hell, allegiance! vows, to the blackest
  devil!   [pit!
Conscience and grace, to the profoundest
I dare damnation:—to this point I stand,—
That both the worlds I give to negligence,
Let come what comes; only I'll be reveng'd
Most throughly for my father.
KING.   Who shall stay you?
LAER. My will, not all the world:
And, for my means, I'll husband them so
  well,
They shall go far with little.
KING.   Good Laertes,
If you desire to know the certainty
Of your dear father's death, is't writ in
  your revenge,
That, sweepstake, you will draw both
  friend and foe,
Winner and loser?
LAER. None but his enemies.
KING.   Will you know them, then?
LAER. To his good friends thus wide I'll
  ope my arms:
And, like the kind life-rendering pelican,
Repast them with my blood.
KING.   Why, now you speak
Like a good child, and a true gentleman.
That I am guiltless of your father's death,
And am most sensibly in grief for it,
It shall as level to your judgment pierce,
As day does to your eye.
DANES. [Within.] Let her come in.
LAER. How now! what noise is that?
          Re-enter OPHELIA.
O heat, dry up my brains! tears seven
  times salt,
Burn out the sense and virtue of mine
  eye!—
By heaven, thy madness shall be paid by
  weight,   [May!
Till our scale turn the beam. O rose of
Dear maid, kind sister, sweet Ophelia!—
O heavens! is't possible, a young maid's
  wits
Should be as mortal as an old man's life?
Nature is fine in love; and, where 'tis fine,
It sends some precious instance of itself
After the thing it loves.

OPH. [Singing.]
    They bore him barefac'd on the bier;
    Hey non nonny, nonny, hey nonny;
    And on his grave rain'd many a tear,—
Fare you well, my dove!
LAER. Hadst thou thy wits, and didst persuade revenge,
It could not move thus.
OPH. You must sing, "Down a-down, an
you call him a-down-a." O, how the wheel
becomes it! It is the false steward, that
stole his master's daughter.
LAER. This nothing's more than matter.
OPH. There's rosemary, that's for remembrance; pray, love, remember: and there
is pansies, that's for thoughts.
LAER. A document in madness,—thoughts
and remembrance fitted.
OPH. There's fennel for you, and colum-
bines:—there's rue for you; and here's
some for me: we may call it herb of grace
o' Sundays:—you may wear your rue with
a difference.—There's a daisy:—I would
give you some violets, but they withered
all when my father died:—they say, he
made a good end,—[Singing.]
    For bonny sweet Robin is all my joy,—
LAER. Thought and affliction, passion,
hell itself,
She turns to favour, and to prettiness.
OPH. [Singing.]
    And will he not come again?
    And will he not come again?
        No, no, he is dead,
        Go to thy death-bed,
    He never will come again.
    His beard was as white as snow,
    All flaxen was his poll:
        He is gone, he is gone,
        And we cast away moan:
    God ha' mercy on his soul!
And of all Christian souls! I pray God.—
God be wi' you!   [Exit.
LAER. Do you see this, O God?
KING. Laertes, I must commune with your
grief,
Or you deny me right. Go but apart,
Make choice of whom your wisest friends
  you will,
And they shall hear and judge 'twixt you
  and me:
If by direct, or by collateral hand
They find us touch'd, we will our kingdom
  give,   [ours,
Our crown, our life, and all that we call
To you in satisfaction; but if not,
Be you content to lend your patience to us,
And we shall jointly labour with your soul
To give it due content.

LAER.　　　　　　Let this be so;
His means of death, his obscure funeral,—
No trophy, sword, nor hatchment, o'er
　his bones,
No noble rite, nor formal ostentation,—
Cry to be heard, as 'twere from heaven to
That I must call't in question.　　[earth,
KING.　　　　　　So you shall;
And, where th' offence is, let the great axe
I pray you, go with me.　　　　　[fall.
　　　　　　　　　　　　[*Exeunt.*

Scene VI.—*Another Room in the Castle.*

Enter HORATIO *and a* Servant.

HOR. What are they that would speak
with me?

SERV. Sailors, Sir: they say, they have
letters for you.

HOR. Let them come in.—
　　　　　　　　　[*Exit* Servant.
I do not know from what part of the world
I should be greeted, if not from lord Ham-
　let.

Enter Sailors.

1 SAIL. God bless you, Sir.

HOR. Let him bless thee too.

1 SAIL. He shall, Sir, an't please him.
There's a letter for you, Sir; it comes from
the embassador that was bound for England; if your name be Horatio, as I am
let to know it is.

HOR. [*Reads.*] "Horatio, when thou shalt
have overlooked this, give these fellows
some means to the king: they have letters
for him. Ere we were two days old at sea,
a pirate of very warlike appointment gave
us chase. Finding ourselves too slow of
sail, we put on a compelled valour: in the
grapple I boarded them: on the instant
they got clear of our ship; so I alone became their prisoner. They have dealt with
me like thieves of mercy: but they knew
what they did; I am to do a good turn for
them. Let the king have the letters I have
sent; and repair thou to me with as much
haste as thou would'st fly death. I have
words to speak in thine ear will make thee
dumb; yet are they much too light for the
bore of the matter. These good fellows will
bring thee where I am. Rosencrantz and
Guildenstern hold their course for England:
of them I have much to tell thee. Farewell.

He that thou knowest thine, HAMLET."
Come, I will give you way for these your
　letters;　　　　　　　　　　　　[me
And do't the speedier, that you may direct
To him from whom you brought them.
　　　　　　　　　　　　[*Exeunt.*

Scene VII.—*Another Room in the Castle.*

Enter KING *and* LAERTES.

KING. Now must your conscience my ac-
　quittance seal,
And you must put me in your heart for
　friend,　　　　　　　　　　　　[ear,
Sith you have heard, and with a knowing
That he, which hath your noble father
Pursu'd my life.　　　　　　　　　[slain,

LAER.　　It well appears:—but tell me
Why you proceeded not against these feats,
So crimeful and so capital in nature,
As by your safety, greatness, wisdom, all
　things else,
You mainly were stirr'd up.

KING.　　　O, for two special reasons;
Which may to you, perhaps, seem much
　unsinew'd,
But yet to me they are strong. The queen,
　his mother,
Lives almost by his looks; and for myself,
(My virtue, or my plague, be it either
　which)
She's so conjunctive to my life and soul,
That, as the star moves not but in his
　sphere,　　　　　　　　　　　　[tive,
I could not but by her. The other mo-
Why to a public count I might not go,
Is the great love the general gender bear
　him;　　　　　　　　　　　　[tion,
Who, dipping all his faults in their affec-
Would, like the spring that turneth wood
　to stone,
Convert his gyves to graces; so that my
　arrows,
Too slightly timber'd for so loud a wind,
Would have reverted to my bow again,
And not where I had aim'd them.

LAER. And so have I a noble father lost;
A sister driven into desperate terms,—
Whose worth, if praises may go back again,—
Stood challenger on mount of all the age
For her perfections:—but my revenge will
　come.

KING. Break not your sleeps for that:
　you must not think
That we are made of stuff so flat and dull,
That we can let our beard be shook with
　danger,
And think it pastime. You shortly shall
　hear more:
I loved your father, and we love ourself;
And that, I hope, will teach you to imag-
　ine,—

Enter a Messenger.

How now! what news?

MESS.　　Letters, my lord, from Hamlet:
This to your majesty; this to the queen.

KING. From Hamlet! who brought them?

MESS. Sailors, my lord, they say; I saw them not:
They were given me by Claudio,—he receiv'd them
Of him that brought them.
KING.   Laertes, you shall hear them.—
Leave us.   [*Exit* Messenger.
[*Reads.*] "High and mighty,—you shall know I am set naked on your kingdom. To-morrow shall I beg leave to see your kingly eyes: when I shall, first asking your pardon thereunto, recount the occasions of my sudden and more strange return.
                                        HAMLET."
What should this mean? Are all the rest come back?
Or is it some abuse, and no such thing?
LAER. Know you the hand?
KING. 'Tis Hamlet's character:—"naked,"
And, in a postscript here, he says, "alone."
Can you advise me?
LAER. I'm lost in it, my lord. But let him come;
It warms the very sickness in my heart,
That I shall live and tell him to his teeth,
"Thus diddest thou."
KING.   If it be so, Laertes,—
As how should it be so? how otherwise?—
Will you be ruled by me?
LAER.   Ay, my lord;
So you will not o'er-rule me to a peace.
KING. To thine own peace. If he be now return'd,—
As checking at his voyage, and that he means   [him
No more to undertake it,—I will work
To an exploit, now ripe in my device,
Under the which he shall not choose but fall: [breathe;
And for his death no wind of blame shall
But even his mother shall uncharge the
And call it accident.   [practice,
LAER.   My lord, I will be rul'd;
The rather, if you could devise it so,
That I might be the organ.
KING.   It falls right.
You have been talk'd of since your travel much,
And that in Hamlet's hearing, for a quality
Wherein, they say, you shine: your sum of parts
Did not together pluck such envy from him,
As did that one; and that, in my regard,
Of the unworthiest siege.
LAER.   What part is that, my lord?
KING. A very riband in the cap of youth,
Yet needful too; for youth no less becomes
The light and careless livery that it wears,
Than settled age his sables and his weeds,

Importing health and graveness.—Two months since,
Here was a gentleman of Normandy,—
I have seen myself, and serv'd against the French,   [gallant
And they can well on horseback: but this
Had witchcraft in't; he grew unto his seat;
And to such wond'rous doing brought his horse,
As he had been incorps'd and demi-natur'd
With the brave beast: so far he topp'd my thought,
That I, in forgery of shapes and tricks,
Come short of what he did.
LAER.   A Norman was't?
KING. A Norman.
LAER. Upon my life, Lamord.
KING.   The very same.
LAER. I know him well: he is the brooch,
And gem of all the nation.   [indeed,
KING. He made confession of you;
And gave you such a masterly report,
For art and exercise in your defence,
And for your rapier most especially,
That he cried out, 'twould be a sight indeed,
If one could match you: the scrimers of their nation,
He swore, had neither motion, guard, nor eye,
If you oppos'd them. Sir, this report of his
Did Hamlet so envenom with his envy,
That he could nothing do, but wish and beg
Your sudden coming o'er, to play with you.
Now, out of this,—
LAER.   What out of this, my lord?
KING. Laertes, was your father dear to you?
Or are you like the painting of a sorrow,
A face without a heart?
LAER.   Why ask you this?
KING. Not that I think you did not love your father;
But that I know love is begun by time;
And that I see, in passages of proof,
Time qualifies the spark and fire of it.
There lives within the very flame of love
A kind of wick, or snuff, that will abate it;
And nothing is at a like goodness still;
For goodness, growing to a plurisy,
Dies in his own too-much: that we would do,
We should do when we would; for this "would" changes,
And hath abatements and delays as many,
As there are tongues, are hands, are accidents;
And then this "should" is like a spend-thrift sigh,
That hurts by easing. But, to the quick o' the ulcer:—

Hamlet comes back: what would you un-
dertake,
To show yourself your father's son in deed,
More than in words?
LAER.   To cut his throat i' the church.
KING. No place, indeed, should murder
sanctuarize;
Revenge should have no bounds. But, good
Laertes,
Will you do this, keep close within your
chamber.   [home:
Hamlet, return'd, shall know you are come
We'll put on those shall praise your excel-
lence,
And set a double varnish on the fame
The Frenchman gave you; bring you, in
fine, together,
And wager on your heads: he, being re-
miss,   [ing,
Most generous, and free from all contriv-
Will not peruse the foils; so that, with
ease,
Or with a little shuffling, you may choose
A sword unbated, and, in a pass of practice,
Requite him for your father.
LAER.   I will do't:
And, for that purpose, I'll anoint my sword.
I bought an unction of a mountebank,
So mortal, that but dip a knife in it,
Where it draws blood no cataplasm so rare,
Collected from all simples that have virtue
Under the moon, can save the thing from
death,   [point
That is but scratch'd withal: I'll touch my
With this contagion, that, if I gall him
It may be death.   [slightly,
KING.   Let's farther think of this;
Weigh, what convenience, both of time
and means,
May fit us to our shape: if this should fail,
And that our drift look through our bad
performance,
'Twere better not assay'd: therefore this
project
Should have a back, or second, that might
hold,
If this should blast in proof. Soft!—let
me see:—
We'll make a solemn wager on your cun-
I ha't: [nings,—
When in your motion you are hot and dry,
(As make your bouts more violent to that
end)
And that he calls for drink, I'll have pre-
par'd him
A chalice for the nonce; whereon but
sipping,
If he by chance escape your venom'd
Our purpose may hold there.   [stuck,
    Enter QUEEN.
            How now, sweet queen!

QUEEN. One woe doth tread upon an-
other's heel,
So fast they follow:—your sister's drown'd,
Laertes.
LAER. Drown'd! O, where?
QUEEN. There is a willow grows aslant
a brook,
That shows his hoar leaves in the glassy
stream;
There with fantastic garlands did she
come
Of crow-flowers, nettles, daisies, and long
purples,
That liberal shepherds give a grosser
name,
But our cold maids do dead men's fingers
call them:
There, on the pendent boughs her coronet
weeds
Clambering to hang, an envious sliver
broke;
When down her weedy trophies, and her-
self,
Fell in the weeping brook. Her clothes
spread wide;
And, mermaid-like, awhile they bore her
up:
Which time, she chanted snatches of old
tunes;
As one incapable of her own distress,
Or like a creature native and indu'd
Unto that element: but long it could not
be,
Till that her garments, heavy with their
drink,
Pull'd the poor wretch from her melodious
To muddy death.   [lay
LAER.   Alas, then, she is drown'd?
QUEEN. Drown'd, drown'd.
LAER. Too much of water hast thou, poor
Ophelia,
And therefore I forbid my tears: but yet
It is our trick; nature her custom holds,
Let shame say what it will: when these
are gone,
The woman will be out.—Adieu, my lord:
I have a speech of fire, that fain would
blaze,
But that this folly douts it.   [*Exit.*
KING.   Let's follow, Gertrude.
How much I had to do to calm his rage!
Now fear I this will give it start again;
Therefore let's follow.   [*Exeunt.*

ACT V.

SCENE I.—*A Church-Yard.*

Enter two CLOWNS, *with spades, &c.*
1 *CLO.* Is she to be buried in Christian
burial, that wilfully seeks her own salvation?

2 *CLO.* I tell thee, she is; and therefore make her grave straight: the crowner hath set on her, and finds it Christian burial.

1 *CLO.* How can that be, unless she drowned herself in her own defence?

2 *CLO.* Why, 'tis found so.

1 *CLO.* It must be *se offendendo*; it cannot be else. For here lies the point: if I drown myself wittingly, it argues an act: and an act hath three branches; it is, to act, to do, and to perform: argal, she drowned herself wittingly.

2 *CLO.* Nay, but hear you, goodman delver,—

1 *CLO.* Give me leave. Here lies the water; good: here stands the man; good: if the man go to this water, and drown himself, it is, will he, nill he, he goes,— mark you that; but if the water come to him, and drown him, he drowns not himself; argal, he that is not guilty of his own death, shortens not his own life.

2 *CLO.* But is this law?

1 *CLO.* Ay, marry, is't; crowner's-quest law.

2 *CLO.* Will you ha' the truth on't? If this had not been a gentlewoman, she should have been buried out of Christian burial.

1 *CLO.* Why, there thou say'st; and the more pity, that great folk should have countenance in this world to drown or hang themselves, more than their even Christian. —Come, my spade. There is no ancient gentlemen but gardeners, ditchers, and grave-makers: they hold up Adam's profession.

2 *CLO.* Was he a gentleman?

1 *CLO.* He was the first that ever bore arms.

2 *CLO.* Why, he had none.

1 *CLO.* What, art a heathen? How dost thou understand the Scripture? The Scripture says, Adam digged: could he dig without arms? I'll put another question to thee: if thou answerest me not to the purpose, confess thyself—

2 *CLO.* Go to.

1 *CLO.* What is he, that builds stronger than either the mason, the shipwright, or the carpenter?

2 *CLO.* The gallows-maker; for that frame outlives a thousand tenants.

1 *CLO.* I like thy wit well, in good faith: the gallows does well; but how does it well? it does well to those that do ill: now, thou dost ill to say the gallows is built stronger than the church: argal, the gallows may do well to thee. To't again, come.

2 *CLO.* Who builds stronger than a mason, a shipwright, or a carpenter?

1 *CLO.* Ay, tell me that, and unyoke.

2 *CLO.* Marry, now I can tell.

1 *CLO.* To't.

2 *CLO.* Mass, I cannot tell.

Enter HAMLET *and* HORATIO, *at a distance.*

1 *CLO.* Cudgel thy brains no more about it, for your dull ass wit will not mend his pace with beating; and, when you are asked this question next, say a gravemaker: the houses that he makes, last till doomsday. Go, get thee to Yaughan; fetch me a stoop of liquor. [*Exit* 2 *Clown.*

[*Digging and singing.*]

> In youth, when I did love, did love,
>   Methought it was very sweet,
> To contract, O, the time, for, ah, my behove,
>   O, methought, there was nothing meet.

HAM. Has this fellow no feeling of his business, that he sings at grave-making.

HOR. Custom hath made it in him a property of easiness.

HAM. 'Tis e'en so: the hand of little employment hath the daintier sense.

1 *CLO.* [*Singing.*]

> But age, with his stealing steps,
>   Hath claw'd me in his clutch,
> And hath shipped me intill the land,
>   As if I had never been such.

[*Throws up a scull.*

HAM. That scull had a tongue in it, and could sing once: how the knave jowls it to the ground, as if it were Cain's jawbone, that did the first murder! This might be the pate of a politician, which this ass now o'er-reaches; one that would circumvent God, might it not?

HOR. It might, my lord.

HAM. Or of a courtier; which could say, "Good-morrow, sweet lord! How dost thou, good lord?" This might be my lord such-a-one, that praised my lord such-a-one's horse, when he meant to beg it,—might it not?

HOR. Ay, my lord.

HAM. Why, e'en so; and now my lady Worm's; chapless, and knocked about the mazard with a sexton's spade: here's fine revolution, an we had the trick to see't. Did these bones cost no more the breeding, but to play at loggats with them? mine ache to think on't.

1 *CLO.* [*Singing.*]

> A pick-axe, and a spade, a spade,
>   For and a shrouding sheet:
> O, a pit of clay for to be made
>   For such a guest is meet.

[*Throws up another scull.*

HAM. There's another: why may not that be the scull of a lawyer? Where be his quiddits now, his quillets, his cases, his tenures, and his tricks? why does he suffer this rude knave now to knock him about the sconce with a dirty shovel, and will not tell him of his action of battery? Hm! This fellow might be in's time a great buyer of land, with his statutes, his recognizances, his fines, his double vouchers, his recoveries: is this the fine of his fines, and the recovery of his recoveries, to have his fine pate full of fine dirt? will his vouchers vouch him no more of his purchases, and double ones too, than the length and breadth of a pair of indentures? The very conveyances of his lands will hardly lie in this box; and must the inheritor himself have no more, ha?

HOR. Not a jot more, my lord.   [skins?

HAM. Is not parchment made of sheep-

HOR. Ay, my lord, and of calf-skins too.

HAM. They are sheep, and calves, which seek out assurance in that. I will speak to this fellow.—Whose grave's this, Sir?

1 *CLO.* Mine, Sir.—[*Singing.*]

    O, a pit of clay for to be made
      For such a guest is meet.

HAM. I think it be thine, indeed; for thou liest in't.

1 *CLO.* You lie out on't, Sir, and therefore it is not yours: for my part, I do not lie in't, and yet it is mine.

HAM. Thou dost lie in't, to be in't, and say it is thine: 'tis for the dead, not for the quick; therefore thou liest.

1 *CLO.* 'Tis a quick lie, Sir; 'twill away again, from me to you.

HAM. What man dost thou dig it for?

1 *CLO.* For no man, Sir.

HAM. What woman, then?

1 *CLO.* For none, neither.

HAM. Who is to be buried in't?

1 *CLO.* One that was a woman, Sir; but, rest her soul, she's dead.

HAM. How absolute the knave is! we must speak by the card, or equivocation will undo us. By the lord, Horatio, these three years I have taken note of it; the age is grown so picked, that the toe of the peasant comes so near the heel of the courtier, he galls his kibe.—How long hast thou been a grave-maker?

1 *CLO.* Of all the days i' the year, I came to't that day that our last king Hamlet overcame Fortinbras.

HAM. How long is that since?

1 *CLO.* Cannot you tell that? every fool can tell that: it was the very day that young Hamlet was born,—he that is mad, and sent into England.

HAM. Ay, marry, why was he sent into England?

1 *CLO.* Why, because he was mad: he shall recover his wits there; or, if he do not, 'tis no great matter there.

HAM. Why?

1 *CLO.* 'Twill not be seen in him there; there the men are as mad as he.

HAM. How came he mad?

1 *CLO.* Very strangely, they say.

HAM. How strangely?

1 *CLO.* 'Faith, e'en with losing his wits.

HAM. Upon what ground?

1 *CLO.* Why, here in Denmark: I have been sexton here, man and boy, thirty years.

HAM. How long will a man lie i' the earth ere he rot?

1 *CLO.* 'Faith, if he be not rotten before he die, (as we have many pocky corses now-a-days, that will scarce hold the laying in) he will last you some eight year, or nine year: a tanner will last you nine year.

HAM. Why he more than another?

1 *CLO.* Why, Sir, his hide is so tanned with his trade, that he will keep out water a great while; and your water is a sore decayer of your whoreson dead body. Here's a scull now; this scull hath lain you i' the earth three and twenty years.

HAM. Whose was it?

1 *CLO.* A whoreson mad fellow's it was: whose do you think it was?

HAM. Nay, I know not.

1 *CLO.* A pestilence on him for a mad rogue! 'a poured a flagon of Rhenish on my head once. This same scull, Sir, was Yorick's scull, the king's jester.

HAM. This?

1 *CLO.* E'en that.

HAM. Let me see.—[*Takes the scull.*] Alas, poor Yorick!—I knew him, Horatio: a fellow of infinite jest, of most excellent fancy: he hath borne me on his back a thousand times; and now, how abhorred in my imagination it is! my gorge rises at it. Here hung those lips, that I have kissed I know not how oft. Where be your gibes now? your gambols? your songs? your flashes of merriment, that were wont to set the table on a roar? Not one now, to mock your own grinning? quite chapfallen? Now get you to my lady's chamber, and tell her, let her paint an inch thick, to this favour she must come; make her laugh at that.—Pr'ythee, Horatio, tell me one thing.

HOR. What's that, my lord?

HAM. Dost thou think, Alexander looked o' this fashion i' the earth?

HOR. E'en so.

HAM. And smelt so? pah!

     [*Puts down the scull.*

HOR. E'en so, my lord.

HAM. To what base uses we may return, Horatio! Why may not imagination trace the noble dust of Alexander, till he find it stopping a bung-hole?

HOR. 'Twere to consider too curiously, to consider so.

HAM. No, faith, not a jot; but to follow him thither with modesty enough, and likelihood to lead it: as thus; Alexander died, Alexander was buried, Alexander returneth into dust; the dust is earth; of earth we make loam; and why of that loam, whereto he was converted, might they not stop a beer-barrel?

  Imperial Cæsar, dead and turn'd to clay,
  Might stop a hole to keep the wind away:
  O, that that earth, which kept the world in awe,
  Should patch a wall t' expel the winter's flaw!—

But soft! but soft! aside:—here comes the king,

Enter Priests, &c. *in procession: the corse of* OPHELIA, LAERTES, *and mourners following;* KING, QUEEN, *their trains,* &c.

The queen, the courtiers: who is that they follow?
And with such maimed rites? This doth betoken,
The corse they follow did with desperate hand
Fordo its own life: 'twas of some estate.
Couch we awhile, and mark.

    [*Retiring with* HORATIO.

LAER. What ceremony else?

HAM.   That is Laertes,
A very noble youth: mark.

LAER. What ceremony else?

1 PRIEST. Her obsequies have been as far enlarg'd
As we have warranty: her death was doubtful;
And, but that great command o'ersways the order,
She should in ground unsanctified have lodg'd,
Till the last trumpet; for charitable prayers,
Shards, flints, and pebbles, should be thrown on her:
Yet here she is allow'd her virgin crants,
Her maiden strewments, and the bringing home
Of bell and burial.

LAER. Must there no more be done?

1 PRIEST.   No more be done!
We should profane the service of the dead,
To sing a *requiem*, and such rest to her
As to peace-parted souls.

LAER.   Lay her i' the earth;
And from her fair and unpolluted flesh,
May violets spring!—I tell thee, churlish priest,
A ministering angel shall my sister be,
When thou liest howling.

HAM.   What, the fair Ophelia!

QUEEN. Sweets to the sweet: farewell!

    [*Scattering flowers.*

I hop'd thou should'st have been my Hamlet's wife;
I thought thy bride-bed to have deck'd, sweet maid,
And not have strew'd thy grave.

LAER.   O, treble woe
Fall ten times treble on that cursed head,
Whose wicked deed thy most ingenious sense
Depriv'd thee of!—Hold off the earth awhile,
Till I have caught her once more in mine arms.   [*Leaping into the grave.*
Now pile your dust upon the quick and dead,
Till of this flat a mountain you have made,
To o'er-top old Pelion, or the skyish head
Of blue Olympus.

HAM. [*Advancing.*] What is he, whose grief
Bears such an emphasis? whose phrase of sorrow
Conjures the wandering stars, and makes them stand,
Like wonder-wounded hearers? this is I,
Hamlet the Dane. [*Leaping into the grave.*

LAER.   The devil take thy soul!

    [*Grappling with him.*

HAM. Thou pray'st not well.
I pr'ythee, take thy fingers from my throat;
For though I am not splenetive and rash,
Yet have I in me something dangerous,
Which let thy wisdom fear: hold off thy hand.

KING. Pluck them asunder.

QUEEN.   Hamlet, Hamlet!

ALL. Gentlemen,—

HOR.   Good my lord, be quiet.

[*The* Attendants *part them, and they come out of the grave.*

HAM. Why, I will fight with him upon this theme,
Until my eyelids will no longer wag.

QUEEN. O my son, what theme?

HAM. I lov'd Ophelia: forty thousand brothers
Could not, with all their quantity of love,
Make up my sum.—What wilt thou do for her?

KING. O, he is mad, Laertes.

QUEEN. For love of God, forbear him.

HAM. 'Swounds, show me what thou'lt
   do:
Woo't weep? woo't fight? woo't fast? woo't
   tear thyself?
Woo't drink up Esil? eat a crocodile?
I'll do't.—Dost thou come here to whine?
To outface me with leaping in her grave?
Be buried quick with her, and so will I:
And, if thou prate of mountains, let them
   throw
Millions of acres on us; till our ground,
Singeing his pate against the burning zone,
Make Ossa like a wart! Nay, an thou'lt
I'll rant as well as thou.   [mouth,
QUEEN.   This is mere madness:
And thus awhile the fit will work on him;
Anon, as patient as the female dove,
When that her golden couplets are dis-
His silence will sit drooping.   [clos'd,
HAM.   Hear you, Sir;
What is the reason that you use me thus?
I lov'd you ever: but it is no matter;
Let Hercules himself do what he may,
The cat will mew, and dog will have his
   day.   [*Exit.*
KING. I pray you, good Horatio, wait
   upon him.—   [*Exit* HORATIO.
[*To* LAERTES.] Strengthen your patience in
   our last night's speech;
We'll put the matter to the present push.—
Good Gertrude, set some watch over your
   son.—
This grave shall have a living monument:
An hour of quiet shortly shall we see;
Till then, in patience our proceeding be.
                                  [*Exeunt.*

SCENE II.—*A Hall in the Castle.*

Enter HAMLET *and* HORATIO.

HAM. So much for this, Sir: now shall
   you see the other:—
You do remember all the circumstance?
HOR. Remember it, my lord!
HAM. Sir, in my heart there was a kind
   of fighting,
That would not let me sleep: methought
   I lay
Worse than the mutines in the bilboes.
   Rashly,—
And prais'd be rashness for it,—let us
   know,
Our indiscretion sometimes serves us well,
When our deep plots do pall: and that
   should teach us,
There's a divinity that shapes our ends,
Rough-hew them how we will.
HOR.   That is most certain.
HAM. Up from my cabin.
My sea-gown scarf'd about me, in the dark
Grop'd I to find out them: had my desire;

Finger'd their packet; and, in fine, with-
   drew
To mine own room again: making so bold,
My fears forgetting manners, to unseal
Their grand commission; where I found,
   Horatio,
O royal knavery! an exact command,—
Larded with many several sorts of reasons,
Importing Denmark's health, and England's
   too,
With, ho! such bugs and goblins in my
   life,—
That, on the supervise, no leisure bated,
No, not to stay the grinding of the axe,
My head should be struck off.
HOR.   Is't possible?
HAM. Here's the commission: read it at
   more leisure.
But wilt thou hear me how I did proceed?
HOR. I beseech you.
HAM. Being thus benetted round with
   villanies,—
Ere I could make a prologue to my brains,
They had begun the play,—I sat me down;
Devis'd a new commission; wrote it fair:—
I once did hold it, as our statists do,
A baseness to write fair, and labour'd
   much
How to forget that learning; but Sir, now
It did me yeoman's service:—wilt thou
The effect of what I wrote?   [know
HOR.   Ay, good my lord.
HAM. An earnest conjuration from the
   king,—
As England was his faithful tributary;
As love between them like the palm might
   flourish;
As peace should still her wheaten garland
   wear,
And stand a comma 'tween their amities;
And many such like as's of great charge,—
That, on the view and know of these
   contents,
Without debatement farther, more or less,
He should the bearers put to sudden death,
Not shriving-time allow'd.
HOR.   How was this seal'd?
HAM. Why, even in that was heaven
   ordinant.
I had my father's signet in my purse,
Which was the model of that Danish seal;
Folded the writ up in form of the other;
Subscrib'd it; gave't th' impression; plac'd
   it safely,
The changeling never known. Now, the
   next day
Was our sea-fight; and what to this was
Thou know'st already.   [sequent
HOR. So Guildenstern and Rosencrantz go
   to't.

HAM. Why, man, they did make love to
this employment;
They are not near my conscience; their
defeat
Does by their own insinuation grow:
'Tis dangerous, when the baser nature
comes
Between the pass and fell incensed points
Of mighty opposites.
HOR.   Why, what a king is this!
HAM. Does it not, think thee, stand me
now upon—
He that hath kill'd my king, and whor'd
my mother;
Popp'd in between th' election and my
hopes;
Thrown out his angle for my proper life,
And with such cozenage—is't not perfect
conscience,
To quit him with this arm? and is't not to
be damn'd,
To let this canker of our nature come
In farther evil?
HOR. It must be shortly known to him
from England,
What is the issue of the business there.
HAM. It will be short: the interim is
mine;
And a man's life's no more than to say, one.
But I am very sorry, good Horatio,
That to Laertes I forgot myself;
For, by the image of my cause, I see
The portraiture of his: I'll count his
favours:
But, sure, the bravery of his grief did put
Into a towering passion.   [me
HOR.   Peace? who comes here?
          Enter OSRICK.
OSR. Your lordship is right welcome back
to Denmark.
HAM. I humbly thank you, Sir.—*Aside to*
HOR.] Dost know this water-fly?
HOR. [*Aside to* HAM.] No, my good lord.
HAM. [*Aside to* HOR.] Thy state is the
more gracious; for 'tis a vice to know him.
He hath much land, and fertile: let a beast
be lord of beasts, and his crib shall stand
at the king's mess: 'tis a chough; but, as I
say, spacious in the possession of dirt.
OSR. Sweet lord, if your lordship were at
leisure, I should impart a thing to you from
his majesty.
HAM. I will receive it, Sir, with all diligence of spirit. Your bonnet to his right
use; 'tis for the head.
OSR. I thank your lordship, 'tis very hot.
HAM. No, believe me, 'tis very cold; the
wind is northerly.
OSR. It is indifferent cold, my lord, indeed.

HAM. But yet, methinks, it is very sultry,
and hot; or my complexion—
OSR. Exceedingly, my lord; it is very
sultry,—as 'twere,—I cannot tell how.—But,
my lord, his majesty bade me signify to
you, that he has laid a great wager on your
head: Sir, this is the matter,—
HAM. I beseech you, remember—
          [HAMLET *moves him to put on his hat.*
OSR. Nay, in good faith; for mine ease,
in good faith. Sir, here is newly come to
court, Laertes; believe me, an absolute
gentleman, full of most excellent differences, of very soft society, and great showing: indeed, to speak feelingly of him, he
is the card or calendar of gentry; for you
shall find in him the continent of what part
a gentleman would see.
HAM. Sir, his definement suffers no perdition in you:—though, I know, to divide
him inventorially, would dizzy the arithmetic of memory; and yet but raw neither,
in respect of his quick sail. But, in the
verity of extolment, I take him to be a
soul of great article; and his infusion of
such dearth and rareness, as, to make true
diction of him, his semblable is his mirror;
and who else would trace him, his umbrage,
nothing more.
OSR. Your lordship speaks most infallibly
of him.
HAM. The concernancy, Sir? why do we
wrap the gentleman in our more rawer
breath?
OSR. Sir?
HOR. Is't not possible to understand in
another tongue? You will do't, Sir, really.
HAM. What imports the nomination of
this gentleman?
OSR. Of Laertes?
HOR. [*Aside to* HAM.] His purse is empty
already; all his golden words are spent.
HAM. Of him, Sir.
OSR. I know you are not ignorant—
HAM. I would you did, Sir; yet, in faith,
if you did, it would not much approve me:
—well, Sir.
OSR. You are not ignorant of what excel-
lence Laertes is—
HAM. I dare not confess that, lest I should
compare with him in excellence; but, to
know a man well, were to know himself.
OSR. I mean, Sir, for his weapon; but in
the imputation laid on him by them, in his
meed he's unfellowed.
HAM. What's his weapon?
OSR. Rapier and dagger.
HAM. That's two of his weapons: but,
well.

OSR. The king, Sir, hath wagered with him six Barbary horses: against the which he has imponed, as I take it, six French rapiers and poniards, with their assigns, as girdle, hangers, and so: three of the carriages, in faith, are very dear to fancy, very responsive to the hilts, most delicate carriages, and of very liberal conceit.

HAM. What call you the carriages?

HOR. [*Aside to* HAM.] I knew you must be edified by the margent, ere you had done.

OSR. The carriages, Sir, are the hangers.

HAM. The phrase would be more german to the matter, if we could carry cannon by our sides: I would it might be hangers till then. But, on: six Barbary horses against six French swords, their assigns, and three liberal-conceited carriages; that's the French bet against the Danish. Why is this imponed, as you call it?

OSR. The king, Sir, hath laid, that in a dozen passes between yourself and him, he shall not exceed you three hits: he hath laid, on twelve for nine; and it would come to immediate trial, if your lordship would vouchsafe the answer.

HAM. How, if I answer, no?

OSR. I mean, my lord, the opposition of your person in trial.

HAM. Sir, I will walk here in the hall: if it please his majesty, it is the breathing time of day with me; let the foils be brought, the gentleman willing, and the king hold his purpose, I will win for him, if I can; if not, I will gain nothing but my shame, and the odd hits.

OSR. Shall I deliver you so?

HAM. To this effect, Sir; after what flourish your nature will.

OSR. I commend my duty to your lordship.

HAM. Yours, yours.—[*Exit* OSRICK.] He does well to commend himself; there are no tongues else for's turn.

HOR. This lapwing runs away with the shell on his head.

HAM. He did comply with his dug, before he sucked it. Thus has he (and many more of the same breed, that, I know, the drossy age dotes on) only got the tune of the time, and outward habit of encounter; a kind of yesty collection, which carries them through and through the most fond and winnowed opinions; and do but blow them to their trial, the bubbles are out.

Enter a Lord.

LORD. My lord, his majesty commended him to you by young Osrick, who brings back to him, that you attend him in the hall: he sends to know, if your pleasure hold to play with Laertes, or that you will take longer time.

HAM. I am constant to my purposes; they follow the king's pleasure: if his fitness speaks, mine is ready; now, or whensoever, provided, I be so able as now.

LORD. The king, and queen, and all are coming down.

HAM. In happy time.

LORD. The queen desires you to use some gentle entertainment to Laertes, before you fall to play.

HAM. She well instructs me. [*Exit* Lord.

HOR. You will lose this wager, my lord.

HAM. I do not think so; since he went into France, I have been in continual practice; I shall win at the odds. But thou would'st not think, how ill all's here about my heart: but it is no matter.

HOR. Nay, good my lord,—

HAM. It is but foolery; but it is such a kind of gain-giving, as would perhaps trouble a woman.

HOR. If your mind dislike any thing, obey it: I will forestal their repair hither, and say you are not fit.

HAM. Not a whit, we defy augury: there is a special providence in the fall of a sparrow. If it be now, 'tis not to come; if it be not to come, it will be now; if it be not now, yet it will come: the readiness is all: since no man, of aught he leaves, knows, what is't to leave betimes? Let be.

Enter KING, QUEEN, LAERTES, Lords, OSRICK, *and* Attendants *with foils, &c.*

KING. Come, Hamlet, come, and take this hand from me.

[*The* KING *puts the hand of* LAERTES *into that of* HAMLET.

HAM. Give me your pardon, Sir: I've done you wrong;
But pardon't, as you are a gentleman.
This presence knows,
And you must needs have heard, how I am punish'd
With sore distraction. What I have done,
That might your nature, honour, and exception,
Roughly awake, I here proclaim was madness.
Was't Hamlet wrong'd Laertes? Never Hamlet:
If Hamlet from himself be ta'en away,
And, when he's not himself, does wrong Laertes,
Then Hamlet does it not; Hamlet denies it.
Who does it, then? His madness: if't be so,
Hamlet is of the faction that is wrong'd;
His madness is poor Hamlet's enemy.

Sir, in this audience,
Let my disclaiming from a purpos'd evil
Free me so far in your most generous
thoughts,
That I have shot mine arrow o'er the
And hurt my brother.   [house,
LAER.   I am satisfied in nature,
Whose motive, in this case, should stir me
most
To my revenge: but in my terms of honour,
I stand aloof; and will no reconcilement,
Till by some elder masters, of known
honour,
I have a voice and precedent of peace,
To keep my name ungor'd. But till that
time,
I do receive your offer'd love like love,
And will not wrong it.
HAM.   I embrace it freely;
And will this brother's wager frankly
play.—
Give us the foils.—Come on.
LAER.   Come, one for me.
HAM. I'll be your foil, Laertes: in mine
ignorance
Your skill shall, like a star i' the darkest
Stick fiery off indeed.   [night,
LAER.   You mock me, Sir.
HAM. No, by this hand.
KING. Give them the foils, young Osrick.
—Cousin Hamlet,
You know the wager?
HAM.   Very well, my lord;
Your grace hath laid the odds o' the
weaker side.
KING. I do not fear it; I have seen you
both:
But since he is better'd, we have therefore
odds.
LAER. This is too heavy, let me see an-
other.
HAM. This likes me well. These foils
have all a length? [*They prepare to play.*
OSR. Ay, my good lord.
KING. Set me the stoops of wine upon
that table.—
If Hamlet give the first or second hit,
Or quit in answer of the third exchange,
Let all the battlements their ordnance fire;
The king shall drink to Hamlet's better
breath;
And in the cup a union shall he throw,
Richer than that which four successive
kings
In Denmark's crown have worn. Give me
the cups;
And let the kettle to the trumpet speak,
The trumpet to the cannoneer without,
The cannons to the heavens, the heavens
to earth,

"Now the king drinks to Hamlet!"—Come,
begin;—
And you, the judges, bear a wary eye.
HAM. Come on, Sir.
LAER. Come, my lord.   [*They play.*
HAM.   One.
LEAR.   No.
HAM.   Judgment.
OSR. A hit, a very palpable hit.
LAER.   Well;—again.
KING. Stay; give me drink.—Hamlet, this
pearl is thine;
Here's to thy health.—
[*Drinks from one of the cups. Trumpets
sound; and cannon shot off within.*
              Give him the cup.
HAM. I'll play this bout first; set it by
awhile.
Come.—Another hit; what say you?
                 [*They play.*
LAER. A touch, a touch, I do confess.
KING. Our son shall win.
QUEEN. He's fat, and scant of breath.—
Here, Hamlet, take my napkin, rub thy
brows:
The queen carouses to thy fortune, Hamlet.
             [*Takes the other cup.*
HAM. Good Madam!
KING.   Gertrude, do not drink.
QUEEN. I will, my lord; I pray you, par-
don me.   [*Drinks.*
KING. [*Aside.*] It is the poison'd cup;
it is too late.
      [QUEEN *offers the cup to* HAMLET.
HAM. I dare not drink yet, Madam; by
and by.
QUEEN. Come, let me wipe thy face.
LAER. My lord, I'll hit him now.
KING.   I do not think it.
LAER. [*Aside.*] And yet 'tis almost 'gainst
my conscience.
HAM. Come, for the third, Laertes: you
but dally;
I pray you, pass with your best violence;
I am afeard you make a wanton of me.
LAER. Say you so? come on. [*They play.*
OSR. Nothing, neither way.
LAER. Have at you now!
[LAERTES *wounds* HAMLET; *then in scuf-
fling they change rapiers, and* HAMLET
wounds LAERTES.
KING.   Part them; they are incens'd.
HAM. Nay, come, again.
              [*The* QUEEN *falls.*
OSR. Look to the queen there, ho!
HOR. They bleed on both sides.—How is
it, my lord?
OSR. How is it, Laertes?
LAER. Why, as a woodcock to mine own
springe, Osrick;
I am justly kill'd with mine own treachery.

HAM. How does the queen?
KING.   She swoons to see them bleed.
QUEEN. No, no, the drink, the drink,—O
my dear Hamlet!—
The drink, the drink;—I am poison'd.
                              [*Dies.*
HAM. O villany!—Ho! let the door be
Treachery! seek it out.   [lock'd:
                              [LAERTES *falls.*
LAER. It is here, Hamlet: Hamlet, thou
art slain;
No medicine in the world can do thee
good;
In thee there is not half an hour of life;
The treacherous instrument is in thy hand,
Unbated, and envenom'd: the foul practice
Hath turn'd itself on me; lo, here I lie,
Never to rise again: thy mother's
poison'd:—
I can no more:—the king, the king's to
blame.
HAM. The point
Envenom'd too!—Then, venom, to thy work.
                              [*Stabs the* KING.
ALL. Treason! treason!
KING. O, yet defend me, friends; I am
but hurt.
HAM. Here, thou incestuous, murderous,
damned Dane,
Drink off this potion:—is thy union here?
Follow my mother.   [KING *dies.*
LAER.   He is justly serv'd;
It is a poison temper'd by himself.—
Exchange forgiveness with me, noble
Hamlet: [thee;
Mine and my father's death come not upon
Nor thine on me!   [*Dies.*
HAM. Heaven make thee free of it! I
follow thee.—
I am dead, Horatio.—Wretched queen,
adieu!—
You that look pale and tremble at this
chance,
That are but mutes or audience to this act,
Had I but time, (as this fell sergeant,
Death,
Is strict in his arrest) O, I could tell you,—
But let it be.—Horatio, I am dead;
Thou liv'st; report me and my cause aright
To the unsatisfied.
HOR.   Never believe it:
I am more an antique Roman than a Dane:
Here's yet some liquor left.
HAM.   As thou'rt a man,
Give me the cup: let go; by heaven, I'll
have it.—
O God!—Horatio, what a wounded name,
Things standing thus unknown, shall live
behind me!
If thou didst ever hold me in thy heart,
Absent thee from felicity awhile,

And in this harsh world draw thy breath
To tell my story.—   [in pain,
          [*March afar off, and shot within.*
          What warlike noise is this?
OSR. Young Fortinbras, with conquest
come from Poland,
To the embassadors of England gives
This warlike volley.
HAM. [*Falls.*]   O, I die, Horatio;
The potent poison quite o'er-crows my
spirit:
I cannot live to hear the news from
England;
But I do prophesy the election 'lights
On Fortinbras: he has my dying voice;
So tell him, with the occurrents, more and
less,
Which have solicited.—The rest is silence.
                              [*Dies.*
HOR. Now cracks a noble heart:—good
night, sweet prince;
And flights of angels sing thee to thy
rest!—   [*March within.*
Why does the drum come hither?
Enter FORTINBRAS, *the English* Embas-
          sadors, *and others.*
FORT. Where is this sight?
HOR.   What is it ye would see?
If aught of woe or wonder, cease your
search.
FORT. This quarry cries on havock.—O
proud death,
What feast is toward in thine eternal cell,
That thou so many princes at a shot
So bloodily hast struck?
1 *EMB.*   The sight is dismal;
And our affairs from England come too
late:
The ears are senseless that should give us
hearing,
To tell him his commandment is fulfill'd,
That Rosencrantz and Guildenstern are
dead:
Where should we have our thanks?
HOR.   Not from his mouth,
Had it th' ability of life to thank you:
He never gave commandment for their
death.
But since, so jump upon this bloody
question,
You from the Polack wars, and you from
England,
Are here arriv'd, give order that these
bodies
High on a stage be placed to the view;
And let me speak to the yet unknowing
world,
How these things came about: so shall you
hear
Of carnal, bloody, and unnatural acts;

Of accidental judgments, casual slaughters;
Of deaths put on by cunning, and forc'd
    cause;
And, in this upshot, purposes mistook
Fall'n on the inventors' heads; all this
Truly deliver.   [can I
FORT.   Let us haste to hear it,
And call the noblest to the audience.
For me, with sorrow I embrace my fortune:
I have some rights of memory in this king-
    dom;
Which, now to claim, my vantage doth
    invite me.
HOR. Of that I shall have also cause to
    speak,
And from his mouth whose voice will draw
    on more:

But let this same be presently perform'd,
Even while men's minds are wild; lest more
    mischance,
On plots and errors, happen.
FORT.   Let four captains
Bear Hamlet, like a soldier, to the stage;
For he was likely, had he been put on,
To have prov'd most royally: and, for his
    passage,
The soldiers' music, and the rites of war,
Speak loudly for him.—
Take up the bodies:—such a sight as this
Becomes the field, but here shows much
Go, bid the soldiers shoot.   [amiss.—
[A dead march. Exeunt, bearing away the
    dead bodies; after which, a peal of
    ordnance is shot off.

Lear cursing his daughters.

KING LEAR

DRAMATIS PERSONÆ.

LEAR, *King of Britain.*
KING OF FRANCE.
DUKE OF BURGUNDY.
DUKE OF CORNWALL.
DUKE OF ALBANY.
EARL OF KENT.
EARL OF GLOSTER.
EDGAR, *Son to* GLOSTER.
EDMUND, *Bastard Son to* GLOSTER.
CURAN, *a Courtier.*
OSWALD, *Steward to* GONERIL.
Old Man, *Tenant to* GLOSTER.

Physician.
Fool.
Captain, *employed by* EDMUND.
Gentleman, *Emissary to* CORDELIA.
A Herald.
Servants *to* CORNWALL.
GONERIL,
REGAN, } *Daughters to* LEAR.
CORDELIA,
Knights of LEAR'S train, Officers, Messengers, Soldiers, *and* Attendants.

SCENE,—BRITAIN.

ACT I.

SCENE I.—*A Room of State in* KING LEAR'S *Palace.*

Enter KENT, GLOSTER, *and* EDMUND.

KENT. I thought the king had more affected the duke of Albany, than Cornwall.

GLO. It did always seem so to us: but now, in the division of the kingdom, it appears not which of the dukes he values most; for equalities are so weighed, that curiosity in neither can make choice of either's moiety.

KENT. Is not this your son, my lord?

GLO. His breeding, Sir, hath been at my charge: I have so often blushed to acknowledge him, that now I am brazed to it.

KENT. I cannot conceive you.

GLO. Sir, this young fellow's mother could; whereupon she grew round-wombed, and had, indeed, Sir, a son for her cradle

481

ere she had a husband for her bed. Do
you smell a fault?

KENT. I cannot wish the fault undone,
the issue of it being so proper.

GLO. But I have a son, Sir, by order of
law, some year elder than this, who yet is,
no dearer in my account: though this knave
came somewhat saucily into the world,
before he was sent for, yet was his mother
fair; there was good sport at his making,
and the whoreson must be acknowledged.
—Do you know this noble gentleman,
Edmund?

EDM. No, my lord.

GLO. My lord of Kent: remember him
hereafter as my honourable friend.

EDM. My services to your lordship.

KENT. I must love you, and sue to know
you better.

EDM. Sir, I shall study deserving.

GLO. He hath been out nine years, and
away he shall again.—The king is coming.
                              [*Sennet within*.

Enter LEAR, CORNWALL, ALBANY, GONERIL,
    REGAN, CORDELIA *and* Attendants.

LEAR. Attend the lords of France and
Burgundy, Gloster.

GLO. I shall, my liege.
            [*Exeunt* GLOSTER *and* EDMUND.

LEAR. Meantime we shall express our
darker purpose.
Give me the map there.—Know, that we
have divided   [intent
In three, our kingdom: and 'tis our fast
To shake all cares and business from our
age;
Conferring them on younger strengths,
while we
Unburden'd crawl toward death.—Our son
of Cornwall,
And you, our no less loving son of Albany,
We have this hour a constant will to pub-
lish   [strife
Our daughters' several dowers, that future
May be prevented now. The princes,
France and Burgundy,
Great rivals in our youngest daughter's
love,   [sojourn,
Long in our court have made their amorous
And here are to be answer'd.—Tell me,
my daughters,
(Since now we will divest us, both of rule,
Interest of territory, cares of state)
Which of you, shall we say, doth love us
most?
That we our largest bounty may extend
Where nature doth with merit challenge.—
Our eldest-born, speak first.   [Goneril,

GON. Sir, I love you more than words
can wield the matter;

Dearer than eye-sight, space, and liberty;
Beyond what can be valued, rich or rare;
No less than life, with grace, health,
beauty, honour:
As much as child e'er lov'd or father
found;   [unable;
A love that makes breath poor, and speech
Beyond all manner of so much I love you.

COR. [*Aside*.] What shall Cordelia do?
Love, and be silent.

LEAR. Of all these bounds, even from
this line to this,
With shadowy forests, and with champains
rich'd,
With plenteous rivers and wide-skirted
meads,
We make thee lady: to thine and Albany's
issue   [daughter,
Be this perpetual.—What says our second
Our dearest Regan, wife to Cornwall?
Speak.

REG. I am made of that self metal as
my sister,   [heart
And prize me at her worth. In my true
I find she names my very deed of love;
Only she comes too short,—that I profess
Myself an enemy to all other joys,
Which the most precious square of sense
possesses;
And find I am alone felicitate
In your dear highness' love.

COR. [*Aside*.]   Then, poor Cordelia!
And yet not so; since, I am sure, my
More richer than my tongue.   [love's

LEAR. To thee and thine, hereditary ever,
Remain this ample third of our fair king-
dom;
No less in space, validity, and pleasure,
Than that conferr'd on Goneril.—Now, our
joy,   [young love
Although our last, not least; to whose
The vines of France, and milk of Bur-
gundy,   [to draw
Strive to be interess'd; what can you say,
A third more opulent than your sisters?
Speak.

COR. Nothing, my lord.

LEAR. Nothing!

COR. Nothing.

LEAR. Nothing will come of nothing:
speak again.

COR. Unhappy that I am, I cannot heave
My heart into my mouth: I love your
majesty
According to my bond; nor more, nor less.

LEAR. How, how, Cordelia! mend your
speech a little,
Lest you may mar your fortunes.

COR.   Good my lord,
You have begot me, bred me, lov'd me: I

Return those duties back as are right fit,
Obey you, love you, and most honour you.
Why have my sisters husbands, if they say
They love you all? Haply, when I shall
    wed,
That lord, whose hand must take my
    plight, shall carry
Half my love with him, half my care, and
    duty:
Sure, I shall never marry like my sisters,
To love my father all.
LEAR. But goes thy heart with this?
COR.   Ay, good my lord.
LEAR. So young, and so untender?
COR. So young, my lord, and true.
LEAR. Let it be so,—thy truth, then, be
    thy dower:
For, by the sacred radiance of the sun,
The mysteries of Hecate, and the night;
By all the operation of the orbs
From whom we do exist, and cease to be;
Here I disclaim all my paternal care,
Propinquity and property of blood,
And, as a stranger to my heart and me,
Hold thee, from this, for ever. The bar-
    barous Scythian,
Or he that makes his generation messes
To gorge his appetite, shall to my bosom
Be as well neighbour'd, pitied, and re-
    liev'd,
As thou my sometime daughter.
KENT.   Good my liege,—
LEAR. Peace, Kent!
Come not between the dragon and his
    wrath.   [rest
I lov'd her most, and thought to set my
On her kind nursery. Hence, and avoid
    my sight!
So be my grave my peace, as here I give
Her father's heart from her!—Call France;
    —who stirs?
Call Burgundy.—Cornwall, and Albany,
With my two daughters' dowers digest the
    third: [her.
Let pride, which she calls plainness, marry
I do invest you jointly with my power,
Pre-eminence, and all the large effects
That troop with majesty. Ourself, by
    monthly course,
With reservation of a hundred knights,
By you to be sustain'd, shall our abode
Make with you by due terms. Only, we
    still retain
The name, and all th' additions to a king;
The sway,
Revenue, execution of the rest,
Beloved sons, be yours: which to confirm,
This coronet part between you.
                        [*Giving the crown.*
KENT.   Royal Lear,

Whom I have ever honour'd as my king,
Lov'd as my father, as my master follow'd,
As my great patron thought on in my
    prayers,—
LEAR. The bow is bent and drawn, make
    from the shaft.
KENT. Let it fall rather, though the fork
    invade   [nerly,
The region of my heart: be Kent unman-
When Lear is mad. What would'st thou
    do, old man?
Think'st thou that duty shall have dread
    to speak,
When power to flattery bows? To plain-
    ness honour's bound,   [doom;
When majesty stoops to folly. Reverse thy
And, in thy best consideration, check
This hideous rashness: answer my life my
    judgment,   [least;
Thy youngest daughter does not love thee
Nor are those empty-hearted, whose low
Reverbs no hollowness.   [sound
LEAR.   Kent, on thy life, no more.
KENT. My life I never held but as a
    pawn   [to lose it,
To wage against thine enemies; nor fear
Thy safety being the motive.
LEAR.   Out of my sight!
KENT. See better, Lear; and let me still
The true blank of thine eye.   [remain
LEAR. Now, by Apollo,—
KENT.   Now, by Apollo, king,
Thou swear'st thy gods in vain.
LEAR. [*Grasping his sword.*] O, vassal!
    miscreant!
ALB. CORN. Dear Sir, forbear.
KENT. Do;
Kill thy physician, and the fee bestow
Upon the foul disease. Revoke thy gift;
Or, whilst I can vent clamour from my
I'll tell thee thou dost evil.   [throat,
LEAR.   Hear me, recreant!
On thine allegiance, hear me!
Since thou hast sought to make us break
    our vow   [strain'd pride,
(Which we durst never yet) and, with
To come betwixt our sentence and our
    power,   [bear)
(Which nor our nature nor our place can
Our potency made good, take thy reward.
Five days we do allot thee, for provision
To shield thee from diseases of the world;
And, on the sixth, to turn thy hated back
Upon our kingdom: if, on the tenth day
    following,
Thy banish'd trunk be found in our do-
    minions,
The moment is thy death. Away! By
    Jupiter,
This shall not be revok'd.

KENT. Fare thee well, king: since thus thou wilt appear,   [here.—
Freedom lives hence, and banishment is
[*To* COR.] The gods to their dear shelter take thee, maid,   [said!—
That justly think'st, and hast most rightly
To [GON. *and* REG.] And your large speeches may your deeds approve,
That good effects may spring from words of love.—
Thus Kent, O princes, bids you all adieu;
He'll shape his old course in a country new.   [*Exit.*
Flourish. Re-enter GLOSTER, *with* FRANCE, BURGUNDY, *and* Attendants.
GLO. Here's France and Burgundy, my noble lord.
LEAR. My lord of Burgundy,
We first address toward you, who with this king   [the least,
Hath rivall'd for our daughter: what, in Will you require in present dower with
Or cease your quest of love?   [her,
BUR.   Most royal majesty,
I crave no more than hath your highness Nor will you tender less.   [offer'd,
LEAR.   Right noble Burgundy,
When she was dear to us, we did hold her so;   [stands:
But now her price is fall'n. Sir, there she If aught within that little seeming substance,
Or all of it, with our displeasure piec'd,
And nothing more, may fitly like your grace,
She's there, and she is yours.
BUR.   I know no answer.
LEAR. Will you, with those infirmities she owes,
Unfriended, new-adopted to our hate,
Dower'd with our curse, and stranger'd with our oath,
Take her, or leave her?
BUR.   Pardon me, royal Sir;
Election makes not up on such conditions.
LEAR. Then leave her, Sir; for, by the power that made me,
I tell you all her wealth.—[*To* FRANCE.]
For you, great king,   [stray,
I would not from your love make such a
To match you where I hate; therefore, beseech you
T' avert your liking a more worthier way,
Then on a wretch whom nature is asham'd
Almost t' acknowledge hers.
FRANCE.   This is most strange,
That she, who even but now was your best object,
The argument of your praise, balm of your age,

The best, the dearest, should in this trice of time
Commit a thing so monstrous, to dismantle So many folds of favour. Sure, her offence
Must be of such unnatural degree,
That monsters it, or your fore-vouch'd affection
Fall into taint: which to believe of her,
Must be a faith that reason, without Could never plant in me.   [miracle,
COR.   I yet beseech your majesty,
(If for I want that glib and oily art,
To speak and purpose not; since what I well intend,   [known
I'll do't before I speak) that you make It is no vicious blot, murder, or foulness,
No unchaste action, or dishonour'd step,
That hath depriv'd me of your grace and favour;
But even for want of that for which I am richer,—
A still-soliciting eye, and such a tongue That I am glad I have not, though not to Hath lost me in your liking.   [have it,
LEAR.   Better thou
Hadst not been born, than not to have pleas'd me better.
FRANCE. Is it but this,—a tardiness in nature,
Which often leaves the history unspoke,
That it intends to do?—My lord of Burgundy,   [love,
What say you to the lady? Love is not When it is mingled with respects, that stand
Aloof from the entire point. Will you have She is herself a dowry.   [her?
BUR.   Royal Lear,
Give but that portion which yourself propos'd,
And here I take Cordelia by the hand,
Duchess of Burgundy.
LEAR. Nothing: I have sworn; I am firm.
BUR. I am sorry, then, you have so lost a father,
That you must lose a husband.
COR.   Peace be with Burgundy!
Since that respects of fortune are his love,
I shall not be his wife.
FRANCE. Fairest Cordelia, that art most rich, being poor;   [despis'd!
Most choice, forsaken; and most lov'd,
Thee and thy virtues here I seize upon:
Be it lawful, I take up what's cast away.
Gods, gods! 'tis strange, that from their cold'st neglect
My love should kindle to inflam'd respect.—   [my chance,
Thy dowerless daughter, king, thrown to

Is queen of us, of ours, and our fair
 France:
Not all the dukes of waterish Burgundy
Shall buy this unpriz'd precious maid of
 me.—
Bid them farewell, Cordelia, though un-
 kind:
Thou losest here, a better where to find.
LEAR. Thou hast her, France: let her be
 thine; for we
Have no such daughter, nor shall ever see
That face of hers again:—therefore, be
 gone
Without our grace, our love, our benison.—
Come, noble Burgundy.

  [*Flourish. Exeunt* LEAR, BURGUNDY,
   CORNWALL, ALBANY, GLOSTER, *and*
   Attendants.

FRANCE. Bid farewell to your sisters.
COR. Ye jewels of our father, with wash'd
 eyes   [are;
Cordelia leaves you: I know you what you
And, like a sister, am most loath to call
Your faults as they are nam'd. Love well
 our father:
To your professed bosoms I commit him:
But yet, alas, stood I within his grace,
I would prefer him to a better place.
So, farewell to you both.
GON. Prescribe not us our duty.
REG.   Let your study
Be to content your lord, who hath receiv'd
 you   [scanted,
At fortune's alms. You have obedience
And well are worth the want that you have
 wanted.
COR. Time shall unfold what plighted
 cunning hides:
Who cover faults, at last shame them de-
Well may you prosper!   [rides.
FRANCE.   Come, my fair Cordelia.

  [*Exeunt* FRANCE *and* CORDELIA.

GON. Sister, it is not little I have to say
of what most nearly appertains to us both.
I think our father will hence to-night.
REG. That's most certain, and with you;
next month with us.
GON. You see how full of changes his age
is; the observation we have made of it hath
not been little: he always loved our sister
most, and with what poor judgment he hath
now cast her off, appears too grossly. ·
REG. 'Tis the infirmity of his age: yet he
hath ever but slenderly known himself.
GON. The best and soundest of his time
hath been but rash; then, must we look to
receive from his age, not alone the imperfections of long-engrafted condition, but,
therewithal, the unruly waywardness that
infirm and choleric years bring with them.

REG. Such unconstant starts are we like
to have from him, as this of Kent's banishment.
GON. There is farther compliment of leave-
taking between France and him. Pray you,
let us hit together: if our father carry authority with such dispositions as he bears,
this last surrender of his will but offend us.
REG. We shall farther think of it.
GON. We must do something, and i' the
heat.   [*Exeunt.*

    ―――――

  SCENE II.—*A Hall in the* EARL OF
    GLOSTER'S *Castle.*

  Enter EDMUND, *with a letter.*

EDM. Thou, nature, art my goddess; to thy
 law
My services are bound. Wherefore should I
Stand in the plague of custom, and permit
The curiosity of nations to deprive me,
For that I am some twelve or fourteen moon-
 shines   [base?
Lag of a brother? Why bastard? wherefore
When my dimensions are as well compact,
My mind as generous, and my shape as true,
As honest madam's issue? Why brand they
 us   [base?
With base? with baseness? bastardy? base,
Who, in the lusty stealth of nature, take
More composition and fierce quality,
Than doth, within a dull, stale, tired bed,
Go to the creating a whole tribe of fops,
Got 'tween asleep and wake?—Well, then,
Legitimate Edgar, I must have your land:
Our father's love is to the bastard Edmund,
As to the legitimate: fine word,—legitimate!
Well, my legitimate, if this letter speed,
And my invention thrive, Edmund the base
Shall top the legitimate. I grow; I pros-
 per:—
Now, gods, stand up for bastards!

    Enter GLOSTER.

GLO. Kent banish'd thus! And France in
 choler parted!
And the king gone to-night! subscrib'd his
 power!
Confin'd to exhibition! All this done
Upon the gad!—Edmund, how now! what
 news?
EDM. So please your lordship, none.

     [*Putting up the letter.*

GLO. Why so earnestly seek you to put up
that letter?
EDM. I know no news, my lord.
GLO. What paper were you reading?
EDM. Nothing, my lord.
GLO. No! What needed, then, that terrible
despatch of it into your pocket? the quality
of nothing hath not such need to hide itself.

Let's see: come, if it be nothing, I shall not need spectacles.

EDM. I beseech you, Sir, pardon me: it is a letter from my brother, that I have not all o'er-read; and for so much as I have perused, I find it not fit for your o'er-looking.

GLO. Give me the letter, Sir.

EDM. I shall offend, either to detain or give it.

The contents, as in part I understand them, Are to blame.

GLO. Let's see, let's see.

EDM. I hope, for my brother's justification, he wrote this but as an essay or taste of my virtue.

GLO. [*Reads.*] "This policy, and reverence of age, makes the world bitter to the best of our times; keeps our fortunes from us, till our oldness cannot relish them. I begin to find an idle and fond bondage in the oppression of aged tyranny, who sways, not as it hath power, but as it is suffered. Come to me, that of this I may speak more. If our father would sleep till I waked him, you should enjoy half his revenue for ever, and live the beloved of your brother, EDGAR."—Hm!—Conspiracy!—"Sleep till I waked him,—you should enjoy half his revenue,"—My son Edgar! Had he a hand to write this? a heart and brain to breed it in?—When came this to you? Who brought it?

EDM. It was not brought me, my lord,—there's the cunning of it; I found it thrown in at the casement of my closet.

GLO. You know the character to be your brother's?

EDM. If the matter were good, my lord, I durst swear it were his; but, in respect of that, I would fain think it were not.

GLO. It is his.

EDM. It is his hand, my lord; but I hope his heart is not in the contents.

GLO. Hath he never heretofore sounded you in this business?

EDM. Never, my lord: but I have often heard him maintain it to be fit, that, sons at perfect age, and fathers declined, the father should be as ward to the son, and the son manage his revenue.

GLO. O villain, villain!—His very opinion in the letter!—Abhorred villain! Unnatural, detested, brutish villain! worse than brutish!—Go, sirrah, seek him; I'll apprehend him:—abominable villain!—Where is he?

EDM. I do not well know, my lord. If it shall please you to suspend your indignation against my brother, till you can derive from him better testimony of his intent, you shall run a certain course; where, if you violently proceed against him, mistaking his purpose, it would make a great gap in your own honour, and shake in pieces the heart of his obedience. I dare pawn down my life for him, that he hath writ this to feel my affection to your honour, and to no other pretence of danger.

GLO. Think you so?

EDM. If your honour judge it meet, I will place you where you shall hear us confer of this, and by an auricular assurance have your satisfaction; and that without any farther delay than this very evening.

GLO. He cannot be such a monster—

EDM. Nor is not, sure.

GLO. To his father, that so tenderly and entirely loves him.—Heaven and earth!—Edmund, seek him out; wind me into him, I pray you: frame the business after your own wisdom. I would unstate myself, to be in a due resolution.

EDM. I will seek him, Sir, presently; convey the business as I shall find means, and acquaint you withal.

GLO. These late eclipses in the sun and moon portend no good to us: though the wisdom of nature can reason it thus and thus, yet nature finds itself scourged by the sequent effects: love cools, friendship falls off, brothers divide; in cities, mutinies; in countries, discord; in palaces, treason; and the bond cracked between son and father. This villain of mine comes under the prediction; there's son against father: the king falls from bias of nature; there's father against child. We have seen the best of our time: machinations, hollowness, treachery, and all ruinous disorders, follow us disquietly to our graves.—Find out this villain, Edmund; it shall lose thee nothing; do it carefully.—And the noble and truehearted Kent banished! his offence, honesty!—Strange! strange!   [*Exit.*

EDM. This is the excellent foppery of the world, that, when we are sick in fortune, (often the surfeit of our own behaviour) we make guilty of our disasters, the sun, the moon, and the stars: as if we were villains by necessity; fools, by heavenly compulsion; knaves, thieves, and treachers, by spherical predominance; drunkards, liars, and adulterers, by an enforced obedience of planetary influence; and all that we are evil in, by a divine thrusting on: an admirable evasion of whore-master man, to lay his goatish disposition to the charge of a star! My father compounded with my mother under the dragon's tail; and my nativity was under *ursa major;* so that, it follows, I am rough and lecherous.—Tut!

I should have been that I am, had the maidenliest star in the firmament twinkled on my bastardizing. Edgar—

Enter EDGAR.

and pat he comes, like the catastrophe of the old comedy: my cue is villanous melancholy, with a sigh like Tom o' Bedlam.— O, these eclipses do portend these divisions! Fa, sol, la, mi.

EDG. How now, brother Edmund! What serious contemplation are you in?

EDM. I am thinking, brother, of a prediction I read this other day, what should follow these eclipses.

EDG. Do you busy yourself with that?

EDM. I promise you, the effects he writes of, succeed unhappily; as of unnaturalness between the child and the parent; death, dearth, dissolutions of ancient amities; divisions in state, menaces and maledictions against king and nobles; needless diffidences, banishment of friends, dissipation of cohorts, nuptial breaches, and I know not what.

EDG. How long have you been a sectary astronomical?

EDM. Come, come; when saw you my father last?

EDG. The night gone by.

EDM. Spake you with him?

EDG. Ay, two hours together.

EDM. Parted you in good terms? Found you no displeasure in him, by word or countenance?

EDG. None at all.

EDM. Bethink yourself, wherein you may have offended him: and at my entreaty forbear his presence, till some little time hath qualified the heat of his displeasure; which at this instant so rageth in him, that with the mischief of your person it would scarcely allay.

EDG. Some villain hath done me wrong.

EDM. That's my fear. I pray you, have a continent forbearance, till the speed of his rage goes slower; and, as I say, retire with me to my lodging, from whence I will fitly bring you to hear my lord speak. Pray you, go: there's my key.—If you do stir abroad, go armed.

EDG. Armed, brother!

EDM. Brother, I advise you to the best; I am no honest man, if there be any good meaning toward you: I have told you what I have seen and heard, but faintly; nothing like the image and horror of it. Pray you, away.

EDG. Shall I hear from you anon?

EDM. I do serve you in this business.—

[*Exit* EDGAR.

A credulous father! and a brother noble, Whose nature is so far from doing harms, That he suspects none; on whose foolish honesty My practices ride easy!—I see the business.— Let me, if not by birth, have lands by wit: All with me's meet, that I can fashion fit.

[*Exit.*

SCENE III.—*A Room in the* DUKE OF ALBANY'S *Palace.*

Enter GONERIL *and* OSWALD.

GON. Did my father strike my gentleman for chiding of his fool?

OSW. Ay, Madam.

GON. By day and night he wrongs me: every hour He flashes into one gross crime or other, That sets us all at odds: I'll not endure it: His knights grow riotous, and himself upbraids us   [hunting, On every trifle.—When he returns from I will not speak with him; say, I am sick:— If you come slack of former services, You shall do well; the fault of it I'll answer.   [*Horns heard.*

OSW. He's coming, Madam; I hear him.

GON. Put on what weary negligence you please   [question: You and your fellows; I'd have it come to If he distaste it, let him to my sister, Whose mind and mine, I know, in that are one, Not to be over-ruled. Idle old man, That still would manage those authorities, That he hath given away!—Now, by my life, Old fools are babes again; and must be us'd With checks as flatteries,—when they are seen abus'd. Remember what I have said.

OSW.   Well, Madam.

GON. And let his knights have colder looks among you; What grows of it, no matter; advise your fellows so: I would breed from hence occasions, and I shall,   [sister, That I may speak:—I'll write straight to my To hold my course.—Prepare for dinner.

[*Exeunt.*

SCENE IV.—*A Hall in the* DUKE OF ALBANY'S *Palace.*

Enter KENT, *disguised.*

KENT. If but as well I other accents borrow, That can my speech diffuse, my good intent May carry through itself to that full issue

For which I raz'd my likeness.—Now, banish'd Kent,
If thou canst serve where thou dost stand condemn'd,
So may it come, thy master, whom thou lov'st,
Shall find thee full of labours.

Horns heard. Enter LEAR, Knights, *and*
Attendants.

LEAR. Let me not stay a jot for dinner; go, get it ready. [*Exit an* Attendant.] How now! what art thou?

KENT. A man, Sir.

LEAR. What dost thou profess? What would'st thou with us?

KENT. I do profess to be no less than I seem; to serve him truly that will put me in trust; to love him that is honest; to converse with him that is wise, and says little; to fear judgment; to fight when I cannot choose; and to eat no fish.

LEAR. What art thou?

KENT. A very honest-hearted fellow, and as poor as the king.

LEAR. If thou be as poor for a subject, as he is for a king, thou art poor enough. What would'st thou?

KENT. Service.

LEAR. Whom would'st thou serve?

KENT. You.

LEAR. Dost thou know me, fellow?

KENT. No, Sir; but you have that in your countenance, which I would fain call master.

LEAR. What's that?

KENT. Authority.

LEAR. What services canst thou do?

KENT. I can keep honest counsel, ride, run, mar a curious tale in telling it, and deliver a plain message bluntly: that which ordinary men are fit for, I am qualified in; and the best of me is diligence.

LEAR. How old art thou?

KENT. Not so young, Sir, to love a woman for singing; nor so old, to dote on her for any thing: I have years on my back forty-eight.

LEAR. Follow me; thou shalt serve me: if I like thee no worse after dinner, I will not part from thee yet.—Dinner, ho, dinner!— Where's my knave? my fool?—Go you, and call my fool hither. [*Exit an* Attendant.

Enter OSWALD.

You, you, sirrah, where's my daughter?

OSW. So please you,— [*Exit.*

LEAR. What says the fellow there? Call the clotpoll back.—[*Exit a* Knight.] Where's my fool, ho?—I think the world's asleep.—[*Re-enter* Knight.] How now! where's that mongrel?

KNIGHT. He says, my lord, your daughter is not well.

LEAR. Why came not the slave back to me, when I called him?

KNIGHT. Sir, he answered me in the roundest manner, he would not.

LEAR. He would not!

KNIGHT. My lord, I know not what the matter is; but, to my judgment, your highness is not entertained with that ceremonious affection as you were wont: there's a great abatement of kindness appears, as well in the general dependants, as in the duke himself also, and your daughter.

LEAR. Ha! sayest thou so?

KNIGHT. I beseech you, pardon me, my lord, if I be mistaken; for my duty cannot be silent, when I think your highness wronged.

LEAR. Thou but rememberest me of mine own conception: I have perceived a most faint neglect of late; which I have rather blamed as mine own jealous curiosity, than as a very pretence and purpose of unkindness: I will look farther into't.—But where's my fool? I have not seen him this two days.

KNIGHT. Since my young lady's going into France, Sir, the fool hath much pined away.

LEAR. No more of that; I have noted it well.—Go you, and tell my daughter I would speak with her.— [*Exit an* Attendant.
Go you, call hither my fool.—
[*Exit an* Attendant.

Re-enter OSWALD.

O, you Sir, you, come you hither, Sir: who am I, Sir?

OSW. My lady's father.

LEAR. My lady's father! my lord's knave! you whoreson dog! you slave! you cur!

OSW. I am none of these, my lord; I beseech your pardon.

LEAR. Do you bandy looks with me, you rascal? [*Striking him.*

OSW. I'll not be struck, my lord.

KENT. Nor tripped neither, you base football player. [*Tripping up his heels.*

LEAR. I thank thee, fellow; thou servest me, and I'll love thee.

KENT. Come, Sir, arise, away! I'll teach you differences: away, away! If you will measure your lubber's length again, tarry: but away! Go to; have you wisdom? so.
[*Pushes* OSWALD *out.*

LEAR. Now, my friendly knave, I thank thee: there's earnest of thy service.
[*Giving* KENT *money.*
Enter Fool.

FOOL. Let me hire him too:—here's my coxcomb.   [*Offering* KENT *his cap.*

LEAR. How now, my pretty knave! how dost thou?

FOOL. Sirrah, you were best take my coxcomb.

KENT. Why, fool?

FOOL. Why, for taking one's part that's out of favour: nay, an thou canst not smile as the wind sits, thou'lt catch cold shortly: there, take my coxcomb: why, this fellow has banished two of his daughters, and did the third a blessing against his will; if thou follow him, thou must needs wear my coxcomb.—How now, nuncle! Would I had two coxcombs, and two daughters!

LEAR. Why, my boy?

FOOL. If I gave them all my living, I'd keep my coxcombs myself. There's mine; beg another of thy daughters.

LEAR. Take heed, sirrah,—the whip.

FOOL. Truth's a dog must to kennel; he must be whipped out, when Lady, the brach, may stand by the fire and stink.

LEAR. A pestilent gall to me!

FOOL. [*To* KENT.] Sirrah, I'll teach thee a speech.

LEAR. Do.

FOOL. Mark it, nuncle:—

> Have more than thou showest,
> Speak less than thou knowest,
> Lend less than thou owest,
> Ride more than thou goest,
> Learn more than thou trowest,
> Set less than thou throwest;
> Leave thy drink and thy whore,
> And keep in-a-door,
> And thou shalt have more
> Than two tens to a score.

KENT. This is nothing, fool.

FOOL. Then, 'tis like the breath of an unfee'd lawyer,—you gave me nothing for't.—Can you make no use of nothing, nuncle?

LEAR. Why, no, boy; nothing can be made out of nothing.

FOOL. [*To* KENT.] Pr'ythee, tell him, so much the rent of his land comes to: he will not believe a fool.

LEAR. A bitter fool!

FOOL. Dost thou know the difference, my boy, between a bitter fool and a sweet one?

LEAR. No, lad; teach me.

FOOL. That lord that counsell'd thee
> To give away thy land,
> Come place him here by me,—
> Do thou for him stand:
> The sweet and bitter fool
> Will presently appear;
> The one in motley here,
> The other found out there.

LEAR. Dost thou call me fool, boy?

FOOL. All thy other titles thou hast given away; that thou wast born with.

KENT. This is not altogether fool, my lord.

FOOL. No, 'faith, lords and great men will not let me; if I had a monopoly out, they would have part on't, and loads too: they will not let me have all fool to myself; they'll be snatching.—Nuncle, give me an egg, and I'll give thee two crowns.

LEAR. What two crowns shall they be?

FOOL. Why, after I have cut the egg i' the middle, and eat up the meat, the two crowns of the egg. When thou clovest thy crown i' the middle, and gavest away both parts, thou borest thine ass on thy back o'er the dirt: thou hadst little wit in thy bald crown, when thou gavest thy golden one away. If I speak like myself in this, let him be whipped that first finds it so.

[*Singing.*]

> Fools had ne'er less grace in a year;
> For wise men are grown foppish;
> And know not how their wits to wear,
> Their manners are so apish.

LEAR. When were you wont to be so full of songs, sirrah?

FOOL. I have used it, nuncle, ever since thou madest thy daughters thy mothers: for when thou gavest them the rod, and puttest down thine own breeches,

[*Singing.*]

> Then they for sudden joy did weep,
> And I for sorrow sung,
> That such a king should play bo-peep,
> And go the fools among.

Pr'ythee, nuncle, keep a school-master that can teach thy fool to lie: I would fain learn to lie.

LEAR. An you lie, sirrah, we'll have you whipped.

FOOL. I marvel what kin thou and thy daughters are: they'll have me whipped for speaking true, thou'lt have me whipped for lying; and sometimes I am whipped for holding my peace. I had rather be any kind o' thing than a fool: and yet I would not be thee, nuncle; thou hast pared thy wit o' both sides, and left nothing i' the middle:—here comes one o' the parings.

Enter GONERIL.

LEAR. How now, daughter! what makes that frontlet on?

Methinks you are too much of late i' the frown.

FOOL. Thou wast a pretty fellow, when thou hadst no need to care for her frowning; now thou art an O without a figure: I am better than thou art now; I am a fool, thou art nothing.—[*To* GON.] Yes,

forsooth, I will hold my tongue; so your
face bids me, though you say nothing. Mum,
mum,

> He that keeps nor crust nor crum,
> Weary of all, shall want some.—

That's a shealed peascod.

> *[Pointing to* LEAR.

GON. Not only, Sir, this your all-licens'd
fool,
But other of your insolent retinue
Do hourly carp and quarrel; breaking forth
In rank and not-to-be-endured riots. Sir,
I had thought, by making this well known
        unto you,   [fearful,
To have found a safe redress; but now grow
By what yourself too late have spoke and
done,
That you protect this course, and put it on
By your allowance; which if you should,
        the fault   [sleep,
Would not 'scape censure, nor the redresses
Which, in the tender of a wholesome weal,
Might in their working do you that offence,
Which else were shame, that then necessity
Will call discreet proceeding.

FOOL. For you trow, nuncle,

> The hedge-sparrow fed the cuckoo so long,
> That it had its head bit off by its young.

So, out went the candle, and we were left
darkling.

LEAR. Are you our daughter?

GON. I would you would make use of your
        good wisdom,   . .   [away
Whereof I know you are fraught; and put
These dispositions, which of late transform
you
From what you rightly are.

FOOL. May not an ass know when the
cart draws the horse?—Whoop, Jug! I love
thee.

LEAR. Does any here know me?—This is
not Lear: does Lear walk thus? speak thus?
Where are his eyes? Either his notion
weakens, or his discernings are lethar-
gied.—Sleeping or waking?—Ha! sure
'tis not so.—Who is it that can tell me who
I am?—

FOOL. Lear's shadow,—

LEAR. I would learn that; for, by the
marks of sovereignty, knowledge, and reason, I should be false persuaded I had
daughters.

FOOL. Which they will make an obedient
father.

LEAR. Your name, fair gentlewoman?

GON. This admiration Sir, is much o' the
favour
Of other your new pranks. I do beseech you
To understand my purposes aright:
As you are old and reverend, should be wise.

Here do you keep a hundred knights and
        squires;
Men so disorder'd, so debauch'd and bold,
That this our court, infected with their man-
ners,
Shows like a riotous inn: epicurism and lust
Make it more like a tavern, or a brothel,
Than a grac'd palace. The shame itself doth
        speak
For instant remedy: be, then, desir'd
By her, that else will take the thing she
        begs,
A little to disquantity your train;
And the remainder, that shall still depend,
To be such men as may besort your age,
Which know themselves and you.

LEAR.   Darkness and devils!—
Saddle my horses; call my train together.—
Degenerate bastard! I'll not trouble thee:
Yet have I left a daughter.

GON. You strike my people; and your
disorder'd rabble
Make servants of their betters.

Enter ALBANY.

LEAR. Woe, that too late repents,—[*To*
ALB.] O, Sir, are you come?
Is it your will? Speak, Sir.—Prepare my
horses.—
Ingratitude, thou marble-hearted fiend,
More hideous, when thou show'st thee in a
        child,
Than the sea-monster!

ALB.   Pray, Sir, be patient.

LEAR [*To* GON.] Detested kite! thou liest:
My train are men of choice and rarest parts,
That all particulars of duty know,
And in the most exact regard support
The worships of their name.—O most small
        fault,
How ugly didst thou in Cordelia show!
Which, like an engine, wrench'd my frame
        of nature   [all love,
From the fix'd place; drew from my heart
And added to the gall. O Lear, Lear, Lear!
Beat at this gate, that let thy folly in,

> *[Striking his head.*

And thy dear judgment out!—Go, go, my
people.

ALB. My lord, I am guiltless, as I am ignorant
Of what hath mov'd you.

LEAR.   It may be so, my lord.—
Hear, nature, hear; dear goddess, hear!
Suspend thy purpose, if thou didst intend
To make this creature fruitful!
Into her womb convey sterility!
Dry up in her the organs of increase;
And from her derogate body never spring
A babe to honour her! If she must teem,
Create her child of spleen; that it may live,

And be a thwart disnatur'd torment to her!
Let it stamp wrinkles in her brow of youth;
With cadent tears fret channels in her
  cheeks;
Turn all her mother's pains and benefits
To laughter and contempt; that she may
  feel
How sharper than a serpent's tooth it is
To have a thankless child!—Away, away!
                       [*Exit*.

ALB. Now, gods that we adore, whereof
  comes this?

GON. Never afflict yourself to know the
  cause;
But let his disposition have that scope
That dotage gives it.

Re-enter LEAR.

LEAR. Well, fifty of my followers, at a
  clap!
Within a fortnight!

ALB.   What's the matter, Sir?

LEAR. I'll tell thee;—[*To* GON.] Life and
  death! I am ashamed
That thou hast power to shake my manhood
  thus;
That these hot tears, which break from me
  perforce,
Should make thee worth them. Blasts and
  fogs upon thee!
Th' untented woundings of a father's curse
Pierce every sense about thee!—Old fond
  eyes,
Beweep this cause again, I'll pluck you out,
And cast you, with the waters that you lose,
To temper clay.—Ha!
Let it be so:—I have another daughter,
Who, I am sure, is kind and comfortable:
When she shall hear this of thee, with her
  nails
She'll flay thy wolfish visage. Thou shalt find
That I'll resume the shape, which thou dost
  think
I have cast off for ever.
    [*Exeunt* LEAR, KENT, *and* Attendants.

GON. Do you mark that?

ALB. I cannot be so partial, Goneril,
To the great love I bear you,—

GON. Pray you, content.—What, Oswald,
  ho!—

[*To the* FOOL.] You, Sir, more knave than
fool, after your master.

FOOL. Nuncle Lear, nuncle Lear, tarry,
and take the fool with thee.

    A fox, when one has caught her,
    And such a daughter,
    Should sure to the slaughter,
    If my cap would buy a halter:
    So the fool follows after.   [*Exit*.

GON. This man hath had good counsel:—
a hundred knights!

'Tis politic, and safe, to let him keep
At point a hundred knights: yes, that, on
  every dream,
Each buz, each fancy, each complaint, dislike,
He may enguard his dotage with their
  powers,
And hold our lives in mercy.—Oswald, I
  say!—

ALB. Well, you may fear too far.

GON.   Safer than trust too far:
Let me still take away the harms I fear,
Not fear still to be taken: I know his heart.
What he hath utter'd I have writ my sister:
If she sustain him and his hundred knights,
When I have showed th' unfitness,—

Re-enter OSWALD.

              How now, Oswald!
What, have you writ that letter to my sister?

OSW. Ay, Madam.

GON. Take you some company, and away
  to horse:
Inform her full of my particular fear;
And thereto add such reasons of your own,
As may compact it more. Get you gone;
And hasten your return.   [*Exit* OSWALD.
           No, no, my lord,
This milky gentleness, and course of yours,
Though I condemn not, yet, under pardon,
You are much more attask'd for want of
  wisdom,
Than prais'd for harmful mildness.

ALB. How far your eyes may pierce, I cannot tell:
Striving to better, oft we mar what's well.

GON. Nay, then—

ALB. Well, well; the event.   [*Exeunt*.

           ———

SCENE V.—*Court before the* DUKE OF
ALBANY's *Palace*.

Enter LEAR, KENT, *and* Fool.

LEAR. Go you before to Gloster with these
letters. Acquaint my daughter no farther
with any thing you know, than comes from
her demand out of the letter. If your diligence be not speedy, I shall be there before
you.

KENT. I will not sleep, my lord, till I
have delivered your letter.   [*Exit*.

FOOL. If a man's brains were in's heels,
were't not in danger of kibes?

LEAR. Ay, boy.

FOOL. Then, I pr'ythee, be merry; thy wit
shall not go slipshod.

LEAR. Ha, ha, ha!

FOOL. Shall see, thy other daughter will
use thee kindly; for though she's as like
this, as a crab is like an apple, yet I can
tell what I can tell.

LEAR. What canst tell, boy?

FOOL. She will taste as like this, as a crab does to a crab. Thou canst tell why one's nose stands i' the middle on's face?

LEAR. No.

FOOL. Why, to keep one's eyes of either side's nose; that what a man cannot smell out, he may spy into.

LEAR. I did her wrong:—

FOOL. Canst tell how an oyster makes his shell?

LEAR. No.

FOOL. Nor I neither; but I can tell why a snail has a house.

LEAR. Why?

FOOL. Why to put his head in; not to give it away to his daughters, and leave his horns without a case.

LEAR. I will forget my nature.—So kind a father!—Be my horses ready?

FOOL. Thy asses are gone about 'em. The reason why the seven stars are no more than seven is a pretty reason.

LEAR. Because they are not eight?

FOOL. Yes, indeed: thou would'st make a good fool.

LEAR. To take it again perforce!—Monster ingratitude!

FOOL. If thou wert my fool, nuncle, I'd have thee beaten for being old before thy time.

LEAR. How's that?

FOOL. Thou shouldst not have been old before thou hadst been wise.

LEAR. O, let me not be mad, not mad, sweet heaven!

Keep me in temper: I would not be mad!—
Enter Gentleman.

How now! Are the horses ready?

GENT. Ready, my lord.

LEAR. Come, boy.

FOOL. She that's a maid now, and laughs at my departure,

Shall not be a maid long, unless things be cut shorter.   [*Exeunt.*

ACT II.

SCENE I.—*A Court within the Castle of the* EARL OF GLOSTER.

Enter EDMUND *and* CURAN, *meeting.*

EDM. Save thee, Curan.

CUR. And you, Sir. I have been with your father, and given him notice, that the duke of Cornwall, and Regan his duchess, will be here with him to-night.

EDM. How comes that?

CUR. Nay, I know not.—You have heard of the news abroad,—I mean the whispered ones, for they are yet but ear-kissing arguments?

EDM. Not I: pray you, what are they?

CUR. Have you heard of no likely wars toward, 'twixt the dukes of Cornwall and Albany?

EDM. Not a word.

CUR. You may then, in time. Fare you well, Sir.   [*Exit.*

EDM. The duke be here to-night? The better! best!

This weaves itself perforce into my business.

My father hath set guard to take my brother;

And I have one thing, of a queasy question,

Which I must act:—briefness, and fortune, work!—

Brother a word;—descend:—brother, I say!
Enter EDGAR.

My father watches:—O Sir, fly this place;

Intelligence is given where you are hid;

You have now the good advantage of the night:—

Have you not spoken 'gainst the duke of Cornwall?   [haste,

He's coming hither; now, i' the night, i' the

And Regan with him: have you nothing said

Upon his party 'gainst the duke of Albany?

Advise yourself.

EDG.   I am sure on't, not a word.

EDM. I hear my father coming:—pardon me;

In cunning, I must draw my sword upon you:—

Draw: seem to defend yourself: now 'quit you well.—

Yield:—come before my father.—Light, ho, here!—

Fly, brother.—Torches, torches!—So, farewell.—   [*Exit* EDGAR.

Some blood drawn on me would beget opinion.   [*Wounds his arm.*

Of my more fierce endeavor: I have seen drunkards

Do more than this in sport.—Father, father!—

Stop, stop!—No help?
Enter GLOSTER, *and* Servants *with torches.*

GLO. Now, Edmund, where's the villain?

EDM. Here stood he in the dark, his sharp sword out,

Mumbling of wicked charms, conjuring the moon

To stand auspicious mistress,—

GLO.   But where is he?

EDM. Look, Sir, I bleed.

GLO. Where is the villain, Edmund?

EDM. Fled this way, Sir. When by no means he could—

GLO. Pursue him, ho!—Go after.—[*Ex-*

eunt some Servants.] "By no means" what?

EDM. Persuade me to the murder of your lordship;

But that I told him, the revenging gods
'Gainst parricides did all their thunders bend;
Spoke, with how manifold and strong a bond   [in fine,
The child was bound to the father;—Sir,
Seeing how loathly opposite I stood
To his unnatural purpose, in fell motion,
With his prepared sword, he charges home
My unprovided body, lanc'd mine arm:
But when he saw my best alarum'd spirits,
Bold in the quarrel's right, rous'd to th' encounter,
Or whether gasted by the noise I made,
Full suddenly he fled.

GLO.   Let him fly far:
Not in this land shall he remain uncaught;
And found—despatch.—The noble duke my master,
My worthy arch and patron, comes to-night:
By his authority I will proclaim it,
That he which finds him shall deserve our thanks,
Bringing the murderous coward to the stake;
He that conceals him, death.

EDM. When I dissuaded him from his intent,   [speech
And found him pight to do it, with curst
I threaten'd to discover him: he replied,
"Thou unpossessing bastard; dost thou think,
If I would stand against thee, would the reposal
Of any trust, virtue, or worth, in thee
Make thy words faith'd? No: what I should deny,
(As this I would; ay, though thou didst produce
My very character) I'd turn it all
To thy suggestion, plot, and damned practice:
And thou must make a dullard of the world,
If they not thought the profits of my death
Were very pregnant and potential spurs
To make thee seek it."

GLO.   Strong and fasten'd villain!
Would he deny his letter?—I never got him.—   [*Tucket within.*
Hark, the duke's trumpets! I know not why he comes.—
All ports I'll bar; the villain shall not 'scape;
The duke must grant me that: besides, his picture
I will send far and near, that all the kingdom

May have due note of him; and of my land,
Loyal and natural boy, I'll work the means
To make thee capable.

Enter CORNWALL, REGAN, *and* Attendants.

CORN. How now, my noble friend! since I came hither,
(Which I can call but now) I have heard strange news.

REG. If it be true, all vengeance comes too short,   [my lord?
Which can pursue th' offender. How dost,

GLO. O Madam, my old heart is crack'd,— it's crack'd!

REG. What, did my father's godson seek your life?
He whom my father nam'd? your Edgar?

GLO. O lady, lady, shame would have it hid!   [ous knights

REG. Was he not companion with the riot-
That tend upon my father?

GLO. I know not, Madam:—'tis too bad, too bad.

EDM. Yes, Madam, he was of that consort.

REG. No marvel, then, though he were ill affected:
'Tis they have put him on the old man's death,   [nues.
To have th' expense and waste of his reve-
I have this present evening from my sister
Been well inform'd of them; and with such cautions,
That if they come to sojourn at my house,
I'll not be there.

CORN.   Nor I, assure thee, Regan.—
Edmund, I hear that you have shown your father
A child-like office.

EDM.   'Twas my duty, Sir.

GLO. He did bewray his practice; and receiv'd
This hurt you see, striving to apprehend him.

CORN. Is he pursued?

GLO.   Ay, my good Lord.

CORN. If he be taken, he shall never more
Be fear'd of doing harm: make your own purpose,   [Edmund,
How in my strength you please.—For you,
Whose virtue and obedience doth this instant
So much commend itself, you shall be ours:
Natures of such deep trust we shall much need;
You we first seize on.

EDM.   I shall serve you, Sir,
Truly, however else.

GLO.   For him I thank your grace.

CORN. You know not why we came to visit you.

REG. Thus out of season, threading dark-ey'd night:

Occasions, noble Gloster, of some poise,
Wherein we must have use of your advice:—
Our father he hath writ, so hath our sister,
Of differences, which I best thought it fit
To answer from our home; the several
    messengers
From hence attend despatch. Our good old
    friend,
Lay comforts to your bosom; and bestow
Your needful counsel to our business,
Which craves the instant use.
GLO.   I serve you, Madam:
Your graces are right welcome. [*Exeunt.*

SCENE II.—*Before* GLOSTER'S *Castle.*
Enter KENT *and* OSWALD, *severally.*
OSW. Good dawning to thee, friend: art
of this house?
KENT. Ay.
OSW. Where may we set our horses?
KENT. I' the mire.
OSW. Pr'ythee, if thou love me, tell me.
KENT. I love thee not.
OSW. Why, then, I care not for thee.
KENT. If I had thee in Lipsbury pinfold, I
would make thee care for me.
OSW. Why dost thou use me thus? I know
thee not.
KENT. Fellow, I know thee.
OSW. What dost thou know me for?
KENT. A knave; a rascal; an eater of
broken meats; a base, proud, shallow, beggarly, three-suited, hundred-pound, filthy,
worsted-stocking knave; a lily-liver'd, ac-
tion-taking knave; a whoreson glass-gazing,
superserviceable, finical rogue; one-trunk-
inheriting slave; one that would'st be a
bawd, in way of good service, and art nothing but the composition of a knave, beggar,
coward, pander, and the son and heir of a
mongrel bitch; one whom I will beat into
clamorous whining, if thou deniest the least
syllable of thy addition.
OSW. Why, what a monstrous fellow art
thou, thus to rail on one, that is neither
known of thee, nor knows thee!
KENT. What a brazen-faced varlet art
thou, to deny thou knowest me! Is it two
days since I tripped up thy heels, and beat
thee, before the king? Draw, you rogue: for,
though it be night, yet the moon shines;
I'll make a sop o' the moonshine of you:
[*Drawing his sword.*] Draw, you whoreson cullionly barbermonger, draw.
OSW. Away! I have nothing to do with
thee.
KENT. Draw, you rascal: you come with
letters against the king; and take Vanity,
the puppet's, part, against the royalty of
her father: draw, you rogue, or I'll so car-

bonado your shanks:—draw, you rascal;
come your ways.
OSW. Help, ho! murder! help!
KENT. Strike, you slave; stand, rogue,
stand; you neat slave, strike. [*Beating him.*
OSW. Help, ho! murder! murder!
        Enter CORNWALL, REGAN, GLOSTER,
                EDMUND, *and* Servants.
EDM. How now! What's the matter?
KENT. With you, goodman boy, if you
please: come, I'll flesh you; come on, young
master.
GLO. Weapons! arms! What's the matter
here?
CORN. Keep peace, upon your lives;
He dies, that strikes again. What is the
matter?
REG. The messengers from our sister and
the king.
CORN. What is your difference? speak.
OSW. I am scarce in breath, my lord.
KENT. No marvel, you have so bestirred
your valour. You cowardly rascal, nature
disclaims in thee: a tailor made thee.
CORN. Thou art a strange fellow: a tailor
make a man?
KENT. Ay, a tailor, Sir: a stone-cutter, or
a painter, could not have made him so ill,
though they had been but two hours at the
trade.
CORN. Speak yet, how grew your quarrel?
OSW. This ancient ruffian, Sir, whose life
    I have spar'd
At suit of his grey beard,—
KENT. Thou whoreson zed! thou unnec-
essary letter!—My lord, if you will give me
leave, I will tread this unbolted villain
into mortar, and daub the wall of a jakes
with him.—Spare my grey beard, you wag-
tail?
CORN. Peace, sirrah!
You beastly knave, know you no reverence?
KENT. Yes, Sir; but anger hath a priv-
    ilege.
CORN. Why art thou angry?
KENT. That such a slave as this should
    wear a sword,
Who wears no honesty. Such smiling rogues
    as these,
Like rats, oft bite the holy cords atwain
Which are too intrinse t'unloose; smooth
    every passion
That in the natures of their lords rebels;
Bring oil to fire, snow to their colder moods;
Renege, affirm, and turn their halcyon
    beaks
With every gale and vary of their masters,
Knowing naught, like dogs, but follow-
    ing.—
A plague upon your epileptic visage!

Smile you my speeches, as I were a fool?
Goose, if I had you upon Sarum plain,
I'd drive ye cackling home to Camelot.
CORN. What, art thou mad, old fellow?
GLO. How fell you out? say that.
KENT. No contraries hold more antipathy,
Than I and such a knave.
CORN. Why dost thou call him knave?
What is his fault?
KENT. His countenance likes me not.
CORN. No more, perchance, does mine,
nor his, nor hers.
KENT. Sir, 'tis my occupation to be plain:
I have seen better faces in my time,
Than stands on any shoulder that I see
Before me at this instant.
CORN.   This is some fellow,
Who, having been prais'd for bluntness,
doth affect
A saucy roughness, and constrains the garb
Quite from his nature: he cannot flatter,
he,—   [truth!
An honest mind and plain,—he must speak
An they will take it, so; if not, he's plain.
These kind of knaves I know, which in this
plainness
Harbour more craft, and more corrupter
ends,
Than twenty silly ducking observants,
That stretch their duties nicely.
KENT. Sir, in good sooth, in sincere verity,
Under th' allowance of your grand aspect,
Whose influence, like the wreath of radiant
fire
On flickering Phœbus' front,—
CORN.   What mean'st by this?
KENT. To go out of my dialect, which you
discommend so much. I know, Sir, I am
no flatterer: he that beguiled you in a plain
accent was a plain knave; which, for my
part, I will not be, though I should win
your displeasure to entreat me to't.
CORN. What was the offence you gave
him?
OSW. I never gave him any:
It pleas'd the king, his master, very late,
To strike at me, upon his misconstruction;
When he, compact, and flattering his dis-
pleasure,
Tripp'd me behind; being down, insulted,
rail'd,
And put upon him such a deal of man,
That worthied him, got praises of the king
For him attempting who was self-subdu'd;
And, in the fleshment of this dread exploit,
Drew on me here again.
KENT. None of these rogues, and cowards,
But Ajax is their fool.
CORN.   Fetch forth the stocks!—

You stubborn ancient knave, you reverend
We'll teach you—   [braggart,
KENT.   Sir, I am too old to learn:
Call not your stocks for me: I serve the
king;
On whose employment I was sent to you:
You shall do small respect, show too bold
malice
Against the grace and person of my master,
Stocking his messenger.
CORN.   Fetch forth the stocks!—
As I have life and honour, there shall he
sit till noon.
REG. Till noon! till night, my lord; and
all night too.
KENT. Why, Madam, if I were your fa-
ther's dog,
You should not use me so.
REG.   Sir, being his knave, I will.
CORN. This is a fellow of the self-same
colour
Our sister speaks of.—Come, bring away
the stocks!   [*Stocks brought out.*
GLO. Let me beseech your grace not to do
so:
His fault is much, and the good king his
master   [correction
Will check him for't: your purpos'd low
Is such, as basest and contemned'st
wretches,
For pilferings and most common trespasses,
Are punish'd with: the king must take it ill,
That he, so slightly valued in his messenger,
Should have him thus restrain'd.
CORN.   I'll answer that.
REG. My sister may receive it much more
worse,
To have her gentleman abus'd, assaulted,
For following her affairs.—Put in his legs.—
                   [KENT *is put in the stocks.*
Come, my lord, away.
          [*Exeunt all except* GLOSTER *and* KENT.
GLO. I am sorry for thee, friend; 'tis the
duke's pleasure,
Whose disposition, all the world well knows,
Will not be rubb'd, nor stopp'd: I'll entreat
for thee.
KENT. Pray, do not, Sir; I have watch'd,
and travell'd hard;
Some time I shall sleep out, the rest I'll
whistle.
A good man's fortune may grow out at
Give you good morrow!   [heels.
GLO. The duke's to blame in this; 'twill
be ill taken.   [*Exit.*
KENT. Good king, that must approve the
common saw,—
Thou out of heaven's benediction com'st
To the warm sun!
Approach, thou beacon to this under globe,

That by thy comfortable beams I may
Peruse this letter!—Nothing, almost, sees
  miracles,
But misery:—I know 'tis from Cordelia,
Who hath most fortunately been inform'd
Of my obscured course; and shall find time
From this enormous state,—seeking to give
Losses their remedies,—All weary and o'er-
  watch'd,
Take vantage, heavy eyes, not to behold
This shameful lodging. Fortune, good night:
Smile once more; turn thy wheel!
                              [*He sleeps.*

SCENE III.—*The open Country.*

Enter EDGAR.

EDG. I heard myself proclaim'd;
And by the happy hollow of a tree
Escap'd the hunt. No port is free; no place,
That guard, and most unusual vigilance,
Does not attend my taking. While I may
  'scape,
I will preserve myself: and am bethought
To take the basest and most poorest shape,
That ever penury, in contempt of man,
Brought near to beast: my face I'll grime
  with filth;
Blanket my loins; elf all my hair in knots;
And with presented nakedness out-face
The winds and persecutions of the sky.
The country gives me proof and precedent
Of Bedlam beggars, who, with roaring
  voices,
Strike in their numb'd and mortified bare
  arms
Pins, wooden pricks, nails, sprigs of rose-
  mary;
And with this horrible object, from low
  farms,
Poor pelting villages, sheep-cotes, and mills,
Sometime with lunatic bans, sometime with
  prayers,
Enforce their charity.—Poor Turlygod! poor
  Tom!
That's something yet:—Edgar I nothing
  am.   [*Exit.*

SCENE IV.—*Before* GLOSTER'S *Castle.* KENT
  in the Stocks.

Enter LEAR, *Fool, and* Gentleman.

LEAR. 'Tis strange that they should so de-
  part from home,
And not send back my messenger.
GENT.   As I learn'd,
The night before there was no purpose in
Of this remove.   [them
KENT.   Hail to thee, noble master!
LEAR. Ha!

Mak'st thou this shame thy pastime?
KENT.   No, my lord.
FOOL. Ha, ha! he wears cruel garters.
Horses are tied by the head, dogs and bears
by the neck, monkeys by the loins, and men
by the legs: when a man is over-lusty at
legs, then he wears wooden nether-stocks.
LEAR. What's he, that hath so much thy
  place mistook,
To set thee here?
KENT.   It is both he and she,—
Your son and daughter.
LEAR. No.
KENT. Yes.
LEAR. No, I say.
KENT. I say, yea.
LEAR. No, no, they would not.
KENT. Yes, they have.
LEAR. By Jupiter, I swear, no.
KENT. By Juno, I swear, ay.
LEAR.   They durst not do't;
They could not, would not do't; 'tis worse
  than murder,
To do upon respect such violent outrage:
Resolve me, with all modest haste, which
  way
Thou might'st deserve, or they impose, this
  Coming from us.   [usage.
KENT.   My lord, when at their home
I did commend your highness' letters to
  them,
Ere I was risen from the place that show'd
My duty kneeling, came there a reeking
  post,
Stew'd in his haste, half breathless, panting
  forth
From Goneril, his mistress, salutations;
Deliver'd letters, spite of intermission,
Which presently they read: on whose con-
  tents,
They summon'd up their meiny, straight
  took horse;
Commanded me to follow, and attend
The leisure of their answer; gave me cold
  looks:
And meeting here the other messenger,
Whose welcome, I perceiv'd, had poison'd
  mine,
(Being the very fellow which of late
Display'd so saucily against your highness)
Having more man than wit about me, drew:
He rais'd the house with loud and coward
  cries.
Your son and daughter found this trespass
  worth
The shame which here it suffers.
FOOL. Winter's not gone yet, if the wild
geese fly that way.
    Fathers, that wear rags,
      Do make their children blind;

But fathers, that bear bags,
  Shall see their children kind.
Fortune, that arrant whore,
Ne'er turns the key to the poor.—
But, for all this, thou shalt have as many
dolours for thy daughters, as thou canst
tell in a year.
LEAR. O, how this mother swells up
  toward my heart!
Hysterica passio,—down, thou climbing sor-
  row,
Thy element's below!—Where is this
  daughter?
KENT. With the earl, Sir, here within.
LEAR.   Follow me not;
Stay here.   [*Exit.*
GENT. Made you no more offence than
  what you speak of?
KENT. None.
How chance the king comes with so small a
  train?
FOOL. An thou hadst been set i' the
stocks for that question, thou hadst well
deserved it.
KENT. Why, fool?
FOOL. We'll set thee to school to an ant,
to teach thee there's no labouring i' the
winter. All that follow their noses are led
by their eyes, but blind men; and there's
not a nose among twenty but can smell him
that's stinking. Let go thy hold when a great
wheel runs down a hill, lest it break thy
neck with following it; but the great one
that goes up the hill, let him draw thee
after. When a wise man gives thee better
counsel give me mine again: I would have
none but knaves follow it, since a fool gives
it.
  That Sir, which serves and seeks for
      gain,
    And follows but for form,
  Will pack when it begins to rain,
    And leave thee in the storm.
  But I will tarry; the fool will stay,
    And let the wise man fly:
  The knave turns fool that runs away;
    The fool no knave, perdy.
KENT. Where learn'd you this, fool?
FOOL. Not i' the stocks, fool.
  Re-enter LEAR *with* GLOSTER.
LEAR. Deny to speak with me? They are
  sick? they are weary?
They have travell'd hard to-night? Mere
  fetches;
The images of revolt and flying off.
Fetch me a better answer.
GLO.   My dear lord,
You know the fiery quality of the duke;
How unremovable and fix'd he is
In his own course.

LEAR. Vengeance! plague! death! con-
  fusion!—
Fiery? what quality? Why, Gloster, Gloster,
I'd speak with the duke of Cornwall and
  his wife.
GLO. Well, my good lord, I have inform'd
  them so.
LEAR. Inform'd them! Dost thou under-
  stand me, man?
GLO. Ay, my good lord.
LEAR. The king would speak with Corn-
  wall; the dear father
Would with his daughter speak, commands
  her service:
Are they inform'd of this?—My breath and
  blood!—
Fiery? the fiery duke?—Tell the hot duke,
  that—
No, but not yet:—may be, he is not well:
Infirmity doth still neglect all office,
Whereto our health is bound; we are not
  ourselves,
When nature, being oppress'd, commands
  the mind
To suffer with the body: I'll forbear;
And am fallen out with my more headier
  will,
To take the indispos'd and sickly fit
For the sound man.—Death on my state!
  wherefore   [*Looking on* KENT.
Should he sit here? This act persuades me,
That this remotion of the duke and her
Is practice only. Give me my servant forth.
Go, tell the duke and's wife, I'd speak with
  them,
Now, presently: bid them come forth and
  hear me,
Or at their chamber door I'll beat the drum,
Till it cry sleep to death.
GLO. I would have all well betwixt you.
            [*Exit.*
LEAR. O me, my heart, my rising heart!—
  but, down!
FOOL. Cry to it, nuncle, as the cockney
did to the eels, when she put them i' the
paste alive; she rapp'd 'em o' the coxcombs
with a stick, and cried, "Down, wantons,
down!" 'Twas her brother, that, in pure
kindness to his horse, buttered his hay.
  Enter CORNWALL, REGAN, GLOSTER, *and*
      Servants.
LEAR. Good morrow to you both.
CORN.   Hail to your grace!
          [KENT *is set at liberty.*
REG. I am glad to see your highness.
LEAR. Regan, I think you are; I know
  what reason
I have to think so: if thou shouldst not
  be glad,

I would divorce me from thy mother's tomb,
Sepulchring an adult'ress.—[*To* KENT.] O,
are you free?
Some other time for that.—Beloved Regan,
Thy sister's naught: O Regan, she hath tied
Sharp-tooth'd unkindness, like a vulture,
here,— [*Points to his heart.*
I can scarce speak to thee; thou'lt not believe,
With how deprav'd a quality—O Regan!
REG. I pray you, Sir, take patience: I
have hope,
You less know how to value her desert,
Than she to scant her duty.
LEAR. Say, how is that?
REG. I cannot think, my sister in the least
Would fail her obligation: if, Sir, perchance,
She have restrain'd the riots of your followers,
'Tis on such ground, and to such wholesome
As clears her from all blame. [end,
LEAR. My curses on her!
REG. O, Sir, you are old;
Nature in you stands on the very verge
Of her confine: you should be rul'd, and led
By some discretion, that discerns your state
Better than you yourself. Therefore, I pray
you,
That to our sister you do make return;
Say, you have wrong'd her, Sir.
LEAR. Ask her forgiveness?
Do you but mark how this becomes the
house: [*Kneeling.*
"Dear daughter, I confess that I am old;
Age is unnecessary: on my knees I beg
That you'll vouchsafe me raiment, bed, and
food."
REG. Good Sir, no more; these are unsightly tricks:
Return you to my sister.
LEAR. [*Rising.*] Never, Regan:
She hath abated me of half my train;
Look'd black upon me; struck me with her
tongue,
Most serpent-like, upon the very heart:—
All the stor'd vengeances of heaven fall
On her ingrateful top! Strike her young
bones,
You taking airs, with lameness!
CORN. Fie, Sir, fie!
LEAR. You nimble lightnings, dart your
blinding flames
Into her scornful eyes! Infect her beauty,
You fen-suck'd fogs, drawn by the power-
To fall and blast her pride! [ful sun,
REG. O the blest gods! So will you wish
on me,
When the rash mood is on.
LEAR. No, Regan, thou shalt never have
my curse:

Thy tender-hefted nature shall not give
Thee o'er to harshness: her eyes are fierce;
but thine
Do comfort, and not burn. 'Tis not in thee
To grudge my pleasures, to cut off my train,
To bandy hasty words, to scant my sizes,
And, in conclusion, to oppose the bolt
Against my coming in: thou better know'st
The offices of nature, bond of childhood,
Effects of courtesy, dues of gratitude;
Thy half o' the kingdom hast thou not
Wherein I thee endow'd. [forgot,
REG. Good Sir, to the purpose.
LEAR. Who put my man i' the stocks?
[*Tucket within.*
CORN. What trumpet's that?
REG. I know't,—my sister's: this approves
her letter,
That she would soon be here.—
Enter OSWALD.
Is your lady come?
LEAR. This is a slave, whose easy-borrow'd pride
Dwells in the fickle grace of her he follows.—
Out, varlet, from my sight! [
CORN. What means your grace?
LEAR. Who stock'd my servant? Regan, I
have good hope
Thou didst not know of't.—Who comes
here? O heavens,
Enter GONERIL.
If you do love old men, if your sweet sway
Allow obedience, if yourselves are old,
Make it your cause; send down, and take
my part!—
[*To* GON.] Art not asham'd to look upon
this beard?—
O Regan, wilt thou take her by the hand?
GON. Why not by the hand, Sir? How
have I offended?
All's not offence, that indiscretion finds,
And dotage terms so.
LEAR. O sides, you are too tough;
Will you yet hold?—How came my man
i' the stocks?
CORN. I set him there, Sir; but his own
disorders
Deserv'd much less advancement.
LEAR. You! did you?
REG. I pray you, father, being weak, seem
If, till the expiration of your month, [so.
You will return and sojourn with my sister,
Dismissing half your train, come then to
me:
I am now from home, and out of that provision
Which shall be needful for your entertainment.
LEAR. Return to her, and fifty men dismiss'd?

No, rather I abjure all roofs, and choose
To wage against the enmity o' the air;
To be a comrade with the wolf and owl,—
Necessity's sharp pinch!—Return with her?
Why, the hot-blooded France, that dower-
less took
Our youngest born, I could as well be
brought
To knee his throne, and, squire-like, pen-
sion beg
To keep base life afoot.—Return with her?
Persuade me rather to be slave and sumpter
To this detested groom.
                    [*Pointing to* OSWALD.
GON.   At your choice, Sir.
LEAR. I pr'ythee, daughter, do not make
me mad:
I will not trouble thee, my child; farewell:
We'll no more meet, no more see one an-
other:—
But yet thou art my flesh, my blood, my
daughter;
Or, rather, a disease that's in my flesh,
Which I must needs call mine: thou art a
boil,
A plague-sore, an embossed carbuncle,
In my corrupted blood. But I'll not chide
thee;   [it:
Let shame come when it will, I do not call
I do not bid the thunder-bearer shoot,
Nor tell tales of thee to high-judging Jove:
Mend when thou canst; be better at thy
leisure:
I can be patient; I can stay with Regan,
I and my hundred knights.
REG.   Not altogether so:
I look'd not for you yet, nor am provided
For your fit welcome. Give ear, Sir, to my
sister;
For those that mingle reason with your
passion,
Must be content to think you old, and so—
But she knows what she does.
LEAR.   Is this well spoken?
REG. I dare avouch it, Sir: what, fifty fol-
lowers?
Is it not well? What should you need of
more?
Yea, or so many, sith that both charge and
danger
Speak 'gainst so great a number? How, in
one house,
Should many people, under two commands,
Hold amity? 'Tis hard; almost impossible.
GON. Why might not you, my lord, re-
ceive attendance
From those that she calls servants, or from
mine?
REG. Why not, my lord? If then they
chanc'd to slack you,

We could control them. If you will come
to me,
(For now I spy a danger) I entreat you
To bring but five and twenty: to no more
Will I give place, or notice.
LEAR. I gave you all—
REG.   And in good time you gave it.
LEAR. Made you my guardians, my de-
positaries;
But kept a reservation to be follow'd
With such a number. What, must I come
to you
With five and twenty, Regan? said you so?
REG. And speak't again, my lord; no more
with me.
LEAR. Those wicked creatures yet do look
well-favour'd,
When others are more wicked; not being
the worst,
Stands in some rank of praise.—[*To* GON.]
I'll go with thee:
Thy fifty yet doth double five and twenty,
And thou art twice her love.
GON.   Hear me, my lord:
What need you five and twenty, ten, or five,
To follow in a house, where twice so many
Have a command to tend you?
REG.   What need one?
LEAR. O, reason not the need: our basest
beggars
Are in the poorest thing superfluous:
Allow not nature more than nature needs,
Man's life is cheap as beast's. Thou art a
lady;
If only to go warm were gorgeous,
Why, nature needs not what thou gorgeous
wear'st,
Which scarcely keeps thee warm. But, for
true need,—
You heavens, give me that patience, pa-
tience I need!
You see me here, you gods, a poor old man,
As full of grief as age; wretched in both!
If it be you that stir these daughters'
hearts
Against their father, fool me not so much
To bear it tamely; touch me with noble
anger!
O, let not women's weapons, water-drops,
Stain my man's cheeks!—No, you unnatu-
ral hags,
I will have such revenges on you both,
That all the world shall—I will do such
things,—
What they are, yet I know not; but they
shall be
The terrors of the earth. You think I'll
weep;
No, I'll not weep:—
I have full cause of weeping; but this
heart

Shall break into a hundred thousand flaws,
Or ere I'll weep.—O fool, I shall go mad!
    [*Exeunt* LEAR, GLOSTER, KENT, *and* Fool.
        Storm heard at a distance.]
CORN. Let us withdraw; 'twill be a storm.
REG. This house is little: the old man and
    his people
Cannot be well bestow'd.
GON. 'Tis his own blame; h'ath put him-
    self from rest,
And must needs taste his folly.
REG. For his particular, I'll receive him
    gladly,
But not one follower.
GON.   So am I purpos'd.
Where is my lord of Gloster?
CORN. Follow'd the old man forth:—he is
    return'd.
                Re-enter GLOSTER.
GLO. The king is in high rage.
CORN.   Whither is he going?
GLO. He calls to horse; but will I know
    not whither.
CORN. 'Tis best to give him way; he leads
    himself.
GON. My lord, entreat him by no means to
    stay.
GLO. Alack, the night comes on, and the
    bleak winds
Do sorely ruffle; for many miles about
There's scarce a bush.
REG.   O, Sir, to wilful men,
The injuries that they themselves procure
Must be their schoolmasters. Shut up your
    doors:
He is attended with a desperate train;
And what they may incense him to, being
    apt
To have his ear abus'd, wisdom bids fear.
CORN. Shut up your doors, my lord; 'tis
    a wild night:
My Regan counsels well: come out o' the
    storm.   [*Exeunt.*

ACT III.

SCENE I.—*A Heath.*

A storm, with thunder and lightning. Enter
    KENT *and* Gentleman, *meeting.*
KENT. Who's here, beside foul weather?
GENT. One minded, like the weather, most
    unquietly.
KENT. I know you. Where's the king?
GENT. Contending with the fretful ele-
    ments;
Bids the wind blow the earth into the sea,
Or swell the curled waters 'bove the main,
That things might change or cease; tears
    his white hair,

Which the impetuous blasts, with eyeless
    rage,
Catch in their fury, and make nothing of;
Strives in his little world of man to out-
    scorn
The to-and-fro-conflicting wind and rain.
This night, wherein the cub-drawn bear
    would couch,
The lion and the belly-pinched wolf
Keep their fur dry, unbonneted he runs,
And bids what will take all.
KENT.   But who is with him?
GENT. None but the fool; who labours to
    outjest
His heart-struck injuries.
KENT.   Sir, I do know you;
And dare, upon the warrant of my note,
Commend a dear thing to you. There is di-
    vision,
Although as yet the face of it be cover'd
With mutual cunning, 'twixt Albany and
    Cornwall;
Who have (as who have not, that their great
    stars
Thron'd and set high?) servants, who seem
    no less,
Which are to France the spies and specula-
    tions
Intelligent of our state; what hath been
    seen,
Either in snuffs and packings of the dukes;
Or the hard rein which both of them have
    borne
Against the old kind king; or something
    deeper,
Whereof, perchance, these are but fur-
    nishings;—
But, true it is, from France there comes a
    power
Into this scatter'd kingdom; who already,
Wise in our negligence, have secret feet
In some of our best ports, and are at point
To show their open banner.—Now to you:
If on my credit you dare build so far
To make your speed to Dover, you shall
    find
Some that will thank you, making just
    report
Of how unnatural and bemadding sorrow
The king hath cause to plain.
I am a gentleman of blood and breeding;
And, from some knowledge and assurance,
This office to you.   [*offer*
GENT. I will talk farther with you.
KENT.   No, do not.
For confirmation that I am much more
Than my out wall, open this purse, and take
What it contains. If you shall see Cordelia,
(As fear not but you shall) show her this
    ring;

[handwritten: analogy → storm controls old man as daughters control him.]

And she will tell you who that fellow is
That yet you do not know. [*Thunder.*] Fie
　on this storm!
I will go seek the king.
GENT. Give me your hand: have you no
　more to say?
KENT. Few words, but, to effect, more
　than all yet,—
That, when we have found the king, (in
　which your pain
That way, I'll this) he that first lights on
　him,
Holla the other.　　　　[*Exeunt severally.*

———

Scene II.—*Another Part of the Heath.
　　Storm continues.*

Enter Lear *and* Fool.

LEAR. Blow, winds, and crack your
　cheeks! rage! blow!
You cataracts and hurricanoes, spout
Till you have drench'd our steeples, drown'd
　the cocks!
You sulphurous and thought-executing fires,
Vaunt-couriers of oak-cleaving thunder-
　bolts,
Singe my white head! And thou, all-shak-
　ing thunder,
Strike flat the thick rotundity o' the world!
Crack nature's moulds, all germins spill at
　once,
That make ingrateful man!
FOOL. O nuncle, court holy-water in a
dry house is better than this rain-water out
o' door. Good nuncle, in, and ask thy
daughter's blessing: here's a night pities
neither wise men nor fools.
LEAR. Rumble thy bellyful! Spit, fire!
　spout, rain!
Nor rain, wind, thunder, fire, are my
　daughters:
I tax not you, you elements, with unkind-
　ness;
I never gave you kingdom, call'd you chil-
　dren,
You owe me no subscription: then, let fall
Your horrible pleasure; here I stand, your
　slave,
A poor, infirm, weak, and despis'd old
　man:—
But yet I call you servile ministers,
That will with two pernicious daughters
　join
Your high-engender'd battles, 'gainst a
　head
So old and white as this. O! O! 'tis foul!
FOOL. He that has a house to put's head
in, has a good head-piece.

The cod-piece that will house,
　Before the head has any,
The head and he shall louse;—
　So beggars marry many.
The man that makes his toe
　What he his heart should make,
Shall of a corn cry woe,
　And turn his sleep to wake.
—for there was never yet fair woman, but
she made mouths in a glass.
LEAR. No, I will be the pattern of all pa-
I will say nothing.　　　　[tience;
　　　Enter Kent.
KENT. Who's there?
FOOL. Marry, here's grace, and a cod-
piece; that's a wise man, and a fool.
KENT. Alas, Sir, are you here? things
　that love night,
Love not such nights as these; the wrathful
　skies
Gallow the very wanderers of the dark,
And make them keep their caves: since I
　was man,
Such sheets of fire, such bursts of horrid
　thunder,
Such groans of roaring wind and rain, I
　never
Remember to have heard: man's nature
　cannot carry
Th' affliction, nor the fear.
LEAR.　　　　Let the great gods,
That keep this dreadful pother o'er our
　heads,
Find out their enemies now. Tremble,
　thou wretch,
That hast within thee undivulged crimes,
Unwhipp'd of justice: hide thee, thou
　bloody hand;
Thou perjur'd, and thou simular of virtue
That art incestuous: caitiff, to pieces shake,
That under covert and convenient seeming
Hast practis'd on man's life: close pent-up
　guilts,
Rive your concealing continents, and cry
These dreadful summoners grace.—I am a
　man
More sinn'd against, than sinning.
KENT.　　　　Alack, bare-headed!
Gracious my lord, hard by here is a hovel;
Some friendship will it lend you 'gainst
　the tempest:
Repose you there; while I to this hard
　house　　　　rais'd;
(More hard than is the stone whereof 'tis
Which even but now, demanding after you,
Denied me to come in) return, and force
Their scanted courtesy.
LEAR.　　　　My wits begin to turn.—
Come on, my boy: how dost, my boy? Art
　cold?

I am cold myself.—Where is this straw,
my fellow?
The art of our necessities is strange,
That can make vile things precious. Come,
your hovel.—
Poor fool and knave, I have one part in my
That's sorry yet for thee.		[heart
FOOL. [Singing.]
> He that has and a little tiny wit,—
>> With hey, ho, the wind and the
>> rain,—
> Must make content with his fortunes
> fit;
> Though the rain it raineth every day.
LEAR. True, boy.—Come, bring us to this
hovel.			[Exeunt LEAR and KENT.
FOOL. This is a brave night to cool a cour-
tezan.—I'll speak a prophecy ere I go:
> When priests are more in word than
> matter;
> When brewers mar their malt with water;
> When nobles are their tailors' tutors;
> No heretics burn'd, but wenches' suitors;
> When every case in law is right;
> No squire in debt, nor no poor knight;
> When slanders do not live in tongues;
> Nor cutpurses come not to throngs;
> When usurers tell their gold i' the field;
> And bawds and whores do churches
> build;—
> Then shall the realm of Albion
> Come to great confusion:
> Then comes the time, who lives to see't,
> That going shall be us'd with feet.
This prophecy Merlin shall make; for I live
before his time.			[Exit.

SCENE III.—A Room in GLOSTER'S Castle.
Enter GLOSTER and EDMUND.
GLO. Alack, alack, Edmund, I like not this
unnatural dealing. When I desired their
leave that I might pity him, they took from
me the use of mine own house; charged me,
on pain of their perpetual displeasure,
neither to speak of him, entreat for him,
nor any way sustain him.
EDM. Most savage, and unnatural!
GLO. Go to; say you nothing. There is
division between the dukes; and a worse
matter than that: I have received a letter
this night;—'tis dangerous to be spoken;—
I have locked the letter in my closet: these
injuries the king now bears will be revenged home: there is part of a power already footed: we must incline to the king.
I will seek him, and privily relieve him: go
you, and maintain talk with the duke, that
my charity be not of him perceived: if he
ask for me, I am ill, and gone to bed. If I die
for it, as no less is threatened me, the king,

my old master, must be relieved. There is
some strange thing toward, Edmund; pray
you, be careful.			[Exit.
EDM. This courtesy, forbid thee, shall
the duke
Instantly know; and of that letter too:—
This seems a fair deserving, and must draw
me
That which my father loses.—no less than
all:
The younger rises, when the old doth fall.
					[Exit.

SCENE IV.—A Part of the Heath, with a
hovel.
Storm continues.
Enter LEAR, KENT, and Fool.
KENT. Here is the place, my lord; good
my lord, enter:
The tyranny of the open night's too rough
For nature to endure.
LEAR.			Let me alone.
KENT. Good my lord, enter here.
LEAR.			Wilt break my heart?
KENT. I'd rather break mine own. Good
my lord, enter.
LEAR. Thou think'st 'tis much that this
contentious storm
Invades us to the skin: so 'tis to thee;
But where the greater malady is fix'd,
The lesser is scarce felt. Thou'dst shun
a bear;
But if thy flight lay toward the roaring sea,
Thou'dst meet the bear i' the mouth. When
the mind's free,
The body's delicate: the tempest in my
mind
Doth from my senses take all feeling else,
Save what beats there.—Filial ingratitude!
Is it not as this mouth should tear this
hand,
For lifting food to't?—But I will punish
home:—
No, I will weep no more.—In such a night
To shut me out!—Pour on; I will endure:—
In such a night as this! O Regan, Gon-
eril!—
Your old kind father, whose frank heart
gave all,—
O, that way madness lies; let me shun that;
No more of that.
KENT.			Good my lord, enter here.
LEAR. Pr'ythee, go in thyself; seek thine
own ease:
The tempest will not give me leave to pon-
der
On things would hurt me more.—But I'll
go in.
[To the Fool.] In, boy; go first.—You
houseless poverty,—

Nay, get thee in. I'll pray, and then I'll
sleep.—   [*Fool goes in.*
Poor naked wretches, whereso'er you are,
That bide the pelting of this pitiless storm,
How shall your houseless heads, and unfed
  sides,
Your loop'd and window'd raggedness, de-
  fend you
From seasons such as these? O, I have ta'en
Too little care of this! Take physic, pomp;
Expose thyself to feel what wretches feel,
That thou may'st shake the superflux to
  them,
And show the heavens more just.
EDG. [*Within.*] Fathom and half, fathom
  and half! Poor Tom!
                [*The Fool runs out from the hovel.*
FOOL. Come not in here, nuncle, here's
  a spirit. Help me, help me!
KENT. Give me thy hand.—Who's there?
FOOL. A spirit, a spirit: he says his
  name's poor Tom.
KENT. What art thou that dost grumble
  there i' the straw?
Come forth.
      Enter EDGAR, *disguised as a madman.*
EDG. Away! the foul fiend follows me!—
Through the sharp hawthorn blows the cold
  wind.—
Hm! go to thy cold bed, and warm thee.
LEAR. Didst thou give all to thy daughters?
And art thou come to this?
EDG. Who gives any thing to poor Tom?
whom the foul fiend hath led through fire
and through flame, through ford and whirl-
pool, o'er bog and quagmire; that hath laid
knives under his pillow, and halters in his
pew; set ratsbane by his porridge; made
him proud of heart, to ride on a bay trot-
ting-horse over four-inched bridges, to
course his own shadow for a traitor.—
Bless thy five wits!—Tom's a-cold,—O,
do de, do de, do de.—Bless thee from whirlwinds, starblasting, and taking! Do poor
Tom some charity, whom the foul fiend
vexes:—there could I have him now,—and
there,—and there again, and there.
                        [*Storm continues.*
LEAR. What, have his daughters brought
  him to this pass?—
Could'st thou save nothing? Did'st thou
  give them all?
FOOL. Nay, he reserved a blanket, else
we had been all shamed.
LEAR. Now, all the plagues, that in the
  pendulous air
Hang fated o'er men's faults, light on thy
  daughters!
KENT. He hath no daughters, Sir.

LEAR. Death, traitor, nothing could have
  subdued nature
To such a lowness, but his unkind daugh-
  ters.—
Is it the fashion, that discarded fathers
Should have thus little mercy on their flesh?
Judicious punishment! 'twas this flesh begot
Those pelican daughters.
EDG.   Pillicock sat on Pillicock-hill:—
Halloo, halloo, loo, loo!
FOOL. This cold night will turn us all to
fools and madmen.
EDG. Take heed o' the foul fiend: obey
thy parents; keep thy word justly; swear
not; commit not with man's sworn spouse;
set not thy sweet heart on proud array.
Tom's a-cold.
LEAR. What hast thou been?
EDG. A serving-man, proud in heart and
mind; that curled my hair; wore gloves
in my cap; served the lust of my mistress's
heart, and did the act of darkness with
her; swore as many oaths as I spake words,
and broke them in the sweet face of heaven:
one, that slept in the contriving of lust,
and waked to do it: wine loved I deeply,
dice dearly; and in woman out-paramoured
the Turk: false of heart, light of ear,
bloody of hand; hog in sloth, fox in stealth,
wolf in greediness, dog in madness, lion in
prey. Let not the creaking of shoes, nor the
rustling of silks, betray thy poor heart to
woman: keep thy foot out of brothels, thy
hand out of plackets, thy pen from lenders'
books, and defy the foul fiend.—Still
through the hawthorn blows the cold wind:
says suum, mun, nonny. Dolphin my boy,
my boy; sessa! let him trot by.
                        [*Storm still continues.*
LEAR. Why, thou wert better in thy grave,
than to answer with thy uncovered body this
extremity of the skies.—Is man no more
than this? Consider him well. Thou owest
the worm no silk, the beast no hide, the
sheep no wool, the cat no perfume.—Ha!
here's three of us are sophisticated! Thou
art the thing itself: unaccommodated man
is no more but such a poor, bare, forked
animal as thou art.— Off, off, you lendings!
—Come, unbutton here.—
                        [*Tearing off his clothes.*
FOOL. Pr'ythee, nuncle, be contented; 'tis
a naughty night to swim in.—Now a little
fire in a wild field were like an old lecher's
heart,—a small spark, all the rest on's body
cold.—Look, here comes a walking fire.
EDG. This is the foul fiend Flibbertigibbet:
he begins at curfew, and walks till the first
cock; he gives the web and the pin, squints
the eye, and makes the hare-lip; mildews

the white wheat, and hurts the poor creature of earth.

    Swithold footed thrice the old;
      He met the night-mare, and her nine-
        fold;
        Bid her alight,
        And her troth plight,
    And aroint thee, witch, aroint thee!

KENT. How fares you grace?

    Enter GLOSTER, *with a torch.*

LEAR. What's he?

KENT. Who's there? What is't you seek?

GLO. What are you there? Your names?

EDG. Poor Tom; that eats the swimming
frog; the toad, the tadpole, the wall-newt,
and the water; that in the fury of his heart,
when the foul fiend rages, eats cow-dung
for sallets; swallows the old rat, and the
ditch-dog; drinks the green mantle of the
standing pool; who is whipped from tything to tything, and stocked, punished, and
imprisoned; who hath had three suits to
his back, six shirts to his body, horse to
ride, and weapon to wear;—

    But mice, and rats, and such small deer,
    Have been Tom's food for seven long
      year.

Beware my follower.—Peace, Smulkin!
peace, thou fiend!

GLO. What, hath your grace no better
company?

EDG. The prince of darkness is a gentleman;
Modo he's call'd, and Mahu.

GLO. Our flesh and blood, my lord, is
grown so vile,
That it doth hate what gets it.

EDG. Poor Tom's a-cold.

GLO. Go in with me: my duty cannot
suffer
To obey in all your daughter's hard commands:
Though their injunction be to bar my
doors,
And let this tyrannous night take hold upon
you,
Yet have I ventur'd to come seek you out,
And bring you where both fire and food is
ready.

LEAR. First let me talk with this philosopher.—
What is the cause of thunder?

KENT. Good my lord, take his offer; go
into the house.

LEAR. I'll talk a word with this same
learned Theban.—
What is your study?

EDG. How to prevent the fiend, and to kill
vermin.

LEAR. Let me ask you one word in private.

KENT. Importune him once more to go,
my lord;
His wits begin to unsettle.

GLO.   Canst thou blame him?
His daughters seek his death:—ah, that
good Kent!—
He said it would be thus,—poor banish'd
man!—
Thou say'st the king grows mad; I'll tell
thee, friend,
I am almost mad myself: I had a son,
Now outlaw'd from my blood; he sought
my life,
But lately, very late: I lov'd him, friend,
No father his son dearer: true to tell thee,
          [*Storm continues.*
The grief hath craz'd my wits.—What a
night's this!—
I do beseech your grace,—

LEAR.   O, cry you mercy, Sir.
Noble philosopher, your company.

EDG. Tom's a-cold.

GLO. In, fellow, there, into the hovel:
keep thee warm.

LEAR. Come, let's in all.

KENT.   This way, my lord.

LEAR.   With him;
I will keep still with my philosopher.

KENT. Good my lord, soothe him; let him
take the fellow.

GLO. Take him you on.

KENT. Sirrah, come on; go along with us.

LEAR. Come, good Athenian.

GLO.   No words, no words:
Hush.

EDG. Child Rowland to the dark tower
came,
    His word was still,—Fie, foh, and fum,
    I smell the blood of a British man.
                 [*Exeunt.*

SCENE V.—*A Room in* GLOSTER'S *Castle.*

    Enter CORNWALL *and* EDMUND.

CORN. I will have my revenge, ere I depart his house.

EDM. How, my lord, I may be censured,
that nature thus gives way to loyalty, something fears me to think of.

CORN. I now perceive, it was not altogether your brother's evil disposition
made him seek his death; but a provoking
merit, set-a-work by a reproveable badness
in himself.

EDM. How malicious is my fortune, that
I must repent to be just! This is the letter
he spoke of, which approves him an intelligent party to the advantages of France. O
heavens! that this treason were not, or not
I the detector!

CORN. Go with me to the duchess.

EDM. If the matter of this paper be certain, you have mighty business in hand.

CORN. True, or false, it hath made thee earl of Gloster. Seek out where thy father is, that he may be ready for our apprehension.

EDM. [*Aside.*] If I find him comforting the king, it will stuff his suspicion more fully.—[*To* CORN.] I will persevere in my course of loyalty, though the conflict be sore between that and my blood.

CORN. I will lay trust upon thee; and thou shalt find a dearer father in my love.
　　　　　　　　　　　　　　　[*Exeunt.*

————

SCENE VI.—*A Chamber in a Farm-House, adjoining the Castle.*

Enter GLOSTER, LEAR, KENT, Fool *and* EDGAR.

GLO. Here is better than the open air; take it thankfully. I will piece out the comfort with what addition I can: I will not be long from you.

KENT. All the power of his wits has given way to his impatience.—The gods reward your kindness!　　　　[*Exit* GLOSTER.

EDG. Fratteretto calls me; and tells me Nero is an angler in the lake of darkness. —Pray, innocent, and beware the foul fiend.

FOOL. Pr'ythee, nuncle, tell me whether a madman be a gentleman, or a yeoman?

LEAR. A king, a king!

FOOL. No, he's a yeoman, that has a gentleman to his son; for he's a mad yeoman, that sees his son a gentleman before him.

LEAR. To have a thousand with red burning spits.
Come whizzing in upon them,—

EDG. The foul fiend bites my back.

FOOL. He's mad, that trusts in the tameness of a wolf, a horse's health, a boy's love, or a whore's oath.

LEAR. It shall be done; I will arraign them straight.—
[*To* EDG.] Come, sit thou here, most learned justicer;—
[*To the* Fool.] Thou, sapient Sir, sit here. —Now, you she foxes!—

EDG. Look, where he stands and glares!— Wantest thou eyes at trial, Madam?
Come o'er the bourn, Bessy, to me,—

FOOL. Her boat hath a leak,
And she must not speak
Why she dares not come over to thee.

EDG. The foul fiend haunts poor Tom in the voice of a nightingale. Hopdance cries in Tom's belly for two white herring. Croak not, black angel; I have no food for thee.

KENT. How do you, Sir? Stand you not so amaz'd:
Will you lie down and rest upon the cushions?

LEAR. I'll see their trial first.—Bring in the evidence.—
[*To* EDG.] Thou robed man of justice, take thy place;—
[*To the* Fool.] And thou, his yoke-fellow of equity,
Bench by his side:—[*To* KENT.] you are o' the commission,
Sit you too.

EDG. Let us deal justly.
Sleepest, or wakest thou, jolly shepherd?
　　Thy sheep be in the corn;
And for one blast of thy minikin mouth,
　　Thy sheep shall take no harm.
Pur! the cat is grey.

LEAR. Arraign her first; 'tis Goneril. I here take my oath before this honourable assembly, she kicked the poor king her father.

FOOL. Come hither, mistress. Is your name Goneril?

LEAR. She cannot deny it.

FOOL. Cry you mercy, I took you for a joint-stool.

LEAR. And here's another, whose warp'd looks proclaim
What store her heart is made on.—Stop her there!
Arms, arms, sword, fire!—Corruption in the place!—
False justicer, why hast thou let her 'scape?

EDG. Bless thy five wits!

KENT. O pity!—Sir, where is the patience now,
That you so oft have boasted to retain?

EDG. [*Aside.*] My tears begin to take his part so much,
They'll mar my counterfeiting.

LEAR. The little dogs and all,
Tray, Blanch, and Sweet-heart, see, they bark at me.

EDG. Tom will throw his head at them.— Avaunt, you curs!
　　Be thy mouth or black or white,
　　Tooth that poisons if it bite;
　　Mastiff, greyhound, mongrel grim,
　　Hound or spaniel, brach or lym,
　　Or bobtail tike, or trundle-tail,—
　　Tom will make them weep and wail:
　　For, with throwing thus my head,
　　Dogs leap the hatch, and all are fled.
Do de, de, de. Sessa! Come, march to wakes and fairs, and market towns.—Poor Tom, thy horn is dry.

LEAR. Then let them anatomize Regan; see what breeds about her heart. Is there

any cause in nature, that makes these hard
hearts?—[*To* EDGAR.] You, Sir, I entertain
you for one of my hundred; only I do not
like the fashion of your garments: you will
say, they are Persian attire; but let them
be changed.

KENT. Now, good my lord, lie here, and
rest awhile.

LEAR. Make no noise, make no noise;
draw the curtains: so, so, so: we'll go to
supper i' the morning: so, so, so.

FOOL. And I'll go to bed at noon.

Re-enter GLOSTER.

GLO. Come hither, friend: where is the
king my master?

KENT. Here, Sir; but trouble him not, his
wits are gone.

GLO. Good friend, I pr'ythee, take him
in thy arms;
I have o'er-heard a plot of death upon him:
There is a litter ready; lay him in't,
And drive toward Dover, friend, where
thou shalt meet   [master:
Both welcome and protection. Take up thy
If thou should'st dally half an hour, his life,
With thine, and all that offer to defend him,
Stand in assured loss: take up, take up;
And follow me, that will to some provision
Give thee quick conduct.

KENT.   Oppress'd nature sleeps:—
This rest might yet have balm'd thy broken
senses,
Which, if convenience will not allow,
Stand in hard cure.—[*To the* Fool.] Come,
help to bear thy master;
Thou must not stay behind.

GLO.   Come, come, away.

[*Exeunt* KENT, GLOSTER, *and the* Fool,
bearing away LEAR.

EDG. When we our betters see bearing our
woes,
We scarcely think our miseries our foes.
Who alone suffers, suffers most i' the mind,
Leaving free things and happy shows
behind;   [o'erskip,
But then the mind much sufferance doth
When grief hath mates, and bearing fellow-
ship.
How light and portable my pain seems now,
When that which makes me bend, makes
the king bow;
He childed, as I father'd!—Tom, away!
Mark the high noises; and thyself bewray,
When false opinion, whose wrong thought
defiles thee,
In thy just proof, repeals and reconciles
thee.   [the king!
What will hap more to-night, safe 'scape
Lurk, lurk.   [*Exit.*

SCENE VII.—*A Room in* GLOSTER'S *Castle.*

Enter CORNWALL, REGAN, GONERIL,
EDMUND, *and* Servants.

CORN. Post speedily to my lord your
husband; show him this letter:—the army
of France is landed.—Seek out the traitor
Gloster.   [*Exeunt some of the* Servants.

REG. Hang him instantly.

GON. Pluck out his eyes.

CORN. Leave him to my displeasure.—
Edmund, keep you our sister company: the
revenges we are bound to take upon your
traitorous father are not fit for your beholding. Advise the duke, where you are
going, to a most festinate preparation: we
are bound to the like. Our posts shall be
swift and intelligent betwixt us.—Farewell,
dear sister:—farewell, my lord of Gloster.—

Enter OSWALD.

How now! Where's the king?

OSW. My lord of Gloster hath convey'd
him hence:
Some five or six and thirty of his knights,
Hot questrists after him, met him at gate;
Who, with some other of the lord's depend-
ants,   [they boast
Are gone with him toward Dover; where
To have well-armed friends.

CORN.   Get horses for your mistress.

GON. Farewell, sweet lord, and sister.

CORN. Edmund, farewell.—

[*Exeunt* GONERIL, EDMUND, *and* OSWALD.
        Go seek the traitor Gloster,
Pinion him like a thief, bring him before
us.   [*Exeunt other* Servants.
Though well we may not pass upon his
life
Without the form of justice, yet our power
Shall do a courtesy to our wrath, which
men
May blame, but not control.—Who's there?
The traitor?

Re-enter Servants, *with* GLOSTER.

REG. Ingrateful fox! 'tis he.

CORN. Bind fast his corky arms.

GLO. What mean your graces? Good my
friends, consider   [friends.
You are my guests: do me no foul play,

CORN. Bind him, I say.
        [Servants *bind him.*

REG.   Hard, hard.—O filthy traitor!

GLO. Unmerciful lady as you are, I am
none.

CORN. To this chair bind him.—Villain,
thou shalt find—
        [REGAN *plucks his beard.*

GLO. By the kind gods, 'tis most ignobly
To pluck me by the beard.   [done

REG. So white, and such a traitor!

GLO.   Naughty lady,
These hairs, which thou dost ravish from
    my chin,   [host:
Will quicken, and accuse thee: I am your
With robbers' hands my hospitable favours
You should not ruffle thus. What will you
    do?
CORN. Come, Sir, what letters had you
    late from France?
REG. Be simple-answer'd, for we know
    the truth.
CORN. And what confederacy have you
    with the traitors
Late footed in the kingdom?
REG. To whose hands have you sent the
    lunatic king? Speak.
GLO. I have a letter guessingly set down,
Which came from one that's of a neutral
And not from one oppos'd.   [heart,
CORN.   Cunning.
REG.   And false.
CORN. Where hast thou sent the king?
GLO.   To Dover.
REG. Wherefore to Dover? Wast thou
    not charg'd at peril—
CORN. Wherefore to Dover? Let him
    answer that.   [stand the course.
GLO. I am tied to the stake, and I must
REG. Wherefore to Dover?
GLO. Because I would not see thy cruel
    nails   [sister
Pluck out his poor old eyes; nor thy fierce
In his anointed flesh stick boarish fangs.
The sea, with such a storm as his bare
    head   [buoy'd up,
In hell-black night endured, would have
And quench'd the stelled fires:
Yet, poor old heart, he holp the heavens
    to rain.   [stern time,
If wolves had at thy gate, howl'd that
Thou should'st have said, "Good porter,
    turn the key,"
All cruels else subscrib'd: but I shall see
The winged vengeance overtake such
    children.
CORN. See it shalt thou never.—Fellows,
    hold the chair.—
Upon these eyes of thine I'll set my foot.
GLO. He that will think to live till he be
    old,
Give me some help!—O cruel!—O ye
    gods!
REG. One side will mock another; the
    other too.
CORN. If you see vengeance,—
1 SERV.   Hold your hand, my lord:
I have serv'd you ever since I was a child,
But better service have I never done you,
Than now to bid you hold.
REG.   How now, you dog!

1 SERV. If you did wear a beard upon
    your chin,   [mean?
I'd shake it on this quarrel. What do you
CORN. My villain!   [Draws.
1 SERV. Nay then, come on, and take the
    chance of anger.
            [Draws. They fight. CORNWALL is
                wounded.
REG. Give me thy sword.—A peasant
    stand up thus!
        [Takes a sword from another Servant,
            and stabs first Servant.
1 SERV. O, I am slain!—My lord, you
    have one eye left
To see some mischief on him.—O! [Dies.
CORN. Lest it see more, prevent it.—
    Out, vile jelly!
Where is thy lustre now?
GLO. All dark and comfortless—Where's
    my son Edmund?
Edmund, enkindle all the sparks of nature,
To quit this horrid act.
REG.   Out, treacherous villain!
Thou call'st on him that hates thee: it was
    he   [us;
That made the overture of thy treasons to
Who is too good to pity thee.
GLO. O my follies! Then Edgar was
    abus'd.—
Kind gods, forgive me that, and prosper
    him!
REG. Go thrust him out at gates, and
    let him smell
His way to Dover.—How is't, my lord?
    How look you?
CORN. I have receiv'd a hurt:—follow me
    lady.—   [slave
Turn out that eyeless villain;—throw this
Upon the dunghill.—Regan, I bleed apace:
Untimely comes this hurt: give me your
    arm.
        [Exit CORNWALL, led by REGAN.—Some
            of the Servants unbind GLOSTER,
            and lead him out.
2 SERV. I'll never care what wickedness
If this man come to good.   [I do,
3 SERV.   If she live long,
And, in the end, meet the old course of
    death,
Women will all turn monsters.
2 SERV. Let's follow the old earl, and get
    the Bedlam
To lead him where he would: his roguish
Allows itself to any thing.   [madness
3 SERV. Go thou: I'll fetch some flax,
    and whites of eggs,
To apply to his bleeding face. Now, heaven
    help him!   [Exeunt severally.

ACT IV.

Scene I.—*The Heath.*

Enter Edgar.

EDG. Yet better thus, and known to be contemn'd,
Than still contemn'd and flatter'd. To be worst, [tune,
The lowest and most dejected thing of for-
Stands still in esperance, lives not in fear:
The lamentable change is from the best;
The worst returns to laughter. Welcome, then,
Thou unsubstantial air, that I embrace!
The wretch, that thou hast blown unto the worst,
Owes nothing to thy blasts.—But who comes here?—

Enter Gloster, *led by an* Old Man.

My father, poorly led?—World, world, O world! [hate thee
But that thy strange mutations make us
Life would not yield to age.
OLD MAN. O my good lord, I have been your tenant, and your father's tenant, these fourscore years.
GLO. Away, get thee away; good friend, be gone:
Thy comforts can do me no good at all;
Thee they may hurt.
OLD MAN. Alack, Sir, you cannot see your way.
GLO. I have no way, and therefore want no eyes;
I stumbled when I saw: full oft 'tis seen,
Our means secure us, and our mere defects
Prove our commodities.—Ah, dear son Edgar,
The food of thy abused father's wrath!
Might I but live to see thee in my touch,
I'd say I had eyes again!
OLD MAN. How now! Who's there?
EDG. [*Aside.*] O gods! Who is't can say, "I am at the worst?"
I am worse than e'er I was.
OLD MAN. 'Tis poor mad Tom.
EDG. [*Aside.*] And worse I may be yet: the worst is not,
So long as we can say, "This is the worst."
OLD MAN. Fellow, where goest?
GLO. Is it a beggar-man?
OLD MAN. Madman, and beggar too.
GLO. He has some reason, else he could not beg. [saw,
I' the last night's storm I such a fellow
Which made me think a man a worm: my son
Came then into my mind; and yet my mind
Was then scarce friends with him: I have heard more since.

As flies to wanton boys, are we to the [gods,—
They kill us for their sport.
EDG. [*Aside.*] How should this be?—
Bad is the trade that must play fool to sorrow,
Angering itself and others.—[*To* Glo.]
Bless thee, master!
GLO. Is that the naked fellow?
OLD MAN. Ay, my lord.
GLO. Then, pr'ythee, get thee gone: if, for my sake, [twain,
Thou wilt o'ertake us, hence a mile or
I' the way toward Dover, do it for ancient love; [soul,
And bring some covering for this naked
Whom I'll entreat to lead me.
OLD MAN. Alack, Sir, he is mad.
GLO. 'Tis the times' plague, when madmen lead the blind.
Do as I bid thee, or rather do thy pleasure;
Above the rest, be gone.
OLD MAN. I'll bring him the best 'parel that I have,
Come on't what will. [*Exit.*
GLO. Sirrah, naked fellow,—
EDG. Poor Tom's a-cold.—[*Aside.*] I cannot daub it farther.
GLO. Come hither, fellow.
EDG. [*Aside.*] And yet I must.—[*To* Glo.] Bless thy sweet eyes, they bleed.
GLO. Know'st thou the way to Dover?
EDG. Both stile and gate, horse-way and foot-path. Poor Tom hath been scared out of his good wits: bless thee, good man's son, from the foul fiend! Five fiends have been in poor Tom at once; of lust, as Obidicut; Hobbididance, prince of dumbness; Mahu, of stealing; Modo, of murder; and Flibbertigibbet, of mopping and mowing,—who since possesses chambermaids and waiting-women. So, bless thee, master!
GLO. Here, take this purse, thou whom the heavens' plagues
Have humbled to all strokes: that I am wretched, [so still!
Makes thee the happier:—Heavens, deal
Let the superfluous and lust-dieted man,
That slaves your ordinance, that will not see [quickly,
Because he doth not feel, feel your power
So distribution should undo excess,
And each man have enough.—Dost thou know Dover?
EDG. Ay, master.
GLO. There is a cliff, whose high and bending head
Looks fearfully in the confined deep:
Bring me but to the very brim of it,
And I'll repair the misery thou dost bear,
With something rich about me: from that

I shall no leading need.   [place
EDG.   Give me thy arm:
Poor Tom shall lead thee.   [Exeunt.

SCENE II.—Before the DUKE of ALBANY's
Palace.

Enter GONERIL and EDMUND; OSWALD
meeting them.

GON. Welcome, my lord: I marvel, our
mild husband
Not met us on the way.—Now, where's
your master?
OSW. Madam, within; but never man so
chang'd.
I told him of the army that was landed;
He smil'd at it: I told him you were
coming;
His answer was, "The worse:" of Gloster's
treachery,
And of the loyal service of his son,
When I inform'd him, then he call'd me
sot,
And told me I had turn'd the wrong side
out:—
What most he should dislike, seems pleas-
What like, offensive.   [ant to him;
GON. [To EDMUND.] Then, shall you go
no farther.
It is the cowish terror of his spirit,
That dares not undertake: he'll not feel
wrongs,   [the way
Which tie him to an answer. Our wishes on
May prove effects. Back, Edmund, to my
brother;   [powers:
Hasten his musters, and conduct his
I must change arms at home, and give the
distaff   [servant
Into my husband's hands. This trusty
Shall pass between us: ere long you are
like to hear,
If you dare venture in your own behalf,
A mistress's command. Wear this; spare
speech;   [Giving a favour.
Decline your head: this kiss, if it durst
speak,
Would stretch thy spirits up into the
Conceive, and fare thee well.   [air:—
EDM. Yours in the ranks of death.
GON.   My most dear Gloster!
[Exit EDMUND.
O, the difference of man and man!
To thee a woman's services are due:
My fool usurps my body.
OSW.   Madam, here comes my lord.
[Exit.
Enter ALBANY.
GON. I have been worth the whistle.
ALB.   O Goneril!

You are not worth the dust which the rude
wind
Blows in your face.—I fear your disposi-
tion:
That nature, which contemns its origin,
Cannot be border'd certain in itself;
She that herself will sliver and disbranch
From her material sap, perforce must
And come to deadly use.   [wither,
GON. No more; the text is foolish.
ALB. Wisdom and goodness to the vile
seem vile:
Filths savour but themselves. What have
you done?   [perform'd?
Tigers, not daughters, what have you
A father, and a gracious aged man,
Whose reverence the head-lugg'd bear
would lick,
Most barbarous, most degenerate! have you
madded.
Could my good brother suffer you to do it?
A man, a prince, by him so benefited?
If that the heavens do not their visible
spirits
Send quickly down to tame these vile
It will come,   [offences,
Humanity must perforce prey on itself,
Like monsters of the deep.
GON.   Milk-liver'd man!
That bear'st a cheek for blows, a head for
wrongs;   [ing
Who hast not in thy brows an eye discern-
Thine honour from thy suffering; that not
know'st,
Fools do those villains pity, who are pun-
ish'd
Ere they have done their mischief. Where's
thy drum?
France spreads his banners in our noise-
less land;   [threats;
With plumed helm thy slayer begins
Whilst thou, a moral fool, sitt'st still, and
"Alack, why does he so?"   [criest,
ALB.   See thyself, devil!
Proper deformity seems not in the fiend
So horrid, as in woman.
GON.   O vain fool!
ALB. Thou changed and self-cover'd thing,
for shame,
Be-monster not thy feature. Were't my
fitness
To let these hands obey my blood,
They are apt enough to dislocate and tear
Thy flesh and bones:—howe'er thou art a
fiend,
A woman's shape doth shield thee.
GON. Marry, your manhood now!
Enter a Messenger.
ALB. What news?
MESS. O, my good lord, the duke of
Cornwall's dead;

Slain by his servant, going to put out
The other eye of Gloster.

ALB.   Gloster's eyes!

MESS. A servant that he bred, thrill'd
with remorse,
Oppos'd against the act, bending his sword
To his great master; who, thereat enrag'd,
Flew on him, and among'st them fell'd
him dead;   [since
But not without that harmful stroke, which
Hath pluck'd him after.

ALB.   This shows you are above,
You justicers, that these our nether crimes
So speedily can venge!—But, O poor
Lost he his other eye?   [Gloster!

MESS.   Both, both, my lord.—
This letter, Madam, craves a speedy
'Tis from your sister.   [answer;

GON. [*Aside.*] One way I like this well;
But being widow, and my Gloster with her,
May all the building in my fancy pluck
Upon my hateful life: another way,
The news is not so tart.—[*To Mess.*] I'll
read, and answer.   [*Exit.*

ALB. Where was his son, when they did
take his eyes?

MESS. Come with my lady hither.

ALB.   He is not here.

MESS. No, my good lord; I met him back
again.

ALB. Knows he the wickedness?

MESS. Ay, my good lord; 'twas he inform'd against him;
And quit the house, on purpose that their
punishment
Might have the freer course.

ALB.   Gloster, I live
To thank thee for the love thou show'dst
the king,   [friend:
And to revenge thine eyes.—Come hither,
Tell me what more thou knowest.
                            [*Exeunt.*

SCENE III.—*The French Camp near* DOVER.

Enter KENT *and* Gentleman.

KENT. Why the king of France is so
suddenly gone back know you the reason?

GENT. Something he left imperfect in the
state,   [of; which
Which since his coming forth is thought
Imports to the kingdom so much fear and
danger,
That his personal return was most requir'd
And necessary.

KENT. Whom hath he left behind him
general?

GENT. The Mareschal of France, Monsieur La Far.

KENT. Did your letters pierce the queen
to any demonstration of grief?

GENT. Ay, Sir; she took them, read
them in my presence;
And now and then an ample tear trill'd
down   [queen
Her delicate cheek: it seem'd she was a
Over her passion; who, most rebel-like,
Sought to be king o'er her.

KENT.   O, then it mov'd her.

GENT. Not to a rage: patience and sor-
row strove   [have seen
Who should express her goodliest. You
Sunshine and rain at once: her smiles and
tears
Were like a better way: those happy
smilets,   [know
That play'd on her ripe lip, seem'd not to
What guests were in her eyes; which
parted thence,
As pearls from diamonds dropp'd.—In
brief, sorrow
Would be a rarity most belov'd, if all
Could so become it.

KENT.   Made she no verbal question?

GENT. 'Faith, once or twice she heav'd
the name of "father"
Pantingly forth, as if it press'd her heart;
Cried, "Sisters! sisters!—Shame of ladies!
sisters!
Kent! father! sisters! What, i' the storm?
i' the night?
Let pity not be believed!"—There she
shook
The holy water from her heavenly eyes,
And clamour moisten'd: then away she
To deal with grief alone.   [started

KENT.   It is the stars,
The stars above us, govern our conditions;
Else one self mate and mate could not
beget
Such different issues. You spoke not with
her since?

GENT. No.

KENT. Was this before the king return'd?

GENT.   No, since.

KENT. Well, Sir, the poor distress'd
Lear's in the town,
Who sometime, in his better tune, remem-
bers
What we are come about, and by no means
Will yield to see his daughter.

GENT.   Why, good Sir?

KENT. A sovereign shame so elbows him:
his own unkindness
That stripp'd her from his benediction,
turn'd her
To foreign casualties, gave her dear rights
To his dog-hearted daughters,—these
things sting
His mind so venomously, that burning
shame
Detains him from Cordelia.

GENT.   Alack, poor gentleman!
KENT. Of Albany's and Cornwall's pow-
ers you heard not?
GENT. 'Tis so, they are afoot.
KENT. Well, Sir, I'll bring you to our
master Lear,
And leave you to attend him: some dear
cause
Will in concealment wrap me up awhile;
When I am known aright, you shall not
grieve   [go
Lending me this acquaintance. I pray you,
Along with me.   [Exeunt.

SCENE IV.—A Tent in the French Camp.

Enter CORDELIA, Physician, and Soldiers.
COR. Alack, 'tis he: why, he was met
even now
As mad as the vex'd sea; singing aloud;
Crown'd with rank fumiter, and furrow
weeds,
With harlocks, hemlock, nettles, cuckoo-
flowers,
Darnel, and all the idle weeds that grow
In our sustaining corn.—A century send
forth;
Search every acre in the high-grown field,
And bring him to our eye.—
                        [Exit an Officer.
               What can man's wisdom,
In the restoring his bereaved sense?
He, that helps him, take all my outward
worth.
PHY. There is means, Madam:
Our foster-nurse of nature is repose,
The which he lacks; that to provoke in
him,
Are many simples operative, whose power
Will close the eye of anguish.
COR.   All bless'd secrets,
All you unpublish'd virtues of the earth,
Spring with my tears! be aidant and
remediate
In the good man's distress!—Seek, seek
for him;
Lest his ungovern'd rage dissolve the life
That wants the means to lead it.
             Enter a Messenger.
MESS.   News, Madam;
The British powers are marching hither-
ward.
COR. 'Tis known before; our preparation
stands
In expectation of them.—O dear father,
It is thy business that I go about;
Therefore great France
My mourning, and important tears, hath
pitied.
No blown ambition doth our arms incite,

But love, dear love, and our ag'd father's
right:
Soon may I hear and see him!   [Exeunt.

SCENE V.—A Room in GLOSTER'S Castle.

          Enter REGAN and OSWALD.
REG. But are my brother's powers set
forth?
OSW. Ay, Madam.
REG. Himself in person there?
OSW.   Madam with much ado:
Your sister is the better soldier.
REG. Lord Edmund spake not with your
lord at home?
OSW. No, Madam.
REG. What might import my sister's let-
ter to him?
OSW. I know not, lady.
REG. 'Faith, he is posted hence on seri-
ous matter.
It was great ignorance, Gloster's eyes being
out,
To let him live: where he arrives he moves
All hearts against us: Edmund, I think, is
gone,
In pity of his misery, to despatch
His nighted life; moreover, to descry
The strength o' the enemy.
OSW. I must needs after him, Madam,
with my letter.
REG. Our troops set forth to-morrow:
stay with us;
The ways are dangerous.
OSW.   I may not, Madam:
My lady charg'd my duty in this business.
REG. Why should she write to Edmund?
Might not you
Transport her purposes by word? Belike
Something—I know not what:—I'll love
thee much;
Let me unseal the letter.
OSW.   Madam, I had rather—
REG. I know your lady does not love her
husband;
I am sure of that: and, at her late being
here,
She gave strange eyeliads, and most speak-
ing looks
To noble Edmund. I know you are of her
bosom.
OSW. I, Madam?
REG. I speak in understanding: you are,
I know it;
Therefore I do advise you, take this note:
My lord is dead; Edmund and I have
talk'd;
And more convenient is he for my hand,
Than for your lady's:—you may gather
more.

If you do find him, pray you, give him this;

And when your mistress hears thus much from you,

I pray, desire her call her wisdom to her.
So, fare you well.

If you do chance to hear of that blind traitor,

Preferment falls on him that cuts him off.

OSW. Would I could meet him, Madam! I would show

What party I do follow.

REG.   Fare thee well.   [*Exeunt.*

———

SCENE VI.—*The Country near* DOVER.

Enter GLOSTER, *and* EDGAR *dressed like a peasant.*

GLO. When shall I come to the top of that same hill?

EDG. You do climb up it now: look, how we labour.

GLO. Methinks the ground is even.

EDG.   Horrible steep.
Hark, do you hear the sea?

GLO.   No, truly.

EDG. Why, then your other senses grow imperfect

By your eyes' anguish.

GLO.   So may it be, indeed.
Methinks thy voice is alter'd; and thou speak'st

In better phrase and matter than thou didst.

EDG. You're much deceiv'd: in nothing am I chang'd,

But in my garments.

GLO.   Methinks you're better spoken.

EDG. Come on, Sir; here's the place: stand still.—How fearful

And dizzy 'tis, to cast one's eyes so low!

The crows, and choughs, that wing the midway air,

Show scarce so gross as beetles: half way down

Hangs one that gathers samphire,—dreadful trade!

Methinks he seems no bigger than his head:

The fishermen that walk upon the beach,

Appear like mice; and yon tall anchoring bark,

Diminish'd to her cock; her cock, a buoy

Almost too small for sight: the murmuring surge,

That on th' unnumber'd idle pebbles chafes,

Cannot be heard so high.—I'll look no more;

Lest my brain turn, and the deficient sight
Topple down headlong.

GLO.   Set me where you stand.

EDG. Give me your hand:—you are now within a foot

Of th' extreme verge: for all beneath the moon

Would I not leap upright.   [moon

GLO.   Let go my hand.
Here, friend, is another purse; in it, a jewel

Well worth a poor man's taking: fairies and gods

Prosper it with thee! Go thou farther off;

Bid me farewell, and let me hear thee going.

EDG. Now fare you well, good Sir.

GLO.   With all my heart.

EDG. [*Aside.*] Why I trifle thus with his despair,

Is done to cure it.

GLO.   O you mighty gods!
This world I do renounce, and, in your sights,

Shake patiently my great affliction off:

If I could bear it longer, and not fall

To quarrel with your great opposeless wills,

My snuff, and loathed part of nature, should

Burn itself out. If Edgar live, O, bless him!

Now, fellow, fare thee well.   [him!

EDG.   Gone, Sir:—farewell.
         [GLOSTER *leaps, and falls along.*

[*Aside.*] And yet I know not how conceit may rob

The treasury of life, when life itself

Yields to the theft: had he been where he thought,

By this, had thought been past.—Alive, or dead?

[*To* GLO.] Ho, you Sir! friend!—Hear you, Sir?—speak!—

[*Aside.*] Thus might he pass indeed;—yet he revives.

[*To* GLO.] What are you, Sir?

GLO.   Away, and let me die.

EDG. Hadst thou been aught but gossamer, feathers, air,

So many fathom down precipitating,

Thou'dst shiver'd like an egg: but thou dost breathe;

Hast heavy substance; bleed'st not; speak'st; art sound.

Ten masts at each make not the altitude,

Which thou hast perpendicularly fell:

Thy life's a miracle. Speak yet again.

GLO. But have I fallen, or no?

EDG. From the dread summit of this chalky bourn.

Look up a-height;—the shrill-gorg'd lark so far

Cannot be seen or heard: do but look up.

GLO. Alack, I have no eyes.—
Is wretchedness depriv'd that benefit,
To end itself by death? 'Twas yet some
    comfort,
When misery could beguile the tyrant's
    rage,
And frustrate his proud will.
EDG.   Give me your arm:
Up:—so.—How is't? Feel you your legs?
    You stand.
GLO. Too well, too well.
EDG.   This is above all strangeness.
Upon the crown o' the cliff, what thing
Which parted from you?   [was that
GLO.   A poor unfortunate beggar.
EDG. As I stood here below, methought
    his eyes
Were two full moons; he had a thousand
    noses,
Horns whelk'd and wav'd like the enridged
    sea:
It was some fiend; therefore, thou happy
    father,
Think that the clearest gods, who make
    them honours
Of men's impossibilities, have preserv'd
    thee.
GLO. I do remember now: henceforth I'll
    bear
Affliction, till it do cry out itself.
"Enough, enough," and die. That thing
    you speak of,
I took it for a man; often 'twould say,
"The fiend, the fiend:" he led me to that
    place.
EDG. Bear free and patient thoughts.—
    But who comes here?

Enter LEAR, *fantastically dressed with wild
            flowers.*

The safer sense will ne'er accommodate
His master thus.
LEAR. No, they cannot touch me for coin-
    ing; I am the king himself.
EDG. O, thou side-piercing sight!
LEAR. Nature's above art in that respect.
—There's your press-money. That fellow
handles his bow like a crow-keeper: draw
me a clothier's yard.—Look, look, a mouse!
Peace, peace;—this piece of toasted cheese
will do't.—There's my gauntlet; I'll prove
it on a giant.—Bring up the brown bills.—
O, well flown, bird!—i' the clout, i' the
clout: hewgh!—Give the word.
EDG. Sweet marjoram.
LEAR. Pass.
GLO. I know that voice.
LEAR. Ha! Goneril!—with a white
beard!—They flatter'd me like a dog; and
told me, I had white hairs in my beard,
ere the black ones were there. To say
"ay," and "no," to every thing I said!—

"Ay" and "no" too, was no good divinity.
When the rain came to wet me once, and
the wind to make me chatter; when the
thunder would not peace at my bidding;
there I found them, there I smelt them out.
Go to, they are not men o' their words:
they told me I was every thing; 'tis a lie,
—I am not ague-proof.
GLO. The trick of that voice I do well re-
Is't not the king?   [member:
LEAR.   Ay, every inch a king:
When I do stare, see how the subject
    quakes.
I pardon that man's life.—What was thy
    cause?—
Adultery?—
Thou shalt not die: die for adultery! No:
The wren goes to't, and the small gilded fly
Does lecher in my sight.
Let copulation thrive; for Gloster's bastard
    son
Was kinder to his father, than my daugh-
Got 'tween the lawful sheets.   [ters
To't, luxury, pell-mell! for I lack soldiers.—
Behold yon simpering dame,
Whose face between her forks presageth
    snow;
That minces virtue, and does shake the
    head
To hear of pleasure's name;—
The fitchew, nor the soiled horse, goes to't
With a more riotous appetite.
Down from the waist they are centaurs,
Though women all above:
But to the girdle do the gods inherit,
Beneath is all the fiends'; there's hell,
there's darkness, there is the sulphurous pit,
burning, scalding, stench, consumption;—
fie, fie, fie, pah, pah! Give me an ounce
of civet, good apothecary, to sweeten my
imagination: there's money for thee.
GLO. O, let me kiss that hand!
LEAR. Let me wipe it first; it smells of
    mortality.
GLO. O ruin'd piece of nature! This great
    world
Shall so wear out to naught.—Dost thou
    know me?
LEAR. I remember thine eyes well enough.
Dost thou squiny at me? No, do thy worst,
blind Cupid; I'll not love.—Read thou
this challenge: mark but the penning of it.
GLO. Were all the letters suns, I could
    not see one.
EDG. [*Aside.*] I would not take this from
    report;—it is,
And my heart breaks at it.
LEAR. Read.
GLO. What, with the case of eyes?

LEAR. O, ho, are you there with me? No eyes in your head, nor no money in your purse? Your eyes are in a heavy case, your purse in a light: yet you see how this world goes.

GLO. I see it feelingly.

LEAR. What, art mad? A man may see how this world goes, with no eyes. Look with thine ears: see how yon justice rails upon yon simple thief. Hark, in thine ear: change places; and handy-dandy, which is the justice, which is the thief?—Thou hast seen a farmer's dog bark at a beggar?

GLO. Ay, Sir.

LEAR. And the creature run from the cur? There thou might'st behold the great image of authority: a dog's obey'd in office.—

Thou rascal beadle, hold thy bloody hand! Why dost thou lash that whore? Strip thine own back;

Thou hotly lust'st to use her in that kind For which thou whipp'st her. The usurer hangs the cozener.

Through tatter'd clothes small vices do appear;

Robes and furr'd gowns hide all. Plate sin with gold,

And the strong lance of justice hurtless breaks;

Arm it in rags, a pigmy's straw doth pierce it.

None does offend, none,—I say, none; I'll able 'em:

Take that of me, my friend, who have the power

To seal th' accuser's lips. Get thee glass eyes;

And, like a scurvy politician, seem To see the things thou dost not.—Now, now, now, now:

Pull off my boots:—harder, harder:—so.

EDG. [*Aside.*] O, matter and impertinency mix'd!

Reason in madness!

LEAR. If thou wilt weep my fortunes, take my eyes.

I know thee well enough; thy name is Gloster:

Thou must be patient; we came crying hither:

Thou know'st, the first time that we smell the air,

We wawl and cry. I will preach to thee: mark me.

GLO. Alack! alack the day!

LEAR. When we are born, we cry that we are come

To this great stage of fools,—this' a good block:—

It were a delicate stratagem, to shoe

A troop of horse with felt: I'll put it in proof;

And when I have stolen upon these sons-in-law,

Then, kill, kill, kill, kill, kill, kill!

Enter Gentleman *with* Attendants.

GENT. O, here he is: lay hand upon him. —Sir,

Your most dear daughter—

LEAR. No rescue? What, a prisoner? I am even

The natural fool of fortune.—Use me well;

You shall have ransom. Let me have a surgeon,

I am cut to the brains.   [surgeon,

GENT.   You shall have any thing.

LEAR. No seconds? All myself?

Why, this would make a man a man of salt,

To use his eyes for garden water-pots,

Ay, and laying autumn's dust.

GENT.   Good Sir,—

LEAR. I will die bravely,

Like a smug bridegroom. What! I will be jovial:

Come, come; I am a king, my masters, know you that?

GENT. You are a royal one, and we obey you.

LEAR. Then there's life in it. Nay, an you get it, you shall get it by running. Sa, sa, sa, sa.   [*Exit.* Attendants *follow.*

GENT. A sight most pitiful in the meanest wretch,

Past speaking of in a king!—Thou hast one daughter,

Who redeems nature from the general curse

Which twain have brought her to.

EDG. Hail, gentle Sir!

GENT. Sir speed you: what's your will?

EDG. Do you hear aught, Sir, of a battle toward?

GENT. Most sure and vulgar: every one hears that

Which can distinguish sound.

EDG.   But by your favour,

How near's the other army?

GENT. Near, and on speedy foot; the main descry

Stands on the hourly thought.

EDG.   I thank you, Sir: that's all.

GENT. Though that the queen on special cause is here,

Her army is mov'd on.

EDG.   I thank you, Sir.

          [*Exit* Gent.

GLO. You ever-gentle gods, take my breath from me;

Let not my worser spirit tempt me again

To die before you please!

EDG.   Well pray you, father.

GLO. Now, good Sir, what are you?

EDG. A most poor man, made tame to fortune's blows;
Who, by the art of known and feeling sorrows,
Am pregnant to good pity. Give me your hand,
I'll lead you to some biding.   [hand,

GLO.   Hearty thanks:
The bounty and the benison of heaven
To boot, and boot!

        Enter OSWALD.

OSW.   A proclaim'd prize! Most happy!
That eyeless head of thine was first fram'd flesh
To raise my fortunes.—Thou old unhappy traitor,
Briefly thyself remember:—the sword is
That must destroy thee.   [out

GLO.   Now let thy friendly hand
Put strength enough to it.

       [EDGAR *interposes.*

OSW.   Wherefore, bold peasant,
Dar'st thou support a publish'd traitor? Hence;
Lest that th' infection of his fortune take
Like hold on thee. Let go his arm.

EDG. Chill not let go, zir, without varther 'casion.

OSW. Let go, slave, or thou diest.

EDG. Good gentleman, go your gait, and let poor volk pass. And ch'ud ha' been zwagger'd out of my life, 'twould not ha' been zo long as 'tis by a vortnight. Nay, come not near the old man; keep out, che vor'ye, or Ise try whether your costard or my ballow be the harder. Ch'ill be plain with you.

OSW. Out, dunghill!

EDG. Ch'ill pick your teeth, zir: come; no matter vor your foins.

   [*They fight and* EDGAR *knocks him down.*

OSW. Slave, thou hast slain me:—villain, take my purse:
If ever thou wilt thrive, bury my body;
And give the letters, which thou find'st about me,
To Edmund earl of Gloster; seek him out
Upon the British party:—O, untimely death!   [*Dies.*

EDG. I know thee well: a serviceable villain;
As duteous to the vices of thy mistress,
As badness would desire.

GLO.   What, is he dead?

EDG. Sit you down, father; rest you.—
Let's see his pockets: these letters, that he speaks of,
May be my friends.—He's dead; I am only sorry
He had no other deathsman.—Let us see:—

Leave, gentle wax; and, manners, blame us not:
To know our enemies' minds, we'd rip their hearts;
Their papers, is more lawful.
[*Reads.*] "Let our reciprocal vows be remembered. You have many opportunities to cut him off: if your will want not, time and place will be fruitfully offered. There is nothing done, if he return the conqueror: then am I the prisoner, and his bed my goal; from the loathed warmth whereof deliver me, and supply the place for your labour.
     "Your (wife, so I would say)
        "affectionate servant,
,   GONERIL."

O undistinguish'd space of woman's will!
A plot upon her virtuous husband's life;
And the exchange, my brother!—Here, in the sands,
Thee I'll rake up, the post unsanctified
Of murderous lechers: and, in the mature time,
With this ungracious paper strike the sight
Of the death-practis'd duke: for him 'tis well,
That of thy death and business I can tell.

GLO. The king is mad: how stiff is my vile sense,
That I stand up, and have ingenious feeling
Of my huge sorrows! Better I were distract:
So should my thoughts be sever'd from my griefs;
And woes, by wrong imaginations, lose
The knowledge of themselves.

        [*Drum afar off.*

EDG.   Give me your hand:
Far off, methinks, I hear the beaten drum:
Come, father, I'll bestow you with a friend.
        [*Exeunt.*

SCENE VII.—*A Tent in the French Camp.*

LEAR *on a bed, asleep; soft music playing:*
Physician, Gentleman, and others, attending. Enter CORDELIA *and* KENT.

COR. O thou good Kent! how shall I live and work,
To match thy goodness? My life will be too short,
And every measure fail me.

KENT. To be acknowledg'd, Madam is o'er-paid.
All my reports go with the modest truth;
Nor more, nor clipp'd, but so.

COR.   Be better suited:
These weeds are memories of those worser
I pr'ythee, put them off.   [hours:

KENT.   Pardon, dear Madam;
Yet to be known shortens my made intent:
My boon I make it, that you know me not,
Till time and I think meet.

COR. Then be't so, my good lord.—[*To the* Phy.]
How does the king?

PHY. Madam, sleeps still.

COR. O you kind gods,
Cure this great breach in his abused nature!
Th' untun'd and jarring senses, O, wind up
Of this child-changed father!

PHY.   So please your majesty,
That we may wake the king: he hath slept long.

COR. Be govern'd by your knowledge, and proceed
I' the sway of your own will. Is he array'd?

GENT. Ay, Madam; in the heaviness of sleep,
We put fresh garments on him.

PHY. Be by, good Madam, when we do awake him;
I doubt not of his temperance.

COR.   Very well.

PHY. Please you, draw near.—Louder the music there!

COR. O my dear father! Restoration, hang
Thy medicine on my lips; and let this kiss
Repair those violent harms, that my two sisters
Have in thy reverence made!   [sisters

KENT.   Kind and dear princess!

COR. Had you not been their father, these white flakes
Had challeng'd pity of them. Was this a face
To be expos'd against the warring winds?
To stand against the deep dread-bolted thunder?
In the most terrible and nimble stroke
Of quick, cross lightning? to watch (poor perdu!)
With this thin helm? Mine enemy's dog,
Though he had bit me, should have stood that night
Against my fire; and wast thou fain, poor father,
To hovel thee with swine, and rogues forlorn,
In short and musty straw? Alack, alack!
'Tis wonder, that thy life and wits at once
Had not concluded all.—He wakes; speak to him.

PHY. Madam, do you; 'tis fittest.

COR. How does my royal lord? How fares your majesty?

LEAR. You do me wrong to take me out o' the grave:—
Thou art a soul in bliss; but I am bound
Upon a wheel of fire, that mine own tears
Do scald like molten lead.

COR.   Sir, do you know me?

LEAR. You are a spirit, I know: when did you die?

COR. Still, still, far wide.   [you die?

PHY. He's scarce awake: let him alone awhile.

LEAR. Where have I been? Where am I?
—Fair day-light?—
I am mightily abus'd.—I should even die with pity,
To see another thus.—I know not what to say.—
I will not swear these are my hands:—let's see;
I feel this pin prick. Would I were assur'd
Of my condition!

COR.   O, look upon me, Sir,
And hold your hands in benediction o'er
No, Sir, you must not kneel.   [me:—

LEAR.   Pray, do not mock me:
I am a very foolish fond old man,
Fourscore and upward, not an hour more
And, to deal plainly,   [nor less;
I fear I am not in my perfect mind.
Methinks I should know you, and know this man;
Yet I am doubtful: for I am mainly ignorant
What place this is; and all the skill I have
Remembers not these garments; nor I know
Where I did lodge last night.   [not
Do not laugh at me;
For, as I am a man, I think this lady
To be my child Cordelia.

COR.   And so I am, I am.

LEAR. Be your tears wet? Yes, 'faith. I pray, weep not:
If you have poison for me, I will drink it.
I know you do not love me; for your sisters
Have as I do remember, done me wrong:
You have some cause, they have not.

COR.   No cause, no cause.

LEAR. Am I in France?

KENT.   In your own kingdom, Sir.

LEAR. Do not abuse me.

PHY. Be comforted, good Madam: the great rage,
You see, is cur'd in him: and yet it is danger
To make him even o'er the time he has lost.
Desire him to go in; trouble him no more,
Till farther settling.

COR. Will't please your highness walk?

LEAR.   You must bear with me:
Pray you now, forget and forgive: I am old and foolish.
[*Exeunt* LEAR, CORDELIA, Physician, *and* Attendants.

GENT. Holds it true, Sir, that the duke of Cornwall was so slain?

KENT. Most certain, Sir.

GENT. Who is conductor of his people?

KENT. As 'tis said, the bastard son of Gloster.

GENT. They say, Edgar, his banished son, is with the earl of Kent in Germany.

KENT. Report is changeable. 'Tis time to look about; the powers of the kingdom approach apace.

GENT. The arbitrement is like to be bloody. Fare you well, Sir.　　　[*Exit.*

KENT. My point and period will be thoroughly wrought,
Or well or ill, as this day's battle's fought.
　　　　　　　　　　　　　　　[*Exit.*

ACT V.

SCENE I.—*The Camp of the British Forces, near* DOVER.

Enter, with drum and colours, EDMUND, REGAN, *Officers, Soldiers, and others.*

EDM. Know of the duke, if his last purpose hold;
Or whether since he is advis'd by aught
To change the course: he's full of alteration,
And self-reproving:—bring his constant pleasure. [*To an* Officer, *who goes out.*

REG. Our sister's man is certainly miscarried.

EDM. 'Tis to be doubted, Madam.

REG.　　　　　　Now, sweet lord,
You know the goodness I intend upon you:
Tell me,—but truly,—but then speak the truth,
Do you not love my sister?

EDM.　　　　　In honour'd love.

REG. But have you never found my brother's way
To the forefended place?

EDM.　　　　That thought abuses you.

REG. I am doubtful that you have been conjunct
And bosom'd with her, as far as we call hers.

EDM. No, by mine honour, Madam.

REG. I never shall endure her: dear my lord,
Be not familiar with her.

EDM.　　　　Fear me not:—
She, and the duke her husband.

Enter ALBANY, GONERIL, *and* Soldiers

GON. [*Aside.*] I had rather lose the battle, than that sister
Should loosen him and me.

ALB. Our very loving sister, well be-met.—
Sir, this I hear,—the king is come to his daughter,

With others, whom the rigour of our state
Forc'd to cry out. Where I could not be honest,
I never yet was valiant: for this business,
It toucheth us, as France invades our land,
Not bolds the king, with others, whom, I fear,
Most just and heavy causes make oppose.

EDM. Sir, you speak nobly.

REG.　　　　Why is this reason'd?

GON. Combine together 'gainst the enemy;
For these domestic and particular broils
Are not the question here.

ALB.　　　　Let's, then, determine
With the ancient of war on our proceedings.

EDM. I shall attend you presently at your tent.

REG. Sister, you'll go with us?

GON. No.

REG. 'Tis most convenient; pray you, go with us.

GON. [*Aside.*] O, ho! I know the riddle.
—[*Aloud.*] I will go.
　　　　　Enter EDGAR, *disguised.*

EDG. If e'er your grace had speech with man so poor,
Hear me one word.

ALB.　　　　I'll overtake you.—Speak.

[*Exeunt* EDMUND, REGAN, GONERIL, Officers, Soldiers, *and* Attendants.

EDG. Before you fight the battle, ope this letter.
If you have victory, let the trumpet sound
For him that brought it: wretched though I seem,
I can produce a champion, that will prove
What is avouched there. If you miscarry,
Your business of the world hath so an end,
And machination ceases. Fortune love you!

ALB. Stay till I have read the letter.

EDG.　　　　I was forbid it.
When time shall serve, let but the herald cry,
And I'll appear again.

ALB. Why fare thee well: I will o'erlook thy paper.　　　　[*Exit* EDGAR.
　　　　Re-enter EDMUND.

EDM. The enemy's in view; draw up your powers.
Here is the guess of their true strength and forces
By diligent discovery;—but your haste
Is now urg'd on you.

ALB.　　We will greet the time. [*Exit.*

EDM. To both these sisters have I sworn my love;
Each jealous of the other, as the stung
Are of the adder. Which of them shall I take?
Both? one? or neither? Neither can be enjoy'd,

If both remain alive: to take the widow,
Exasperates, makes mad, her sister Goneril;
And hardly shall I carry out my side,
Her husband being alive. Now, then, we'll
  use
His countenance for the battle; which be-
  ing done,
Let her, who would be rid of him, devise
His speedy taking off. As for the mercy
Which he intends to Lear, and to Cor-
  delia,—
The battle done, and they within our
  power,
Shall never see his pardon; for my state
Stands on me to defend, not to debate.
                                        [*Exit.*

_____

SCENE II.—*A Field between the two
              Camps.*

*Alarum within. Enter, with drum and
  colours,* LEAR, CORDELIA, *and their
  forces; and exeunt. Enter* EDGAR *and*
  GLOSTER.

EDG. Here, father, take the shadow of this
  tree
For your good host; pray that the right
  may thrive:
If ever I return to you again,
I'll bring you comfort.
GLO.   Grace go with you, Sir!
                                  [*Exit* EDGAR.
Alarum; afterwards a retreat. Re-enter
              EDGAR.
EDG. Away, old man! give me thy hand,
  away!
King Lear hath lost, he and his daughter
Give me thy hand; come on.   [ta'en:
GLO. No farther, Sir; a man may rot
  even here.
EDG. What, in ill thoughts again? Men
  must endure
Their going hence, even as their coming
  hither:
Ripeness is all. Come on.
GLO.   And that's true too.
                                      [*Exeunt.*

_____

SCENE III.—*The British Camp near
              DOVER.*

Enter, in conquest, with drum and colours,
  EDMUND; LEAR *and* CORDELIA, *as prison-
  ers;* Captain, Officers, Soldiers, *&c.*
EDM. Some officers take them away; good
  guard,
Until their greater pleasures first be known,
That are to censure them.
COR.   We are not the first,
Who, with best meaning, have incurr'd the
  worst.

For thee, oppressed king, am I cast down;
Myself could else out-frown false fortune's
  frown.
Shall we not see these daughters, and these
  sisters?
LEAR. No, no, no, no! Come, let's away
  to prison:
We two alone will sing like birds i' the
  cage:
When thou dost ask me blessing, I'll kneel
  down,
And ask of thee forgiveness: so we'll live,
And pray, and sing, and tell old tales, and
  laugh
At gilded butterflies, and hear poor rogues
Talk of court news; and we'll talk with
  them too,—
Who loses, and who wins; who's in, who's
  out;
And take upon's the mystery of things,
As if we were God's spies: and we'll wear
  out,   [ones,
In a wall'd prison, packs and sets of great
That ebb and flow by the moon.
EDM.   Take them away.
LEAR. Upon such sacrifices, my Cordelia,
The gods themselves throw incense. Have
  I caught thee?
He that parts us shall bring a brand from
  heaven,
And fire us hence like foxes. Wipe thine
  eyes;   [fell,
The goujeers shall devour them, flesh and
Ere they shall make us weep: we'll see
  them starve first.
Come.   [*Exeunt* LEAR *and* CORDELIA,
                                      guarded.
EDM. Come hither, captain; hark.
Take thou this note; [*Giving a paper.*] go
  follow them to prison:
One step I have advanc'd thee; if thou dost
As this instructs thee, thou dost make thy
  way   [men
To noble fortunes: know thou this,—that
Are as the time is: to be tender-minded
Does not become a sword:—thy great em-
  ployment
Will not bear question; either say thou'lt
Or thrive by other means.   [do't,
CAPT.   I'll do't, my lord.
EDM. About it; and write happy, when
  thou'st done.
Mark,—I say, instantly; and carry it so,
As I have set it down.
CAPT. I cannot draw a cart, nor eat dried
If it be man's work, I will do it. [oats;
                                    [*Exit.*
Flourish. Enter ALBANY, GONERIL, REGAN,
              Officers, *and* Attendants.
ALB. Sir, you have shown to-day your
  valiant strain,

And fortune led you well: you have the
   captives
Who were the opposites of this day's strife:
We do require them of you, so to use them,
As we shall find their merits and our safety
May equally determine.
EDM.   Sir, I thought it fit
To send the old and miserable king
To some retention, and appointed guard;
Whose age has charms in it, whose title
   more,
To pluck the common bosom on his side,
And turn our impress'd lances in our eyes,
Which do command them. With him I
   sent the queen;
My reason all the same; and they are ready
To-morrow, or at farther space, to appear
Where you shall hold your session. At this
   time
We sweat and bleed: the friend hath lost
   his friend;
And the best quarrels, in the heat, are
   curs'd
By those that feel their sharpness:—
The question of Cordelia, and her father,
Requires a fitter place.
ALB.   Sir, by your patience,
I hold you but a subject of this war,
Not as a brother.
REG.   That's as we list to grace him.
Methinks our pleasure might have been
   demanded,   [powers,
Ere you had spoke so far. He led our
Bore the commission of my place and per-
   son;
The which immediacy may well stand up,
And call itself your brother.
GON.   Not so hot:
In his own grace he doth exalt himself,
More than in your addition.
REG.   In my rights,
By me invested, he compeers the best.
GON. That were the most, if he should
   husband you.
REG. Jesters do oft prove prophets.
GON.   Holla, holla!
That eye, that told you so, look'd but
   a-squint.
REG. Lady, I am not well; else I should
   answer
From a full-flowing stomach.—General,
Take thou my soldiers, prisoners, patri-
   mony;   [thine:
Dispose of them, of me; the walls are
Witness the world, that I create thee here
My lord and master.
GON.   Mean you to enjoy him?
ALB. The let-alone lies not in your good
   will.
EDM. Nor in thine, lord.

ALB.   Half-blooded fellow, yes.
REG. [To EDMUND.] Let the drum strike,
   and prove my title thine.
ALB. Stay yet; hear reason.—Edmund, I
   arrest thee
On capital treason; and, in thy arrest,
[Pointing to GON.] This gilded serpent.—
   For your claim, fair sister,
I bar it in the interest of my wife;
'Tis she is sub-contracted to this lord,
And I, her husband, contradict your bans.
If you will marry, make your love to me,
My lady is bespoke.
GON.   An interlude!
ALB. Thou art arm'd, Gloster:—let the
   trumpet sound:
If none appear to prove, upon thy person,
Thy heinous, manifest, and many treasons,
There is my pledge; [Throwing down a
   glove.] I'll prove it on thy heart,
Ere I taste bread, thou art in nothing less
Than I have here proclaim'd thee.
REG.   Sick, O, sick!
GON. [Aside.] If not, I'll ne'er trust poi-
   son.
EDM. There's my exchange: [Throwing
   down a glove.] what in the world he is
That names me traitor, villain-like he lies:
Call by thy trumpet: he that dares ap-
   proach,   [tain
On him, on you, (who not?) I will main-
My truth and honour firmly.
ALB. A herald, ho!
EDM.   A herald, ho, a herald!
ALB. Trust to thy single virtue; for thy
   soldiers,
All levied in my name, have in my name
Took their discharge.
REG.   My sickness grows upon me.
ALB. She is not well; convey her to my
   tent.   [Exit REGAN, led.
         Enter a Herald.
Come hither, herald,—let the trumpet
And read out this.   [sound,—
OFF. Sound, trumpet! [A trumpet sounds.
         Herald reads.
"If any man of quality, or degree, within
the lists of the army, will maintain upon
Edmund, supposed earl of Gloster, that he
is a manifold traitor, let him appear at
the third sound of the trumpet: he is bold
in his defence."
EDM. Sound!   [1 Trumpet.
HER. Again!   [2 Trumpet.
HER. Again!   [3 Trumpet.
      [Trumpet answers within.
   Enter EDGAR, armed, preceded
       by a trumpet.
ALB. Ask him his purposes, why he ap-
Upon this call o' the trumpet.   [pears

HER.   What are you?
Your name? your quality? and why you
This present summons?   [answer
EDG.   Know, my name is lost;
By treason's tooth bare-gnawn, and canker-
Yet am I noble as the adversary   [bit:
I come to cope.
ALB.   Which is that adversary?
EDG. What's he that speaks for Edmund
  earl of Gloster?
EDM. Himself:—what say'st thou to him?
EDG.   Draw thy sword,
That, if my speech offend a noble heart,
Thy arm may do thee justice: here is mine.
Behold, it is the privilege of mine honours,
My oath, and my profession: I protest,—
Maugre thy strength, youth, place, and
  eminence,   [tune,
Despite thy victor sword and fire-new for-
Thy valour and thy heart,—thou art a
  traitor;   [father;
False to thy gods, thy brother, and thy
Conspirant 'gainst this high illustrious
  prince;   [head,
And, from th' extremest upward of thy
To the descent and dust below thy foot,
A most toad-spotted traitor. Say thou
  "No,"
This sword, this arm, and my best spirits,
  are bent
To prove upon thy heart, whereto I speak,
Thou liest.
EDM. In wisdom, I should ask thy name;
But, since thy outside looks so fair and
  warlike,   [breathes,
And that thy tongue some 'say of breeding
What safe and nicely I might well delay
By rule of knighthood, I disdain and
  spurn:
Back do I toss these treasons to thy head;
With the hell-hated lie o'erwhelm thy
  heart;
Which,—for they yet glance by, and scarce-
  ly bruise,—
This sword of mine shall give them instant
  way,   [speak!
Where they shall rest for ever.—Trumpets,
     [*Alarums. They fight.* EDMUND *falls.*
ALB. Save him, save him!
GON.   This is practice, Gloster:
By the law of arms, thou wast not bound
  to answer
An unknown opposite; thou art not van-
But cozen'd and beguil'd.   [quish'd,
ALB.   Shut your mouth, dame;
Or with this paper shall I stop it:—hold,
  Sir;   [evil:—
Thou worse than any name, read thine own
No tearing, lady: I perceive you know it.
     [*Gives the letter to* EDMUND.

GON. Say, if I do,—the laws are mine, not
Who can arraign me for't?   [thine:
ALB.   Most monstrous!
Know'st thou this paper?
GON.   Ask me not what I know.
                 [*Exit.*
ALB. Go after her: she's desperate; gov-
  ern her.   [*To an* Officer, *who goes out.*
EDM. What you have charg'd me with,
  that have I done;
And more, much more; the time will bring
  it out:
'Tis past, and so am I.—But what art thou,
That hast this fortune on me? If thou'rt
I do forgive thee.   [noble,
EDG.   Let's exchange charity.
I am no less in blood than thou art, Ed-
  mund;
If more, the more thou hast wrong'd me.
My name is Edgar, and thy father's son.
The gods are just, and of our pleasant
Make instruments to plague us: [vices
The dark and vicious place where thee he
Cost him his eyes.   [got,
EDM. Thou hast spoken right, 'tis true;
The wheel is come full circle; I am here.
ALB. Methought thy very gait did proph-
  esy
A royal nobleness:—I must embrace thee:
Let sorrow split my heart, if ever I
Did hate thee, or thy father!
EDG.   Worthy prince, I know't.
ALB. Where have you hid yourself?
How have you known the miseries of your
  father?
EDG. By nursing them, my lord.—List a
  brief tale;—
And, when 'tis told, O, that my heart would
  burst!—
The bloody proclamation to escape,
That follow'd me so near, (O, our lives'
  sweetness!   [die,
That we the pain of death would hourly
Rather than die at once!) taught me to
  shift   [blance
Into a madman's rags; to assume a sem-
That very dogs disdain'd: and in this habit
Met I my father with his bleeding rings,
Their precious stones new lost; became his
  guide,   [despair;
Led him, begg'd for him, sav'd him from
Never (O fault!) reveal'd myself unto him,
Until some half hour past, when I was
  arm'd;   [cess,
Not sure, though hoping, of this good suc-
I ask'd his blessing, and from first to last
Told him my pilgrimage: but his flaw'd
  heart,
(Alack, too weak the conflict to support!)
'Twixt two extremes of passion, joy and
Burst smilingly.   [grief,

EDM. This speech of yours hath mov'd me,
And shall, perchance, do good: but speak
you on;
You look as you had something more to say.
ALB. If there be more, more woful, hold
it in:
For I am almost ready to dissolve,
Hearing of this.
EDG.   This would have seem'd a period
To such as love not sorrow; but another,
To amplify too-much, would make much
And top extremity.   [more,
Whilst I was big in clamour, came there
a man,
Who, having seen me in my worst estate,
Shunn'd my abhorr'd society; but then,
finding   [arms
Who 'twas that so endur'd, with his strong
He fasten'd on my neck, and bellow'd out
As he'd burst heaven; threw him on my
father;   [him,
Told the most piteous tale of Lear and
That ever ear receiv'd: which in recount-
ing,   [life
His grief grew puissant, and the strings of
Began to crack; twice then the trumpet
And there I left him tranc'd.   [sounded,
ALB.   But who was this?
EDG. Kent, Sir, the banish'd Kent; who
in disguise
Follow'd his enemy king, and did him
Improper for a slave.   [service
Enter a Gentleman *hastily, with a
bloody knife.*
GENT. Help, help, O help!
EDG.   What kind of help?
ALB.   Speak, man.
EDG. What means that bloody knife?
GENT.   'Tis hot, it smokes;
It came even from the heart of—O, she's
dead!
ALB. Who dead? speak, man.
GENT. Your lady, Sir, your lady: and her
sister
By her is poison'd; she hath confess'd it.
EDM. I was contracted to them both: all
Now marry in an instant.   [three
ALB. Produce the bodies, be they alive
or dead:—   [*Exit* Gentleman.
This judgment of the heavens, that makes
Touches us not with pity.   [us tremble,
EDG.   Here comes Kent.
Enter KENT.
ALB. O, it is he:—
The time will not allow the compliment,
Which very manners urges.
KENT.   I am come
To bid my king and master aye good night:
Is he not here?
ALB.   Great thing of us forgot!—

Speak, Edmund, where's the king? and
where's Cordelia?—
        [*The bodies of* GONERIL *and* REGAN *are
brought in.*
Seest thou this object, Kent?
KENT. Alack, why thus?
EDM.   Yet Edmund was belov'd:
The one the other poison'd for my sake,
And after slew herself.
ALB. Even so.—Cover their faces.
EDM. I pant for life:—some good I mean
to do,   [send,—
Despite of mine own nature. Quickly
Be brief in it,—to the castle; for my writ
Is on the life of Lear, and on Cordelia:—
Nay, send in time.
ALB.   Run, run, O, run!
EDG. To whom, my lord?—Who has the
Thy token of reprieve.   [office? send
EDM. Well thought on: take my sword,
Give it the captain.
ALB.   Haste thee, for thy life.
                           [*Exit* EDGAR.
EDM. He hath commission from thy wife
and me
To hang Cordelia in the prison, and
To lay the blame upon her own despair,
That she forbid herself.
ALB. The gods defend her!—Bear him
hence awhile.   [EDMUND *is borne off.*
Re-enter LEAR, *with* CORDELIA *dead in his
arms;* EDGAR, *Officer, and others.*
LEAR. Howl, howl, howl, howl!—O, you
are men of stones: [so
Had I your tongues and eyes, I'd use them
That heaven's vault should crack.—She's
gone for ever!—
I know when one is dead, and when one
lives;   [glass;
She's dead as earth.—Lend me a looking-
If that her breath will mist or stain the
Why, then she lives.   [stone,
KENT.   Is this the promis'd end?
EDG. Or image of that horror?
ALB.   Fall, and cease!
LEAR. This feather stirs; she lives! if it
be so,
It is a chance which does redeem all sor-
That ever I have felt.   [rows
KENT. [*Kneeling.*] O, my good master!
LEAR. Pr'ythee, away.
EDG.   'Tis noble Kent, your friend.
LEAR. A plague upon you, murderers,
traitors all!
I might have sav'd her; now, she's gone
for ever!—
Cordelia, Cordelia! stay a little. Ha!
What is't thou say'st?—Her voice was ever
soft,   [woman.—
Gentle, and low,—an excellent thing in
I kill'd the slave that was a hanging thee.

OFF. 'Tis true, my lords, he did.
LEAR.   Did I not, fellow?
I have seen the day, with my good biting
    faulchion   [now,
I would have made them skip: I am old
And these same crosses spoil me.—Who
    are you?
Mine eyes are not o' the best:—I'll tell
    you straight.
KENT. If fortune brag of two she lov'd
    and hated,
One of them we behold.
LEAR. This is a dull sight:—are you not
    Kent?
KENT.   The same,
Your servant Kent. Where is your servant
    Caius?
LEAR. He's a good fellow, I can tell you
    that;
He'll strike, and quickly too:—he's dead
    and rotten.
KENT. No, my good lord; I am the very
    man—
LEAR. I'll see that straight.
KENT. That, from your first of difference
    and decay,
Have follow'd your sad steps,—
LEAR.   You are welcome hither.
KENT. Nor no man else.—All's cheerless,
    dark, and deadly.—
Your eldest daughters have fordone them-
And desperately are dead.   [selves,
LEAR.   Ay, so I think.
ALB. He knows not what he says; and
    vain is it,
That we present us to him.
EDG.   Very bootless.
            Enter an Officer.
OFF. Edmund is dead, my lord.
ALB.   That's but a trifle here.—
You lords, and noble friends, know our
    intent.
What comfort to this great decay may
    come,

Shall be applied: for us, we will resign,
During the life of this old majesty,
To him our absolute power:—[*To* EDGAR
    and KENT.] you, to your rights;
With boot, and such addition as your hon-
    ours   [taste
Have more than merited.—All friends shall
The wages of their virtue, and all foes
The cup of their deservings.—O, see, see!
LEAR. And my poor fool is hang'd! No,
    no, no life!
Why should a dog, a horse, a rat, have
    life,   [no more,
And thou no breath at all? Thou'lt come
Never, never, never, never, never!—
Pray you, undo this button:—thank you,
    Sir.—   [*her lips,—*
Do you see this? Look on her,—look,—
Look there, look there!—   [*Dies.*
EDG.   He faints!—My lord, my lord!—
KENT. Break, heart; I pr'ythee, break!
EDG.   Look up, my lord.
KENT. Vex not his ghost: O, let him
    pass! he hates him,
That would upon the rack of this tough
Stretch him out longer.   [world
EDG.   He is gone, indeed.
KENT. The wonder is, he hath endur'd
He but usurp'd his life.   [so long:
ALB. Bear them from hence.—Our pres-
    ent business
Is general woe.—[*To* KENT *and* EDGAR.]
    Friends of my soul, you twain
Rule in this realm, and the gor'd state
    sustain.
KENT. I have a journey, Sir, shortly to go;
My master calls me,—I must not say no.
ALB. The weight of this sad time we
    must obey;
Speak what we feel, not what we ought to
    say.   [young,
The oldest hath borne most: we, that are
Shall never see so much, nor live so long.
            [*Exeunt with a dead march.*

Death of Othello. Act V. S.2.

OTHELLO, THE MOOR OF VENICE

DRAMATIS PERSONÆ.

DUKE OF VENICE.
BRABANTIO, *a Senator.*
Other Senators.
GRATIANO, *Brother to* BRABANTIO.
LODOVICO, *Kinsman to* BRABANTIO.
OTHELLO, *A noble Moor; General in the Venetian Service.*
CASSIO, *his Lieutenant.*
IAGO, *his Ancient.*
RODERIGO, *a Venetian Gentleman.*
MONTANO, OTHELLO'S *predecessor in the Government of* CYPRUS.

Clown, *Servant to* OTHELLO.
Herald.

DESDEMONA, *Daughter to* BRABANTIO, *and Wife to* OTHELLO.
EMILIA, *Wife to* IAGO.
BIANCA, *Mistress to* CASSIO.

Officers, Gentlemen, Messengers, Musicians, Sailors, Attendants, &c.

SCENE,—*The first Act, in* VENICE; *during the rest of the Play, at a Sea-Port in* CYPRUS.

ACT I.

SCENE I.—VENICE. *A Street.*

Enter RODERIGO *and* IAGO.

ROD. Never tell me; I take it much unkindly
That thou, Iago, who hast had my purse
As if the strings were thine, should'st know
of this.
IAGO. 'Sblood, but you will not hear
me:—

If ever I did dream of such a matter,
Abhor me.
ROD. Thou told'st me thou didst hold him
in thy hate.
IAGO. Despise me, if I do not. Three great
ones of the city,
In personal suit to make me his lieutenant,
Off-capp'd to him:—and, by the faith of
man,
I know my price, I am worth no worse a
place:—

523

But he, as loving his own pride and
  purposes,
Evades them, with a bombast circumstance
Horribly stuff'd with epithets of war;
And, in conclusion,
Nonsuits my mediators; for, "Certes,"
  says he,
"I have already chose my officer." And
  what was he?
Forsooth, a great arithmetician,
One Michael Cassio, a Florentine,
A fellow almost damn'd in a fair wife;
That never set a squadron in the field,
Nor the division of a battle knows
More than a spinster; unless the bookish
  theorick,
Wherein the toged consuls can propose
As masterly as he: mere prattle, without
  practice,
Is all his soldiership. But he, Sir, had th'
  election:
And I,—of whom his eyes had seen the
  proof,
At Rhodes, at Cyprus, and on other
  grounds,
Christian and heathen,—must be be-lee'd
  and calm'd
By debitor-and-creditor, this counter-caster;
He, in good time, must his lieutenant be,
And I, (God bless the mark!) his Moor-
  ship's ancient.
ROD. By heaven, I rather would have been
  his hangman.
IAGO. Why, there's no remedy; 'tis the
  curse of service,
Preferment goes by letter and affection,
Not by the old gradation, where each
  second
Stood heir to the first. Now, Sir, be judge
  yourself.
Whether I in any just term am affin'd
To love the Moor.
ROD.   I would not follow him, then.
IAGO. O, Sir, content you;
I follow him to serve my turn upon him:
We cannot all be masters, nor all masters
Cannot be truly follow'd. You shall mark
Many a duteous and knee-crooking knave,
That, doting on his own obsequious
  bondage,
Wears out his time, much like his master's
  ass,
For naught but provender; and when he's
  old, cashier'd:
Whip me such honest knaves. Others there
  are,
Who, trimm'd in forms and visages of
  duty,
Keep yet their hearts attending on them-
  selves;

And, throwing but shows of service on
  their lords,
Do well thrive by them, and, when they
  have lin'd their coats
Do themselves homage: these fellows have
  some soul;
And such a one do I profess myself.
For, Sir,
It is as sure as you are Roderigo,
Were I the Moor, I would not be Iago:
In following him, I follow but myself;
Heaven is my judge, not I for love and
  duty,
But seeming so, for my peculiar end:
For when my outward action doth dem-
  onstrate
The native act and figure of my heart
In compliment extern, 'tis not long after
But I will wear my heart upon my sleeve
For daws to peck at: I am not what I am.
ROD. What a full fortune does the thick-
If he can carry't thus!   [lips owe,
IAGO.   Call up her father;
Rouse him: make after him, poison his
  delight,
Proclaim him in the streets; incense her
  kinsmen;
And, though he in a fertile climate dwell,
Plague him with flies: though that his joy
  be joy,
Yet throw such changes of vexation on't,
As it may lose some colour.
ROD. Here is her father's house; I'll call
  aloud.
IAGO. Do; with like timorous accent, and
  dire yell,
As when, by night and negligence, the fire
Is spied in populous cities.
ROD. What, ho, Brabantio! signior Bra-
  bantio, ho!
IAGO. Awake! what, ho, Brabantio!
  thieves! thieves! thieves!
Look to your house, your daughter, and
  Thieves! thieves!   [your bags!
    Enter BRABANTIO, above, at a window.
BRA. What is the reason of this terrible
  summons?
What is the matter there?
ROD. Signior, is all your family within?
IAGO. Are your doors lock'd?
BRA.   Why, wherefore ask you this?
IAGO. 'Zounds, Sir, you are robb'd; for
  shame, put on your gown;
Your heart is burst, you have lost half your
  soul;
Even now, now, very now, an old black ram
Is tupping your white ewe. Arise, arise;
Awake the snorting citizens with the bell,
Or else the devil will make a grandsire of
Arise, I say.   [you:

BRA.   What, have you lost your wits?
ROD. Most reverend signior, do you know my voice?
BRA. Not I: what are you?
ROD. My name is Roderigo.
BRA.   The worse welcome:
I have charg'd thee not to haunt about my doors:
In honest plainness thou hast heard me say,
My daughter is not for thee; and now, in madness,
Being full of supper and distempering draughts,
Upon malicious bravery, dost thou come
To start my quiet.
ROD. Sir, Sir, Sir,—
BRA.   But thou must needs be sure,
My spirit and my place have in them power
To make this bitter to thee.
ROD.   Patience, good Sir.
BRA. What tell'st thou me of robbing? this is Venice;
My house is not a grange.
ROD.   Most grave Brabantio,
In simple and pure soul I come to you.
IAGO. 'Zounds, Sir, you are one of those, that will not serve God, if the devil bid you. Because we come to do you service, and you think we are ruffians, you'll have your daughter covered with a Barbary horse; you'll have your nephews neigh to you; you'll have coursers for cousins, and gennets for germans.
BRA. What profane wretch art thou?
IAGO. I am one, Sir, that comes to tell you, your daughter and the Moor are now making the beast with two backs.
BRA. Thou art a villain.
IAGO.   You are—a senator.
BRA. This thou shalt answer; I know thee, Roderigo.
ROD. Sir, I will answer any thing. But, I beseech you,
If't be your pleasure, and most wise consent,
(As partly, I find, it is) that your fair daughter,
At this odd-even and dull watch o' the night,
Transported, with no worse nor better guard,
But with a knave of common hire, a gondolier,
To the gross clasps of a lascivious Moor,—
If this be known to you, and your allowance,
We then have done you bold, and saucy wrongs;
But, if you know not this, my manners tell me,

We have your wrong rebuke. Do not believe,
That, from the sense of all civility,
I thus would play and trifle with your reverence:
Your daughter,—if you have not given her leave,—
I say again, hath made a gross revolt;
Tying her duty, beauty, wit, and fortunes,
In an extravagant and wheeling stranger,
Of here and every where. Straight satisfy yourself:
If she be in her chamber, or your house,
Let loose on me the justice of the state
For thus deluding you.
BRA.   Strike on the tinder, ho!
Give me a taper!—call up all my people!—
This accident is not unlike my dream:
Belief of it oppresses me already.—
Light, I say! light!   [*Exit above.*
IAGO.   Farewell; for I must leave you:
It seems not meet, nor wholesome to my place,
To be produc'd (as, if I stay, I shall)
Against the Moor: for, I do know, the state,—
However this may gall him with some check,—
Cannot with safety cast him; for he's embark'd
With such loud reason to the Cyprus wars,
(Which even now stand in act) that, for their souls,
Another of his fathom they have none,
To lead their business: in which regard,
Though I do hate him as I do hell pains,
Yet, for necessity of present life,
I must show out a flag and sign of love,
Which is indeed but sign. That you shall surely find him,
Lead to the Sagittary the raised search;
And there will I be with him. So, farewell.   [*Exit.*
Enter below, BRABANTIO, *and* Servants *with torches.*
BRA. It is too true an evil: gone she is;
And what's to come of my despised time,
Is naught but bitterness.—Now, Roderigo,
Where didst thou see her?—O unhappy girl!—
With the Moor, say'st thou—Who would be a father!
How didst thou know 'twas she?—O, she deceives me
Past thought!—What said she to you?—Get more tapers;
Raise all my kindred.—Are they married, think you?
ROD. Truly, I think, they are.
BRA. O heaven!—How got she out?—O, treason of the blood!—

Father's from hence trust not your daughters' minds
By what you see them act.—Are there not charms,
By which the property of youth and maidhood
May be abus'd? Have you not read, Roderigo,
Of some such thing?
ROD.   Yes, Sir, I have indeed.
BRA. Call up my brother.—O, that you had had her!—
Some one way, some another.—Do you know
Where we may apprehend her and the Moor?
ROD. I think I can discover him, if you please
To get good guard, and go along with me.
BRA. Pray you, lead on. At every house I'll call;
I may command at most.—Get weapons, ho!
And raise some special officers of night.—
On, good Roderigo;—I'll deserve your pains.   [*Exeunt.*

SCENE II.—VENICE. *Another Street.*
Enter OTHELLO, IAGO, *and* Attendants, *with torches.*

IAGO. Though in the trade of war I have slain men,
Yet do I hold it very stuff o' the conscience
To do no contriv'd murder: I lack iniquity
Sometimes to do me service: nine or ten times
I had thought to have yerk'd him here under the ribs.
OTH. 'Tis better as it is.
IAGO.   Nay, but he prated,
And spoke such scurvy and provoking terms
Against your honour.
That, with the little godliness I have,
I did full hard forbear him. But, I pray, Sir,
Are you fast married? for, be sure of this,
That the magnifico is much beloved;
And hath, in his effect, a voice potential
As double as the duke's: he will divorce you;
Or put upon you what restraint and grievance   [on)
The law (with all his might to enforce it
Will give him cable.
OTH.   Let him do his spite:
My services, which I have done the signiory,
Shall out-tongue his complaints. 'Tis yet to know,—
Which, when I know that boasting is an honour,

I shall promulgate,—I fetch my life and being
From men of royal siege; and my demerits
May speak, unbonneted, to as proud a fortune
As this that I have reach'd: for know, Iago,
But that I love the gentle Desdemona,
I would not my unhoused free condition
Put into circumscription and confine
For the sea's worth. But, look! what lights come yonder?
IAGO. Those are the raised father, and his friends:
You were best go in.   [friends:
OTH.   Not I; I must be found:
My parts, my title, and my perfect soul,
Shall manifest me rightly. Is it they?
IAGO. By Janus, I think no.
Enter CASSIO, *and certain* Officers, *with torches.*
OTH. The servants of the duke, and my lieutenant.—
The goodness of the night upon you, friends!
What is the news?   [friends!
CAS.   The duke does greet you, general;
And he requires your haste-post-haste appearance,
Even on the instant.   [pearance,
OTH.   What is the matter, think you?
CAS. Something from Cyprus, as I may divine:
It is a business of some heat: the galleys
Have sent a dozen sequent messengers
This very night at one another's heels;
And many of the consuls, rais'd and met,
Are at the duke's already: you have been hotly call'd for;
When, being not at your lodging to be found,   [quests
The senate hath sent about three several
To search you out.
OTH.   'Tis well I am found by you.
I will but spend a word here in the house,
And go with you.   [*Exit.*
CAS.   Ancient, what makes he here?
IAGO. 'Faith, he to-night hath boarded a land carrack:
If it prove lawful prize, he's made for ever.
CAS. I do not understand.
IAGO.   He's married.
CAS.   To whom?
Re-enter OTHELLO.
IAGO. Marry, to—Come, captain, will you go?
OTH.   Have with you.
CAS. Here comes another troop to seek for you.
IAGO. It is Brabantio:—general, be advis'd;
He comes to bad intent.   [vis'd;
Enter BRABANTIO, RODERIGO, *and* Officers, *with torches and weapons.*
OTH.   Holla! stand there!
ROD. Signior, it is the Moor.

BRA. 　　　　　Down with him, thief!
　　　　[*They draw on both sides.*
IAGO. You, Roderigo! come, Sir, I am for
　　you.
OTH. Keep up your bright swords, for the
　　dew will rust them.—
Good signior, you shall more command with
Than with your weapons. 　　　[years,
BRA. O thou foul thief, where hast thou
　　'stow'd my daughter?
Damn'd as thou art, thou hast enchanted
　　her;
For I'll refer me to all things of sense,
If she in chains of magic were not bound,
Whether a maid so tender, fair, and happy,
So opposite to marriage, that she shunn'd
The wealthy curled darlings of our nation,
Would ever have, to incur a general mock,
Run from her guardage to the sooty bosom
Of such a thing as thou,—to fear, not to
　　delight.
Judge me the world, if 'tis not gross in
　　sense,
That thou hast practis'd on her with foul
　　charms;
Abus'd her delicate youth with drugs, or
　　minerals,
That weaken motion.—I'll have't disputed
　　on:
'Tis probable, and palpable to thinking.
I therefore apprehend and do attach thee,
For an abuser of the world, a practiser
Of arts inhibited and out of warrant.—
Lay hold upon him: if he do resist,
Subdue him at his peril.
OTH. 　　　　Hold your hands,
Both you of my inclining, and the rest:
Were it my cue to fight, I should have
　　known it
Without a prompter.—Where will you that
To answer this your charge? 　　[I go
BRA. 　　　To prison; till fit time
Of law, and course of direct session,
Call thee to answer.
OTH. 　　　　What if I do obey?
How may the duke be therewith satisfied,
Whose messengers are here about my side,
Upon some present business of the state,
To bring me to him?
OFF. 　'Tis true, most worthy signior;
The duke's in council, and your noble self,
I am sure, is sent for.
BRA. 　　　How! the duke in council!
In this time of the night!—Bring him
　　away:
Mine's not an idle cause: the duke himself,
Or any of my brothers of the state,
Cannot but feel this wrong, as 'twere their
　　own;

For if such actions may have passage free,
Bond-slaves and pagans shall our statesmen
　　be. 　　　　　　　　　　[*Exeunt.*

SCENE III.—VENICE. *The Council-*
Chamber.

The DUKE, *and* Senators, *sitting at a table;*
　　Officers *attending.*

DUKE. There is no composition in these
That gives them credit. 　　　[news,
1 SEN. Indeed, they are disproportion'd;
My letters say, a hundred and seven galleys.
DUKE. And mine, a hundred and forty.
2 SEN. 　　　　And mine, two hundred:
But though they jump not on a just account,
(As in these cases, where the aim reports,
'Tis oft with difference) yet do they all
　　confirm
A Turkish fleet, and bearing up to Cyprus.
DUKE. Nay, it is possible enough to judg-
　　ment:
I do not so secure me in the error,
But the main article I do approve
In fearful sense.
SAILOR. [*Within.*] What, ho! what, ho!
　　what, ho!
OFF. A messenger from the galleys.
　　　　　Enter a Sailor.
DUKE. 　　　　Now,—the business?
SAIL. The Turkish preparation makes for
　　Rhodes;
So was I bid report here to the state,
By signior Angelo.
DUKE. How say you by this change?
1 SEN. 　　　　　This cannot be,
By no assay of reason: 'tis a pageant,
To keep us in false gaze. When we con-
　　sider
The importancy of Cyprus to the Turk;
And let ourselves again but understand,
That, as it more concerns the Turk than
　　Rhodes, 　　　　　　　　　　[it,
So may he with more facile question bear
For that it stands not in such warlike brace,
But altogether lacks th' abilities
That Rhodes is dress'd in:—if we make
　　thought of this,
We must not think the Turk is so unskilful,
To leave that latest which concerns him
　　first,
Neglecting an attempt of ease and gain,
To wake and wage a danger profitless.
DUKE. Nay, in all confidence, he's not for
　　Rhodes.
OFF. Here is more news.
　　　　　Enter a Messenger.
MESS. The Ottomites, reverend and gra-
　　cious, 　　　　　　　　　[of Rhodes,
Steering with due course toward the isle

Have there injointed them with an after
fleet.

1 *SEN.* Ay, so I thought.—How many, as
you guess?

MESS. Of thirty sail: and now they do
re-stem

Their backward course, bearing with frank
appearance

Their purposes toward Cyprus.—Signior
Montano,

Your trusty and most valiant servitor,

With his free duty recommends you thus,

And prays you to believe him.

DUKE. 'Tis certain, then, for Cyprus.—
Marcus Luccicos, is not he in town?

1 *SEN.* He's now in Florence.

DUKE. Write from us to him; post-post-
haste despatch.

1 *SEN.* Here comes Brabantio, and the
valiant Moor.

Enter BRABANTIO, OTHELLO, IAGO, RODER-
IGO, *and* Officers.

DUKE. Valiant Othello, we must straight
employ you

Against the general enemy Ottoman.—

[*To* BRA.] I did not see you; welcome,
gentle signior;

We lack'd your counsel and your help to-
night.

BRA. So did I yours. Good your grace,
pardon me;

Neither my place, nor aught I heard of
business,

Hath rais'd me from my bed; nor doth the
general care

Take hold of me; for my particular grief

Is of so flood-gate and o'erbearing nature,

That it engluts and swallows other sorrows,

And it is still itself.

DUKE. Why, what's the matter?

BRA. My daughter! O, my daughter!

DUKE AND SENATORS.   Dead?

BRA.   Ay, to me;

She is abus'd, stol'n from me, and corrupted

By spells and medicines bought of mounte-
banks;

For nature so preposterously to err,—

Being not deficient, blind, or lame of
sense,—

Sans witchcraft could not.   [sense,—

DUKE. Whoe'er he be that, in this foul
proceeding,

Hath thus beguil'd your daughter of herself,

And you of her, the bloody book of law

You shall yourself read in the bitter letter,

After your own sense; yea, though our
proper son

Stood in your action.

BRA.   Humbly I thank your grace.

Here is the man, this Moor; whom now, it
seems,

Your special mandate, for the state affairs,

Hath hither brought.

DUKE AND SENATORS. We are very
sorry for it.

DUKE. [*To* OTH.] What, in your own
part, can you say to this?

BRA. Nothing, but this is so.

OTH. Most potent, grave, and reverend
signiors,

My very noble and approv'd good masters,—   [daughter,

That I have ta'en away this old man's

It is most true; true, I have married her:

The very head and front of my offending

Hath this extent, no more. Rude am I in
my speech,

And little bless'd with the soft phrase of
peace;

For since these arms of mine had seven
years' pith,

Till now some nine moons wasted, they
have us'd

Their dearest action in the tented field;

And little of this great world can I speak,

More than pertains to feats of broil and
battle;

And therefore little shall I grace my cause,

In speaking for myself. Yet, by your
gracious patience,

I will a round unvarnish'd tale deliver

Of my whole course of love; what drugs,
what charms,

What conjuration, and what mighty
magic,—

For such proceeding I am charg'd withal,—

I won his daughter.

BRA.   A maiden never bold;

Of spirit so still and quiet, that her motion

Blush'd at herself; and she,—in spite of
nature,

Of years, of country, credit, every thing—

To fall in love with what she fear'd to
look on!

It is a judgment maim'd, and most imperfect,

That will confess perfection so could err

Against all rules of nature; and must be
driven

To find out practices of cunning hell,

Why this should be. I therefore vouch
again,   [the blood,

That with some mixtures powerful o'er

Or with some dram conjur'd to this effect,

He wrought upon her.

DUKE.   To vouch this, is no proof:

Without more certain and more overt test,

These are thin habits, and poor likelihoods

Of modern seeming, you prefer against

1 *SEN.* But, Othello, speak: [him.

Did you by indirect and forced courses

Subdue and poison this young maid's af-
   fections?   [tion
Or came it by request, and such fair ques-
As soul to soul affordeth?
OTH.   I do beseech you,
Send for the lady to the Sagittary,
And let her speak of me before her father:
If you do find me foul in her report,
The trust, the office, I do hold of you,
Not only take away, but let your sentence
Even fall upon my life.
DUKE.   Fetch Desdemona hither.
OTH. Ancient, conduct them; you best
   know the place.—
          [*Exeunt* IAGO *and* Attendants.
And, till she come, as truly as to heaven
I do confess the vices of my blood,
So justly to your grave ears I'll present
How I did thrive in this fair lady's love,
And she in mine.
DUKE. Say it, Othello.
OTH. Her father lov'd me; oft invited me;
Still question'd me the story of my life,
From year to year,—the battles, sieges,
   fortunes,
That I have pass'd.
I ran it through, even from my boyish
   days,
To the very moment that he bade me tell it:
Wherein I spake of most disastrous chances,
Of moving accidents by flood and field;
Of hair-breadth scapes i' th' imminent
   deadly breach;
Of being taken by the insolent foe,
And sold to slavery; of my redemption
   thence,
And portance in my travel's history:
Wherein of antres vast, and deserts idle,
Rough quarries, rocks, and hills whose
   heads touch heaven,
It was my hint to speak,—such was the
   process;
And of the Cannibals that each other eat,
The Anthropophagi, and men whose heads
Do grow beneath their shoulders. This to
   hear,
Would Desdemona seriously incline:
But still the house affairs would draw her
   thence;
Which ever as she could with haste des-
   patch,
She'd come again, and with a greedy ear
Devour up my discourse:—which I observ-
   ing,   [means
Took once a pliant hour; and found good
To draw from her a prayer of earnest heart,
That I would all my pilgrimage dilate,
Whereof by parcels she had something
   heard,
But not intentively: I did consent;
And often did beguile her of her tears,

When I did speak of some distressful
   stroke
That my youth suffer'd. My story being
   done,
She gave me for my pains a world of sighs:
She swore,—in faith, 'twas strange, 'twas
   passing strange;
'Twas pitiful, 'twas wondrous pitiful:
She wish'd she had not heard it; yet she
   wish'd
That heaven had made her such a man:
   she thank'd me;
And bade me, if I had a friend that lov'd
   her,
I should but teach him how to tell my
   story,
And that would woo her. Upon this hint
   I spake:
She lov'd me for the dangers I had pass'd;
And I lov'd her that she did pity them.
This only is the witchcraft I have us'd:—
Here comes the lady; let her witness it.
   Enter DESDEMONA, IAGO, *and* Attendants.
DUKE. I think this tale would win my
   daughter too.—
Good Brabantio,
Take up this mangled matter at the best:
Men do their broken weapons rather use,
Than their bare hands.
BRA.   I pray you, hear her speak:
If she confess that she was half the wooer,
Destruction on my head, if my bad blame
Light on the man!—Come hither, gentle
   mistress:
Do you perceive in all this noble company,
Where most you owe obedience?
DES.   My noble father,
I do perceive here a divided duty:
To you, I am bound for life and education;
My life and education both do learn me
How to respect you; you are the lord of
   duty,—
I am hitherto your daughter: but here's my
   husband;
And so much duty as my mother show'd
To you, preferring you before her father,
So much I challenge that I may profess
Due to the Moor my lord.
BRA. God be with you!—I have done.—
Please it your grace, on to the state affairs:
I had rather to adopt a child than get it.—
Come hither, Moor:
I here do give thee that with all my heart,
Which, but thou hast already, with all my
   heart   [jewel,
I would keep from thee.—For your sake,
I am glad at soul I have no other child;
For thy escape would teach me tyranny,
To hang clogs on them.—I have done, my
   lord.

DUKE. Let me speak like yourself; and lay a sentence,
Which, as a grise, or step, may help these
Into your favour.   [lovers
When remedies are past, the griefs are ended
By seeing the worst, which late on hopes depended.
To mourn a mischief that is past and gone,
Is the next way to draw new mischief on.
What cannot be preserv'd when fortune takes,
Patience her injury a mockery makes.
The robb'd, that smiles, steals something from the thief;
He robs himself, that spends a bootless grief.
BRA. So let the Turk of Cyprus us beguile:
We lose it not, so long as we can smile.
He bears the sentence well, that nothing bears   [he hears,
But the free comfort which from thence
But he bears both the sentence and the sorrow,
That, to pay grief, must of poor patience borrow.
These sentences, to sugar, or to gall,
Being strong on both sides, are equivocal:
But words are words; I never yet did hear,
That the bruis'd heart was pierced through the ear.—
Beseech you, now to the affairs of state.
DUKE. The Turk with a most mighty preparation makes for Cyprus:—Othello, the fortitude of the place is best known to you; and though we have there a substitute of most allowed sufficiency, yet opinion, a sovereign mistress of effects, throws a more safer voice on you: you must, therefore, be content to slubber the gloss of your new fortunes with this more stubborn and boisterous expedition.
OTH. The tyrant custom, most grave senators,
Hath made the flinty and steel couch of war
My thrice-driven bed of down: I do agnize
A natural and prompt alacrity
I find in hardness: and do undertake
These present wars against the Ottomites.
Most humbly, therefore, bending to your state,
I crave fit disposition for my wife;
Due reference of place and exhibition;
With such accommodation, and besort,
As levels with her breeding.
DUKE.   If you please,
Be't at her father's.
BRA.   I'll not have it so.
OTH. Nor I.

DES.   Nor I; I would not there reside,
To put my father in impatient thoughts,
By being in his eye. Most gracious duke,
To my unfolding lend your prosperous ear;
And let me find a charter in your voice,
To assist my simpleness.
DUKE. What would you, Desdemona?
DES. That I did love the Moor to live with him,
My downright violence and storm of fortunes   [subdued
May trumpet to the world: my heart's
Even to the very quality of my lord:
I saw Othello's visage in his mind;
And to his honours, and his valiant parts,
Did I my soul and fortunes consecrate.
So that, dear lords, if I be left behind,
A moth of peace, and he go to the war,
The rites for which I love him are bereft me,
And I a heavy interim shall support
By his dear absence. Let me go with him.
OTH. Your voices, lords: 'beseech you, let
Have a free way.   [her will
Vouch with me, heaven, I therefore beg it not,
To please the palate of my appetite;
Nor to comply with heat (the young affects
In me defunct) and proper satisfaction;
But to be free and bounteous to her mind:
And heaven defend your good souls, that you think
I will your serious and great business scant,
For she is with me: no, when light-wing'd toys
Of feather'd Cupid seel with wanton dulness
My speculative and offic'd instruments,
That my disports corrupt and taint my business,
Let housewives make a skillet of my helm,
And all indign and base adversities
Make head against my estimation!
DUKE. Be it as you shall privately determine,
Either for her stay, or going: th' affair cries haste,
And speed must answer it.
1 SEN. You must away to-night.
OTH.   With all my heart.
DUKE. At nine i' the morning here we'll meet again.—
Othello, leave some officer behind,
And he shall our commission bring to you;
With such things else of quality and re-
As doth import you.   [spect,
OTH.   Please your grace, my ancient;
A man he is of honesty and trust:
To his conveyance I assign my wife,
With what else needful your good grace
To be sent after me.   [shall think

DUKE. 　　　　Let it be so.—

Good night to every one.—[*To* BRA.] And,
　noble signior,
If virtue no delighted beauty lack,
Your son-in-law is far more fair than black.

1 SEN. Adieu, brave Moor! use Desdemona well.

BRA. Look to her, Moor, if thou hast eyes
　to see:
She has deceiv'd her father, and may thee.

　　　[*Exeunt* DUKE, Senators, Officers, &c.

OTH. My life upon her faith!—Honest
　Iago,
My Desdemona must I leave to thee:
I pr'ythee, let thy wife attend on her;
And bring them after in the best advan-
　tage.—

Come, Desdemona; I have but an hour
Of love, of worldly matters and direction,
To spend with thee: we must obey the
　time.

　　　[*Exeunt* OTHELLO *and* DESDEMONA.

ROD. Iago,—

IAGO. What say'st thou, noble heart?

ROD. What will I do, thinkest thou?

IAGO. Why, go to bed, and sleep.

ROD. I will incontinently drown myself.

IAGO. Well, if thou dost, I shall never
love thee after. Why, thou silly gentleman!

ROD. It is silliness to live, when to live
is torment; and then have we a prescription
to die, when death is our physician.

IAGO. O villanous! I have looked upon
the world for four times seven years; and
since I could distinguish betwixt a benefit
and an injury, I never found man that
knew how to love himself. Ere I would
say, I would drown myself for the love of
a Guinea-hen, I would change my humanity
with a baboon.

ROD. What should I do? I confess it is
my shame to be so fond; but it is not in
my virtue to amend it.

IAGO. Virtue! a fig! 'tis in ourselves that
we are thus, or thus. Our bodies are gar-
dens; to the which, our wills are gardeners:
so that if we will plant nettles, or sow let-
tuce; set hyssop, and weed up thyme;
supply it with one gender of herbs, or distract it with many; either to have it sterile
with idleness, or manured with industry;
why, the power and corrigible authority of
this lies in our wills. If the balance of our
lives had not one scale of reason to poise
another of sensuality, the blood and baseness of our natures would conduct us to
most preposterous conclusions: but we have
reason to cool our raging motions, our
carnal stings, our unbitted lusts; whereof I
take this, that you call—love, to be a sect,
or scion.

ROD. It cannot be.

IAGO. It is merely a lust of the blood, and
a permission of the will. Come, be a
man: drown thyself! drown cats, and blind
puppies. I have professed me thy friend,
and I confess me knit to thy deserving
with cables of perdurable toughness; I
could never better stead thee than now.
Put money in thy purse; follow these wars;
defeat thy favour with a usurped beard; I
say, put money in thy purse. It cannot
be, that Desdemona should long continue
her love to the Moor,—put money in thy
purse,—nor he his to her: it was a violent
commencement, and thou shalt see an
answerable sequestration;—put but money
in thy purse.—These Moors are changeable
in their wills;—fill thy purse with money:
—the food that to him now is as luscious
as locusts, shall be to him shortly as bitter
as coloquintida. She must change for
youth: when she is sated with his body,
she will find the error of her choice: she
must have change, she must: therefore put
money in thy purse.—If thou wilt needs
damn thyself, do it a more delicate way
than drowning. Make all the money thou
canst: if sanctimony and a frail vow, betwixt an erring barbarian and a super-
subtle Venetian, be not too hard for my
wits, and all the tribe of hell, thou shalt
enjoy her; therefore make money. A pox
of drowning thyself! it is clean out of the
way: seek thou rather to be hanged in
compassing thy joy, than to be drowned
and go without her.

ROD. Wilt thou be fast to my hopes, if I
depend on the issue?

IAGO. Thou art sure of me:—go, make
money:—I have told thee often, and I re-
tell thee again and again, I hate the Moor:
my cause is hearted; thine hath no less
reason. Let us be conjunctive in our revenge against him: if thou canst cuckold
him, thou dost thyself a pleasure, me a
sport. There are many events in the womb
of time, which will be delivered. Traverse;
go; provide thy money. We will have more
of this to-morrow. Adieu.

ROD. Where shall we meet i' the morning?

IAGO. At my lodging.

ROD. I'll be with thee betimes.

IAGO. Go to; farewell. Do you hear, Roderigo?

ROD. What say you?

IAGO. No more of drowning, do you hear?

ROD. I am changed: I'll sell all my land.

IAGO. Go to; farewell: put money enough
　in your purse.—　　　　[*Exit* RODERIGO.

Thus do I ever make my fool my purse;

For I mine own gain'd knowledge should profane,
If I would time expend with such a snipe,
But for my sport and profit. I hate the Moor;
And it is thought abroad, that 'twixt my sheets
He has done my office: I know not if't be true;
But I, for mere suspicion in that kind,
Will do as if for surety. He holds me well;
The better shall my purpose work on him.
Cassio's a proper man: let me see now;
To get his place, and to plume up my will,
In double knavery,—How, how?—Let's see:—
After some time, to abuse Othello's ear
That he is too familiar with his wife:—
He hath a person, and a smooth dispose,
To be suspected; fram'd to make women false.
The Moor is of a free and open nature,
That thinks men honest that but seem to be so;
And will as tenderly be led by the nose,
As asses are.—
I have't;—it is engender'd:—hell and night
Must bring this monstrous birth to the world's light.   [*Exit.*

ACT II.

SCENE I.—*A Sea-port Town in* CYPRUS. *A Platform.*

Enter MONTANO *and two* Gentlemen.

MON. What from the cape can you discern at sea?

1 GENT. Nothing at all: it is a high-wrought flood;
I cannot, 'twixt the heaven and the main,
Descry a sail.

MON. Methinks the wind hath spoke aloud at land;
A fuller blast ne'er shook our battlements:
If it hath ruffian'd so upon the sea,
What ribs of oak, when mountains melt on them,
Can hold the mortise? what shall we hear of this?

2 GENT. A segregation of the Turkish fleet:
For do but stand upon the foaming shore,
The chidden billow seems to pelt the clouds;
The wind-shak'd surge, with high and monstrous mane,
Seems to cast water on the burning bear,
And quench the guards of th' ever-fixed pole:
I never did like molestation view
On the enchafed flood.

MON.   If that the Turkish fleet
Be not enshelter'd and embay'd, they are drown'd;
It is impossible to bear it out.

Enter a third Gentleman.

3 GENT. News, lads! our wars are done.
The desperate tempest hath so bang'd the Turks,   [of Venice
That their designment halts: a noble ship
Hath seen a grievous wreck and sufferance
On most part of their fleet.

MON. How! is this true?

3 GENT.   The ship is here put in,
A Veronessa; Michael Cassio,
Lieutenant to the warlike Moor Othello,
Is come on shore: the Moor himself's at sea,
And is in full commission here for Cyprus.

MON. I am glad on't; 'tis a worthy governor.

3 GENT. But this same Cassio,—though he speak of comfort,
Touching the Turkish loss,—yet he looks sadly,
And prays the Moor be safe; for they were parted
With foul and violent tempest.   [parted

MON.   Pray heaven he be;
For I have serv'd him, and the man commands
Like a full soldier. Let's to the sea-side, ho!
As well to see the vessel that's come in,
As to throw out our eyes for brave Othello,
Even till we make the main, and th' aerial
An indistinct regard.   [blue,

3 GENT.   Come, let's do so;
For every minute is expectancy
Of more arrivance.

Enter CASSIO.

CAS. Thanks, you, the valiant of this war-like isle,
That so approve the Moor! O, let the heavens
Give him defence against the elements,
For I have lost him on a dangerous sea!

MON. Is he well shipp'd?

CAS. His bark is stoutly timber'd, and his pilot
Of very expert and approv'd allowance;
Therefore my hopes, not surfeited to death,
Stand in bold cure.

[*Within.*]   A sail, a sail, a sail!

Enter a fourth Gentleman.

CAS. What noise?

4 GENT. The town is empty; on the brow o' the sea
Stand ranks of people, and they cry, "a sail!"

CAS. My hopes do shape him for the governor.   [*Guns heard.*

2 GENT. They do discharge their shot of
Our friends, at least.   [courtesy:
CAS.   I pray you, Sir, go forth,
And give us truth who 'tis that is arriv'd.
2 GENT. I shall.   [*Exit.*
MON. But, good lieutenant, is your general wiv'd?
CAS. Most fortunately: he hath achiev'd a maid
That paragons description and wild fame;
One that excels the quirks of blazoning pens,
And in th' essential vesture of creation,
Does bear all excellency.—
          Re-enter second Gentleman.
          How now! who has put in?
2 GENT. 'Tis one Iago, ancient to the general.
CAS. He has had most favourable and happy speed:
Tempests themselves, high seas, and howling winds,
The gutter'd rocks, and congregated sands,—
Traitors ensteep'd to clog the guiltless keel,—
As having sense of beauty, do omit
Their mortal natures, letting go safely by
The divine Desdemona.
MON.   What is she?
CAS. She that I spake of, our great captain's captain,
Left in the conduct of the bold Iago;
Whose footing here anticipates our thoughts,
A se'nnight's speed.—Great Jove, Othello guard,   [ful breath,
And swell his sail with thine own power-
That he may bless this bay with his tall ship,   [arms,
Make love's quick pants in Desdemona's
Give renew'd fire to our extincted spirits,
And bring all Cyprus comfort!—O, behold,
Enter DESDEMONA, EMILIA, IAGO, RODERIGO, *and* Attendants.
The riches of the ship is come on shore!
Ye men of Cyprus, let her have your knees.—
Hail to thee, lady! and the grace of heaven,
Before, behind thee, and on every hand,
Enwheel thee round!
DES.   I thank you, valiant Cassio.
What tidings can you tell me of my lord?
CAS. He is not yet arriv'd: nor know I aught
But that he's well, and will be shortly here.
DES. O, but I fear—How lost you company?

CAS. The great contention of the sea and
Parted our fellowship:—   [skies
          [*Within,* "A sail, a sail!"
but, hark! a sail.   [*Guns heard.*
2 GENT. They give their greeting to the
This likewise is a friend.   [citadel:
CAS.   See for the news.—
          [*Exit* Gentleman.
Good ancient, you are welcome:—[*To*
EMILIA.] welcome, mistress:—
Let it not gall your patience, good Iago,
That I extend my manners; 'tis my breeding
That gives me this bold show of courtesy.
          [*Kissing her.*
IAGO. Sir, would she give you so much of her lips,
As of her tongue she oft bestows on me,
You'd have enough.
DES.   Alas, she has no speech.
IAGO. In faith, too much;
I find it still, when I have list to sleep:
Marry, before your ladyship, I grant,
She puts her tongue a little in her heart,
And chides with thinking.
EMIL. You have little cause to say so.
IAGO. Come on, come on; you are pictures out of doors,
Bells in your parlours, wild cats in your kitchens,
Saints in your injuries, devils being offended,   [wives in your beds.
Players in your housewifery, and house-
DES. O, fie upon thee, slanderer!
IAGO. Nay, it is true, or else I am a Turk:
You rise to play, and go to bed to work.
EMIL. You shall not write my praise.
IAGO.   No, let me not.
DES. What would'st thou write of me, if thou should'st praise me?
IAGO. O gentle lady, do not put me to't;
For I am nothing, if not critical.
DES. Come on; assay.—There's one gone to the harbour?
IAGO. Ay, Madam.
DES. I am not merry; but I do beguile
The thing I am, by seeming otherwise.—
Come, how would'st thou praise me?
IAGO. I am about it; but, indeed, my invention
Comes from my pate, as birdlime does from frize,—
It plucks out brains and all: but my muse
And thus she is deliver'd.   [labours,
If she be fair and wise,—fairness and wit,
The one's for use, the other useth it.
DES. Well prais'd! How if she be black and witty?
IAGO. If she be black, and thereto have a wit,

She'll find a white that shall her blackness
DES. Worse and worse.   [fit.
EMIL. How if fair and foolish?
IAGO. She never yet was foolish that was
fair;
For even her folly help'd her to an heir.
DES. These are old fond paradoxes, to
make fools laugh i' the alehouse. What
miserable praise hast thou for her that's
foul and foolish?
IAGO. There's none so foul, and foolish
thereunto,
But does foul pranks which fair and wise
ones do.
DES. O heavy ignorance! thou praisest the
worst best. But what praise could'st thou
bestow on a deserving woman indeed,—
one that, in the authority of her merit, did
justly put on the vouch of very malice
itself?
IAGO. She that was ever fair, and never
proud;
Had tongue at will, and yet was never
loud;
Never lack'd gold, and yet went never gay;
Fled from her wish, and yet said, "now I
may;"
She that, being anger'd, her revenge being
nigh,   [fly;
Bade her wrong stay, and her displeasure
She that in wisdom never was so frail,
To change the cod's head for the salmon's
tail;
She that could think, and ne'er disclose her
mind;
See suitors following, and not look behind;
She was a wight,—if ever such wight
were,—
DES. To do what?
IAGO. To suckle fools, and chronicle small
beer.
DES. O most lame and impotent conclusion!—Do not learn of him, Emilia, though
he be thy husband.—How say you, Cassio?
is he not a most profane and liberal counsellor?
CAS. He speaks home, Madam: you may
relish him more in the soldier, than in the
scholar.
IAGO. [Aside.] He takes her by the palm:
ay, well said, whisper: with as little a web
as this, will I ensnare as great a fly as
Cassio. Ay, smile upon her, do; I will
gyve thee in thine own courtship. You say
true; 'tis so, indeed: if such tricks as these
strip you out of your lieutenantry, it had
been better you had not kissed your three
fingers so oft, which now again you are
most apt to play the sir in. Very good;
well kissed! an excellent courtesy! 'tis so,
indeed. Yet again your fingers to your lips?

would they were clyster-pipes for your
sake!—[A trumpet heard.] The Moor! I
know his trumpet.
CAS. 'Tis truly so.
DES. Let's meet him, and receive him.
CAS. Lo, where he comes!
       Enter OTHELLO and Attendants.
OTH. O my fair warrior!
DES.   My dear Othello!
OTH. It gives me wonder great as my
content,
To see you here before me. O my soul's
joy!
If after every tempest come such calms,
May the winds blow till they have waken'd
death!
And let the labouring bark climb hills of
seas,
Olympus-high, and duck again as low
As hell's from heaven! If it were now to
die,
'Twere now to be most happy; for, I fear,
My soul hath her content so absolute,
That not another comfort like to this
Succeeds in unknown fate.
DES.   The heavens forbid
But that our loves and comforts should
increase,
Even as our days do grow!
OTH.   Amen to that, sweet powers!—
I cannot speak enough of this content;
It stops me here; it is too much of joy:
And this, and this, [Kissing her.] the
greatest discords be,
That e'er our hearts shall make!
IAGO. [Aside.]   O, you are well tun'd
now!
But I'll set down the pegs that make this
As honest as I am.   [music.
OTH.   Come, let us to the castle.—
News, friends; our wars are done, the
Turks are drown'd.
How does my old acquaintance of this
isle?—
Honey, you shall be well desir'd in Cyprus;
I have found great love amongst them. O
my sweet,
I prattle out of fashion, and I dote
In mine own comforts.—I pr'ythee, good
Iago,
Go to the bay, and disembark my coffers:
Bring thou the master to the citadel;
He is a good one, and his worthiness
Does challenge much respect.—Come, Des
demona,
Once more well met at Cyprus.
      [Exeunt all except IAGO and RODERIGO.
IAGO. Do thou meet me presently at the
harbour. Come hither. If thou be'st vali
ant,—as, they say, base men, being in love
have then a nobility in their natures more

than is native to them,—list me. The lieutenant to-night watches on the court of guard:—first, I must tell thee this,—Desdemona is directly in love with him.

ROD. With him! why, 'tis not possible.

IAGO. Lay thy finger thus, and let thy soul be instructed. Mark me with what violence she first loved the Moor, but for bragging, and telling her fantastical lies: and will she love him still for prating? let not thy discreet heart think it. Her eye must be fed; and what delight shall she have to look on the devil? When the blood is made dull with the act of sport, there should be,—again to inflame it, and to give satiety a fresh appetite,—loveliness in favour, sympathy in years, manners, and beauties; all which the Moor is defective in: now, for want of these required conveniences, her delicate tenderness will find itself abused, begin to heave the gorge, disrelish and abhor the Moor; very nature will instruct her in it, and compel her to some second choice. Now, Sir, this granted, —as it is a most pregnant and unforced position,—who stands so eminently in the degree of this fortune, as Cassio does? a knave very voluble; no farther conscionable, than in putting on the mere form of civil and humane seeming for the better compassing of his salt and most hidden loose affection? why, none; why, none: a subtle slippery knave; a finder-out of occasions; that has an eye can stamp and counterfeit advantages, though true advantage never present itself: a devilish knave! besides, the knave is handsome, young, and hath all those requisites in him, that folly and green minds look after: a pestilent complete knave; and the woman hath found him already.

ROD. I cannot believe that in her; she is full of most blessed condition.

IAGO. Blessed fig's end! the wine she drinks is made of grapes: if she had been blessed, she would never have loved the Moor: blessed pudding! Didst thou not see her paddle with the palm of his hand? didst not mark that?

ROD. Yes, that I did; but that was but courtesy.

IAGO. Lechery, by this hand; an index and obscure prologue to the history of lust and foul thoughts. They met so near with their lips, that their breaths embraced together. Villanous thoughts, Roderigo! when these mutualities so marshal the way, hard at hand comes the master and main exercise, the incorporate conclusion: pish!— But, Sir, be you ruled by me: I have brought you from Venice. Watch you to-

night; for the command, I'll lay't upon you: Cassio knows you not:—I'll not be far from you: do you find some occasion to anger Cassio, either by speaking too loud, or tainting his discipline; or from what other course you please, which the time shall more favourably minister.

ROD. Well.

IAGO. Sir, he is rash, and very sudden in choler, and, haply, may strike at you: provoke him, that he may; for even out of that will I cause these of Cyprus to mutiny; whose qualification shall come into no true taste again, but by the displanting of Cassio. So shall you have a shorter journey to your desires, by the means I shall then have to prefer them; and the impediment most profitably removed, without the which there were no expectation of our prosperity.

ROD. I will do this, if I can bring it to any opportunity.

IAGO. I warrant thee. Meet me by and by at the citadel: I must fetch his necessaries ashore. Farewell.

ROD. Adieu.   [*Exit.*

IAGO. That Cassio loves her, I do well believe it;

That she loves him, 'tis apt, and of great credit:

The Moor—howbeit that I endure him not,—

Is of a constant, loving, noble nature;

And, I dare think, he'll prove to Desdemona

A most dear husband. Now, I do love her too;   [venture,

Not out of absolute lust, (though, perad-I stand accountant for as great a sin)

But partly led to die at my revenge,

For that I do suspect the lusty Moor

Hath leap'd into my seat: the thought whereof

Doth, like a poisonous mineral, gnaw my inwards;

And nothing can or shall content my soul,

Till I am even'd with him, wife for wife;

Or, failing so, yet that I put the Moor

At least into a jealousy so strong

That judgment cannot cure. Which thing to do,—

If this poor trash of Venice, whom I trash

For his quick hunting, stand the putting on,—

I'll have our Michael Cassio on the hip;

Abuse him to the Moor in the rank garb,—

For I fear Cassio with my night-cap too;—

Make the Moor thank me, love me, and reward me,

For making him egregiously an ass,

And practising upon his peace and quiet,

Even to madness. 'Tis here, but yet confus'd:
Knavery's plain face is never seen, till us'd.   [*Exit.*

SCENE II.—*A Street.*

Enter a Herald, *with a proclamation; people following.*

HER. It is Othello's pleasure, our noble and valiant general, that, upon certain tidings now arrived, importing the mere perdition of the Turkish fleet, every man put himself into triumph; some to dance, some to make bonfires, each man to what sport and revels his addiction leads him: for, besides these beneficial news, it is the celebration of his nuptial:—so much was his pleasure should be proclaimed. All offices are open; and there is full liberty of feasting, from this present hour of five, till the bell have told eleven. Heaven bless the isle of Cyprus, and our noble general Othello!   [*Exeunt.*

SCENE III.—*A Hall in the Castle.*

Enter OTHELLO, DESDEMONA, CASSIO, *and* Attendants.

OTH. Good Michael, look you to the guard to-night:
Let's teach ourselves that honourable stop,
Not to out-sport discretion.
CAS. Iago hath direction what to do;
But, notwithstanding, with my personal eye
Will I look to't.
OTH.   Iago is most honest.
Michael, good night: to-morrow, with your earliest,
Let me have speech with you.—[*To* DES.]
Come, my dear love,—
The purchase made, the fruits are to ensue;
That profit's yet to come 'tween me and you.—
Good night.   [you.—
        [*Exeunt* OTH., DES. *and* Attend.
        Enter IAGO.
CAS. Welcome, Iago: we must to the watch.
IAGO. Not this hour, lieutenant; 'tis not yet ten o'clock. Our general cast us thus early for the love of his Desdemona; whom let us not therefore blame: he hath not yet made wanton the night with her; and she is sport for Jove.
CAS. She's a most exquisite lady.
IAGO. And, I'll warrant her, full of game.
CAS. Indeed, she is a most fresh and delicate creature.

IAGO. What an eye she has! methinks it sounds a parley of provocation.
CAS. An inviting eye; and yet methinks right modest.
IAGO. And when she speaks, is it not an alarum to love?
CAS. She is, indeed, perfection.
IAGO. Well, happiness to their sheets! Come, lieutenant, I have a stoop of wine; and here without are a brace of Cyprus gallants, that would fain have a measure to the health of black Othello.
CAS. Not to-night, good Iago: I have very poor and unhappy brains for drinking: I could well wish courtesy would invent some other custom of entertainment.
IAGO. O, they are our friends; but one cup: I'll drink for you.
CAS. I have drunk but one cup to-night, and that was craftily qualified too, and, behold, what innovation it makes here: I am unfortunate in the infirmity, and dare not task my weakness with any more.
IAGO. What, man! 'tis a night of revels: the gallants desire it.
CAS. Where are they?
IAGO. Here at the door; I pray you, call them in.
CAS. I'll do't; but it dislikes me. [*Exit.*
IAGO. If I can fasten but one cup upon him,
With that which he hath drunk to-night already,
He'll be as full of quarrel and offence
As my young mistress' dog. Now, my sick fool Roderigo,
Whom love has turn'd almost the wrong side out,
To Desdemona hath to-night carous'd
Potations pottle deep; and he's to watch:
Three lads of Cyprus,—noble swelling spirits,
That hold their honours in a wary distance,
The very elements of this warlike isle,—
Have I to-night fluster'd with flowing cups,
And they watch too. Now, 'mongst this flock of drunkards,
Am I to put our Cassio in some action
That may offend the isle:—but here they come:
If consequence do but approve my dream,
My boat sails freely, both with wind and stream.
Re-enter CASSIO, *with him* MONTANO, *and* Gentlemen. Servant *following with wine.*
CAS. 'Fore heaven, they have given me a rouse already.
MON. Good faith, a little one; not past a pint, as I am a soldier.

IAGO. Some wine, ho!
[*Singing.*]

> And let me the canakin clink, clink;
> And let me the canakin clink;
>   A soldier's a man;
>   A life's but a span;
> Why, then let a soldier drink.

Some wine, boys!
CAS. 'Fore heaven, an excellent song.
IAGO. I learned it in England, where, indeed, they are most potent in potting: your Dane, your German, and your swag-bellied Hollander,—Drink, ho!—are nothing to your English.
CAS. Is your Englishman so exquisite in his drinking?
IAGO. Why, he drinks you with facility, your Dane dead drunk; he sweats not to overthrow your Almain; he gives your Hollander a vomit, ere the next pottle can be filled.
CAS. To the health of our general!
MON. I am for it, lieutenant; and I'll do you justice.
IAGO. O sweet England!

> King Stephen was a worthy peer,
>   His breeches cost him but a crown;
> He held them sixpence all too dear,
>   With that he call'd the tailor lown.
>
> He was a wight of high renown,
>   And thou art but of low degree:
> 'Tis pride that pulls the country down;
>   Then take thine auld cloak about thee.

Some wine, ho!
CAS. Why, this is a more exquisite song than the other.
IAGO. Will you hear it again?
CAS. No; for I hold him to be unworthy of his place, that does those things.—Well, —heaven's above all; and there be souls must be saved, and there be souls must not be saved.
IAGO. It's true, good lieutenant.
CAS. For mine own part,—no offence to the general, nor any man of quality,—I hope to be saved.
IAGO. And so do I too, lieutenant.
CAS. Ay, but, by your leave, not before me; the lieutenant is to be saved before the ancient. Let's have no more of this; let's to our affairs.—Forgive us our sins! —Gentlemen, let's look to our business. Do not think, gentlemen, I am drunk: this is my ancient;—this is my right hand, and this is my left hand:—I am not drunk now; I can stand well enough, and speak well enough.
ALL. Excellent well.

CAS. Why, very well, then; you must not think, then, that I am drunk.   [*Exit.*
MON. To the platform, masters; come, let's set the watch.
IAGO. You see this fellow that is gone before;—
He is a soldier fit to stand by Cæsar
And give direction: and do but see his vice;
'Tis to his virtue a just equinox,
The one as long as th' other: 'tis pity of him.
I fear, the trust Othello puts him in,
On some odd time of his infirmity,
Will shake this island.
MON.   But is he often thus?
IAGO. 'Tis evermore the prologue to his sleep:
He'll watch the horologe a double set,
If drink rock not his cradle.
MON.   It were well,
The general were put in mind of it.
Perhaps he sees it not; or his good nature
Prizes the virtue that appears in Cassio,
And looks not on his evils: is not this true?
            Enter RODERIGO.
IAGO. [*Aside to him.*] How now, Roderigo!
I pray you, after the lieutenant; go.
                    [*Exit* ROD.
MON. And 'tis great pity, that the noble Moor
Should hazard such a place as his own second,
With one of an ingraft infirmity:
It were an honest action to say
So to the Moor.
IAGO.   Not I, for this fair island:
I do love Cassio well; and would do much
To cure him of this evil. But hark! what noise?   [*Cry within,* "Help! Help!"
Re-enter CASSIO, *driving in* RODERIGO.
CAS. You rogue! you rascal!
MON.   What's the matter, lieutenant?
CAS. A knave!—teach me my duty?
I'll beat the knave into a twiggen bottle.
ROD. Beat me!
CAS.   Dost thou prate, rogue?
                [*Striking* RODERIGO.
MON. [*Staying him.*] Nay, good lieutenant;
I pray you, Sir, hold your hand.   [ant;
CAS.   Let me go, Sir,
Or I'll knock you o'er the mazard.
MON.   Come, come, you're drunk.
CAS. Drunk!   [*They fight.*
IAGO. [*Aside to* ROD.] Away, I say: go out, and cry a mutiny!   [*Exit* ROD.
Nay, good lieutenant,—alas, gentlemen;—
Help, ho!—Lieutenant,—Sir,—Montano,—Sir;—

Help, masters!—Here's a goodly watch, indeed!
                [*Bell rings.*

Who's that that rings the bell?—Diablo,
ho!   [hold!
The town will rise: God's will, lieutenant,
You will be sham'd for ever.
Re-enter OTHELLO *and* Attendants.
OTH.   What is the matter here?
MON. 'Zounds, I bleed still; I am hurt to
the death.
OTH. Hold, for your lives!
IAGO. Hold, hold, lieutenant!—Sir,—
Montano,—gentlemen,—
Have you forgot all sense of place and
duty?
Hold! the general speaks to you, hold, for
shame!
OTH. Why, how now, ho! from whence
ariseth this?
Are we turn'd Turks, and to ourselves do
that
Which heaven hath forbid the Ottomites?
For Christian shame, put by this barbarous
brawl:
He that stirs next to carve for his own
rage,
Holds his soul light; he dies upon his
motion.—
Silence that dreadful bell! it frights the
isle
From her propriety.—What is the matter,
masters?—
Honest Iago, that look'st dead with griev-
ing,   [charge thee.
Speak, who began this? on thy love, I
IAGO. I do not know:—friends all but
now, even now,
In quarter, and in terms like bride and
groom
Devesting them for bed; and then, but
now,
(As if some planet had unwitted men)
Swords out, and tilting one at other's
breast,
In opposition bloody. I cannot speak
Any beginning to this peevish odds;
And would in action glorious I had lost
Those legs, that brought me to a part of it!
OTH. How comes it, Michael, you are thus
forgot?
CAS. I pray you, pardon me; I cannot
speak.
OTH. Worthy Montano, you were wont be
civil;
The gravity and stillness of your youth
The world hath noted, and your name is
great   [matter.
In mouths of wisest censure; what's the
That you unlace your reputation thus,
And spend your rich opinion, for the name
Of a night-brawler? give me answer to it.
MON. Worthy Othello, I am hurt to dan-
ger:

Your officer, Iago, can inform you,—
While I spare speech, which something now
offends me,—
Of all that I do know: nor know I aught
By me that's said or done amiss this night;
Unless self-charity be sometimes a vice,
And to defend ourselves it be a sin,
When violence assails us.
OTH.   Now, by heaven,
My blood begins my safer guides to rule;
And passion, having my best judgment
collied,
Assays to lead the way:—if I once stir,
Or do but lift this arm, the best of you
Shall sink in my rebuke. Give me to know
How this foul rout began, who set it on;
And he that is approv'd in this offence,
Though he had twinn'd with me, both at a
birth,
Shall lose me.—What! in a town of war,
Yet wild, the people's hearts brimful of
fear,
To manage private and domestic quarrel,
In night, and on the court and guard of
safety!
'Tis monstrous.—Iago, who began it?
MON. If partially affin'd, or leagu'd in
office,
Thou dost deliver more or less than truth,
Thou art no soldier.
IAGO.   Touch me not so near:
I had rather have this tongue cut from my
mouth,
Than it should do offence to Michael
Cassio;
Yet, I persuade myself, to speak the truth
Shall nothing wrong him.—Thus it is, gen-
eral.
Montano and myself being in speech,
There comes a fellow, crying out for help;
And Cassio following him with determin'd
sword,
To execute upon him. Sir, this gentleman
Steps in to Cassio, and entreats his pause
Myself the crying fellow did pursue,
Lest by his clamour (as it so fell out)
The town might fall in fright: he, swift of
foot,
Outran my purpose; and I return'd, the
rather
For that I heard the clink and fall of
swords,
And Cassio high in oath; which till to
night   [back
I ne'er might say before. When I came
(For this was brief) I found them close
together,   [were
At blow and thrust; even as again they
When you yourself did part them.
More of this matter can I not report:—

But men are men; the best sometimes forget:—
Though Cassio did some little wrong to him,—
As men in rage strike those that wish them best,—
Yet, surely, Cassio, I believe, received
From him that fled some strange indignity,
Which patience could not pass.
OTH.   I know, Iago,
Thy honesty and love doth mince this matter,   [thee;
Making it light to Cassio.—Cassio, I love
But never more be officer of mine.—
          Re-enter DESDEMONA, *attended.*
Look, if my gentle love be not rais'd up!—
[*To* CAS.] I'll make thee an example.
DES.   What's the matter?
OTH. All's well now, sweeting; come away to bed.—
Sir, for your hurts, myself will be your surgeon.—
Lead him off.—   [MONTANO *is led off.*
Iago, look with care about the town,
And silence those whom this vile brawl distracted.—
Come, Desdemona: 'tis the soldiers' life,
To have their balmy slumbers wak'd with strife.
          [*Exeunt all except* IAGO *and* CASSIO.
IAGO. What, are you hurt, lieutenant?
CAS. Ay, past all surgery.
IAGO. Marry, heaven forbid!
CAS. Reputation, reputation, reputation! O, I have lost my reputation! I have lost the immortal part of myself, and what remains is bestial.—My reputation, Iago, my reputation!
IAGO. As I am an honest man, I thought you had received some bodily wound; there is more offence in that, than in reputation. Reputation is an idle and most false imposition; oft got without merit, and lost without deserving: you have lost no reputation at all, unless you repute yourself such a loser. What, man! there are ways to recover the general again: you are but now cast in his mood, a punishment more in policy than in malice; even so as one would beat his offenceless dog, to affright an imperious lion: sue to him again, and he's yours.
CAS. I will rather sue to be despised, than to deceive so good a commander, with so slight, so drunken, and so indiscreet an officer. Drunk? and speak parrot? and squabble? swagger? swear? and discourse fustian with one's own shadow?—O thou invisible spirit of wine, if thou hast no name to be known by, let us call thee devil!

IAGO. What was he that you followed with your sword? What had he done to you?
CAS. I know not.
IAGO. Is't possible?
CAS. I remember a mass of things, but nothing distinctly; a quarrel, but nothing wherefore.—O God, that men should put an enemy in their mouths, to steal away their brains! that we should, with joy, pleasance, revel, and applause, transform ourselves into beasts!
IAGO. Why, but you are now well enough: how came you thus recovered?
CAS. It hath pleased the devil drunkenness, to give place to the devil wrath: one unperfectness shows me another, to make me frankly despise myself.
IAGO. Come, you are too severe a moraler: as the time, the place, and the condition of this country stands, I could heartily wish this had not befallen; but, since it is as it is, mend it for your own good.
CAS. I will ask him for my place again,—he shall tell me I am a drunkard! Had I as many mouths as Hydra, such an answer would stop them all. To be now a sensible man, by and by a fool, and presently a beast! O strange!—Every inordinate cup is unblessed, and the ingredient is a devil.
IAGO. Come, come, good wine is a good familiar creature, if it be well used: exclaim no more against it. And, good lieutenant, I think you think I love you.
CAS. I have well approved it, Sir.—I drunk!
IAGO. You, or any man living, may be drunk at some time, man. I'll tell you what you shall do. Our general's wife is now the general;—I may say so in this respect, for that he hath devoted and given up himself to the contemplation, mark, and denotement of her parts and graces:—confess yourself freely to her; importune her; she'll help to put you in your place again. She is of so free, so kind, so apt, so blessed a disposition, that she holds it a vice in her goodness, not to do more than she is requested: this broken joint between you and her husband, entreat her to splinter; and, my fortunes against any lay worth naming, this crack of your love shall grow stronger than it was before.
CAS. You advise me well.
IAGO. I protest, in the sincerity of love and honest kindness.
CAS. I think it freely; and, betimes in the morning, I will beseech the virtuous Desdemona to undertake for me: I am desperate of my fortunes, if they check me here.

IAGO. You are in the right. Good night,
lieutenant; I must to the watch.
CAS. Good night, honest Iago.   [*Exit.*
IAGO. And what's he, then, that says I
play the villain?
When this advice is free I give, and honest,
Probal to thinking, and, indeed, the course
To win the Moor again? For 'tis most easy
The inclining Desdemona to subdue
In any honest suit: she's fram'd as fruitful
As the free elements. And, then, for her
To win the Moor,—were't to renounce his
baptism,
All seals and symbols of redeemed sin,—
His soul is so enfetter'd to her love,
That she may make, unmake, do what she
list,
Even as her appetite shall play the god
With his weak function. How am I, then,
a villain,
To counsel Cassio to this parallel course,
Directly to his good? Divinity of hell!
When devils will the blackest sins put on,
They do suggest at first with heavenly
shows,
As I do now: or while this honest fool
Plies Desdemona to repair his fortunes,
And she for him pleads strongly to the
Moor,
I'll pour this pestilence into his ear,—
That she repeals him for her body's lust;
And, by how much she strives to do him
good,
She shall undo her credit with the Moor.
So will I turn her virtue into pitch;
And out of her own goodness make the net
That shall enmesh them all.—
        Re-enter RODERIGO.
                How now, Roderigo!
ROD. I do follow here in the chase, not
like a hound that hunts, but one that fills
up the cry. My money is almost spent; I
have been to-night exceedingly well cudg-
elled; and I think the issue will be—I
shall have so much experience for my
pains; and so, with no money at all, and a
little more wit, return again to Venice.
IAGO. How poor are they that have not
patience!
What wound did ever heal, but by degrees?
Thou know'st we work by wit, and not by
witchcraft;
And wit depends on dilatory time.
Does't not go well? Cassio hath beaten
thee,   [*Cassio*
And thou, by that small hurt, hast cashier'd
Though other things grow fair against the
sun,   [*ripe:*
Yet fruits that blossom first will first be
Content thyself a while.—By the mass, 'tis
morning;

Pleasure and action make the hours seem
                        [short.—
Retire thee; go where thou art billeted:
Away, I say; thou shalt know more here-
after:
Nay, get thee gone. [*Exit* ROD.] Two
things are to be done,—
My wife must move for Cassio to her mis-
I'll set her on: [*tress;*
Myself, the while, to draw the Moor apart,
And bring him jump when he may Cassio
find
Soliciting his wife:—ay, that's the way;
Dull not device by coldness and delay.
                        [*Exit.*

ACT III.

SCENE I.—CYPRUS. *Before the Castle.*
    Enter CASSIO, *and some* Musicians.
CAS. Masters, play here,—I will content
your pains,—
Something that's brief; and bid good-
morrow, general.   [*Music.*
        Enter Clown.
CLO. Why, masters, have your instruments been in Naples, that they speak i'
the nose thus?
1 MUS. How, Sir, how?
CLO. Are these, I pray you, wind instruments?
1 MUS. Ay, marry, are they, Sir.
CLO. O, thereby hangs a tail.
1 MUS. Whereby hangs a tale, Sir?
CLO. Marry, Sir, by many a wind instrument that I know. But, masters, here's
money for you: and the general so likes
your music, that he desires you, for love's
sake, to make no more noise with it.
1 MUS. Well, Sir, we will not.
CLO. If you have any music that may not
be heard, to't again: but, as they say, to
hear music the general does not greatly
care.
1 MUS. We have none such, Sir.
CLO. Then put up your pipes in your bag,
for I'll away. Go; vanish into air; away!
                    [*Exeunt* Musicians.
CAS. Dost thou hear, mine honest friend?
CLO. No, I hear not your honest friend;
I hear you.
CAS. Pr'ythee, keep up thy quillets.
There's a poor piece of gold for thee: if
the gentlewoman that attends the general's
wife be stirring, tell her there's one Cassio
entreats her a little favour of speech: wilt
thou do this?
CLO. She is stirring, Sir: if she will stir
hither, I shall seem to notify unto her.
CAS. Do, good my friend.— [*Exit* Clown.

Enter IAGO.

        In happy time, Iago.

IAGO. You have not been a-bed, then?

CAS. Why, no; the day had broke
Before we parted. I have made bold, Iago,
To send in to your wife: my suit to her
Is, that she will to virtuous Desdemona
Procure me some access.

IAGO.   I'll send her to you presently;
And I'll devise a mean to draw the Moor
Out of the way, that your converse and
May be more free.   [business

CAS. I humbly thank you for't.—
              [*Exit* IAGO.
        I never knew
A Florentine more kind and honest.

Enter EMILIA.

EMIL. Good morrow, good lieutenant: I
   am sorry
For your displeasure; but all will soon be
   well.
The general and his wife are talking of it;
And she speaks for you stoutly: the Moor
   replies,   [prus,
That he you hurt is of great fame in Cy-
And great affinity, and that in wholesome
   wisdom
He might not but refuse you; but he pro-
   tests he loves you,
And needs no other suitor but his likings,
To take the saf'st occasion by the front,
To bring you in again.

CAS.   Yet, I beseech you,—
If you think fit, or that it may be done,—
Give me advantage of some brief discourse
With Desdemona alone.

EMIL.   Pray you, come in:
I will bestow you where you shall have
To speak your bosom freely.   [time

CAS.   I am much bound to you.
              [*Exeunt.*

Scene II.—*A Room in the Castle.*

Enter OTHELLO, IAGO, *and* Gentlemen.

OTH. These letters give, Iago, to the pilot;
And, by him, do my duties to the senate:
That done, I will be walking on the works;
Repair there to me.

IAGO.   Well, my good lord, I'll do't.

OTH. This fortification, gentlemen,—shall
   we see't?

GENT. We'll wait upon your lordship.
              [*Exeunt.*

Scene III.—*Before the Castle.*

Enter DESDEMONA, CASSIO, *and* EMILIA.

DES. Be thou assur'd, good Cassio, I will
All my abilities in thy behalf.   [do

EMIL. Good Madam, do: I warrant it
   grieves my husband,
As if the case were his.

DES. O, that's an honest fellow.—Do not
   doubt, Cassio,
But I will have my lord and you again
As friendly as you were.

CAS.   Bounteous Madam,
Whatever shall become of Michael Cassio,
He's never any thing but your true servant.

DES. I know't,—I thank you. You do love
   my lord: [assur'd,
You have known him long; and be you well
He shall in strangeness stand no farther off
Than in a politic distance.

CAS.   Ay, but, lady,
That policy may either last so long,
Or feed upon such nice and waterish diet,
Or breed itself so out of circumstance,
That, I being absent, and my place sup-
   plied,   [ice.
My general will forget my love and serv-

DES. Do not doubt that; before Emilia
   here,
I give thee warrant of thy place: assure
   thee,
If I do vow a friendship, I'll perform it
To the last article: my lord shall never
   rest;   [patience;
I'll watch him tame, and talk him out of
His bed shall seem a school, his board a
   shrift;
I'll intermingle every thing he does
With Cassio's suit: therefore be merry,
   Cassio;
For thy solicitor shall rather die,
Than give thy cause away.

EMIL. Madam, here comes my lord.

CAS. Madam, I'll take my leave.

DES. Why, stay, and hear me speak.

CAS. Madam, not now: I am very ill at
Unfit for mine own purpose.   [ease,

DES. Well, do your discretion.
           [*Exit* CASSIO.

Enter OTHELLO *and* IAGO.

IAGO. Ha! I like not that.

OTH.   What dost thou say?

IAGO. Nothing, my lord: or if—I know
   not what.

OTH. Was not that Cassio parted from
   my wife?

IAGO. Cassio, my lord? No, sure, I can-
   not think it,
That he would steal away so guilty-like,
Seeing you coming.

OTH.   I do believe 'twas he.

DES. How now, my lord!
I have been talking with a suitor here,
A man that languishes in your displeasure.

OTH. Who is't you mean?

DES. Why, your lieutenant, Cassio. Good
my lord,
If I have any grace or power to move you,
His present reconciliation take;
For if he be not one that truly loves you,
That errs in ignorance, and not in cunning,
I have no judgment in an honest face:
I pr'ythee, call him back.
OTH. Went he hence now?
DES. Ay, sooth; so humbled,
That he hath left part of his grief with me,
To suffer with him. Good love, call him
back.
OTH. Not now, sweet Desdemona; some
other time.
DES. But shall't be shortly?
OTH. The sooner, sweet, for you.
DES. Shall't be to-night at supper?
OTH. No, not to-night.
DES. To-morrow dinner, then?
OTH. I shall not dine at home;
I meet the captains at the citadel.
DES. Why then, to-morrow night; or
Tuesday morn;
On Tuesday noon, or night; on Wednes-
day morn:—
I pr'ythee, name the time; but let it not
Exceed three days: in faith, he's penitent.
And yet his trespass, in our common rea-
son,   [examples
(Save that, they say, the wars must make
Out of their best) is not almost a fault
To incur a private check. When shall he
come?
Tell me, Othello: I wonder in my soul,
What you could ask me that I should deny,
Or stand so mammering on. What! Mi-
chael Cassio,
That came a wooing with you; and so
many a time,
When I have spoke of you dispraisingly,
Hath ta'en your part; to have so much to
do   [much,—
To bring him in! Trust me, I could do
OTH. Pr'ythee, no more: let him come
when he will;
I will deny thee nothing.
DES. Why, this is not a boon;
'Tis as I should entreat you wear your
gloves,   [warm,
Or feed on nourishing dishes, or keep you
Or sue to you to do a peculiar profit
To your own person: nay, when I have a
suit
Wherein I mean to touch your love indeed,
It shall be full of poise and difficult weight,
And fearful to be granted.
OTH. I will deny thee nothing:
Whereon, I do beseech thee, grant me this,
To leave me but a little to myself.

DES. Shall I deny you? no: farewell, my
lord.
OTH. Farewell, my Desdemona: I'll come
to thee straight.
DES. Emilia, come.—Be as your fancies
teach you;
Whate'er you be, I am obedient.
             [*Exit, with* EMILIA.
OTH. Excellent wretch! Perdition catch
my soul,
But I do love thee! and when I love thee
Chaos is come again.   [not,
IAGO. My noble lord,—
OTH. What dost thou say, Iago?
IAGO. Did Michael Cassio, when you
woo'd my lady,
Know of your love?
OTH. He did, from first to last: why dost
thou ask?
IAGO. But for a satisfaction of my
No farther harm.   [thought;
OTH. Why of thy thought, Iago?
IAGO. I did not think he had been ac-
quainted with her.
OTH. O, yes; and went between us very
oft.
IAGO. Indeed!
OTH. Indeed! ay, indeed:—discern'st thou
aught in that?
Is he not honest?
IAGO. Honest, my lord?
OTH. Honest? ay, honest.
IAGO. My lord, for aught I know.
OTH. What dost thou think?
IAGO. Think, my lord?
OTH. Think, my lord!
By heaven, he echoes me,   [thought
As if there were some monster in his
Too hideous to be shown.—Thou dost mean
something: [that,
I heard thee say but now,—thou lik'dst not
When Cassio left my wife: what didst not
like?
And when I told thee he was of my counsel
In my whole course of wooing, thou criedst,
"Indeed!"
And didst contract and purse thy brow
together,
As if thou then hadst shut up in thy brain
Some horrible conceit: if thou dost love me,
Show me thy thought.
IAGO. My lord, you know I love you.
OTH. I think thou dost;
And,—for I know thou art full of love
and honesty,
And weigh'st thy words before thou giv'st
them breath,—
Therefore these stops of thine fright me
the more:
For such things, in a false disloyal knave,

Are tricks of custom; but in a man that's just,   [heart,
They are close delations, working from the
That passion cannot rule.
IAGO.   For Michael Cassio,
I dare be sworn, I think that he is honest.
OTH. I think so too.
IAGO.   Men should be what they seem;
Or, those that be not, would they might
     seem none!
OTH. Certain, men should be what they
     seem.
IAGO. Why, then, I think Cassio's an hon-
     est man.
OTH. Nay, yet there's more in this:
I pray thee, speak to me as to thy think-
     ings,
As thou dost ruminate; and give thy worst
The worst of words.   [of thoughts
IAGO.   Good my lord, pardon me:
Though I am bound to every act of duty,
I am not bound to that all slaves are free
     to.
Utter my thoughts? Why, say, they are
     vile and false,—
As where's that palace whereinto foul
     things   [so pure,
Sometimes intrude not? who has a breast
But some uncleanly apprehensions
Keep leets and law-days, and in session sit
With meditations lawful?
OTH. Thou dost conspire against thy
     friend, Iago,
If thou but think'st him wrong'd, and
     mak'st his ear
A stranger to thy thoughts.
IAGO.   I do beseech you,—
Though I, perchance, am vicious in my
     guess,
(As, I confess, it is my nature's plague
To spy into abuses; and oft my jealousy
Shapes faults that are not)—that your wis-
     dom yet,
From one that so imperfectly conceits,
Would take no notice; nor build yourself
     a trouble   [ance.
Out of his scattering and unsure observ-
It were not for your quiet, nor your good,
Nor for my manhood, honesty, or wisdom,
To let you know my thoughts.
OTH.   What dost thou mean?
IAGO. Good name in man and woman,
     dear my lord,
Is the immediate jewel of their souls:
Who steals my purse, steals trash; 'tis
     something, nothing;
'Twas mine, 'tis his, and has been slave to
     thousands;   [name,
But he, that filches from me my good
Robs me of that, which not enriches him,
And makes me poor indeed.

OTH. By heaven, I'll know thy thoughts.
IAGO. You cannot, if my heart were in
     your hand;
Nor shall not, whilst 'tis in my custody.
OTH. Ha!
IAGO.   O, beware, my lord, of jealousy;
It is the green-ey'd monster, which doth
     mock   [in bliss,
The meat it feeds on: that cuckold lives
Who, certain of his fate, loves not his
     wronger;
But, O, what damned minutes tells he o'er,
Who dotes, yet doubts; suspects, yet
     strongly loves!
OTH. O misery!
IAGO. Poor and content is rich, and rich
     enough;
But riches fineless is as poor as winter
To him that ever fears he shall be poor:—
Good heaven, the souls of all my tribe de-
From jealousy!   [fend
OTH.   Why, why is this?
Think'st thou I'd make a life of jealousy,
To follow still the changes of the moon
With fresh suspicions? No; to be once in
     doubt,   [goat,
Is once to be resolv'd: exchange me for a
When I shall turn the business of my soul
To such exsufflicate and blown surmises,
Matching thy inference. 'Tis not to make
     me jealous,
To say my wife is fair, feeds well, loves
     company,   [well;
Is free of speech, sings, plays, and dances
Where virtue is, these are more virtuous:
Nor from mine own weak merits will I
     draw
The smallest fear, or doubt of her revolt;
For she had eyes, and chose me. No, Iago;
I'll see before I doubt; when I doubt,
     prove;   [this,—
And, on the proof, there is no more but
Away at once with love, or jealousy!
IAGO. I am glad of it; for now I shall
     have reason
To show the love and duty that I bear you
With franker spirit: therefore, as I am
     bound,   [proof.
Receive it from me:—I speak not yet of
Look to your wife; observe her well with
     Cassio;
Wear your eye thus,—not jealous, nor se-
     cure: [ture,
I would not have your free and noble na-
Out of self-bounty, be abus'd; look to't:
I know our country disposition well;
In Venice they do let heaven see the pranks
They dare not show their husbands; their
     best conscience
Is, not to leave undone, but keep unknown.
OTH. Dost thou say so?

IAGO. She did deceive her father, marrying you;
And, when she seem'd to shake, and fear
She lov'd them most.   [your looks,
OTH.   And so she did.
IAGO.   Why, go to, then;
She that, so young, could give out such a seeming,
To seel her father's eyes up, close as oak,—
He thought 'twas witchcraft:—but I am much to blame;
I humbly do beseech you of your pardon,
For too much loving you.
OTH.   I am bound to thee for ever.
IAGO. I see, this hath a little dash'd your spirits.
OTH. Not a jot, not a jot.
IAGO.   Trust me, I fear it has.
I hope you will consider what is spoke
Comes from my love:—but, I do see you are mov'd:—
I am to pray you, not to strain my speech
To grosser issues, nor to larger reach,
Than to suspicion.
OTH. I will not.
IAGO.   Should you do so, my lord,
My speech should fall into such vile success
As my thoughts aim not at. Cassio's my worthy friend:—
My lord, I see you are mov'd.
OTH.   No, not much mov'd:—
I do not think but Desdemona's honest.
IAGO. Long live she so! and long live you to think so!
OTH. And yet, how nature erring from itself,—
IAGO. Ay, there's the point:—as,—to be bold with you,—
Not to affect many proposed matches
Of her own clime, complexion, and degree,
Whereto, we see, in all things nature tends,—   [rank,
Foh! one may smell in such a will most
Foul disproportion, thoughts unnatural:—
But pardon me: I do not in position
Distinctly speak of her; though I may fear
Her will, recoiling to her better judgment,
May fall to match you with her country
And happily repent.   [forms,
OTH.   Farewell, farewell:
If more thou dost perceive, let me know more;
Set on thy wife to observe: leave me, Iago.
IAGO. My lord, I take my leave. [*Going.*
OTH. Why did I marry?—This honest creature, doubtless,
Sees and knows more, much more, than he unfolds.
IAGO. [*Returning.*] My lord, I would I might entreat your honour

To scan this thing no farther; leave it to time: [place,—
Although 'tis fit that Cassio have his
For, sure, he fills it up with great ability,—
Yet, if you please to hold him off a while,
You shall by that perceive him and his means:
Note, if your lady strain his entertainment
With any strong or vehement importunity;
Much will be seen in that. In the mean time,
Let me be thought too busy in my fears,—
As worthy cause I have to fear I am,—
And hold her free, I do beseech your honour.
OTH. Fear not my government.
IAGO. I once more take my leave. [*Exit.*
OTH. This fellow's of exceeding honesty,
And knows all qualities with a learned spirit   [gard,
Of human dealings. If I do prove her haggard,
Though that her jesses were my dear heart-strings,   [wind,
I'd whistle her off, and let her down the wind,
To prey at fortune. Haply, for I am black,
And have not those soft parts of conversation
That chamberers have; or, for I am declin'd
Into the vale of years,—yet that's not much;—
She's gone; I am abus'd; and my relief
Must be to loathe her. O curse of marriage,   [ours,
That we can call these delicate creatures ours
And not their appetites! I had rather be a toad,
And live upon the vapour of a dungeon,
Than keep a corner in the thing I love,
For others' uses. Yet, 'tis the plague of great ones;
Prerogativ'd are they less than the base;
'Tis destiny unshunnable, like death:
Even then this forked plague is fated to us,
When we do quicken.—Desdemona comes:
If she be false, O, then heaven mocks itself!   [self!—
I'll not believe it.
Re-enter DESDEMONA *and* EMILIA.
DES.   How now, my dear Othello!
Your dinner and the generous islanders,
By you invited, do attend your presence.
OTH. I am to blame.
DES. Why is your speech so faint? are you not well?
OTH. I have a pain upon my forehead here.
DES. Faith, that's with watching; 'twill away again:
Let me but bind it hard, within this hour
It will be well.

OTH.   Your napkin is too little;
     [*Puts the handkerchief from him, and
          it drops.*
Let it alone. Come, I'll go in with you.
DES. I am very sorry that you are not
well.   [*Exeunt* OTH. *and* DES.
EMIL. I am glad I have found this nap-
kin: [Moor:
This was her first remembrance from the
My wayward husband hath a hundred times
Woo'd me to steal it; but she so loves the
token,—   [it,—
For he conjur'd her she should ever keep
That she reserves it evermore about her,
To kiss, and talk to. I'll have the work
ta'en out,
And give't Iago: what he will do with it,
Heaven knows, not I;
I nothing, but to please his fantasy.
          Re-enter IAGO.
IAGO. How now! what do you here alone?
EMIL. Do not you chide; I have a thing
for you.
IAGO. A thing for me!—it is a common
EMIL. Ha?   [thing—
IAGO. To have a foolish wife.
EMIL. O, is that all? What will you give
me now
For that same handkerchief?
IAGO.   What handkerchief?
EMIL. What handkerchief!
Why, that the Moor first gave to Desde-
mona;
That which so often you did bid me steal.
IAGO. Hast stolen it from her?
EMIL. No, 'faith; she let it drop by negli-
gence;   [up.
And, to th' advantage, I, being here, took't
Look, here it is.
IAGO.   A good wench; give it me.
EMIL. What will you do with't, that you
have been so earnest
To have me filch it?
IAGO.   Why, what's that to you?
          [*Snatching it.*
EMIL. If it be not for some purpose of
import,
Give't me again: poor lady, she'll run mad
When she shall lack it.
IAGO. Be not acknown on't; I have use
for it.
Go, leave me.—   [*Exit* EMILIA.
I will in Cassio's lodging lose this napkin,
And let him find it. Trifles, light as air,
Are to the jealous confirmations strong
As proofs of holy writ. This may do some-
thing.   [son:—
The Moor already changes with my poi-
Dangerous conceits are, in their natures,
poisons,   [taste;
Which at the first are scarce found to dis-

But, with a little act upon the blood,
Burn like the mines of sulphur.—I did say
so:—   [mandragora,
Look, where he comes! Not poppy, nor
Nor all the drowsy syrups of the world,
Shall ever medicine thee to that sweet
sleep
Which thou ow'dst yesterday.
          Re-enter OTHELLO.
OTH.   Ha! ha! false to me?
IAGO. Why, how now, general! no more
of that.
OTH. Avaunt! be gone! thou hast set me
on the rack:—
I swear, 'tis better to be much abus'd,
Than but to know't a little.
IAGO.   How now, my lord!
OTH. What sense had I of her stolen
hours of lust?
I saw't not, thought it not, it harm'd not
me: [merry;
I slept the next night well, was free and
I found not Cassio's kisses on her lips:
He that is robb'd, not wanting what is
stolen,   [at all.
Let him not know't, and he's not robb'd
IAGO. I am sorry to hear this.
OTH. I had been happy, if the general
camp,   [body,
Pioneers and all, had tasted her sweet
So I had nothing known. O, now, for ever
Farewell the tranquil mind! farewell con-
tent!   [wars,
Farewell the plumed troop, and the big
That make ambition virtue! O, farewell!
Farewell the neighing steed, and the shrill
trump,   [fife,
The spirit-stirring drum, the ear-piercing
The royal banner, and all quality,
Pride, pomp, and circumstance of glorious
war!   [throats
And, O you mortal engines, whose rude
Th' immortal Jove's dread clamours coun-
terfeit,
Farewell! Othello's occupation's gone!
IAGO. Is it possible, my lord?
OTH. Villain, be sure thou prove my love
a whore,—
Be sure of it; give me the ocular proof;
          [*Seizing him by the throat.*
Or, by the worth of mine eternal soul,
Thou hadst been better have been born a
Than answer my wak'd wrath.   [dog,
IAGO.   Is't come to this?
OTH. Make me to see't; or, at the least,
so prove it,
That the probation bear no hinge nor loop
To hang a doubt on; or woe upon thy life!
IAGO. My noble lord,—
OTH. If thou dost slander her, and tor-
ture me,

Never pray more; abandon all remorse;
On horror's head horrors accumulate;
Do deeds to make heaven weep, all earth
    amaz'd;
For nothing canst thou to damnation add
Greater than that.
IAGO.   O grace! O heaven defend me!
Are you a man? have you a soul, or
    sense?—
God be wi' you; take mine office.—O
    wretched fool,
That liv'st to make thine honesty a vice!—
O monstrous world! Take note, take note,
    O world,
To be direct and honest is not safe.—
I thank you for this profit; and, from
    hence,   [offence.
I'll love no friend, since love breeds such
OTH. Nay, stay:—thou shouldst be honest.
IAGO. I should be wise; for honesty's a
And loses that it works for.   [fool,
OTH.   By the world,
I think my wife be honest, and think she
    is not;
I think that thou art just, and think thou
    art not:
I'll have some proof: her name, that was
    as fresh
As Dian's visage, is now begrim'd and black
As mine own face. If there be cords, or
    knives,
Poison, or fire, or suffocating streams,
I'll not endure it.—Would I were satisfied!
IAGO. I see, Sir, you are eaten up with
    passion:
I do repent me that I put it to you.
You would be satisfied?
OTH.   Would! nay, I will.
IAGO. And may; but how? how satisfied,
    my lord?
Would you, the supervisor, grossly gape
Behold her tupp'd?   [on,—
OTH.   Death and damnation! O!
IAGO. It were a tedious difficulty, I think,
To bring them to that prospect. Damn
    them, then,
If ever mortal eyes do see them bolster,
More than their own! What then? how
    then?
What shall I say? Where's satisfaction?
It is impossible you should see this,
Were they as prime as goats, as hot as
    monkeys,   [gross
As salt as wolves in pride, and fools as
As ignorance made drunk: but yet, I say,
If imputation, and strong circumstances,—
Which lead directly to the door of truth,—
Will give you satisfaction, you may have it.
OTH. Give me a living reason she's dis-
    loyal.

IAGO. I do not like the office:
But, sith I am enter'd in this cause so
    far,—
Prick'd to't by foolish honesty and love,—
I will go on. I lay with Cassio lately;
And, being troubled with a raging tooth,
I could not sleep.
There are a kind of men so loose of soul,
That in their sleeps will mutter their af-
One of this kind is Cassio: [fairs:
In sleep I heard him say, "Sweet Desde-
    mona,
Let us be wary, let us hide our loves;"
And then, Sir, would he gripe and wring
    my hand,
Cry, "O, sweet creature!" and then kiss
    me hard,
As if he pluck'd up kisses by the roots,
That grew upon my lips: then laid his leg
Over my thigh, and sigh'd, and kiss'd; and
    then   [Moor!"
Cried, "Cursed fate, that gave thee to the
OTH. O monstrous! monstrous!
IAGO.   Nay, this was but his dream.
OTH. But this denoted a foregone con-
    clusion: [dream.
'Tis a shrewd doubt, though it be but a
IAGO. And this may help to thicken other
That do demonstrate thinly.   [proofs,
OTH.   I'll tear her all to pieces.
IAGO. Nay, but be wise: yet we see noth-
    ing done;
She may be honest yet. Tell me but this,—
Have you not sometimes seen a handker-
    chief,   [hand?
Spotted with strawberries, in your wife's
OTH. I gave her such a one; 'twas my
    first gift.
IAGO. I know not that: but such a hand-
    kerchief,
(I am sure it was your wife's) did I to-day
See Cassio wipe his beard with.
OTH.   If it be that,—
IAGO. If it be that, or any that was hers,
It speaks against her with the other proofs.
OTH. O, that the slave had forty thou-
    sand lives!
One is too poor, too weak for my revenge.
Now do I see 'tis true.—Look here, Iago;
All my fond love thus do I blow to heaven:
'Tis gone.—
Arise, black vengeance, from the hollow
    hell!   [throne,
Yield up, O love, thy crown, and hearted
To tyrannous hate! swell, bosom, with thy
For 'tis of aspics' tongues!   [fraught,
IAGO. Pray, be content.
OTH.   O, blood, Iago, blood!
IAGO. Patience, I say; your mind, per-
    haps, may change.

OTH. Never, Iago. Like to the Pontick sea,
Whose icy current and compulsive course
Ne'er feels retiring ebb, but keeps due on
To the Propontick, and the Hellespont;
Even so my bloody thoughts, with violent
pace,   [love,
Shall ne'er look back, ne'er ebb to humble
Till that a capable and wide revenge
Swallow them up.—Now, by yond' marble
heaven,
In the due reverence of a sacred vow,
                              [*Kneeling.*
I here engage my words.
IAGO.   Do not rise yet.—
                              [*Kneeling.*
Witness, you ever-burning lights above,
You elements that clip us round about,—
Witness, that here Iago doth give up
The execution of his wit, hands, heart,
To wrong'd Othello's service! Let him
command,
And to obey shall be in me remorse,
What bloody work soever.
OTH.   I greet thy love,
Not with vain thanks, but with acceptance
bounteous,
And will upon the instant put thee to't:
Within these three days let me hear thee
That Cassio's not alive.   [say
IAGO. My friend is dead; 'tis done at
But let her live.   [your request:
OTH. Damn her, lewd minx! O, damn her!
Come, go with me apart; I will withdraw,
To furnish me with some swift means of
death   [tenant.
For the fair devil. Now art thou my lieu-
IAGO. I am your own for ever. [*Exeunt.*

SCENE IV.—*The Same.*

Enter DESDEMONA, EMILIA, *and* Clown.
DES. Do you know, sirrah, where lieuten-
ant Cassio lies?
CLO. I dare not say he lies any where.
DES. Why, man?
CLO. He is a soldier; and for one to say
a soldier lies, is stabbing.
DES. Go to: where lodges he?
CLO. To tell you where he lodges, is to
tell you where I lie.
DES. Can any thing be made of this?
CLO. I know not where he lodges; and for
me to devise a lodging, and say he lies
here, or he lies there, were to lie in mine
own throat.
DES. Can you enquire him out, and be
edified by report?
CLO. I will catechize the world for him;
that is, make questions, and by them answer.

DES. Seek him, bid him come hither: tell
him I have moved my lord in his behalf,
and hope all will be well.
CLO. To do this is within the compass
of man's wit; and therefore I will attempt
the doing it.   [*Exit.*
DES. Where should I lose that handker-
chief, Emilia?
EMIL. I know not, Madam.
DES. Believe me, I had rather have lost
my purse
Full of cruzadoes: and, but my noble Moor
Is true of mind, and made of no such base-
ness
As jealous creatures are, it were enough
To put him to ill thinking.
EMIL.   Is he not jealous?
DES. Who, he? I think the sun, where
he was born,
Drew all such humours from him.
EMIL.   Look, where he comes.
DES. I will not leave him now, till Cassio
Be call'd to him.—
        Enter OTHELLO.
            How is't with you, my lord?
OTH. Well, my good lady.—[*Aside.*] O,
hardness to dissemble!—
How do you, Desdemona?
DES.   Well, my good lord.
OTH. Give me your hand. This hand is
moist, my lady.
DES. It yet has felt no age, nor known
no sorrow.
OTH. This argues fruitfulness, and liberal
heart:—   [quires
Hot, hot, and moist: this hand of yours re-
A sequester from liberty, fasting and pray-
er,
Much castigation, exercise devout;
For here's a young and sweating devil
here,
That commonly rebels. 'Tis a good hand,
A frank one.
DES.   You may, indeed, say so;
For 'twas that hand that gave away my
heart.
OTH. A liberal hand: the hearts of old
gave hands;
But our new heraldry is—hands, not hearts.
DES. I cannot speak of this. Come now,
your promise.
OTH. What promise, chuck?
DES. I have sent to bid Cassio come speak
with you.
OTH. I have a salt and sullen rheum of-
Lend me thy handkerchief.   [fends me:
DES.   Here, my lord.
OTH. That which I gave you.
DES.   I have it not about me.
OTH. Not?
DES.   No, indeed, my lord.

OTH.   That is a fault.
That handkerchief
Did an Egyptian to my mother give;
She was a charmer, and could almost read
The thoughts of people: she told her, while
  she kept it,
'Twould make her amiable, and subdue my
  father
Entirely to her love; but if she lost it,
Or made a gift of it, my father's eye
Should hold her loathed, and his spirits
  should hunt   [me;
After new fancies: she, dying, gave it
And bid me, when my fate would have me
  wive,   [on't;
To give it her. I did so: and take heed
Make it a darling like your precious eye;
To lose or give't away, were such perdition,
As nothing else could match.
DES.   ·   Is't possible?
OTH. 'Tis true: there's magic in the web
  of it:
A sibyl, that had number'd in the world
The sun to course two hundred compasses,
In her prophetic fury sew'd the work;
The worms were hallow'd that did breed
  the silk;
And it was dy'd in mummy, which the skil-
Conserv'd of maidens' hearts.   [ful
DES.   Indeed! is't true?
OTH. Most veritable; therefore look to't
  well.
DES. Then would to heaven that I had
  never seen it!
OTH. Ha! wherefore?
DES. Why do you speak so startingly and
  rash?
OTH. Is't lost? is't gone? speak, is it out
  o' the way?
DES. Heaven bless us!
OTH.   Say you?
DES. It is not lost; but what an if it
OTH. How!   [were?
DES. I say, it is not lost.
OTH.   Fetch't, let me see't.
DES. Why, so I can, Sir; but I will not
  now.
This is a trick, to put me from my suit:
Pray you, let Cassio be receiv'd again.
OTH. Fetch me the handkerchief: my
DES. Come, come;   [mind misgives.
You'll never meet a more sufficient man.
OTH. The handkerchief!
DES.   I pray, talk me of Cassio.
OTH. The handkerchief!
DES.   A man that, all his time,
Hath founded his good fortunes on your
Shar'd dangers with you;—   [love;
OTH. The handkerchief!
DES. In sooth, you are to blame.
OTH. Away!   [*Exit.*

EMIL. Is not this man jealous?
DES. I ne'er saw this before.
Sure, there's some wonder in this hand-
  kerchief:
I am most unhappy in the loss of it.
EMIL. 'Tis not a year or two shows us a
  man;   [food;
They are all but stomachs, and we all but
They eat us hungerly, and when they are
  full,
They belch us.—Look you,—Cassio, and
  my husband.
            Enter IAGO *and* CASSIO.
IAGO. There is no other way; 'tis she
  must do't:
And, lo, the happiness! go, and importune
  her.
DES. How now, good Cassio! what's the
  news with you?
CAS. Madam, my former suit: I do be-
  seech you,
That by your virtuous means I may again
Exist, and be a member of his love,
Whom I, with all the office of my heart,
Entirely honour: I would not be delay'd.
If my offence be of such mortal kind,
That nor my service past, nor present sor-
  rows,
Nor purpos'd merit in futurity,
Can ransom me into his love again,
But to know so must be my benefit,
So shall I clothe me in a forc'd content,
And shut myself up in some other course,
To fortune's alms.
DES.   Alas, thrice-gentle Cassio!
My advocation is not now in tune;
My lord is not my lord; nor should I know
  him,
Were he in favour, as in humour, alter'd.
So help me every spirit sanctified,
As I have spoken for you all my best,
And stood within the blank of his dis-
  pleasure,
For my free speech! You must a while
  be patient:
What I can do, I will; and more I will,
Than for myself I dare: let that suffice
  you.
IAGO. Is my lord angry?
EMIL.   He went hence but now;
And, certainly, in strange unquietness.
IAGO. Can he be angry? I have seen the
  cannon,
When it hath blown his ranks into the air,
And, like the devil, from his very arm
Puff'd his own brother;—and can he be
  angry?   [him:
Something of moment, then: I will go meet
There's matter in't, indeed, if he be angry.
DES. I pr'ythee, do so,—[*Exit* IAGO.]
Something, sure, of state,—

Either from Venice, or some unhatch'd
practice   [him,—
Made demonstrable here in Cyprus to
Hath puddled his clear spirit; and, in
such cases,
Men's natures wrangle with inferior things,
Though great ones are their object. 'Tis
even so;
For let our finger ache, and it indues
Our other healthful members ev'n to that
sense   [gods,
Of pain: nay, we must think men are not
Nor of them look for such observances
As fit the bridal.—Beshrew me much,
Emilia,
I was (unhandsome warrior as I am)
Arraigning his unkindness with my soul!
But now I find, I had suborn'd the witness,
And he's indicted falsely.

EMIL. Pray heaven, it be state matters,
as you think,
And no conception, nor no jealous toy,
Concerning you.

DES. Alas the day! I never gave him
cause.

EMIL. But jealous souls will not be an-
swer'd so;
They are not ever jealous for the cause,
But jealous for they are jealous: 'tis a
monster,
Begot upon itself, born on itself.

DES. Heaven keep that monster from
Othello's mind!

EMIL. Lady, amen.

DES. I will go seek him.—Cassio, walk
hereabout:
If I do find him fit, I'll move your suit,
And seek to effect it to my uttermost.

CAS. I humbly thank your ladyship.

[*Exeunt* DESDEMONA *and* EMILIA.
Enter BIANCA.

BIAN. Save you, friend Cassio.

CAS.   What make you from home?
How is it with you, my most fair Bianca?
I' faith, sweet love, I was coming to your
house.   [Cassio,

BIAN. And I was going to your lodging,
What, keep a week away? seven days and
nights?   [hours,
Eight score eight hours? and lovers' absent
More tedious than the dial eight score
O weary reckoning!   [times?

CAS.   Pardon me, Bianca:
I have this while with leaden thoughts been
press'd;
But I shall, in a more continuate time,
Strike off this score of absence. Sweet
Bianca,
    [*Giving her* DESDEMONA'S *handkerchief.*
Take me this work out.

BIAN.   O Cassio, whence came this?
This is some token from a newer friend:
To the felt absence, now, I feel a cause:
Is't come to this? Well, well.

CAS.   Go to, woman!
Throw your vile guesses in the devil's
teeth,
From whence you have them. You are
jealous now,
That this is from some mistress, some re-
membrance:
No, in good troth, Bianca.

BIAN.   Why, whose is it?

CAS. I know not, sweet: I found it in
my chamber.
I like the work well: ere it be demanded,
(As like enough it will) I'd have it copied:
Take it, and do't; and leave me for this
time.

BIAN. Leave you! wherefore?

CAS. I do attend here on the general;
And think it no addition, nor my wish,
To have him see me woman'd.

BIAN.   Why, I pray you?

CAS. Not that I love you not.

BIAN.   But that you do not love me.
I pray you, bring me on the way a little;
And say if I shall see you soon at night.

CAS. 'Tis but a little way that I can bring
you;
For I attend here: but I'll see you soon.

BIAN. 'Tis very good; I must be cir-
cumstanc'd.   [*Exeunt.*

ACT IV.

SCENE I.—CYPRUS. *Before the Castle.*

Enter OTHELLO *and* IAGO.

IAGO. Will you think so?

OTH.   Think so, Iago!

IAGO.   What,
To kiss in private?

OTH.   An unauthoriz'd kiss.

IAGO. Or to be naked with her friend
abed
An hour or more, not meaning any harm?

OTH. Naked abed, Iago, and not mean
harm!
It is hypocrisy against the devil:
They that mean virtuously, and yet do so,
The devil their virtue tempts, and they
tempt heaven.

IAGO. If they do nothing, 'tis a venial
slip:
But if I give my wife a handkerchief,—

OTH. What then?

IAGO. Why, then, 'tis hers, my lord; and,
being hers,
She may, I think, bestow't on any man.

OTH. She is protectress of her honour too:
May she give that?
IAGO. Her honour is an essence that's not
seen;
They have it very oft, that have it not:
But, for the handkerchief,—
OTH. By heaven, I would most gladly
have forgot it:—
Thou saidst,—O, it comes o'er my memory,
As doth the raven o'er the infected house,
Boding to all,—he had my handkerchief.
IAGO. Ay, what of that?
OTH.   That's not so good, now.
IAGO. What, if I had said I had seen him
do you wrong?
Or heard him say,—as knaves be such
abroad,
Who having, by their own importunate
suit,
Or voluntary dotage of some mistress,
Convinced or supplied them, cannot choose
But they must blab,—
OTH.   Hath he said any thing?
IAGO. He hath, my lord, but be you well
No more than he'll unswear.   [assur'd,
OTH.   What hath he said?
IAGO. 'Faith, that he did,—I know not
what he did.
OTH. What? what?
IAGO. Lie—
OTH. With her?
IAGO.   With her, on her; what you
will.
OTH. Lie with her! lie on her!—We say,
lie on her, when they belie her. Lie with
her! that's fulsome.—Handkerchief,—con-
fessions,—handkerchief!—To confess, and
be hanged for his labour:—first, to be
hanged, and then to confess:—I tremble at
it. Nature would not invest herself in such
shadowing passion, without some instruction. It is not words that shake me thus:
——Pish!—Noses, ears, and lips.—Is it
possible?—Confess!—Handkerchief!—O
devil!—   [*Falls in a trance.*
IAGO. Work on,
My medicine, work! Thus credulous fools
are caught;
And many worthy and chaste dames, even
thus,
All guiltless, meet reproach.—What, ho!
my lord!
My lord, I say! Othello!—
          Enter CASSIO.
          How now, Cassio!
CAS. What's the matter?
IAGO. My lord is fallen into an epilepsy:
This is his second fit; he had one yester-
day.
CAS. Rub him about the temples.

IAGO.   No, forbear;
The lethargy must have his quiet course:
If not, he foams at mouth; and, by and
by,
Breaks out to savage madness. Look, he
stirs:—
Do you withdraw yourself a little while,
He will recover straight: when he is gone,
I would on great occasion speak with
you.—   [*Exit* CASSIO.
How is it, general? have you not hurt
your head?
OTH. Dost thou mock me?
IAGO.   I mock you! no, by heaven.
Would you would bear your fortune like
a man!
OTH. A horned man's a monster, and a
beast.
IAGO. There's many a beast, then, in a
populous city,
And many a civil monster.
OTH. Did he confess it?
IAGO.   Good Sir, be a man;
Think every bearded fellow, that's but
yok'd,
May draw with you: there's millions now
alive,
That nightly lie in those unproper beds,
Which they dare swear peculiar: your case
is better.
O, 'tis the spite of hell, the fiend's arch-
mock,
To lip a wanton in a secure couch,
And to suppose her chaste! No, let me
know;
And, knowing what I am, I know what
she shall be.
OTH. O, thou art wise; 'tis certain.
IAGO. Stand you awhile apart;
Confine yourself but in a patient list.
Whilst you were here, o'erwhelmed with
your grief,
(A passion most unsuiting such a man)
Cassio came hither: I shifted him away,
And laid good 'scuse upon your ecstasy;
Bade him anon return, and here speak
with me;
The which he promis'd. Do but encave
yourself,
And mark the fleers, the gibes, and notable
scorns,
That dwell in every region of his face;
For I will make him tell the tale anew,—
Where, how, how oft, how long ago, and
when
He hath, and is again to cope your wife:
I say, but mark his gesture. Marry,
patience;
Or I shall say you are all in all in spleen,
And nothing of a man.

OTH.   Dost thou hear, Iago?
I will be found most cunning in my
  patience;
But (dost thou hear?) most bloody.
IAGO.   That's not amiss;
But yet keep time in all. Will you with-
  draw?   [OTHELLO *retires*.
Now will I question Cassio of Bianca,
A housewife, that, by selling her desires,
Buys herself bread and clothes: it is a
  creature
That dotes on Cassio,—as 'tis the strumpet's
  plague
To beguile many, and be beguil'd by
  one:—
He, when he hears of her, cannot refrain
From the excess of laughter:—here he
  comes:—
As he shall smile, Othello shall go mad;
And his unbookish jealousy must construe
Poor Cassio's smiles, gestures, and light
Quite in the wrong.—   [behaviour
          Re-enter CASSIO.
          How do you now, lieutenant?
CAS. The worser, that you give me the
Whose want even kills me.   [addition,
IAGO. Ply Desdemona well, and you are
  sure on't.
[*Speaking lower.*] Now, if this suit lay in
  Bianca's power,
How quickly should you speed!
CAS.   Alas, poor caitiff!
OTH. [*Aside.*] Look, how he laughs al-
  ready!
IAGO. I never knew woman love man so.
CAS. Alas, poor rogue! I think, i' faith,
  she loves me.
OTH. [*Aside.*] Now he denies it faintly,
  and laughs it out.
IAGO. Do you hear, Cassio?
OTH. [*Aside.*]   Now he importunes him
To tell it o'er:—go to; well said, well said.
IAGO. She gives it out that you shall
Do you intend it?   [marry her:
CAS.   Ha, ha, ha!
OTH. [*Aside.*] Do you triumph, Roman?
  do you triumph?
CAS. I marry her!—what, a customer! I
  pr'ythee, bear some charity to my wit; do
  not think it so unwholesome. Ha, ha, ha!
OTH. [*Aside.*] So, so, so, so:—they laugh
  that win.
IAGO. 'Faith, the cry goes, that you shall
  marry her.—
CAS. Pr'ythee, say true.
IAGO. I am a very villain else.
OTH. [*Aside.*] Have you scored me? Well.
CAS. This is the monkey's own giving
  out: she is persuaded I will marry her,
  out of her own love and flattery, not out
  of my promise.

OTH. [*Aside.*] Iago beckons me; now he
  begins the story.
CAS. She was here even now; she haunts
  me in every place. I was, the other day,
  talking on the sea-bank with certain Vene-
  tians, and thither comes this bauble; and,
  by this hand, she falls me thus about my
  neck,—
OTH. [*Aside.*] Crying, "O dear Cassio!"
  as it were: his gesture imports it.
CAS. So hangs, and lolls, and weeps upon
  me; so hales, and pulls me:—ha, ha, ha!
OTH. [*Aside.*] Now he tells, how she
  plucked him to my chamber. O, I see that
  nose of yours, but not that dog I shall
  throw it to.
CAS. Well, I must leave her company.
IAGO. Before me! look, where she comes.
CAS. 'Tis such another fitchew! marry, a
  perfumed one.—
          Enter BIANCA.
What do you mean by this haunting of me?
BIAN. Let the devil and his dam haunt
  you! What did you mean by that same
  handkerchief, you gave me even now? I
  was a fine fool to take it. I must take out
  the work!—A likely piece of work, that
  you should find it in your chamber, and
  not know who left it there! This is some
  minx's token, and I must take out the
  work! There, give it your hobby-horse:
  wheresoever you had it, I'll take out no
  work on't.
CAS. How now, my sweet Bianca! how
  now, how now!
OTH. [*Aside.*] By heaven, that should be
  my handkerchief!
BIAN. An you'll come to supper to-night,
  you may; an you will not, come when you
  are next prepared for.   [*Exit.*
IAGO. After her, after her.
CAS. 'Faith, I must; she'll rail in the
  street else.
IAGO. Will you sup there?
CAS. 'Faith, I intend so.
IAGO. Well, I may chance to see you; for
  I would very fain speak with you.
CAS. Pr'ythee, come; will you?
IAGO. Go to; say no more. [*Exit* CASSIO.
OTH. [*Advancing.*] How shall I murder
  him, Iago?
IAGO. Did you perceive how he laughed
  at his vice?
OTH. O, Iago!
IAGO. And did you see the handkerchief?
OTH. Was that mine?
IAGO. Yours, by this hand: and to see
  how he prizes the foolish woman your wife!
  she gave it him, and he hath given it his
  whore.

OTH. I would have him nine years a killing.—A fine woman! a fair woman! a sweet woman!

IAGO. Nay, you must forget that.

OTH. Ay, let her rot, and perish, and be damned to-night; for she shall not live. No, my heart is turned to stone; I strike it, and it hurts my hand.—O, the world hath not a sweeter creature: she might lie by an emperor's side, and command him tasks.

IAGO. Nay, that's not your way.

OTH. Hang her! I do but say what she is:—so delicate with her needle! An admirable musician! O, she will sing the savageness out of a bear! Of so high and plenteous wit and invention!

IAGO. She's the worse for all this.

OTH. O, a thousand thousand times. And then, of so gentle a condition!

IAGO. Ay, too gentle.

OTH. Nay, that's certain:—but yet the pity of it, Iago! O, Iago! the pity of it, Iago!

IAGO. If you are so fond over her iniquity, give her patent to offend; for, if it touch not you, it comes near nobody.

OTH. I will chop her into messes:—cuckold me!

IAGO. O, 'tis foul in her.

OTH. With mine officer!

IAGO. That's fouler.

OTH. Get me some poison, Iago; this night:—I'll not expostulate with her, lest her body and beauty unprovide my mind again:—this night, Iago.

IAGO. Do it not with poison, strangle her in her bed, even the bed she hath contaminated.

OTH. Good, good: the justice of it pleases: very good.

IAGO. And for Cassio,—let me be his undertaker: you shall hear more by midnight.

OTH. Excellent good.—[*A trumpet heard.*] What trumpet is that same?

IAGO. Something from Venice, sure. 'Tis Lodovico,

Come from the duke: and, see, your wife is with him.

> *Enter* LODOVICO, DESDEMONA, *and* Attendants.

LOD. 'Save you, worthy general!

OTH.   With all my heart, Sir.

LOD. The duke and senators of Venice greet you.   [*Giving him a packet.*

OTH. I kiss the instrument of their pleasures. [*Opens the packet, and reads.*

DES. And what's the news, good cousin Lodovico?

IAGO. I am very glad to see you, signior; Welcome to Cyprus.

LOD. I thank you. How does lieutenant Cassio?

IAGO. Lives, Sir.

DES. Cousin, there's fallen between him and my lord

An unkind breach: but you shall make all well.

OTH. Are you sure of that?

DES. My lord?

OTH. [*Reading.*] "This fail you not to do, as you will"—

LOD. He did not call; he's busy in the paper.

Is there division 'twixt my lord and Cassio?

DES. A most unhappy one: I would do much

To atone them, for the love I bear to Cassio.

OTH. Fire and brimstone!

DES.   My lord?

OTH.   Are you wise?

DES. What, is he angry?

LOD.   May be, the letter mov'd him;

For, as I think, they do command him home, Deputing Cassio in his government.

DES. Trust me, I am glad on't.

OTH.   Indeed!

DES.   My lord?

OTH. I am glad to see you mad.

DES.   How, sweet Othello?

OTH. Devil!   [*Striking her.*

DES.   I have not deserv'd this.

LOD. My lord, this would not be believ'd in Venice,

Though I should swear I saw it: 'tis very much:

Make her amends; she weeps.

OTH.   O devil, devil!

If that the earth could teem with woman's tears,

Each drop she falls would prove a crocodile.—

Out of my sight!

DES.   I will not stay to offend you.
                                        [*Going.*

LOD. Truly, an obedient lady:—

I do beseech your lordship, call her back.

OTH. Mistress!

DES.   My lord?

OTH.   What would you with her, Sir?

LOD. Who, I, my lord?

OTH. Ay; you did wish that I would make her turn:

Sir, she can turn, and turn, and yet go on,

And turn again; and she can weep, Sir, weep;

And she's obedient, as you say,—obedient,—

Very obedient.—Proceed you in your tears.—

Concerning this, Sir,—O well-painted passion!—

I am commanded home.—Get you away;
I'll send for you anon.—Sir, I obey the mandate,
And will return to Venice.—Hence, avaunt!
                              [Exit DESDEMONA.
Cassio shall have my place. And, Sir, to-night,
I do entreat that we may sup together:
You are welcome, Sir, to Cyprus.—Goats
  and monkeys!   [Exit.
LOD. Is this the noble Moor whom our
  full senate
Call all-in-all sufficient? this the noble
  nature
Whom passion could not shake? whose
  solid virtue
The shot of accident, nor dart of chance,
Could neither graze nor pierce?
IAGO.   He is much chang'd.
LOD. Are his wits safe? is he not light of
  brain?
IAGO. He's that he is: I may not breathe
  my censure.
What he might be,—if, what he might,
  he is not,—
I would to heaven he were!
LOD.   What, strike his wife!
IAGO. 'Faith, that was not so well; yet
  would I knew
That stroke would prove the worst.
LOD.   Is it his use?
Or did the letters work upon his blood,
And new-create this fault?
IAGO.   Alas, alas!
It is not honesty in me to speak
What I have seen and known. You shall
  observe him;
And his own courses will denote him so,
That I may save my speech: do but go after,
And mark how he continues.
LOD. I am sorry that I am deceiv'd in
  him.   [Exeunt.

_____

SCENE II.—*A Room in the Castle.*

Enter OTHELLO *and* EMILIA.

OTH. You have seen nothing, then?
EMIL. Nor ever heard, nor ever did
  suspect.
OTH. Yes, you have seen Cassio and her
  together.
EMIL. But then I saw no harm; and then
  I heard
Each syllable that breath made up be-
  tween them.
OTH. What, did they never whisper?
EMIL.   Never, my lord.
OTH. Nor send you out o' the way?
EMIL.   Never.
OTH. To fetch her fan, her gloves, her
  mask, nor nothing?

EMIL. Never, my lord.
OTH.   That's strange.
EMIL. I durst, my lord, to wager she is
  honest,
Lay down my soul at stake: if you think
  other,
Remove your thought; it doth abuse your
  bosom.
If any wretch have put this in your head,
Let heaven requite it with the serpent's
  curse!
For, if she be not honest, chaste, and true,
There's no man happy; the purest of their
Is foul as slander.   [wives
OTH.   Bid her come hither:—go.—
                              [Exit EMILIA.
She says enough;—yet she's a simple bawd
That cannot say as much. This is a subtle
  whore,
A closet-lock-and-key of villainous secrets:
And yet she'll kneel and pray; I have seen
  her do't.
    Re-enter EMILIA, *with* DESDEMONA.
DES. My lord, what is your will?
OTH.   Pray, chuck, come hither.
DES. What is your pleasure?
OTH.   Let me see your eyes;
Look in my face.
DES.   What horrible fancy's this?
OTH. [*To* EMIL.] Some of your function,
  mistress;
Leave procreants alone, and shut the door;
Cough, or cry hem, if any body come:
Your mystery, your mystery;—nay, des-
  patch.   [Exit EMILIA.
DES. Upon my knees, what doth your
  speech import?
I understand a fury in your words,
But not the words.
OTH. Why, what art thou?
DES.   Your wife, my lord; your true
And loyal wife.
OTH.   Come, swear it, damn thyself;
Lest, being like one of heaven, the devils
  themselves
Should fear to seize thee: therefore be
  double-damn'd,—
Swear thou art honest.
DES.   Heaven doth truly know it.
OTH. Heaven truly knows that thou art
  false as hell.
DES. To whom, my lord? with whom?
  how am I false?
OTH. O Desdemona!—away! away! away!
DES. Alas the heavy day!—Why do you
  weep?
Am I the occasion of these tears, my lord?
If, haply, you my father do suspect
An instrument of this your calling back,
Lay not your blame on me: if you have
Why, I have lost him too.   [lost him,

OTH.   Had it pleas'd heaven
To try me with affliction; had he rain'd
All kinds of sores, and shames, on my bare
  head;
Steep'd me in poverty to the very lips;
Given to captivity me and my utmost
  hopes;
I should have found in some part of my
  soul
A drop of patience: but, alas, to make me
A fixed figure, for the time of scorn
To point his slow unmoving finger at!—
Yet could I bear that too; well, very well:
But there, where I have garner'd up my
  heart,
Where either I must live, or bear no life,—
The fountain from the which my current
  runs,
Or else dries up; to be discarded thence!
Or keep it as a cistern, for foul toads
To knot and gender in!—turn thy com-
  plexion there,
Patience, thou young and rose-lipp'd
  cherubim,—
Ay, there, look grim as hell!
DES. I hope, my noble lord esteems me
  honest.
OTH. O, ay; as summer flies are in the
  shambles,
That quicken even with blowing. O thou
  weed,
Who art so lovely fair, and smell'st so
  sweet,
That the sense aches at thee,—would thou
  hadst ne'er been born!
DES. Alas, what ignorant sin have I com-
  mitted?
OTH. Was this fair paper, this most goodly
  book,
Made to write whore upon? What com-
  mitted!
Committed!—O thou public commoner!
I should make very forges of my cheeks,
That would to cinders burn up modesty,
Did I but speak thy deeds.—What com-
  mitted!
Heaven stops the nose at it, and the moon
  winks;
The bawdy wind, that kisses all it meets,
Is hush'd within the hollow mine of earth,
And will not hear it.—What committed!—
Impudent strumpet!
DES.   By heaven, you do me wrong.
OTH. Are not you a strumpet?
DES.   No, as I am a Christian:
If to preserve this vessel for my lord,
From any other foul unlawful touch,
Be not to be a strumpet, I am none.
OTH. What, not a whore?
DES.   No, as I shall be saved.
OTH. Is it possible?

DES. O, heaven forgive us!
OTH.   I cry you mercy, then;
I took you for that cunning whore of
  Venice,
That married with Othello.—You, mistress,
That have the office opposite to Saint Peter,
And keep the gate of hell!
          Re-enter EMILIA.
                    You, you, ay, you!
We have done our course; there's money
  for your pains.
I pray you, turn the key, and keep our
  counsel.   [*Exit.*
EMIL. Alas, what does this gentleman
  conceive?—
How do you, Madam? how do you, my
  good lady?
DES. 'Faith, half asleep.
EMIL. Good Madam, what's the matter
  with my lord?
DES. With whom?
EMIL.   Why, with my lord, Madam.
DES. Who is thy lord?
EMIL.   He that is yours, sweet lady.
DES. I have none: do not talk to me,
  Emilia;
I cannot weep; nor answer have I none,
But what should go by water. Pr'ythee,
  to-night
Lay on my bed my wedding sheets,—re-
And call thy husband hither. [member;—
EMIL.   Here is a change indeed!
                              [*Exit.*
DES. 'Tis meet I should be us'd so, very
  meet.
How have I been behav'd, that he might
  stick
The small'st opinion on my least misuse?
          Re-enter EMILIA, *with* IAGO.
IAGO. What is your pleasure, Madam?
  How is it with you?
DES. I cannot tell. Those that do teach
  young babes,
Do it with gentle means and easy tasks:
He might have chid me so; for, in good
I am a child to chiding.   [faith,
IAGO.   What's the matter, lady?
EMIL. Alas, Iago, my lord hath so be-
  whor'd her,
Thrown such despite and heavy terms upon
As true hearts cannot bear.   [her,
DES. Am I that name, Iago?
IAGO.   What name, fair lady?
DES. Such as, she says, my lord did say
  I was.
EMIL. He call'd her whore: a beggar, in
  his drink,
Could not have laid such terms upon his
IAGO. Why did he so?   [callat.
DES. I do not know; I am sure I am
  none such.

IAGO. Do not weep, do not weep:—alas the day!

EMIL. Has she forsook so many noble matches,
Her father, and her country, and her friends,
To be call'd whore? would it not make one weep?

DES. It is my wretched fortune.

IAGO.   Beshrew him for it!
How comes this trick upon him?

DES.   Nay, heaven doth know.

EMIL. I will be hang'd, if some eternal villain,
Some busy and insinuating rogue,
Some cogging, cozening slave, to get some office,
Have not devis'd this slander; I'll be hang'd else.

IAGO. Fie, there is no such man; it is impossible.

DES. If any such there be, heaven pardon him!

EMIL. A halter pardon him! and hell gnaw his bones!
Why should he call her whore? who keeps her company?
What place? what time? what form? what likelihood?
The Moor's abus'd by some most villainous knave,
Some base notorious knave, some scurvy fellow:—
O heaven, that such companions thou'dst unfold,
And put in every honest hand a whip,
To lash the rascals naked through the world,
Even from the east to the west!

IAGO.   Speak within door.

EMIL. O, fie upon them! some such squire he was,
That turn'd your wit the seamy side without,
And made you to suspect me with the Moor.

IAGO. You are a fool; go to.

DES.   O good Iago,
What shall I do to win my lord again?
Good friend, go to him; for, by this light of heaven,
I know not how I lost him. Here I kneel:—
If e'er my will did trespass 'gainst his love,
Either in discourse of thought, or actual deed;
Or that mine eyes, mine ears, or any sense,
Delighted them in any other form;
Or that I do not yet, and ever did,
And ever will,—though he do shake me off
To beggarly divorcement,—love him dearly,
Comfort forswear me! Unkindness may do much;

And his unkindness may defeat my life,
But never taint my love. I cannot say whore,—
It does abhor me, now I speak the word;
To do the act that might the addition earn,
Not the world's mass of vanity could make me.

IAGO. I pray you, be content; 'tis but his humour:
The business of the state does him offence,
And he does chide with you.

DES.   If 'twere no other,—

IAGO. 'Tis but so, I warrant.
                    [*Trumpets heard.*
Hark, how these instruments summon to supper!
The messengers of Venice stay the meat.
Go in, and weep not; all things shall be well. [*Exeunt* DESDEMONA *and* EMILIA.
                    Enter RODERIGO.
How now, Roderigo!

ROD. I do not find that thou deal'st justly with me.

IAGO. What in the contrary?

ROD. Every day thou daff'st me with some device, Iago; and rather, as it seems to me now, keep'st from me all conveniency, than suppliest me with the least advantage of hope. I will, indeed, no longer endure it; nor am I yet persuaded, to put up in peace what already I have foolishly suffered.

IAGO. Will you hear me, Roderigo?

ROD. 'Faith, I have heard too much; for your words, and performances, are no kin together.

IAGO. You charge me most unjustly.

ROD. With naught but truth. I have wasted myself out of my means. The jewels you have had from me, to deliver to Desdemona, would half have corrupted a votarist: you have told me she has received them, and returned me expectations and comforts of sudden respect and acquaintance; but I find none.

IAGO. Well; go to; very well.

ROD. Very well! go to! I cannot go to, man; nor 'tis not very well: by this hand, I say, it is very scurvy; and begin to find myself fobbed in it.

IAGO. Very well.

ROD. I tell you, 'tis not very well. I will make myself known to Desdemona: if she will return me my jewels, I will give over my suit, and repent my unlawful solicitation; if not, assure yourself, I will seek satisfaction of you.

IAGO. You have said now.

ROD. Ay, and I have said nothing, but what I protest intendment of doing.

IAGO. Why, now I see there's mettle in thee; and even, from this instant, do build

on thee a better opinion than ever before.
Give me thy hand, Roderigo: thou hast
taken against me a most just exception; but
yet, I protest, I have dealt most directly
in thy affair.

ROD. It hath not appeared.

IAGO. I grant, indeed, it hath not appeared; and your suspicion is not without
wit and judgment. But, Roderigo, if thou
hast that in thee indeed, which I have
greater reason to believe now than ever,—
I mean, purpose, courage, and valour,—this
night show it: if thou the next night following enjoy not Desdemona, take me from
this world with treachery, and devise
engines for my life.

ROD. Well, what is it? is it within
reason, and compass?

IAGO. Sir, there is especial commission
come from Venice, to depute Cassio in
Othello's place.

ROD. Is that true? why, then Othello and
Desdemona return again to Venice.

IAGO. O, no, he goes into Mauritania, and
takes away with him the fair Desdemona,
unless his abode be lingered here by some
accident: wherein none can be so determinate, as the removing of Cassio.

ROD. How do you mean, removing of him?

IAGO. Why, by making him uncapable of
Othello's place,—knocking out his brains.

ROD. And that you would have me do?

IAGO. Ay, if you dare do yourself a profit,
and a right. He sups to-night with a harlotry, and thither will I go to him:—he
knows not yet of his honourable fortune.
If you will watch his going thence, (which
I will fashion to fall out between twelve
and one) you may take him at your
pleasure: I will be near to second your
attempt, and he shall fall between us.
Come, stand not amazed at it, but go along
with me; I will show you such a necessity
in his death, that you shall think yourself
bound to put it on him. It is now high
supper-time, and the night grows to waste:
about it.

ROD. I will hear farther reason for this.

IAGO. And you shall be satisfied.

[*Exeunt.*

SCENE III.—*Another Room in the Castle.*

Enter OTHELLO, LODOVICO, DESDEMONA,
EMILIA, *and* Attendants.

LOD. I do beseech you, Sir, trouble yourself no farther.

OTH. O, pardon me; 'twill do me good
to walk.

LOD. Madam, good night; I humbly thank
your ladyship.

DES. Your honour is most welcome.

OTH.   Will you walk, Sir?—
O,—Desdemona,—

DES.   My lord?

OTH. Get you to bed on the instant; I
will be returned forthwith: dismiss your
attendant there: look it be done.

DES. I will, my lord.

[*Exeunt* OTHELLO, LODOVICO, *and*
Attendants.

EMIL. How goes it now? he looks gentler
than he did.

DES. He says he will return incontinent:
He hath commanded me to go to bed,
And bade me to dismiss you.

EMIL.   Dismiss me!

DES. It was his bidding; therefore, good
Emilia,
Give me my nightly wearing, and adieu:
We must not now displease him.

EMIL. I would you had never seen him!

DES. So would not I: my love doth so
approve him,
That even his stubbornness, his checks, his
frowns,—
Pr'ythee, unpin me,—have grace and favour
in them.

EMIL. I have laid those sheets you bade
me on the bed.

DES. All's one.—Good father! how foolish
are our minds!—
If I do die before thee, pr'ythee, shroud
In one of those same sheets.   [me

EMIL.   Come, come, you talk.

DES. My mother had a maid call'd Bar-
bara:
She was in love; and he she lov'd prov'd
mad,
And did forsake her: she had a song of
"willow;"
An old thing 'twas, but it express'd her
fortune,
And she died singing it: that song, to-night,
Will not go from my mind; I have much
to do,
But to go hang my head all at one side,
And sing it like poor Barbara.—Pr'ythee,
despatch.

EMIL. Shall I go fetch your night-gown?

DES.   No, unpin me here.—
This Lodovico is a proper man.

EMIL. A very handsome man.

DES. He speaks well.

EMIL. I know a lady in Venice would
have walked barefoot to Palestine for a
touch of his nether lip.

DES. [*Singing.*]
    The poor soul sat sighing by a syca-
        more tree,
        Sing all a green willow;

Her hand on her bosom, her head
on her knee,
Sing willow, willow, willow:
The fresh streams ran by her, and
murmur'd her moans;
Sing willow, willow, willow:
Her salt tears fell from her, and
soften'd the stones;—

Lay by these:—
Sing willow, willow, willow:

Pr'ythee, hie thee; he'll come anon:—
Sing all a green willow must be
my garland.
Let nobody blame him; his scorn
I approve,—

Nay, that's not next.—Hark! who is it
that knocks?

EMIL. It is the wind.

DES. [*Singing.*]
I call'd my love false love; but what
said he then?
Sing willow, willow, willow:
If I court mo women, you'll couch
with mo men.

So, get thee gone: good night. Mine eyes
Doth that bode weeping?   [do itch;

EMIL.   'Tis neither here nor there.

DES. I have heard it said so.—O, these
men, these men!—
Dost thou in conscience think,—tell me,
Emilia,—
That there be women do abuse their
In such gross kind?   [husbands

EMIL. There be some such, no question.

DES. Would'st thou do such a deed for
all the world?

EMIL. Why, would not you?

DES.   No, by this heavenly light!

EMIL. Nor I neither by this heavenly
light;
I might do't as well i' the dark.

DES. Would'st thou do such a deed for
all the world?

EMIL. The world is a huge thing: 'tis a
great price
For a small vice.

DES. In troth, I think thou would'st not.

EMIL. In troth, I think I should; and
undo't, when I had done. Marry, I would
not do such a thing for a joint-ring, nor
for measures of lawn, nor for gowns, petticoats, nor caps, nor any petty exhibition;
but, for the whole world,—why, who would
not make her husband a cuckold, to make
him a monarch? I should venture purgatory
for't.

DES. Beshrew me, if I would do such a
wrong for the whole world.

EMIL. Why, the wrong is but a wrong i'
the world; and, having the world for your
labour, 'tis a wrong in your own world, and
you might quickly make it right.

DES. I do not think there is any such
woman.

EMIL. Yes, a dozen; and as many
To the vantage, as would store the world
they play'd for.
But I do think it is their husbands' faults,
If wives do fall. Say, that they slack their
duties,
And pour our treasures into foreign laps;
Or else break out in peevish jealousies,
Throwing restraint upon us; or, say, they
strike us,
Or scant our former having in despite;
Why, we have galls; and, though we have
some grace,
Yet have we some revenge. Let husbands
know,
Their wives have sense like them: they see,
and smell,
And have their palates, both for sweet and
sour,
As husbands have. What is it that they do,
When they change us for others? Is it
sport?
I think it is; and doth affection breed it?
I think it doth. Is't frailty that thus errs?
It is so too:—and have not we affections,
Desires for sport, and frailty, as men have?
Then, let them use us well: else, let them
know,
The ills we do, their ills instruct us so.

DES. Good night, good night: heaven me
such usage send,
Not to pick bad from bad, but by bad
mend!   [*Exeunt.*

———

ACT V.

Scene I.—Cyprus. *A Street.*

Enter Iago *and* Roderigo.

IAGO. Here, stand behind this bulk;
straight will he come:
Wear thy good rapier bare, and put it
home:
Quick, quick; fear nothing; I'll be at thy
elbow:
It makes us, or it mars us; think on that,
And fix most firm thy resolution.

ROD. Be near at hand; I may miscarry
in't.

IAGO. Here, at thy hand: be bold, and
take thy stand.
      [*Retires to a little distance.*

ROD. I have no great devotion to the
deed;

And yet he has given me satisfying reasons:—

'Tis but a man gone:—forth, my sword; he dies.   [*Goes to his stand.*

IAGO. I have rubb'd this young quat almost to the sense,

And he grows angry. Now, whether he kill Cassio,

Or Cassio him, or each do kill the other,

Every way makes my game: live Roderigo,

He calls me to a restitution large

Of gold and jewels that I bobb'd from As gifts to Desdemona;   [him,

It must not be: if Cassio do remain,

He hath a daily beauty in his life,

That makes me ugly; and, besides, the Moor

May unfold me to him; there stand I in much peril:

No, he must die:—be't so; I hear him coming.

Enter CASSIO.

ROD. I know his gait, 'tis he.—Villain, thou diest!

[*Rushing forth, and making a pass at* CASSIO.

CAS. That thrust had been mine enemy indeed,

But that my coat is better than thou know'st:

I will make proof of thine.

[*Draws, and wounds* RODERIGO.

ROD.   O, I am slain!

[IAGO *rushes forth, cuts* CASSIO *behind in the leg, and exit.*

CAS. I am maim'd for ever.—Help, ho! murder! murder!   [*Falls.*

Enter OTHELLO, *at a distance.*

OTH. The voice of Cassio:—Iago keeps his word.

ROD. O, villain that I am!

OTH.   It is e'en so.

CAS. O, help, ho! light! a surgeon!

OTH. 'Tis he:—O brave Iago, honest and just,

That hast such noble sense of thy friend's wrong!

Thou teachest me.—Minion, your dear lies dead,

And your unblest fate hies:—strumpet, I come!

Forth of my heart those charms, thine eyes, are blotted;

Thy bed, lust-stain'd, shall with lust's blood be spotted.   [*Exit.*

Enter LODOVICO *and* GRATIANO, *at a distance.*

CAS. What, ho! no watch? no passage? murder! murder!

GRA. 'Tis some mischance; the voice is very direful.

CAS. O, help!

LOD.   Hark!

ROD.   O wretched villain!

LOD. Two or three groan:—it is a heavy night:

These may be counterfeits; let's think 't unsafe

To come in to the cry, without more help.

ROD. Nobody come? then shall I bleed to death.

LOD. Hark!

GRA. Here's one comes in his shirt, with light and weapons.

Re-enter IAGO, *with a light.*

IAGO. Who's there? whose noise is this, that cries on murder?

LOD. We do not know.

IAGO.   Did not you hear a cry?

CAS. Here, here! for heaven's sake, help me!

IAGO.   What's the matter?

GRA. This is Othello's ancient, as I take it.

LOD. The same indeed; a very valiant fellow.

IAGO. What are you here, that cry so grievously?

CAS. Iago? O, I am spoil'd, undone by Give me some help.   [villains!

IAGO. O me, lieutenant! what villains have done this?

CAS. I think that one of them is here—And cannot make away.   [about,

IAGO.   O treacherous villains!—

[*To* LOD. *and* GRA.] What are you there? come in, and give some help.

ROD. O, help me here!

CAS. That's one of them.

IAGO.   O murderous slave! O villain!

[*Stabs* RODERIGO.

ROD. O damn'd Iago! O inhuman dog!

IAGO. Kill men i' the dark!—Where be these bloody thieves?—

How silent is this town!—Ho! murder! murder!—

What may you be? are you of good, or evil?

LOD. As you shall prove us, praise us.

IAGO. Signior Lodovico?

LOD. He, Sir.

IAGO. I cry you mercy. Here's Cassio hurt by villains.

GRA. Cassio!

IAGO. How is it, brother?

CAS. My leg is cut in two.

IAGO.   Marry, heaven forbid!—

Light gentlemen:—I'll bind it with my shirt.

Enter BIANCA.

BIAN. What is the matter, ho? who is 't that cried?

IAGO. Who is't that cried!

BIAN. O my dear Cassio! my sweet Cassio!
O Cassio, Cassio, Cassio!

IAGO. O notable strumpet!—Cassio, may you suspect
Who they should be, that have thus mangled you?

CAS. No.

GRA. I am sorry to find you thus: I have been to seek you.

IAGO. Lend me a garter:—so.—O, for a [chair,
To bear him easily hence!

BIAN. Alas, he faints!—O Cassio! Cassio! Cassio!

IAGO. Gentlemen all, I do suspect this [trash
To be a party in this injury.—
Patience a while, good Cassio.—Come, come;
Lend me a light.—Know we this face, or no?
Alas, my friend, and my dear countryman,
Roderigo? no:—yes, sure; O heaven!
Roderigo.

GRA. What, of Venice?

IAGO. Even he, Sir: did you know him?

GRA. Know him! ay.

IAGO. Signior Gratiano? I cry you gentle pardon;
These bloody accidents must excuse my [manners,
That so neglected you.

GRA. I am glad to see you.

IAGO. How do you, Cassio?—O, a chair,

GRA. Roderigo! [a chair!

IAGO. He, he, 'tis he.—O, that's well said;—the chair:— [*A chair brought in.*
Some good man bear him carefully from hence;
I'll fetch the general's surgeon.—[*To* BIANCA.] For you, mistress,
Save you your labour.—He that lies slain here, Cassio,
Was my dear friend: what malice was between you?

CAS. None in the world; nor do I know the man.

IAGO. [*To* BIANCA.] What, look you pale?—O, bear him out o' the air.— [*Cassio and* ROD. *are borne off.*
Stay you, good gentlemen.—Look you pale, mistress?—
Do you perceive the gastness of her eye?—
Nay, if you stare, we shall hear more anon.—
Behold her well; I pray you, look upon her:
Do you see, gentlemen? nay, guiltiness will speak,
Though tongues were out of use. [*Enter* EMILIA.

EMIL. Alas, what's the matter? what's the matter, husband?

IAGO. Cassio hath here been set on in the dark
By Roderigo, and fellows that are scap'd:
He's almost slain, and Roderigo dead.

EMIL. Alas, good gentleman! alas, good Cassio!

IAGO. This is the fruit of whoring.—Pr'ythee, Emilia,
Go know of Cassio where he supp'd to-night.—
What, do you shake at that?

BIAN. He supp'd at my house; but I therefore shake not.

IAGO. O, did he so? I charge you, go with me.

EMIL. Fie, fie upon thee, strumpet!

BIAN. I am no strumpet; but of life as honest,
As you that thus abuse me.

EMIL. As I? foh! fie upon thee!

IAGO. Kind gentlemen, let's go see poor Cassio dress'd.—
Come, mistress, you must tell's another tale.—
Emilia, run you to the citadel,
And tell my lord and lady what hath happ'd.—
Will you go on, I pray?—[*Aside.*] This is the night
That either makes me, or fordoes me quite. [*Exeunt.*

SCENE II.—*A Bedchamber in the Castle.*

DESDEMONA *in bed asleep. A light burning.*
Enter OTHELLO.

OTH. It is the cause, it is the cause, my soul,—
Let me not name it to you, you chaste stars!—
It is the cause.—Yet I'll not shed her blood;
Nor scar that whiter skin of hers than snow,
And smooth as monumental alabaster.
Yet she must die, else she'll betray more men.
Put out the light, and then—Put out the light!
If I quench thee, thou flaming minister,
I can again thy former light restore,
Should I repent me:—but once put out thy light,
Thou cunning'st pattern of excelling nature,
I know not where is that Promethean heat,
That can thy light relume. When I have pluck'd thy rose,
I cannot give it vital growth again,
It needs must wither:—I'll smell it on the tree.— [*Kissing her.*
O balmy breath, that dost almost persuade
Justice to break her sword!—One more, one more:—

Be thus when thou art dead, and I will
  kill thee,
And love thee after:—one more, and this
  the last:
So sweet was ne'er so fatal. I must weep,
But they are cruel tears: this sorrow's
  heavenly;
It strikes, where it doth love.—She wakes,—
DES. Who's there? Othello?
OTH.   Ay, Desdemona.
DES. Will you come to bed, my lord?
OTH. Have you pray'd to-night, Desde-
  mona?
DES.   Ay, my lord.
OTH. If you bethink yourself of any
  crime,
Unreconcil'd as yet to heaven and grace,
Solicit for it straight.
DES. Alas, my lord! what may you mean
  by that?
OTH. Well, do it, and be brief; I will
  walk by:
I would not kill thy unprepared spirit;
No,—heaven forfend!—I would not kill thy
DES. Talk you of killing?   [soul.
OTH.   Ay, I do.
DES.   Then, heaven
Have mercy on me!
OTH.   Amen, with all my heart!
DES. If you say so, I hope you will not
OTH. Hm!   [kill me.
DES. And yet I fear you; for you are fatal
  then,
When your eyes roll so: why I should fear
  I know not,
Since guiltiness I know not; but yet, I feel
  I fear.
OTH. Think on thy sins.
DES.   They are loves I bear to you.
OTH. Ay, and for that thou diest.
DES. That death's unnatural, that kills for
  loving.—
Alas! why gnaw you so your nether lip?
Some bloody passion shakes your very
  frame:
These are portents; but yet, I hope, I hope,
They do not point on me.
OTH.   Peace, and be still!
DES. I will so. What's the matter?
OTH. That handkerchief, which I so lov'd,
  and gave thee,
Thou gav'st to Cassio.
DES.   No, by my life and soul!
Send for the man, and ask him.
OTH.   Sweet soul, take heed,
Take heed of perjury; thou'rt on thy death-
  bed.
DES. Ay, but not yet to die.
OTH.   Yes, presently:
Therefore confess thee freely of thy sin;
For to deny each article with oath,

Cannot remove, nor choke, the strong con-
  ception
That I do groan withal. Thou art to die.
DES. Then, Lord have mercy on me!
OTH.   I say, amen.
DES. And have you mercy too!—I never
  did
Offend you in my life; never lov'd Cassio,
But with such general warranty of heaven
As I might love; I never gave him token.
OTH. By heaven, I saw my handkerchief
  in's hand.
O perjur'd woman! thou dost stone my
  heart,
And mak'st me call, what I intend to do,
A murder, which I thought a sacrifice:
I saw the handkerchief.
DES.   He found it, then;
I never gave it him:—send for him hither;
Let him confess a truth.
OTH.   He hath confess'd.
DES. What, my lord?
OTH. That he hath—us'd thee.
DES.   How? unlawfully?
OTH. Ay.
DES.   He will not say so.
OTH.   No, his mouth is stopp'd;
Honest Iago hath ta'en order for't.
DES. O, my fear interprets!—what, is he
  dead?
OTH. Had all his hairs been lives, my
  great revenge
Had stomach for them all.
DES. Alas, he is betray'd, and I undone!
OTH. Out, strumpet! weep'st thou for him
  to my face?
DES. O, banish me, my lord, but kill me
  not!
OTH. Down, strumpet!
DES. Kill me to-morrow; let me live to-
  night!
OTH. Nay, if you strive,—
DES.   But half an hour!
OTH.   Being done,
There is no pause.
DES.   But while I say one prayer!
OTH. It is too late.   [Smothers her.
EMIL. [Within.] My lord, my lord! what,
  ho! my lord, my lord!
OTH. What noise is this?—Not dead? not
  yet quite dead?
I, that am cruel, am yet merciful;
I would not have thee linger in thy pain:—
So, so.
EMIL. [Within.] What, ho! my lord, my
  lord!
OTH.   Who's there?
EMIL. [Within.] O, good my lord, I would
  speak a word with you!
OTH. Yes:—'tis Emilia:—by and by.—
  She's dead.—

'Tis like she comes to speak of Cassio's
death;
The noise was high.—Ha! no more mov-
ing?   [Were't good?
Still as the grave.—Shall she come in?
I think she stirs again:—no.—What's best
to do?
If she come in, she'll sure speak to my
wife:
My wife! my wife! what wife?—I have no
wife.
O, insupportable! O heavy hour!
Methinks it should be now a huge eclipse
Of sun and moon, and that th' affrighted
Should yawn at alteration.   [globe
EMIL. [*Within.*]   I do beseech you
That I may speak with you, O, good my
lord!
OTH. I had forgot thee: O, come in,
Emilia:—
Soft,—by and by:—let me the curtains
draw.—
Where art thou?   [*Unlocks the door.*
What's the matter with thee now?
Enter EMILIA.
EMIL. O, my good lord, yonder's foul
murder done!
OTH. What, now?
EMIL.   But now, my lord.
OTH. It is the very error of the moon;
She comes more near the earth than she
was wont,
And makes men mad.
EMIL. Cassio, my lord, has kill'd a young
Call'd Roderigo.   [Venetian,
OTH.   Roderigo kill'd!
And Cassio kill'd?
EMIL.   No, Cassio is not kill'd.
OTH. Not Cassio kill'd! then murder's
out of tune,
And sweet revenge grows harsh.
DES. O, falsely, falsely murder'd!
EMIL.   Alas, what cry is that?
OTH. That! what?
EMIL. Out, and alas! that was my lady's
voice:—
Help! Help, ho! help!—O lady, speak
again!
Sweet Desdemona! O sweet mistress,
speak!
DES. A guiltless death I die.
EMIL.   O, who hath done
This deed?
DES.   Nobody; I myself. Farewell:
Commend me to my kind lord: O farewell!
                                    [*Dies.*
OTH. Why, how should she be murder'd?
EMIL.   Alas, who knows?
OTH. You heard her say herself, it was
not I.

EMIL. She said so: I must needs report
the truth.
OTH. She's, like a liar, gone to burning
'Twas I that kill'd her.   [hell:
EMIL.   O, the more angel she,
And you the blacker devil!
OTH. She turn'd to folly, and she was a
whore.
EMIL. Thou dost belie her, and thou art
a devil.
OTH. She was false as water.
EMIL.   Thou art rash as fire, to say
That she was false: O, she was heavenly
true!
OTH. Cassio did tup her; ask thy hus-
band else.
O, I were damn'd beneath all depth in hell,
But that I did proceed upon just grounds
To this extremity. Thy husband knew it
all.
EMIL. My husband!
OTH. Thy husband.
EMIL. That she was false to wedlock?
OTH. Ay, with Cassio. Nay, had she been
true,
If heaven would make me such another
world
Of one entire and perfect chrysolite,
I'd not have sold her for it.
EMIL. My husband!
OTH.   Ay, 'twas he that told me first:
An honest man he is, and hates the slime
That sticks on filthy deeds.
EMIL.   My husband!
OTH. What needs this iterance, woman?
I say, thy husband.
EMIL. O mistress, villany hath made
mocks with love!—
My husband say that she was false!
OTH.   He, woman;
I say, thy husband: dost understand the
word?
My friends, thy husband, honest, honest
Iago.
EMIL. If he say so, may his pernicious
soul
Rot half a grain a day! he lies to the
heart:
She was too fond of her most filthy bargain.
OTH. Ha!
EMIL.   Do thy worst:
This deed of thine is no more worthy
heaven,
Than thou wast worthy her.
OTH.   Peace! you were best.
EMIL. Thou hast not half the power to
do me harm,
As I have to be hurt. O gull! O dolt!
As ignorant as dirt! thou hast done a
deed,—

I care not for thy sword; I'll make thee known,
Though I lost twenty lives.—Help! help, ho! help!
The Moor has kill'd my mistress! Murder! murder!

Enter MONTANO, GRATIANO, *and* IAGO.

MON. What is the matter?—How now, general!
EMIL. O, are you come, Iago? you have done well,
That men must lay their murders on your neck.
GRA. What is the matter?
EMIL. Disprove this villain, if thou be'st a man:
He says thou told'st him that his wife was false:
I know thou didst not, thou'rt not such a villain:
Speak, for my heart is full.
IAGO. I told him what I thought; and told no more
Than what he found himself was apt and true.
EMIL. But did you ever tell him she was false?
IAGO. I did.   [false?
EMIL. You told a lie; an odious, damned lie;
Upon my soul, a lie; a wicked lie:—
She false with Cassio!—Did you say with Cassio?
IAGO. With Cassio, mistress. Go to, charm your tongue.
EMIL. I will not charm my tongue; I am bound to speak:
My mistress here lies murder'd in her bed,—
ALL. O heavens forfend!
EMIL. And your reports have set the murder on.
OTH. Nay, stare not, masters: it is true, indeed.
GRA. 'Tis a strange truth.
MON. O monstrous act!
EMIL.   Villany, villany, villany!
I think upon't,—I think,—I smell't; O villany!
I thought so then;—I'll kill myself for grief:—
O villany, villany!
IAGO. What, are you mad? I charge you, get you home.
EMIL. Good gentlemen, let me have leave to speak:
'Tis proper I obey him, but not now.—
Perchance, Iago, I will ne'er go home.
OTH. O! O! O!   [*Falling on the bed.*
EMIL.   Nay, lay thee down and roar;
For thou hast kill'd the sweetest innocent,
That e'er did lift up eye.

OTH.   O, she was foul!—
                                [*Rising.*
I scarce did know you, uncle: there lies your niece,
Whose breath, indeed, these hands have newly stopp'd:
I know, this act shows terrible and grim.
GRA. Poor Desdemona! I am glad thy father's dead.
Thy match was mortal to him, and pure grief
                                [live now,
Shore his old thread in twain: did he
This sight would make him do a desperate turn,
Yea, curse his better angel from his side,
And fall to reprobance.
OTH. 'Tis pitiful; but yet Iago knows
That she with Cassio hath the act of shame
A thousand times committed; Cassio confess'd it:
And she did gratify his amorous works
With that recognizance and pledge of love
Which I first gave her; I saw it in his hand:
It was a handkerchief, an antique token
My father gave my mother.
EMIL. O heaven! O heavenly powers!
IAGO.   Come, hold your peace.
EMIL. 'Twill out, 'twill out:—I hold my peace, Sir? no;
I'll be in speaking liberal as the air:
Let heaven, and men, and devils, let them all,
All, all, cry shame against me, yet I'll speak.
IAGO. Be wise, and get you home.
EMIL.   I will not.
                [IAGO *offers to stab his wife.*
GRA.   Fie!
Your sword upon a woman?
EMIL. O thou dull Moor! that handkerchief thou speak'st of,
I found by fortune, and did give my husband;
For often, with a solemn earnestness,—
More than, indeed, belong'd to such a trifle,—
He begg'd of me to steal it.
IAGO.   Villanous whore!
EMIL. She give it Cassio! no, alas, I found it,
And I did give't my husband.
IAGO.   Filth, thou liest!
EMIL. By heaven, I do not, I do not, gentlemen.—
O murderous coxcomb! what should such a fool
Do with so good a wife?
                        [IAGO *stabs* EMILIA.

OTH.   Are there no stones in heaven,
But what serve for the thunder?—Precious
     villain!
          [*Assaults* IAGO, *and is disarmed by*
               MONTANO. IAGO *runs out.*
GRA. The woman falls; sure, he has kill'd
     his wife.
EMIL. Ay, ay:—O, lay me by my mistress'
     side!
GRA. He's gone, but his wife's kill'd.
MON. 'Tis a notorious villain. Take you
     this weapon,
Which I have here recover'd from the
     Moor:
Come, guard the door without; let him not
     pass,   [villain,
But kill him rather. I'll after that same
For 'tis a damned slave.
          [*Exeunt* MONTANO *and* GRATIANO.
OTH.   I am not valiant neither,
But every puny whipster gets my sword:—
But why should honour outlive honesty?
Let it go all.
EMIL. What did thy song bode, lady?
Hark, canst thou hear me? I will play the
     swan,
And die in music:—"Willow, willow, wil-
     low."—   [Moor;
Moor, she was chaste; she lov'd thee, cruel
So come my soul to bliss, as I speak true;
So speaking as I think, I die,—I die.
                         [*Dies.*
OTH. I have another weapon in this cham-
     ber;   [per:—
It is a sword of Spain, the ice-brook's tem-
O, here it is.—Uncle, I must come forth.
GRA. [*Within.*]. If thou attempt it, it will
     cost thee dear:
Thou hast no weapon, and perforce must
     suffer.
OTH. Look in upon me, then, and speak
     with me,
Or, naked as I am, I will assault thee.
          Re-enter GRATIANO.
GRA. What is the matter?
OTH.   Behold, I have a weapon;
A better never did itself sustain
Upon a soldier's thigh: I have seen the day,
That, with this little arm and this good
     sword,
I have made my way through more impedi-
     ments   [boast!
Than twenty times your stop:—but, O vain
Who can control his fate? 'tis not so
     now.—   [pon'd;
Be not afraid, though you do see me wea-
Here is my journey's end, here is my butt,
And very sea-mark of my utmost sail.
Do you go back dismay'd? 'tis a lost fear;
Man but a rush against Othello's breast,

And he retires:—where should Othello
     go?—
Now, how dost thou look now? O ill-starr'd
     wench!
Pale as thy smock! when we shall meet at
     compt,   [heaven,
This look of thine will hurl my soul from
And fiends will snatch at it. Cold, cold,
Even like thy chastity.—   [my girl!
O, cursed, cursed slave!—Whip me, ye
     devils,
From the possession of this heavenly sight!
Blow me about in winds! roast me in sul-
     phur!   [fire!
Wash me in steep-down gulfs of liquid
O Desdemona! Desdemona! dead! O!
O! O!
Enter LODOVICO, MONTANO, CASSIO *carried
     in a chair, and* Officers, *with* IAGO,
               prisoner.
LOD. Where is this rash and most unfor-
     tunate man?
OTH. That's he that was Othello;—here
     I am.
LOD. Where is that viper? bring the vil-
     lain forth.
OTH. I look down towards his feet,—but
     that's a fable.—
If that thou be'st a devil, I cannot kill thee.
                    [*Wounds* IAGO.
LOD. Wrench his sword from him.
IAGO.   I bleed, Sir; but not kill'd.
OTH. I am not sorry neither: I'd have thee
     live;
For, in my sense, 'tis happiness to die.
LOD. O thou Othello! that wert once so
     good,
Fall'n in the practice of a damned slave,
What shall be said to thee?
OTH.   Why, any thing:
An honourable murderer, if you will;
For naught I did in hate, but all in honour.
LOD. This wretch hath part confess'd his
     villany:
Did you and he consent in Cassio's death?
OTH. Ay.
CAS. Dear general, I never gave you
     cause.
OTH. I do believe it, and I ask your par-
     don.—
Will you, I pray, demand that demi-devil,
Why he hath thus ensnar'd my soul and
     body?
IAGO. Demand me nothing: what you
     know, you know:
From this time forth I never will speak
     word.
LOD. What, not to pray?
GRA.   Torments will ope your lips.

OTH. Well, thou dost best.

LOD. Sir, you shall understand what hath befall'n,
Which, as I think, you know not. Here is a letter,
Found in the pocket of the slain Roderigo;
And here another: the one of them imports
The death of Cassio to be undertook
By Roderigo.

OTH. O villain!

CAS.   Most heathenish, and most gross!

LOD. Now, here's another discontented paper,
Found in his pocket too; and this, it seems,
Roderigo meant to have sent this damned villain;
But that, belike, Iago in the interim
Came in and satisfied him.

OTH.   O, the pernicious caitiff!—
How came you, Cassio, by that handker-
That was my wife's?   [chief,

CAS.   I found it in my chamber:
And he himself confess'd, but even now,
That there he dropp'd it, for a special purpose,
Which wrought to his desire.

OTH.   O fool! fool! fool!

CAS. There is, besides, in Roderigo's let-
ter,
How he upbraids Iago, that he made him
Brave me upon the watch; whereon it came   [spake,
That I was cast: and even but now he
After long seeming dead,—Iago hurt him,
Iago set him on.

LOD. You must forsake this room, and go with us:
Your power and your command is taken off,
And Cassio rules in Cyprus. For this slave,—
If there be any cunning cruelty
That can torment him much, and hold him long,
It shall be his. You shall close prisoner rest,
Till that the nature of your fault be known
To the Venetian state.—Come, bring away.

OTH. Soft you; a word or two, before you go.
I have done the state some service, and they know it;—
No more of that.—I pray you, in your letters,
When you shall these unlucky deeds relate,
Speak of me as I am; nothing extenuate,
Nor set down aught in malice: then, must you speak
Of one that lov'd, not wisely, but too well;
Of one not easily jealous, but, being wrought,
Perplex'd in the extreme; of one, whose hand,
Like the base Indian, threw a pearl away,
Richer than all his tribe; of one, whose subdued eyes,
Albeit unused to the melting mood,
Drop tears as fast as the Arabian trees
Their medicinal gum. Set you down this;
And say, besides,—that in Aleppo once,
Where a malignant and a turban'd Turk
Beat a Venetian, and traduc'd the state,
I took by the throat the circumcised dog,
And smote him—thus.   [*Stabs himself.*

LOD. O bloody period!

GRA.   All that's spoke is marr'd.

OTH. I kiss'd thee, ere I kill'd thee:—no way but this, [*Falling upon* DESDEMONA.
Killing myself, to die upon a kiss. [*Dies.*

CAS. This did I fear,—but thought he had no weapon;
For he was great of heart.

LOD. [*To* IAGO.]   O Spartan dog,
More fell than anguish, hunger, or the sea!
Look on the tragic loading of this bed;
This is thy work:—the object poisons sight;
Let it be hid.—Gratiano, keep the house,
And seize upon the fortunes of the Moor,
For they succeed on you.—To you, lord governor,
Remains the censure of this hellish villain;
The time, the place, the torture;—O, enforce it!
Myself will straight aboard; and to the state
This heavy act with heavy heart relate.
        [*Exeunt.*

Antony taking leave of Cleopatra. Act I. S. 3.

ANTONY AND CLEOPATRA

DRAMATIS PERSONÆ.

M. ANTONY,
OCTAVIUS CÆSAR, } *Triumvirs.*
M. ÆMIL. LEPIDUS,

SEXTUS POMPEIUS.

DOMITIUS ENOBARBUS,

VENTIDIUS,
EROS,
SCARUS,
DERCETAS, } *Friends to* ANTONY
DEMETRIUS,
PHILO,

MECÆNAS,
AGRIPPA,
DOLABELLA, } *Friends to* CÆSAR
PROCULEIUS,
THYREUS,
GALLUS,

MENAS,
MENECRATES, } *Friends to* POMPEY.
VARRIUS,

TAURUS, *Lieutenant-General to* CÆSAR.
CANIDIUS, *Lieutenant-General to* ANTONY.
SILIUS, *an Officer under* VENTIDIUS.
EUPHRONIUS, *Embassador from* ANTONY *to* CÆSAR.
ALEXAS, MARDIAN, SELEUCUS, *and* DIOMEDES, *Attendants on* CLEOPATRA.
A Soothsayer. A Clown.

CLEOPATRA, *Queen of Egypt.*
OCTAVIA, *Sister to* CÆSAR, *and Wife to* ANTONY.
CHARMIAN, } *Attendants on* CLEOPATRA.
IRAS,
Officers, Soldiers, Messengers, *and other* Attendants.

SCENE,—*In several Parts of the* ROMAN EMPIRE.

ACT I.

SCENE I.—ALEXANDRIA. *A Room in* CLEOPATRA'S *Palace.*

Enter DEMETRIUS *and* PHILO.

PHI. Nay, but this dotage of our general's

O'erflows the measure: those his goodly [eyes,
That o'er the files and musters of the war
Have glow'd like plated Mars, now bend, now turn,
The office and devotion of their view
Upon a tawny front: his captain's heart,

Which in the scuffles of great fights hath
burst   [per,
The buckles on his breast, reneges all tem-
And is become the bellows and the fan
To cool a gipsy's lust. [*Flourish within.*]
Look, where they come:
Take but good note, and you shall see in
him
The triple pillar of the world transform'd
Into a strumpet's fool: behold and see.

Enter ANTONY *and* CLEOPATRA, *with their
trains; Eunuchs fanning her.*

CLEO. If it be love indeed, tell me how
much.
ANT. There's beggary in the love that
can be reckon'd.
CLEO. I'll set a bourn how far to be belov'd.
ANT. Then must thou needs find out new
heaven, new earth.

Enter an Attendant.

ATT. News, my good lord, from Rome.
ANT.   Grates me:—the sum.
CLEO. Nay, hear them, Antony:
Fulvia, perchance, is angry; or, who knows
If the scarce-bearded Cæsar have not sent
His powerful mandate to you, "Do this, or
this;   [that,
Take in that kingdom, and enfranchise
Perform't, or else we damn thee."
ANT.   How, my love!
CLEO. Perchance,—nay, and most like,—
You must not stay here longer; your dis-
mission   [Antony.—
Is come from Cæsar; therefore hear it,
Where's Fulvia's process? Cæsar's, I would
say?—Both?—
Call in the messengers.—As I am Egypt's
queen,   [thine
Thou blushest, Antony; and that blood of
Is Cæsar's homager: else so thy cheek pays
shame,   [messengers!
When shrill-tongu'd Fulvia scolds. — The
ANT. Let Rome in Tiber melt, and the
wide arch   [space.
Of the rang'd empire fall! Here is my
Kingdoms are clay: our dungy earth alike
Feeds beast as man: the nobleness of life
Is to do thus; [*Embracing.*] when such a
mutual pair,
And such a twain can do't, in which I bind,
On pain of punishment, the world to weet,
We stand up peerless.
CLEO.   Excellent falsehood!
Why did he marry Fulvia, and not love
her?—
I'll seem the fool I am not; Antony
will be himself.
ANT.   But stirr'd by Cleopatra.—
Now, for the love of Love, and her soft
hours,

Let's not confound the time with confer-
[ence harsh:
There's not a minute of our lives should
stretch   [to-night?
Without some pleasure now: what sport
CLEO. Hear the embassadors.
ANT.   Fie, wrangling queen!
Whom every thing becomes,—to chide, to
laugh,
To weep; whose every passion fully strives
To make itself, in thee, fair and admir'd!
No messenger; but thine, and all alone,
To-night we'll wander through the streets,
and note
The qualities of people. Come, my queen;
Last night you did desire it:—speak not to
us.
              [*Exeunt* ANT. *and* CLEO. *with their train.*
DEM. Is Cæsar with Antonius priz'd so
slight?
PHI. Sir, sometimes, when he is not An-
tony,
He comes too short of that great property
Which still should go with Antony.
DEM.   I am full sorry
That he approves the common liar, who
Thus speaks of him at Rome: but I will
hope
Of better deeds to-morrow. Rest you happy.
                                  [*Exeunt.*

———

SCENE II.—ALEXANDRIA. *Another Room
in the Palace.*

Enter CHARMIAN, IRAS, *and* ALEXAS.

CHAR. Lord Alexas, sweet Alexas, most
any thing Alexas, almost most absolute
Alexas, where's the soothsayer that you
praised so to the queen? O! that I knew
this husband, which, you say, must charge
his horns with garlands!
ALEX. Soothsayer!

Enter a Soothsayer.

SOOTH. Your will?
CHAR. Is this the man?—Is't you, Sir,
that, know things?
SOOTH. In nature's infinite book of se-
A little I can read.   [crecy
ALEX.   Show him your hand.

Enter ENOBARBUS.

ENO. Bring in the banquet quickly; wine
Cleopatra's health to drink.   [enough
CHAR. Good Sir, give me good fortune.
SOOTH. I make not, but foresee.
CHAR. Pray, then, foresee me one.
SOOTH. You shall be yet far fairer than
you are.
CHAR. He means, in flesh.
IRAS. No, you shall paint when you are
old.
CHAR. Wrinkles forbid!

ALEX. Vex not his prescience; be attentive.

CHAR. Hush!

SOOTH. You shall be more beloving, than
belov'd.

CHAR. I had rather heat my liver with
drinking.

ALEX. Nay, hear him.

CHAR. Good now, some excellent fortune!
Let me be married to three kings in a
forenoon, and widow them all: let me have
a child at fifty, to whom Herod of Jewry
may do homage: find me to marry me with
Octavius Cæsar, and companion me with
my mistress.

SOOTH. You shall outlive the lady whom
you serve.

CHAR. O excellent! I love long life better than figs.

SOOTH. You have seen, and proved a
fairer former fortune,
Than that which is to approach.

CHAR. Then, belike, my children shall
have no names:—pr'ythee, how many boys
and wenches must I have?

SOOTH. If every of your wishes had a
womb,
And fertile every wish, a million.

CHAR. Out, fool! I forgive thee for a
witch.

ALEX. You think none but your sheets
are privy to your wishes.

CHAR. Nay, come, tell Iras hers.

ALEX. We'll know all our fortunes.

ENO. Mine, and most of our fortunes, to-
night, shall be,—drunk to bed.

IRAS. There's a palm presages chastity, if
nothing else.

CHAR. Even as the o'erflowing Nilus pres-
geth famine.

IRAS. Go, you wild bedfellow, you cannot
soothsay.

CHAR. Nay, if an oily palm be not a
fruitful prognostication, I cannot scratch
mine ear.—Pr'ythee, tell her but a worky-
day fortune.

SOOTH. Your fortunes are alike.

IRAS. But how? but how? give me particulars.

SOOTH. I have said.

IRAS. Am I not an inch of fortune better
than she?

CHAR. Well, if you were but an inch of
fortune better than I, where would you
choose it?

IRAS. Not in my husband's nose.

CHAR. Our worser thoughts heavens
mend!—Alexas,—come, his fortune, his fortune!—O, let him marry a woman that cannot go, sweet Isis, I beseech thee: and let

her die too, and give him a worse! and let
worse follow worse, till the worst of all
follow him laughing to his grave, fifty-fold
a cuckold! Good Isis, hear me this prayer,
though thou deny me a matter of more
weight; good Isis, I beseech thee!

IRAS. Amen. Dear goddess, hear that
prayer of the people! for, as it is a heart-
breaking to see a handsome man loose-
wived, so it is a deadly sorrow to behold
a foul knave uncuckolded: therefore, dear
Isis, keep decorum, and fortune him accordingly!

CHAR. Amen.

ALEX. Lo, now, if it lay in their hands
to make me a cuckold, they would make
themselves whores, but they'd do't!

ENO. Hush! here comes Antony.

CHAR.   Not he; the queen.

Enter CLEOPATRA.

CLEO. Saw you my lord?

ENO. No, lady.

CLEO. Was he not here?

CHAR. No, Madam.

CLEO. He was dispos'd to mirth; but on
the sudden,
A Roman thought hath struck him.—
Enobarbus,—

ENO. Madam?

CLEO. Seek him, and bring him hither.
Where's Alexas?

ALEX. Here, at your service.—My lord
approaches.

CLEO. We will not look upon him: go
with us.
[*Exeunt* CLEOPATRA, ENOBARBUS, ALEXAS,
IRAS, CHARMIAN, *and* Soothsayer.

Enter ANTONY, *with a* Messenger *and*
Attendants.

MESS. Fulvia, thy wife, first came into the

ANT. Against my brother Lucius?   [field.

MESS. Ay:
But soon that war had end, and the time's
state
Made friends of them, jointing their force
'gainst Cæsar;
Whose better issue in the war, from Italy,
Upon the first encounter, drave them.

ANT.   Well, what worst?

MESS. The nature of bad news infects
the teller.

ANT. When it concerns the fool, or
coward.—On:—
Things, that are past, are done, with me.—
'Tis thus;
Who tells me true, though in his tale lie
I hear him as he flatter'd.   [death,

MESS.   Labienus

(This is stiff news) hath, with his Parthian force,

Extended Asia from Euphrates;
His conquering banner shook, from Syria
To Lydia, and to Ionia; whilst—
ANT. Antony, thou would'st say,—
MESS. O, my lord!
ANT. Speak to me home, mince not the
general tongue:
Name Cleopatra as she is call'd in Rome;
Rail thou in Fulvia's phrase; and taunt
my faults
With such full licence, as both truth and
malice
Have power to utter. O, then we bring
forth weeds,
When our quick winds lie still; and our ills
told us,
Is as our earing. Fare thee well awhile.
MESS. At your noble pleasure.   [*Exit.*
ANT. From Sicyon, ho, the news! Speak
there!
1 *ATT.* The man from Sicyon,—is there
such a one?
2 *ATT.* He stays upon your will.
ANT.   Let him appear.—
These strong Egyptian fetters I must break,
Or lose myself in dotage.—
        Enter another Messenger.
                 What are you?
2 *MESS.* Fulvia thy wife is dead.
ANT.   Where died she?
2 *MESS.* In Sicyon:
Her length of sickness, with what else
more serious
Importeth thee to know, this bears.
                [*Giving a letter.*
ANT.   Forbear me.—
              [*Exit second* Messenger.
There's a great spirit gone! Thus did I
desire it:
What our contempts do often hurl from us,
We wish it ours again; the present pleasure,
By revolution lowering, does become
The opposite of itself: she's good, being
gone;
The hand could pluck her back, that shov'd
her on.
I must from this enchanting queen break
off:
Ten thousand harms, more than the ills
I know,
My idleness doth hatch.—Ho, Enobarbus!
        Enter ENOBARBUS.
ENO. What's your pleasure, Sir?
ANT. I must with haste from hence.
ENO. Why, then, we kill all our women:
we see how mortal an unkindness is to
them; if they suffer our departure, death's
the word.
ANT. I must be gone.
ENO. Under a compelling occasion, let
women die: it were pity to cast them away

for nothing; though, between them and
a great cause, they should be esteemed
nothing. Cleopatra, catching but the least
noise of this, dies instantly; I have seen
her die twenty times upon far poorer
moment: I do think there is mettle in
death, which commits some loving act upon
her, she hath such a celerity in dying.
ANT. She is cunning past man's thought.
ENO. Alack, Sir, no; her passions are
made of nothing but the finest part of pure
love: we cannot call her winds and waters
sighs and tears; they are greater storms
and tempests than almanacs can report:
this cannot be cunning in her; if it be, she
makes a shower of rain as well as Jove.
ANT. Would I had never seen her!
ENO. O, Sir, you had then left unseen a
wonderful piece of work; which not to
have been blessed withal, would have dis-
credited your travel.
ANT. Fulvia is dead.
ENO. Sir?
ANT. Fulvia is dead.
ENO. Fulvia!
ANT. Dead.
ENO. Why, Sir, give the gods a thankful
sacrifice. When it pleaseth their deities to
take the wife of a man from him, it shows
to man the tailors of the earth; comforting
therein, that when old robes are worn out,
there are members to make new. If there
were no more women but Fulvia, then had
you indeed a cut, and the case to be
lamented: this grief is crowned with consolation; your old smock brings forth a new
petticoat:—and, indeed, the tears live in
an onion that should water this sorrow.
ANT. The business she hath broached in
the state
Cannot endure my absence.
ENO. And the business you have broached
here cannot be without you; especially that
of Cleopatra's, which wholly depends on
your abode.
ANT. No more light answers. Let our
officers
Have notice what we purpose. I shall break
The cause of our expedience to the queen,
And get her love to part. For not alone
The death of Fulvia, with more urgent
touches,
Do strongly speak to us; but the letters
too,
Of many our contriving friends in Rome
Petition us at home: Sextus Pompeius
Hath given the dare to Cæsar, and com-
mands
The empire of the sea: our slippery people
(Whose love is never link'd to the deserver
Till his deserts are past) begin to throw

'ompey the great, and all his dignities,
Jpon his son; who, high in name and
  power,
ligher than both in blood and life, stands
  up
'or the main soldier; whose quality, going
  on,
.he sides o' the world may danger: much
  is breeding,
Vhich, like the courser's hair, hath yet but
  life,
ᴀnd not a serpent's poison. Say, our
  pleasure,
'o such whose place is under us, requires
)ur quick remove from hence.

:NO.   I shall do it.
                   [*Exeunt.*

Sᴄᴇɴᴇ III.—*Another Room in the Palace.*
Enter Cʟᴇᴏᴘᴀᴛʀᴀ, Cʜᴀʀᴍɪᴀɴ, Iʀᴀs, *and*
             Aʟᴇxᴀs.

:LEO. Where is he?
'HAR.   I did not see him since.
'LEO. See where he is, who's with him,
  what he does:—
did not send you.—If you find him sad,
ay I am dancing; if in mirth, report
'hat I am sudden sick: quick, and return.
                 [*Exit* Aʟᴇx.
'HAR. Madam, methinks, if you did love
  him dearly,
'ou do not hold the method to enforce
he like from him.
'LEO.   What should I do, I do not?
HAR. In each thing give him way, cross
  him in nothing.
LEO. Thou teachest like a fool,—the way
  to lose him.
HAR. Tempt him not so too far; I wish,
  forbear:
ᴀ time we hate that which we often fear.
ᴜt here comes Antony.
LEO.   I am sick, and sullen.
          Enter Aɴᴛᴏɴʏ.
NT. I am sorry to give breathing to my
  purpose,—
LEO. Help me away, dear Charmian; I
  shall fall:
cannot be thus long, the sides of nature
'ill not sustain it.
NT.   Now, my dearest queen,—
LEO. Pray you, stand farther from me.
NT.   What's the matter?
LEO. I know, by that same eye, there's
  some good news.   [go:
'hat says the married woman?—You may
'ould she had never given you leave to
  come!
ᴇt her not say 'tis I that keep you here,—
have no power upon you; hers you are.

ANT. The gods best know,—
CLEO.   O, never was there queen
So mightily betray'd! yet at the first
I saw the treasons planted.
ANT.   Cleopatra,—
CLEO. Why should I think you can be
  mine, and true,   [gods,
Though you in swearing shake the throned
Who have been false to Fulvia? Riotous
  madness,   [vows,
To be entangled with those mouth-made
Which break themselves in swearing!
ANT.   Most sweet queen,—
CLEO. Nay, pray you, seek no colour for
  your going,
But bid farewell, and go: when you sued
  staying,
Then was the time for words: no going
  then;—
Eternity was in our lips and eyes,   [poor,
Bliss in our brows' bent; none our parts so
But was a race of heaven: they are so still,
Or thou, the greatest soldier of the world,
Art turn'd the greatest liar.
ANT.   How now, lady!
CLEO. I would I had thy inches; thou
  should'st know
There were a heart in Egypt.
ANT.   Hear me, queen:
The strong necessity of time commands
Our services a while; but my full heart
Remains in use with you. Our Italy
Shines o'er with civil swords: Sextus Pom-
  peius
Makes his approaches to the port of Rome:
Equality of two domestic powers
Breeds scrupulous faction: the hated, grown
  to strength,   [Pompey,
Are newly grown to love: the condemn'd
Rich in his father's honour, creeps apace
Into the hearts of such as have not thriv'd
Upon the present state, whose numbers
  threaten;   [purge
And quietness, grown sick of rest, would
By any desperate change: my more
  particular,
And that which most with you should safe
Is Fulvia's death.   [my going,
CLEO. Though age from folly could not
  give me freedom,
It does from childishness:—can Fulvia die?
ANT. She's dead, my queen:
Look here, and, at thy sovereign leisure,
  read
The garboils she awak'd; at the last,—
  best,—
See when and where she died.
CLEO.   O most false love!
Where be the sacred vials thou should'st
  fill
With sorrowful water? Now I see, I see,

In Fulvia's death, how mine receiv'd shall
be.
ANT. Quarrel no more, but be prepar'd to
know
The purposes I bear; which are, or cease,
As you shall give the advice: by the fire
That quickens Nilus' slime, I go from
hence
Thy soldier, servant; making peace, or
As thou affect'st.   [war,
CLEO. Cut my lace, Charmian, come:—
But let it be:—I am quickly ill, and well;
So Antony loves.
ANT. My precious queen, forbear;
And give true evidence to his love, which
An honourable trial.   [stands
CLEO. So Fulvia told me.
I pr'ythee, turn aside, and weep for her;
Then bid adieu to me, and say the tears
Belong to Egypt: good now, play one scene
Of excellent dissembling; and let it look
Like perfect honour.
ANT. You'll heat my blood: no more.
CLEO. You can do better yet; but this is
ANT. Now, by my sword,—   [meetly.
CLEO. And target.—Still he mends;
But this is not the best:—look, pr'ythee,
Charmian,
How this Herculean Roman does become
The carriage of his chafe.
ANT. I'll leave you, lady.
CLEO. Courteous lord, one word.
Sir, you and I must part,—but that's not it:
Sir, you and I have lov'd,—but there's not
it;
That you know well: something it is I
would,—
O, my oblivion is a very Antony,
And I am all forgotten.
ANT. But that your royalty
Holds idleness your subject, I should take
For idleness itself.   [you
CLEO. 'Tis sweating labour
To bear such idleness so near the heart,
As Cleopatra this. But, Sir, forgive me;
Since my becomings kill me, when they
do not
Eye well to you: your honour calls you
hence;
Therefore be deaf to my unpitied folly,
And all the gods go with you! upon your
sword
Sit laurel'd victory! and smooth success
Be strew'd before your feet!
ANT. Let us go. Come;
Our separation so abides, and flies,
That thou, residing here, go'st yet with me,
And I, hence fleeting, here remain with
Away!   [thee.
     [*Exeunt.*

SCENE IV.—ROME. *An Apartment in*
CÆSAR'S *House.*

Enter OCTAVIUS CÆSAR, LEPIDUS, *and*
Attendants.

CÆS. You may see, Lepidus, and henc‖
forth know,
It is not Cæsar's natural vice to hate
Our great competitor: from Alexandria
This is the news:—he fishes, drinks, a‖
wastes
The lamps of night in revel: is not mo‖
manlike
Than Cleopatra; nor the queen of Ptolem‖
More womanly than he: hardly give auc
ence, or
Vouchsaf'd to think he had partners: y‖
shall find there
A man, who is the abstract of all faults
That all men follow.
LEP. I must not think there a‖
Evils enow to darken all his goodness:
His faults, in him, seem as the spots ‖
heaven,
More fiery by night's blackness; hereditar‖
Rather than purchas'd; what he cann‖
Than what he chooses.   [chang‖
CÆS. You are too indulgent. Let ‖
grant, it is not
Amiss to tumble on the bed of Ptolemy;
To give a kingdom for a mirth; to sit
And keep the turn of tippling with a slav‖
To reel the streets at noon, and stand t‖
buffet
With knaves that smell of sweat: say, th‖
becomes him,
(As his composure must be rare indeed,
Whom these things cannot blemish) y‖
must Antony
No way excuse his soils, when we do be‖
So great weight in his lightness. If he fil‖
His vacancy with his voluptuousness,
Full surfeits and the dryness of his bon‖
Call on him for't: but, to confound su‖
time,
That drums him from his sport, and spea‖
as loud
As his own state and ours,—'tis to be ch‖
As we rate boys; who, being mature ‖
knowledge,
Pawn their experience to their prese‖
And so rebel to judgment.   [pleasu‖
Enter a Messenger.
LEP. Here's more nev‖
MESS. Thy biddings have been done; a‖
every hour,
Most noble Cæsar, shalt thou have rep‖
How 'tis abroad. Pompey is strong at se‖
And it appears, he is belov'd of those
That only have fear'd Cæsar: to the po‖

The discontents repair, and men's reports
Give him much wrong'd.
CÆS.   I should have known no less:
It hath been taught us from the primal
  state,
That he which is, was wish'd, until he
  were;
And the ebb'd man ne'er lov'd, till ne'er
  worth love,
Comes dear'd by being lack'd. This common
  body,
Like to a vagabond flag upon the stream,
Goes to and back, lackeying the varying
To rot itself with motion.   [tide,
MESS.   Cæsar, I bring thee word,
Menecrates and Menas, famous pirates,
Make the sea serve them, which they ear
  and wound
With keels of every kind: many hot inroads
They make in Italy; the borders maritime
Lack blood to think on't, and flush youth
  revolt:
No vessel can peep forth, but 'tis as soon
Taken as seen; for Pompey's name strikes
Than could his war resisted.   [more,
CÆS.   Antony,
Leave thy lascivious wassails. When thou
  once   [slew'st
Wast beaten from Modena, where thou
Hirtius and Pansa, consuls, at thy heel
Did famine follow; whom thou fought'st
  against,   [more
Though daintily brought up, with patience
Than savages could suffer: thou didst drink
The stale of horses, and the gilded puddle,
Which beasts would cough at: thy palate
  then did deign
The roughest berry on the rudest hedge;
Yea, like the stag, when snow the pasture
  sheets,   [Alps,
The barks of trees thou browsed'st; on the
It is reported, thou didst eat strange flesh,
Which some did die to look on: and all
  this
(It wounds thine honour, that I speak it
  now)
Was borne so like a soldier, that thy cheek
So much as lank'd not.
LEP.   'Tis pity of him.
CÆS. Let his shames quickly
Drive him to Rome: 'tis time we twain
Did show ourselves i' the field; and, to that
  end,
Assemble we immediate council: Pompey
Thrives in our idleness.
LEP.   To-morrow, Cæsar,
I shall be furnish'd to inform you rightly,
Both what by sea and land I can be able,
To front this present time.
CÆS.   Till which encounter,
It is my business too. Farewell.

LEP. Farewell, my lord: what you shall
  know mean time
Of stirs abroad, I shall beseech you, Sir,
To let me be partaker.
CÆS. Doubt not, Sir; I knew it for my
  bond.   [*Exeunt.*

Scene V.—Alexandria. *A Room in the
  Palace.*

Enter Cleopatra, Charmian, Iras, *and*
  Mardian.

CLEO. Charmian,—
CHAR. Madam.
CLEO. Ha, ha!—
Give me to drink mandragora.
CHAR.   Why, Madam?
CLEO. That I might sleep out this great
My Antony is away.   [gap of time,
CHAR.   You think of him too much.
CLEO. O, 'tis treason!
CHAR.   Madam, I trust, not so.
CLEO. Thou, eunuch, Mardian,—
MAR.   What's your highness' pleasure?
CLEO. Not now to hear thee sing; I take
  no pleasure
In aught a eunuch has: 'tis well for thee,
That, being unseminar'd, thy freer thoughts
May not fly forth of Egypt. Hast thou
MAR. Yes, gracious Madam. [affections?
CLEO. Indeed?
MAR. Not in deed, Madam; for I can do
  nothing
But what in deed is honest to be done:
Yet have I fierce affections, and think
What Venus did with Mars.
CLEO.   O Charmian,
Where think'st thou he is now? Stands he,
  or sits he?
Or does he walk? or is he on his horse?
O happy horse, to bear the weight of
  Antony!
Do bravely, horse! for wot'st thou whom
  thou mov'st?
The demi-Atlas of this earth, the arm
And burgonet of men.—He's speaking now,
Or murmuring, "Where's my serpent of old
  Nile?"
For so he calls me:—now I feed myself
With most delicious poison:—think on me,
That am with Phœbus' amorous pinches
  black,
And wrinkled deep in time? Broad-fronted
  Cæsar,
When thou wast here above the ground,
  I was
A morsel for a monarch: and great Pompey
Would stand, and make his eyes grow in
  my brow;
There would he anchor his aspect, and die
With looking on his life.

Enter ALEXAS.

ALEX.   Sovereign of Egypt, hail!

CLEO. How much unlike art thou Mark
Antony!
Yet, coming from him, that great medicine
With his tinct gilded thee.—   [hath
How goes it with my brave Mark Antony?

ALEX. Last thing he did, dear queen,
He kiss'd,—the last of many doubled
kisses,—
This orient pearl:—his speech sticks in
my heart.

CLEO. Mine ear must pluck it thence.

ALEX. "Good friend," quoth he,
"Say, the firm Roman to great Egypt sends
This treasure of an oyster; at whose foot,
To mend the petty present, I will piece
Her opulent throne with kingdoms; all the
east,
Say thou, shall call her mistress." So he
nodded,
And soberly did mount an arm-gaunt steed,
Who neigh'd so high, that what I would
have spoke
Was beastly dumb'd by him.

CLEO.   What, was he sad, or merry?

ALEX. Like to the time o' the year between the extremes
Of hot and cold; he was nor sad, nor
merry.

CLEO. O well-divided disposition!—Note
him,
Note him, good Charmian, 'tis the man;
but note him:
He was not sad,—for he would shine on
those
That make their looks by his; he was not
merry,—
Which seem'd to tell them, his remem-
brance lay
In Egypt with his joy; but between both:
O heavenly mingle!—Be'st thou sad, or
merry,
The violence of either thee becomes,
So does it no man else.—Met'st thou my
posts?

ALEX. Ay, Madam, twenty several messengers:
Why do you send so thick?

CLEO.   Who's born that day
When I forget to send to Antony,
Shall die a beggar.—Ink and paper,
Charmian.—
Welcome, my good Alexas.—Did I, Char-
Ever love Cæsar so?   [mian,

CHAR.   O, that brave Cæsar!

CLEO. Be chok'd with such another
Say, the brave Antony.   [emphasis!

CHAR.   The valiant Cæsar!

CLEO. By Isis, I will give thee bloody
teeth,

If thou with Cæsar paragon again
My man of men.

CHAR.   By your most gracious pardon,
I sing but after you.

CLEO.   My sallad days,
When I was green in judgment:—cold in
blood,
To say as I said then!—But come, away;
Get me ink and paper:
He shall have every day a several greeting,
Or I'll unpeople Egypt.   [*Exeunt.*

ACT II.

SCENE I.—MESSINA. *A Room in* POMPEY'S
House.

Enter POMPEY, MENECRATES, *and* MENAS.

POM. If the great gods be just, they shall
The deeds of justest men.   [assist

MENE.   Know, worthy Pompey,
That what they do delay, they not deny.

POM. Whiles we are suitors to their
throne, decays
The thing we sue for.

MENE.   We, ignorant of ourselves,
Beg often our own harms, which the wise
powers
Deny us for our good; so find we profit,
By losing of our prayers.

POM.   I shall do well:
The people love me, and the sea is mine;
My power's a crescent, and my auguring
hope
Says it will come to the full. Mark Antony
In Egypt sits at dinner, and will make
No wars without doors: Cæsar gets money
where
He loses hearts: Lepidus flatters both,
Of both is flatter'd; but he neither loves,
Nor either cares for him.

MEN.   Cæsar and Lepidus
Are in the field: a mighty strength they
carry.

POM. Where have you this? 'tis false.

MEN.   From Silvius, Sir.

POM. He dreams: I know they are in
Rome together,
Looking for Antony. But all the charms of
love,
Salt Cleopatra, soften thy wan'd lip!
Let witchcraft join with beauty, lust with
both!
Tie up the libertine in a field of feasts,
Keep his brain fuming; Epicurean cooks,
Sharpen with cloyless sauce his appetite;
That sleep and feeding may prorogue his
Even till a Lethe'd dulness!—   [honour,

Enter VARRIUS.

How now, Varrius!

VAR. This is most certain, that I shall
deliver:—

Mark Antony is every hour in Rome
Expected: since he went from Egypt, 'tis
A space for farther travel.
POM.   I could have given less matter
A better ear.—Menas, I did not think
This amorous surfeiter would have donn'd
    his helm
For such a petty war: his soldiership
Is twice the other twain: but let us rear
The higher our opinion, that our stirring
Can from the lap of Egypt's widow pluck
The ne'er lust-wearied Antony.
MEN.   I cannot hope,
Cæsar and Antony shall well greet to-
    gether:
His wife, that's dead, did trespasses to
    Cæsar;
His brother warr'd upon him; although,
Not mov'd by Antony.   [I think,
POM.   I know not, Menas,
How lesser enmities may give way to
    greater.
Were't not that we stand up against them
    all,
'Twere pregnant they should square be-
    tween themselves;
For they have entertained cause enough
To draw their swords: but how the fear
    of us
May cement their divisions, and bind up
The petty difference, we yet not know.
Be it as our gods will have't! It only stands
Our lives upon, to use our strongest hands.
Come, Menas.   [*Exeunt.*

————

SCENE II.—ROME. *A Room in* LEPIDUS'
House.

Enter ENOBARBUS *and* LEPIDUS.

LEP. Good Enobarbus, 'tis a worthy deed,
And shall become you well, to entreat your
To soft and gentle speech.   [captain
ENO.   I shall entreat him
To answer like himself: if Cæsar move
    him,
Let Antony look over Cæsar's head,
And speak as loud as Mars. By Jupiter,
Were I the wearer of Antonius' beard,
I would not shave't to-day.
LEP.   'Tis not a time
For private stomaching.
ENO.   Every time
Serves for the matter that is then born in't.
LEP. But small to greater matters must
    give way.
ENO. Not if the small come first.
LEP.   Your speech is passion:
But, pray you, stir no embers up. Here
The noble Antony.   [comes

Enter ANTONY *and* VENTIDIUS.

ENO.   And yonder, Cæsar.

Enter CÆSAR, MECÆNAS, *and* AGRIPPA.

ANT. If we compose well here, to Parthia:
Hark you, Ventidius.
CÆS.   I do not know,
Mecænas; ask Agrippa.
LEP.   Noble friends,
That which combin'd us was most great,
    and let not
A leaner action rend us. What's amiss,
May it be gently heard: when we debate
Our trivial difference loud, we do commit
Murder in healing wounds: then, noble
    partners,—
The rather, for I earnestly beseech,—
Touch you the sourest points with sweetest
    terms,
Nor curstness grow to the matter.
ANT.   'Tis spoken well.
Were we before our armies, and to fight,
I should do thus.
CÆS. Welcome to Rome.
ANT.   Thank you.
CÆS. Sit.
ANT. Sit, Sir.
CÆS. Nay, then—
ANT. I learn, you take things ill, which
    are not so;
Or, being, concern you not.
CÆS.   I must be laugh'd at,
If, or for nothing, or a little, I
Should say myself offended; and with you
Chiefly i' the world: more laugh'd at, that
    I should
Once name you derogately, when to sound
    your name
It not concern'd me.
ANT.   My being in Egypt, Cæsar,
What was't to you?
CÆS. No more than my residing here at
    Rome
Might be to you in Egypt: yet, if you
    there
Did practise on my state, your being in
Might be my question.   [Egypt
ANT.   How intend you, practis'd?
CÆS. You may be pleas'd to catch at
    mine intent,
By what did here befall me. Your wife,
    and brother,
Made wars upon me; and their contestation
Was theme for you,—you were the word
    of war.
ANT. You do mistake your business; my
    brother never
Did urge me in his act: I did enquire it;
And have my learning from some true
    reports,
That drew their swords with you. Did he
    not rather

Discredit my authority with yours;
And make the wars alike against my
stomach,
Having alike your cause? Of this my letters
Before did satisfy you. If you'll patch a
quarrel,
As matter whole you have to make it with,
It must not be with this.

CÆS. You praise yourself
By laying defects of judgment to me; but
You patch'd up your excuses.

ANT. Not so, not so;
I know you could not lack, I am certain
on't,
Very necessity of this thought, that I,
Your partner in the cause 'gainst which
he fought,
Could not with graceful eyes attend those
wars
Which fronted mine own peace. As for
my wife,
I would you had her spirit in such another:
The third o' the world is yours; which
with a snaffle
You may pace easy, but not such a wife.

ENO. Would we had all such wives, that
the men might go to wars with the women!

ANT. So much uncurbable, her garboils,
Cæsar,
Made out of her impatience, (which not
wanted
Shrewdness of policy too) I grieving
grant,
Did you too much disquiet: for that, you
But say, I could not help it. [must

CÆS. I wrote to you,
When rioting in Alexandria; you
Did pocket up my letters, and with taunts
Did gibe my missive out of audience.

ANT. Sir,
He fell upon me, ere admitted: then
Three kings I had newly feasted, and did
want
Of what I was i' the morning: but, next
day,
I told him of myself; which was as much
As to have ask'd him pardon. Let this
fellow
Be nothing of our strife; if we contend,
Out of our question wipe him.

CÆS. You have broken
The article of your oath; which you shall
never
Have tongue to charge me with.

LEP. Soft, Cæsar.

ANT. No, Lepidus, let him speak:
The honour's sacred which he talks on
now,
Supposing that I lack'd it.—But on, Cæsar;
The article of my oath.

CÆS. To lend me arms and aid when I
requir'd them;
The which you both denied.

ANT. Neglected, rather;
And then, when poison'd hours had bound
me up
From mine own knowledge. As nearly as
I may,
I'll play the penitent to you: but mine
honesty
Shall not make poor my greatness, nor my
power
Work without it. Truth is, that Fulvia,
To have me out of Egypt, made wars here;
For which myself, the ignorant motive, do
So far ask pardon, as befits mine honour
To stoop in such a case.

LEP. 'Tis nobly spoken.

MEC. If it might please you, to enforce
no farther
The griefs between ye: to forget them
quite,
Were to remember that the present need
Speaks to atone you.

LEP. Worthily spoken, Mecænas.

ENO. Or, if you borrow one another's love
for the instant, you may, when you hear
no more words of Pompey, return it again:
you shall have time to wrangle in, when
you have nothing else to do.

ANT. Thou art a soldier only: speak no
more.

ENO. That truth should be silent, I had
almost forgot.

ANT. You wrong this presence; therefore
speak no more.

ENO. Go to, then; your considerate stone.

CÆS. I do not much dislike the matter,
but
The manner of his speech; for it cannot be,
We shall remain in friendship, our con-
ditions
So differing in their acts. Yet, if I knew
What hoop should hold us stanch, from
edge to edge
O' the world I would pursue it.

AGR. Give me leave, Cæsar,—

CÆS. Speak, Agrippa.

AGR. Thou hast a sister by the mother's
side,
Admir'd Octavia: great Mark Antony
Is now a widower.

CÆS. Say not so, Agrippa:
If Cleopatra heard you, your reproof
Were well deserv'd of rashness.

ANT. I am not married, Cæsar: let me
hear
Agrippa farther speak.

AGR. To hold you in perpetual amity,
To make you brothers, and to knit your
hearts

With an unslipping knot, take Antony
Octavia to his wife; whose beauty claims
No worse a husband than the best of men;
Whose virtue and whose general graces
　　speak
That which none else can utter. By this
　　marriage,
All little jealousies, which now seem great,
And all great fears, which now import their
　　dangers,
Would then be nothing: truths would be
　　but tales,
Where now half tales be truths: her love
　　to both,
Would, each to other, and all loves to both,
Draw after her. Pardon what I have spoke;
For 'tis a studied, not a present thought,
By duty ruminated.
ANT.　　　　　　　　Will Cæsar speak?
CÆS. Not till he hears how Antony is
With what is spoke already.　　[touch'd
ANT.　　　What power is in Agrippa,
If I would say, "Agrippa, be it so,"
To make this good?
CÆS.　　　　　The power of Cæsar, and
His power unto Octavia.
ANT.　　　　　　　　May I never
To this good purpose, that so fairly shows,
Dream of impediment!—Let me have thy
　　hand:
Farther this act of grace; and from this
　　hour
The heart of brothers govern in our loves,
And sway our great designs!
CÆS.　　　　　　There is my hand.
A sister I bequeath you, whom no brother
Did ever love so dearly: let her live
To join our kingdoms, and our hearts; and
Fly off our loves again!　　　　[never
LEP.　　　　　　　　Happily, amen!
ANT. I did not think to draw my sword
'gainst Pompey;
For he hath laid strange courtesies, and
　　great,
Of late upon me: I must thank him only,
Lest my remembrance suffer ill report;
At heel of that, defy him.
LEP.　　　　　　Time calls upon us:
Of us must Pompey presently be sought,
Or else he seeks out us.
ANT.　　　　　　　Where lies he?
CÆS. About the Mount Misenum.
ANT.　　　　　　What's his strength
By land?
CÆS. Great, and increasing: but by sea
He is an absolute master.
ANT.　　　　　　　So is the fame.
Would we had spoke together! Haste we
　　for it:
Yet, ere we put ourselves in arms, despatch
The business we have talk'd of.　　[we

CÆS.　　　　　　With most gladness;
And do invite you to my sister's view,
Whither straight I'll lead you.
ANT.　　　　　　Let us, Lepidus,
Not lack your company.
LEP.　　　　　　　Noble Antony,
Not sickness should detain me.

[*Flourish. Exeunt* CÆSAR, ANTHONY, *and*
　　LEPIDUS.

MEC. Welcome from Egypt, Sir.
ENO. Half the heart of Cæsar, worthy
Mecænas!—my honourable friend, Agrippa!—
AGR. Good Enobarbus!
MEC. We have cause to be glad, that
matters are so well digested. You stay'd
well by it in Egypt.
ENO. Ay, Sir; we did sleep day out of
countenance, and made the night light with
drinking.
MEC. Eight wild boars roasted whole at
a breakfast, and but twelve persons there;
is this true?
ENO. This was but as a fly by an eagle:
we had much more monstrous matter of
feast, which worthily deserved noting.
MEC. She's a most triumphant lady, if
report be square to her.
ENO. When she first met Mark Antony,
she pursed up his heart, upon the river of
Cydnus.
AGR. There she appeared indeed; or my
reporter devised well for her.
ENO. I will tell you.
The barge she sat in, like a burnish'd
　　throne,
Burn'd on the water: the poop was beaten
　　gold;
Purple the sails, and so perfumed, that
The winds were love-sick with them; the
　　oars were silver,
Which to the tune of flutes kept stroke,
　　and made
The water, which they beat, to follow
　　faster,
As amorous of their strokes. For her own
　　person,
It beggar'd all description: she did lie
In her pavilion, (cloth-of-gold of tissue)
O'er-picturing that Venus, where we see
The fancy out-work nature: on each side
　　her
Stood pretty dimpled boys, like smiling
　　Cupids,
With divers-colour'd fans, whose wind did
　　seem
To glow the delicate cheeks which they did
And what they undid, did.　　　　[cool.
AGR.　　　　　　O, rare for Antony!

ENO. Her gentlewomen, like the Nereids,
So many mermaids, tended her i' the eyes,
And made their bends adornings: at the
helm
A seeming mermaid steers: the silken tackle
Swell with the touches of those flower-
soft hands,
That yarely frame the office. From the
barge
A strange invisible perfume hits the sense
Of the adjacent wharfs. The city cast
Her people out upon her; and Antony,
Enthron'd i' the market-place, did sit alone,
Whistling to the air; which, but for
vacancy,
Had gone to gaze on Cleopatra too,
And made a gap in nature.
AGR.   Rare Egyptian!
ENO. Upon her landing, Antony sent to
her,
Invited her to supper: she replied,
It should be better he became her guest;
Which she entreated: our courteous Antony,
Whom ne'er the word of "No" woman
heard speak,
Being barber'd ten times o'er, goes to the
feast;
And, for his ordinary, pays his heart
For what his eyes eat only.
AGR.   Royal wench!
She made great Cæsar lay his sword to bed:
He plough'd her, and she cropp'd.
ENO.   I saw her once
Hop forty paces through the public street;
And having lost her breath, she spoke, and
panted,
That she did make defect perfection,
And, breathless, power breathe forth.
MEC. Now Antony must leave her utterly.
ENO. Never; he will not:
Age cannot wither her, nor custom stale
Her infinite variety: other women cloy
The appetites they feed, but she makes
hungry
Where most she satisfies: for vilest things
Become themselves in her; that the holy
Bless her when she is riggish.   [priests
MEC. If beauty, wisdom, modesty, can
settle
The heart of Antony, Octavia is
A blessed lottery to him.
AGR.   Let us go.—
Good Enobarbus, make yourself my guest
Whilst you abide here.
ENO.   Humbly, Sir, I thank you.
                                        [*Exeunt.*

————

SCENE III.—ROME. *A Room in CÆSAR'S
House.*

Enter CÆSAR, ANTONY, OCTAVIA *between
them; and* Attendants.

ANT. The world, and my great office, will
sometimes
Divide me from your bosom.
OCT.   All which time,
Before the gods my knee shall bow my
prayers
To them for you.   [prayers
ANT.   Good night, Sir.—My Octavia,
Read not my blemishes in the world's
report:
I have not kept my square; but that to
come
Shall all be done by the rule. Good night,
dear lady.—
OCT. Good night, Sir.
CÆS. Good night.
                [*Exeunt* CÆSAR *and* OCTAVIA.
                Enter Soothsayer.
ANT. Now, sirrah,—you do wish yourself
in Egypt?
SOOTH. Would I had never come from
thence, nor you thither!
ANT. If you can, your reason?
SOOTH. I see it in my motion, have it
not in my tongue: but yet hie you to Egypt
again.
ANT. Say to me, whose fortunes shall rise
higher, Cæsar's, or mine?
SOOTH. Cæsar's.
Therefore, O Antony, stay not by his side:
Thy demon,—that's thy spirit which keeps
thee,—is
Noble, courageous, high, unmatchable,
Where Cæsar's is not; but, near him, thy
angel
Becomes a fear, as being o'erpower'd:
therefore,
Make space enough between you.
ANT.   Speak this no more.
SOOTH. To none but thee; no more, but
when to thee.
If thou dost play with him at any game,
Thou art sure to lose; and, of that natural
luck,
He beats thee 'gainst the odds: thy lustre
thickens,
When he shines by: I say again, thy spirit
Is all afraid to govern thee near him;
But, he away, 'tis noble.
ANT.   Get thee gone:
Say to Ventidius, I would speak with
him.—   [*Exit* Soothsayer.
He shall to Parthia.—Be it art, or hap,
He hath spoken true: the very dice obey
him;
And, in our sports, my better cunning
faints
Under his chance: if we draw lots, he
speeds;
His cocks do win the battle still of mine,
When it is all to naught; and his quails
ever

Beat mine, inhoop'd, at odds. I will to
Egypt:
And though I make this marriage for my
I' the east my pleasure lies.—   [peace,
Enter VENTIDIUS.

O, come, Ventidius,
You must to Parthia: your commission's
Follow me, and receive it.   [ready;
[*Exeunt.*

SCENE IV.—ROME. *A Street.*

Enter LEPIDUS, MECÆNAS, *and* AGRIPPA.

LEP. Trouble yourselves no farther: pray
you, hasten
Your generals after.
AGR.   Sir, Mark Antony
Will e'en but kiss Octavia and we'll follow.
LEP. Till I shall see you in your soldier's
dress,
Which will become you both, farewell.
MEC.   We shall,
As I conceive the journey, be at the Mount
Before you, Lepidus.
LEP.   Your way is shorter;
My purposes do draw me much about:
You'll win two days upon me.
MEC. AGR.   Sir, good success!
LEP. Farewell.   [*Exeunt.*

SCENE V.—ALEXANDRIA. *A Room in the
Palace.*

Enter CLEOPATRA, CHARMIAN, IRAS,
ALEXAS, *and* Attendant.

CLEO. Give me some music,—music,
moody food
Of us that trade in love.
ATTEND.   The music, ho!
Enter MARDIAN.

CLEO. Let it alone; let's to billiards:
come, Charmian.
CHAR. My arm is sore; best play with
Mardian.
CLEO. As well a woman with a eunuch
play'd,
As with a woman.—Come, you'll play with
me, Sir?
MAR. As well as I can, Madam.
CLEO. And when good will is show'd,
though't come too short,
The actor may plead pardon. I'll none
now:—
Give me mine angle,—we'll to the river:
there,
My music playing far off, I will betray
Tawny-finn'd fishes; my bended hook shall
pierce
Their slimy jaws; and, as I draw them up,
I'll think them every one an Antony,

And say, "Ah, ha! you're caught."
CHAR.   'Twas merry, when
You wager'd on your angling; when your
diver
Did hang a salt-fish on his hook, which he
With fervency drew up.
CLEO.   That time,—O times!—
I laugh'd him out of patience; and that
night
I laugh'd him into patience: and next morn,
Ere the ninth hour, I drunk him to his bed;
Then, put my tires and mantles on him,
whilst
I wore his sword Philippan.—
Enter a Messenger.
     O, from Italy!—
Ram thou thy fruitful tidings in mine ears,
That long time have been barren.
MESS.   Madam, Madam,—
CLEO. Antony's dead!—if thou say so,
villain,
Thou kill'st thy mistress: but well and free,
If thou so yield him, there is gold, and
here
My bluest veins to kiss,—a hand that kings
Have lipp'd, and trembled kissing.
MESS. First, Madam, he is well.
CLEO.   Why, there's more gold.
But, sirrah, mark, we use
To say, the dead are well: bring it to that,
The gold I give thee will I melt, and pour
Down thy ill-uttering throat.
MESS. Good Madam, hear me.
CLEO.   Well, go to, I will;
But there's no goodness in thy face: if
Antony
Be free, and healthful,—so tart a favour
To trumpet such good tidings! if not well,
Thou should'st come like a fury crown'd
with snakes,
Not like a formal man.
MESS.   Will't please you hear me?
CLEO. I have a mind to strike thee ere
thou speak'st:
Yet, if thou say Antony lives, is well,
Or friends with Cæsar, or not captive to
him,
I'll set thee in a shower of gold, and hail
Rich pearls upon thee.
MESS.   Madam, he's well.
CLEO.   Well said.
MESS. And friends with Cæsar.
CLEO.   Thou'rt an honest man.
MESS. Cæsar and he are greater friends
than ever.
CLEO. Make thee a fortune from me.
MESS.   But yet Madam,—
CLEO. I do not like "but yet," it does
allay
The good precedence; fie upon "but yet!"
"But yet" is as a gaoler to bring forth

Some monstrous malefactor. Pr'ythee, friend,
Pour out the pack of matter to mine ear,
The good and bad together: he's friends with Cæsar,
In state of health, thou say'st; and thou say'st, free.

MESS. Free, Madam! no; I made no such
He's bound unto Octavia.   [report:

CLEO.   ^T For what good turn?

MESS. For the best turn i' the bed.

CLEO.   I am pale, Charmian.

MESS. Madam, he's married to Octavia.

CLEO. The most infectious pestilence upon thee!   [*Strikes him down.*

MESS. Good Madam, patience.

CLEO.   What say you?—Hence,
          [*Strikes him again.*
Horrible villain! or I'll spurn thine eyes
Like balls before me; I'll unhair thy head:
          [*She hales him up and down.*
Thou shalt be whipp'd with wire, and stew'd in brine,
Smarting in lingering pickle.

MESS.   Gracious Madam,
I, that do bring the news, made not the match.

CLEO. Say, 'tis not so, a province I will give thee,
And make thy fortunes proud: the blow thou hadst
Shall make thy peace, for moving me to rage;
And I will boot thee with what gift beside
Thy modesty can beg.

MESS.   He's married, Madam.

CLEO. Rogue! thou hast liv'd too long.
          [*Draws a dagger.*

MESS.   Nay, then I'll run.—
What mean you, Madam? I have made no fault.   [*Exit.*

CHAR. Good Madam, keep yourself within yourself:
The man is innocent.

CLEO. Some innocents 'scape not the thunderbolt.—
Melt Egypt into Nile! and kindly creatures
Turn all to serpents!—Call the slave again:—
Though I am mad, I will not bite him:—

CHAR. He is afeard to come.   [call.

CLEO.   I will not hurt him.—
          [*Exit Attendant.*
These hands do lack nobility, that they strike
A meaner than myself; since I myself
Have given myself the cause.—
          Re-enter Attendant *with* Messenger.
          Come hither, Sir.
Though it be honest, it is never good

To bring bad news: give to a gracious message
A host of tongues; but let ill tidings tell
Themselves, when they be felt.

MESS. I have done my duty.

CLEO.   Is he married?
I cannot hate thee worser than I do,
If thou again say, "Yes."

MESS.   He's married, Madam.

CLEO. The gods confound thee! dost thou hold there still?

MESS. Should I lie, Madam?

CLEO.   O, I would thou didst,
So half my Egypt were submerg'd and made
A cistern for scal'd snakes! Go, get thee hence:
Hadst thou Narcissus in thy face, to me
Thou would'st appear most ugly. He is married?

MESS. I crave your highness' pardon.

CLEO.   He is married?

MESS. Take no offence, that I would not offend you:
To punish me for what you make me do,
Seems much unequal. He is married to Octavia.

CLEO. O, that his fault should make a knave of thee,
That art not! What, thou'rt sure of't?—
Get thee hence:
The merchandise which thou hast brought from Rome,
Are all too dear for me: lie they upon thy hand,
And be undone by 'em!   [*Exit* Messenger.

CHAR.   Good your highness, patience.

CLEO. In praising Antony, I have dispraisd' Cæsar.

CHAR. Many times, Madam.

CLEO.   I am paid for't now.
Lead me from hence;
I faint. O Iras! Charmian!—'Tis no matter.—
Go to the fellow, good Alexas; bid him
Report the feature of Octavia, her years,
Her inclination, let him not leave out
The colour of her hair:—bring me word quickly.—   [*Exit* ALEXAS.
Let him for ever go:—let him not—Charmian,
Though he be painted one way like a Gorgon,
The other way he's a Mars.—[*To* MARDIAN.] Bid you Alexas
Bring me word, how tall she is.—Pity me, Charmian,
But do not speak to me.—Lead me to my chamber.   [*Exeunt.*

SCENE VI.— *Near* MISENUM.

Flourish. Enter POMPEY *and* MENAS, *from one side, with drum and trumpet: from the other,* CÆSAR, ANTONY, LEPIDUS, ENOBARBUS, MECÆNAS, *with* Soldiers *marching.*

POM. Your hostages I have, so have you mine;
And we shall talk before we fight.
CÆS.   Most meet,
That first we come to words; and therefore have we
Our written purposes before us sent;
Which, if thou hast consider'd, let us know
If 'twill tie up thy discontented sword,
And carry back to Sicily much tall youth,
That else must perish here.
POM.   To you all three,
The senators alone of this great world,
Chief factors for the gods,—I do not know
Wherefore my father should revengers want,
Having a son and friends; since Julius Cæsar,
Who at Philippi the good Brutus ghosted,
There saw you labouring for him. What was't
That mov'd pale Cassius to conspire? and what
Made the all-honoured, honest Roman, Brutus,
With the arm'd rest, courtiers of beauteous freedom,
To drench the Capitol; but that they would
Have one man but a man? And that is it
Hath made me rig my navy; at whose burden
The anger'd ocean foams; with which I meant
To scourge th' ingratitude that despiteful
Cast on my noble father.   [Rome
CÆS.   Take your time.
ANT. Thou canst not fear us, Pompey, with thy sails;
We'll speak with thee at sea: at land, thou know'st
How much we do o'er-count thee.
POM.   At land, indeed,
Thou dost o'er-count me of my father's house:
But, since the cuckoo builds not for himself,
Remain in't as thou may'st.   [self,
LEP.   Be pleas'd to tell us
(For this is from the present) how you
The offers we have sent you.   [take
CÆS.   There's the point.
ANT. Which do not be entreated to, but weigh
What it is worth embrac'd.

CÆS.   And what may follow,
To try a larger fortune.
POM.   You have made me offer
Of Sicily, Sardinia; and I must
Rid all the sea of pirates; then, to send
Measures of wheat to Rome: this 'greed upon,
To part with unhack'd edges, and bear
Our targes undinted.   [back
CÆS. ANT. LEP.   That's our offer.
POM.   Know, then,
I came before you here, a man prepar'd
To take this offer: but Mark Antony
Put me to some impatience:—though I lose
The praise of it by telling, you must know,
When Cæsar and your brother were at blows,
Your mother came to Sicily, and did find
Her welcome friendly.
ANT.   I have heard it, Pompey;
And am well studied for a liberal thanks,
Which I do owe you.
POM.   Let me have your hand:
I did not think, Sir, to have met you here.
ANT. The beds i' the east are soft; and thanks to you,
That call'd me, timelier than my purpose,
For I have gain'd by it.   [hither;
CÆS.   Since I saw you last,
There is a change upon you.
POM.   Well, I know not
What counts harsh fortune casts upon my face;
But in my bosom shall she never come,
To make my heart her vassal.
LEP.   Well met here.
POM. I hope so, Lepidus.—Thus we are agreed:
I crave, our composition may be written,
And seal'd between us.
CÆS.   That's the next to do.
POM. We'll feast each other, ere we part; and let's
Draw lots who shall begin.
ANT.   That will I, Pompey.
POM. No, Antony, take the lot: but, first
Or last, your fine Egyptian cookery
Shall have the fame. I have heard, that Julius Cæsar
Grew fat with feasting there.
ANT.   You have heard much.
POM. I have fair meanings, Sir.
ANT.   And fair words to them.
POM. Then, so much have I heard:
And I have heard, Apollodorus carried—
ENO. No more of that:— he did so.
POM.   What, I pray you?
ENO. A certain queen to Cæsar in a mattress.

POM. I know thee now: how far'st thou,
soldier?
ENO. Well;
And well am like to do; for, I perceive,
Four feasts are toward.
POM. Let me shake thy hand;
I never hated thee: I have seen thee fight,
When I have envied thy behaviour.
ENO. Sir,
I never lov'd you much; but I have prais'd
you,
When you have well deserv'd ten times as
As I have said you did. [much
POM. Enjoy thy plainness,
It nothing ill becomes thee.—
Aboard my galley I invite you all:
Will you lead, lords?
CÆS. ANT. LEP. Show us the way, Sir.
POM. Come.
[*Exeunt all except* MENAS *and* ENOBARBUS.
MEN. [*Aside.*] Thy father, Pompey, would
ne'er have made this treaty.—[*Aloud.*]
You and I have known, Sir.
ENO. At sea, I think.
MEN. We have, Sir.
ENO. You have done well by water.
MEN. And you by land.
ENO. I will praise any man that will
praise me; though it cannot be denied
what I have done by land.
MEN. Nor what I have done by water.
ENO. Yes, something you can deny for
your own safety: you have been a great
thief by sea.
MEN. And you by land.
ENO. There I deny my land service. But
give me your hand, Menas: if our eyes had
authority, here they might take two thieves
kissing.
MEN. All men's faces are true, whatso'er
their hands are.
ENO. But there is never a fair woman has
a true face.
MEN. No slander,—they steal hearts.
ENO. We came hither to fight with you.
MEN. For my part, I am sorry it is turned
to a drinking. Pompey doth this day laugh
away his fortune.
ENO. If he do, sure, he cannot weep it
back again.
MEN. You have said, Sir. We looked not
for Mark Antony here: pray you, is he
married to Cleopatra?
ENO. Cæsar's sister is call'd Octavia.
MEN. True, Sir; she was the wife of
Caius Marcellus.
ENO. But she is now the wife of Marcus
Antonius.
MEN. Pray you, Sir?
ENO. 'Tis true.

MEN. Then is Cæsar, and he, for ever
knit together.
ENO. If I were bound to divine of this
unity, I would not prophesy so.
MEN. I think, the policy of that purpose
made more in the marriage, than the love
of the parties.
ENO. I think so too. But you shall find,
the band that seems to tie their friendship
together will be the very strangler of their
amity: Octavia is of a holy, cold, and still
conversation.
MEN. Who would not have his wife so?
ENO. Not he, that himself is not so;
which is Mark Antony. He will to his
Egyptian dish again: then, shall the sighs
of Octavia blow the fire up in Cæsar; and,
as I said before, that which is the strength
of their amity, shall prove the immediate
author of their variance. Antony will use
his affection where it is: he married but
his occasion here.
MEN. And thus it may be. Come, Sir, will
you aboard? I have a health for you.
ENO. I shall take it, Sir: we have used
our throats in Egypt.
MEN. Come, let's away. [*Exeunt.*

SCENE VII.—*On board* POMPEY'S *Galley,*
lying near MISENUM.

Music. Enter two or three Servants, *with*
a banquet.

1 *SERV.* Here they'll be, man. Some o'
their plants are ill-rooted already; the least
wind i' the world will blow them down.
2 *SERV.* Lepidus is high-coloured.
1 *SERV.* They have made him drink alms-
drink.
2 *SERV.* As they pinch one another by
the disposition, he cries out, "no more;"
reconciles them to his entreaty, and himself
to the drink.
1 *SERV.* But it raises the greater war between him and his discretion.
2 *SERV.* Why, this it is to have a name in
great men's fellowship: I had as lief have
a reed that will do me no service, as a
partisan I could not heave.
1 *SERV.* To be called into a huge sphere,
and not to be seen to move in't, are the
holes where eyes should be, which pitifully
disaster the cheeks.

A sennet sounded. Enter CÆSAR, ANTONY,
LEPIDUS, POMPEY, AGRIPPA, MECÆNAS,
ENOBARBUS, MENAS, *with other* Captains.
ANT. [*To* CÆSAR.] Thus do they, Sir:
they take the flow o' the Nile
By certain scales i' the pyramid; they
know,

By the height, the lowness, or the mean,
if dearth,
Or foison, follow: the higher Nilus swells,
The more it promises: as it ebbs, the seeds-
man
Upon the slime and ooze scatters his grain,
And shortly comes to harvest.

LEP. You have strange serpents there.

ANT.   Ay, Lepidus.

LEP. Your serpent of Egypt is bred, now,
of your mud by the operation of your sun:
so is your crocodile.

ANT. They are so.

POM. Sit,—and some wine!—A health to
Lepidus.

LEP. I am not so well as I should be, but
I'll ne'er out.

ENO. Not till you have slept; I fear me,
you'll be in, till then.

LEP. Nay, certainly, I have heard, the
Ptolemies' pyramises are very goodly
things; without contradiction, I have heard
that.

MEN. [*Aside to* Pom.] Pompey, a word.

POM. [*Aside to* Men.] Say in mine ear:
what is't?

MEN. [*Aside to* Pom.] Forsake thy seat,
I do beseech thee, captain,
And hear me speak a word.

POM. [*Aside to* Men.] Forbear me till
anon.—
This wine for Lepidus.

LEP. What manner o' thing is your crocodile?

ANT. It is shaped, Sir, like itself; and it
is as broad as it hath breadth; it is just
so high as it is, and moves with its own
organs; it lives by that which nourisheth
it; and the elements once out of it, it
transmigrates.

LEP. What colour is it of?

ANT. O its own colour too.

LEP. 'Tis a strange serpent.

ANT. 'Tis so: and the tears of it are wet.

CÆS. Will this description satisfy him?

ANT. With the health that Pompey gives
him, else he is a very epicure.

POM. [*Aside to* Men.] Go hang, Sir,
hang! Tell me of that? away!
Do as I bid you.—Where's this cup I call'd
for?

MEN. [*Aside to* Pom.] If for the sake of
merit thou wilt hear me,
Rise from thy stool.

POM. [*Aside to* Men.] I think, thou'rt
mad. The matter?

         [*Rises; and walks aside with* Menas.

MEN. I have ever held my cap off to thy
fortunes.

POM. Thou hast serv'd me with much
faith. What's else to say?—
Be jolly, lords.

ANT.   These quick-sands, Lepidus,
Keep off them, for you sink.

MEN. Wilt thou be lord of all the world?

POM.   What say'st thou?

MEN. Wilt thou be lord of the whole
world? That's twice.

POM. How should that be?

MEN.   But entertain it,
And though thou think me poor, I am the
Will give thee all the world.   [man

POM.   Hast thou drunk well?

MEN. No, Pompey, I have kept me from
the cup.
Thou art, if thou dar'st be, the earthly
Jove:
Whate'er the ocean pales, or sky inclips,
Is thine, if thou wilt have't.

POM.   Show me which way.

MEN. These three world-sharers, these
competitors,
Are in thy vessel: let me cut the cable;
And, when we are put off, fall to their
All there is thine.   [throats:

POM.   Ah, this thou should'st have done,
And not have spoke on't! In me, 'tis
villany;
In thee, 't had been good service. Thou
must know,
'Tis not my profit that does lead mine
honour;
Mine honour, it. Repent that e'er thy
tongue
Hath so betray'd thine act: being done
unknown,
I should have found it afterwards well
done;
But must condemn it now. Desist, and
drink.   [*Returns to his guests.*

MEN. [*Aside.*] For this,
I'll never follow thy pall'd fortunes more.
Who seeks, and will not take, when once
'tis offer'd,
Shall never find it more.

POM.   This health to Lepidus!

ANT. Bear him ashore.—I'll pledge it for
him, Pompey.

ENO. Here's to thee, Menas!

MEN.   Enobarbus, welcome!

POM. Fill, till the cup be hid.

ENO. There's a strong fellow, Menas.
[*Pointing to the* Attendant *who carries
off* Lepidus.

MEN.   Why?

ENO.   He bears
The third part of the world, man; see'st
not?

MEN. The third part, then, is drunk: would it were all,
That it might go on wheels!
ENO. Drink thou; increase the reels.
MEN. Come.
POM. This is not yet an Alexandrian feast.
ANT. It ripens towards it.—Strike the vessels, ho!—
Here is to Cæsar!
CÆS.   I could well forbear't.
It's monstrous labour, when I wash my brain,
And it grows fouler.
ANT.   Be a child o' the time.
CÆS. Possess it, I'll make answer: but I had rather fast
From all four days, than drink so much in one.
ENO. [*To* ANT.] Ha, my brave emperor!
Shall we dance now the Egyptian Bacchanals,
And celebrate our drink?
POM.   Let's ha't, good soldier.
ANT. Come, let's all take hands,
Till that the conquering wine hath steep'd our sense
In soft and delicate Lethe.
ENO.   All take hands.—
Make battery to our ears with the loud music:—
The while I'll place you: then, the boy shall sing;
The holding every man shall bear, as loud
As his strong sides can volley.
            [*Music plays.* ENOBARBUS *places them hand in hand.*

SONG.

Come, thou monarch of the vine,
Plumpy Bacchus, with pink eyne!
In thy vats our cares be drown'd;
With thy grapes our hairs be crown'd;
Cup us, till the world go round;
Cup us, till the world go round!

CÆS. What would you more?—Pompey, good night.—Good brother,
Let me request you off: our graver business
Frowns at this levity.—Gentle lords, let's part;
You see, we have burnt our cheeks: strong Enobarbe
Is weaker than the wine; and mine own tongue
Splits what it speaks: the wild disguise hath almost
Antick'd us all. What needs more words? Good night.—
Good Antony, your hand.

POM.   I'll try you on the shore.
ANT. And shall, Sir: give's your hand.
POM.   O, Antony!
You have my father's house,—But, what? we are friends.
Come, down into the boat.
ENO.   Take heed you fall not.—
            [*Exeunt* POMPEY, CÆSAR, ANTONY, *and Attendants.*
Menas, I'll not on shore.
MEN.   No, to my cabin.—
These drums!—these trumpets, flutes! what!—
Let Neptune hear, we bid a loud farewell
To these great fellows: sound, and be hang'd! sound out!   [*A flourish.*
ENO. Hoo! says 'a.—There's my cap.
MEN.   Hoo!—noble captain, come.
            [*Exeunt.*

ACT III.

SCENE I.—*A Plain in* SYRIA.

Enter VENTIDIUS, *in triumph, with* SILIUS, *and other* Romans, Officers, *and* Soldiers; *the dead body of* PACORUS *borne before him.*

VEN. Now, darting Parthia, art thou struck; and now
Pleas'd fortune does of Marcus Crassus' death
Make me revenger.—Bear the king's son's body
Before our army.—Thy Pacorus, Orodes,
Pays this for Marcus Crassus.
SIL.   Noble Ventidius,
Whilst yet with Parthian blood thy sword is warm,
The fugitive Parthians follow; spur through Media,
Mesopotamia, and the shelters whither
The routed fly: so thy grand captain, Antony,
Shall set thee on triumphant chariots, and
Put garlands on thy head.
VEN.   O Silius, Silius,
I have done enough: a lower place, note well,
May make too great an act; for learn this, Silius,—
Better to leave undone, than by our deed acquire
Too high a fame, when him we serve's away.
Cæsar and Antony have ever won
More in their officer, than person: Sossius,
One of my place in Syria, his lieutenant,
For quick accumulation of renown,
Which he achiev'd by the minute, lost his favour.

Who does i' the wars more than his captain
    can,
Becomes his captain's captain: and am-
    bition,
The soldier's virtue, rather makes choice
    of loss,
Than gain which darkens him.
I could do more to do Antonius good,
But 'twould offend him; and in his offence
Should my performance perish.
SIL.   Thou hast, Ventidius, that
Without the which a soldier, and his
    sword,
Grants scarce distinction. Thou wilt write
    to Antony?
VEN. I'll humbly signify what in his
    name,
That magical word of war, we have ef-
    fected;
How, with his banners and his well-paid
    ranks,
The ne'er-yet-beaten horse of Parthia
We have jaded out o' the field.
SIL.   Where is he now?
VEN. He purposeth to Athens: whither,
    with what haste
The weight we must convey with us will
    permit,
We shall appear before him.—On, there;
    pass along!   [Exeunt.

SCENE II.—ROME. An Ante-Chamber in
    CÆSAR'S House.

Enter AGRIPPA and ENOBARBUS, meeting.
AGR. What, are the brothers parted?
ENO. They have despatch'd with Pompey;
    he is gone;
The other three are sealing. Octavia weeps
To part from Rome; Cæsar is sad; and
    Lepidus,
Since Pompey's feast, as Menas says, is
With the green sickness.   [troubled
AGR.   'Tis a noble Lepidus.
ENO. A very fine one: O, how he loves
    Cæsar!
AGR. Nay, but how dearly he adores
    Mark Antony!
ENO. Cæsar? Why, he's the Jupiter of
    men.
AGR. What's Antony? The god of Jupiter.
ENO. Spake you of Cæsar? Hoo! the non-
    pareil!
AGR. O Antony! O thou Arabian bird!
ENO. Would you praise Cæsar, say,
    "Cæsar,"—go no farther.
AGR. Indeed, he plied them both with ex-
    cellent praises.
ENO. But he loves Cæsar best;—yet he
    loves Antony:

Hoo! hearts, tongues, figures, scribes,
    bards, poets, cannot
Think, speak, cast, write, sing, number,—
    hoo!—
His love to Antony. But as for Cæsar,
Kneel down, kneel down, and wonder.
AGR.   Both he loves.
ENO. They are his shards, and he their
    beetle.—So,—   [Trumpets heard.
This is to horse.—Adieu, noble Agrippa.
AGR. Good fortune, worthy soldier; and
    farewell.
    Enter CÆSAR, ANTONY, LEPIDUS, and
                OCTAVIA.
ANT. No farther, Sir.
CÆS. You take from me a great part of
    myself;
Use me well in't.—Sister, prove such a
    wife
As my thoughts make thee, and as my
    farthest band
Shall pass on thy approof.—Most noble
    Antony,
Let not the piece of virtue, which is set
Betwixt us as the cement of our love,
To keep it builded, be the ram to batter
The fortress of it; for better might we
Have loved without this mean, if on both
This be not cherish'd.   [parts
ANT.   Make me not offended
In your distrust.
CÆS.   I have said.
ANT.   You shall not find,
Though you be therein curious, the least
    cause
For what you seem to fear: so, the gods
    keep you,
And make the hearts of Romans serve
    your ends!
We will here part.
CÆS. Farewell, my dearest sister, fare
    thee well:
The elements be kind to thee, and make
Thy spirits all of comfort! fare thee well.
OCT. My noble brother!—
ANT. The April's in her eyes: it is love's
    spring,
And these the showers to bring it on.—
    Be cheerful.
OCT. Sir, look well to my husband's
    house; and—
CÆS. What, Octavia?
OCT. I'll tell you in your ear.
ANT. Her tongue will not obey her heart,
    nor can
Her heart inform her tongue; the swan's
    down feather,
That stands upon the swell at the full of
    tide,
And neither way inclines.
ENO. [Aside to AGR.] Will Cæsar weep?

AGR. [*Aside to* ENO.] He has a cloud in's
face.

ENO. [*Aside to* AGR.] He were the worse
for that, were he a horse;
So is he, being a man.

AGR. [*Aside to* ENO.] Why, Enobarbus,
When Antony found Julius Cæsar dead,
He cried almost to roaring; and he wept
When at Philippi he found Brutus slain.

ENO. [*Aside to* AGR.] That year, indeed,
he was troubled with a rheum;
What willingly he did confound, he wail'd:
Believe't, till I weep him.

CÆS.   No, sweet Octavia,
You shall hear from me still; the time shall not
Out-go my thinking on you.   [shall not

ANT.   Come, Sir, come;
I'll wrestle with you in my strength of
love:
Look, here I have you; thus I let you go,
And give you to the gods.

CÆS.   Adieu; be happy!

LEP. Let all the number of the stars give
light
To thy fair way!

CÆS.   Farewell, farewell!
               [*Kisses* OCTAVIA.

ANT.   Farewell!
          [*Trumpets heard. Exeunt.*

SCENE III.—ALEXANDRIA. *A Room in the
          Palace.*

Enter CLEOPATRA, CHARMIAN, IRAS, *and*
          ALEXAS.

CLEO. Where is the fellow?

ALEX.   Half afeard to come.

CLEO. Go to, go to.—
          Enter a Messenger.
          Come hither, Sir.

ALEX.   Good majesty,
Herod of Jewry dare not look upon you,
But when you are well pleas'd.

CLEO.   That Herod's head
I'll have: but how, when Antony is gone,
Through whom I might command it?—
     Come thou near.

MESS. Most gracious majesty,—

CLEO.   Didst thou behold
Octavia?

MESS. Ay, dread queen.

CLEO.   Where?

MESS.   Madam, in Rome
I look'd her in the face; and saw her led
Between her brother and Mark Antony.

CLEO. Is she as tall as me?

MESS.   She is not, Madam.

CLEO. Didst hear her speak? Is she
shrill-tongu'd, or low?

MESS. Madam, I heard her speak: she is
low-voiced.

CLEO. That's not so good:—he cannot
like her long.

CHAR. Like her! O Isis! 'tis impossible.

CLEO. I think so, Charmian: dull of
tongue and dwarfish!—
What majesty is in her gait? Remember,
If e'er thou look'dst on majesty.

MESS.   She creeps;
Her motion and her station are as one:
She shows a body rather than a life;
A statue, than a breather.

CLEO.   Is this certain?

MESS. Or I have no observance.

CHAR.   Three in Egypt
Cannot make better note.

CLEO.   He's very knowing;
I do perceive't:—there's nothing in her
yet.—
The fellow has good judgment.

CHAR.   Excellent.

CLEO. Guess at her years, I pr'ythee.

MESS.   Madam,
She was a widow,—

CLEO.   Widow!—Charmian, hark.

MESS. And I do think, she's thirty.

CLEO. Bear'st thou her face in mind?
is't long, or round?

MESS. Round, even to faultiness.

CLEO. For the most part, too, they are
foolish that are so.—
Her hair, what colour?

MESS. Brown, Madam; and her forehead
As low as she would wish it.

CLEO.   There's gold for thee.
Thou must not take my former sharpness
ill:—
I will employ thee back again; I find thee
Most fit for business: go, make thee ready;
Our letters are prepar'd.
          [*Exit.* Messenger.

CHAR.   A proper man.

CLEO. Indeed, he is so: I repent me
much,
That so I harried him. Why, methinks, by
This creature's no such thing.   [him,

CHAR. Nothing, Madam.

CLEO. The man hath seen some majesty,
and should know.

CHAR. Hath he seen majesty? Isis else
defend,
And serving you so long!

CLEO. I have one thing more to ask him
yet, good Charmian:
But 'tis no matter; thou shalt bring him
to me
Where I will write. All may be well enough.

CHAR. I warrant you, Madam.   [*Exeunt.*

SCENE IV.—ATHENS. *A Room in* ANTONY'S *House.*

Enter ANTONY *and* OCTAVIA.

ANT. Nay, nay, Octavia, not only that,—
That were excusable, that and thousands more
Of semblable import,—but he hath wag'd
New wars 'gainst Pompey; made his will,
To public ear: [and read it
Spoke scantly of me: when perforce he could not
But pay me terms of honour, cold and sickly
He vented them; most narrow measure lent me:
When the best hint was given him, he not took't,
Or did it from his teeth.   [took't,
OCT.   O my good lord,
Believe not all; or, if you must believe,
Stomach not all. A more unhappy lady,
If this division chance, ne'er stood between,
Praying for both parts:
The good gods will mock me presently,
When I shall pray, "O, bless my lord and husband!"
Undo that prayer, by crying out as loud,
"'O bless my brother!" Husband win, win brother,
Prays, and destroys the prayer; no midway
'Twixt these extremes at all.
ANT.   Gentle Octavia,
Let your best love draw to that point, which seeks
Best to preserve it: if I lose mine honour,
I lose myself: better I were not yours,
Than yours so branchless. But, as you requested,
Yourself shall go between us: the mean time, lady,
I'll raise the preparation of a war
Shall stain your brother: make your soonest haste:
So, your desires are yours.
OCT.   Thanks to my lord.
The Jove of power make me most weak, most weak,   [would be
Your reconciler! Wars 'twixt you twain
As if the world should cleave, and that slain men
Should solder up the rift.
ANT. When it appears to you where this begins,
Turn your displeasure that way; for our faults
Can never be so equal, that your love
Can equally move with them. Provide your going;
Choose your own company, and command what cost
Your heart has mind to.   [*Exeunt.*

SCENE V.—ATHENS. *Another Room in* ANTONY'S *House.*

Enter ENOBARBUS *and* EROS, *meeting.*

ENO. How now, friend Eros!
EROS. There's strange news come, Sir.
ENO. What, man?
EROS. Cæsar and Lepidus have made wars upon Pompey.
ENO. This is old: what is the success?
EROS. Cæsar, having made use of him in the wars 'gainst Pompey, presently denied him rivality; would not let him partake in the glory of the action: and not resting here, accuses him of letters he had formerly wrote to Pompey; upon his own appeal, seizes him: so the poor third is up, till death enlarge his confine.
ENO. Then, world, thou hast a pair of chaps, no more;
And throw between them all the food thou hast,
They'll grind the one the other. Where's Antony?
EROS. He's walking in the garden—thus; and spurns
The rush that lies before him; cries, "Fool, Lepidus!"
And threats the throat of that his officer,
That murder'd Pompey.
ENO.   Our great navy's rigg'd.
EROS. For Italy, and Cæsar. More, Domitius;
My lord desires you presently: my news
I might have told hereafter
ENO.   'Twill be naught:
But let it be.—Bring me to Antony.
EROS. Come, Sir.   [*Exeunt.*

SCENE VI.—ROME. *A Room in* CÆSAR'S *House.*

Enter CÆSAR, AGRIPPA, *and* MECÆNAS.

CÆS. Contemning Rome, he has done all this, and more,
In Alexandria: here's the manner of it:—
I' the market-place, on a tribunal silver'd,
Cleopatra and himself in chairs of gold
Were publicly enthron'd: at the feet sat
Cæsarion, whom they call my father's son,
And all the unlawful issue, that their lust
Since then hath made between them. Unto her
He gave the 'stablishment of Egypt; made
Of lower Syria, Cyprus, Lydia,   [her
Absolute queen.
MEC.   This in the public eye?
CÆS. I' the common show-place, where they exercise.
His sons he there proclaim'd the kings of kings:

Great Media, Parthia, and Armenia,
He gave to Alexander; to Ptolemy he
assign'd
Syria, Cilicia, and Phœnicia: she
In the habiliments of the goddess Isis
That day appear'd; and oft before gave
As 'tis reported, so. [audience,
MEC. Let Rome be thus
Inform'd.
AGR. Who, queasy with his insolence
Already, will their good thoughts call from
him.
CÆS. The people know it; and have now
His accusations. [receiv'd
AGR. Whom does he accuse?
CÆS. Cæsar: and that, having in Sicily
Sextus Pompeius spoil'd, we had not rated
him
His part o' the isle: then does he say, he
lent me
Some shipping unrestor'd: lastly, he frets
That Lepidus of the triumvirate
Should be depos'd; and, being, that we
All his revenue. [detain
AGR. Sir, this should be answer'd.
CÆS. 'Tis done already, and the mes-
senger gone.
I have told him, Lepidus was grown too
cruel;
That he his high authority abus'd,
And did deserve his change: for what I
have conquer'd,
I grant him part; but then, in his Ar-
menia,
And other of his conquer'd kingdoms, I
Demand the like.
MEC. He'll never yield to that.
CÆS. Nor must not, then, be yielded to
in this.

Enter OCTAVIA, *with her train.*

OCT. Hail, Cæsar, and my lord! hail, most
dear Cæsar! [away!
CÆS. That ever I should call thee cast-
OCT. You have not call'd me so, nor have
you cause.
CÆS. Why have you stol'n upon us thus?
You come not
Like Cæsar's sister: the wife of Antony
Should have an army for an usher, and
The neighs of horse to tell of her approach,
Long ere she did appear; the trees by the
way, [fainted,
Should have borne men, and expectation
Longing for what it had not; nay, the dust
Should have ascended to the roof of
heaven,
Rais'd by your populous troops: but you
are come [vented
A market-maid to Rome, and have pre-

The ostentation of our love, which, left
unshown, [you
Is often left unlov'd: we should have met
By sea and land; supplying every stage
With an augmented greeting.
OCT. Good my lord
To come thus was I not constrain'd, but
did it
On my free-will. My lord, Mark Antony,
Hearing that you prepar'd for war, ac-
quainted
My grieved ear withal; whereon, I begg'd
His pardon for return.
CÆS. Which soon he granted,
Being an obstruct 'tween his lust and him.
OCT. Do not say so, my lord.
CÆS. I have eyes upon him,
And his affairs come to me on the wind.
Where is he now?
OCT. My lord, in Athens.
CÆS. No, my most wronged sister; Cleo-
patra [his empire
Hath nodded him to her. He hath given
Up to a whore; who now are levying
The kings o' the earth for war: he hath
assembled
Bocchus, the king of Lybia; Archelaus,
Of Cappadocia; Philadelphos, king
Of Paphlagonia; the Thracian king,
Adallas;
King Malchus of Arabia; king of Pont;
Herod of Jewry; Mithridates, king
Of Comagene; Polemon and Amintas,
The kings of Mede, and Lycaonia,
With a more larger list of sceptres.
OCT. Ah me, most wretched,
That have my heart parted betwixt two
That do afflict each other! [friends,
CÆS. Welcome hither:
Your letters did withhold our breaking
forth;
Till we perceiv'd, both how you were
wrong led, [heart:
And we in negligent danger. Cheer your
Be you not troubled with the time, which
drives
O'er your content these strong necessities;
But let determin'd things to destiny
Hold unbewail'd their way. Welcome to
Rome;
Nothing more dear to me. You are abus'd
Beyond the mark of thought: and the high
gods,
To do you justice, make their ministers
Of us and those that love you. Best of
And ever welcome to us. [comfort;
AGR. Welcome, lady.
MEC. Welcome, dear Madam.
Each heart in Rome does love and pity
you:

Only the adulterous Antony, most large
In his abominations, turns you off;
And gives his potent regiment to a trull,
That noises it against us.
OCT.   Is it so, Sir?
CÆS. Most certain. Sister, welcome: pray
 you,
Be ever known to patience: my dearest
 sister!   [Exeunt.

SCENE VII.—ANTONY'S *Camp, near the
 Promontory of* ACTIUM.
Enter CLEOPATRA *and* ENOBARBUS.
CLEO. I will be even with thee, doubt it
 not.
ENO. But why, why, why?
CLEO. Thou hast forspoke my being in
 these wars,
And say'st, it is not fit.
ENO.   Well, is it, is it?
CLEO. If not denounc'd against us, why
Be there in person? [should not we
ENO. [*Aside.*] Well, I could reply:—
If we should serve with horse and mares
 together,
The horse were merely lost: the mares
A soldier, and his horse. [would bear
CLEO.   What is't you say?
ENO. Your presence needs must puzzle
 Antony;   [from's time,
Take from his heart, take from his brain,
What should not then be spar'd. He is
 already
Traduc'd for levity; and 'tis said in Rome,
That Photinus a eunuch, and your maids,
Manage this war.
CLEO. Sink Rome; and their tongues rot,
That speak against us! A charge we bear
 i' the war,
And, as the president of my kingdom, will
Appear there for a man. Speak not against
I will not stay behind.   [it;
ENO.   Nay, I have done.
Here comes the emperor.
Enter ANTONY *and* CANIDIUS.
ANT.   Is it not strange, Canidius,
That from Tarentum, and Brundusium,
He could so quickly cut the Ionian sea,
And take in Toryne?—You have heard
 on't, sweet?
CLEO. Celerity is never more admir'd,
Than by the negligent.
ANT.   A good rebuke,
Which might have well become the best
 of men,
To taunt at slackness.—Canidius, we
Will fight with him by sea.
CLEO.   By sea! What else?
CAN. Why will my lord do so?
ANT.   For that he dares us to't.

ENO. So hath my lord dar'd him to single
 fight.
CAN. Ay, and to wage this battle at Phar-
 salia,
Where Cæsar fought with Pompey: but
 these offers,
Which serve not for his vantage, he shakes
And so should you.   [off;
ENO. Your ships are not well mann'd,—
Your mariners are muleteers, reapers,
 people
Ingross'd by swift impress; in Cæsar's fleet
Are those, that often have 'gainst Pompey
 fought;   [grace
Their ships are yare; yours, heavy: no dis-
Shall fall you for refusing him at sea,
Being prepar'd for land.
ANT.   By sea, by sea.
ENO. Most worthy Sir, you therein throw
 away
The absolute soldiership you have by land;
Distract your army, which doth most con-
 sist
Of war-mark'd footmen; leave unexecuted
Your own renowned knowledge; quite
 forego
The way which promises assurance; and
Give up yourself merely to chance and
From firm security.   [hazard,
ANT.   I'll fight at sea.
CLEO. I have sixty sails, Cæsar none
 better.
ANT. Our overplus of shipping will we
 burn;
And, with the rest, full-mann'd, from the
 head of Actium
Beat th' approaching Cæsar: but if we fail,
We then can do't at land.
Enter a Messenger.
     Thy business?
MESS. The news is true, my lord; he is
Cæsar has taken Toryne. [descried;
ANT. Can he be there in person? 'tis
 impossible;   [idius,
Strange, that his power should be.—Can-
Our nineteen legions thou shalt hold by
 land,   [our ship:
And our twelve thousand horse.—We'll to
Away, my Thetis!—
Enter a Soldier.
   How now, worthy soldier!
SOLD. O noble emperor, do not fight by
 sea;
Trust not to rotten planks: do you mis-
 doubt   [the Egyptians,
This sword, and these my wounds? Let
And the Phœnicians, go a ducking: we
Have used to conquer, standing on the
And fighting foot to foot.   [earth,
ANT.   Well, well:—away!

[Exeunt ANTONY, CLEOPATRA, *and*
ENOBARBUS.

SOLD. By Hercules, I think I am i' the
right.

CAN. Soldier, thou art; but his whole
action grows
Not in the power on't: so our leaders led,
And we are women's men.

SOLD. You keep by land
The legions and the horse whole, do you
not?

CAN. Marcus Octavius, Marcus Justeius,
Publicola, and Cælius, are for sea:
But we keep whole by land. This speed
Carries beyond belief. [of Cæsar's

SOLD. While he was yet in Rome,
His power went out in such distractions, as
Beguil'd all spies.

CAN. Who's his lieutenant, hear you?

SOLD. They say, one Taurus.

CAN. Well I know the man.

Enter a Messenger.

MESS. The emperor calls Canidius.

CAN. With news the time's with labour;
and throes forth,
Each minute, some. [Exeunt.

———

SCENE VIII.—*A Plain near* ACTIUM.

Enter CÆSAR, TAURUS, Officers, *and others.*

CÆS. Taurus,—

TAUR. My lord?

CÆS. Strike not by land; keep whole:
Provoke not battle, till we have done at
sea.
Do not exceed the prescript of this scroll:
Our fortune lies upon this jump. [Exeunt.

Enter ANTONY *and* ENOBARBUS.

ANT. Set we our squadrons on yon side
o' the hill,
In eye of Cæsar's battle; from which place
We may the number of the ships behold,
And so proceed accordingly. [Exeunt.

Enter CANIDIUS, *marching with his land
army one way; and* TAURUS, *the Lieutenant of* CÆSAR, *with his army, the
other way. After they are gone, the noise
of a sea-fight is heard.*

Alarum. Re-enter ENOBARBUS.

ENO. Naught, naught, all naught! I can
behold no longer:
The Antoniad, the Egyptian admiral,
With all their sixty, fly, and turn the rud-
To see't, mine eyes are blasted. [der:

Enter SCARUS.

SCAR. Gods and goddesses,
All the whole synod of them!

ENO. What's thy passion?

SCAR. The greater cantle of the world is
lost

With very ignorance; we have kiss'd away
Kingdoms and provinces.

ENO. How appears the fight?

SCAR. On our side like the token'd
pestilence, [of Egypt,—
Where death is sure. Yon ribald-rig nag
Whom leprosy o'ertake!—i' the midst o'
the fight,
When vantage like a pair of twins ap-
pear'd,
Both as the same, or rather ours the
elder,—
The brize upon her, like a cow in June,—
Hoists sails, and flies.

ENO. That I beheld:
Mine eyes did sicken at the sight, and
Endure a farther view. [could not

SCAR. She once being loof'd,
The noble ruin of her magic, Antony,
Claps on his sea-wing, and like a doting
mallard,
Leaving the fight in height, flies after her:
I never saw an action of such shame;
Experienced, manhood, honour, ne'er before
Did violate so itself.

ENO. Alack! alack!

Enter CANIDIUS.

CAN. Our fortune on the sea is out of
breath,
And sinks most lamentably. Had our
general
Been what he knew himself, it had gone
well:
O, he has given example for our flight,
Most grossly, by his own!

ENO. Ay, are you thereabouts! Why, then,
Indeed. [good night

CAN. Towards Peloponnesus are they fled.

SCAR. 'Tis easy to't; and there I will
What farther comes. [attend

CAN. To Cæsar will I render
My legions, and my horse: six kings
already
Show me the way of yielding.

ENO. I'll yet follow
The wounded chance of Antony, though
my reason
Sits in the wind against me. [Exeunt.

———

SCENE IX.—ALEXANDRIA. *A Room in the
Palace.*

Enter ANTONY *and* Attendants.

ANT. Hark! the land bids me tread no
more upon't,—
It is asham'd to bear me!—Friends, come
hither:
I am so lated in the world, that I
Have lost my way for ever:—I have a ship
Laden with gold; take that, divide it; fly,
And make your peace with Cæsar.

ATTENDANTS. Fly! not we.

ANT. I have fled myself; and have in-
structed cowards
To run, and show their shoulders.—Friends,
be gone;
I have myself resolv'd upon a course,
Which has no need of you; be gone:
My treasure's in the harbour, take it.—O,
I follow'd that I blush to look upon:
My very hairs do mutiny; for the white
Reprove the brown for rashness, and they
them
For fear and doting.—Friends, be gone:
you shall
Have letters from me to some friends, that
will
Sweep your way for you. Pray you, look
not sad,
Nor make replies of loathness: take the
hint
Which my despair proclaims; let that be
left
Which leaves itself: to the sea-side straight-
way:
I will possess you of that ship and treasure.
Leave me, I pray, a little: 'pray you now:—
Nay, do so; for, indeed, I have lost
command,
Therefore I pray you:—I'll see you by
and by.　　　　　　　　　　　[*Sits down.*

Enter CLEOPATRA, *led by* CHARMIAN *and*
IRAS; EROS *following.*

EROS. Nay, gentle Madam, to him,—com-
fort him.
IRAS. Do, most dear queen.
CHAR. Do! Why, what else?
CLEO. Let me sit down. O Juno!
ANT. No, no, no, no, no.
EROS. See you here, Sir?
ANT. O fie, fie, fie!
CHAR. Madam,—
IRAS. Madam, O good empress,—
EROS. Sir, Sir,—
ANT. Yes, my lord, yes;—he, at Philippi,
kept
His sword e'en like a dancer; while I struck
The lean and wrinkled Cassius; and 'twas I
That the mad Brutus ended: he alone
Dealt on lieutenantry, and no practice had
In the brave squares of war: yet now—No
matter.
CLEO. Ah, stand by.
EROS. The queen, my lord, the queen.
IRAS. Go to him, Madam, speak to him:
He is unqualitied with very shame.
CLEO. Well then,—sustain me:—O!
EROS. Most noble Sir, arise; the queen
approaches;
Her head's declin'd, and death will seize
her, but
Your comfort makes the rescue.

ANT. I have offended reputation,—
A most unnoble swerving.
EROS.　　　　　　　　　　Sir, the queen.
ANT. O, whither hast thou led me, Egypt?
See,
How I convey my shame out of thine eyes,
By looking back what I have left behind
'Stroy'd in dishonour.
CLEO.　　　　　　　　O my lord, my lord,
Forgive my fearful sails! I little thought
You would have follow'd.
ANT. Egypt, thou knew'st too well,
My heart was to thy rudder tied by the
strings,
And thou should'st tow me after: o'er my
spirit
Thy full supremacy thou knew'st, and that
Thy beck might from the bidding of the
gods
Command me.　　　　　　　　　　[*gods*
CLEO.　　　　　　　　　O, my pardon!
ANT.　　　　　　　　　　　　Now I must
To the young man send humble treaties,
dodge
And palter in the shifts of lowness; who
With half the bulk o' the world play'd as
I pleas'd,
Making and marring fortunes. You did
know
How much you were my conqueror; and
that
My sword, made weak by my affection,
Obey it on all cause.　　　　　　　　[*would*
CLEO.　　　　　　　　Pardon, pardon!
ANT. Fall not a tear, I say; one of them
rates
All that is won and lost: give me a kiss;
Even this repays me.—We sent our school-
master;
Is he come back?—Love, I am full of
lead.—
Some wine, within there, and our viands!—
Fortune knows,
We scorn her most when most she offers
blows.　　　　　　　　　　　　[*Exeunt.*

SCENE X.—CÆSAR'S *Camp in* EGYPT.

Enter CÆSAR, DOLABELLA, THYREUS,
and others.

CÆS. Let him appear that's come from
Know you him?　　　　　　　[Antony.—
DOL.　　　　　Cæsar, 'tis his schoolmaster:
An argument that he is pluck'd, when
hither
He sends so poor a pinion of his wing,
Which had superfluous kings for mes-
Not many moons gone by.　　　[sengers,
Enter EUPHRONIUS.
CÆS.　　　　　　　Approach, and speak.
EUPH. Such as I am, I come from
Antony:

I was of late as petty to his ends,
As is the morn-dew on the myrtle leaf
To his grand sea.
CÆS. Be it so:—declare thine office.
EUPH. Lord of his fortunes he salutes
thee, and
Requires to live in Egypt: which not
granted,
He lessens his requests; and to thee sues
To let him breathe between the heavens
and earth,
A private man in Athens: this for him.
Next, Cleopatra does confess thy greatness;
Submits her to thy might; and of thee
craves
The circle of the Ptolemies for her heirs,
Now hazarded to thy grace.
CÆS. For Antony,
I have no ears to his request. The queen
Of audience, nor desire, shall fail; so she
From Egypt drive her all-disgraced friend,
Or take his life there: this if she perform,
She shall not sue unheard. So to them
EUPH. Fortune pursue thee! [both.
CÆS. Bring him through the bands.
[*Exit* EUPHRONIUS.
[*To* THYR.] To try thy eloquence, now 'tis
time; despatch:
From Antony win Cleopatra: promise,
And in our name, what she requires; add
more,
From thine invention, offers: women are
not
In their best fortunes strong; but want will
perjure
The ne'er-touch'd vestal: try thy cunning,
Thyreus;
Make thine own edict for thy pains, which
Will answer as a law. [we
THYR. Cæsar, I go.
CÆS. Observe how Antony becomes his
flaw,
And what thou think'st his very action
In every power that moves. [speaks
THYR. Cæsar, I shall.
[*Exeunt.*

SCENE XI.—ALEXANDRIA. *A Room in
the Palace.*

Enter CLEOPATRA, ENOBARBUS, CHARMIAN,
and IRAS.

CLEO. What shall we do, Enobarbus?
ENO. Think, and die.
CLEO. Is Antony, or we, in fault for this?
ENO. Antony only, that would make his
will
Lord of his reason. What though you fled
From that great face of war, whose several
ranges
Frighted each other,—why should he follow?

The itch of his affection should not then
Have nick'd his captainship; at such a
point,
When half to half the world oppos'd, he
being
The mered question: 'twas a shame no less
Than was his loss, to course your flying
And leave his navy gazing. [flags,
CLEO. Pr'ythee, peace.
Enter ANTONY, *with* EUPHRONIUS.
ANT. Is that his answer?
EUPH. Ay, my lord.
ANT. The queen shall, then, have courtesy, so she
Will yield us up?
EUPH. He says so.
ANT. Let her know it.—
To the boy Cæsar send this grizzled head,
And he will fill thy wishes to the brim
With principalities.
CLEO. That head, my lord?
ANT. To him again: tell him, he wears
the rose
Of youth upon him; from which the world
should note
Something particular: his coin, ships, legions, [prevail
May be a coward's; whose ministers would
Under the service of a child, as soon
As i' the command of Cæsar: I dare him,
therefore,
To lay his gay comparisons apart,
And answer me declin'd; sword against
sword,
Ourselves alone. I'll write it: follow me.
[*Exeunt* ANTONY *and* EUPHRONIUS.
ENO. [*Aside.*] Yes, like enough, highbattled Cæsar will
Unstate his happiness, and be stag'd to
the show
Against a sworder! I see, men's judgments
are [ward
A parcel of their fortunes; and things outDo draw the inward quality after them,
To suffer all alike. That he should dream,
Knowing all measures, the full Cæsar will
Answer his emptiness! Cæsar, thou hast
His judgment too. [subdu'd
Enter an Attendant.
ATT. A messenger from Cæsar.
CLEO. What, no more ceremony?—See,
my women!
Against the blown rose may they stop their
nose,
That kneel'd unto the buds.—Admit him,
Sir. [*Exit* Attendant.
ENO. [*Aside.*] Mine honesty and I begin
to square.
The loyalty well held to fools does make
Our faith mere folly: yet he, that can
endure

To follow with allegiance a fallen lord,
Does conquer him that did his master conquer,
And earns a place i' the story.

Enter THYREUS.

CLEO.　　　　　Cæsar's will?

THYR. Hear it apart.

CLEO.　None but friends: say boldly.

THYR. So, haply, are they friends to Antony.

ENO. He needs as many, Sir, as Cæsar has;　　　　　　　[master
Or needs not us. If Cæsar please, our
Will leap to be his friend: for us, you know,
Whose he is, we are, and that is Cæsar's.

THYR.　　　　　　　　So.—
Thus then, thou most renown'd: Cæsar entreats,
Not to consider in what case thou stand'st,
Farther than he is Cæsar.

CLEO.　　　　Go on: right royal.

THYR. He knows, that you embrace not Antony
As you did love, but as you fear'd him.

CLEO.　　　　　　　　　O!

THYR. The scars upon your honour, therefore, he
Does pity, as constrained blemishes,
Not as deserv'd.

CLEO.　　　He is a god, and knows
What is most right: mine honour was not
But conquer'd merely.　　　[yielded,

ENO. [*Aside.*]　　To be sure of that,
I will ask Antony.—Sir, Sir, thou'rt so leaky,　　　　　　[for
That we must leave thee to thy sinking,
Thy dearest quit thee.　　　[*Exit.*

THYR.　Shall I say to Cæsar
What you require of him? for he partly begs
[please him,
To be desir'd to give. It much would
That of his fortunes you should make a staff
To lean upon: but it would warm his spirits,
To hear from me you had left Antony,
And put yourself under his shroud,
The universal landlord.

CLEO.　　　　What's your name?

THYR. My name is Thyreus.

CLEO.　　　　Most kind messenger,
Say to great Cæsar this:—in disputation
I kiss his conqu'ring hand: tell him, I am prompt
To lay my crown at's feet, and there to kneel:
Tell him, from his all-obeying breath I
The doom of Egypt.　　　[hear

THYR.　　　　'Tis your noblest course.
Wisdom and fortune combating together,

If that the former dare but what it can,
No chance may shake it. Give me grace
My duty on your hand.　　　[to lay

CLEO.　　　　Your Cæsar's father oft,
When he hath mus'd of taking kingdoms in,
Bestow'd his lips on that unworthy place,
As it rain'd kisses.

Re-enter ANTONY *and* ENOBARBUS.

ANT.　Favours, by Jove that thunders!—
What art thou, fellow?

THYR.　　　One, that but performs
The bidding of the fullest man, and worthi-
To have command obey'd.　　　[est

ENO. [*Aside.*]　You will be whipp'd.

ANT.　Approach, there!—Ay, you kite!
—Now, gods and devils!
Authority melts from me: of late, when I cried, "ho!"
Like boys unto a muss, kings would start forth,
And cry, "Your will?"—Have you no ears?
Antony yet.　　　　　　[I am

Enter Attendants.
Take hence this Jack, and whip him.

ENO. [*Aside.*] 'Tis better playing with a lion's whelp,
Than with an old one dying.

ANT.　　　　　Moon and stars!—
Whip him.—Were't twenty of the greatest tributaries
That do acknowledge Cæsar, should I find them
So saucy with the hand of—she here, what's her name,
Since she was Cleopatra?—Whip him, fellows,
Till, like a boy, you see him cringe his face,
And whine aloud for mercy: take him hence.

THYR. Mark Antony,—

ANT.　Tug him away: being whipp'd,
Bring him again:—this Jack of Cæsar's
Bear us an errand to him.—　　　[shall

[*Exeunt* Attendants *with* THYREUS.
You were half blasted ere I knew you:—ha!
Have I my pillow left unpress'd in Rome,
Forborne the getting of a lawful race,
And by a gem of women, to be abus'd
By one that looks on feeders?

CLEO.　　　　Good my lord,—

ANT. You have been a boggler ever:—
But when we in our viciousness grow hard,
(O misery on't!) the wise gods seel our eyes;
In our own filth drop our clear judgments; make us
Adore our errors; laugh at us, while we
To our confusion.　　　　[strut

CLEO.　　　O, is it come to this?

ANT. I found you as a morsel, cold upon
Dead Cæsar's trencher; nay, you were a
　fragment
Of Cneius Pompey's; besides what hotter
　hours,
Unregister'd in vulgar fame, you have
Luxuriously pick'd out: for, I am sure,
Though you can guess what temperance
　should be,
You know not what it is.

CLEO.　　　　　　Wherefore is this?

ANT. To let a fellow that will take re-
　wards,
And say, "God quit you!" be familiar with
My playfellow, your hand; this kingly seal,
And plighter of high hearts!—O, that I
　were
Upon the hill of Basan, to outroar
The horned herd! for I have savage cause;
And to proclaim it civilly, were like
A halter'd neck, which does the hangman
For being yare about him.—　　　[thank

Re-enter Attendants, *with* THYREUS.

　　　　　　　　Is he whipp'd?

1 ATT. Soundly, my lord.

ANT.　Cried he? and begg'd he pardon?

1 ATT. He did ask favour.

ANT. If that thy father live, let him
　repent
Thou wast not made his daughter; and be
　thou sorry
To follow Cæsar in his triumph, since
Thou hast been whipp'd for following him:
　henceforth,
The white hand of a lady fever thee;
Shake thou to look on't.—Get thee back
　to Cæsar,
Tell him thy entertainment: look, thou say,
He makes me angry with him; for he seems
Proud and disdainful, harping on what I
　am,　　　　　　　　　　　　[angry;
Not what he knew I was: he makes me
And at this time most easy 'tis to do't,
When my good stars, that were my former
　guides,　　　　　　　　　　　[fires
Have empty left their orbs, and shot their
Into the abysm of hell. If he mislike
My speech, and what is done, tell him, he
　has
Hipparchus, my enfranchis'd bondman,
　whom　　　　　　　　　　　[ture,
He may at pleasure whip, or hang, or tor-
As he shall like, to quit me: urge it thou:
Hence with thy stripes, begone!

　　　　　　　　　[*Exit* THYREUS.

CLEO. Have you done yet?

ANT.　　　　Alack, our terrene moon
Is now eclips'd; and it portends alone
The fall of Antony!

CLEO.　　　I must stay his time.

ANT. To flatter Cæsar, would you mingle
With one that ties his points?　　[eyes

CLEO.　　　　　Not know me yet?

ANT. Cold-hearted toward me?

CLEO.　　　　　　　Ah, dear, if I be so,
From my cold heart let heaven engender
　hail,
And poison it in the source; and the first
　stone
Drop in my neck: as it determines, so
Dissolve my life! The next Cæsarion smite!
Till, by degrees, the memory of my womb,
Together with my brave Egyptians all,
By the discandying of this pelleted storm,
Lie graveless,—till the flies and gnats of
Have buried them for prey!　　　[Nile

ANT.　　　　I am satisfied.
Cæsar sits down in Alexandria; where
I will oppose his fate. Our force by land
Hath nobly held; our sever'd navy, too,
Have knit again, and fleet, threat'ning most
　sea-like.
Where hast thou been, my heart?—Dost
　thou hear, lady?
If from the field I shall return once more
To kiss these lips, I will appear in blood;
I and my sword will earn our chronicle:
There's hope in't yet.

CLEO.　　　That's my brave lord!

ANT. I will be treble-sinew'd, hearted,
　breath'd,
And fight maliciously: for when mine hours
Were nice and lucky, men did ransom lives
Of me for jests; but now I'll set my teeth,
And send to darkness all that stop me:—
　come,
Let's have one other gaudy night: call to
　me　　　　　　　　　　　　　[more
All my sad captains; fill our bowls; once
Let's mock the midnight bell.

CLEO.　　　　　It is my birthday:
I had thought to have held it poor; but,
　since my lord
Is Antony again, I will be Cleopatra.

ANT. We will yet do well.

CLEO. Call all his noble captains to my
　lord.

ANT. Do so, we'll speak to them; and to-
　night I'll force
The wine peep through their scars.—Come
　on, my queen;
There's sap in't yet. The next time I do
　fight,
I'll make death love me; for I will contend
Even with his pestilent scythe.

　　　　　[*Exeunt all except* ENOBARBUS.

ENO. Now he'll outstare the lightning. To
　be furious,
Is to be frighted out of fear; and in that
　mood,　　　　　　　　　　　　[still,
The dove will peck the estridge; and I see

A diminution in our captain's brain
Restores his heart: when valour preys on
reason,
It eats the sword it fights with. I will seek
Some way to leave him.   [*Exit.*

ACT IV.

SCENE I.—CÆSAR'S *Camp at* ALEXANDRIA.

Enter CÆSAR, *reading a letter;* AGRIPPA,
MECÆNAS, *and others.*

CÆS. He calls me boy; and chides, as he
had power
To beat me out of Egypt; my messenger
He hath whipp'd with rods; dares me to
personal combat,
Cæsar to Antony:—let the old ruffian know,
I have many other ways to die; meantime,
Laugh at his challenge.
MEC.   Cæsar must think,
When one so great begins to rage, he's
hunted   [now
Even to falling. Give him no breath, but
Make boot of his distraction:—never anger
Made good guard for itself.
CÆS.   Let our best heads
Know, that to-morrow the last of many
battles
We mean to fight:—within our files there
are,
Of those that serv'd Mark Antony but late,
Enough to fetch him in. See it done:
And feast the army; we have store to do't,
And they have earn'd the waste.—Poor
Antony!   [*Exeunt.*

SCENE II.—ALEXANDRIA. *A Room in the
Palace.*

Enter ANTONY, CLEOPATRA, ENOBARBUS,
CHARMIAN, IRAS, ALEXAS, *and others.*

ANT. He will not fight with me, Domi-
tius.
ENO.   No.
ANT. Why should he not?   [ter fortune,
ENO. He thinks, being twenty times of bet-
He is twenty men to one.
ANT.   To-morrow, soldier,
By sea and land I'll fight: or I will live,
Or bathe my dying honour in the blood
Shall make it live again. Woo't thou fight
well?
ENO. I'll strike, and cry, "Take all."
ANT.   Well said; come on.—
Call forth my household servants: let's to-
Be bounteous at our meal.—   [night
Enter Servants.
                    Give me thy hand,
Thou hast been rightly honest;—so hast
thou;—

Thou,—and thou,—and thou:—you have
serv'd me well,
And kings have been your fellows.
CLEO. [*Aside to* ENO.] What means this?
ENO. [*Aside to* CLEO.] 'Tis one of those
odd tricks, which sorrow shoots
Out of the mind.
ANT.   And thou art honest too.
I wish I could be made so many men,
And all of you clapp'd up together in
An Antony, that I might do you service,
So good as you have done.
SERVANTS.   The gods forbid!
ANT. Well, my good fellows, wait on me
to-night:
Scant not my cups; and make as much of
me,
As when mine empire was your fellow too,
And suffer'd my command.
CLEO. [*Aside to* ENO.]   What does he
mean?
ENO. [*Aside to* CLEO.] To make his fol-
lowers weep.
ANT.   Tend me to-night;
May be, it is the period of your duty:
Haply, you shall not see me more; or if,
A mangled shadow: perchance, to-morrow
You'll serve another master. I look on you,
As one that takes his leave. Mine honest
friends,
I turn you not away; but, like a master
Married to your good service, stay till
death:
Tend me to-night two hours, I ask no more,
And the gods yield you for't!
ENO.   What mean you, Sir,
To give them this discomfort? Look, they
weep;
And I, an ass, am onion-ey'd: for shame,
Transform us not to women.
ANT.   Ho, ho, ho!
Now, the witch take me, if I meant it thus!
Grace grow where those drops fall! My
hearty friends,
You take me in too dolorous a sense;
For I spake to you for your comfort,—did
desire you   [my hearts,
To burn this night with torches: know,
I hope well of to-morrow; and will lead
you,
Where rather I'll expect victorious life,
Than death and honour. Let's to supper,
come,
And drown consideration.   [*Exeunt.*

SCENE III.—ALEXANDRIA. *Before the
Palace.*

Enter two Soldiers, *to their guard.*

1 *SOLD.* Brother, good night: to-morrow
is the day.

2 *SOLD.* It will determine one way: fare you well.
Heard you of nothing strange about the streets?
1 *SOLD.* Nothing. What news?
2 *SOLD.* Belike, 'tis but a rumour. Good night to you.
1 *SOLD.* Well, Sir, good night.
Enter two other Soldiers.
2 *SOLD.* Soldiers, have careful watch.
3 *SOLD.* And you. Good night, good night.
[*The first and second place themselves at their posts.*
4 *SOLD.* Here we:
[*The third and fourth take their posts.*
and if to-morrow
Our navy thrive, I have an absolute hope
Our landmen will stand up.
3 *SOLD.* 'Tis a brave army,
And full of purpose.
[*Music as of hautboys under ground.*
4 *SOLD.* Peace! what noise?
1 *SOLD.* List! list!
2 *SOLD.* Hark!
1 *SOLD.* Music i' the air.
3 *SOLD.* Under the earth.
4 *SOLD.* It signs well, does it not?
3 *SOLD.* No.
1 *SOLD.* Peace, I say! What should this mean?
2 *SOLD.* 'Tis the god Hercules, whom Antony lov'd,
Now leaves him.
1 *SOLD.* Walk; let's see if other watch-
Do hear what we do. [men
[*They advance to another post.*
2 *SOLD.* How now, masters!
SOLDIERS. [*Speaking together.*] How now!
How now! do you hear this?
1 *SOLD.* Ay; is't not strange?
3 *SOLD.* Do you hear, masters? do you hear?
1 *SOLD.* Follow the noise so far as we have quarter;
Let's see how it will give off.
SOLDIERS. [*Speaking together.*] Content.
'Tis strange. [*Exeunt.*

SCENE IV.—ALEXANDRIA. *A Room in the Palace.*

Enter ANTONY *and* CLEOPATRA; CHARMIAN, *and others, attending.*

ANT. Eros! mine armour, Eros!
CLEO. Sleep a little.
ANT. No, my chuck.—Eros, come; mine armour, Eros!
Enter EROS, *with armour.*
Come, good fellow, put mine iron on:—

If fortune be not ours to-day, it is
Because we brave her:—come.
CLEO. Nay, I'll help too. What's this for?
ANT. Ah, let be, let be! thou art
The armourer of my heart:—false, false; this, this.
CLEO. Sooth, la, I'll help: thus it must be.
ANT. Well, well;
We shall thrive now.—Seest thou, my good Go, put on thy defences. [fellow?
EROS. Briefly, Sir.
CLEO. Is not this buckled well?
ANT. Rarely, rarely:
He that unbuckles this, till we do please
To doff't for our repose, shall hear a storm.—
Thou fumblest, Eros; and my queen's a squire [O love,
More tight at this, than thou: despatch.—
That thou could'st see my wars to-day, and knew'st
The royal occupation! thou should'st see
A workman in't.—
Enter an Officer, *armed.*
Good morrow to thee; welcome!
Thou look'st like him that knows a warlike charge:
To business that we love, we rise betime,
And go to't with delight.
OFF. A thousand, Sir,
Early though't be, have on their riveted And at the port expect you. [trim,
[*Shout. Flourish of trumpets heard.*
Enter Captains *and* Soldiers.
CAPT. The morn is fair.—Good morrow, general.
ALL. Good morrow, general.
ANT. 'Tis well blown, lads:
This morning, like the spirit of a youth
That means to be of note, begins betimes.—
So, so; come, give me that: this way; well said. [me:
Fare thee well, dame, whate'er becomes of
This is a soldier's kiss:—[*Kisses her.*] rebukable,
And worthy shameful check it were, to stand
On more mechanic compliment; I'll leave thee [fight,
Now, like a man of steel.—You that will
Follow me close; I'll bring you to't.—Adieu.
[*Exeunt* ANTONY, EROS, Officers, *and* Soldiers.
CHAR. Please you, retire to your chamber.
CLEO. Lead me.
He goes forth gallantly. That he and Cæsar might
Determine this great war in single fight!

Then, Antony,—but now,—well, on.
                                        [*Exeunt.*

SCENE V.—ANTONY'S *Camp near*
                ALEXANDRIA.

Trumpets sound. Enter ANTONY *and* EROS;
        a Soldier *meeting them.*

SOLD. The gods make this a happy day to
Antony!
ANT. Would thou, and those thy scars,
    had once prevail'd
To make me fight at land!
SOLD.   Hadst thou done so,
The kings that have revolted, and the
    soldier
That has this morning left thee, would
Follow'd thy heels.   [have still
ANT. Who's gone this morning?
SOLD.   Who!
One ever near thee: call for Enobarbus,
He shall not hear thee; or from Cæsar's
    camp
Say, "I am none of thine."
ANT.   What say'st thou?
SOLD.   Sir,
He is with Cæsar.
EROS.   Sir, his chests and treasure
He has not with him.
ANT.   Is he gone?
SOLD.   Most certain.
ANT. Go, Eros, send his treasure after;
    do it;
Detain no jot, I charge thee: write to him
(I will subscribe) gentle adieus, and greet-
    ings;
Say, that I wish he never find more cause
To change a master.—O, my fortunes have
Corrupted honest men!—Despatch.— Eno-
    barbus!   [*Exeunt.*

SCENE VI.—CÆSAR'S *Camp before*
                ALEXANDRIA.

Flourish. Enter CÆSAR, *with* AGRIPPA,
        ENOBARBUS, *and others.*

CÆS. Go forth, Agrippa, and begin the
Our will is, Antony be took alive;   [fight:
Make it so known.
AGRI. Cæsar, I shall.   [*Exit.*
CÆS. The time of universal peace is near:
Prove this a prosperous day, the three-
    nook'd world
Shall bear the olive freely.
        Enter a Messenger.
MESS.   Antony
Is come into the field.
CÆS.   Go, charge Agrippa
Plant those that have revolted in the van;
That Antony may seem to spend his fury
Upon himself.
        [*Exeunt all except* ENOBARBUS.

ENO. Alexas did revolt; and went to
Jewry on
Affairs of Antony; there did persuade
Great Herod to incline himself to Cæsar,
And leave his master Antony: for this
    pains,   [the rest
Cæsar hath hang'd him. Canidius, and
That fell away, have entertainment, but
No honourable trust. I have done ill;
Of which I do accuse myself so sorely,
That I will joy no more.
        Enter a Soldier *of* CÆSAR'S
SOLD.   Enobarbus, Antony
Hath after thee sent all thy treasure, with
His bounty overplus: the messenger
Came on my guard; and at thy tent is now
Unloading of his mules.
ENO.   I give it you.
SOLD. Mock not, Enobarbus.
I tell you true: best you saf'd the bringer
Out of the host; I must attend mine office,
Or would have done't myself. Your em-
Continues still a Jove.   [peror
                                [*Exit.*

ENO. I am alone the villain of the earth,
And feel I am so most. O Antony,
Thou mine of bounty, how would'st thou
    have paid
My better service, when my turpitude
Thou dost so crown with gold! This blows
    my heart:
If swift thought break it not, a swifter
    mean
Shall outstrike thought: but thought will
    do't, I feel.
I fight against thee!—No: I will go seek
Some ditch, wherein to die; the foul'st .
    best fits
My latter part of life.   [*Exit.*

SCENE VII.—*Field of Battle between the*
                Camps.

Alarum. Drums and trumpets. Enter
        AGRIPPA *and others.*

AGR. Retire, we have engag'd ourselves
    too far:
Cæsar himself has work, and our oppres-
Exceeds what we expected.   [sion.
                            [*Exeunt.*
Alarum. Enter ANTONY *and* SCARUS,
                wounded.

SCAR. O my brave emperor, this is fought
    indeed!
Had we done so at first, we had driven
    them home
With clouts about their heads.
ANT.   Thou bleed'st apace.
SCAR. I had a wound here that was like
    a T,
But now 'tis made an H.

ANT.   They do retire.
SCAR. We'll beat 'em into bench-holes: I
    have yet
Room for six scotches more.
                    Enter EROS.
EROS. They are beaten, Sir; and our ad-
    vantage serves
For a fair victory.
SCAR.   Let us score their backs,
And snatch 'em up, as we take hares, be-
'Tis sport to maul a runner.   [hind:
ANT.   I will reward thee
Once for thy sprightly comfort, and ten-
    fold
For thy good valour. Come thee on.
SCAR.   I'll halt after.
                    —————   [*Exeunt.*

SCENE VIII.—*Under the Walls of*
                    ALEXANDRIA.

Alarum. Enter ANTONY, *marching;* SCARUS,
                    and forces.
ANT. We have beat him to his camp:—
    run one before,
And let the queen know of our gests.—
    To-morrow,
Before the sun shall see us, we'll spill the
    blood
That has to-day escap'd. I thank you all;
For doughty-handed are you, and have
    fought
Not as you serv'd the cause, but as't had
    been   [all Hectors.
Each man's like mine; you have shown
Enter the city, clip your wives, your friends,
Tell them your feats; whilst they with joy-
    ful tears   [and kiss
Wash the congealment from your wounds,
The honour'd gashes whole.—[*To* SCARUS.]
    Give me thy hand;
                    Enter CLEOPATRA, *attended.*
To this great fairy I'll commend thy acts,
Make her thanks bless thee.—O thou day
    o' the world!
Chain mine arm'd neck; leap thou, attire
    and all,
Through proof of harness to my heart, and
Ride on the pants triumphing.   [there
CLEO.   Lord of lords!
O infinite virtue! com'st thou smiling from
The world's great snare uncaught?
ANT.   My nightingale,
We have beat them to their beds. What,
    girl! though grey
Do something mingle with our younger
    brown; yet have we
A brain that nourishes our nerves, and can
Get goal for goal of youth. Behold this
    man;   [hand:—
Commend unto his lips thy favouring
Kiss it, my warrior:—he hath fought to-day,

As if a god, in hate of mankind, had
Destroy'd in such a shape.
CLEO.   I'll give thee, friend,
An armour all of gold; it was a king's.
ANT. He has deserv'd it, were it car-
    buncled
Like holy Phœbus' car.—Give me thy
    hand:
Through Alexandria make a jolly march;
Bear our hack'd targets like the men that
    owe them:
Had our great palace the capacity
To camp this host, we all would sup to-
    gether,
And drink carouses to the next day's fate,
Which promises royal peril.—Trumpeters,
With brazen din blast you the city's ear;
Make mingle with our rating tabourines;
That heaven and earth may strike their
    sounds together,
Applauding our approach.   [*Exeunt.*

SCENE IX.—CÆSAR'S *Camp.*

Sentinels *on their post.*
1 *SOLD.* If we be not reliev'd within this
    hour,   [night
We must return to the court of guard: the
Is shiny; and, they say, we shall embattle
By the second hour i' the morn.
2 *SOLD.*   This last day was
A shrewd one to us.
                    Enter ENOBARBUS.
ENO. O, bear me witness, night,—
3 *SOLD.* What man is this?
2 *SOLD.*   Stand close, and list him.
ENO. Be witness to me, O thou blessed
    moon!
When men revolted shall upon record
Bear hateful memory, poor Enobarbus did
Before thy face repent.—
1 *SOLD.*   Enobarbus!
3 *SOLD.*   Peace!
Hark farther.
ENO. O sovereign mistress of true melan-
    choly!
The poisonous damp of night dispunge
    upon me,
That life, a very rebel to my will,
May hang no longer on me: throw my
    heart
Against the flint and hardness of my fault;
Which, being dried with grief, will break
    to powder,
And finish all foul thoughts. O Antony!
Nobler than my revolt is infamous,
Forgive me in thine own particular;
But let the world rank me in register
A master-leaver, and a fugitive.
O Antony! O Antony!   [*Dies.*
2 *SOLD.* Let's speak to him.

1 *SOLD.* Let's hear him; for the things
May concern Cæsar.   [he speaks
3 *SOLD.*   Let's do so. But he sleeps.
1 *SOLD.* Swoons rather; for so bad a
prayer as his
Was never yet for sleep.
2 *SOLD.*   Go we to him.
3 *SOLD.* Awake, Sir, awake; speak to us.
2 *SOLD.*   Hear you, Sir?
1 *SOLD.* The hand of death hath raught
him.   [*Drums afar off.*
                    Hark! the drums
Demurely wake the sleepers. Let us bear
him
To the court of guard; he is of note: our
Is fully out.   [hour
3 *SOLD.*   Come on, then;
He may recover yet. [*Exeunt with the body.*

SCENE X.—*Ground between the two
Camps.*

Enter ANTONY *and* SCARUS, *with forces,
marching.*

ANT. Their preparation is to-day by sea;
We please them not by land.
SCAR.   For both, my lord.
ANT. I would they'd fight i' the fire, or i'
the air;
We'd fight there too. But this it is; our
foot
Upon the hills adjoining to the city
Shall stay with us: order for sea is given;
They have put forth the haven: farther on,
Where their appointment we may best dis-
cover,
And look on their endeavour.   [*Exeunt.*
Enter CÆSAR, *and his forces, marching.*
CÆS. But being charg'd, we will be still
by land,
Which, as I take't, we shall; for his best
force
Is forth to man his galleys. To the vales,
And hold our best advantage!   [*Exeunt.*
Re-enter ANTONY *and* SCARUS.
ANT. Yet they are not join'd. Where
yond' pine does stand,
I shall discover all: I'll bring thee word
Straight, how 'tis like to go.   [*Exit.*
SCAR.   Swallows have built
In Cleopatra's sails their nests: the au-
gurers
Say, they know not,—they cannot tell;—
look grimly,
And dare not speak their knowledge.
Antony
Is valiant, and dejected; and, by starts
His fretted fortunes give him hope, and
Of what he has, and has not.   [fear,
     [*Alarum afar off, as at a sea-fight.*

Re-enter ANTONY.

ANT.   All is lost!
This foul Egyptian hath betrayed me:
My fleet hath yielded to the foe; and
yonder
They cast their caps up, and carouse to-
gether   [whore! 'tis thou
Like friends long lost. — Triple-turn'd
Hast sold me to this novice; and my heart
Makes only wars on thee.—Bid them all
fly;
For when I am reveng'd upon my charm,
I have done all:—bid them all fly; be
gone.   [*Exit* SCARUS.
O sun! thy uprise shall I see no more:
Fortune and Antony part here; even here
Do we shake hands.—All come to this?—
The hearts
That spaniel'd me at heels, to whom I gave
Their wishes, do discandy, melt their sweets
On blossoming Cæsar; and this pine is
bark'd,
That overtopp'd them all. Betray'd I am:
O this false soul of Egypt! this grave
charm,—
Whose eye beck'd forth my wars, and
call'd them home;
Whose bosom was my crownet, my chief
end,—
Like a right gipsy, hath, at fast and loose,
Beguil'd me to the very heart of loss.—
What, Eros! Eros!

Enter CLEOPATRA.

               Ah, thou spell! Avaunt!
CLEO. Why is my lord enrag'd against
his love?
ANT. Vanish, or I shall give thee thy
deserving,
And blemish Cæsar's triumph. Let him take
thee,   [ians—
And hoist thee up to the shouting plebe-
Follow his chariot, like the greatest spot
Of all thy sex; most monster-like, be
shown
For poor'st diminutives, for doits; and let
Patient Octavia plough thy visage up
With her prepared nails.   [*Exit* CLEO.
               'Tis well thou'rt gone,
If it be well to live: but better 'twere
Thou fell'st into my fury; for one death
Might have prevented many.—Eros, ho!—
The shirt of Nessus is upon me:—teach me,
Alcides, thou mine ancestor, thy rage:
Let me lodge Lichas on the horns o' the
moon;
And with those hands, that grasp'd the
heaviest club,
Subdue my worthiest self. The witch shall
die:

To the young Roman boy she hath sold me,
and I fall
Under this plot; she dies for't.—Eros, ho!
                                    [*Exit.*

———

SCENE XI.—ALEXANDRIA. *A Room in the
Palace.*

Enter CLEOPATRA, CHARMIAN, IRAS, *and*
MARDIAN.

CLEO. Help me, my women! O, he is
more mad
Than Telamon for his shield; the boar of
Was never so emboss'd.   [Thessaly,
CHAR.   To the monument!
There lock yourself, and send him word
you are dead.
The soul and body rive not more in part-
Than greatness going off.   [ing,
CLEO.   To the monument!—
Mardian, go tell him I have slain myself;
Say, that the last I spoke was, "Antony,"
And word it, pr'ythee, piteously: hence,
Mardian and bring me how he takes my
death.—
To the monument!   [*Exeunt.*

———

SCENE XII.—*Another Room in the Palace.*

Enter ANTONY *and* EROS.

ANT. Eros, thou yet behold'st me?
EROS.   Ay, noble lord.
ANT. Sometime we see a cloud that's
dragonish;
A vapour sometime like a bear or lion,
A tower'd citadel, a pendent rock,
A forked mountain, or blue promontory
With trees upon't, that nod unto the world,
And mock our eyes with air: thou hast seen
these signs;
They are black vesper's pageants.
EROS.   Ay, my lord.
ANT. That which is now a horse, even
with a thought
The rack dislimns, and makes it indistinct,
As water is in water.
EROS.   It does, my lord.
ANT. My good knave, Eros, now thy cap-
tain is
Even such a body: here I am Antony,
Yet cannot hold this visible shape, my
knave.   [queen,—
I made these wars for Egypt; and the
Whose heart I thought I had, for she had
mine;   [unto't
Which, whilst it was mine, had annex'd
A million more, now lost,—she, Eros, has
Pack'd cards with Cæsar, and false play'd
my glory
Unto an enemy's triumph.—

Nay, weep not, gentle Eros; there is left us
Ourselves to end ourselves.—
          Enter MARDIAN.
                    O, thy vile lady!
She has robb'd me of my sword.
MAR.   No, Antony;
My mistress lov'd thee, and her fortunes
With thine entirely.   [mingled
ANT.   Hence, saucy eunuch! peace!
She hath betray'd me, and shall die the
death.
MAR. Death of one person can be paid but
once,
And that she has discharg'd: what thou
would'st do,
Is done unto thy hand: the last she spake
Was, "Antony! most noble Antony!"
Then, in the midst, a tearing groan did
break
The name of Antony; it was divided
Between her heart and lips: she render'd
Thy name so buried in her.   [life,
ANT.   Dead, then?
MAR.   Dead.
ANT. Unarm, Eros; the long day's task is
done,   [hence safe,
And we must sleep.—That thou depart'st
Does pay thy labour richly; go.—
                    [*Exit* MARDIAN.
                    Off, pluck off:—
The seven-fold shield of Ajax cannot keep
The battery from my heart. O, cleave, my
sides!
Heart, once be stronger than thy continent,
Crack thy frail case! — Apace, Eros,
apace.—
No more a soldier:—bruised pieces, go;
You have been nobly borne.—From me a
while.—   [*Exit* EROS.
I will o'ertake thee, Cleopatra, and
Weep for my pardon. So it must be, for
now   [out,
All length is torture:—since the torch is
Lie down, and stray no farther: now all
labour
Mars what it does; yea, very force entangles
Itself with strength: seal then, and all is
done.—
Eros!—I come, my queen.—Eros!—Stay
for me:
Where souls do couch on flowers, we'll
hand in hand,
And with our sprightly port make the
ghosts gaze:
Dido and her Æneas shall want troops,
And all the haunt be ours.—Come, Eros!
Eros!
          Re-enter EROS.
EROS. What would my lord?
ANT.   Since Cleopatra died,

I have liv'd in such dishonour, that the
gods
Detest my baseness. I, that with my sword
Quarter'd the world, and o'er green Nep-
tune's back
With ships made cities, condemn myself to
lack
The courage of a woman; less noble mind
Than she, which by her death our Cæsar
tells,   [sworn, Eros,
"I am conqueror of myself." Thou art
That, when the exigent should come,
(which now
Is come indeed) when I should see behind
The inevitable prosecution of   [me
Disgrace and horror, that, on my com-
mand,   [time is come:
Thou then would'st kill me: do't; the
Thou strik'st not me, 'tis Cæsar thou de-
Put colour in thy cheek.   [feat'st.
EROS.   The gods withhold me!
Shall I do that, which all the Parthian
darts,
Though enemy, lost aim, and could not?
ANT.   Eros,
Would'st thou be window'd in great Rome,
and see
Thy master thus with pleach'd arms, bend-
ing down
His corrigible neck, his face subdued
To penetrative shame, whilst the wheel'd
seat   [branded
Of fortunate Cæsar, drawn before him,
His baseness that ensued?
EROS.   I would not see't.
ANT. Come, then; for with a wound I
must be cur'd.
Draw that thy honest sword, which thou
hast worn
Most useful for thy country.
EROS.   O, Sir! pardon me.
ANT. When I did make thee free, swor'st
thou not then
To do this when I bade thee? Do it at
once;
Or thy precedent services are all
But accidents unpurpos'd. Draw, and come.
EROS. Turn from me, then, that noble
countenance,
Wherein the worship of the whole world
lies.
ANT. Lo thee!   [Turning from him.
EROS. My sword is drawn.
ANT.   Then let it do at once
The thing why thou hast drawn it.
EROS.   My dear master,
My captain, and my emperor, let me say,
Before I strike this bloody stroke, farewell.
ANT. 'Tis said, man;—and farewell.
EROS. Farewell, great chief. Shall I
strike now?

ANT.   Now, Eros.
EROS. Why, there then:—
                    [Falls on his sword.
                    thus do I escape the sorrow
Of Antony's death.   [Dies.
ANT.   Thrice nobler than myself!
Thou teachest me, O valiant Eros, what
I should, and thou could'st not. My queen
and Eros
Have, by their brave instruction, got upon
A nobleness in record: but I will be   [me
A bridegroom in my death, and run into't
As to a lover's bed. Come, then; and,
Eros,
Thy master dies thy scholar: to do thus
                    [Falling on his sword.
I learn'd of thee.—How! not dead? not
dead?—
The guard,—ho!—O, despatch me!

          Enter DERCETAS and Guard.

1 GUARD.   Whats' the noise?
ANT. I have done my work ill, friends: O,
make an end
Of what I have begun.
2 GUARD.   The star is fallen.
1 GUARD. And time is at his period.
ALL.   Alas, and woe!
ANT. Let him that loves me, strike me
dead.
1 GUARD.   Not I.
2 GUARD. Nor I.
3 GUARD. Nor any one. [Exeunt Guard.
DER. Thy death and fortunes bid thy
followers fly.   [tidings,
This sword but shown to Cæsar, with this
Shall enter me with him.

          Enter DIOMEDES.

DIO. Where's Antony?
DER. There, Diomed, there.
DIO. Lives he?
Wilt thou not answer, man?
                    [Exit DERCETAS.
ANT. Art thou there, Diomed? Draw thy
sword, and give me
Sufficing strokes for death.
DIO.   Most absolute lord,
My mistress, Cleopatra, sent me to thee.
ANT. When did she send thee?
DIO.   Now, my lord.
ANT.   Where is she?
DIO. Lock'd in her monument. She had
a prophesying fear   [saw
Of what hath come to pass: for when she
(Which never shall be found) you did sus-
pect   [your rage
She had dispos'd with Cæsar, and that
Would not be purg'd, she sent you word
she was dead;
But, fearing since how it might work, hath
sent

Me to proclaim the truth; and I am come,
I dread, too late.

ANT. Too late, good Diomed:—call my
    guard, I pr'ythee.

DIO. What, ho, the emperor's guard! The
    guard, what, ho!
Come, your lord calls!

    Enter some of the Guard.

ANT. Bear me, good friends, where Cleo-
    patra bides;   [you.
'Tis the last service that I shall command

1 GUARD. Woe, woe are we, Sir, you may
    not live to wear
All your true followers out.

ALL.   Most heavy day!

ANT. Nay, good my fellows, do not please
    sharp fate   [welcome
To grace it with your sorrows: bid that
Which comes to punish us, and we punish
    it
Seeming to bear it lightly. Take me up:
I have led you oft: carry me now, good
And have my thanks for all.   [friends,
    [*Exeunt, bearing* ANTONY.

SCENE XIII.—ALEXANDRIA. *A Monument.*

Enter, above, CLEOPATRA, CHARMIAN, *and*
    IRAS.

CLEO. O Charmian, I will never go from
    hence.

CHAR. Be comforted, dear Madam.

CLEO.   No, I will not:
All strange and terrible events are welcome,
But comforts we despise: our size of sor-
    row,
Proportion'd to our cause, must be as great
As that which makes it.—

    Enter, below, DIOMEDES.

            How now! is he dead?

DIO. His death's upon him, but not dead.
Look out o' the other side your monument;
His guard have brought him thither.

Enter, below, ANTONY, *borne by the* Guard.

CLEO.   O sun,
Burn the great sphere thou mov'st in!—
    darkling stand
The varying shore o' the world.—O Antony,
Antony, Antony!—Help, Charmian, help,
Iras, help;—
Help, friends below;—let's draw him
    hither.

ANT.   Peace!
Not Cæsar's valour hath o'erthrown An-
    tony,
But Antony's hath triumph'd on itself.

CLEO. So it should be, that none but
    Antony
Should conquer Antony; but woe 'tis so!

ANT. I am dying, Egypt, dying; only
I here importune death a while, until

Of many thousand kisses the poor last
I lay upon thy lips.

CLEO.   I dare not, dear,—
Dear my lord, pardon,—I dare not,
Lest I be taken: not the imperious show
Of the full-fortun'd Cæsar ever shall
Be brooch'd with me; if knife, drugs,
    serpents, have
Edge, sting, or operation, I am safe:
Your wife Octavia, with her modest eyes,
And still conclusion shall acquire no
    honour
Demuring upon me.—But come, come,
    Antony,—
Help me, my women,—we must draw thee
Assist, good friends.   [up;—

ANT.   O, quick, or I am gone.

CLEO. Here's sport indeed!—How heavy
    weighs my lord!
Our strength is all gone into heaviness,
That makes the weight: had I great Juno's
    power,   [thee up,
The strong-wing'd Mercury should fetch
And set thee by Jove's side. Yet come a
    little,—
Wishers were ever fools.—O, come, come,
    come;   [*They draw* ANTONY *up.*
And welcome, welcome! die where thou
    hast liv'd: [power,
Quicken with kissing: had my lips that
Thus would I wear them out.

ALL.   A heavy sight!

ANT. I am dying, Egypt, dying:
Give me some wine, and let me speak a
    little.

CLEO. No, let me speak; and let me rail
    so high,
That the false housewife Fortune break her
    wheel,   [wheel,
Provok'd by my offence.   [wheel,

ANT.   One word, sweet queen:
Of Cæsar seek your honour, with your
    safety.—O!

CLEO. They do not go together.

ANT.   Gentle, hear me:
None about Cæsar trust, but Proculeius.

CLEO. My resolution and my hands I'll
None about Cæsar.   [trust;

ANT. The miserable change now at my
    end   [thoughts,
Lament nor sorrow at; but please your
In feeding them with those my former
    fortunes
Wherein I liv'd, the greatest prince o' the
    world,
The noblest; and do now not basely die,
Not cowardly put off my helmet to
My countryman,—a Roman by a Roman
Valiantly vanquish'd. Now my spirit is
I can no more.   [going;

CLEO.   Noblest of men, woo't die?
Hast thou no care of me? shall I abide

In this dull world, which in thy absence is
No better than a sty?—O, see, my women,
                                    [Antony *dies.*
The crown o' the earth doth melt:—my
  lord!—
O, wither'd is the garland of the war,
The soldier's pole is fallen: young boys
  and girls
Are level now with men; the odds is gone,
And there is nothing left remarkable
Beneath the visiting moon.   [*Faints.*
CHAR.   O, quietness, lady!
IRAS. She is dead too, our sovereign.
CHAR.   Lady!—
IRAS.   Madam!—
CHAR. O Madam, Madam, Madam!—
IRAS.   Royal Egypt!
  Empress!—
CHAR. Peace, peace, Iras!
CLEO. No more, but e'en a woman; and
  commanded   [milks,
By such poor passion as the maid that
And does the meanest chares.—It were for
  me
To throw my sceptre at the injurious gods;
To tell them that this world did equal
  theirs,
Till they had stolen our jewel. All's but
  naught;
Patience is sottish, and impatience does
Become a dog that's mad: then, is it sin
To rush into the secret house of death,
Ere death dare come to us?—How do you,
  women?   [Charmian!
What, what! good cheer! Why, how now,
My noble girls!—Ah, women, women!
  look,   [take heart:—
Our lamp is spent, it's out!—Good sirs,
We'll bury him; and then, what's brave,
  what's noble,
Let's do it after the high Roman fashion,
And make death proud to take us. Come,
  away:—
This case of that huge spirit now is cold:
Ah, women, women! come; we have no
  friend
But resolution, and the briefest end.
[*Exeunt; those above bearing off* Antony's
  body.

ACT V.

Scene I.—Cæsar's *Camp before* Alexandria.

Enter Cæsar, Agrippa, Dolabella,
Mecænas, Gallus, Proculeius, *and others.*

CÆS. Go to him, Dolabella, bid him
  yield;
Being so frustrate, tell him, he mocks us by
The pauses that he makes.
DOL. Cæsar, I shall.   [*Exit.*

Enter Dercetas, *with the sword of*
  Antony.

CÆS. Wherefore is that? and what art
  thou, that dar'st
Appear thus to us?
DER.   I am call'd Dercetas;
Mark Antony I serv'd, who best was
  worthy   [spoke,
Best to be serv'd: whilst he stood up and
He was my master; and I wore my life
To spend upon his haters. If thou please
To take me to thee, as I was to him
I'll be to Cæsar; if thou pleasest not,
I yield thee up my life.
CÆS.   What is't thou say'st?
DER. I say, O Cæsar, Antony is dead.
CÆS. The breaking of so great a thing
  should make
A greater crack: the round world
Should have shook lions into civil streets,
And citizens to their dens:—the death of
  Antony
Is not a single doom; in the name lay
A moiety of the world.
DER.   He is dead, Cæsar;
Not by a public minister of justice,
Nor by a hired knife; but that self hand,
Which writ his honour in the acts it did,
Hath, with the courage which the heart
  did lend it,
Splitted the heart. This is his sword;
I robb'd his wound of it; behold it stain'd
With his most noble blood.
CÆS.   Look you sad, friends?
The gods rebuke me, but it is tidings
To wash the eyes of kings.
AGR.   And strange it is,
That nature must compel us to lament
Our most persisted deeds.
MEC.   His taints and honours
Waged equal with him.
AGR.   A rarer spirit never
Did steer humanity: but you, gods, will
  give us   [touch'd.
Some faults to make us men. Cæsar is
MEC. When such a spacious mirror's set
  before him,
He needs must see himself.
CÆS.   O Antony!
I have follow'd thee to this;—but we do
  lance
Diseases in our bodies: I must perforce
Have shown to thee such a declining day,
Or look on thine; we could not stall to-
  gether
In the whole world: but yet let me lament,
With tears as sovereign as the blood of
  hearts,
That thou, my brother, my competitor
In top of all design, my mate in empire,

Friend and companion in the front of war,
The arm of mine own body, and the heart
Where mine his thoughts did kindle,—that
   our stars,
Unreconcileable, should divide
Our equalness to this.—Hear me, good
   friends,—
But I will tell you at some meeter season:
         Enter a Messenger.
The business of this man looks out of him;
We'll hear him what he says.—Whence are
   you?
MESS. A poor Egyptian yet. The queen
   my mistress,
Confin'd in all she has, her monument,
Of thy intents desires instruction,
That she preparedly may frame herself
To the way she's forced to.
CÆS.   Bid her have good heart:
She soon shall know of us, by some of ours,
How honourable and how kindly we
Determine for her; for Cæsar cannot live
To be ungentle.
MESS.   So the gods preserve thee!
                      [*Exit.*
CÆS. Come hither, Proculeius. Go and
   say,   [comforts
We purpose her no shame: give her what
The quality of her passion shall require;
Lest, in her greatness, by some mortal
   stroke
She do defeat us; for her life in Rome
Would be eternal in our triumph. Go,
And, with your speediest, bring us what
   she says,
And how you find of her.
PRO.   Cæsar, I shall.   [*Exit.*
CÆS. Gallus, go you along.—
                 [*Exit* GALLUS.
            Where's Dolabella,
To second Proculeius?
AGR. MEC.   Dolabella!
CÆS. Let him alone for I remember now
How he's employed: he shall in time be
   ready.
Go with me to my tent where you shall see
How hardly I was drawn into this war;
How calm and gentle I proceeded still
In all my writings: go with me and see
What I can show in this.   [*Exeunt.*

———

SCENE II.—ALEXANDRIA. *The Monument.*

Enter, above, CLEOPATRA, CHARMIAN, *and*
         IRAS.

CLEO. My desolation does begin to make
A better life. 'Tis paltry to be Cæsar;
Not being Fortune, he's but Fortune's
   knave,
A minister of her will: and it is great

To do that thing that ends all other deeds;
Which shackles accidents, and bolts up
   change;
Which sleeps, and never palates more the
The beggar's nurse and Cæsar's.   [dung,
Enter, below, to the gates of the monu-
   ment, PROCULEIUS, GALLUS, *and* Soldiers.
PRO. Cæsar sends greeting to the queen
   of Egypt;
And bids thee study on what fair demands
Thou mean'st to have him grant thee.
CLEO.   What's thy name?
PRO. My name is Proculeius.
CLEO.   Antony
Did tell me of you, bade me trust you; but
I do not greatly care to be deceiv'd,
That have no use for trusting. If your
   master   [tell him,
Would have a queen his beggar, you must
That majesty, to keep decorum, must
No less beg than a kingdom: if he please
To give me conquer'd Egypt for my son,
He gives me so much of mine own, as I
Will kneel to him with thanks.
PRO.   Be of good cheer;
You are fallen into a princely hand, fear
   nothing:
Make your full reference freely to my lord,
Who is so full of grace, that it flows over
On all that need: let me report to him
Your sweet dependancy; and you shall
   find
A conqueror that will pray in aid for kind-
   ness,
Where he for grace is kneel'd to.
CLEO.   Pray you, tell him
I am his fortune's vassal, and I send him
The greatness he has got. I hourly learn
A doctrine of obedience; and would gladly
Look him i' the face.
PRO.   This I'll report, dear lady.
Have comfort, for I know your plight is
Of him that caus'd it.   [pitied
GAL. You see how easily she may be
   surpris'd.
     [PROCULEIUS, *and two of the* Guard,
    ascend the monument by a ladder,
    and come behind CLEOPATRA. *Some*
    of the Guard *unbar and open the*
    gates, discovering the lower room of
    the monument.
[*To* PRO.] Guard her till Cæsar come.
                      [*Exit.*
IRAS. Royal queen!
CHAR. O Cleopatra! thou art taken,
   queen!
CLEO. Quick, quick, good hands.
            [*Drawing a dagger.*
PRO.   Hold, worthy lady, hold!
            [*Seizes and disarms her.*

Do not yourself such wrong, who are in
Reliev'd, but not betray'd.   [this
CLEO.   What, of death too,
That rids our dogs of languish?
PRO.   Cleopatra,
Do not abuse my master's bounty, by
Th' undoing of yourself: let the world see
His nobleness well acted, which your death
Will never let come forth.
CLEO.   Where art thou, death?
Come hither, come! come, come, and take
    a queen
Worth many babes and beggars!
PRO.   O, temperance, lady!
CLEO. Sir, I will eat no meat, I'll not
    drink, Sir,
(If idle talk will once be necessary)
I'll not sleep neither: this mortal house
    I'll ruin,
Do Cæsar what he can. Know, Sir, that I
Will not wait pinion'd at your master's
    court;
Nor once be chastis'd with the sober eye
Of dull Octavia. Shall they hoist me up,
And show me to the shouting varletry
Of censuring Rome? Rather a ditch in
    Egypt   [mud
Be gentle grave to me! rather on Nilus'
Lay me stark nak'd, and let the water-flies
Blow me into abhorring! rather make
My country's high pyramides my gibbet,
And hang me up in chains!
PRO.   You do extend
These thoughts of horror farther, than you
Find cause in Cæsar.   [shall

        Enter DOLABELLA, *below.*

DOL.   Proculeius,
What thou hast done thy master Cæsar
    knows,   [queen,
And he hath sent for thee: as for the
I'll take her to my guard.
PRO.   So, Dolabella,
It shall content me best:—

    [*Brings* CLEOPATRA *down into the lower
    room of the monument, and delivers
    her to* DOLABELLA.
                be gentle to her.—
[*To* CLEO.] To Cæsar I will speak what
    you shall please,
If you'll employ me to him.
CLEO.   Say, I would die.
        [*Exeunt* PROCULEIUS *and* Soldiers.
DOL. Most noble empress, you have heard
CLEO. I cannot tell.   [of me?
DOL.   Assuredly, you know me.
CLEO. No matter, Sir, what I have heard,
    or known.   [dreams;
You laugh when boys or women tell their
Is't not your trick?
DOL.   I understand not, Madam.

CLEO. I dream'd there was an emperor
    Antony:—
O, such another sleep, that I might see
But such another man!
DOL.   If it might please you,—
CLEO. His face was as the heavens; and
    therein stuck
A sun and moon, which kept their course,
    and lighted
The little O, the earth.
DOL.   Most sovereign creature,—
CLEO. His legs bestrid the ocean: his
    rear'd arm
Crested the world: his voice was propertied
As all the tuned spheres, and that to
    friends;
But when he meant to quail and shake
    the orb,
He was as rattling thunder. For his bounty,
There was no winter in't; an autumn 'twas,
That grew the more by reaping: his de-
    lights   [above
Were dolphin-like; they show'd his back
The element they liv'd in: in his livery
Walk'd crowns, and crownets; realms and
    islands were
As plates dropp'd from his pocket.
DOL.   Cleopatra,—
CLEO. Think you there was, or might be,
As this I dream'd of?   [such a man
DOL. Gentle Madam, no.
CLEO. You lie, up to the hearing of the
    gods.
But, if there be, or ever were, one such,
It's past the size of dreaming: nature
    wants stuff   [imagine
To vie strange forms with fancy; yet, to
An Antony, were nature's peace 'gainst
Condemning shadows quite.   [fancy,
DOL. Hear me, good Madam.
Your loss is as yourself, great; and you
    bear it   [might never
As answering to the weight: would I
O'ertake pursu'd success, but I do feel,
By the rebound of your's, a grief that
My very heart at root.   [smites
CLEO.   I thank you, Sir.
Know you what Cæsar means to do with
    me?
DOL. I am loath to tell you what I would
    you knew.
CLEO. Nay, pray you, Sir,—
DOL. Though he be honourable,—
CLEO. He'll lead me, then, in triumph?
DOL. Madam, he will; I know it.
Within. Make way there!—Cæsar!
Enter CÆSAR, GALLUS, PROCULEIUS, ME-
    CÆNAS, SELEUCUS, *and* Attendants.
CÆS. Which is the queen of Egypt?

DOL. It is the emperor, Madam.
                    [CLEOPATRA *kneels.*
CÆS. Arise, you shall not kneel.
I pray you, rise; rise, Egypt.
CLEO.   Sir, the gods
Will have it thus; my master and my lord
I must obey.
CÆS. Take to you no hard thoughts:
The record of what injuries you did us,
Though written in our flesh, we shall
    remember
As things but done by chance.
CLEO.   Sole Sir o' the world,
I cannot project mine own cause so well
To make it clear; but do confess I have
Been laden with like frailties, which before
Have often sham'd our sex.
CÆS.   Cleopatra, know,
We will extenuate rather than enforce:
If you apply yourself to our intents,
(Which towards you are most gentle) you
    shall find
A benefit in this change; but if you seek
To lay on me a cruelty, by taking
Antony's course, you shall bereave your-
    self   [children
Of my good purposes, and put your
To that destruction which I'll guard them
    from,
If thereon you rely. I'll take my leave.
CLEO. And may, through all the world:
    'tis yours; and we,
Your scutcheons, and your signs of con-
    quest, shall
Hang in what place you please. Here, my
    good lord.
CÆS. You shall advise me in all for
    Cleopatra.
CLEO. [*Giving a scroll.*] This is the brief
    of money, plate, and jewels,
I am possess'd of: 'tis exactly valued;
Not petty things admitted.—Where's Seleu-
    cus?
SEL. Here, Madam.
CLEO. This is my treasurer: let him
    speak, my lord,
Upon his peril, that I have reserv'd
To myself nothing.—Speak the truth,
SEL. Madam,   [Seleucus.
I had rather seal my lips, than, to my peril,
Speak that which is not.
CLEO.   What have I kept back?
SEL. Enough to purchase what you have
    made known.
CÆS. Nay, blush not, Cleopatra; I ap-
Your wisdom in the deed.   [prove
CLEO.   See, Cæsar! O, behold,
How pomp is follow'd! mine will now be
    yours;   [be mine.
And, should we shift estates, yours would

The ingratitude of this Seleucus does
Even make me wild:—O slave, of no more
    trust
Than love that's hir'd!—What, goest thou
    back? thou shalt
Go back, I warrant thee; but I'll catch
    thine eyes,
Though they had wings: slave, soul-less
O rarely base!   [villain, dog!
CÆS.   Good queen, let us entreat you.
CLEO. O Cæsar, what a wounding shame
    is this,—
That thou, vouchsafing here to visit me,
Doing the honour of thy lordliness
To one so meek, that mine own servant
    should
Parcel the sum of my disgraces by
Addition of his envy! Say, good Cæsar,
That I some lady trifles have reserv'd,
Immoment toys, things of such dignity
As we greet modern friends withal; and
    say,
Some nobler token I have kept apart
For Livia, and Octavia, to induce
Their meditation; must I be unfolded
With one that I have bred? The gods! it
    smites me
Beneath the fall I have.—[*To* SEL.] Pr'y-
    thee, go hence;
Or I shall show the cinders of my spirits
Through th' ashes of my chance:—wert
    thou a man,
Thou would'st have mercy on me.
CÆS.   Forbear, Seleucus.
                    [*Exit* SELEUCUS.
CLEO. Be it known, that we, the greatest,
    are misthought   [fall,
For things that others do; and, when we
We answer others' merits in our name,—
Are therefore to be pitied.
CÆS.   Cleopatra,
Not what you have reserv'd, nor what
    acknowledg'd,   [yours,
Put we i' the roll of conquest: still be it
Bestow it at your pleasure; and believe,
Cæsar's no merchant, to make prize with
    you
Of things that merchants sold. Therefore
    be cheer'd;   [dear queen;
Make not your thoughts your prisons: no,
For we intend so to dispose you, as
Yourself shall give us counsel. Feed, and
    sleep:
Our care and pity is so much upon you,
That we remain your friend; and so, adieu.
CLEO. My master, and my lord!
CÆS.   Not so. Adieu.
        [*Flourish. Exeunt* CÆSAR *and his train.*
CLEO. He words me, girls, he words me,
    that I should not

Be noble to myself: but, hark thee, Char-
mian. [*Whispers* CHARMIAN.
IRAS. Finish, good lady; the bright day
And we are for the dark. [is done,
CLEO. Hie thee again:
I have spoke already, and it is provided;
Go, put it to the haste.
CHAR. Madam, I will.
Re-enter DOLABELLA.
DOL. Where is the queen?
CHAR. Behold, Sir. [*Exit.*
CLEO. Dolabella!
DOL. Madam, as thereto sworn by your
command,
Which my love makes religion to obey,
I tell you this: Cæsar through Syria
Intends his journey; and, within three
days,
You with your children will he send
before: [form'd
Make your best use of this: I have per-
Your pleasure, and my promise.
CLEO. Dolabella,
I shall remain your debtor.
DOL. I your servant.
Adieu, good queen; I must attend on
Cæsar.
CLEO. Farewell, and thanks. [*Exit* DOL.]
Now, Iras, what think'st thou?
Thou, an Egyptian puppet, shalt be shown
In Rome, as well as I: mechanic slaves
With greasy aprons, rules, and hammers,
shall
Uplift us to the view; in their thick
breaths,
Rank of gross diet, shall we be enclouded,
And forc'd to drink their vapour.
IRAS. The gods forbid!
CLEO. Nay, 'tis most certain, Iras:—saucy
lictors [rhymers
Will catch at us, like strumpets; and scald
Ballad us out o' tune: the quick comedians
Extemporally will stage us, and present
Our Alexandrian revels; Antony
Shall be brought drunken forth, and I
shall see
Some squeaking Cleopatra boy my great-
I' the posture of a whore. [ness
IRAS. O, the good gods!
CLEO. Nay, that is certain.
IRAS. I'll never see it; for, I am sure,
my nails
Are stronger than mine eyes.
CLEO. Why, that's the way
To fool their preparation, and to conquer
Their most absurd intents.—
Re-enter CHARMIAN.
Now, Charmian?—
Show me, my women, like a queen:—go
fetch

My best attires;—I am again for Cydnus,
To meet Mark Antony:—sirrah Iras, go.—
Now, noble Charmian, we'll despatch in-
deed;
And, when thou hast done this chare, I'll
give thee leave
To play till dooms-day.—Bring our crown
and all. [*Exit* IRAS. *A noise heard.*
Wherefore's this noise?
Enter one of the Guard.
GUARD. Here is a rural fellow,
That will not be denied your highness'
He brings you figs. [presence:
CLEO. Let him come in.—[*Exit* Guard.]
What poor an instrument
May do a noble deed! he brings me liberty.
My resolution's plac'd, and I have nothing
Of woman in me: now from head to foot
I am marble-constant; now the fleeting
No planet is of mine. [moon
Re-enter Guard, *with a* Clown *bringing in*
a basket.
GUARD. This is the man.
CLEO. Avoid, and leave him.—
[*Exit* Guard.
Hast thou the pretty worm of Nilus there,
That kills and pains not?
CLOWN. Truly, I have him: but I would
not be the party that should desire you to
touch him, for his biting is immortal;
those that do die of it, do seldom or never
recover.
CLEO. Remember'st thou any that have
died on't?
CLOWN. Very many, men and women too.
I heard of one of them no longer than
yesterday: a very honest woman, but something given to lie; as a woman should not
do, but in the way of honesty: how she
died of the biting of it, what pain she
felt,—truly, she makes a very good report
o' the worm; but he that will believe all
that they say, shall never be saved by half
that they do: but this is most fallible, the
worm's an odd worm.
CLEO. Get thee hence; farewell.
CLOWN. I wish you all joy of the worm.
[*Sets down the basket.*
CLEO. Farewell.
CLOWN. You must think this, look you,
that the worm will do his kind.
CLEO. Ay, ay; farewell.
CLOWN. Look you, the worm is not to
be trusted but in the keeping of wise
people; for, indeed, there is no goodness
in the worm.
CLEO. Take thou no care; it shall be
heeded.
CLOWN. Very good. Give it nothing, I
pray you, for it is not worth the feeding.

CLEO. Will it eat me?

CLOWN. You must not think I am so simple, but I know the devil himself will not eat a woman: I know that a woman is a dish for the gods, if the devil dress her not; but, truly, these same whoreson devils do the gods great harm in their women; for in every ten that they make, the devils mar five.

CLEO. Well, get thee gone; farewell.

CLOWN. Yes, forsooth: I wish you joy of the worm.   *[Exit.*

Re-enter IRAS, *with a robe, crown, &c.*

CLEO. Give me my robe, put on my crown; I have

Immortal longings in me: now no more

The juice of Egypt's grape shall moist this lip:—   [I hear

Yare, yare, good Iras; quick.—Methinks

Antony call; I see him rouse himself

To praise my noble act; I hear him mock

The luck of Cæsar, which the gods give men

To excuse their after wrath:—husband, I come: [title!

Now to that name my courage prove my

I am fire, and air; my other elements

I give to baser life.—So,—have you done?

Come then, and take the last warmth of my lips.   [well.

Farewell, kind Charmian;—Iras, long fare-
        [Kisses them. IRAS *falls and dies.*

Have I the aspick in my lips? Dost fall?

If thou and nature can so gently part,

The stroke of death is as a lover's pinch,

Which hurts, and is desir'd. Dost thou lie still?   [world

If thus thou vanishest, thou tell'st the

It is not worth leave-taking.

CHAR. Dissolve, thick cloud, and rain; that I may say,

The gods themselves do weep.

CLEO.   This proves me base:

If she first meet the curled Antony,

He'll make demand of her, and spend that kiss,

Which is my heaven to have.—Come, thou mortal wretch,
        [To an asp, *which she applies to her breast.*

With thy sharp teeth this knot intrinsicate

Of life at once untie: poor venomous fool,

Be angry, and despatch. O, could'st thou speak,   [ass

That I might hear thee call great Cæsar Unpolicied!

CHAR.   O eastern star!

CLEO.   Peace, peace!

Dost thou not see my baby at my breast,

That sucks the nurse asleep?

CHAR.   O, break! O, break!

CLEO. As sweet as balm, as soft as air, as gentle,—

O Antony!—Nay, I will take thee too.—
        [Applying another asp to her arm.

What should I stay—
        [Falls on a bed, and dies.

CHAR. In this wild world?—So, fare thee well.—

Now boast thee, death, in thy possession lies   [close;

A lass unparallel'd.—Downy windows,

And golden Phœbus never be beheld

Of eyes again so royal!—Your crown's awry;

I'll mend it, and then play—

        Enter the Guard, *rushing in.*

1 GUARD. Where is the queen?

CHAR. Speak softly, wake her not.

1 GUARD. Cæsar hath sent—

CHAR.   Too slow a messenger.
        [Applies an asp

O, come apace, despatch: I partly feel thee.   [Cæsar's beguil'd.

1 GUARD. Approach, ho! All's not well:

2 GUARD. There's Dolabella sent from Cæsar; call him.

1 GUARD. What work is here!—Charmian, is this well done?

CHAR. It is well done, and fitting for a princess

Descended of so many royal kings.

Ah, soldier!   [Dies.

        Re-enter DOLABELLA.

DOL. How goes it here?

2 GUARD.   All dead.

DOL.   Cæsar, thy thoughts

Touch their effects in this: thyself art coming

To see perform'd the dreaded act, which thou

So sought'st to hinder.

WITHIN. A way there! a way for Cæsar!

        Re-enter CÆSAR *and his train.*

DOL. O Sir, you are too sure an augurer;

That you did fear, is done.

CÆS.   Bravest at the last;

She levell'd at our purposes, and, being royal,   [deaths?

Took her own way.—The manner of their

I do not see them bleed.

DOL.   Who was last with them?

1 GUARD. A simple countryman, that brought her figs;

This was his basket.

CÆS.   Poison'd then.

1 GUARD.   O Cæsar,

This Charmian lived but now; she stood, and spake:

I found her trimming up the diadem

On her dead mistress; tremblingly she
   stood,
And on the sudden dropp'd.
CÆS.   O noble weakness!—
If they had swallow'd poison, 'twould ap-
   pear   [sleep,
By external swelling: but she looks like
As she would catch another Antony
In her strong toil of grace.
DOL.   Here, on her breast,
There is a vent of blood, and something
   blown:
The like is on her arm.
1 *GUARD.* This is an aspick's trail; and
   these fig leaves
Have slime upon them, such as the aspick
   leaves
Upon the caves of Nile.

CÆS.   Most probable
That so she died; for her physician tells
   me
She hath pursu'd conclusions infinite
Of easy ways to die.—Take up her bed;
And bear her women from the monument:
She shall be buried by her Antony:
No grave upon the earth shall clip in it
A pair so famous. High events as these
Strike those that make them; and their
   story is
No less in pity, than his glory, which
Brought them to be lamented. Our army
   shall,
In solemn show, attend this funeral;
And then to Rome:—come, Dolabella, see
High order in this great solemnity.
                           [*Exeunt.*

A

ABATE. To curtail, Mids. N. iii. 2.

ABHOR. To reject, Henry VIII, ii. 4.

ABODE. To bode or forebode, Hen. VIII. i. 1.

ABRIDGMENT. A term for a dramatic performance, Mids. N. v. 1. Applied in a similar sense to an actor, Ham. ii. 2.

ABY. To abide, Mids. N. iii. 2.

ACKNOWN. Acknowledgly acquainted, Oth. iii. 3.

ADAMANT. The old term for the magnet, Mids. N ii. 2.

ADDICTION. Inclination ; being given or addicted to, Oth. ii. 2.

ADDITION. Title, or mark of distinction, Ham. i. 4, Lear ii. 2.

ADDREST. Ready, prepared, Mids. N. v. 1.

AFFECTION. Used for constitutional inclination, tendency ; involuntary sympathy or antipathy, Mer. Ven. iv. 1.

AFFECTIONED. Affected, Tw. N. ii. 3.

AFFECTS. Affections, passions, Oth. i. 3. [In some editions effects.]

AFFEER'D. Confirmed, substantiated, Macb. iv. 3.

AFFIN'D. Joined by affinity, bound, Oth. i. 1 & ii. 3, Ham. iv. 1.

AFFRONT. To confront ; meet face to face, Ham. iii. 1.

AGATE. Used in allusion to a small person ; referring to the figures cut upon agates for rings, Much Ado iii. 1, 2.

AGLET-BABY. A point for fastening dress, Tam. S. i. 2.

AGLET-BABY. From Fr. *Aiguillette*, a tag ; and from the tags, or points, being frequently in the form of small figures. Tam. S. i. 2.

AGNIZE. To recognize, or acknowledge, Oth. i. 3.

AIERY. (Spelt also Eyry, from *Eyren*, eggs.) A brood of eagles, or hawks, Rich. III. i. 3, Ham. ii. 2.

AIM. "Cry aim" : a term in archery, Mer. W. ii. 3 & iii. 2.

AIM. Guess, conjecture, Jul. Cæs. i. 2, Oth. i. 3.

ALLOW. To approve, Lear ii. 4.

ALL-THING. Every way, Macb. iii. 1.

AMAIMON. The name of a Fiend, Mer. W. ii. 2.

AMORT. Dead, dispirited, Tam. S. iv. 3.

ANCHOR. Abbreviation of Anchoret, Hermit, Ham. iii. 2.

ANCIENT. Ensign ; also ensign-bearer, Oth. i. 1 & ii. 3.

ANDREN. Holinshed (Shakespeare's authority) gives this as the name for the valley of Ardren ; which, lying between Guynes and Ardres (the former then belonging to the English, and the latter to the French), was a fitting spot for the interview between Henry VIII. and Francis I., Hen. VIII. i. 1.

ANGEL. A coin, value near ten shillings. Used in Tam. S. iv. 2 ("ancient Angel") for a good old soul.

ANGLE. Fishing apparatus ; used metaphorically. Ham. v. 2.

ANTRE. A cavern, Oth. i. 3.

APPREHENSION. Used in the sense of brain-conceit, or faculty for sarcastic sayings, Much Ado iii. 4.

APPROOF. Approbation, Ant. Cl. iii. 2.

AQUA-VITAE. An old term for Brandy, or other spirituous liquor, Tw. N. ii. 5, Rom. J. iii. 2 & iv. 5.

ARCH. Principal, leader, chief, Lear ii. 1.

ARGAL. A corruption of the Lat. word *ergo*, therefore, Ham. v. 1.

ARGIER. The old name for Algiers, Temp. i. 2.

ARGOSIES. Merchant vessels, Mer. Ven. i. 1 & v. 1, Tam. S. ii. 1.

ARM-GAUNT. If Shakespeare's word, (and none suggested as a substitute is satisfactory,) its poetical sense, —conveying a grim image, —can be better felt than defined. Ant. Cl. i. 5.

ARM-GAUNT. It has since struck me that this word is a misprint for "rampant," formerly spelt "rampaunt," Ant. Cl. i. 5.

AROINT. Avaunt, Macb. i. 3, Lear iii. 4, (Song.)

ASCAUNT. Aslant, across, Ham. iv. 7.

ATOMIES. Atoms, As you L. iii. 2 & iii. 5, Rom. J. i. 4.

ATONE. To make at one, to agree, to reconcile, As you L. v. 4, Ant. Cl. ii. 2.

ATONEMENT. Reconciliation, Mer. W. i. 1, Rich. III. i. 3.

ATTACHED WITH. Overpowered by, Temp. iii. 3.

AVOUCH. Proof, testimony, Ham. i. 1.

B

BACCARE. A cant phrase, meaning, "Go back !" Tam. S. ii. 1.

BAFFLE. A punishment of recreant knights, by hanging them up by the heels, and beating them with sticks. From the Fr. "*Baffouer*," or "*Baffoler*," Tw. N. ii. 5.

BALDRICK. A belt, Much Ado i. 1.

BALLOW. A provincial word for a pole or staff, Lear iv. 6.

BAN. (Spelt also Bann.) To curse, Lear ii. 3, Ham. iii. 2.

BAND. Used for Bond, Ant. Cl. iii. 2, Ham. i. 2.

BANDY. To strike to and fro ; a term used in the game of Tennis, Rom. J. ii. 5.

BARBASON. The name of a Fiend, Mer. W. ii. 2.

BARBED. A corruption of barded ; barbe (or more properly barde) being a term for horse-armour, Rich. III. i. 1.

BARN. (Spelt also Barne.) A child, Much Ado iii. 4.

BASTA. An Italian term for enough, Tam. S. i. 1.

BATED. Bating, a term in falconry; to flutter, to beat the wings, from the Fr. *battre*, Rom. J. iii. 2.

BATLET. A small bat, used in clothes-washing, As you L. ii. 4.

BATTEN. To feed, or fatten, Ham. iii. 4.

BAUBLE. The fool's toy-badge of office, Rom. J. ii. 4.

BAWCOCK. From the Fr. *Beaucoq*. A fine, dashing fellow, Tw. N. iii. 4.

BAY. Bay-window, or bow-window, Tw. N. iv. 2.

BAYNARD'S. A residence of Rich. III. in London, and still gives name to one of the wards in that city—"Castle Baynard Ward," Rich. III. iii. 5.

BEAR IN HAND. To lure on, to keep in false expectation. Much Ado iv. 1, Tam. S. iv. 2.

BEAVER. The front of the helmet, used for covering the face. Fr. *Bavière*, the vizor, Ham. i. 2.

BECK. A signal for citing and summoning, Ham. iii. 1, Tam. S. 2, (Ind.)

BECOME. In the sense of embellish, adorn, As you L. iii. 2.

BEDLAM. A corruption of Bethlehem, an asylum for lunatics; hence the term was applied to the individuals, Lear i. 2 & ii. 3 & iii. 7.

BENISON. Blessing, Macb. ii. 4, Lear i. 1 & iv. 6.

BERGOMASK. A clownish Italian dance; in imitation of the people of *Bergomasca*, a district in the Venetian States, Mids. N. v. 1.

BERMOOTHES. The old name for Bermudas, Temp. i. 2.

BESHREW. To curse. A shrewish woman was called a curst woman, Mid. N. ii. 3, Oth. iv. 3.

BESMIRCH. To soil, Ham. i. 3.

BESORT. To suit, or befit, Lear i. 4.

BESORT. Attendance, escort, Oth. i. 3.

BESTRAUGHT. Distracted, Tam. S. 2, (Ind.)

BETEEM. To allow, afford, Ham. i. 2, Mid. N. i. 1.

BEVIS. A hero of chivalry; for whose marvellous exploits (amounting to the incredible) William the Conqueror created him Earl of Southampton, Hen. VIII. i. 1.

BEVY. A flock of birds; applied to a company of ladies, Hen. VIII. i. 4.

BEWRAY. To betray, to discover, Lear ii. 1.

BID. Past tense of bided, or abided, endured, Rich. III. iv. 4.

BILBO. A sword; from Bilboa, a town in Spain famous for steel manufacture, Mer. W. i. 1 & iii. 5.

BILBOES. Fetters, used at sea to confine prisoners; same derivation as above, Ham. v. 2.

BILL. A halbert, used by watchmen, Much Ado iii. 3.

BILL. A placard publicly set up by challengers, Much Ado i. 1.

BIRD-BOLT. A short, thick arrow, blunt at the end, to kill birds by the blow only, Much Ado i. 1.

BISSON. Blind, Ham. ii. 2.

BITE THE EAR. Formerly used as a playful expression of loving kindness, Rom. J. ii. 4.

BITE THE THUMB. An insulting action. In this position the thumb represented a fig; meaning 'A fig for you,' Rom. J. i. 1.

BITE THE THUMB. An insulting action, performed by letting the thumb-nail jerk from the upper teeth with a clicking noise, as a challenge to quarrel, Rom. J. i. 1.

BITTER SWEETING. SEE SWEETING, Rom. J. ii. 4.

BLACK-MONDAY. Easter Monday. So named from the bitter cold of that day, on the 14th Ap. 1360, which carried off many of Edw'd III's soldiers, then before Paris, (Stowe,) Mer. Ven. ii. 5.

BLANK. The centre of the target, Lear i. 4, Oth. iii. 4.

BLENT. Blended, Tw. N. i. 5, Mer. Ven. iii. 2.

BLIND-WORM. A small snake, believed to be venomous; but it is harmless, Mid. N. ii. 3, (Song), Macb. iv. 1.

BLOCK. Formerly used for the shape or fashion of a hat; Much Ado i. 1, Lear iv. 6.

BLOOD. Used for disposition, impulse, Lear iv. 2.

BLOOD-BOLTERED. Sprinkled with blood as if from a sieve, or bolter, Macb. iv. 1.

BLOWN. Swollen, over-charged, puffed up, tumid, Lear iv. 4, Oth. iii. 3, Ant. Cl. v. 2.

BLOWS. Swells to bursting, Ant. Cl. iv. 6.

BOB. To cheat, or obtain by fraud, Oth. v. 1. Also, a taunt, or scoff, As you L. ii. 7.

BODKIN. A small dagger, Ham. iii. 1. In Stowe's Chron. it is said that Jul. Cæsar was slain with 'bodkins.'

BOGGLER. A swerver from the right path; a vicious woman, Ant. Cl. iii. 11.

BOLDS. Emboldens, Lear v. 1.

BOLT. A peculiar kind of arrow, pointed instead of blunted, like the bird-bolt, Mids. N. ii. 2.

BOMBARD. (Sometimes spelt Bumbard.) A species of cannon; also (on account of its similar appearance) a huge drinking vessel, made of leather, Temp. ii. 2, Hen. VIII. v. 3.

BOMBAST. Stuffing. Doublets were stuffed out with cotton; hence applied metaphorically, Oth. i. 1.

BOOT. Something given over and above, Rich. III. iv. 4.

BORE. The calibre of a cannon; used metaphorically, Ham. iv. 6. Also, to pierce, to injure, Hen. VIII. i. 1.

BORE, *or* BORNE IN HAND. Kept in expectation, Ham. ii. 2.

BOSKY. Low Latin, *Boscus*; Ital. *Bosco*, woody, (sometimes spelt Busky,) Temp. iv. 1.

BOSOM, TO THE. A not unusual address upon letters to ladies, Ham. ii. 2, (Let.)

BOSSED. Embossed, or studded, Tam. S. ii. 1.

BOTTLE OF HAY. A truss of hay, Mid. N. iv. 1.

BOUGHT AND SOLD. To be over-reached, or disposed of out-and-out, Rich. III. v. 3. (Scroll.)

BOURN. Boundary, limit, Temp. ii. 1, Ant. Cl. i. 1. Also a rivulet, Lear iii. 6, (Song.)

BOW. A yoke for oxen; called still, oxbow, As you L. iii. 3.

BRABBLE. Brawl, quarrel, Tw. N. v. 1.

BRACH. A scent-hound, Tam. S. 1, (Ind.), Lear i. 4 & iii. 6.

BRAIN. To beat out the brains, Temp. iii. 2.

BRAKE. A thicket or thorny path, Hen. VIII. i. 2.

BRAVE, BRAVED, BRAVERY. Finely apparelled; also, flouted, dared; used punningly, Tam. S. iv. 3.

BRAVERY. Bravado, Oth. i. 1.

BREAK UP. To carve. Used metaphorically for opening a letter, Mer. Ven. ii. 4.

BREAST. Used to signify a musical voice, Tw. N. ii. 3.

BREATHED. Well exercised; kept in breath, Tam. S. 2, (Ind.)

BREATHING. Action, exertion, exercise, Ham. v. 2.

BREED-BATE. A hatcher of quarrels, Mer. W. i. 4.

BRING ON THE WAY. To accompany, Oth. iii. 4.

BRIZE. The gad-fly, (also spelt Breese.) Ant. Cl. iii. 8.

BROCK. Badger; frequently used as a term of abuse. Tw. N. ii. 5.

BROKE CROSS. It was reckoned disgraceful, at tilting, to have the lance broken across the person of the antagonist, instead of by a straight thrust, Much Ado v. 1.

BROKEN. For broken their minds to, communicated, Hen. VIII. v. 1.

BROKEN MUSIC. Mr. Chappell, in his valuable work on "English Minstrelsy," states that "broken music" meant what we now term "a stringed band;" probably because stringed instruments (being formerly played without a bow) were incapable of giving *sustained* notes. It affords the poet punning allusion, As you L. i. 2.

BROOCH'D. Ornamented, Ant. Cl. iv. 13.

BROWNIST. A religious sectarian, Tw. N. iii. 2.

BRUITED. Noised abroad, proclaimed, Macb. v. 7.

BUCK-BASKET. The basket used for carrying linen to be washed, Mer. W. iii. 3 & 5.

BUCKING. Washing, Mer. W. iii. 3.

BUCKLERS. "To give the bucklers," to yield the victory, Much Ado v. 2.

BUCKLERSBURY. A street in London, in former times chiefly inhabited by druggists, who sold medicinal herbs, or simples, Mer. W. iii. 3.

BUG, BUG-BEAR. Hob-goblin, Tam. S. i. 2, Ham. v. 2.

BULK. The person, or body of a man, Rich. III. i. 4.

BURGONET. A species of helmet, Ant. Cl. i. 5.

BURN DAY-LIGHT. A proverbial phrase, meaning, to use superfluous actions, Mer. W. ii. 1, Rom. J. i. 4.

BURST. Formerly used for to break, Tam. S. 1, (Ind.)

BUT. In the sense of only, unless, except, Temp. i. 2, Macb. i. 7, Ant. Cl. iii. 9.

BUTT-SHAFT. An arrow, without a barb, to shoot at butts; so that it may be easily drawn out, Rom. J. ii. 4.

BUTTERY-BAR. The place where the meat and drink were dispensed, Tw. N. i. 3.

'BY. Abbreviation of aby; to abide the consequences; to pay the penalty, Mids. N. iii. 2.

BY AND BY. Immediately. Soon, Rom. J. iii. 4.

C

CADENT. Falling. Lat. *Cadens,* Lear i. 4.

CAKE. "My cake is dough," an old proverb: meaning, a cake from the oven spoiled; and implying defeated expectation, Tam. S. i. 1 & v. 1.

CALLAT, *or* CALLET. A worthless woman, Oth. iv. 2.

CAMELOT. A town in Somersetshire (now called Camel, or rather, Queen Camel) where King Arthur held his court. Shakespeare's allusion to the place refers to its being famous for a breed of geese, Lear ii. 2.

CAN. To be capable, able. To know, to be skilful in, Ham. iv. 7.

CANARY, *or* CANARIES. A sprightly dance. Mrs. Quickly confuses it with 'Quandary,'—a vulgar word for perplexity, Mer. W. ii. 2. The name of a wine (from the Canary Islands), Mer. W. iii. 2, Tw. N. i. 3.

CANDLE-WASTERS. Night-revellers, Much Ado v. 1.

CANE-COLOURED. A farther definition of the *"yellow* beard," mentioned as Master Slender's; yet some editors print "Cain-coloured," explaining it to mean *red;* that hue of hair being popularly ascribed to both Cain and Judas, as the colour held to be ugliest, Mer. W. i. 4.

CANKER. The dog-rose, or common single wild rose, Much Ado i. 3.

CANKER. A caterpillar, Mids. N. ii. 3.

CANON. Law, or rule, Ham. i. 2.

CANTLE. A portion, Ant. Cl. iii. 8.

CANTONS. Songs, Tw. N. i. 5.

CAPABLE. Susceptible, Hen. VIII. v. 2.

CAPRICIOUS. Goat-like, whimsical, wanton. Lat. *Caper,* As you L. iii. 3.

CARD OF TEN. An old proverbial term, implying success; ten being the highest card, Tam. S. ii. 1.

CARDUUS BENEDICTUS. The blessed thistle, Much Ado iii. 4.

CAREIRES. To pass the carriere, was a military phrase, for running a charge, or career, in a tournament. Used metaphorically — say whimsically, Mer. W. i. 1.

CARLOT. The same meaning As you L. iii. 5.

CARPET CONSIDERATION. A carpet knight was one created during a time of peace, and by favour, Tw. N. iii. 4.

CARPET-MONGER. The same sort of person, Much Ado v. 2.

CARPING. Querulously catching at trifles; petulantly censuring, Much Ado iii. 1, Rich. III. iii. 5.

CARRACK. A ship, a Spanish galleon; named so from *Carico,* a lading or freight, Oth. i. 2.

CARRIAGE. Import, intention, Ham. i. 1.

CART. Formerly used for car, or chariot, Ham. iii. 2.

CARVE. To carve seems to have been an accomplishment of peculiar significance in gallantry, Mer. W. i. 3.

CASTILIAN. Used contemptuously, after the defeat of the Armada, Mer. W. ii. 3.

CASTILIANO VULGO. Possibly a hint from Sir Toby to Maria, to put on a grave, or "Castilian" manner, at the approach of Sir Andrew; the Castilians being famed for staid bearing, Tw. N. i. 3.

CATAIAN. A thief, or sharper. Cataia, or Cathay, the old name for China; the Chinese being reputed acute thieves, Mer. W. ii. 1. Sir Toby calls his niece thus, as we playfully call those we like 'rogue,' Tw. N. ii. 3.

CATER-COUSINS. From the Fr. *"quatre-cousin;"* a word in ridicule of claiming kindred even to remotest degree, Mer. Ven. ii. 2.

CATES. Delicate viands, Tam. S. ii. 1.

CATLING. A small violin string made of catgut. Simon Catling, is the name for a fiddler, Rom. J. iv. 5.

CAUSE. Motive, impellent, incitement, Macb. v. 2, Ham. v. 2.

CAUSE, FIRST AND SECOND. A term used in the science of duelling, Rom. J. ii. 4. "The Seventh Cause," As you L. v. 4.

CAUTEL. From the Roman law-term, *Cautela,* a caution, or security. Used in a crafty sense, Ham. i. 3.

CAUTELOUS. Cautious, artful, deceitful, Jul. Cæs. ii. 1.

CAVALEROES. Cavaliers; gay dashing fellows. "Cavalero-justice," Mer. W. ii. 1.

CAVIARE. A delicacy made of the roe of sturgeon, salted and dried. It comes from Russia; and being a rarity in Shakespeare's time, he applied the word metaphorically, as being unknown to the generality of people, Ham. ii. 2.

CENSER. The censer was used by barbers to perfume their shops, Tam. S. iv. 3.

CENSURE. Judgment, opinion, Rich. III. ii. 2. A judicial sentence, Oth. v. 2.

CENTURY. A company of a hundred men, Lear iv. 4.

CEREMENTS. Waxed cloths, in which embalmed **b o d i e s** were wrapped, Ham. i. 4.

CEREMONIES. Regal and pompous ornaments, Jul. Cæs. i. 1. Also, prodigies, Jul. Cæs. ii. 1 & 2.

CERTES. Of a truth, certainly, Temp. iii. 3.

CHAIN. A chain was a badge of various dignities and callings, Much Ado ii. 1, Tw. N. ii. 3.

CHAIR. Public rostrum for orations: from the Fr. *Chaire,* pulpit, Jul. Cæs. iii. 2.

CHAMBER. Mr. Payne Collier says London was called "The King's **C h a m b e r**," *"Camera Regis,"* from the time of the Conquest downwards, Rich. III. iii. 1.

CHAMBERER. A dangler, an idler, Oth. iii. 3.

CHAMBERLAIN. A servant who has the care of chambers, Macb. i. 7.

CHAMPAIGN, **C H A M P A I N**, CHAMPIAN. Open country, Tw. N. ii. 5, Lear i. 1.

CHARACTER. H a n d-writing, Lear i. 2, Tw. N. v. 1. Also, to imprint, Ham. i. 3.

CHARACTERY. That which is legible by **c h a r a c t e r s**, marks, or traces, Mer. W. v. 5, Jul. Cæs. ii. 1.

CHARE. Char-work, common, casual, task-labour. Still used in the form of charwoman, Ant. Cl. iv. 13 & v. 2.

CHARIEST. The most reserved and scrupulous, Ham. i. 3.

CHARINESS. Discretion, caution, Mer. W. ii. 1.

CHARM. To conjure, invoke, or evoke by fascinating means, Jul. Cæs. ii. 1.

CHAUDRON. The entrails of a beast, Macb. iv. 1.

CHEATER. Used punningly for escheater ; an officer in the Exchequer, whose duty was to exact forfeitures, Mer. W. i. 3.

CHECK. A term in falconry. To change from one prey to another, Tw. N. iii. 1.

CHERRY-PIT. A boy's game, consisting of **p i t c h i n g** cherry-stones into a hole, Tw. N. iii. 4.

CHEVERIL. **L e a t h e r** made from kid's skin, Fr. *Chevreau.* Being pliable, the term was used metaphorically. Tw. N. iii. 1, Rom. J. ii. 4. Hen. VIII. ii. 3.

CHEW. To ruminate, Jul. Cæs. i. 2.

CHIDING. Resounding : the cry of hounds, Mids. N. iv. 1.

CHILD. A youth trained to arms. Used as a title, Lear iii. 4, (Song.)

CHILDING. Bearing children, or offspring ; fruitful, Mids. N. ii. 2.

CHOPINE. A high shoe, or clog, Ham. ii. 2.

CHOUGH. A sea-side crow, Lear iv. 6, Temp. ii. 1, Mids. N. iii. 1.

CINQUE-PACE. A dance ; (called also a Galiard), the steps of which were regulated by the number five, Much Ado ii. 1.

CIRCUMSTANCED. Submissive to circumstances, Oth. iii. 4.

CLAW. To flatter ; from to scratch, or tickle, Much Ado i. 3.

CLEAR STORIES. A term in architecture for a row of windows running along the upper part of the wall of an apartment, Tw. N. iv. 2.

CLEPE. To call, to name, Macb. iii. 1, Ham. i. 4.

CLING. To shrivel, to shrink up ; to waste, consume, Macb. v. 5.

CLINQUANT. Glittering. Fr. *Clinquant,* tinsel, Hen. VIII i. 1.

CLOUD IN HIS FACE. Said of a horse that has a dark coloured spot between the eyes ; a mark supposed to be indicative of bad temper, Ant. Cl. iii. 2.

CLOUT. A cloth, or towel, Rich. III. i. 3, Ham. ii. 2.

CLUBS. In an affray in London, the cry used to be, "Clubs ! Clubs !"—whether to part, or join the combatants, As you L. v. 2, Hen. VIII. v. 3.

COACH-FELLOW. A horse employed to draw with another. By metaphor, a close companion, Mer. W. ii. 2.

COALS. "To carry coals ;" to submit to any degradation ; the lowest menials being the carriers of wood and coal, Rom. J. i. 1.

COCK. A subterfuge oath, used instead of the name of the Deity, Ham. iv. 5, (Song.)

COCK. The name of a small boat ; a cock-boat, Lear iv. 6.

COCKATRICE. A fabulous serpent, crested like a cock ; supposed to kill with its looking, Tw. N. iii. 4, Rom. J. iii. 2, Rich III. iv. 1.

COCKLE HAT. A cockle shell worn in the hat was the distinction of a pilgrim, Ham. iv. 5, (Song.)

COCKNEY. The ordinary use of the word is as a cant name for a Londoner, Shakespeare uses the word for a cook, Lear ii. 4 ; and for an affected, conceited fellow, Tw. N. iv. 1.

COCKREL. A young cock, Temp. ii. 1, Rom. J. i. 3.

COCK-SHUT TIME. Twilight. The time for ensnaring woodcocks. that then come out to feed, Rich. III. v. 3.

COFFIN. The raised crust of a pie. "C u s t a r d-coffin," Tam. S. iv. 3.

COG. To cheat, to play falsely with dice, Mer. W. iii. 3.

COIGNE. The corner-stone of a building, Macb. i. 6.

COIL. Bustle, tumult, confusion, Temp. i. 2, Much Ado v. 2.

COLLECTION. Conclusion, or consequence drawn, Ham. iv. 5.

COLBRAND. A Danish giant, overcome by Guy Earl of Warwick, Hen. VIII. v. 3.

COLLIED. Smudged with coal, blackened, discolored, darkened, Mids. N. i. 1, Oth. ii. 3.

COLLIER. Formerly a word of insult, Tw. N. iii. 4, Rom. J. i. 1.

COLMES-KILL. An island in the Hebrides, Macb. ii. 4.

COLOURS. "Fear no colours." A military term, meaning Fear not the enemy, Tw. N. i. 5.

CO-MART. Bargain, covenant, treaty, Ham. i. 1.

COME OFF. In modern vulgar parlance, to "come down with" [money], Mer. W. iv. 3.

COMMA. Used to indicate the smallest stop and as a link of connection, Ham. v. 2.

COMPANION. Used as a term of contempt, Jul. Cæs. iv. 3.

COMPETITOR. Used in the sense of a confederate, a colleague, Ant. Cl. i. 4 & ii. 7 & v. 1.

COMPLEMENT. Full observance, Mer. W. iv. 2.

COMPLEXION. Temperament, constitutional **t e n d e n c y**, Ham. i. 4.

COMPROMISED. Used in the sense of promised with each other, or mutually agreed, Mer. Ven. i. 3.

COMPTIBLE. Sensitive, susceptible, Tw. N. i. 5.

CON. To know, to learn, Tw. N. i. 5, Mids. N. i. 2.

CONCEAL. Simple's blunder for 'reveal.' It would be gratuitous to explain this, but that one of the commentators gravely proposed inserting what he called the correct word,—to the despoiling us of that pleasant passage, Mer. W. iv. 5.

CONCEIT. Fanciful contrivance, thought, Mids. N. i. 1, Ham. v. 2.

CONCLUSION. Experiment. Used for that whence conclusion may be drawn, Ham. iii. 4.

CONDUCT. Used as conductor, Temp. v. 1.

CONEY-CATCHING. Swindling, cheating. From Coney, the name of a rabbit, esteemed a simple animal, Mer. W. i. 1. Used also for jocular tricking, Tam. S. iv. 1.

CONFECT. Sweetmeat. "Count Confect," a sugary gentleman, Much Ado iv. 1.

CONFINELESS. Boundless, Macb. iv. 3.

CONFUSIONS. Launcelot's blunder for 'Conclusions,' Mer. Ven. ii. 2.

CONTAIN. Used in the sense of retain, Mer. Ven. v. 1.

CONTEMPTIBLE. Commonly used formerly for contemptuous, or s c o r n f u l, Much Ado ii. 3.

CONTINENT. That which contains, or encloses, Ham. iv. 4.

CONTINUATE. Uninterrupted, Oth. iii. 4.

CONTRIVE. To pass, spend, or wear away, Tam. S. i. 2.

CONVENTS. Comes together, accords, agrees, suits, Tw. N. v. 1.

CONVENTED. S u m m o n e d, Hen. VIII. v. 1.

CONVEY. A polite verb, for, to steal, Mer. W. i. 3.

CONVINCE. To overcome, overwhelm, Macb. i. 7 & iv. 3.

COPATAIN HAT. A tall, high-crowned hat, Tam. S. v. 1.

COPE. To engage. Lear v. 3, Ham. iii. 2.

COPHETUA. An ideal African king. Rom. J. ii. 1.

CORAGIO. From the Ital.; an encouraging exclamation, Temp. v. 1.

CORANTO. A brisk dance, Tw. N. i. 3.

CORKY. Dry, withered, Lear iii. 7.

COROLLARY. A crowning number or quantity; amply, or even more than enough, Temp. iv. 1.

COSTARD. The head, Mer. W. iii. 1, Lear iv. 6.

COTED. Overtook; came side by side with. From Fr. Coté, Ham. ii. 2.

COT-QUEAN. A coddler, a potterer in household affairs, Rom. J. iv. 4.

COTSALL. Cotswold, in Gloucestershire, Mer. W. i. 1.

COUNTENANCE. To do honour to, to pay hospitable attention to, Tam. S. iv. 1.

COUNTER. To "run counter," in hunting, is to trace the scent backwards, Ham. iv. 5.

COUNTERFEIT. Resemblance, likeness, portrait, Mer. Ven. iii. 2, Ham. iii. 4.

COUNTERPOINTS. Counterpanes, Tam. S. ii. 1.

COUNTERS. These were formerly used as aids in reckoning and casting accounts. "Counter-caster." Oth. i. 1.

COUNTY. Count, or Earl, Tw. N i. 5, Rom. J. i. 3.

COURSER'S HAIR. An allusion to the superstition that horse-hair laid in water, would become alive, and turn to venomous reptiles, Ant. Cl. i. 2.

COURT-CUPBOARD. A moveable buffet, or closet, Rom. J. i. 5.

COURT HOLY-WATER. A proverbial expression, signifying flattery; also, words, not deeds, Lear iii. 2.

COY. To smooth, or caress, Mids. N. iv. 1.

COYSTRIL, or COISTREL. A low fellow, Tw. N. i. 3.

COZIER. A cobbler, a tailor; also a botcher, Tw. N. ii. 3.

CRAB. A wild apple roasted, and put into ale; a favourite old indulgence, Mids. N. ii. 1.

CRANTS. Garlands, Ham. v. 1.

CRAVEN. A dastard, a recreant, Tam. S. ii. 1.

CREDENT. Credible, to be believed, Ham. i. 3.

CREDIT. Belief, Tw. N. iv. 3.

CRISP. Winding, curled, curved, Temp. iv. 1, Mer. Ven. iii. 2.

CROSSES. Coin. So called, because stamped with the cross, As you L. ii. 4.

CROSS-ROW. The Alphabet was formerly printed in the form of a cross; and used to be called the Christcross, cris-cros, or crossrow, Rich. III. i. 1.

CROW-KEEPER. A scare-crow, Rom. J i. 4, Lear iv. 6.

CROWNER'S-QUEST. The grave-digger's corruption of coroner's inquest, Ham. v. 1.

CRUSH A CUP. A drinking phrase. As we now say, 'Crack a bottle,' Rom. J. i. 2.

CRUZADO. A Portuguese gold coin; stamped with a cross, and varying in value at different periods, Oth. iii. 4.

CRY AIM. See AIM.

CRY ON. To cry on Victory, to cry on Havock, to cry on Murder, are used by Shakespeare; and the verb seems to stand for hailing, invoking, or proclaiming, Rich. III. v. 3, Ham. v. 2, Oth. v. 1.

CUE. Theatrical term. The last word of a preceding speech, Mids. N. iii. 1.

CULLION. A despicable fellow, a stupid lout, Tam. S. iv. 2.

CULLIONLY. Base, rascally, Lear ii. 2.

CUNNING. Skill, skilful, knowing, Ham. iv. 7.

CURB. To crouch, truckle, bend; Fr. Courber, Ham. iii. 4.

CURFEW. The 8 o'clock evening bell (Fr. Couvre feu) instituted by William I. of England, Temp. v. 1, Rom. J. iv. 4, Lear iii. 4.

CURIOSITY. Scrupulousness, Lear i. 2.

CURIOUS. Scrupulous, precise, Tam. S. iv. 4.

CURST. Ill-tempered, cross, vicious, Tam. S. i. 1 & 2, Much Ado ii. 1, Lear ii. 1, Rich. III. i. 2.

CURTAIL DOG. Primarily, a dog belonging to one not qualified for the chase; and therefore obliged to have its tail docked; subsequently, applied to a dog unfit for sport, Mer. W. ii. 1.

CURTLE-AX. A cutlass, or short, broad-bladed sword; Fr. Coutelas, As you L. i. 3.

CUSTOMER. A name for a common woman, Oth. iv. 1.

CUT. A term of contempt, Tw. N. ii. 3.

CUT AND LONG TAIL. Meaning every sort of dog. Used metaphorically for men of all degrees, under that of Esquire, Mer. W. iii. 4.

CUTLERS' POETRY. Mottoes inscribed by cutlers on their knives, Mer. Ven. v. 1.

CUT-PURSE. A thief: the purse formerly hung from the girdle, Ham. iii. 4.

CYPRUS. Spelt also, Cypress. The stuff which is now called crape, Tw. N. iii. 1.

D

DAFF. A form of "Doff." To dash off, to put away, Much Ado ii. 3 & v. 1.

DAGGER. The dagger was formerly worn behind the back, Rom. J. v. 3.

DAGGER OF LATH. The wooden weapon used by the 'Vice' in the old 'Moralities,' Tw. N. iv. 2, (Song.)

DAINTY. To "make dainty," was to be delicate or fastidious in consenting, Rom. J. i. 5.

DAMN. To condemn to death, Jul. Cæs. iv. 1, Ant. Cl. i. 1.

DANGER. To be in a person's "danger," meant, to be in his debt, Mer. Ven. iv. 1.

DANK. Damp, moist, Mids. N. ii. 3, Jul. Cæs. ii. 1, Rom. J. ii. 2.

DANSKERS. Danes, Ham. ii. 1.

DARE. To daunt, to scare. Larks are frightened or bewildered, and caught by a mirror put upon a piece of scarlet cloth, Hen. VIII. iii. 2. Also used in the sense of a challenge, or defiance, Ant. Cl. i. 2.

DARNEL. A pertinacious weed : Botanice *Lolium perenne;* called also 'Ray grass,' Lear iv. 4.

DAUB. To smear, Lear ii. 2. Also to feign, to put on a manner, Lear iv. 1.

DAUBERY. Imposture by trumpery shows, Mer. W. iv. 2.

DAW. Used to signify a silly fellow, as well as the bird so called, Oth. i. 1.

DAY-BED. A couch or sofa, Tw. N. ii. 5, Rich. III. iii. 7.

DEAR. From the Sax. *Dere,* —dire, or hurtful, Tw. N. v. 1.

DEAREST. *Derest,* direst, Ham. i. 2.

DEARTH. Formerly was used for dearness, Ham. v. 2. Elsewhere, in its usual sense of scarcity, Ant. Cl. ii. 7.

DEATHSMAN. The Executioner, Lear iv. 6.

DEBITOR-AND-CREDITOR. The title of certain old treatises upon commercial book-keeping. Used as a sneering nickname, Oth. i. 1.

DEBOSHED. Debauched, degraded, Temp. iii. 2.

DECEIVABLE. Deceptious, Tw. N. iv. 3.

DECKED. Sprinkled. To deg is still in provincial use for to sprinkle. *Daeg,* Icelandic, means a shower, Temp. i. 2.

DECLINE. To pass through various forms, as in the grammar, Rich. III. iv. 4.

DEFEAT. "Defeat thy favour," is, obliterate thy natural look, Oth. i. 3.

DEFEND. To forbid ; Fr. *Défendre,* Much Ado ii. 1, Oth. i. 3.

DEFTLY. Dexterously, cleverly, Macb. iv. 1.

DEFY. To disdain, refuse, renounce, Mer. W. ii. 2. As you L. (Epil.)

DELATIONS. Intimations, informations, Oth. iii. 3.

DELIGHTED. For delightful, Oth. i. 3.

DEMERITS, and 'Merits,' formerly had sometimes the same signification : Demerit being classically derived from *demereo,* which had an even stronger meaning than *mereo,* Oth. i. 2. Shakespeare uses the word in its more ordinary and modern sense, Macb. iv. 3.

DEMISE. To grant, Rich. III. iv. 4.

DEMURELY. Gravely, solemnly, Ant. Cl. iv. 9.

DEMURING. Looking demurely, with sobriety, Ant. Cl. iv. 13.

DEN. "Good den," a corruption of 'Good e'en.' It was formerly proper to say 'evening' any time after mid-day, Much Ado iii. 2, Rom. J. ii. 4.

DENAY. Denial, Tw. N. ii. 4.

DENIER. A French piece of money of lowest value, Tam. S. i. (Ind.), Rich. III. i. 2.

DEPART. Depart and Part were formerly used indiscriminately, Rom. J. iii. 1.

DEPRIVE. To disinherit, Lear i. 2.

DEROGATE. Degenerate, degraded, Lear i. 4.

DESCANT. An antiquated term in music, meaning to make variations upon a given theme, or ground, Rich. III. i. 1 & iii. 7.

DESIRE. For desire the delay of. To pray for a longer or more distant day, is still a term in legal use, Hen. VIII. ii. 4.

DESPATCHED. Despoiled, bereft, Ham. i. 5 .

DETERMINATE. Brought to a crisis, or conclusion, Oth. iv. 2.

DEVESTING. Undressing ; Lat. *Devestio,* Fr. *Devêtir,* Oth. ii. 3.

DICKON. The familiar of Richard : like the modern, 'Dick,' Rich. III. v. 3, (Scroll.)

DIE. Used in the sense of suffer, undergo, Lear v. 3.

DIFFUSED. Irregular, disorderly, Mer. W. iv. 4, Lear i. 4.

DISABLE. Disparage, undervalue, As you L. iv. 1.

DISAPPOINTED. Unappointed, not prepared, Ham. i. 5.

DISCANDYING. Melting like sugar, uncandying, Ant. Cl. iii. 11 & iv. 10.

DISCERN. This is the word, in the original ; which Theobald altered to "deserve,"—an alteration adopted by all editors since. But in restoring the word "discern," I feel that it gives the sense consistent both with what Malcolm has previously said of Macbeth's having "once been thought honest," and with what he afterwards says in taxing himself with vices. Moreover, it supplies the verb required before "wisdom," which all the editors miss, —they themselves having banished it. Shakespeare often makes one verb do double duty in a sentence ; thus the present passage appears to me to mean "you may discern something of Macbeth's once-believed virtue in me, and [may discern] the wisdom of betraying me to him," Macb. iv. 3.

DISCLOSED. Hatched, Ham. v. 1.

DISCOURSE. Used for power of discursive ratiocination, Ham. iv. 4.

DISEASE. Uneasiness, inconvenience, discomfort, discontent, Lear i. 1.

DISLIMNS. Obliterates, dissolves, Ant. Cl. iv. 12.

DISNATURED. Unnatural, Lear i. 4.

DISPOSE. Disposition, deportment, Oth. i. 3.

DISPOSED. In the mood for mirth, Tw. N. ii. 3.

DISPUNGE. Discharge, spunge-like, Ant. Cl. iv. 9.

DISSEAT. To unseat, dethrone, Macb. v. 3.

DISTEMPERATURE. Disarrangement, perturbation. Mids. N. ii. 2, Rom. J. ii. 3.

DISTRACTIONS. Detachments, separate parties, Ant. Cl. iii. 7.

DISTRAUGHT. The old participle for distracted, Rom. J. iv. 3, Rich. III. iii. 5.

DIVISION. A term in music. A florid passage of sequent notes, Rom. J. iii. 5.

DIVULGED. Publicly reported, or spoken of, Tw. N. i. 5.

DOFF. To do off, or put off, Tam. S. iii. 2.

DOLE. A lot or portion dealt out, Mer. W. iii. 4. In the sense of grief or dolour, Ham. i. 2.

DON. Do on, put on, Ham. iv. 5, (Song,) Ant. Cl. ii. 1.

DOUT. Do out, put out, Ham. i. 4 & iv. 7.

DOWLE. A feather ; the downy fibre of a feather, Temp. iii. 3.

DOWN-GYVED. Hanging, like fetters, or gyves about the ankles, Ham. ii. 1.

DRABBING. Following bad women, Ham. ii. 1.

DRAFF. Refuse, hog-wash, Mer. W. iv. 2.

DROLLERY. A puppet-show, Temp. iii. 3.

DRUMBLE. To boggle, to dawdle, Mer. W. iii. 2.

DUDGEON. The handle of a dagger, made of box-wood, Macb. ii. 1.

DUELLO. The code of laws for duelling, Tw. N. iii. 4.

DULLARD. An insensible lout, Lear ii. 1.

DUMB. To make dumb, Ant. Cl. i. 5.

DUMP. A mournful song, Much Ado ii. 3, (Song.)

DUN'S THE MOUSE. A proverbial saying, of which the meaning is obsolete, and remains 'dun,' or dark to all the commentators, Rom. J. i. 4.

DUN'S THE MOUSE. In the line following, there is an allusion to an old rural sport called "Dun is in the mire;" where Dun is the name for a carthorse, represented by a log of wood, hauled at by the company to extricate him from his supposed sticking in the mire. Rom. J. i. 4.

DUNG. Used contemptuously to signify productions of earth needful for the nourishment of man, Ant. Cl. v. 2.

DUNGY. Employed with similar signification; the one passage serving to elucidate the other, in the poet's use of the words "dung'" and "dungy" in this play, Ant. Cl. i. 1.

DUP. To do up, to lift open; some doors formerly requiring to be raised in opening, like port-cullises, Ham. iv. 5, (Song.)

E

EACH. "At each," here stands for 'each at end of each;' and has the sense of the word ECHE, Lear iv. 6.

EAGER. Sour; Fr. Aigre, Ham. i. 5. Keen, piercing, Ham. i. 4.

EANING. The season for producing off-spring, Mer. Ven. i. 3.

EANLINGS. Young lambs just born, Mer. Ven. i. 3.

EAR. To till, or plough. Metaphorically used, Ant. Cl. i. 4.

EARING. Cultivation; figuratively employed, Ant. Cl. i. 2.

ECSTASY. Madness, Macb. iv. 3, Temp. iii. 3, Ham. iii. 1 & 4.

EDWARD SHOVEL-BOARD. A shilling of Edward the Sixth's reign; a broad coin; and used in playing the game of Shovel-board, Mer. W. i. 1. See SHOVEL-GROAT.

EFFECTS. Intended actions, Ham. iii. 4.

EFTEST. Readiest, quickest, easiest, Much Ado iv. 2.

EGLANTINE. The sweet brier, Mids. N. ii. 2.

EGYPTIAN THIEF. An allusion to the story of Thyamis, a robber-chief and native of Memphis; who, knowing he must die, would have stabbed his captive, Chariclea, the woman he loved, Tw. N. v. 1.

EKE. To add to, As you L. i. 2.

EKE. Also, likewise, Mer. W. i. 3 & ii. 3.

ELD. Old age, Mer. W. iv. 4.

ELEMENT. Used formerly to express the whole visible expanse of air and heaven, Tw. N. i. 1, Jul. Cæs. i. 3.

ELEMENT. Elementary knowledge, initiation, Hen. VIII. i. 1. Shakespeare has satirized the fantastic use of the word "element" in his time. Tw. N. iii. 1, and has given an instance of that fashionable whim. Tw. N. iii. 4. He alludes to another then-prevailing idea respecting the "elements" as forming (morally and physically) component parts of human beings, Tw. N. ii. 3, Jul. Cæs. v. 5, Ant. Cl. v. 2.

ELF. To twist or entangle the hair, Lear ii. 3. "Elf-locks," hair thus matted, Rom. J. i. 4.

EMBALLING. Carrying the ball at a coronation, Shakespeare's invented word, Hen. VIII. ii. 3.

EMBOSSED. Run down, foaming, swollen, raised, Ant. Cl. iv. 11.

EMBOWELLED. Exhausted, emptied, Rich. III. v. 2.

EMPERY. Sovereign command, empire, kingdom, Rich. III. iii. 7.

ENACTURE. Action, or effect, Ham. iii. 2.

ENCAVE. To hide, Oth. iv. 1.

ENGINE. A warlike machine; also of torture, the rack, Lear i. 4.

ENGROSS. To enlarge, heap up together, or make fat, Rich. III. iii. 7.

ENKINDLE. To excite, to stimulate, Macb. i. 3, Lear iii. 7.

ENSCONCE. To hide: to protect as with a fort. Mer. W. ii. 2 & iii 3.

ENSEAMED. Gross, rank. The fat, or grease of an animal is called seam; and a hawk was said to be enseamed, when too fat for flight, Ham. iii. 4.

ENTERTAIN. To keep in service, Mer. W. i. 3.

ENVIOUSLY. Pettishly, wrathfully, Ham. iv. 5.

ENVY. In sense of hatred, or ill will, Hen. VIII. ii. 1 & iii 1, Mer. Ven. iv. 1.

EPHESIANS. Jolly comrades, Mer. W. iv. 5.

EQUIPAGE. Supposed to be a cant term for stolen goods, Mer. W. ii. 2.

ERRING. In its Latin sense of erratic, wandering, Ham. i. 1, Oth. i. 3.

ERST. Heretofore, As you L. iii. 5.

ESCHEWED. Shunned, avoided, Mer. W. v. 5.

ESCOTED. Paid. From the Fr. Escot, a shot, or reckoning, Ham. ii. 2.

ESIL. By some supposed to mean Yssell, Issell, or Izel, a river near Denmark; by others, to be the same word as Eisel. But, in both instances, used by the poet to indicate a difficult, or disagreeable draught, Ham. v. 1.

ESPERANCE. Hope, Fr., regularly adopted by Shakespeare, Lear iv. 1.

ESPIALS. Spies, Ham. iii. 1.

ESTRIDGE. Ostrich; which was formerly spelt Ostridge, and previously, Estridge, Ant. Cl. iii. 11.

ETERNE. Eternal, Macb. iii. 2, Ham. ii. 2.

EVEN. To level, to make equal, or plain, Lear iv. 7.

EVEN CHRISTIAN. A term used for Fellow-Christian, Ham. v. 1.

EVER. "Not ever;" not always; not on all occasions, Hen. VIII. v. 1.

EVIL. The 'Evil,' or 'King's Evil,' a scrofulous disease, supposed to be cured by the royal touch.—Dr. Johnson, when a child, was touched by Queen Anne. The pretension to the power is said to have originated with Edward the Confessor, Macb. iv. 3.

EXCREMENT. From the Lat. Excresco, to grow out of. Applied to the hair and the beard, Mer. Ven. iii. 2, Ham. iii. 4.

EXERCISE. The week-day sermon of the Puritans was called an 'Exercise,' Rich. III. iii. 2.

EXHIBITION. A college term. A stipend, an allowance of money, or maintenance, Oth. i. 3, Lear i. 2.

EXIGENT. For exigence, Jul. Cæs. v. 1.

EXORCISMS. Conjurations. "Exorcist," Jul. Cæs. ii. 1.

EXPEDIENCE. Enterprise, undertaking, Ant. Cl. i. 2.

EXPEDIENT. Quick, expeditious, As you L. iii. 1.

EXPIATE. Elapsed, closed, Rich. III. iii. 3.

EXPOSTULATE. To question, to discuss, Ham. ii. 2.

EXSUFFLICATE. Despicable, contemptible, abhorred, Oth. iii. 3.

EXTENDED. Law term. Seized, Ant. Cl. i. 2.

EXTENT. Ditto. Seizure, As you L. iii. 1. Assault, Tw. N. i. 5.

EXTERN. For external, Oth. i. 1.

EXTRACTING. Shakespeare uses this word (as he frequently uses words) in the strict sense of its classical derivation. By an "extracting frenzy," Olivia means a frenzy (her infatuation for Viola) which drew her out of all thoughts but one, Tw. N. v. 1.

EXTRAVAGANT. Used in its strict etymological sense; wandering out of, Ham. i. 1, Oth. i. 1.

EYASES. Nestling hawks, Ham. ii. 2.

EYAS-MUSKET. A young sparrow-hawk, Mer. W. iii. 3.

EYE OF GREEN. A tender hint of green, Temp. ii. 1.

EYELIADS. Eye-glances; Fr. Œillades, Mer. W. i. 3, Lear iv. 5.

EYNE. Eyes, Mids. N. i. 1.

F

FADGE. To answer, suit, fit, Tw. N. ii. 2.

FAIN. Glad, gladly, Temp. i. 2.

FAITHED. Believed, given credence to, Lear ii. 1.

FALL. As an active verb. To let drop, Ant. Cl. iii. 9.

FANCY. Love, Mids. N. iv. 1, Mer. Ven. iii. 2, (Song,) Tw. N. v. 1.

FANCY-FREE. Love-free, Mids. N. ii. 2.

FANTASTICAL. Fanciful, imaginary, Macb. i. 3, Tw. N. i. 1.

FANTASTICOES. Coxcombs, Rom. J. ii. 4.

FAP. Cant term for drunk, Mer. W. i. 1.

FARDEL. A burden; Ital. Fardello, Ham. iii. 1.

FASHIONS. A corruption from Fr. Farcins. Farcy, a sort of leprosy in horses, Tam, S. iii. 2.

FAST AND LOOSE. A cheating game, practised by vagrants and gipsies, Ant. Cl. iv. 10.

FATHOM. Depth, capacity, Oth. i. 1.

FAVOUR. Countenance, feature, appearance, look, Tw. N. ii. 4, Jul. Cæs. i. 2, Macb. i. 5, Oth. i. 3.

FAY. Faith. "By my fay," a common oath, Tam. S. 2. (Ind.), Rom. J. i. 5, Ham. ii. 2.

FEAR. Alluding to the personage so called in some of the old Moralities, Ant. Cl. ii. 3.

FEAR. Used actively. To scare, to frighten, Ant. Cl. ii. 6.

FEALTY. Cleverly, Temp. i. 2, (Song.)

FEATURE. Countenance, general appearance, Ant. Cl. ii. 5.

FEE. A regular stipend, Ham. ii. 2.

FEEDERS. Servants, retainers, Ant. Cl. iii. 11. Caterer, or provider of food, As you L. ii. 4.

FEE-GRIEF. A sorrow peculiar to one person exclusively, Macb. iv. 3.

FEE-SIMPLE. A tenant in fee-simple, was one holding lands and tenements, and to his heirs forever, Mer. W. iv. 2.

FELL. Hide, or skin with hair, As you L. iii. 2, Lear v. 3. The skin of the head, the scalp, Macb. v. 5.

FELLIES. The outer circles of wheels, Ham. ii. 2.

FELLOW. Equal in companionship, whether male or female, Temp. iii. 1, Tw. N. iii. 4.

FELLOWLY. Sympathetic, Temp. v. 1.

FENNEL. An inflammatory herb. Fennel was also held to be emblematic of flattery, Ham. iv. 5.

FESTINATE. Quick, speedy; Lat. Festinatus, Lear iii. 7.

FESTIVAL TERMS. Holiday, or florid language, Much Ado v. 2.

FETCH OR WARRANT. A sanctioned trick or pretence, Ham. ii. 1.

FETTLE. To prepare, to make ready; to adjust, to put in order; still in provincial use, Rom. J. iii. 5. [In most editions, "settle."]

FICO, or FIGO. Fig. A term of contempt and defiance; said to be of Spanish origin, Mer. W. i. 3.

FIGHTS. Cloths hung round a ship when in action, to conceal the men. Mer. W. ii. 2.

FILE. Number, list, catalogue, Macb. iii. 1 & v. 2.

FILED. Contraction of defiled, Macb. iii. 1. Also, kept an equal pace with, Hen. VIII. iii. 2.

FILLY. A young mare; opposed to colt, a young horse, Mids. N. ii. 1.

FINE. Conclusion, Much Ado i. 1.

FINE AND RECOVERY. This was formerly the strongest assurance known to the English law, Mer. W. iv. 2.

FINELESS. Endless, Oth. iii. 3.

FIRAGO. For Virago. A double wilful blunder of Sir Toby's, applying the term to a man; instead of, as is usual, to a turbulent woman, Tw. N. iii. 4.

FIRE-DRAKE. A fiery dragon. Humorously, a man with a flaming nose, Hen. VIII. v. 3.

FIT OF THE FACE. An affected look, a grimace, Hen. VIII. i. 3.

FITCHEW. A pole-cat. Applied to a musk-scented, bad woman, Oth. iv. 1.

FIVES. A corruption of the Fr. Avives. An inflammatory disease in the neck of horses, Tam. S. iii. 2.

FLAW. A sudden wind-storm, Ham. v. 1.

FLECKED. Spotted, speckled, Rom. J. ii. 3.

FLESHMENT. Pride, stimulated by newly-achieved success. A soldier is said to 'flesh his sword,' when first he draws blood with it, Lear ii. 2.

FLEWED. Having overhanging chaps, like a hound; called 'Flews,' Mids. N. iv. 1.

FLIBBERTIGIBBET. The name of a fiend, Lear iii. 4.

FLICKERING. Fluttering, as flame, Lear ii. 2.

FLIGHT. A light, slender arrow for shooting at long distances, Much Ado i. 1.

FLIRT-GILL. A light-charactered wench, Rom. J. ii. 4.

FLOTE. A poetical name for the sea, as waves; Fr. Flot, a wave, Temp. i. 2.

FLUSH. Ripe, full, luxuriant, Ant. Cl. i. 4. Ham. iii. 3.

FLUSHING. Springing; and moreover, the redness occasioned by weeping, Ham. i. 2.

FOIN. To thrust fiercely in fencing, Mer. W. ii. 3, Lear iv. 6.

FOISON. Abundance, especially applicable to harvest, Temp. ii. 1 & iv. 1, (Song,) Macb. iv. 3, Ant. Cl. ii. 7.

FOND. Weakly loving, foolish, Rom. J. iii. 3, Ham. i. 5, Lear i. 4 & iv. 7.

FOND AND WINNOWED. Esteemed and choice, Ham. v. 2.

FOOLS' ZANIES. Fools' baubles; which had a fool's head on them, Tw. N. i. 5. See BAUBLE.

FOOT. To kick, to spurn, Mer. Ven. i. 3.

FOOT-CLOTH. The housing to a horse; used on state occasions, Rich. III. iii. 4.

FOR. Used in the sense of 'because,' or 'since,' Oth. i. 3.

FORCED. Supplied with forces, manned, strengthened, Macb. v. 5.

FORDO. To undo, to destroy, Ham. v. 1, Oth. v. 1, Lear v. 3.

FOREHAND. Previous, Much Ado iv. 1.

FORMAL. Sedate, rational, sane, Tw. N. ii. 5.

FORMER. Used for foremost, Jul. Cæs. v. 1.

FORSPOKE. Anticipated, forbidden, Ant. Cl. iii. 7.

FORTHRIGHT. A direct path, Temp. iii. 3.

FOUR. This word (like "forty") seems to have been occasionally used to express an indefinite number, Ham. ii. 2, Ant. Cl. ii. 6 & 7.

FRAMPOLD. Vexatious, uncomfortable, Mer. W. ii. 2.

FRANKED UP. Styed, like swine, Rich. III. i. 3 & iv. 5.

FRAY. An affray, a fight, Mer W. ii. 1, Much Ado v. 1, Mids. N. iii. 2.

FREE. Shakespeare, Chaucer, and other early poets, use this word for free from vicious taint, pure, chaste. Tw. N. ii. 4.

FRENCH CROWN. The term has three significations : — a piece of French money ; the head of a Frenchman ; and a disease in the scalp, said to be French. Shakespeare plays upon the words, Mids. N. i. 2.

FRETS. The stopping-points in a lute or guitar, Tam. S. ii. 1, Ham. iii. 2.

FRIPPERY. Originally meaning an old clothes-shop ; now confined to its contents. Temp. iv. 1.

FRIZE. A coarse woollen cloth, made in Wales, Mer. W. v. 5, Oth. ii. 1.

FRONTLET. A forehead-band, metaphorically meaning a scowling look, Lear i. 4.

FULLAMS. Loaded dice so named. They were called 'high fullams,' or 'low fullams,' according as they were required. They were chiefly made at Fulham, in Middlesex ; hence the name, Mer. W. i. 3.

FUMITER. A rampant weed in corn, Lear iv. 4.

FURNISHINGS. Appendages, Lear iii. 1.

FUST. To mould, or grow fusty, Ham. iv. 4.

G

GABERDINE. A coarse cloak, or gown ; Span. *Gavardina*, Temp. ii. 2, Mer. Ven. i. 3.

GAD. A sharp point, a spur. "Upon the gad," on the spur of the occasion, Lear i. 2.

GAGE. Pledge. Used also for 'gauge,' to measure, Mer. Ven. i. 1.

GAGED. Laid as a wager, Ham. i. 1.

GAIN-GIVING. Uncertainty of mind, misgiving, Ham. v. 2.

GAIT. Procedure, Ham. i. 2.

GALLIARD. A French dance, lively and nimble. Tw. N. i. 3.

GALLIASSES. Galleys of large construction, Tam. S. ii. 1.

GALLOW. To scare, to frighten, Lear iii. 2.

GALLOWGLASSES. Heavy-armed foot-soldiers of Ireland and the Western Isles, Macb. i. 2.

GALLY-MAWFRY. A heterogeneous jumble, Mer. W. ii. 1.

GAMESTER. A familiar term for a debauchee of either sex, Hen. VIII. i. 4.

GAPING. Bawling, Hen. VIII. v. 3.

GARBOILS. Uproars, commotions, Ant. Cl. i. 3 & ii. 2. Fr. *Garbouille*.

GASKINS. Wide hose, or breeches, Tw. N. i. 5.

GASTED. Ghasted, made aghast, affrighted, Lear ii. 1.

GASTNESS. Ghastness, or ghastliness, Oth. v. 1.

GAUDY NIGHT. A 'gaudy day' is a day of rejoicing and festivity. Still used in the English universities and inns of court, Ant. Cl. iii. 11.

GAWDS. Toys, finery, gewgaws, Mids. N. i. 1.

GEAR. Matter in hand, Mer. Ven. i. 1.

GECK. A fool, a dupe, Tw. N. v. 1.

GENERAL. The populace, Ham. ii. 2.

GENERAL GENDER. The common race of people, Ham. iv. 7.

GENEROUS. Noble in birth and rank, Oth. iii. 3.

GENNET. A Jennet, a Spanish or Barbary horse, Oth. i. 1.

GENTILITY. High birth, and breeding, As you L. i. 1.

GENTLE. Belonging to gentry, noble, high-minded, Temp. i. 2.

GENTLES. Gentlemen, Tam. S. iii. 2.

GENTRY. Used for urbanity, politeness, Ham. ii. 2.

GERMANE, *or* GERMAN. Akin, allied, Ham. v. 2.

GERMANS. Relations, Oth. i. 1.

GERMINS. Seeds, germinations, Macb. iv. 1, Lear iii. 2.

GESTS. Deeds, exploits ; Lat. *Gesta*, Ant. Cl. iv. 7. [In some editions, given "guests."]

GHOSTED. Haunted, ghost-like, Ant. Cl. ii. 6.

GIB. A male cat. The gib cat is now called the tom cat ; gib being the abbreviation of Gilbert, Ham. iii. 4.

GING. A gang, Mer. W. iv. 2.

GIRDLE. To turn the girdle, meant, that when a man intended to challenge another at wrestling, he turned the buckle of his belt behind ; that his adversary might have a good gripe of his girdle, Much Ado v. 1.

GIS. Supposed to be a substituted form of asseveration for 'Jesus,' Ham. iv. 5, (Song.)

GLEEK. To joke, to scoff, or beguile, Mids. N. iii. 1, Rom. J. iv. 5.

GLUT. To swallow up, to englut ; Fr. *Engloutir*, Temp. i. 1.

GO TO THE WORLD. Meaning to be married, Much Ado ii. 1.

GODFATHERS. Formerly the twelve jurymen used to be jocosely called the prisoner's godfathers, Mer. Ven. iv. 1.

GOD 'ILD, *or* 'IELD. Corruption of God yield, or reward you, Ham. iv. 5.

GOD'S SONTIES. Thought to be a corruption of God's saints ; anciently written *sanctes*, Mer. Ven. ii. 2.

GONGARIAN. Pistol's more sonorous form of 'Hungarian,' Mer. W. i. 3.

GOOD DEN. Good even, or evening. (See DEN.) Much Ado iii. 2.

GOOD MY LORD, *and* GOOD MADAM. A form of polite acknowledgment, equivalent to our modern, 'You are very good,' Ham. ii. 1 & ii. 2 & v. 2.

GOSS, *or* GORSE. Furze. A heath plant, bearing yellow blossoms, Temp. iv. 1.

GOSSAMER. (Spelt also, Gossomer.) The webs of a particular kind of spider, that float in the air during the latter summer season, Lear iv. 6, Rom. J. ii. 6.

GOURDS. False dice. (See FULLAM.) Mer. W. i. 3.

GOUTS. Drops ; Fr. *Gouttes*, Macb. ii. 1.

GOVERNMENT. Mildness and gentle submission, with self-control and reticence, Hen. VIII. ii. 4.

GRAMERCY. Great thanks ; Fr. *Grand merci*, Mer. Ven. ii. 2, Rich. III. iii. 2. "Gramercies," Tam. S. i. 1.

GRANGE. The farm-house, or granary to a monastery, Oth. i. 1.

GRAVE. Deadly, fatal, Ant. Cl. iv. 10.

GRISE. (Spelt also, Grize.) A step, a degree, Tw. N. iii. 1, Oth. i. 3.

GROUND. A term in music. The subject, or air upon which variations, or descants are made, Rich. III. iii. 7.

GROUNDLINGS. The audience in the pit of a theatre, which was also called the 'Ground;' and the seats, 'ground-stands,' Ham. iii. 2.

GUARDED. Ornamented with trimmings, Mer. Ven. ii. 2, Hen. VIII. (Prol.)

GUARDS. Embroideries, or lace trimmings on dress, Much Ado i. 1.

GUDGEON. The Gudgeon is a common bait for fish. It is itself, also, easily caught; and therefore esteemed foolish, Mer. Ven. i. 3.

GUERDON. Recompense, Much Ado v. 3, (Scroll.)

GUINEA HEN. A cant term for a purchasable woman, Oth. i. 3.

GULES. A term in heraldry for the colour of red, Ham. ii. 2.

GULF. Throat, gullet; that which gulps, or engulfs, Macb. iv. 1.

GULL. A trick, Much Ado ii. 3. To dupe, to trick, Tw. N. ii. 3.

GUST. Zest, relish, Tw. N. i. 3.

GYVE. To fetter, Oth. ii. 1.

H

HAGGARD. An untrained hawk, Tw. N. iii. 1, Much Ado iii. 1, Tam. S. iv. 1 & iv. 2. In the sense of irreclaimable, Oth. iii. 3.

HAIR. Quality, texture, character. 'Against the hair,' is a saying equivalent to 'Against the grain,' Mer. W. ii. 3.

HALCYON. The king fisher. It was believed that when hung up in a room, this bird would always turn its beak to the point of the wind, Lear ii. 2.

A HALL, A HALL! An exclamation, to clear a space in a crowd, Rom. J. i. 5.

HAND. "At any hand;" or "In any hand." A phrase or idiom, for 'At all events,' 'In any case,' Tam. S. i. 2. "Of his hands," was a technical phrase, for 'Of his height,' Mer. W. i. 4.

HANGER. The loop of the belt in which the sword was suspended, Ham. v. 2.

HAPPILY. Used for haply, perchance, Oth. iii. 3, Ham. i. 1.

HARLOCK. Supposed to be Charlock, the wild mustard, — a common field weed, Lear iv. 4.

HARNESS. Armour; Fr. Harnois, Macb. v. 5, Ant. Cl. iv. 8.

HARRIED. The same meaning as Harrowed. To harass, torment, ill-treat, Ant. Cl. iii. 3.

HAVING. Used as a substantive, for possession, or property, Mer. W. iii. 2, Macb. i. 3. "Havings," Hen. VIII. iii. 2.

HAVOCK. A word of signal for general slaughter; for no quarter to be given, Jul. Cæs. iii. 1, Ham. v. 2.

HEBENON. Ebony. The juice was said to be a poison, Ham. i. 5.

HEDGE. To swerve, to deviate; still a sporting term, Mer. W. ii. 2.

HEFTS. "Tender-hefted," i. e. moved, or heaved tenderly, Lear ii. 4.

HENCHMAN. An attendant page. The etymology contested, Mids. N. ii. 2.

HENT. Seized. Used for occasion, or opportunity to be seized, Ham. iii. 3.

HERB OF GRACE. Rue, Ham. iv. 5.

HEST. Injunction, command, Temp. i. 2, iii. 1, iv. 1.

HIDE FOX AND ALL AFTER. A commonly-known boys' game, called 'All-hid,' and 'Hide and seek,' Ham. iv. 2.

HIGH AND LOW. A cant phrase for false dice, Mer. W. i. 3.

HIGHT. Called, named, Mids. N. v. 1.

HILDING. A low, cowardly rascal; a mean woman, Tam. S. ii. 1, Rom. J. ii. 4 & iii. 5.

HIP. To "have on the hip;" i. e. at complete advantage, Mer. Ven. i. 3, Oth. ii. 1.

HIS. Almost always used for 'its' by old writers. "His grand sea," Ant. Cl. iii. 10.

HOBBIDIDANCE. The name of a fiend, Lear iv. 1.

HOBBY-HORSE. A mimic horse, that figured in the morris-dance. Latterly, omitted; which gave rise to the almost proverbial expression, "The hobby-horse is forgot," Ham. iii. 2.

HOB, NOB. Derived from 'Hab, nab;' which means have, or not have; German, Haben. Hob, or nob, is a drinking expression; 'Will you have a glass or not?' It was used to signify a choice of any kind, Tw. N. iii. 4.

HOLDING. Burden, or (in modern parlance) Chorus, Ant. Cl. ii. 7.

HOLIDAME. An exclamation, thought to mean,—'By the Virgin Mary,' Tam. S. v. 2.

HOLP. Perfect tense of to help, Temp. i. 2.

HOODMAN-BLIND. The game of blind-man's buff, Ham. iii. 4.

HOP-DANCE. The name of a fiend, Lear iii. 6.

HORN IS DRY. A horn was carried by the Bedlam beggars, which they wound when arriving at a house to ask alms, and into which they put what drink they were given. Shakespeare, in making Edgar exclaim "Poor Tom, thy horn is dry," not only assigns him a speech which is a last attempt to preserve the character he has assumed, as containing a mendicant hint that his horn needs replenishing, but which possesses an exquisite double significance, as allusive to his powers of "counterfeiting" being exhausted at sight of Lear's condition, Lear iii. 6.

HOROLOGE. A clock; Lat. Horologium, Oth. ii. 3.

HOSE. Breeches and stockings, both in one, Mer. W. iii. 1.

HOUSE. Used in the sense of the head of the house, Lear ii. 4.

HUGGER-MUGGER. Low, unworthy hiding, or concealment, Ham. iv. 5.

HULL. To float listlessly on the waves, Rich. III. iv. 4. Tw. N. i. 5. "Hulling," Hen. VIII. ii. 4.

HUMOROUS. Humid, damp, Rom. J. ii. 1. Also used for humorsome, or capricious, As you L. i. 1.

HUMOUR. Any peculiarity or eccentricity of conduct or manner, was termed a man's humour. Shakespeare ridiculed the coxcombry of the application in the character of Nym, Mer. W. ii. 1.

HUNDRED MERRY TALES. An old jest-book so titled, Much Ado ii. 1.

HUNTS-UP. A song to rouse hunters in a morning, Rom. J. iii. 5.

HURLY. Tumult, uproar, confusion, Tam. S. iv. 1. "Hurly-burly," Macb. i. 1.

HURRICANO. A water-spout, Lear iii. 2.

HURTLED. Clashed, struggling together; Fr. Heurter, Jul. Cæs. ii. 2, As you L. iv. 3.

HUSBANDRY. Household government, Mer. Ven. iii. 4. Thrift, frugality, economy, Macb. ii. 1. Industry, Ham. i. 3.

HYEM. Winter, Mids. N. ii. 2.

HYEN. The hyena, As you L. iv. 1.

I

I. In Shakespeare's time the personal pronoun, I, was constantly used for the word of assent, "Ay ;"—hence the tendency to pun upon the term, Rom. J. iii. 2.

I. Used to be repeated, for emphasis sake, at the end of a phrase, Rom. J. iii. 1 & 5.

IMMEDIACY. Absolute representation. Lear v. 3.

IMMOMENT. Unimportant, not momentous, Ant. Cl. v. 2.

IMPARTMENT. Imparting, making a communication, Ham. i. 4.

IMPONE. To lay down by way of wager ; from the Lat. *Impono.* It may represent Osric's affected way of pronouncing 'impawned,' Ham. v. 2.

IMPORTANCE. Importunity, Tw. N. v. 1.

IMPORTANT. Importunate, urgent, Much Ado ii. 1.

IMPRESS. Forcible enlistment, Ant. Cl. iii. 7, Ham. i. 1. To compel to subjection, Macb. iv. 1.

IMPUTATION. For imputed excellence. Ham. v. 2.

INCARDINATE. Ague-Cheek's ignorant use of the word 'incarnate,' Tw. N. v. 1.

INCARNARDINE. To stain of a carnation-red colour, Macb. ii. 2.

INCENSED. Prompted, urged, instructed, Much Ado v. 1, Rich. III. iii. 1, Hen. VIII. v. 1.

INCH. An island. An Erse word, Macb. i. 2.

INCH-MEAL. By an inch at a time ; as we now say, piecemeal, Temp. ii. 2.

INCISION. Literally, cutting ; Lat. *Incido.* 'To make incision,' was a surgical phrase for bleeding ; humorously employed as a wish for letting some of the foolish blood out of the person addressed, As you L. iii. 2.

INCLIPS. Embraces, encircles, Ant. Cl. ii. 7.

INCONTINENT,. INCONTINENTLY. Immediately, suddenly, Oth. i. 3.

INCORPSED. Incorporated, made one body, Ham. iv. 7.

INDEX. Used in the sense of pre-indication, as well as subject-matter, Rich. III. ii 2 & iv. 4, Ham. iii. 4, Oth. ii. 1.

INDIFFERENT. Impartial, Hen. VIII. ii. 4. Moderately, Tw. N. i. 3 & 5, Ham. iii. 1, "Indifferent children of the earth ;" generality of mortals, Ham. ii. 2.

INDIGN. Unworthy. Lat. *Indignus,* Oth. i. 3.

INDIRECTION. Wrong, or crooked course, Jul. Cæs. iv. 3.

INDIRECTLY. Wrongfully, Rich. III. iv. 4.

INDITE. To summon, to convict, Rom. J. ii. 4, Ham. ii. 2.

INDUED. Invested, endowed, provided, Ham. iv. 7.

INDURANCE. For durance, confinement, imprisonment, Hen. VIII. v. I.

INHERIT. Used simply for to obtain, or possess, with no reference to inheritance, Rom. J. i. 2.

INHIBITED. Prohibited, forbidden, Oth. i. 2.

INHOOPED. Cocks and quails, when matched for fighting, were confined within hoops, Ant. Cl. ii. 3.

INIQUITY. The 'Vice,' or Buffoon, in the old dramas or moralities, went also by the title of "Iniquity," Rich. III. iii. 1.

INLAND BRED. Meaning, gently, or well bred ; in opposition to upland bred, which meant rough and unpolished, As you L. ii. 7 & iii. 2.

INSANE ROOT. Probably henbane, Macb. i. 3.

INSTANCE. Motive, Rich. III. iii. 2, Ham. iii. 2.

INSUPPRESSIVE. Not to be restrained, Jul. Cæs. ii. 1.

INTEND. To pretend, Tam. S. iv. 1. "Intending," Rich. III. iii. 5.

INTENDMENT. Intention, As you L. i. 1.

INTENTIVELY. Attentively, heedfully, Oth. i. 3.

INTERESS'D. Become of interest, prove acceptable, Lear i. 1.

INTERGATORIES. Interrogatories, Mer. Ven. v. 1.

INTRENCHANT. That which may not be cut, Macb. v. 7.

INTRINSE. Intricate, Lear ii. 2. "Intrinsicate," Ant. Cl. v. 2.

INVECTIVELY. Abusively, As you L. ii. 1.

INWARD. Intimate, closely confiding, Rich. III. iii. 4.

INWARDNESS. Familiarity, attachment, Much Ado iv. 1.

IRK. To vex, to distress, As you L. ii. 1.

ITERANCE. Iteration, Oth. v. 2.

J

JACK-A-LENT. A puppet thrown at during Lent, as were cocks on Shrove Tuesday, Mer. W. iii. 3 & v. 5.

JACK O' THE CLOCK. A figure on the outside of public clocks. Rich. III. iv. 2.

JAY. An ill-charactered woman, Mer. W. iii. 3.

JESSES. The thongs which held the hawks to the fist, Oth. iii. 3.

JET. To strut, to throw forth the body in walking, Tw. N. ii. 5.

JEW. Used humorously as a term of endearment, Mids. N. iii. 1.

JOHN-A-DREAMS. A sleepyheaded, lumpish fellow, Ham. ii. 2.

JOINT-RING. A united, or jointed ring, Oth. iv. 3.

JUMP. Precisely, coincident with, immediately upon, Oth. ii. 3, Ham. v. 2. To run a risk, a hazard. Macb. i. 7. A chance, turn of fortune, Ant. Cl. iii. 8.

JUNKET, *or* **JUNCATE.** Ital. *Giuncata.* A sweetmeat, or dainty, Tam. S. iii. 2.

JUSTICERS. Magistrates, or justices of the peace were so called, Lear iii. 6.

JUT. To intrude or encroach upon, Rich. III. ii. 4.

JUTTY. A projecting portion of a building, Macb. i. 6.

JUVENAL. A playful name for a youth, Mids. N. iii. 1.

K

KEECH. A lump of fat made into a roll ; a mass of grossness, Hen. VIII. i. 1.

KEISAR. An old form of Cæsar, Mer. W. i. 3.

KERCHIEF. A covering for the head ; which it was an old English custom to wear in illness, Jul. Cæs. ii. 1.

KERNES. Peasants, Irish foot-soldiers, Macb. i. 2 & v. 7.

KIBE. A sort of chilblain, Temp. ii. 1, Ham. v. 1.

KID-FOX. The fox known to be hidden ; 'kidde being a word for 'known,' 'detected,' in Chaucer's time, Much Ado ii. 3.

KILL, KILL, KILL! This was the ancient onset-cry in the English army, Lear iv. 6.

KIND. Nature, Jul. Cæs. i. 3, Ant. Cl. v. 2.

KINDLE. To incite, to induce, As you L. i. 1.

KINDLESS. Unnatural, Ham. ii. 2.

KINDLY. Punningly for amiably and for appositely or aptly, Rom. J. ii. 4.

KNAPPED. Snapped, or broke, Mer. Ven. iii. 1.

KNAVE. A boy, or servant lad ; Sax. *Knabe,* Ant. Cl. iv. 12 & v. 2, Lear i. 4. The meaning has now wholly subsided into the synonyme of rogue.

KNIFE. Often used for dagger, or sword, Macb. i. 5 & 7.

KNOT-GRASS. Formerly reputed to have the power of stopping growth, when taken in infusion, Mids. N. iii. 2.

L

LABRAS. Spanish for lips, Mer. W. i. 1.

LACKEYING. Servilely following, or obeying, Ant. Cl. i. 4.

LAG. Late, last, tardy; also, by metaphor, the lowest or commonest people, Rich, III. ii. 1.

LAKIN. A diminutive, for Ladykin, or Little Lady; "By'r Lakin," is, by our Lady, Temp. iii. 3, Mids. N. iii. 1.

LAMPASS. A disorder in cattle; a tumour in the gums, Tam. S. ii. 1.

LANCES. Used upon one occasion for Lancers, or Lancemen, Lear v. 3.

LANGUISH. For languishment, Rom. J. i. 2, Ant. Cl. v. 2.

LAPSED. Shakespeare seems to use this word as expressive of inadvertency; negligently straying, thoughtlessly lost, Tw. N. iii. 3, Ham. iii. 4.

LAPWING. Plover, and Peewit; all names for the same bird. Believed to lure strangers from its nest by crying and limping, as if wounded. Much Ado iii. 1, Ham. v. 2.

LARGE. Used for coarse, free, Much Ado iv. 1.

LASS-LORN. Mistress-bereft, Temp. iv. 1.

LATCH. To catch hold of, Macb. iv. 3.

LATCHED. Anointed, smeared, Mids. N. iii. 2.

LATED. Overtaken by the night, Macb. iii. 3, Ant. Cl. iii. 9.

LATTEN. An old word for brass; Fr. Laiton, Mer. W. i. 1.

LAY. A wager, Oth. ii. 3.

LEA. A field, or meadow, Sax. Temp. iv. 1.

LEAD APES. An uncomplimentary phrase respecting the vocation assigned to those old maids in the next world who have been coquettes in this, Much Ado ii. 1.

LEASING. Lying, Tw. N. i. 5.

LEER. Complexion, look, As you L. iv. 1.

LEET. A court of jurisdiction for petty offences, Tam. S. 2, (Ind.) Oth. iii. 3.

LEMAN. A paramour, a lover, Mer. W. iv. 2, Tw. N. ii. 3.

LENTEN. Spare, fasting, pertaining to Lent time, Tw. N. i. 5, Rom. J. ii. 4, Ham. ii. 2.

LET. To hinder, Tw. N. v. 1, Ham. i. 4. Hindrance, Rom. J. ii. 2.

LETHE. Oblivion. Lethe, the river of oblivion in the Greek mythology, Tw. N. iv. 1, Rich. III. iv. 4, Ant. Cl. ii. 7, Ham. i. 5.

LETHE. Death, from the Lat. Lethum, Jul. Cæs. iii. 1. In this sense, Lethe seems to have been used and sounded as a monosyllable by our old writers.

LEWD. Wicked. Much Ado v. 1. Idle, obnoxious, Rich. III. i. 3.

LIBERAL. Coarse-spoken, free-spoken, Much Ado iv. 1, Ham. iv. 7, Oth. ii. 1.

LIBERTY. Used to express the licence of employing the actors' own words in extempore performance, in opposition to the "law of writ" —the written words set down for them by an author in a regularly composed play, Ham. ii. 2.

LIEGEMAN. One bound to do feudal service, Ham. i. 1.

LIGHT O' LOVE. A dance-tune, Much Ado iii. 4.

LIGHTLY. In common course, usually, Rich. III. iii. 1.

LIKED. Pleased, As you L. (Epil.)

LIMBECK. An alembic, or distilling vessel, Macb. i. 7.

LIMBO PATRUM. The name of the place where the Fathers of the church awaited their resurrection; used jocosely for a prison, Hen. VIII. v. 3.

LIME. Put into wine for adulteration, Mer. W. i. 3.

LINE OF LIFE. The lines in the palm of the hand expounded by gipsies, and other cheats in palmistry, Mer. Ven. ii. 2.

LINED. Drawn, delineated, As you L. iii. 2, (verses.)

LINK. A torch of pitch. Incredible as it may appear, the smoke of a link was used to blacken rusty hats, Tam. S. iv. 1.

LIST. Limit, or boundary. A term derived from the lists at a tournament, Tw. N. iii. 1, Ham. iv. 5, Oth. iv. 1. Also, desire, inclination, Oth. ii. 1.

LIST. To listen, Mer. W. v. 5, Oth. ii. 1, Also, to like, to prefer. Oth. ii. 3.

LIVELIHOOD. Living appearance, liveliness, Rich. III. iii. 4.

LOB. A lubber, a clown. Puck was the jester (or 'clown') to King Oberon, Mids. N. ii. 1.

LOCK, or LOVE-LOCK. A long lock of hair, worn at the side of the head; often plaited with ribband, Much Ado iii. 3.

LODE-STAR. The pole-star, and guide to mariners, Mids. N. i. 1.

LODGED. Layed by the wind, Macb. iv. 1.

LOFFE. An old form of laugh, Mids. N. ii. 1.

LOGGATS. The diminutive of logs. A game formerly played by rustics, somewhat resembling nine-pins, Ham. v. 1.

'LONGS. "Longing," for belonging, Hen. VIII. i. 2.

LONGLY. For longingly, Tam. S. i. 1.

LOOFED. Now spelt luffed. A ship brought close to the wind, Ant. Cl. iii. 8.

LOON. A stupid fellow, a clown, Macb. v. 3.

LOP. A cutting from a tree, Hen. VIII. i. 2.

LOVER. Formerly meant any one who was beloved of another, male or female. Between men, it signified a bosom-friend, Mer. Ven. iii. 4.

LOWN. Another form of Loon. Oth. ii. 3. (Song.)

LUCE. A pike fish, or jack, Mer. W. i. 1.

LUNES. Lunacy, frenzy, Mer. W. iv. 2, Ham. iii. 3.

LURCH. To win from, to gain by distancing, Mer. W. ii. 2.

LURE. The bait for a hawk, Tam. S. iv. 1. To entice, to tempt, Rom. J. ii. 2.

LUSH. Of rich or luxuriant vegetation; hence, probably 'luscious,' Temp. ii. 1.

LUXURIOUS. Wanton, unchaste, Much Ado iv. 1.

LYM. A sporting-hound led by a thong, called a Leam or Leash, Lear iii. 6.

M

MAGGOT-PIES. Now called Magpies; Fr. Magot, a chatterer. Macb. iii. 4.

MAGNIFICO. The title of the Venetian nobles, Oth. i. 2, Mer. Ven. iii. 2.

MAKE. "What make you here?" for, what are you doing here? As you L. i. 1 & 3. Ham. ii. 2. "Make the doors," to fasten, or shut them close, As you L. iv. 1.

MALT-HORSE. A heavy cart-horse, like a brewer's horse, Tam. S. iv. 1.

MAMMERING. Stammering, hesitating, Oth. iii. 3.

MAMMETS. Dolls, or puppets, Rom. J. iii. 5.

MANAGE. A term originating in the tilt-yard. A career, or course run. Likewise for horse-training; Fr. Manège, As you L. i. 1.

MANDRAGORA, *or* MANDRAKE. A root possessing strong soporific qualities; superstitiously believed to utter groans when torn up; and that the uprooter died mad, Ant. Cl. i. 5, Oth. iii. 3, Rom. J. iv. 3.

MARCH-PANE. A confectionary compounded of sugar and pounded almonds, Rom. J. i. 5.

MARGENT *or* MARGIN. Alluding to the margins of old books, which contained a commentary on the subject-matter of the page, Rom. J. i. 3, Ham. v. 2.

MARRY TRAP. A cant exclamation, when likely to be caught, Mer. W. i. 1.

MART. To traffic, or deal; from the substantive, Mart, a market, Jul. Cæs. iv. 3.

MATED. To bewilder, stupefy, confound, or overpower, Macb. v. 1.

MAUGRE. In spite of; Fr. *Malgré*, Tw. N. iii. 1, Lear v. 3.

MAW. The stomach, Macb. iv. 1.

MAZZARD. A familiar word for the head, Ham. v. 1, Oth. ii. 3.

MEACOCK. A sneak and a coward, Tam. S. ii. 1.

MEASURE. A grave and stately dance, Much Ado ii. 1, As you L. v. 4.

MEED. Reward, desert, Ham. v. 2.

MEET WITH. An idiom, for to frustrate, or counteract, Temp. iv. 1. "To be meet with," was equivalent to, 'To be even with,' Much Ado i. 1.

MEINY. A lord's household retinue, or train of menials, Lear ii. 4.

MEPHOSTOPHILUS. The name of the familiar spirit, or the Devil, in Marlowe's play of 'Faustus,' Mer. W. i. 1.

MERCATANTE. A merchant, Tam. S. iv. 2.

MERCHANT. Sometimes employed as a term of familiarity, also of contempt, Rom. J. ii. 4.

MERED. Bounded, limited, defined, Ant. Cl. iii. 11.

METAL. Used in its legitimate sense as a mineral, and sometimes blendedly with the sense which it has obtained, from its oral resemblance with the word Mettle, which means temper, temperament, courage, Jul. Cæs. i. 1, Much Ado ii. 1.

METAPHYSICAL. Formerly used in the sense of supernatural, Macb. i. 5.

METE-YARD. A yard-measure, Tam. S. iv. 3.

METHEGLIN. Mead; a beverage made of honey, Mer. W. v. 5.

METTLE. See METAL.

MEWED. Confined, shut up, Mids. N. i. 1, Tam. S. i. 1, Rich. III. i. 1 & 3, Rom. J. iii. 4.

MICHING MALLECHO. Lurking malice, or mischief. To 'mich,' means to skulk, to act stealthily; and 'malheco' is a Spanish word, signifying misdeed, or evil-doing, Ham. iii. 2.

MICKLE. Still the Scotch term for much, or great, Rom. J. ii. 3.

MIDDLE EARTH. Formerly a term in frequent use for our globe, Mer. W. v. 5.

MIDDLE SUMMER'S SPRING. The season when vegetation puts forth its second shoot, Mids. N. ii. 1.

MIEN. Countenance. "The revolt of mien," is the 'change of countenance' which Nym hopes Page will betray when made jealous; and which will make him dangerously vengeful, Mer. W. i. 3.

MILL-SIXPENCES. Queen Elizabeth first introduced the coining by the mill into England about 1562, Mer. W. i. 1.

MILLSTONES. To "weep millstones" was an old saying of those not given to the melting mood, Rich. III. i. 3 & 4.

MINCE. To make affectedly small steps, to trip along, Mer. W. v. 1.

MINIKIN. Very diminutive, Lear iii. 6, (Song.)

MISPRISED. Mistaken, Mids. N. iii. 2. Undervalued, As you L. i. 1 & 2.

MISPRISING. Underrating, not estimating, Much Ado iii. 1.

MISSIVES. Messengers, Macb. i. 5, (let.), Ant. Cl. ii. 2.

MISTAKEN. Misinterpreted, misconstrued, Hen. VIII. i. 1.

MISTEMPERED. Wrathful, ill-conditioned, Rom. J. i. 1.

MISTRESS. A title often appended to a woman's name formerly, whether she were a maiden or a wife. "Mistress Anne Page," Mer. W. i. 1. We find that Mistress Quickly is unmarried, Mer. W. ii. 2.

MOBLED. Muffled, or negligently covered on the head. Mob-cap is a modern term for an undress cap, Ham. ii. 2.

MODERN. Common, trite, ordinary, Ant. Cl. v. 2, Rom. J. iii. 2, As you L. ii. 7 & iv. 1.

MOE. To ridicule by making mouths, Temp. ii. 2.

MOIETY. A part, not merely a half, Lear i. 1.

MOMENTANY. Used by others as well as Shakespeare for momentary, Mids. N. i. 1.

MONTANT. Abbreviation of *Montanto*, a term in fencing, Mer. W. ii. 3. Beatrice gives the latter as a mocking title to Benedick, Much Ado i. 1.

MOON-CALF. A lumpish and shapeless mass; a monster, Temp. ii. 2 & iii. 2.

MOONISH. Changeable, As you L. iii. 2.

MOONSHINE. "A sop o' the moonshine" was a sippet in a dish of eggs, dressed after a peculiar fashion, called 'Eggs in moonshine,' Lear ii. 2.

MORAL. Formerly meant the sense or signification of a thing, Much Ado iii. 4, Tam. S. iv. 4.

MORALIZE. To expound, to deduce a meaning from, Rich. III. iii. 1.

MORTIFIED. Ascetic, devoted to self-denial, Macb. v. 2.

MORTISE. A joint in timber-work, Oth. ii. 1.

MOSE. "To mose in the chine," is a disease in horses, somewhat varying from the glanders; which consists of a discharge from the nose, Tam. S. iii. 2.

MOST. Was frequently used by the old writers with adjectives already in the superlative degree, in order to add emphasis to the meaning. "Most poorest," Lear ii. 3. "Most best," Ham. ii 2. "Most unkindest," Jul. Cæs. iii. 2. The comparative, "More," was applied in the same way. "More corrupter," Lear ii. 2. "More better," Temp. i. 2.

MOTHER. There was a disease known by this name, and by that of *hysterica passio*, Lear ii. 4.

MOTION. A name for a puppet, and puppet-show. Also used to signify wishes, or desires, Tw. N. ii. 4. And indignation, Hen. VIII. i. 1. Likewise for divinatory agitation, Ant. Cl. ii. 3.

MOTLEY. The Fool or Jester's parti-coloured dress. As you L. ii. 7, Hen. VIII. (Prol.)

MOUSE. A term of endearment, Ham. iii. 4.

MOUSED. Mammocked, torn in pieces, Mids. N. v. 1.

MOW. Used in the same way as MOE, Temp. iv. 1, Ham. ii. 2.

MUCH. An exclamation of disdain and denial. Used adjectively in the same sense ; "Here much Orlando," As you L. iv. 3.

MUFFLER. A sort of veil to cover the lower part of the face and throat, Mer. W. iv. 2.

MUM BUDGET. A cant signal, or nay-word, implying silence, Mer. W. v. 2.

MUMMY. A liquor, or balsam, prepared from the embalmed Egyptian bodies, Oth. iii. 4.

MURDERING-PIECE. A small piece of artillery so called, Ham. iv. 5.

MURKY. Dark, Macb. v. 1.

MURRAIN. A plague in cattle, Temp. iii. 2, Mids. N ii. 2.

MUSCADEL. A rich French wine ; so named from its possessing a musk flavour, Tam. S. iii. 2.

MUSCLE-SHELL. Falstaff's name for Simple, as a hint that he stands with his mouth open, Mer. W. iv. 5.

MUSE. To admire or wonder, Temp. iii. 3. Also to consider, to reflect upon, Mer. W. v. 5.

MUSS. A scramble for things thrown down to be snatched up, Ant. Cl. iii. 11.

MUTINES. Mutineers, Ham. v. 2.

N

NAPKIN. An old word for handkerchief, Ham. v. 2, Oth. iii. 3.

NAUGHT. "Be naught awhile." A phrase formerly in use, tantamount to 'Be hanged to you,' As you L. i. 1.

NAUGHTY. Formerly, this word had a much stronger signification than at present. It held its primitive force ; and meant worthless, worth naught or nothing, Much Ado v. 1, Mer. Ven. iii. 3, Lear iii. 7.

NAY-WORD. A watch-word, Mer. W. i. 2 & v. 2. Also, a bye-word, Tw. N. ii. 3.

NEAT. Oxen, horned cattle, Lear ii. 2.

NEEDLY. Needfully, necessarily, Rom. J. iii. 2.

NEELD. A form of the word, 'Needle,' where the measure required a monosyllable, Mids. N. iii. 2.

NEEZE. An old word for sneeze, Mids. N. ii. 1.

NEIF. Fist, or hand, Mids. N. iv. 1.

NETHER-STOCKS. Stockings ; nether meaning lower. The upper-stocks were the breeches. (See HOSE.) Lear ii. 4.

NETTLE. There is allusion in books of Shakespeare's period to the "nettle of India" being peculiarly smarting ; and this word far better suits the epithet Sir Toby applies to Maria than "metal," which some editors have printed instead of the "mettle" of the Folio edition. "Metal of India," as a mode of expression for gold, is far less characteristic of both Sir Toby's diction and Maria's stinging qualities than "nettle," Tw. N. ii. 5.

NEW-FANGLED. Frivolously new-fashioned, As you L. iv. 1.

NICE. Dainty, particular, precise, Much Ado v. 1. Trifling, foolish, Tam. S. iii, 1, Rom. J. v. 2.

NICKED. To score, or set a mark of folly upon, Ant. Cl. iii. 11.

NIGHT-RULE. Order of revelry, Mids. N. iii. 2.

NINEFOLD. A form of 'nine foals,' for the sake of rhyme, Lear iii. 4, (Song.)

NINE-MEN'S MORRIS. An old game played with nine holes, cut upon a square in a turf. There were nine players on a side ; one side using wooden pegs, the other stones. It is a rustic variation of an old French game, called *Mérelles*, which was played on a board, Mids. N. ii. 2.

NONCE. Purpose, occasion, Ham. iv. 7.

NONNY. and NONINO. Burdens to old songs ; as Fal-lal-la, As you L. v. 3, Ham. iv. 5, (Song,) Much Ado ii. 3, (Song.)

NOR. The old writers considered that the doubling of the negative strengthened the affirmation. "Nor never," Tam. S. iv. 3. "Nor no," and "Nor to no," Jul. Cæs. iii. 1.

NOTE. Knowledge, information, Lear iii. 1 & iv. 5.

NOVICE. One fresh and inexperienced, Tam. S. ii. 1, Rich. III. i. 4, Ant. Cl. iv. 10.

NOWL. The head, Mids. N. iii. 2.

NURTURE. Education, As you L. ii. 7.

NUTHOOK. A bailiff who hooks thieves, Mer. W. i. 1.

O

O. The single letter O was formerly employed to signify things circular. The earth, the world, Ant. Cl. v. 2. "Oes," refer to the stars, Mids. N. iii. 2.

OBLIGATION. Requirement, duty, bond, Lear ii. 4, Ham. i. 2 & ii. 2. Motive, inducement, Hen. VIII. ii. 3. Bond, in a legal sense ; a paper of contract, Mer. W. i. 1.

OBSEQUIOUS. Appertaining to funeral obsequies, Ham. i. 2. "Obsequiously," Rich. III. i. 2.

OCCUPATION. Used for mechanics, operatives, Jul. Cæs. i. 2.

O'ERCOUNT. To out-number, and to outdo by unfair means, Ant. Cl. ii. 6.

O'ERLOOKED. Bewitched, enchanted, Mer. W. v. 5, Mer. Ven. iii. 2.

O'ERRAUGHT. Caught up, or overtook, Ham. iii. 1.

OF ALL LOVES. For love's sake ; by all means, or, I entreat you, Mer. W. ii. 2, Mids. N. ii. 3.

OFFICES. Those apartments in the house appropriated to the domestics, and to where refreshments are prepared and served out, Macb. ii. 1. Oth. ii. 2.

OLD. An ancient form of the word 'wold,' a wild open plain, Lear iii. 4.

OLD. Frequently used in a humorous sense, signifying abundant, excessive, Mer. W. i. 4, Much Ado v. 2, Mer. Ven. iv. 2.

ONCE. In the sense of once for all, Much Ado i. 1.

ONCE. Used in the sense of 'one time or other,' 'sometime,' Mer. W. iii. 4, Hen. VIII. i. 2.

OPAL. A precious stone, varying in colour in various lights, Tw. N. ii. 4.

OPERANT. Operating, potent, Ham. iii. 2.

OPPOSITE. Antagonist, opponent, Tw. N. iii. 2 & 4.

ORBS. Fairies' circles on the grass, Mids. N. ii. 1.

ORDINANCE. Ordination, appointment, decree, Rich. III. iv. 4 & v. 4, Jul. Cæs. i. 3, Lear iv. 1.

ORDINANT. Swaying, directing, Ham. v. 2.

ORDINARY. A public dining-table, where each man pays his score, Ant. Cl. ii. 2.

'ORT. Sir Hugh Evans's Welsh abbreviation of 'Word.' Mer. W. i. 1.

OSTENT. Show, appearance, display, Mer. Ven. ii. 2.

OTHERGATES. In another manner, Tw. N. v. 1.

OTTOMITES. Turks, Ottomans, Oth. i. 3 & ii. 3.

OUPHES. Goblins, fairies, Mer. W. iv. 4 & v. 5.

OUSEL. The black-bird, Mids. N. iii. 1.

OUT. Fully, completely. "Out three years old," Temp. i. 2.

OWE. Frequently used for to own, have, or possess, Temp. i. 2, Mids. N. ii. 3.

OXLIP. The large cowslip, Mids. N. ii. 2.

O-YES. Old French, *Oyez,*— 'Hear ye !' The exclamation of the town-cryer, even at the present day, in England, Mer. W. v. 5.

P

PACKED. Sorted, or shuffled cards unfairly, Ant. Cl. iv. 12.

PACKINGS. Contrivances, underhand dealings, Lear iii. 1.

PADDOCK. The name for a toad : and hence, for an evil spirit, Ham. iii. 4, Macb. i. 1.

PAINTED CLOTH. Chamberhangings, similar to tapestry ; representing devices. with mottoes, and moral sentences, As you L. iii. 2.

PALABRAS. The Spanish for words. The B and the V being used in Spanish indiscriminately, the English word 'Palaver' is thence derived ; a term of contempt for over-much speech, Much Ado iii. 4. Corrupted into "Pallabris," Tam. S. 1. (Ind.)

PALE. To encircle, to confine, as within a paling, Ant. Cl. ii. 7.

PALL. To decline, wane, fall away, Ham. v. 2. To invest, as with a funereal pall, Macb. i. 5.

PALLED. Cloyed, waned, faded, dwindled, Ant. Cl. ii. 7.

PALMY. Victorious, triumphant : the Palm being the symbol of victory, Ham. i. 1.

PAPERS. Used as a verb ; for puts down in his paper, or "letter," Hen. VIII. i. 1.

PARCEL. A portion, part of, Mer. W. i. 1.

PARIS GARDEN. The celebrated beargarden in Southwark, London ; near to the Globe Theatre. So named from Robert of Paris, who had a house there in the reign of Rich. II. Hen. VIII. v. 3.

PARISH-TOP. A large whip-top was formerly kept in most towns and parishes for the amusement of the commonalty in winter, Tw. N. i. 3.

PARLE. The same signification as "Parley." A discussion or treaty, by word of mouth, Ham. i. 1.

PARLOUS. A common version of perilous. Mids. N. iii, 1, As you L. iii. 2, Rich. III. ii. 4 & iii. 1, Rom. J. i. 3.

PARTISAN. (Spelt also Partizan.) A pike, or halberd. Ant. Cl. ii. 7, Rom. J. i. 1, Ham. i. 1.

PASSADO. A thrust. An old fencing term, Rom. J. ii. 4 & iii. 1.

PASSAGE. One passing, a passenger, Oth. v. 1.

PASSED. "It passed." An expression implying, 'it passed belief,' Mer. W. i. 1.

PASSES. "This passes." i. e. exceeds all bounds, Mer. W. iv. 2.

PASSING. Extremely, Mids. N. ii. 1, Tam. S. ii. 1.

PASSION. To suffer, to feel passion, Temp. v. 1.

PASSY-MEASURE. A stately-stepping dance. Sir Toby in his drunken ire calls its object "a Passy-measures pavin," bungling up the names of two solemn dances into one, as a fitting epithet for a pompous fellow, Tw. N. v. 1.

PASTRY. The confectionary, or pastry-room, Rom. J. iv. 4.

PATCH. A fool. Ital. *Pazzo*; Temp. iii. 2, Mer. Ven. ii. 5, Macb. v. 3.

PATH. To go, as in a path, to walk, Jul. Cæs. ii. 1.

PATHETICAL. Affectedly lamentable, As you L. iv. 1.

PATINE. From the Latin *Patina;* the gold plate with which the priest covers the chalice at high mass. Poetically applied to the stars, Mer. Ven. v. 1.

PAUCA. Lat., *few.* Adopted as a cant expression for 'Let's have few words,' or 'Be brief,' Mer. W. i. 1.

PAUL'S. In St. Paul's Cathedral, London, was formerly transacted almost every description of business ; and even some amusements or games, Rich. III. iii. 6.

PAVIN. From the Latin *Pavo,* a peacock. A grave and stately dance, Tw. N. v. 1.

PEARL. A term used for whatever is highly valued. Here meaning the chief nobility, Macb. v. 7.

PEASCOD. The pea-shell, now called the pod, Tw. N. i. 5, As you L. ii. 4, Lear i. 4.

PEAT. A small, delicate, and favorite person : the origin of 'Pet.' Fr. *Petit;* Tam. S. i. 1.

PEDANT. A schoolmaster, Tam. S. iv. 2.

PEDASCULE. A whimsical name for a preceptor, or pedant, Tam. S. iii. 1.

PEEVISH. Silly, trifling, foolish, Mer. W. i. 4. Wayward, Tw. N. i. 5, Ham. i. 2, Oth. iv. 3. Fretful, cross, Mer. Ven. i. 1.

PEG-A-RAMSEY. The subject of an old ballad, Tw. N. ii. 3.

PEIZE. To weigh, or bear down. Fr. *Peser;* Mer. Ven. iii. 2, Rich. III. v. 3.

PELTING. Paltry, trifling, unimportant, Mids. N. ii. 2, Lear ii. 3.

PERDU. Fr., lost. *'Enfant perdu,'* was a soldier on a forlorn hope, Lear iv. 7.

PERDURABLE. Very durable, Oth. i. 3.

PERDY. A vulgarized French oath, *'Par Dieu,'* Ham. iii. 2.

PERPEND. Ponder, mentally weigh, Mer. W. ii. 1, Ham. ii. 2.

PERPLEXED. In Shakespeare's time this word had greater force than at present ; meaning, as he uses it, bewildered, distracted, maddened, Oth. v. 2.

PERSPECTIVE. A glass so contrived as to produce an optical deception, Tw. N. v. 1.

PETAR. A kind of mortar, used to blow up gates, Ham. iii. 4.

PEW-FELLOW. Originally, one who sat in the same pew. Metaphorically, a partner, a companion, Rich. III. iv. 4.

PHEESE. To chastise, and to humble, Tam. S. i. (Ind.)

PIA MATER. The membrane which covers the brain, Tw. N. i. 5.

PICK. To pitch, or toss, Hen. VIII. v. 3.

PICKT-HATCH. A house of ill resort, Mer. W. ii. 2.

PICKED. Spruce, coxcombical, Ham. v. 1.

PICKERS AND STEALERS. A caustic name for the hands, Ham. iii. 2. To pickeer was a word for to pillage.

PIERCED. Reached, penetrated, Oth. i. 3.

PIGHT. Pitched, fixed, settled, decided, Lear ii. 1.

PILCHER. A covering of leather, a scabbard, Rom. J. iii. 1.

PILL. To pillage or rob. "Pilled," Rich III. i. 3.

PIN. The centre of a target, now called the bull's eye, Rom. J. ii. 4.

PIN AND WEB. The old term for a cataract in the eye, Lear iii. 4.

PINK EYNE. Small, close-shut. peering eyes, Ant. Cl. ii. 7, (Song.)

PINNACE. A small ship, Mer. W. i. 3.

PIP. A pip is a spot on the cards ; and "a pip out," signified more than the number that sufficed to win the game. The phrase came into jocose usage to signify one or two more than needful, Tam. S. i. 2.

PITCH. The extreme ascent of a hawk before he stooped upon his prey, Jul. Cæs. i. 1.

PLAIN. For complain, Lear iii. 1.

PLAIN-SONG. The simple notes of an air or melody, Mids. N. iii. 1, (Song,) Hen. VIII. i. 3.

PLANTS. Feet. From the Latin *Planta;* Ant. Cl. ii. 7.

PLASH. A puddle, or small pool of water, Tam. S. i. 1.

PLATES. Silver money. Span. *Plata;* Ant. Cl. v. 2.

PLEACHED. Intertwined, Much Ado iii. 1, Ant. Cl. iv. 12.

PLEASANCE. Pleasure, delight, Oth. ii. 3.

PLIGHTED. Folded in. Fr. *Plié.* Metaphorically, close, complicated, sly, Lear i. 1.

PLOT. A space of ground; usually of turf, Mids. N. iii. 1.

PLUMMET. The plumb-line, for ascertaining the soundings at sea, Temp. iii. 3. Metaphorically used to imply, 'Ignorance itself can take my depth,' Mer. W. v. 5.

PLURISY. Excess of blood; Plethora, Ham. iv. 7.

POINTS. The metal tags, at the end of the laces, used for fastening up the hose, Tw. N. i. 5.

POINT-DE-VICE. (Spelt also Point-de-vise.) With punctilious nicety, without defect, As you L. iii. 2, Tw. N. ii. 5.

POISE. Weight, moment, importance, Lear ii. 1.

POLACK. A Polander, Ham. i. 1 & iv. 4.

POOR JOHN. A fish (Hake) salted and dried, Temp. ii. 2, Rom. J. i. 1.

PORT. State, attendance, Tam. S. i. 1.

PORTANCE. Deportment, conduct, Oth. i. 3.

POSSESS. To make understand, to inform distinctly and accurately, Tw. N. ii. 3, Much Ado v. 1.

POSSESSED. Insane, Tw. N. iii. 4.

POSSET. A night-drink, composed of hot milk and some strong infusion, curdled, Mer. W. i. 4 & v. 5, Macb. ii. 2; used as a verb, Ham. i. 5.

POST. At the doors of sheriffs, posts were set up, on which proclamations were placed, Tw. N. i. 5.

POSY. A motto; from poesy, Mer. V. v. 1, Ham. iii. 2.

POTTLE. A measure holding two quarts. But often used for a drinking vessel, without reference to the measure, Mer. W. ii. 1 & iii. 5, Oth. ii. 3.

PRACTICE. Art, deceit, treachery, Lear ii. 4 & v. 3, Oth. v. 2.

PRÆMUNIRE. The first words of, and signifying the writ which puts an offender out of the king's protection,— all his goods, chattels, &c., becoming forfeit to the crown, Hen. VIII. iii. 2.

PRANK. To dress gaily and daintily, Tw. N. ii. 4.

PRECEDENT. The first draught, or rough copy of a writing, Rich. III. iii. 6, Hen VIII. i. 2.

PRECISIAN. A restrainer within precise limits, Mer. W. ii. 1. (Letter.)

PREGNANT. Apprehensive, fertile in perception, Tw. N. iii. 1. Rich in evidence, convincing, Oth. ii. 1. Full of mischievous ingenuity, Tw. N. ii. 2. Apt, meaning, replete with intelligence, Ham. ii. 2. Promptly subservient, Ham. iii. 2. Susceptible of, open to, capable of receiving, Lear iv. 6.

PRENOMINATE. Heretofore named, Ham. ii. 1.

PRESCRIPT. Prescribed, or previously written injunction, Ant. Cl. iii. 8.

PRESENCE. The receiving-room of the sovereign, Hen. VIII. iii. 1. Hence, it came to be used for any state room, Rom. J. v. 3.

PRESENTLY. Immediately, Temp. iv. 1.

PRESS. A crowd, Hen. VIII. iv. 1 & v. 3, Jul. Cæs. i. 2. Fr. *Presse.*

PREST. Ready. Old Fr. *Prest;* Mer. Ven. i. 1.

PRETENCE. Intention, Macb. ii. 3, Lear i. 2.

PREVENT. To anticipate, to be beforehand with. Lat. *Prevenio,* to come before, Jul. Cæs. v. 1.

PRICK-SONG. Written music; from its being marked down with points or dots, Rom. J. ii. 4.

PRIME. First, Temp. i. 2. Youth, spring, morning. Rich. III. i. 2.

PRIMERO. A game at cards, Mer. W. iv. 5, Hen. VIII. v. 1.

PRIMY. Early, spring-like, Ham. i. 3.

PRINCOX. From the Latin *Præcox,* a forward, pert youngster. According to the modern cant, a 'fast young gent,' Rom. J. i. 5.

PRINT. "In print," meant, to speak, or act with precision, As you L. v. 4.

PRIVATE. Privacy, Tw. N. iii. 4.

PROBAL. A contraction of probable, Oth. ii. 3.

PROCESS. A law term for a summons, a citation, Ant. Cl. i. 1.

PRODIGIOUS. Unnatural, portentous, Rich. III. i. 2, Rom. J. i. 5.

PROGRESS. The journey of a sovereign, when visiting his dominions in state. Sarcastically applied, Ham. iv. 3.

PROJECT. To pre-arrange, or shape out, Ant. Cl. v. 2.

PRONE. Addicted, Hen. VIII. i. 1.

PROOF. For approof, in the sense of approval, Tam. S. iv. 3.

PROPER. Comely, well-shaped, Temp. ii. 2, Mids. N. i. 2. Also, one's own, or belonging to, Ham. v. 2, Oth. i. 3.

PROPERTIED. Made a property of, made use of, Tw. N. iv. 2. Gifted with qualities, or properties, Ant. Cl. v. 2.

PROPERTIES. Theatrical necessaries, Mer. W. iv. 4. Mids. N. i. 2.

PROPOSE. Talk, conversation. Fr. *Propos,* Much Ado iii. 1. Harangue, holding forth, Oth. i. 1.

PROROGUE. Suspend, Ant. Cl. ii. 1. Lengthen out, or prolong, "Prorogued," Rom. J. ii. 2.

PUCK. Robin Goodfellow. A waggish sprite, of Celtic origin. Puke, in Icelandic, means a demon, Mids. N. ii. 1.

PUNTO. A hit. A term in fencing, Mer. W. ii. 3. "Punto reverso," a backhanded stroke, Rom. J. ii. 4.

PURPLES. "Long Purples." A common English flower, *orchis mascula,* Ham. iv. 7.

PUSH. An old form of 'Pish,' or 'Pshaw,' Much Ado v. 1.

PUT ON. Instigated, induced, Ham. v. 2.

PUTTER-OUT. One who places money out at interest, Temp. iii. 3.

Q

QUAIL. To give way, to faint, Mids. N. v. 1, As you L. ii. 2.

QUAINT. Agreeably fantastical, graceful, Temp. i. 2. Tasteful, well-fancied, Much Ado iii. 4, Tam. S. iv. 3. Ingeniously contrived, Mer. Ven. iii. 4.

QUAINT MAZES. Fairy rings, Mids. N. ii. 2.

QUALITY. Qualification, gift, Temp. i. 2. Used technically of the theatrical profession, Ham. ii. 2.

QUARREL. A square-headed arrow. Making Fortune the arrow which divides or divorces, Hen. VIII. ii. 3.

QUARRY. A heap of dead game, Macb. iv. 3, Ham. v. 2. Shakespeare makes the soldier use the words "his damned quarry" for Macdonwald's heap of Kernes and Gallow glasses doomed to become the slaughtered prey of Macbeth, Macb. i. 2.

QUAT. A pimple on the skin. Applied metaphorically to mean a little common fellow, Oth. v. 1.

QUEAN. A slut, an ill-famed woman, Mer. W. iv. 2.

QUEASY. Squeamish, fastidious, delicate, Much Ado ii. 1, Lear ii. 1. Disgusted, Ant. Cl. iii. 6.

QUELL. To subdue, to destroy, to murder. Mids. N. v. 1. Used as a noun for murder, assassination, Macb. i. 7.

QUERN. A hand-, or horsemill for grinding corn, Mids. N. ii. 1.

QUEST. A common abbreviation of inquest, Rich. III. i. 4, Ham. v. 1. (See CROWNER'S-QUEST.)

QUESTRISTS. Searchers, those in quest, Lear iii. 7.

QUICK. Alive, living, Mer. W. iii. 4.

QUIDDIT. A contraction of quiddity. A refinement in reasoning, usually applied to legal quibblings, Ham. v. 1.

QUILLETS. Sophisms, chicanery, Ham. v. 1, Oth. iii. 1.

QUINTAIN. A post in the form of a man, used as a mark, at which riders tilted in pretended tournament, As you L. i. 2.

QUIPS. Scoffs, jokes, smart repartees, Mer. W. i. 3, Much Ado ii. 3, As you L. v. 4.

QUIRE. A choir, a company of singers. Used for any assembly, Mids. N. ii. 1.

QUIT. To answer, requite, avenge, Rich. III. v. 3, Ham. v. 2, Lear iii. 7.

QUITTANCE. Acquittance, release, discharge, Mer. W. i. 1, As you L. iii. 5.

R

RABATO. A collar, or fallingback ruff for the neck; Fr. Rabat, Much Ado iii. 4.

RACE. Progeny, Ant. Cl. i. 3.

RACK. A long range of clouds, Temp. iv. 1, Ant. Cl. iv. 12, Ham. ii. 2.

RAG. An opprobrious name for a beggarly person; a Raggamuffin, Mer. W. iv. 2, Tam. S. iv. 3, Rich. III. v. 3.

RAIED. Striped, Fr. Raie, Tam. S. iii. 2.

RANK. Pace, or rate of going, As you L. iii. 2.

RAPT. Mentally caught up, filled with admiration, Macb. i. 3 & 5.

RASCAL. Lean, degenerate; applied chiefly to deer, As you L. iii. 3.

RASE. To strike, as a boar with his tusks, Rich. III. iii. 4.

RASED. Torn, as by a boar, Rich. III. iii. 2.

RAT. Alluding to a legend in Ireland, that rats could be rhymed to death, As you L. iii. 2.

RAVIN. To gorge, or devour greedily, Macb. ii. 4.

RAW. Unskilful, Ham. v. 2.

RAWER. More unskilful; with a punning involvement of another meaning of the word "Raw,"—cold with damp, Ham. v. 2.

RAWLY. "Rawness," Macb. iv. 3.

RAYED. For berayed; soiled, muddled, made filthy, Tam. S. iv. 1.

RAZED. Slashed; Fr. Raser, to cut, Ham. iii. 2.

READ. Counsel, precept, monition, Ham. i. 3.

REAR-MICE. Bats, Mids. N. ii. 3.

RECEIVING. Prompt perception, Tw. N. iii. 1.

RECHEAT. The note of recall for the dogs in hunting, sounded on the horn, Much Ado i. 1.

RECK. To care for, As you L. ii. 4, Ham. i. 3.

RECORDER. A small pipe, a flageolet. Thus named from the instrument being used for teaching birds to sing tunes,—when their first essays are termed 'recording,' Mids. N. v. 1, Ham. iii. 2.

RECURE. Literally, to cure again; simply, to cure, to heal, Rich. III. iii. 7.

RED-LATTICE. A lattice window so painted; common to public houses in Shakespeare's time. "Red-lattice phrases" therefore meant ale-house language, Mer. W. ii. 2.

REDUCE. To bring back; Lat. Reduco, Rich. III. ii. 2 & v. 4.

REECHY. Smoky, filthy, foul, Much Ado iii. 3, Ham. iii. 4.

REEK. To stream forth as vapour or breath. Used metaphorically for to sweat as beneath a burden, Hen. VIII. ii. 4. Vaporous effluvia, Mer. W. iii. 3.

REGIMENT. Government, sway. The old signification of the word. Lat. Regimen, Ant. Cl. iii. 6.

RELUME. To light again, Oth. v. 2.

REMORSE. Not unfrequently used for pity, compassion, Mer. Ven. iv. 1.

REMOTION. Removal, withdrawal, Lear ii. 4.

REMOVED. Secluded, sequestered, As you L. iii. 2, Ham. i. 4.

RENDER. To render an account, declare, state, or describe, As you L. iv. 3.

RENEGE. To deny, (Lat. Renego), to renounce, Lear ii. 2, Ant. Cl. i. 1. [Coleridge suggests spelling it 'reneague,' to obtain the hard-sounded g required by the measure, where the verb takes a final s.]

RENT. An old form of the verb to rend, Mids. N. iii. 2, Macb. iv. 3.

REPROBANCE. Reprobation; the state of being reprobate, lost to virtue, Oth. v. 2.

REPUTE. To esteem, account, or hold, Oth. ii. 3.

RESOLVED. Convinced, satisfied, Jul. Cæs. iii. 1.

RESPECTIVE. Regardful, Mer. Ven. v. 1. Considerate, circumspect, Rom. J. iii. 1.

RESPECTS. Considerations, Rich. III. iii. 7, Lear i. 1.

REST. To "set up one's rest," is a metaphor borrowed from the game of Primero, when a player resolved to abide by the cards he held; thence used to express making up one's mind, or coming to a determination, Rom. J. iv. 5.

RIVAL. An associate, or companion in office, Ham. i. 1.

RIVALITY. Equality of honour, Ant. Cl. iii. 5.

ROMAGE. Bustle, tumult, Ham. i. 1.

RONYON. A mangy, or scabby animal; Fr. Rogneux, Mer. W. iv. 2, Macb. i. 3.

ROOD. The cross, the crucifix, Rich. III. iii. 2, Rom. J. i. 3. Ham. iii. 4.

ROPERY. Fit for the rope, roguery, Rom. J. ii. 4.

ROPE-TRICKS. Knavish jests, Tam. S. i. 2.

ROSE. A house then belonging to the duke of Buckingham; now the Merchant Tailors' School, Suffolk lane, Thames street, Hen. VIII. i. 2.

ROSEMARY. A symbol of remembrance, formerly used at funerals, weddings, and various social meetings, Rom. J. iv. 5, Ham. iv. 5.

ROUNDEL. Roundelay; a merry song, or catch. Fr. Rondelet. Also, a dance, Mids. N. ii. 3.

ROUSE. Carousal, Ham. i. 2 & ii. 1. A jovial draught, Oth. ii. 3.

ROYAL MERCHANT. A term applied to commercial traders of the highest grade; erectors of principalities, like the Grimaldi, &c., of Venice, and the Medici of Florence. Sir Thomas Gresham, of London, was an English Royal Merchant, Mer. Ven. iii. 2 & iv. 1.

ROYNISH. Scurvy, paltry, As you L. ii. 3.

RUBIOUS. Ruby-red, Tw. N. i. 4.

RUDESBY. An ill-bred, rude person, Tw. N. iv. 1, Tam. S. iii. 2.

RUE. Called "Herb of grace," from its being used in exorcisms against evil spirits. Ham. iv. 5.

RUFFLE. To agitate, excite, rouse, Jul. Cæs. iii. 2. To rifle, pillage, Lear iii. 7.

RULE. Behaviour, Tw. N. ii. 3.

RUNAWAYS. Speeders, fugitives, wanderers, truants, vagabonds, As you L. ii. 2, Rom. J. iii. 2. [In the last passage, its allusive signification has been variously explained by different editors; and, by some, discarded for other substituted words. None are satisfactory; and "Runaways" has been retained in the text, assuming it to allude to the horses of the sun (the "fiery-footed steeds") as a poetical embodiment of Day. The nearest that could be proposed to the original lection is, 'Sunny day's,' — according well with the whole speech,
{ Runnawayes,]
{ Sunny day's.]

RUSHES STREWED. The usual covering for state-room floors, before the invention of carpets, Tam. S. iv. 1, Rom. J. i. 4.

S

SABA. The form of her name under which Sheba, Solomon's queenly visitor usually appears in the pages of our early writers, Hen. VIII. v. 4.

SACK. Sherris sack is a dry rough sherry wine. Hence its being commonly drunk with sugar, Mer. W. ii. 1 & iii. 5.

SACKERSON. A famous bear of that period. It was customary to call the bears by the names of their leaders, Mer. W. i. 1.

SACRING BELL. The bell sounded at mass, or in processions, at the elevation, or approach of the Host, Hen. VIII. iii. 2.

SAD. Sedate, serious, grave, Much Ado i. 3, Mer. Ven. ii. 2, Tw. N. iii. 4. "Sadly;" "sadness," Rom. J. i. 1.

SAFE. To make secure, Ant. Cl. i. 3. "Safed," Ant. Cl. iv. 6.

SAGG. To droop or flag, Macb. v. 3.

SAGITTARY. The residence of the military officers at the arsenal at Venice; over the door of which, is the figure of an archer, Oth. i. 1 & 3.

SAID. "Well said," was not unfrequently used for well done, As you L, ii. 6.

SALLETS. Phrases, seasoned with salt, or gross and ribald meanings, Ham. ii. 2.

SALT. Sometimes used in the sense of salacious, licentious, gross, Ant. Cl. ii. 1, Oth. ii. 1 & iii. 3.

SALUTE. Excite, stimulate, exhilarate, Hen. VIII. ii. 3.

SAND-BLIND. Bad sight, as if sand were floating in the eyes, Mer. Ven. ii. 2.

SANDED. Marked with sand-coloured spots, Mids. N. iv. 1.

SARUM. The old name for Salisbury, Lear ii. 2.

SAW. A saying, As you L. ii. 7, Lear ii. 2.

'SAY. From assay; taste, relish, or sample. "Some 'say of breeding," Lear v. 3.

SCALD. Scabby, particularly in the head; hence used as a term of loathing and contempt, Ant. Cl. v. 2.

SCAMBLING. A form of scrambling, Much Ado v. 1.

'SCAPE. A contraction of escape, Mer. W. iii. 5.

SCARF. To veil, or bandage, Macb. iii. 2.

SCARFED. Adorned with streamers and pennons, Mer. Ven. ii. 6. Loosely wrapped, Ham. v. 2.

SCATH. Injury, Rich. III. i. 3, Rom. J. i. 5.

SCATHFUL. Hurtful, destructive, Tw. N. v. 1.

SCONCE. Still used as a term for the head, Ham. v. 1.

SCOTCHED. Cut, hacked, maimed, Macb. iii. 2. "Scotches," Ant. Cl. iv. 7.

SCRIMERS. Fencers; Fr. Escrimeurs, Ham. iv. 7.

SCRIP. From script, a writing, Mids. N. i. 2.

SCRIP AND SCRIPPAGE. Touchstone's diminutive of "Bag and baggage," As you L. iii. 2.

SEA-MELLS. Waterfowl; a species of gull. The best that can be made of the word in the old editions, ("Scamels'") is that it may mean small limpets; but Caliban would scarcely offer to get "young" little shell-fish as a tempting prize; whereas nestling birds are poetically appropriate, Temp. ii. 2.

SEAR. (Spelt also Sere.) To dry, to wither, to scorch, Macb. iv. 1 & v. 3, Rich. III. iv. 1.

SEASON. To preserve, Tw. N. i. 1. To temper, Mer. Ven. iv. 1, Ham. i. 1.

SECT. A section, a cutting in horticulture, Oth. i. 3.

SEEL. To close the eyes; metaphorically, to render blind, Ant. Cl. iii. 11, Oth. i. 3 & iii. 3.

SEELING. Closing the eye-lids. A term in falconry, Macb. iii. 2.

SEEN. "Well seen," well skilled, Tam. S. i. 2.

SEETH. "Seething," boiling, working, fermenting, Mids. N. v. 1.

SEGREGATION. The dispersing of a company, Oth. ii. 1.

SEIZED. Possessed. A law-term in use at the present day, Ham. i. 1.

SEMBLABLE. Resemblance, likeness, Ham. v. 2. Resembling, similar, Ant. Cl. iii. 4.

SEMBLATIVE. Seemingly, apparently, Tw. N. i. 4.

SENSIBLY. Feelingly, Ham. iv. 5.

SERE. "Tickled o' the sere," may be interpreted, 'Troubled with dryness,'—probably of old age, Ham. ii. 2.

SESSA. Supposed to be derived from the French Cessez,—cease, Tam. S. i. (Ind.), Lear iii. 4 & 6.

SETEBOS. A fabled god, mentioned in books of travel in Shakespeare's time, Temp. i. 2 & v. 1.

SEWER. The attendant who placed and removed the dishes on table. Stage direction to Macb. i. 7.

SHARD. Fragments of tile, or earthen pots, Ham. v. 1. Scaly covering of a wing, Ant. Cl. iii. 2. "Shard-borne," Macb. iii. 2.

SHARKED. Picked up, as prey, Ham. i. 1.

SHEEN. Lustre, brightness, shining, Mids. N. ii. 1, Ham. iii. 2.

SHEER. Mere, pure, (in the sense of simply, only) Tam. S. i. (Ind.)

SHENT. Chidden, scolded, ruined, Mer. W. i. 4, Tw. N. iv. 2, Ham. iii. 2.

SHIP-TIRE. A high, flaunting head-dress, with streamers, Mer. W. iii. 3.

SHOUGHS. Shaggy dogs, Macb. iii. 1.

SHOVE-GROAT or SHOVEL-BOARD. A game played upon a table by pushing certain coins to a prescribed mark, Mer. W. i. 1.

SHRIFT. Confession, Rich. III. iii. 4. Absolution, Rom. J. ii. 3. The office of hearing confession, and giving absolution, Rom. J. ii. 4 & 5.

SHROUD. Shelter, protecting cover, Ant. Cl. iii. 11.

SIDE-SLEEVES. Long hanging sleeves, Much Ado iii. 4.

SIEGE. (Fr.) Station, Ham. iv. 7, Oth. i. 2.

SIGHTLESS. Imperceptible, invisible, Macb. i. 5 & 7.

SIGN. To exhibit, to signalize, Hen. VIII. ii. 4.

SIGNIORY. The state, the government, Oth. i. 2.

SILENCE. Used as a verb for hiding silently, Ham. iii. 4.

SILLY SOOTH. Simple truth, Tw. N. ii. 4.

SIMULAR. Counterfeit, seeming, Lear iii. 2.

SINK-A-PACE. Sir Toby's corruption of CINQUE-PACE, Tw. N. i. 3.

SIR. An early designation of a Bachelor of arts, or Priest in orders, Mer. W. i. 1, Tw. N. iii. 4, Rich. III. iii. 2 & iv. 5. Used also substantively for a gentleman, Oth. ii. 1. Also (and by other of the elder dramatists) as a form of address to women, Ant. Cl. iv. 13.

SIRRAH. Sometimes a term of deference, or familiar courtesy, As you L. iv. 3. Rom. J. i. 5. Also to women, Ant. Cl. v. 2.

SITH. Since, Mer. W. ii. 2.

SIZES. Allowances, allotted portions of food; a college term, Lear ii. 4.

SKAINS-MATES. Free companions, Rom. J. ii. 4.

SKILLS NOT. Signifies not, makes no difference, Tam. S. iii. 2.

SKIRR. To scour, to ride furiously, Macb. v. 3.

SLAB. Moist and adhesive, sticky, Macb. iv. 1.

SLEAVE. Raw silk, ready for weaving, Macb. ii. 2.

SLEDDED. Borne in a sled, or sledge, Ham. i. 1.

SLEIGHT. (Sometimes spelt Slight.) Cunning practice, art, Macb. iii. 5, 3.

'SLIGHT. Contraction of 'by this light,' Tw. N. ii. 5 & iii. 2.

SLIP. A name for counterfeit coin;—and, to 'Give the slip,' is a familiar expression for stealing away, Rom. J. ii. 4.

SLIVER. A portion, broken, or cut off, Lear iv. 2, Ham. iv. 7. "Slivered," Macb. iv. 1.

SLOP, or SLOPS. Loose trousers, or breeches, Much Ado iii. 2, Rom. J. ii. 4.

SLOUGH. The cast-off skin of a snake, Tw. N. ii. 5, (Letter.)

SLUBBER. To sloven, or neglect, Mer. Ven. ii. 8. To soil, or make dim, Oth. i. 3.

SMACK. To have a tinge, or taste of, Mer. Ven. ii. 2, Macb. i. 2.

SMATCH. A taste, a tincture, a twang, Jul. Cæs. v. 5.

SMIRCHED. Dirtied, soiled, obsured, Much Ado iii. 3 & iv. 1.

SMULKIN. (Spelt also Smolkin.) The name of a spirit, or fiend, Lear iii. 4.

SMOOTHING. Flattering, Rich. III. i. 2.

SNECK UP. An exclamation of contemptuous defiance, Tw. N. ii. 3.

SNUFF. To "take in snuff," meant to be angry, to take offence. Punningly used in this sense; and in the sense of candle-snuff, Mids. N. v. 1.

SNUFFS. Mutual offence-takings, and dislikes, Lear iii. 1.

SO-FORTH. Used for expressing additional, or unwillingly uttered enumerations, Ham. ii. 1.

SOILED. Pampered, high-fed, full of blood, Lear iv. 6.

SOLICITED. Incited, occasioned, Ham. v. 2.

SOLICITING. Prompting, temptation, incitement, Macb. i. 3.

SOMETIME. Heretofore, Mer. W. iv. 4.

SONTIES. Supposed corruption of 'Saints,' (in old language 'Saunctes,') Mer. Ven. ii. 2.

SOOTH. Truth, Temp. ii. 2, Macb. i. 2 & v. 5. Oth. iii. 3 & 4.

SORT. Distinction, rank, Much Ado i. 1.

SORT. A set of people, used contemptuously, Rich. III. v. 3. To fit, or suit, Much Ado v. 4. Ham. i. 1.

SOUD, SOUD. An expressive word of Shakespeare's to convey the noise made by an impatient person, heated and fatigued, Tam. S. iv. 1.

SOWTER. The name of a hound, Tw. N. ii. 5.

SPAVIN. A disease in horses' legs, Tam. S. iii. 2, Hen. VIII. i. 3.

SPECIALTIES. Legal papers containing particulars, or special points of agreement, Tam. S. ii. 1.

SPLEEN. Shakespeare uses this word for violent emotion, as well of humour, as of anger, Tw. N. iii. 2, Tam. S. i. (Ind.) Also for haste, hurry, Mids. N. i. 1.

SPLEENY. Irritable, ill-tempered, Hen. VIII. iii. 2.

SPLINTER'D. Shakespeare uses this word in the sense of splinted; secured, held firmly adjusted, Rich. III. ii. 2. To splinter, Oth. ii. 3.

SPOONS. A present formerly given at christenings, by the sponsors; called Apostle Spoons, from their having the apostles' heads on them, Hen. VIII. v. 2 & 3.

SPOTTED. Polluted, stained, Mids. N. i. 1.

SPRAG. Sir Hugh's pronunciation of 'Sprack.' Nimble, alert, Mer. W. iv. 1.

SPRINGHALT. A lameness in horses, from being overridden: shown in twitching up their legs, Hen. VIII. i. 3.

SPURS. The longest lateral roots of trees, Temp. v. 1.

SQUARE. To quarrel. The action of pugilists preparing to strike, is still called 'squaring,' Mids. N. ii. 1, Ant. Cl. ii. 1 & iii. 11. "Squarer," Much Ado i. 1.

SQUASH. The unripe pod of a pea, Tw. N. i. 5, Mids. N. iii. 1.

SQUINNY. A familiar use of the word squint, Lear iv. 6.

STAGGERS. A disease in horses, like apoplexy, Tam. S. iii. 2.

STAIN. To throw into shade, to eclipse, Ant. Cl. iii. 4.

STALE. A decoy, a bait, Temp. iv. 1. A pun upon a term at chess, Tam. S. i. 1. An ill-famed woman, Much Ado iv. 1.

STALE. To make stale, flat, vapid, worn out, Jul. Cæs. i. 2. Ant. Cl. ii. 2.

STALK. To pursue game by means of the stalking-horse, Much Ado ii. 3.

STANYEL. An inferior kind of hawk, Tw. N. ii. 5.

STAR. In the sense of ruling star of destiny, Ham. ii. 2.

START-UP. Now, 'up-start,' Much Ado i. 3.

STATE. Throne, or seat of dignity, Tw. N. ii. 5.

STATION. Standing position, Ham. iii. 4. State of repose, Ant. Cl. iii. 3.

STAVES. The wood of the lances, of which, the lightest, as well as the soundest, was the best, Rich. III. v. 3.

STEAD. To aid, benefit, or support, Tam. S. i. 2, Rom. J. ii. 3, Oth. i. 3.

STELLED. Starry, Lear iii. 7.

STINTED. Ceased, stopped. Rom. J. i. 3.

STITHY. Now called 'Smithy.' The place where the anvil stands; Stith being an old name for an anvil, Ham. iii. 2.

STOCCATA. A thrust in fencing. Mercutio calls Tybalt "*A la Stoccata*," as a nickname, Rom. J. iii. 1. "Stoccadoes," Mer. W. ii. 1.

STOCK. A fencing term: to hit in attack, Mer. W. ii. 3.

STOMACH. Haughtiness, arrogance, Hen. VIII. iv. 2, Tam. S. v. 2. To resent, to bear in angry remembrance, Ant. Cl. iii. 4.

STOMACHING. Ill-will, resentment, Ant. Cl. ii. 2.

STONE-BOW. A cross-bow for discharging stones, Tw. N. ii. 5.

STOOP. (Spelt also Stoup.) A measure of about half a gallon in quantity; a cup, bowl, or flagon, Tw. N. ii. 3, Ham. v. 1 & 2, Oth. ii. 3.

STORIES. See CLEAR STORIES.

STOVER. Fodder of all kinds, Temp. iv. 1.

STRACHY. A title, or designation of unknown import: but implying superior rank. Tw. N. ii. 5.

STRAIN. Family, descent, lineage, Much Ado ii. 1. Nature, disposition, Lear v. 3.

STRANGENESS. Shyness, coyness, reserve, Tw. N. iv. 1, Oth. iii. 3.

STUCK. (See STOCK.) Ham. iv. 7.

SUBMERGED. Whelmed under water, Ant. Cl. ii. 5.

SUBSCRIBED. Surrendered, Lear i. 2 & iii. 7.

SUBSCRIPTION. Obedience, Submission, Lear iii. 2.

SUCCESS. Sequel, consequence, following conclusion. Oth. iii. 3.

SUFFICIENCY. Ability, efficiency. Much Ado. v. 1, Oth. i. 3.

SUGGEST. To tempt, prompt, instigate, Oth. ii. 3.

SUGGESTION. Temptation, wicked prompting, Temp. ii. 1. A cunning device, Hen. VIII. iv. 2.

SUIT. A petition to royalty, Rom. J. i. 4.

SUMPTER. A horse or mule to carry baggage or provision, Lear ii. 4.

SURCEASE. Completion, Macb. i. 7. To cease, Rom. J. iv. 1.

SWASHING. Bold, dashing, Rom. J. i. 1.

SWATH. The quantity of grass laid by one stroke of the scythe. Finely applied to the sentences of a big talker. Tw. N. ii. 3.

SWEET AND TWENTY. A term of endearment, Tw. N. ii. 3, (Song.)

SWEETING. An apple so called, Rom. J. ii. 4.

SWINGED. Beat, or beaten; thrashed, Mer. W. v. 5.

SWOOP. The rush down of a bird of prey, Macb. iv. 3.

SWORN BROTHERS. Originally, and according to the rules of chivalry, meant brothers in arms; but it came to be applied to close friends, or associates, Much Ado i. 1.

T

TABLE. The lines in the hand, and its general appearance for interpretation by palmistry, and chiromancy, Mer. Ven. ii. 2.

TABLES. The same as Tablebook, or Tablets; meaning memorandum-book, Ham. i. 5.

TABOR. A little drum, like a tambourine, with a pipe fixed to it, Temp. iv. 1, Much Ado ii. 3. It formed part of the clown, or jester's paraphernalia, Tw. N. iii. 1.

TABOURINE. A military drum, Ant. Cl. iv. 8.

TAG and TAG-RAG. The commonest people, Jul. Cæs. i. 2.

TAIL. A witch, transformed to any tailed animal, was believed to be always tailless, Macb. i. 3.

TAILOR. It was an old custom to cry out 'Tailor,' when any one fell backward, Mids. N. ii. 1.

TAKE IN. To occupy, or conquer, Ant. Cl. iii. 7.

TAKE OUT. To copy, Oth. iii. 4 & iv. 1.

TAKES. Blasts, strikes, infects, Mer. W. iv. 4, Ham. i. 1.

TAKING. Blasting, blighting, infectious. Lear ii. 4 & iii. 2.

TALE. Reckoning. "As thick as tale;" as fast as they can be counted, Macb. i. 3.

TALL. Valiant, bold, Mer. W. i. 4 & ii. 1 & 2, Tw. N. i. 3, Rom. J. ii. 4.

TANG. A clanging sound like a bell, Temp. ii. 2, (Song.) To ring out loudly, Tw. N. ii. 5, (Letter.)

TARGES. (Sounded with a hard g, to make it a monosyllable, for the sake of the metre.) An abbreviation of targets, Ant. Cl. ii. 6.

TARRE. To set on, to incite, Ham. ii. 2.

TARTAR. For Tartarus; the Pagan Hell, Tw. N. ii. 5.

TASSEL-GENTLE. The male Goss-hawk, Rom. J. ii. 2.

TASTE. To prove, try; Old Fr. *Taster*. In modern English to test, Tw. N. iii. 1 & iii. 4.

TAXATION. Satirical speech; taxing foibles too sharply. It was the custom to whip fools when they were overfree in their sarcasms, As you L. i. 2.

TEEN. Grief, trouble, Temp. i. 2, Rich. III. iv. 1, Rom. J. i. 3.

TEMPER. Used for temperament, constitution, Jul. Cæs. i. 2.

TENDER-HEFTED. See HEFTS.

TENT. To probe, to search, Ham. ii. 2.

TERMAGANT. A saracen god: the character was introduced into the old plays and moralities as a roaring and ranting woman, Ham. iii. 2.

TESTER. A coin, value sixpence; from the old Fr. *Teste*, because it had a head on it, Mer. W. i. 3.

TETCHY. A corruption of touchy; testy, captious, peevish, Rich. III. iv. 4, Rom. J. i. 3.

THEORICK. Theory; opposed to practick, or practice, Oth. i. 1.

THEWES. Brawny proportions, muscular strength, Jul. Cæs. i. 3, Ham. i. 3.

THICK. Thickly, rapidly, closely together. "Thickcoming," Macb. v. 3.

THICK-SKIN. A coarse lout, Mer. W. iv. 5, Mids. N. iii. 2.

THILL-HORSE. The shafthorse, Mer. Ven. ii. 2.

THOU'ST. The pronoun used as a verb. The French have *Tutoyer*; and, to thee and thou a person still implies extreme familiarity; or, upon occasion, contempt, Tw. N. iii. 2.

THRASONICAL. Boastful; from *Thraso*, a boaster in old comedy, As you L. v. 2.

THREAD AND THRUM. In weaving, the thread is the substance of the warp; the thrum, the small tuft beyond, where it is tied, Mids. N. v. 1.

THRIFT. Prosperity, Mer. Ven. i. 1. Gain, profit, Mer. W. i. 3, Mer. Ven. i. 3, Hen. VIII. iii. 2. Saving, parsimony, Ham. i. 2.

THRIFTLESS. Profitless, Macb. ii. 4. Fruitless, useless, Two. N. ii. 2.

THRIFTY. Economical, prudent, frugal, sparing, Mer. Ven. ii. 5, As you L. ii. 3.

THROSTLE. The thrush, Mids. N. iii. 1, (Song,) Mer. Ven. i. 2.

THROW. An ancient word, for a point of time, Tw. N. v. 1.

THRUMMED HAT. A hat made of the tufts, or thrums of the coarsest cloth, Mer. W. iv. 2.

THUNDER-STONE. A solid body, formerly supposed to be discharged from the thunder-cloud, Jul. Cæs. i. 3.

TIKE. A large, rough shepherd's dog, Lear iii. 6. Falstaff dubs Simple "Sir Tike," by way of politely calling him a cur, Mer. W. iv. 5.

TILTH. The word will apply to either tillage or tilled land, as Shakespeare employs it here. But the parallel passage in Montaigne, makes the former more probable, Temp. ii. 1.

TIMELESS. Uniformly employed by Shakespeare in the sense of untimely, Rich. III. i. 2, Rom. J. v. 3.

TIRE. A head-dress, Mer. W. iii. 3, Much Ado iii. 4.

TIRING-HOUSE. (Spelt also Tyring-house.) The dressing-room of a theatre, Mids. N. iii. 1.

TOAD. It was supposed to have a precious stone in its head; which would cure the bite of venomous reptiles, As you L. ii. 1.

TOGED. Gowned, robed. Oth. i. 1.

TOM O' BEDLAM. Wandering mendicants, so called, whose cure from lunacy being doubtful, were discharged from Bethlem Hospital. Their style and title were assumed by impostors, known as "Abram men" (whence is derived the phrase still current, "to sham Abram"); but both sorts went by the name of "Bedlam beggars," Lear i. 2 & ii. 3.

TOP. See PARISH-TOP.

TOUCH. Test, or trial; employed for touchstone, Rich. III. iv. 2, Denotement, indication, Tw. N. ii. 1. A sense, a perception, Temp. v. 1. "Touches;" hints, points, As you L. v. 4.

TOWARD. In preparation, approaching, Tam. S. i. 1 & v. 1, Rom. J. i. 5, Ham. i. 1 & v. 2. Tractable, docile, Tam. S. v. 2.

TOYS. Trifles, light songs, Mer. W. i. 4. Fantastic sprites, Mer. W. v. 5. Fancies, freaks of imagination, Mids. N. v. 1.

TRAIL. The scent left behind by game, Mer. W. iv. 2, Ham. ii. 2 & iv. 5. Slimy track, Ant. Cl. v. 2.

TRAIN. Lure, snare, stratagem, Macb. iv. 3.

TRAMMEL. To enfold, to enclose, Macb. i. 7.

TRANECT. From this word it is likely that the ancient ferry between Venice and the main land was passed in a boat drawn through the water by a process still in use at some places: as the editor once witnessed at Rotterdam; where a rope, strained across the canal, afforded the means of traversing, Mer. Ven. iii. 4.

TRASH. Rubbish, Oth. iii. 3. A worthless person, Oth. ii. 1 & v. 1. To check, or keep back; a hunting term, Temp. i. 2, Tam. S. 1, (Ind.) Oth. ii. 1.

TRAVERSE. An ancient military term for march, Oth. i. 3.

TRAY-TRIP. A game played with dice. Tw. N. ii. 5.

TREACHERS. Traitors. Lear i. 2.

TRENCHED. Carved, or cut; Fr. Trancher, Macb. iii. 4.

TRIBULATION. A society of Puritans so named; whose patience might be expected to bear any amount of uproar, Hen. VIII. v. 3.

TRICE. A very minute space of time, Temp. v. 1, Tw. N. iv. 2, (Song.) Lear i. 1.

TRICK. A peculiarity of countenance. Peculiarity of tone, Lear iv. 6.

TRICKING. Dress, finery, Mer. W. iv. 4.

TRICKSY. Nimble, fairy-like, Temp. v. 1. Sportive, fanciful, Mer. Ven. iii. 5.

TRIPLE. Used for one of three, Ant. Cl. i. 1. An epithet applied to Hecate, to express her three-fold character of Luna in Heaven, Diana on Earth, and Hecate in the infernal regions, Mids. N. v. 2.

TRIUMPH. The trump at cards. Corrupted from the French word Triomphe. Ant. Cl. iv. 12.

TROLL. To sing trippingly, Temp. iii. 2.

TROPICALLY. Figuratively. From trope, a term in rhetorick, Ham. iii. 2.

TROT. A contemptuous name for an old woman, Tam. S. i. 2.

TROW. To know, As you L. iii. 2, Lear i. 4. To believe, to think, Rom. J. i. 3 & ii. 5. Used for, 'I should like to know,' Much Ado iii. 4, Mer. W. ii. 1.

TRUCKLE-BED. A small bed, made to slide under a larger. The latter was called a "Standing-bed," Mer. W. iv. 5, Rom. J. ii. 1. From this term, the modern expression, to 'truckle,' to be subservient, is doubtless derived.

TRUE-PENNY. A mining term; signifying an indication in the soil, of the direction in which ore is to be found, Ham. i. 5.

TRUNDLE-TAIL. A dog with a curly tail, Lear iii. 6.

TUCK. A small sword, or rapier, Tw. N. iii. 4.

TURK. To "turn Turk," was a phrase of the time for a total change of condition, Ham. iii. 2.

TURLYGOD. or TURLYGOOD. A crazy mendicant, Lear ii. 3.

TWIGGEN BOTTLE. A bottle cased with a wicker work of twigs, Oth. ii. 3.

TWINK. A twinkle of the eye, Temp. iv. 1, Tam. S. ii. 1.

TYPE. Referring to the symbol of sovereignty, the crown, Rich. III. iv. 4.

U

UMBER. A brown earth, used as a colour, or pigment, As you L. i. 3.

UNANELED. Not having received the sacrament of extreme unction. Ele is the Saxon for oil. Ham. i. 5.

UNAVOIDED. For unavoidable, not to be avoided, Rich. III. iv. 4.

UNBATED. Sharp, not blunted with the button, as fencing-foils are, Ham. iv. 7 & v. 2. Used for unabated, unslackened, Mer. Ven. ii. 6.

UNBOLTED. Not sifted, coarse, Lear ii. 2.

UNBONNETED. Openly, unconcealedly, Oth. i. 2.

UNBOOKISH. Unpractised, unversed, Oth. iv. 1.

UNBREATHED. Unexercised, Mids. N. v. 1.

UNCAPE. A sporting term; to unearth the fox, Mer. W. iii. 3.

UNCHARGE. Leave unarraigned, uncharged, Ham. iv. 7.

UNCONFIRMED. Unpractised in the ways of the world, Much Ado iii. 3.

UNCOUTH. The old meaning is, uncommon, unusual, unknown. Strange, wild, As you L. ii. 6. The modern acceptation of the word is, unaccustomed, awkward, ungainly.

UNDERBORNE. Underlaid, undertrimmed, Much Ado iii. 4.

UNDERGOES. Is subject to, Much Ado v. 2.

UNDERTAKER. One who undertakes another man's quarrel, Tw. N. iii. 4. Dispatcher, Oth. iv. 1.

UNEXPRESSIVE. Ineffable, not to be expressed, As you L. iii. 2.

UNGARTERED. Formerly, gentlemen profoundly amorous, denoted their mental condition by going ungartered, As you L. iii. 2, Ham. ii. 1.

UNHAPPILY. Roguishly, archly, mischievously, Hen. VIII. i. 4.

UNHATCH'D. Not hacked; Fr. *Hacher*, Tw. N. iii. 4.

UNHOUSELED. Not having received the sacrament of the Eucharist as a Viaticum, Ham. i. 5.

UNIMPROVED. Unpractised, unproved, Ham. i. 1.

UNION. A pearl of fine quality, Ham. v. 2.

UNLUCKY. Ill-omened. To dream of being at banquets was deemed inauspicious, Jul. Cæs. iii. 3.

UNMANNED. A term in falconry; meaning a bird not tamed, Rom. J. iii. 2.

UNMASTERED. Ungoverned, Ham. i. 3.

UNPREGNANT. Inapt, incapable, unfit to perceive, or to cope with, Ham. ii. 2.

UNPROPER. Not appropriated to one individual; common to others, Oth. iv. 1.

UNQUALITIED. Deprived of his faculties, Ant. Cl. iii. 9.

UNQUESTIONABLE. Not choosing to be questioned, or talked with, As you L. iii. 2.

UNRESPECTIVE. Inattentive, uninquisitive, Rich. III. iv. 2.

UNREST. Uneasiness, discomfort, unhappiness, Rich. III. iv. 4 & v. 3, Rom. J. i. 5.

UNROUGH. Smooth-faced, beardless, Macb. v. 2.

UNSMIRCHED. Pure, undefiled, Ham. iv. 5.

UNSTATE. To degrade, or descend from rank, Ant. Cl. iii. 11, Lear i. 2.

UNTENTED. Unrelieved, unalleviated, as by a surgeon's tenting, Lear i. 4.

UNTHRIFT. Lavish, unsparing, Mer. Ven. v. 1.

UNVALUED. In the sense of invaluable, Rich. III. i. 4.

UPSPRING. Upstart, Ham. i. 4.

UPWARD. Summit, Lear v. 3.

URCHINS. Evil sprites, wicked fairies, Temp. i. 2 & ii. 2, Mer. W. iv. 4.

USANCE. Usurious interest, Mer. Ven. i. 3.

USE. Interest, Tw. N. iii. 1.

USE. In the sense of possession, power over, Mer. Ven. iv. 1, Ant. Cl. i. 3.

USURER'S CHAIN. See CHAIN.

UTTERANCE. Fr. *Outrance*. Extremity of opposition, Macb. iii. 1.

V

VAIL. To lower, Tam S. v. 2. "Vailed;" lowered, Ham. i. 2. "Vailing;" lowering, Mer. Ven. i. 1.

VALANCED. Fringed with a beard, Ham. ii. 2.

VALIDITY. Value. Tw. N. i. 1, Lear i. 1, Rom. J. iii. 3, Ham. iii. 2.

VANITY. A technical term for a magical show, or illusion, Temp. iv. 1. The name for one of the characters in the old Moralities and Puppet-shows, Lear ii. 2.

VANTAGE. For advantage, Macb. i. 6. Surplus, addition, Oth. iv. 3.

VARY. Variation, caprice, Lear ii 2.

VAST. Employed as a substantive to signify great or desolate space, Temp. i. 2, Ham. i. 2.

VASTY. For vast, Mer. Ven. ii. 7.

VAWARD. Early part, Mids. N. iv. 1.

VELURE. Velvet; Fr. *Velours*, Tam. S. iii. 2.

VENEW, *or* VENEY. Fr. *Venue*. A hit in fencing, Mer. W. i. 1.

VENGEANCE. Mischief, harm, As you L. iv. 3, (Letter.)

VENTAGES. The holes or stops in a flute, Ham. iii. 2.

VIA. An exclamation, meaning literally, 'away!' Mer. Ven. ii. 2. Used exultingly; or encouragingly, Mer. W. ii 2.

VICE. (See INIQUITY.) The Vice was dressed in particoloured scraps: hence Hamlet's words, "A king of shreds and patches," Ham. iii. 4, Tw. N. iv. 2, (Song.)

VICE'S DAGGER. The Vice, or Jester was armed with a wooden dagger. Falstaff applies the name to Shallow when he was a slim lath of a lad, Tw. N. iv. 2, (Song.)

VIED. A term at cards: staked, played, Tam. S. ii. 1.

VIOL-DE-GAMBOYS. A musical instrument, smaller than the violoncello, with six strings, Tw. N. i. 3.

VULGAR. Common, general, plebeian, Tw. N. iii. 1, As you L. v. 1. Of common report, Lear iv. 6.

W

WAFT. To beckon with the hand. For wafted. Mer. Ven. v. 1. [In some editions, "waved."]

WAGE. To carry on, maintain, Ant. Cl. iii. 7. To stake in wager, Lear i. 1. To strive, Lear ii. 4. To encounter and prosecute, Oth. i. 3.

WAGED. Stood as stakes in a wager, Ant. Cl. v. 1.

WAIST. The middle part of a vessel, Temp. i. 2.

WAKE. To keep a night festival, Ham. i. 4.

WALK. A path, glade, or district in a forest, Mer. W. v. 5.

WALLS ARE THINE. A camp metaphor, signifying, to surrender at discretion, Lear v. 3.

WANTON. "Make a wanton;" to trifle with, Ham. v. 2.

WARD. A guard or posture of defence, Temp. i. 2.

WARDER. Sentinel, or guard, Macb. i. 7 & iv. 1.

WARN. To summon, Jul. Cæs. v. 1, Rich. III. i. 1, Rom. J. v. 3.

WARE. The great bed at Ware, in Hertfordshire, is still in existence at the chief inn of the town. It is square, and large enough to contain 24 persons, Tw. N. iii. 2.

WASSAIL. To 'wish health.' The Saxon ejaculation when drinking at festivals: afterwards applied to the festivity itself, Macb. i. 7, Ant. Cl. i. 4, Ham. i. 4.

WATCH. A watch-light, Rich. III. v. 3.

WAX. To grow, Ham. iii. 1.

WAXEN. Increase, Mids. N. ii. 1.

WAY. This is the word in the original text. It has been altered to "day" and "May;" though without satisfactory explanation of either substituted word. "A better way" seems to me to mean that Cordelia's mingled "smiles and tears" expressed her feelings in a better way than either "patience" or "sorrow" could do separately; who each "strove who should express her goodliest," Lear iv. 3.

WEAR. The fashion of the time, that which is most popularly worn, As you L. ii. 7.

WEATHER. To "make fair weather," was an idiom for flattering, insinuating oneself into favour; or for accommodating oneself to circumstances, Much Ado i. 3.

WEAVER. Weavers being a sedentary people, were generally good singers; like the cotton spinners in Lancashire, who are excellent chorus-singers. Many of the weavers in Elizabeth's time were Flemings, who had fled, for faith's sake, from the persecution of the Duke of Alva; and were great psalm-singers, Tw. N. ii. 3.

WEB. See PIN AND WEB.

WEEDS. Dress, clothing, garments, T.w. N. v. 1, Much Ado v. 3.

WEEN. To think, to imagine, Hen. VIII. v. 1.

WEET. To know, Ant. Cl. i. 1.

WEIRD. From the Saxon, Witch. "The weird sisters" were the northern Fates, Macb. i. 3 & 5 (Letter,) ii. 1, iii. 1, iii. 4. iv. 1.

WELKIN. The sky, Mer. W. i. 3, Mids. N. iii. 2.

WELL-SEEN. Accomplished, proficient, well-skilled, Tam. S. i. 2.

WENCH. This term had not always formerly the degrading signification that it now bears, Oth. v. 2.

WEND. To go. Hence the present perfect tense, went, Mids. N. iii. 2, As you L. iii. 3. [In some editions "wind."]

WHEEL. The burden of a ballad : so called from its rotatory character, in frequently recurring, Ham. iv. 5.

WHELKED. Marked with protuberances, Lear iv. 6.

WHEN. An exclamation, denoting restlessness, or impatience. "Why, when, I say !" Tam. S. iv. 1.

WHERE. Used in the sense of place. "A better where to find," Lear i. 1.

WHILE. Used for until. "While then, God be with you," Macb. iii. 1. Still, a very common North-British provincialism.

WHILES. Long used for while, Tw. N. iv. 3.

WHILE-ERE. A short time ago. The form is now reversed to erewhile, Temp. iii. 2.

WHIPSTOCK. The stock or handle of a whip, Tw. N. ii. 3.

WHIST. Were hushed, or silent. Formed from the exclamation, 'hist !' or 'hush !' Temp. i. 2. (Song.)

WHISTLE OFF. The hawk was dismissed from the fist, to pursue its prey, by a whistle. When in chase, against the wind ; and when it was "haggard,"—ill-tamed, and unserviceable, — with, or down the wind, Oth. iii. 3.

WHITE. To "hit the white," in archery ; the centre of the target, Tam. S. v. 2.

WHITING-TIME. Bleaching-time, Mer. W. iii. 3.

WHITSTER, or WHITESTER. A bleacher of linen, Mer. W. iii. 3.

WHOOPING. "Out of all whooping," out of reach of hearing ; beyond measure, As you L. iii. 2.

WIFE. Taken in its ordinary sense, this word occasions difficulty in the passage, "a fellow almost damn'd in a fair wife," applied to Cassio,—who is unmarried. But the epithet may have been used for "woman" as well as for a spouse, like the French *femme* or the German *frau*; and if so, the phrase would bear this interpretation :— "a fellow who'd give himself to perdition for a handsome woman." "Good wife" seems to have been a title for a woman generally, whether wedded or unwedded. Falstaff addresses Mistress Quickly thus : and though she answers disclaiming the rank of married woman which she assumes him to attribute to her, it is by no means clear that he intended such attribution, Mer. W. ii. 2. Shakespeare uses the word "wives" in passages where it may mean merely "women," without regard to their being married. Jul. Cæs. iii. 1.

WIGHT. A person, male or female, Mer. W. i. 3, Oth. ii. 1 & 3.

WINDS. Used as in collective metaphor to signify the wholesomely searching, and brisk winds that prosper the crops ; and equally wholesome, though rough breath of public censure, and private candour, producing moral harvest, Ant. Cl. i. 2.

WIS. To know, to be aware. Mer. Ven. ii. 9, (Scroll,) Tam. S. i. 1, Rich. III. i. 3.

WISH. Used in the sense of to recommend, Tam. S. i. 1 & 2.

WITTOL. A tame submitter to conjugal shame. Mer. W. ii. 2. "Wittolly," Mer. W. ii. 2.

WOLD. An open and bare district, Lear iii. 4, (Song.)

WOMANED. Accompanied, or haunted by a woman, Oth. iii. 4.

WONDERED. Able to achieve wonders, wonder-gifted, Temp. iv. 1.

WONT. Custom, habit, Ham. i. 4.

WOODCOCK. A bird having the character of being stupid ; and, therefore, the name was applied to simpletons, Tw. N. ii. 5, Much Ado v. 1, Tam. S. i. 2.

WOODMAN. A forester ; chiefly a hunter. Applied equivocally, Mer. W. v. 5.

WOO'T. An old (and still provincial) form of 'Wilt thou,' Ant. Cl. iv. 2 & 13, Ham. v. 1.

WORLD. "To go to the world." A phrase which meant to be married, Much Ado ii. 1. A "woman of the world ;" a married woman, As you L. v. 3 ; a "world to see," i. e. wonderful to see, Tam. S. ii. 1.

WORM. The superstition was fostered that lazy maids had worms grow at the ends of their fingers, Rom. J. i. 4.

WORTS. Plants of the cabbage species. Falstaff's jeer at Sir Hugh's Welsh pronunciation of "words," Mer. W. i. 1.

WOT. To know, Mer. W. ii. 2. Mids. N. iv. 1.

WREST. A tuning-key for drawing up the strings of instruments to correct pitch. To twist, wrench, force, or sway, Much Ado iii. 4. Mer. Ven. iv. 1.

WRETCH. Used occasionally as an epithet of tenderness, and softest pity, Ham. iv. 7, Rom. J. i. 3, Oth. iii, 3.

WROTH. Misfortune : that which causes writhing, Mer. Ven. ii. 9. [In some editions "Wrath ;" to the injury of sense and rhyme.]

Y

YARE. Prompt, alert, quick, Temp. i. 1, Tw. N. iii. 4. Trim, ready for service, Temp. v. 1, Ant. Cl. iii. 7.

YEARN. To grieve, Mer. W. iii. 5. Jul. Cæs. ii. 2.

YELLOWS. A disorder in horses. The gall-pipe being stopped, the matter returns to the blood, and tinctures the skin and eyes. In the human being it is called jaundice. Tam. S. iii. 2.

YELLOWNESS. Jealousy, Mer. W. i. 3.

YESTY. Frothy, like yeast, Macb. iv. 1, Ham. v. 2.

YOUNKER. A youth, a youngster, Mer. Ven. ii. 6.

Z

ZANY. A fool, buffoon. "Zanies," Tw. N. i. 5.

ZED. Called an "unnecessary letter," because S would answer its purposes, Lear ii. 2.

ZENITH. The point in the heavens directly overhead ; hence used, astrologically, to mean the highest point of a man's fortune, Temp. i. 2.